FROMMER'S
MEXICO
ON $20 A DAY™

PLUS BELIZE AND GUATEMALA

Tom Brosnahan

1987-88 Edition

Published by Prentice Hall Press
A Division of Simon & Schuster, Inc.
Gulf + Western Building
One Gulf + Western Plaza
New York, NY 10023

ISBN 0–671–62351-6

Manufactured in the United States of America

*Although every effort was made to ensure the accuracy
of price information appearing in this book,
it should be kept in mind that prices
can and do fluctuate in the course of time.*

CONTENTS

MAPS

For Juanita Pescadora

Special thanks to Marge Marchak, Bill Bjork, Debby Drong-Bjork, and Nancy Keller for their help.

While I was updating this guide, the situation for tourists in Guatemala and Belize improved dramatically. Though there was not enough time to do the weeks of research necessary to fully cover these destinations, I wanted to give you as much help as I could, so I've added Part Two to this guide.

You'll find Part Two extremely helpful as you tour Guatemala and Belize, even though it does not cover all of the budget lodging and dining places in depth. For the next edition of this guide, I'll have the time to re-explore these wonderful places in detail. And you can help! Send notes on your experiences and discoveries, addressed to me, personally: Tom Brosnahan, Prentice Hall Press, One Gulf + Western Plaza, New York, NY 10023. And thanks for helping future readers in their travels.

For up-to-the-minute information on traveling in Guatemala and Belize, you can call the U.S. Department of State's Citizens' Emergency Center in Washington, D.C. at 202/647-5225, during business hours (Eastern time).

Important to remember: In Mexico, the dollar sign is used to denote pesos, and a Mexican sign reading "$500" means 500 pesos, not 500 dollars. To eliminate confusion, the dollar sign in this book is used only to indicate U.S. dollars.

It's good to have $25 or so in cash dollars of small denominations with you at all times for emergencies (most places will take them if you don't have the proper local currency).

Mexico has a Value Added Tax (*Impuesto de Valor Aggregado,* or "IVA," pronounced *ee*-bah) on almost everything, including hotel rooms, restaurant meals, bus tickets, and souvenirs. In 1985 the Mexican government passed a law requiring this tax to be included, or "hidden," in the price of goods and services, not added at the time of sale. Thus, prices quoted to you should be *IVA incluido,* "tax included." All prices given in this book already include the tax.

The $20 daily budget, which provides the title for this book, is intended to cover only the cost of your hotel room and three meals, and not your entertainment and transportation expenses. As a result, the accommodations listed in this book are, in my opinion, generally moderately priced, and not rock-bottom. The book can be used with safety by persons of both sexes and of all ages. These days, it's easily possible to tour Mexico on $10 a day, so $20 daily can include *all* your expenses.

Although every effort is made to ensure that the information given is accurate and up-to-date at press time, keep in mind that some transportation schedules, museum opening hours, telephone numbers, and *prices* (in this age of inflation) may change by the time you reach Mexico. Mexico's economic situation is chaotic these days, with inflation running nearly 100% a year. But foreign tourists going to Mexico benefit from the frequent devaluations of the peso, so a trip to Mexico is now more of a bargain than ever. Use my dollar prices as a more reliable guide than the peso prices.

As of this writing, the rate of exchange in Mexico is 500 pesos for US $1. This may well change by the time you visit Mexico, but any commercial bank will be glad to provide you with the current rate.

MEXICO ON $20 A DAY

**1. A Brief History
2. The $20-a-Day Way
3. Preparing for Your Trip
4. About This Book
5. The $25-a-Day Travel Club—How
to Save Money on All Your Travels**

EVERYONE NORTH OF THE RIO GRANDE has at least some idea (usually an old-fashioned one) about what Mexico is like, but only those who go there can know the real Mexico, for the country is undergoing fast-paced and far-reaching change, as are most countries touched by modern technology. Being so close to the United States and Canada, she is so forcefully affected by what goes on in her neighboring countries to the north that the Old Mexico of cowboy songs and movies has long ago been replaced by a land full of the familiar signs of 20th-century life. But this does not mean that a trip to Mexico will reveal people, sights, and sounds just like home, for Mexico is very much her own country, the result of a particular blending of the land itself and of ancient Indian, colonial European, and modern industrial influences. These three elements have produced a tradition and a culture unique in all the world.

To discover this unique Mexico you must look beyond the many modern conveniences—good roads, luxury hotels, frequent air and bus service, and the like—back to the basis of the culture.

First there is the land: it includes seemingly trackless desert, thousands of miles of lush seacoast, tropical lowland jungle, snow-capped mountains; from the breathtaking gorges of Chihuahua to the flat coastal plain of Yucatán, from the Pacific at California to the Caribbean at Quintana Roo, Mexico stretches 2,000 miles from sea to sea.

Then there are the peoples: Indians descended from the founders of many civilizations—Olmec, Toltec, Mayan, Aztec; the Spanish Conquistadores; Africans brought as slaves; European merchants and soldiers of fortune; a French influence left from the time of the abortive venture at New World empire by Maximilian of Habsburg and Napoléon III. All these influences have combined to create a particularly Mexican cast of mind, which you will see revealed in the art and architecture of the cities and towns, the cuisine, the costumes and habits of the people.

Mexican history goes back over 10,000 years, and is crucial to your under-

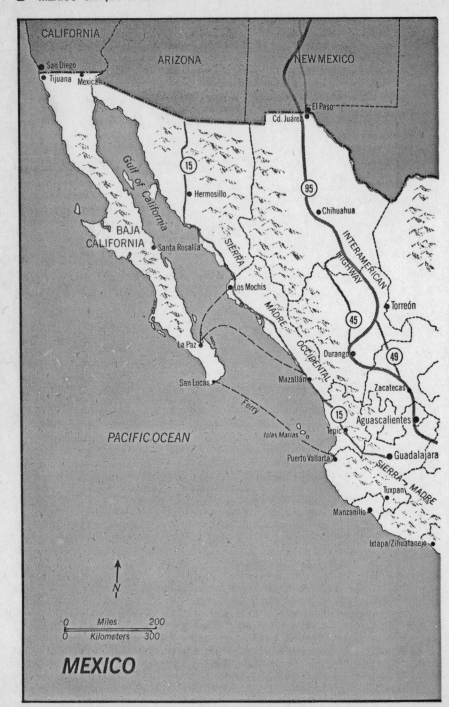

MEXICO

standing of the country and its people. To whet your appetite, here follows a summary of those 10,000 years.

1. A Brief History

The earliest "Mexicans" were Stone Age men and women, descendants of the race that had crossed the Bering Strait and reached North America prior to about 10,000 B.C. These were *Homo sapiens* who hunted mastodons, bison, and the like, and gathered other food as they could. Later (Archaic Period, 5200–1500 B.C.), signs of agriculture and domestication appear: baskets were woven; corn, beans, squash, and tomatoes were raised; turkeys and dogs were kept for food. By 2400 B.C. the art of potting had been discovered (the use of pottery was a significant advance). Life in these times was still very primitive, of course, but there were "artists" who made clay figurines for use as votive offerings or household "gods." Actually, goddesses is a better term, for all the figurines found so far have been female, and are supposed to be symbols of Mother Earth or Fertility in a very primitive sense. (Use of these figurines predates any belief in well-defined gods.)

THE PRECLASSIC PERIOD: It was in the Preclassic Period (2000 B.C.–A.D. 300) that the area known by archeologists as Middle America (from the northern Mexico Valley through Guatemala) began to show signs of a farming culture. They farmed either by the "slash-and-burn" method of cutting grass and trees, then setting fire to the area to clear it for planting; or by constructing terraces and irrigation ducts, this latter method being the one used principally in the highlands around Mexico City, where the first large towns developed. At some time during this period, religion became an institution as certain men took the role of *shaman,* or guardian of the magical and religious secrets. These were the predecessors of the folk healers and nature priests still to be found in modern Mexico and Guatemala.

The most highly developed culture of this Preclassic Period was that of the Olmecs, flourishing a full millennium before that of the Mayas. From 1200 to 400 B.C. the Olmecs lived in what is today the state of Tabasco, south of Veracruz, and it was to this coastal land that they transported colossal 40-ton blocks of basalt, carved as roundish heads. These sculptures still present problems to archeologists: How were they cut and carved with only the primitive implements the Olmecs had? How and why were they transported the many miles from the source of the basalt to the Gulf Coast at La Venta (near Villahermosa)? What do they signify? The heads seem infantile in their roundness, but all have the peculiar "jaguar mouth" with a high-arched upper lip that is the identifying mark of the Olmecs, and that was borrowed and adapted by many later cultures. The artists seemed obsessed with deformity, and many smaller carved or clay figures are of monstrosities or misshapen forms. Besides their achievements in sculpture, the Olmecs were the first in Mexico to use a calendar of 365 days.

THE CLASSIC PERIOD: Most of the real artistic and cultural achievement came during the Classic Period (A.D. 300–900), when life was no longer centered in the villages but rather in cities. Class distinctions, absent from village life, arose as the military and religious aristocracy took control, a class of merchants and artisans grew, and the farmer who had been independent became the serf under a landlord's control. The cultural centers of the Classic Period were the Yucatán and Guatemala (home of the Maya), the Mexican Highlands at Teotihuacán, the Zapotec cities of Monte Albán and Mitla (near Oaxaca), and the Totonac cities of Tajín and Zempoala on the Gulf Coast.

The Mayas are at the apex of pre-Columbian cultures. Besides their superior artistic achievements, the Mayas made significant discoveries in science, including the use of the zero in mathematics and their famous, complex calendar with which their priests could predict eclipses and the movements of the stars for centuries to come. The Mayas were warlike, and although one group or another might raid its neighbors from time to time, their sacrifices—some of them human—were on a very small scale compared to those of their successors, the bloodthirsty Aztecs. All considered, the Mayas seem to have been an admirable people: fairly peaceable, artistically gifted, imaginative, although also conservative and superstitious.

Teotihuacán is thought to have been a Toltec city of 85,000 or more inhabitants. At its height, Teotihuacán was the greatest cultural center in Mexico. Its layout is certainly of religious significance; on the tops of its pyramids consecrated to the sun and moon, high priests performed human sacrifices, attended but not observed by the masses of the people at the foot of the pyramid. Some of the magnificent reliefs and frescoes that decorated the religious monuments can be seen in Mexico City's museums.

The Zapotecs, influenced by the Olmecs, raised an impressive culture in the region of Oaxaca. Their two principal cities were Monte Albán, inhabited by an elite of merchants and artisans, and Mitla, reserved for the high priests. Both cities exhibit the artistic and mathematical genius of the people: characteristic geometric designs, long-nosed gods with feathered masks, hieroglyph stelae, a bar-and-dot numerical system, and a 52-cycle calendar. Like the Olmecs, the Zapotecs favored grotesque and fantastic art, of which the frieze of the "Danzantes" at Monte Albán—naked figures of distorted form and contorted position—is an outstanding example.

Of these important Classic Period cultures, perhaps least is known of the Totonacs, a small tribe centered in Tajín and Zempoala on the Gulf Coast. The Pyramid of the Niches which they built at Tajín is unique of its kind, and the numerous clay figures they crafted of men at play, smiling, dancing, and clowning, bespeak a joyfulness best described by a 16th-century Spaniard: "They were fun-loving with no affront of words, no ugly or unjust thing." Be sure to see their art in the museum at Villahermosa.

THE POSTCLASSIC PERIOD: In the Postclassic Period (900–1520), warlike cultures in time developed impressive societies of their own, although they never surpassed the Classic peoples. All paintings and hieroglyphs of this period show war, migration, and disruption. Somehow the glue of society became unstuck, people wandered from their homes in search of a better life, the religious hierarchy lost influence over the people.

Finally, in the 1300s, the most warlike people of all, the Aztecs, settled in the Mexico Valley on Lake Texcoco (site of Mexico City), with the island city of Tenochtitlán as their capital. Legend has it that as the wandering Aztecs were passing the lake they saw a sign that their prophets had told them to look for: an eagle perched on a cactus plant with a snake in its mouth. They built their city where they saw the sign, and in time it grew to become a huge (pop. 300,000) and impressive capital. The empire that grew up with it was a more or less loosely united congeries of states and territories of great size. The high lords of the capital became fabulously rich in gold, stores of food, cotton, and perfumes; the artisans were skilled and prosperous; events of state were occasions of elaborate ceremony. But the other part of the picture was that of the victorious Aztecs returning from battle to sacrifice thousands of captives on the altars atop the pyramids, cutting their chests open with stone knives and ripping the living hearts out to offer to their gods.

QUETZALCÓATL: The legend of Quetzalcóatl, a holy man who appeared during the time of troubles at the end of the Classic Period, is one of the most important tales in Mexican history and folklore. Quetzalcóatl means "feathered serpent," but seems to have been a religious title during later Mayan times. Like the young Jesus, wise and learned beyond his years, he became the high priest and leader of the Toltecs at Tula, and did a good deal to "civilize" them and stop or ameliorate the bad effects of sacrifice. He stopped human sacrifice altogether. His influence completely changed the Toltecs from a group of spartan warriors to peaceful and fabulously productive farmers, artisans, and craftsmen. But his success upset the old priests who had depended on human sacrifice for their own importance, and they called upon their ancient god of darkness, Texcatlipoca, to degrade Quetzalcóatl in the eyes of the people. One night the priests conspired to dress Quetzalcóatl in a ridiculous garb, get him drunk, and tempt him to break his vow of chastity. The next morning they offered him a mirror, and the horror of what he saw after this night of debauch drove him in shame out of his own land and into the wilderness, where he lived for 20 years. He emerged in Coatzacoalcos, in the Isthmus of Tehuantepec, constructed a boat of feathers, bade his few followers farewell, and sailed away, having promised to return in a future age. But artistic influences noted at Chichén-Itzá in the Yucatán suggest that in fact he landed there and began his "ministry" again, this time with much success among the peaceable Mayas. He died there, but the legend of his return in a future age remained.

THE SPANISH CONQUISTADORES: When Hernán Cortés and his men landed in 1519 in what would become Veracruz, the Aztec empire was ruled by Moctezuma (also, misspelled, Montezuma) in great splendor. The emperor thought the strangers might be Quetzalcóatl and his followers, returning at last, in which case no resistance must be offered; on the other hand, if the strangers were not Quetzalcóatl, they might be a threat to his empire. Moctezuma tried to bribe them with gold to go away, but this only whetted their appetites. Despite the fact that Moctezuma and his ministers received the Conquistadores with full pomp and glory when they reached Mexico City, Cortés pronounced the Aztec chief to be under arrest and had him tortured. Moctezuma never did reveal where he had hidden his fabulous treasure, which had been seen by a Spaniard earlier.

Actually the Spaniards were living on bravado at this point, for they were no match for the hundreds of thousands of Aztecs; but they skillfully kept things under their control until a revolt threatened Cortés's entire enterprise. He retired to the countryside, made alliances with non-Aztec tribes, and finally marched on the empire when it was governed by the last Aztec emperor, Cuauhtémoc. He was victorious; Cuauhtémoc defended himself and his people furiously, but was finally captured, tortured, and made a prisoner. He was ultimately executed.

The Spanish conquest had started out as an adventure by Cortés and his men, unauthorized by the Spanish crown or its governor in Cuba, but the conquest was not to be reversed and soon Christianity was being spread through "New Spain." Guatemala and Honduras were explored and conquered, and by 1540 the territory of New Spain included Spanish possessions from Vancouver to Panama. In the two centuries that followed, Franciscan and Augustinian friars converted great numbers of Indians to Christianity, and the Spanish lords built up huge feudal estates on which the Indian farmers were little more than serfs. The silver and gold which Cortés had sought made Spain the richest country in Europe.

INDEPENDENCE: Spain ruled Mexico through a viceroy until 1821, when Mexico finally gained its independence after a decade of upheaval. The independence movement had begun in 1810 when a priest, Fr. Miguel Hidalgo, gave the cry for independence from his pulpit in the town of Dolores, Gto. With the help of a military officer named Ignacio de Allende, who had had revolutionary thoughts even earlier than had Hidalgo, the priest assembled a mob army and sought redress of grievances against the Spanish. The revolt soon became a revolution, and Hidalgo and Allende were joined by another priest, Father José María Morelos, as their "army" threatened Mexico City. Ultimately the revolt failed, and Hidalgo was executed, but he is honored as Mexico's foremost patriot, "the Father of Modern Mexico." Morelos kept the revolt alive until 1815, when he too was caught and executed.

When independence finally came, one Agustín Iturbide was ready to take over. Iturbide founded a short-lived "empire" with himself as emperor in 1822. The next year it fell and was followed by the proclamation of a republic with Gen. Guadalupe Victoria as first president. A succession of presidents and military dictators followed Guadalupe Victoria until one of the most bizarre and extraordinary episodes in modern times: the French intervention. In the 1860s, certain factions among the Mexican upper class offered the Archduke Maximilian of Habsburg the crown of Mexico, and with the support of the ambitious French emperor, Napoléon III, the young Austrian actually came to Mexico and "ruled" for three years (1864–1867) while the country was in a state of civil war. This move for European interference in New World affairs was not welcomed by the United States, and as Napoléon's support became more and more extensive without good results, the French emperor finally withdrew his troops, leaving the brave but misguided Maximilian to be captured and executed by firing squad in Querétaro. His adversary and successor (as president of Mexico) was a Zapotec Indian lawyer named Benito Juárez, one of the most powerful and heroic figures in Mexican history. After victory over Maximilian, Juárez did his best to unify and strengthen his country, but it was not long before the stresses of the struggle gave him a heart attack. He died in 1872. His effect on the future of Mexico was profound, however, and his plans and visions continued to bear fruit for decades to come.

From 1877 to 1911, a period now called the "Porfiriato," the prime role in the drama of Mexico was played by one of Juárez's generals, and emotional strongman named Porfirio Díaz. Hailed by some as a modernizer, he was a terror to his enemies and to anyone who stood in his way or challenged his absolute power. He was finally forced to step down in 1911 by Francisco Madero and the greater part of public opinion.

The fall of the Porfirist dictatorship only led to more trouble, however. The country was split among several factions, including those led by "Pancho Villa" (real name Doroteo Arango), Alvaro Obregón, Venustiano Carranza, and Emiliano Zapata. The turbulent era from the fall of Porfirio Díaz through the next ten years is referred to as the Mexican Revolution. Drastic reforms were proposed and carried out by the leaders in this period, and the surge of vitality and progress from this exciting if turbulent time has inspired Mexicans down to the present day. Succeeding presidents have invoked the spirit of the Revolution, and it is still studied and discussed.

THE TWENTIETH CENTURY: After the turmoil of the revolution, Mexico sought stability. It came in the form of the *Partido Revolucionario Institucional* *(el PRI*, pronounced ell-*pree)*, the country's dominant political party. With the aim of "institutionalizing the revolution," the PRI literally engulfed Mexican society, leaving little room for vigorous, independent opposition. For over half a century, the monolithic party has had control of the government, labor unions, trade organizations, and other centers of power in Mexican society.

The most outstanding Mexican president of the century is without doubt General Lázaro Cárdenas (1934–1940). A vigorous and effective leader, Cárdenas broke up vast tracts of agricultural land and distributed parcels to small cooperative farms called ejidos; reorganized the labor unions along democratic lines; and provided funding for village schools. His most famous action was the expropriation of Mexico's oil industry from U.S. and European interests. The expropriated assets became Petroleros Mexicanos (Pemex), the enormous government petroleum monopoly.

The PRI has selected Mexico's president (and, in fact, virtually everyone else on the government payroll) from its own ranks after Cárdenas, the national election being only a confirmation of the choice. Among these men have been Avila Camacho, who continued many of Cárdenas's policies; Miguel Alemán, who expanded national industrial and infrastructural development; Adolfo López Mateos, who expanded the highway system and increased hydroelectric power sources; and Gustavo Díaz Ordaz, who provided credit and technical help to the agricultural sector.

In 1970, Luis Echeverría came to power, followed in 1976 by José López Portillo. During their presidencies there emerged a studied coolness in relations with the United States and an activist role in international affairs. This period also saw an increase in charges of large-scale corruption in the upper echelons of Mexican society. The corruption, though endemic to the system, may have been fostered by the river of money that began to flow into Mexican banks (and Mexican pockets) because of the precipitous rise in oil prices. As oil income skyrocketed, Mexican borrowing and spending did likewise. Virtually all bankers, economists and politicians saw the rise in oil prices as permanent. When, in the 1980's, oil prices dropped as fast as they had risen, Mexico was left with an enormous debt to foreign banks, and serious deficiencies in its infrastructure.

MEXICO TODAY: When oil wealth was paying all the bills, Mexico neglected its agricultural and industrial sectors to concentrate on petroleum production and marketing. Now that oil is no longer king, the country has the difficult and painful job of rebuilding these sectors, cutting government expenditures, taming corruption, and keeping creditors at bay. President Miguel de la Madrid Hurtado, who assumed the presidency in 1982, has struggled with these problems, and has made important progress. But the economy, and society, are still under tremendous economic pressure, and charges of government corruption still abound.

MEXICAN FACTS AND FIGURES: The United Mexican States today is headed by an elected president and a bicameral legislature. It's divided into 31 states, plus the Federal District (Mexico City). The population of about 70 million is 15% white (descendants of the Spaniards); 60% mestizo, or mixed Spanish and Indian blood; and 25% pure Indian (descendants of the Mayas, Aztecs, and other peoples). Although Spanish is the official language, about 50 Indian languages are still spoken, mostly in the Yucatán peninsula and the mountainous region of Oaxaca. Economically, Mexico is not by any means a poor country. Only about a sixth of the economy is in agriculture. Mining, which made the Spanish colonists and their king fabulously rich, is still fairly important. Gold and silver account for some of it, and there are many other important minerals still mined, but the big industry today is oil. Mexico is also well industrialized, manufacturing textiles, food products, everything from tape cassettes to automobiles.

In short, Mexico is well into the 20th century, with all the benefits and problems that contemporary life brings, and although vast sums are spent on education and public welfare (much, much more than is spent on implements of war), a high birth rate, high unemployment, and unequal distribution of wealth show that much remains to be done.

This is the Mexico you'll get to know.

2. The $20-a-Day Way

A trip to Mexico can be the most reasonably priced foreign vacation you'll ever experience if you abide by the philosophy and recommendations of this book. As a reader of this book you'll have a better chance to discover the truly fascinating Mexico, for many times the guests at the posh hotels are tempted to stay there and not risk discomfort or inconvenience, while the readers of *Mexico on $20 a Day* will have at their fingertips the information needed to get the basics of travel—hotels, meals, and transportation—out of the way as quickly and as cheaply as possible so they can plunge into the Mexico of the Mexicans. In fact, it's amazing how much of a country you can miss by going through it luxury class. The luxurious hotel room, the taxi or chauffeur-driven car, the plush restaurant with "local and international cuisine" all cater to an imaginary wealthy stereotype who, it seems, is always pleased to live in the midst of smiling and subservient staff, bland meals, canned music, and picturesque sights kept at a respectful distance—all at a greatly padded price. Think of the difference if you can say "Buēnos días!" to the cheerful señora who runs your pension, happy in her work and confident of her position in society; eat in local restaurants where the cuisine is designed to please residents of the neighborhood, and presents the outsider with new delights (and some perils!); rub shoulders with the real Mexican, the man in the street, in the subway, on buses, or in colectivos (shared taxis). What you give up is standardization: rooms are different in each hotel and pension, whereas a luxury hotel chain will give you almost exactly the same room, in Baghdad or Bombay. The staff in a small hotel can be super-friendly or indifferent, whereas in the big places they are always polite but distant.

Our $20-a-Day budget is intended to cover only the expenses of room and three meals each day. Thus I will recommend hotels where you will be able to stay for about $10 per person per night, and restaurants in which it will be possible to have three meals for the other $10: breakfast for about $2.50, lunch (the largest meal in the Mexican's day) for about $4.50, and supper for about $3. (Actually, you can easily get along well nowadays on $15 a day per person.) Spend a few dollars more, and you can live a good deal more comfortably—even luxuriously—for $25 a day.

In fact, your vacation to Mexico may cost you well over $20 a day, but that will be your choice, and will be much affected by your personal preferences: if you like air travel, expect to pay a good deal more; if you don't mind buses (and in Mexico they are the easiest and cheapest way to go), your extra cost for transportation will be minimal. Add a few dollars a day for entertainment if you're a nightclub fan, but add only a quarter or two if you are satisfied with going to museums and exhibitions. Of course there are those who want to do Mexico as cheaply as possible and will gladly pass up comforts rather than part with dollars, so under my "Starvation Budget" heading I'll give some tips on how to do it as cheaply as possible—as low as $5 a day—short of sleeping in cornfields, bumming rides, and singing for supper. Therefore the hotels generally recommended in this book will be clean, respectable places, sometimes with some comforts and conveniences such as multilingual staff, swimming pools, or bathrooms in the rooms, suitable for any traveler except the luxury-minded. You will not find these hotels standardized into sterility, as are many luxury places; each will have its own special treats—and surprises—and as some readers may like certain features more than others, descriptions of each establishment are given. Let's say you want a room with a view over the lovely plaza in the center of Querétaro. Then you must next consider, as you look over the hotel descriptions and also when you look at the hotel itself, how seriously you might be bothered by motorcycles buzzing under your window. If motor noise is your weak point, it'd be best to look into someplace on a side street, perhaps with rooms around an inner court; or even a motel on the outskirts of town, which may not have a view and which may be slightly more expensive but will be easier on your nerves.

There will be times when you'd like to get away from it all, when the buses and motorcycles (most of which have no mufflers in order to save gas) so assault your ears and nose that the scented, soundproof, air-conditioned, and be-Muzak'ed halls of a luxury hotel seem like a piece of heaven, or when the 25¢ "calculation error" on your budget lunch bill makes you wish the proprietor would simply charge an extortionate rate at the start (as luxury places do) and get it over with. These are the daily fatigues that go with strenuous travel in a strange land, and for those times when you want to escape to cushioned comfort I have included hotel and restaurant choices under the heading "The Big Splurge." American-style eateries are also noted now and then so you may, if you wish, give your stomach a respite from unfamiliar food. But the reason you bought this book is so that you can live closer to things authentically Mexican, and have a memorable trip at a reasonable price, so travel the way I do.

MONEY-SAVING TIPS, OR HOW TO STRETCH YOUR $$$: What you spend on your trip to Mexico depends a lot on how you operate. Here, first, are some tips to save you money on hotel bills.

Saving on Hotels

At the outset, remember that rooms with bath or air conditioning are always more expensive. Don't deny yourself these comforts if you want them, but ask yourself "Do I really want/need it today?" Second, in many hotels rooms in the back of the hotel with no view (except of an airshaft) are cheaper *and quieter* than rooms with a view of the street. How much time will you be spending looking out your hotel window at the street? Third, two people sharing a room always pay less than two people in single rooms, and two people sharing a double bed (called a *cama matrimonial* in Mexico) pay least of all. When the desk clerk asks "How many beds?" don't necessarily answer "Two." Or if the clerk shows you a room with two beds, ask if he has one with a double bed. Fourth, often the price the desk clerk quotes you for a room *won't* be the cheapest room he has available, but rather what he thinks to be the most desirable—which is bound to be more expensive. Ask to see a cheaper room (*"Quiero ver un cuarto mas barato, por favor"*)—it can't hurt, and if the cheap room turns out to be a dungeon you can always take the more expensive room.

Saving on Food

More money can be saved by how you eat than on any other expense of your trip, but I rush to add that eating well is one of the most important things you can do to make your trip enjoyable. Wholesome food—good bread, milk, meat, fish, fresh vegetables, and fruit—is always a bargain, because you get your money's worth in nutrition. If a soft drink costs 30¢ and an equal amount of milk or fruit juice costs 35¢, get in the habit of drinking the milk or juice—it'll keep you going longer. Avoid snacky "junk" foods, a luxury item in Mexico, and eat nuts or fruit instead. This pays off not only in having to eat less, but also in getting sick less, as good nutrition is one of the keys to avoiding or mitigating the dread "Turista" diarrhea (see below under "Health").

Now some specifics on eating cheaply. **Breakfast:** Breakfast is the most overpriced meal in the world for travelers, and in Mexico it is no exception. Big-breakfast eaters should not refrain from buying the bacon and eggs they want, but if you can exist until lunchtime on a light breakfast, consider this. In most Mexican cities you can drop by a *panadería or pastelería* (bakery or pastry shop) and get delicious rolls and sweet rolls or pastry for incredibly cheap prices, and a few of these, plus perhaps a glass of milk or a piece of cheese (available in the markets), can keep you going until you have your big lunch at noon. Also, a $5 immersion coil, plus a heat-resistant plastic cup, a jar of instant coffee or a tea bag, and some powdered milk will enable you to make your own coffee or tea in the morning at a cost of about 16¢ a cup. Coffee in Mexico normally costs 25¢ to 40¢ a cup. The electrical current throughout Mexico is 110-volt and the plugs and sockets are American style. Some of my more fanatic money-saving readers pack small, lightweight aluminum percolators in their bags, with which they can brew fresh coffee or even make soup. Having a coil or a hot pot is also very handy if you come down with diarrhea and can only stomach tea, herb tea (chamomile tea is a specific for queasy stomach), or bouillon. Coffee (ground and instant), tea bags, powdered milk *(leche en polvo)*, and bouillon cubes are all readily available in Mexico, and I've indicated the whereabouts of pastry shops in most cities covered in this book.

Lunch: Now for lunch. Your best value by far will be to eat a big meal at noon, and if you're not inflexible it shouldn't be too hard to fit in the rest of the day around this meal rather than vice-versa. For instance, most parts of Mexico that you will be visiting will be warm or hot during most of the day, so plan to be up early and out to the things you want to see early in the morning after a light breakfast. Then, after some exercise, relax and collect your thoughts over a largish lunch at about one o'clock, amble back to your hotel for a nap (or escape to a shady place if your hotel's a good distance away), and take it easy during the hottest part of the day. Then, rested and replenished, set out again in the late afternoon and evening for more exploration, and have a light supper before returning to your hotel. This is what Mexicans invariably do, and so most restaurants offer a *comida corrida,* or special lunch of several courses at a special, low price, served between about 1 and 4 p.m. Usually the meal will be of soup, pasta, a main course, dessert, and coffee, and will cost anywhere from $1 to $4, depending on the class of the restaurant, but it will always be much cheaper than the total for the individual items offered. Often there is some choice of soup and entree. Many of the cheaper restaurants will advertise their comida corrida on blackboards hung by the door, and that will be your only look at a menu; slightly more expensive places will attach a slip to the menu listing the comida and its price. The comida corrida is the biggest meal bargain in Mexico, so you should try to take advantage of it.

Dinner: For dinner you'll want to eat lightly, having eaten heavily at one or two o'clock, and if you can make do on a good bowl of soup and a plate of enchiladas you will need to spend very little. Avoid by all means the long, luxurious dinners so popular in Europe and the U.S., unless you've decided to splurge or are celebrating a special occasion. Such evening meals are not truly Mexican, and are therefore more expensive.

Markets: Some other eating tips: Every town in Mexico has a market, the ones in the cities being fabulous affairs, often modern, in which the full range of local produce, cheese, eggs, bread, etc., is for sale. I've bought pineapples for as little as 20¢, bananas for a song. The location of the market (indicated by "M" or "Market" on my city maps) is given for most towns covered in this book; if in doubt, ask for the *mercado*. Avoid milk and cream in open containers. In most places you should be able to find modern factory-packaged milk; if not, the powdered whole milk sold everywhere is almost as good, much more delicious than the powdered skim milk available at home.

THE WAGES OF CHANGE: On the subject of money, it might be good to put in a word about prices and inflation. Back in the halcyon days (several decades ago) when prices throughout the world changed at a rate of about 3% a year, a traveler could take dad's copy of a good travel book abroad and make a mental adjustment for a small price rise. But recently the inflation rate for Mexico has been in the neighborhood of 100% per annum; some businesses (hotels and restaurants included) will hold off as long as they can, perhaps two years, and then raise prices by even more than this factor to compensate for *future* inflation! Every effort is made to provide the most accurate and up-to-date information in this book, even to the point of predicting price increases that I feel are on the way and that will arrive before the book reaches the reader's hands; but changes are inevitable and uncontrollable with inflation. Keep in mind when you look at price lists that even though the peso price may have risen over that given in the book, the dollar price will still be fairly accurate, and *the establishments recommended will still be the best value for the money.*

Speaking of currency, don't forget that the dollar sign ($) is used by Mexicans and some other Latin Americans to denote their own national currencies, and thus a Mexican menu will have "$300" for a glass of orange juice and mean 300 pesos. To avoid confusion I will use the dollar sign in this book *only* to denote U.S. currency. Peso prices will be listed merely with figures or with the qualifying word "pesos."

3. Preparing for Your Trip

Preparation means information—you must know what you're preparing for. Below are some hints on how to get ready, so you can avoid unpleasant surprises when you arrive. Keep in mind the entire time you're reading this book that there is a wealth of classified information at your fingertips in Chapter XVII, "Latin Listings." When you have a question, look there first.

WHERE SHOULD I GO? People often ask me, "Where should I go in Mexico? It's so big, and I've heard so much about it, but what places are really worth visiting?" Here's what I tell them:

You have to travel as much as 1,000 miles south of the border to find the "real" Mexico of your dreams: gorgeous colonial mountain towns, bustling modern cities, sleek coastal resorts. Northern Mexico is arid but rich, hard-working, vast, and heavily influenced by its great neighbor to the north.

The Mexico of the travel brochures begins south of the Tropic of Cancer. Of the resorts, Puerto Vallarta is without doubt my favorite. Of the major cities, Guadalajara is nice, but is a pale second to the great capital, Mexico City, which you definitely should see. The silver mining towns of the northern Valley of Mexico are the undiscovered treasures of Mexican tourism: Guanajuato is a spellbinding place, San Miguel de Allende is charming, Querétaro and

San Luis Potosí clean and pleasant, with a wealth of colonial architecture. Zacatecas, at the border of the desert, has a rugged charm enhanced by great palaces and churches from centuries ago.

Between Mexico City and Guadalajara, Pátzcuaro is the town to visit, as close to an authentic, remote Spanish mountain town as you'll find north of Central America.

South of Mexico City, Taxco is a must-see, Oaxaca too. You can spend a day in Veracruz pleasantly enough if you're passing through. Puerto Escondido and Puerto Angel, south of Oaxaca on the Pacific Coast, are the relatively undiscovered coastal hideaways which, in a decade, will be the new Acapulco and Puerto Vallarta. See them before it's too late.

East of the Isthmus of Tehuantepec, everybody wants to see San Cristóbal de las Casas. It's cool up there in the mountains, the wild scenery is beautiful, and the Indians largely retain their traditional way of life.

And then there's Yucatán. For my money, Yucatán—along with the Valley of Mexico—represents the most fascinating area to visit. Perfect beaches, ancient ruins, interesting local cuisine, friendly people—Yucatán has it all. You must see Palenque (near Villahermosa), Mérida, Uxmal, and Chichén-Itzá. Cancún is for the charter-group sun-seekers, although you might try out the beaches for a day or two. Much more interesting resorts, in my way of thinking, are Isla Mujeres and Cozumel.

How long will it take? You could see a lot in two weeks, based in Mexico City or Mérida, traveling by bus. To see all of these favorite places you'd need a month at least, for Mexico is a huge and mountainous place, and the twisty roads take much longer to negotiate than do Interstate highways. If you can afford the occasional airplane ride, you'll be able to fit more sightseeing into your vacation.

TRAVELING WITH CHILDREN: With Mexico's high birth rate, small children make up a large part of the population. The Mexican government has big programs to promote children's well-being. It even develops such unique children's delights as Acapulco's Centro Internacional de Convivencia Infantil (International Center for Children's Fellowship). So your child will feel very welcome in Mexico.

As for more practical matters, you should check with your doctor at home, and get advice on medicines to combat diarrhea, etc. Bring a supply, just to be sure. If your child is an infant, you'll be happy to know that disposable diapers are made and sold in Mexico (one popular brand is Kleen Bebé). The price is about the same as at home, though the quality is not quite so high. Also, Gerber's baby foods are on sale in many stores. In addition to the foods you're used to, you'll see "exotic" ones such as mango and papaya. Dry cereals, powdered formulas, baby bottles, purified water—they're all available easily in the larger cities.

The one problem you may encounter is with cribs. Except for the largest and most luxurious hotels, few Mexican hotels will have cribs, so you should be prepared to manage some other way.

A NEWSLETTER: Lloyd Wilkins, a keen and witty observer of the Mexican scene, publishes a bimonthly newsletter called *AIM (Adventures in Mexico)*, directed at those who may be planning to retire south of the border. But the contents prove useful—and entertaining—to just about anyone planning more than a short trip to Mexico. The current price for a year's subscription is U.S.

$12 ($14 Canadian); send a check or money order to AIM, Apdo. 31-70, Gua-dalajara, Jalisco, México 45050.

BOOKS: "What you take away from a country depends on what you bring," so you may want to do some reading before you go. There are endless numbers of books written on the history, culture, and archeology of Mexico and Central America. I have listed those that I especially enjoyed or those that have been recommended by readers.

History: *A Short History of Mexico* by J. Patrick McHenry (Doubleday), a concise historical account. *The Conquest of New Spain* by Bernal Díaz (Penguin), the famous story of the Mexican conquest written by Cortés's lieutenant. *The Crown of Mexico* by Joan Haslip, a biography of Maximilian and Carlotta that reads like a novel. *Sons of the Shaking Earth* (University of Chicago Press) by Eric Wolf, the best single-volume introduction to Mexican history and culture I know of. Maurice Collis's *Cortés and Montezuma* (New York: Avon Books, 1954, 1978) is as exciting as an adventure novel—even more so—because of the real-life drama experienced by its two main characters.

Culture: *Five Families* (Basic Books) and *Children of Sanchez* (Random House) by Oscar Lewis, is a sociological study written in the late 1950s of a typical Mexican family (somewhat outdated but still a very valuable source of information to understand the Mexican culture). *Mexican and Central American Mythology* by Irene Nicholson (Paul Hamlyn, 1973). *A Guide to Tequila, Mescal and Pulque* by Virginia B. de Barrios (Minutiae Mexicana), a very interesting account of the agave agriculture that includes the history and culture surrounding this industry. Three more specialized works devoted to art are: *My Art, My Life* by Diego Rivera; *Mexican Muralists* by Alma Reed; *Mexico South* by Miguel Covarrubias.

Archeology: *The Ancient Sun Kingdoms of the Americas* by Victor Wolfgang Von Hagen (Paladin), an easy-to-read, concise account of Mexican cultures from the Maya to the Aztec—recommended! A must for any traveler visiting the Maya ruins is *The Maya* by Michael Coe (Praeger); it is easy to understand and will help the archeology buff to relate art and architecture with the different periods of Maya life. *National Geographic* subscribers who save back copies should look through the last ten years issues for the interesting articles on the Maya, as well as the society's book, *Discovering Man's Past in the Americas*. C. Bruce Hunter's *A Guide to Ancient Maya Ruins* (University of Oklahoma Press) covers most of the major Maya sites in Mexico and Central America. Last, a book that tells the story of the Indians' "painted books" is *The Mexican Codices and Their Extraordinary History* by Maria Sten (Ediciones Lara).

On Yucatán: Anyone heading for Yucatán should first read the wonderfully entertaining accounts of travel in that region by the 19th-century Yucatán traveler, New York lawyer, and amateur archeologist John L. Stephens. His books, *Incidents of Travel in Central America, Chiapas and Yucatan,* and also the account of his second trip, *Incidents of Travel in Yucatan,* have been reprinted by Dover Publications. Stephens's adventures are part of Dover's fascinating series of reprints on Mayan archeology, history, and culture, which are available at bookstores or from Dover by mail at 31 E. 2nd St., Mineola, NY 11501-3582.

The series also includes Friar Diego de Landa's *Yucatan Before and After the Conquest,* written in the 1560s. Friar Diego's account is a detailed description of Maya daily life, much of which has remained the same from his time until today. Dover even has a book on learning to read Maya hieroglyphs.

LEGAL DOCUMENTS: You'll need a Mexican Tourist Card, issued free, available at the border, at a Mexican consulate, or at any of the Mexican tourist offices listed below. Those flying to Mexico can ask their travel agent or airline to get them a Tourist Card; most agents will do so at no extra charge.

The Tourist Card is more important than a passport in Mexico, so hold onto it carefully—if you lose it, you may not be able to leave the country until you can replace it, and that bureaucratic hassle takes several days or a week at least.

READERS' TIP—VISAS: "For non-U.S. citizens going to Mexico, we suggest getting a visa even if your local consulate considers a tourist card sufficient. Immigration officials at Mexican airports had different rules for admitting my Austrian wife. Border crossings by land (El Paso / Cd. Juárez, etc.) are, by contrast, quick and easy in both directions" (Senta and Charles Hoge, Santa Fe, N.Mex.).

Important Note: A Mexican Tourist Card can be issued for up to 180 days, and although your stay south of the border will doubtless be less than that, you should get the card for the maximum time, just in case. When the official who fills out your card asks you how long you intend to stay, say "six months," or at least *twice* as long as you really plan to be there. Who knows? You may find the perfect stretch of beach and not want to leave, or you may have to stay for some reason, and you'll save yourself *a lot* of hassle if you don't have to renew your papers. This hint is especially important for people who take cars into Mexico.

Mexican government tourist offices abroad include those in the following cities in the United States and Canada:

Chicago: Two Illinois Center, 233 N. Michigan Ave., Suite 1413, Chicago IL 60601 (tel. 312/565-2785).
Houston: 2707 N. Loop West, Suite 450, Houston TX 77008 (tel. 713/880-5153).
Los Angeles: 10100 Santa Monica Blvd., Suite 225, Los Angeles CA 90067 (tel. 213/203-8151).
Montréal: One Place Ville Marie, Suite 2409, Montréal QC H3B 3M9 (tel. 514/871-1052).
Toronto: 181 University Ave., Suite 1112, Toronto ON M5H 3M7 (tel. 416/364-2455).

Offices in Europe are as follows:

Frankfurt: Weisenhuettenplatz 26, 6000 Frankfurt A/Main 1 (tel. 925-3413).
London: 7 Cork St., London W1X 1PB (tel. 734-1058 or 734-1059).
Madrid: Calle de Velázquez 126, Madrid 6 (tel. 261-3520).
Paris: 34 Av. George V, Paris 75008 (tel. 720-6907 or 720-6911).
Rome: Via Berberini 3, 00187 Roma (tel. 474-2986).

To get your Tourist Card, be sure to bring along a birth certificate, passport, or naturalization papers when you apply, and when you travel in Mexico. You'll also need this proof of citizenship to reenter the U.S. or Canada. Minors under the age of 18 when traveling alone must have a notarized statement of parental consent *signed by both parents* before they can get a permit. One parent entering Mexico with a minor child must have written consent from the other parent. Check with the nearest Mexican tourist office for details.

Special Note for Car Drivers: Those who have visited Mexico before by car know that a car driver is issued a Temporary Importation Permit for his car. It used to be that this document was issued in addition to the Tourist Card, also required; but sometimes there's a new procedure by which a car driver turns in his Tourist Card as he enters Mexico, and is issued a *single document* that serves as both Tourist Card and Temporary Importation Permit. When you walk out of the border station, don't think you've lost your Tourist Card, or that the officials have forgotten to give it back to you: the one-page document you're carrying does double duty.

RESERVE IN ADVANCE FOR HOLIDAYS: Those planning to be in resort areas like Mazatlán, Acapulco, Puerto Vallarta, Manzanillo, Cozumel, Isla Mujeres, and similar spots should definitely write ahead for hotel reservations on major holidays (Mexican as well as international). Christmas and New Year's are the worst for crowding. If you discover you're up against a holiday when you're almost there, plan to arrive in the resort early in the day—before noon—and see what you can find.

Several readers have written to say that they've encountered difficulties in making reservations by mail, and even by toll-free reservation number: no answer, no record of their request (or deposit check) when they've arrived, and such like. I've experienced the same frustrations. Here's a suggestion: write for reservations in plenty of time, saying in your letter that you'll forward a deposit upon receipt of a confirmation. Or, instead, place a telephone call to the hotel concerned, make the reservation, get the name of the person who takes the reservation, and then send your deposit by registered mail, return receipt requested. Remember that the process can take a good deal of time.

WEATHER, CLOTHING, PACKING: As for your clothing needs, Mexico City is high up, and so you'll need a topcoat in winter and preferably a couple of sweaters. In summer, it gets warm during the day and cool, but not cold, at night. It also rains almost every afternoon or evening between May and October (this is common all over Mexico)—so take a raincoat.

In sea-level areas, there is considerable difference between climates on the Gulf and West Coast. This is particularly true in winter. The tropic latitude zone of the Pacific Coast, bounded on the north by Puerto Vallarta and on the south by Puerto Angel, Oaxaca, furnishes one of the world's most perfect winter climates—dry, balmy, with temperatures ranging from the 80s by day to the 60s at night. (Although geographically within the tropic zone, Mazatlán is excluded from this perfect weather belt. From Puerto Vallarta south you can swim year round; in Mazatlán you'll encounter winter days when dips would appeal only to the hardiest.) But it's an entirely different scene on the gulf. While high mountains shield Pacific beaches from *nortes* (freezing blasts out of Canada via the Texas Panhandle), the gulf enjoys no such immunity. The most disconcerting thing about nortes is that they strike so suddenly. You can be luxuriating on a Veracruz beach, enjoying Montego Bay weather, when all of a sudden you'll notice a slight haze obscuring the sun. That's all the warning you'll get. Within an hour it's like March in New York—gray skies, a boisterous wind, chilly rain whipping your cheeks. In that brief hour the temperature will have dropped as much as 40 degrees. But here's an interesting twist. While nortes hit Veracruz (latitude 19) with vicious intensity, their sting is far less severe in the most northerly Yucatán peninsula. This is because these gales hit Veracruz overland and Mérida over water, the gulf having a warming effect.

So much for winter climate. In summer the difference between West Coast and Gulf Coast temperatures lessens considerably, both areas becoming warm and rainy. Of the two regions the gulf is far rainier, particularly in the states of Tabasco and Campeche.

Look in the Appendix to this book for a handy temperature conversion chart. Bring your own washcloth if you use one regularly—you'll rarely find one in a hotel room. If you plan on visiting archeological sites, a small flashlight will aid you in seeing the interior parts of the ruins.

HEALTH AND MEDICAMENTS: Of course, the very best ways to avoid illness or to mitigate its effects are to make sure that you're in top health and that you *don't overdo it*. Travel, strange foods, upset schedules, overambitious sightseeing tend to take more of your energy than a normal working day, and missed meals provide less of the nutrition you need. Make sure you get three good, wholesome meals a day, get *more* rest than you normally do, don't push yourself if you're not feeling in top form, and you'll be able to fight off the "turista."

How to Prevent Turista

Turista is the name given to the pervasive diarrhea, often accompanied by fever, nausea, and vomiting, that attacks so many travelers to Mexico on their first trip. Doctors, who call it Travelers' Diarrhea, say it's not just one "bug," or factor, but a combination of different food and water, upset schedules, overtiring, and the stresses that accompany travel. I've found that I get it when I'm tired and careless about what I eat and drink. A good high-potency (or "therapeutic") vitamin supplement, and even extra vitamin C, is a help; yogurt is good for a healthy digestion, but it is not available everywhere in Mexico.

The U.S. Public Health Service recommends the following measures for prevention of Travelers' Diarrhea:

Drink only purified water. This means tea, coffee, and other beverages made with boiled water; canned or bottled carbonated beverages, including carbonated water; beer and wine; or water that you yourself have brought to a rolling boil or otherwise purified. To purify water you can add five drops of 2% tincture of iodine to clear water; for cloudy water, strain it through a clean cloth, then add ten drops of 2% tincture of iodine. You can also purify water with tetraglycine hydroperiodide tablets sold under brand names such as Globaline, Potable-Agua, or Coughlan's. Pick them up in a pharmacy or sporting goods store.

Choose food carefully. In general, avoid salads, uncooked vegetables, and unpasteurized milk or milk products (including cheese). Choose food that is freshly cooked and still hot. Peel fruit yourself. Don't eat undercooked meat, fish, or shellfish.

What To Do If You Get It

The Public Health Service does not recommend that you take any medicines as preventatives. All the applicable medicines, including antibiotics, bismuth subsalicylate (as in Pepto-Bismol) and difenoxine (as in Lomotil), can have nasty side-effects if taken for long periods of several weeks. The best way to prevent illness is to take care with food and water, get rest, and don't overdo it.

Should you get sick, there are lots of medicines available in Mexico which can harm more than help. You should talk with your doctor before you go, and ask what medicine he recommends for Travelers' Diarrhea. Ask the doctor's opinions of these treatments:

Bismuth subsalicylate ("Pepto-Bismol"), one ounce of liquid or the equivalent in tablets, every half hour, for four hours (if you have kidney problems, or are allergic to salicylates, this can be dangerous).

Diphenoxylate and loperamide (Lomotil, Imodium), synthetic opiates known as antimotility agents, should not be used if you have a high fever, or blood in the stool, and should not be used longer than two full days.

As for antibiotics, the Public Health Service guidelines are these: if there are three or more loose stools in an eight-hour period, especially with other symptoms such as nausea, vomiting, abdominal cramps and fever, it might be time to go to a doctor and get an antibiotic. The ones usually prescribed, both available in Mexico if you haven't brought a supply, are doxycycline (100 mg twice daily); or trimethoprim (160 mg) / sulfamethoxazole (800 mg), known as TMP/SMX and sold in Mexico as Bactrim F (Roche), taken twice daily.

If someone recommends any other drug, be suspicious and get another opinion. These antibiotics are strong medicine, they can have significant and even dangerous side-effects, which is why you should consult with a doctor before taking them. Remember that what you have may not be Travelers' Diarrhea at all, and that such an antibiotic might not be the appropriate treatment. Also, antibiotics can cause reactions such as painful rashes when the skin is exposed to sunlight. In sunny Mexico, the last thing you want is hands that can't be exposed to the sun.

How To Get Well

Should you come down with "turista," the first thing to do is go to bed, stay there, and don't move on until it runs its course. Traveling with the illness only makes it last longer, whereas you can be over it in a day or so if you take it easy. Drink lots of liquids: tea without milk or sugar, or the Mexican *té de manzanilla* (chamomile tea), is best. Eat only *pan tostada* (dry toast rusks), sold in grocery stores and *panaderías* (bakeries). Keep to this diet for at least 24 hours, and you'll be well over the worst of it. If you fool yourself into thinking that a plate of enchiladas can't hurt, you'll be back at square one as far as the turista is concerned.

The Public Health Service advises that you be especially careful to replace fluids and electrolytes (potassium, sodium, etc.) during a bout of diarrhea. Do this by drinking glasses of fruit juice (high in potassium) with honey and a pinch of salt added; and also a glass of pure water with 1/4 teaspoon of sodium bicarbonate (baking soda) added.

Altitude Sickness

Also called Acute Mountain Sickness, this ailment results from the relative lack of oxygen and decrease in barometric pressure which come from being at high altitudes (5,000 feet / 1,500 meters, or more). Mexico City is at an altitude of more than 7,000 feet, as are a number of other central Mexican cities, so it's very possible you'll find yourself experiencing the discomfort of altitude sickness. Symptoms include shortness of breath, fatigue, headache, even nausea.

The way to avoid altitude sickness is to take it easy for the first few days after you arrive at high altitude. Drink extra fluids; but avoid alcoholic beverages, which not only tend to dehydrate you, but also are more potent in a low-oxygen environment. If you have any heart or lung problems, talk to your doctor before going above 8,000 feet.

Bugs and Bites

Another thing you should consider is the bugs and bites. Mosquitoes and gnats are quite prevalent along the coast and in the lowlands of Yucatán. Insect repellent *(rapellante contra insectos)* is a must, and it's not always available in Mexico. Also, those sensitive to bites should pick up some antihistamine cream from a drugstore at home ("Di-Delamine" is available without a prescription). Rubbed on a fresh mosquito bite, the cream keeps down the swelling and reduces the itch. In Mexico, ask for "Camfo-Fenicol" (Camphophenique), a second-best remedy.

Most readers won't ever see a scorpion, but they are found in most parts of Mexico. Stings can be painful to dangerous (if you're particularly sensitive to the venom), and it's best to go to a doctor if you get stung.

More Serious Diseases

Mexico has a tropical climate, and it has tropical diseases. You don't have to worry about these too much if your journey is for less than three months, and if you stay to the normal tourist routes (that is, you don't head out into the boondocks to camp with the locals for a week).

You can also protect yourself by taking some simple precautions. Besides being careful about what you eat and drink, do not go swimming in polluted waters. This includes any stagnant water such as in ponds, slow-moving rivers, and Yucatecan cenotes. Avoid mosquitoes because they carry malaria, dengue fever, and other serious illnesses. Cover up, avoid going out when mosquitoes are active, use repellant, sleep under mosquito netting if you camp, and stay away from places that seem to have a lot of mosquitoes. The most dangerous areas seem to be on Mexico's west coast, away from the big resorts (which are relatively safe).

To prevent against contracting malaria, you must get a prescription for antimalarial drugs, and you must begin taking them *six weeks before* you enter a malarial area. You must also continue to take them for a certain amount of time after you leave the malarial area. Talk to your doctor about this.

It's a good idea to be inoculated against tetanus, typhoid, and diptheria, but *this does not guarantee you won't get the disease.* I heard about a case of typhoid contracted by a person who had been inoculated against it.

The following list of diseases should not alarm you, as their incidence is rare among tourists. But if you become ill with something more virulent than Travelers' Diarrhea, I want you to have this information ready at hand:

Dengue Fever: It's transmitted by mosquitoes, and comes on fast with high fever, severe headache, joint and muscle pain. Three or four days after the onset of the disease, there's a skin rash. Highest risk is during July, August, and September. Risk for normal tourists is low, but keep away from mosquitoes all the same.

Dysentery: Caused by contaminated food or water, either amebic or bacillary in form, it is somewhat like Travelers' Diarrhea, but more severe. Risk for tourists is low.

Hepatitis, Viral: This virus is spread through contaminated food and water (often in rural areas), and through intimate contact with infected persons. Risk for tourists is normally low, but if, say, you wander into the bush and have sex with a local, risk is high.

Malaria: In this disease spread by mosquito bites, symptoms are headache, malaise, fever, chills, sweats, anemia, and jaundice. Mexico does not have chloroquine-resistant malaria strains. Weekly prophylaxis with chloroquine can help prevent the disease, but even taking the drug it is possible to contract the illness. Malaria can be effectively treated if treatment begins soon after the disease is contracted.

Rabies: This is a virus almost always passed by bites from infected animals, occasionally through broken skin or the mucous membranes (as from breathing rabid-bat-contaminated air in a cave). If you are bitten by an animal, wash the wound at once with large amounts of soap and water—this is important! Retain the animal, alive if possible, for rabies quarantine. Contact local health authorities to get rabies immunization. This is essential, as rabies is a potentially fatal disease which can be cured by prompt treatment.

Schistosomiasis: This is a parasitic worm, passed by a fresh-water snail larva which can penetrate unbroken human skin. You get it by wading or swimming in fresh water where the snails are, such as in stagnant pools, streams, or cenotes. Two or three weeks after exposure, there's fever, lack of appetite, weight loss, abdominal pain, weakness, headaches, joint and muscle pain, diarrhea, nausea, and coughing. Six to eight weeks after infection, the microscopic snail eggs can be found in the stools. Once diagnosed (after a very unpleasant month or two), treatment is fast, safe, effective, and cheap. If you think you've accidentally been exposed to schistosomiasis-infected water, rub yourself vigorously with a towel, and/or spread rubbing alcohol on the exposed skin.

Typhoid Fever: You can protect yourself by having a typhoid vaccination (or booster, as needed), but protection is not total. You can still get this disease from contaminated food and water. Symptoms are like those for Travelers' Diarrhea, but much worse. If you get typhoid fever, you'll need close attention by a doctor, perhaps hospitalization for a short period. This is a very serious disease, but it can be cured efficiently if caught early.

Typhus Fever: Risk is very low. If you go to a mountain town and get lice, you can get typhus. Tetracycline or chloramphenicol cures it.

4. About This Book

THE FUTURE OF THIS BOOK: *Mexico on $20 a Day* has become a clearinghouse for the low-cost hotel and restaurant "finds" discovered by its readers. If you have come across any particularly appealing hotel, restaurant, store, beach, you-name-it, don't keep it to yourself. Send your find to Tom Brosnahan, c/o Frommer Books, Prentice Hall Press, One Gulf + Western Plaza, New York, NY 10023.

By the way, I *personally* read every single letter sent in, although it is sometimes impossible to answer every letter. Be assured: I'm listening!

5. The $25-a-Day Travel Club—How to Save Money on All Your Travels

In this book we'll be looking at how to get your money's worth in Mexico, but there is a "device" for saving money and determining value on *all* your trips. It's the popular, international $25-a-Day Travel Club, now in its 24th successful year of operation. The Club was formed at the urging of numerous readers of the $$$-a-Day and Dollarwise Guides, who felt that such an organization could provide continuing travel information and a sense of community to value-minded travelers in all parts of the world. And so it does!

In keeping with the budget concept, the annual membership fee is low and is immediately exceeded by the value of your benefits. Upon receipt of $18 (U.S. residents), or $20 U.S. by check drawn on a U.S. bank or via international postal money order in U.S. funds (Canadian, Mexican, and other foreign residents) to cover one year's membership, we will send all new members the following items.

(1) *Any two* of the following books

Please designate in your letter which two you wish to receive:

Europe on $25 a Day
Australia on $25 a Day
England on $35 a Day
Eastern Europe on $25 a Day
Greece including Istanbul and Turkey's Aegean Coast on $25 a Day

Hawaii on $45 a Day
India on $15 & $25 a Day
Ireland on $35 a Day
Israel on $30 & $35 a Day
Mexico on $20 a Day (plus Belize and Guatemala)
New York on $45 a Day
New Zealand on $35 a Day
Scandinavia on $40 a Day
Scotland and Wales on $35 a Day
South America on $25 a Day
Spain and Morocco (plus the Canary Is.) on $35 a Day
Turkey on $25 a Day (avail. May '87)
Washington, D.C., on $40 a Day

Dollarwise Guide to Austria and Hungary
Dollarwise Guide to Benelux (Belgium, the Netherlands, and
Luxembourg) (avail. June '87)
Dollarwise Guide to Bermuda and The Bahamas
Dollarwise Guide to Canada
Dollarwise Guide to the Caribbean
Dollarwise Guide to Egypt
Dollarwise Guide to England and Scotland
Dollarwise Guide to France
Dollarwise Guide to Germany
Dollarwise Guide to Italy
Dollarwise Guide to Japan and Hong Kong
Dollarwise Guide to Portugal, Madeira, and the Azores
Dollarwise Guide to the South Pacific (avail. June '87)
Dollarwise Guide to Switzerland and Liechtenstein
Dollarwise Guide to Alaska (avail. April '87)
Dollarwise Guide to California and Las Vegas
Dollarwise Guide to Florida
Dollarwise Guide to New England
Dollarwise Guide to New York State (avail. May '87)
Dollarwise Guide to the Northwest
Dollarwise Guide to Skiing USA-East
Dollarwise Guide to Skiing USA-West
Dollarwise Guide to the Southeast and New Orleans
Dollarwise Guide to the Southwest
Dollarwise Guide to Texas
(Dollarwise Guides discuss accommodations and facilities in all price
ranges, with emphasis on the medium-priced.)

A Guide for the Disabled Traveler
(A guide to the best destinations for wheelchair travelers and other disabled
vacationers in Europe, the United States, and Canada by an experienced wheelchair traveler. Includes detailed information about accommodations, restaurants, sights, transportation, and their accessibility.)

A Shopper's Guide to Best Buys in England, Scotland, and Wales
(Describes in detail hundreds of places to shop—department stores, factory
outlets, street markets, and craft centers—for great quality British bargains.)

A Shopper's Guide to the Caribbean
(A guide to the best shopping in the islands. Includes full descriptions of what to look for and where to find it.)

Bed & Breakfast—North America
(This guide contains a directory of over 150 organizations that offer bed & breakfast referrals and reservations throughout North America. The scenic attractions, businesses, and major schools and universities near the homes of each are also listed.)

Dollarwise Guide to Cruises
(This complete guide covers all the basics of cruising—ports of call, costs, fly-cruise package bargains, cabin selection booking, embarkation and debarkation and describes in detail over 60 or so ships cruising the waters of Alaska, the Caribbean, Mexico, Hawaii, Panama, Canada, and the United States.)

Dollarwise Guide to Skiing Europe
(Describes top ski resorts in Austria, France, Italy, and Switzerland. Illustrated with maps of each resort area plus full-color trail maps.)

How to Beat the High Cost of Travel
(This practical guide details how to save money on absolutely all travel items—accommodations, transportation, dining, sightseeing, shopping, taxes, and more. Includes special budget information for seniors, students, singles, and families.)

Marilyn Wood's Wonderful Weekends
(This very selective guide covers the best mini-vacation destinations within a 175-mile radius of New York City. It describes special country inns and other accommodations, restaurants, picnic spots, sights, and activities—all the information needed for a two- or three-day stay.)

Motorist's Phrase Book
(A practical phrase book in French, German, and Spanish designed specifically for the English-speaking motorist touring abroad.)

Museums in New York
(A complete guide to all the museums, historic houses, gardens, zoos, and more in the five boroughs. Illustrated with over 200 photographs.)

Swap and Go—Home Exchanging Made Easy
(Two veteran home exchangers explain in detail all the money-saving benefits of a home exchange, and then describe precisely how to do it. Also includes information on home rentals and many tips on low-cost travel.)

The Fast 'n' Easy Phrase Book
(French, German, Spanish, and Italian—all in one convenient, easy-to-use phrase guide.)

The New York Urban Athlete
(The ultimate guide to all the sports facilities in New York City for jocks and novices.)

Travel Diary and Record Book
(A 96-page diary for personal travel notes plus a section for such vital data as passport and traveler's check numbers, itinerary, postcard list, special people and places to visit, and a reference section with temperature and conversion charts, and world maps with distance zones.)

Where to Stay USA
(By the Council on International Educational Exchange, this extraordinary guide is the first to list accommodations in all 50 states that cost anywhere from $3 to $30 per night.)

(2) A one-year subscription to *The Wonderful World of Budget Travel*

This quarterly eight-page tabloid newspaper keeps you up-to-date on fast-breaking developments in low-cost travel in all parts of the world bringing you the latest money-saving information—the kind of information you'd have to pay $25 a year to obtain elsewhere. This consumer-conscious publication also features columns of special interest to readers: **Hospitality Exchange** (members all over the world who are willing to provide hospitality to other members as they pass through their home cities); **Share-a-Trip** (offers and requests from members for travel companions who can share costs and help avoid the burdensome single supplement); and **Readers Ask . . . Readers Reply** (travel questions from members to which other members reply with authentic firsthand information).

(3) A copy of *Arthur Frommer's Guide to New York*

This is a pocket-size guide to hotels, restaurants, nightspots, and sightseeing attractions in all price ranges throughout the New York area.

(4) Your personal membership card

Membership entitles you to purchase through the Club all Arthur Frommer publications for a third to a half off their regular retail prices during the term of your membership.

So why not join this hardy band of international budgeteers and participate in its exchange of travel information and hospitality? Simply send your name and address, together with your annual membership fee of $18 (U.S. residents) or $20 U.S. (Canadian, Mexican, and other foreign residents), by check drawn on a U.S. bank or via international postal money order in U.S. funds to: $25-A-Day Travel Club, Inc., Frommer Books, Gulf + Western Building, One Gulf + Western Plaza, New York, NY 10023. And please remember to specify which *two* of the books in section (1) above you wish to receive in your initial package of members' benefits. Or, if you prefer, use the last page of this book, simply checking off the two books you select and enclosing $18 or $20 in U.S. currency.

Once you are a member, there is no obligation to buy additional books. No books will be mailed to you without your specific order.

Part One

MEXICO

Chapter I

GETTING THERE

1. By Air
2. By Train
3. By Bus
4. By Car

THERE IS NO VAST DIFFERENCE in price among the various means of getting to Mexico from points in the United States and Canada. It used to be that flying was expensive, taking the train or driving was moderate, and going by bus was low in price. Those distinctions are not so distinct anymore.

Airline deregulation has produced a bumper crop of bargain airfares to various points. Mexico's economic crisis has kept transportation costs within the country especially low. You may discover that the cheapest way to go is by charter flight, or by scheduled airline to the border at a bargain fare, switching to a Mexican airline once you're in the country. Today there are many choices.

In the sections that follow, you'll find these alternative methods of transportation discussed separately and in greater detail. This information is meant to serve as a helpful guide, not as a timetable. Let me emphasize that it is important to check schedules *every* time you plan to travel. They change often and without notice.

1. By Air

TO MEXICO: Air fares to Mexico are an indisputable bargain. Many airlines operate direct or nonstop flights to points in Mexico from Chicago, Dallas / Fort Worth, Denver, Houston, Los Angeles, Miami, New Orleans, New York, Philadelphia, San Antonio, San Francisco, Seattle, Toronto, and Tucson. Excursion and package plans proliferate, getting cheaper and cheaper as the Mexican peso continues its inexorable fall in value.

For information on saving money in every aspect of travel, but especially air fares and tours, you might want to pick up a copy of *How to Beat the High Cost of Travel* (New York: Frommer/Pasmantier). If you can add to the considerable wealth of time- and money-saving information already contained in that book, the publisher will send you a free copy of the next edition.

The Mexican national carriers, AeroMéxico and Mexicana, are both top-flight operations with high standards. Of the two, Mexicana is thought by many to have the edge in service. These two companies are marketing their destinations very aggressively, at very good prices for you. A travel agent will be able to give you all the latest details, prices, and schedules, at no cost to you.

Here are a few sample fares to give you some idea of what it may cost to fly to Mexico City. These excursion fares are round trip, with some restrictions on when you can fly, how long you can stay, and how far in advance you must buy your ticket:

Air Fares Between Mexico City and	
Atlanta	$412
Chicago	$402 to $437
Dallas	$277 to $342
Denver	$449
Detroit	$425
Houston	$175
Kansas City	$345
London (U.K.)	$1357 to $1500
Los Angeles	$325 to $369
Miami	$260 to $300
Minneapolis	$419 to 439
New York	$400 to $425
Philadelphia	$468 to $488
St. Louis	$300
San Antonio	$221 to $300
San Francisco	$409 to $439
Seattle	$459 to $499
Toronto	$515
Tucson	$331

Important Note

Mexico charges an airport tax on international departures. When it comes time to leave the country, you'll need about U.S. $10 *in cash pesos* to get out of the country, so don't spend every last centavo until you have your boarding pass and have paid the tax.

TO MEXICO CITY FROM THE BORDER:

In addition to the flights to Mexico City from U.S. cities, there are flights from border cities on the Mexican side by Mexican airlines. Many people, particularly those living in the southern and western parts of the United States, find it convenient to take a bus or to drive to border towns, cross the border into Mexico, and then fly to the capital from there. This can be a considerable money-saver, because domestic Mexican air fares may be lower than their U.S. counterparts.

For instance, a regular, one-way flight from Los Angeles or San Diego to Mexico City is quoted in the Mexicana schedule as costing $230. But if you go across the border and get a flight from Tijuana, the price in pesos is equivalent to less than $90! Similarly, a regular one-way ticket from San Antonio, Texas, to Mexico City costs $130 to $162, but if you can just get across the border to Nuevo Laredo, three hours by road from San Antonio, the price goes down to $76. Here are a few fares (in U.S. dollars) from northern Mexican cities (subject to change, of course):

Air Fares Between Mexico City and

City	One way	Excursion
Ciudad Juárez	$85	—
Guaymas	$80	—
Hermosillo	$82	$147
Mexicali	$87	$154
Monterrey	$40	—
Nuevo Laredo	$56	$98
Tijuana	$90	$165

You don't have to be approaching Mexico from border points to take advantage of cheap internal Mexican airfares. For instance, if you were to buy a regular one-way ticket from Miami to Mexico City, the cost would be $200. But if you flew from Miami to Mérida, and then Mérida to Mexico City, the total cost would be $110 + $60 =$170 and you got a stopover in Mérida!

Remember that Mexican domestic flights are charged in pesos, so your savings (in terms of U.S. dollars) will depend to some extent on the exchange rate. If the airlines have not changed fares in several months, and the peso has been devaluing all that time, you will get fantastic bargains. But if you fly just after a fare revision takes effect, your savings will be less—but still considerable.

You should also know that you can benefit from Mexican domestic excursion fares and packages. Why not? If you get a cheap excursion from Miami to Cancún and back, look into buying a Mexican cheap excursion from Cancún to, say, Mexico City. All this information should be available from a good travel agent.

2. By Train

TO MEXICO: What condition are you in when you start your vacation? If you've been under a great deal of pressure or stress, consider this: you can make a phone call and get a reservation on a train departing from a nearby major city; and if you're on a main line you might be able to climb into a sleeping car and into your own little compartment, and for several days do nothing but unwind, look at the scenery, and every now and then amble on down to the dining car or bar for sustenance. Personally, I think it's a piece of heaven, not claustrophobic like the bus, not hectic like the plane, not tiresome like a car. But it is not cheap. To get a sleeper (called in the trade a "roomette"), you will have to travel first class and pay a supplement—but the point is you're buying a piece of limbo so you can get it together and begin your vacation in the right frame of mind. Should you want some adventure on the way, you may be eligible for stopovers at no extra charge (ask about the requirements when you buy your ticket). In fact, several New York-Los Angeles express trains spend part of a day and a night in New Orleans, and if you have a sleeper the car becomes your hotel at no extra charge. You can buy a through ticket to Mexico City (see below for train travel in Mexico), or you can get off at a border town, cross the border, and take a bus or plane to Mexico City. This sort of luxury train travel is similar in price to air fare, and remember that you have the cost of meals to consider.

Call Amtrak (in the white pages of your phone book) toll free for fares, information, and reservations.

IN MEXICO: Train travel is a matter of economics or personal preference; for although it is safer and also cheaper than going by bus (in some cases *half* the very reasonable bus fare), it is slower and schedules are liable to be a bit more inconvenient. I would not recommend train travel east of the Isthmus of Tehuantepec (that is, into Yucatán or Chiapas), or traveling *segunda* (second class) anywhere as it is usually hot, overcrowded, dingy, and generally unpleasant. *Primera* (first class) can be the same way unless you are sure to ask for *primera especial:* that is, a first-class reserved seat that you buy a day or so in advance if possible. In primera especial there is rarely the crowding and disorder of other classes. The top-of-the-line accommodations on trains, cheaper than flying but more expensive than the bus, are Pullman compartments for overnight travel.

Sleeping cars are called *coche dormitorio,* and have several different types of accommodation. Cheapest is the upper berth (*cama alta),* next is the lower berth (*cama baja),* then a private compartment for one or two persons (*camarín),* and finally, larger, more deluxe compartments for two, three, or four (*alcoba* and *gabinete).* You must make sure in advance that the specific train you plan to take hauls sleeping cars on the date you want to take it. You should reserve your accommodations a day or more in advance if you can. You must have a first-class sleeping-car ticket (*primera coche), plus* you must have a ticket for the sleeping accommodations you desire.

More detailed information on trains from the border is given in Chapter II, "Heading South Overland." From Nuevo Laredo, it's a 25-hour, 735-mile ride to Mexico City. Other border towns are farther from the capital, though. The trip from Ciudad Juárez, across from El Paso, takes over 35 hours to Mexico City. Buy your ticket at least two hours in advance. There is a daily train from Matamoros, across from Brownsville, Texas, to Monterrey. This trip takes eight hours and then a change of trains is made. There is an overnight (6 p.m. to 9 a.m.) sleeper train daily between Monterrey and Mexico City.

In addition to the Mexican National Railways (Ferrocarriles Nacionales de México), there's the Pacific Railroad Company (Ferrocarriles del Pacífico), which operates daily service between the border and Guadalajara. From Nogales, the trip takes 26 or 36 hours, depending on which train you take. From Mexicali, the fast train takes 30 hours to Guadalajara, 45 to Mexico City, and is several hours faster on the northbound run. It leaves Mexicali around noon daily, connecting later with the train from Nogales.

Information, Tickets, Schedules, Stations

If you plan to travel by train into Mexico from one of the border towns, it would be advisable to check the schedules first.

The Pacific Railroad Company maintains its headquarters at Tolsa 336, Guadalajara, Jal., but has branch offices both in Mexico City (Avenida Lázaro Cárdenas 13-701) and in Nogales. For information, contact the New York office of the Mexican National Railways.

Mexico City has a modern railroad station, Estación Buena Vista, on Avenida Insurgentes Norte at Mosqueta, eight blocks north of the Insurgentes-Reforma intersection.

Note: If you want train fares and schedule information in Mexico City, just phone 547-6593 or 547-1084.

You can also get fairly reliable schedule information by consulting the passenger travel edition of the *Official Railway Guide* or the *Thomas Cook Overseas Timetable.* Better travel agents will have a recent edition.

READER'S TRANSPORTATION TIP: "It's important to reserve Pullman compartments according to the number of beds required, not the number of people travelling. Mexican railroad officials seem to have decided that compartment beds originally designed for one are appropriate for 2½. We found out the hard way" (Donna Radtke, Athabasca, Alberta, Canada).

3. By Bus

TO MEXICO: Traveling to Mexico by bus is fine from southern California, but it's a long, tiring trip from northern cities and is economical only at first glance. From New York, for example, you could be on the bus three days and three nights if you rode straight through, closer to a week if you spent the nights in hotels. Add the price of hotels, meals, and incidentals (think of how many newspapers, magazines, books, and snacks you'll need on that ride!), and that "expensive" plane fare looks a lot more reasonable.

Advantages of bus travel are that you do get to see the countryside, and you can usually make any stopovers you want along the way for no extra charge. Those out to make their vacation a Pan-American one, seeing both Mexico and U.S., will appreciate this feature.

A bus operated by a U.S. company (mostly Greyhound and Trailways) will take you to the border, where you change to a Mexican bus for the remainder of the trip to your Mexican destination. Greyhound has offices in Mexico City, and will book you straight through to a Mexican destination (that is, you needn't buy another ticket at the border) in some cases.

Greyhound and Trailways are usually neck-and-neck when it comes to special promotional fares, but it's advisable to call both and see what's currently being offered. Some of the short-term special fares are incredible bargains: as of this writing, the one-way fare from New York City or Chicago to the border at Laredo, Texas, is only $99 from either company; from Los Angeles to El Paso it's a mere $79. But these fares change all the time, so call to keep current. Here is the essential data:

From New York City
Both companies operate out of the Port Authority Bus Terminal at Eighth Avenue and 41st Street (tel. Greyhound, 212/635-0800; Trailways, 212/564-8320). Each company has a daily bus headed for the border at Laredo; the trip takes around 60 hours, depending on the route.

From Chicago
Greyhound is at Clark and Randolph Streets (tel. 312/781-2882), with daily service to Laredo. The trip takes about 55 hours, straight through. Trailways, at 20 E. Randolph St. (tel. 312/726-9500), has similar service in a similar number of hours.

From Los Angeles
Greyhound is at 6th and Los Angeles Streets (tel. 213/620-1200), and has frequent daily buses to the border at El Paso, as well as frequent service to Tijuana and Laredo. Trailways, again, has similar service; they're located at 601 S. Main St. (tel. 213/742-1200). The trip from Los Angeles to El Paso takes about 50 hours.

Remember that in summer U.S. buses (Mexican ones too) tend to be powerfully air-conditioned, and so a sweater or warm jacket is essential even in the blazing heat of the Texas desert.

Take along things to eat and to read for the Mexican part of the journey especially. Also toilet paper—because the area you're passing through is one of the most sparsely populated in the whole country, and the rest stops aren't exactly up to Howard Johnson standards. Also, don't forget that tickets on a Mexican bus entitle you to a specific seat; you don't just sit anywhere. Keep your eye on your luggage and stay in sight of the bus driver at meal stops, because when he's finished eating he'll go—in spite of what he says about stopping for 20 minutes.

Good luck! You'll need it for this usually exhausting trip.

IN MEXICO: Within Mexico, large air-conditioned Greyhound-type buses operated by a dozen private companies roll over the intercity routes at a very reasonable cost, working out to only about 2¢ a mile (1½¢ a kilometer), or roughly $6 for the seven-hour trip from Mexico City to Acapulco. No longer is bus travel the *mañana* pastime of Malcolm Lowry's day when the village bus growled and wheezed into motion as soon as it was sufficiently overloaded. Today it's best to buy your reserved-seat ticket (all seats are reserved) a day in advance, and to be at the terminal on time for departure, as schedules are fairly dependable. Many Mexican cities now have new central bus stations rather than the bewildering and constantly changing array of tiny private company offices scattered all over town. For long trips, carry some food and a sweater for overpowerful air conditioning, and always a good amount of toilet paper.

Where feasible in this book I've included information on bus routes along my suggested itineraries. Keep in mind that routes, times, and prices are liable to change, and as there is no central directory of schedules for the whole country, current information must be obtained from local bus stations or travel offices.

4. By Car

TO MEXICO: With deregulation of the airline industry, and partial deregulation of the buses, driving is certainly not the cheapest way to get to Mexico. But it is still a wonderful way to see the country.

You can cut costs on the way to the border by staying in the popular budget motels such as **Motel 6, Susse Chalet,** and **Days Inn.** For a list of budget motel chains and their reservation numbers, plus lots of other money-saving information on all aspects of travel, pick up a copy of Frommer's *How to Beat the High Cost of Travel* (see the last page of this book for an order blank).

IN MEXICO: Using your own car in Mexico is no longer the cheapest, or even best way to see the country. For instance, Mexican fuel prices, though lower than those in the U.S. and Canada, are in reality not that much lower because the fuel tends to be of much lower octane. Remember, it's not just how much a gallon of gas costs, it's how far you can go on that gallon that's important; and 82-octane Mexican Nova doesn't get you as far as 91-octane American regular. As for unleaded gasoline, the Mexican government says it is going to make sure that it is available along the major tourist routes from the border to Mexico City, but let's wait and see. Actual availability can be an ever-changing thing.

Insurance costs are now very high (about $100 for two months of the minimum liability coverage—collision coverage is extra, a lot extra), although gas is a bit cheaper than at home, and parking is a problem in the cities (isn't it everywhere?). Unless you have a full carload, the bus and train come out cheaper per person, and with public transport you don't have to undertake the tedious amount of driving needed to see a country this big. More and more North Americans are using public transport in Mexico, but if you cherish the privacy and independence only a private automobile can give you, and are willing to pay for it, by all means take your car.

But one last note: Should you want to drive to the Mexican border, but not *into* Mexico, several readers have had good luck in striking bargains with garage and parking lot managers in U.S. border towns such as El Paso and Nogales. They paid a small sum to leave their cars in a lot or garage while they were seeing Mexico by bus or train, and then picked up their cars upon leaving Mexico for the drive home.

READER'S DRIVING TIP: "Unleaded 'Extra' gasoline was always difficult to find, and often unavailable. I had a Mexican muffler shop remove the catalytic converter from my car, and replace it with a piece of pipe. I saved the converter and had it welded back in place just prior to our return to the U.S. The 350 engine in my Olds 88 ran just fine on 81-octane 'Nova' gas as long as we were above 3,000 feet altitude. At lower altitudes we got a little 'ping' when accelerating because we did not bother with having the timing adjusted" (Dr. Wilber E. Scoville, Oshkosh, Wis.). [*Note from T.B.:* Having the catalytic converter removed in the U.S. is illegal, but having it done in Mexico as Dr. Scoville suggests is an excellent plan. Just make sure to have it reinstalled before reentering the U.S. Virtually any Mexican mechanic should be able to do this little job quickly and inexpensively.]

Mexican Roads

Most Mexican roads, although quite sufficient, are not up to northern standards of smoothness, hardness, width of curve or grade of hill, or safety marking. You will have to get used to the spirited Latin methods, which tend to depend more on flair and good reflexes than on system and prudence. Be prepared for new procedures, as when a truck flips on his left-turn signal when there's not a crossroad for miles. He's probably telling you that the road's clear ahead for you to pass—after all, he's in a position to see better than you are. How do you tell that's what he means, and not that he intends to pull over on the left-hand shoulder? Hard to say. More about trucks: They're very important to the country's economy, but the government is only in the first stages of building a system of divided, limited-access highways so that truck and car traffic is easy for both. You may follow trucks without mufflers and pollution-control devices for miles. Under these conditions it's best to drop back and be patient, take a side road, or stop for a break when you feel tense or tired.

Your Car

It's important to know the condition of your car before you cross the border. Parts and service in Mexico, while often of the very best quality, are usually a good deal more expensive than at home. Your cooling system should be in good condition, with the proper mixture of coolant and water, and no old radiator hoses. Carry a spare fan belt. In summer for long drives an air conditioner is not a luxury but nearly a necessity. You might want a spare belt for this too, just in case. Remember that Mexico is a big country, and that you may put several thousand miles on your tires before you return home—can your tires last a few thousand on Mexican roads? Mexican gasoline is not up to high standards, even the best of it, so it's good to be sure your car is in tune to handle it. By the way, Mexican filling stations are not as frequent as those up north, but I've never run out of gas. Plan ahead: don't leave a city for a long drive through the mountains or the desert with a half-full tank. Take simple tools along if you're handy with them, also a flashlight or spotlight, a cloth to wipe the windshield, toilet paper, and a tire gauge (saves tread wear to have the pressure right).

Car Papers

You will have to provide proof that you own the car, of course. Registration papers are sufficient for this. Then, you will turn in your Tourist Card and an official will type out a new document that serves as a Temporary Import Permit for your car, and also as your Tourist Card. *You may not receive two separate documents,* as in years past. The car papers will be issued for the same length of time as your Tourist Card was issued for. It's a very good idea to greatly overestimate the time you'll spend in Mexico, *when applying for your Tourist Card,* so that if something unforeseen happens and you have to (or want to) stay longer, you don't have to go through the long, long hassle of getting your papers renewed. The maximum term for Tourist Card and Temporary Importation Permit is three months. When the official who is filling out your Tourist Card asks how long you intend to stay, tell him three months.

Mexican Auto Insurance

You might want to buy your Mexican auto insurance before you cross the border. It costs no more on the American side, and the various agencies that handle it are often helpful in handing out free travel literature or in changing small amounts of dollars to pesos. You must purchase Mexican insurance, as U.S. or Canadian insurance is not valid in Mexico, and any party involved in an accident who has no insurance is automatically clapped into jail and his car is impounded until all claims are settled. Those with insurance are assumed to be good for claims and are released. The agency will show you a full table of current rates and will recommend the coverage it thinks adequate. The policies are written along lines similar to those north of the border. The agents usually tell you that it's best to *overestimate* the amount of time you plan to be in Mexico, for should you plan to stay longer than originally expected, it's a real runaround to get your policy term lengthened in Mexico; whereas any part of the term unused will be prorated and that part of your premium refunded to you in cash at the office on the American side as you come out, or by mail to your home.

Another hint on saving money: If you go through Guatemala and Belize, you'll have to pick up local insurance there as well—your Mexican insurance isn't good in these countries—so as you leave Mexico, have the Customs official stamp your policy with the date and time of exit from Mexico. When you reenter, have the official stamp you in again, and the portion of your time spent out of the country will be refunded to you.

After you cross the border into Mexico from the U.S., stop at the first Customs post you come to. If you don't have a Tourist Card, you'll have to pick one up here. Then you may be told to proceed down the road a ways (depending on the border crossing point) to the auto inspection station. Here you must park and lock your car and go into the office. Forms will be filled out, you wait your turn to be called, the car will be registered on the driver's Tourist Card, a sticker will be put on the window, and an inspection will be carried out. Theoretically the Tourist Card, the auto permit, and the inspection are not subject to charge, but you may have to learn about saying no to the uniformed officer when he says politely, "That will be one dollar, please." See Chapter XVI, "Bribes."

Remember that the driver of the car will not be able to leave the country without the car (even if it's later wrecked or stolen) unless he or she satisfies Customs that the import duty will be paid. This means that if you must suddenly fly home, you've got to go through the procedure at the airport of putting the car under Customs seal and having your tourist permit stamped to that effect. There may be storage fees. Check into it.

A last word: Mexican border officials are human, and I've found that if you look presentable (from a Mexican point of view, which means neat and clean), and are friendly and patient, the officials will treat you the same and make it all as easy as possible. Incidentally, when you cross back into the U.S. after an extended trip in Mexico, the American Customs officials will more often than not inspect *every* nook and cranny of your car, your bags, even your person, all very quickly, efficiently, and politely. They're looking for drugs, of course.

Driving in Mexico

Cardinal rule: **Never drive at night if you can avoid it.** The roads aren't good enough, the trucks and carts and pedestrians and bicycles usually have no lights, you can hit potholes, animals, rocks, dead ends, bridges out with no warning. Enough said.

Indeed, get used to the fact that people in the countryside are not good at judging the speed of an approaching car, and often panic in the middle of the road even though they could easily have reached the shoulder. It's not rude to use your horn if it may save someone from injury.

Road Signs

Here are the most common ones:

Camino en Reparación	Road Repairs
Conserva Su Derecha	Keep Right
Cuidado con el Ganado, el Tren	Watch Out for Cattle, Trains
Curva Peligrosa	Dangerous Curve
Derrumbes	Earthquake Zone
Despacio	Slow
Desviación	Detour
Disminuya Su Velocidad	Slow Down
Entronque	Highway Junction
Escuela	School (Zone)
Grava Suelta	Loose Gravel
Hombres Trabajando	Men Working
No Hay Paso	Road Closed
Peligro	Danger
Puente Angosto	Narrow Bridge
Raya Continua	Continuous (solid) White Line
Tramo en Reparación	Road Under Construction
Un Solo Carril a 100 m.	One-lane Road 100 Meters Ahead
Zona Escolar	School Zone

Also *Topes,* or a sign with a drawing of a row of little bumps on it, means that there's a row of speed bumps across the road placed there by the authorities to slow you down through towns or villages. Slow down when coming to a village whether you see the sign or not—sometimes they install the bumps but not the sign!

Kilometer stones on main highways register the distance from local population centers. There is always a shortage of directional signs, so check quite frequently that you are going on the right road.

Road and Bridge Tolls

Mexico has a number of toll highways and bridges, and you should know that tolls are at high rates. You can pay as much, or even more, to use an expressway or a bridge in Mexico than you would to use similar services in the U.S.

The word for "toll" in Spanish is *cuota.*

The Green Patrols

The Mexican government sponsors an admirable service whereby green, radio-equipped repair trucks manned by uniformed, English-speaking officers patrol the major highways during daylight hours to aid motorists with troubles.

Minor repairs and adjustments should be free of charge, although you pay for parts and materials if you have need of these "Green Angels."

Minor Accidents

Most motorists think it best to drive away from minor accidents if possible. You are at a distinct disadvantage without fluent Spanish when it comes to describing your version of what happened. Sometimes the other descriptions border on mythology, and you may end up spending days straightening out things that were not even your fault. In fact, fault often has nothing to do with it.

Parking

I use pay parking lots in cities, especially at night, to avoid annoyances such as broken antennas, swiped emblems, or break-ins. Never leave anything within view inside your locked car on the street (day or night), for Mexico has thieves like everyplace else. Another good reason to use pay parking lots is that you avoid parking violations, and when a cop in Mexico finds you parked illegally, and knows you may ignore a ticket, he'll take out his pliers and screwdriver and remove your license plate and take it to the station house. When pay lots are not available, dozens of small boys will surround you as you stop, wanting to "watch your car for you." Pick the leader of the group, let him know you want him to guard it, and give him a peso or two when you leave. Kids may be very curious about the car and may look in, crawl underneath, or even climb on top, but they rarely do any damage.

Getting Gas

Along with Mexico's economic difficulties has come a return to highway robbery at the pumps. Though many service station attendants are honest and above-board, a surprising number are not. Here's what to do when you have to fuel up:

Drive up to the pump and get close enough so that you will be able to watch the pump run as your tank is being filled. Check that the pump is turned back to zero, go to your fuel filler cap and unlock it yourself, and watch the pump and the attendant as the gas goes in. By the way, it's good to ask for a specific peso amount rather than saying "full." This is because the attendants tend to overfill, splashing gas on the car and anything within range.

As there are always lines at the gas pumps, attendants often finish fueling one vehicle, turn the pump back quickly (or don't turn it back at all), and start on another vehicle. You've got to be looking at the pump when the fueling is finished, because it may show the amount for only a few seconds. This "quick draw" from car to car is another good reason to ask for a certain peso-amount of gas. If you've asked for 1,000 pesos' worth, the attendant can't charge you 1,300 for it.

Once the fueling is complete, *then* you can let the attendant check your oil, or radiator, or put air in the tires. Do only one thing at a time, be with him as he does it, and don't let him rush you. Get into these habits, or it'll cost you.

If you get oil, make sure that the can that is tipped into your engine is a full one. If in doubt, have the attendant check the dipstick again after the oil has supposedly been put in.

Check your change, and again, don't let them rush you.

Check that your locking gas cap is back in place.

Don't depart from a major town or city except with a full or near-full tank of gas. Mexico is a big country, and service stations are not quite as frequent as in other countries. It's wise to keep the gas tank pretty full at all times.

All gasoline in Mexico is sold by the government-owned **Pemex** (Petroleras

Mexicanas) company. Nova (81 octane) costs about 70¢ per gallon. Nova is leaded gasoline *(con plomo),* and comes from the blue pump; Extra is a high-octane unleaded *(sin plomo)* gasoline, from the silver pump, but you will rarely find it available; the red pump is for diesel fuel, which costs about 45¢ a gallon. In Mexico fuel and oil are sold by the liter, so, a liter being slightly more than a quart, 40 liters equal about 10½ gallons.

No credit cards are accepted for gas purchases, so be prepared to pay in cash.

CAMPING: The *Rand McNally Campground and Trailer Park Guide: United States/Canada/Mexico* (New York, published every year) covers camping areas in Mexico, with full descriptions of facilities. Sanborn's, which sells Mexican insurance in the U.S., also hands out a list of camping places, free, to its insurance customers.

READER'S CAMPING TIP: "The **Mexico Camping Directory** by Carlos A. Melendez, published by Club Monarca de Acampadores, Apdo. Postal 31-750, Guadalajara, Jalisco 45050, is far better than all of the alternatives. I purchased my copy from the Sanborn's Insurance Agency in El Paso, Texas, for about $4" (Wilber E. Scoville, Oshkosh, Wis.).

THE AVAILABLE ROUTES: Depending on where you live in the United States, you will drive to Mexico by one of four basic routes.

Approaching from the West, the most likely border-crossing towns are either Nogales or El Paso; approaching from the East, the most popular entry point is Nuevo Laredo. This latter town also draws much of the traffic from the Chicago area and the Midwest. The fourth route is via Eagle Pass, Texas, just across the border from Piedras Negras in the Mexican state of Coahuila. This route to Mexico City travels one of the country's newest and best roads (Route 57), and you won't have to contend with either hot weather or dizzying mountain passes.

The following chapter deals with all four of these routes, first the West Coast route, entering at Nogales, then the route from El Paso, and finally the Laredo and Eagle Pass routes.

Chapter II

HEADING SOUTH OVERLAND

1. The West Coast Route: Hermosillo to Culiacán
2. The El Paso Route: Chihuahua to Fresnillo
3. The Eastern Route via Monterrey and Saltillo

ALTHOUGH AIR TRAVEL IS a very popular way to get to Mexico, and although flying is a good choice because of the great distances to be covered, the traveler who enters Mexico by road sees parts of the country and ways of life that the air traveler will miss for good. The northern regions of the country, while only sparsely furnished with what might be called "tourist attractions," are of critical importance to Mexico's economy. Mining, fishing, manufacturing, farming, and cattle ranching make these vast semi-arid regions among the wealthiest in the country.

The scenery and customs of the people change gradually as the kilometers click by. Soon the tall buildings of Americanized Chihuahua, the farmers in cowboy hats and pickup trucks, the fuming smokestacks of Monterrey give way to the lusher country of the Valley of Mexico or to the incredibly fertile tropics of the Gulf and Pacific Coasts.

Herewith I provide hints for stops along the way south, no matter what route you take, no matter whether your destination is Acapulco, Mexico City, Veracruz, or beyond.

1. The West Coast Route: Hermosillo to Culiacán

If you're coming to Mexico from the western United States, you'll probably cross the border at Nogales, near the Gulf of California. This west coast route to Mexico's capital is an attractive one, as it heads straight down to Mexico's Pacific beach resorts (see Chapter III). Well traveled by Mexican and American tourists, truckers and locals, the route poses no problems—if you stick to the route. But you should know that the Pacific Coast state of Sinaloa has long been known as a center of drug trafficking and other unsavory activities. You won't see any of this if you stick to the beaten path and the main highway, with no adventurous side trips to little out-of-the-way villages.

Coming from California by car, it's not really worth it to cross the border at Tijuana and drive over bad roads through the desert to pick up Mexican Route 15. Take my word for it, you'd be much better off taking I-10 or I-8 to Tucson and then I-19 to Nogales.

If you're traveling from California by bus or train, however, it's a different story; you may want to cross over the border as soon as possible, entering Mexico at Tijuana or Mexicali, since travel by either bus or train in Mexico costs only a fraction of what it costs in the U.S. to cover the same distance. For example, at this writing, to go from San Diego to Calexico, Calif., costs $15.60 on the Greyhound bus; to go from Tijuana to Mexicali on the Mexican side, the cities just across the border from San Diego and Calexico respectively, costs only 1,070 pesos ($2.14) on the Mexican bus line.

To cross over by bus from San Diego or Calexico, do this: buy your Greyhound ticket through to the destination on the Mexican side, either Tijuana or Mexicali. The Greyhound bus crosses the border, stopping at the border station for you to obtain your tourist card. Make sure you get your card at the time you cross the border! The Greyhound will go to the bus station in *downtown* Tijuana; from here you'll take a bus to the *central camionera* (central bus station) on the *outskirts* of Tijuana, which is the departure point for long-distance buses of every major Mexican bus line, both first and second class, serving Tijuana. From here you can buy your ticket to wherever your destination may be.

If you're in downtown San Diego without a bus ticket through to Tijuana, do this: take the electric trolley to San Ysidro for $1.50, walk through the border station, and pick up a "Centro" or "Central Camionera" local city bus—tell the driver you want to get to the central camionera. You can also take a taxi from the fleet of taxis you see waiting just across the border.

To travel by train, you can catch the southbound train at the beginning of the line, either in Mexicali or in Nogales. (If you want to switch over from the bus to the train in Mexicali, you can walk the few blocks from the central camionera to the train station, or take a taxi.) The faster train, "El Costeño," departs daily from Mexicali around 3 p.m. (check the time on this one), from Nogales at 3:30 p.m.; the slower train, "El Mexicali," which stops off at many little towns along the way, leaves daily from Mexicali at 8 a.m., from Nogales at 7:15 a.m. (Do check these schedules to be sure they're still the same; see the section "Getting There By Train" in the beginning of the book for details.)

After crossing the border, your first major destination is the coastal resort city of Mazatlán. 735 miles to the south. Much of this stretch is desert country, boiling hot in the summer. Here first are the towns you'll pass through en route, with suggestions for food and lodging.

Remember, if you're driving, to stop at the border station and pick up your Tourist Card, if you don't already have one. The cars that are zipping right through the border station are not heading south, but are just crossing over for the day—that's why they don't have to stop. A few miles farther along the road south, Customs officials will check your Tourist Card and/or car entry permit (if you have a car), and will inspect your luggage.

HERMOSILLO: This city (alt. 720 feet; pop. 300,000), capital of the state of Sonora, is the center of a fruit- and vegetable-farming area. You enter on a lovely tree-lined boulevard, which in summer is vibrant with the orange flowers of the yucateros.

Where to Stay and Eat
Highway 15 goes straight through the center of Hermosillo, becoming Avenida Rosales and passing the university. At the corner of Serdan and Rosales, Hermosillo, Sonora 83000, you'll see the **Hotel San Alberto** (tel. 621/2-1800), on the right-hand side as you come from the north, across the street from the Telegraph Office. It's an older, five-story structure on the outside, but a warm and well-run hotel on the inside. The 175 comfy air-conditioned rooms with private bath in this prime downtown location cost 7,085 pesos ($14.17) single, 8,005 pesos ($16) double, with 400 pesos (80¢) more for a color TV if you

request one; prices include a complete breakfast served from 7 to 9:30 a.m. Other services include swimming pool, off-street parking, cafeteria, bar, discothèque, and even a beauty parlor and tobacco shop.

The **Hotel Washington,** at Dr. Noriega Pte. 68, Hermosillo, Sonore 83000 (tel. 621/3-1183), has 35 simple but acceptable rooms stacked along narrow courts. All are air-conditioned, with clean bathrooms, and cost 3,300 pesos ($6.60) single, 4,000 pesos ($8) double. For those sharing a room but not a bunk, there are two double beds in each room.

Another good choice is the **Hotel Monte Carlo,** at one corner of the Plaza Juárez, on the corner of Juárez and Sonora (no number), Hermosillo, Sonora 83000 (tel. 621/2-0853). You can save yourself some steps by telephoning first to see if there is a vacancy at this very busy hotel. The 38 units are all air-conditioned and bright, with single rooms priced at 3,800 pesos ($7.60), doubles at 4,025 pesos ($8.05). Adjoining the Monte Carlo is a corner restaurant, open 7 a.m. to 10 p.m. daily except Saturdays, that is simple, inexpensive, and filled with hungry Mexicans who recognize a good deal at lunchtime. The comida corrida, served from noon to 3 p.m., offers soup, salad, a meat entree varying daily, beverage, and dessert for 800 pesos ($1.60). If you need some help or information, ask for Sr. Gilberto Villa Martinez, who speaks a little English and who has infinite patience with those who speak only a little Spanish.

Around the corner from the Monte Carlo is the **Hotel San Andres,** Oaxaca 14 Ore., Hermosillo, Sonora 83000 (tel. 621/2-0653, 2-2663, or 2-2664), which is a little more expensive, with singles at 5,750 pesos ($11.50), doubles at 6,900 pesos ($13.80). It offers off-street parking and a restaurant open from 7 a.m. to 11 p.m.

If you'd like to be in a bit quieter location, but still near the center of things, an excellent choice is the 31-room **Hotel America Colonial,** Juárez 171 Sur, Hermosillo, Sonora 83000 (tel. 621/2-2448), where single rooms are 3,000 pesos ($6), doubles 3,500 pesos ($7) with one bed, 4,000 pesos ($8) with two double beds. Rooms here are dark, but the air conditioners are powerful and the people at the front desk very friendly and helpful. The lobby has a TV and supply of good cold drinking water; there's off-street parking in front of the hotel. Meals are available at the Crazy Horse Restaurant next door, open 6 a.m. to 11 p.m., with the comida corrida served noon to 4 p.m. for 700 pesos ($1.40), breakfast or dinner for 400 pesos (80¢). To get to the Colonial, follow Highway 15 through town and turn left on the "Bulevar Transversal," a divided road. Look for Avenida Juárez; turn left on Juárez and go nine blocks to no. 171 Sur (which is in the direction of the mountains). It is about six blocks from the Plaza Juárez.

You will note that there are many expensive hotels in Hermosillo, as befits a state capital, and in extreme cases you may have to search one of them out. Or, conversely, you'll see several **casas de huespedes** (guesthouses) around town, especially in the area near the Plaza Juárez; these are cheaper in price, but also inferior in accomodations.

As for meals, **El Rodeo Rosticeria** (tel. 2-1395), Dr. Noriega Pte. 92, is a fine choice. The specialty of the house is broiled beef served hot at your table on a Mexican "hibachi" for 1,750 pesos ($3.50). Half a roasted chicken, or a quarter chicken prepared any one of several fancy ways, costs 1,100 pesos ($2.20), as do several shrimp and fish entrees. All come with chips and salsa, and you can get guacamole dip for 350 pesos (70¢).

The **Mercado Municipal,** on the block bordered by Plutarco Elias Calles, Calle Guerrero, Avenida Monterrey, and Matamoros, is a great place to go for a low-cost breakfast or lunch. Many little cafés offer sit-down counter service, and you can get anything from licuados to tamales or a sandwich, plus a wide variety of fresh produce at good prices.

If you're in the mood for something quieter, however, you might try the **Café San Cesar** (tel. 3-8450), half a block down from the mercado at Plutarco Elias Calles Pte. 71, open 7 a.m. to 10 p.m. Ham and eggs or a cheese omelette will cost 700 pesos ($1.40), with many chicken dinners offered for 875 pesos ($1.75) on the bilingual menu.

A cool, nutritious snack can be had at the **Casa del Yogurt** (no phone), a few blocks up from the mercado on Plutarco Elias Calles near the corner of Juárez. With space for only about four people to sit down on stools at the counter, it is nonetheless a very popular little place, offering service for there or to go. A big cup of yogurt with lots of assorted chopped fruit and a nice sauce costs 340 pesos (68¢), half a liter comes for 540 pesos ($1.08), and a whole liter for 900 pesos ($1.80), with plain yogurt at 240 pesos (48¢) a big cup, 540 pesos ($1.08) per liter. Fresh orange and carrot juice are also offered. Open 8 a.m. to 8 p.m.

Another good place to go for a refreshing cool treat is **Jugos Chapala,** at Aquiles Serdán 105, a couple of blocks up from the telegraph office. Here 300 pesos (60¢) will get you any of five pure freshly-made fruit juices or 14 flavors of *licuado* (a milk drink blended with fresh fruit), and for 350 pesos (70¢) you can get a good, big cup of *escamochas* (crushed mixed fruit topped with raisins, nuts, coconut, and a thick, sweetened milk sauce).

About my favorite snack in Hermosillo—or in all of the state of Sonora for that matter—is a chili dog from the vendors who stroll around Hermosillo with little carts, selling hot dogs on steamed buns topped with onions, tomatoes, beans, mayonnaise, mustard, and hot sauce for a mere 180 pesos (36¢). You'll see them in several of the little parks around town.

Side Trips

Sixty-seven miles west of Hermosillo on a fairly good road lies **Kino Bay.** Actually there are two Kinos: **Kino Viejo,** a small, somnolent fishing village, and **Kino Nuevo,** an area that has become popular with wealthy Americans and condominium owners. Part of the attraction is due to the good fishing, and in June the International Sport Fishing Tournament draws crowds. The beach too is beautiful, with miles of white sand and gorgeous houses lining it. Many public *palapas* (open palm-roofed shelters) dot the shore, available for shade against the glittering sun. If you feel like spending some time in total relaxation, enjoying pure tranquility, sparkling water, fishing, and sun before you continue on into Mexico, Kino is a good place to do it.

Although prices in Kino Nuevo are out of our range, you can stay at the **Islandia Marina** (tel. 624/2-0080) in Old Kino. To find it, just follow the sign on the left side of the highway as you're heading past Old Kino. You'll see white cabins surrounded by a low stone wall, with trailers in the middle. Islandia Marina is a combination trailer park/beach facility, with eight cabins for rent at $10 a day single, $12 for 2 to 5 persons, with discounts of 10% per week or 25% per month for longer stays. The cabins have hot water baths, kitchens, one double bed and three large *catres* (cots), and some are just yards from the gentle waves. The English-speaking owner deals in dollars, not pesos, keeping the same dollar price for many years. You can write ahead to the Islandia Marina at Apdo. Postal 2000, Bahia Kino, Sonora 83340.

Next to the Islandia Marina is the **Restaurant Marlin** (tel. 624/2-0111), which also has a sign out on the highway (although when I was there, only an old, yellow "Carta Blanca" beer sign was there to identify the low white stucco restaurant). Inside, the restaurant is very pleasant, clean and cool, with an adjoining bar under a large round palapa roof where you can dance until midnight if you like. The house specialty is a seafood platter at 3,000 pesos ($6), and for this you receive lobster, shrimp, abalone, clams, scallops, octopus, and turtle.

You may request substitutes. Otherwise, prices range from 1,400 pesos ($2.80) for filet of fish dinners, 1,800 pesos ($3.60) for shrimp or lobster dinners, down to a good sandwich for 400 pesos (80¢). All the seafood is certifiably fresh: ask the bilingual waiter to show you one of the live sea turtles out back, and you'll get to know what fresh is. Open 2 to 10 p.m.

A short walk into "downtown" Kino Viejo brings you to the **Restaurant Palapa** (tel. 2-0210 or 2-0219), with the same menu and management as the Marlin. Unlike the air-conditioned Marlin, however, the Palapa is under a huge round palapa roof, with open-air, waist-high walls. The restaurant/bar is open from 7 a.m. to 8 p.m.

On the other side of the farmacia from the Palapa is the **Restaurant Lupita** (tel. 2-0011), open 8 a.m. to midnight, where breakfasts come for 600 pesos ($1.20), antojitos for 600 pesos ($1.20), *carne asada* (roast meat) for 900 pesos ($1.80), fried fish for 400 pesos (80¢), and shrimp dinners for 1,500 pesos ($3).

Just a block from here, the fishermen come to beach their little boats. Many little open-air shacks offer their wares, and the carvings of the Seris. Occasionally a group of Seri Indians will be camped beyond the end of the road in Kino Nuevo on their way to or from Desemboque. The Seri are known for their ironwood carvings; you can find them at work in Kino Viejo as well. Today, the ancient tool kit contains power carving tools as well.

For nondrivers there are daily second-class buses from Hermosillo to Kino Bay, leaving from the station of Autobuses de Municipio de Hermosillo (tel. 621/2-6924), one and a half blocks up Calle Sonora from the Hotel Monte Carlo, at Sonora and Manuel González, no. 44. Buses leave Hermosillo at 5:45, 9:30, and 11:30 a.m.; 1:30, 3:30, and 5:30 p.m. They depart from Kino at 9 and 11 a.m., 2, 4, and 6 p.m. for the return trip to Hermosillo. Travel time is roughly two hours. If you don't want to stay over in Kino, there's nothing to prevent you from getting an early start, making a day of it at the beach, and returning to Hermosillo in the late afternoon.

GUAYMAS: Guaymas (pronounced why-*mass;* pop. 152,000), on the coast, owes its reputation to fishing, both commercial and sport. Runs of marlin and sailfish generally occur between February 15 and August 15. Lobster, sea turtles, and clams abound in nearby waters as well.

The town is divided by a hilly range, the port on one side and the resort plus Miramar Beach on the other. Unfortunately, it's not much of a resort. The beach is unexceptional and the majority of the hotels and motels in the area customarily charge *more* in the scorching off-season summer months than they do in winter. Explanation: You pay extra for the electrical current used by the air conditioner (which you must take advantage of).

The town's **Tourism Office** (tel. 622/2-2932) is on the main boulevard, Aquiles Serdán, at no. 437, between Calles 12 and 13. The English-speaking staff has lots of helpful and interesting information printed in both English and Spanish, covering Guaymas, San Carlos, and the entire state of Sonora. Open Monday through Friday, 9 a.m. to 1 p.m. and 3 to 6 p.m.

The bus station here is right downtown on Calle 14, and there are taxis available to take you anywhere in the city.

Where to Stay

There are a number of nice places to stay in Guaymas, in various price ranges. First, the medium-priced.

The **Del Puerto Motel** (tel. 622/2-3408) is right downtown at the corner of Yanez and Calle 19 (no number), Guaymas, Sonora 85400, one block from the big *mercado* (market). The 72 rooms all have air conditioning, and are nice and clean. Prices are 4,000 pesos ($8) for one person, 5,000 pesos ($10) for two, 6,000 pesos ($12) for three, and so on. The owners of the Del Puerto also operate the 40-room **Malibu Motel** (tel. 622/2-2244), located north of town on the International Highway, km. 1983, with similar services and rates.

Also a block away from the mercado, but in the other direction, is the **Hotel Impala** (tel. 622/2-1335 or 2-0922), at Calle 20, no. 40, Guaymas, Sonora 85400, on the corner of Calle 20 and Avenida A.L. Rodriguez. The 60-room hotel is old and a little dark, but the rooms are clean, air-conditioned, and come with their own phone. Prices are 4,000 pesos ($8) single, 5,000 pesos ($10) double, 6,000 pesos ($12) triple, etc. Attached is the air-conditioned **Restaurant Mandarin,** specializing in Chinese food, with an ample à la carte menu of Oriental, meat and seafood dishes, with three Chinese combination plates priced at 1,650, 2,100, and 2,500 pesos ($3.30, $4.20, and $5) and three breakfast specials at 510, 615, and 790 pesos ($1.02, $1.23, and $1.58).

Near here, but in a little quieter part of town a couple of blocks from the cathedral, is the spotless and pleasant **Hotel Ana,** Calle 25, no. 135, Guaymas, Sonora 85400 (tel. 622/2-3048). The 42 air-conditioned, simple but very clean rooms, with red-and-white-checked tile floors, have barred windows opening onto the fresh air of the central patio. Single rooms go for 4,000 pesos ($8), doubles 5,000 ($10), triples 6,000 pesos ($12), etc.

Right on the main boulevard is the **Hotel Santa Rita** (tel. 622/2-8100 or 2-6463), at the corner of Aquiles Serdán and Calle Mesa (no number), Guaymas, Sonora 85400. Prices are the same—singles 4,000 pesos ($8), doubles 5,000 pesos ($10), triples 6,000 pesos ($12), etc.—and the decor is pleasant, with dark Spanish-style heavy wooden furniture, red curtains and red-and-black bedspreads set against white walls and white tile floors. Rooms come with air conditioning and TV.

A higher-priced, more luxurious choice is the **Motel Armida** (tel. 622/2-3050), on the International Highway just as you enter Guaymas from the north (no number), Guaymas, Sonora 85400. The special winter price here is 8,625 pesos ($17.25) single or double, with the normal rate for the rest of the year being 10,177 pesos ($20.35) single or double. The large, 82-room motel has a swimming pool, parking, air conditioning, phone and TV in the rooms, as well as a bar, discothèque, steak house, international restaurant, and cafeteria.

On the cheaper end of the spectrum, three **casas de huespedes** (guesthouses), all near the bus stations, offer basic but clean rooms for those traveling on a tighter budget. At **Casa de Huespedes Lupita** (no phone), on Calle 15, no. 125, Guaymas, Sonora 85400, between Avenidas 10 and 12, the 20 rooms open onto an inner patio with lots of shady trees, sharing bathrooms and hot water showers (separate for men and women). Rooms with one bed cost 1,500 pesos ($3); those with two beds cost 3,000 pesos ($6).

Three blocks up from the bus station, on the corner of Calle 14 and Avenida 8 (no number), Guaymas, Sonora 85400, is **Casa de Huespedes La Colimense** (tel. 622/2-0845), with 60 rooms and more in construction. Rooms with private cold-water bathrooms cost 1,600 pesos ($3.20) single, 1,900 pesos ($3.80) double; with shared bathroom facilities (men and women separate), the prices are 1,300 pesos ($2.60) single and 1,600 pesos ($3.20) double.

A block closer to the bus stations is the **Casa de Huespedes Esperanza,** on Calle 14, no. 209, Guaymas, Sonora 85400, at the corner of Calle 14 and Avenida 9 (tel. 622/2-0593). There's no sign, but the door is right next to the little restaurant Yoremita on the southwest corner. Prices here are 1,000 pesos ($2) single, 1,500 pesos ($3) double; the seven rooms all have private cold-water bathroom and shower, with one double bed. The birds in the aviary under the stairs make a cheerful music that can be heard from all the rooms in this tiny guesthouse.

Where to Eat

Being a fishing town, most of Guaymas's good restaurants specialize in the seafood the town is famous for.

One good all-purpose restaurant in downtown Guaymas is the **Restaurant El Paradise** (tel. 2-1184), at Rodriguez 34, right across from the ancient Hotel Impala and one block from the market. In Paradise you'd expect to find those little extra touches: English menu, waiters who can speak your lingo, air conditioning, big portions. What I'd want from Paradise is seafood, and they have it here, fresh from Guaymas harbor. A wide variety of fish and seafood specialties, served with rice, vegetables, and rolls, comes for 2,100 pesos ($4.20), 12 kinds of shrimp dishes for 2,600 pesos ($5.20), and a whole lobster (in season) for 3,800 pesos ($7.60). The house extravagance, a seafood combo with deviled crab, fish filets, broiled shrimp, clams ranchero style, French fries, vegetables, and rolls with butter, comes for 3,500 pesos ($7). Posters on the wall display fishes, mollusks, and crustaceans of the North Pacific labeled in several languages. Open daily from noon until 11 p.m.

Another fine all-purpose selection is the **Restaurant Sonorense** (tel. 2-5180), right on the main street, Aquiles Serdán, between Calles 12 and 13 (no number), specializing in seafood and charcoal-broiled meats. There are two menus here: the "menu económico" with seafood, meat and chicken dishes for 1,200 to 1,600 pesos ($2.40 to $3.20), beef stew for 800 pesos ($1.60); and also the specialty menu, with breakfasts from 650 to 800 pesos ($1.30 to $1.60), antojitos from 900 to 1,200 pesos ($1.90 to $2.40), steak cuts at 2,400 pesos ($4.80), and fish filets for 1,900 pesos ($3.80). Sea animals are painted on the window out front. Open 8 a.m. to 10 p.m.

The **Restaurant/Bar Del Rio** (tel. 2-7400), is a little further down Avenida Serdán, between Calles 9 and 10 (no number), open 10 a.m. to 2 a.m. It's a beautiful place, located in an old mansion with all kinds of deluxe touches in the decor. You can eat inside or out on the terrace. The house specialty is shrimp mignon for 2,800 pesos ($5.60), while shrimp del Rio—large shrimps stuffed with yellow cheese, rolled in bacon and served with a special sauce—come for 2,600 pesos ($5.20) on the bilingual menu. Live music for dancing or listening is played every night except Monday from 9 p.m. to 2 a.m.

Also on Avenida Serdán, between Calles 16 and 17 (no number), is another very fancy restaurant, the **Restaurant/Bar Del Mar** (tel. 2-0226 or 2-4650), open from 12:30 p.m. to midnight. Refreshingly air-conditioned, with a marine decor of fishes swimming on the wall, poster-size photos of Guaymas harbor, real sea turtle shells for lightshades, and heavy Spanish chairs, the bilingual menu sports fish entrees such as fish amandine sautéed in butter and Spanish almonds for 2,750 pesos ($5.50), up to a combo plate with fish, shrimp, and crab meat au gratin for 3,250 pesos ($6.50), and steak and lobster for 5,500 pesos ($11).

The nice **Restaurant El Sarape,** facing the cathedral on Calle 23 and Alfonse Iberri (tel. 2-3140), has a special Sunday buffet that is probably the best deal in town: for 1,500 pesos ($3) for adults and less for children under 10, you can get all you can eat between 1 and 4 p.m., with four choices of entrees, two soups, beans, tortillas, bread, and dessert. Dance music is played by a combo Tuesdays through Sundays from 8 p.m. to 1 a.m. On the à la carte menu, meat and fish dishes come with soup and salad, with carne asada à la Tampiqueña for 1,835 pesos ($3.67), steaks for 2,395 pesos ($4.79), and Guaymas shrimp for 2,300 pesos ($4.60).

For a cool snack, **Jugos Chapalita,** on Rodriguez in the same block as the Restaurant El Paradise and the Hotel Impala, is one of those juice shops that seems to have just about every kind of fruit you can think of. Licuados of fresh fruit blended with milk come in 11 tropical flavors for 280 to 320 pesos (56¢ to 64¢), charging 50 pesos (10¢) extra if they're made with two eggs. Large-size freshly made juices of carrot, orange, grapefruit, papaya, or pineapple come for 280 to 500 pesos (56¢ to $1), with escamochas for 350 pesos (70¢).

You can get just about anything you want at the **mercado** (market) located on Avenida A.L. Rodriguez on the entire block between Calle 19 and Calle 20, including economical breakfasts and lunches, licuados, vegetables and fruits, meats and groceries, clothes, sombreros (hats), shoes and juaraches (sandals). Watch out for the prices on the clothes, however. You may get a good deal or two, and if you're not going much further south, you can buy beautiful Mexican embroidered dresses, blouses, etc. here at the Guaymas market. But by and large, these things are bought for a fraction of their marked price at places like Mexico City and Guadalajara and brought up to Guaymas to be sold at exorbitant prices; if you're planning to go further south, you'd do better to wait until you get down there to make your purchases.

On Playa Miramar

Guaymas' beach area, north of town across the hills, is called **Playa Miramar,** on Bocochibampo Bay. The city bus ("Miramar") will take you the 25-minute ride from Guaymas for 45 pesos (9¢), driving north along the beach past beachfront homes and finally terminating at a small beachfront complex of shops, little restaurants, a trailer park, and **Leo's Inn,** North Miramar Beach, Calle 28, no. 133, Guaymas, Sonora 85400 (tel. 622/2-9490 at the Inn, or 622/2-1337 at the reservation office in Guaymas). Leo's is a nice, modern little place with a verdant garden on one side and two floors of tidy air-conditioned rooms with bug screens and even screen doors. Rooms with two double beds cost 8,550 pesos ($17.10) single or double, with discounts of 5% to 10% for longer stays. The attractive, large, and homey lobby/sitting room has a TV and a video cassette recorder for movies, and faces out onto a lovely seaside terrace. Parking is to one side of the hotel.

In the little complex right next to Leo's is the **Restaurant La Bocana** (tel. 622/2-4822), an airy glassed-in room with a view of the sea, an informal ambience, and seafood. Cheapest and best is the filete de pescado al mojo de ajo (fish filet in garlic sauce) for 1,800 pesos ($3.60), with abalone for 1,400 pesos ($2.80), sea turtle for 1,800 pesos ($3.60), meat dishes 2,500 to 2,800 pesos ($5 to $5.60), up to 2,200 pesos ($4.40) for shrimp and 3,500 pesos ($7) for lobster. The house specialty, a seafood platter of breaded *and* grilled shrimp, fried fish filet, fried perch, clams, rice, and salad, comes for 3,000 pesos ($6). A variety of breakfasts are priced at 670 pesos ($1.34). Open 8 a.m. to 10 p.m. (You can also get information here regarding the **Escalante Trailer Park** next door, which rents spaces for $6 U.S. per night, or $150 U.S. per month.)

Side Trip to San Carlos

About 12 miles north of Guaymas off Highway 15 is the resort area of San Carlos. The beaches are nice, for sure, but the hotels and restaurants are pretty expensive. You drive east seven miles from the highway through a riot of billboards advertising house lots for sale, condos, time-sharing, trailer parks, and all types of *bienes raices* (real estate).

Set in the midst of striking scenery—pinnacled mountains on a beautiful bay—San Carlos is not at all like Puerto Vallarta or Acapulco. Rather, it's new, growing, and aimed not at the casual tourist but at the condo crowd. Restaurants tend to be expensive. If you want to see San Carlos, I'd recommend it being only a day trip. You can take the Guaymas city bus ("San Carlos") for 150 pesos (30¢).

CIUDAD OBREGÓN: The best way to describe Ciudad Obregón (pop. 173,000) is by asking the reader to picture a typical old colonial hill town with narrow cobblestone streets—and then imagine the polar opposite. Ciudad Obregón, a model city founded in 1928, has probably the flattest location, widest streets, and least colonial atmosphere of any community in Mexico. With 20th-century buildings, and oozing modernity at every pore, it differs from such settlements as San Cristóbal de Las Casas and Guanajuato as the Yukon does from the Congo.

Best choice in Obregón is the **Hotel Imperial,** on the corner of Sinaloa and Guerrero (no number), Ciudad Obregón, Sonora 85000 (tel. 641/3-5062), a pastel-green tile edifice located unfortunately at the opposite side of town from the bus station. The Imperial is rather large, and is graced with a cool central court and simplistic modern curved stairway. The reception desk is enclosed in a refrigerated glass box, but the amiable gentleman behind the desk will be happy to come out into the sticky heat and show you one of the simple air-conditioned rooms. They all have bath, telephone, bare walls, and venetian blinds, and are blessedly cool. Singles are 3,200 pesos ($6.40); doubles, 3,500 pesos ($7).

Right around the corner from the Imperial is the **Hotel Kuraika,** Calle 5 de Febrero no. 211 Sur, Ciudad Obregón, Sonora 85000 (tel. 641/3-5047), a good low-budget choice. Rates are 1,700 pesos ($3.40) single, 2,400 pesos ($4.80) double. It's bare and a bit run-down looking, with its bright-green paint starting to peel off the walls, and fluorescent lights. But it has what you need, with air conditioning in the summer, a hot water bath in all the rooms, a restaurant next door, and a convenient downtown location near banks and all other services. A good deal for the price.

The little **Hotel Jardín,** Galeana Pte. 411, Ciudad Obregón, Sonora 85000 (tel. 641/3-5490), is only about half the distance from the bus station as the aforementioned hotels, and it's in a quieter part of town, right across the street from a park. The lobby is no great shakes, but you'll probably forget what it looked like once you settle into one of the air-conditioned rooms. Rooms are small, with multicolored bath with walls that go only two-thirds of the way to the ceiling! Singles are 2,700 pesos ($5.40); doubles, 3,200 pesos ($6.40).

NAVOJOA: There's no real reason to stop in Navojoa, Sonora (alt. 125 feet; pop. 43,817), about 42 miles south of Ciudad Obregón. An agricultural town, there's not much for the tourist to see; about the most interesting quality Navojoa holds for tourists is its proximity to other, more attractive places, such as Alamos and the beach at Huatabampito. But if you should be in the area and need a place to stay for the night, there are a few recommendable spots.

Where to Stay and Eat

The **Hotel Colonial** (tel. 642/2-1919), right on the highway on the south end of town as you leave Navojoa, is the fancy choice in town, with rates at 6,555 pesos ($13.11) single, 7,992 pesos ($15.98) double. Rooms have air conditioning, carpets, phone, and color TV with cablevision and parabolic antenna. The restaurant is open 7 a.m. to 11 p.m., charging 940 to 1,040 pesos ($1.88 to $2.08) for breakfast specials, 820 to 890 pesos ($1.64 to $1.78) for Mexican antojitos, and 1,150 to 1,840 pesos ($2.30 to $3.68) for supper meat entrees. There's also a bar and a discothèque which is open Tuesday through Sunday from 8 p.m. until everyone leaves. The address is Pesqueira Prolongación Sur (no number), Navojoa, Sonora.

The **Motel El Mayo** (tel. 642/2-0099) has a large white neon sign on the main highway to direct you to its location one block off the highway at the corner of Otero and Jiménez (no number), Navojoa, Sonora. A pleasant and quiet place, the 39 air-conditioned rooms go for 5,200 pesos ($10.40) single, 5,900 pesos ($11.80) double. (The new section of bungalows rents for 6,900 pesos ($13.80) single or double, but the older "economy" rooms are just as nice.) Although the rooms are a bit on the colorful side, with walls painted bright green, shocking pink, or the like, they all have windows facing the garden outside and are very clean. There's plenty of purified water around.

Crossing the main highway downtown is Calle Allende, where the Transportes Norte de Sonora bus station is. On Allende, over on the other side of the highway from the bus station, are two other less expensive (but not quite as nice) hotel choices. The **Hotel Gema,** at Allende 213, Navojoa, Sonora (tel. 642/2-0591 and 2-0691), charges 4,887 pesos ($9.77) single and 5,750 pesos ($11.50) double for its 24 smallish, plain, but fairly clean rooms, equipped with air conditioning, phone, and TV. The restaurant attached, also air-conditioned, is open from 7 a.m. to 11 p.m.

Motel Aduana, on Allende between the main highway (called Calle Pesquiera) and Otero (no number), Navojoa, Sonora (tel. 642/2-0069), has small, simple but clean rooms with air conditioning and hot water bath for 3,500 pesos ($7) single, 4,000 pesos ($8) double. If you call here in the evening and receive no answer, don't be discouraged; the telephone usually works only between 7 a.m. and 6 p.m.

As for eating, the **Restaurant Margarita** (tel. 2-0417), on the main highway at Pesqueira 503 Sur, is open 24 hours a day and is recommended by locals as a good place to eat. The specialty is the comida corrida, served from noon until 5 p.m. for 1,200 pesos ($2.40). Otherwise, breakfast specials come for 300 to 600 pesos (60¢ to $1.20), with your choice of eggs, beans, flour or corn tortillas, toast, and coffee. Enchiladas are 600 pesos ($1.20) per order, and carne asada comes for 1,200 pesos ($2.40).

Back on Allende, the restaurant **Mariscos El Pescador** (tel. 2-4102) at Allende 102, open 8 a.m. to 6 p.m., specializes in seafood and serves most meals in the 1,200- to 1,500-peso ($2.40 to $3) range. You may see a big shrimp, fish, octopus, and oyster painted in bright colors on the windows outside.

TO HUATABAMPO AND ALAMOS: You can catch local buses leaving Navojoa for Huatabampo and Alamos from the bus station near the corner of Calle Guerrero and Rincón, just a few blocks west of the main highway. They leave for Huatabampo, on the seacoast, every 30 minutes between 6 a.m. and 8:30 p.m., costing 210 pesos (42¢). It's 274 pesos (54¢) for the 40-minute ride to Alamos, with buses leaving hourly between 6:30 a.m. and 7 p.m.

By car, you can get to Huatabampo from Navojoa by driving 21 miles south on Calle Talamante, running parallel to Calle Pesquiera six blocks to the west. To drive to Alamos, turn east on Avenida Abasolo and go straight ahead for 34 miles.

Side Trip to Alamos

From the turnoff from Rte. 15 in Navojoa (see above), it is 34 miles on a dead-end road to reach the ancient silver city of Alamos. This city was already more than a century old when the king of Spain sent out a surveyor-general to plan out the main streets in 1750. Early Catholic missions were maintained in this isolated valley as early as 1613, and by 1685 some of the richest silver mines in the world were operating nearby.

Before the year 1800 the population had increased to 14,000 and Spain was benefiting by millions of pesos' worth of silver each year from the city and its industrious workers. Beautiful homes and government buildings were erected, and although the city changed hands many times in subsequent wars and the silver finally gave out (around 1900), there were very few physical changes. Today, Alamos is a National Monument and cannot be altered. It is an impressive sight.

Cobbled streets wind aimlessly around arcaded porticos, and the visitor quickly becomes affected by the isolation. Because of the valley's sheltered location, 1,400 feet above sea level, it has an excellent climate and flowers are abundant. There is a branch of the National Museum of Arts and Crafts and an American colony of enterprising souls who have bought old houses for a song and remodeled them into mansions.

Where to Stay and Eat: As this is a tourist town, most hotels are expensive, but there are several choices within our range. You can stay at the **Hotel Enriquez,** next to the Hotel Los Portales on the main square (Calle Juárez, no. 4, Alamos, Sonora; no phone), for 1,000 pesos ($2) per person—and less than that for longer stays. Of the 15 high-ceilinged rooms in the elegant old building, all of which open onto the arched inner courtyard, eight have a private hot-water bathroom, and the rest share baths; prices are the same either way. Attached is the **Restaurant OK,** right on the corner of the plaza, open 7 a.m. to 9 p.m., where you can get a variety of simple meals, with an order of quesadillas, beans and vegetables coming for 600 pesos ($1.20).

The aforementioned **Hotel Los Portales,** on the church plaza at Calle Juárez, no. 6, Alamos, Sonora (tel. 642/8-0221), is a much fancier place in the same basic style, very beautifully done, with a lovely courtyard boasting plants, decorated arches, and a large fireplace. The 11 rooms all have fireplace, overhead fan, and private bath. Singles here are 8,000 pesos ($16), doubles 11,000 pesos ($22).

As you enter Alamos from Navojoa, you'll see two acceptable motels just before you enter town. **Motel Somar,** Madero 10, Alamos, Sonora (tel. 642/8-0195), is a new motel, eager to please guests, and at this writing still in the planning stages for a restaurant, bar, and swimming pool. Present already are 28 very clean rooms, all with one double bed and one single bed, which rent for 3,000 pesos ($6) for one to four people. The motel is just across the street from the Parque Madero, which has facilities for sports and children's play.

Motel Dolisa, also on Madero (no number), Alamos, Sonora (tel. 642/8-0131), has eight rooms, with 28 trailer spaces out back. Rates are 3,500 pesos ($7) single, 4,600 pesos ($9.20) double, for rooms with a fireplace; firewood is an additional 600 pesos ($1.20). In summer, when air conditioning must be used, the rates are set 1,000 pesos ($2) higher to cover the cost of the cooling.

Alamos has a number of nice little places to eat. As you enter town either by bus or car, you find yourself on a grassy strip with a snack bar at one end; at the other end is the town's **mercado.** Lining the mercado, not inside but on the *outside* of the building, are several small cafés, some with only a couple of tables; you might walk along here and see what appeals to you. On the right-hand side as you face towards the market, is the **Loncheria Naturista Arco Iris** (tel. 8-0183) on Calle Aurora (no number). There's no sign outside, but when the doors are open they reveal (painted on their insides) lovely scenes of natural foods with blue mountains in the background, with two large rattan tables inside the small café. Service here is informal: Mario, the friendly owner, tells you what he has on hand right then and you make your selection.

For a more formal, sit-down meal, try the cheerful, colorfully decorated **Restaurant Las Palmeras** (tel. 8-0065), located on one corner of the church plaza at no. 9, Calle Lázaro Cárdenas. Open 6:30 a.m. to 10 p.m., the restaurant serves breakfasts for 700 to 750 pesos ($1.40 to $1.50), dinners for 1,250 to 2,000 pesos ($2.50 to $4), hamburgers for 1,000 pesos ($2), and a banana split for 500 pesos ($1). The house specialties are milanesa (breaded beef) for 1,400 pesos ($2.80), fried fish from the nearby reservoir Presa Macúsare for 1,250 pesos ($2.50), and a Sunday special of oven-roasted leg of pork for 1,250 pesos ($2.50).

What to Do: As Alamos is a small town, there's not a whole lot of big-city-type excitement, but it's a beautiful place for relaxing and strolling around. It's estimated that about 300 Americans, mostly retired, have made Alamos their permanent home, and a sizeable part of this colony came here when the town was isolated and inexpensive, bought old mansions and remodeled them into beauties. You can spend a lovely day just strolling around the streets of Alamos and seeing what you can glimpse of these, while you enjoy the overall beauty of the whole Spanish town. For a more intimate view of the mansions, be at the bank side of the church plaza any Saturday at 10 a.m. for the **Home and Garden Tour** sponsored by Alamos's Friends of the Library. Cost is 1,000 pesos ($2), and includes coffee and cookies served at the library in the government palacio just behind the cathedral at the end of the tour.

The **Palacio,** built in 1899, is a lovely building, as is the **cathedral** in the block just before it. Also on the cathedral plaza is the **museum,** open Wednesday through Sunday, 9 a.m. to 1 p.m. and 3 to 7 p.m. You can find beautiful art and craft work for sale in Alamos at several shops. Prices here are higher than in some other places, but quality tends to be very high as well. If your hotel doesn't give you a map of Alamos, pick one up at a crafts store for 100 pesos (20¢); it will help you as you walk around, alerting you to the many interesting sights tucked away all over town.

Outside of town, eight miles to the south on Carretera Guirocoba, the natural springs / swimming hole at **Cuchujaki** draws visitors year round, but especially in summer, when in addition to swimmers there are American students come to camp out. If you don't have a car, a taxi will take you from Alamos for 3,000 pesos ($6), returning for you at the time you specify if you ask the driver.

To the west of Alamos, the park **El Chalotón** is about 1¼ miles from downtown, especially popular during the months of June through October. A half mile farther on is **Solipasos,** another popular swimming hole. The presa (reservoir) **Macúsare** on the highway between Navojoa and Alamos, about equidistant between the two, is another fine place for swimming—and for fishing, too.

I've never been in Alamos in June, but they say that one of the most delightful pastimes all year takes place around then in the hills west of town. Twenty-one days after the first rain of the season, usually coming sometime in June, people take to the hills (the Sierra de Alamos) to hunt **Mexican jumping beans**—*los brincadores.* Early in the morning, when the sun begins to warm them up, they start jumping, and they say you can find them on the ground or rustling around in little piles of dry leaves. I've never yet been blessed with the chance to go hunting for the jumping beans of Alamos, but I hope to someday, so if you find any, please write and let me know how it was.

LOS MOCHIS: Los Mochis, Sinaloa (alt. 243 feet; pop. 111,800), is in a fertile agricultural area and, aside from the enormous sugar mill at the northwest end of town, there is not much of note. It is from here that you can board the Ferrocarril Chihuahua al Pacifico, which makes the 13-hour trip through the spectacular Copper Canyon to Chihuahua (see Section 2 of this chapter, under Chihuahua).

Where to Stay and Eat

A good place to stay is the two-story, 44-room **Hotel America,** two blocks south of Obregón on Allende Sur, at no. 655 Los Mochis, Sinaloa 81200 (tel. 681/2-1355). The second floor has an open sitting area with chairs, purified water, and an ice-making machine. Rooms are all air-conditioned and equipped with a telephone, and are priced at 3,500 pesos ($7) single, 4,000 pesos ($8) double with one bed, or 4,300 pesos ($8.60) double with two beds. (Try to get a room away from the street; the local buses, often without mufflers, pass by on Allende first thing in the morning.) The hotel has off-street parking. It's clean, friendly, and central, being only a block south of the Tres Estrellas de Oro bus station (with other bus stations nearby), and two blocks from the Hotel Catalina, which is pretty much the center of town. The America is operated by the same people who run the Hotel Beltran (see below).

Attached to the Hotel America is a restaurant with the same name. Most entrees range from 600 to 1,000 pesos ($1.20 to $2), while the comida corrida costs 800 pesos ($1.60). Open 7 a.m. to 11 p.m., except Sundays, when it closes at 3 p.m.

A block down from the Tres Estrellas de Oro bus station is the three-story **Hotel Lorena,** at the corner of Obregón and Guillermo Prieto 186 Pte., Los Mochis, Sinaloa 81200 (tel. 681/2-2039 or 2-0958). Very clean rooms priced at 3,500 pesos ($7) single, 4,300 pesos ($8.60) double, open onto large hallways with big rocking chairs all along the walls, and sitting groups of tables and chairs at the end of the hall. A restaurant up on the third floor is open from 7 to 11 a.m. and 7 to 11 p.m.

The **Hotel Fenix,** Angel Flores 365, Los Mochis, Sinaloa 81200 (tel. 681/2-2623), is another good downtown choice, with singles at 3,500 pesos ($7), doubles at 4,300 pesos ($8.60). The 35 clean, carpeted, air-conditioned rooms have TV, phone, and laundry and dry cleaning service. A 24-hour restaurant, the **Restaurant Jaramillo** (tel. 2-4137 and 5-1868), opens onto the hotel lobby. Breakfast combination specials at 1,000 pesos ($2) are served from 5 to 11 a.m., with the comida corrida, priced at 1,200 pesos ($2.40), served between 2 and 4 p.m. Dinner entrees are priced around 1,300 pesos ($2.60). You can order anything anytime from the extensive à la carte menu.

The six-story **Hotel Catalina,** Obregón Pte. 36 at Allende Sur, Los Mochis, Sinaloa 81200 (tel. 681/2-1240), is another possibility. All 50 rooms show signs of wear. Singles go for 3,500 pesos ($7), doubles with one or two beds for 4,300 pesos ($8.60). The lobby is spartan but functional, and includes a restaurant specializing in Oriental food. And there's air conditioning throughout.

The three-story Hotel Beltran, on the corner of Hidalgo and Zaragoza 281 Pte., Los Mochis, Sinaloa 81200 (tel. 681/2-0039, 2-0010, and 2-0688), has had its ups and downs in this book, but is now very much on the up. The 42 rooms, some with views of the city, all have air conditioning and telephone. Singles are 3,500 pesos ($7), doubles with one bed 4,075 pesos ($8.15), and doubles with two beds 4,300 pesos ($8.60). Purified water and an ice-making machine can be found on each floor, along with pleasant sitting rooms complete with rocking chairs.

The most luxurious hotel in Los Mochis is the **Hotel Santa Anita,** at the corner of Leyva and Hidalgo (no number), Los Mochis, Sinaloa 81200, (tel. 681/

2-0046); it's the six-story edifice you'll see a block down from the Hotel Beltran. Prices are higher here, of course, with singles at 9,143 pesos ($18.28), doubles 10,868 pesos ($21.73). Services correspond to the luxury of the hotel, with uniformed waiters for room service from the attached restaurant and bar, color cable TV and telephone in each of the 133 rooms, parking, laundry, etc. Perhaps best of all are the travel services offered, with information available about airlines, side trips, and any other travel arrangements you may want to make. Even if you're not staying here, you can still come here to avail yourself of the travel services.

Aside from the restaurants at the above hotels, Los Mochis hosts several other good places to dine. If your budget can stand a small splurge, try the finest restaurant in Los Mochis, **El Farallon** (tel. 2-1273 or 2-1428), on Obregón (no. 495—if it had a number) at Flores, down the block from the Restaurant Madrid (see below). The walls are painted with murals depicting the wealth of the Sea of Cortés and also the new agricultural pride of the area: the dam on the Fuerte River. Fish nets strung about, seashells, sharks' jaws, and glass fishing floats complete the nautical decor. The restaurant is air-conditioned and holds about 40 tables. The bilingual menu sports a wide selection of seafood dishes, including exotica such as frogs' legs, marlin, and sea turtle. For a seafood dinner of soup, fish or shrimp, dessert, and coffee, you pay about 2,070 pesos ($4.14). For dessert, try the fresh fruit displayed in the refrigerated case near the cashier. An alternative, melon with ice cream, will cool you on even the hottest summer day.

The **Restaurant Madrid** (tel. 2-3461), Obregón 414 at Leyva, is plain but nice, its tables covered with white cloths, and the white cloths thriftily covered with plate-glass tops. The air conditioning is powerful, the food is good, the portions are big, and the prices are low: the comida corrida, served noon to 4 p.m., is 1,260 pesos ($2.52) daily, with the Sunday special at 1,600 pesos ($3.20). The extensive dinner menu includes seafood dishes as well as a wide variety of entrees, with Chateaubriand for two at 3,000 pesos ($6), filet mignon with mushrooms at 1,800 pesos ($3.60), and breakfasts around 600 pesos ($1.20). Open 7 a.m. to midnight. (If you don't find the Madrid at the address above, look for it at Obregón 520 Pte. A new location is being built, with space for a larger restaurant, a bar, and a discothèque.)

Just down the block from the Hotel Beltran is another good restaurant specializing in seafood, **Restaurant Henry** (tel. 2-3959), at Hidalgo 147 Pte., open 9 a.m. to 8 p.m. You'll see fresh oysters being opened in the window out front. The wide variety of seafood entrees come for 800 to 1,000 pesos ($1.60 to $2).

There are many places around town to get a licuado or jugo (fruit juice). One place with a good selection is **Jugos Gema** at Hidalgo 161. You can get a good variety of licuados with a little wheat germ sprinkled in for 250 pesos (50¢), yogurt with fruit for 300 pesos (60¢), and escamochas for 350 pesos (70¢). Open 7 a.m. to 8 p.m.

Side Trips

The Ferrocarril Chihuahua al Pacifico station is about three miles from the center of town on a street with the unpronounceable name of Netzahualcóyotl. Trains leave from here daily for Copper Canyon and Chihuahua at 6 a.m., Mountain Time. Take note: The railroad runs on Central Time, although Los Mochis is on Mountain Time! This means that if the train is scheduled to depart Los Mochis at 7 a.m. railway time, it pulls out at 6 a.m. local time! (See Section 2 of this chapter, on Chihuahua, for more details.) You can buy your first-class train ticket at the Viajes Flamingo travel agency (tel. 681/2-1613 and 2-1929), located on the ground floor of the Hotel Santa Anita, for 3,980 pesos ($7.96).

Viajes Flamingo is open daily except Sunday, from 8 a.m. to 1 p.m. and 3 to 6 p.m.

At Viajes Flamingo you can also get tickets for a city tour of Los Mochis, which includes a boat ride on nearby Topolobampo Bay, for 4,000 pesos ($8).

From Topolobampo, a ferry leaves for La Paz, Baja California, every Monday, Tuesday, Thursday, and Friday, at 10 a.m. The cost is 500 pesos ($1), and the trip takes about eight hours. Bring your own food and drink. The bus from Los Mochis to Topolobampo leaves from the Pemex gas station around the corner from the Tres Estrellas de Oro bus station (across the boulevard from the Hotel America) every 20 minutes throughout the day, starting at 5:45 a.m., but to get the one that goes all the way to the ferry terminal about two miles outside the town of Topolobampo, be there for the bus that leaves between 7:30 and 8 a.m.

CULIACÁN: Almost equidistant between Los Mochis and Mazatlán (130 miles from the former, 140 miles from the latter) is Culiacán, capital of Sinaloa. The surrounding region, located between the foothills of the Sierra Madre and the Pacific, is a rich agricultural one abounding in cotton, peanuts, and some of the world's finest tomatoes. The last are regularly exported to the U.S., as is that illegal commodity derived from the sector's abundant poppy fields. Along with Southeast Asia, the Culiacán area is one of the world's greatest producers of crude opium.

On a happier note, Culiacán itself is a humming, progressive city of 560,000, where modern buildings stand cheek-by-jowl with structures dating back to colonial times. Examples of both can be seen on Plaza Obregón, where a lovely old cathedral looks across the park at some of the most futuristic architecture in Mexico.

Where to Stay and Eat

The bus station is about a mile from the center of town, but right across the street from the first-class station is the **Hotel Salvador,** Boulevard L. Solano (the main highway) at Calle Ramón Corona 287 Pte., Culiacán, Sinaloa (tel. 671/3-7466). The 40 rooms all have air conditioning, bath, black-and-white TV, and carpeting, for 6,325 pesos ($12.65) single, 7,475 pesos ($14.95) double.

A block along the street from the Salvador is the snazzier **Hotel del Valle,** Boulevard Leyva Solano 180 Ore., Culiacán, Sinaloa (tel. 671/3-9020). It's right at a traffic circle, an odd mod-colonial building with spikes along the top of the façade as the colonial touch, but with carpeting and air conditioning inside, plus services including laundry, dry cleaning, telephone and TV in the rooms, a nice restaurant attached, and enclosed parking across the street for an extra 400 pesos (80¢) every 12 hours. The restaurant, open 7 a.m. to 11 p.m., offers various breakfast specials from 560 to 900 pesos ($1.12 to $1.80), a comida corrida for 1,200 pesos ($2.40), and meat entrees priced from 1,300 to 1,800 pesos ($2.60 to $3.60). The del Valle looks as if it had once been pretty fancy, but now it's a bit worn.

At both of the above hotels, you'll have to beware of the noise inherent in their location right on the main highway. But not at the spacious, quiet **Hotel 3 Rios,** on the Carretera Internacional, km. 1423, Calidad Norte, Culiacán, Sinaloa (tel. 671/5-4440). Rooms here are all spread out around a large garden acreage at the side of one of the three rivers flowing through Culiacán, from which the hotel gets its name. You'll see an arched wall out front, with a restaurant and bar inside completing the hotel complex. Rooms at this luxury hotel go for 10,580 pesos ($21.16) single, 11,385 pesos ($22.77) double.

Three blocks up from the bus station, past the Hotel del Valle, is an outdoor plaza where you'll see about 50 umbrellaed tables spread around a **snack bar** located across from the fountain, with lots of shady trees. This is the corner of Boulevard Leyva Solano and Avenida Obregón, one of Culiacán's principal thoroughfares. The snack bar, open 7 a.m. to 10 p.m., offers escamochas, licuados, and cool drinks. Be sure to see the statue of the opulent Indian woman in the fountain at the other side of the snack bar, putting to shame the American idea that to be beautiful a woman must be shaped like a pencil. (Culiacán, by the way, is famous for the beauty of its women.)

Going down Avenida Obregón you will come to Culiacán's large, beautiful **cathedral,** dedicated in 1842, with its two white bell towers and high round dome towering over the plaza and street below, a cool oasis of tranquillity, timelessness, spirituality, and powerful artwork in this thriving, busy city.

Down this stretch of Avenida Obregón you will see many little cafés where you can get antojitos, snacks, tortas, sandwiches, jugos, escamochas, and so on. But if you feel like a treat, why not try the pizza at **La Távola Pizza** (tel. 3-8561), "la buena mesa" at Obregón and Colón (no number), where you see the round red-and-white-striped awning out over the sidewalk. It's air-conditioned, has a nice wooden and rattan decor with pictures and posters of American movie stars all around, plays happy music, and has good pizza at a good price. A basic cheese pizza comes for 550 pesos ($1.10) small size, 900 pesos ($1.80) medium, and 1,150 pesos ($2.30) for the large "familiar"—large enough to feed the whole family. In all, 17 combinations are offered, with most large-size combos priced around 1,900 pesos ($3.80). Spaghetti and cheese fondue are also served from the bilingual menu, at 800 and 900 pesos ($1.60 and $1.80) apiece. Open noon to midnight.

Onward to the Resorts

From Culiacán it's an easy three-hour drive to Mazatlán, the most northerly of Mexico's fabulous Pacific resorts. Pretty country separates the two cities, with rolling uplands gradually yielding to fertile tropic savannahs.

Not far to the south of where you are now, some of Mexico's most exciting attractions await you. Refer to Chapter III for the rundown on the resort towns along the coast, from Mazatlán all the way to Puerto Angel in the state of Oaxaca. Chapter IV is devoted to Guadalajara, Mexico's second-largest city, and the towns and sights around it. From Guadalajara you can journey to the fascinating Silver Cities of the northern Valley of Mexico (Chapter V), or on to the largest (and in my opinion also the greatest) city in the world—México, D.F. (Chapters VI through XII).

2. The El Paso Route: Chihuahua to Fresnillo

An alternate route to the Valley of Mexico from the southwestern U.S. is through El Paso, Texas (Ciudad Juárez on the Mexican side), and down either Highway 45 through Durango or Highway 49 through Torreón. The Durango way offers no particular advantage unless you're heading for Mazatlán and the Pacific Coast resorts. Highway 49 via Torreón, on the other hand, takes you straight into the Colonial Silver Cities (see Chapter V) in the northern part of the Valley of Mexico. The bus will undoubtedly follow 49 to Fresnillo, near where the two highways merge to become Highway 45/49, parting ways again east of Zacatecas.

Although the range of the Sierra Madre Occidental divides this route from the one in the previous section, there are several points at which it is practical to cross over. The Chihuahua al Pacifico Railroad (described below) will take you from Chihuahua to Los Mochis, and will take your car as well, for a price. You can drive or bus over the mountains from Durango if your goal is Mazatlán.

Border formalities at the Ciudad Juárez Customs and Immigration station take between 30 minutes and an hour, the longer period if you're bringing in a car. Then it's a four-hour ride along a straight, fast road to Chihuahua, 230 miles to the south.

Readers have mentioned that if you're going by bus, it's much easier if you get your Mexican bus ticket in El Paso, before you cross the border, rather than waiting until you get to Ciudad Juárez on the other side, where the bus station is often very crowded. They say the Omnibus de México buses depart from the Trailways bus station, while Transportes Chihuahuenses depart from the Greyhound terminal. By doing it this way, you are assured of getting a reserved seat through to your destination, and a speedy crossover through the border station.

CHIHUAHUA: This American-style city (alt. 4,700 feet; pop. 700,000) is the capital of the state of Chihuahua, the largest and richest state in Mexico. The money comes from mining, timber, and cattle-raising besides the industry in the city, and you'll notice lots of well-dressed businessmen striding purposefully through its streets. Somehow, they manage to impart their aura of hardworking prosperity to the rest of the city.

Aside from its industry, Chihuahua boasts a modern university, a museum in the house where Pancho Villa lived, and those tiny, hairless Chihuahua dogs. According to many Chihuahuans, the little dogs are rapidly becoming extinct around here, but a few kennels still raise them and sell them in the Sunday market.

Getting to and from Chihuahua

There's air service from Mexico City, but if you're going through Chihuahua you're undoubtedly going by land.

By Bus: Transportes Chihuahuenses is the big local line, but Omnibus de México and Autobuses Estrella Blanca also run big buses from the border through Chihuahua to points south. Check with them at the Central Camionera.

From the Central Camionera (bus station, "BUS" on map), you can see the several tall buildings which mark Chihuahua's center. If you feel like going downtown, you can walk, and it's easy to orient yourself from anywhere in the city if you keep an eye on the tall buildings—I use the tall tower "El Presidente," on the corner of Juárez and Independencia, easy to spot even at night with its flashing lights, about 20 stories tall. If you're not up for a long walk, however, I recommend taking a taxi. City buses easily bring you *back* to the Central Camionera (look for "C. Camionera" in white paint on the bus windshield) from downtown, but for some reason it's not so easy to go from the bus station to the city's center.

By Train: Two daily trains in each direction connect Chihuahua and Ciudad Juárez, at the border, departing Juárez at 10 a.m. and 5 p.m. From Chihuahua to Juárez the trains leave at 8 a.m. and 6 p.m. Trains from Chihuahua south to Mexico City depart every night at 11:25 p.m. The main station (11) in Chihuahua is at the northeastern end of Avenida División del Norte. Leave the center of town by Avenida Universidad (going northwest), and turn right at Avenida División del Norte.

And then there's the famous **Chihuahua al Pacifico Railway,** in a class by itself, one of the world's great train rides (described later in this section).

Where to Stay

As you bypass the town, coming in from the north on Route 45, you'll see the **Santa Rita Motel (1),** Avenida Tecnológico 4702, Chihuahua, Chih. 31310 (tel. 141/17-4047), whose 30 roomy units are nestled among shade trees and flowering plants. Rates are average—singles 3,105 pesos ($6.21), doubles 3,910 pesos ($7.82)—but the entire motel is in the process of being remodeled, and as they are completed, with new furniture, carpet, bathroom tile, etc., the refurbished rooms are given price tags of about 5,000 pesos ($10) single and 7,325 pesos ($14.65) double. There's a beautiful, giant-size pool in the back, open April through September, and the rooms are spacious and pleasant, with both heat and air conditioning—and a bonus is the convenience of staying right on the highway.

Starvation Budget Hotels: Very inexpensive in price, but actually a quite enjoyable place to stay, is the **Hotel Reforma (5),** Calle Victoria 809, Chihuahua, Chih. 31300 (tel. 141/12-5808), just a few doors down from Ocampo. It's an old mansion, evidently a really fancy place when it was built in 1913. The rooms facing the street have French doors opening onto little balconies; the others face an inner courtyard, now covered, which serves as the lobby. Rooms are very basic, but clean, with private hot water bath. Rooms with one double bed (for one or two people) go for 1,265 pesos ($2.53); it's 1,380 pesos ($2.76) for two twin-size beds, and 1,495 pesos ($2.99) for a room with one double bed and one twin (two or three people).

The **Hotel Santa Regina (12),** at Calle 3a between Juárez and Doblado (no number), Chihuahua, Chih. 31300 (tel. 141/15-3889), is an economical choice right downtown. Single rooms here go for 2,000 pesos ($4) basic up to 3,500 pesos ($7) for a room with both carpet and TV; doubles are priced at 2,200 to 3,700 pesos ($4.40 to $7.40) with one bed, 2,800 to 4,500 pesos ($5.60 to $9) with two beds.

The **Motel Nieves (1)** on Route 45, at the corner of Technológico and Ahuehuete, Chihuahua, Chih. 31310 (tel. 141/13-2516), is just a few blocks south of the older, aforementioned Santa Rita and is another good on-the-highway choice. Despite its arctic name (*nieves* could mean "snow" or "ice cream"), you will find no polar bears at the Nieves, but after a hot drive across the state of Chihuahua the clean, air-conditioned rooms and the two swimming pools (open April to September) will do very nicely. You will pay 5,106 pesos ($10.21) single, 6,383 pesos ($12.76) double to stay here, but that includes a staff which speaks some English, a nice shady poolside copse, and 70 rooms to choose from. The motel has a restaurant, and smaller, less expensive eateries are nearby. For campers, the motel provides a bare but hookup-equipped lot in the rear.

Halfway between in-town and on-the-road is the grand and pleasant **Hotel Victoria** at the corner of Avenidas Juárez and Colón, Chihuahua, Chih. 31300 (tel. 141/12-8893), only a few blocks from the highway and ten blocks from the main plaza. The Victoria is a substantial place richly decorated with colored tiles, run by a soft-spoken and attentive staff, and patronized by well-to-do Mexican businessmen who drive big cars. Room doors open onto mezzanine-like walkways that tower in tiers above the lobby-courtyard, an early version of the Hyatt Regency design. The entire place is air-conditioned, and rooms cost 6,382 pesos ($12.75) single or double, with bath. A bar, restaurant, disco, swimming pool, car-rental agency, and private parking lot fill out the services. Two travel agencies in the lobby provide information on the Copper Canyon Railway and various tours, with information also on how to connect to other points from Los Mochis when you disembark the train. You can walk, drive, or take a bus or cab straight down Juárez into the heart of town.

A good place to stay in the downtown area is the **Hotel Bal-Flo (3),** at the corner of Niños Héroes and Calle 5a, no. 702 (tel. 141/16-0300). All 91 rooms

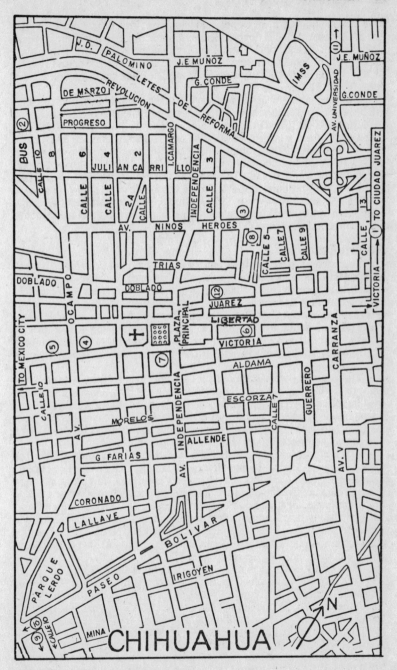

have air conditioning, heat, carpet, and telephone, for 4,025 pesos ($8.05) single, 5,175 pesos ($10.35) double. The proprietor, Sr. Baltazar Flores, speaks English and is quite helpful. There is underground parking and a cafeteria serving a variety of good food. Breakfasts range from 575 to 1,150 pesos ($1.15 to $2.30), antojitos 690 to 1,380 pesos ($1.38 to $2.76), and hamburgers 402 to 690 pesos (80¢ to $1.38).

Over by the central camionera are two other hotel choices, both of which can be seen as you exit the door of the bus station. The **Hotel del Cobre (2)**, on the corner of Calle 10 and Progreso, Chihuahua, Chih. 31300 (tel. 141/15-1660), is the better deal, with singles at 3,060 pesos ($6.12), doubles 3,824 pesos ($7.64), for clean, modern rooms with air conditioning, carpeting, and phone, some with TV, and a restaurant open 7 a.m. to 11 p.m. There's also the **Hotel El Dorado**, at the corner of Calle 14 and Julian Carrillo, Chihuahua, Chih. 31300 (tel. 141/12-5770), similar to the del Cobre but a little more expensive at 4,150 pesos ($8.30) single, 4,715 pesos ($9.43) double. There's a restaurant here, too, open 7 a.m. to 10 p.m., and a separate ladies' bar open nightly from 8 p.m. to 4 a.m. with a variety show.

Where to Eat

The cafeteria in the Central Camionera is as good a place as any to have an informal lunch or dinner or some quick breakfast eggs. Prices are kept at a reasonable level because you do the serving (it's a real cafeteria line) and the problem of choosing unfamiliar dishes from a foreign-language menu is not present—you choose the unfamiliar dishes by sight from the hot table in the line. (When in doubt, ask *"Es piquante?"*—eys-pee-kahn-teh—"Is it spicy?") Prices are marked near the dishes: stews and soups are 330 to 830 pesos (66¢ to $1.66), a quarter chicken 850 pesos ($1.70); free seconds on coffee. Open 24 hours a day.

Those out for a walk in the center of the city might try the **Cafetería Liveer (6),** (tel. 15-4902), at Libertad 318 between Calles 3 and 5, another walk-down-the-line style cafeteria. Bright and clean, it serves a variety of main dishes, side dishes, salads, desserts, and drinks at reasonable prices: chicken 530 pesos ($1.06), chiles with rice and corn 600 pesos ($1.20), enchiladas 180 pesos (36¢). You can get hot snacks "to go" from the window out front.

A few blocks east of the main plaza is **El Herradero (8)** (tel. 16-9404), on Calle 5a between Trías and Niños Héroes (no number). Open 7 a.m. to 11 p.m., it serves good food—and lots of it—for a very good price, in a pleasant atmosphere. There are five breakfast specials offered from 360 to 500 pesos (72¢ to $1); for example, for 400 pesos (80¢) you can get eggs a la Mexicana (or any way you like), beans, hearty homemade flour tortillas, buttered toast with jam, plus fruit juice and coffee. The comida corrida, for only 800 pesos ($1.60), is served daily from noon until 4:30 p.m. Many antojitos come for 500 pesos ($1) per order, and steak and potatoes is 850 pesos ($1.70).

For a really nice, fancy meal, try the restaurant **Degá (4)** (tel. 16-7550 or 16-7770), located beside the Hotel San Francisco at Calle Victoria 409, just off Ocampo. The hotel is beyond our budget, at 13,455 pesos ($26.91) single, 14,375 pesos ($28.75) double, but the restaurant/cafeteria/bar is surprisingly economical for the good quality it offers. For dinner, try the T-bone, sirloin, or filet mignon steaks for 2,070 pesos ($4.14), Mexican specialties priced from 748 pesos ($1.49) for chiles rellenos (stuffed peppers) up to 2,000 pesos ($4) for the special house filet, black bass for 1,587 pesos ($3.17), or shrimp al Pernod for 2,700 pesos ($5.40), in the restaurant section with a Scottish decor of matching red plaid on tables and wall and scenes of European fox hunting. There are fully 20 breakfast combinations to choose from, priced at 575 to 1,500 pesos ($1.15 to

$3), and a special Sunday buffet, served 1 to 5 p.m., for 2,015 pesos ($4.03). Live music is featured in the bar. Open 7 a.m. to 1:30 a.m.

What to Do

For a diversion in Chihuahua, take a drive past the statue of Pancho Villa at Division del Norte and Avenida Universidad. To your right, you'll see **Chihuahua University,** a series of rather unimaginative modern buildings against a backdrop of dry, rocky mountains. Note the cattle-raising school and meteorological institute—evidences that Mexico is well aware of the importance of its money-making industries and of the necessity for systematizing knowledge that once passed informally from generation to generation. The university also has an extensive "sports city," whose special pride is the basketball court (basketball is popular in these parts); it includes a swimming pool, baseball stadium, and, to relieve your fears of too much Americana, a jai alai court.

The **Museum of Pancho Villa (9)** (tel. 141/16-2958), at Calle 10 no. 3014, on the corner of Calle 10 and Mendez, is located in Villa's former house on what was once the outskirts of the city. Luz Corral de Villa, Villa's legitimate wife (he had others, they say), lived in the house until her death in 1981. Exhibits include Villa's weapons, some personal effects, lots of period photos, and the 1922 Dodge in which he was shot in 1923, complete with bullet holes. Open every day 9 a.m. to 1 p.m. and 3 to 7 p.m.; admission 20 pesos (4¢). To get to the Villa house, first thing to do is to ignore the street address, for Calle 10 is not simply one street but in fact a discontinuous assortment of streets, alleys, thoroughfares, etc., now on the west side of Ocampo, later on the southeast side. Do this: From downtown, go down Ocampo until you get to the intersection of 20 de Noviembre, just a few blocks past Parque Lerdo; you'll see a large traffic circle in the middle of the intersection with a tall statue bearing a clock, and a big church will be on the corner to your right. Go two blocks further on Ocampo, bringing you to Mendez; turn left here and go another two blocks, and you'll be there at the corner of Calle 10 and Mendez, just outside Pancho Villa's walled garden. The entrance is around the corner to your left, on Calle 10. If you're starting from downtown, you can walk, but it's several blocks; you might want to take the city bus "Colonia Dale" which heads west down Juárez, turning south onto Ocampo, and will let you off on the corner of Ocampo and Mendez.

You can get information at any travel agency—the ones in the lobby of the Hotel Victoria are fine—about a number of interesting side trips to places near Chihuahua. For example, there's a **Mennonite colony** in the town of Cuauhtémoc, about two hours' ride west of Chihuahua; you can go by train (the Chihuahua al Pacifico railway passes by there), by car or bus west on Hwy. 16, or you can take one of the tours offered by Viajes Cañon del Cobre (tel. 141/12-8893, ext. 607) at the Hotel Victoria. The Mennonites still live as they did in Germany 150 years ago, costume and all. Another worthwhile side trip is to the **ruins of Paquimé** near Casas Grandes, about three hours to the north of Chihuahua on Hwy. 10. Here you will find the archeological excavations of northern Mexico's most important pre-Hispanic city, with many-storied architecture and step pyramids built before the city was attacked by Aztecs in the 14th century. (You can see this as a side trip from Chihuahua, or you can stay over in the nearby town of Nuevo Casas Grandes, about five miles to the northeast of the ruins.)

THE CHIHUAHUA AL PACIFICO RAILROAD: If you're headed west from Chihuahua rather than south, you have a scenic treat in store for you on one of the world's most unique train rides. The Ferrocarril Chihuahua al Pacifico runs Vistadome trains daily from Chihuahua to Los Mochis. The distance covered is

406 miles and the trip, taking about 12½ hours, is as fascinating culturally as it is scenically. The high spot, literally and figuratively, is a 9,000-foot elevation called **Divisadero,** where the train makes a 15-minute stop and passengers are allowed to get off and take pictures. Divisadero is in the heart of the Tarahumara country, land of those cave-dwelling Indians who wear a costume resembling a diaper and are world-famous long-distance runners. It also overlooks the incredible **Barranca de Cobre,** 1,500 feet deeper than the Grand Canyon and four times as wide. Citizens who painfully scrimp for that jet vacation in the Caribbean would envy the way the Tarahumaras "go south" for the winter. Leaving the snowy pine forests of the rimrock country, they simply descend to the base of the canyon where orchids bloom and the climate is balmily subtropical. The train leaves Chihuahua at 7 a.m. and makes the return trip from Los Mochis the same time (7 a.m. Mountain Time, 6 a.m. Central Time) daily.

For this long trip, it's best to get tickets in the first-class, reserved section (the "Vistatren") at 4,702 pesos ($9.40), as these areas are roomy with reclining seats. A dining/bar car is attached offering breakfast, lunch, and dinner, but you'd be better off bringing picnic supplies.

A conventional train, called the "Mixto," leaves Chihuahua at 7:20 a.m. Monday, Wednesday, and Friday, and at 2,017 pesos ($4.03), it costs less than half the Vistatren price. (The same train leaves Los Mochis at the same time— 7:20 a.m. Central Time, 6:20 a.m. Mountain Time, on Tuesday, Thursday, and Saturday.) However, most travelers say that the small amount of money saved in no way makes it worthwhile to take this train, which is described as dirty, crowded, and without the large windows for viewing that the Vistatren offers. Also, the Mixto train covers the distance more slowly, stopping off in every little village along the way, meaning that you may be in the dark for part of the journey, missing the breathtaking scenery. I haven't tried the Mixto train myself, but after hearing all this from so many travelers, I'd recommend taking the Vistatren.

You can take the same line to or from the U.S.-Mexico border at Ojinaga-Presidio, Texas. Trains leave Chihuahua for Ojinaga at 7 a.m. Monday, Wednesday, and Friday.

Note that the entire railroad operates on Central Time, despite the fact that Los Mochis is in the Mountain Time Zone.

Note too that the Ferrocarril de Chihuahua al Pacifico has its own stations (no. 10 on map) in both Chihuahua and Los Mochis—these trains do *not* leave from the "main" stations. Tickets are available at the stations (in Chihuahua at the station in the southern part of town, behind the penitentiary; go out Ocampo or 20 de Noviembre to the intersection of these two main streets, where you'll see a large church and a traffic circle with a tall clock tower in the middle of the intersection. From here, it's two blocks down 20 de Noviembre to the prison, a huge walled building with towers; the train station is one block behind the prison, right beside the tracks).

You can reserve tickets in advance through your hotel, the travel agency in the lobby of Hotel Victoria (Viajes Cañon del Cobre, tel. 141/12-8893, ext. 607), or by writing Superintendent General de Tráfico, F.C. Chihuahua al Pacifico, Apdo. Postal 46, Chihuahua, Chih. 31300, México (tel. 141/12-2284 or 12-3867), but you must still buy your reserved tickets at the train station. I must warn you that several readers have written to say that ticketing on this railroad is a hassle, especially the purchase in advance of round-trip, reserved-seat tickets. It's best to get your tickets at the station, where they are on sale Monday through Friday from 5:30 to 9 a.m. and 11 a.m. to 2 p.m., Saturday 5:30 to 8:30 a.m., and Sunday from 6 to 9 a.m.

In recent years, it has become popular to make a stopover somewhere along the way between Chihuahua and Los Mochis, rather than always forging straight through. You'll see why when you travel this route: the 15 minute pause at Divisadero is nowhere near enough time to savor the mysterious beauty of the canyon, but with the Vistatren running only once a day, you must stay at least one night to gain more time—a very pleasant prospect here.

When you buy a ticket between Chihuahua and Los Mochis, it is good for one month and you can get on and off the train as many times as you want in that month; the catch is that you must specify dates and locations of getting off and on again at the time you purchase your ticket. This is fine if you know exactly what your plans are, and it reserves your seat for your entire trip. But it does mean that you must stick to that schedule, since the ticket is good only for the dates specified and once you've bought it, you cannot change it. You may wish to buy the ticket for shorter distances along the way, enabling you to spend as much time as you like in any location, continuing on when you are ready to do so.

Creel

One popular spot to stop over along the Chihuahua al Pacifico Railroad is the village of **Creel** (alt. 8,400 feet; pop. 7,000), a five-hour ride west of Chihuahua. Creel is located right in the heart of Tarahumara Indian country, about 30 miles from the Divisadero; it makes a fine place to stay while making explorations of the surrounding canyons. There are many scenic spots nearby, including several canyons, waterfalls, a lake, a hot springs, Tarahumara villages and cave dwellings, the Divisadero, and an ancient Jesuit mission. You can ask for information about these and other things to do from your hotel; at the time of this writing, the best deal in a variety of tours was being offered by the Motel Parador de la Montaña, with more economical (also more irregular and informal) tours offered through the Casa de Huespedes Margarita, and yet others organized by the Hotel Nuevo.

If you're planning to do any strenuous hiking, rock climbing, or adventuring, it's strongly recommended that you take someone with you who knows the area—you're in the wilderness out here, and you can't count on anyone coming along to rescue you should an accident occur far from civilization.

For being such a small town, Creel has quite a number of places to stay. The only industries in town are lumber and the international tourism attracted to the region. You may see travelers from every country in the world, especially if you're coming during the busy tourist seasons of December, Semana Santa (the week before Easter), or July and August. If you're coming at these times, be sure to reserve a room in advance if at all possible—and clarify the price, since prices in Creel are subject to being higher during these busy seasons. (They may also be lower during the off-seasons, when the available inns must compete for customers. It never hurts to ask for a lower price at these times.)

Getting to and from Creel: You can get to Creel on any of the Chihuahua al Pacifico trains. If you're coming from Chihuahua, you can take the Vistatren for 2,118 pesos ($4.23), the Mixto for 908 pesos ($1.81), or the special nonstop Autovia, running only between Chihuahua and Creel, also for 2,118 pesos ($4.23), leaving Chihuahua at 8 a.m. Monday, Wednesday, Friday, Saturday, and Sunday.

Where to Stay and Eat: One of the nicest places to stay in Creel is the **Casa de Huespedes Margarita,** the private home of a gracious hostess, Margarita, and her family. There's no sign, but it's easy to find, right on the zócalo, between the two churches, at no. 11 Lopez Mateos. You'll likely find Margarita in the kitchen cooking—she's well known as an excellent cook, and the 2,500 pesos ($5) she charges per person per night includes two home-cooked meals into the bargain. There are four rooms with their own private hot-water bath, plus six more guest rooms in both Margarita's own home and the house next door in which guests share bathrooms. Look in the guest book and you'll find comments written by travelers from every country in Europe, plus Mexico, the U.S.A., Canada, Australia, and New Zealand, and even some writing in Japanese. For advance reservations, send a check to Sra. Margarita Quinteros de González, Avenida Lopez Mateos y Parróquia No. 11, Estación Creel, Chih. 33200, México. (To telephone ahead, call the general phone—the *caseta*—for the town of Creel, and ask for Margarita.)

The **Hotel Korachi,** right across from the train station at Avenida Ferrocarril 116, Creel, Chih. 33200 (tel. 145/6-0207), offers 14 rooms sharing sex-segregated bathrooms, with prices at 1,500 pesos ($3) single, 2,000 pesos ($4) for two sharing a bed, and 2,500 pesos ($5) for two with two beds. There are also eight cabañas (cabins) out back, with private bath, wood stove for heat, a balcony with table and chairs, and two double beds; cabaña prices are 3,000 pesos ($6) single, 5,000 pesos ($10) double. Inspect the facilities before you pay for a room here: I've heard reports that housekeeping standards have varied quite a bit, sometimes fine and sometimes not.

Also across from the train station on Avenida Ferrocarril, Creel, Chih. 33200, is the **Hotel Nuevo** (tel. 145/6-0022). The listed price is 3,000 pesos ($6) single, 6,000 pesos ($12) double, but it can vary a lot with the seasons. There's a restaurant attached serving breakfast for 800 pesos ($1.60), comida for 1,750 pesos ($3.50), and dinner for 1,500 pesos ($3). The Nuevo also offers a number of tours to many places, ranging in length from 2 to 12 hours, with prices set at 3,450 pesos ($6.90) *per hour* for a group of 1 to 6 people, with additional people an extra 500 pesos ($1) per hour each.

The luxury accommodation in town is the **Motel Parador de la Montaña** (tel. 145/6-0075 or 6-0085), a few blocks west of the zócalo on Avenida Lopez Mateos (no number). There's a discothèque, bar, and restaurant, numerous daily tours, and 35 very large, clean, and fancy rooms, with two big double beds, high wood-beamed ceilings, and a beautifully tiled private bathroom entered through a brick archway. Prices here are higher, of course: singles cost 8,855 pesos ($17.71), doubles 10,120 pesos ($20.24). Even if you're not staying here, you can still come by for a tour or a delicious meal in the restaurant; selections on the bilingual menu include steak with soup, salad, and potatoes for 2,000 to 2,500 pesos ($4 to $5), black bass for 1,250 pesos ($2.50), enchiladas for 720 pesos ($1.44), and a Mexican combination with tostada, taco, chile relleño, quesadilla, and beans for 875 pesos ($1.75). You can reserve a room by calling or writing either to the motel itself in Creel, or to its Chihuahua office at Calle Allende 114, Chihuahua, Chih. 31300 (tel. 141/12-2062 and 15-5408).

Stretched along the blocks between the zócalo and the Motel Parador are several small family restaurants, all serving roughly the same type of typical Mexican dishes for about the same prices. The one most often recommended is the **Restaurant El Metate** (no phone or street number), serving eggs as you like them or a hamburger with ham and cheese for 500 pesos ($1), fried chicken for 700 pesos ($1.40), burritos for 200 pesos (40¢), and beef or shrimp entrees for 1,200 pesos ($2.40).

Other Stopoffs

Aside from Creel, there are several other places along the Chihuahua al Pacifico railway where one can spend the night or a few days; you can ask at travel agents in either Chihuahua or Los Mochis and get the rundown on them. One that is especially well recommended by travelers is the **Posada Barranca del Cobre,** just a five-minute walk from the edge of the canyon, with its own railroad stop an eight-minute ride west of the Divisadero. It's a great starting place for excursions into the canyon on foot or horseback. The price of $25 per person for the large, luxurious rooms with fireplaces hewn of local stone includes three meals. For reservations and current rates, you can contact the office at Calle Mina 1403, Apdo. Postal 725, Chihuahua, Chih. 31300 (tel. 141/16-5950), or the Hotel Santa Anita in Los Mochis on the corner of Leyva and Hidalgo (tel. 681/2-0046), or a travel agent. You also might want to ask a travel agent about "the hotel that is perched right on the cliffs at Divisadero."

JIMÉNEZ: The small city of Jiménez (pop. 18,095) is located at the bifurcation of Hwys. 45 and 49, about 140 miles south of Chihuahua. If you want an overnight stop away from the big cities, the best you can do here is the **Motel Florido** (tel. 154/2-0400), a modern motel with 42 rooms built around a central swimming pool. Rooms have air conditioning, heat, phone, and carpet, and are quite clean and pleasant. Rates are 4,140 pesos ($8.28) single, 5,060 pesos ($10.12) double, with about another 600 pesos ($1.20) added if you request a TV. The restaurant (open 7:30 a.m. to 11 p.m.) does a big business, with 16 breakfast specials to choose from at 450 to 2,170 pesos (90¢ to $4.34), a comida corrida served for 1,200 pesos ($2.40) from 1 to 3 p.m., and an à la carte menu with antojitos at 650 to 1,050 pesos ($1.30 to $2.10), hamburgers 460 pesos (92¢), and dinner meat entrees from 1,575 to 2,220 pesos ($3.15 to $4.44). As you enter Jiménez the motel is to the right (follow the signs on the highway); from Hwy. 45 it's about five blocks going toward town; and from the bus station, it's about four blocks back the other way (to your left as you exit the bus station).

HIDALGO DEL PARRAL: Hidalgo del Parral (alt. 5,430 feet; pop. 57,619), on the way to Durango, was the spot where the famous revolutionary Pancho Villa was ambushed and killed. For centuries before that, it was famous as a rich mining area.

DURANGO: Durango (alt. 6,210 feet; pop. 321,148) was at the time of the conquest the land of the Chichimecas. In 1562 an expedition under the direction of Francisco de Ibarra went in search of minerals and by 1563 a rich mining center had been established at Durango. It is still a mining town today but in recent years its claim to fame has been as a mecca for Mexican and American western-movie makers. This town is fairly modern and there are some interesting 16th-century churches, convents, and houses.

You needn't make a special trip to Durango, but if you are here for an overnight stay, head for the **Tourism Office** (tel. 181/1-2139 and 1-1107) and pick up their mimeographed information sheet and map. It's located at Calle Hidalgo 508, near the corner of Hidalgo and 5 de Febrero, in an old colonial building bearing a plaque announcing it as the birthplace of poet and revolutionary Antonio Gaxiola (1890–1917). To get there from the main plaza, just go three blocks west down 5 de Febrero until you come to Hidalgo, and it will be on your left. Open 9 a.m. to 3 p.m. and 6 to 8 p.m. Monday through Friday.

As you're heading down 5 de Febrero, you'll see the **Government Palace,** built as a private residence in the 17th century, one block south of the Plaza de Armas. In the courtyard are some very fine murals painted by Montoya de la Cruz.

It's not hard to orient yourself in downtown Durango: just find the central

Plaza de Armas, bounded by 20 de Noviembre, 5 de Febrero, Constitución, and Juárez, and you'll have no trouble finding all the spots mentioned here. (If you have a car, you might consider parking it and walking, since it is much easier to walk within the few blocks of the downtown area than it is to negotiate all the one-way streets.)

If you are arriving by bus you'll be on the northeast end of town near the junction of Routes 40 and 45; if by train you'll be north of town on Avenida Felipe Pescador. From the bus station you can take the Central Camionera bus, which will take you to the intersection of 20 de Noviembre and Juárez, right on the zócalo. Any bus traveling down Constitución, which is the street directly in front of the railroad station, will also take you to the main plaza.

Where to Stay and Eat

I enjoyed the **Posada Duran,** on the corner of 20 de Noviembre and Juárez, Durango, Dgo. 34000 (tel. 181/1-2412), a small, simple but elegant hotel with a sparkling fountain in the central courtyard. There are 15 rooms, all with beautiful tile bath and tasteful decorations, and price tags of 2,600 to 3,500 pesos ($5.20 to $7) single, 3,100 to 4,000 pesos ($6.20 to $8) double.

On 20 de Noviembre, at no. 811, Durango, Dgo. 34000, is the **Hotel Casablanca** (tel. 181/1-3599), two blocks from the main plaza. It's modern and comfortable, and just within our budgetary limits. The 50 rooms are spacious and colorful and most cost 4,240 pesos ($8.48) single, 5,300 pesos ($10.60) double; media suites are priced a little higher, at 5,500 pesos ($11) single and 6,900 pesos ($13.80) double. Parking in rear. The hotel's restaurant is small and pleasant, and offers quite adequate meals from a menu that lists filet mignon with mushrooms and potatoes at 1,725 pesos ($3.45), a daily special entree for 975 pesos ($1.95), a quarter chicken with mushroom gravy and potatoes for 805 pesos ($1.61), and a comida corrida for 1,400 pesos ($2.80). Open 8 a.m. to midnight daily, until 1 a.m. on Fridays.

The old **Posada San Jorge,** Constitución Sur 102, Durango, Dgo. 34000 (tel. 181/1-4866), is a sturdy forest-green colonial inn that you enter through a handsome 20-foot stone gate. Inside is a large stone court decorated with iron railings and good-looking leather furniture. The San Jorge is clean—and singles run 3,300 pesos ($6.60); doubles, 3,800 pesos ($7.60). Some rooms have a balcony; all have a bath.

Eating in Durango is not easy, for most of the restaurants I checked out were either way overpriced or dumpy. One place to try is the **Restaurant La Terraza** (tel. 2-6851), facing the plaza on 5 de Febrero up on the second floor. Part of the restaurant is an outdoor patio with brightly colored umbrellas over the tables. The pizzas are popular items on the menu ranging from 1,050 to 2,765 pesos ($2.10 to $5.53), served by tuxedo-clad waitresses. Breakfast specials are priced from 460 to 1,510 pesos (92¢ to $3.02). Open 8 a.m. to midnight.

The **Cafe Neveria "La Bohemia"** suggests Central European cuisine, but in fact the menu turns out to be quite international, with spaghetti, German-style pork shank or sausage with potatoes and cabbage, various traditional Mexican dishes, and even vegetarian salads. Prices range from 700 to 2,100 pesos ($1.40 to $4.20) per entree, with hamburgers priced at only about 500 pesos ($1). The comida corrida, served 1 to 4 p.m., costs 800 pesos ($1.60) with a meat entree, 850 pesos ($1.70) with chicken. Soup comes to your table in a handsome big kettle so you can serve yourself. La Bohemia is open every day from 8 a.m. until midnight. Look for it at no. 907 on Avenida 20 de Noviembre (tel. 1-5422).

TORREÓN: Torreón, Coahuila (alt. 3,700 feet; pop. 363,886), is a modern city, built less than a century ago. It offers little for the tourist—no old churches or breathtaking artwork. By admission of the locals, in fact, there is nothing to see in Torreón. This is mainly a businessman's city.

Though there's not much to see, there's certainly something to read about Torreón. One Patrick O'Hea, an Englishman who dropped out of Cambridge, came to Mexico in 1905 just in time to witness the end of the Porfiriato (reign of dictator Porfirio Díaz) and the conflagrations of the Mexican Revolution. He managed a country hacienda near Torreón, and wrote an account of the tragicomic events of that turbulent period, entitled *Reminiscences of the Mexican Revolution* (London: Sphere Books, 1981). The book is not for sale in the United States, but if you see a copy in Mexico, grab it—particularly if you can read it while whizzing through Torreón.

The city does have a pretty main plaza, though, lined with the tall, slender royal palm trees usually found only in Acapulco or other coastal towns. The city is also a center for mining, smelting, and viniculture. The Mexican wine industry, all but nonexistent a decade ago, is now flourishing and producing enjoyable vintages and drinkable brandies. Tours of Torreón's wineries can be arranged by asking at the town's **Tourist Information Office** (tel. 171/18-5530), open Monday through Friday from 9 a.m. to 4 p.m., more easily accessible by phone than by going there since it's moved to Claveles 160-A, well out of the central district. The staff at this office is knowledgeable and eager to help the tourist; it's well worth it to give them a call. They offer printed or personal information and advice, including data on hotels, stores, tourist discounts, and guides, and will help in solving any kind of problem the traveler may encounter.

Where to Stay

The **Hotel Río Nazas** at Morelos 732 Pte., Torreón, Coah. 27000 (tel. 171/16-1212), is Torreón's old reliable hostelry, and as it towers above the intersection of Morelos and Trevino it is visible from practically the entire city. All the standard luxuries are to be found in its 170 modern rooms: air conditioning, wall-to-wall carpeting, some bathtubs along with the showers, telephone, and TV; and big hotel services, such as a garage, laundry, bar, and restaurant, are all available, even down to a car-rental agency and airline ticket sales right in the lobby. Rates are not wildly unreasonable for all this plushness: 7,000 pesos ($14) single, 7,500 pesos ($15) double.

The 97-room **Hotel Calvete,** located on the corner of Juárez and Corona at Corona 320 Sur, Torreón, Coah. 27000 (tel. 171/16-1010, 16-1530, or 12-0378), is another luxury choice, with singles going for 5,500 pesos ($11) and doubles for 6,500 pesos ($13). All rooms have air conditioning, phone, and TV; some come with a nice outside balcony, some with carpeting, some with bathtub. Next door is the nice **Restaurant/Cafetería Alcala,** open 7 a.m. to 10 p.m., with a comida corrida for 1,300 pesos ($2.60) served 1 to 5 p.m., antojitos from 425 to 975 pesos (85¢ to $1.95), and supper entrees from 950 to 1,700 pesos ($1.90 to $3.40).

Close to the Río Nazas is the **Hotel del Paseo,** Morelos 560 at the corner of Ildefonso Fuentes, Torreón, Coah. 27000 (tel. 171/16-0303), which has 86 rooms with bath, carpet, TV, telephone, and central air conditioning, for which you pay 3,200 pesos ($6.40) single, 3,800 pesos ($7.60) double. The rooms are adequate, having few windows, but this in fact helps to keep rooms quiet. There is a restaurant next to the hotel, open 7:30 a.m. to 10:30 p.m., with six breakfast specials all at 550 pesos ($1.10), sandwiches or orders of four tacos for 500 pesos ($1), and a comida corrida served from 1:30 to 3 p.m. for 1,000 pesos ($2).

The **Hotel Savoy,** Manuel Acuña Sur 257, Torreón, Coah. 27000 (tel. 171/16-0777), is close to the main Plaza, between Morelos and Juárez. Its spare, modern lobby leads to 68 bright, clean, air-conditioned, telephone-equipped rooms, with lots of windows and freshly tiled bathrooms. Singles cost 3,335 pesos ($6.67), doubles 3,910 pesos ($7.82) with one large bed, 4,485 pesos ($8.97) with two beds.

The owners of the Savoy are also in the process of remodeling the **Hotel Plaza,** at Rodriguez Sur 153, Torreón, Coah. 27000 (tel. 171/16-0669), one block from the Plaza de Armas. When the remodeling is completed, which it should be by the time you're reading this book, the intention is for it to be just as nice as the Hotel Savoy, with all the same features, only more economical, with the 30 rooms priced at 2,000 pesos ($4) single, 2,500 pesos ($5) for two people sharing a bed, and 3,000 pesos ($6) for two beds.

The **Hotel Galicia,** on the main plaza at Cepeda Sur 273, Torreón, Coah. 27000 (tel. 171/16-1111), was for many years my budget favorite, but is now a bit behind the times in everything but price. Still, it's a fascinating place to stay: the lobby is full of old leather chairs, stained-glass windows, and fanciful carved animals at the foot of the stairs. The decor may be straight out of *Alice in Wonderland,* but the little rooms are clean, if very basic, and all have a bath. Design allows for good cross-ventilation—the Galicia is clearly a pre-air conditioning establishment. Rooms cost 2,369 pesos ($4.73) single, 2,875 pesos ($5.75) double.

Where to Eat

For those of you in town in the afternoon, I can recommend an excellent restaurant: the **Restaurant Español "El Hórreo"** (tel. 12-2671), in what looks like a large old Spanish house on the corner of Rodriguez and Matamoros at Matamoros 1094, two blocks from the main plaza. The restaurant is practically an institution; it's been in the same spot for 38 years, and until recently didn't even have a sign, attracting totally by word of mouth. It was known as Casa Doña Julia, named for the Spanish woman who made it famous with her delicious Spanish cooking.

Doña Julia died in 1985, well into her 80s, but the tradition of her restaurant is preserved by the people who run it now. They come from the town of Torazo, in the province of Asturias in northern Spain, bringing their own spices, excellent culinary knowledge, and European hospitality with them. The restaurant is open only from 1 to 6 p.m. daily, serving a set meal for the day to the house full of happy customers. The courses are served at your table in large bowls and platters, so that you can serve yourself as much as you want of every dish. The large meal costs 1,100 pesos ($2.20) during the week, except for Thursdays when the house specialty, paella valenciana, is served, and that's 1,250 pesos ($2.50); the huge Sunday feast is 1,600 pesos ($3.20). The beautifully European decor, with maps, paintings, and pictures of Spain all around, the prompt, friendly service, and delicious food all combine to make this one of the most pleasurable dining experiences I've had in Mexico. Highly recommended.

For more general fare at various times of the day, try the **Café Los Globos** (tel. 12-0734), at the northeast corner of the main plaza (Cepeda 193 Sur). Almost always bustling with hungry-but-busy types, Los Globos is the perfect place for a light meal served quickly in modern, air-conditioned surroundings. The comida corrida, served 12:30 to 3:30 p.m., costs 800 to 1,000 pesos ($1.60 to $2), depending on the entree you order, with the antojito plates mostly in the 700-peso ($1.40) range. A hamburger with salad and French fries costs 650 pesos ($1.30); there are five other burger specials, ranging from 650 to 1,140 pesos ($1.30 to $2.28), and a variety of soups and soda-fountain treats. Eleven ample breakfast specials are priced from 530 to 1,200 pesos ($1.06 to $2.40). Open 7 a.m. to 10 p.m.

Also on the main plaza, at Calle V. Carillo 258 Sur, is the **Apolo Palacio** (tel. 12-0436 and 12-0774), a large air-conditioned restaurant with leather booths, tables, and a varied clientele of workers, politicos from the nearby government buildings, and people coming downtown for every reason. Service is good, and so are the ten varieties of breakfast specials priced from 355 to 1,075 pesos (71¢ to $2.15). You can get three kinds of spaghetti for 310 pesos (62¢), or something from the soda fountain. On the six-course comida corrida you get a selection of about seven entrees, and the price depends on the entree you choose; the day I was there, prices ranged from 699 pesos ($1.40) for enchiladas of chicken in mole sauce up to 1,225 pesos ($2.45) for fried shrimp. Open 7 a.m. to 2 a.m.

If it's just a snack you're after, try the bakery on Juárez 809 Pte., near the corner of Falcon, open 7 a.m. to 10 p.m., called the **Central Panificadora y Pasteleria** (no phone). You can get a slice of jelly roll with coconut on the outside for 60 pesos (12¢), or slices of delicious chocolate or vanilla cake rolls filled with icing for 125 pesos (25¢). Doughnuts, butterhorn rolls, big sugar cookies, and conchas (sweet rolls) all cost only 30 pesos (6¢), pineapple or strawberry turnovers go for 40 pesos (8¢), and you can get big white "torta" sandwich rolls for only 20 pesos each (4¢).

Torreón Miscellany

The city of Torreón is easy to get around if you orient yourself by the main plaza (zócalo), which is bounded on the south by Juárez and on the north by Morelos, on the west by Valdez Carrillo and on the east by Cepeda. . . . There is a good **market** on Juárez, two blocks east of the plaza between Acuña and Blanco, with what seem like hundreds of inexpensive, counter-style eateries, fresh produce, meats, fish, and a million other things. . . . The **post office** is located nine blocks east of the plaza on Juárez and Galeana, in the rear part of the federal building. It's open 8 a.m. to 7 p.m. Monday through Friday, 9 a.m. to 1 p.m. Saturday, closed Sunday. . . . The **bus stations** (A.D.O., Estrella Blanca, Omnibus de México, Trailways, Chihuahuenses, Transportes del Norte) are located two blocks south of the plaza, on the two blocks bordered by Cepeda, Zaragoza, Carranza, and Blvd. Revolución. . . . The town closes down between 2 and 4 p.m. for siesta. . . . The **bank** on the southeast corner of the main plaza will change your money for you Monday through Friday between 9 a.m. and noon.

What to Do

Should you be stuck in Torreón for a few days with car troubles or ticket difficulties, wander down to the **Casa de la Cultura,** at Blvd. Constitución 279 Pte. (tel. 16-3340), and see what's doing in the way of art exhibits, recitals, and other cultural offerings.

The **Museo Regional** (tel. 13-9545), open 9 a.m. to 5 p.m. with exhibits of local Indian culture, is found on Avenida Juárez, within the Bosque Venustiano Carranza (Carranza Forest); you can take the bus "Campo Alianza" down Avenida Juárez, or just drive down Juárez to the west until you reach the park. The tiny **Museo de la Revolución** is just one small room, built right on top of the bridge that once served as an aqueduct, at the end of Blvd. Constitución, which was once a canal. The museum is open only on Sundays from 11 a.m. to 2 p.m. Although it's very small, it's dedicated to a proud purpose, honoring General Francisco ("Pancho") Villa and his Division of the North: "He opened the doors to the Mexico of today," the plaque outside proclaims. Despite Torreón's unimpressive façade in terms of tourist attractions, it holds a special place in Mexican history, being the place where **Pancho Villa** was made the General of the North after he took Torreón.

From Torreón it's a short drive to the nearby suburb of **Lerdo,** where, standing facing an elementary school on one side and a public park on the other, you can see a plaque commemorating the exact spot on which the first shots of the Mexican revolution were fired on November 20, 1910. Looking around you at the suburban sprawl, the elementary school and park, and past it at the dry hills not too far off in the distance, it gives you pause to consider how different is the Mexico of today from the Mexico of that day. And when you realize that it was not really so long ago, that the old folks you see walking around today still remember the suspense they felt while waiting for Pancho Villa and his Division of the North to come and liberate their little towns, you can get a better feeling for what really is the spirit of the developing Mexico you see today, where people's rights to free enterprise, to education, and to own their own land, are so recently won.

On your way out of Torreón, follow Morelos heading west to regain the highway.

FRESNILLO: Heading south from Torreón you cross the Tropic of Cancer just before arriving in Fresnillo, Zacatecas (alt. 7,370 feet; pop. 140,000). This is a silver-mining town at the northern edge of the Valley of Mexico, not quite so fancy or attractive as many of the other silver towns in the region (see Chapter V), but a pleasant place with an unhurried, small-town atmosphere, good for a relaxing stay after a long day on the road. The town boasts the distinction of being located at the halfway point between Ciudad Juárez and Mexico City.

Where to Stay

If you're coming by car from the north, the first lodging you'll see will be the **Motel La Fortuna,** at Carretera Panamericana km. 724, Fresnillo, Zac. 99000 (tel. 493/2-0694), with large blue neon signs announcing Motel and Restaurant. At 6,000 pesos ($12) single, 7,500 pesos ($15) double, the prices are higher than some other selections in town, but it's a nice enough place, the 61 rooms equipped with TV (parabolic antenna receives many channels) and phone, and also offering a swimming pool, bar, and restaurant open 7 a.m. to 11 p.m. The rooms are lined up out back, with parking in front of each room.

Coming by bus, you'll arrive in Fresnillo just a few blocks from downtown and a hotel with a lot more charm. Coming out of the bus station, go to your left and you'll see a small plaza; on the far side of this is Calle Garcia Salinas, one of Fresnillo's main downtown streets. Take this street and go about six blocks towards town, and you'll reach the **Hotel Casa Blanca,** at García Salinas 103, Fresnillo, Zac. 99000 (tel. 493/2-0014 and 2-1288), where Greek columns jut out over the sidewalk. Inside the older, 37-room hotel is a comfortable lobby with a big stone fireplace, Oriental rug and leather furniture. The rooms, equipped with telephone, TV, and carpeting, are similarly old-style elegant, and cost 4,500 pesos ($9) single, 5,650 pesos ($11.30) for a double room with two beds. Parking in a supervised garage costs an extra 130 pesos (26¢). You can sit in front of the fireplace of an evening and listen to the lovely piano music drift in from the hotel's restaurant, one of the nicer places to eat in Fresnillo.

The **Hotel del Mineral,** at Garcia Salinas 501, Fresnillo, Zac. 99000 (tel. 493/2-1833), is right next door to the Hotel Casa Blanca. Some of the 80 simple but clean rooms have TV; all have phone and carpeting. Parking is provided. Singles go for 3,950 pesos ($7.90), doubles for 4,770 pesos ($9.54).

Two blocks further up the street is the **Hotel del Fresno,** Avenida Hidalgo 411, Fresnillo, Zac. 99000 (tel. 493/2-1120 and 2-1126), facing the Jardín Hidalgo. Prices here are higher, with singles at 7,000 pesos ($14), doubles 8,000 pesos

($16), but the hotel is very modern and stylish. All rooms have color TV, phone, large mirror and dresser, fancy tile in the bathroom, and private parking, with plenty of purified water and ice available. A powerful TV antenna brings in two channels from the U.S., and the hotel even has a channel of its own for showing movies.

Where to Eat

All of the above hotels have nice restaurants, quite adequate for a short stay in Fresnillo. Especially pleasant is the **Restaurant Hotel Casa Blanca,** open 8 a.m. to midnight, with its live piano music played by Don Pascual from 3 to 5 p.m. and 9 to 11 p.m. When I was there he was playing a variety ranging from classical Mexican, Spanish, and European music to waltzes to hits by Stevie Wonder. Spanish watercolor paintings on the walls, fresh flowers, and white linen tablecloths complete the decor. An ample comida corrida is served from 1:30 to 4:30 p.m. for 1,400 pesos ($2.80); entrees of antojitos, seafood, and meats range in price from 400 pesos (80¢) for tostadas Jalisco style to 3,170 pesos ($6.34) for Italian style shrimp or shrimp brochette; T-bone steak comes for 1,900 pesos ($3.80). The owner of both the hotel and restaurant, Sr. Ismael Monreal, speaks English and tries to make everything as nice as possible for the traveler; try to meet him if you can.

The **Hotel del Fresno** also has a nice restaurant/bar, open 7 a.m. to 11:30 p.m., with a variety of complete breakfast specials for 1,200 pesos ($2.40), a comida corrida served 1 to 4 p.m. for 2,000 pesos ($4), international entrees from 1,000 to 1,700 pesos ($2 to $3.40), and a variety of soups for 400 pesos (80¢) including corn, onion, garlic, and asparagus soups.

The specialty of the restaurant at the **Hotel del Mineral** is pork chops *(chuletas),* which come with soup and salad for 1,320 pesos ($2.64). The comida corrida, served 1:30 to 3:30 p.m., costs 1,200 pesos ($2.40); an order of Italian spaghetti, 755 pesos ($1.51). Open 7 a.m. to 11 p.m. The adjoining bar is open to both sexes.

What to Do

If you'll be in Fresnillo a while, take a stroll down to the **tourism office** (tel. 493/2-0382), open 10 a.m. to 3 p.m. at the **Agora Cultural Center,** about five blocks down from the Jardín Hidalgo on Prolongación Avenida Hidalgo (no number). The large building, originally built as a mining school in 1883, now houses Fresnillo's art museum (with special salons for Manuel M. Ponce, pianist, and paintings by Francisco Goítia, among others), university, library, and cultural center. The large inner courtyard, once used for bullfights, now hosts summertime concerts.

Out behind the Ágora building is La Companía Fresnillo, a huge **silver mine** still in operation, extending 110 "stories" down under the ground. This is a working mine, not a tourist attraction, but it's said that permission to descend below is often granted to visitors. If you're interested, you might go and ask permission.

Side Trips

If you're in the Fresnillo area, you definitely shouldn't miss a visit to **El Santuário de Plateros,** about 6 km. (3.7 miles) to the north of Fresnillo. About 2,500,000 pilgrims come every year to the little village of Plateros to ask miracles of **El Niño de Santa Maria de Atocha,** patron of miners, housed in the large sanctuary. It's said that the little Niño (a figure of the Christ child) began granting miracles there in 1621; construction of the present temple was started in 1789, and in 1977 devotees erected a three-story hospice to give shelter to the millions of pilgrims coming from all over the western hemisphere. The really amazing thing about this temple is the literally *thousands* of *retablos* lining the walls and ceilings of the right side of the courtyard; each one depicts, both in words and in color illustration, the miracle the artist received from the Niño de Atocha. You'll see scenes of hospital operations, of people surviving all manner of perilous accidents, of people being shot with rifles; and all these people lived to be able to make their own retablo as a witness to the miracle of salvation received from the Niño.

The traditional way to get to Plateros is on foot, and a large walkway stretches out beside the road for the *peregrinos* (pilgrims) to walk on. For a few pesos you can catch the local bus at Fresnillo's centro, or you can get to Plateros in a taxi from Fresnillo for 1,000 pesos ($2).

Another interesting side trip is a visit to the thermal hot springs at **Valparaiso,** 91 kilometers (56.4 miles) from Fresnillo on Hwy. 54. If you don't have a car, you can take the bus from Fresnillo to Valparaiso, get off and take the local Valparaiso city bus the extra 3 kilometers (1.8 miles) to the springs. Look for the baths named **Atotonilco.** Use of the baths is about 150 pesos (30¢).

3. The Eastern Route via Monterrey and Saltillo

The two Texas towns of Eagle Pass and Laredo are only about 120 miles apart on the Rio Grande, and the Mexican highways that run southward from them are roughly parallel, running down either side of a mountain range, and offer several opportunities for crossover from one to the other, first at Saltillo-Monterrey, then at San Roberto-Linares, later on at Huizache and Antigua Morelos, and finally at San Luis Potosí-Ciudad Valles. The route from Laredo (85) is one of the most popular for visitors from the north because it can be reached conveniently from the northern and eastern United States via Interstate highways and also because it goes directly to the large Mexican city closest to the border: Monterrey.

You might try this if you enter at Laredo: go to Monterrey, then take Mex. 40 to Saltillo and then go south on Mex. 57 to San Luis Potosí; the towns along 85 south of Monterrey are not of great interest, and if you go via San Luis Potosí you can stop in Guanajuato. San Miguel de Allende, Querétaro, and Tula ruins before entering Mexico City (see Chapter V). This is by far a more interesting route.

If you cross at Eagle Pass you can take a shortcut to Monterrey via Mex. 53 south of Monclova, then return via Mex. 40 to Saltillo and Mex. 57 south. I'll describe Monterrey, Saltillo, and the preferred Rte. 57 first, and then tell you what's in store on the alternate road, Rte. 85.

READER'S HOTEL SELECTION—NUEVO LAREDO: "In Nuevo Laredo we stayed in the **Don Antonio Motel,** Gonzalez 2435 (tel. 871/2-1140). This is well recommended for an overnight stay; it is, I am sure, comparable to any motel on the U.S. side of the border in every way except price. We paid 4,664 pesos ($9.33) for two in a modern, twin-bedded room with bathroom and the usual conveniences" (Martin Lister, Saltash, Cornwall, England).

READER'S TRAVEL TIP—LEAVE YOUR CAR IN LAREDO: "We drove to Laredo and found an excellent place to leave the car: the **Hamilton Hotel Garage** (tel. 512/723-3833), 1211 Houston St., is about four blocks west of the end of I-35, very near the International Bridge. The garage is open every day except Sunday, from 8 a.m. to 7 p.m. Rates are $26.28 per week or $52.56 per month for dead storage. The garage is covered, locked at night, and attended during the day. If you already have your Tourist Cards, a taxi will take you across the bridge to the train station for $5 per person" (Dr. Irwin Rovner, Raleigh, N.C.).

TAKING THE TRAIN: Though the bus offers many advantages (speed, more departure times), you may want to take the train. Here are some tips.

You can make advance reservations by calling the Mexican National Railways (Ferrocarriles Nacionales de México) in Nuevo Laredo, Tamaulipas, at 871/2-8097. They will quote you prices for a first-class sleeping-car ticket, and for the sleeping-car supplement. Find out the current exchange rate for the peso, compute the prices, and then send two cashier's (bank) checks for the two amounts. For the ticket, the check should be made out to National Railways of Mexico; for the sleeping-car supplement, it must be made out to Sleeping Car Service, Mexican Railways. Mail the checks to National Railways of Mexico, P.O. Box 595, Laredo, TX 78042. Having done all this, you will have had your first encounter with Mexican bureaucratic ways.

Now for some more useful details: Trains run on Central Standard Time, *all year.* Daylight Saving Time is never used. The ticket window at the station is open from 10:50 to 11:50 a.m. and from 5:30 to 6:55 p.m., Monday through Saturday, but only from 5:30 to 6:55 p.m. on Sunday. Go to the "Dormitorio" window if you're going to buy a sleeping-car ticket. If you encounter any problems, ask for the gracious Foreign Agent, Mrs. Guadelupe Contreras de López.

Renting a *camarín* sleeping compartment on the train works out to be the cheapest and best way to move a family from the border to Mexico City (if you don't plan to drive). Have reservations, if possible. Also, pack food *and beverages* (as I advised in Chapter I, Section 2), and toilet paper. Be advised that the air conditioning and the electrical outlets on the train may not work. The trip between Nuevo Laredo and Mexico City takes about 25 hours, with arrival time about 8:04 p.m. the following night.

By the way, the train is not the best way to get to Monterrey, since you arrive late in the evening, leaving little time to find a hotel. It's better to spend the night in Laredo (there are many motels in town, including an inexpensive Motel 6) and start out early the next morning.

If you go by road, it takes no more than three hours to cover the 146 miles (235 kilometers) between Nuevo Laredo and Monterrey, once you've cleared the various Customs *(Aduana)* and Immigration *(Migración)* stops.

MONTERREY: This city, capital of the state of Nuevo León, is Mexico's third-largest city (alt. 1,770 feet; pop. 2,250,000) and its main industrial center. Its setting is spectacular: hemmed in by towering, craggy mountains, one of which (Cerro de la Silla, "Saddle Mountain") has become a symbol of the city. This beautiful modern city, also known as the Sultana of the North (La Sultana Del Norte), now "holds court" in the recently completed Gran Plaza. Its gardens, fountains, monuments, and buildings breathe new life into the city center. No stopover in Monterrey is complete without at least two visits to the Gran Plaza. A daytime excursion to enjoy the monuments, fountains, and innovative architecture, and an evening visit to see the laser slice the night sky should be sufficient to appease the Sultana of the North.

They seem to make everything here: steel, beer, cement, glass, cigarettes, chemicals, textiles, building materials, and on and on. With the industrial sprawl has come some serious noise and air pollution, the latter often in the form of a pall that hangs in the valley 24 hours a day. But Monterrey, named in 1596 for the Count of Monterrey, Viceroy of New Spain, retains some colonial touches among its shiny new buildings and factories: the town hall, the Government Palace (state house of Nuevo León), mansions and hotels, churches and monasteries, and the parks and squares that the colonial planners always put into the new towns they laid out.

I might mention that Monterrey is hardly the best introduction to Mexican urban life. Crowded, polluted, noisy, and expensive, it's hardly the stereotypical Mexican town: laid back, charming, colonial, filled with flowers all year and mariachis each evening. Monterrey is Monterrey, a raw, muscular city that produces a great deal of Mexico's wealth. Save your visions of charm for Guanajuato, Zacatecas, and Querétaro, which have it in abundance.

Now before you start, hotel hunters take note: the intersection of **Juárez** and **Aramberri** divides Monterrey's street addresses. All numbers north or south of Aramberri are norte (north) and sur (south) respectively. All numbers east or west of Juárez are oriente (east) and poniente (west) respectively; and the numbers *start* at this intersection (you might call it the "zero point") and go up.

Getting to and from Monterrey

The country's third-largest city is easily reached by all means of transportation. Check times and fares, and make reservations atleast a day in advance, no matter how you plan to travel.

By Bus: Autobuses Anáhuac, in the Central de Autobuses (tel. 75-3238), will get you to Mexico City in 10½ hours; they also run to San Luis Potosí, as does Transportes del Norte (tel. 74-3775). Tres Estrellas de Oro (tel. 74-2410) also operates from Monterrey to points all over Mexico, and, like Transportes del Norte, connects with Greyhound at the Texas border. Autobuses Estrella Blanca (tel. 75-7216) and Transportes Frontera (tel. 75-7557) too operate from Monterrey to points south and west. Transportes Monterrey-Saltillo (tel. 75-5744) heads out to the Garcia Caves and Saltillo. Drop by the Central de Autobuses a day before you plan to leave and arrangements to almost anywhere will be a snap to make.

By Rail: The way to get to Mexico City by rail is to catch **El Regiomontano**, an express leaving Monterrey every day at 6 p.m., arriving in the capital at 9 a.m. the next morning. Times for the Mexico City to Monterrey train are the same. El Regiomontano will drop you in Saltillo at 8:10 p.m., in San Luis Potosí at 1:50 a.m. There's another night train, leaving at 10:05 a.m., and in Mexico City at 8:04 p.m. Between Monterrey and the U.S. border (Nueva Laredo) there is one train a day, leaving Monterrey at 2:20 a.m. and arriving in Nuevo Laredo at 7:20 a.m. (to connect with Amtrak's thrice-weekly train to San Antonio, Dallas, and St. Louis). From Nuevo Laredo to Monterrey, a daily train runs at 6:55 p.m. and arrives in Monterrey at 11:30 p.m.

By Air: Monterrey has good air connections with Mexico City (9 to 12 flights a day), two daily flights to Chihuahua, and four flights daily to Guadalajara. Texas International Airlines runs daily flights between Monterrey and Dallas / Forth Worth and Houston. AeroMéxico has two daily flights between Monterrey and Los Angeles, California. Look into excursion fares on the Dallas / Forth Worth and Houston flights. AeroMéxico is at Padre Mier and Cuauhtémoc (tel. 83/40-8760); Mexicana is at Avenida Hidalgo 922 Pte. (tel. 83/44-1122).

Aeropuerte Transportaciones (tel. 40-3840) remains the cheapest way to get to and from the airport; cost is 1,000 pesos ($2). A cab may cost you as much as 8,500 pesos ($17) if you're not careful; the airport is 30 kilometers (19 miles) away.

Getting Around

City bus travel for destinations I describe can be accomplished on the many Ruta 1 buses. The trip from the bus station to the Zona Rosa is easy on Ruta 1. Catch the bus along Pino Suárez, fare 25 pesos (5¢). You will pass the lovely Alameda Park, then watch the blocks tick off until Hidalgo. The return trip to the bus terminal is also a Ruta 1 bus, only catch it along Juárez. Get off along Colón for a short two-block walk to the bus station. Route 1 San Nicholas goes past the Cuauhtémoc Brewery (22) and north on Hwy. 85 to the Royal Court and Alamo Hotels. Get off when you see the Holiday Inn, fare 50 pesos (10¢). Return to downtown on (did you guess?) a Ruta 1 bus, catch it on the Holiday Inn side of Hwy. 85.

The State Tourist Bureau (tel.83/40-1080) has moved to a location that insures few people will journey to it. The office is on the sixth floor of the San Francisco Building at the corner of San Francisco and Loma Grande in the Loma Larga suburb. Perhaps as an act of contrition for the above-mentioned indiscretion, a recorded message called Divertel (the fun line) is available. Call 43-5060 for a Spanish message or 43-5059 for the same message in English. Call at any hour, the message is updated daily.

Where to Stay

Unfortunately for those on a tight budget, the cheaper hotels in Monterrey are a good distance from the center of the town's culture and nightlife. In fact, as the city grows and prospers it gets harder and harder to find good, clean hotels within our budget range. As this is one of the three largest cities in Mexico and thus relatively high priced (compared to a provincial town), you may want to allow yourself a splurge for a day or two here, and plan to make up the deficit in a smaller, cheaper city later on in your trip. The prime area for accommodations for those who really want to enjoy their stay in Monterrey is in and around the Zona Rosa (Pink Zone), the plush downtown district centered on the Plaza Zaragoza, Monterrey's main square, and the Plaza Hidalgo, a small but very lovely park nearby. I'll give the low-down on places to stay in and around the Zona Rosa, and will then list the cheaper hotels near the bus and train stations, 15 long blocks north of downtown.

Zona Rosa Area: The premier hotel of the Zona Rosa is the 300-room **Gran Hotel Ancira (1),** at Hidalgo and Escobedo on the southwest corner of Plaza Hidalgo (tel. 83/42-2040). The hotel has as much turn-of-the-century atmosphere and elegance as any in Mexico. All the amenities of a fine five-star hotel are in place. Summer prices (high season) hover around $60 U.S. (30,000 pesos) single or double regardless of the prevailing exchange rate; winter rates are 23,000 pesos ($46).

The **Hotel Ambassador (2)** (tel. 83/42-2040), next door to the Ancira (1), is nearly the same size but lacks the colonial aura. This posh commercial hotel has all the expensive services that can drain one's pockets with astonishing speed. Expect to pay 26,450 pesos ($52.90) single or double.

The third splurge hotel in the Zona Rosa is the 200-room **Hotel Monterrey (31),** facing the Gran Plaza on Morelos and Zaragoza (tel. 83/43-5120). All services are available. Prices are the same as at the Hotel Ambassador.

A few blocks from the Plaza Hidalgo are two high-rise hotels with less of the snazz of the top places, but with all of the luxury facilities. The mammoth 17-story **Hotel Río (28)** (tel. 83/44-9040) is a block long, has 400 rooms, and a garage for 400 cars, plus central air conditioning, TV sets in the rooms, tile baths with tubs, nice modern furnishings, and a large swimming pool surrounded by a big sunbathing area, high above the street. Prices are 14,835 pesos ($29.67) in a double, but this is for a luxury room with two double beds; less luxurious rooms are often available at correspondingly lower prices. The Hotel Río fills the block along Garibaldi between Morelos and Padre Mier; there are two high-rise towers to the hotel, and two lobbies: Hotel Río Norte is on Padre Mier, Hotel Río Sur is on Morelos.

Almost across the street from the Río's Padre Mier entrance is the **Hotel Jolet (29),** Padre Mier Pte. 201 (tel. 83/40-5504), a very modern seven-story building with 120 rooms and prices several thousand pesos lower than those at the Río 10,977 pesos ($21.96) single or double to be exact—the one big difference being that the Jolet lacks a swimming pool. To make up for the lack, the Jolet has a bar in its lobby.

Going down in price, but actually going closer to the Plaza Hidalgo, the **Hotel Colonial (13),** Hidalgo Ote. 475 (tel. 83/43-6791), is an older place that has 90 rooms redecorated in an interesting but ghastly imitation of colonial style. Rooms are air-conditioned and many have two double beds, and prices are 5,820 pesos ($11.64) single, 5,952 pesos ($11.91) double—but there's a catch: housekeeping standards are pretty low. They can get away with it because of their location right next to the Plaza Hidalgo and right across the street from the Gran Hotel Ancira. The trick is to take a good look at a few rooms before you move in.

If you are determined to stay in the Zona Rosa, the stone-front **Hotel Fronterizo (11),** Hidalgo Ote. 206 (tel. 83/42-8800), could help balance your budget. The hotel seems to be chronically under renovation that is never accomplished, but prices are cheap. The 50 rooms clustered around a small, parched courtyard show signs of past hard use and rent for 2,185 pesos ($4.37) single, 2,415 pesos ($4.83) double. Limited free parking is available. Does this sound too good to be true? It may be. When I checked the Fronterizo, water was only available from 6 a.m. to 3 p.m. due to a problem pump. Be sure to ask about water and look at a few rooms before signing in.

Avenida Madero Area: If you arrive in Monterrey by bus or train you'll come into either the train station on Avenida Reyes or the Central de Autobuses on Avenida Colón, about 20 blocks to the north of the downtown Zona Rosa. The bus depot is a few blocks south of the railroad station; Avenida Madero, with its Independence Arch monument, is two blocks south of the bus station and parallel to Avenida Colón. Madero is a lively, noisy boulevard full of outdoor life and once replete with cheap, fairly good hotels. Most hotel business has moved downtown, however, and so proximity to the bus station and the city's cheapest eateries is about your only advantage here. But since decent and cheap hotel rooms are getting hard to find all over Monterrey, this is still your best bet if you must stick rigidly to your budget.

If you're staying in this older part of Monterrey, a walk up Avenida Madero, starting at the arch that commemorates Mexico's independence from Spain, is a good way to start your day. The street is one of the liveliest in Mexico—girls will be furiously washing windows . . . music will blare at you from all sides. . . briefcased businessmen will pause to admire the prettier señoritas . . . the current total of Monterrey's car accidents will be inscribed on the arch. It's a capsule view of Mexican life.

The **Hotel Posada (23),** at Amado Nervo Nte. 1138 (tel. 83/72-3908), half a block from the bus station, is the newest place to check out. Your company within will be businessmen and tired families. It's difficult to escape the growling of the buses in this area, but here at least the rooms have no exterior windows and

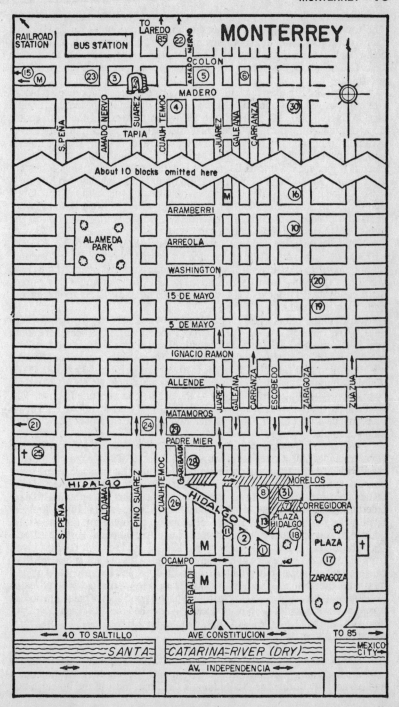

instead face the beginnings of an interior courtyard hosting one potted plant. The rooms, with singles at 2,530 pesos ($5.06) and doubles for 2,990 pesos ($5.98), are very small but sport new mattresses and box springs, and either a ceiling or table fan. If you are on the claustrophobic side, be sure to see a room first. The minuscule restaurant next door can serve your needs until you head for town.

Almost the cheapest and still the best choice in the area, only two blocks from the bus station, is the **Hotel Nuevo León (3)**, on a quietish side street called Amado Nervo Nte., at no. 1007 (tel. 83/74-1900). Walk out the front center door of the Central de Autobuses, take the left-hand pedestrian bridge over Avenida Colón, and you'll find Amado Nervo a bit more to the left; the hotel is a block down on the left-hand side. The 72 rooms are all doubles with bath, are clean and modern if a bit small, and come without air conditioning. Rates are 2,200 pesos ($4.40) single, 2,500 pesos ($5) double, tax included. No English is spoken. The emphasis is on cleanliness with taste of a sort; although the lobby and reception desk sport a lot of whitish Formica, the hallways have brick accents that make the place very attractive. Make sure you get a room off the street. This is my first choice in the area.

Compact but clean and neat is the **Hotel Patricia (5)**, Madero Ote. 123 (tel. 83/75-0750), on the other side of Avenida Juárez and therefore in the "oriente" numbering (zero's at Juárez). If you don't mind somewhat cramped quarters, you'll find their tidy rooms are quite serviceable and not impossibly priced: 3,105 pesos ($6.21) single, 3,450 pesos ($6.90) double. All 30 rooms have a bath; most have ceiling fans.

Also on the oriente portion of Madero, at no. 243 Ote. (corner of Galeana), is the **Hotel 5a Avenida (6)** (tel. 83/75-6565), which has been here some years but is still one of the most respectable places in the neighborhood. All the rooms upstairs have fairly modern furniture, private bath, and telephone, and all 70 of them rent for 5,462.50 pesos ($10.93) single, 6,612.50 pesos ($13.23) double; although not all rooms have windows, this includes all taxes *and* air conditioning—not available in most of the rooms recommended above. This would make the 5a Avenida a "weather choice," and you might head for it in the scorching days of summer. Commercial travelers make up most of the 5a Avenida's clientele.

Just south of Madero on Calle Zaragoza is the 11-story, 106-room, **Gran Hotel Yamallel (30)**, Calle Zaragoza Nte. 912 (tel. 83/75-3598), a big modern place with its own garage and pretensions to plushness that make it seem a good bargain, in a way. Perhaps the hotel was built before the Zona Rosa became the fashionable area to stay in. In any case, it was built for luxury, although it's a bit faded now; and it offers good value: singles are 6,325 pesos ($12.65); doubles, 6,440 pesos ($12.88). With 11 floors of rooms to choose from, get one with a good view and not much noise. All rooms are air-conditioned. Parking is free.

The **Hotel Madero (4)**, Madero Pte. 428 (tel. 83/75-5471), is a half block from the Independence Arch on Avenida Madero. It's my last choice here because it's older, because it's right on the main drag, and because it has a good number of quiet rooms. The Madero has a plain lobby decorated with red leather chairs and star-painted walls. The rooms have a good coat of paint and decent furniture—not brand-new, but serviceable—and the rates are reasonable: singles with bath for 1,840 pesos ($3.68), doubles for 2,070 pesos ($4.14); several rooms with air conditioning go for more.

Motel Area: All in all, with the current trend in urban renewal, accommodations are becoming more and more difficult to find. During peak vacation times and particularly during the school holidays in June, most of the hotels in our favorite budget range may be booked. The choices then are to go up in price, way down in quality, or out of the city proper. This is not as despairing as it may sound, for at least you won't have to walk. The Ruta 1 bus that stops all along Avenida Juárez will transport you to the northern fringes of Monterrey for 50 pesos (10¢). Here in the land of Holiday Inn at 27,500 pesos ($55) you can make your last stand at the Alamo.

The **Motel Alamo** (tel. 83/52-5890), J. S. Pronceda 100 (really on the main highway), is only half a block from the city bus stop. If you are coming from the center of town and don't spot this motel in time, get off at the Holiday Inn and walk south on the same side of the street. The Alamo is no urban gem, but it does have a few amenities, be they worn, noisy, or drippy. The dark rooms all face a parking courtyard, so the highway noise is minimal. There's a murky pool outside and individual air conditioners inside, so 4,500 pesos ($9) for a single or 5,860 pesos ($11.72) for a double is a fair price. A bonus here is that the owner speaks English and can give excellent directions.

For a bit more in pleasantness and a bit more out of the pocket, try the **Royal Court** (tel. 83/52-5868), across the street and two blocks north. The official address is Carr. a Laredo Nte. 314, and rooms rent for 7,475 pesos ($14.95) single, 7,647.50 pesos ($15.30) double.

Remember, out here you are also away from the area of down-home Mexican cooking and into the land of fast food with Kentucky Fried Chicken and Pizza Hut reigning. A large American-style pizza runs between 1,800 to 2,450 pesos ($3.60 to $4.90), and beer is 300 pesos (60¢) a bottle including the frosted mug.

Where to Eat

Most of the fun, adventurous, and reasonably priced dining—and there's lots of it—used to be found in the Zona Rosa. As Monterrey is a cosmopolitan city, you'll still find all kinds of restaurants: Mexican, American, and some with a European flair. However, with the city's new outlook, restaurants are a bit more scattered and a lot more expensive. My favorite mom-and-pop family-run affairs have given way to chic boutiques and shoe stores. Most of the eateries I recommend are near Plaza Hidalgo, so make your way there for a meal and a wistful last look at a plaza of the past.

There are now numerous American-type eateries in the Zona Rosa where you can find tacos, hamburgers, and fried chicken at a reasonable price. **VIPS (13)**—modern, clean, and busy—is a reflection of Monterrey's downtown shopping and business district. This restaurant (of the VIPS chain), on the corner of Carranza and Hidalgo (tel. 42-5073), is open 24 hours a day and is always jammed. Imitation stained glass gives the ceiling a kaleidoscopic effect, very trendy. The menu is a combination of fast-food, regional, and international fare. Hamburgers are in the 500-pesos ($1) category, Mexican dishes in the 450- to 1,150-peso (90¢ to $2.30) range; and good pie and ice cream won't destroy the budget at 350 to 500 pesos (70¢ to $1.00).

Bordering Plaza Hidalgo is **Picos (13)**, the local answer to a fast-food hamburger joint. True to its name, colorful artificial parrots lurk among the potted trees. Ronald of the golden arches chain may feel a wisp of jealousy here. Picos is sleek and clean, decked out with bright-yellow tables, track lighting, hanging table lamps (good for writing or reading), and a slick fast-food counter. Grab a burger frijoles, and cup of coffee for a grand total of 500 pesos ($1.00).

Later, for dessert, continue around the square to **Helados Danesa (7),** one in a chain of ice-cream parlors. It's open 10 a.m. to 10 p.m., and with its 33 different flavors, you're bound to find your favorite here. A one-scoop cone costs 350 pesos (70¢).

By the way, there's also **Luisiana,** right off the plaza. Service and food here have more of an international flair, with prices also flaring beyond our budget.

For those of you who want to feel even more at home, go around the corner to Escobedo 920 where you'll find a branch of **Sanborn's (8),** a large store with cosmetics, magazines, bric-a-brac, etc., as well as a restaurant and coffeeshop. The restaurant is always full so you may have to wait if you are there during peak periods. The menu (same in the restaurant and at the lunch counter) offers a variety of items priced from 1,200 to 1,500 pesos ($2.40 to $3.00), but that's for a very full platter, with drink and tip included. There is also an entrance to San-born's at Morelos 464.

For another back-home-type meal there's always **Kentucky Fried Chicken.** Eleven branches have opened in Monterrey and you're bound to stumble across one in your wanderings around the city. Though still expensive for chicken, prices are about one-third less than in the States, with a nine-piece thrift box, for example, going for 1,685 pesos ($3.37).

If fast-food has become a drag, you may be ready for **Restaurant Regio (7)** (tel. 43-6250), on Plaza Hidalgo at Corregidora 523 Ote. Regio (that's *Ray*-hee-oh) is housed in a long, quite narrow room, so sit at least in the middle to catch the action in the kitchen. The place is a series of contrasting features. Heavy wooden chandeliers set off bright red table cloths and stoneware stamped "Regio." The steaming tortillas are served in white Styrofoam containers, but the spicy sauce is served in the three-legged *molcajete,* made of volcanic rock and used in ancient times to crush the main ingredients of chiles and tomatoes. Under the last stuccoed arch is a huge ceramic-tile kitchen out of which explode waiters bearing plates of sizzling meat (peek into the kitchen to learn the secret of the hot plates). A meal here can be a serving of cream of asparagus soup for 414 pesos (83¢), puchero (vegetable and meat stew) for 632 pesos ($1.27), and a beer for 345 pesos (69¢), or a more expensive grilled meat dish for 2,300 to 2,760 pesos ($4.60 to $5.52). Although the cabrito is excellent, it is expensive here so save that treat for elsewhere. Also, any little desserts you didn't order but arrive at the table are not donations to your cause. If you indulge you will be charged. Regio is open from noon until 11 p.m.

A good cheap seafood restaurant is **La Pesca (11),** Hidalgo 126, about a block west of the elegant Ambassador Hotel. Although the place is totally un-pretentious (something of a cafeteria ambience), it's clean and very easy on the budget. Have a fish filet and the bill will be about 900 pesos ($1.80). Shrimp dinners are more, at 900 to 1,100 pesos ($1.80 to $2.20).

La Puntada, across from La Pesca (11) at Hidalgo no. 123 Ote., is another budget eatery serving tacos for 380 pesos (76¢), breakfast for 380 to 450 pesos (76¢ to 90¢), and nothing topping 550 pesos ($1.10) on the entire menu.

The **York Restaurant** (tel. 75-6565) adjoining the Hotel 5a Avenida (6), has been completely remodeled from the tile floor and new pine tables to the gleam-ing white walls decked out with artwork in pastels of pink, blue, and gray. You can enter from the hotel lobby. Clean and shiny, it's all right for a quick but pleasant breakfast at 300 to 600 pesos (60¢ to $1.20), perhaps an egg dish for lunch, antojitos (snacks) for 570 to 800 pesos ($1.14 to $1.60), a sandwich or a hamburger steak for supper. They have more expensive things, like meat dishes for 1,100 to 1,850 pesos ($2.20 to $3.70), but I'd save the money for a splurge, as the prices for these items are almost the same wherever you go, and this is quin-tessentially a light-lunch place with nothing on the midday menu more than the 900-peso ($1.80) comida.

Walking down Calle Zaragoza, you'll find the **Restaurant Mérida (16),** Za-ragoza Norte 522, a very attractive modern restaurant, with a huge mosaic of the Chichén-Itzá pyramids—and napkin holders in the form of little pyramids.

A popular place for businessmen, it offers soup, Mexican plates, meats, and a whole page of Yucatán specialties. You can have a drink here too, if you like, and a generous comida corrida need cost only 700 pesos ($1.40), an excellent value, served by the friendly proprietress, Amanda Silva de Reyes.

For the Local Specialty: The local specialty, cabrito (roast kid), is to be found in many places around town. Usually restaurants serving it will have a fire of glowing coals in the window, with the meat stretched out on spits.

You won't be able to just walk by **El Cabritero (10)** (tel. 43-6834), on the corner of Zaragoza and Arreola (just a few blocks north of the Federal Palace). You literally walk into the aroma of roasting kid and your senses will lead you to the spectacle in the window. Red-hot charcoal along all 15 feet of the grill hisses with the spatter and drippings of roasting kid. Chopping blocks the size of giant tree stumps are not just for decoration at El Cabritero. Inside, the decor is stylish western from the one large menu carved out of a solid piece of wood, to the wagon wheels, lantern-style lighting, and old rifles on the walls. Your meal, served by waiters in white shirts and ties, will include a salad, onions, and of course your favorite cut of cabrito for 1,300 to 1,650 pesos ($2.60 to $3.30).

One of the first restaurants in Monterrey to serve cabrito is still one of the best—as evidenced by the lunchtime family crowds that keep the friendly waiters scurrying back and forth. This is **El Pastor (15)** (tel. 74-0480), Madero Pte. 1067, at Alvarez (five blocks west of Pino Suárez), a thoroughly unclassy and democratic place. Sit anywhere and order cabrito in any of a dozen ways (*al pastor* is roasted). There's no menu, but a price card is by the kitchen, so no need to worry about excessive charges; it comes, depending on what part of the animal you eat, to around 1,300 to 1,750 pesos ($2.60 to $3.50) per order. Further on at Madero Pte. 3126 is **El Pastor del Norte** (tel. 46-8559), with the same menu and prices.

What to Do

The crown jewel of the Sultana of the North is the **Gran Plaza** or **Macro Plaza (17),** dedicated to the new wealth of Monterrey. Covering over 40 acres (16 hectares) of downtown, from the City Hall (A) to the State Capitol Building (19), the Gran Plaza has been called the largest in the world; it may well be. Construction was accomplished in the record time of three years, albeit long ones, a fact city fathers are proud of.

I cannot help but feel that Monterrey, spurred to action by envy for the parks and fountains of Mexico City, set out on a course of plaza one-upmanship. Unlike the nation's capital where the parks teem with life, Monterrey seems to be protecting its plaza like the dowager who refuses to remove the slipcovers on the furniture. Street vendors are noticeably absent and in fact are hustled off the plaza by police. In time, surely the Gran Plaza will become the true "living room" of Monterrey.

Orient yourself with your back to the City Hall (A) and the Commerce Beacon ahead and to your right. Padre Mier is the only street that crosses the plaza between you and the State Capitol Building (19). The following streets pass under the raised plaza and are indicated on the map with dashed lines: Zaragoza (southbound), Zuazua (northbound), Matamoros, Allende and Ramón. Parking for 900 vehicles is available under the plaza.

On the east side of the plaza is the town's **cathedral,** begun in 1600 but not finished until 150 years later. The lavish paintings, sculpture, and decoration inside are typical of colonial Catholicism, and if you think it over, give some insight into the function and position of the church in the colonial period.

The steel and glass **City Hall (A)** (Palacio Municipal) contains little of interest for the tourist but serves as a reference point for an exploratory walk north.

By far the tallest attraction is the vivid-orange, 70-meter (230-foot) **Commerce Beacon (B)** (Faro de Comercio). The well-known architect Luis Barragan designed the monolith to commemorate the 100th anniversary of the Monterrey Chamber of Commerce. The bright orange color was chosen to signify the influence of the folklore of Mexico and is used frequently in exclusive homes in the area. Atop the tower is a green laser that rotates about, slicing the night air every evening except Monday, from 7 to 11 p.m. The fine green beam is barely detectable in the air until it strikes a far-off radio tower or tall building creating a flash of brilliant green sparks.

Across Padre Mier and down the stairs is the **Commercial Mall (C)**. The gleaming shops below offer everything from antiques to hot dogs. Exits on this level lead to parking areas.

Back atop the plaza, notice the innovative architecture of the **City Theater (E), Infonavit Building (F)**, and the **Legislative Palace (G)**, all built with a single theme. The **Fountain of Life (H)**, designed by sculptor Luis Sanguino, is the major water-works on the plaza. Neptune with trident, the central figure of the fountain, was designed to symbolically end the water shortage that has plagued Monterrey throughout history. A great fountain; unfortunately, the water problem persists.

The **Central Library (I)** should be finished soon, as the walls are up and some glass is already installed.

The **Hidden Garden** (Bosque Hundido) separates the Fountain of Life from the **Héroes Esplanade (J)**. The small fountains, artworks, large trees, and man-made waterfalls make this green space one of the most comfortable niches in all of Monterrey. Monuments to Hidalgo, Juárez, Escobedo, and Morelos are the largest works in the Esplanade of Heroes.

Further on is the imposing façade of the **State Capitol Building of Nuevo León (19),** interesting for its Spanish-style patio and decorated hallways. The art-deco **Federal Building (20),** which contains the post office, seems strangely out of sync with its surroundings. A good view over the city can be had by climbing the stairs and looking out one of the windows.

Plaza Hidalgo is the center of the Zona Rosa (Pink Zone). If you're just wandering around town and are hot, or maybe want to write a few postcards, drop into the stately **Gran Hotel Ancira (1)** on the southwest corner of Jardín Hidalgo. The ceiling is about 60 feet high, the floor is alternating squares of black and white marble, and the place is filled with patio-style tables and chairs giving it a French-café atmosphere. In the center of all is a magnificent grand staircase that coils down from an ornate gallery on the mezzanine. Both food and lodging here are expensive but this is certainly the prime place to write postcards or pick up bus tour (Osetur) information.

The best view of Monterrey is from the Bishop's Palace, **El Obispado (21)**—perched atop a hill at the western end of Avenida Padre Mier. Built in the late 18th century to provide employment for the poor during a famine, it has played a part in almost every aspect of Monterrey's history. It has been, at various times, a bishop's palace, a fort, a hospital, and now a museum. During the Mexican-American War it served as a barracks for U.S. troops until their exodus from Mexico. During the yellow fever epidemics of 1898 and 1901 it was used as a hospital. In 1913 Pancho Villa stormed it and it was used again as a fort. It's in a commanding position, and the cannons mounted around it emphasize how easy it must have been to defend in those days of small arms. Many historical objects, including the first printing press brought to northern Mexico, in 1813, have been moved here. There is a small admission charge. Its chief asset, however, is its view of the city—excellent.

When approaching El Obispado by car, head west on Padre Mier to the end of the street. Turn right, go one block, turn left, and follow the signs to El Obispado.

Another thing to do in town: Go on a free tour of the **Cuauhtémoc Brewery (22),** Avenida Universidad Nte. 2202, Tuesday through Friday at 11 a.m., noon, and 3 p.m. An added bonus Tuesday through Sunday from 10:30 a.m. to 6:30 p.m. is the beer garden where you can sit and sip free Carta Blanca. You can reach the brewery by taxi, or you can take any Ruta 1 bus from Avenida Juárez.

Bullfights can be seen on Sunday at the **Plaza Monterrey,** southwest of the city off Avenida Chapultepec. Tickets can be bought from the Tourist Office (see above). The **Charras Rodeo,** every Sunday at 11 a.m., is held in Villa de Guadalupe, off Rte. 85. You can take a bus, which will leave you in the town plaza. From there it's a bit of a walk to the Charras, but worth it to see cowboys pulling steers off their feet by galloping past and grabbing their tails!

Monterrey is famous for its lead crystal, and there is one factory with two showrooms specializing in the manufacture and sale of this beautiful product. Tours through the **Kristaluxus** factory are held Monday through Friday at 10:30 a.m. and 3 p.m., but you must call ahead to make arrangements (tel. 83/51-8447). The glittering showrooms (all sales final) are open Monday through Friday from 8:30 a.m. to 12:45 p.m. and 2 to 5 p.m. Although there are no bargain-basement deals to be made at either place, there are many pieces displayed as "promotional specials." You can do well if you know a bit about crystal beforehand. Actually, prices are only slightly lower than in the stores handling it in town, but the selection is much greater. One store is located at Doblado and Progreso, and the other at Prol. Zuazua and José Ma. Vigil. There is no satisfactory bus service to either place, so plan to take a taxi or the city tour, as it's quite a distance from anywhere else.

Markets

There are three main markets in Monterrey that are open every day of the week. They are all similar in terms of merchandise and prices, although bargaining is a bit easier at the Indian Market. The **Colón Market (M)** is a large, semi-covered bazaar extending several blocks from Juárez and Hidalgo south to Avenida Constitución. The **Juárez Market (M)** is a closed market at the corner of Aramberri and Juárez. The **Indian Market (M),** is outside the downtown area at Simón Bolívar and Madero. You can get there by taking bus 4 from Plaza Zaragoza.

Lest you head off to market with visions of the wealth of the Indies in your head, I hasten to mention that Monterrey's markets are pretty uninspired collections of the mundane and the ridiculous. They have their moments, of course: an artist's stall from which you can buy a recently completed oil painting (if you like the style), or the shop of the *bruja* ("witch," or, more nicely, "herbal healer") in which you can buy an aerosol can of African Power Oil—guaranteed to give you all sorts of powers and bottled in Connecticut. But for a truly superb collection of Mexican arts and crafts, stop in and browse through the shop called **Carapan,** Hidalgo Ote. 305 (tel. 83/42-4360), not far from the Plaza Hidalgo, open Monday through Saturday from 9 a.m. to 1 p.m. and 3 to 7 p.m.; closed Sunday. Antiques and modern items, silver and tin, glass and pottery, textiles and toys—the collection is eclectic and obviously done with an expert's eye. Sr. Profiero Sosa, the owner, has created a work of art—his shop—from works of art—the best of Mexican crafts—and I would be remiss if I didn't mention it. I must add that prices are fairly high, and if you expect to head farther south and you want to buy in quantity, you may decide to put off your purchases until later. It's a gamble: if you find an item you may find it cheaper—but then again you may not be able to find it at all.

One-Day Trips from the City

About 25 miles south of Monterrey, on Rte. 85, are **La Boca Dam** (near the little village of Santiago) and **Horsetail Falls (Cola de Caballo).** La Boca has facilities for waterskiing, swimming, and boating, and features boat races almost every Sunday. There are picnic areas and restaurants nearby. Horsetail Falls (small fee to enter) is located on a private hacienda named Vista Hermosa. Turn right off Rte. 85 to the village of El Cercado, and travel about four miles up a rough but passable road. The road winds around for about three miles from the main road (making the falls accessible only by car or taxi), and leads to a car park where horses and burros can be hired for the final half mile to the falls. If you walk it, it's hard to resist the blandishments of the children who accompany you on burros, making reduced offers all the way until, when you're nearly there, they start bargaining about the return trip. I walked both ways and found it no particular strain.

On the road to Saltillo, there are several more things to see. Taking Hwy. 40 in the Saltillo direction, you'll find **Chipinque Mesa** about 13 miles from Monterrey. Turn left at Colonia del Valle, pay a toll of 100 pesos (20¢) per person, and you're on your way. The trip is up the pine-covered slopes of the Sierra Madre and culminates in a breathtaking view of Monterrey from a 4,200-foot plateau. The **Motel and Restaurant Chipinque** here is a very glamorous place, with volleyball courts, badminton, archery range, Ping-Pong, croquet, and expensive rooms; and guided excursions by horseback, burro, or on foot to **Los Manantiales** (The Springs), **Bosque Encantado** (The Enchanted Forest) or into the Sierra Madre Mountains.

You can also travel 15 miles along the road to Saltillo until you reach the village of Santa Catarina. Turn left here, go two miles more, and you'll find yourself at **Huasteca Canyon,** a massive rock formation framing dangerously deep ravines. This trip can be hazardous to the car as well as to the nerves.

On the road to Saltillo too, about 27 miles from Monterrey, are the **Garcia Caves** (Grutas de Garcia), with the usual stalactites and stalagmites, huge chambers, and a subterranean lake.

Monterrey Nightlife

The Zona Rosa tends to be the center of Monterrey's social life. This being a big college town, you'll see lots of students as well as nonscholarly types hanging around, leaning on cars, filling store doorways, and winking, whistling, and flirting. On Sunday in summer there are band concerts in Hidalgo Plaza and other days of the week there are night concerts at City Hall.

Most of the bars in town discourage women—it's a real "macho" man's world in there. For men alone, Monterrey offers good opportunities to practice that old Spanish custom of bar-hopping—whose popularity is best evidenced by the fact that there are at least three colloquial ways of saying "bar-hopping." Of course, to really *ir de tascas* in proper style, one should plan a visit to at least five places, have a drink and some tapas (hors d'oeuvres) in every one, make sure you're seen, greet everybody, and then plow on to the next. The casual tourist, however, will find this ritual rather trying if not impossible, so you can consider yourself excused.

There are a few places where women, in groups or alone, are perfectly welcome. One such place is **La Cabaña (24),** at Matamoros 318 Pte. between Pino Suárez and Cuauhtémoc (tel. 42-9523). It's a very nice, air-conditioned beer garden with wooden booths and woven grass-seated chairs. The food is excellent and Cabaña now specializes in some nice meat and fish dishes with a special local touch. If you're not a nighttime carouser this is also a popular afternoon restaurant. Beer is 300 pesos (60¢), a light meal goes for about 400 to 900 pesos (80¢ to $1.80). They are open from 11 a.m. to 1 a.m. every day of the week with the exception of Friday and Saturday when they keep the beer flowing until 2 a.m.

The downtown hotel lounges and bars are the other places where a lady can enjoy a drink and "still keep her title," as they say in Monterrey!

A word about **Purísima Square (25):** This used to be the place where young people gathered for the nighttime paseo; on my last visit there seemed to be little going on in this neighborhood. It's worth a visit, however, preferably in daylight, to see the famous modernistic **Purísima Church,** built in 1946, with parabolas of concrete and an adjoining tower of brown stone topped with a blue neon cross. The church façade is decorated with a crucified Christ and 12 stone Apostles.

Cinemas: Luckily for gringos (and gringas), most foreign films screened in Mexico are in the original language. This doesn't help you if the movie was made in Spain, but if it was made in Hollywood you'll be able to catch the original English soundtrack. They turn the sound down in some places, though, so don't sit too far back.

Monterrey's cinemas are dotted throughout the city, but there are three movie houses on the Avenida Zaragoza within six blocks of the Gran Plaza, and these three tend to show recent first-run American films. Seven and nine o'clock are common screening times, but take your stroll slightly earlier, just to be sure.

Monterrey Miscellany

Guided Tours: Walk down along Hidalgo near the Plaza Hidalgo, and every taxi driver you encounter will offer to take you on a tour of Monterrey's sights—for a price. The way to handle it is to talk for a while and see how good his English is, and whether his personality appeals or not. Then, set down exactly what the tour will cover. A good city tour should take you to the Palacio del Gobierno, the Palacio Federal, Purísima Church, El Obispado, University City, and perhaps to the markets, all in about three hours. The "official" rate is $35 U.S. (regardless of the value of the peso) for the carload. See if you can round up several people to share the cost. It's good to compare prices with several drivers and the official rates before making a commitment.

I've always wished there would be an easier way to do this, and now there is—Osetur to the rescue! Osetur (tel. 83/43-6616) operates out of the San Francisco Building (same location as the tourist office), but you don't have to travel way out there for information as the major downtown hotels (Ancira, etc.) provide information and sell tickets. You do not have to be a guest in any particular hotel to get in on this deal. The Osetur bus plies Monterrey's hotspots Tuesday through Saturday. The morning tour begins at 9:30 a.m. and takes a slightly different, but equally pleasing, route each day—including the Gran Plaza and Kristaluxus, and either the museums or craft shops. The bilingual Osetur brochure includes a daily schedule. The afternoon trips, which are further afield, begin at 1:30 p.m. Again, check the brochure as it indicates exactly where each tour goes. For example, on Tuesday you can visit Garcia Caves, while on Wednesday it's La Boca Dam (Bahia Escondido Resort) and Horsetail Falls. On Sunday there is a special tour beginning at 9:30 a.m. which includes the Gran Plaza, the mall area, two large handcraft shops, and Horsetail Falls.

Best of all is the price of 2,000 pesos ($4) per person for either a morning or afternoon tour. This price includes the tour, door-to-door pick up at the major hotels, entrance tickets at all visits, and the services of a bilingual host.

For those who for some reason want a completely private tour, this can be had—but so can you! The free-lance tour guides are knowledgeable and really will take you where you want to go, but it's an expensive proposition which leaves you dealing with the details of the trip. These "official" guides carry identification vouching for their authenticity, which they will flourish upon approaching you. They also carry an official rate sheet, which you will see as soon as you attempt to bargain for a lower price. The rates include city tours as well as day trips as far as Saltillo—in your car, the guide's car, or a bus. An example at the time of this writing is a four-hour tour in the guide's car to Horsetail Falls for one to five people at $40.00 U.S. (20,000 pesos).

Sports: The state government has ingeniously converted the dry bed of the Santa Caterina River, which runs through the center of the city, into over two miles of playing fields of every conceivable type: soccer, baseball, tennis, track —you name it, it's there.

Further Information: Pick up copies of "Where to Go, What to Know," "Hola Monterrey," and "Spotlight," tourist publications available for free in tourist offices, hotels, and bus depots; there's much useful information in them, and you can't beat the price.

Bus Information: Your best source of up-to-date information is, of course, the Central de Autobuses (main bus depot) on the Avenida Colón, roughly two blocks north of the Independence Arch.

SALTILLO: This is the mile-high capital (alt. 5,280 feet; pop. 330,000) of the state of Coahuila, and holds both the State College of Coahuila and also the International University, both of which attract American students during the summer. The climate is excellent, with gentle breezes that sweep down from the mountains to dispel lingering heat and humidity in midsummer; in winter, it's chillier than you'd expect—note that most of the budget hotels are not heated.

The main tower of the two-century-old cathedral, on the Plaza de Armas, offers a good view of the city, but this, together with the tree- and lake-filled Alameda Park, present just about the only diversions for the wanderer in this once-colonial-now-industrial city. Sadly, noise and air pollution have become quite a problem.

If you visit Saltillo in August, you may be in time for the big fair and exposition, an annual event to display local achievements in agriculture and industry.

The **bus station** is inconveniently located on the bypass loop (Calzado L. Echeverría) on the southern edge of town. Count on a brisk 30-minute walk up and down the hilly Saltillo side streets to get to the center of the city. As for the **railroad station,** it's at the southwest corner of town on Avenida Carranza (Hwy. 57), which runs parallel to Allende. To get to Allende from Carranza, walk along the latter to Ramos Arizpe and turn right, going until you abut on Allende, the town's main axis.

Where to Stay

The hotel situation in Saltillo is bad—and getting worse. The half-dozen downtown hostelries that once surrounded guests with at least a modicum of colonial charm—at low prices—have lost business to the new Rodeway Inn and Camino Real hotels on the outskirts of town. As the trade moved out, downtown hotels got careless with housekeeping and service. Short of settling into one of the out-of-town hotels at exorbitant prices, here's what you can check out downtown:

To guide you to our hotel and restaurant choices, I'll use the lively **Plaza Acuña,** next to the market, as a central point, as it's within easy walking distance of all the places listed below. The plaza is bounded by Allende, Aldama, Padre Flores, and the market.

The **Hotel Urdinola** (tel. 841/4-0940) has been one of Saltillo's better budget lodging choices for many years. Originally built in colonial style many years ago, it has undergone periodic renovation to keep it presentable. Some of its nicer features have escaped the ravages of modernization, though: the huge white granite stairway that leads to the second floor and a large stained-glass window, a lovely long sunny patio onto which the rooms open, and a fine tile fountain at the patio's end. All rooms have bath, telephone, and individual lights over the beds, and are priced at 4,600 pesos ($9.20) single, 5,175 pesos ($10.35) double. The Urdinola's location at Calle Victoria 427 is ideal: Victoria is the city's main shopping street for handcrafts, and it's only two blocks from the Plaza Acuña. Parking is available next door to the Urindola for a very high 1,200 pesos ($2.40).

At Victoria 418 you'll find the rather elegant (if pricey) **Hotel Arizpe-Sainz** (tel. 841/4-0404), right across the street from the Urdinola. Not among the lowest priced of budget choices, the Arizpe-Sainz charges 6,750 pesos ($13.50) single, 7,875 pesos ($15.75) double, but for this price you get a delightful and well-maintained colonial-style building with two pretty courtyard patios, big and old-fashioned but fairly luxurious rooms, a good restaurant, a coffeeshop, and a bar. Sandwiches will run 700 to 850 pesos ($1.40 to $1.70), and a basic meal costs 800 to 1,200 pesos ($1.60 to $2.40). Again the location on Calle Victoria is ideal.

In keeping with the reputation of downtown Saltillo hotels, the **Hotel Premier,** Allende Nte. 508 (tel. 841/2-1050), charges a bit too much for what you get: single rooms with bath here run 4,200 pesos ($8.40), doubles are 4,700 pesos ($9.40). Be sure to look at a few rooms before you choose one. The downstairs rooms have been remodeled and are a better value than the rooms upstairs which are scheduled to be remodeled in the future.

If you roll into Saltillo very late in the evening and find yourself standing outside the bus station, just cross the street to the **Hotel Central** on L. Echeverría 231 (tel. 841/2-8410). This is a no-frills place inside and out. The exterior is plain unfinished wood, rivaled only by the starkness of the lobby with its five "waiting room"—style chairs lined up against the wall and a TV pressed against the opposite wall. The 48 rooms, though small, are adequate and clean, with ceiling fans and nice bathrooms too. Singles here go for 1,500 pesos ($3) and doubles for 3,000 pesos ($6). The Panificadora next door makes delicious sugar doughnuts.

Where to Eat

Café y Arte on the Plaza de Armas at Zaragoza Nte. 200 is a delightful haunt for Saltillo's university crowd. The menu is to the point—100% pure Mexican coffee for 160 pesos (32¢), many alcohol-coffee combinations such as the reasonably priced Kahlúa and anis combinations priced between 300 and 450 pesos (60¢ and 90¢), lemonade for 200 pesos (40¢), and desserts for 400 pesos (80¢). The cappuccino is great, the local weaving and contemporary artwork on the walls are a nice touch; but here the real adventure is a trip back in time to the coffeehouse ambiance of the 1960s. By 9 p.m. the tables are crammed and the entertainment is in full swing. The night I was there a male vocalist with guitar sang his own songs of love mixed with popular Mexican folksongs and a sprinkling of requests which included quite a few '60s ballads. "Teen Angel" really is quite pleasant in Español! An added attraction on the way out is an awesome view of the lighted cathedral across the plaza.

Restaurant Arcasa, one block west of Café y Arte on Allende (no phone), is a typical, unpretentious eatery interested only in serving a good, basic meal. Usual breakfast fare ranges in price from 180 to 310 pesos (36¢ to 62¢). Sandwiches are made for our budget at 225 to 360 pesos (45¢ to 72¢). Meat dishes, priced at not more than 1,100 pesos ($2.20), are the only selections available in the evening. The steak is chewy, but servings are generous. Down it with a refresco for 90 pesos (18¢) or a cold beer for 200 pesos (40¢).

For the local specialty, cabrito (roast kid), the best place around is the **Restaurant Principal** (tel. 4-3384), Allende Nte. 710, on the corner of Allende and Alessio Robles, four blocks north (down the hill) from the Plaza Acuña on the right-hand side. Bright and modern, with brick arches and a tile kitchen open to view, it's a pleasant place to try the succulent (although a bit greasy) kids cooking over coals in the window. The price for a portion is a standard 1,380 pesos ($2.76) and while you can have other things here—(chicken, for instance, is 1,035 pesos ($2.07)—you should come here to have the specialty of the house.

Saltillo has a seafood restaurant that serves up marine delicacies for moderate prices. The **Boca del Río,** (tel. 841/2-4105), Acuña Nte. 533 has moved since the last edition. The new building is one block west of Allende and is well worth the short walk from the Plaza Acuña. Parking is provided alongside the glass-front building. Considerate touches set off this clean restaurant, including comfortable woven leather chairs, the huge copper sailfish on one wall (also moved from the old building), fresh flowers on every table, and black-and-white-clad waiters who are out to please. A delicious fish cocktail (ceviche) costs 564 pesos ($1.13); octopus with shrimp and rice is a moderate 920 pesos ($1.84) and is very good, if somewhat spicy. Most entree plates are moderately priced between 725 to 900 pesos ($1.45 to $1.80). The Boca del Río's star performance is the jumbo shrimp en brochette, a tremendous helping of food which is almost heavenly, and might well be for 1,645 pesos ($3.29). Large portions are the rule here.

What to Do

The **Plaza Acuña** might be called the "People's Park" of Saltillo, for all throughout the day there's action: sellers of boiled corn, tacos, candies, and other treats; an army of shoeshine boys; a car being raffled; a public photographer with an antediluvian camera; another man with a more modern camera taking pictures of children astride a plaster horse; a kiddie's rocketship ride; old men sunning on benches; young men checking out the hotrods and the girls; pitchmen selling gizmos of every conceivable type. Don't miss this microcosm.

The "formal" park is all that Acuña is not. This is the **Plaza de Armas,** bounded on one side by the government palace, on the opposite side by the 17th-century cathedral, and on a third by the local headquarters of the **PRI,** Mexico's leading political party. A graceful fountain plays in the evening when Saltillo's more sedate citizens fill the wrought-iron benches to take the air. Take a close look at the **cathedral,** actually two separate naves with a façade that's truly an eyeful. The style is churrigueresque, a 17th-century Spanish mutation of baroque that carries the style to even more ornate extremes than usual. The nave on the left is quite impressive, but walk all the way to the altar in the nave on the right to see the elaborate side altars of gilded wood. You can climb the cathedral's main tower for a good view of the city.

Saltillo's third park is the **Alameda,** a tree-and-pond oasis at the opposite (west) end of Victoria from Allende, a good place for a late afternoon stroll.

Shopping

The town's main market, **Mercado Juárez,** next to the Plaza Acuña, has been modernized but is worth a quick stroll. The main floor is mostly fresh food and is of little interest if you're looking for souvenirs, but the lower floor has a good selection of baskets at very reasonable prices. The shops on the second story carry an amazing assortment of piñatas during the Christmas season. After a brief visit to the market, serious shoppers should direct their steps to the main shopping street, the **Calle Victoria.** One door away from the town's **post office** (at no. 453, open every day including Sunday) is one of the big stores that sell the products that give Saltillo its claim to fame, namely the colorful wool or cotton serapes. In my opinion the best of the stores is **El Saltillero,** at Victoria 469, where the serapes (displayed up front) come in every shape, size, and pattern, and are very reasonably priced. The store also holds an amazing assortment of other handcrafts, including embroidered blouses and shirts, articles in painted paper-mâché (including intricate candelabra), things made from copper, brass, alabaster, leather, glass, and tin. One of the wildest offerings is a row of milk cans decorated with scenic views—heaven knows what you'd use them for. Some of the staff speak English, and all are very helpful and polite.

A new competitor to El Saltillero is the attractive store called **El Serape de Saltillo,** across from the cathedral. Take a look in here as well.

One store you shouldn't miss, even if you're not in a buying mood, is the **Saltillo Silver Factory,** located near the Hotel Arizpe-Sainz at Calle Victoria 404, and offering some of the finest handcrafts in all of Mexico. Prices even by U.S. standards are rather high, but you can admire wares that include huge, striking paper flowers in every color from turquoise to black; papier-mâché bracelets; oddly shaped wall decorations; wrought-iron chandeliers; sculptured candles; and almost every other imaginable objet d'art. You can see the same type of things elsewhere (at San Angel's Bazar Sabado in Mexico City, for instance) but these are done with special skill and imagination.

The last shopping area to look at is on Allende near the market, especially if you're interested in a fine pair of boots at a reasonable price. The ones I liked best were in the shoe store *(zapatería)* at no. 348.

BACK ON THE HIGHWAY: Off to Monterrey? By road it's about an hour and a half over a divided highway with beautiful mountain vistas. Those going south to Mexico City via Hwy. 57 will first go through Matehuala.

Matehuala

There's desert almost all the way from Saltillo to San Luis Potosí, but the town of Matehuala, San Luis Potosí (alt. 5,085 feet; pop. 50,000), almost halfway, is a welcome oasis. Matehuala is the second-largest city in the state of San Luis Potosí, but it's hard to believe it's more than a small town. If you're looking for a quiet, nontouristy, south-of-the-border town, this is it! Nothing happens here, but that's why I like it.

There is a very inexpensive hotel near a quiet plaza, the **Hotel Matehuala,** Bustamente 134 (tel. 488/2-0680). From Rte. 57 bear to the right under the arch that leads into town. Follow this road until you come to the zócalo, go right, and continue on this road until you come to Hidalgo (about four blocks). Turn left and the hotel is straight ahead. The hotel is presently a plain, ancient yellow and looks worse on the outside than it does on the inside. There is a mammoth court furnished with kitchen furniture and absolutely quiet. There are 40 rooms on two levels off the court. They are plain, with high ceilings and bare walls. However, the hotel has recently come into the capable hands of new owner/manager Estella L. Cavazos, and one by one the rooms are being remodeled. With bath, rooms are 2,075 pesos ($4.50) single, 2,875 pesos ($5.75) double; without bath, 1,375 to 1,750 pesos ($2.75 to $3.50). Strike up a conversation (English or Spanish) with this enthusiastic businesswoman; she's better than a tourist office.

If you're looking for creature comforts, try the **Motel Oasis** (tel. 488/2-

0742), on Rte. 57 just north of Matehuala, next to the large "Gasolinera" sign. The rates are reasonable—singles are 2,750 to 5,000 pesos ($5.50 to $10); doubles, 3,500 to 6,250 pesos ($7 to $12.50)—and the situation is beautiful, with lots of grass and trees and a refreshing pool. The clientele is mostly Mexican, which tends to keep the rates reasonable. They also have a restaurant on the premises; a complete breakfast is 750 pesos ($1.50) and a full meal costs 875 to 1,500 pesos ($1.75 to $3.00) with grilled meat. All in all, a good bet for the weary traveler.

The **Restaurant Tokio** is off the plaza, two blocks from the hotel Matehuala, on the street to the right of the church on the main plaza. It is bright and modern and offers a good comida corrida for 1,000 pesos ($2.00).

Restaurant Sante Fe, also near the main plaza at Morelos 709, is another inexpensive place to eat. With its cooling ceiling fans, bright-orange chairs, and lots of windows, you can enjoy almost any meal on the menu for 750 pesos ($1.50) or less. Omelets range from 200 to 500 pesos (40¢ to $1.00), pigeon is 500 pesos ($1.00), and rice pudding runs 250 pesos (50¢).

La Playa Frontera, on the plaza, is the local ice-cream parlor and the place to hang out in the evening.

If you end up with an extra day in Matehuala, you might consider a side trip up the mountain to the old silver-mining ghost town of **Real de Catorce.** It's a 30-mile excursion, but can be made by bus for 1,000 pesos ($2.00). Catch the bus around the corner from the Hotel Matehuela, right by the plaza. Be prepared for an entire day as this is a six-hour trip leaving at 8 a.m. The history is boom and bust, with excessive luxury followed by empty, dusty streets. Robert Service may have paused here had he been in the area.

HIGHWAY 85, THE ALTERNATIVE ROUTE: As mentioned above, the route
due south of Monterrey following Hwy. 85 is not as interesting as the aforementioned trip via Hwy. 57, but if you decide that Hwy. 85 is for you, here's what you'll encounter:

Montemorelos
You'll see the name of Montemorelos, Nuevo León (alt. 1,609 feet; pop. 18,000), described as "Naranjiera Capital" (Orange Capital). Montemorelos is hot in summer and doesn't ever have too much to offer, except the mid-July fiesta, the pecan fair in mid-September, and the sight of the orange and lemon trees in bloom from February to March.

Linares
Fifty-one kilometers (30 miles) south of Montemorelos is Linares, Nuevo León (alt. 1,272 feet; pop. 50,000), a clean, pleasant town that is the center of a farming area and some small industry (bricks, furniture).

Right in the center of downtown Linares, at Hidalgo 102, is the **Hotel Plaza Mira** (tel. 821/2-0025), on the main street and only a block from the first-class bus station. Rooms at the Plaza Mira were redecorated—virtually rebuilt—during 1978 and now have piped-in music (who needs it?), new tile baths, shiny air conditioning units, satellite TV, and a swimming pool. Prices reflect this luxury: singles cost 4,750 to 5,905 pesos ($9.50 to $11.81); doubles run 5,705 to 7,465 pesos ($11.41 to $14.93). Free parking.

When you get hungry, just follow the smell to **Super Pollo** on Morelos, a scant half block from the cathedral. Here half a chicken, charcoal broiled, costs 600 pesos ($1.20) with a plate of warm tortillas. This is enough for two. On a typical afternoon the cook will be grilling 30 to 40 chickens, creating an almost irresistible aroma!

Between Linares and Ciudad Victoria the road is mostly straight and fast, with plenty of greenery and the majestic Sierra Madre range towering up on the right (west). There's little else to be seen, however, except an occasional passing car, bus, or cyclist, and lazy cattle grazing by the road. This is sugarcane country.

Ciudad Victoria

Victoria (alt. 1,471 feet; pop. 155,000), capital of the state of Tamaulipas, was named in 1825 for Mexican revolutionary Guadalupe Victoria, who became the country's first president. Today, far from being a one-burro town, it has modern architecture, open-air snackbars, and a town square complete with fountain.

On the northern edge of town is the 66-room **San Antonio Motel** (tel. 131/2-0311), which has a large modern dining room and very high prices. Rooms are simple, clean, and bright, and cost 6,900 pesos ($13.80) single, 8,050 pesos ($16.10) double. Quiet, plenty of shade trees, a restful place. You might have a bite to eat here: sandwiches are 770 to 920 pesos ($1.54 to $1.84), and most entrees are in the 1,000- to 1,600-pesos ($2.00 to $3.20) range.

Farther north on Hwy. 85 at the intersection with Mateos is the **Motel Jardin** (tel. 131/2-1124). Although worn, the rooms are adequate and come with a car port and individual air conditioner (be sure yours works). Rooms cost 2,000 pesos ($4.00) single or double.

The town's main plaza holds three major hotels. Most modern and suitable is the 100-room **Hotel Everest** (tel. 131/2-4050) which, like its mountain namesake, is blissfully air-conditioned. All rooms have private bath, of course. Prices are too high at 7,475 pesos ($14.95) single, 8,625 pesos ($17.25) double. The Everest's official address is Hidalgo 9 and Colón 126.

The **Hotel Sierra Gorda** (tel. 131/2-2280) used to hold the place of Victoria's prime hostelry, but has lost it to the Everest. Rooms cost 3,450 to 5,865 pesos ($6.90 to $11.73) single and 4,050 to 6,900 pesos ($8.10 to $13.80) double. The less expensive rooms have ceiling fans while the others are air-conditioned. One gets the distinct feeling that these prices are only for those who will pay them, however, and that a bit of bargaining will get very dramatic reductions. Ask for the "promotional" rates. Once you've bargained for a price, your room will have a private bathroom, piped-in music, a telephone, and even a TV set. Parking costs extra.

Right next door, still on the plaza, is the **Hotel Los Monteros** (tel. 131/2-0300), a simple gem of colonial architecture with rooms for half the price. The Monteros' lobby is a vast symmetrical court, edged with pillars and dominated by a sweeping stone staircase; fortunately no one seems to have considered "modernizing" the place, because its downstairs is lit by graceful old chandeliers instead of the standard neon. The rooms are super-clean and face a series of bright interior courts bordered by elaborate iron balconies; all have comfortable beds, carved wooden bedsteads, and private bath. The price is the best part: 2,935 pesos ($5.87) single, 3,462 pesos ($6.93) double, 3,738 pesos ($7.48) triple. The big difference in price between the Sierra Gorda and the Monteros comes from the difference in climate control: the Sierra Gorda has air conditioning, while the Monteros has only fans.

Adjoining the Hotel Los Monteros is a good restaurant where prices run 700 pesos ($1.40) or less for a sandwich and drink, or 520 to 800 pesos ($1.04 to $1.60) for a more substantial tuck-in.

The old mom-and-pop standbys have generally retreated here, making way for the new-breed of good but less personal restaurants such as **Daddy's,** located next to the Everest on the main square (no phone). Modern, mirrored, and shiny-clean, Daddy's does a rush-hour business at midday and all evening.

The menu includes such delicacies as turtle soup for 380 pesos (76¢), Mexican specialties for 633 to 800 pesos ($1.27 to $1.60), and tangy mangoes and cream for 322 pesos (65¢).

Twenty-four miles south the road starts to drop considerably; before Ciudad Mante, 85 miles south of Victoria, it falls 1,000 feet. Watch for a place to pull off on the left-hand side of the road, and stop for the magnificent views across a miles-wide canyon with startling rock buttes like those in Colorado. Giant cactus and tropical fruit grow all around this tropical area (you're in the Tropic of Cancer now). Continue for another 56 miles (94 kilometers) and you'll reach Ciudad Valles.

Ciudad Valles
This town, in the state of San Luis Potosí (pop. 240,000), doesn't have much to recommend it in my view, but it is a good place to take a break in your journey to other places. Relax and do what the local people do in the evening. Walk the zócalo and enjoy the fountain and the view over the River Valles. There are several good hotels in Cuidad Valles. The first two are on Rte. 85 (now officially called Boulevard in town), and the third is downtown.

The best is the **Hotel Valles** (tel. 138/2-0050), an elaborate hacienda-style motor hotel garnished with quantities of palm trees and gardens and a splendid 100-foot swimming pool. Rooms are large and comfortably furnished; prices are a little high for its being out in the middle of nowhere—singles run 4,428 to 5,635 ($8.86 to $11.27); doubles, 5,635 to 6,900 pesos ($11.27 to $13.80); air conditioning is in only the more expensive rooms. The Valles also has a thatched cathedral-ceilinged restaurant-bar which is nice to look at but expensive. You can camp here for 1,150 pesos ($2.30) if you have the necessary equipment.

Two blocks closer to town on Rte. 85 is the **Posada Don Antonio** (tel. 138/2-0066). The official address is Boulevard 15. Rooms cost 2,950 to 6,400 pesos ($5.90 to $12.80) single, 3,750 to 7,700 pesos ($7.50 to $15.40) double, with ceiling fans in the cheaper rooms, air conditioning in the more expensive. Rooms face interior courtyards, one of which is for parking and the other has a garden and swimming pool. Rooms have all modern conveniences, huge bathrooms, and televisions. Some rooms even have neat little window box gardens by the bathroom vent windows. Restaurant and Bar Don Antonio is attached to the motel, and is slick, modern, and clean. The daily comida is 950 pesos ($1.90), with other meals in the 850- to 1,400-pesos ($1.70 to $2.80) range, and a Sunday buffet for 1,400 pesos ($2.80).

A centrally located choice only two blocks from the zócalo and the bus depot is the **Hotel Piña**, at Juárez 210 (tel. 138/2-0183). The 55-room hotel offers free courtyard parking, fairly large, clean rooms, plain dark-wood furniture, and ceiling fans. Singles cost 2,000 pesos ($4.00), doubles in one or two beds run 2,360 pesos ($4.72), and triples go for 2,710 pesos ($5.42).

Restaurant Malibu, at Hidalgo 109, less than half a block from the zócalo, is a plain but pleasant air-conditioned oasis complete with espresso machine. You can enjoy the comida at midday for 700 pesos ($1.40), 800 pesos ($1.60) on Sunday, with most à la carte meals in the 600- to 1,200-pesos ($1.20 to $2.40) range. Long-distance phone calls can also be made from here.

If you are looking for a light meal, stop at the corner of Juárez and Madero at the tin-roofed **Mariscos de Veracruz** (no phone). Ease onto a folding chair and order the passable stone crab ceviche for 350 pesos (70¢). If you're put off by the casual kitchen, pop next door to Café Marianna (no phone) on Madero. Here you'll pay to sit inside, with shrimp cooked in garlic going for 1,500 pesos ($3.00).

Heading West: Going west to San Luis Potosí? The road is wonderfully scenic, even magnificent, joining 9,000-foot highlands to tropics, but the 170 miles of road are full of twists and turns and rough-ish pavement, so allow about four hours to drive it unless you plan to push hard. See Chapter V for details of San Luis Potosí and other Silver Cities.

Heading South: For a real treat, make sure to be alert for the stretch of road south of Ciudad Valles. From Valles to Mexico City, you pass about 250 miles of unusually beautiful sights, and the trip should definitely be made in daylight. The hillsides are a patchwork quilt of fields, patterned irregularly with different crops and colors. In late summer and fall, clouds of tiny yellow butterflies fill the road and the sun sets early and plays tricks with your eyes.

Heading East to Tuxpan: You can drive to Tuxpan from Ciudad Valles, taking a pretty but fantastically misshapen roadbed from Tamuin through Tancuayalab to El Higo. (Be sure to check road conditions before setting out.) Before you get to the Río Tampaon you'll have to leave the paved road and turn left onto a dirt track which goes through a village and then descends to a little rickety toll ferry (which may not be operating during high water). No sign marks the turnoff. El Higo has a big sugar mill, and so the road surface between the town and the intersection with Hwy. 105 is pretty beat-up. Turn left onto Hwy. 127 after Tempoal, and head for Tuxpan. This interesting trip is full of surprises and bone-jaggles, and takes about 4½ hours. Don't expect deliverance from rough roads when you reach Hwys. 105, 127, and 180. Most of the mileage all the way to Tuxpan is similar to a minefield after the war. You really may not want to do this to your vehicle.

Pachuca

Pachuca, the last major stop before the capital (alt. 8,000 feet; pop. 132,000), is an attractive old town that is swept by cooling breezes. The women selling socks, handkerchiefs, and scarves in the plaza are constantly having to get up to retrieve items of clothing blown into the street by sudden gusts of wind. In the hills around the town, silver has been mined for at least five centuries, and is still produced in large quantities.

It is well worth the effort to climb one of the narrow, precipitous streets up the hillside, from which there is an excellent view not only of the forest of TV aerials, but of the irregular surrounding terrain.

Pachuca has a small, clean **market** through which it is pleasant to stroll. One section appears to specialize in making funeral wreaths with dozens of different white flowers woven into the greenery. There are many **bake shops** with appetizing cookies and pastries on show.

For a place to stay, home-in on the **Plaza Independencia.** There are several other plazas in town, each quite unique. You won't miss this one if you look for the massive clock and bell tower. The remainder of the plaza is bare concrete. However, under the bell tower is a subterranean complex housing the cinema El Reloj, where it costs 100 pesos (55¢) to watch a film, a few shops, public bathrooms, and parking.

First choice for a room is the **Hotel Emily,** on Plaza Independencia (tel. 771/5-6122). The entrance faces the clock and bell tower and the marquee for the cinema. Walk up half a flight of stairs to this sparkling new hotel. An upholstered lounge area furnished only with pillows spruces up the lobby. The large rooms, accented with natural pine touches, are absolutely spotless. Singles are 3,400 pesos ($6.80); doubles in one bed, 3,800 pesos ($7.60); in two beds, 4,200 pesos ($8.40). The deluxe suite sports a sitting room and one of the largest king-size beds in Mexico for 5,000 pesos ($10).

Nearby is the old but well-kept 62-room **Hotel de los Baños,** Calle de Matamoros 205, two blocks from the Plaza Independencia (tel. 771/3-0700). Here one finds a vast, tile court for a lobby, guarded by sturdy wooden gates. The central court has several tiers of balconies leading to the rooms, some with elaborately carved Spanish furniture, Oriental rugs, and chandeliers; other rooms have modernish, functional hotel furniture. It's a businesslike place, kept quite clean. Singles are 2,600 pesos ($5.20), with doubles for 3,200 pesos ($6.40). Six tiny tables, set to one side in the lobby, serve as a restaurant.

Another choice for a room is the **Hotel Noriega,** Calle de Matamoros 305 (tel. 771/2-5000), just a few minutes' stroll from the main plaza. A dazzlingly rich old colonial place, the Noriega boasts lots of gleaming glass, red tiles, and carved wood, but also lays on the modern comforts: all rooms come with TV. Expect to see a huge rubber tree in the courtyard. For a single you'll pay 2,750 pesos ($5.50), and for a double 3,000 pesos ($6).

In the same building is the Noriega Restaurant. Fine service, cloth napkins and tablecloths, and lace curtains are a few of the niceties here. Sandwiches range in price from 400 to 600 pesos (80¢ to $1.20), and the comida is set at 775 pesos ($1.55).

There is no lack of other good restaurants in town; you'll find most either on the plaza or the Calle de Matamoros. The **Restaurant La Fogata,** Calle de Matamoros 203, has a comida corrida that includes soup, entrees, dessert, and beverages for 650 pesos ($1.30). Competition has had a positive effect in Pachuca, as you can buy a great breakfast consisting of a ham and cheese omelet and toast for 500 pesos ($1) or tacos anytime for the same price.

On the same street, the **Restaurant La Blanca,** Calle de Matamoros 201, offers chicken, steak, and a comida for 700 pesos ($1.40). Almost anything else on the menu goes for 650 pesos ($1.30). While you're here, take a look at the large wall painting, which captures a moment of Pachuca's mining history.

The **Casino Español,** Calle de Matamoros 207, which is classier and looks rather like a gilded men's room, is open daily 8 a.m. to 9 p.m., but unless you push open the heavy exterior door and walk up the stairs you could miss this one on a cool Pachucan evening. Once up, proceed through the ballroom, resplendent with chandeliers, and into a smaller room with arches and the standard fluorescent lighting. The tab for an excellent comida will be 1,000 pesos ($2); children's plates are less.

Chip's Restaurant, on Plaza Independencia, is attached to the Emily Hotel. Lots of mirrors and bright tablecloths highlight this modern dining room. The up-and-coming young Pachucans gather here to sip steaming cappuccino and indulge in gooey desserts in the cool evenings. If it's a meal you need, take a table by the windows facing the plaza and enjoy one for an average price of 1,600 pesos ($3.20).

Things to Do: Something new in something old describes Mexico's first regional history museum, recently opened in Pachuca. The museum, the **Hidalgo Cultural Center,** is located in what used to be the Convent of San Francisco on Bartolomé de Medina Plaza, about five blocks south of the main square (ask for directions). The former convent, considered to be the most important and original building in Pachuca, is an architectual gem itself. Built in 1596, it has seen a progression of uses: first as a mission base, then as a mining school, city hospital, penitentiary, home for photographic archives, and today the Hildago Cultural Center. Take the time to stop in at this promising first-of-its-kind regional museum and browse through the historical and cultural past of this area. Open 9 a.m. to noon and 3 to 5 p.m. Admission 40 pesos (8¢).

Chapter III

PACIFIC COAST RESORTS

MEXICO'S PACIFIC COAST is over 2,000 miles long. Although the northern reaches of the coast are the western edges of the Sonoran Desert, once you get south of Culiacán the lush tropical climate takes over and provides the perfect milieu for beach resorts.

Visitors from North America discovered how perfectly this stretch lent itself to sunning and swimming and a general laid-back lifestyle long before their Mexican neighbors did. A half-century ago Acapulco was a sleepy fishing port with only a few renegade *norteamericanos* living on low budgets and doing odd things such as lying on the beach half-naked for hours.

Since then, things have changed. Although the small fishing ports still exist, you have to forge ever southward to find them. The more northerly ones have come of age as glittering resorts served by jet aircraft and guarded from the sea by towering walls of high-rise luxury hotels. But for all this modernity each resort retains an older downtown section of reasonably priced hotels and restaurants.

Each of Mexico's fabled Pacific resorts has its own special *ambiente,* which you will discover more readily by traveling on $20 a day than if you zip in by Lear-Jet and stay at El Presidente. Here, then, is this fabulous lineup, starting with some information on up-and-coming Baja, then on to the most northerly of the resort cities—Mazatlán—and continuing all the way down to the tiny tropical hideaways of Puerto Escondido and Puerto Angel, in the state of Oaxaca.

1. Baja California

The long finger of land extending southward from Tijuana is a unique area of Mexico. Populated for centuries by only a few hardy fishermen and their families, Baja is finally coming into its own. The road from Tijuana in the north to Cabo San Lucas on the peninsula's southern tip is finished and open, and the Mexican government has decided to rush development of a mammoth Cancún-style resort complex here.

The peninsula is actually two Mexican states, the northern one of Baja California, with its capital at Mexicali, and the southern one of Baja California Sur, the capital city of which is La Paz. Besides fishing and tourism, Baja's industries include viticulture and winemaking. The sandy soil and bright sun yield crisp, dry white wines of excellent quality.

But Baja is not for everyone. The trip by car from the American state of California is long, often dull, certainly tiring, and perhaps not worth it. From Tijuana to Cabo San Lucas is 1,700 kilometers (1,054 miles). Once you get to the peninsula's southern tip, you can delight in watching the sun rise over the water each morning, and set into the water each night. But you usually pay for the privilege, as Baja's price structure is definitely upper crust. As the peninsula, and particularly the southern end between La Paz and Cabo San Lucas, becomes more developed and populated, there will doubtless be more establishments within our price range. As it is now, the few budget establishments which exist are mostly in La Paz, with a few others scattered in towns to the north and south.

BAJA ACTIVITIES: People go to Baja to relax on the beach, ride the surf, and hunt for the big game fish. That's about all there is to do. The parched landscape, forested with giant saguaro cacti, is interesting for the first 50 miles, but then it becomes monotonous. Traveling to Baja on a budget, there's even less to do, as big game fishing and many of the other water sports cost big money.

I'd recommend that you spend a day in La Paz, to get the flavor of Baja life; another day or two in San José del Cabo and Cabo San Lucas, the peninsula's two premier beach resorts; and perhaps, if you come anywhere near it, several days in the beautiful oasis of Mulegé. Loreto, by the way, has little to offer except its famous Tenicentro (tennis center), of interest mostly to those coming on package tours. As for Santa Rosalía, it is a port for mainland ferries and a mining center. The concession to exploit the mineral wealth is owned by a French firm, so don't be surprised when you hear French spoken in the streets.

If, during your Baja travels, you find an inexpensive place to dig in and stay awhile, by all means do so, then write and tell me about it so I can spread the news to other readers.

A Note on Taxes

Baja is a special duty-free zone, a status given it by the government to bolster its commerce. This means that you may be subject to a customs check as you pass from Baja to the mainland; this goes for your car as well.

A bonus in Baja is that Mexico's value-added tax (IVA), rather than being the norm of 10%, 15%, or 20%, is only 6%, 8%, or 10% in Baja (percentage depends on the type of item you're buying). You may not notice the difference, as the tax is normally included in the prices marked.

GETTING THERE: If you're not one of those hardy folk who come by road, you'll be coming by air or sea.

By Air

Unless you're flying to Tijuana, your plane trip by **AeroMéxico** to Baja will terminate at one of the three "L's": La Paz, Los Cabos, or Loreto.

La Paz: The capital of Baja Sur has direct or nonstop flights to and from: Culiacán, one daily; Guaymas, one daily; Guadalajara, daily except Tuesday; Los Angeles, two or three daily; Mazatlán, one daily; Mexico City, five daily; San Diego, one daily; Tijuana, three daily; and Tucson, one daily.

All of these flights are on **AeroMéxico** (tel. 682/2-0091, 2-0093, or 2-1636), Paseo Alvaro Obregón, La Paz; except for one flight to Tijuana and one to Mexico City on **Mexicana** (tel. 682/2-4999 or 2-4010), Paseo Alvaro Obregón 340, La Paz.

Los Cabos: This little airport, a few miles northwest of San José del Cabo, serves both that town and Cabo San Lucas, which has only a small landing strip; it's 22 miles (35 km) from Los Cabos airport to Cabo San Lucas.

In San José del Cabo, **AeroMéxico** (tel. 684/2-0398) is at the corner of Zaragoza and Hidalgo; **Mexicana** (tel. 684/3-0411, 3-0412, or 2-0230) is at Zaragoza and Niños Héroes, also at Bulevar Mijares no. 4-B.

Air routes connecting Los Cabos include: Denver, Mexicana, daily nonstop; Guadalajara, Mexicana, daily nonstop; Los Angeles, AeroMéxico, at least two nonstops daily; Manzanillo, AeroMéxico, daily nonstop; Mazatlán, Mexicana, one or more daily nonstops; Mexico City, three daily direct flights, two of them by Mexicana; Puerto Vallarta, Mexicana, daily nonstop; San Francisco, Mexicana, four direct flights per week; and Tijuana, AeroMéxico, one daily nonstop.

Loreto: This town, midway up the eastern coast of Baja Sur, has direct flights to and from Guadalajara, Los Angeles, and Tijuana, all by AeroMéxico (tel. 683/3-0205). Make reservations and buy tickets at the airport.

The Regional Carrier: Aero California (tel. 682/2-1113 or 2-1114), Paseo Alvaro Obregón 220, La Paz, offers flights connecting La Paz with Cabo San Lucas (daily), Ciudad Obregón (three a week), Guadalajara (daily), Hermosillo (three a week), Los Mochis (daily), and Tijuana (daily). They also have flights to and from Ciudad Constitución, the farming town 130 miles (210 km) northwest of La Paz on Hwy. 1.

Contact them at these addresses:

Ciudad Obregón: Avenida Miguel Aleman 398–3 (tel. 641/4-6233 or 5-0454).

Culiacán: Hidalgo 30, corner of Obregón (tel. 671/5-1155 or 5-1135).

Guadalajara: López Cotilla 1423 (tel. 36/26-1901 or 26-1962).

Guaymas: Serdán 265 Pte. (tel. 622/2-6410).

Hermosillo: Bulevar Abelardo M. Rodríguez 24 (tel. 621/2-6938).

Loreto: Paseo Hidalgo s/n (tel. 683/3-0204).

Los Mochis: Hidalgo 440 Pte. (tel. 681/2-8466 or 2-6790).

Tijuana: Paseo Héroes no. C–19–1, Centro Comercial Plaza Río Tijuana (tel. 66/84-2006, 84-2007, or 84-2008).

By Sea

Ferryboats supposedly operate between Guaymas and Santa Rosalía (8 hours); Topolobampo (Los Mochis) and Pichilingue (La Paz) (10 hours); Mazatlán and Pichilingue (La Paz) (16 hours); and Puerto Vallarta and Cabo San Lucas (18 hours). Refer to the sections on those departure cities for more information.

Schedules and operations tend to be erratic, and you can never really be sure the ferries are running as they should be. If they are running, be prepared to pay very low fares for a somewhat long and pretty uncomfortable journey.

The most comfortable way to go is in a cabin. Reserve one of these as early as possible. When you try to make your reservations, you might be told that all the cabins are taken. In this situation, an extra amount of money over and above the cabin fare often miraculously results in a cabin being "found."

You'd be well advised to pack some food for the ferry trip. Meals are available aboard, but you'll be far better off with your own supplies.

By the way, taking your car on the ferry to Baja, while theoretically possible, may not be easy. Think it over carefully, as you'll have big hassles with officialdom, several bribes to pay, and long waits, perhaps days. Is this the way you want to spend your vacation?

GETTING AROUND: Public transportation is not highly developed in Baja; you may be in for some inconvenience and/or extra expense.

By Bus

Two companies, **Tres Estrellas de Oro** and **Aguila,** operate about eight return-trip buses per day north from La Paz to Ciudad Constitución (3½ hours), Loreto (5 hours), Mulegé (7 hours), Santa Rosalía (9 hours), and on to Tijuana (21 hours, more or less).

As for the southern route to San José del Cabo (3 hours) and Cabo San Lucas (3½ hours), there are about seven buses daily.

By Rental Car

Rental cars in Baja are breathtakingly expensive, upwards of $60 per day, all included for a Volkswagen Beetle. Rental cars are readily available at La Paz and Los Cabos airports. Be prepared to pay. Also, be sure to check that you have a spare tire (*llanta extra,* one that holds air, and is up to pressure), a jack (*gato),* and a lug wrench (*llave).* Lots of cars come incomplete, and you don't want to be stranded out in the blistering Baja desert. Unless you have enough people to fill the car, consider flying rather than renting a car. It's cheaper!

By Air

Aero California (see above) will provide air-taxi service to or from any point in Baja. Most settlements, and even some of the luxury hotels, have their own little airstrips. This service costs plenty. If you have enough people to fill the little plane (five, or nine, people), the price is lowest.

ORIENTATION: Distances are large in Baja. Here are some mileages from La Paz so you'll know what to expect:

Cabo San Lucas, 215 km (133 miles)
Ciudad Constitución, 210 km (130 miles)
Loreto, 355 km (220 miles)
Mulegé, 490 km (304 miles)
San José del Cabo, 183 km (114 miles)
Santa Rosalía, 550 km (340 miles)
Villa Insurgentes, 235 km (146 miles).

LA PAZ: The capital city (pop. 120,000) of Baja Sur is mostly new. It's a transportation center, a duty-free port, government center, and in general the "metropolis" of southern Baja. You'll see lots of shops selling imported goods such as clothing, toys, electronics, and cameras, because of Baja's special tax status.

Orientation

This city sprawls well inland, though you'll spend most of your time in the older, more congenial downtown section along the waterfront. The seaside boulevard, or Malecón, is called the Paseo Alvaro Obregón.

The **bus station** (Central Camionera) is at Jalisco and Héroes de la Independencia, about 25 blocks southwest of the center of town.

The **airport** is several miles southwest of town along the highway to Ciudad Constitución and Tijuana. Airport minibuses to the center cost 605 pesos ($1.21) per person, or 1,630 pesos ($3.26) for a private (taxi) trip.

Though La Paz has a nice waterfront and a few beaches, the better beaches are 18 km (11 miles) north at Pichilingue. The dock for mainland ferries is in Pichilingue as well. If you arrive by ferry, you'll probably find it necessary to take a taxi (2,800 pesos, $5.60) to get to La Paz.

Look for the **state tourist office** (Dirección de Turismo del Gobierno del Estado de B.C.S., tel. 682/2-1199 or 2-7975) near the main intersection of 16 de Septiembre and Paseo Alvaro Obregón, in downtown La Paz, a few steps from the dock. Hours are 8 to 1 and 2 to 7 daily, but don't bet on it.

Most of what you'll need in town is located between the tourism office at the northeast, and the Hotel Los Arcos to the southwest.

Where to Stay

The **Hotel Perla,** Paseo Obregón 1570 (P.O. Box 640), La Paz, B.C.S. 23500 (tel. 682/2-0777), overlooks the water in the very center of town, and boasts an airy local-favorite streetside restaurant. Though it is one of the town's upscale hotels, you pay only 4,863 pesos ($9.72) for an air-conditioned double room here.

The **Hotel Plaza Real de La Paz,** at the corner of Esquerro and Callejón La Paz (tel. 682/2-9333), is one-half block in from the water near the Hotel Perla. It has four storys of modern rooms equipped with telephones, television sets, and air-conditioners, for 5,777 pesos ($11.55) double, a bit less for one person in a room.

Other than these, the hotels in La Paz are downscale. The best of the budget choices is the simple but congenial **Hotel Lori,** Calle Bravo 110 Pte. (tel. 682/2-1819), some distance southwest of the center, a cross between a small hotel and a casa de huespedes. You get a hotel room, but also the personal service of a casa (and the noise of the water pump in the courtyard). Rooms are well used, water pressure is erratic, but it's quiet, friendly, and clean for 2,268 pesos ($4.53) single, 2,882 pesos ($5.76) double, with private bath and air conditioner.

The **Hotel Posada San Miguel,** facing the Palacio Municipal at the corner of Madero and 16 de Septiembre (tel. 682/2-1802), is smack in the middle of the downtown commercial district. Decoration—primitive, and lots of it!—is the forte here. If there is such a style as arts-and-crafts baroque, this is it. All is tidy, the proprietors are friendly, a double with bath goes for a mere 1,500 pesos ($3), and, as you might have guessed, the San Miguel is often booked solid.

Two small pensions, near one another, have similar basic accommodations within old colonial houses. The **Pension California,** Degollado 209, at Madero, across from the big "MAS" department store (no phone), has primitive paintings in the lobby, a plant-filled courtyard, and doubles with bath going for 1,100 pesos ($2.20).

Around the corner, heading downhill on Madero, at no. 85, the **Hostería El Convento** (no phone) has similar rooms at similar prices.

The Big Splurge: About the nicest place to stay right downtown in La Paz is the **Hotel Los Arcos,** Paseo Obregón 498 (P. O. Box 112), La Paz, B.C.S. 23500 (tel. 682/2-2744). The renovated and modernized three-story colonial-style structure gives you the benefits of a downtown location, plus two bars, two swimming pools, a sauna, restaurant, and cafeteria. Actually, there are two parts to the hotel; the main building, and the Cabañas (bungalows) de Los Arcos, across the street. In the hotel proper, you'll pay 17,250 pesos ($34.50) single, 18,400 pesos ($36.80) double for an air-conditioned room. In the delightful and shady air-conditioned cabañas, set amid a virtual forest of tropical shrubbery, the price is 16,100 pesos ($32.20) double.

READERS' HOTEL SELECTIONS: "**La Purísima Hotel,** 16 de Septiembre and Serdán (tel. 682/2-3444), is clean and convenient, on the main street (16 de Septiembre) about six blocks from the Malecón. A single costs about 5,800 pesos ($11.60)"(Duke Rank, University Park, Ill.). . . . "The **Hotel San Bernardino,** Abasolo 436 near 5 de Febrero (tel. 682/2-9220 or 2-9210), is a tidy place with a good shower and an inside bolt on the door. There is a small inner courtyard for parking a car. The rate for a single was 4,500 pesos ($9)"(Charlotte McMurray, Palm Springs, Calif.).

Where to Eat

La Paz is no culinary mecca—far from it. In fact, the food is pretty terrible, in general, despite the availability of fresh seafood. I suppose we can attribute this to its status as a developing area.

The **Restaurant Terraza** in the Hotel Perla (tel. 2-0777), Paseo Obregón 1570, is among the most appealing restaurants because of its central location and view of the bay. It's big, airy, and comfortable. Service is okay. Most main course dishes are priced around 1,500 pesos ($3); figure twice that amount for a full dinner. Open every day, for every meal.

Very near the tourism office on the waterfront esplanade is the restaurant **El Yate** (tel. 2-1492), which specializes in seafood and sea views. Perched right at the edge of the water, it serves lunch and dinner daily except Sundays. Figure between 2,500 and 3,500 pesos ($5 and $7) for a three-course fish dinner.

For that early-morning breakfast before heading out on the road or the waves, drop by the **cafeteria** at the Hotel Los Arcos, (tel. 2-2744), Paseo Obregón 498 Sur. It's a real American-style cafeteria. It is not particularly cheap, and a full breakfast may cost you 1,800 pesos ($3.60), but it's open and serving at 6 or 6:30 a.m. You can, of course, avail yourself of the air-conditioned convenience for lunch or dinner, any day.

SAN JOSÉ DEL CABO: If you follow Avenida Zaragoza in from Hwy. 1, here's what you'll find: a charming, typical little Mexican town with narrow streets, church painted white, and scenes of small-town daily life. That's San José, and it's straight out of a tourist brochure.

But San José has another character as well. Follow Zaragoza to its end, turn right, and you'll be on Avenida Lázaro Cárdenas, which widens to become the four-lane divided Bulevar Antonio Mijares before joining the Paseo San José, a similarly grand waterfront drive which winds past a half-dozen fancy tourist hotels on the beach. This is also San José.

The beach area boasts a salt-water estuary *(estero)* preserved as a bird sanctuary. It's just east of the Hotel El Presidente. If you spend any time in town, wander along the estuary shore and admire the winged residents.

Orientation

The problem with this idyllic setting is that the town presently has only four small budget-class hotels, three of them worth your consideration, none of them with telephones. So you must arrive in town and take pot luck, unless you want to stay in a luxury hotel on the beach.

The **bus station** *(Terminal de Autobuses)* is on Doblado at Colegio Militar, about two blocks east of the highway. The **municipal market** *(mercado munici-*

pal) is a block southeast of the bus station on Mauricio Castro. There are two **banks** on Zaragoza.

Tourist Information: San José's Chamber of Commerce *(Camara de Comercio),* just off Zaragoza on Hidalgo, hands out good, simple, free maps of the town, and can help you with information.

Transportation: Local bus service is very limited, and you may find yourself taking a taxi, or hitchhiking, to the beach.

Where to Stay and Eat

The newish **Hotel Colli** (no phone), on Hidalgo near Zaragoza not far from the AeroMéxico office, is the best budget lodging in town. Double rooms with bath are priced at 3,180 pesos ($6.36).

On Zaragoza at the side of the church is the **Hotel Ceci** (no phone), an extremely plain and basic place where a room with bath costs 2,120 pesos ($4.24) double.

The **Hotel Central** (no phone), on Zaragoza beside the church, likes to rent its spartan rooms by the month, and charges 15,000 pesos ($30) double for thirty days. You can rent one by the day if there is a room available.

As for restaurants, most are angling for the luxury crowd staying in the big beachfront hotels, and so their prices tend to be high according to Mexican village standards. This being so, and quality being what it is, I didn't find any which I thought were recommendable. As time goes by and the tourist trade in Baja develops, there will be some. If you find a newly opened place, please write and let me know.

CABO SAN LUCAS: If you've heard anything about this resort town, it probably runs like this: beautiful rock formations, the sun rising out of the Sea of Cortez and setting into the Pacific, lots of sport fishermen, and a half-dozen very expensive ($90-per-night) resort hotels. It's all true. The safe, pretty little harbor of Cabo San Lucas was discovered by sport fishermen decades ago, and it soon became a base for voyages in search of sailfish, spearfish, and swordfish. With these well-to-do sports enthusiasts came their $150-a-day price structure.

Cabo San Lucas today is a study in contrasts. Though the rock eminences surrounding the town are crowned with dramatic and sprawling luxury hotels, the center of the village itself has dusty, unpaved streets, chickens pecking in back yards, and the occasional somnolent souvenir stand or dive shop. The sheen, polish, and prices of Cancún may be on the way to Cabo, but they sure haven't arrived yet.

Again, the problem for the budget traveler is lack of budget services. The handful of small pensions usually have no vacancies. Your best bet is to call for reservations from La Paz, or take an early bus, getting to Cabo when some visitors are checking out and moving on.

Where to Stay

The **Hotel Marina,** on the Paseo de la Marina at Guerrero (tel. 684/3-0030), is at a curve in the highway as it approaches the harbor. The two-story structure has some rooms overlooking a courtyard planted with trees and flowering shrubs, others overlooking the harbor. The ones on the harbor side can be a bit noisy, but you do get the view. A double room, air-conditioned, costs 4,100 pesos ($8.20) in winter, less in summer when it's blazing hot.

The **Hotel Casablanca,** Morelos and Revolución (Apdo. Postal 79) (tel. 684/3-0260), charges 4,200 pesos ($8.40) for a double room with bath. The hotel is about three blocks inland from the harbor, very simple, but with a parking lot and restaurant.

LORETO: Once touted as Mexico's newest resort, Loreto, 355 km. (220 miles) north of La Paz, has not yet caught on with hordes of tourists. The beach on the Sea of Cortez is beautiful, the backdrop of jagged mountains is dramatic, and the Tenicentro (tennis center) has John McEnroe as its sometime pro (usually during the annual tennis festival in early December). Besides the Tenicentro, facilities include a jet airport and the very nice Hotel El Presidente, but that's about it. The town is dusty and sleepy, with nothing else to do.

READER'S HOTEL SELECTION—CABO SAN LUCAS: "Most of the hotels here are jet-set, ranging from $70 to $100 daily. Try the **Hotel Mar de Cortez,** Lázaro Cárdenas and Guerrero (tel. 684/3-0032), a good hotel, primarily Mexican clientele, with a swimming pool and courtyard for $25 single, $29 double in the older section of rooms; for U.S. reservations, phone Monterrey, Calif., tel. 408/375-4755" (Duke Rank, University Park, Ill.).

Where to Stay and Eat

Luckily for travelers to Loreto, the **Hotel El Presidente,** Bulevar Misión de Loreto s/n, Loreto 23880, B.C.S. (tel. 683/3-0700), is lavish, well run, friendly, located right next to the Tenicentro, and moderately priced. Except for when the Tenicentro has some special program attracting crowds, prices for the 250 plush, air-conditioned, satellite TV–equipped rooms are only US$32 to $44 single, US$34 to $48 double, US$39 to $52 triple, tax included. Prices here are normally quoted in U.S. dollars; the higher prices are for the winter season from mid-December through April. Though it is a bit of a splurge given our budget, it is also the best value for money in all of Baja.

When it comes to dining, El Presidente is also your best—virtually your only—choice, unless you're content to buy snacks from a tienda in town.

MULEGÉ: The coast of the Sea of Cortez (or, Gulf of California) north from Loreto to Santa Rosalía is extremely scenic, if barren. Rough mountains come right to the water's edge, and any open places may have only cacti as greenery, but here and there, especially on the shore of the Bahía de Concepción, you'll come across coves and inlets with palm trees, great swimming, and a collection of beach shacks, tents, and camping vehicles (with U.S. and Canadian license plates) occupied by some of the most contented people in the world. The entire stretch of coast is completely undeveloped and unspoiled, and perfect for al fresco lodging.

Mulegé itself is very "un-Baja-like." In the midst of this arid landscape, Mulegé is a bit of the lush tropics. An emerald river winds slowly from a valley through groves of palms to the sea, cutting right through the center of town. Some of the local homes have thatched roofs, and a jungle, oasis ambience prevails.

Where to Stay

Though it's a bit of paradise, Mulegé is most useful for the traveler who wants to settle down and vegetate on a nearby beach for a few weeks. Overnight accommodations are scarce in town, and very simple, unless you want to pay the resort prices charged at the Hotel Las Casitas.

For air-conditioned rooms, your choice is the **Hotel Vieja Hacienda** (no phone), east of the main plaza, where doubles are priced at 5,750 pesos ($11.50).

If you can get along with just a ceiling fan, the **Casa de Huespedes Manuelita** (no phone) will fill the bill, with double rooms with bath for 3,750 pesos ($7.50).

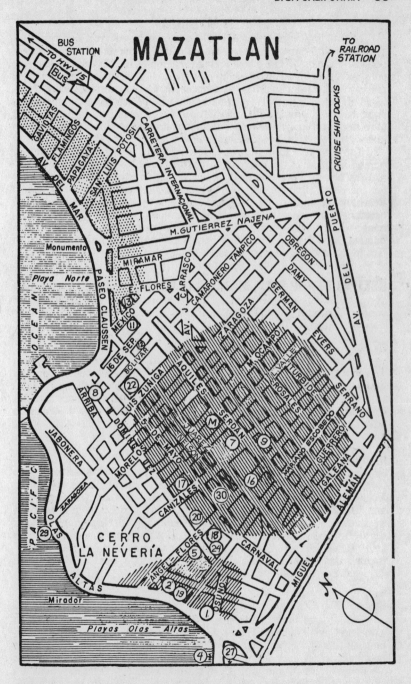

MAZATLAN

2. Mazatlán

Mazatlán, Sinaloa (pop. 200,000), was once best known as a resort for sportsmen who came to hunt sailfish and marlin, some weighing hundreds of pounds. You can still hire a boat for big-game fishing (at $200-plus per day), or guns and guide for a game expedition to the countryside, but Mazatlán today makes its living from industry and resort hotels. Once almost the exclusive preserve of visitors from California, Mazatlán, with its beaches and resort ambience, has been promoted by the Mexican government into an international attraction. Still, you'll see lots of recreational vehicles with California plates under the palms that shade the local trailer parks.

Travel writers have been kind to Mazatlán, dreaming up such sugary phrases as "jewel of the West," "pearl of the Pacific," and "place of the deer" (this last being a literal translation of the Nahuatl word). The beaches aren't as big and beautiful as Acapulco's, but they are nice enough, especially Sabalo Beach, to the north of the town and accessible by bus from the zócalo. The beach right downtown is good for watching sunsets but not so good for swimming, which might explain why Mazatlán is more popular with souvenir-hunters, window-shoppers, diners-and-dancers than it is with swimmers. In fact, it's good for all these activities.

GETTING TO AND FROM MAZATLÁN: Almost any land transport coming down the Pacific coast goes by Mazatlán, and there are many direct flights from various Mexican cities and from several in the United States.

By Bus

Transportes del Norte, Tres Estrellas de Oro, Autobuses Estrella Blanca, Transportes Norte de Sonora, Transportes del Pacifico—all these major lines have service to and from Mazatlán; most of them touch here on their way to and from the U.S.-Mexico border at Nogales or Mexicali. All these lines have onward service from Mazatlán to Guadalajara and Mexico City as well. Reserve in advance and you'll have no trouble finding space.

By Train

Ferrocarriles del Pacifico runs two trains a day through Mazatlán on the Nogales—Guadalajara run (see map for station location). Trains arrive from Nogales at 4 a.m. and 8:25 a.m., leaving for Guadalajara at 4:30 a.m. and 8:35 a.m. The trip to Guadalajara takes 13½ hours on the earlier train, 11 hours on the later one (named *El Costeno*). Trains heading north to Nogales and Mexicali depart from Mazatlán at 1 a.m. (the slower) and 6:05 p.m. (the faster, *El Costeno*). Remember when figuring schedules that there's a time zone change between Mazatlán and Guadalajara. For information (and to check these changeable times), call 678/1-2036.

By Air

From Mazatlán there are three or four flights a day to Mexico City, three a week to Ciudad Juárez (El Paso), and daily flights to Monterrey and Guadalajara, all run by AeroMéxico and Mexicana airlines. Hughes Air West runs two flights a day each from San Francisco and Los Angeles. You can take advantage of an excursion fare if you fly from San Francisco. For reservations and information in Mazatlán, call AeroMéxico (tel. 1-3096) or Mexicana (tel. 1-3414).

By Ferryboat

There is a ferry (27) that connects Mazatlán with La Paz, Baja California Sur, leaving at about 5 or 6 p.m. daily except Sunday; for more information, call 678/1-7020. A seat in the salon with the peasants for the 16-hour voyage costs 500 to 1,000 pesos ($1 to $2), while a private cabin will be about 1,800 to 3,000 pesos ($3.60 to $6). Prices to ship a car start at 5,500 pesos ($11).

ORIENTATION: From being just a small port town on a peninsula, Mazatlán has spread northward along the coast for miles. The older part, **downtown,** has several good budget hotel and restaurant choices, and it is also the center of daily life for the townfolk. From the center, **a waterfront drive** heads northward, starting out as Avenida Olas Altas, changing names to Paseo Claussen, Avenida del Mar, Avenida Camaron-Sabalo, and Avenida Sabalo-Cerritos. The bus station (Central Camionera) is about 2½ miles from downtown, but only a few blocks from the waterfront drive and the Hotel Sands.

Four miles north of downtown is **a traffic circle** at Punta Camaron, a restaurant (El Camaron) built on a rocky outcrop over the water, and the Motel San Diego. From this point, the resorts continue to spread ever northward. Between the traffic circle and the huge **El Cid** Touristic Complex you'll find the American Express office, rental car offices, a golf course, several trailer parks, and Sabalo Beach, one of Mazatlán's best.

It's another five miles north to **Los Cerritos** (or El Cerrito, the Little Hill[s]), the northern limit of the resort. The northern limits are still under development, and fancy hotels alternate with older trailer parks, vacant lots, the rubble of construction, and a few posh private homes.

Keep in mind, then, that this resort is fully ten miles long, and use the landmarks of downtown, Sabalo traffic circle, El Cid, and Los Cerritos to find your way. Street numbers are of little practical use.

GETTING AROUND: Buses run along the waterfront drive, and since virtually the entire resort is right on the water, they provide easy transport to any point.

Besides taxis, Mazatlán has a moderately priced alternative. Little three-wheel, open-air motorscooters putt and sputter along the waterfront, carrying up to four passengers anywhere for less than taxi fare. Called *pulmonías* (pneumonias), they have a surrey-like top to protect you from the beating sun, but no sides to keep off the cool night breezes. Be sure to haggle for a good price *before* you clamber in the back of the pulmonía.

The downtown transportation center, for buses, taxis, and pulmonías, is the main square with its basilica (look for "Basilica" on bus signboards, if you want to get downtown.)

INFORMATION AND EMERGENCY HELP: The **Federal Tourism Office (29)** (tel. 678/1-4966) is on the waterfront drive, Olas Altas, open from 9 a.m. to 2 p.m. and 4 to 7 p.m. daily except Sunday.

The **Municipal Tourism Office (30)** (tel. 678/2-2111) is in the Palacio Municipal on Angel Flores, downtown, one block from the main plaza.

The **post office** (Correos) is on the east side of the main plaza, on Calle Juárez just off Angel Flores.

There's an **American Consulate** (tel. 678/1-2685) in town, on Carranza near the Hotel La Siesta.

Mazatlán's central **market (M)** is located in the block between Aquiles Serdan and Juárez, and Ocampo and Leandro Valle.

By the way, if you arrive in Mazatlán in the week before Lent, carnival will be in full swing. It's barrels of fun—so long as you already have a room reservation locked up tight. Beware: pressure on rooms, and their prices, is intense at this time.

HOTELS IN MAZATLÁN: The hotels in Mazatlán are of two types, generally speaking: those downtown, which are older, cheaper, and some of which are suitable; and those along the beachfront heading north, most of which are new, flashy, and expensive, though others fit our budget nicely. These latter extend in an almost unbroken row for miles and miles. The hotels downtown are in two areas, the Downtown Seafront and the Midtown areas.

Hotels—Downtown Seafront

The **Hotel Belmar (1)**, Olas Altas Boulevard 166 (tel. 678/1-4299), is right on the waterfront drive, and is actually two hotels in one. A recent addition of air-conditioned deluxe rooms is more expensive, but the older rooms, which the management refers to rather grandly as the "colonial section," are within our range: singles are 4,025 pesos ($8.05) and doubles are 5,290 pesos ($10.58), without air conditioning but with bath. The hotel is very pleasant, built around a central court and entered through huge wooden gates. A new pool, tennis court, and lots of tiles, color, and colonial effect make it a pleasant place to stay —try here first.

The next block north houses the huge, squat, cement **Hotel La Siesta (2)**, Olas Altas Boulevard 11 (tel. 678/1-2640), one of the most attractive hotels in the area. Tasteful and well-appointed rooms open onto a lush central palm court lined with green balconies. The court, which is long and narrow, sports both a jungle of colorful umbrellas and the restaurant El Shrimp Bucket, which I'll mention later. Singles run from 5,860 pesos ($11.72), doubles from 7,302 pesos ($14.60). All rooms are air-conditioned and telephone equipped.

Continuing along the coastline and a few blocks up the hill brings you to the 30-room **Hotel Olas Altas (4)**, Calle Centenario 14 (tel. 678/1-3192). The upstairs lobby, with white wicker chairs and an airy balcony overlooking the ocean, is a cool delight. The rooms are a bit worn and have no air conditioning, but the hotel's prices sell the rooms. Singles are 3,200 to 4,000 pesos ($6.40 to $8); doubles, 4,000 to 5,000 pesos ($8 to $10). High-priced rooms have an ocean view, and perhaps two double beds; extra persons pay 750 pesos ($1.50), and there's a 10% discount for weekly stays.

Hotels—Midtown

The largest shaded area on our map comprises the center of the town and its southern limits (as far as hotels are concerned). This area includes the commercial hub of the town with bustling streets, countless shops, chronic parking problems, and continued activity, music and shouting, seasoned with exotic aromas that waft into the streets from a hundred little Mexican restaurants.

Try the **Hotel Central (5)**, three very long blocks from the ocean at B. Dominguez Sur 2, near the corner of Calle A. Flores (tel. 678/2-1888). The prices are a bit steep, but such is fate in a resort town, and the rooms are all very nice, with good beds, air conditioning, and phone: singles are 5,520 pesos ($11.04); doubles with two double beds, 6,900 pesos ($13.80). The upstairs lobby shares space with a small café.

Nearby is the **Hotel Milan (7)**, Canizales Pte. 717, corner of Flores (tel. 678/1-3588). Rooms here aren't quite as good, tend to be dark, but are adequate and each has a private bath. Downstairs there's a lunch counter in the lobby and an amiable staff with a *mañana* outlook on life, with singles at 2,560 pesos ($5.12) and doubles at 3,145 pesos ($6.29).

There are two more places which are in a location roughly between the

Midtown area and the Northern Beach area. The first is **Joncol's Hotel (8)**, Belisario Dominguez Nte. 2701 (tel. 678/1-2131), a big (36-room) modern multi-windowed place about a block from the ocean. Rooms are quite adequate: large, clean, all with private balconies and sea view, and well-appointed furnishings. Rates are not bad—3,740 pesos ($7.48) single, 4,960 pesos ($9.92) double —but Joncol's is highly recommended mainly because of its consistent performance.

In spite of its beachy name, the 22-room **Hotel Villa del Mar (9)**, Aquiles Serdan Nte. 1506, near the corner of 31 de Mayo (tel. 678/1-3426), is about as dead center in town as you can get. But motorists will be pleased to know that they have parking space for seven cars. Nor will lobby sitters be disappointed; they go in for rocking chairs here and cursory inspection revealed no fewer than six of these comfortable accessories. Rooms are adequate, and all have ceiling fans and hot water. Singles are 2,400 pesos ($4.80), and doubles are 3,200 pesos ($6.40).

There are quite a few small, acceptable, less-than-top-notch hotels in the midtown area. Generally speaking, each shares a typical description: small but clean rooms, lazy ceiling fans, and intermittent service.

The **Hotel Beltran (11)**, A. Serdan Nte. 2509 (tel. 678/2-2776), is the cheapest of these with singles at 1,700 pesos ($3.40), doubles at 2,200 pesos ($4.40). Enter the Beltran through the archway and choose a room from among the 28 along the long open patio.

Next in price is the **Hotel Santa Barbara (12)**, on the corner of Juárez and 16 de Septiembre (tel. 678/2-2120). The homey lobby with a piano on one side and a group of avid television viewers on the other is perhaps a more comfortable place to sit than in the tiny rooms. Singles here are 2,200 pesos ($4.40); doubles, 3,000 pesos ($6).

Hotels—Northern Beach

Finally, there's the Northern Beach area, an elegant arc of golden sand serviced by a palm-lined, dual-lane boulevard and bordered by flashy hotels and a sprinkling of elaborate beach houses complete with high walls and watchdogs. In winter this is Mazatlán's reason for existence, and charter flights fill the big hotels with eager sun-seekers from colder climates. Prices, in winter, are high with little compromise. In summer and in the neither-here-nor-there months of May and September, some of the more modest hotels along this beach cut their prices, usually advertising the fact boldly by a signboard on the sidewalk— customers before pride.

Here's the rundown of the affordable places, starting from downtown and heading north. Street numbers are little help in finding a place, so I'll mention landmarks and prominent establishments so you can spot your chosen hotel as you whiz along the waterfront.

The **Hotel Aqua Marina** (tel. 678/1-3748) is at Avenida del Mar 110 (Apdo. Postal 301), and you'll recognize it as a two-story motel-type structure with a parking lot, palm trees, and little pool in front. The beach is right across the street, and if you get a room on the preferable second floor of the motel, you'll be able to sit out on a little private terrace and enjoy the view. Prices for the 100 air-conditioned rooms are 10,350 pesos ($20.70) single, 12,075 pesos ($24.15) double. The Aqua Marina has a restaurant and bar.

Not far along is the **Hotel Cabinas al Mar** (tel. 678/1-5752), Avenida del Mar 123 (Apdo. Postal 444), a little five-story building with a thatched palapa on top, a good place from which to watch the sunsets. Rooms on the front have little balconies, sea views, and higher price tags. Other rooms come in a variety of sizes and shapes, tend to be darker, but quieter and cheaper. Several rooms have one double bed and two singles, perfect for a family. Basic prices are 2,875 pesos ($5.75) single, 3,680 pesos ($7.36) double.

The **Hotel Sands** (tel. 678/2-0000 or 2-0600) is right between the bus station and the beach, and right next door to Señor Frog's restaurant (see below) and an outlet for Kentucky Fried Chicken. With three stories, balconies with a sea view, air conditioning, a pool, and private baths, it's an excellent choice in all regards. The prices aren't bad, either: 6,555 pesos ($13.11) single, 9,200 pesos ($18.40) double, 10,350 pesos ($20.70) triple.

The **Motel del Sol** (tel. 678/1-4712) is a modernistic brown place with shuttered windows. It looks small from the street, but actually extends a way back, sheltering a warren of various rooms, most of which are modern, small, and nice. Many have a kitchenette; all have air conditioning, private bath, and use of the swimming pool and restaurant. The last time I visited I was quoted a price of 4,025 pesos ($8.05) single and 4,255 pesos ($8.51) double. By the way, there's a Pizza Hut just past the Motel del Sol.

For a bit of a splurge, you can stay in the imposing 100-room **Posada de Don Pelayo** (tel. 678/3-1977), Avenida del Mar 1111 (Apdo. Postal 1088), a few blocks south of the traffic circle. Every room has a king-size bed or two double beds, a telephone, private bath, and air conditioning, and those on the front have sea views. The price for a single is 10,350 pesos ($20.70), and a double runs 12,075 pesos ($24.15). There's a swimming pool here too.

The budget choice in the area is on the traffic circle about four miles along the waterfront drive toward Sabalo Beach. It's the **Motel San Diego** (tel. 678/3-5703), mailing address Apdo. Postal 295. Take a "Sabalo" bus from the zócalo, midtown at the cathedral, and get off at the circle where you'll see the motel on your right. The ten rooms are clean, comfortable, and feature exposed stone walls in the rooms. You can park for free under the palms in front. Rates for the ground-floor are 4,500 pesos ($9) single, 4,500 to 5,500 pesos ($9 to $11) double (with two double beds), and that includes a ceiling fan. You can walk to beach areas from here, and although you'll still have to take the bus to get to Sabalo, you have only half as far to go as if you'd stayed downtown.

Hotels—Near the Bus Station

If you've just arrived by bus, the aforementioned **Hotel Sands** is the one you want to look at first. It's only one (long) block from the Central Camionera.

READER'S HOTEL SELECTION: "The **Hotel Zaragoza,** on Calle Zaragoza between Avenidas Benito Juárez and Aquiles Serdan, is exceptionally clean, with lots of light and fresh air. I paid 1,500 pesos ($3) single for one night, but the price is lower if you stay longer. There are a few retired Americans who stay there for several months at a time. The *dueño* (owner) and his family are very helpful" (Nancy Keller, Forestville, Calif.).

EATING IN MAZATLÁN: Sad to say, prices for seafood in this seaside town have kept up with the rise of seafood prices the world over. As in most Mexican towns, Mexican plates (enchiladas, burritos, tacos, etc.) are your best bargain, but those are available anywhere. I'll give you some hints on where to find the most reasonably priced fish dishes.

The **Restaurant Mamucas (22),** Simón Bolívar Pte. 404 (tel. 1-3490), is 1½ short blocks from Joncol's Hotel. Behind a modest entrance is a big, interesting dining room, with the kitchen to one side. Darkly clad señoras cook away, waiters scurry here and there, and a mariachi band trumpets above the clatter of dishes and silverware. The specialty here is seafood, good and fresh, at moderate prices, and the restaurant keeps busy from 10 a.m. to 10 p.m. every day serving it up. Have a feast beginning with shrimp cocktail or oysters, then grilled fish, coffee, and dessert, and you'll pay about 3,000 pesos ($6). With beer or wine (bottles reasonably priced), it may be a bit more.

You won't find poi on the menu at the **Restaurant Aloha** but there are some great alternatives. One American couple I met regularly come here for the shrimp with garlic at 1,400 pesos ($2.80). A huge salad of fresh fruit goes for 400 pesos (80¢) and there's a comida corrida daily for 775 pesos ($1.55). Make sure you try the pineapple empañadas (turnovers), made fresh daily. Go to Canizales 6B, next to the Hotel Milan.

An air-conditioned restaurant, which is one of the older establishments with a tried-and-true clientele, is **Joncol's (18),** located two blocks inland on Angel Flores at no. 608. They have a comida for 1,200 pesos ($2.40), three courses and good. Meat and fish entrees range from 1,000 to 1,800 pesos ($2 to $3.60). They are open for breakfast, and if you want an afternoon *refresca,* stop here for ice cream 450 pesos (90¢). *Note:* There have been a few complaints about the service.

The **Madrid (19),** Olas Altas Boulevard 25, is a Spanish restaurant, with stucco walls and arches. A few outdoor tables overlook the Malecón and the ocean. This restaurant is in the older section of town. Bullfight posters decorate the walls, ceiling fans keep the air moving, and waiters will bring you, say, a nice fruit salad and a garnished platter of fried fish, plus a soft drink, for 1,700 pesos ($3.40). The Madrid is one in a row of restaurants.

Another in the row is the **Restaurant Fito's (19),** Olas Altas 166D, to the right of the Restaurant Madrid. Smaller and less fancy, with only two rows of tables plus a few out on the sidewalk, Fito's is ruled by a señora busy in the kitchen. Prices are similar to those at the Madrid, but Fito's also offers an afternoon comida corrida of soup, fish, dessert, and coffee for 1,200 pesos ($2.40). The clients are mostly Mexican families, who know a bargain when they see one.

On North Beach

North Beach is crowded with eateries, everything from elegant places specializing in shrimp to Pizza Hut and Colonel Sanders'. You'll do better for seafood downtown, where the local people go.

A block from the Hotel Sands, and thus near the bus station as well, is **Los Norteños.** A shaded patio overlooks the street, and a glassed-in, air-conditioned dining room is behind that. It's not fancy, but serves good food at good prices: a varied plate of Mexican delicacies, or a fried filet of fish, for 1,187 pesos ($2.37) or so. They feature exotic repasts as well, like cabrito al pastor (roast kid), partridge, and lobster, for a good deal more. You can spend over 3,500 pesos ($7) if you go exotic, less than half that if you don't.

You'll spot **La Parrillada** on the Avenida del Mar (no. 1004) because it's a small corner place with a square, tile-roofed grill-cum-kitchen surrounded by high stools. A dozen little umbrella-shaded tables surround the grill area. The specialty here is grilled meat, served in soft tacos. Order bistek (steak) or chuletas (chop) tacos, some frijoles, and a beer; or perhaps quesadillas (melted cheese in a grilled, folded tortilla) or sinchronizadas (cheese-and-meat tacos). You can eat well here for less than 1,100 pesos ($2.20).

Splurge and Specialty Restaurants

Now for a few places that will cater to your need, every now and then, for a nicer dinner in a nicer place.

Everyone has a good time at **Señor Frog's** (tel. 1-4367), next to the Hotel Sands. A sign over the door says "Just Another Bar & Grill," but the line waiting to get in says just the opposite. It's a Carlos Anderson restaurant of course, and one cannot help but wonder where he got all those little panes of beveled glass for the front windows. The decor is similarly interesting, original, and expensive; the food and music are great; the company is upbeat and cheerful. The price is not low, but it's good for what you get. Seafood, meat, whatever—expect to pay something like 4,500 pesos ($9) per person for dinner, somewhat less for lunch. Open till midnight.

Casa de Bruno Restaurant is another great place to dine. The ambience of this stucco and brick establishment is created by the friendly staff, wandering minstrels, and lively clientele, whether you choose to sit indoors or outside. Lobster is guaranteed to be fresh. Shrimp entrees are priced from 2,975 to 3,400 pesos ($5.95 to $6.80) and fish is 1,475 to 1,600 pesos ($2.95 to $3.20). Specialties are the barbecue dishes, priced in between. In addition, Mexican dishes are available, including a fabulous combination plate for 1,950 pesos ($3.90). If Bruno, the owner, is around (you'll know him by the apron bearing his name), ask him to mix up his special concoction called "Bruno's Kiss for the Ladies"—I leave you to take care of it after that. Bruno's is open from noon to 1 a.m. at the intersection of Sabalo and Loaiza.

For the real bullfight aficionado, **El Camaron** is the place to eat. The indoor dining room is the traditional rendezvous of matadores and aficionados after the bullfights. The dining area is actually a display of hundreds of items of bullfight memorabilia. Oceanside dining is the real treat, and you are likely to have a beautiful view of the beach from your table. Food is excellent, in the range of, say, 3,500 pesos ($7) for shrimp—figure 5,000 pesos ($10) for the full dinner. El Camaron is also a good place just for a drink. It's across from the Motel San Diego on the Avenida del Mar at the traffic circle.

El Shrimp Bucket (2) (tel. 1-6350), in the Hotel La Siesta, is probably your best bet for a splurge, for they not only have good food, but live music and dancing nightly to go with it. Most entrees cost between 2,700 and 4,200 pesos ($5.40 to $8.40). If you've never visited a Carlos Anderson restaurant, start with this one and then move on to the ones in Mexico City, Acapulco, Cuernavaca, etc. Each has its own eccentric personality and guaranteed good times.

Starvation Budget

If you're really low on bucks, try one of Mazatlán's most popular downtown taco houses, **El Potrero (24)**, located on the corner of Dominguez and Escobedo. Guests enter this restored colonial mansion through wrought-iron gates to have plates of traditional food for about 200 pesos (40¢), à la carte. The bean soup is justly famous. El Potrero is open only in the evenings, from 6 p.m. to midnight.

Los Comales (16), Angel Flores 908, right downtown, is an odd old place with high ceilings, funky down-home decor, and local cooking that couldn't be called fancy but could be called good. The daily comida corrida goes for just 900 pesos ($1.80), and a plate of enchiladas is only 750 pesos ($1.50). They serve a decent fish soup. Order Pacifico, the local beer, and you'll save a few pesos over national brands. Open most of the time.

An alternative to restaurant-eating is to stop at one of the many loncherías scattered throughout downtown Mazatlán. Here, one can purchase a torta (sandwich) for about 250 pesos (50¢). Tortas come stuffed with a variety of meats, cheese, chilis, tomatoes, onions, etc.

READER'S RESTAURANT SELECTIONS: "Our big finds were these: **Doney's,** two blocks from the cathedral at the dead-end of Cinco de Mayo, where they have Mexican dishes such as enchiladas for 850 pesos ($1.70); large, well lit, air-conditioned, good service, English-speaking. **Los Faroles,** at the corner of Angel Flores and Carneval, has huge plates of shrimp for 1,800 pesos ($3.60), a comida corrida for 950 pesos ($1.90), very good cooking and service, and ceiling fans" (Yvonne Donner, Martinez, Calif.).

WHAT TO DO IN MAZATLÁN: Mazatlán is a beach resort, so most of the entertainment is along these lines. Herewith, a rundown of the beaches.

The Beaches

Right downtown is the rocky, pebbly **Playa Olas Altas,** not the best for swimming when the northern beaches are so much better. Around a rocky promontory to the north of Olas Altas is **Playa Norte,** several miles of good sand beach.

At the traffic circle, a point (Punta Camaron) juts into the water, and on either side of the point is **Playa Las Gaviotas. Playa Sabalo** is yet farther north, and is perhaps the very best of all. The next point jutting into the water is Punta Sabalo, past which is a bridge over the channel that flows in and out of the lagoon. North of the bridge, even more beach, all the way to Los Cerritos. Enjoy! And remember that *all* beaches in Mexico are public property, so feel free to wander where you like.

Cruises and Rentals

The **Fiesta Yacht Cruise (27)** runs a large double-deck boat every morning at 11:00 a.m., leaving from the south beach near the lighthouse. You can purchase your tickets from any of the big hotels. The cruise is three hours around the harbor and bay; they have bilingual guides to explain the marine activity as well as a musical group to entertain. They stop for a short swim at one of the small islands so be sure to bring your suit.

You can **rent a fishing boat (27)** on the south side of town, at the base of the 515-foot hill that supports the lighthouse. Rates range from $200 and up a day for deep-sea cruises including all equipment. A fishing license is necessary; you can write to Unifleet, P.O. Box 1035, Mazatlán, Sinaloa, México, or call 678/1-5121 for information. There are also places that rent skindiving and waterskiing equipment, but the prices vary from shop to shop so be sure to check around for the lowest offer (bargaining may be necessary).

If you want to **rent bicycles, motor scooters, sailboats,** or take a flying leap over the Pacific on **a parachute,** go to the Hotel Playa Mazatlán, four miles north of downtown, past the traffic circle.

Arrangements for **city tours,** or tours to any part of Mexico, can be made at the front desk of any major hotel.

A good place to go for primitive **camping,** unspoiled beaches, and pleasant picnics, is the **Isla de la Piedra (27).** From the center of town, board a *circunvalación* bus from the north side of the zócalo for the ride to the boat landing. Talk to the pilot of a small launch for the trip to the island. Take whatever you'll need on the island as there are no services at all.

Other Things to Do

There is a bullring in town where they have scheduled **bullfights** every Sunday, but *only* in the winter. The rest of the year, the ring is used for rodeos, an equally interesting spectacle.

Looking for a **disco?** Those out for dining-and-dancing need only take a stroll along the northern beach to run into the city's assorted discos, all fun, new, loud, and relatively expensive: **Elephant, La Jirafa, Ney's,** and **Valentino's** are only a few.

The **Arts and Crafts Center,** north of the traffic circle at Punta Camaron, is a modern bazaar with numerous artists' stalls. They sell all types of crafts from all over Mexico. Open daily from 9 a.m. to 6 p.m.

Activities for Children

Mazatlán has two outstanding attractions for children. Besides the beaches, children interested in the sea will love the **Acuario Mazatlán** (the aquarium), a brand-new government-run building one block off Avenida del Mar (look for the turn near the Motel del Sol and the Pizza Hut). Open 10 a.m. to 6 p.m. Tuesday through Sunday, closed Monday, the admission charge is 500 pesos ($1) for adults, half price for kids age 3 to 14.

Still in the realm of the aquatic, Mazatlán has a water slide called **Aqua Sport,** north of El Cid and just before the Holiday Inn, on the waterfront drive. You'll see a low hill, and lots of kids milling about on top, carrying plastic mats. They'll plop down their mats in the chute and come slushing down into the three-foot-deep pool at the base. Here's how it works: you pay 750 ($1.50) for a 30- or 40-minute period, and your child receives a mat of a certain color. The color identifies the period, so the kid shouldn't swap mats with anyone. Shady chairs and a refreshments stand cater to waiting parents while the kids glide down from the hilltop, past bushes and around boulders, to the little pool. Aqua Sport is open daily from 10 a.m. to 8 p.m.

3. San Blas and Tepic

The road from the highway to the coast at San Blas, Nayarit (pop. 35,000), is better than you'd expect. It takes about one hour to drive and winds through ever-lusher tropical country, finally emerging into the sleepy town on the Pacific. Although there are better hotels in Tepic, my advice would be to stay here overnight as San Blas is more interesting. In fact, if you can manage to get here by noon, it makes a delightful break to rest on the beach, drink coconut milk, and have a plate of fish at one of the beach shacks that pass for restaurants.

Many of the Pacific beach towns have been pretty well developed and consequently the prices for food and accommodations are high. San Blas is the exception. You will still find the tourists but thus far the developers have not taken over, so you'll be able to find hotels and restaurants at very reasonable prices. By the way, San Blas is famous for its biting gnats. The government sprays periodically, which seems to help a bit, but bug repellent is necessary.

Note: The peak season for San Blas, as well as for the other Pacific Coast resorts, is Christmas, from mid-December through February, and Easter, end of March through April. Advance reservations are recommended. Off-season, the hotel rates are quite flexible, so you can almost always bargain for a cheaper rate.

GETTING TO AND FROM SAN BLAS: Transportes del Noroeste de Nayarit has four buses a day between San Blas and Tepic, two a day to Guadalajara and back (morning and evening).

SAN BLAS ORIENTATION: As you rumble into the village of San Blas, you'll come to the main square. At the far end is the old church, and a new one a building next to it. Next to this is the town's bus station.

The main street into and through town is Avenida Juárez. After passing the square on your right, the first street to the left is Calle Battalion, an important thoroughfare that passes a bakery, the Estrella de Oro bus ticket office, the tourism office, a medical clinic; farther on, the street passes several hotels and trailer parks before coming to the beach.

WHERE TO STAY IN SAN BLAS: San Blas's selection of hotels is not a particularly good one. The tropical heat and relative lack of customers during the summer months encourage owners to sit back and "let things go" at the hotel, although this condition is somewhat alleviated in winter. If the list presented below seems to be too inclusive, it's only because I don't want you to get to San Blas and have no place to stay. The town is attractive. Soon, let's hope more of the hotels will be too.

Hotels

San Blas's newest and tidiest hostelry is the **Motel Posada del Rey,** Calle Campeche 10 (tel. 321/5-0123). A few blocks from the main square, the Posada has a dozen rooms arranged around a tiny courtyard taken up entirely by a nice little swimming pool. Rooms have private baths and ceiling fans, and rent for 3,400 pesos ($6.80) single, 4,500 pesos ($9) double. Nice!

The **Posada Casa Morales** (tel. 321/5-0023), on the beach and walking distance from town, is one of the newer hotels in San Blas. To get there, walk or drive to the end of Juárez, past the old Flamingo Hotel, and turn left. Follow this unpaved road for about three blocks and look for a sign pointing off to the right to the Casa Morales. The complex of bungalows, pool, and garden is on the ocean; some rooms have an ocean view, others look onto the pool and garden. All rates *include* breakfast and dinner during the winter season: singles are 10,000 pesos ($20); doubles, 12,000 to 14,000 pesos ($24 to $28). Summer rates are without meals: singles are 6,000 pesos ($12); doubles, 8,800 pesos ($17.60). Parking is included.

Across the street from the Casa Morales is the equally nice **Motel Las Brisas** (tel. 321/5-0112), also with a garden and pool, and 36 new units, but here the rates are 5,750 pesos ($11.50) single, 6,900 pesos ($13.80) double. The rooms, with table fans, are modern, bright, and airy. Parking is available next to the rooms. They also have a small garden restaurant where you can get breakfast.

Apartments

San Blas is not a big enough town in which to find "apartments"—most of the villagers still live in houses made of sticks. But there are establishments here that Mexicans call "suites," what I'd call housekeeping rooms, efficiencies, or self-catering flats.

The **Suites San Blas** (tel. 321/5-0047), Apdo. Postal 12, is a big new building off Calle Battalion, with "suites" renting for 5,200 pesos ($10.40) single, 6,900 pesos ($13.80) double. Each suite has a ceiling fan, kitchenette, and private bath. In addition, the complex has a swimming pool, disco, and dining room.

For other places and their daily and monthly rates, check the ads in McDonald's Restaurant.

Camping

Should you have camping gear, you'll want to know that San Blas has two trailer parks: **Los Cocos,** on Battalion near the beach, and **El Dorado,** across the street from El Alteño. Los Cocos has a wonderful luxury: an automatic laundry which advertises "Wash and dry in two hours!"

EATING IN SAN BLAS: Eating is not only good but cheap in San Blas. There are quite a number of newer restaurants, but I will stick by my favorites. The two best budget restaurants in town are on Juárez, just off the plaza. You can't go wrong at either one, and in fact the fare and prices seem just about the same; perhaps the **McDonald's** is a bit cheaper. McDonalds is open every day and features delicious fried fish for 800 pesos ($1.60), a fruit cocktail plate for 350 pesos (70¢), shrimp cocktail and most meat items in the 850-peso ($1.70) area. All meals come with fresh hot tortillas. Just down the street, on the same side, is the **Diligencias,** open 8 a.m. to 11 p.m. daily, closed Monday. They have a full breakfast for 450 pesos (90¢). The dinners are excellent: huge portions of fish and meat at 800 to 1,000 pesos ($1.60 to $2), served with frijoles and hot toasted rolls with butter.

One block down the street extending from the southeast corner of the main plaza (parallel to Battalion), the restaurant **La Isla** provides pleasurable dining outdoors. The hanging shark jawbones and fish nets set the mood for their excellent shrimp, oysters, lobster, and fish. You'll pay 1,200 pesos ($2.40) for a good dinner here. All eight tables extend from the kitchen in back where the owners diligently prepare the food.

For a light snack, homemade bread, granola, yogurt, and honey are on sale at **La Tumba de Yako,** two blocks from La Isla on Battalion. While munching, browse the store, which features a variety of Mexican and Guatemalan artwork. They sell yogurt-to-go after 3:30 p.m. each day at the Tumba.

For those on a starvation budget I can recommend the little shacks on the beach that serve fresh grilled fish. A fairly large fish with hot tortillas and a coco to drink will cost only 800 pesos ($1.60). I have eaten at several of these little places and found them satisfactory. The best seem to be those shacks a bit off the beach, on the road leading into town. From town, take the street south from the zócalo; about half a mile down you'll smell grilling fish.

READER'S RESTAURANT SELECTION: "We discovered the **Restaurant 'Tomas,'** owned by Thomas Yee, a Chinese-American. The food is absolutely delicious, and quite cheap. For example, we had chicken with mushrooms and wine sauce for 900 pesos ($1.80), and chop suey with chicken and shrimp for even less. The restaurant is on Calle Sinaloa just one block off the main square. Bring your own beer or wine. They also serve Mexican dishes and a few other things such as hamburgers" (Laurence Martin, Punta Gorda, Fla.).

WHAT TO DO: There is nothing to do here but relax, swim, read, walk the beach, and eat fish. But such an existence! I love this little town for just these reasons. The best **beaches** are those about one mile from town; driving or walking (there's also a town bus that runs down morning and evening), take Calle Battalion from the main plaza. The road west, along Juárez, will also take you to the Pacific, but the beaches are not as nice here.

For those hunting a secluded place to swim I have a suggestion: rent a canoe and head out to the island. Beach your craft, walk to the other side, and there you are . . . *maybe* all by yourself. It's worth a try. No trees, so bring your own shade.

Almost the moment you hit San Blas, you'll be approached by a "guide" who offers **"a boat ride into the jungle."** This can be exciting, but it can be expensive as well, depending on how many people you're able to get together to share expenses. The rates are controlled by the Tourism Office now, and are set at about 6,000 pesos ($12) for a three-hour trip, this being the *price for the boatload* of one to four persons; a fifth person pays an extra 1,000 pesos ($2). The guide will offer to take you to "The Plantation" during your voyage; this will cost another 3,000 pesos ($6), and, in my opinion, is not worth it. But getting to Elias and Chinche for the birdwatching *is* worth it. Try to depart as early as possible because the first boat on the river in the morning encounters the most wildlife.

The boat winds through the beautiful freshwater jungle maze, arriving finally at a spring which is San Blas's water supply. Swimming is permitted here, so you should have your suit along—the water is luxurious and refreshing. Although I can't recommend the restaurant at the spring, I'll permit you to buy a soft drink or beer there.

The Beach at Mantachen

Three miles from the square in San Blas is Mantachen. Head out Avenida Juárez as though you were returning to the main highway, and turn right, following the signs to Mantachen. Buses run this route at 9 and 11 a.m., 1 and 3 p.m. There's a little settlement here where you can have a snack or a meal, rent a boat for the jungle river cruise, etc. A half mile past the settlement is a dirt road to Las Islitas, which has a magnificent swath of sand beach. Beach-shack eateries provide sustenance, Mexican families on vacation are your company, and the beach is yours for miles and miles. Sometimes there's even transport out here from the square in San Blas.

Port of San Blas

Why San Blas? What determined that this small village should have a collection of good hotels? The fact is that San Blas was a very important port, like Acapulco, for New Spain's trade with the Philippines. Pirates would attempt to intercept the rich Spanish galleons headed for San Blas, and so the town had to be fortified. Ruins of the fortifications, on a hill east of town, of the old Spanish customs house, and of various foreign consulates are still visible down at the beach end of Avenida Juárez. Take a stroll down and have a look.

ON TO TEPIC: The country from San Blas to Tepic, capital of the small state of Nayarit, is lush and tropical, with many banana plantations and coconut palms. Heavy, warm rain falls almost every day in the summer.

Orientation

Highway 15, the main coastal highway, passes through Tepic as Avenida Insurgentes, but it skirts the edge of town. Motels and restaurants aimed at the tourist trade are lined up along the highway, but the real budget choices are in the center of town, about eight or nine blocks off Hwy. 15 / Avenida Insurgentes.

Follow the signs into the center of town and you'll pass two large squares. The first one has an impressively gaudy Palacio de Gobierno (state government building) at one end. The second one, the main square, has a hemicycle of columns at its center and a huge Gothic church at one end. One doesn't see many Gothic churches in Mexico, with all that churrigueresque stuff around.

My hotel and restaurant choices are grouped around the second, or main square, within sight of the Gothic church.

Where to Stay and Eat

Top marks for budget hotel finds I encountered on my latest visit go to the 84-room **Hotel San Jorge,** Lerdo Pte. 124 (tel. 321/2-1324). Gleaming and spotless, it offers maximum comfort for the very modest tab of 5,174 pesos ($10.34) single, 6,774 pesos ($13.59) double. There I enjoyed a palatial twin-bedded room for a fraction of what I'd have paid in Mexico City. Location is also good, 1½ blocks west of the main square. Highly recommended.

Another good hotel is the **Hotel Sierra de Alica** (tel. 321/2-0322 or 2-0324),

Avenida México Norte 180, half a block south of the Gothic church and the main square. It's an older place, centrally located, big with lots of space in corridors and rooms. Plumbing fixtures are old too, and one gets a shower, not a tub, but all is fairly well kept. Prices are 5,096 pesos ($10.19) single, 6,580 pesos ($13.16) double.

On the square itself, the **Hotel Fray Junipero,** Lerdo 23 Pte., Tepic, Nay. 63000 (tel. 321/2-2175 or 2-2051), may draw your eye. A double here costs a cool 8,325 pesos ($16.65).

As for dining, most of the town's decent restaurants are out on the main highway in order to catch the transient crowd. Downtown you can try **Wendy's Cafeteria,** right next to the Hotel Sierra de Alica at Avenida México Nte. 170. Open virtually all the time. Wendy's has Formica tables, ceiling fans, pictures of Peter Pan characters on the walls, and a portrait of Wendy (Disney style) over the short cafeteria line. Have a big breakfast of ham and eggs, a muffin, milk, and coffee; or a lunch of enchiladas, frijoles, and soft drink; or a sandwich or burger and salad, and the bill in any case will be less than 800 pesos ($1.60).

A popular and established local restaurant is **La Terraza,** Hwy. 15/Avenida Insurgentes Pte. 98 (tel. 2-2521). As unpretentious as you could imagine, it looks like nothing more than a good Stateside diner on a well-traveled highway. Also furnishing an American touch is a rack filled with the latest U.S. magazines. Fare is cheap and nourishing, with four tamales and beverage for 600 pesos ($1.20), and the costliest dish, filet mignon, at 1,200 pesos ($2.40). Try one of the excellent pies—I prefer the lemon—or cakes. Ice cream addicts will like the banana split; in fact, I'll wager nonaddicts will like it too.

I do it only as a prescription against homesickness, but here it is: Tepic has a branch of the **Kentucky Fried Chicken** chain on the main highway. (If you compare prices, you'll find this rather expensive.)

4. Puerto Vallarta

Of all the Pacific seacoast resorts in Mexico, this is my favorite. The beaches are not as magnificent as those at Acapulco, not everybody speaks English as at Mazatlán, and it's not "unspoiled" as are Puerto Escondido and Puerto Angel. But Puerto Vallarta is gorgeous, with its tropical mountains tumbling right into the sea, its coves and beaches, and its Mexican town. Yes! Unlike Acapulco and Mazatlán, where the town has withered as the resort has grown, Puerto Vallarta's development—mostly on the outskirts of the original town—has lent prosperity without robbing charm.

Puerto Vallarta, Jalisco (pop. 90,000), started out as a little primitive settlement on the Bay of Banderas, far from roads, airports, electricity, prosperity, and tourism. With the making of *Night of the Iguana,* Puerto Vallarta ceased to be a well-kept secret. Elizabeth Taylor returned to the place where the movie had been shot. With the passing years and Mexico's economic development came a good highway, a jetport, prosperity, and renown.

Today, Nuevo Vallarta is the focus of charter tour activity. It's a planned resort development to the north of the old town, with golf links, high-rise hotels, yacht marina, airport, cruise-ship wharf, a convention center, and all the other accoutrements of a touristic megadevelopment. But, luckily for you, the old town has remained a charming place, spanning the Río Cuale, nestled into the emerald hills. If anything, the wealth brought by the tourist boom has helped to spruce up old Puerto Vallarta and make it even more attractive.

GETTING TO AND FROM PUERTO VALLARTA: When Elizabeth Taylor first spied Puerto Vallarta it was still a pretty remote and pristine Pacific fishing village. *Night of the Iguana* did its work, however, and a road was built. Today big jets stream in and out of the burgeoning town. This is no doubt being greeted with mixed emotions, as some mourn the increased accessibility of a once-remote resort.

By Air

Mexicana Airlines (in Guadalajara at Avenida 16 de Septiembre 495, tel. 36/13-2222; in Puerto Vallarta at Juárez 202, tel. 322/2-1808) has daily flights on jet aircraft between Puerto Vallarta and Guadalajara, Mexico City, Mazatlán, Denver, and Dallas / Fort Worth. For information regarding the flights call Mexicana's Puerto Vallarta office or the Mexico City operation at Juárez and Balderas (tel. 905/585-2666).

AeroMéxico has flights from Puerto Vallarta to Mexico City, Guadalajara, and (with one stop en route) to Chihuahua, Ciudad Juárez, and Houston. Offices are in Puerto Vallarta at Juárez 255 (tel. 322/2-0031), in Guadalajara at Avenida Corona 196 (tel. 322/5-1010), and in Mexico City at Reforma 445 (tel. 905/553-1577).

To get into Puerto Vallarta from the airport, take the airport minibus (a VW) for 620 pesos ($1.25), or walk the block out to the highway and get a city bus for 50 pesos (10¢).

By Bus

Autotransportes del Pacifico will get you from Guadalajara to Puerto Vallarta on any of their hourly buses that run throughout the day. This is the most convenient service. They make the return run just as frequently.

Tres Estrellas de Oro will take you to Puerto Vallarta from Guadalajara six times a day (should you want to go that often). Catch the bus at the Central Camionera. Buses from Tepic run several times a day as well, but here you must wait for the bus to arrive before they sell you a seat on it—assuming there's one vacant. Time from Guadalajara is about seven hours, from Tepic about three hours.

Bus stations for most major lines—Transportes del Pacifico, Tres Estrellas de Oro, Norte de Sonora, and Estrella Blanca—are along Avenida Insurgentes between Serdan and the Río Cuale.

By Ferryboat to Baja

Boats operate between Puerto Vallarta and Cabo San Lucas, Baja California, a trip of 18 hours at a cost of 600 to 1,200 pesos ($1.20 to $2.40) for a seat, 2,600 to 4,200 pesos ($5.20 to $8.40) for a cabin. Departure from Puerto Vallarta is at 4 p.m. on Tuesday and Saturday; from Cabo San Lucas, at 4 p.m. on Wednesday and Sunday.

ORIENTATION: Once in the town, everything is within walking distance. The main promenade, the **Malecón,** follows the rim of the bay from north to south, and the town stretches back into the hills for no farther than about four or five blocks. Coming in from the airport, north of town, you'll pass the Holiday Inn and the Sheraton; in the town the Malecón is lined with more hotels. The area north of the Río Cuale is the older part of town—the original Puerto Vallarta, you might say. South of the Río Cuale used to be only beach, but in the last decade it has gotten as built up as the old town. Today, the best budget lodgings are to be found south of the river and inland. The several bus stations are here as well. No doubt the bus stations will all be moved to a unified terminal, a "Central Camionera" on the outskirts when Puerto Vallarta finally gets its long-awaited "Libramiento," or bypass. This will take coastal Hwy. 200 around behind the town, rather than right through the center of it.

Tourism Information

The **Tourism Office** is at the corner of Juárez and Independencia (tel. 322/2-2042). It's near the AeroMéxico offices.

WHERE TO STAY: To facilitate your search for a suitable hotel room, I'll divide the town into areas, and start with the one boasting the best lodging bargains. When you arrive in Puerto Vallarta, you may descend from your bus in the perfect locale for finding a clean, cheery, inexpensive room.

Note: During the winter season (mid-December to May), the rooms in Puerto Vallarta are all booked. It's best to have reservations, but if you want to chance it, get to town early in the day and start your search. If you are told that the rooms are full, ask if you can leave your name and return at check-out time to see if anyone has vacated.

South of the Río Cuale

The corner of Madero and Insurgentes is the center of Puerto Vallarta's bus activity, and this means that some clean, decent hotels will be nearby. The buses aren't really a nuisance either; there's not a lot of noise and hubbub because it's not that big a town.

On Francisco I. Madero: The **Hotel Villa del Mar (10),** Madero 440 at Jacarandas (tel. 322/2-0785), is a simple, three-story place with big windows in the front rooms. Its 28 rooms are arranged around a tidy slot-like courtyard that manages to nurture several tall bamboo plants. Pretty tile picture panels brighten the public areas, and although the rooms are simple (naked lightbulbs, etc.) they are not what you'd call bare. The Villa del Mar is run by industrious señoras who see to its upkeep and propriety, and who charge 2,300 pesos ($4.60) single, 3,100 pesos ($6.20) double.

At Madero 473, up past Jacarandas, is the 46-room **Hotel Azteca (15)** (tel. 322/2-2750), which you'll recognize from its low brick arches, standard slot-like courtyard, and pretty garden. Prices are about the lowest on the street: 2,000 pesos ($4) single, 3,000 pesos ($6) double.

On Basilio Vadillo: Three blocks south of, and parallel to, Calle Madero is Calle Basilio Vadillo (or Badillo—there's no pronunciation difference in Spanish). Here you will find some more budget and moderately priced hotels (restaurants, too).

The **Hotel Posada de Roger (1),** Basilio Vadillo 237, near the corner of Ignacio Vallarta (tel. 322/2-0836), has come up quite a ways in the world since its first inclusion in this book years ago. Once a pension, it has now become a hotel with very simple but spotless rooms at very good prices: 5,000 pesos ($10) single, 6,000 pesos ($12) double, 7,000 pesos ($14) triple, and all 52 rooms have private bath. The hotel keeps the same friendly *ambiente,* and guests still gather in the attractive courtyard for conversation, entertainment, and general fun.

Farther down Basilio Vadillo at no. 168 is the **Hotel Yazmin (2)** (tel. 322/2-0087). Although the Yazmin lacks the charged atmosphere of Roger's, it does have a very nice courtyard, and quite suitable rooms with bath for 3,220 pesos ($6.45) single, 4,025 pesos ($8.05) double.

By the way, if you're looking for an apartment and you know well in advance when you'll be in this city, try writing for reservations at the **Apartments La Peña (22)** at Apdo. Postal 177 (tel. 322/2-1213). There're only ten apart-

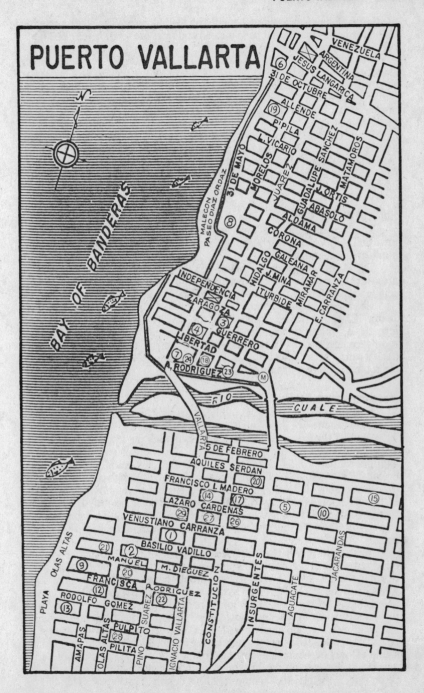

PUERTO VALLARTA

ments but all have open-air kitchenettes on the balconies. The apartments are up on the rocks (that's what *peña* means) and rates are 4,600 pesos ($9.20) for two and 8,050 pesos ($16.10) for four.

Next door to the Apts. La Peña at Fca. Rodríguez 168 is the new **Hotel Costa Alegre** (tel. 322/2-4793). The 28 clean rooms with ceiling fans are decorated with a country flair—flowered bedspreads and wooden trunks against hardwood floors. A small swimming pool borders a well-tended garden. Singles are priced at 5,000 pesos ($10) and doubles are 6,000 pesos ($12). Some kitchenettes are available.

If you can't find a room anywhere else, try the **Hotel Bernal** on Francisco Madero 423 (tel. 322/2-3605). Although the 34 rooms are clean, they are a bit worn and you'll probably have a shower curtain for a bathroom door. All come with ceiling fans and bath for 2,300 pesos ($4.60) single and 3,100 pesos ($6.20) double.

North of the Río Cuale

This is the real center of town, with the market (M), squares, church, and town hall. A few choices for budget lodgings still exist here, although most of the hotels are moderately priced.

The **Hotel Chulavista (4),** Juárez 263 (tel. 322/2-0290), has been modernized and renovated at least once in its present incarnation. Simple rooms with ceiling fans and bath go for 3,220 pesos ($6.45) single, 4,025 ($8.05) double.

Head down Hidalgo almost to the river to find the new **Hotel Encino (18),** Juárez 122 between A. Rodriguez and the river (tel. 322/2-0051). One might term this a "budget resort hotel," as it tries to be mod and stylish although the rooms are small and darkish. It seems to have been built by unskilled workmen, but it's run by better sorts who charge 12,075 pesos ($24.15) double for most of the rooms; a few cost more.

More Expensive Hotels

Now for some hotel choices at higher prices, but with the addition of sea views, kitchenettes, or other small luxuries.

South of the River: For ocean-loving splurgers, the **Hotel Marsol (9)** (tel. 332/2-1365; Apdo. Postal 4) is located on the Playa del Sol beach. Its rooms, all with private bath (hot and cold water), rent for 5,980 pesos ($12) single with balcony, 7,475 pesos ($14.95) double. It's a big airy place with nothing but a row of coconut palms (and a retaining wall) between its open veranda and the beach. It should be noted that they offer only rooms with breakfast included, and also that the staff tends to be grouchy. The beach restaurants are a scant 50 yards away. *Note:* Only apartments face the sea; rooms without kitchen are all in the back.

North of the River: The **Hotel Oceano (8)** (tel. 322/2-1322; Apdo. Postal 45) is located on the Malecón next to a tiny black-and-white lighthouse that is operative but actually pretty useless—a ship would have to be halfway across the Malecón to see it. The 52-room Oceano is notable for its bar (well patronized) and its location (very central). Rooms are small, with substantial wood furniture, colorful bedspreads, and stained wood shutters instead of windows, which can be adjusted to let in more or less light. Construction is of sun-bleached stucco and dark wood, and since it's right on the ocean, there's a continual soothing sound of low surf. Unfortunately, the Oceano's location at the corner of Ordaz and Morelos guarantees the unsoothing sound of traffic as well. Rates are 8,280 pesos ($16.56) single, 10,350 pesos ($20.70) double, 12,430 pesos ($24.86) triple. All rooms come with ceiling fans.

With the exception of the Oceano, you don't get all you should at the moderately priced hotels. If rooms are tight, try these:

In the northern reaches of town, at no. 901 on the waterfront street variously named El Malecón, Paseo Díaz Ordaz, and Calle 31 de Mayo, corner of 31 de Octubre, is the **Nuevo Hotel Rosita (6)** (tel. 322/2-1033; Apdo. Postal 32). It is among the oldest in town, popular with Americans because of its pool and its view from the open-air bar facing the ocean. The building is huge, white, built in 1948 and recently remodeled (downstairs) à la Spanish colonial with pleasing results. The Rosita is divided into an old wing, where rooms are small, a bit weather-beaten, have frosted windows, tiny balconies, and cost 5,290 pesos ($10.58) single or double (12 such rooms); and a spiffier new wing where the remaining 79 rooms are 6,440 pesos ($12.88) single, 7,015 to 10,500 pesos ($14 to $21) for a double. There's a pleasant restaurant on the ground floor and a bar with marvelous burled wood chairs.

The Rosita recently opened another place, **Hotel El Pescador,** four blocks away at Paraguay 1117 near the intersection of Uruguay (tel. 322/2-2169). Entrances to the 42 spacious rooms all face the ocean with a price range of 6,440 pesos ($12.90) with fan to 7,705 pesos ($15.40) with air conditioning, single; 7,050 pesos ($14.10) to 8,280 pesos ($16.60), double. There is a swimming pool and a restaurant/bar as well.

Next to the Río Cuale is the **Hotel Río (7),** Morelos 170 (tel. 322/2-0366; Apdo. Postal 23), which is a sort of condensed version of the Hotel Rosita—the same white cement architecture topped with an exotic-looking sign that reads "RIO" in striped letters set askew apparently on purpose. The court is shady and lush and contains a kidney-shaped pool modeled after someone's very small kidneys. However, it's used, and guests can be seen lying precariously on its narrow, raised periphery catching rays. Rooms are several cuts above the low-cost models at the Rosita—all outside, all with bath. Rates are not bad: singles cost 4,500 pesos ($9); doubles, 5,100 pesos ($10.20). Large rooms with extra-spacious balconies and corner locations are more expensive.

READERS' HOTEL SELECTIONS: "The **Posada Río Cuale** was a nice place to stay, at 7,000 pesos ($14) for two. It's on the main street just south of the river, very handy to the beach and the town; rooms are nicely decorated. Meals are considered among the best in Puerto Vallarta. Also, **Roger's Apartments,** at Olas Altas 385, was a referral from his hotel up the street. On the third floor, we had two bedrooms and a huge living-dining-kitchen area, and two bathrooms, for $350 per month for four" (Mrs. F. E. Shields, Victoria, B.C., Canada). . . . "We got one of the 13 rooms at the **Casa Corazón** (no phone), Apdo. Postal 66, Puerto Vallarta, Jalisco 48300, which is really a villa, for $200 double, per month; rates per night were $12.50 single, $20 double, including breakfast. These are summer rates, and I don't know if they're as cheap in winter. The villa is beautiful, with a family-type atmosphere. It's run by Americans, who also run the Barba Roja on Los Muertos Beach, directly in front of the villa" (Ann Schultz, Toronto, Ontario, Canada).

EATING IN PUERTO VALLARTA: One of the beauties of Puerto Vallarta is its

collection of small, homey restaurants aimed at the Mexican family on vacation. Moderate prices, big portions, decent service, long hours—these restaurants are a welcome alternative to the expensive and pretentious places with hyped-up tropical "atmosphere," high-decibel Muzak, and sassy waiters. I'll start our explorations of dining places south of the Río Cuale.

South of the River

We'll look first at an eatery near the hotels and bus stations on the south side, and then wander on down to the beach.

Near Hotels and Buses: The **Restaurant Gilmar (10),** Madero 418, is a small place with brick arches, rickety wooden chairs, bright colors, and a blackboard menu. The good, simple Mexican food is whipped up by the owner-señora, who features a comida corrida for less than 400 pesos (80¢). It's nothing spectacular, just good, convenient, and low-priced.

Down Near Playa Olas Altas: On Olas Altas near the Hotel Marsol, **Las Tres Huastecas (12)** is a tried-and-true place heavily patronized by both local and foreign tourists (menus in Spanish and English). The unpretentious Formica tables are usually packed with happy diners having such high-ticket items as huachinango (red snapper) or carne asada (grilled beef) for a mere 900 pesos ($1.80).

When you first look at **Los Pinguinos (20),** on Olas Altas more or less across from **Las Tres Huastecas,** you'll think it's a real low-budget place. But enter the big, airy dining room (with kitchen to one side) and you'll see that thought was given to the decoration, from the painted border of flowering vines that's painted along the walls to the small flower print tablecloths and the nice paintings hung here and there. The menu has a good variety of items in all price ranges, and you can satisfy your hunger with a huge fruit salad for 450 pesos (90¢) or a big Mexican combination plate at 1,800 pesos ($3.60). Service, when I was there, was surprisingly professional.

Across the street from Los Pinguinos, in the Hotel Los Arcos, the **Restaurant Los Arcos (21)** has a standard selection of dishes at moderate prices, and provides a more formal atmosphere than you might otherwise find on Olas Altas, a beachcombers' street.

Speaking of beachcombers, they're the reason the **Restaurant La Palapa (13)** was established many years ago. But this thatched place, right on the beach near the Hotel Marsol, has graduated at least to tourist class, and now serves sandwiches and main courses—seafood's the specialty, naturally—for slightly more than the eateries on Olas Altas. You can get by on 1,250 pesos ($2.50) for a sandwich and soft drink, 1,550 to 2,600 pesos ($3.10 to $5.20) for a more substantial three-course repast. Other, similar beachfront restaurants are nearby.

Beachcombers' Fare: About the cheapest palatable food on the beach is sold by boys who catch or buy small fish, and then cook them on a stick over a driftwood fire. You buy what amounts to a pescado-lollipop, preferably hot off the fire, for about 400 pesos (80¢), after haggling for a few seconds.

Dessert, anyone? **La Casita de Postres y Muffins** at 342 Basilio Badillo concocts a delicious Puerto Vallarta brownie (with peanut butter) in addition to cheesecake (chocolate, amaretto or plain), which is sold in area restaurants, pies, muffins (bran, carrot, or banana) and homemade yogurt. Belly up to the small tile counter and make your selection which will cost you from 175 to 500 pesos (35¢ to $1).

North of the River

Just tell the taxi driver, **"Tony's,** please," and he'll whisk you to a popular eatery at Juárez and A. Rodríguez (tel. 2-0757). The decor, with its nautical themes interposed with wine and fruit still lifes, is as eclectic as the choice of entrees. Frogs' legs provençal, fish sautéed in wine sauce, or tenderloin tips, all priced at 1,900 pesos ($3.80), or even the Mexican combination plate at 1,300 pesos ($2.60) are all excellent choices.

Sea bass and fries? Well, at **Antojenia** it's known as fish and chips and the aroma will guide your nose to this restaurant at Morelos 657, near Abasolo. The price for the above is 850 pesos ($1.70), hamburgers are 650 pesos ($1.30), and tacos and enchiladas are 150 pesos (30¢) each. Eat to the beat of the music at the counter or at one of the five tables.

For Pizza: **Pietro Pastas & Pizzas** (tel. 2-3233), at Zaragoza 245 offers a variety of 12-inch pizzas on the trilingual menu (English, Spanish, Italian) ranging from 1,417 to 2,551 pesos ($2.83 to $5.10). The pasta is also good and you can order "ravioli just like mama used to make" for 1,275 pesos ($2.55).

More Expensive Places

For a marginally more expensive dinner, but still within our budget range, try one of these places.

For Spanish Fare: **Las Cazuelas (14),** Basilio Badillo 479 (tel. 2-1658), is by far one of my favorite eating spots in Puerto Vallarta. Cazuela in Spanish means "earthenware cooking pot," and it is here that you can sample the savory food from such pots. It is distinctly Spanish in all ways, from the smells to the hustle and bustle. A full dinner might cost 6,000 to 7,500 pesos ($12 to $15): appetizer (soup, guacamole), fried cheese, choice of entree, dessert, and Mexican cinnamon coffee. Open daily from 6 until 11 p.m. Call to reserve one of the 23 tables. *(Note:* Las Cazuelas sometimes closes down in summer.)

A Chinese Restaurant: Hunting for Peking on the Río Cuale? The place to look is Avenida Lázaro Cárdenas 302, corner of Constitución, where you'll find the **Restaurant Palacio Oriental (26).** The proprietor, Carlos Chong, serves up combination dinners of five or six courses for 2,100 to 2,600 pesos ($4.20 to $5.20). Should you order one of the à la carte delicacies such as butterfly shrimp, your bill could soar to 3,000 pesos ($6) or so. Chinese trinkets and decorations turn what would otherwise be a plain Mexican restaurant into a palacio oriental (well, sort of), complete with ceiling fans.

For Oysters or Beef: On Calle Libertad (no. 171) and across from the Hotel Río, is El Ostión Feliz, **The Happy Oyster,** which serves the oyster and also a host of his nautical associates. Squid, octopus, frogs' legs, conch, and shark are tossed right into salad makings and served up for 1,900 pesos ($3.80); more commonly encountered dishes such as shrimp, lobster, and crab are there as well. The seafood casserole is highly recommended. Oh, yes: oysters come as a cocktail for 2,800 pesos ($5.60), breaded or deviled for 3,800 pesos ($7.60). The extra-specialty of the house can be commanded for extra-special occasions: it's barbecued white whale, and the minimum order is for 1,000 servings.

A block away from The Happy Oyster is the **Restaurant Los Venados (24),** Calle Rodriguez 177, around the corner from the Hotel Río. Fixed up with brick arches, tablecloths, and a country-ish decor, Los Venados will serve you any of the standard Mexican repasts, including a beefsteak dinner for 1,322 pesos ($2.65), or a big avocado salad for much less.

A Lobster Splurge: It's not difficult to guess the specialty at the **Lobster House (27),** Lázaro Cárdenas 254, corner of Ignacio Vallarta (tel. 2-0676). Besides lobster, they serve fish, jumbo shrimp, and (much cheaper) octopus and squid. A big restaurant with many bright dining rooms, all done in quaint colonial style, the Lobster House has a lively atmosphere, and a piano player to make sure it stays that way. Expect to spend 5,000 pesos ($10) per person, more or less. Come between 6 and 7 p.m. and you can enjoy Happy Hour, with two drinks (all brands) for the price of one. Open for lunch and dinner every day.

A Mexican Fiesta: If you want a real extravaganza, go to **La Iguana (17)** (tel. 2-0105), a couple of blocks south of the river at Lázaro Cárdenas 311, between Constitutición and Insurgentes, where a full dinner will cost 8,050 pesos ($16.10), but that includes an *open bar,* and an all-you-can-eat buffet. The owner-chef, Gustavo Salazar, was born to Mexican parents in Hong Kong, where he later managed the American Club. La Iguana's atmosphere is as eclectic as its owner's experience. You'll cross a Mexican version of a Chinese moon bridge over a wishing pool, enter a thick-walled adobe-arched pavilion, where you'll be entertained by mariachis and a Ballet Folklorico. Fiesta nights are only on Thursday and Sunday. It's definitely for tourist trade and rarely visited by locals.

Although I readily admit that all Mexican food is good, there are restaurants that rise above the most, such as **La Cabaña de Pancho Villa,** V. Carranza 248, at I. Vallarta (tel. 2-2311). Pancho Villa opens at 9:00 p.m. and doesn't stop serving excellent carne asada and pollo a la parilla until 5:00 a.m. Marinated cauliflower and carrots with peppers are served at every table and entrees come with frijoles charros (beans, cowboy style), grilled onions, and radishes. Just about everything is grilled here, such as beef for 2,200 pesos ($4.40) and chicken for 1,800 pesos ($3.60), or try the best quesadillas I've tasted for 800 pesos ($1.60).

READERS' RESTAURANT SELECTIONS: "**Orphans Bar 'n Wok** (no phone), on Basilio Badillo across from the bakery, serves delicious oriental-style dishes, including a good selection of vegetarian dishes. The chef used to be John Huston's personal cook. Open only for dinner from 6:30 to 11:30 p.m., prices are reasonable at 1,500 to 2,500 pesos ($3 to $5) for main courses. Wonderful service! Also, we enjoyed gourmet dining at the **Manatial Restaurant** (tel. 2-3881), corner of Allende and Morelos, elegant dining for very reasonable prices (6,000 to 7,500 pesos, $12 to $15, for two). It has a good selection of vegetarian appetizers and main courses" (Monica Levine, New Rochelle, N.Y.). . . . "We were looking for breakfast, and though their sign didn't show it, for 750 pesos ($1.50) we got eggs, beans, bacon, tortillas, salsa, coffee, and fresh-squeezed OJ at the **Restaurant Vallarta Cuale,** on Isla Río Cuale (the island in the river). It was great, with a view of the river and the ocean" (Kai McCarthy, Baldwin Park, Calif.). . . . "For the nightspot, I would highly recommend the **Zapata Restaurant** (tel. 2-4748), Paseo Díaz Ordaz 522. A restaurant and bar with a fine menu, very personable staff, live Latin music, and 'revolutionary' ambience. It absolutely made our vacation" (Jean Ranc, Chapel Hill, N.C.).

SUNNING AND STROLLING: The beaches in Puerto Vallarta, of course, take up most people's time. They start well to the north of town, out by the airport, with Playa de Oro, and extend all around the bay. The most popular ones are **Playa Olas Altas,** off the street of the same name south of the Río Cuale; and **Playa Mismaloya,** in a beautiful sheltered cove a kilometer or so south of town along Hwy. 200.

Susan Bates-Harbuck of Sandpoint, Idaho, has written to say, "Around the rocky point south of Playa Olas Altas are quite a number of small, sheltered coves that get very little use, and then mostly from Mexican families out for the weekend. It's much nicer than the Coney Island atmosphere of the main beach. No peddlers either." Sounds good to me.

Playa Yelapa

About the best beach around is Playa Yelapa, a two-hour trip by boat down the coast. Go to the Terminal Maritima north of town past the Holiday Inn (but before the airport), and get the 9 a.m. boat to Yelapa for 5,000 pesos ($10) round trip, returning at 4:30 p.m.

Besides the beach, Yelapa has a hotel, called the **Hotel Lagunitas.** It's not fancy, and services are unpredictable, but you can spend a blissful night or two if you make reservations in advance at Mexitours (Apdo. Postal 395, Puerto Vallarta, Jalisco, México). A double room costs about 9,000 pesos ($18), depending on demand. Accommodations are in little cottages-with-bath.

Cheaper accommodations at Yelapa? Ask around to see if any of the Americans living there is putting up rooms for rent; or rent a palapa hut with a dirt floor—some go for as low as $100 for a half *year*. The cheapest way of all, of course, is to sleep on the beach, but don't plan this during the rainy season!

There's absolutely nothing to do at Yelapa except lie in the sun, eat, play darts, and trudge 'round the bay to a tiny Indian village of the same name.

PUERTO VALLARTA NIGHTLIFE: An interesting place to sit around, see, and be seen is the lounge of the **Hotel Oceano (8).** A band often plays there for dancing, and there's a good deal of table-hopping by both strangers and friends. Girls from the University of Guadalajara are sometimes in Puerto Vallarta on vacation; don't think that a Mexican girl won't speak English, many of them do. Plenty of guys around too.

These days, the swinging after-dark crowds have succumbed to disco madness. The discos are very much like those at home, being high-volume, high-price, and high-times places. Expect a cover charge of about 1,500 pesos ($3), and then you'll pay about 700 pesos ($1.40) for a margarita, 800 pesos ($1.60) for whisky and a mix.

Wander down the Malecón after dark and your ears will lead you to **Carlos O'Brien's (19),** or **Casablancas.** Here you can sit amid jungle animals dangling from the ceiling, or you can shoulder your way up to the Cuckoo's Nest.

Walk up behind the Hotel Delfin, south of the Río Cuale on Olas Altas at Francisca Rodríguez, to find **Capriccio (28).** It's up those steep steps on what would be the continuation of Pulpito, were it not for the hill interrupting the street. Another disco to check out, especially if you're young and single, is the **City Dump (29),** Vallarta 278, corner of Lázaro Cárdenas, open 10:30 p.m. to 4 a.m.—dark, low-key, semi-chic.

The beach doesn't go to sleep at night, for the shady palapas that provided refuge during the heat of the day provide room for bands at night. The locale and the band can change with the phases of the moon, or even every day, but the twang of the electric guitar will draw you to the spot where the carefree and budget-minded are dancing on the beach.

SHOPPING TIPS: Puerto Vallarta's **municipal market (M)** is just north of the Río Cuale where Libertad and A. Rodríguez meet. You can pick up very inexpensive fruit, vegetables, and picnic fixings here.

Should you be in the market for those wonderfully comfy and practical sandals called *huaraches,* made of leather strips and rubber-tire soles, head for Calle Libertad between Juárez and the market. This is huarache city, with a dozen shops. Shop around, and buy a pair that fits very tightly—they stretch out almost immediately, and can become too floppy.

5. San Patricio and Barra de Navidad

Just to show that those tiny Pacific Coast villages, laid back and lovely, are still to be found, I'll take you on a tour through San Patricio and Barra de Navidad, two small villages on the beach of the Bahía de Navidad, sometimes called Melaque Bay.

The road south from Puerto Vallarta, Hwy. 200, joins the road from Guadalajara (Hwy. 80) at Barra de Navidad, and then Hwy. 200 heads southeast to Manzanillo. It's a three-hour ride from Puerto Vallarta to San Patricio, over five hours from Guadalajara. The distance from Barra to Manzanillo is about 30 miles.

These villages are easy of access because so much bus traffic runs between Puerto Vallarta and Manzanillo, and between Guadalajara and Manzanillo. Any bus on these routes will drop you near San Patricio. Coming from Manzanillo, Autotransportes Cihuatlán operates buses to San Patricio.

SAN PATRICIO: The most northwesterly of these communities, and the first one you'll encounter if you're coming from Puerto Vallarta, is San Patricio. On a crescent-shaped bay with curious rock outcrops at the points of the crescent, San Patricio can boast a perfect beach and an easy mood in which fishermen and beachcombers blend without difficulty. Unlike Zihuatanejo, this village hasn't been tarted up to meet jet-setters' expectations of what a Mexican fishing village should look like—this is the real thing. The paved road ends where the town begins. A few yachts bob at anchor in the harbor.

San Patricio is not exactly big enough to get lost in, but a word of orientation will help. Coming into town from the main road, you'll be on the town's main street, Avenida López Mateos. You'll pass the main square and come right down to the waterfront, where there's a trailer park. The street going left (southeast) along the bay is Avenida Gómez Farías; the one going right (northwest) is Avenida de las Palmas.

The **Tourism Office** is on Avenida de las Palmas just past the Hotel Melaque, open 9 a.m. to 3 p.m. and 5 to 7 p.m. Monday through Friday, on Saturday from 9 a.m. to 1 p.m. Once you get to know San Patricio, you'll understand not to trust those hours too much.

Where to Stay

Come into town, down to the water, and turn right onto Avenida de las Palmas, and this is what you'll find:

On the left-hand side, about a block down Palmas, is the **Motel Vista Hermosa** (tel. 333/7-0002). An attractive three-story hotel built around a nice courtyard, it has little of the motel about it. Rooms are not fancy, but newish, adequate, and clean. The court is shady, with a little red-tile gazebo in the center from which refreshments are sometimes served. Although you're right on the beach here, don't expect your room to have much of a sea view, as most rooms don't. Prices are 3,960 pesos ($7.95) single, 4,950 pesos ($9.90) double.

The **Posada de Legazpi** (tel. 333/7-0109), all the way down at the end of Avenida de las Palmas, is well worn and somewhat carelessly kept, but in a way that seems to fit the tropical climate. Rooms are clean, the beach is right out front, and the management is sympathetic. Double rooms with bath cost 5,500 pesos ($11) here.

Now for a look in the other direction. If you turn left onto Gómez Farías in the center of town, you'll come to the **Posada Las Gaviotas** (tel. 333/7-0129), entered from a side street called Calle Hidalgo (at no. 4). Long arches stretch from Gómez Farías all the way down to the beach, and beneath the arches are simple, cool rooms with no real sea view, but private baths. The cost is 3,979 pesos ($7.95) single, 4,973 pesos ($9.95) double.

Next along the street is the attractive (for San Patricio, even chic) **Posada Pablo de Tarso,** Gómez Farías 408 (tel. 333/7-0117). This two-level, 19-room place is exceptionally tidy, with brilliantly green grass and plants in the courtyard, shaded parking places, and neat, comfy rooms which rent for 4,974 pesos ($9.95) single or 5,969 pesos ($11.95) double. Again, you're right on the beach here.

Where to Eat

Avenida López Mateos has several little eateries here and there along its length, and these will do for light meals or snacks. For a substantial meal in pleasant surroundings, find your way to the **Restaurant Fonda Los Portales,** on Gómez Farías almost next to the Posada Las Gaviotas. A small palapa-shaded place, you can tuck into any of a dozen seafood platters here, and your entire meal will cost less than 1,500 pesos ($3).

BARRA DE NAVIDAD: About three miles (five km.) east of San Patricio along the road to Manzanillo is Barra de Navidad, an even smaller village with equally fine beaches and an identical easy lifestyle. Also like San Patricio, Barra has been discovered, but only by a very small number of people. You'll see tanned gringos and gringas circulating on the streets leading to the beach, fishermen and townfolk going about their business.

Where to Stay and Eat

Barra is small enough that ten minutes of wandering will give you the town's entire layout. When you find Calle Morelos, make your way to no. 23 and the **Hotel Delphin** (tel. 333/7-0068), a relatively new four-story hotel surrounded by verdure. Rooms, as befits such a beach town, are very basic, cooled by sea breezes through cross-ventilation, but they're equipped with private bath. Rates are 3,979 pesos ($7.95) single, 4,974 pesos ($9.95) double.

Coming in from the highway, follow the road almost to its end at the beach and you'll see the **Hotel Tropical** (tel. 333/7-0020) on the right-hand side. This is Barra's fancy address, with well-equipped, sea-view rooms going for 6,647 pesos ($13.30) single, 8,309 pesos ($16.60) double.

As for food, it's pretty much catch-as-catch-can in this little place. Very basic eateries will provide for your needs, or you can do what most visitors do: pick up picnic goods and make your own meals.

READER'S FOOD AND LODGING SELECTIONS: "The **Hotel San Lorenzo**—come in on the highway, turn left on the street that the Banco de México Somex is on (I didn't see any street signs), go one block. It's clean, and costs 2,300 pesos ($4.60) single, 2,875 pesos ($5.75) double, 4,025 pesos ($8.05) for a four-person room. The water is a little sporadic, but generally seems to be working in *some* rooms at any given time. . . . **Eloy's** was our favorite restaurant. It's on the same street as the Tropical. The friendly owner speaks enough English to recite the menu with his recommendations. The squid and huachinango (red snapper) were delicious at 1,300 pesos ($2.60) each" (Susan Bates-Harbuck, Sandpoint, Idaho).

ONWARD TO MANZANILLO: At Barra, Hwy. 80 heads up into the hills of Guadalajara, but if you're bound ever southward in your tour of Mexican Pacific Coast resorts, start for Manzanillo, about 30 miles down the road. On the way you'll pass Playa de Oro and Manzanillo's airport (which is actually midway between Barra and Manzanillo), then Santiago, then the fabulous Las Hadas resort complex, then the Las Brisas district, and finally you'll pull into the city itself.

6. Manzanillo to Playa Azul

MANZANILLO: In the 17th century Manzanillo's major role was that of a harbor for segments of the Spanish fleet, and it was from there, in 1654, that galleons set off to conquer the Philippines. Today, Manzanillo, Colima (pop. 36,000), relies on fishing and a fairly thriving resort business from Mexican tourists.

The town, which is rather less attractive than you might expect, is situated at one end of a seven-mile-long curving beach, the Playa Azul, whose northern terminus is the Santiago Peninsula. In Santiago are located some beautiful private homes as well as the best hotel in the area, the Hotel Playa de Santiago. There are two lagoons, one almost behind the city and the other behind the beach. A bus runs from town to Santiago every 20 minutes and it's a pleasant area in which to stay, if you don't mind being seven miles from downtown life and shopping.

Downtown activity centers around the plaza, which is separated from the waterfront by railroad and ship yards. The plaza sports a brilliant poinciana tree, whose red blossoms always seem to be in bloom, and a kiosk serving all kinds of delicious fruit drinks *(licuados)*.

In the daytime, the major attractions are the beaches, of course. **La Audiencia Beach,** on the way to Santiago, offers the best swimming, but **San Pedrito,** shallow for a long way out, is the most popular because it is much nearer the downtown area. The major part of the Playa Azul drops off a little too steeply for safe swimming, and is not recommended for waders.

Taxis don't have meters in Manzanillo, so agree on the price in advance before you set out on any ambitious trips. Much cheaper are the local buses (called *camionetas*). These make a circuit back along the lagoon behind the downtown area, and out along the Bay of Manzanillo to the Santiago Peninsula. This is a lovely way to see the coast and the cost is only a few pesos.

Manzanillo is famous for its fishing—marlin, sailfish, dolphin, sea bass, and manta ray—and competitions are held in late November and late January. Many charter boats are available along the waterfront.

Getting to and from Manzanillo

A good list of choices by all three means:

By Bus: You rarely go wrong riding a bus run by Tres Estrellas de Oro or one of the other big lines such as Transportes Norte de Sonora or Transportes del Pacifico. They all run daily buses to Manzanillo from Guadalajara and Mexico City. Other lines operating to Manzanillo out of Guadalajara include Flecha Amarilla, Autobuses de la Piedad, and Transportes Unidos de la Costa, although a reader advises us that the last-mentioned line makes no rest stops in the six-hour drive, and several of its drivers fancy themselves the Latin incarnation of Emerson Fittipaldi. If in doubt, you can always go . . .

By Train: A train leaves Guadalajara's main station every morning and heads toward the Pacific, stopping at Colima (see Chapter IV), to Manzanillo.

By Plane: AeroMéxico has daily flights from Guadalajara and Mexico City to Manzanillo, and also three flights a week to and from Los Angeles. The Manzanillo office of AeroMéxico, and of Continental, is in the Centro Comercial "Carrillo Puerto" on Avenida México (tel. 333/2-1267 or 2-1711). Mexicana is at Avenida México 382.

Arriving in Manzanillo

Manzanillo's **Central Camionera** (bus station) is located east of town just off the road to Colima. Follow Hidalgo east till you come to Galeana, and the Camionera will be off to the right.

The **airport** is quite a way northwest of town, at a place called Playa de Oro.

The **Tourism Office** (tel. 333/2-2090) is at Avenida Juárez 111 (fourth floor), corner of 21 de Marzo, open 9 a.m. to 3 p.m. daily except Sunday.

If you need a **laundromat,** there's one at the junction of the Manzanillo-Las Brisas-Santiago roads called Lavandería Automática Gissy (that's "*Hee*-see"), in a little complex of shops.

Hotels in Downtown Manzanillo

The strip of coastline on which Manzanillo is located can be divided into three areas: **downtown,** with its shops, markets, and continual activity; **Las Brisas,** the motel-lined beach area immediately to the north of the city; and **Santiago,** which is virtually a suburb situated at the northern end of Playa Azul. All areas are reasonably convenient to one another by either bus or taxi. *Note:* Reservations are recommended for the Christmas and New Year holidays.

Downtown Hotels: In the downtown area, one place to stay is the **Hotel Colonial,** Calle México 100 and Gonzales Bocanegra, one short block inland from the center of the main square (tel. 333/2-1080 or 2-1134). It's a fairly involved colonial-style affair, much carved, beamed, and chandeliered. It lists its well-furnished rooms for 4,140 to 4,600 pesos ($8.30 to $9.20) single, 4,600 to 5,175 pesos ($9.20 to $10.35) double.

At the east end of the plaza is the four-story, 46-room **Hotel Miramar,** Juárez 122 (tel. 333/2-1008). Although the rates—2,500 pesos ($5) single, 3,500 pesos ($7) double—are reasonable enough, one drawback is that only some of the rooms have ceiling fans. While you can get by without this convenience in breezy Las Brisas, the hotter nights downtown can be decidedly uncomfortable. Rooms are clean, if worn, and all have bath (although you may lack a toilet seat).

With prices the way they are in Manzanillo, the **Hotel Savoy** (tel. 333/2-0754) may be just the place to stay. I'll warn you at the outset that this is the sort of hotel where one screws in the light bulb to turn on the light. But that having been said, here's the good part: many of the rooms higher in the building have beautiful views of the city and the harbor, and prices are reasonable, with singles and doubles at 3,220 pesos ($6.40). The Savoy is at Carrillo Puerto 60, at the southwest corner of the plaza.

The **Hotel Flamingos,** at Madero and 10 de Mayo (tel. 333/2-1037), is one short block off the main plaza, across the street from a hospital. The ample rooms are fairly clean and bright, and rent for 2,865 pesos ($5.75) single, 4,255 pesos ($8.50) double.

Hotels at Las Brisas

Buses run out to Las Brisas from downtown. Look for "Brisas Direc" on the signboard. It's a six-mile trundle around Manzanillo Bay, ultimately curving southward. You're not all that far from town here—except that town is across the bay.

If you decide to stay in Las Brisas, your best choice is the tree-shaded, pink stucco **Hotel La Posada** (tel. 333/2-2404), which is built around a large arch that leads to a broad, tile patio looking out on the sea and beach. Inside are 24 rooms with natural brick walls and simple but very tasteful furnishings. The cost is 20,010 pesos ($40) double, breakfast included. For reservations, write to Apdo. Postal 135, Manzanillo, Colima, México.

A little farther up the beach is **Club Vacacional Las Brisas** (tel. 333/2-1951), a collection of 21 attractive bungalows with kitchenettes, recently reconstructed. Of these, 16 fit six people and five accommodate four. The bungalows rent for 13,800 pesos ($27.60) with two beds. Parking, large pool, well-kept grounds—a good choice. For reservations write Avenida L. Cárdenas s/n, Fracc. Las Brisas.

The eight units of the **Bungalows Jaragua** (no phone) all face the beach through floor-to-ceiling glass louvers, and have clean tile floors. Outside, the building is notable for its wood louvers to deflect the sun, small swimming pool, pastel walls, and spiral staircase on the corner. Rates for a day are 10,000 pesos ($20) double; for one month, 100,000 ($200).

Hotels in Santiago

Three miles north of Las Brisas is the peninsula and village of Santiago, which is home to several other hostelries. Three hotels range in price from splurge level to budget. **Hotel Playa de Santiago** (tel. 333/3-0055) is gorgeous and overpriced: singles are 9,200 pesos ($18.40); doubles, 11,500 pesos ($23). Services include free parking, a swimming pool, restaurant, convention room, and an assortment of activities. It's located at the end of the road along Santiago Bay. You'll enjoy the playroom for children, and the spacious grounds, too.

Right next to the Hotel Playa de Santiago is the new **Hotel Marlin** (also spelled Marlyn) (tel. 333/3-0107; Apdo. Postal 288). White, breezy, and open, it's right on the beach, and has a nice little swimming pool and beachfront café. You pay a few dollars more for rooms with a sea view: these cost 4,000 pesos ($8) single, 4,500 to 8,000 pesos ($9 to $16) double. If you're willing to look at the street instead, a reduction is in order.

You'll notice the old **Hotel Anita** (tel. 333/3-0161) next to the Marlin. Although it's the oldest and most well-worn of the lot here, some rooms are still suitable, especially for 2,300 pesos ($4.60) single and 3,700 pesos ($7.40) double.

Eating in Manzanillo

The dining room of the **Hotel Colonial,** Calle México 100, at the corner of Bocanegra, offers a 1,127-peso ($2.65) lunch (comida) which is excellent and usually includes some sort of fish appetizer as well as a choice of fish entree. À la carte entrees range from 1,000 to 4,000 pesos ($2.50 to $8) in the evening.

The **Chantilly,** at the corner of Juárez and Madero, across from the plaza, has a large international menu with good cheap food. Hamburgers range from 375 to 600 pesos (75¢ to $1.20); fried fish plates are twice as much. They also have safe-to-eat ice cream. Club sandwiches, carne asada à la Tampiqueña, vegetable salads—the menu is wonderfully eclectic, and the place is dependably good.

On the southwest corner of the main plaza is Restaurant Babieca at Balvino Davalos 25, a modern and even vaguely stylish place (for Manzanillo) where you can get a hamburger and soft drink for less than 850 pesos ($1.70).

The **Restaurant Savoy,** in the hotel of the same name at the southwest corner of the plaza, is as unpretentious as the hotel, which is to say pretty darn unpretentious. But it does have white tablecloths (well, not precisely white), full breakfasts for 400 pesos (80¢), and lunches or suppers for less than double that amount.

On Sunday, **El Camaron Despierto,** in the shopping mall off Avenida Cuauhtémoc between Avenidas México and Puerto, serves a delicious paella for 1,000 pesos ($2.50). Outside, the locals sit and sip beverages. Inside, leather-strapped wooden chairs with high backs face tables with checkered tablecloths. A fish dinner costs 1,000 pesos ($2.50) and shrimp is 1,600 pesos ($3.20), or have a sandwich and a beer for 500 pesos ($1).

Eating at Las Brisas

El Sombrero, owned by Carmen and Otto Meyer, is one of the cheeriest restaurants in all of Mexico. The setting is simple but attractive, being in a palapa (thatched "hut"), and the food is Mexican and delicious (nothing outrageously spicy): three enchiladas will cost you 600 pesos ($1.20), quesadillas (the cheese-filled wheat tortillas) are 600 pesos ($1.20), or the filling hominy-and-meat stew called pozole is 450 pesos (90¢). El Sombrero is open only in the evenings from 7 p.m. to 11 p.m. It's right near the end of the bus line—turn down the street by the old Ralph's Super, following signs to the Hospital Naval.

Las Hadas

Brainchild of the South American entrepreneur Antenor Patino, Las Hadas is a self-contained little jet-set Eden with its own hotel and condominiums, three restaurants, four bars, two pools, a marina, a golf course, and lots of posh shops. Having done a somewhat languid business for years, Las Hadas got a boost when it figured prominently in the movie *10,* Bo Derek's sensational picture. Whether the boost will be long lasting remains to be seen. But you can have a look around this fascinating resort-cum-movie set; go out Hwy. 80 to Santiago Bay, turn left at the golf course (follow the signs to "Club Las Hadas"), and then left again at the sign to El Tesoro. Buses ("Las Hadas") run out from town.

HEADING SOUTHEAST: Highway 200 is now complete between Manzanillo and the resort towns to the southeast, Playa Azul, Barra de Navidad, and Ixtapa-Zihuatanejo. This used to be a bad stretch of unpaved road, washed-out bridges (in the rainy season from May to October), and no gas stations. Now it is reportedly fine, a nice new highway with sufficient services along all its length.

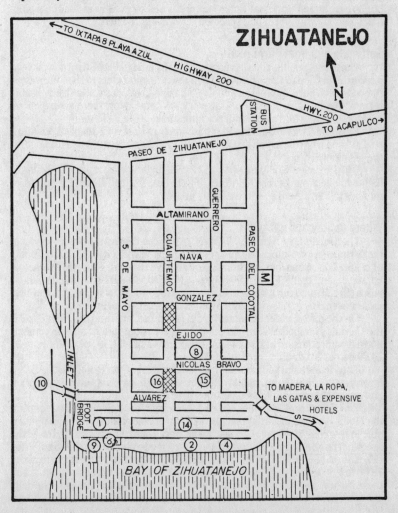

PLAYA AZUL: Playa Azul (pop. 6,000) is Michoacán's entry into the offbeat tropical paradise derby. Facing open ocean rather than a bay, the town lies on a coastal plain dominated by row after row of magnificent coconut palms. The highway from Uruapán is good, but it's literally one curve after another for its entire 147-mile length to the coast. At some point in the future Playa Azul will very possibly experience a tourist boom, but until then it figures to remain off the "gran turismo" circuit. There are no phones, bus service is irregular, and you have to take pot luck on cabs that originate from sitios (cab stands) in neighboring towns.

But I don't want to depict Playa Azul as the sort of primitive place that only Albert Schweitzer could have appreciated. Although luxury accommodations have only recently come to Playa Azul, prices are high enough to make you think they've been there and building trade for decades. Who knows? What with the rage of development in Ixtapa-Zihuatanejo, the crowds may fill the hotels here soon. Note that things are pretty sleepy here in the summertime, and hotels are running at half speed on service and facilities.

Getting to and from Playa Azul

Those using public transport and coming by land to Playa Azul may have to pass through Ciudad Lázaro Cárdenas, a town 20 kilometers to the southeast of Playa Azul. Until a number of years ago Lázaro Cárdenas was a sleepy fishing town with a mañana mood, but discovery has come. Now there are expensive oceanfront hotels and a steel mill belching smoke.

By Bus: Tres Estrellas runs four buses daily to Lázaro Cárdenas from Mexico City, and from there you take a local bus for a 30-minute trip or a minibus for the 15-minute trip.

By Air: Líneas Coaloman (tel. 452/3-5990 in Uruapán) makes daily Cessna flights to and from Lázaro Cárdenas. Flight time is a half hour. Take a bus or minibus to Playa Azul as noted directly above.

Where to Stay and Eat

The **Hotel Playa Azul** (tel. 743/6-0024), in the center of town, is a sympathetic three-story complex with 80 rooms equipped with either air conditioning or ceiling fans, clean and functional. Rooms have two beds each, and perpetual hot water, and cost 5,175 to 6,900 pesos ($10.35 to $13.80) single, 5,750 to 8,050 pesos ($11.50 to $16.10) double. The ocean is 500 yards away, but the *powerful undertow* makes it sort of unsafe. Swim in the hotel's pool instead.

On the paved street between the old Hotel La Loma and the Playa Azul is the **Casa de Huespedes Silva** (no phone), where rooms are small, the cement-floored bathrooms are also small, and the price is a small 1,500 pesos ($3) single, 2,000 pesos ($4) double.

The **Hotel Delfin** (no phone), half a block west of the Hotel Playa Azul, is newish, mustard-colored, filled with palms and banana plants around the pool, and reasonably priced at 4,500 pesos ($9), single or double.

The **Restaurant Marthita**, around the corner and down a side street from the Hotel Playa Azul, is the type of small-town diner that still seems comfortable in this coastal village. No beachfront prices here, and the fish is fresh: the señora even showed me her catch and asked me to choose what I liked! Price depends on your selection, but most seafood meals served here come to about 1,000 to 1,800 pesos ($2 to $3.60). Lobster, the only really expensive item, is half the price here that it is in most restaurants. You can get steak here too. The daily comida corrida costs 1,000 pesos ($2).

The palapa-type eateries on the beach, once to be found in every Pacific Coast town, are still thriving (as of this writing) in Playa Azul. Straw thatched roofs, dirt floors, and surrounding coconut palms create a South Seas atmosphere. Prices should be dirt-cheap, but in fact turn out to be moderate.

As for swimming, remember that the beaches here front on open surf—not on sheltered bays as in Acapulco—and therefore there is a constant, *deadly danger of undertow.* Don't go too far out. By the time you realize what's happened, it's too late.

7. Ixtapa-Zihuatanejo

As modern road and air communications expand throughout Mexico, the secluded hideaways that made the Pacific Coast an intrepid tourist's dream-come-true are being discovered en masse. Such is the fate of Zihuatanejo, in the state of Guerrero, a town that shut off its electricity at 11 p.m. only a few years ago. Now the lights are on 24 hours a day, and the primitive airstrip has been turned into a jetport welcoming daily flights from Mexico City, only 1¾ hours away by air. The draw is not Zihuatanejo itself so much as it is Ixtapa, sister development to Cancún, a planned resort catering to the charter crowd at a beautiful spot ten kilometers northwest of Zihuatanejo.

In 1972 Zihuatanejo had a population of about 4,000 souls; now it is over 16,000. Pardon me if I regret the passing of Zihuatanejo's innocence. In my view there are plenty of super-expensive tourist complexes in Mexico—Acapulco, Manzanillo, Cancún, Cozumel—but fewer and fewer beautiful little seaside villages good for budget travelers.

The coast road from Acapulco or Playa Azul is new, good, and fairly fast. Zihuatanejo itself is absolutely beautiful. The beach curves around a small, natural bay in which fishing boats and an occasional sailboat bob at anchor, and in the town there's still a feeling of village life despite the boom.

Special Note: During the winter season from mid-December through mid-April, the rooms in Zihuatanejo are *all filled, every day.* February seems to be the worst month of all for finding rooms. If you can't get reservations and you want to chance it, get to town as early in the day as possible and find a room, any room. Then, with more time, you can search for the room that suits you best.

If there are simply no rooms vacant, you'll have to search in high-priced Ixtapa (see below), or—worse—in the next town (Petatlán) along the road, 22 miles to the southeast.

GETTING TO ZIHUATANEJO: Buses from Acapulco, Lázaro Cárdenas/Playa Azul, and Uruapán; planes from Mexico City.

By Bus

Three Estrella de Oro buses run daily from Acapulco, two express and one first-class (normal) service. Flecha Roja has buses every hour on the hour. See below under "Getting to Acapulco" for more details.

When you leave Zihuatanejo, you can choose from three departures per day to Acapulco by Estrella de Oro; six departures daily to Lázaro Cárdenas and Uruapán by Tres Estrellas and Autobuses del Occidente. Flecha Roja buses to Acapulco leave each half hour from 4 a.m. to 10 p.m., plus a bus at 11 p.m. and one at midnight. Flecha Roja is by far the less desirable line.

Note: The Tres Estrella de Oro bus station (tickets and information) is on Ejido near the intersection of Guerrero, although you board the buses on Paseo del Cocotal at Ejido. The rest of the bus lines operate from the bus station on Paseo de Zihuatanejo.

By Air

AeroMéxico has four daily flights from Mexico City to Ixtapa-Zihuatanejo, from early in the morning to late in the evening. Mexicana has one morning and one early-evening flight from the capital to Zihuatanejo. Offices are in these locations: Calle Juan N. Alvarez 34 (tel. 743/4-2018); Centro Comercial "La Puerta" (tel. 743/4-2929); Cinco de Mayo 14 (tel. 743/3-0853).

Mexicana has the same number of daily flights. In Zihuatanejo, they're at Vicente Guerrero and Nicolás Bravo (tel. 743/4-2208).

WHERE TO STAY: Even though it is no longer a sleepy little fishing village, almost everything in Zihuatanejo is either on the main street (which runs from the highway to the beach through the center of town), or on the beach itself. The more expensive hotels and nightspots are a 20-minute walk from the main street.

The hotels and pensions near the Playa Principal (main beach) are some of the best low-budget beachfront buys left on the Pacific. The beaches themselves, as yet unladen with touristic trappings such as parachutes, horses, and motorized water toys, are a real pleasure for the plain old sunbather, swimmer, or snorkler.

An old budget standard is the **Hotel Raúl Tres Marias (10)** (tel. 743/4-2191), all the way at the west end of town just past the boat dock and over a wooden footbridge. The hotel was here a decade ago when Zihuatanejo was at the end of a dirt road; like the village, the hotel has grown, but it retains the same friendly atmosphere of previous years. There are 25 rooms, and from here you can see the whole town. The rooms are very bare and simple but bright and clean; all have a shower and rent for 2,500 pesos ($5) single, 3,500 pesos ($7) double, in summer. For this you get screens, a fan, and the largest bar of complimentary soap I have ever seen in any hotel anywhere. To get there from the bus station, walk down the main street to the beach, turn right onto the last street before the beach proper, and follow it to the end. The only disadvantage of the hotel is that it's not directly on the beach.

On down the beach is the **Hotel Avila (4)** (tel. 743/4-2010), quite nice but decidedly overpriced. The 25 rooms are all fairly attractive and equipped with showers and ceiling fans, and the porch-patio opening onto the main beach is a luxury. Upstairs rooms, considered more desirable, are 7,600 pesos ($15.20) single, 9,250 pesos ($18.50) double in winter. Downstairs rooms are a bit more reasonable at 6,950 pesos ($13.90) single, 8,600 pesos ($17.20) double in winter. Bargain for the price of your room here in summer.

Right around the corner from the Avila on Vincente Guerrero are two modest hotels each offering 14 bright rooms with fans. **Hotel Susy**, at V. Guerrero 1 (tel. 743/4-2339), has singles for 5,000 pesos ($10) and doubles for 7,000 pesos ($14). Next door, **Posada Citlali** (tel. 743/4-2043) has smaller rooms and thus, smaller prices of 4,000 pesos ($8) single and 6,000 pesos ($12) double.

Another hotel not on the ocean, but within running distance, is the **Hotel El Dorado (14)** (tel. 743/4-2052). The El Dorado is half a block from the beach, just up from the square. Singles are the regulation 3,500 pesos ($7); doubles, 5,000 pesos ($10). A warning is in order here: check to see that your ceiling fan works before taking the room.

The small, plain **Hotel Flores** (tel. 743/4-2252), has 29 small, bare, clean rooms with private baths and ceiling fans—and prices a bit higher than they should be. Double rooms here cost 3,000 pesos ($6) on "first ask," but if you turn away you may just get another, lower, quotation. The pleasant couple who run the Flores are not unreasonable. You'll find the hotel back from the beach more or less on the road to the expensive hotels mentioned below.

At the **Casa Aurora (8),** on Nicolás Bravo (no phone), two people pay 5,000 pesos ($10) in summer, 6,000 pesos ($12) in winter, for a small and rather airless room away from the beach (only a few minutes away, though). Some rooms are better than others—check before you buy.

The High-Rent District

Separated from each other only by a craggy shoreline are the two other beaches accessible by road. The next one, Playa Madera, holds several small resort hotels, which are at the top limit of our housing budget.

At the **Hotel Posada Caracol** (tel. 743/4-2035), the 57 rooms are mostly air-conditioned, and other extra services (two restaurants, a small nightclub, two pools, etc.) bring the room prices to 8,050 pesos ($16.10) single and 11,500 pesos ($23) double.

Slightly farther along the coast from the center of Zihuatanejo is Playa La Ropa, and two more hotels that make sense to explore during the summer slow season. The 26-room **Hotel Catalina** (tel. 743/4-2137 or 4-2032) is the smaller of the two, with less variety in its collection of rooms. For 4,000 to 5,200 pesos ($8 to $10.40) single, 5,200 to 6,400 pesos ($10.40 to $12.80) double, 7,600 pesos ($15.20) triple, you'll have a room with private bath "cooled by refreshing sea breezes" (that is, without fan or air conditioner). For another 5,600 pesos ($11.20) per person you can have breakfast and dinner each day. The Catalina's sister hotel next door is the larger (44-room) **Hotel Sotavento** (same phones as Catalina), with three categories of rooms. The best rooms are in the newer building with the best sea views; cheapest are the older, bare rooms, which at least get you a place to sleep near the beach. Summer prices here range from 8,000 to 9,200 pesos ($16 to $18.40) single, 10,000 to 11,200 pesos ($20 to $22.40) double, 13,200 pesos ($26.40) triple. I should mention that there are only three rooms at the very lowest prices. An extra bed costs 2,000 pesos ($4). For best value, get three or four people together and rent a triple (with an extra bed, if needed). Rooms at the Sotavento have fans and private baths; a few are air-conditioned.

Finally, farthest away from town to the southeast, is Playa Las Gatas. Least "touristy" of all the beaches, Las Gatas bears a collection of modest houses and beach shacks as well as the rather posh **Las Gatas Beach Club.** Consider this one only if you're coming in summer, as winter rates are about 25,875 pesos ($51.75) per person, and a minimum stay of three days is often required. You're a longish way from town here too, although launches ply the seas between Las Gatas and Zihuatanejo throughout the day.

Staying at Ixtapa

Strictly speaking, a place like Ixtapa has no place in a book such as this, but just so you'll know: the lowest priced hotel rents its cheapest double room for about 22,500 pesos ($45) *during the summer;* winter rates are a lot higher. Ixtapa was built for the charter tour or package tour visitor, and is really enjoyable only if you buy an all-inclusive package, which will be expensive, but actually a lot cheaper than making all the separate arrangements for flight, hotel, and meals yourself. By all means, don't wander into one of the fancy hotels and ask for a room for a night or two. "Rack rates," the prices given to the casual, un-programmed guest, are the highest rates ever charged by any hotel. Buy a package if you buy at all.

There's nothing to stop you from having a look, and there's no reason why you can't put on your best tatami-sandals and mingle with the beach crowd there —an empty lounge chair is an invitation to sit down. In fact, you shouldn't miss having a look as the situation of Ixtapa is simply magnificent.

Local buses trundle between the two towns of Zihuatanejo and Ixtapa frequently (buses leave from across the market in Zihuatanejo). As you come up over the rise from Zihuatanejo, the bay of Ixtapa is spread out before you. If you've ever had dreams of paradise, they'll probably coincide with what you see. Palms line the wide beach which fronts a sea always alive with surf. The high-rise hotels are very new, modern, and ever increasing in number. Although plans call for a total of 16 high-rises, not all have gone up to date. You'll ride along past the hotels, through well-kept grounds and a golf course, and if you get the feeling you're outclassed, remember this: all beaches in Mexico are public property, open to everyone.

READERS' HOTEL SELECTIONS: "After one night at the Hotel Irma (nice but more expensive than we expected), we found **Bungalows Allec** on Playa Madera (tel. 743/4-2002). These are two-bedroom units built terrace-like so each unit has a sea view. Right on the beach, we had cooking facilities and most obliging hosts: Klaus and Nickolaus Errodt, Germans who speak excellent English. Cost of the apartment for four people was 22,500 pesos ($45) which includes breakfast." (Mrs. F. E. Shields, Victoria, B.C., Canada). . . . "The **Posada Colve,** Hermenegildo Galeana no. 5 (tel. 743/4-2047), is a new casa de huespedes, very clean, with ten large rooms, some with three or four beds, and fans, good for families. It's right next to the Larga Distancia (long-distance telephone office) in the center of town" (Liz Fraser, Vancouver, B.C., Canada).

WHERE TO EAT:
The days are gone when Zihuatenejo offered only beach-shack seafood stands or bus station greasy spoons. Besides the hotel restaurants, there are a number of attractive places to dine. **La Bocana (2),** close to where the main street hits the beach, is a reasonably priced restaurant serving red snapper for 1,500 pesos ($3), half a chicken for the same, beef entrees for 1,600 pesos ($3.20), snails for the same. You dine inside the restaurant or on the open patio, with the romance of native recorded music in the background, and at some seasons, unfortunately, the hum of lazy afternoon flies. When I last ate here, a light lunch for two consisting of one ceviche, a big salad (which was shared), a plate of red snapper, three beers, and one coffee, came to 4,000 pesos ($8).

A block down, but on the beach, is the **Canaima (6).** The view is through airy wrought-iron or bamboo "walls" to the beach, and you get full benefit of the breeze. The snapper here is excellent, and a meal of snapper filet, oyster cocktail, beer, coffee, and dessert will cost 4,700 pesos ($9.40). By the way, you must enter the Canaima from near the beach; if you enter from the street, that's a totally different restaurant, called the Taboga.

The **Kapi-Cofi (16),** once highly recommended in this book, is not the bright and shiny place it was a few years ago. Still, the blessed cool from the air conditioner packs 'em in during the hot months, and the omelets, sandwiches, hamburgers, and full breakfasts are reasonably priced from 450 to 600 pesos (90¢ to $1.20); a daily set-price lunch goes for 700 pesos ($1.40).

Besides the hotel restaurants on Madera Beach, this area has one other appealing eatery. The **Kon-Tiki,** across the street from the Hotel Posada Caracol, is a fun pizza place up the hill overlooking the beach. An average price for any of the 12 types of pizzas is 2,300 pesos ($4.60); shish kebab is 2,500 pesos ($5); a big vegetable salad is 750 pesos ($1.50). It's open 2 to 11 p.m. I have but one question: How does a pizza-and-hamburger joint in Zihuatanejo, Mexico, get the name Kon-Tiki?

More Elegant Dining
Zihuatanejo has fortunately retained the village flavor and still managed to attract a few unobtrusive high-budget restaurants. **La Mesa del Capitán (15),**

Nicolás Bravo 18 (tel. 4-2027), is simply furnished with dark wooden chairs and tables. The extensive menu includes such entrees as shrimp, natural or sweet-and-sour, for 3,700 pesos ($7.40); fish for 2,200 to 2,400 pesos ($4.40 to $4.80); and T-bone steak for 2,950 pesos ($5.90). All meat orders come with a delicious baked potato with lots of tasty cheese. La Mesa serves from 2 p.m. until midnight.

Coconuts, at V. Guerrero 4 (tel. 4-2518), is about the most expensive independent (non-hotel) restaurant in town. It's very atmospheric, however, to dine al fresco under twinkling, white lights in the lush garden setting. You can order red snapper sautéed or fried, 2,900 to 3,600 pesos ($5.80 to $7.20), or shrimp, prepared a variety of ways, for 3,800 to 4,200 pesos ($7.60 to $8.40). With drinks, appetizer, and dessert, your bill for two could easily run 12,000 pesos ($24). If you're not hungry, stop for a drink in the adjoining bar which is usually full.

With the burgeoning of Ixtapa, Zihuatanejo has seen even more expensive restaurants open up. Mariano's, Don Juan, etc., all will serve you decent meals in pleasant surroundings, but for about 4,400 to 6,600 pesos ($8.80 to $13.20) per person. They can get these prices because (1) their clients are mostly from Ixtapa, (2) they're all on short but expensive vacations.

Cheap Eats

As always in Mexican towns, there's one place where the food is always basic but tasty, and the prices are dependably low: the **central market.** Located on **Paseo del Cocotal (M),** Zihuatanejo's market has been nicely fixed up in recent years (at least, over what it was before). Local señoras always set up rough-and-ready cookshops to serve the villagers who come to market daily. The food is best at lunchtime, as most marketing is finished by early afternoon. A big bowl of pozole (meat-and-hominy stew), grilled chicken, or tacos is sure to be filling, and $2 is about all you'll have to spend.

For another inexpensive snack location, walk down to **Calle Ejido** between Cuauhtémoc and Guerrero, where rows of little taco shops line the street. Their savory concoctions satisfy tourist and local alike, for about 200 pesos (40¢) apiece. Also here is the **Expendio de Pan "El Buen Gusto,"** a bakery sales shop, and a juguería (juice stand)—in short, all you need for a low-budget feast.

BEACHES: Besides the tranquil town beach, there are three other main beaches. The town is protected from the main surge of the Pacific, but the **Madera** beach (below the Madera Hotel) and **La Ropa** beach (below the Catalina Hotel) are both open to the surf. La Ropa is the largest and most beautiful beach on the bay, and buses run to it, leaving from near the market (M).

Along a rocky seaside path that leads from La Ropa is **Las Gatas,** which is unusually beautiful and secluded. You might plan a splurge-type lunch here, as there are several open-air restaurants specializing in red snapper, clams, oysters, and lobster.

For those not up to the walk around the bay, charter boats are available to take you to Las Gatas and pick you up later in the day. For fares, see the price list posted at the **Embarcadero (9).** Theoretically, you can specify at what hour you wish to be picked up, but just remember that Mexicans are not noted for watching the clock very closely.

There is a fourth beach on the bay, about a third of a mile to the north, and accessible either by boat or footpath. Nestled between stone cliffs, and only about 100 yards wide, it is composed entirely of large stone blocks blocking the mouth of a (usually dry) river.

Bigger boats are available at the town pier for more adventurous expeditions: for instance, you can combine deep-sea fishing with a visit to the near-deserted ocean beaches that extend for miles along the coast from Zihuatanejo. As a final note, you might want to explore the small islands to the north, accessible only by boat, and noted for two small secluded beaches which make them a favorite day-excursion.

The most popular is **Ixtapa Island,** about ten miles from the mainland. Here are golden sand beaches and brilliant blue water joined to an unfenced wildlife "park" filled with exotic birds and animals. The one restaurant there is expensive, but good. The excursion launch going to Ixtapa Island from Zihuatanejo is expensive too. It stays all day, returning to the Embarcadero by 5 p.m. You might want to go to the Ixtapa Resort area or Playa Quieta and scout around for launches leaving from there for Ixtapa Island—sometimes they do, and they cost less.

Another of the main islands, **Morro de los Pericos,** is known for the great variety of birds that nest on rocky points jutting out into the blue Pacific. You'll have to rent a boat for this one, as outlined above.

ZIHUATANEJO MISCELLANY: The **market (M)** still serves as the place to go for basic food and clothing items, although a few shops now sell stuff in some ways more suitable to the tourist.

Of the nightlife places, **Los Alpes** has a lively jukebox, fluorescent lighting, and the patronage of local young bloods—cover charge is 400 pesos (80¢), and no booze is served. The **Ibiza Discothèque,** on the highway along Playa La Ropa, swings to the beat from 10 p.m. to 4 a.m. with a cover charge of 1,500 pesos ($3).

The drive-in theater has come to Zihuatanejo—well, in a way. The only difference in the theater here is that you walk in rather than drive in, and you sit outside on a bench to watch the movie that is flashed onto the wall of a nearby building, painted white for the purpose. Gather up 200 pesos (40¢) on Saturday night and enjoy a Mexican film here.

The **Tourism Office (1)** is on the beach, Paseo del Pescador, near the municipal pier, open from 9 a.m. to 2 p.m. and 4 to 6 p.m., on Saturday from 9 a.m. to 1 p.m.; closed Sunday. Sr. Hernandez Abaunza here is most helpful.

8. Acapulco

The truly astounding thing about Acapulco (pop. 600,000) is not its perennial romantic reputation—or even its jet-set status—but its variety. To a local businessman, staunch member of the Lions Club, Acapulco is probably as thrilling as Dubuque. To the "beautiful people," Acapulco is an exciting playground. To the aware traveler, Acapulco is not only a bustling commercial center and jet-set haven but one of those fascinating multiracial localities on the order of Trinidad and Rio. In most of Mexico, the prevailing ethnic mix is Spanish-Indian; in Acapulco it's Afro-Spanish-Indian. And this adds an extra dimension to Acapulco's charm.

A word about climate. Although it's fashionable to talk about six dry months and six wet months here, this is an oversimplification. June—when the rains begin—is extremely wet, but July and August considerably less so. In that interim you have what amounts to a "little dry season." The rains increase in September and October, ending at the beginning of *la seca* (the dry season) in November.

While the city is not typically Mexican, it's futile to indulge in comparisons with other places, such as the French Riviera, the Florida Gold Coast, or whatever. You'll encounter, as you survey local housing, expensive exquisite taste, expensive atrocious taste, drab suburbia, and some of the foulest slums this side of Rio's "favelas." The accent is ever on variety.

Even more than other places in Mexico, Acapulco is what you make of it; and what you make of it depends, to some degree, on how much you spend. Compared to a place like Mexico City, Acapulco's hotels and restaurants charge more and give less: such is the lure of resorts and romance.

I should warn you about street names and numbers in this city: the jumbled maze of streets and alleys that lace the city's hilltops and hillsides are badly marked, if they're marked at all, and street numbers are also hard to find. I've done my best to tell you how to find your way around, but you'll have to ask repeatedly to get to any destination except the most obvious ones.

GETTING TO ACAPULCO: This is an easy task because Acapulco is well served by public transportation. What follows is a brief listing of the major means of conveyance.

By Bus

Remember that buses from Mexico City to Acapulco leave from the Terminal Central de Autobuses del Sur (Metro Taxqueña) and *not* from the giant Central del Norte. The trip to Acapulco costs about 2,800 pesos ($5.60) and takes about seven hours.

Estrella de Oro (tel. 905/549-8520) has hourly buses from Mexico City to Acapulco, but you should try to reserve your seat a few days in advance. (See Chapter VI, "Arriving in Mexico City," for information on making reservations.) Deluxe service costs only about 100 pesos (20¢) more than express service; the difference is a larger bus of equal comfort. As the difference in cost is not much, I'd suggest you pick your bus by departure time (that most convenient for you) and ignore the deluxe or express part of it. All the buses are air-conditioned and have toilets, which may or may not be usable. I might note that the road between Acapulco and Mexico City is pretty curvy and makes for a tedious journey.

Lineas Unidas del Sur / Flecha Roja also runs 24 daily buses to Acapulco from the Central del Sur, but their equipment is not generally up to the same standards as that of Estrella de Oro.

By Air

Acapulco has a *very* busy airport, and there are direct flights between this city and Los Angeles (daily), Atlanta (Eastern Airlines, two per weekend), Chicago (six a day), Dallas / Fort Worth (four a day), New York (two a day), and Guadalajara (daily). All these flights offer special low excursion rates. Operators are AeroMéxico, Eastern, Mexicana, American Airlines, and Western Airlines. There are a dozen flights daily to Mexico City, mostly by AeroMéxico, a few by Mexicana.

ARRIVING IN ACAPULCO: This city has one of the most confusing layouts in Mexico, and it's growing so fast even the natives can't keep up with it.

By Bus

Coming by bus from Taxco or Mexico City, you ride past the new working-class development called Renaissance City (Ciudad Renacimiento), through the seamier parts of town to the north of the hills ringing the bay, but then rise to a pass in these hills for a glorious change from squalor to magnificence. The bus then descends the hills to the station: in the case of Lineas Unidas del Sur /

Flecha Roja (tel. 748-3763), the bus station is in the market area only about six blocks from the zócalo; the Estrella de Oro bus station, however, is at Avenida Cuauhtémoc 1490 (5-5282). Cuauhtémoc is the major artery inland from and roughly parallel to the Costera Aleman. A taxi from the bus station of the Estrella de Oro line to the zócalo will cost about 650 pesos ($1.30); to any of the larger hotels, about the same amount. Local buses pass the terminal in both directions, and are a very inexpensive way of getting to your hotel.

There are several hotels within walking distance of the bus station, and you should be able to get to them even if your luggage is pretty heavy (see below under "Where to Stay").

If these are full, you should know that the bus station runs a service that will help you find a room. Here's how it works: as you get off the bus, men will ask you if you have a hotel room. Say "no," and one will escort you to a telephone. After asking how much you want to pay, he'll make some calls, find a place, get in a cab with you, and take you to it. He gets a commission from the hotel for bringing you there, of course (he'll collect it after you've registered and gone to your room). You must pay for the taxi, and you may tip the hotel-finder if you wish, but you really needn't give him much as he gets that commission from the hotel.

The drawback is that the hotel-finder may aim for a hotel that costs more than you want to pay (his commission is bigger that way), and he'll try to stick to a few hotels that he knows. You may ask him to call a particular hotel that you've chosen from this book. He may oblige, and get you a room there; or he may say "They're full up" after the call, when in fact they may have rooms—you don't do the talking, so you don't know!

Look upon this business not as a scam but as a service for which you pay a service charge. If you don't like the hotel he takes you to, you can always change after one night.

By Air

Acapulco's airport is 14 miles out of town, over the hills lying to the east of the bay. In front of the airport you will see several desks staffed by personnel of the **Transportaciones de Pasajeros** company (tel. 748/5-2332 or 5-2591). They'll sell you a ticket for transportation into town by bus (815 pesos, $1.63, per person), by Volkswagen minibus (1,250 pesos, $2.50, per person), or by taxi (3,500 pesos, $7, for two people, slightly more for three or four). Kids pay half-price. You can, if you like, buy a round-trip ticket for twice the one-way fare.

For your return to the airport at the end of your stay, call the number listed above at least a day (24 hours) in advance of your departure, and make a reservation for a seat back to the airport. The bus, minibus, or car (depending on demand) will pick you up about 90 minutes (domestic flights) or 120 minutes (flights to other countries) before your flight's departure time, and whisk you back to the airport.

GETTING AROUND: Acapulco, the town and its resorts, now stretches for four miles all around the bay, and so walking to see it all is not practical unless you're an Olympic type. Taxis charge between 400 and 1,000 pesos (80¢ and $2) for a ride within the city, more if you go farther out. Before you get a cab, ask to see the list of prices (*lista de precios*) in the dispatcher's booth at the cab stand (*sitio*) to be sure you're paying the legally authorized fare. Report any trouble or overcharges to the Procuraduría del Turista (State Advocates' Office for Tourists, tel. 748/4-6134 or 4-6136), Costera Aleman near Caleta.

For transport in town you'll find the city buses best, and cheapest. Best place near the zócalo to catch buses is beside Sanborn's, two blocks east. "Caleta Directo" buses will take you to Caleta and Caletilla beaches along the Costera Aleman; some buses return along the same route, others ("Caleta Flamingos") go around the southwest side of the peninsula to return to the zócalo. As for the beaches of Hornos, Condesa, and the restaurants and night spots in the posh hotel district to the east, catch a "Cine Río-La Base" bus beside Sanborn's. It'll go along Cuauhtémoc, a block inland and *not* along Costera Aleman, to the Estrella de Oro terminal; it then turns at the terminal and heads down to the beach at the Ritz hotel, turns left, and continues east along Costera Aleman through the Diana Circle, and out past El Presidente. "Zócalo Directo" and "Caleta Directo" buses follow the same route in the opposite direction to get you back to the zócalo or Caleta area.

USEFUL FACTS: Though Acapulco is operated with the foreign tourist in mind, you'll find the following facts essential for saving money, time, and trouble:

Anyone, even perhaps the beggars, will change dollars to pesos for you. But the only places in which you get full value for your dollar are the **banks.** Hours are usually 8:30 or 9 a.m. to 1 or 1:30 p.m., Monday through Friday. Outside of these hours, you can easily change money at casas de cambio (currency exchange booths or offices), restaurants, your hotel, travel agencies, taxi drivers, etc., but you'll lose money on the deal. Try to get to a bank. They're scattered all along the Costera Aleman, with a particularly dense concentration near the zócalo.

The **American Express** representative is at Costera Aleman 709 (tel. 4-6375 or 4-5051).

Acapulco has few **consulates,** but many consular representatives at the ends of telephone lines. Try these: Canada (tel. 5-6621 or 5-4978), United Kingdom (tel. 4-1650 or 4-6605), and U.S.A. (tel. 5-6600 or 3-1969).

The **central post office** is near the zócalo, on Costera Aleman, very near Sanborn's. There's a branch in the Estrella de Oro bus station on Avenida Cuauhtémoc, inland from the Acapulco Ritz hotel; and another branch on Costera Aleman near Caleta beach.

Tourist Information

Acapulco has several tourist offices, but perhaps the most convenient source of an answer to a quick question can be found at one of the little booths scattered along the **Costera Aleman,** staffed from mid-morning till early evening.

The national **Secretaría de Turismo** (SECTUR) office is on Costera Aleman at Río de Camarón (tel. 748/2-2170 or 2-2246), on Hornos beach.

The **State of Guerrero** maintains a tourist office (tel. 748/4-1014) in the state government building on Costera Aleman across from the entrance to CICI, the children's aquatic park. The state also has a **Tourist's Assistance Bureau** (Procuraduría del Turista, tel. 748/4-6134 or 4-6136) on Costera Aleman between the zócalo and Caleta beach.

If you see policemen in uniforms of white and light blue, they're from a special corps of English-speaking Tourist Police.

WHERE TO STAY: I used to recommend mostly small and inexpensive downtown hotels in this section. But with the fall of the peso, numerous hotels out on the beaches have come within our budget (or very close—this is Acapulco!); and the downtown section, like much of Mexico, has seen a slight increase in bothersome petty crime. So I'd now like to recommend two things. First, that

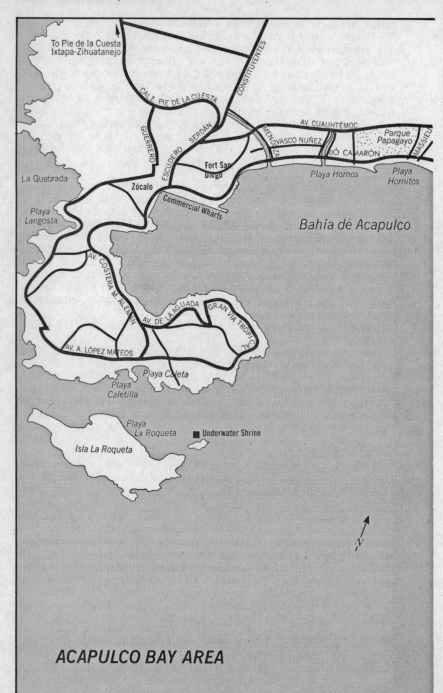

To Pie de la Cuesta
Ixtapa-Zihuatanejo

CALZ. PIE DE LA CUESTA

CONSTITUYENTES

GUERRERO

ESCUDERO

SERDÁN

MENDIZA

AV. CUAUHTÉMOC

VASCO NUÑEZ

RÍO CAMARÓN

MASSIEU

Parque
Papagayo

La Quebrada

Fort San
Diego

Zócalo

Playa Hornos

Playa
Hornitos

Playa
Langosta

Commercial Wharfs

Bahía de Acapulco

AV. COSTERA M. ALEMÁN

AV. DE LA AGUADA

GRAN VIA TROPICAL

AV. A. LÓPEZ MATEOS

Playa Caleta

Playa
Caletilla

Playa
La Roqueta

Underwater Shrine

Isla La Roqueta

N

ACAPULCO BAY AREA

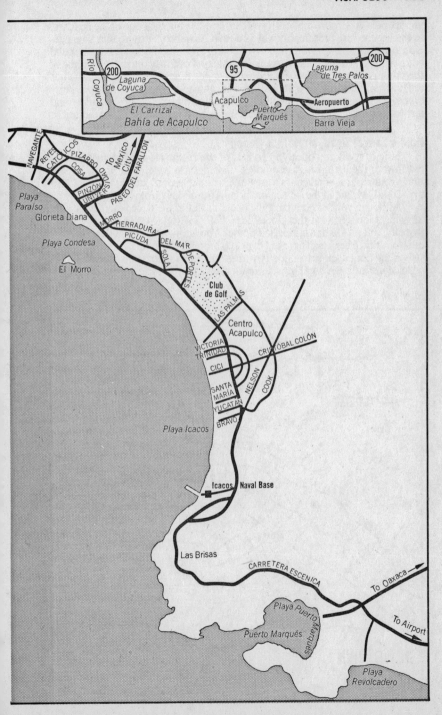

you spend a little more money, if you can, and stay out near one of the beaches, as the beaches are presumably why you're in Acapulco. Second, that if you decide to stay downtown, you choose your hotel carefully. The ones I recommend below should be fine, with no problems (though I can't say the same for some of the other places downtown). The good downtown hotels constitute marvelous lodging bargains, and you should take advantage of them. As for that petty crime, it's actually present in any city (including other parts of Acapulco) and any country, so don't be paranoid, just use normal common sense and caution.

Hotels East of Town, on Hornos Beach

Strictly speaking, once you go east of the zócalo along Costera Aleman, out toward the luxury high-rise hotels, lodgings are largely out of our budget range, but several hotels in this area offer rates that don't do great violence to my $20-a-Day rule in the off-season months from May through October.

Although you may not have the bucks to stay at the Ritz, you may be able to swing a few nights at the **Autotel Ritz,** C.P. 257 (tel. 748/5-8023 or 5-8075), just off Costera Aleman inland half a block from its high-rise namesake on Avenida Wilfrido Massieu. There are over 100 rooms here, in an L-shape around a swimming pool itself surrounded by trees and green arbors and set with tables which constitute the hotel's restaurant, called El Jardín. Elevators take you up

DOWNTOWN ACAPULCO

to the comfortable, almost luxurious modern motel rooms which feature flower boxes on the little balconies (a few of which have sea views—ask for them on the seventh floor). Prices are 13,800 pesos ($27.60) single, 16,100 pesos ($32.20) double, these prices being for the winter season.

Also in this area, a few blocks back from the beach up on the hillside, is the new and shiny **Hotel Villa Rica,** Avenida Universidad at the corner of Avenida Dr. Chavez / Reyes Católicos (tel. 748/5-6024). Front rooms have balconies with grand bay views; all rooms are spacious, tasteful, modern, and air-conditioned. Good, firm beds, a few parking spaces inside the gates, and a quiet location are extras, but the biggest extra of all is the beautiful swimming pool. Prices are a bit high, but the hotel is fairly new: 8,050 pesos ($16.10) single, 9,085 pesos ($18.17) double, in the winter season. If they're not full or if you're staying for a few days, bargain for a reduction.

Near Paraíso Beach

The small **Hotel Jacqueline,** just across the Costera Aleman from the Paraíso Hotel (tel. 748/5-9338), has only a half-dozen rooms, and you must check one out before you check in. All are arranged around a lush little plot of grass and shrubs, and if the room is acceptable to you, you'll pay 5,000 pesos ($10) single, 6,000 pesos ($12) double, with reductions for longer stays.

Every now and then I come upon a small hotel near the expensive beaches such as Paraíso that has incredibly good prices. Such a hotel is the **Hotel del Valle,** Gonzalo G. Espinoza 150, Z.P.7., just off the Costera along the eastern side of Papagayo Park (tel. 748/5-8336 or 5-8388). As you go along the Costera, look for the tiny Hotel Jacqueline and you'll find the Hotel del Valle just behind it. Simple and well kept, the del Valle is a mere half block from Paraíso beach, and charges only 4,025 pesos ($8.05) for a double room with fan, 6,325 pesos ($12.65) for a double with air conditioning. Can't go wrong here.

Near the Bus Station

If you're taking the Estrella de Oro bus to Acapulco from Mexico City or Taxco, you'll be glad to know that there are several budget-to-moderate hotels within easy walking distance of the bus station.

Right behind the Estrella de Oro bus station is the **Hotel Inn** [sic], Calle Alvaro de Amezquita Z10, corner of Wilfrido Massieu/Magellanes (tel. 748/5-8649 or 5-8652). The rooms come with private bath and with fans (no air conditioning), and the hotel has a little swimming pool. A single costs 9,500 pesos ($19), a double is 10,500 pesos ($21).

Just past the aforementioned hotel in the direction of the beach is the Autotel Ritz, described with the hotels near Hornos beach. The Autotel Ritz (not to be confused with its plushy sister establishment, the Ritz Acapulco Hotel) is only 2½ blocks from the bus station, and half a block from the beach.

Near the Glorieta Diana

Up the hill from the traffic circle bearing the statuette of Diana the Huntress is the little **Hotel Paraíso Escondido,** Privada del Caracol 137, Fracc. El Farallon, Acapulco, Gro. 39690 (tel. 748/4-2063). It truly is "secret." Here's how to find it: a block east of the Diana circle is Calle del Morro, heading inland up the hill. Walk or drive up this road past the club called La Condesa (on the right), and turn left. Follow the hotel's signs. Another way is to walk inland from the Diana circle, past the Pemex station (on the left), and take the first street on the right, which goes uphill. Turn left at the first opportunity, which is a dirt track between two walls, at the end of which is a stairway to the hotel. Once you arrive, you'll find a small, simple hotel hugging the hillside. A few rooms have good views, all have ceiling fans and tile shower; some have two double beds. There's a slightly murky little swimming pool. Prices in winter are 6,900 pesos ($13.80) single, 8,050 pesos ($16.10) double, all included.

Near Icacos Beach

These hotels are all in the southeastern reaches of the bay, not far from the Centro Acapulco (convention center), and the Centro Internacional de Convivencia Infantil (CICI), Acapulco's fabulous children's water amusement park.

A few blocks southeast of CICI, toward the airport, is a hotel called Romano's Le Club, on the beach side of Costera Aleman. Right beside Romano's is a little street called Calle Cañonero Bravo, and a half-block down it at no. 5 is the **Hotel Sol-i-Mar,** Fracc. Costa Azul, Acapulco, Gro. 39850 (tel. 748/4-1534 or 4-1356). The hotel is in several two-story neocolonial buildings with lots of brick, tile, and wrought ironwork. Two small swimming pools provide cool dips, though the beach is only a block away. Rates for air-conditioned, bathroom-equipped double rooms are 11,500 pesos ($23) in winter, about 23% less in summer.

Well out toward the eastern limits of the bay is the **Best Western Hotel El Tropicano,** Costera Aleman 510 (tel. 748/4-1100). This motel-style 136-room place has many little extras in the rooms: tub-and-shower combination bath, servi-bar refrigerator, air conditioning, television set. Two swimming pools are located within the hotel's inner courtyard. The hotel is on the landward side of the Costera, but the beach is less than five minutes' walk away. In winter two pay 22,500 pesos ($45) about 25% less in summer.

Right next to CICI is the tidy little **Motel Quinta Mica,** Calle Cristóbal Colón 115, Fracc. Costa Azul, Acapulco, Gro. 39850 (tel. 748/4-0121 or 4-0122). The three-story motel has 25 rooms, each with kitchenette, refrigerator, and air conditioning. A wading pool is provided for kids, and a swimming pool for their parents. The beach is only half a block away. Because you have a kitchenette in your room, the prices here are a bit higher than normal: 15,000 pesos ($30) single, 16,000 pesos ($32) double. When you figure this place against our daily budget, remember that in the kitchenette you'll be able to prepare many of your meals cheaply.

Downtown—On La Quebrada

West of the zócalo and up the hillside to where the famous high divers do their thing stretches a warren of busy little streets where only the occasional resort-wear shop reminds one that Acapulco lives mainly on visitors. The hotels are simple and cheap—much the same standard. The one disadvantage to the Quebrada area is that four times each evening big tour buses roar up the hill for the high divers' act, some leaving their engines running until it's over. The last dive is at 11:30 p.m., so it's not really quiet until midnight. But even so, La Quebrada and neighboring La Paz and Juárez harbor the best buys in the city.

The **Hotel Angelita,** Quebrada 37, Acapulco, Gro. 39300 (tel. 748/3-5734), advertises *limpieza absoluta,* or absolute cleanliness, and that's what you'll find in this bright place. White rooms are adjoined by blue tile baths, all rooms have ceiling fans, and the sympathetic patron charges 4,000 pesos ($8) single, 5,000 pesos ($10) double, 2,000 pesos ($4) per person for triples and quadruples. If you stay any length of time you get a 10% reduction. Recommended.

Right next door is the **Hotel Pachis,** Quebrada 39, Acapulco, Gro. 39300 (tel. 748/2-1256), another clean and tidy place offering rooms with fans for 4,000 pesos ($8) double during the busy winter season, and about the same price during the summer.

At the top of the hill, La Quebrada opens into the Plaza La Quebrada, where you'll see the Hotel El Mirador (described below). You'll also see the older **Hotel El Faro,** Quebrada 83, Acapulco, Gro. 39300 (tel. 748/2-1365 or 2-1366). Once among Acapulco's top hotels (a long time ago), El Faro still has those big old rooms with louvered shutters, and some rooms have big terrace-balconies overlooking the square. The family who run the hotel are friendly and kind, and they charge only 3,328 pesos ($6.65) single, 3,508 pesos ($7.01) double for a room with bath. Look at the room before you register; if it's not exactly what you had in mind, ask to see another.

Perched on the hillside overlooking the Plaza La Quebrada is the tidy **Hotel La Torre Eiffel,** Inalámbrica 110, Acapulco, Gro. 39300 (tel. 748/2-1683). The climb from the plaza up to the hotel is not as long or as wearisome as it looks, except perhaps on blistering summer afternoons. A family-run place, the hotel has a kidney-shaped pool the size of a hot tub and rooms with ceiling fans and private bath for 4,000 pesos ($8) single, 5,000 pesos ($10) double in winter, less in summer.

The Big Splurge

The **Hotel El Mirador,** Quebrada 74, Acapulco, Gro. 39300 (tel. 748/3-1155 or 3-1221), right at the top of the Avenida La Quebrada overlooking the high divers' perch, is in the competent hands of Hoteles El Presidente, the quasi-governmental chain. El Presidente hotels are usually luxurious and therefore expensive, but several members of the chain skirt the upper limits of our daily budget. Especially in summer, you should be able to stay here without going too far overboard—and you'll certainly get your money's worth.

El Mirador is still one of Acapulco's most delightful moderately priced hotels with its walkways and gardens, its various levels of lodgings built into the hillside, its restaurant-bar (La Perla) with spectacular views of the sunset and of the high divers. Rooms cost 17,000 pesos ($34) single, 19,000 pesos ($38) double during the high season, in winter. An extra person in the room pays a low 4,600 pesos ($9.20). One or two children 12 years of age or younger can stay with their parent or parents for no extra charge. These prices do not include meals. In summer, you can expect reductions of 20% to 25% in these prices. For reservations in the U.S., call toll free 800/472-2427.

Downtown—The La Paz Area

La Paz is one of the streets that runs back into the zócalo and it, too, is a good area for budget hotels. Try the **Hotel California,** La Paz 12 (tel. 748/2-2893), where the rooms, built around an open paved patio, all have nice white drapes and Formica furniture (private bath, hot water). Singles here, without meals, cost 6,000 pesos ($12), and doubles run 7,500 pesos ($15), 1,000 pesos ($2) more for air conditioning. You'll find the zócalo and the city bus stops only one block away.

A fine, centrally located budget buy is the **Hotel Colimense,** Iglesias 11 (tel. 748/2-2890). All eight rooms are on the second floor and overlook a shaded courtyard supporting such homey features as swings and rocking chairs. Rooms are clean and well screened with ceiling fans to cut the heat. Rates are 4,000 pesos ($8), single or double.

An older hotel that has been completely—but completely—redone is the **Hotel Mision,** Felipe Valle 12 (tel. 748/2-3643). A dusty and none-too-handsome courtyard has been turned into a wonderland of colonial-style tiles, furniture, arches, all centered on an enormous and magnificent mango tree. In the rooms, the tile washbasin is outside the toilet/shower area, a thoughtful addition. White brick walls, ceiling fans (no air conditioning), and screens are in all rooms, as is constant hot water (so they say). The price is 6,000 pesos ($12) single, 7,000 pesos ($14) double, high for this area, but not for the style of the hotel.

Hotels Out of Town, Near Playa Langosta

If you stand in the zócalo and face the water, to your right the waterfront boulevard called Costera Miguel Aleman will take you to the next budget hotel areas. This peninsula hooks to the south and east, and hotels dot the slopes of its several hills. You can get to the bottom of any hill easily—any bus along Costera Aleman will take you there—but then you must hoof it to the top, or take a cab. But the distances are not really that great, and you get the extra bonus of good views of the bay from the ones higher up. Taxis from the zócalo or anywhere downtown cost a dollar or two to any of these hotels. Take a taxi up with your bags when you arrive; walk after that.

Not too far along the Costera Aleman will be a turn to the right across the isthmus of the peninsula (a distance of 100 yards) to a small beach called the Playa Langosta, at the head of a pretty little inlet. Facing the playa is the **Hotel Mozimba,** Av. López Mateos at Las Palmas (Apdo. Postal 88) (tel. 748/2-2785), an attractive, family-type place with 41 rooms, plenty of hot water, and excellent meals. This is the kind of hotel that people return to every year, so there's always a crowd that knows one another. In the winter season they tend to run on American Plan (you must buy your meals there), at $12 per person, two meals included; but in the off-season of May to December 10% discounts are in order.

A Motel Near Caleta and Caletilla

Whether or not you drive to Acapulco, you should consider staying at the **Motel La Jolla,** Costera Aleman and Avenida López Mateos, (tel. 748/2-5862; in Mexico City, tel. 905/566-2377), where a bright and modern double room costs 9,500 pesos ($19) off-season, 12,085 pesos ($24.17) in season. This L-shaped, two-story motel surrounds a swimming pool bordered with coconut palms, and although there is no view of the sea whatsoever, there is a flying-saucer-shaped restaurant. You are quite near the beach here, although you can't see it.

Near Caletilla Beach

The beaches of Caleta and Caletilla are side by side, so access to one is access to the other. Several hotels offer good accommodations within walking distance of the water—no need to catch a bus along Costera Aleman as there was for the above choices.

The layout of streets in the peninsula is confusing, and the disorganization in street names and numbers is enough to drive one to tears: a street will be named Avenida López Mateos, but so will the street meeting it at a 90-degree angle; some streets have two names, while others have none; many buildings have two street numbers, so here are explicit directions to my hotel choices in this area. Fronting on Caletilla beach is a semicircular array of little restaurants, and behind this semicircle and across the street is a large, tree-lined parking lot for the Jai Alai Fronton, a peeling yellowish building at the far end of the parking lot. As you face the parking lot (your back to the water), a street runs along the left side of the lot up the hill. This is supposedly Avenida López Mateos (also marked as Avenida Flamingos) and along it, on the left-hand side of the street, are several good hotels only a few minutes' walk from the beach.

Right at the base of the hill is the small new **Hotel Bonanza,** Av. López Mateos 14 (tel. 748/3-7765), with a little fountain in the entry court, and a tiny swimming pool (though you're only steps from the beach). Rooms have ceiling fans and louvered windows for good cross-ventilation. Though you may hear noise from the parking lot in front, this is the closest to the beach. Singles are 4,000 pesos ($8), doubles are 5,000 pesos ($10) in winter.

Several shiny new hostelries have opened in the Caleta-Caletilla area, among them the **Hotel Suites Dalia's Caleta,** Avenida López Mateos 45 (tel. 748/2-3420 or 2-5364). Dalia's is a warren of modern little rooms, all enclosed within a wall, a favorite with Mexican families. It has its own little swimming pool. Rooms with private bath and air conditioning cost 8,500 pesos ($17) single, 10,000 pesos ($20) double in winter. Look for Dalia's right across the street from the more visible Motel Caribe.

The 26-room **Motel Caribe,** López Mateos 10, at Enseñada (tel. 748/2-1550), with music going constantly in the lobby, has rooms arranged around an open garden. Dark stained doors and slatted windows open off the rooms to terraces: private on one side, public walkways on the other. All rooms have private bath with hot and cold water. Rates are 5,750 pesos ($11.50); the winter price includes a continental breakfast.

Now in a slightly different location is an exceptionally good place to stay: facing the Hotel de la Playa between Caleta and Caletilla beaches, take the street to your left up the hill. About 1½ blocks up the hill you'll find the sinuous façade of the 70-room **Hotel Belmar,** Gran Via Tropical and Av. de las Cumbres (tel. 748/2-1525 or 2-1526), an older hotel well kept up and very pleasant. Two small pools and shady patios fill the grassy lawn in front of the hotel. The four-story hotel was built in the '50s, with air conditioning added later. The cool, breezy rooms cost 6,000 pesos ($12) single, 7,500 pesos ($15) double in winter.

Only a few steps from Caleta beach, to the left of the enormous Hotel Caleta, is the **Hotel Lindavista** (tel. 748/2-2783 or 2-5414), at the far end of the Caleta parking lot. Snuggled into the hillside, the old-style Lindavista does indeed provide a good view of the beach and its hinterland. The hotel's pace is out of a bygone age, a favorite with older Mexican couples, who also like the very good prices: 8,000 pesos ($16) for a double room with fan, or 12,000 pesos ($24) for the same room plus three meals a day! The hotel does have some rooms with air conditioning at a markup. There's a little pool. You will find yourself spending a good deal of time at the simple terrace-restaurant, enjoying the view.

Back toward the center of town on the Costera, across the street from the Motel Las Palmas, is the **Casa de Huespedes Walton,** Costera Aleman 223 (tel. 748/2-0452). This congenial little pension set back from the busy street is run by a bevy of happy señoras who want everything to go right: signs in the courtyard admonish people "For the love of God, park correctly and obey the lines!" and "Don't ruin tourism with loud horns and mufflers!" Rooms at the Casa Walton rent at the reasonable price of 2,500 pesos ($5) per person in winter. The small but pleasant Playa Langosta (or Angosta) is only five minutes' walk from your door.

A Splurge Hotel at Caleta

Were I to arrive in Acapulco with pockets full of cash, rather than blowing it in the Empire State Buildings arrayed along the eastern beaches I'd head for the **Hotel Boca Chica,** C.P. 1211 (tel. 748/2-6014), overlooking Caletilla beach at the end of the Costera Aleman. The five-story hotel fits into the hillside fairly unobtrusively. Lawns, terraces, the pool, the bar and restaurant are on different levels. The hotel's location on the headland of the beach allows for 180-degree panoramic views. All 45 air-conditioned rooms have a little veranda, fine marble-and-tile bath, lots of windows, and room to unfold in. The hotel can also provide facilities for waterskiing, sailing, scuba-diving, deep-sea fishing, surfing, golf, and tennis. During the winter you must take breakfast and dinner in the hotel, and the cost is a hefty 17,710 pesos ($35.42) single, 28,175 pesos

($56.35) double. But during the rest of the year (May 1 to December 15) prices are about 18% lower, and you needn't include the meals in the price.

READERS' HOTEL SELECTION: "We chose the **Hotel Monte Alegre,** Calle San Marcos 52, off Gran Vía Tropical, (tel. 748/2-0429), managed by Sr. and Sra. Caso. Sra. Caso speaks English. Since we were staying a month, they agreed to a price of 9,000 pesos ($18) per day for a suite with large bedroom (three beds), complete kitchen with cookware, and view of the ocean. The hotel has a beautiful swimming pool" (Rick and Jeanne Rinear, Fairbanks, Alaska).

WHERE TO EAT:
Some of the budget hotels recommended above will insist that you take your meals in the hotel during high season in the winter (this is euphemistically called the American Plan—forced purchase), but many have no restaurant. Here are my choices of places to eat.

Near the Diana Glorieta

The stretch of Costera Aleman between Papagayo Park and the Glorieta Diana traffic circle has numerous restaurants. Some of the places in this high-rent district, believe it or not, are within our price range, even in the winter high season.

The **Restaurant-Cantina La Flor de Acapulco** (tel. 4-3628) is just a few steps west of the Diana circle, across from the Hyatt Continental hotel. Decor is Mexican ranch, with a few tables having a view of the sidewalk. Mexican cooking, especially charcoal-grilled dishes, are featured. The tacos al carbon are authentic but plain—just bits of steak on dry tortillas—but the steak is really savory and delicious. Many main courses such as chicken, a club sandwich, a steak-and-cheese omelette, or a small beefsteak, cost only 1,000 pesos ($2). There's seafood, too. Open every day, for all three meals.

For breakfasts, snacks, and lunches with the natural touch, try the **Cafetería Flamboyant** (tel. 4-3565), Costera Aleman 180 in the Centro Comercial Flamboyant across from the Acapulco Plaza Holiday Inn. This tiny place bears a sign reading "100% Melendez, Comidas Corridas" and offers an air-conditioned room in which you can order pastries and sandwiches for around 250 pesos (50c), steaks and chicken dishes for 600 to 1,000 pesos ($1.20 to $2), and nine assorted breakfasts for 700 pesos ($1.40) each. It's open from 8 a.m. to 5 p.m., Monday through Saturday.

Down near Papagayo Park is the pleasant little **Taquería** (taco house) **El Torito,** Costera Aleman 236 across from the Paraíso hotel. The breezy, shady sidewalk tables stay cool, and so do you. I had two chicken burritos with refried beans, cheese, and avocado, and two soft drinks, for 1,000 pesos ($2), tip included.

East of the Diana circle a few steps, toward Condesa beach, is **Lalo's Grill** (tel. 4-0426), a funny place carved out of the rocky hillside and favored by Canadians, particularly those who speak French. Not surprisingly, onion soup heads the menu, and a bowl of that plus some fried fish or chicken will set you back about 3,500 pesos ($7). The Mexican combination plate, though a bit pricey at 3,000 pesos ($6), is still filling and fun. Hours here are 1 p.m. to 12 midnight every day.

On Condesa Beach

Condesa beach is hardly a budget-priced area. You could blow our entire daily budget on one dinner here. But I've uncovered a few places that should serve our purposes very well, and still keep the budget intact.

You'll notice **Blackbeard's** (tel. 4-2549) on the beach side of the Costera

Aleman just before the Hotel Condesa del Mar (if you're coming from town). Well, Blackbeard's itself is too expensive for us, but its annex, called **Mimi's Chili Bar,** serves burgers, salads, and bowls of chili in a funky Old West decor. You can chow down heartily here for under 2,500 pesos ($5).

In the evening it's pleasant to sit outdoors at the **Restaurant Cocula** (tel. 4-2244), in the complex called El Patio, on the landward side of Costera Aleman across from the Exelaris Hyatt Continental Hotel. Several circular patios make up the open-air restaurant: one serves as the dining area, another as the barbecue pit, yet another as the bar. All are set well back from the busy street. Prices are moderate for Acapulco: have a steak or a mixed grill, plus a bottle of cidra rosada (Mexican sparkling cider), or one of the good Mexican wines (try Urbiñon or Los Reyes), and two people will spend less than 6,000 pesos ($12)—that's only $6 apiece.

Farther east along the Costera, across from La Torre de Acapulco at the corner of Avenida Lomas del Mar (there's a Denny's restaurant on the corner) is **La Tortuga** (no phone), a small and very congenial outdoor restaurant at no. 5-A. Located half a block from the Costera, it's quiet and shady, with tables set out on numerous terraces filled with greenery. Order from the full restaurant menu, or just have a sandwich or a plate of tacos and a beer. The large Mexican combination plate costs 3,500 pesos ($7), beer, tax, and tip included, but you can easily dine for only half that amount. Recommended.

On Icacos Beach

You may be surprised to find **Restaurant Fersato's** (tel. 4-3949) in this area, on the landward side of the Costera between CICI and the Hotel La Palapa, because it doesn't fit the image, or the price structure. Fersato's is a little set of palapas, open to the breeze (which is helped along by ceiling fans). Beneath the palapa thatch, pinned to its underside, is an extraordinary collection of . . . T-shirts! Suspended up there among the funny, wry, and naughty T-shirt imprints are a few California license plates, presumably from vacationers who drove down and decided never to drive back. Fersato's menu, cuisine, and service are hardly elegant. For instance, milanesa con papas is translated as "piece of cattle meat and potatoes," which is literally accurate, if hardly appetizing. Prices are good, though: less than 2,000 pesos ($4) for said piece of cattle meat (which is a breaded cutlet), plus a beer, and tax and tip.

Most Acapulco restaurants serve seafood, and many specialize in it. One of the latter is **Mariscos Pipo** (tel. 4-0165) Costera Aleman and Calle Victoria, near CICI and Icacos Beach in the eastern bay. Pipo's is a famous downtown seafood restaurant with a reputation spanning decades. The downtown location (see below) is quite modest. But here on the Costera, things are a bit fancier and certainly more comfortable. Even so, prices in the attractive new Pipo's are low, and you should be able to have a full meal of soup, grilled red snapper (huachinango à la parrilla), dessert, and wine or beer for 3,750 to 5,000 pesos ($7.50 to $10), tax and tip included.

In the Downtown (Zócalo) Area

The place to go is Calle Juárez, the street running west off the zócalo beside the local incarnation of Denny's restaurant chain. On Juárez, at no. 5, is the **San Carlos** (tel. 2-6459), with a western motif—lots of brick and wood—and food served in pleasant surroundings at chuck-wagon prices: charcoal-broiled meats for 500 to 800 pesos ($1 to $1.60), fish for about the same. A comida corrida costs only 650 pesos ($1.30). The San Carlos is only a few steps from the zócalo.

Right next door at Juárez 7 is the **Restaurant Ricardo's** (no phone). Small, plain, and usually jammed with happy, hungry customers, Ricardo's offers a popular daily set-price lunch of, say, fish soup, rice or noodles, a green pepper stuffed with cheese, and ice cream or coffee for a mere 500 pesos ($1).

There are many other good, astoundingly inexpensive places on Juárez. Have a look at **El Amigo Juan** (no phone), Juárez 4-I. A courtyard allows you to get away from the street noise, and a blackboard menu announces a daily comida corrida priced at less than 750 pesos ($1.50).

Mariscos Pipo (tel. 2-2452) is a diminutive place that specializes in seafood and, while not dirt-cheap, gives good value for money. An order of ceviche, which comes with lemon and lots of Saltine crackers, plus a beer, makes a light lunch for 850 pesos ($1.70). Tuna, octopus, snails, and other delectables come in various combination plates for 1,100 to 1,600 pesos ($2.20 to $3.20). Red snapper is a bit expensive, but almendrado (fish baked with cheese and almonds) is usually quite cheap. Tables stand in an airy, vine-draped room off the sidewalk five short blocks from the zócalo. Walk along Costera Aleman west toward Caleta, past the market stalls and down a passageway by the Farmacía Santa Lucia; or walk along Juárez and at the fork in the road, bear left. Legal address of the Pipo (as though any of these streets are marked!) is Almirante Breton 3. Menu in English. Pipo is open every day from 10 a.m. to 6 p.m.

Very similar to Pipo, but cheaper and a bit closer to the zócalo, at the corner of Juárez and Almirante Breton, is **El Amigo Miguel** (no phone), a large inside dining room very plainly furnished. Usually it's filled to brimming with seafood lovers taking advantage of the fish at low prices.

Mariscos Milla (no phone), at the corner of Azueta and Carranza, might fool you at first into thinking prices are high here. Although the decor is upbeat and pleasant, this doesn't seem to affect the low prices. The kitchen is occupied by a platoon of hard-working señoras who will serve you ceviche (fish cocktail) for a mere 400 pesos (80¢). A delicious meal of fish filet and a beer need cost only 1,200 pesos ($2.40). Mariscos Milla is open seven days a week from 7 a.m. to 8 p.m. You'll recognize it—an airy corner restaurant—across the street from the Hotel Sacramento, and not far from the Casa Anita.

Sanborn's, a block or two off the zócalo east along Costera Aleman, and **Denny's,** right on the zócalo (on the west side), offer American-style food and popular Mexican plates at rather high prices, but in clean and comfortable surroundings (air-conditioned!). Prices are about the same in both. If they're offering a daily special plate when you're there, order it—that's the best value-for-money, at about 1,700 pesos ($3.40). Everything is modern and quite sanitary. Breakfast is about 1,500 pesos ($3) for hotcakes, an egg, juice, and coffee—and you get free seconds on coffee.

Terraza Las Flores (tel. 3-9463), entered via Calle Juárez across from Denny's, has menus in English, Spanish, and German; the friendly and engaging owner speaks Spanish and English, and his son speaks Spanish and German. Full meals cost 7,000 to 8,500 pesos ($14 to $17) complete if you have meat or fish, a good deal less if you have something like enchiladas. You always seem to find a few exotic (for Acapulco) dishes such as pork and cabbage offered. The Terraza has about two dozen tables overlooking the square on two levels, lots of potted plants, and is open from 11 a.m. to 11 p.m. every day.

Rock-Bottom Prices

Restaurant Carmon's at Juárez 8 is certainly low on the price scale. You don't get so much atmosphere here, for the Carmon is pretty plain, but you don't pay for it either. The comida corrida is only 425 pesos (85¢) for five courses, and the noise from the TV that thrums to itself in a corner costs nothing extra.

Acapulco's lowest prices of all are concentrated along the street named **Azueta,** near La Paz. Comidas corridas at the humble eateries along the way average 400 to 550 pesos (80¢ to $1.10). Follow Juárez until it meets the Costera Aleman, and tiny hole-in-the-wall cookstands will serve you a four-course lunch for as little as 360 pesos (72¢). The food will be very simple.

Caleta-Caletilla Beach Area

The area around Caleta and Caletilla beaches used to be rather down-at-the-heels, but not long ago the municipal authorities pumped lots of money into public facilities here. Now the beaches have nice shady palapas and beach chairs, clean sand, and fine palm trees. Three neo-native buildings were built to house "vestidores, regarderas" (changing rooms, showers, and lockers) and restaurants. Little dining places line the outer periphery of the buildings, and the kitchen work is done at the center (peek around to the kitchen to see boys cutting up fish for the pot).

The best way to find a good meal here is to wander along the rows of restaurants, looking for busy spots where people are eating (and not just sipping drinks). Pore over menus, which will either be displayed or handed to you with a smile, on request. Although the restaurants may tend to look all the same, you'll be surprised at the difference in prices. Filete de pescado (fish filet) might be 750 pesos ($1.50) at one place, and 1,200 ($2.40) at another; beer can cost anywhere from 250 to 450 pesos (50¢ to 90¢). Some offer inexpensive set-price meals for little over a dollar.

Starvation Budget (Caleta-Caletilla)

To get a good, but inexpensive, meal you'll have to leave the beach and go back along the Costera Aleman to the Pemex station (crossroads with Avenida Americas—there's a Tastee-Freez across from the gas station). Now, behind the Pemex station and across the street from the Club de Yates under a low thatched roof and hidden by much vegetation and verdure is the **Restaurant Mitla** (no phone), a comely if humble establishment run by several hefty señoras who serve up a full comida corrida for 625 pesos ($1.25), or a plate of bifstek for even less. Nothing fancy—the garden terraces are artfully hedged by rows of beer bottles to support the soil—still it's a pleasant, open-air place. Jukebox, cheap cold beer, good smells, tasty food, low price. Go there from 7 a.m. to 11 p.m. every day.

The Big Splurge

Although it's probably an oversimplification to say that if you've seen one Carlos Anderson restaurant you've seen them all, I couldn't help being struck by the similarity between **Carlos 'n Charlie's** (tel. 4-0039), Costera, opposite Las Torres Gemelas, and Harry's Bar in Cuernavaca. Same revolutionary posters, same sassy waiters, same ponderous humor in the menu listings ("splash" for seafood, "moo" for beef) . . . well, you get the idea. But the food is good and the place is always packed, which is a good indication that people like what they get for the price they pay. A full meal with a fish or meat main course will cost about 7,000 pesos ($14), chicken a bit less, shrimp a bit more. Come early and get a seat on the terrace overlooking the sidewalk. While there may be many similarities among Anderson's restaurants, they also have in common the fact that virtually everyone comes away having had a good meal and a good time.

There's now another Carlos Anderson branch in Acapulco. Called **Huachinango Charlie's** (tel. 748/4-0493), it's at Costera Aleman, just east of the Diana circle in the Eve Discothèque building. Prices, mood, and service are similar to that at Carlos 'n Charlie's, so you should plan to spend about 7,000 pesos ($14) for dinner. Remember to watch out for those high drink prices!

THE BEACHES: Here's the rundown, from west to east around the bay. **Playa Langosta (or Angosta)** is a small, sheltered cove just around the bend from La Quebrada, often deserted, and worth a try anytime. On the peninsula south of the downtown area are **Caleta** and **Caletilla** beaches, each in its own cove. In recent years Caleta and Caletilla have been favored by budget-wise Mexican families, as these are the beaches closest to the city's collection of inexpensive hotels. In the old days, these beaches were what Acapulco was all about.

Nowadays, the beaches and the resort development stretch the entire four-mile length of the bay's shore. Going east from the zócalo, you pass **Terraplen, Clavelito, Carabali,** and **Hornos.** Past the Parque Altamirano (also called Papagayo Park) is **Paraíso,** then you continue along the Costera Aleman and pass the Diana Circle (with a statue/fountain of the goddess) to get to **Condesa** beach, and later **Icacos** beach, the naval base ("La Base"), and **Guitarrón.** After Guitarrón the road climbs the hillside to the fabulous hotel called **Las Brisas,** where many of the bungalow-type rooms have their own swimming pools (there are 200 pools in all!) and cost about $160 per day with a shared pool, $235 per day for a double room with private pool in winter. Past Las Brisas, the road continues on to **Puerto Marques,** about 12 miles from the zócalo, and in a way, spiritually removed from the rest of Acapulco. The fabulous Acapulco and Pierre Marques Princess Hotels dominate the landscape.

The bay of Puerto Marques is an attractive area in which to bathe. The water is calm, the bay is sheltered, and waterskiing is available.

Past the bay, there's an open beach called **Revolcadero,** and a fascinating jungle lagoon. Take a bus to Puerto Marques and then a canoe through the lagoon to Revolcadero. But don't plan to swim on any beach that fronts on open sea. Each year in Acapulco at least one (and usually two or three) unwary swimmers drown because of deadly rip tides and undertow. *Swim only in Acapulco Bay or Puerto Marques Bay.*

There are other beaches, but they're less practical without a car. One, **La Pie de la Cuesta,** about eight miles west of town (buses leave town every five or ten minutes) is not for swimming as it's an open-sea beach, but it is a popular spot from which to watch the sunset—they're big on sunsets in Acapulco—and every sundown the beach is jumping with hammock-swinging sunset aficionados sipping gin-filled coconuts and watching the waves break along the shore. Beware that boys will try to collect money from you to sit under the thatched palapas on the public beach—you needn't pay it.

If you drive, continue right out along the peninsula, passing the lagoon on your right, until you have almost reached the small air base at the tip. All the way along, you'll be invited to drive into different sections of beach by various private entrepreneurs, mostly small boys.

Parasailing

If you've never tried this, you're in for a fantastic thrill. The operators strap you into a parachute harness that is attached by a tow rope to a fast motorboat. A few seconds later your feet leave the beach as the specially designed parachute lifts you up toward the rooftops of the giant hotels. Soon you're above them, floating, soaring, with the entire bay and the mountains in view, and although you don't stay up for more than a few minutes, it seems like about a half hour. It looks like a daredevil act, but the operators put people aloft dozens of times each day, with nary a mishap. How they manage to have you land right where they want you, into the arms of the waiting "landing men," is a sight in itself. The thrill is yours for 7,500 pesos ($15) with an enlarged color portrait (optional) delivered to your hotel the next day for an additional fee. Most of the parachute rides operate on Condesa beach.

OTHER THINGS TO DO: During the day, it's pleasant to take a walk (early, before it gets too hot) around the zócalo (officially, Plaza Alvarez) area. Pop into the cathedral, whose big, blue, bulbous spires make it look more like a Russian Orthodox church; and then turn east along the side street going off at right angles. It has no marker, but it's the Calle Carranza and its arcade includes newsstands, shops selling swimsuits, and such-like attractions.

A fabulous view of Acapulco is had by taking a taxi or by driving (no buses) up the hill directly behind the cathedral in the zócalo, following the signs leading to La Mira. The view is well worth the drive.

Yacht Cruises

You can see the whole bay from the deck of a yacht, the *Fiesta*, which leaves from the pier of Bono Batani, on the waterfront just west of the zócalo. There are two basic cruises: 4:30 p.m. is castoff time for the regular afternoon cruise (about $7.50); and the moonlight cruise with dancing (about $10) leaves at 10:30 p.m. The two other motor yachts, the *Sea Cloud* (4:30 and 10:30 p.m.) and the *Bonanza* (4:30 p.m.) make similar trips daily.

La Roqueta Island

Just across Acapulco Bay from Caletilla beach, the small island of **La Roqueta** is accessible by boat, at 200 pesos (40¢) from Caleta beach. On Roqueta itself, there's nothing to do but lie on the beach, but if you can spare the energy, take the paved path up through the woods to the lighthouse. The walk through the woods from the beach takes about 20 minutes.

Fort San Diego

East of the zócalo along the Costera Aleman, you might have noticed the little fortress crowning a hill opposite the cargo docks. This is **El Fuerte de San Diego,** which dates from 1616, when it was built to protect the town from pirate attacks. Acapulco at that time was a fairly wealthy port in the trade with the Philippine islands; both Mexico and the Philippines were part of Spain's enormous empire. What you see of the fort today is actually later construction, as the fort was rebuilt after extensive damage by an earthquake in 1776.

As of this writing, the fort is closed, being refurbished and converted into a museum by the city. It should be completed and open by the time you arrive. Even if the fort is not open, the view from the hilltop is very pretty.

You can reach the fort by a roadway through a military zone; coming from the zócalo, look for the road on the left, landward side of the Costera. Or, if your legs are in shape, you can climb a cascade of stairs opposite the cargo docks.

Cultural Center

The State of Guerrero's Instituto Guerrerense de la Cultura sponsors the **Centro Cultural de Acapulco,** a complex of little buildings in a shady grove across from the Twin Dolphin Hotel and Fersato's Restaurant, near the eastern end of the Costera. Among the center's buildings you'll find a small **Museo de Arqueología** (Archeological Museum) with quite an interesting, though limited, collection of pre-Columbian artifacts. It's open from 9 a.m. to 2 p.m. and 5 to 8 p.m. seven days a week. Other buildings hold displays of crafts (many for sale), or host classes in painting or guitar, poetry readings, and performances of music and dance.

Bullfights

Traditionally termed the **Fiesta Brava,** the bullfights are held during Acapulco's winter season at a ring up the hill from Caletilla beach. Tickets are sold by most travel agents, and at the Kennedy Center box office on Costera Aleman (tel. 5-8540). The festivities begin each Sunday in winter at 5:30 p.m.

The Soft Life

Take a bus out past the Diana Circle and check out any of the high-rise palaces lining the beach. In fact, in sunglasses, bathing trunks, and a sport shirt, or a bikini and smock or beach jacket, carrying an English-language newspaper or a current bestseller, who's to know you aren't staying there? Somehow it's delicious to sit in the beach chairs and sip a drink, observing the local fauna, or even to try out the pool. Think: even the most observant of lackeys can't keep straight the faces of the people who inhabit his 400 rooms, and who come and go day by day.

ACAPULCO NIGHTLIFE: Up on La Quebrada each day at 1, 7:15, 8:15, 9:15, and 10:30 p.m. the **high diver** performs. From a spotlit ledge just below the Hotel El Mirador's terraces the solitary diver plunges into the roaring surf 130 feet below after praying at a small shrine nearby. To the applause of the crowd that has gathered, he then climbs up the rocks and accepts congratulations and gifts of money from onlookers.

Sitting in the **zócalo,** which is closed to vehicular traffic and furnished with lots of benches and trees, is a very pleasant pastime and costs nothing. As you're sitting there, all kinds of pitchmen will approach you: men with barrel organs, women offering rebozos, mariachis, small boys selling gum or puppets or matches, beggars, and so on.

The Clubs

I might almost venture to say that Acapulco is more famous for its nightclubs than it is for its beaches. The problem is that the clubs open and close with revolving-door regularity, making it very difficult for me to make specific recommendations that will be accurate when you arrive. Some general tips will help: every club seems to have a cover charge of about $5 to $7, drinks can cost anywhere from 1,250 to 2,500 pesos ($2.50 to $5).

Clubs seem to have their preferred clientele. **Disco 9** (tel. 4-3399), at Costera Aleman 78, for instance, is gay. The most infuriatingly exclusive spot when I was last in town was **Baby-O** (tel. 4-7474), across from Romano's Le Club, open from 10 p.m. to 4 a.m., where you can not only dance but also tingle in a Jacuzzi. At **The Gallery** (tel. 4-3497), across from the Acapalco Plaza Holiday Inn, the attraction is "Les Femmes," a group of talented entertainers who—surprise!—aren't women at all. The place for those with buckets of cash and tremendous wardrobes is **Eve** (tel. 4-4777), Costera Aleman 115—be dressed in your best when you go, and take one of those buckets along.

Several nightspots are grouped around the shopping complex called El Patio, across the Costera Aleman from the Hyatt Continental hotel. **Jackie'O** (tel. 4-0843) is the oldest of these, having survived more than two years! **Midnight** (tel. 4-8295) is just behind Jackie'O. Behind them both, down the little side street, is the newest disco in the area, called **Cat's** (tel. 4-7235), which has yet to prove that it has nine lives.

Among the longest-running old favorites which attract a yuppie-type crowd are the flashy **Le Dome** (tel. 4-1190), across from the Calinda Quality Inn, famous for the variety and activity of its lights; and **Boccaccio** (tel. 4-1900), near the Best Western El Tropicano, which is cozier (read smaller), but with the same sort of clientele.

For live Latin music on Friday and Saturday nights, try **El Palacio de la Salsa** (tel. 4-6302), facing the Acapulco Plaza Holiday Inn. Another place with live music (sometimes) is **Ninas** (tel. 4-2400), more or less across the street from the Centro Acapulco entrance. Here the music is "tropical" and the bar serving beer and Mexican drinks is free and open once you've paid your $7 admission fee. (Don't expect the world's most luscious drinks.)

The high-rise hotels each have their own bars, supper clubs, and nightclubs with floor shows. At least once a week many of these feature a "Noche Mexicana" with Ballet Folklorico—type entertainment. Also a good bet are the informal lobby or poolside cocktail bars, often with live entertainment. As of this writing, the **Exelaris Hyatt Regency Acapulco** (tel. 4-2888), all the way at the eastern end of the bay near La Base, is sponsoring performances of the authentic Ballet Folklorico de México, but if it happens in the future it will no doubt be a winter-season phenomenon.

The Centro Acapulco

Acapulco has its own spectacular culture and convention center, called the Centro Acapulco, on the eastern reaches of the bay between Condesa and Icacos beaches. Done with fine and extravagant Mexican taste, the Centro has rolling lawns dotted with a copy of an Olmec head, another of the Quetzalcóatl of Teotihuacán, etc.; you enter up a grand promenade with a central row of pools and high-spouting fountains. Within the gleaming modern building are all the services and diversions one could want: a mariachi bar, a piano bar, a disco, a movie theater, a legitimate theater, a café, a nightclub, several restaurants, and outdoor performance areas. Should you want to buy a stamp, make a phone call, dress a wound, buy a dress, or tape a TV show, all you need is right here. During the day you can stroll around the grounds for free; at night you pay a few pesos for admission to the floodlit grounds. After that, you're free to stroll around as you wish. If, however, you *sit* at one of the café tables to watch a performance, you must order something to eat or drink, and the minimum is several dollars per person.

Programs with the center's current offerings are given away around town, at hotel desks and the like, or call 4-7050 for latest word.

9. Puerto Escondido and Puerto Angel

Last of Mexico's fabulous resort towns are two fairly secluded little seaside villages in the wild and mountainous state of Oaxaca. Both are still small and relatively undiscovered—relative to, say, Zihuatanejo or Puerto Vallarta. But although Puerto Escondido (pop. 25,000) means "Hidden Port," this and its sister town a short ride away will not remain hidden much longer: a new jetport is now complete, and the Mexican government plans to turn the sleepy hamlet of Santa Cruz Huatulco, east of Puerto Angel, into a Cancún-style mega-resort.

PUERTO ESCONDIDO: There are two villages here, actually. On the inland side of the coastal highway is the Mexican village, with pottery and produce markets, plus lots of little ma-and-pa eateries and general town life. The other village is the tourist strip on the seashore side of the highway. As you walk from west to east on the tourist strip's main thoroughfare, you cannot help but notice the recent changes here. No longer the quaint seaside resort with dirt streets. No! Avenida Alfonso Perez Gasga is paved and contains a three-block pedestrian mall. The mall is very pleasant in the evenings; informal groups gather to discuss the day's events without the dust of the pre-pavement days. However, woe be to anyone who wanders across the barren, shadeless bricks in the midday heat. Even the plastic pelicans on the trash barrels seem to wilt. Fortunately, cool liquid refreshment is plentiful at every turn. Continue along Avenida Perez Gasga until you reach the Neptune trailer park, and turn right for the beach. Here are Puerto Escondido's greatest attractions.

Ahead of you, on a range of low hills overlooking the bay, is a cluster of army barracks. Beyond that, nothing . . . nothing except palm groves and a stretch of the most glorious beach you'e ever seen. This is particularly true if you're facing east. The bay is irregular in shape; its western promontory consists of a tiny beach followed by rocks jutting into the sea. By way of contrast, the eastern peninsula is about a mile long with low green hills descending to meet a long stretch of bone-white sand.

Getting to and from Puerto Escondido

One of the reasons this idyllic spot remained hidden was inaccessibility. As of this writing, access is easy if you're coming by air from Oaxaca, or by road from Acapulco or Salina Cruz. But should you plan to come by road from Oaxaca, you're in for a long, bumpy ride, unless you travel on Hwy. 175 via Pochutla; then you are in for a long, winding ride.

By Road: It's 230 miles (370 km) from Acapulco to Puerto Escondido by Hwy. 200, a fairly good and fast road. Whether you go by bus or car you will undergo frequent army inspections (they're looking for drugs and firearms). It's a good idea to keep your eyes open and to inspect along with the soldiers. Most are intent on doing their duty; a few have sticky fingers, and these have no right to take advantage of you. They know it, and if you let them know that you know it, you'll be treated with nothing but deference and respect.

The road from Salina Cruz to Puerto Escondido, 150 miles (243 km), can be driven in four or five hours but shouldn't be rushed through. This route takes you right past the Bahías de Huatulco and the turnoff for Puerto Angel.

Coming from Oaxaca, Autobuses La Solteca make the fairly arduous trip to Puerto Escondido six times a day in second-class equipment. The trip takes from eight to nine hours, although it is less than 150 miles; a ticket costs 1,162 pesos ($2.33) one way. A few stretches are paved, but a good two-thirds of it is not paved, and is dusty and rutty in the dry season, muddy and rutty—and even perhaps washed out—in the rainy season.

By Air: A shining new airport capable of handling jets is now in service. The bad news is that it is about four kilometers (2.5 miles) from the center of town. The good news is that the new airport is user-friendly. The restrooms are sparkling clean, waiting space is ample, most signs are bilingual, and prices for the minibus to town are posted: 420 pesos (84¢) per person. If you elect to make the scorching trip to town on foot, walk out to Hwy. 200 and turn left.

You can fly to Puerto Escondido from Oaxaca in a 28-passenger DC-3 if you buy a ticket from either one of these little airlines: **Aerovias Oaxaqueñas S.A.,** Armenta y Lopez 209 (between Hidalgo and Guerrero), Oaxaca (tel. 951/6-3824 or 6-3833; at the airport 951/6-1600; in Mexico City, Balderas 32, no. 514 tel. 905/510-0162); or **Lineas Aereas Oaxaqueñas,** Avenida Hidalgo 503, Oaxaca (tel. 951/6-5362 or 6-5243; in Mexico City at Calle 28 no. 20, Colonia Federal, tel. 905/571-2882 or 784-4043). The first-mentioned airline has two flights to Puerto Escondido each day with slightly different times on Sunday, the second airline only one flight a day, seven days a week. Cost for a one-way ticket is 7,900 pesos ($15.80).

Important Note: Your flight from Oaxaca to Puerto Escondido may touch down in the little coastal town of Pinotepa Nacional on the way to Puerto Escondido. There will be no sign, and no announcement of where you have landed. Be careful! *Don't get off in Pinotepa by mistake!* Ask the flight attendant "Puerto Escondido?" before you deplane, just to be sure.

AeroMéxico flies a Boeing 727-200 from Mexico City to Puerto Escondido on Monday, Wednesday, and Friday. The jet departs Mexico City at 9:45 and arrives in Puerto Escondido at 10:40. The return trip departs Puerto Escondido at 11:05. A one-way ticket is 12,036 pesos ($24.07); double this for roundtrip.

Where to Stay

For my money, the best hotel in town is the **Hotel Santa Fe,** C.P. 96, on Calle del Morro (tel. 958/2-0170). Walk from Avenida Alfonso Perez Gasga down to the beach, follow the shoreline to the left, and in the distance you'll see a Spanish villa-style structure—that's the Hotel Santa Fe. Prices are a bit high for our budget, but you get a lot for your money: single rooms cost 8,860 to 10,510 pesos ($17.72 to $21.05), and doubles are 11,250 to 14,750 pesos ($22.50 to $29.50). Triple rooms cost only 2,400 to 3,000 pesos ($4.80 to $6.00) more than doubles. An extra bed in a room is 750 pesos ($1.50). For these prices, you get a shiny new hotel with a nice little swimming pool, a restaurant-bar overlooking the ocean, well-kept grounds, screens on the windows, and fans in the rooms. A constant sea breeze does away with the need for air conditioning. Highly recommended.

In town near the beach, the best choice is the 40-room **Hotel Las Palmas,** Avenida Alfonso Perez Gasga (tel. 958/2-0230). Similar to neighboring establishments, Las Palmas is a U-shaped building facing the ocean, the "U" becoming a delightful palm-shaded courtyard. There are three floors of rooms with ceiling fans, and prices are 5,380 pesos ($10.76) single, 6,417 pesos ($12.84) double, for a room with bath. The courtyard holds a nice patio restaurant, nothing fancy, but very pleasant.

The **Hotel Rincon del Pacifico,** on Avenida Alfonso Perez Gasga, right next to the Hotel Las Palmas (tel. 958/2-0056), has two floors of rooms built in a U-shape around a patch of sand shaded by a few tremendous palms and fronting right on the Pacific. The sea breeze cools all of the glass-fronted modern rooms, and jalousies allow the breeze to come straight through. They advertise that they have constant hot water in the tile baths. Prices are 3,243 pesos ($6.49) single, 4,053 pesos ($8.11) double. The hotel has a restaurant on the beach level, open from 7 a.m. to 11 p.m. daily.

The **Hotel Rocamar** (tel. 958/2-0339), on the landward side of Avenida Alfonso Perez Gasga, is newish and tidy. Screens on the windows keep the bugs out; all rooms come with shower and cost 3,000 pesos ($6.00) single, 4,000 pesos ($8.00) double. Though the hotel is not facing the beach, you're only 90 seconds away from the surf.

Up on the hill, on the road into town at the west, is the **Hotel Nayar** (tel. 958/2-0113), where 24 rooms are built into two floors around a central court. Here you have a modern place with good beds, good cross-ventilation, table-top fans, tile baths, and some fabulous views. It looks as though it should charge much more than it does: 3,243 pesos ($6.49) single, 4,053.75 pesos ($8.11) double; 4,864.50 pesos ($9.73) triple. Why so cheap? The Mexican government's star-rating system gives the Nayar only two stars (it has no swimming pool), and that keeps prices delightfully low. Even if you don't stay here, you should come for a meal in the patio restaurant, which has a fabulous view.

The 12-room **Hotel Loren** (tel. 958/2-0057), located at the western end of Avenida Alfonso Perez Gasga, is a bit pricey for what you get. With three floors (the top one a sun roof offering the best view in town), the hotel looks bigger than it is. Rooms are stark but clean, and although they may betray a slight mustiness, that is the fate of all rooms in salt-breeze resorts—you'll be hard put to find a room without it. Rates are 4,715 pesos ($9.43) double, with a sometime seasonal rise in winter.

Starvation-Budget Rooms: The **Hotel Los Crotos,** on Avenida Alfonso Perez Gasga (tel. 958/2-0025), is perhaps the town's most basic lodging. But prices are delightfully basic as well: 2,500 pesos ($5.00) single, 3,000 pesos ($6.00) double. Check your room before you move in.

The Big Splurge: You can spend more than our budget in Puerto Escondido. If you stay at the luxurious **Castel Puerto Escondido** (tel. 958/2-0133), about a mile and a half northwest of town on the Acapulco road, you'll spend up to 11,700 pesos ($23.40) for a double room.

But closer to town and to the beaches is the small but very nice **Hotel Paraíso Escondido,** Calle Union 1 (tel. 958/2-0444). This quaint little place is built in hacienda style with lots of stairs, patios, tiny lawns, a little swimming pool, and views of the bay. Rooms come with air conditioning and private bath, and are priced at 8,850 pesos ($17.70) double. Look for the hotel behind the more prominent and visible Hotel Nayar.

Camping: Puerto Escondido has a few fairly primitive camping areas for hammocks, tents, or camping vehicles. Try the **Neptuno,** in the southern part of the beach, on the way to the Hotel Santa Fe, or try the **Trailer Park Carrizalillo** on a steep bank above the beach with same name. Playa Carrizalillo is the beach where nude bathing is tolerated. Remember, the police may bust you if they choose.

READERS' HOTEL SELECTION: "We stayed at **Fatima's** (no phone), which is just a few rooms behind an ice cream factory—everybody in town knows where it is. Further from the beach you cannot be, but we paid just 2,400 pesos ($4.80) for three persons, and a 15-minute walk won't hurt you. We had three enormous beds, a fan, and a bathroom with shower (lukewarm water). On Sunday we were awakened by a choir of children having Sunday school in the yard behind" (Mary Ann Jongenelen and Wouter van Furth, Utrecht, Netherlands).

Where to Eat

Most hotels in Puerto Escondido have their own little restaurants. They're all simple, family-run affairs with modest cuisine and laid-back if friendly service at fairly exorbitant resort prices. Some are better than others. Here are my picks:

A substantial restaurant not connected to any hotel is the **Restaurant El Dorado** (no phone), around the northwestern edge of the bay. You'll recognize it as a handsome bamboo building, its vine-covered archways overlooking the bay; no sign identifies it. From a distance, it looks a bit fancier than it is. Food and service are similar to those at the hotel restaurants, but prices here are lower: fish plates for 1,500 pesos ($3.00) and up, full meals for under 2,000 pesos ($4.00). Open 8 a.m. to 11 p.m.

Of the hotel restaurants, I like the one at the **Hotel Nayar** best. The panoramic view of the bay and the town is itself sufficient reason to dine here at least once. Prices are not bad. A meal of shrimp cocktail, fried fish, or steak with french fries, with dessert, drink, tax, and tip should cost around 3,000 pesos ($6.00). You can easily fill up for half that price, though. The Nayar's restaurant is open from 7:30 a.m. till 10 p.m., but it's closed between 4 and 6 p.m. Wear at least a shirt and shorts when you go here. Men or women in brief bathing suits (bikinis) are not admitted.

The restaurants in the courtyards of the hotels **Las Palmas** and **Rincon del Pacifico** are very pleasant, shaded by palm trees, cooled by sea breezes. Expect prices from 800 pesos ($1.60) for fried fish to 1,200 pesos ($2.40) for other seafood, and don't go for great cuisine.

The **Spaghetti House** (no phone), Avenida Alfonso Perez Gasga s/n, is open daily from 8:30 a.m. to 11 p.m. One can enjoy the spaghetti for 800 pesos ($1.60) or a cheesy pizza for between 900 and 1,300 pesos ($1.80 to $2.60). The pizzas are large enough to feed two persons unless both are ravenous. The most coveted tables here are on the second level; the thatched roof and split bamboo rails make this an excellent place to enjoy the evening breeze.

The cheapest eats in town are to be found, naturally, away from the beach, though not necessarily away from the water. Walk a few steps past the aforementioned Restaurant El Dorado to the little boat harbor, and you will find two extremely basic and inexpensive eateries. Prices will be somewhat lower, and cuisine about the same, as at the town's other places.

But for a greater selection of dishes and the lowest prices of all, wander in the upper reaches of town, on the landward side of the macadam highway, until you find the **market** square. At mealtimes, local señoras fuel up their cookfires for the commercial trade. The dishes may be unfamiliar, but with a discreet point of the finger you can get what you want. Before you order, *ask the price*. You'll be sorry if you ignore this advice!

READERS' RESTAURANT SELECTIONS: "There is now a really good restaurant in Puerto Escondido, the **Restaurant Papagayo,** open 7 a.m. to 11 p.m. It's not cheap, but it's beautifully run, with a young waitress who dashes around and serves everybody at New York speed. Great seafood, and the *best coffee* I had *anywhere* in Mexico" (Callie Angell, New York, N.Y.). . . . "The best restaurant in town is **Los Crotos,** next to the Hotel Las Palmas on the beach. We had broiled lobster (two per serving), for 3,500 pesos ($7). The shrimp is good also. Each morning before 10 a.m. the fisherman drives his pick-up truck by the various restaurants and we watched as the owner of Los Crotos inspected and selected his meals for the day" (Bruce Martin, San Antonio, Tex.).

What to Do

The three-block mall area of Avenida Alfonso Perez Gasga has now sprouted a row of tourist shops selling straw hats, Puerto Escondido T-shirts, and cold drinks, as well as a busy branch of the Oaxaca state Tourism Office, (tel. 958/2-0175) between hotels Las Palmas and Rincon del Pacifico. The office has, while supplies last, an excellent free map of Puerto Escondido, Puerto Angel, and the Bahías de Huatulco project. Get your map Monday through Saturday from 8 a.m. to 1 p.m. or 5 to 8 p.m. and Sunday morning from 8 to 11 a.m.

The restaurant/bar **La Estancia** (no phone), Avenida Gasga (s/n), offers drinks and a live band most evenings.

After that, there are the beaches, which speak for themselves and need no introduction—you'll see. Laziness here is a state of mind, sipping a cool bottle of something refreshing, feeling the sea breeze, watching the pelicans soar and wheel and then come down to race across the surface of the water. Anyone who wandered into Acapulco a half century ago might have found a similar scene and a similar ambience. The thing to do while you're in Puerto Escondido is to catch it before it's gone forever. Then, of course, there's the surfing. . . .

Puerto Angelito: Take a launch from the beach below Avenida Alfonso Perez Gasga, and you'll end up at Puerto Angelito, a small cove popular with Mexican families (no surf, safe for kids) and snorkelers. If you're up for a walk, it's less than half an hour.

At the risk of repeating myself, but in the interests of saving a life, I'll repeat my warning about open surf. To swim at a beach that fronts on open sea is to risk your life. After the first few people died at Puerto Escondido beaches, the authorities put up big warning signs, but still someone dies every year. Swim at the beach in town, or at other sheltered beaches in bays and coves, but *never swim where a rip tide or undertow can take you out to sea*. You may see surfers; it's safer for them because they have surfboards to cling to, and they know waves and tides. Obey the signs. If you see a sign, that probably means someone has already alerted the authorities to the danger on that particular beach . . . the hard way.

READER'S SIGHTSEEING SELECTION: "The State Tourism Office offers a **day trip** for 7,500 pesos ($15). They take about six people, pick you up at your hotel early in the morning, drive to Puerto Angel for breakfast, then continue down the coast through dramatic valleys and lush jungle to Santa Cruz. There they rent a 15- or 20-foot boat and captain to navigate the coast to hidden coves and inlets with clean water and little surf. We snorkeled for two hours, had the lunch we had ordered earlier, and got back to Puerto Escondido at 7 p.m. It's a long day, but an incredible memory for the price" (Bruce Martin, San Antonio, Tex.).

PUERTO ANGEL: Fifty miles southeast of Puerto Escondido along Hwy. 200 is the tiny fishing port of Puerto Angel (pop. 6,000), known to a handful of vacationers who come here regularly, mostly from Mexico City. A small, beautiful bay and several inlets provide rough-and-ready swimming (watch out for the undertow if the beach you choose is washed by open surf), and the village's position at the end of every road assures a sleepy tranquil atmosphere.

Every now and then a naval boat will pull in for a visit at the small naval station, and the village bestirs itself a bit. Otherwise, it's fishing as usual.

Getting to and from Puerto Angel

The situation here is much like that of Puerto Escondido, mentioned above. The bus trip from Oaxaca is only a bit less arduous. As of this writing there is plane service only to Puerto Escondido.

Puerto Angel is 11 kilometers (7 miles) south of Hwy. 200 on Hwy. 175. The most direct and most expensive route to Puerto Angel is a taxi from Puerto Escondido for 10,000 pesos ($20). The bus situation can be confusing although not insurmountable. Ten buses a day leave Puerto Escondido for Patchutla where one must transfer for the remaining brief ride to Puerto Angel. Colectivos depart every 20 minutes.

Where to Stay

Although Puerto Angel only has a few hundred meters of paved streets, mostly along the waterfront, there are three suitable hotels. One right downtown on a small cliff is the **Hotel Soraya** (no phone), which rents its clean, motel-style rooms for 3,450 pesos ($6.90) single, 3,795 pesos ($7.59) double, 4,600 pesos ($9.20) triple; all rooms have fans. The hotel has recently installed window air conditioners in a few rooms and charges 5,784 pesos ($11.57) double. You may get a view if you choose your room right. The restaurant has a panoramic view.

The second place offers rooms that are a bit tattered and are expensive for what you get. The **Hotel Angel del Mar** (tel. 6) stands atop a promontory with panoramic views of the town, the surrounding region, and the sea. Rooms have tile shower, marble washbasin, two large beds, and fantastic views. There is also, for your delectation, a restaurant, bar, and swimming pool, not to mention cobbled paths and drives. Prices are 7,245 pesos ($14.49) single, 8,000 pesos ($16.00) double; detached bungalows cost the same as rooms in the main building and are less noisy. Even if you do not stay here, enjoy a sunrise or sunset from the hotel grounds. The taxi ride from the pier will cost 1,000 pesos ($2.00). The early morning sun bursts from the ocean east of Puerto Angel in your full view. The sunset is equally spectacular as one can observe the last sunlight on Puerto Angel, then turn around and watch the sun's fireball dip into the Pacific. The view probably sells the rooms here.

Of the many posadas scattered around Puerto Angel, I like the tiny ten-room **Posada Cañon Devata** (no phone), a three-minute walk from Playa Pantheon; watch for the sign. The Posada is run by Suzanne and Mateo Lopez, whose business cards say "A Place to Rest from the World." Mateo has created a cool oasis by reforesting a narrow, formerly denuded, canyon. Hammocks are hung on the top level providing a wonderfully breezy place to laze in the midday heat. A fixed-menu evening meal is available featuring fish or vegetarian fare. Conversation around the table during these communal meals is one of the more delightful attractions here. Because of the communal atmosphere this place may not be for everyone. Rooms rent from 2,500 pesos ($5.00) for a double without private bath to 4,800 pesos ($9.60) for a huge double-bedded room with private bath. All the rooms are unique. Reservations can be made by mail. Apartado Postal No. 74, Pochutla, Oaxaca.

What to Do

The white sands of Puerto Angel are the attraction here so in the "Where to Soak" section let's begin with **Playa Principal,** directly in front of you as you come down the hill from the Pochutla intersection. You can't miss it as the beach lies between the pier from which the bulk of the local fishing fleet works and a Mexican Navy camp. Unfortunately, this beach is somewhat polluted, thus does not afford the finest swimming. A 15-minute walk along the dirt continuation of Puerto Angel's main street will bring you around the rock outcropping that separates the Playa Principal from **Playa Panteón** (follow the signs for Hotel Angel del Mar). This is the premium beach close to town. The water is luxuriously warm and the swimming is safe in this sheltered bay. Panteón Beach is so closely lined with eateries that it is difficult to tell which you are patronizing. The many palapas are perfect to escape the hot sun and reconstitute yourself with a cold drink.

I have saved the best beach for last. The 6 kilometers (3.7 miles) of rough road to **Playa Zipolite,** (that's *See*-poh-*lee*-teh) can be negotiated on foot in 45 minutes or by taxi for 1,500 pesos ($3.00). The partially shaded road can sap the last bit of your energy if you attempt to walk back to town in the midday heat; a hat will be a much appreciated piece of apparel. Zipolite is a beach without protection from the open surf. Consequently, *swimming can be very dangerous.* The beach's main claim to fame is surfing, with many surfers ensconced in hammocks under numerous palapas along the beach. Beyond a large rock outcropping at the far end of the beach is an area where nude bathing has been tolerated for several years. One caveat: police could roust au naturel bathers at any time as they are technically breaking the law. Beyond the nude beach in several white buildings is a macabre attraction, a turtle farm. Large turtles are slaughtered here Monday through Saturday. (In case you were wondering, yes, turtles can cry.)

10. Bahías de Huatulco

"The next Cancún!" trumpets the tourist literature. Development has begun on the next megaresort. Forty kilometers (25 miles) east of Pochutla or

140 kilometers (87 miles) west of Salina Cruz on Hwy. 200 is the community of Santa Cruz de Huatulco. This village is now a sleepy hamlet of less than 500 persons strung along Santa Cruz Bay. The present village further defines sleepy. Enough fishing is done to feed the community which leaves plenty of time for eating and relaxing in the breezy hammocks under shady palapas. A small crop of pigs wallow in the sometimes wet arroyo behind buildings a mere 50 meters (54 yards) from the beach. All of this is about to change. The current village will be leveled as soon as the new location, approximately one mile inland, is ready. Already the large shovels are transforming the old pig wallow into a small boat harbor, and prestressed concrete beams are being delivered. Owners of the Hotel Victoria in Oaxaca are planning to develop a hotel here.

The development of the Bahías de Huatulco is an ambitious project which includes 50,000 hectares (124,000 acres) of land bounded by Hwy. 200 and the Pacific Ocean on the north and south and the Río Copalita and Río Coyula on the east and west. Construction of an international airport has begun on a site 25 kilometers (15 miles) east of Pochutla and is scheduled for completion in early 1988.

The final portion of the Bahías de Huatulco project that will require extensive earthmoving is a road through Santa Cruz parallel to Hwy. 200 but nearer the coast. The new road will provide access to eight additional bays including San Agustín, Chachacual, Cacaluta, El Maguey, El Organo, Chahue, Tangolunda, and Conejos. Only Bahía Tangolunda is currently accessible from Hwy. 200, six kilometers (3.6 miles) east of the Santa Cruz intersection. A bumpy 4-kilometer (2.3 miles) trail, which will be closed when the new road along the coast is complete, winds along a dry arroyo to the unspoiled jewel of a bay. The gem is soon to be cut however as three large hotels are slated for completion in early 1988; these include a 500-bed Club Med, a 400-bed El Presidente, and another as yet unnamed 400-bed hotel.

As you may have noticed, budget travelers, no cheap accommodations are in the works, but don't despair. Once the development gets off the ground reasonable priced accommodations are sure to appear. Stay tuned for future developments.

Chapter IV

GUADALAJARA AND NEARBY CITIES

1. Guadalajara
2. Lake Chapala
3. Colima
4. Uruapán
5. Pátzcuaro
6. Morelia

VIRTUALLY EVERYONE WHO has heard anything about Mexico has heard the sonorous name of her second-largest city, Guadalajara, and the fame of this great metropolis is well deserved. But several nearby cities, including two state capitals, come as surprises to the visitor who stays in Guadalajara and who later sets out for Manzanillo or Playa Azul on the Pacific Coast, or for Mexico City. The region encompassed by the states of Jalisco, Colima, and Michoacán is one rich in local crafts, local culture, and local delicacies, not to mention splendid scenery, beautiful lakes and mountains—including one recently active volcano. Everything centers on the "City of Roses," so I'll start our explorations there.

1. Guadalajara

Guadalajara (alt. 5,209 feet; pop. 2,500,000), capital of the state of Jalisco, has a long and brilliant history. Given its charter as *muy leal y muy noble ciudad* ("most loyal and noble city") in 1539 by none other than Emperor Charles V, it has held a prominent place in Mexican events ever since that time. Charles, who ran most of Europe and a lot of the world at the time, certainly knew what he was doing.

As though to emphasize the great things that were expected of it, Guadalajara's Spanish builders gave the city not one but *four* beautiful plazas in its center. Today the city's leaders are giving it a fifth, the enormous Plaza Tapatía, an ambitious swath of urban redevelopment stretching for what seems a mile through the urban landscape. Scattered with trees and monuments, sprinkled with fountains, the new super-plaza links the city's major colonial buildings, opens new perspectives for viewing them, and joins the past with the great new buildings of the present. It's an ambitious project, very Mexican in its grand scope, and that's as it should be: many people consider this the most "Mexican" of cities.

By the way, *tapatío* (or *tapatía*) is a word you'll come across often in this city. No one is certain quite where it originated, but tapatío means "Guadalajaran"—a thing, a person, even an idea. The way a *charro* (Mexican cowboy) gives his all, or the way a mariachi sings his heart out. That's tapatío!

GETTING TO AND FROM GUADALAJARA: No trouble getting to or from this big city. Go to the Central Camionera and you can book a seat on a bus to virtually any point in North America and parts of Central America. Several airlines have direct flights to and from foreign countries. Trains go to the Pacific coast, Mexico City, and the U.S. border. Here are some tips.

By Bus

All of the big lines operating in this area run very frequent buses to this transportation hub. Omnibus de México has connections with U.S. companies at the border; Tres Estrellas de Oro, Transportes Norte de Sonora, and Estrella Blanca run buses both up the coast to the border and inland to the capital. Buses to Aguascalientes, Guanajuato, Puerto Vallarta, Querétaro, Patzcuaro, Morelia, etc., are all available from the Central Camionera. Remember to buy your ticket in advance (a day in advance should be enough). By the way, the Mexico City–Guadalajara trip takes about eight hours.

By Rail

The National Railways run three trains a day in each direction between the capital and Guadalajara, one in the morning early, and two in the evening suitable for sleeping-car travel. Take the later evening train, which leaves about 9 p.m., for it's an express and gets you to Mexico City in slightly over 12 hours rather than the 13½ of the earlier evening train. There are also trains to Colima and Manzanillo (one morning train a day), six hours to Colima, eight to Manzanillo; and of course the two daily trains between the U.S. border and Guadalajara, one of which is the famous *El Costeño*. These are run by the Pacific Railways with connections to the National Railways. They operate morning and noon from Guadalajara, morning and evening from Nogales (connections from Mexicali), and run via Hermosillo, Ciudad Obregón, Mazatlán, and Tepic. Time from Guadalajara to the border is about 36 hours.

By Air

International service direct to Guadalajara includes a daily flight to and from Houston, and seven flights a day to and from Los Angeles. To travel between Guadalajara and Mexico City (a 50-minute flight) you can choose from any of 17 daily flights; there are also flights to these cities: Monterrey (two daily), Mazatlán (one a day), Puerto Vallarta (three or four a day), Manzanillo (one daily), Acapulco (one daily). Aero México operates the bulk of these flights; Mexicana runs most of the rest. Both operate to and from Los Angeles. Any airline office or travel bureau can give you current flight times and fares.

Money-savers: Look into the excursion fares on flights between Guadalajara and Acapulco or Los Angeles.

ORIENTATION: Guadalajara is not a difficult city to find your way around in. But it certainly is big, so some hints on arrival might be of use to you. The numbers in parentheses in the text refer to locations on the map of Guadalajara on page 164.

Arriving by Bus or Train

Should you arrive by bus in Guadalajara's modern Central Camionera (bus terminal), you'll find several respectable hotel choices a few blocks away (see below). The easiest way to get downtown is to walk the several blocks out the bus station's front door down Calle Estadio to the Calzada Independencia. Any bus traveling from left to right will take you to the central market (Mercado Libertad), San Juan de Dios church (30), and the Plaza de Mariachis, from which it's a short walk to the Degollado Theater (35) and other points of interest.

From the railroad station, at the south end of Calzada Independencia, take a no. 2 bus ("San Juan de Dios—Retiro Directo") from directly in front of the station to get to the central market. Other buses tend to wind through suburban quarters before finally coming to the downtown area. It's easier to get back to the depots than it is to get from them to the downtown section. Just take any bus that has "Estación" (for the train station) or "Camion" or "Camionera" (for the bus station) on the signboard or painted in white on the windshield. The Ruta 61, 62, 63, or 2 buses are good choices and go from the main squares and the market to the terminals.

Arriving by Air

When you arrive at Guadalajara's modern airport, you'll walk outside to find minibuses operated by Auto Transportaciones Aeropuerto (tel. 11-5469 and 11-1855), with offices at Avenida Federalismo Sur 915, Colonia Moderna. They'll ask you where in the city you want to go; say *centro* or *zona uno* (Zone 1) if you're headed to any of the downtown hotels recommended in this book. In fact, if you've already picked your prospective hotel, they'll drop you off right at the door for no additional charge. If you haven't chosen a hotel, say *catedral,* as the cathedral is the center of everything. The cost is about 670 pesos ($1.35) per person in a full minibus, 1,385 pesos ($2.75) per person for only two or three in a minibus, and 2,215 pesos ($4.45) if you want a minibus all to yourself—a private taxi.

Tourism Information

The state of Jalisco maintains a tourism office, open every now and again, in the ex-Convento del Carmen, on Calle 8 de Julio off Avenida Juárez.

The federal government's Tourism Office is at Avenida Juárez 638 (tel. 36/14-0156). Hours are 9 a.m. to 3 p.m. Monday through Friday, to 1 p.m. on Saturday.

GETTING AROUND: Two bus routes will fill 90% of your intracity transportation needs. Buses bearing the sign "Par Vial" run a circle route going east along Hidalgo to the Mercado Libertad and then west along Hidalgo to the Glorieta Minerva, near the western edge of the city.

For north-south travel along the Calzada Independencia, there are many buses, but the "San Juan de Dios—Estación" bus goes between the points you want: San Juan de Dios church, next to the Mercado Libertad, and the railroad station past Parque Agua Azul. This bus is best because most other buses on Independencia have longer routes (out to the suburbs, for instance) and thus tend to be more heavily crowded at all times. Buses that pass the intercity bus terminal have "Camion" written in soap on the windshield.

HOTELS IN GUADALAJARA: Guadalajara does not have the great number of budget hotels to be found in Mexico City. In fact, the number of recommendable hotels here seems small in relation to the city's size and tourist flow. But the

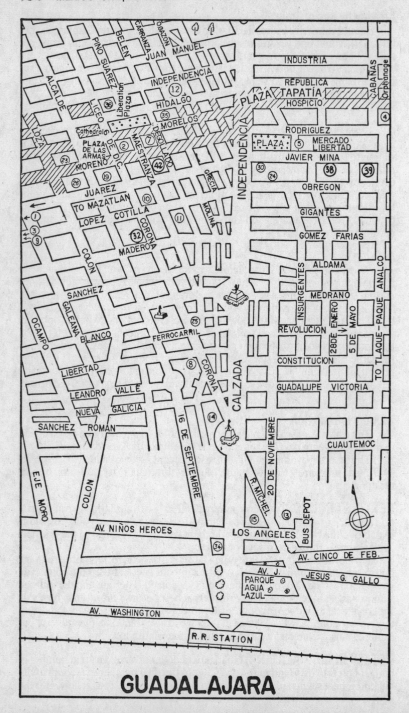

GUADALAJARA

room situation does not seem to be particularly tight. I'll look at some moderately priced hotels downtown at first, and then suggest where to go if you want to upgrade or downgrade your accommodations.

Downtown Hotels

For a new hotel with a touch of class, try the **Hotel San Francisco Plaza,** Degollado 267 near Priciliano Sanchez (tel. 36/13-8954). Stone arches, brick tile floors, bronze sculptures, and potted plants complement one another in the lobby under the skylight. The rooms are large and are well-appointed in beige tones and blond furniture. A single is priced at 4,600 pesos ($9.20) and doubles range from 5,160 to 5,985 pesos ($10.35 to $12). A small restaurant in the lobby serves breakfast and lunch.

The newish **Hotel Universo (11),** López Cotilla 161 (tel. 36/13-2815), can boast of a private garage and clean double rooms costing 4,800 to 6,500 pesos ($9.60 to $13), and singles for 4,000 to 5,000 pesos ($8 to $10). Added comforts are exceptionally nice bathrooms, piped-in music (which can be piped back out with the turn of a switch), a telephone in each room, a parking lot, and carpeted hallways.

The **Hotel Frances (7),** Maestranza 35 (tel. 36/13-6293), is on a very quiet side street right off the Plaza Libertad and near the Degollado Theater. The lobby on the ground level has crystal chandeliers, and a wonderful marble statue in a pool. The guest rooms on the second and third levels all have new private bath, telephone, good beds, and comfy furnishings for 8,050 pesos ($16.10) double. Newly refurbished, tidy, and even a bit stylish, and exceptionally well located—that's the Frances.

The modern **Hotel Continental (8),** Avenida Corona 450 at Libertad (tel. 36/14-1117), is halfway between downtown and the bus station. For its modernity, the Continental is surprisingly well worn, but prices reflect the loss of its gleam: singles are 3,450 pesos ($6.90); doubles, 4,140 to 4,370 pesos ($8.30 to $8.75); triples, 5,520 pesos ($11).

Sharing some aspects with the Continental is the **Hotel Nueva Galicia (14),** Avenida Corona 610 (tel. 36/14-8780). It's a tall, wedge-shaped building that has seen its glory days pass and is now sensible rather than snazzy. The rooms are priced at 3,864 pesos ($7.75) single, 4,830 pesos ($9.65) double. The restaurant is even better known and better patronized than the hotel; its afternoon lunch is a big event in the neighborhood.

Near the Bus Station

There is scant advantage to staying near Guadalajara's new bus station unless you're planning to leave from it early, or from the railroad station nearby—and then only if you're the kind of sleeper who snoozes blissfully through hurricanes. The mighty behemoths of the highway prowl and growl around the terminal all night, and at dawn invariably the jukebox in some all-night café coughs out Mexican rock'n'roll. The only advantages are that you'll save the taxi fare from the hotel to station, providing you can carry your bags, and you'll be able to sleep the 10 or 15 minutes longer than it would otherwise have taken to get to the station. However, if you're dead at the end of a long day on the bus and too tired to go anywhere but to the closest quiet bed, go straight to the **Hotel Praga (13),** 28 de Enero 733A (tel. 36/17-3760), a block from the bus station, to the right as you walk down the station steps. It's a fairly large (70 rooms), blue-tile building with pine siding paneling the lower part of a large, bright lobby. The lunch counter in the lobby is the dominant feature of the decor, plus the semicircular reception desk. Rooms are clean, simple, often dark, lit by fluorescent ceiling lights; they cost 2,300 pesos ($4.60) single, 2,691 to 3,084 pesos ($5.40 to $6.20) for a double, more for a twin-bedded room.

If you have no luck at the Praga, you might try the **Hotel Canada (15),** Estadio 77 (tel. 36/19-4014)—not to be confused with the new Gran Hotel Canada (which faces the bus station and is slightly more expensive). All rooms at the Canada have private bath and cost 2,200 pesos ($4.40) single, 3,000 pesos ($6) double. The place is nondescript, but clean.

The newest and most deluxe of hotels in the bus station area is the **Hotel Flamingos Guadalajara (15),** Calzada Independencia Sur 725, at the corner of Balderas (tel. 36/18-0003). It's an eight-minute walk from the bus station, out the front doors, down Los Angeles, and right. Modern and almost posh, with air conditioning, it looks as though it must be expensive, but it's not: singles are 1,725 pesos ($3.45); doubles, 1,955 to 2,070 pesos ($3.90 to $4.15).

Starvation-Budget Lodgings

Like the moderately priced hotels, Guadalajara's low-budget line-up is a mixed bag. Here are the tried-and-true places.

An excellent choice for those wishing to stay close to the Mercado is the **Hotel Ana-Isabel (38),** Calle Javier Mina 164 (tel. 36/17-7920), just across from La Libertad market. The lobby is one flight up and overlooks the bustling buying and selling. Because the rooms open onto the interior, street noise is not a problem. With cheerful staff, newly painted walls, and nice blue bathrooms, this is an excellent choice: singles are 1,700 pesos ($3.40); doubles with two double beds, 2,200 pesos ($4.40). They offer free parking too.

A block down the street on Javier Mina, at no. 230, is the **Hotel México 70 (39)** (tel. 36/17-9978). Tunnel-dark halls lead to 80 average-size rooms with clean baths. Rooms facing the street have small balconies, but watch out for the street noise. One person pays 1,700 pesos ($3.40), and two pay 2,200 pesos ($4.40) for two double beds.

Take a look at the **Posada España,** López Cotilla 594, corner of 8 de Julio (tel. 36/13-5377). The rooms here are well used, but clean and extremely inexpensive.

The Big Splurge

Stepping up a notch is easy in Guadalajara, and a few of the city's higher priced hotels offer good value for money.

The new and modern 500-room **Hotel Aranzazu (25),** Avenida Revolución 110, near the meeting-point of Corona and Degollado (tel. 36/13-3232), not only has a fine location, but a long list of luxuries as well, including color televisions in the rooms, air conditioning, two swimming pools (one for kids). Prices for all this, and for the hotel's high sheen, are not bad: 9,120 pesos ($18.25) single, 11,400 pesos ($22.80) double.

The 175-room **Hotel Calinda Roma (42),** Avenida Juárez 170 at Degollado (tel. 36/14-8650), is hooked into the Quality Inn system, so you can call their toll-free numbers for reservations. An older but well-refurbished downtown hotel, the Roma is semi-posh and quite comfy, with a rooftop swimming pool and patio bar, private parking lot, television sets (and even some refrigerators) in the rooms. The location is excellent, and the prices aren't bad: 11,625 pesos ($23.25) single, 13,225 pesos ($26.45) double.

One of this city's most popular upper-bracket hotels with foreigners is the **Hotel de Mendoza (12)** (tel. 36/13-4646), Carranza 16, corner of Hidalgo, only steps from Liberation Plaza and the Degollado Theater. Gringos and gringas seem to enjoy the colonial atmosphere, the beautifully restored building, and the modern conveniences, not to mention the prime location. Rooms come with

TV, big bed (or two big beds), air conditioning; they have a pool and a garage. You pay 10,350 pesos ($20.70) single, 11,385 pesos ($22.80) double, for any of the 100-odd rooms.

Motels

Most of the best motels are on the two highways—to Mexico City and to Mazatlán—that funnel into the Glorieta Minerva. Good English is spoken at the **Motel Chapalita,** López Mateos 1617 Sur (tel. 36/21-0607), which is modern and flashy and also has a pool in the central court. Rooms are well furnished but prices are a little high: 5,500 pesos ($11) for singles, 6,500 pesos ($13) for doubles. The motel's first-class restaurant is on the ground floor.

The road from Mazatlán is lined with motels too, all advertising pretty competitive rates. On Vallarta, the selection resembles a budget-motel grouping at home, only here the rates are a lot less.

READERS' HOTEL SELECTIONS: "I chose the **Motel del Bosque** (tel. 36/21-4650), López Mateos Sur 265, right off the Glorieta Minerva. It is ideal for those who don't want to stay amid the noise and dirt of a large city's downtown. The motel is walking distance from the Tequila Sauza plant (tours), and many small cafés and restaurants. Prices are quite reasonable: 5,750 pesos ($11.50) for a single room, or 6,900 pesos ($13.80) for two persons. The motel has a 'country club'–type garden and swimming pool; one should request an interior room facing the pool" (Shelley Harris, San Francisco, Calif.). . . . "We stayed at the **Suites Bernini,** at the corner of Vallarta and Union. We had a large bedroom with lots of closet and drawer space, tile bath with large shower, and kitchen with eating nook. It is carpeted and boasts excellent views from floor-to-ceiling windows on two sides. The typical Mexican lack of attention to maintenance shows, but the maid service is good and the place is clean. It's at Avenida Vallarta 1885 (tel. 36/16-6736), and we paid 6,900 pesos ($13.80) per day" (Jean and Bruce Wallenberg, Santa Barbara, Calif.). . . . "The **Hotel Las Americas,** Avenida Hidalgo 76 (tel. 36/13-9622 or 14-1604), has a quiet location, and clean lobby and rooms; the desk clerks speak some English. It's very well located for sightseeing on foot. Prices are 2,150 pesos ($4.30) for one person, 3,330 pesos ($6.70) for two" (Wilma Lomastro, Fairmont, Minn.). . . . "The **Posada Regis,** Av. Corona 171, at the corner of López Cotilla (tel. 36/13-3026), is in the center of downtown, but inside one would not know it because of its tranquil, friendly atmosphere. The hotel is a restored mansion, and charges $10 double ($16 double with meals)" (Mark Herman, Davis, Calif.).

READER'S LODGING TIP: "We contacted Mr. Philip Hersey, a retired Texan who is a partner in **Guadalajara Homefinders,** Rentas y Ventas S.A. (tel. 36/25-5844), c/o Motel Isabel, Room 601, Montenegro 1572, Guadalajara, Jal. 44100. He helped us to find a two-bedroom furnished apartment for $300 per month. His fee is a one-time charge of 10.15% of the first month's rent" (Prof. Irwin Rovner, Raleigh, N.C.).

EATING IN GUADALAJARA: For a really authentic Mexican meal, which is a risky thing to promise given the variety of styles in Mexican cooking, go to **El Farol (23),** Pedro Moreno 466, at Galeana, partly open to the street. Just inside the door, after you've elbowed your way past waitresses and women flapping out tortillas, you'll pass a table loaded with beautiful fruit gelatin desserts (try gelatina de frutas—as a salad). Each table is equipped with bowls of pickled carrots and lime rinds to nibble on while you wait—first for the waitress, then for the menu, then for the food, then for the check, then for the change. You can save at least ten minutes by knowing in advance what to order: tacos, four for 360 pesos (75¢), or tamales. But save some room for the cheese pie for which the restaurant is famous. Pleasantly, and perhaps uniquely, El Farol is open very late—I've passed at 2 a.m. and seen the place full of people happily munching tacos.

A very fine place to dine in the central business and shopping district is the **Café Madrid (19),** Juárez 264, a couple of doors from the corner of Juárez and Corona. The café is always full, any time of the day, and waiters in white jackets and black ties move quickly from table to kitchen and back again. For a light and inexpensive lunch, I order the generous fruit cocktail at 400 pesos (90¢), and a sandwich at 520 pesos ($1.05), which comes with a slice of tomato, some "safe" lettuce, and fried potatoes (when you order, ask for the potatoes—they seem to cost no extra). When the front section of the restaurant is crowded, there's still usually some room way in the back, next to the big mural.

It's no trouble to find restaurants offering standard breakfast fare, but if you get the urge for pastries, try the **Acropolis Café and Restaurant,** Corona 175. Feast your eyes and waistline on the colorful array of neopolitans, fresh fruit tarts, cream puffs, tortes, cakes, and pies that occupy the front of the restaurant. For the more disciplined, there are 15 standard breakfast specials, averaging 1,250 pesos ($2.50), in addition to a full menu. Hours are 8 a.m. to 10 p.m.; closed Sunday.

Thinking of late-night places, the city market is traditionally the place for all-night eats. Down by Guadalajara's Mercado Libertad and Plaza de Mariachis, it's **Mi Ranchito (24),** Obregón 21 (Obregón is the street that runs east off Independencia starting at the huge Cine Alameda). It's open "dia y noche," and serves pickled pigs' feet for 650 pesos ($1.30) in a red vinyl and Formica dining room. Other entrees include enchiladas for 350 to 650 pesos (70¢ to $1.30).

For a snack or light supper, try one of the many *loncherías* along Juárez (open for "lonch" or supper). About the nicest I found is the **Lonchería La Playita (19),** Juárez 242, where you get a receipt from the cashier, then present it to the waitress/cook for perhaps a sliced pork sandwich (torta de pierna), garnished with onions, tomatoes, and a single, easily retrievable hot pepper, at 350 pesos (70¢). Soft drinks are 80 pesos (16¢). Point to what you want—the waitress will catch on and assemble it on the spot.

One block from the Tourism Office on Juárez at no. 590 is **Balcones Mi Tierra.** It appears to have been fashioned after La Copa de Leche, lacking only the high prices and tuxedo-clad waiters of the latter establishment. The five-course comida, served on the balcony or downstairs, is 650 pesos ($1.30), tea or coffee included. The menu keeps the budget-minded customer happy by offering nothing over 1,600 pesos ($3.20): filet mignon with mushrooms is 1,600 pesos ($3.20); fish is 1,100 pesos ($2.20).

By the way, if you're looking for something a bit fancier in this area, look at the **Restaurant Agora,** in the ex-Convento del Carmen.

For Chinese Food

Guadalajara has several Chinese restaurants, but the most convenient one is the **Palacio Chino (10),** Corona 145 at López Cotilla. One large, modern room looking onto the street, the Palacio Chino is no lunch counter, but a full-fledged restaurant. As in most Chinese places, the thing to do here is to order one of the set-price meals. Number two, for instance, provides small portions of wonton soup, a fried shrimp, two spare ribs, fried rice, good pork chop suey, dessert, and tea for 1,350 pesos ($2.70). Other set-price meals go from 1,200 to 2,250 pesos ($2.40 to $4.50). Open every day for lunch and dinner.

Splurge Restaurants

Perhaps the most famous and long-lived restaurant in Guadalajara is **La Copa de Leche (26),** Juárez 414 (tel. 14-5347). A sidewalk café, plus upstairs and downstairs dining rooms, give La Copa lots of space in which to serve a varied, eclectic menu filled with Mexican, American, and continental specialties. Just for coffee and cake you might pay 880 pesos ($1.75); a full-course dinner will run as high as 2,000 pesos ($4). Open daily.

Those willing to travel from downtown for a good meal should go to Chapultepec Nte. 110 where **Los Itacates Fonda** (tel. 25-1106) is located. The brightly colored Mexican decor in pink, powder blue, and sea green will indicate the fare available here. Chicken in mole sauce or a beef brochette will cost 1,200 pesos ($2.40) and appetizers, such as queso fundido, guacamole, or aztec soup are in the range of 800 pesos ($1.60). Besides terrific food, there's a full bar and you may dine indoors or on the patio.

For lunch, especially on a hot day, whiz up the elevator to the rooftop **Restaurant Terrazza Romana** of the Hotel Roma, at Juárez 170. Here you dine at poolside on the set-price lunch for about 1,400 pesos ($2.80), from soup through dessert. Otherwise, one can dine from the bottom of the à la carte menu for about the same, all in: pork chops with a pineapple glaze, for instance, cost 1,800 pesos ($3.60). Beer, wine, and liquor are served.

If you're planning to visit Tlaquepaque in the morning, save lunch for the **Restaurant Los Cazadores,** Golfo de México 606, the last of the great patio restaurants. It will be an expensive lunch—figure 6,000 pesos ($12) per person—but well worth it. The grounds are extensive, with several arcades and rooms to dine in if it rains; otherwise you dine on the shady patio. Service and food are very good, and the easy ambience is even better. Patrons start drifting in about 1:30 p.m., and the place is full by 3. The large mariachi group is one of the best I've heard, and plays for free. The only fly in the soup (so to speak) is that one or two of the waiters are not above slight overcharges, charging for an item you didn't ask for or kindly bringing appetizers you didn't remember ordering. They all speak English, so make sure they know what you want and *don't* want. Also, booze can be outrageously expensive and cocktail prices are not on the menu. Ask the price before you order!

Now that you've been forewarned, don't miss the chance to dine at Los Cazadores. To get to the Tlaquepaque branch, leave *el parian* (the square in the village) via Independencia (which is one way). At the end of this street, turn left onto Revolución, and drive back toward Guadalajara nine-tenths of a mile. At the traffic circle, go down the street to the right of the Pemex station for two blocks. Cazadores is on the right; drive into the parking lot.

Starvation-Budget Restaurants

El Nuevo Faro, at López Cotilla 24 near Independencia, offers a great six-course comida corrida for 500 pesos ($1). (I might add that with this last revision I found that more and more restaurants are no longer offering the comidas.) Try El Nuevo Faro: the food and service are good, the prices right. It's open every day from 7 a.m. to 2 a.m.

READERS' RESTAURANT SELECTIONS: "The second floor at the **Mercado Libertad** is packed with mini restaurants serving authentic if generally undistinguished Mexican foods. Stews are cooked in huge clay bowls placed directly on the fire. You can get cabrito (roast kid) here. Most dishes are 250 to 460 pesos (50¢ to 95¢), plus a few pesos more for a stack of fresh, hot tortillas" (Norriss, Edith, and Elizabeth Hetherington, Berkeley, Calif.). . . . "I stayed at the new Fiesta Americana, and discovered **El Abajeno,** right on the circle where the Fiesta is, at the intersection of López Mateos and Vallarta. It was typically Mexican, a steak dinner plus beer for 1,500 pesos ($3), a roving band of mariachis, just delightful, highly recommended" (Fred H. Hoon, Williamsville, N.Y.). . . . "A real treasure of a place is just two doors up from the Hotel Ana-Isabel, Calle Javier Mina 164; it's called **El Buen Gusto.** It's a bakery that serves food too. Potato omelets, scrambled eggs, enchiladas were all priced under 320 pesos (65¢); fresh rolls—all you want—are served with every meal. A big glass of puréed canteloupe, papaya, or watermelon is 150 pesos (30¢). The service is friendly and quick" (Susan Bates-Harbuck, Sandpoint, Idaho).

"Our budget-priced restaurant find is **Las Margaritas**, López Cotilla 1477 (tel. 16-8906), a few doors from Chapultepec. The cuisine is vegetarian, with a three-course comida corrida priced at 850 pesos ($1.70), beverage extra (no alcohol). The comida seems to run out early on weekdays, so get there not much after 1 p.m. From the cathedral area, take the bus along Juárez to Chapultepec and walk one block to López Cotilla; the Ruta 1 bus stops at the corner; the Ruta 40 bus crosses Chapultepec three blocks away" (John H. Canavan, Queens Village, N.Y.). . . . "In a charming small plaza at Juárez and Colón is a cheerful outdoor cafe by the name of **Las Paraguas.** Dinner, consisting of chicken tacos, beans, salad, and beer was only 1,550 pesos ($3.10). A bonus is being entertained by the mimes and musicians in the plaza" (Bob Marlin, Los Angeles, Calif.).

WHAT TO SEE: Downtown Guadalajara is becoming a district ever more congenial to pedestrians. Streets are being closed to through traffic, other streets are set aside for a few buses only, still others are left only to strollers. It's simply wonderful for the sightseer.

The Spaniards started it all 4½ centuries ago when they laid out the city with a cluster of four plazas. The **Plaza de Armas,** with its ornate central bandstand, is perhaps the favorite of *tapatíos* and *tapatías* (not to mention *tapatititos*). Shopping arcades line two sides, the cathedral forms another, and the ornate **Palacio de Gobierno (2),** built in 1774, fills the last. You'll want to duck into the palacio's courtyard to view Clemente Orozco's enormous mural of Hidalgo, and various scenes portraying the Mexican fight for liberty (1937). Orozco, who lived in Guadalajara, is the city's favorite artist—more on him later.

South of the Plaza de Armas is the charming **Plaza de la Universidad,** with its huge fountain (a children's favorite) and its outdoor café (an adults' favorite). The café has food and beverages, is moderately priced, and is usually full of weary shoppers resting their limbs.

The immense **cathedral,** on the north side of the Plaza de Armas, begun in 1558 and finished 60 years later, is impressive and eclectic in style. Inside, over the doorway in the sacristy, is a painting thought to be by Bartolomé Murillo (1617–1682). In front of the cathedral is the second of the four plazas, called **Plaza de los Laureles.** One look tells you why.

KEY TO MAP OF GREATER GUADALAJARA: 1.—Minerva Fountain; 2.—Arches; 3.—Niños Héroes Monument; 4.—Juárez Square; 5.—House of Art & Crafts, and Agua Azul Park; 6.—House of Culture; 7.—Bus Depot; 8.—Technological Stadium; 9.—Baseball Park; 10.—Cockfight Arena; 11.—Revolution Square; 12.—Cathedral; 13.—Government Palace; 14.—Liberation Square; 15.—Museum; 16.—Post Office; 17.—Degollado Theater; 19.—Libertad Municipal Market; 20.—Cabañas Orphanage; 21.—Alcalde Park; 22.—Public City's High School; 23.—Morelos Park; 24.—Football Stadium; 25.—New Cemetery; 26.—Estación F.F.C.C. (train station).

On the opposite side of the cathedral from the Plaza de Armas is the **Plaza de los Martires,** with a circle of columns to commemorate Guadalajarans who fought and died for their country. East of the plaza is the museum.

The **Museo Regional de Guadalajara (Regional Museum) (36)** is open daily

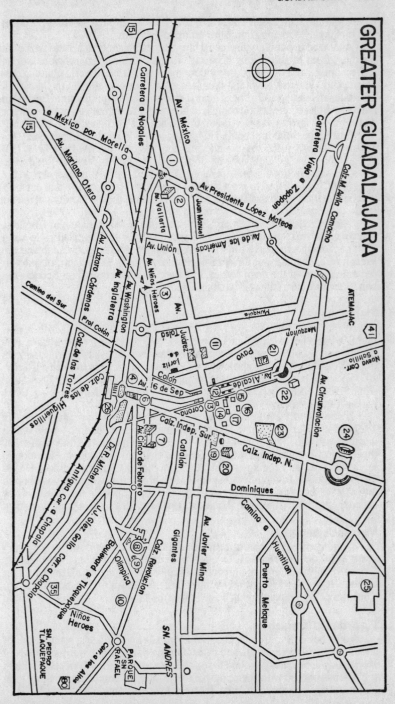

except Monday; admission is 50 pesos (10¢) Tuesday through Saturday, 25 pesos (5¢) on Sunday. Opening hours are 9 a.m. to 3:45 p.m.

Arranged around an airy courtyard, the exhibit rooms are stocked with paintings from Mexico's long history: 17th- and 18th-century religious works, folk paintings, and works by the modern masters Orozco, Rivera, Quiroga, Vizcarra, and Figueroa. Several rooms (nos. 6 and 7) are devoted to the history of the state of Jalisco, and others hold displays of ethnography and European painting. At least one exhibit room is held open for temporary shows of crafts or works by local artists. It's well done, this place, and worth a visit by all means.

East of the cathedral, behind it, is the spacious **Plaza de la Liberación** (Liberation Plaza), with the wonderful neoclassical **Teatro Degollado (35)** (Degollado—that's "Deh-goh-*yah*-doh"—Theater) at its far (east) end. The two streets that bound the plaza, Hidalgo on the left (north) and Morelos on the right (south), are closed to most traffic. Look down Morelos for a fine perspective view of the great **Plaza Tapatía,** with the domed Hospicio Cabañas at the far end.

The Degollado, Guadalajara's prime theater for legitimate plays, operas, and concerts, was built in the 1850s and named for Santos Degollado. He was a local patriot who supported Juárez in the struggle against Maximilian and the French (Guadalajara was Juárez's capital for a time). Degollado, despite his fervent support of the great Juárez, lost every fight he entered on Benito's behalf. So what? He's still a hero in this city!

Plaza Tapatía

Walk down Morelos from the theater. Behind the Degollado is a new mural in bas relief, with a fountain, entitled *The Founding of Guadalajara*. Farther along is a sculpture of a tree with lions, then two huge slabs bearing the texts of Charles V's proclamations that gave Guadalajara the right to call itself a city.

Soon the concourse opens into a fine big plaza, complete with dedication stone (1982). Fountains are everywhere, and giant department stores and office blocks frame the plaza.

It's not far to the **Hospicio Cabañas,** or Cabañas Orphanage (4), founded in 1829 and used for just that purpose—housing homeless children—until only a decade or so ago. The orphanage is a huge and complex structure with many inner courts, but what you want to see is the main building with the fine dome. Here, the walls and ceiling are covered in murals by Clemente Orozco (1883–1949), brooding, frightening, magnificent paintings that will take your breath away. Wide benches allow you to lie on your back to view the murals. Now called the Instituto Cultural Cabañas, it's open from 9 a.m. to 4 p.m. every day.

Mercado Libertad

Coming out of Gabañas, turn left and find a stairway down to the mammoth Mercado Libertad (5), Guadalajara's modern central market building. One can easily wander in this great blur of color, smells, sights, and activities for an hour. If you need a quiet break, duck into the San Juan de Dios church (30). The interior's baroque, having been built in the 1700s.

Plaza de los Mariachis

Right beside San Juan de Dios is the Plaza de los Mariachis, actually a short street lined with restaurants and cafés. During daylight hours, small bands of mariachis will be loafing around here and there, sipping a cool one. But at night the place is packed with them, bashing away at their guitars and singing their hearts out for love and/or money. It's a sight you must not miss.

Parque Agua Azul

The Parque Agua Azul (near the bus station at the south end of Calzada Independencia) is filled with plants, trees, shrubbery, statues, fountains, etc. This is the perfect refuge from the bustling city. Pay the admission fee, wander in, and visit the zoo (you may be lucky enough to see the hippopotamus getting his daily bath—with a firehose—or the lions their monster lunch). For kids there's "El Chuku Chuku," a rubber-tire minitrain that circulates through the grounds. "Los Espejos Magicos" is the house of mirrors. Lots more to explore and discover.

Also within the park is the **Instituto de las Artesanías de Jalisco,** the state-run crafts market, with a good selection.

Near the entrance to the park is the **flower market.** It's not difficult, after a glimpse here, to see why Guadalajara is sometimes called the City of Roses. A tremendous bouquet of three or four dozen roses sells for only a few dollars. Half a block north is the modern building of the **Experimental Theater of Jalisco,** which is well worth the admission charge, even for those who don't speak Spanish.

The state-run **Casa de la Cultura (34)** is near the entrance to the park, across from the flower market. Besides a permanent deep-relief mural they have exhibitions of contemporary art.

Rodeos

Also in the region of Agua Azul, actually to the east of it, is the **Aceves Galindo Lienzo,** or rodeo ring, where you can see a *charreada,* or Mexican rodeo, each Sunday during the summer at noon. Riding, roping and rope tricks, and a traditional grand promenade are all part of the action at the charreada.

Orozco Museum

Clemente Orozco's Guadalajara studio (3) was turned into a museum after the artist's death, and it makes for a fascinating hour's visit. Take a Par Vial bus, or no. 40, "Plaza del Sol," on Avenida Juárez all the way to the Glorieta Minerva (1), the large traffic circle with statue and fountain on the main highway north. See the arches? The studio is at Calle Aurelio Aceves 27, just beside the arches, open Tuesday through Saturday from 10 a.m. to 2 p.m. and 3:30 to 5 p.m., on Sunday to 2 p.m., for 150 pesos (30¢) admission. A modern cement building, it contains many examples of the artist's violent but bewitching work: magnificent character studies, portraits of the artist's family, and a room devoted entirely to sketches of the 1910 revolution (Orozco was 27 years old in 1910). By the way, Orozco died in 1949, in Mexico City.

Side Trip to the Tequila Plant

Now that you're out here, you might want to take a tour of the Tequila Sauza bottling plant, just a bit farther (walking distance) along Avenida Vallarta (no. 3213, on the left) on the way out of town. They're open weekdays during business hours, and if you're there between noon and 1:30 p.m. you can join in the "Happy Hour," with fantastic creamy tequila drinks. By the way, this is just a bottling plant. The distillery is—where else?—in the town of Tequila, off Highway 15 about 40 kilometers (25 miles) east of Guadalajara.

Tlaquepaque and Tonalá

The suburbs of Tlaquepaque and Tonalá are of special interest to pottery aficionados, for here is where some of Mexico's best is made. You should consider a day trip to these towns. For details, see below under "Shopping in Guadalajara."

NIGHTTIME ACTIVITIES: Center of cultural activities in the evening is the **Degollado Theater (35)** in the Plaza de la Liberación, where concerts by the State Symphony Orchestra and visiting groups, opera performances, recitals, and ballet folklorico performances by the university's Grupo Folkiorico (every Sunday) take place. Tickets to most events cost from 400 to 1,500 pesos (90¢ to $3), the second balcony seats being just about right. Note that the theater is not air-conditioned.

Nearby in the **Plaza de las Armas,** the Jalisco State Band puts on free concerts every Sunday evening starting about 6 p.m. during the summer.

Don't forget the **Plaza de los Mariachis (3),** down by San Juan de Dios and the Libertad Market, junction of Calzada Independencia and Juárez/Javier Mina. Every evening the colorfully clad mariachis of the city, in various tuneful keys and states of inebriation, hold forth for money (if they can get it) or for free. You can have a meal here, or a snack, or a soft drink, or just stand around spending nothing but time, and no one will bother you, except perhaps the itinerant vendors who abound in such places. Do this for sure one evening; it's fun and it's free.

Ever been to a cockfight? The local "pit" is the **Plaza de Gallos, "La Tapatía,"** on the way to Tlaquepaque (take a Tlaquepaque bus from along Calzada Independencia). Profits from the blood-sport go to charity, oddly enough; matches are held every Sunday, Monday, and Tuesday evening. Be there by about 7 p.m.

Most of the downtown music-and-dance scene takes place in hotel clubs. The **Sheraton** (tel.14-7272), Avenida 16 de Septiembre and Niños Héroes, is typical. The Bar Chinaco has a trio playing music nightly until midnight; 1,200 pesos ($2.40) cover charge, no minimum. The disco here is called Delirium. There's a rooftop supper club too, La Rondalla, on the 20th floor, with shows at 11 p.m. and 1 a.m.

SHOPPING IN GUADALAJARA: Besides the mammoth **Mercado Libertad (5),** described above, in which you can find almost anything, Guadalajara now boasts the largest modern shopping center in Latin America. It's the **Plaza del Sol** megacomplex, sprawling over 120,000 square yards in an area at the junction of Avenidas López Mateos and Mariano Otero, outside the center of town. Here you can buy anything from a taco to a Volkswagen; you can also cash a check, make a plane reservation, or buy a lottery ticket. There are even hotels and restaurants for weary shoppers! Take the no. 40 bus from Calzada Independencia near the Libertad Market.

Right by the junction of Juárez and 16 de Septiembre is a branch of the worldwide chain of Woolworth's. There's a convenient pedestrian passageway that runs under Juárez where there are many stalls selling candied fruits, leather belts, and other goods. A better place to purchase leather goods, however, is down on **Pedro Moreno,** a street that runs parallel to Juárez, and for shoes, go to **E. Alatorre** where 70 shoe stores are located.

Tlaquepaque and Tonalá
Apart from the regular around-the-streets shopping downtown, Guadalajara holds a special treat for shoppers—an excursion to the neighboring suburb of **Tlaquepaque** (pronounced "*Tla*-kay-*pah*-kay"). You'll find buses labeled

"Tlaquepaque" or "Tonalá" constantly along the Calzada Independencia. It's a two-mile ride. To drive, go south on Calzada Independencia (toward the Agua Azul Park) and turn left onto the Avenida Revolución. This main thoroughfare goes all the way to Tlaquepaque. You'll get to a traffic circle by a Pemex station. Revolución continues along the left side of this station. Nine-tenths of a mile from the circle, just as the tree-lined median in the road comes to an end, turn right onto the street that will take you to *el parian,* the main plaza in Tlaquepaque.

Tlaquepaque is famous for two things: its sidewalk cafés with innumerable mariachis (Sunday evenings, you can sit and hear about six different groups around you); and its pottery and glass "factories." The latter are an absorbing sight. In a score of private houses are rooms off the patio devoted to racks and racks of glazed and unglazed bowls, jars, figurines, glass and pottery animals, bathtubs big and old enough for Roman emperors to have bathed in, tiles, jugs, and miniature figures of priests, soldiers, brides, and bulls. The street on which to find all these factories is Independencia. Stop in at the **Regional Ceramics Museum** (hours are 10 a.m. to 4 p.m.; closed Monday) at Independencia 237. There is no entrance fee and the display of ceramics is worth the visit. Don't miss the figurines in clay of Mexican presidents from Díaz to Echeverría, a delightful cross between caricature and statuary.

Across the street from the museum is the **glass factory.** In a room at the rear of the patio, a dozen scurrying men and boys heat glass bottles and jars on the end of hollow, steel poles. Then, blowing furiously, they'll chase across the room, narrowly missing spectators and fellow workers alike as they swing the red-hot glass within an inch of a man who sits placidly rolling an elaborate jug out of another chunk of the cooling glass. Nonchalantly, the old man will leave his own task long enough to clip off the end of the boy's vase at the exact moment at which it comes within reach of his hand. Then he drops the clippers and returns once more to his own task as the urchin charges back across the room to reheat the vase in the furnace.

Tlaquepaque has become "refined" in the past years, and prices have risen considerably, making shopping there a dubious bargain. If you see something you can't resist, be *sure* to bargain for it. Perhaps due to the deluge of American tourists, prices are artificially high—sometimes even by American standards—and cash withdrawn from your wallet at the proper psychological moment or a mock exit from the store will normally bring them down to a proper level. If you purchase something, take it with you, or else you might find yourself having paid for shipping and then receiving a notice after you return home, informing you that $10 is owed in innumerable fees and shipping charges.

Final hint: Get to Tlaquepaque in the morning or evening, for the shops close between 2 and 4 p.m.

By the way, the village of **Tonalá,** three miles farther along the road, is no longer the "poor man's Tlaquepaque." The tourist traffic has finally arrived, and the town really differs from Tlaquepaque only in that it's harder to get to. There is, however, an interesting factory in which you can see the artisans painting delicate designs on their pottery. Park in the zócalo (or disembark from any no. 6 bus), and at least three boys will offer to take you there.

READER'S RESTAURANT SELECTION—TLAQUEPAQUE: "We had one of the best splurge meals ever at the **Restaurant With No Name,** Madero 80, in Tlaquepaque. The food was superb, large servings, vegetables washed in pure water. Our lunch of soup, salad, and main course came to $8. Two white male peacocks 'perform' on the patio" (William H. Brickner, Los Altos, Calif.). [*Note from T.B.:* Other readers have also written to recommend the No Name Restaurant.]

2. Lake Chapala

Mexico's largest lake has long been popular with foreign vacationers. The climate is perfect, the scenery gorgeous; several charming or quaint little towns border the lake; and the big city is only 26 miles away.

There's not a lot to see or do here unless you stay a while, renting a house or apartment. If you do stay, anything can happen. D. H. Lawrence ended up writing *The Plumed Serpent* during his stay in Ajijic. Those of us who are less ambitious might be satisfied to make some new friends among Ajijic's expatriate community, and enjoy the lake views.

Three towns—Chapala, Ajijic, and Jocotepec—border the lake and draw tourists. Each has a different ambience.

GETTING TO CHAPALA: Buses run several times a day from Guadalajara's Central Camionera (bus station) on the 45-minute run to the town of Chapala. If you're lucky enough to have a car, you'll be able to enjoy the lake and its towns more fully. Here's how to drive there:

Although you can get to Lake Chapala via Hwy. 15/80, be advised that most heavy truck traffic also uses this route to the south. If you're driving, I'd suggest you leave Guadalajara via Avenida Gonzalez Gallo, which intersects with Calzada Independencia just before Playa Azul Park. Going south on Independencia, you turn left onto Gallo and follow it all the way out of town past the airport, where it becomes Hwy. 44, the main road to Chapala. The 42-kilometer drive is through peaceful farming country, and you don't really get a view of the lake until you're almost in Chapala.

CHAPALA: With a wide but dusty main street (Avenida Madero) leading down to the lakeshore, Chapala, Jalisco, is the district's business and administrative center as well as its oldest resort. Not that there's much business, or even resort activity. Much of the town's prosperity comes from wealthy retirees who live on the outskirts and come into Chapala to change money, buy groceries, check the stock ticker, etc. It can be a pretty sleepy place. If laid-back is what you like, you'll like Chapala.

The **Tourist Information Office** (tel. 376/5-2279) is at 200A Madero, on the same street as the Hotel Nido. They speak English, and have maps and brochures. Around the corner from the tourist office, at Hidalgo 202, is **Libros y Revistas,** a shop that carries English-language newspapers, magazines, and books.

Where to Stay and Eat

For transients, the best budget hotel in town is the **Nido,** right in the center of town a half block from the water at Madero 202 (tel. 376/5-2116). On the premises you'll find bar, pool, and a well-tended garden. The 30 rooms are spacious, with those facing the street even larger than the interior rooms. Rates for rooms alone: 2,400 pesos ($4.80) single, 2,950 to 3,910 pesos ($5.90 to $7.85) double.

The restaurant in the Nido is also very popular. Many of the retired people living in Chapala eat all three meals here and highly recommend the fare. For the casual visitor, the comida corrida is 1,500 pesos ($3), and will constitute the main meal of the day.

Just up Madero at no. 412 is the **Superior,** a more modest establishment very popular with locals, both *gringo* and *indigeno*. Known for its soups, the Superior serves an excellent caldo miche (a savory fish chowder) for 600 pesos ($1.20). With a tuna salad plate, your lunch will cost 900 pesos ($1.80).

Still on Madero at 421 is the **Café Paris,** a small, bright-orange plastic table and chair place. Prices are competitive with the neighbors': have a sandwich for 400 to 750 pesos (80¢ to $1.50), or go elegant and dine on whitefish for 700 pesos ($1.40). A good breakfast of ham and eggs, toast, and coffee, served 8 a.m. to midnight, is only 500 pesos ($1).

La Viuda, around the corner from the wonderfully garish city hall at Hidalgo 217B, is Chapala's class act: wall-to-wall carpeting, baby-grand piano, cool and dark interior. The specialty in the evening is steak, but in the afternoon you can enjoy good red snapper here for only 1,550 pesos ($3.10).

Of the numerous lakeside restaurants, the most attractive and popular is the **Beer Garden Restaurant,** where fish tacos cost 900 pesos ($1.80), sandwiches are around 320 pesos (65¢), and pescado blanco (white fish) is 2,000 pesos ($4). This place is generally crammed with old and young who are chatting, listening to music, or just watching the people. It's a good place day or night to catch the local activity, or to take in the superb lake view. During peak season, **El Tubo,** a disco upstairs, offers weekend dancing. By the way, the Hotel Nido restaurant and El Mirador share the same kitchen.

Located several kilometers outside of Chapala on Hidalgo (which becomes the lake drive) is the handsome 20-room **Chula Vista Hotel** (tel. 376/5-2213), with singles at 5,000 pesos ($10) and doubles at 6,300 pesos ($12.60). You have to have a car to enjoy this place; without one, you're isolated. The hotel is not right on the lake, by the way, but across the highway a short distance from the shore.

AJIJIC: Past the Chula Vista Hotel, the road continues past luxurious houses and open country to Ajijic, Jalisco. As you reach this town, the highway becomes a wide, tree-lined boulevard through an obviously wealthy residential district called La Floresta. One of Ajijic's best places to stay is here, to the left, down by the lake (watch for signs); the others are in the town proper, a place of narrow, cobbled streets, a small church and square, and sunny dispositions.

Where to Stay and Eat

The aforementioned lodging in the luxury district is the **Villa Formoso** (tel. 376/5-2369), at Paseo de las Olas and Boulevard Camino Real, owned and operated by Reg and Mickey Church (Apdo. Postal 193, Ajijic, Jalisco, México). Although accommodations and service are American style, the grounds capture the essence of Mexican charm and Jalisco architecture. The studio and bedroom apartments, both with complete kitchen facilities, and the bedrooms, are all in an enclosed, 200-year-old mango grove. Other facilities include a swimming pool, a hydro-massage pool, meeting and exercise rooms, and a laundry room. Prices are in U.S. dollars: studio apartments are $325 per month; two-bedroom apartments are $375 per month.

The best hotel right in town is the **Posada Ajijic,** on Calle 16 de Septiembre (tel. 376/5-3395). It is a posh collection of Mexican-style bungalows set in tropical gardens rampant with coffee bushes, poinsettias, and banana trees around a turquoise pool. Rates are 4,500 pesos ($9) single, 5,200 to 6,300 pesos ($10.40 to $12.60) double—not at all outlandish. Service, liquor, and food here are magnificent, and the whole place rather reminds one of the expensive summer houses city people go to and pretend to be roughing it. Whether you stay or not, you'll enjoy a stroll around the grounds or the conversation in the lounge. By the way, the bulletin board at the Posada has all sorts of news about rentals, sales of furniture and appliances, lessons, rides and riders, etc.

The **Motel Las Casitas,** located just outside of town on the main highway at Carretera Pte. 20 (no phone), has singles at 3,500 pesos ($7) and doubles at

4,000 pesos ($8). You just can't go wrong here, considering these are truly *casitas* ("little houses") with separate kitchen, large dining and sitting room, bath, and bedroom. The 11 apartments aren't located in the classy lake section, but they are clean, the grounds and teardrop-shaped pool are well kept, and parking is no problem. Weekly and monthly rates are available.

Very near the aforementioned hotel is the **Posada Las Calandrias** (tel. 376/ 5-2819), on the main highway, a brick, two-story building surrounding a nice pool, bougainvillea everywhere, and on the cars, license plates from everywhere: Rhode Island, Montana, British Columbia. The very comfy rooms-with-bath cost 4,600 pesos ($9.20), single or double.

As for dining, the **Posada Ajijic** is your best bet, featuring a comida corrida at lunchtime every day for 1,600 pesos ($3.20), a bit more on Sunday. Brunch on Sunday is from 11 a.m. to 2 p.m., a set-price repast with wine.

What to Do

Ajijic is a quiet place, the main occupations being drinking, reading, and loafing, and the main inhabitants (apart from local fishermen) being good, bad, and indifferent writers and painters, with, recently, a sprinkling of retirees. Social life centers around the cantina at the Posada Ajijic, where a band (of sorts) plays for dancing on weekends. Recently, an **anthropological museum** opened with numerous pre-Columbian ceramic pieces. It's open every day from 10 a.m. to 6 p.m.; admission is 150 pesos (30¢). It's located on the lake drive outside of town.

In the same building complex is a small shop displaying and selling regional craft items made by students who are busily at work upstairs above the shop in a school for artisans.

In the evening (except Monday) you can drop in at **El Tapanco Bar and Disco,** on Calle 16 de Septiembre in the same block as the Posada Ajijic, on the other side of the street. They always have conversation and libations, sometimes food and music. Open at 4 p.m.

JOCOTEPEC: This pretty town a few kilometers west of Ajijic has less of a tourist trade, despite its large arts-and-crafts, bar-and-restaurant establishment called the **Casa de Las Naranjitos.**

Just east of Jocotepec is the pretty motor inn called the **Posada del Pescador** (tel. 28; Apdo. Postal 67). The 14 colonial-style bungalows are scattered around the pool in surroundings that would be great for a flower garden, although one has yet to be developed. Each separate apartment has kitchenette, dining area, fireplace, bedroom, and bath. The bungalows go for 4,600 pesos ($9.20), single or double.

3. Colima

Due south of Guadalajara lies the state of Colima. Although one of Mexico's smallest, it has an incredible range of climate and topography. Northern Colima is pine and lumber country, containing half of the 13,000-foot Volcan de Colima, the northern portion of which lies in Jalisco. This is Mexico's second-highest active volcano, which last erupted in 1941. Yet less than 100 linear miles south of these bleak uplands is a palm-fringed tropic littoral that could pass for the shores of Bali.

Many Americans, who think Colima begins and ends with the popular port of Manzanillo, are missing a bet by overlooking the state's attractive capital. This city, also named Colima, is a balmy metropolis of 80,000 that dates back to 1523. Its founder was the conquistador Gonzalo de Sandoval, youngest member of Cortés's general staff.

While Colima lies virtually at the foot of the volcano, its 1,640-foot altitude makes for a climate that far more resembles Manzanillo's than that of the immediately adjacent mountain area.

Only 165 miles from Guadalajara, Colima can be reached by a picturesque road that skirts the volcano. Also visible on this trip is an even higher mountain, the 14,000-foot Nevado de Colima, which, in spite of its name, lies entirely in the state of Jalisco. Leaving Guadalajara, you take Rte. 80 until you reach Acatlán. Then turn left off Rte. 54, passing through Sayula and Ciudad Guzman until you reach Rte. 110. There you turn right and after a few miles right again. You're now on a state road that takes you to Colima on the route closest to the volcano. On the way you'll go through Atentique, a highland community where lumber is king.

HOTELS IN COLIMA: Colima's best budget hotel is on the zócalo, also known as the Jardín Libertad. It's the **Hotel Casino,** Portal Morelos 11 (tel. 331/2-1406), a beautiful building with classic white façade and open arches. Singles are 2,070 pesos ($4.15) and doubles go for 2,530 pesos ($5.10) in one bed, for 2,875 pesos ($5.75) in two beds. All 55 rooms have ceiling fans and overlook either the zócalo or the interior patio. The Casino's main visual attraction is a large semi-open lounge separated from the street only by grillwork. The hotel also boasts an interior patio with a fountain. Both patio and lounge are generously endowed with potted plants.

Not nearly as nice is the **Hotel Ceballos,** on the eastern side of the Jardín at Portal Medellin 16 (tel. 331/2-1354); singles are 4,025 to 4,370 pesos ($8.05 to $8.75), and doubles cost 5,175 to 6,900 pesos ($10.35 to $13.80), top price going for the hotel's three air-conditioned rooms. Frankly, although it looks great from the outside, they've done a lot of squeezing to make more rooms, and the interior has lost its courtyard as well as its charm.

READER'S HOTEL SELECTION: "Our hotel was the **San Cristóbal,** one block west of the zócalo. It's not fancy but it's clean, with fantastic maid service, for 2,530 pesos ($5.10) double" (Susan Bates-Harbuck, Sandpoint, Idaho).

RESTAURANTS IN COLIMA: The leading restaurant downtown is **Las Naranjas** (The Orange Trees). From the zócalo you walk down Madero (which is left of the cathedral) and take the first street on your left. Your destination, no. 32, is a handsomely decorated place with orange and white linens, light-blue walls, and orange fruit designs hand-painted on the chairs. There's a patio in the rear, blessedly cool on those hot summer days; excellent carne asada for 1,300 pesos ($2.60), plus an assortment of tacos for 150 pesos (30¢). The comida costs 1,100 pesos ($2.20)—a bit of elegant dining for a low price.

Just one block from the zócalo (main square), near the corner of Hidalgo and Medellin, is the **Restaurant Boca de Pascuales,** a hole-in-the-wall diner serving breakfast, lunch, and dinner at bargain-basement prices.

WHAT TO DO: An absolute must activity here is a visit to the city's extraordinary **antique car collection.** The entrance is through the auto-parts store on Parque Nuñez, Colima's largest park. A 150-peso (30¢) entrance fee entitles you to visit three lots that house 350 immaculately restored cars ranging in model year from 1912 to 1941. If, as legend states, all good Americans go to Paris, when they die, it would appear that all good Pierce-Arrows go to Colima.

Also, you should journey to the end of Calle 27 de Septiembre, to Colima's university, for a look at their **Cultural Anthropological Museum.** Besides a fascinating collection of Indian costumes and crafts, there's a good gift store, with prices for some goods much lower than in, say, Guadalajara. Entry to the museum is free.

ONWARD FROM COLIMA: From Colima, it's almost 140 miles to the junction of Hwy. 15, which goes west to Lake Chapala, a resort lake popular with gringoes (see Section 2 in this chapter). Going on to Mexico City, though, you head east, toward Zamora, Uruapán, Patzcuaro, and Morelia.

All the countryside around this region, and onward right into Morelia, is lush and beautiful. It's a major agricultural area and many cattle and sheep graze in fields beside the road.

Continuing south on Rte. 15, the next major town is **Zamora,** Michoacán (alt. 5,275 feet; pop. 85,822), an agricultural center where an overnight stop can be made. The **Hotel Mendoza,** Avenida Morelos Sur 190 (tel. 351/2-1540), is a fairly new building decorated with a heavy colonial touch, whose cool lobby has lots of dark-stained woodwork and a delightful patio with fountain in a manicured grass square. Rooms are on the small side, very clean, with substantial furniture and private baths. The cost is 4,600 pesos ($9.20) for singles, 5,750 pesos ($11.50) for doubles. Downstairs, there's a colonial-type restaurant with blue ceiling, heavy black beams, and a 1,200-peso ($2.40) comida corrida that is an endless procession of food, seven full courses plus coffee.

The **Hotel Fenix** (tel. 351/2-0266) is the biggest in town, with a large new addition. There are two entrances now: the old at Corregidora 54, the new at Madero 401 as you enter town. It is difficult to describe; suffice it to say that the place sprawls, makes ample use of stained glass, and is dominated by a tower (resembling a minaret . . . sort of), which houses the stairs and is encrusted with a series of yellow galleries and pillars. The accommodations range from 1920s-style rooms without bath for 3,450 pesos ($6.90) single, 4,025 pesos ($8.05) double, to the newer section surrounding a kidney-shaped pool. Here the rooms—tucked away behind wooden doors—are simple and clean, with private bath. These rooms are more expensive, of course. There's also a restaurant, bar, two pools, steambath, and nightclub.

4. Uruapán

Uruapán, Michoacán (alt. 5,500 feet; pop. 150,000), has long been famous for the lacquered boxes and trays turned out in the region, and in 1943 became even better known when Paricutin, a brand-new volcano, suddenly erupted in the middle of a cornfield, pouring lava over two nearby villages and forcing thousands from their homes. The volcano, active only a short time, is now extinct and can be seen from a long way away.

Although this town in itself has little to offer in the way of dazzling tourist sights, there are a few side trips that are quite worthwhile. Because of its dearth of tourist attractions, hotels and restaurants in Uruapán tend to be reasonably priced. In fact, it's not madly unreasonable to spend the night in Uruapán and then take a day trip to more touristy (and admittedly more attractive) Pátzcuaro, less than an hour's ride away.

GETTING TO AND FROM PÁTZCUARO AND URUAPÁN: Being slightly off the main highway, most transportation is via Morelia.

By Bus

Autotransportes La Piedad Cabadas and Autobuses de la Piedad operate first-class buses from Pátzcuaro to Morelia or Guadalajara, two buses daily to each destination. If you're headed for Guadalajara and you miss the direct bus, it's best to backtrack to Morelia and get a direct Guadalajara bus from there.

By Train

Three trains run daily in each direction between Uruapán and Mexico City, calling at Pátzcuaro and Morelia. The third train's schedule requires that you spend the night in Acambaro, so it's not really worth considering. The station in Pátzcuaro is down near the lake just off the main highway, and is connected with the town by municipal bus service.

ORIENTATION: Once you find your way to Uruapán's long main square, about 20 blocks from the bus station, you're all set. The "square" is actually a very long rectangle running east-west. The churches are on the north side; the Hotel Victoria, etc., on the south. The market is behind the churches, and in short, everything you need is within a block or two of the square.

WHERE TO STAY AND EAT: One of the nicest hotels in town is 1½ blocks southwest of the plaza on E. Carranza, at no. 15. The **Hotel Villa de Flores** (tel. 452/2-1650) is not fancy, just clean and neat and highly recommended by those who visit here frequently. The 29 good-size rooms open on the typical patio or court full of huge potted plants. Rates are 2,950 pesos ($5.90) single, 3,700 pesos ($7.40) double. The restaurant in the back is also highly recommended, particularly for its regional dishes, which usually include corn fixed in some unusual way. For something different, try the buñuelos, or tamales con atole for 320 pesos (65¢).

The most advertised hotel in town, but not quite worth all the trumping, is the **Hotel Victoria,** Cupatitzio 11, a block southeast of the main plaza (tel. 452/3-6700). Five-storied, modern, and equipped with bar and restaurant, the Victoria charges a steep 5,750 pesos ($11.50) for singles, 7,130 pesos ($14.25) for doubles. It's undistinguished, but the top floor has a nice terrace with a pretty view of Uruapán and surrounding countryside.

Perhaps the city's newest and most modern hotel is the **Nuevo Hotel Alameda,** Avenida 5 de Febrero no. 11, a half block south from the east end of the square (tel. 452/3-4100). Telephones, TV sets, parking lot, slick and tidy bathrooms—all the niceties are here, and are yours for 3,750 pesos ($7.50) single, 4,725 pesos ($9.45) double.

The **Hotel Mirador,** at the southwest end of the plaza (tel. 452/2-0473), is some 50 years old and looks it. The lobby is decked out with random tubes of fluorescent lighting hanging from mustard-colored beams and, upstairs, there's wood instead of the usual stone and tile. Some of the rooms are rather big and all have a private bath—of sorts—and some even have steps up to the windows. The rooms without windows at all should be avoided; some of the others will do, and even lay claim to a certain charm. After, say, 30 hours on a bus, the Mirador will do. Singles are cheap at 1,500 pesos ($3); doubles, equally so for 2,500 pesos ($5).

The **Restaurant Las Palmas** is one short block north of the west end of the square, in a low building at the end of the block. You'll see an arts-and-crafts shop next door. Bright-gold furniture, pleasant señora, moderate prices: a lunch of soup, carne asada, dessert, and coffee need cost only 1,100 pesos ($2.20), and if you prefer antojitos (the traditional Mexican dishes such as tacos, enchiladas, quesadillas, etc.) you can dine for much less.

A restaurant that attracts young and old as an evening meeting place is the **Emperador Restaurant,** Matamoros 18, right on the square (south side). The very polite waiters here wear white jackets and black bow ties, and bring you beef prepared in a variety of ways—filet emperador, at 1,700 pesos ($3.40), is tops. Less fancy tacos, chilaquiles, and club sandwiches, however, are substantially lower in price. Coffee drinkers—and the place is full of them after dark—can indulge their habit for hours at 135 pesos (27¢) per cup. Stronger drinks are served upstairs at a bar called **La Naranja.**

Although you'll think you're entering a fast-food restaurant when you see the white tile counter and yellow booths, **El Rincon del Burrito Real** surprises you with good, solid meals. Located at Portal Matamoros 7, this restaurant has a variety of Mexican dishes from 790 to 1,125 pesos ($1.60 to $2.25). The flauta campechana, at 990 pesos ($2), is a large flour tortilla stuffed with chicken, onions, and peppers, topped with cheese, sour cream, and sauce, and then served with beans and rice—what a meal!

Holanda Helados, an ice-cream parlor, is at Cupatitzio 28, down the same side street as the Hotel Victoria. Single scoops are 130 pesos (26¢), and they say they have 50 different flavors—who could ever eat even a single-dip cone of each, at a total cost 6,000 pesos ($12), to prove there were duplications?

READER'S HOTEL SELECTION: "There is a cheap, clean, quiet, and extremely cheerful hotel near the Casa de los Estudiantes and the Museo. It's the **Hotel Misolar,** Calle Juan Delgado 10 (tel. 452/2-0912). A double is 3,000 pesos ($6) a night. The style is traditional Mexican, with a sunny indoor patio; some rooms have mountain views" (Marlene Engel, New York, N.Y.).

WHAT TO DO: Although I wouldn't make a special trip to Uruapán to go to the market, it's worth a look when you're in town. Look behind the cathedral on Vasco de Quiroga to find the products of Michoacán, including the famous lacquered trays, dishes, and boxes.

All markets are attended by shoppers who get hungry, and the rows of food counters here are particularly clean and appealing, bearing heavy loads of the wherewithal to make such regional specialties as huchepos (green corn with sauce), atole de grano or atole blanco (a liquid refreshment), or churipo con corundas (chicken, dried beef, pork, and vegetables in a soup). Little eateries in the market area specialize in these dishes, and a ten-minute rest on one of the three stools (they hardly ever have more) with a bowl of food and a view of the market is a real slice of Uruapán.

Uruapán also has a small museum, a reason for local pride. **La Huatapera** was set up for citizens, obviously, and not for tourists, and thus has a charm born of authenticity. Attached to the cathedral, La Huatapera was once (1565–1965) a hospital—one of the first in Latin America. Exhibits are mostly of regional ceramic work and dinnerware. Hours are 9:30 a.m. to 1:30 p.m. and 3:30 to 6 p.m. Tuesday through Sunday, closed Monday; no charge for admission.

READER'S SIGHTSEEING TIP—FESTIVALS: "I went to Uruapán to attend a *fería* of regional craftwork which is held every year on the Saturday before Palm Sunday and continuing through Holy Week—an overwhelming display of pottery, embroidery, lacquered and carved woodwork, weavings, baskets, hats, handmade toys, copper work, and most wonderful of all, extraordinary painted clay statues and sculptures of devils, Last Suppers, etc., that I have only seen equalled in the work of Hieronymus Bosch. The displays filled the zócalo and the churchyards around it. Needless to say, all of this wonderful stuff can be acquired at very low prices, which get lower as the week goes on. Since all hotel prices go up on Monday, with the beginning of Holy Week, I recommend arriving on Friday" (Callie Angell, New York, N.Y.).

SIDE TRIPS TO THE VOLCANO AND NATIONAL PARK: Get up early, go down to the Central de Autobuses (city buses will take you there), and hop a bus to Angahuan, a small Tarascan village about 34 kilometers from Uruapán. Once there, you will be besieged by guides/hustlers ready to take you, for a price—about 2,500 pesos ($5)—to the half-buried village of Paricutin, or for about three times that price to the very crater of the volcano. Actually, you don't need a guide or a steed to get to the buried church in Paricutin; the walk takes only a little over a half hour. You may want to rent a horse and guide to get to the summit, though, as this can be perilous, and the journey can take six to seven hours. Plan an entire day for the trip from Uruapán, the ride to the summit, the return, and the trip back to Uruapán.

A less exacting side trip is that to the Parque Nacional Eduardo Ruíz, a botanical delight only eight blocks west of the main plaza (a Plaza Toros Quinta or a Toros Centro Parque bus, which stops in front of the telegraph office on the main square, will even run you down to the park). You may want to "hire" one of the juvenile guides who will offer their services—just to keep the rest at bay. Then you're free to wander in a semitropical paradise of jungle paths, deep ravines, rushing water, and almost-spectacular waterfalls.

The waterfall at Tzararacua, ten kilometers from the main plaza (catch the bus of that name in the main plaza) is the most impressive of all. The Río Cupatitzio originates as a bubbling spring in the National Park, and then runs down to cascade toward the Pacific and form these falls. A trip to Tzararacua and to the National Park can be made in a day, even in an afternoon.

5. Pátzcuaro

Pátzcuaro, Michoacán (alt. 7,250 feet; pop. 40,000), has always been of interest to Mexican history buffs because this attractive town featured in the careers of the two most diametrically opposed figures of colonial times. One was Nuño de Guzman, the infamous conquistador whose lust for riches led him to terrorize the local Tarascan population and burn their chief alive because he wouldn't—or couldn't—disclose the location of gold deposits. The other, a humane bishop named Vasco de Quiroga, was sent to the region to undo the havoc wreaked by Guzman after the latter had been arrested by the Spanish authorities. So extensive was Don Vasco's work of reconstruction that his memory is revered in Pátzcuaro to this day. Streets and hotels are named after him; his statue stands in the main plaza.

The town is also known for its lake, one of the world's highest, where fishermen catch delicious whitefish with nets of such delicate texture and widewinged shape that they have been compared to butterflies. Although the lake is over a mile from town, buses make the run regularly from the market plaza.

Pátzcuaro is an old colonial town with many nice buildings and two lovely plazas. The climate is pleasant most of the year and, being near a lake, the surroundings are lush. As Mexican towns go, Pátzcuaro is pretty, clean, and quiet.

WHERE TO STAY: A small railroad station (daily trains to and from Mexico City) is near the lake. The nearest hotel to the station is the **Posada de Don Vasco Hotel and Motel (1)** (tel. 454/2-0227 or 2-0262), which has recently been taken over by Best Western. Unless you're in the mood for a big splurge, don't stay here: it's elegant—sprawling colonial-style architecture, crystal chandeliers, antique telephones, velvet drapes, bowling alleys, pool, etc.—but out of our price range, as the cheapest single goes for 9,925 pesos ($19.85), and the cheapest double for 11,305 pesos ($22.60).

On the elegant main plaza—not to be confused with the smaller market plaza—is the **Posada San Rafael (3)** (tel. 454/2-0770), which is an excellent copy of a colonial inn. Very new and very nice, the San Rafael has 104 modern rooms with Holiday Inn-type baths and traditional furnishings grouped around a hand-

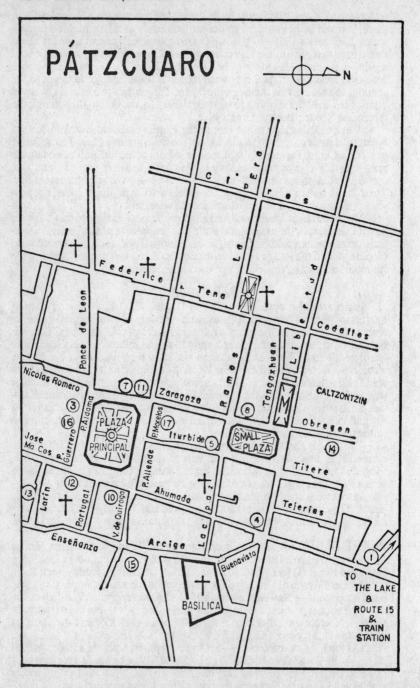

some wood colonnade, the type we're told "they don't build anymore." Pets are welcome, kids under 12 stay free in the same room as their parents, plus lots of garage space, and superb whitefish in the hotel restaurant. Rates are not outlandish: singles are 5,100 pesos ($10.20), twin-bedded rooms, 6,382 pesos ($12.75).

Moving down the price scale slightly is the 17-room **Hotel Valmen (4),** Avenida Lloreda 34 (tel. 454/2-1161), which is likely to be the first hotel you'll see as you ride into the downtown section. The façade is old-fashioned and subdued, but accommodations are modern and extremely comfortable, and located above a colorful pink and yellow glass-roofed court. It's an excellent value for 1,500 pesos ($3) single, 2,500 pesos ($5) double, 3,500 pesos ($7) triple.

Also inexpensive, and on the busy market plaza, is the commercial-looking **Gran Hotel (5),** Bocanegra 6 (tel. 454/2-0443). The 27 rooms are clean, decorated in circa-1950 low-cost modern. Not much style, but bright at least, and functional: singles are 3,220 pesos ($6.45); doubles run 4,025 pesos ($8.05) with one or two beds. The restaurant is pretty good as well, with a 1,150-peso ($2.30) comida served daily.

Back on the main plaza, another highly recommendable hotel is the **Mansion Iturbide (17)** (tel. 454/2-0368). Spacious rooms with wooden floors and huge pieces of solid-looking colonial furniture combine to create an aura of simple elegance. The baths are large, nicely tiled, and are even equipped with shower curtains. Rooms surround a small, simple patio that also serves as a dining area. Singles are 4,600 pesos ($9.20), and doubles are 5,750 pesos ($11.50); add 1,150 pesos ($2.30) for an extra person.

Also on the main plaza is the 30-room **Hotel Los Escudos (11),** Portal Hidalgo 73 (tel. 454/2-0138), a cozy colonial-style hostelry with a grillwork balcony overlooking a slanting tile patio, whitewashed walls, and a beamed ceiling. It's bright, open, and very nice, with singles for 2,500 pesos ($5), doubles for 4,500 pesos ($9); some rooms have a fireplace here.

The **Hotel Pito Perez (7),** Portal Hidalgo 76, is housed in a renovated old mansion on the main square, and offers rooms with bath at 2,500 pesos ($5) single and 3,500 pesos ($7) double.

Starvation-Budget Hotels

Hotel Posada de la Rosa (8), Portal Juárez 29 (tel. 454/2-0811), a second-floor establishment on the market plaza, is very small and very cheerful. Bright flowers in wooden boxes line the open-air patio; rooms are clean and do not have bathrooms, but go for 1,000 pesos ($2) single, 1,200 pesos ($2.40) double. The common bathrooms are rather large, and also clean. There are some rooms with shower, by the way, for a bit more.

Motels and Trailer Parks

Those of you traveling by car might want to know about the **Motel Pátzcuaro,** Avenida de las Americas (tel. 454/2-0767), just 100 yards down the road from the Posada de Don Vasco. It's a relatively new place with only 11 rooms, a small swimming pool, and two tennis courts. The management describes the accommodations as "clean, attractive, and rustic," and they all have private bath and fireplace. The cost? Singles are 2,000 pesos ($4), and doubles (one bed) are 3,500 pesos ($7); with two beds it's slightly more. Furnished houses—price negotiable—are also rented here. Buses will take you into town from the motel every 15 minutes.

Campers with tent or trailer can stay on the lake at **El Pozo Trailer Park,** where spaces rent for 2,000 pesos ($4). Clean facilities, cement pads, lots of grass, and pleasant management.

WHERE TO EAT: One of the best comidas I've ever had was served at the **Restaurant Los Escudos (11)** (tel. 2-1290), adjacent to the hotel of the same name. I ordered the Tarascan soup, vegetable plate, and whitefish, and the entire meal was superb, right through dessert—worth every centavo of the 2,260 pesos ($4.50) I paid. Whatever you have, start off with the Tarascan soup—it's the best!

The restaurant **El Patio (16)** (tel. 2-0484), on the plaza at Plaza Vasco de Quiroga 19, offers live dinner music in addition to good, inexpensive meals. Hot bread and butter are served with meals ranging from carne asada at 800 pesos ($1.60) to whitefish or filet for 1,500 to 1,800 pesos ($3 to $3.60). The five-course comida is delicious and plentiful.

For those with their own transportation and a splurge in mind, the **Hostería de San Felipe,** on the Avenida de las Americas (tel. 2-1298), is recommended by locals who often hold receptions and group dinners there. The menu is highly rarified: the whitefish costs 1,500 pesos ($3) a plate, and other entrees are slightly cheaper. The hotel here, by the way, is only a moderate splurge, with singles for 2,990 pesos ($6), doubles for 5,290 pesos ($10.60).

Down by the Lake

Numerous restaurants line the road to the docks on the lake, and this is the traditional place to dine on the famous whitefish.

You can have lunch or dinner at the **Restaurant Las Redes,** Avenida de Las Americas 6 (tel. 2-1275), about 500 feet from the lakeshore. For 2,400 pesos ($4.80) I recently had a meal of soup, rice, a whole whitefish, salad, and coffee. If you get there in time for the set-price lunch, you save money.

Near the railroad tracks on the road to the lake is **El Gordo,** housed in a long, narrow building. Besides whitefish, El Gordo is good for breakfast (opens at 8 a.m.), and inexpensive meals the rest of the day. For just whitefish, salad, and a soft drink you'll pay 1,950 pesos ($3.90) here.

The cheapest way to enjoy the lake's prime product is to wander right down to the wharf (embarcadero). At little stands right next to it, señoras fry up the delicious fish before your eyes. For a rough-and-ready plate including fish, garnishes, and a soft drink, the price will be less than 1,000 pesos ($2.50).

ACTIVITIES IN PÁTZCUARO: Pátzcuaro is a beautiful town and well worth leisurely strolls about its ancient, unchanged streets and plazas. The **market plaza** is particularly interesting and it is here, among the myriad stalls and vendors, that you can buy the varied pottery, rebozos, and serapes of the region. Market days are Sunday, Tuesday, Thursday, and Friday, the last being the day for the all-Indian market. Just a few blocks away is the splendid main plaza, a vast tree-shaded expanse of manicured lawns and elaborate stone fountains bordered by shops, hotels, and the former mansions of rich merchants. The town is much like Colonial Williamsburg from the standpoint of authenticity, and it enjoys a similar monument status. No new buildings interfere with the time-worn harmony of the colonial roofline.

One of the oldest buildings in Pátzcuaro is the **House of the Giant (10),** on the east side of the main plaza at 40 Portal de Matamoros, so called for the 12-foot-high painted statue that supports one of the arches around the patio. This residence was built in 1663 by a Spanish count and certainly represents the colonial taste of that period: carved stone panels, thick columns, and open courtyards.

The **basilica,** which is located east of the small plaza on top of a small hill, was built in the 16th century at the instigation of Don Vasco, then bishop. It opened for services in 1554, but unfortunately Don Vasco never lived to see it completed. The cathedral has been through many catastrophes, from earthquakes to the civil war of the mid-19th century (Juarists against the imperalists who followed Maximilian). There has been some reconstruction. Of note is the Virgin on the main altar, which is made of "corn-stalk pulp and a mucilage obtained from a prized orchid of the region." She is a very sacred figure to the Indians of this area, and on the 8th day of each month they come from the villages to pay homage to her, particularly for her miraculous healing power.

One block to the south of the basilica is the **Museum of Popular and Regional Arts (15).** It's yet another beautiful colonial building (1540), originally Don Vasco's College of San Nicolás. The rooms with regional crafts and costumes are located off the central courtyard.

There are many old churches in Pátzcuaro but the one which I found most interesting is the **Temple of the Compañía de Jesus (12),** near the museum. This church was Don Vasco's cathedral before the basilica was built. After the basilica was finished, it was given to the Jesuits, but the building was neglected after the Jesuits were expelled from Mexico in 1667. The buildings to the south of the church were once part of the complex containing hospital, soup kitchen, and living quarters for religious scholars.

Last but not least is the **House of the Eleven Patios (13),** located between José Maria Cos and Enseñanza. This edifice is one of the most outstanding architectural achievements of the colonial period. It was formerly a convent of the Catherine nuns, but now the **Tourism Office** and art-craft galleries are located in the building. Supposedly open 9 a.m. to 2 p.m. and 4 to 8 p.m., they are not overly conscientious about observing the hours. Another office (same hours) is in the main plaza. The **post office (14)** is located half a block north of the small plaza, on the right-hand side of the street.

No visit to Pátzcuaro is complete without a trip on the lake, preferably across to the isolated island village of **Janitzio,** on which a hilltop statue of Morelos dominates all the surrounding countryside. The village church is the scene of an annual ceremony called the Day of the Dead, held at midnight on November 1, when villagers climb to the churchyard carrying lighted candles in memory of all their dead relatives.

While there are no fewer than 13 categories of trips to Janitzio, ranging from the special price for island residents only to the price for a special trip to Janitzio and other islands, best bet is the *colectivo,* that is, round-trip group fare. A complete price list is posted at the pier (follow signs saying "Embarcadero").

An ancient dance originated by the Tarascans to ridicule the Spaniards during the Conquest can be seen in its almost original form today. The **Dancers of the Viejitos** perform at the Hotel Posada de Don Vasco every Wednesday and Saturday at 9:00 p.m.

Side Trips

For a good view of the town and the lake, head for **El Estribo,** a lookout two miles from town (leave the main square on Calle Ponce de León, and follow signs.) It's a fine place for a picnic, and in good weather the walk will take you less than 45 minutes.

Take a short jaunt to Tzintzuntzan, ten miles from Pátzcuaro on the road to Quiroga, known for its straw mobiles, baskets, and figures. In earlier centuries

Tzintzuntzan was the capital of a Tarascan empire that controlled over a hundred other towns and villages. Pyramids upon pyramids still remind the casual visitor of a glorious, if also rather bloody, past. The old market is now housed in a new neocolonial building—a lot snazzier with prices to match. Also in town is a nice lake that has a footpath along it should you need a reprieve from shopping.

Santa Clara del Cobre (Villa Escalante), famous for its copper products, can be reached by a bus caught in front of the Church of San Francisco, or at the far corner of the Plaza San Agustín. Although the copper mines that existed during pre-Conquest times seem to have been forever lost, local craftsmen still make copper vessels by the age-old methods, each piece being pounded out by hand from pieces of scrap pipe, radiators, and bits of electrical wire.

BACK ON THE HIGHWAY: Once back on the main highway, there is a 27-mile run through lovely country to Morelia. Red-roofed houses cluster together on the softly sloping hillsides and from time to time the ubiquitous burro, heavily laden with firewood, can be seen followed closely by another laden with two small boys. Many of the men around here carry or wear serapes made of straw to protect them cheaply and efficiently from the heavy rain that makes the countryside so green.

6. Morelia

Morelia (alt. 6,368 feet; pop. 220,000), the capital of the wildly beautiful state of Michoacán, is a lovely colonial city. Over the years it has earned a reputation as one of Mexico's more cultural cities, serving as an intellectual and artistic center for the region. As with much of Mexico, there is layer upon layer of fascinating history here. The area was inhabited first by Indians, notably the Tarascans. Founded by the Spanish in 1541, the city was originally named Valladolid, but the name was later changed in honor of the revolutionary hero José Morelos, who once lived here. The Morelos house (at Morelos 323) is ostensibly a museum housing relics of the old hero—his bed, clerical robe, several portraits of him and his parents, and the table on which the first Mexican independence documents were signed.

Many of the original colonial buildings remain in Morelia, adding that touch of ancient Mexican/Spanish elegance. In an attempt to preserve the architectural harmony, the city government has decreed that all new major construction be in the colonial style. Thus, parts of the city remind one of those reconstructions of Merrie Old English towns that Hollywood prepares so authentically for the movies about Robin Hood. The main movie theater itself, in fact, continues this motif with its oaken doors and chandeliers.

GETTING TO AND FROM MORELIA: Those arriving by bus in Morelia will want to break their journey with a night in a hotel before continuing on to Mexico City. For train information, see above under "Getting to Pátzcuaro."

WHERE TO STAY: Next door to the theater, in the main plaza, the Plaza de los Martires (there are two such plazas, separated by the cathedral) is one of the nicest hotels in town, the **Virrey de Mendoza,** Portal Matamoros 16 (tel. 451/2-0633), which is way out of our price range at 8,694 pesos ($17.40) single, 9,269 pesos ($18.55) double, but worth taking a look at. A lovely old colonial mansion built on the grand scale, the two-story lobby, somehow monastic with its stone arches, is dominated by a life-size portrait of one of the Mendoza forebears gazing down from the wall above the fireplace. The rooms have beautiful, highly waxed hardwood floors, Mexican "Oriental" rugs, carved colonial furniture, monogrammed bed-throws and towels, and old-fashioned telephones that would drive antique dealers to fits of avarice. The hotel's restaurant, once a marvelous baronial dining hall, has been converted into four luxury suites for the very well-heeled. The courtyard, which doubles as the lobby, is now also the restaurant Sic Transit Splendor.

One block from the main plaza on Zaragoza at Ocampo is the **Posada de la Soledad** (tel. 451/2-1888), even more beautiful than the Virrey de Mendoza. Again, the rates are out of our price range—singles are 10,718 pesos ($21.45), doubles, 13,470 pesos ($26.95)—but worth looking at, especially if you need a little help to get into the colonial mood in Morelia. An aura of tranquility actually emanates from the unspoiled courtyard; stone arches heavy with vines, and a stone fountain, dominate the courtyard without overpowering it.

The **Hotel Catedral,** Zaragoza 37, a few steps north of the main plaza (tel. 451/3-0783 or 3-0467), is still fairly posh and still out of our price range. Rooms here are quite comfortable, and grouped around an interior court three stories high. The old-style rooms have been redone during the last few years, and now rent for 8,190 pesos ($16.40) single, 10,120 pesos ($20.25) double.

Moving down the price scale, the **Hotel Casino,** Portal Hidalgo 229 (tel. 451/3-1005), is housed in a fine old building laced with good touches—beams, chandeliers, columns—but tied together with rather unfortunate modernization (the central court has been filled in with a glass-brick ceiling between the first and second floors). Aesthetics aside, the Casino has an excellent location practically across the street from the Mendoza, and 50 cheerful, immaculate rooms-with-bath costing 4,071 pesos ($8.15) single, 5,118 pesos ($10.25) double. Downstairs is a large restaurant and bar, and upstairs is an enclosed court bordered by classical railings which look suspiciously like plywood cutouts.

If you are arriving by bus, you may be interested in the **Hotel Concordia,** just around the corner (left out the bus station door, then left again) from the station at Valentín Gómez Farías 328 (tel. 451/2-3052). The Hotel Concordia was recommended by several readers and on checking it I found it to be an excellent choice: modern, spacious rooms with bath; friendly staff; a quiet situation. The rates are 2,500 pesos ($5) single, 3,200 pesos ($6.40) double.

A hotel just one-half block from the bus depot on V. Gómez Farías at E. Ruíz is the **Hotel Plaza** (tel. 451/2-3095). The 33 rooms are small and exceptionally clean and tidy. Rates are agreeably low, at 2,700 pesos ($5.40) for a single, 3,400 pesos ($6.80) for a double. The restaurant downstairs has the same name, but is actually under separate management; prices are moderate, though.

Hotel San Jorge is on a corner of Madero Pte., at no. 719 (tel. 451/2-4610). Rooms are small and almost devoid of furniture, but clean and nice enough, and the most important piece of furniture—the bed—is of good quality and firm. The private baths are surprisingly large and well kept. Prices are 2,760 pesos ($5.55) single, 3,450 pesos ($6.90) double with one or two beds.

WHERE TO EAT: The restaurants in Morelia that are not associated with the fancy hotels are all well within our budget range. Food is, well, only fair, but then so are the prices. Here they are, not listed in any particular order.

Sandor's Restaurant, Madero Ote. 422C, is a clean open-fronted café-cum-luncheonette with red tablecloths and French chansons playing in the background that's good for a light lunch of chicken tacos with salad, fried chicken, hamburger, salad, and fried potatoes for only about 374 to 820 pesos (75¢ to $1.65). It's cheap and clean and cheerful and good. To find it, walk east past the cathedral out of the main square on Madero, and after about six uneven blocks you'll see it on the right—a street called Serapio Rendon is opposite it.

Across from the magnificent cathedral at Portal de la Nevería 103 is **El Pa-**

raíso de Morelia. This place is always crowded with college students, business people, and those waiting in line to use the phone. (Note that for a small fee someone will place a call for you while you wait.) Pescado blanco here is 750 pesos ($1.50), beefsteak is slightly more; the daily set-price breakfast is 500 pesos ($1), and that includes a beverage. With each meal comes a basket overflowing with bread, pastries, rolls, and tempting cookies. I ate quite a variety of these for a mere 150 pesos (30¢) and I still have no idea how the waiter settled on that small amount.

Morelia's dependable comida corrida restaurant is **El Tracadero,** Hidalgo 63 (Hidalgo runs south from the middle of the main plaza), about half a block from the square on the left-hand side. One high-ceilinged room here is festooned with bullfight posters and other such memorabilia, and filled with chunky pseudo-colonial tables and chairs. Service is slow but friendly—shall I say leisurely?—but the food is good and the price right. I recently had a delicious five-course lunch for 750 pesos ($1.50), and I could have ordered a huge Mexican plate for even a bit less. Open for dinner too.

For espresso coffee, head to the **Café Catedral** on the main plaza, the best place to restore your constitution.

Across from the square and cathedral and on the same side of the street as the Hotel Casino is an entire block filled with sidewalk cafés. All of them seem to enjoy about the same degree of popularity, all are pretty crowded, and prices are competitive. A breakfast of fruit, eggs, toast, and coffee is less than 900 pesos ($1.80). A comida lunch is 1,750 pesos ($3.50) almost anywhere along the block. These daytime cafés become Morelia's nightlife after dark: then the coffee is hot, the beer cold, the setting peaceful, and the college crowd lively, even exuberant.

Near the bus station and in the same building as the Hotel Plaza is the **Hotel Plaza Restaurant.** This eatery is run by an American who came to Morelia years ago and decided to stay. The comida in this plain, clean diner is 721 pesos ($1.45); a banana split is 450 pesos (90¢), and comes topped with fresh strawberries in season. Open from 7 a.m. to 11 p.m.

READERS' RESTAURANT SELECTIONS: "The best vegetarian restaurant I encountered in Mexico is **La Fuente,** Avenida Madero Ote. 493B, just beyond the post office. I bought a monthly meal ticket that entitled me to large, tasty comidas at less than a dollar each. It's open only from 1:30 to 5 p.m.; closed Sunday" (John Donahue, Dalton, Minn.). . . . "The most wonderful restaurant in Morelia is well worth the splurge. It's the **Grill de Enrique,** Hidalgo 54, near the church of San Agustin. Wonderful, elegant atmosphere, fresh rolls and butter, and excellent food. The flan was even better than my mother's (high praise)"(Sonia Fraser, Independence, Calif.).

A WALK AROUND TOWN:
Besides being a way-station on the road to Mexico City, Morelia has a personality and charm all its own. Those planning to spend a day or two here can see what there is to see with a few well-planned walking and city bus tours.

Heading eastward toward the cathedral from the Hotel Virrey de Mendoza, walk up Madero past the plaza, call in at the **cathedral,** and then continue along Madero. The cathedral took 104 years to build (1640–1744) and has two impressive spires which can be climbed (the doors are locked but the man with the key is usually hanging around at midday). The interior of the church is awesome, particularly if you are fortunate enough to be there when the resident organist is playing or practicing.

The **Government Palace,** across the street (Madero) from the cathedral, is worth a brief examination. Most interesting here are the grand murals depicting the history of the state of Michoacán and of Mexico. Some of them were done by a well-known local artist named Alfredo Zalce.

A "must" stop for regional arts fans is the **Palacio del Artesano.** Here, crafts are displayed in an old colonial structure attached to the Church of San Francisco, on the Plaza de San Francisco, one block south of Madero on Fray de San Miguel. To get there, walk east on Madero and then turn south onto Vasco de Quiroga for a block. The church is on the east side of the square; admission is free and visitors are welcome Monday through Saturday from 10 a.m. to 7:30 p.m., on Sunday from 10 a.m. to 2:30 p.m. The three large rooms hold lacquer-ware from Pátzcuaro and Uruapán: delicately flowered trays inlaid with gold, plus several types of trays done in *embutido,* the original process of inlay which involves treating the completed trays with a preparation of colored earth, axle oil, and linseed oil to create a waterproof finish. Also you'll see beautiful deep-green, brown, and black glazed pottery from San José de Gracia and Patam-bam; items with cross-stitch embroidery from Taracuato; lovely handworked pine furniture, and smaller portable items such as boxes and breadboards from Cuanejo; close woven hats from the Isla de Jaracuaro; lots of copperware, and even more. Everything on display is for sale at reasonable prices.

Across the street from the Plaza de San Francisco is the market. South to Avenida Lázaro Cárdenas will take you near the huge Mercado Independencia, actually not all that interesting except on Sunday, the big market day.

In the other direction from the cathedral, going west on Madero, is the "campus" of the **College of San Nicolás de Hidalgo,** a beautiful colonial universi-ty that lays claim to the somewhat frayed title of "Oldest in the Western Hemi-sphere." Founded in Pátzcuaro in 1540, it was moved to Valladolid (that is, Morelia) in 1580 and incorporated into the University of Michoacán in 1957.

The **Tourism Office** is in the same area, in the Palacio Clavijero, staffed by a friendly enough crew. English is spoken and there is a charge for maps and leaf-lets.

A little farther along, a block off Madero on Farías, is the delightful mer-cado de dulces, a jumble of shops laden with *cubitos de ate* (candied fruit wedges), jelly candies, honey, goats' milk, strawberry jam, and chongos (a com-bination of milk, sugar, cinnamon, and honey).

A BUS RIDE THROUGH TOWN: Begin at the zócalo on Madero and board a bus marked "Directo" for the trip east, and soon you'll see the results of the city-hall order to build in colonial style: banks, office buildings, even Wool-worth's, are all in that style.

Six blocks from the zócalo on the left is the massively impressive **Palacio Federal,** which houses the post and telegraph offices: impressive to think that this huge pile is your instrument for mailing postcards.

Leave the bus at the corner of Madero and Avenida Acueducto and walk along the Bosque Cuauhtémoc, which holds the **Museum of Contemporary Art.** Across the street is the three-mile-long aqueduct, constructed in 1785.

Turn right on Calzada Ventura Puente and board a bus labeled "Alberca," which will take you south to the Paseo de La Camelina, and then west (right). The city's **Planetarium** is at this intersection, with shows nightly at 6:30 p.m.; admission is 200 pesos (40¢). The bus will continue west to the Parque Juárez, which has a nice little zoo complete with elephants and tigers for only a few pesos admission.

Outside the park, board the bus marked "Santa Maria" for the ride north to the zócalo along Calzada Juárez and on Abasolo. This last leg of the tour presents an enjoyable view of the narrow streets in the residential quarters of the city's interior. On the corner of Abasolo and Allende is the **Museo Michoacano,** the place to go for an introduction to local history.

The bus will take you right to the zócalo. Fares are so low that you can ride along this route, hopping off at every interesting prospect, and still end up paying a good deal less than a dollar for the entire trip.

READER'S TIP—LAUNDRY: "The best **laundry** is on the bottom level of the Plaza de los Rebullones shopping center, just past where Calzada Madero splits, to the right, just past the traffic circle. The charge (by the kilo) is very reasonable, and they are careful not to damage delicate fabrics" (Sonia Fraser, Independence, Calif.).

BACK ON THE HIGHWAY: From Morelia to Mexico City is a comfortable

day's ride of a little less than 200 miles. You wind up and down through lush mountain country with some breathtaking vistas before leveling off on the plateau. It'll take you about four hours to get to Toluca (see Chapter XI) and another hour to get to the center of Mexico City. The route takes you right down the capital's main drag, the Paseo de la Reforma, which winds through lush and wealthy residential districts before entering Chapultepec Park and the center of town.

Before going on to the capital, however, I'd advise a detour north to one of the most beautiful areas in all Mexico—the northern reaches of the Valley of Mexico, dotted with several magnificent colonial silver cities.

Chapter V

THE COLONIAL SILVER CITIES

1. Zacatecas
2. Aguascalientes
3. San Luis Potosí
4. Guanajuato
5. San Miguel de Allende
6. Querétaro

BETWEEN THE MOUNTAIN RANGES of the Sierra Madre lies the heartland of Mexico, a high plateau sculpted by rains and rivers over the eons and now a maze of highlands, lakes, and valleys. This is Anáhuac, the center of ancient Mexican civilization, today called the Valley of Mexico.

When the Conquistadores had subdued Tenochtitlán (Mexico City) in the early 1500s, they sent their armies and colonists into the other parts of the Valley of Mexico in search of mineral wealth. They found it: lead, tin, zinc, iron, and antimony were found in abundance, and also gold. But what made the fortunes of the early Spanish governors, and of the cities of the northern valley, was silver. So rich were the mines here that the silver cities of the northern Valley of Mexico became incredibly wealthy, and stayed that way for centuries.

Today these cities, more than any others, are Mexico's colonial showpieces, with architectural beauty rivaled by none. Guanajuato is almost a fairytale town; San Luis Potosí exudes wealth and civic pride from its grand government buildings, cathedral, churches, and monasteries. Each city has a lot to offer and a visitor who has not made the rounds of the silver cities hasn't seen colonial Mexico.

No matter how you're traveling in Mexico, the silver cities are easily accessible despite their locations, nestled in mountain valleys. Coming overland from El Paso, Zacatecas is the first real colonial city you'll encounter; from Monterrey and Saltillo, Hwy. 57 goes straight to San Luis Potosí; from Guadalajara it's only a few hours' drive to Aguascalientes. Mexico City is linked to Querétaro by a fast, limited-access toll highway, and from Querétaro one can drive to any other of the silver cities in a few hours' time. Bus service is fast, frequent, and comfortable.

1. Zacatecas

Zacatecas (alt. 8,200 feet; pop. 120,000), capital of tne state of the same name, was already an old town when the Spaniards arrived in 1548. A city made rich by silver mines, it has picturesque, cobbled streets ascending the hillsides, a plaza watched over by a white marble angel atop a column, and a real dearth of tourists.

The façade of the wildly churrigueresque cathedral is the first sight which visitors want to see—you might say they're going for baroque—but many other sights right in town, plus the less obvious Convento de Guadalupe, a short way from town, and the ruins at La Quemada are also good for a look. You can see it all from the hilltops that dominate the town, most notably the Cerro de la Bufa.

One of the first things you might want to do upon arriving in Zacatecas is pay a visit to the **Office of Tourism** (tel. 492/2-0170), located right beside the cathedral in the Plaza Hidalgo. English-speaking staff will supply you with maps and lots of printed information in English, and can answer any questions you may have about Zacatecas and the surrounding area.

During your time in Zacatecas, be aware of two things: first, that it's very hilly here, and you'll be doing a lot of climbing. Second, that you're at more than 8,000 feet altitude in this town, so you'll become winded very quickly going up those hills.

GETTING TO AND FROM ZACATECAS: The bus station, once near the center of town, was moved in early 1986 to a hilltop outside of town. From the station, however, it's easy to hop on a *central camionera* bus which will take you downtown for 45 pesos (9¢). A line of taxis is also standing by, and will take you for 500 pesos ($1).

As Zacatecas is on the main highway between Ciudad Juárez/Mexico City and Monterrey/Guadalajara, buses buzz in and out of town all during the day and night, and there is hardly ever a problem finding a seat to any destination. Make your arrangements at least a few hours in advance, just to be sure.

From Zacatecas to her sister city of Aguascalientes, it is barely a two-hour ride. Those going to Guadalajara on Hwy. 54 will get a chance to stop at the **ruins of Chicomostoc,** also called La Quemada.

WHERE TO STAY: The busiest corner in town is the intersection of Avenidas Juárez and Hidalgo, next to the telegraph office. A few steps from this corner is a good hotel choice, the **Posada de los Condes,** at Juárez 107, Zacatecas, Zac. 98000 (tel. 492/2-1412). The building's façade is about 300 years old, but the inside was remodeled in 1968. Rooms facing the street have French doors opening onto small iron-railed balconies; other rooms have no windows, but do have ceiling ventilation, and these rooms are quieter. Be sure to specify which you prefer. The 58 rooms are in good shape, clean, carpeted, with phone, TV (a parabolic antenna picks up two U.S. channels), and hot water from 6:30 a.m. to midnight. Prices are 4,300 pesos ($8.60) single, 5,500 pesos ($11) double.

Right across the street is the **Hotel Condesa,** at Avenida Juárez 5, Zacatecas, Zac. 98000 (tel. 492/2-1160). Prices here are cheaper, with singles at 2,990 pesos ($5.98), doubles 3,737 pesos ($7.47), but unfortunately, unlike the Posada de los Condes, the Condesa has become somewhat run-down. Still, it does offer all the basics, with hot water morning and evening, telephones, purified water, and a black-and-white TV which can be rented for 125 pesos (25¢) extra per day. The rooms on all three floors open onto a bright, glass-topped courtyard. There is a ladies' bar on the ground floor, and the hotel's restaurant is one of the more popular places to dine in Zacatecas (see listing below). The travel agency located in the lobby—**Turismo Marxal** (tel. 492/2-1160), open weekdays 10 a.m. to 2 p.m. and 4 to 7 p.m., Saturdays 10 a.m. to 3 p.m. and Sundays 1 to 3 p.m.—is also a good resource to be aware of, with a helpful, English-speaking staff.

The **Hotel Reina Cristina,** at Jardín Hidalgo 703, Zacatecas, Zac. 98000, facing the plaza beside the cathedral (tel. 492/2-1130 and 2-1437), is another colonial, once-luxurious hotel which has seen its better days. Still, if worn carpeting and peeling wallpaper don't offend you, you might want to give it a try. Ask to see several rooms—those facing the street have large French windows opening onto the plaza, while those facing the courtyard are very sunny with windows covering almost one entire wall. A few rooms have a big bathtub in addition to a shower, a real luxury for bathtub-lovers. All rooms come with telephone and black-and-white TV; prices are 2,622 pesos ($5.25) single, 3,280 pesos ($6.55) double. A bar and a restaurant open from 8 a.m. to 10:30 p.m. are on the premises, and subterranean parking is also available.

One block south of the cathedral, at Avenida Hidalgo 413, Zacatecas, Zac. 98000, is the **Posada de la Moneda** (tel. 492/2-0881), another good choice. Rooms have telephone, carpet, and hot water all day, with a bar and restaurant open 8 a.m. to 10 p.m. Single rooms go for 4,547 pesos ($9.10), doubles 5,684 pesos ($11.36).

Over on Boulevard López Mateos, near where the bus station used to be, are several hotels. The problem here is that they tend to be loud, being right on the main highway. For my money, I'd rather stay downtown. But if you need a room, all three of these are clean and acceptable, and they're not too far a walk from downtown.

Motel Zacatecas (tel. 492/2-0328), also called **Zacatecas Courts,** sits right between two main streets, Boulevard López Mateos and Avenida López Velarde, with a sign on both sides (the address is López Velarde 602, Zacatecas, Zac. 98000). It's modern and very clean, with phones, TV, carpeting, hot water 24 hours a day, enclosed parking, laundry and dry cleaning services, a travel agency, and even a pharmacy and medical services. The restaurant is open from 7 a.m. to 10:30 p.m. Prices here are 4,600 pesos ($9.20) single, 5,750 pesos ($11.50) double.

Just a little further up the hill is the **Hotel Colón** (tel. 492/2-0464), at López Velarde 508, Zacatecas, Zac. 98000, also situated between the two busy streets, with signs facing both. It's very basic, but clean, with singles priced at 2,012 pesos ($4.02) and doubles at 2,516 pesos ($5.03).

For a real splurge, you could go to the luxury **Best Western Hotel,** just up the hill at the corner of López Mateos and Callejón del Barro, Zacatecas, Zac. 98000 (tel. 492/2-3311). It has every luxury you could desire, right down to uniformed room service, bar, restaurant, discothèque, and even a glass-roofed penthouse swimming pool. Prices are 9,200 pesos ($18.40) single, 10,180 pesos ($20.36) double.

Finally, if you'd prefer to be a bit removed from all the hubbub of downtown, by all means try the **Motel del Bosque** (tel. 492/2-0745) on Paseo Díaz Ordaz (no number), perched high above town with 60 rooms in various positions which give them various views of the city below. You should definitely ask to see several rooms, and be specific in your request for a room with a view, for that is the del Bosque's great advantage over downtown places. When you've chosen one, you'll find that a modern *cuarto con baño* will cost 4,347 pesos ($8.70) for a room with one double bed for one or two people, 5,433 pesos ($10.86) for a room with two double beds. Rooms are nice and clean, with carpet, TV, phone, and hot water 24 hours, lined up in rows stretching along the hillside, with parking on the cobblestone driveway between rows. It's quiet and pleasant up here overlooking the city, and you're located near several of Zacatecas's main tourist attractions: the teleférico, the mine, and the hilltop discothèque El Elefante Blanco.

A Starvation-Budget Hotel

The **Hotel del Parque,** on Prolongación González Ortega, Zacatecas, Zac. 98000 (tel. 492/2-0479), is just a few doors up the hill from Cerro de Alica Park. It's spartan, but clean and quiet. The hot water is not so hot sometimes, and in fact the water goes out altogether in the evening once in a while, but the price is definitely a plus at 1,500 pesos ($3) single, 2,500 pesos ($5) double.

WHERE TO EAT: All the aforementioned hotels have their own restaurants. The one at the **Hotel Condesa** (tel. 2-1160) is popular despite its spartan decoration. Prices are okay: 11 types of egg dishes come for 300 pesos (60¢), antojito dishes for 360 to 415 pesos (72¢ to 83¢). A hearty comida corrida is served for only 685 pesos ($1.37), including soft drink, from 1:30 p.m. until it's gone. Daily specials are also offered. Open 7:30 a.m. to 11 p.m., closed Mondays.

The latest "in" place in Zacatecas seems to be the **Restaurant Mesón La Mina,** (tel. 2-2773), Juárez 15, just a few doors up from the Condesa. Broad stone arches, white walls, red tile floor, fluorescent lights—very Mexican mountain town. It's not elegant or refined, but the food's hearty. Have a plate of bístec de res con papas and a bottle of beer, and your bill will be 680 pesos ($1.35). There's also full bar service, and cappuccino and espresso for 180 pesos (36¢).

The Plaza de la Independencia is the park just down from the Hotel Condesa. Facing this plaza on the south side, across from the library building, up on the second floor at no. 218 is the **Rosticeria El Pastor** (tel. 2-1635), featuring "Super Pollos Rostizados" (super roast chicken). You'll likely find it packed with people who know good food at a good price. The only thing served here is chicken, and it's excellent: 500 pesos ($1) brings you a quarter roasted chicken, barbecued potato chips, salad, salsa, and tortillas; a soda is another 50 pesos (10¢). You can also get a half chicken for 1,000 pesos ($2), a whole one for 2,000 pesos ($4), or a large bowl of chicken soup for 200 pesos (40¢). A plaque on the wall out front proclaims this house as the birthplace of the first journalist in America.

Between the Plaza de la Independencia and Boulevard López Mateos runs Calle Ventura Salazar, a winding little street where the bus station used to be, simply lined with taco shops, snack stands, and hole-in-the-wall eateries just fine for a quick or light bite at a ridiculously low price. For example, **Tacolandia,** at Ventura Salazar 405, open 8 a.m. to 4 p.m. Monday through Saturday, specializes in tacos with any of 14 different stuffings; you can get *five* tacos for 200 pesos (40¢), and a soda for another 40 pesos (8¢). Stroll down this little street and see what appeals to you.

Also along here is the **Restaurant Villa del Mar** (tel. 492/2-5004), at Ventura Salazar 338, where seafood is the only thing served. There's a wide variety, with several combination specials priced at 2,000 to 2,500 pesos ($4 to $5). The specialty of the house is the "Mosaico Villa del Mar," which includes a breaded fish filet, filet of pike, stuffed crab, frogs' legs, onion rings, and french-fried potatoes, all for 2,200 pesos ($4.40). Open 8 a.m. to 8 p.m.

With the money you've saved at the taco stands, treat yourself to an enjoyable dining experience at **El Campanario,** López Velarde 327 (tel. 2-2089). Inside, dark wooden tables accommodating six diners are clothed in yellow and white and are set with copper plates. Paintings of old Zacatecas are displayed amid the green potted plants. The chicken in wine sauce is excellent at 1,293 pesos ($2.60). The waiters will flame a variety of dishes at your table: filets with wine at 2,156 pesos ($4.31), shrimp with tequila at 3,306 pesos ($6.61), or crêpes

Suzette for two at 1,896 pesos ($3.80). For the more adventurous, try the house specialty, paillard Quetzalcoatl, filet of beef with chiles and sauce, flamed with tequila, at 2,530 pesos ($5.06). Open noon to 11 p.m. Monday through Saturday, noon to 8 p.m. Sunday.

One place I enjoyed almost more than any other in Zacatecas was the **Café y Neveria Acropolis** (tel. 2-1284), right across from the cathedral. It's one of the most popular places in town for students and university types, being a soda fountain, sweets and ice cream parlor in the daytime, and a hip coffeehouse in the evening. Whether or not you come here to eat, you shouldn't miss seeing the "saucer art" display on the wall, made by patrons using the sludge left over from the rich Turkish coffee. You'll see street and country scenes, bullfights, portraits, famous persons and more—really inspired artwork!—painted onto the white saucers with the dark brown coffee. See what you can do. The Turkish coffee comes for 120 pesos (24¢) small, 140 pesos (28¢) large. There's a surprisingly extensive menu of ice creams, sodas, cakes and other desserts, fruit delights, and specialty coffees. You can also order a snack of a hamburger and fries for 500 pesos ($1), or a hot dog for 250 pesos (50¢).

WHAT TO DO: Zacatecas is a fine place to take a day (or a few days) off for sightseeing, should you be barreling southward from the U.S. border. A walk around town reveals, first of all, the **cathedral** with its fantastically ornate façade which has earned it the name of "Parthenon of Mexican Baroque" (whatever that means). It took 22 years to build (1730–1752). Take a close look at the zig-zag carving along the lower surfaces, the huge stone pillars inside, and the quaint motif of ears of corn on the ceiling.

The **Jardín Hidalgo,** the town's main square, is where you'll find the state and city government buildings. In the city hall is a modern mural (1970) by Antonio Rodriguez.

Walking down Avenida Hidalgo toward the south you'll pass the **Teatro Calderón** (inaugurated in 1891), a fine and stately building now being remodeled to regain its former glory.

Continue on Hidalgo, across Juárez, and mount the hill to **Cerro de Alica park** (the street changes names up the hill and becomes Avenida Gral. Jesus González Ortega). The equestrian statue (1898) is none other than General González Ortega himself, hero of the Battle of Calpulalpan. Behind it is a gazebo with marvelous acoustics, and a green, lush, and shady park good for a picnic or a romantic stroll, well-lit and pleasant even in the evening.

Behind the park is the **Museo F. Goitía,** a former governor's palace built in 1945. Having been occupied by three governors, each for a four-year term, it was converted into a high school, and then a very fine museum. Exhibits on the ground floor are the work of Francisco Goitía (1882–1960), including *Tata Jesucristo,* one of the artist's most famous, internationally known works. Upstairs are changing exhibits featuring other modern Mexican artists. Ask to meet the guide, Sr. Feliciano Espítia, born in 1910, who still remembers how it was around Zacatecas at the time of the Revolution, and remembers some English from his days in the U.S. during WWII. You can visit the museum without paying a thing, Tuesday through Sunday, 9 a.m. to 2 p.m. and 5 to 8 p.m.

Beginning at Alica Park and extending southward, the famous **Aqueduct of Zacatecas** looms over the street. The wealth of this mining city at the turn of the 18th-19th century allowed it to undertake such impressive public works. Water passed along the aqueduct to a large cistern downtown.

Right downtown, beside the ornate and well-worth-seeing church of **Santo Domingo,** is a museum you shouldn't miss even if you don't like museums. It's the **Museo Pedro Coronel,** which might perhaps have been better named the

World Art Museum, since it contains exhibits from Africa, India, China, Tibet, Thailand, Japan, Oceania, Egypt (even a mummy case!), and ancient Greece and Rome, plus works of European artists such as Picasso, Miró, Chagall, Daumier, William Hogarth (what a sense of humor!), and others, in addition to the work of Coronel. Especially notable is the large collection of native pre-Hispanic art and masks downstairs, matched by a similar display of African masks directly above. The museum is free, open Tuesday through Sunday from 10 a.m. to 5 p.m.

There is also the massive **ex-Templo de San Agustin,** just a short block up the hill east of the cathedral, open Monday through Friday 10 a.m. to 5 p.m. and weekends 10 a.m. to 2 p.m. Behind it is the building of **El Congreso Local del Estado de Zacatecas,** opened in 1985, a replica of the Real Caja (state bank) built in 1763 and destroyed in an explosion during the Revolution.

Down by the Plaza de la Independencia, on the south side where you see "Super Pollos Rostizados El Pastor," you'll see a plaque on the wall announcing it as the birthplace of the **first journalist in America,** Dr. D. Juan Ignacio Maria de Casterena Ursua y Coyeneche Villareal, "en fecha como hoy" (on a day like today) in 1668.

It's hard to miss Zacatecas's market as it's right downtown very near the cathedral. As Mexican markets go it's a fairly good one, and that means fabulous by most other standards. The hundreds of colors and the thousand little vignettes of Mexican daily life could fascinate an "outsider" for days.

To take it all in at once, climb (slowly, please! remember the altitude!) up to the Motel del Bosque on the Cerro Grillo hill, and take the cable car across the valley to the **Cerro de la Bufa.** When the sun is low in the sky, turning the sandstone town to a golden wonder, and the lights begin to twinkle on, it'll all seem magical. Watch your time, though, as the teléferico (cable car) is in operation only Tuesday through Sunday, 12:30 to 7:30 p.m. The cost for a ride is 500 pesos ($1) round trip, or 250 pesos (50¢) one way; or you can hike up either hill and walk down the other if you wish. Before you make that long climb, look: Are the cars actually running? Beware of breakdowns!

Up on **Cerro de la Bufa** you'll find several interesting attractions. Here is the **Museo de la Toma de Zacatecas** (the taking of Zacatecas), founded in 1984, with pictures and exhibits explaining the battle between the Federales and the Revolutionarios in all the hills surrounding Zacatecas in June 1914, when Pancho Villa arrived from the north to seal the fate of the Federales in this battle which marked the turning point in the victory of the Revolution. The museum is fascinating and free, open Tuesday through Sunday, 10 a.m. to 2 p.m. and 4 to 6 p.m.

Beside the museum is the beautiful church **La Capilla de la Virgen del Patrocinio,** patron of Zacatecas, and at the very top of the hill, an **observatory** used for meteorological purposes. Around the far side of the hill is the **Mausoleo de los Hombres Ilústrios de Zacatecas,** where many of the city's important revolutionary fighters still keep watch over their town below.

Back on Cerro Grillo (Cricket Hill), near the teleférico departure and the Hotel del Bosque, is one of the entrances to Zacatecas's mine, **La Mina "El Eden"** (tel. 492/2-3002). The other entrance can be found by walking a few blocks up Avenida Juárez, which becomes Avenida Torreón; turn right at the large Seguro Social building, and in about a block you'll come to the cavernous mine. Opened in 1586, the mine was carved by hand by the indigenous population, forced into slavery by the Spanish. The Indians began working in the mine at age 10 or 12, and lived to a maximum of about 30 years of age, dying of accidents, tuberculosis, or silicosis. The mine was one of the richest, yeilding gold, copper, zinc, iron, and lead in addition to the famous silver, but was closed after only 60 years when an attempt to use explosives rather than manual methods resulted in an inundation of water into the lower shafts. You can still see the water down there. The mine is open Tuesday through Sunday, 1 to 8 p.m., and a guide will take you through for 300 pesos (60¢).

Of Zacatecas's churches, many are notable: San Agustín dates from 1613, when construction was started, although dedication had to wait until 1782; San Francisco was the church of a convent, begun in 1567; the Templo de Jesus was built between 1887 and 1913. But the most famous religious edifice besides the cathedral is about four miles east of Zacatecas on Hwys. 45/49. In the town of Guadalupe, look for a red-brick church and steeple, and turn right just past it onto Calle Independencia. A few blocks down this street is the **Convento de Guadalupe.** It's open daily from 10 a.m. to 5 p.m.; entry to the museum costs 50 pesos (10¢), 25 pesos (5¢) on Sunday. You enter through a small park or court-yard with stone mosaics—look up at the different domes and doorways of the convent. The museum building is to your right. Inside the convent proper, every wall seems to be covered in paintings, with series of huge paintings describing the life of St. Francis de Assisi on the ground floor, and the life of Christ above.

Remember as you tour that these cloistered premises were reserved for the men of the cloth, and that normal folk were not meant to see the paintings. Less were they meant to see the sumptuous "cells" in which the Franciscan monks—or, rather, students and teachers, as this was a sort of college—spent their spare time. You may catch a glimpse of the brown-robed monks through a slatted wooden door, for the building is still in use today as a college of instruction in the Franciscan order, with only a part of it used for the museum. Here at the third Franciscan monastery established in the New World missionaries were educated and sent northward into what is now northern Mexico and the southwestern U.S. in the cultural conquest of the Spaniards. (The Dominican order, also important in the conquest, appears in the artwork of the convent, too; but it's the brown-robed Franciscans that are the more familiar figures, with the three knots of their sashes signifying their vows of obedience, penitence, and poverty.)

The chapel to the left of the main building (as you face the convent from the front court/park) is called the Capilla de Napoles. You will note with a gasp that it must have taken a king's ransom in gold to decorate it, with gold ranging in quality from 6 karat on the lower walls up to 22 karat in the dome above. You can get a guide to show you around, or to open the chapel, which you can see either from the organ loft or from the ground floor—give him a tip for opening the doors and turning on the lights.

Those without cars can get a bus to the town of Guadalupe from Callejón de Tampico, just up from the Best Western Hotel, which drops you off right in front of the convent, leaves about every 15 minutes or so, and costs 45 pesos (9¢) for the 20-minute ride. A taxi to Guadalupe will run about 1,000 pesos ($2).

NIGHT LIFE: Have you ever been to a discothèque located in a silver mine 320 meters underground? That's where you'll be if you go to **El Eden,** open 9:30 p.m. to 2:30 a.m. Fridays and Saturdays, 9:30 p.m. to 2 a.m. Thursdays and Sundays. Cost to enter is 800 pesos ($1.60) per person.

Another unusual spot is the discothèque **El Elefante Blanco** (the White Elephant) perched on the mountaintop with the Hotel del Bosque, right behind the teleférico departure. The side facing the city is almost round, with windows floor-to-ceiling, and needless to say, a magnificent view. It's open from 9 p.m. to 2:30 a.m. Thursday through Saturday, with a 1,000-peso ($2) entrance fee (couples only). You might want to call ahead for reservations (tel. 2-1104); it's a very popular place.

The **Hotel Aristos** and the **Best Western Hotel,** which cater to a more upper-class clientele, also have nightclubs with shows, open to guests and visitors alike.

ZACATECAS MISCELLANY: The **Casa Jaquez,** Avenida Hidalgo 202, is a convenient supermarket and wine shop, open seven days a week, 9 a.m. to 4 p.m. and 6 to 10 p.m.; it's four blocks from the cathedral, heading south. . . . Directly across from the Teatro Calderón is the **Mercado González Ortega,** home of Zacatecan handcrafts. . . . The **post office (Correos)** is *not* in the building with the Telegrafos at the corner of Juárez and Hidalgo, but rather on the side street called Allende, half a block down from Avenida Hidalgo. . . . Zacatecas has its **National Fair** from late August through mid-September each year. Cockfights, bullfights, band concerts, and general hoopla prevail; particularly famous toreadores are laid on, and bullfight tickets go for 1,000 pesos ($2); buses leave from downtown for the gigantic Plaza de Toros (and also for the nearby cockpit) on days when fights are held. . . . Zacatecas is famous, among craftsmen, for its sarapes, its carvings in stone and wood, and its leatherwork.

SIDE TRIPS: Chicomostoc, 34 miles south of Zacatecas on Hwy. 54, about 1¼ miles off the highway, is the archeological site of a 12th-century Indian culture developed by the Nahuatlacas tribe. The pyramids here resemble somewhat the ones at Mitla and Monte Alban, much farther to the south. The largest pyramid, called the Temple, has been restored and offers you your first glimpse of this fascinating aspect of Mexico's past. The rest of the site is not very well preserved, but the 11 pillars built of granite stones serve to give you an idea of the grandiose palace that once stood here. Stone-paved avenues and terraces crowded with foundations of houses mark the Ciudadela, atop which is an observatory from which the Nahuatlacas studied the movements of stars and planets and—who knows?—tracked the course of early extraterrestrial visitors. You can visit the ruins from sunup to sundown daily.

For those without cars, getting to Chicomostoc may present more of a challenge, since at this writing the bus from Zacatecas directly to the ruins had just been discontinued when the central camionera changed locations. If you're vigorous, you could walk the 2 kilometers from the highway to the ruins, but at this writing there is no bus transportation to take you directly there. However, a guided tour is available through Zacatecas's Hotel Aristos (tel. 492/2-1788), and the English-speaking travel agency Turismo Marxal (tel. 492/2-1160) in the lobby of the Hotel Condessa is planning to form a tour as well. You might want to call for current information and prices.

Several **hot springs** are within bus distance of Zacatecas. Those at **Valparaiso,** mentioned as being 91 kilometers (56.4 miles) from Fresnillo, are 151 kilometers (93.6 miles) from Zacatecas. Others around are **San Miguel Atotomlco** in Apozól, in the south of the state of Zacatecas, and **Balneario Agua Azul,** 40 minutes by bus along the road heading to Jeréz. You can get more information about these hot springs at the Tourism Office beside the cathedral in Zacatecas (tel. 492/2-0170) or at the aforementioned Turismo Marxal; or, you might prefer to wait until you get to Aguascalientes or San Luis Potosí and use the hot springs nearer there.

2. Aguascalientes

Aguascalientes (alt. 6,000 feet; pop. 430,000) means "hot waters," so it isn't hard to figure out that the city has hot springs. Underneath the town there's a maze of tunnels believed to have been excavated by some ancient peoples who left no explanation of their feats; the tunnels are not open to the public.

Today Aguascalientes is known for its copper mining as well as for its embroidery and knitwear. Most of the town women are involved in this craft and those who aren't are humming away on their sewing machines. In the streets beside and behind the cathedral and the Plaza Principal you'll note several stores selling the products of this industry.

As this city has grown it has lost some of its colonial charm. The residents no doubt revel in the modernity that progress has brought, but the tourist in search of colonial treasures will find them between newer and less interesting buildings. Aguascalientes is still a nice place to visit, but only as a stop in passing, really.

In recent years, the Mexican government has shown a tendency to move its **tourism offices** well beyond the reach of tourists, and the one in this city is no exception. It's located at Avenida las Americas 413, Suite 103, Aguascalientes, Ags. (tel. 491/6-0123), with an auxiliary office at the Plaza Vestir, on Blvd. José Maria Chavez (no number). It offers maps and tourist information of all kinds.

WHERE TO STAY: The best budget choice in town is the **Hotel Maser (9)**, just a couple of blocks from the Plaza Principal at Juan de Montoro 303, Aguascalientes, Ags., on the corner of 16 de Septiembre (tel. 491/5-3562). It's spotlessly clean, and with its red mosaic tile floors, white walls, and ceramic-potted plants all around, it's really very nice. Some of its 44 bright, cheerful rooms face the covered courtyard forming the lobby, others the open courtyard behind. Single rooms go for 2,500 pesos ($5), doubles 3,000 pesos ($6).

Just a short block away is another good budget hotel, the **Hotel San José (2)**, at Hidalgo 207, Aguascalientes, Ags. (tel. 491/5-5130). The outside is pretty plain, but inside it's just fine. The 31 small, spare but clean rooms open onto narrow hallways. It's a popular, friendly place, with singles at 2,500 pesos ($5), doubles 3,000 pesos ($6). Parking included.

In the same price range is the **Hotel Rosales (7)**, at Calle Gral. Guadalupe Victoria 104 (tel. 491/5-2165). The lobby itself is a visual adventure, with something for everyone including a picture of Rin Tin Tin gazing down on a huge potted plant, a statue of the well-loved Mexican comedian Cantinflas, and a variety of staircases (with every style from a small circular set to those resembling a miniature of the Spanish Steps). Getting to your room may be a bit like being in a life-size version of Chutes and Ladders, but it's all in good fun. All 45 rooms have bath, TV, warm water during the day, and one or two beds. The rooms are small and slightly stuffy, but quiet. The bathrooms are minuscule; you could surely perform all functions in two strides. However, the place is clean and the price is right at 2,600 pesos ($5.20) for a room with one bed (for one or two people), 2,990 pesos ($5.98) for a room with two beds. You can ask for a discount here and probably get it.

Right on the main plaza, there are four very nice hotels to choose from. One is the **Hotel Imperial (3)**, (tel. 491/5-1664 or 491/5-1650), housed in a once-imposing stone building on the Plaza Principal across the street from the cathedral. The Imperial "lobby" is a tiny little entranceway at the side of the building, the original lobby having been converted into a Bancomer branch. Guest rooms are big, and the outside ones are cheerful and especially bright; but beware of the unmerciful street noise. Rooms facing the pleasant inner courtyard are much quieter. The price for these inner rooms is 2,162 pesos ($4.32) single, 2,705 pesos ($5.41) double. For the outer rooms with French doors opening onto wrought-iron balconies with a view of the magnificent cathedral, and for the entire new upper story, prices are 3,956 pesos ($7.91) single and 4,945 pesos ($9.89) double.

Kitty-corner across the plaza from the cathedral is the **Hotel Senorial (4)**, at Colón 104 on the corner of Juan de Montoro, Aguascalientes, Ags. (tel. 491/5-

1630 or 491/5-1473). When I was there the entire hotel looked as if no speck of dust had ever entered. Some of the 32 rooms face the street, with French doors opening onto tiny balconies; you might try to get one of these, especially the one right on the corner facing the plaza, as they are all bright and cheerful. (The rooms on the interior are, of course, quieter.) All go for 3,500 pesos ($7) single, 4,500 pesos ($9) double. There's a cafeteria open 8 a.m. to 11 p.m., a ladies' bar noon to midnight, and long-distance phone service.

On another corner of the plaza, above the restaurant Las Bugambilias, is the **Hotel Río Grande (5),** José Maria Chavez 101, Aguascalientes, Ags (tels. 491/6-1666, or 6-1889). The Río Grande boasts 75 air-conditioned rooms with color TV (U.S. channels received by parabolic antenna), FM radio, telephone, carpeting, and all the other luxuries you could ask for, with underground parking also available for an extra 69 pesos (14¢). This is quite a fancy place. Single rooms here are priced at 6,555 pesos ($13.10), doubles at 6,900 pesos ($13.80).

The elegant **Hotel Francia (6),** Avenida Madero and Plaza Principal, Aguascalientes, Ags. (tel. 491/5-6080), is the high-class place in town—when I was there they were preparing to receive the President of Mexico the following day. It has a synthetic tile floor that looks absolutely like marble and a huge blow-up print of Aguascalientes's Plaza Principal as it looked a century ago. Its huge, modern rooms are air-conditioned and very well appointed, but are at the high end of our range at 8,395 pesos ($16.79) single, 10,350 pesos ($20.70) double. Parking costs 345 pesos (69¢) extra. The clientele at the Francia tend to be well-groomed business types, with the occasional wealthy farmer in sleek cowboy hat. The restaurant downstairs is open from 7 a.m. to 10:30 p.m.

WHERE TO EAT: A nice place in town to eat is the **Restaurant Mitla (10),** Madero 220 (tel. 5-3770), a bar-and-grill restaurant which is spotlessly clean and has such good service that the waiter brings you a plate of rolls, butter, and cheese (cheese at a slight charge) the moment you sit down. Lots of selection in edibles: kidneys and onions, chicken dishes, and excellent chilaquiles (chunks of pork and corn tortillas covered with a hot sauce and sprinkled with cheese) for 500 to 750 pesos ($1 to $1.50), up to 1,600 pesos ($3.20) for filete especial Mitla. Open 7:30 a.m. to midnight.

Enter the **Cafetería Catedral (3),** right below the Hotel Imperial on the corner of 5 de Mayo and Moctezuma, and take a table by the window for a good view of the cathedral, the plaza, and the busiest street corner in Aguascalientes. There are a lot of locals here reading the paper and enjoying a cup of coffee, but while you snack on a sandwich priced at 170 pesos (34¢), a banana split for 300 pesos (60¢), or an espresso for 100 pesos (20¢), gaze out the window for a slice of life. Open 9 a.m. to 10 p.m.

Right around the corner is **Danny-Yo (3),** open 10 a.m. to 9 p.m., where you can get frozen yogurt sundaes to go, priced from 190 pesos (38¢) small size to 390 pesos (78¢) large size for a sundae with a choice of two flavors of frozen yogurt, fresh fruit, and several toppings and sprinkles which you can select as it's being made.

Since you probably didn't stay at the Hotel Río Grande you can eat in the hotel restaurant, **Las Bugambilias (5)** (tel. 5-1666), overlooking the plaza. Popular as a businessmen's lunch hangout, you can dine in style with tablecloths, cloth napkins, and more than one fork. Meals on the à la carte menu will be in the 1,320 to 1,960 pesos range ($2.65 to $3.92), with antojitos priced from 525 to 1,780 pesos ($1.05 to $3.56). Open 7:30 a.m. to 10:30 p.m.

The **Cafetería & Bar Cielo Vista (8)** (tel. 5-3000), a scant half block off the Plaza Principal at Plaza Principal 101, open 8 a.m. to 11:30 p.m., is the place to be in the evening if you are young, or in love, or both. The café and bar are located in the same large room with a travel agency and a perfume shop; clocks along one wall show you the time in Mexico City, New York, Madrid, Tokyo, and "Zulu Time." Prices are a little high, but the atmosphere is amiable and pleasant, with the live guitar music from the bar's corner of the room spilling out into the rest of the busy café. A sandwich will set you back 710 pesos ($1.42), or there are lots of desserts in the 300 to 390 price range (60¢ to 78¢) to enjoy with a cup of coffee as you listen to the music and enjoy the friendly atmosphere.

Off the main plaza, over on Avenida López Mateos, are a couple of good restaurants to try, for very different reasons. One is the **Chicken & Pizza Palace (13),** at López Mateos 207 Pte. (tel. 5-2841), where you can probably get the most filling lunch for the cheapest price in town—an all-you-can-eat buffet of pizza, spaghetti, various chilled vegetables, and several potato and pasta salads to choose from, all for 800 pesos ($1.60), served 1 to 5 p.m. The food's not exactly gourmet, but it's not bad either, and it sure will fill you up. The decor is nice, too, with red cloth tablecloths and dark wooden paneling. Open 10 a.m. to 1 a.m.

The **Restaurant El Pastor (12),** a couple of blocks away at López Mateos 314 (tel. 5-7390), is a fancy gourmet restaurant with a variety of decors in the several parts of the building, all superbly designed. You can dine in the garden on intricate white wrought-iron tables covered by their own individual palapa umbrellas, listening to the birds singing in the little aviary; or try the inside dining room, with its maroon-on-white cloths and matching cloth napkins folded into long-stemmed wine glasses. Specialties are antojitos (priced at 500 to 1,000 pesos, $1 to $2) and meat dinners, which aren't priced half bad for the delicious meals you get; Chateaubriand comes for 1,800 pesos ($3.60), and a variety of other familiar quality meat cuts are priced at 1,750 to 2,000 pesos ($3.50 to $4). Music is played in the ladies' bar from 3 to 5 p.m. daily. Open 1 to 11 p.m.

WHAT TO DO: You might find it relaxing just to walk along the Avenida Carranza to the attractive **Jardín de San Marcos,** a lovely enclosed park where the only sounds are those of hundreds of birds in the treetops and the shouts and laughter of children playing around the bandstand.

The only other sight of the quiet town is the **State Palace (1)** on the Plaza Principal. As you enter you'll be stopped short by the astonishing perspective of carved stone pillars and arches, a sweeping staircase, and the general grandeur of the interior patio. A glorious mural by the Chilean painter Ualdo Ibarra was completed in 1957 and depicts much of the history and sociology of the region. Industry mingles with pastoral scenes, long-haired maidens displaying embroidery, miners climbing from the depths, cannons booming, and succulent grapes overflowing their vases. The ceramic plaque in the palace's lobby notes that the building was erected in 1665, but it has obviously been redone on many subsequent occasions. The **Municipal Palace (14)** next door is a more modern construction in the same style, with a lovely fountain just inside the entrance; it, also, is arresting in its beauty.

Visiting Aguascalientes without sampling its thermal facilities is like going to Blarney Castle and leaving the Blarney Stone unbussed. Principal local spa is **Ojo Caliente (11)** on the eastern outskirts of town (tel. 491/5-4721), whose waters are highly recommended for rheumatism, arthritis, and liver ailments. The water in the hot springs here isn't really *hot,* as the name implies, but you'll find it pleasantly warm, like a heated swimming pool. The spa is open every day from 7 a.m. to 7 p.m. The sum of 250 pesos (50¢), children 150 pesos (30¢), permits you to dip in the Olympic-size general pool, and smaller "family pools"

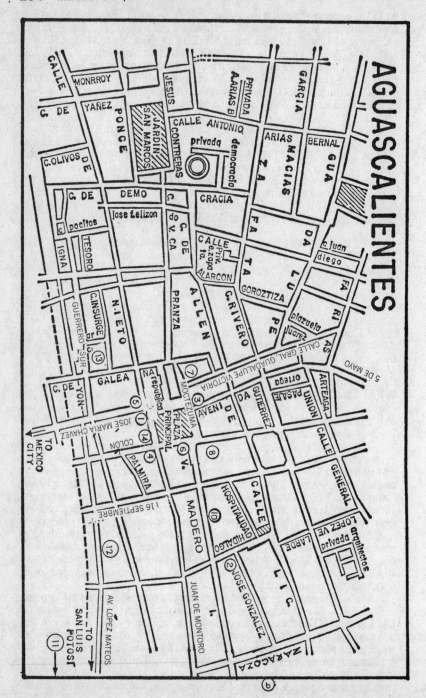

are available at the rate of 1,500 to 2,500 pesos ($3 to $5) per hour. Steam baths cost 400 to 500 pesos (80¢ to $1) per hour, saunas 600 pesos ($1.20) per hour, and squash and tennis courts can also be rented for 500 pesos ($1) per hour. All of these facilities are located where you see the sign "Centro Deportive Ojocaliente" (Ojocaliente Sports Center) out front. You can get to Ojocaliente by taking the Emiliano Zapata bus down Avenida López Mateos, or a taxi will take you from downtown for 350 to 400 pesos (70¢ to 80¢).

Another popular bathing spot is the **Balneario Valladolid,** 22 kilometers (13.6 miles) north of Aguascalientes, a much larger, more decoratively constructed park/hot springs. Entrance is 350 pesos (70¢) per person, and you can get there by taking the Valladolid bus on Avenida López Mateos, heading northward onto Hwy. 45, for another 35 pesos (7¢).

The last week in April—or actually a bit longer, from around April 12 to May 5 (you can check with the Tourist Office for exact dates)—a **fiesta** is held to honor the town's patron saint, San Marcos, and craft exhibits, fireworks, rodeos, and bullfights entertain the townspeople. People come from all over to celebrate, so if you want to join in the festivities you should make your hotel reservations early and pay in advance, to be sure you get a space.

Bulls, incidentally, are bred in the area, and you can make arrangements to visit two well-known breeding ranches, the **Hacienda Chichimeco** and the **Hacienda Penuelas.** Proprietors can be contacted via the Tourist Office.

Finally, a reader from St. Louis, Missouri, Dorothy Schmieder, has written to recommend a side trip (or at least a stop) to **Encarnación de Díaz,** a charming little town 26 miles south of Aguascalientes on Hwy. 45, to see the central plaza, which contains some amazing artwork in the form of living cedar trees. These trees have been pruned into beautiful and unlikely shapes: there is Columbus with his three ships (the *Nina, Pinta,* and *Santa Maria),* kings and queens with ermine robes, zebras, and lions, among others, all created by José Cervantes, who has been tending the trees for 40 years. Sounds pretty interesting, doesn't it?

3. San Luis Potosí

The most picturesque and prosperous mining towns of Mexico include San Luis Potosí among their number, and once you visit this bustling city (alt. 6,200 feet; pop. 400,000) you'll see why. Rich, beautiful colonial architecture abounds, accented by the city's long (400 years) and momentous history. The San Luis of the name is Louis, the saintly king of France; Potosí is the Quechua Indian word for richness, borrowed from the incredibly rich Potosí mines of Bolivia, which San Luis's mines were thought to rival. The colonial city was founded in 1583 by Fray Magdalena and Captain Caldera on the site of the Chichimec Indian town of Tanga-Manga—Indians had been living in a town on this spot for three centuries before the Spaniards arrived. The Spaniards came in search of silver and found it, mostly at a small town called San Pedro some 25 miles from San Luis Potosí. But the mineral springs at San Luis made it a better place to settle than San Pedro, so this became the center of the mining region.

Along with the prospectors came the friars in search of converts: the Franciscans were the first, followed by the Jesuits and the Carmelites. San Luis owes much of its architectural heritage to the vigor—and lavish expenditure—of these groups.

Later, during the Mexican Revolution, the "Plan of San Luis" was proclaimed here. The city has in fact been twice the capital of Mexico—in 1863 and 1867—when Benito Juárez led the fight against European intervention, governing the country from the Palacio de Gobierno (on the Plaza de Armas). From this palace he pronounced the death sentence on Maximilian and his two generals.

Today San Luis Potosí lives on industry rather than silver. Everything from automobiles to mezcal is produced in the factories ringing the city, but happily the colonial center has been preserved intact. It's the capital city of the state of San Luis Potosí, as well.

GETTING TO AND FROM SAN LUIS POTOSÍ: Being a state capital, and right in the geographical center of Mexico, San Luis Potosí is well served by a large number of bus lines. It's an easy day's bus ride (eight hours) from Monterrey or Saltillo, only three hours from Zacatecas or Aguascalientes. There are several daily buses to Guanajuato and San Miguel de Allende, and many to Mexico City via Querétaro. Get tickets in advance at the Central Camionera.

Trains run from Monterrey and Saltillo to San Luis. The same train continues on to Mexico City. There is a morning train from the capital's Buenavista Station to San Luis. These are the "Rápidos"; slower trains, including a night train from the capital with sleeping cars, also run daily. It's best to have a first-class reserved seat, so check in at the station the day before you plan to leave.

ORIENTATION: San Luis is today a big city, but transportation and accommodation present no great problems, as most of what you'll want to see is in the downtown section which holds a good selection of older hotels in a range of prices. Meals are also easy to come by, from snacks to elegant dinners.

The city's **Central Camionera** is a short distance from town, near the grand Benito Juárez Monument. As you exit from either the first- or second-class parts of the bus terminal you'll see bus stops for city buses that will run you to the **Jardín Hidalgo** (the main square, also called the Plaza de Armas, or just the Zócalo).

From the railroad station you can walk—providing your bags are not super-heavy—to most of the hotel selections listed below, the lower priced choices being by and large not more than two or three blocks from the station door.

For information, a map showing the whole town, or answers to questions, head for the **Tourism Office (14),** located upstairs in the old building at Manuel José Othón 130, San Luis Potosí, S.L.P. 78000 (tel. 481/2-3143 and 4-2994), across the street from the cathedral. The staff is knowledgeable and ready to help, and at least one person there will speak English. The office is open from 9 a.m. to 8 p.m. Monday through Friday, 9 a.m. to 2 p.m. Saturdays.

WHERE TO STAY: The area south of the Jardín Hidalgo is a grid of narrow streets lined with graceful and for the most part unmodernized old mansions. These low, elaborate, and ancient homes are built in the Spanish style and each contains a lush central garden courtyard. It's well worth a stroll down here to peek through the delicate iron traceries that cover the windows, and if you're lucky you can catch glimpses of cool, aristocratic rooms lined with gilt and velvet, looking as they have for almost a century.

The modern **Hotel Maria Cristina (3),** Juan Sarabia 110, San Luis Potosí, S.L.P. 78000 (tel. 481/2-9408), is one of San Luis Potosí's most substantial downtown hostelries, with the deluxe touches some love to have, although others would rather not pay for them. If you like the comforts, you'll find them here: a rooftop restaurant and swimming pool, elevators to take you there, lots of carpeting and lots of telephones, and a comfortable lobby that looks just like a European living room, with comfy leather furniture, crystal chandelier, a gas fireplace, and even an antique French clock on the mantelpiece. Singles cost

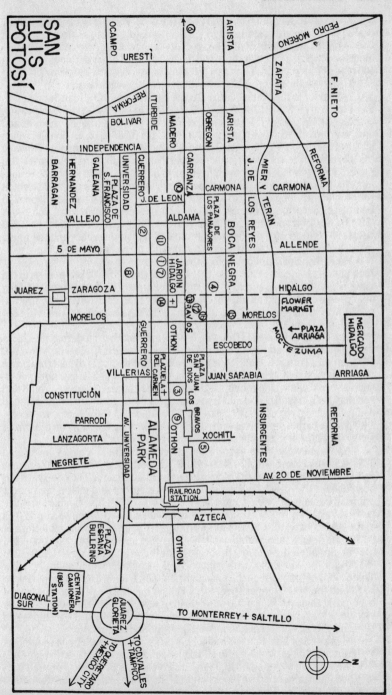

5,400 pesos ($10.80), doubles 6,383 pesos ($12.75). Parking is an additional 400 pesos (80¢). The little restaurant, open 7:30 a.m. to 11 p.m., is up on the ninth floor with the swimming pool. The specialty is enchiladas Potosinas con guacamole for 400 pesos (80¢), and you will find a variety of other antojitos for 360 to 600 pesos (72¢ to $1.20), meat and chicken dishes for 520 to 980 pesos ($1.05 to $1.96), and sandwiches for 250 pesos (50¢) on the bilingual menu.

Next door to the Maria Christina is the **Hotel Napoles (3),** Juan Sarabia 120, San Luis Potosí, S.L.P. 78000 (tel. 481/2-8418), in somewhat stiff competition with the Maria Cristina. Rooms at the Napoles are, again, quite modern and nice, and are priced at 5,405 pesos ($10.81) single, 6,382 ($12.76) double, which includes parking, TV, phone, and some with bathtub as well as shower. Some of the 84 rooms face the street, others an airshaft, so do ask for whichever you prefer. There's a ladies' bar open from noon to 2 a.m., and a very nice restaurant, **La Colomba,** with a bilingual menu and gourmet dishes prepared right at your table, including cheese fondue for 900 pesos ($1.80), Chateaubriand with Béarnaise sauce for 5,500 pesos ($11), and cherries jubilee for 1,265 pesos ($2.53). Seafood, poultry, and meat entrees are priced from 1,800 to 2,800 pesos ($3.60 to $5.60); the decor, coordinated brown-on-white, and the music make it a nice, fancy place to dine out. Open 7 a.m. to 11 p.m.

Hotel Principal, directly across the street from the Maria Cristina (3), at Juan Sarabia 145, San Luis Potosí, S.L.P. 78000 (tel. 481/2-0874), may be in the same neighborhood, but that is the only similarity. This family hotel with an unimpressive lobby but an impressive occupancy rate, occasionally has a vacancy in one of its 18 pleasant and clean rooms. A single here is 1,300 pesos ($2.60) and a double runs 1,800 pesos ($3.60).

The **Hotel de Gante (1)** (tel. 481/2-1492), yet another modern hotel, has a very good location and moderate prices. The entrance is Calle 5 de Mayo no. 140 (San Luis Potosí, S.L.P. 78000), but in fact the building is right at the corner of 5 de Mayo and Madero, on the Plaza de Armas. Although its exterior appearance is very modern, the rooms are a bit older, having seen long use. You'll find you may get a crystal chandelier in exchange for putting up with a little chipped paint. Singles here cost 3,248 pesos ($6.50), doubles 3,823 ($7.65), for rooms with phone, carpet, and some with a bathtub. Ask to see the room on the corner facing the plaza, if it's available, but beware of the plaza's noise.

Another lovely place to try is the **Hotel Filher (8),** Avenida Universidad 375, San Luis Potosí, S.L.P. 78000 (tel. 481/2-1562), at the corner of Zaragoza and Universidad, three short blocks from the main square. The courtyard has been glassed over, but the hotel still whispers elegance and charm, and prices are reasonable with single rooms at 4,105 pesos ($8.21) and doubles at 4,830 pesos ($9.66). The hotel's restaurant, **Los Candiles** (open 7 a.m. to 11 p.m.), is in the large courtyard, and with its lovely decor of yellow-on-white tablecloths it makes the hotel a nice, comfortable place to dine as well as stay. Six breakfast specials are offered, from 350 pesos (70¢) for the continental up to 1,250 pesos ($2.50) for the Mexicano, with fruit cocktail, steak and beans, coffee or milk. Three kinds of spaghetti on the bilingual menu come for 350 to 400 pesos (70¢ to 80¢), and the house dinner specialty, a Pampa meat plate with various cuts of beef, pork, sausage, french fries, and salad, is served for 1,800 pesos ($3.60). A box lunch for travelers is also offered, which for 950 pesos ($1.90) includes two ham and cheese sandwiches, a boiled egg, fruit, and dessert.

Many of San Luis Potosí's budget hotels are as much colonial monuments as the grand edifices on the Jardín Hidalgo. Such a place is the **Hotel Progreso (2)** (tel. 481/2-0366), at Aldama 415, (San Luis Potosí, S.L.P. 78000), between Iturbide and Guerrero, only two blocks south of the Jardín Hidalgo and kitty-corner to the Plaza de San Francisco. Like many other hotels in the city, it's an old mansion converted to a hotel. The lofty court (now the lobby) is filled with heavy colonial wood furniture, and two voluptuous but woebegone caryatids support the arch at the bottom of the grand staircase leading to the rooms. All with bath and phone, the 45 rooms are an odd lot, old-fashioned but comfortable. Singles are 2,800 pesos ($5.60); doubles, 3,300 pesos ($6.60). The desk clerk can help you with parking. This is not the nicest or most refined of the mansions-turned-hotels, but it is certainly one of the most curious ones, and is the best for the money.

Right near the Hotel Jardín is the modern and only slightly weather-beaten **Hotel Anáhuac (5),** at Calle Xochitl 140, San Luis Potosí, S.L.P. 78000 (tel. 481/2-6504). As there are few street numbers on this street, look for the second big (four-story) white building on the right-hand side of the street as you walk down Xochitl from Calle de los Bravos. You'll spot the Anáhuac's cavernous, bare lobby. Rooms are equally without frills, but clean and suitable, renting for 1,886 pesos ($3.77) single, 2,357 pesos ($4.71) double. The hotel has its own big parking lot. A dark café in the hotel lobby brightened by orange and white tablecloths serves a comida for a reasonable 600 pesos ($1.20), egg breakfasts from 350 to 400 pesos (70¢ to 80¢), and antojitos from 350 to 600 pesos (70¢ to $1.20). The area around the Jardín and the Anáhuac is only a few steps from the railroad station. Once it was pretty run-down, but urban renewal has swept away the crumbling buildings and replaced them with parks, public buildings, and a mammoth public parking garage.

Finally, if you prefer older buildings with the wistful air of better days, try the small **Hotel Plaza (7),** Jardín Hidalgo 22, San Luis Potosí, S.L.P. 78000 (tel. 481/2-4631), conveniently located on the south side of the main plaza. The Plaza's 30 rooms are dark and old-fashioned (except for the few facing the plaza), but are clean and quiet, since most face one of two inner courtyards (one covered, the other open) well back from the street. Rates are 1,800 pesos ($3.60) single, 2,800 pesos ($5.60) double. The restaurant downstairs is open from 7 a.m. to 11 p.m.

A Starvation-Budget Hotel

Speaking of older buildings, if funds are stretched to the limit but you're not quite into park benches, head for the **Gran Hotel (12),** at Los Bravos 235, San Luis Potosí, S.L.P. 78000 (tel. 481/2-2119). Although the rooms are washed down each day, no amount of scrubbing is going to put the shine back into the rather dark and desperate Gran Hotel. When all else fails, you can catch a night's sleep here for less than anywhere else in town. Singles without a private bath (sink in room) are 800 pesos ($1.60), doubles 1,000 pesos ($2); the shared bathrooms are separated for men and women. With private bath it's 1,000 pesos ($2) single and 1,500 pesos ($3) double.

WHERE TO EAT: Many of the hotel restaurants listed above are well worth a try (see individual hotels for descriptions), in addition to the restaurants listed here.

Right at the northeast corner of the Jardín Hidalgo, corner of Los Bravos and Hidalgo, is the **Tanga-Manga (13)** (tel. 2-8555). Modern and shiny-bright, its colorful booths and imitation brick contrast with the weighty solidity of the surrounding architecture. The comida corrida, served from 1 to 6 p.m., costs 753 pesos ($1.50), with meat entrees from the grill for 600 to 850 pesos ($1.20 to $1.70); for hanging out at night, there's cappuccino for 120 pesos (24¢), espresso for 109 pesos (21¢), and a bar attached. Scan the menu by the entrance before you walk in and sit down.

The **Restaurant-Café Tokio (9)** (tel. 2-5899), facing the Alameda at Othon

415, is not far from the railroad station. Indeed, it looks sort of like a station inside: bright and bare, always busy with waiters and customers scurrying. It's open 7 a.m. to midnight and serves sandwiches to filet mignon. A good bargain is the enchiladas Potosiñas plate: five enchiladas topped with chopped onions, cheese, generous dollops of refried beans, and guacamole, all for 500 pesos ($1). Other complete meals are priced from around 400 pesos (80¢) and go up to 1,300 pesos ($2.60) for carne a la tampiqueña (roast beef with salad and guacamole). Breakfast dishes come for 350 pesos (70¢), and the comida corrida, served from 1 to 4 p.m., is only 450 pesos (90¢). The Tokio has been dependably good for decades.

A good place for a light lunch or snack is the **Restaurant/Bar El Castillo (11)** (tel. 2-4221), open 8 a.m. to 11 p.m., a bright and comfy modern place just off the Jardín Hidalgo at Madero 145 between Aldama and 5 de Mayo. The walls are splashed with scenes that would make a Parisian feel right at home. Enjoy a view of Montmartre or the Eiffel Tower while checking out the menu. Breakfast huevos rancheros here cost 400 pesos (80¢), with hot dogs, tortas, and sandwiches at 215 pesos (43¢), hot cakes or hamburgers for 350 pesos (70¢), and meat or chicken entrees for 800 to 925 pesos ($1.60 to $1.85). El Castillo is patronized by business-suited types in the morning and late afternoon, by mod young people in the evening, when there's more of a hip coffeehouse atmosphere, and a variety of specialty coffees priced at 170 to 220 pesos (34¢ to 44¢), in addition to full bar service.

La Parroquia, (10) (tel. 2-6681), at Carranza 950 on the corner of Carranza and Díaz de León, is one of several café/restaurant/ice-cream parlors patronized by the business set. Breakfast for 300 to 475 pesos (60¢ to 95¢), pizzas for 600 pesos ($1.20), fish and chicken dishes for 700 to 850 pesos ($1.40 to $1.70), with the most expensive thing in the house being only 1,450 pesos ($2.90) for brochettes de filet, are a few of the drawing cards here. Also, when the cinema next door lets out, the café tables fill up for conversation, seeing and being seen, people-watching—the food is definitely less important than the social life. It's fun, and the menus offer everything from steaks to banana splits. Walk up here for dessert after dinner to take in the nightlife.

Finally there's **La Cigarra (6)** (tel. 2-3984), at least a ten-minute walk west of the main plaza to the middle of the 900 block on Carranza, where you'll find La Cigarra at no. 950. But the prices are economically right and the food is delicious. The house specialty, a delicious *pozole* (a hearty soup of pork and chicken, corn and other vegetables, served with lime to squirt on top) comes for 600 pesos ($1.20); an omelet with ham, potatoes, and beans comes for 500 pesos ($1), a burger and fries for 400 pesos (80¢), chicken or steak dishes for 600 pesos ($1.20), and for the record, nothing on the menu is over 800 pesos ($1.60), the price for the carne Tampiqueña. To walk off this very filling fare, wend your way back to the plaza through the quiet, narrow, residential streets of San Luis Potosí. Open 8 a.m. to 4 a.m. weekdays, weekends until 5 a.m.

Right across from here is the restaurant **Lafayette (6)** (tel. 2-7439), at Carranza 915, specializing in pizza. Prices for a pizza with cheese and one additional topping (there are 11 to choose from) are 350 pesos (70¢) for mini size, 550 pesos ($1.10) individual, 750 pesos ($1.50) medium, and 1,200 pesos ($2.40) family size. Many salads are served from 220 to 495 pesos (44¢ to 99¢), and antojitos are priced at only 120 to 500 pesos (24¢ to $1), with tortas at 160 pesos (32¢).

Starvation-Budget Restaurants

Where can you get a full comida corrida for 400 pesos (80¢) in San Luis? Right on the Jardín Hidalgo, of all places, at the above-mentioned **Hotel Plaza (7).** Served in the courtyard restaurant from noon until it's gone, the comida does indeed seem to be the hotel's reason for existence these days, and is enjoyed by many more people than the number that stay at the hotel.

Another excellent bargain are the restaurants **Las Tortugas,** serving very rich, satisfying *tortas* (sandwiches on a small French roll) for 120 to 160 pesos (24¢ to 32¢) and hamburgers for 350 to 400 pesos (70¢ to 80¢). There are many kinds of tortas to choose from, put together with all the trimmings: avocado, egg, ham, sausage, and two kinds of cheese, to name a few. From its humble beginning of one little sandwich shack, Las Tortugas has become more and more popular for the good food it serves, and now there are several Tortugas: **Las Tortugas Morelos (16)** at the corner of Morelos and Obregón, **Las Tortugas del Charco Verde (4)** on the corner of Obregón and Hidalgo, and yet another, **Las Tortugas del Correo (15),** on the corner of Morelos and Boca Negra. Open 7 a.m. to 11 p.m. At all the Tortugas the atmosphere is friendly and informal, the kitchens clean, the service fast, and the ingredients of good quality. They also feature free delivery—call 2-0029, the phone number of yet another **Tortugas,** this one on the corner of Obregón and Allende.

WHAT TO SEE: The place to begin a walk around town is the **Jardín Hidalgo.** The plaza itself dates from the mid-1700s—before that it was a bullring. After the plaza was laid out, the **Palacio de Gobierno** was begun. What you see today of this building has been much repaired, restored, and added to through the centuries—the back and the south façade were redone as recently as 1973. The front of the building retains much of the original 18th-century decoration, at least on the lower floors.

Across the plaza from the Government Palace is the **cathedral.** The original building had only one bell tower, so another one—the one on the left—was built in 1910 to match, although today the newer tower looks to be the older. The **palace** on the north side of the cathedral was built in 1850 by the Count of Monterrey and was loaded with great wealth—paintings and sculpture—little of which has survived the plaza's stormy history. When the count died in 1890 the palace was taken over by the bishop, and later in 1921 by the city government. Since that year it's been San Luis's City Hall, living in peace for many years until it was firebombed on January 1, 1986, due to political differences. See if it's been restored again by the time you visit San Luis.

By the way, the bandstand in the center of the plaza was built in 1947 (although in colonial style), using the pink stone famous to the region. You'll see the stone throughout San Luis. The band plays here Thursday and Sunday evenings, for free.

From the Jardín Hidalgo, stroll along the **Calle Hidalgo,** heading north out of the plaza. This street's reserved for pedestrians, and it's a treat to walk from the Jardín almost all the way to the city's Central Market.

The Plazuela del Carmen and the Alameda

Southeast of the Jardín Hidalgo is one of the city's most famous and pretty squares, the Plazuela del Carmen, named for the **Templo del Carmen** church. From the Jardín, walk east along Madero-Othon to Escobedo and the Plazuela. The entire area you see was once part of the lush grounds of the Carmelite monastery, built in the 17th century. The church survives from that time, and is perhaps the Potosiños' favorite place of worship, but the convent has been destroyed. In 1857 the government confiscated the convent building and used it as a jail for a time before it was destroyed. The **Teatro de la Paz** now stands on the site, having been built there in 1889.

The square is a fine place to take a rest by one of the fountains before heading on a few more blocks east to get to the **Alameda,** the city's largest downtown park. This is the coolest park as well, because of the shade trees; walk all the way to the center and you barely notice the traffic on the busy streets surrounding the Alameda. All around the side of Alameda park are vendors selling handcrafts, fruits and all manner of snacks: try a hot fried banana with butter and sugar for 125 pesos (25¢), or wrapped tortillas filled with *cajeta,* a wonderful butterscotch made from goat's milk, for only 100 pesos (20¢).

On one side of Alameda park you'll see a modern, futuristic building, and that's the **Sala de Arte,** with exhibits of paintings and other art; right next door is the **Templo de San José.**

Other Plazas

San Luis Potosí has a lot more plazas than the two most famous ones mentioned above. The **Plaza de San Francisco** (also called the Plaza de Guerrero) is south of the Palacio de Gobierno along Aldama, between Universidad and Galeana. The square takes its name from the huge monastery of the Franciscan order at the south side of the plaza. The church on the west side is dated 1799, and next to the church is the interesting **Museo Regional de Arte Popular,** housed in a turn-of-the-century (20th century!) building, renovated to hold the museum in 1953. You can visit the museum Monday to Saturday from 11 a.m. to 2 p.m. and from 5 to 8 p.m. to see the exhibits in glassed-in rooms around the open court. The displays run the gamut of Potosiño crafts: ceramics, inlaid wood, paper-mâché "sculpture," the local designs in rebozos, and so forth. Right now the price is right—the museum's free.

Another square with a church to visit is the **Plaza de los Panadores,** at the intersection of Obregón and Aldama (northwest of the Jardín Hidalgo). You'll want to take a peek through the baroque doorway of the **Loreto Chapel,** dating from the 16th century, and the neighboring headquarters of the **Compañía de Jesus**—the Jesuit order. In the chapel is a magnificent golden sunburst over the altar, a reminder of past glories.

Markets

It's several blocks along the pedestrian Calle Hidalgo from the Jardín Hidalgo to the city's new **Mercado Hidalgo,** a mammoth building devoted mostly to food but also carrying some baskets, rebozos, and straw furniture. While here, be sure to try some *queso de tuna,* a specialty of the region. Although called a "cheese," in fact it's a sweet paste—something like dried figs or dates with a molasses or burnt-sugar taste—made from the prickly pear cactus fruit. It's delicious, and comes in various size pieces ranging from 10 to 350 pesos (2¢ to 70¢), with a whole kilo (2.2 pounds) costing 1,200 pesos ($2.40).

But the walk along Calle Hidalgo is itself an introduction to the city's commercial life. Hardware stores, craftspeople's shops, groceries, and taverns all crowd the street—and have you ever seen so many shoe stores in your life? How on earth do they all survive?

Off to the right (as you walk along Hidalgo from the Jardín Hidalgo) is a large and well-worn building that is San Luis Potosí's **flower market,** a joyous riot of colors and scents anytime of day.

Tangamanga Park

It's a ways from downtown, but if you have transportation you might be interested in a visit to **Parque Tangamanga,** one of the largest parks in all Mexico, located on the Boulevard Diagonal Sur at the intersection of Tata Nacho (tel. 481/3-3274). It covers acres and acres, with three lakes, a Hollywood Bowl–type outdoor theatre, planetarium and observatory, library, children's playground, every kind of sports field you can think of, and many picnic sites set up with barbecue pit, tables, and benches, with slatted shelters for shade. The park is open daily from 6 a.m. to 6 p.m. (admission free).

Side Trip to Gogorrón

For a real treat, you can either make a day trip or stay overnight at the **Balneario de Gogorrón,** an hour's ride to the south of San Luis Potosí on the highway heading towards Guanajuato, where you see the sign saying "Centro Vacacional Gogorrón." The attraction here is the thermal water; unlike many hot springs in the region which have only lukewarm water, the water here is really quite hot, with one small pool of really hot water and a larger, Olympic-size pool where it's still very warm. There are also private Roman baths. Day rates for the large mineral pools are 400 pesos (80¢); the private Roman baths cost 450 pesos (90¢) per person. A sign in the information house tells the mineral content of the water, known for its health-giving qualities.

The springs area has been made into a complete "vacation center," with a restaurant open 9 a.m. to 9 p.m., a bar, horseback riding, a wide lawn, and a children's playground in addition to the mineral pools. It's full of happy Mexican families out for a holiday, and all in all it's a happy, pleasant, and relaxing place to be.

Gogorrón has 20 cabañas (cabins) for rent, with 12 more in construction, spotlessly clean, each with its own private sunken tile tub (large enough for several people to lounge around in the mineral water), two double beds, carpet, and phone in a spacious, very nice room. Prices, including three meals at the restaurant, are 7,100 pesos ($14.20) single, 11,100 pesos ($22.20) double, and 14,500 pesos ($29) for three. During the week (Monday through Friday only) you can pay for just the cabins (no meals) if you wish, and in that case it's 4,300 pesos ($8.60) single and 5,500 pesos ($11) double. (If you want to stay a few days, ask about the discounted rates for a "Paquete Especial," a package deal for 3 days and 2 nights.) There's no extra charge to use any of the mineral water facilities if you're staying overnight. You can make reservations or get additional information by calling Gogorrón at 481/4-6655, or by contacting their office in San Luis Potosí, Jardín Hidalgo 20, Apdo. Postal 700, San Luis Potosí, S.L.P. 78000 (tel. 481/2-9435, 481/2-3636 or 481/2-1550).

To get to Gogorrón from San Luis Potosí, take the highway heading to Mexico City, and turn off to the right on the highway heading towards León and Guanajuato; the balneario is right on this highway, with lots of trees on your left and a big sign on your right. It's also easy to get there by bus: from the central camionera, take the bus line "Flecha Amarilla," leaving every hour or so, for 335 pesos (67¢), and get off the bus right at the entrance to the balneario. Wait at the entrance and flag down a bus when you're ready to go back after a long, relaxing day.

4. Guanajuato

Guanajuato (alt. 6,724 feet; pop. 80,000) is one of Mexico's hidden gems. Like the other Silver Cities, it harbors architectural treasures to be discovered, oddities of man and nature to be explored, very attractive cityscapes to be admired (and photographed), and a wealth of cultural offerings to be enjoyed. Yet the city's fame has not spread beyond Mexico's borders. In my opinion, Guanajuato should be high up on anyone's list of Mexico's finest places to visit.

Guanajuato is an unusually attractive town with an inexplicable air of isolation about it. It was built in 1559 around the Río Guanajuato, and the narrow winding streets of today reflect the meanderings of the past. The river itself was diverted from the town after the last flood in 1905, leaving an excellent bed for

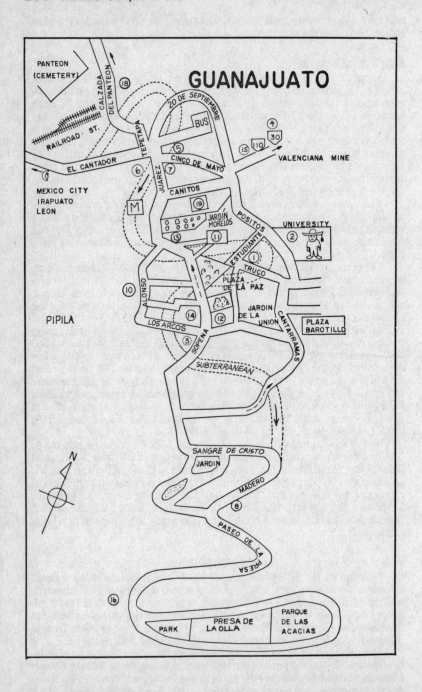

GUANAJUATO

what has now become a subterranean highway. Most of the stonework and arches you'll see were already there in the 17th century. All that was needed was stone pavement and street lights.

Guanajuato has a rich history, being one of the most important colonial cities (along with Querétaro and Zacatecas) in the 16th, 17th, and 18th centuries. Here was mined over a third of all the silver in the world; and like the gold rush towns in the U.S., it bloomed overnight with elaborate churches and mansions, many in the Moorish style. Today, Guanajuato seems like an old Spanish city that has been dumped lock, stock, and barrel into a Mexican river valley.

GETTING TO GUANAJUATO: It's not difficult to get to Guanajuato, despite its mountain location. After all, it is a state capital and a popular tourist sight.

By Bus

From Mexico City's Terminal Norte, the **Flecha Amarilla** line runs 15 buses a day to Guanajuato. Go to area no. 6 ("6 Espera") to find the company's ticket desk and bus platforms. The trip can take as long as six hours if you get a local bus that stops in San Juan del Río, Querétaro, Dolores Hidalgo, and San Miguel de Allende. Ask for the express.

From Guanajuato, Flecha Amarilla runs 6 buses a day to San Luis Potosí, 6 to Aguascalientes, 15 a day to Mexico City, 10 to San Miguel de Allende, 15 to Querétaro, and 17 daily to Guadalajara.

Omnibus de México serves Guanajuato with three daily buses to/from Guadalajara, three to Querétaro, and two each to Dolores Hidalgo and San Miguel de Allende.

Other lines serving Guanajuato include Estrella Blanca, Transportes Chihuahuenses, Transportes La Piedad, Tres Estrellas de Oro, La Altena, and Autobuses de Occidente.

By Rail

Rail connections for the spur to Guanajuato are very inconvenient. Bus is the way to go.

ORIENTATION: The **Tourism Office (5)**, at the intersection of Juárez and Cinco de Mayo (tel. 473/2-0086), will be glad to give you a free and detailed map of the city, with a map of the entire state of Guanajuato on the back. Walking is the only way really to get to know this labyrinthine town. For longer stretches of travel in the city, just hop on the main bus, marked "Presa-Estación," which operates from one end of town at the railroad station to the other end at Presa de la Olla, using the subterranean highway when going south (subterranean bus stops are along the way; you'll need to know of the one near the Teatro Juárez, off the Jardín de la Union).

A Note on Reservations: Guanajuato is a popular tourist destination for both Mexicans and foreign visitors, and the room situation is a bit tight most of the year. During the International Cervantes Festival held from late April to mid-May, and in October, rooms are very hard—virtually impossible—to find unless reserved, and even if you have a reservation it's good to come claim your room early in the day. Some visitors have to stay in places as far away as Querétaro and San Miguel de Allende, coming over to Guanajuato for the day.

WHERE TO STAY: There has been little change in the selection of in-town hotels of Guanajuato for the past decade or so, probably because there is nowhere to build. But these days, with the peso so low, even the luxury hotels are within our range.

On the Jardín de la Union, Guanajuato's prettiest park graced with the Teatro Juárez, is the **Posada Sante Fe (12)** (tel. 473/2-0084). Here you have a bright and almost gaudy display of tiles, chandeliers, colonial decoration, and classical urns. The immense tiled murals get you in the colonial mood, however, and the place itself is very sympathetic. As the demand for rooms here is constantly high, the men at the front desk may treat you with less than effusive politeness, and they may—if it's really busy—require that you take three meals with your room at 8,970 pesos ($17.95) single, 10,235 pesos ($20.50) double.

If the Posada's full, and it may well be, wander across the street to the **Hotel San Diego (14)** (tel. 473/2-1300), a less aggressively colonial establishment but still very pleasant, and priced about the same except that here at the San Diego there's no need to take meals with your room. Prices are 5,750 pesos ($11.50) single, 6,677 pesos ($13.35) double.

A newer addition to the Jardín de la Union's collection of "colonial" hotels is the **Hostería del Frayle (3)** (tel. 473/2-1179), actually a few doors out of the square, past the Teatro Juárez and up the hill on Calle Sopena, at no. 3. Nicely done, although hardly authentic, the Hostería offers pretty much the standard room of a Mexican tourist hotel, at reasonable prices: 6,900 pesos ($13.80) single and 8,165 pesos ($16.35) double.

If you are not opposed to taking a bus to and from the city center, I would recommend your staying outside of town. There are several good choices with reasonable rates, and out here you have the quiet tree-lined streets instead of the city bustle. These hotels are easily reached by taking the Presa-Estación bus from the corner of Cinco de Mayo and Juárez, just north of the Mercado and less than a block from the bus station.

The best choice out of town is the **Motel de Las Embajadoras (8),** Paseo Madero 44 (tel. 473/2-0081). It's very quiet, the rooms small but clean and going for 2,760 pesos ($5.55) single, 4,370 pesos ($8.75) double. The nicest thing, however, is the surrounding grounds. The only daytime sounds are birds chirping, a radio playing, and chairs being scraped across the floors as maids clean the pretty little rooms. There's a patio at the rear, with tables, chairs, and a hammock, and climbing geraniums complete the tranquil scene. A nice little restaurant takes care of meals.

Just a block from the bus station is the recently redone **Hotel El Insurgente (6),** Juárez 226 (tel. 473/2-2294). All the nice old stone doorways have been left intact, and the little lobby fixed up with attractive wood and stone. The rooms-with-bath here are quite small, and could be claustrophobic—look before you buy. Those with windows onto the busy street don't have this problem, but do have the problem of noise; better take a small but quiet one on the glassed-in central court, on the third or fourth floors. Rooms with private bath and cable TV cost 3,450 pesos ($6.90) single, 5,290 pesos ($10.60) double.

Those looking for a European-style pension should seek out the **Casa Kloster (10),** Calle de Alonso 32 (tel. 473/2-0088), on this quiet side street, across the street from Telefonos de México. This 15-room *casa de huespedes,* run by a sympathetic old couple, has a large central courtyard brilliant with birds and flowers, around which are ranged the very plain, but clean, bathless rooms. Showers are available for a small fee, but no meals are served. You pay 1,200 pesos ($2.40) per person per night.

Two more hotels worth a look if everything else if full are on Hwys. 110/30, the road to Dolores Hidalgo, the Valenciana Mine, just two blocks from the Tourism Office. The **Hotel Mineral de Rayas (4),** Alhondiga 7 y Callejón del Apartado (tel. 473/2-1967), is a labyrinthine building which you enter through a ground-floor restaurant. Ascending to the second floor, you'll find the reception desk is at the end of a long corridor. Rooms are plain, done in black and white or in solid colors, and the large number of rooms (46 in all) come in various price ranges from 2,800 pesos ($5.60) single, 3,500 pesos ($7) double; some rooms have three and four beds, good for families and friends traveling together. The Mineral de Rayas takes groups and may be filled with a busload when you visit. Nearby, the **Hotel Alhondiga (15),** Insurgencia 49 (tel. 473/2-0525), is a similar hotel with 33 rooms right off the Plaza Alhondiga, not far from the bus station or the market. Front rooms are the nicest, but also, remember, the noisiest. A single person pays 2,300 pesos ($4.60), two persons pay 3,450 pesos ($6.90), in a room with private bath.

Top of the Budget

With the peso so weak, even some of Guanajuato's upper-bracket hotels have come within the reach of our budget—or almost.

The **Hotel El Presidente Guanajuato (17)** (tel. 473/2-3980) is three kilometers (two miles) from the center of town, set in a pretty valley next to the crumbling remains of several mining barons' haciendas. Flower-covered terraces, a spacious lobby and restaurant, large attractive rooms overlooking a tidy swimming pool, and very friendly staff are what you get; 8,050 pesos ($16.10) single, 10,200 pesos ($20.40) double, 12,750 pesos ($25.50) triple is what you pay. Transportation does present something of a problem. Cabs cost 500 pesos ($1) from town to the hotel, 600 pesos ($1.20) from the hotel to town (they must be called). You can pay only a few pesos by taking a bus ("Noria Alta" or "Marfil") to Noria Alta, then walking five or ten minutes. Catch the same bus back into town; even though the bus goes right by the hotel, it is not allowed to stop on the twisty road, so you must board or descend at Noria Alta.

You will no doubt wonder what it costs to stay at the striking **Hotel Castillo de Santa Cecilia** (tel. 473/2-0485), about a kilometer up the hill from town on the road to Dolores Hidalgo. The place truly is a castle, and the 100 comfortable rooms in this stone labyrinth go for 7,130 pesos ($14.25) single, 8,280 pesos ($16.60) double. You can enjoy a heated swimming pool, restaurant, bar, and lounge with entertainment.

READER'S HOTEL SELECTION: "We stayed at the **Hotel Posada Señorial,** Paseo de la Presa 79 (tel. 473/2-1421). This small hotel is a bargain—2,400 pesos ($4.80), including tax, for a cama matrimonial. It is quiet and very clean, has plenty of hot water, and the folks behind the desk are extremely friendly and helpful" (Deborah Ozga, Washington, D.C.).

WHERE TO EAT: Cheap burgers are yours at **La Hamburguesa Feliz,** Sopena 10, right near Teatro Juárez. A single burger costs a mere 200 pesos (40¢); a jumbo, 300 pesos (60¢). With french fries and a drink, your supper should cost less than 460 pesos (92¢). There are good, cheap, set-price breakfasts too. Self-service, no tipping.

Las Palomas, Calle de la Campaña 19 (tel. 2-4936), is right next to the post office (Correos). Newish and modern, this split-level place will serve you a full lunch for 900 pesos ($1.80), a big Mexican combination plate for a good deal less, and antojitos such as chilaquiles for 460 pesos (92¢).

The best inexpensive lunch in town is the 700-peso ($1.40) one served at the peaceful **Café El Retiro** (tel. 2-0622), opposite the Oficina Federal de Hacienda, just past the Teatro Juárez at Sopena 12. The meal consists of soup, rice with cheese, steak or pork, pastry, coffee. With its vases of flowers on the sideboard, cafeteria-modern furniture, El Retiro seems more like somebody's living room than a restaurant, and the service is just as informally friendly.

Also on the Jardín de la Union, just across from the Teatro Juárez, is **Casa Valadez (12),** a combination restaurant-soda-fountain-film-shop that has reasonable prices. Lunch is 690 pesos ($1.40), but isn't served until after 2 p.m. The Valadez stays open fairly late.

The **Restaurant La Union,** on the corner of the Jardín across from the Santa Fe, is a nothing-special eatery that's popular with students because of its cheap prices. They offer a comida for 700 pesos ($1.40), chicken for 650 pesos ($1.30), and tortilla dishes for half that.

If this is still too high for your budget, I have just the place for you: the **University Cafeteria** offers an excellent set lunch from noon to 4 p.m. for 450 pesos (90¢) (a few pesos more with a drink) that includes soup, pasta, meat, frijoles, salad, and dessert. Although it is supposedly only for students, I've never been questioned so I doubt you'll have any problem—it's certainly the best bargain in town. To get to the cafeteria, take the middle entrance to the university on the ground level off Calle Positos. Turn right immediately after you enter, and go downstairs to the small but nice cafeteria.

Young sophisticates and students with a little cash patronize **Pizza Piazza (11)** (tel. 2-4259) which is—surprise!—a colonial pizza parlor right in the Plazue-la San Fernando. Comfy niche-booths and roughish furniture provide a sympa-thetic ambience for romantic encounters or easy camaraderie: this is one of the best places in town to meet young Mexicans of both sexes. I have no idea how the colonial viceroys of Mexico liked their pizza, but here you can get it small, medium, or large for 700 to 1,500 pesos ($1.40 to $3). The large pizza can feed five or six people. Beer and sangría are also served, either in the dining room or at the tables under the tree in the plazuela. They serve up lots of spaghetti too. Open from noon to midnight every day. Now there's another Pizza Piazza, just out of the Jardín de la Union.

One of Guanajuato's snazzier restaurants is **Tasca de los Santos** (tel. 2-2320) on Juárez, about three blocks north of Hotel San Diego. They do not serve a comida corrida here—everything's à la carte—but the food and service and decor (heavy, colonial furniture, wine racks on the wall, etc.) will please you. Paella, a house specialty, is 2,500 pesos ($5) and chicken in white wine sauce goes for 1,800 pesos ($3.60). Bottles of wine range from 1,800 to 4,800 pesos ($3.60 to $9.60), or order by the glass.

Starvation-Budget Restaurants

How you can do better than the aforementioned university cafeteria I don't know, but if the university's not in session when you're there, head for the little row of eateries (7) facing the parking lot in front of the Hotel El Insurgente. From the hotel all the way to the market, on the opposite side of the plaza/parking lot from these two buildings, are half a dozen very inexpensive home-style cookshops offering four-course set lunches at 500 to 600 pesos ($1 to $1.20), or sandwiches and daily special plates for even less. **El Cedro** is typical, and perhaps the best.

READER'S RESTAURANT SELECTION: "The **Centro Nutricional Vegetariano,** Aguilar 45 (kind of between the university and Jardín de la Union) has good vegetarian food and very good prices—a good place for those who crave whole wheat" (Shel Horowitz, Northampton, Mass.).

AROUND THE TOWN: Walking around the city, it's almost hard to believe that the outside world knows of its existence, and certainly Guanajuatans them-selves don't want it to change (the **Church of San Diego [1]** stands as it did in 1633). An exception to this is the magnificent **university (2)** founded in 1732, but whose entrance was rebuilt in 1945 in a stately manner that makes the building dominate the whole town. The university (Diego Rivera was a graduate), which is just behind the Plaza de la Paz, is open every day and nobody objects to visitors looking around. There's a cafeteria (open 8 a.m. to 10 p.m.) on the ground floor, also an excellent Spanish bookstore.

While you're around this part of town, the **post office (3)** is just to your left, at the end of the block as you come out of the university. The **birthplace of painter Diego Rivera (4)** is to your right, at Calle Positos 47. The crumbling house has been refurbished and made into a museum; on the wall is a plaque commemorating *"el pintor magnifico."* That Rivera was an "unperson" in his hometown for so long is not happenstance or coincidence. Guanajuato, strongly clerical and conservative, sympathized with the rebels during the Catholic counterrevolution of 1926-1929; later the town was an important base for the neofascist Sinarquista movement. Given this atmosphere, it is easy to understand the unpopularity of the city's most illustrious native son, an avowed Marxist whose most famous mural proclaims that "God does not exist." The museum is open from 10 a.m. to 2 p.m. and 4 to 6 p.m. Monday to Saturday. The house has been completely redone and, unfortunately, it is more like a museum than a home. Upstairs there's a fine collection of Rivera's early paintings. Diego began painting when he was 12 years old, and moved to Paris where he became a Marxist during World War I. You can see the cubist influence in his painting of this period. There are sketches of some of his earlier murals, the ones that made his reputation, but most of his works on display are paintings from 1902 to 1956. On the third floor is a small auditorium where lectures and conferences are held.

The Cervantes Festival

Partly because of the university and, in part, because of long traditions, Guanajuato is a fairly cultural place. Every year, in the autumn, the state of Guanajuato sponsors the International Cervantes Festival, which offers two weeks of performing arts from all over the world. Recently they had marionettes from Czechoslovakia, the Elliot Feld dance company from New York, the Cuban National Ballet, and a host of Mexican artists. The shows are held at various places—the **Plazuela San Roque** and two attractive theaters: the **Teatro Principal (13)**, just off the Jardín de la Union (where aside from the Cervantes Festival you can hear a good piano recital for 500 pesos or $1), and the magnificently ornate **Teatro Juárez (14)**, across the same plaza, which, with its columns, friezes, and velvet-draped interior, is a relic of the past century when a theater represented all that was elegant. The foundations for the theater were laid in 1873, but money soon ran out so construction was stopped until 1893 when Porfirio Díaz supplied the wherewithal to finish it. You can browse through this beautiful building daily from 9 a.m. to 2 p.m. and 4 to 7 p.m.

Pipila

High above the town, with a great view overlooking the Jardín de la Union, is the city's monument to José Barajas, also known as Pipila, a brave young miner who, on the orders of Hidalgo, set fire to the strategically situated grain warehouse, the Alhondiga de Granaditas, in which the Royalists were hiding during the War of Independence. Hidalgo, a young priest who had appealed for Mexico's independence from Spain, on September 16, 1810, led an army that captured Guanajuato. In this bloody battle 600 inhabitants and 2,000 Indians were killed, but the revolution was on its way. Guanajuato became the rebel capital, but its history was short. For ten months later, the revolutionary leader, Hidalgo, was captured, shot in Chihuahua, and his head sent to Guanajuato to be exhibited.

The climb up to Pipila can be made via automobile or bus ("Pipila"), but I highly recommend that you try it on foot. Walk up Calle Sopena from the Jardín de la Union, and turn to the right up the Callejón del Calvario. A sign on the wall reads: "Al Pipila." (No, his name wasn't "Al.") A rugged winding pathway (wear comfortable shoes) wends past little homes and gardens perched precariously on the hillside. In one garden you'll see cows; in another, giant cacti. It's a tiring trip, but well worth it.

From the statue at the top (you can climb inside the statue too, if you wish), the lovely city unfolds below. Churches appear everywhere, bronze figures atop the Teatro Juárez appear to be gesturing to the crowd in the Jardín, and it is easy to see how well the massive university, despite its newness, integrates perfectly with the landscape. There's a little park, nicely landscaped, beside the statue. Kids play ball, families picnic, and the atmosphere (and view) is delightful.

The Alhondiga

The **Alhondiga de Granaditas (15),** the doors of which Pipila burned, was a prison from 1864 to 1949, and before that it was the granary. Here the heads of Hidalgo, Allende, Aldama, and Jimenez hung from 1811 to 1821, to remind the populace of what happens to revolutionaries. On the four corners of the building the name-plaques below the cornice commemorate the four heroes of this stormy period.

The Alhondiga is now a museum, and one of the best in Mexico. It is open Tuesday to Sunday from 9 a.m. to 2 p.m. and 4 to 6 p.m.; closed Monday. There are two levels to the museum, with rooms off the courtyard. The lower level (on which you enter) has rooms of regional crafts and several rooms of the pre-Hispanic art collection of Chavez Morado, the artist responsible for the murals on both stairwells. There is also a long corridor that contains bronze masks of the revolutionary heroes as well as an eternal flame in their honor. Upstairs is a Bellas Artes section with shows (both temporary and permanent) of national and international artists. Following are several rooms showing the history of the state of Guanajuato and its dozen mines, the first one begun in 1557 on orders of Charles V. There are some interesting lithographs showing the city as it was in the 18th and 19th centuries, as well as 20th-century photographs. You'll also see numerous pre-Columbian relics: pots, decorative seals and stamps, terracotta figurines, and stone implements.

The Markets

The **Mercado Hidalgo (M),** housed in a building that resembles a Victorian railroad station (built 1909), has a cavernous lower level and an upper balcony that encircles the whole building. It is stacked with every conceivable kind of pottery and ceramic ware, even including ones imported from Japan. From this balcony you can look down onto one of the neatest layouts in Mexico: symmetrical rows of stalls and counters providing splashes of orange, green, red, brown, or black in tones of the fruits and vegetables with which they are covered. Very few people sprawl around on the floor or in the aisles, unlike most markets, but whether this is due to the local ordinance or an untypical sense of orderliness, I can't say. The market is open every day, from morning to evening.

One item worth trying, in the market or elsewhere, is the brightly colored candy called *charramusca*. It's sort of a poor imitation of England's peppermint rock. Among the most popular charramuscas, by the way, are those in the shape of mummies. They're up to a foot long, wrapped in colored cellophane, have raisins for eyes, and are stuffed with coconut.

Right beside the Mercado Hidalgo is the **Mercado Gavira,** which is a very different sort of place. Modern, soiled, and bustling with cookshops à la Marrakesh, this is a good place for the fearless to try native cuisine. If your stomach is beyond insult, launch into a serving of birria, barbacoa (barbecue), pozole (stew), menudo (tripe). Choose kettles that are boiling and you should do all right. As for prices, observe the sign that says (in Spanish): "Avoid disappointments, ask to see the price list!"

The Mummies

At the northwest end of town is the Calzada del Panteon, which leads up to the municipal cemetery. It's a steep climb on foot, but the bus labeled "Presa-Estación" runs along Juárez and this will take you to the foot of the cobbled hill. Guanajuato's cab drivers, for this trip, will invariably tend to charge what the traffic will bear.

When you reach your destination, the cemetery, you'll find there's a cavern with a long hallway along which the mummies are displayed in glass showcases. It seems that the dryness in certain sections of the Panteon is such that decomposition is virtually halted. Due to the lack of space in the cemetery, people are buried for only five years and if at the end of that time there are no relatives to continue paying for the grave, the bodies are exhumed to make room for more. At this juncture, the authorities look at the corpses and if they have become mummified, they are displayed in the underground chamber; if not, they are burnt. Don't ask whether gravesites that are proven mummifiers cost more, because I don't know. The mummies, or *momias* as they are called, are not wrapped Egyptian style, but are just standing in glass cases, grinning, choking, or staring. It's impossible to resist the temptation to go up and look at them—everybody does—and this is the only graveyard I've ever seen with souvenir stands next to the main gate. There are even special hours to see the mummies: 9 a.m. to 6 p.m. every day. Entrance fee is 50 pesos (10¢); cameras, the same.

More Cheerful Destinations

Guanajuato is a strangely colorful town with all kinds of enchanting sights to be seen in the side streets and tiny plazas. Try to see the **Plazuela del Baratillo,** just off the Jardín de la Union. A beautiful fountain (a gift from Emperor Maximilian) is its pride and joy and you'll always find people sitting around peacefully, some in the shade and others in the sun, for late in the afternoon the plazuela is almost exactly divided between *sol* and *sombra*. **Plazuela San Fernando (11)** is larger and has a stone platform where very often there will be local Mexican dances with the younger generation decked out in bright costumes.

The **Church of La Compañía de Jesus,** next door to the university, was built in 1747 by the Jesuit order and was the biggest of their churches at that time. It is distinctly churrigueresque on the outside but the interior, which was restored in the 19th century, is not. This church was built as part of the Jesuit university, founded in 1732 on orders of Philip V, on the site of the present university, the last of 23 universities built by the Jesuit order in Mexico.

If you want to go on a suburban outing, why not hop any bus that says "Presa" (try at the bus stop in the Subterranean near Jardín de la Union) to the **Parque de la Acacias** and the **Presa de la Olla,** the artificial lake? There are several parks, lots of trees: a good place for a lazy afternoon.

While in the neighborhood, you might note the **Government Palace (16)** on Paseo de la Presa, with its pink stone front and green tile interior. The neighborhood around here is residential and will give you another glimpse of Guanajuato, away from the bustle of the plazas.

Last but not least are the **silver mines** in the surrounding mountains. The most famous is **La Valenciana,** said to have produced a fifth of the silver circulating in the world from 1558 to 1810. It can be reached by taking Rte. 30, the Dolores Hidalgo road, three miles northeast of town (buses are "J. Perones-Marfil" with "Valenciana" in soap on the windshield). The mine was closed about 40 years ago, but then reopened, and a caretaker is there to show you the eight-sided vertical shaft (1,650 feet deep) and the once-grandiose courtyard. While you're there, visit the magnificent church built in 1765 by the first Count of Valencia. It is one of the most beautiful of the colonial churches in churrigue-resque style—a true masterpiece. Also nearby, in **Marfil,** are restored mansion-haciendas of wealthy colonial mine owners.

Entremeses

The word *entremeses* means, literally, "intermissions," and it's the term given to short sketches that were written to be presented between perfor-mances. In Guanajuato, it means a very special entertainment: an evening under the stars in a medieval-style courtyard, the **Plazuela de San Roque (19),** with about 90 minutes of acting and action by students and faculty of the Univer-sity of Guanajuato. The entremeses are presented on weekend nights (with the exception of those weekends that fall on a fiesta) and are some of the best thea-ter you'll ever see. Tickets (which must be bought in advance) can be bought at the Teatro Juárez. The Tourist Office (tel. 473/2-0086) can give you a list of dates for which the performances are scheduled.

Let me emphasize again that these are no ordinary amateur theatricals. If you are in the vicinity, or conceivably can arrange to be in the vicinity of Guana-juato, when a performance is scheduled—drop everything and buy, beg, bor-row, or steal a ticket. You'll never regret it. The fact, also, that the show takes place in a real courtyard with galloping horses, water thrown from windows, church bells ringing, gusts of wind blowing out the candles, and people in au-thentic period costumes looking not too out of place in 20th-century Guanajua-to, makes it all the more impressive. Don't miss it.

Guided Tours

Perhaps your best bet for obtaining information or for seeing Guanajuato is to go to **Transportes Turisticos de Guanajuato,** next door to the church of San Diego (1). They offer free information in English as well as an excellent tour of the city that includes the Panteon, the Valencia mines, and Pipila, all of which are otherwise hard to reach. The cost is 1,000 pesos ($2.50); there are three tours (3½ hours long) daily, morning, noonish, and afternoon. They have bilin-gual guides. Passengers are picked up at various hotels, so check to see at what time and where you can catch the minibus. This is one of the best tours offered in all of Mexico.

NIGHTLIFE: A bit posh, with an older, sedate crowd, are the bars at the **Hotel San Diego** and the **Hostería del Frayle.** Even posher is the **Cantarranas Bar** at the Hotel Real de Minas, on the road to Mexico City. There is a piano player who entertains on weekends. You can get there by cab from the city.

DOLORES HIDALGO: For the most scenic route onward to Mexico City, con-tinue on the road to Dolores Hidalgo, then stop in San Miguel de Allende. Dol-ores Hidalgo (pop. 80,000) has little to offer. It is famous because it's where the local priest, Miguel Hidalgo, first made his proclamation for the independence of Mexico, the "Cry of Dolores," on September 16, 1810. The church on the main plaza was the site of the proclamation and Hidalgo's house, at Morelos 1 (one block from the bus station), is now a museum filled with flags, photos, and documents. Since the drive from San Miguel to Guanajuato takes only about two hours, an overnight stop isn't really necessary. If you just want refreshments, stop in at the town's cleanest restaurant, which is located right on the plaza.

5. San Miguel de Allende

San Miguel de Allende (alt. 6,134 feet; pop. 16,000) may well be the prettiest town in Mexico and, like Taxco, has been declared a national monument, which means that even Frank Lloyd Wright would have had to go through plenty of red tape before he'd be allowed to build so much as a hot-dog stand.

San Miguel has cobbled streets reminiscent of Cornwall or Nantucket, and the best known view of the town, where the highway enters it from the south, has been featured in innumerable movies and picture postcards. As mentioned, a sizable colony of American students and pensioners has established itself here, although the major portion of this group tends to turn over about twice a year. Apart from the financially successful, which includes those who have retired here to live relatively well on incomes ranging upward of $500 per month, the town's American colony is always composed of teachers, painters, writers, and others who have saved up enough to buy themselves six months in the sun.

You'll awake early in San Miguel. On the stroke of eight, and often before, the bells of a score of churches will simultaneously begin clanging like a score of hammers on a score of different-shaped anvils and soon the booming of the **parroquía** (cathedral) will superimpose itself as the others begin to fade away. If you're lucky, you'll arrive at the time of a festival (San Miguel loves festivals; the main one is on September 29).

If you can, try to get a look around at least one of the houses in which resident Americans are living. Shabby and almost universally drab from the outside, they open inside onto pretty, cool, flower-filled patios with French doors, lily ponds, and breathtaking views.

GETTING TO AND FROM SAN MIGUEL: You can drive easily to San Miguel, or you can take a train or bus. For the train, catch the *Aztec Eagle* from Mexico City or Nuevo Laredo, or points en route. It arrives in San Miguel in the afternoon. Bus service, however, is the most frequent service to this beautiful town. The bus station in San Miguel is down near the river off Calle de los Organos.

By Bus

Tres Estrellas de Oro has one bus a day to and from Mexico City via Querétaro, a four-hour trip, and two buses a day between San Miguel and Guanajuato.

Autotransportes Corsairos de Bajío also has several buses between San Miguel and Mexico City and Guanajuato.

Omnibus de México has two buses a day to and from Mexico City, and also one bus a day to and from Guadalajara (via Guanajuato).

Flecha Amarilla has the greatest number of buses daily to and from Mexico City: 17 trips in all, counting all the buses in both directions.

To get from Guadalajara to San Miguel, take a bus from the central bus terminal in Guadalajara to the town of Celaya; in Celaya catch a Turismo Allende bus for the last hour of the trip. Turismo Allende operates buses between San Miguel and Celaya every hour from 7 a.m. to 9 p.m.

ORIENTATION: Virtually everything in San Miguel is quite lovely, but there aren't many particular landmarks around town worth seeking out. The best fun is just to wander up and down the cobbled streets, peeping into doorways and

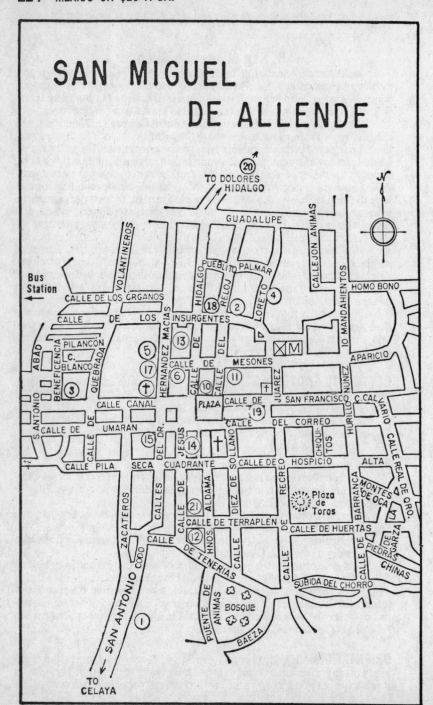

SAN MIGUEL DE ALLENDE

haggling in the stores. The town's biggest draw, apart from the excellent scenery and climate, is the **Instituto Allende (1),** an accredited arts-and-crafts school in what was once a large convent. The Instituto has a predominantly American enrollment.

The Instituto is a beautiful and interesting place, with big grounds, elegant patios and gardens, and murals on some of the walls. You can wander past classrooms where weavers, sculptors, and painters are at work. The notice board in the entrance lobby carries interesting offers ("Ride offered to L.A."; "Paperbacks for sale, Shayne to Schopenhauer"), and the office maintains a list of local families who rent rooms for stays of a month or more.

The Instituto also gives Spanish classes, but for these you're really better off at the charming little **Academia Hispano Americana (2),** situated around a pretty patio on Calle Insurgentes, just below the market. The registrar writes: "This is a language school, teaching Spanish, history and literature of Spain and Mexico. It's small, with classes limited to 12 people; instructors are rotated; grammar is presented and absorbed through example, application, and usage, rather than by rule. It's a serious school, the work is intensive, and we are particularly interested in students who plan to use Spanish in their future careers, people who sincerely feel the need to communicate and understand the other Americas." The school has winter, spring, summer, and fall sessions, and a brochure is available by writing to: Registrar, Academia Hispano Americana, Insurgentes 21, San Miguel de Allende, Gto., México. These people are extremely serious about what they're doing and they even try to find homes for students with Mexican families as a part of their total immersion program. By the way, if you come to San Miguel to study either here or at the Instituto, come with a tourist visa, *not* a student visa, the latter having vastly complicated red tape involved with it.

READERS' SUGGESTION—LANGUAGE SCHOOLS: "We found a language school called **Inter-Idiomas,** situated at Mesones 15. The classes are small (average six), and the lessons are intensive at reasonable prices" (Monika Reul and Felicitas Rohrmoser, Marienheide, West Germany).

WHERE TO STAY: There are ample accommodations for visitors in San Miguel, but the problem is that most hotelkeepers insist on renting rooms only on the American Plan (three meals included). Theoretically, the American Plan rates are only for "in season," but in practice almost the whole year turns out to be considered in season, with the exception of the month of November, and sometimes March through June. Some hotels do rent rooms without meals all year, however.

Right on San Miguel's main square is the **Posada de San Francisco (10),** Plaza Principal 2 (tel. 465/2-1466). A converted colonial mansion with a very pretty courtyard, the San Francisco has large, high-ceilinged, bathroom-equipped rooms (with tubs) and colonial touches for 5,960 pesos ($11.95) single, 7,450 pesos ($14.90) double, 8,960 pesos ($17.95) triple, tax included. The furniture is a bit worn in some rooms, but still quite serviceable. The large windows have screens to keep out bugs. Bar service is available in the courtyard, and the hotel restaurant serves three meals a day. There's even an elevator.

The 34-room **Posada de las Monjas (3),** Canal 37 (tel. 465/2-0171), is a charming little inn and a former convent of pink stone construction with its name emblazoned in relief stone letters over the front door. Inside, it is as quaint as you'd expect: bold colors, heavy wood furniture and lots of beams, arches, and the like. The rooms are quite pleasant and done with simplicity and good taste—double rooms are the best as they have windows and views, but even the tiny singles are good. Best buys are the rooms with a double bed at 3,335 pesos ($6.70) single, 4,830 pesos ($9.65) double. The big rooms with twin beds and fireplaces cost 4,830 pesos ($9.65) single, 7,475 pesos ($14.95) double.

Tucked away amid cobbled lanes and well-tended gardens is the **Quinta Loreto (4),** Callejón Loreto 13 (tel. 465/2-0042), a fairly new motel-type place with a large pool, excellent restaurant, and simple but pleasantly bright rooms. Lunch or dinner here is a bargain, and the owners are extremely nice and friendly. Thirty-one rooms altogether rent for 2,400 pesos ($4.80) single, 3,000 pesos ($6) double. *Warning:* The Loreto is very popular and is often booked up months in advance.

The 25-room **Hotel Sautto (5)** at Hernandez Macias 59, (tel. 465/2-0052), has a very large courtyard and grounds, lemon and lime trees, a fountain, and sweet-smelling flowers everywhere. The hotel itself is an old colonial mansion somewhat fixed up, with single rooms with bath renting for 2,250 pesos ($4.50) and doubles with bath for 3,200 pesos ($6.40). Meals are served in the modest restaurant.

The **Hotel Mesón de San Antonio (6),** at Mesones 80, near the intersection with Hernandez Macias (tel. 465/2-0580), has 14 rooms arranged around two nice clean courtyards and an entrance graced by mustard-yellow tiles. Cast-iron garden furniture adds romance. Because rooms look onto the courtyards, they're a bit dark, and although plain, are still quite acceptable. With bath, rooms go for 3,450 pesos ($6.90) single, 4,370 pesos ($8.75) double. In the dining room are little circular tables with white cloths at which you consume breakfast, lunch, or dinner.

For a long stay in San Miguel (more than a month), it's advisable to check at the **Institute** or the **Academia** for their list of apartments or rooms to rent. The apartments are equipped with kitchens and bedding, some with maid service.

READERS' HOTEL SELECTIONS: "The **Parador San Sebastián,** Calle de Mesones 7 (tel. 465/2-0707), has huge, clean rooms with shower (one double bed and one single) for 2,500 pesos ($5)" (Petrien Uniken Venema and Anton van Enst, Utrecht, Holland). . . . "Finding the downtown places full-up, we went to **Villas El Molino** for a room. It was excellent in all respects. We even liked the meals. Cost was 8,960 pesos ($17.95) double" (Robert E. Struthers, Lakewood, Colo.). . . . "I strongly recommend the **Pension Casa Carmen,** Calle Correo 21 (tel. 465/2-0844). Kitty-corner from the post office, it is only one block from the plaza. Sra. Natalie Morring is the charming bilingual hostess. The tastefully-decorated rooms surround the typical tropical courtyard. Three delicious meals are served each day and all of this for the astounding low price of $30 per day per couple" (A. W. Porter, Coroapolis, Pa.).

WHERE TO EAT: Because of its large foreign colony, and its popularity with Mexicans as a tourist destination, San Miguel has an interesting assortment of restaurants—but it changes frequently. New places open all the time, while eateries only a few years old close down overnight. Part of the reason for the bad survival rate can be ascribed to the town's hostelries, many of which require that guests purchase meals with their rooms. But you won't starve in San Miguel.

A good, attractive and all-around suitable restaurant is **Bugambilia** at Hidalgo 42. The tables, with wicker chairs, are set in a covered courtyard surrounded by, what else—bugambilias. Be sure to start with the aztec soup, a chicken based stock with avocado, tomatoes, onions, and tortillas. Complimentary tostadas are served and most entrees range from 1,300 to 1,900 pesos ($2.60 to $3.80); Mexican dishes are 750 to 1,300 pesos ($1.50 to $2.60).

For a light dinner, fill up on the salad bar at **Barrio Latino,** Calle de Jesus 23, where the vegetables are washed in purified water. Sandwiches are served on baguettes (French bread) in the 650-peso ($1.30) range. They also offer three types of raclette, a Swiss dish involving melting cheese and scraping it onto other food items (it also refers to the type of cheese used).

Biggest bargain for eating? That's **Quinta Loreto (4),** Callejón Loreto 13; go down the very cobbled street and turn right through a gate and then left into an expansive garden on the right. Tucked away at the back is a swimming pool, and adjoining the pool is a terraced café that serves some of the best home cooking in Mexico. The comida corrida is 1,500 pesos ($3) and excellent. The dining room tends to be a bit noisy.

The decor at **El Carrusel (7)** is whimsical, to say the least. As you enter the restaurant on Calle Canal half a block west of the plaza and across from the Casa Maxwell, you'll plunge into a small courtyard filled with café tables topped by colorful umbrellas. You don't get to dine on a merry-go-round, but nonetheless a carnival air is unmistakable. The fare is light and upbeat: chili, lima-bean-and-ham soup, and various sorts of burgers priced from 800 to 1,300 pesos ($1.60 to $2.60). Lunch and dinner are the meals served.

Casual and hip—that sums up the atmosphere at **Mama Mia (15),** Umaran 8, and the cuisine is less important than the clientele. Although the menu is limited to such things as quesadillas, pastas, and meat, the conversation and interaction range freely in this comfy spot. Service is slow, but while you're waiting for your quesadillas and mineral water, at 1,700 pesos ($3.40), all in, you meet the most wonderful people. Open daily from 11 a.m. to 1 a.m., there's jazz nightly except Monday and Tuesday.

Some Splurges

The **Villa Jacaranda (21)** (tel. 2-1015 or 2-0811), Aldama 53, is San Miguel's poshest: dinner is served each evening by appointment only; the restaurant closes at 10 p.m. You can have lunch from noon on, however. Plan to spend about 3,480 to 5,300 pesos ($6.95 to $10.60) for a fine, full-course meal including soups and, say, filet mignon, stuffed shrimp, or chicken Cordon Bleu. You'll enjoy it: the soft music, twittering birds, ivy, vines, exotic flowers, and the elegance of the restaurant's decor all make it so. Remember to call for those dinner reservations, though.

At **Señor Plato (14)** (tel. 2-0626), Calle de Jesus 7, you enter a fine old courtyard with a graceful gazebo at its center. All around are white-clothed tables and dark-blue director's chairs. Yellow and red carnations brighten each table, and soft jazz wafts in from somewhere. Brick walls and arches, myriads of plants, provide visual interest. Elegant and comfortable at the same time, Señor Plata caters to American appetites with barbecued spare ribs, prime rib au jus, or shrimp stuffed with cheese. The many Mexican dishes are priced much lower, however—just over half these prices. A meal for two, with wine, will come to something like 4,680 pesos ($9.35) if you order neither the cheapest nor the most expensive items on the menu. Señor Plato is open from 1 p.m. to midnight every day but Monday. Look for the restaurant's name painted on the side of the building when you're walking along Calle de Jesus.

WHAT TO DO: San Miguel, being an artsy tourist town, is full of shops and galleries. The biggest and best of the shops is **Casa Maxwell,** which has recently expanded to take up the entire block between Canal 14 and Umaran. It's a beautiful house and garden with every imaginable craft displayed, some high-priced, others fairly reasonable. It's well worth a look around; open 9 a.m. to 2 p.m. and 4 to 7 p.m.; closed Sunday. These hours, by the way, are standard for San Miguel, as all shops and galleries close between 2 and 4 p.m.

FONART has a shop at Calle Macias 95.

The best of the art galleries is the **Gallery San Miguel,** Plaza Principal 14. It is run by a charming Mexican woman, fluent in English, who is a well-known art dealer and exhibits the work of local residents, both Mexican and American. The salons hold a wide variety of art, most at fairly high prices. Open 9 a.m. to 2 p.m. and 4 to 7 p.m.; closed Sunday.

Next door to the Gallery San Miguel is the **Tourism Office,** San Francisco 23 in the Oficinas del Gobierno. They have brochures and a map of the city as well as a helpful staff (same hours as the gallery).

The **Centro Cultural Ignacio Ramírez (17)** is a center for instruction in arts such as drawing, jewelry making, guitar, batik, etc. Housed in the beautiful old Convent of the Conception, built in 1775, it contains a courtyard of lush trees, fountain, and murals, as well as numerous rooms on two levels housing art exhibits and classrooms. The major attractions here are several murals by Siqueiros as well as memorabilia of the artist, all very interesting, plus a student gallery and cafeteria, frequent films, and you get to enjoy the grounds as well. The center is located at Hernandez Macias 75 near the corner of Canal; open all day every day for free. They have a bulletin board listing concerts and lectures given at this institute, and elsewhere in the city.

If you're in town on a Sunday, you might be interested in a tour through some of the colonial houses in San Miguel. The tour starts at noon, leaving from the Instituto Allende or Posada San Francisco. The **Biblioteca (18),** Insurgentes 25, is a useful place to know about as it is the gathering point for the American community. It has a good selection of books, some to rent and some to buy. Here too is a courtyard with tables where you can relax and read a book or magazine (open 10 a.m. to 2 p.m. and 4 to 7 p.m. daily; closed Sunday).

The town's movie theater, the **Aldama,** is on San Francisco, in the block between the Jardín and the San Francisco church. The **Post Office and Telegraph (19)** are at Calle Correo 18 (closed 1 to 4 p.m. daily and all day Sunday).

There are several **hot springs** just outside San Miguel on the road northward to Dolores Hidalgo, about five miles out of town. The **Hotel Balneario Taboada** is out of the range for this book, but it does have a delightful hot springs swimming pool which you can use for a small fee. There are buses that leave from Calle San Francisco several times a day (the schedules change frequently so check with the Tourism Office for times).

A Side Trip

About the most pleasant three-hour excursion you can make from San Miguel is to **Atotonilco el Grande,** an Indian town that contains a wonderful 16th-century oratorio (the church of an Augustinian monastery). The frescoes are very imaginative and animated, and although they've been ravaged by time, restoration is under way.

The trip itself is an introduction to Mexican country life: hop a bus on Calle Llamas ("Oratorio") and you'll trundle out of San Miguel on the road to Taboada. Past Taboada you'll take a left at signs reading "Manantiales de la Gruta" and "La Flor del Cortijo." The road passes two large mansions that are now spas (see below), then an aqueduct and a little narrow bridge. It's all superpicturesque, and in no time you're in the small town square of Atotonilco with the Oratorio in front of you.

READER'S SUGGESTION—HOT SPRINGS: "Forget Taboada! Go to the bus station in San Miguel and ask for a bus to **Cortijo,** a hotel and spa on the road to Dolores Hidalgo. When you get off the bus after 15 minutes, you will see a sign for **La Gruta,** and this is where you want to go. Walk a few hundred feet up the road, pay 1,000 pesos ($2) for a ticket, proceed past the large pool, and you will find a smaller pool and simple changing cubicles. After you change, a woman will take your belongings and give you a key. The hot springs are a series of three increasingly warm pools. The last pool is reached by a fairly dark tunnel that opens into a circular cave. This is La Gruta (the Grotto), the source of the spring. It's heavenly! Go during the week; Sunday is family day, and a bit crowded" (Jill Augenblick, San Marcos, Tex.). [*Note from T.B.:* You can combine your spa trek with a visit to the aforementioned Oratorio at Atotonilco—the two sites are within walking distance of one another.]

NIGHTLIFE: I approach the subject of San Miguel's nightlife with trepidation, as clubs and discos here tend to spring up and to die with great rapidity. Still, here are some tips:

The disco called **El Ring,** 25 Hidalgo, in a lovely old building on the right side of the street as you come from the main plaza (Jardín), has a very elaborate layout including strobe lights and other visual hallucinogens (but visual *only*). Cover is 1,200 pesos ($2.40) on weekends; composition of the crowd changes according to the seasons, depending on who's in town for the Spanish courses.

The **Club Tiovivo,** in the Restaurant El Carrusel, opens at 1 p.m., and caters mostly to a local clientele with various floor shows and entertainments. Cover here is the same 1,200 pesos ($2.40) on weekends.

The new hot spot in town? No doubt the response elicited is **Pancho y Lefty's** at Mesones 99. There's dancing nightly to a live band and the place is always packed. Cover charge of 500 pesos ($1) includes a drink during the week (try the frozen Margarita). A light menu for noshing is also available.

MISCELLANEOUS: A good **laundromat** (where they do the washing and drying) is Lavandería Automatica de San Miguel at Potranca 18, Col. Guadiana, located just past the Institute down the street facing the Red Cross.

6. Querétaro

After San Miguel de Allende, you'll come upon Querétaro (alt. 5,873 feet; pop. 250,000), a state capital and a prosperous city with a fantastic history. It was here that Mexico's fight for independence was instigated by Hidalgo in 1810; here that, with the treaty of Guadalupe, Hidalgo sealed the peace of the Mexican War; here that the Emperor Maximilian was executed in 1866; and finally, here that the present Mexican constitution was drafted in 1916.

GETTING TO AND FROM QUERÉTARO: As Querétaro is on the main toll road between Mexico City and points north and east, transportation is a snap. During daylight hours, and in some cases afterward, lots of buses roll in and out of the Central Camionera by the Alameda on the three-hour trip from the capital. In fact, **Flecha Amarilla,** in Mexico City's Terminal Norte at "6 Espera," runs a bus to Querétaro every ten minutes, 24 hours a day. Return service is just as frequent. Other companies run buses about every 20 minutes.

You can also get to the capital by train from Querétaro, leaving slightly before noon or in the early evening. Trains in the opposite direction (Mexico City to Querétaro) are best caught early in the morning at about 7 and 8 a.m. The trip takes between 3½ and 5 hours, depending on the train. Rumor has it that the government is planning to establish a fast electric-train rail link between Mexico City and Querétaro. Ask and see how it's coming along.

From the central bus station near Querétaro's lovely Alameda Park you can walk to several hotels or, in 15 minutes, to the main square *(plaza principal)*. Those in a real hurry or with heavy luggage can take a cab.

STAYING IN QUERÉTARO: You can choose between two lodging areas in Querétaro. Right near the bus station are some beautiful new hotels in the upper reaches of our price range. Downtown near the main square are a few charming old places with very down-to-earth prices.

Near the Bus Station

As your bus pulls into Querétaro's bus station, you will no doubt notice a sign atop the building right next door: "Hotel." Walk out the front door of the bus station, turn left, and walk to the entrance of the new **Hotel Mirabel,** Avenida Constituyentes no. 2 Oriente (tel. 463/4-3535 or 4-3585). Inside the big, dark building is a bright and shiny lobby, a newsstand, a restaurant with snowy tablecloths and glittering stemware, and near-luxurious rooms with private bath and television for 4,600 pesos ($9.20) single, 4,935 to 7,930 pesos ($9.90 to $15.85) double; an extra person pays 500 pesos ($1). Once you've dumped your luggage in your room here, it's an easy walk to most of Querétaro's sights.

The **Hotel Amberes,** Avenida Corregidora Sur no. 188 (tel. 463/2-8604), is one long block from the bus station. Walk out the front door, turn left, then right at the first intersection, and the hotel is halfway down the *long* block on the left-hand side. The hotel is new and well equipped, with private parking, elevators, two bars, a restaurant, and 140 rooms with telephone, television set, piped-in music, and private bath. Prices are good, at 3,800 pesos ($7.60) single, 4,600 pesos ($9.20) double, 7,250 pesos ($14.50) triple; suites cost just a little more.

Between the Bus Station and the Main Square

A modern hotel providing Querétaro with accommodations two long blocks from the bus station is the **Hotel Impala** (tel. 463/2-2570), next to the Alameda park at Colón 1, corner of Zaragoza and Corregidora. The 108 rooms here are all nice and clean, with blue-tile baths, and even (in some rooms) TV. Beds can be a bit spongy or rocky, so pick your room by the bed and by the noise factor: quietest rooms are those that look into the Alameda, or that open onto an airshaft. Prices are reasonable: singles cost 2,070 pesos ($4.15); doubles are 3,590 pesos ($7.20).

Near the Main Square

About a block from the main square is the **Hotel Hidalgo,** Madero Ote. 11 (tel. 463/2-0081), with a central patio, paved and arched with heavy stones, that doubles as a parking lot. Accommodations aren't exactly luxurious but are quite clean. Tiny bathless singles cost 1,150 pesos ($2.30), and doubles run 1,495 to 1,645 pesos ($3 to $3.30); rooms with bath cost 1,840 pesos ($3.70) single, 2,700 pesos ($5.40) double. The Hidalgo's restaurant, toward the back of its patio, is a bit gloomy, but menu prices are reasonable.

The little **Hotel Plaza,** Juárez Norte 23, right on the main square (tel. 463/2-1138), has been fixed up and now offers simple but suitable rooms for 2,300 pesos ($4.60) single, 2,645 pesos ($5.30) double. This used to be a noisy place, but now that the square has been fairly well closed to vehicular traffic, it's much quieter.

EATING IN QUERÉTARO: In addition to the above-mentioned hotel restaurants, all of which stay open all day every day, several pleasant eating places are on or near Querétaro's main plaza.

La Flor de Querétaro, Juárez Norte 5, a few doors down from the Hotel Plaza, is one of the best budget choices in town. Its tablecloths are spotless, the wood-paneled walls are adorned with old scenic photos, and a TV set, always tuned to the bullfight on Sunday, occupies an unobtrusive corner. A large selection of food is offered here, including soups at about 500 pesos ($1), meats at 900 to 2,400 pesos ($1.80 to $4.80). Open daily 9 a.m. to midnight.

A block from the main square along Corregidora, then left, is the **Cafetería La Mariposa,** Angela Peralta 7 (tel. 2-1166); look for the wrought-iron butterfly sign. It's a good place for light lunches such as enchiladas and a fruit salad or club sandwich at 625 pesos ($1.25), or pastries, ice cream, coffee. Right next door is a wickedly tempting sweet shop featuring such irresistibles as candied figs, peaches, bananas, and papaya. You can order these in the restaurant, as the two enterprises are under the same management.

The **Ostioneria Tampico** is Querétaro's answer to a seafood craving. Just off the main square at Corregidora Norte 3, you can chow down on ceviche, fried fish, salad, and soft drink for 1,300 pesos ($2.60). Semi-fancy, darkish, with a lunch counter and some Formica tables, it's busy and handy.

The **Restaurant Café Viena,** Avenida 16 de Septiembre Pte. no. 8, is a bright and modern place serving a set-price lunch for 600 pesos ($1.20). For that price one gets fruit cocktail, soup, rice, "ropa vieja" ("old clothes!"—a savory stewed meat dish), dessert, and coffee. Located half a block off the main square, on the right, set back from the street, it is open seven days a week from 8 a.m. to 10 p.m.

The Big Splurge

Querétaro's most elegant restaurant is a lively place a block from the main square, on the small square at the intersection of Calle de Juan Caballero y Ogio and Calle Angela Peralta. It's called **Truchuelo's Restaurant and Bar** (tel. 4-0880), and has a turn-of-the-century air about it. Table settings are well done in blue and white, with fresh flowers and gleaming wine glasses. Full meals run 3,000 to 5,500 pesos ($6 to $11). Truchuelo's is closed Tuesday, but open for lunch and dinner every other day of the week.

QUERÉTARO SIGHTS: Walking up the pedestrian way off the main plaza, with its pleasant little Jardín Obregón, you'll soon reach the **Plaza de la Independencia,** graced by manicured, umbrella-shaped trees and pretty fountains. And leading off almost any street, you'll find well-tended little plazas and various cobblestone streets reserved for pedestrians.

To the south of the main plaza, walking along **Calle Juárez,** you'll find the **Plaza de la Constitución,** which used to house the town's market on its raised central square. Nowadays, it's a pastel pink piazza boasting a large statue of Venustiano Carranza, who gazes up the polished stones bordering the square and bearing the names of the states of Mexico. A few blocks farther, Juárez meets Avenida Reforma—lined with red-brick, colonial-style homes.

Querétaro is the proper place to send off that long-postponed card to the folks back home because doing so brings you a bonus: the town's **post office** is housed in a former bishop's palace that must be seen to be believed. To find it, walk west out of the main square along Madero for one block to Calle Allende; turn left on Allende and the **Correos** is down the block on the left-hand side, next to the church.

Follow Reforma two blocks west, and you'll hit Calle Guerrero. Four more long blocks south down Guerrero will bring you to Fernando de Tapia and the town's **market.** The market isn't as interesting as it used to be—once the Plaza de la Constitución offered odd-shaped balustrades on which birdcages could be hung—but there's still enough color and noise to intrigue you. Among other things, you can buy very cheap cloth for shirts, skirts, blouses, and dresses if you know a tailor who'll make it up cheaply (three meters for a shirt).

The hills around Querétaro are rich in semiprecious stones, and in town you'll find several little **lapidary shops,** specializing in setting the stones into jewelry boxes', and other objets d'art.

Other places of interest in Querétaro include the **cathedral,** or **Temple of San Francisco,** on Calle Madero with its Moorish-style tile cupola, and various sculptures and pictures inside; and the **Hill of Bells** (Cerro de las Campañas) outside of town, topped by a titanic statue of Juárez. Just below the statue is the site of the execution of Maximilian, ruler of the short-lived Empire of Mexico. In 1901 the Austrian government built an Expiatory Chapel on the side of the hill. The caretaker (who is rarely around to let you in) takes pleasure from showing you the three small columns in front of the altar, and telling you that the stones mark the exact spot where Maximilian and his generals Miramon and Mejia stood before the firing squad. (Maximilian was in the middle, but he ended by giving that place of honor to Miramon.) The caretaker will also inform you that Maximilian gave each member of the firing squad a gold coin so that they would aim at his chest instead of his head. They complied.

Definitely worth seeing is the **Regional Museum** at Corregidora 3, a few steps west of the main square (open every day except Monday from 10 a.m. to 3:30 p.m. and 4 to 6 p.m.; to 4 p.m. on Sunday). The building was built as the Grand Convent (monastery, that is) of Saint Francis of Assisi, and is the oldest such building in the city—the order for its construction was given in 1540. In 1861 it was used as a fortress by the Imperialists who backed Maximilian. The structure is one of those palatial edifices which the "humble" friars favored, replete with arches and Corinthian columns. The first room as you enter holds fascinating memorabilia. Here, several Mexican paintings are informatively compared with European works of the same time; various classical paintings are presented together with modern ones, accompanied by well-written (in Spanish) texts pointing out similarities in form, theme, color, and so forth. Unfortunately, most visitors skip this room and gape at the much duller colonial paintings and furniture in other rooms. In a far wing of the museum is the Sala de Historia, which contains numerous items of (perhaps morbid) interest, including Maximilian's coffin, and countless period photographs.

Around the corner from the museum at Avenida Independencia 58 (half a block up the hill from the Plaza de la Constitución) is the interesting **Artesanías** shop, which holds a good selection of local lapidary creations as well as conventional jewelry and folk art objects.

Querétaro has more colonial monuments, among them the **Palacio Municipal,** where Dona Josefa Ortiz de Dominguez (the mayor's wife who advised Hidalgo to start the revolution) lived; ask the guard, who stands at the doorway on the Plaza de la Independencia, to show you the Dona's rooms *(quartos)*—a tip is customary. The **Neptune Fountain** on Calle Allende just off Madero; the **Convent of Santa Rosa de Viterbo,** built in the 18th century by Mexico's greatest religious architect, Eduardo Tresguerras; and other old churches are all worth a look.

A SIDE TRIP TO TEQUISQUIAPAN: Seventy-five kilometers (46½ miles) from Querétaro, a short distance off the toll road to Mexico City, is the resort town of Tequisquiapan, Querétaro. From a little farming town in the rich Bajío ("lowlands") region, Tequisquiapan has grown to become a favorite weekend getaway destination for residents of the great metropolis only two hours' drive away.

Besides farming, "Tequis" was famous for its crafts, and for some hot springs, and a few big hotels capitalize on the waters today. As the flow of visitors increased, Tequis underwent a good deal of "charm enhancement," whereby dusty streets were replaced with fanciful paving blocks, the native market was moved to the outskirts, and boutiques sprang up in its place.

Despite this clever fakery, Tequis is still a pretty place. The best time to visit is when you can indulge in the region's two choicest products: wine and cheese. Every year at the end of May and beginning of June these two bounties come together and set off the town's **Fería Nacional del Queso y el Vino**—a grand wine and cheese festival. Day and night the festivities rage as sports matches, rodeos, cockfights, even exhibits of children's paintings keep one and all on the go. Wine- and cheese-tasting parties are provided—many of them free of charge— by the big dairies and wineries, and so the gaiety is full-blown and long-lived. If you're in or around Querétaro during the festival, go catch some of its color and fun. Buses run to "Tequis" frequently from Querétaro's Central Camionera, with a lot of extra buses laid on during the wine and cheese festival.

The **Hotel San Alberto** is new and charges $30 for two with three meals. This is not bad, as the rooms are spacious, the water hot, the dinners good, and the dozen or so colonial-style rooms wrap around a nice pool and spot of lawn. The manager, Ms. Castellanos, speaks reasonably good English. **Posada Tequis-quiapan** is older and a little cheaper and has a natural pool.

A SIDE TRIP TO TULA: The ancient Toltec capital of Tula is one of Mexico's most awe-inspiring archeological sites, well worthy of a visit. It's 20 kilometers north from the Querétaro-Mexico City toll road, Hwy. 57D, on State Hwy. 126. The bus from Querétaro's Central Camionera will go through Tepeji del Río, where you may have to change to another bus for Tula. Look below in Chapter XI for full details of this "City of Atlantean Men."

Chapter VI

MEXICO CITY: ORIENTATION

1. Arriving in Mexico City
2. Public Transportation
3. Organized Tours
4. Tourism Information

MEXICO CITY GLITTERS with all the fascination and excitement of a world capital. It's a vital, romantic place of monuments, palaces, parks, broad boulevards, tall buildings, and smart boutiques. It's the fountainhead of government, from which all orders flow, and in every way the center of Mexican life. It's not even "Mexico City" but simply "Mexico" in the lexicon of every Mexican who talks about it.

The region of Mexico City (alt. 7,240 feet; pop. 18,000,000) has held the most important place in the country's history since the rise of Teotihuacán in 300 B.C. Later, in A.D. 1300 the Aztecs built their great capital of Tenochtitlán on an island in the middle of Lake Texoco following a prophecy that they should build where they saw a "sign": an eagle perched on a cactus with a serpent in its beak. Lake Texoco, now shrunken in size, used to fill the entire valley right to the base of Chapultepec ("Grasshopper Hill" in the Aztec language), and the island was reached from the shore by broad causeways built by Aztec engineers. Little remains of this magnificent city of 300,000 inhabitants. What we know of Tenochtitlán is from the 16th-century chronicles of the Spanish conquerors, especially of Bernal Díaz del Castillo who saw "the great towers and temples and buildings rising from the water—it was like the enchantments."

After the Aztec defeat, the Spanish made the city their capital, and in the centuries that followed the lake was filled in and the city limits were greatly extended. Maximilian of Habsburg did much to beautify the city and make it the capital of an empire during his short and stormy tenure. He remodeled Chapultepec Palace, built by a Spanish viceroy in 1783, and established the grand boulevard now named the Paseo de la Reforma.

You can see many signs of Mexico City's varied history: the pyramids of Teotihuacán are a short ride from downtown; Xochimilco, a reminder of the Aztec Floating Gardens in Lake Texoco, is close by; the Zócalo with its cathedral and National Palace is Spain's standard contribution to colonial town planning. And the Mexican Republic has made the city what it is today.

In more ways than these the city is still a creature of its history. In fact, it's literally *sinking* into it, for the soft lake bottom gives easily under the weight of such formidable structures as the marble palace of the Bellas Artes or the sky-scraping Latin American Tower. But it gives only an inch a year, so you needn't worry—take your time in visiting one of the most fascinating capital cities in the world.

You've undoubtedly heard about Mexico City's pollution problem. It is as immense as the city itself. But for the visitor, dealing with the pollution is a matter of luck. On some days you won't notice it, on other days it will make your nose run and your eyes water and your throat rasp. They say that breathing Mexico City air, when it's bad, is equivalent to smoking two packs of cigarettes a day.

If you have respiratory problems, you must be very careful; being at an altitude of 7,200 feet makes things even worse. Minimize your exposure to the fumes by refraining from walking busy streets during rush hour. Make Sunday, when many factories are closed and many cars escape the city, your prime sightseeing day. One positive note: the air in the evenings is usually deliciously cool and relatively clean.

1. Arriving in Mexico City

Tackling one of the world's most enormous cities is enough to give the most experienced traveler nightmares, but fortunately Mexico City is quite well organized for the arriving traveler. Try to arrive during daylight hours, but if you can't, don't worry. You won't have to spend the night in some terminal. The following information will help you glide through, and will also help you when you depart from the metropolis, no matter in what direction.

ARRIVING BY BUS: Mexico City has a bus terminal for each of the four points of the compass: north, east, south, and west. You can't necessarily tell which terminal serves which area of the country by looking at a map, however. Below you'll find descriptions of the terminals and the exact destinations they serve. Some destinations are served from more than one terminal. For a handy list of bus rider's terms and translations, see Chapter XVII, under "Buses."

Terminal Norte	T.A.P. Oriente	Terminal Sur	Terminal Poniente
Aguascalientes	Amecameca	Acapulco	Colima
Casas Grandes	Campeche	Cuernavaca	Culiacán
Chapala, Lake	Cancún	Ixtapa	Ensenada
Chihuahua	Chetumal	Taxco	Guadalajara
Ciudad Juárez	Cholula	Zihuatanejo	Hermosillo
Colima	Cozumel		Los Mochis
Durango	Cuautla		Manzanillo
Guadalajara	Ixta-Popo Park		Mazatlán
Guanajuato	Jalapa		Mexicali
Guaymas	Mérida		Morelia
Hermosillo	Oaxaca		Nogales
Los Mochis	Palenque		Pátzcuaro
Manzanillo	Puebla		Playa Azul
Matamoros	Salina Cruz		Querétaro

Terminal Norte	**T.A.P. Oriente**	**Terminal Sur**	**Terminal Poniente**
Mazatlán	San Cristóbal de las Casas		San Luis Potosí
Monterrey	Tehuacán		Tepic
Morelia	Tehuantepec		Tijuana
Nogales	Tuxpan, Ver.		Toluca
Nuevo Laredo	Tuxtla Gutierrez		Uruapán
Pachuca	Veracruz		
Papantla	Villahermosa		
Pátzcuaro			
Piedras Negras			
Poza Rica			
Puerto Vallarta			
Querétaro			
Reynosa			
Saltillo			
San Juan Teotihuacán			
San Luis Potosí			
San Miguel de Allende			
Teotihuacán			
Tepic			
Torreón			
Tula			
Tuxpan, Ver.			
Zacatecas			

Terminal Central de Autobuses del Norte

Called by shorter names such as "Camiones Norte," "Terminal Norte," or "Central del Norte," or even just "C.N.," this is Mexico's largest bus station, on Avenida de los 100 ("Cien") Metros. It handles most buses coming from the U.S.—Mexican border. All buses from the Pacific Coast as far south as Puerto Vallarta and Manzanillo, from the Gulf Coast as far south as Tampico and Veracruz, and such cities as Guadalajara, San Luis Potosí, Durango, Zacatecas, and Colima arrive and depart from here: in short, this is the terminal for all buses dealt with in Chapters II, IV, V, and XII of this book. You can get out to the Pyramids of San Juan Teotihuacán and Tula from here.

Here are some useful facts and words: a **Tourism Information Booth** is set up at the center of the terminal's crescent-shaped façade, and nearby there's a hotel reservations booth. Both can be very helpful. Words you'll encounter are: *Taquilla* (ticket window), *Recibo de Equipajes,* or simply *Equipajes* (baggage claim), *Llegadas* (gates), *Sanitarios* (toilets), *Sala Espera* (waiting room).

The Central del Norte is a mammoth place, a small city in itself where you can change money (during normal banking hours), buy a shirt, have a meal or a drink, take out insurance, rent a car, etc., etc. There's even a post office and a long-distance phone installation. All of Mexico's major bus companies have desks here where they sell tickets, give information on routes, times, and prices, and check you in for your journey. After you alight from your bus, check the times and prices of the trip to your next destination—you needn't buy your ticket yet unless you're leaving within a day or so.

To get downtown from the Terminal Norte, you have a choice of modes.

The Metro has a station (Estación Terminal de Autobuses del Norte, or T.A.N.) right here. And hop a train and connect for all points.

Walk to the center of the terminal, go out the front door, straight ahead, down the steps, and to the Metro station. This is Linea 5. Follow the signs that say "Dirección Pantitlán." For downtown, you can change trains at either "La Raza" or "Consulado" (see the Metro map in this book). But note! If you change at "La Raza," you will have to walk for about 15 minutes, and you'll encounter stairs. The walk is through a nice marble-lined underground corridor, but it's still long if you have heavy luggage.

Another way to get downtown is by trolleybus. The stop is on Avenida de los Cien Metros, in front of the terminal. The trolleybus runs right down Avenida Lázaro Cárdenas, the "Eje Central" (Central Artery). Or the no. 17-B bus ("Central Camionera del Norte—Villa Olimpica") goes all the way down Avenida Insurgentes, past the university.

Finally, there's a taxi system based on set-price tickets to various zones within the city, operated from a kiosk in the terminal. Locate your destination on the zone map, buy a ticket (boleto) for that zone, and present it to the driver when you get there. A ticket to the center of town costs 1,200 pesos ($2.40).

Terminal de Autobuses de Pasajeros de Oriente ("TAPO")

The terminal for eastern routes has a very long name but a conveniently short acronym: TAPO. Take a no. 20 ("Hipodromo-Pantitlán") bus east along Alvarado, Hidalgo, or Donceles to get there. If you take the Metro, go to the San Lázaro station on the eastern portion of Line 1 (Dirección Pantitlán).

As you emerge from the bus or Metro station, the translucent green dome of TAPO will catch your eye. (If it doesn't, ask anyone, "¿Donde es el TAPO?") Underneath the dome you might expect to find anything from an immense toad to an Olympic swimming pool, but instead there are ticket counters, toilets, a post office, a cafeteria, bookstalls, and snack shops. Enter along "Tunel 1" to the Terminal de Salidas under the central dome.

Companies that sell tickets here include Autobuses Unidos, Autobuses de Oriente, Fletes y Pasajes, Estrella Roja, and Cristobál Colón. Once in possession of a ticket, a growling mammoth machine will whiz you off to any of those points covered in Chapters XII, XIII, XIV, XV, and XVI of this book, and also to Amecameca and Ixta-Popo Park (Chapter XI), and Pachuca (Chapter II). Looking for a bus to Oaxaca, Yucatán, or Guatemala? This is the place to look.

Terminal Central de Autobuses del Sur

Mexico City's southern bus terminal is the Terminal Central de Autobuses del Sur, right next to the Taxqueña Metro stop, last stop on that line. The Central del Sur handles buses to Cuernavaca, Taxco, Acapulco, Zihuatanejo, and intermediate points. Easiest way to get to or from the Central del Sur is on the Metro, all the way to Taxqueña (or Tasqueña, as it's also spelled). Or take a trolleybus down Avenida Lázaro Cárdenas.

By the way, the same taxi ticket system as at the Central del Norte applies when you travel from the Central del Sur into the city. Buy your ticket in the terminal before you exit. A ticket to the Zócalo will cost about 1,400 pesos ($2.80).

This terminal is fairly easy to figure out. If you're going to Cuernavaca, head straight for the ticket counters of Autobuses Pullman de Morelos, as their buses depart every 10 or 15 minutes throughout the day for that destination.

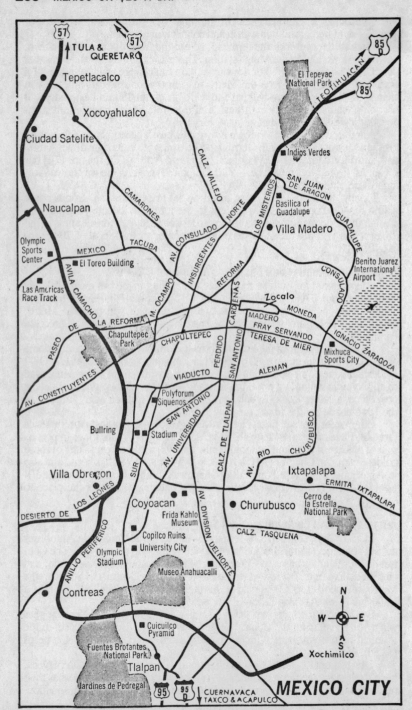

There's hardly ever a problem getting a seat. If, however, you're headed for Taxco, Acapulco, or Zihuatanejo, go to the first-class line named Estrella de Oro. At their ticket counter, you can choose your bus seat on a computer screen!

Other service from the Terminal Sur is by Lineas Unidas del Sur / Flecha Amarilla, a second-class line which will save you a minuscule sum of money over Estrella de Oro. If I were you, I'd go first class.

Terminal Poniente de Autobuses

The western bus terminal is conveniently located right next to the Observatorio Metro station, which you can reach by no. 76 "Zócalo-km. 13" buses (see below) as well. Smallest of the terminals, the Terminal Poniente's main reason for being is the route between Mexico City and Toluca, but some other cities to the west and northwest are served as well. In general, if your chosen destination is also served from the Terminal Norte, you'd be better off going there. The Terminal Norte simply has more buses and better bus lines.

Buying Bus Tickets Downtown

It used to be easy to get bus tickets in the center of Mexico City, but no more. Greyhound (tel. 905/591-0338) has an office at Paseo de la Reforma 27, and they'll sell you tickets on their buses and Mexican connecting lines.

ARRIVING BY TRAIN: The Buena Vista railroad station, three blocks north of the Revolución Metro station along Insurgentes, is called officially the **Terminal de Ferrocarriles Nacionales de México.** You can get away with **Estación Buena Vista.** Walk out the right-hand set of front doors in the terminal, and get your bearings on the front steps. You're facing south. That big boulevard on the right is Avenida Insurgentes, the city's main north-south axis. You can catch a no. 17 "Indios Verdes-Tlalpan" bus south along Insurgentes to get to the Plaza de la República, Paseo de la Reforma, and the Zona Rosa; catch one north to get to the Terminal Norte (main bus station). Straight ahead of you about 12 blocks away, the dome of the Monument to the Revolution floats on the skyline from its site in the Plaza de la República. To the left of it, the spire of the Latin American Tower just skyward from the intersection of Avenida Juárez and Avenida Lázaro Cárdenas.

Bus no. 22 "Cuatro Caminos-Economia" runs east along Mosqueta (the street in front of the station), and you can catch this bus to the intersection with Avenida Lázaro Cárdenas, then transfer to a trolleybus (no. 27 "Reclusorio Norte-Ciudad Jardín") heading south into the center of town, but these buses are often jam-packed. You may feel better taking a taxi to your chosen hotel.

ARRIVING BY PLANE: The ground transportation situation at Mexico City's airport seems to change more frequently than an airline's flight schedule. As of this writing, the red SETTA minibuses which once got you downtown inexpensively are gone, and there are no longer any airport buses, either. The authorized airport taxis (Transportacion Terrestre) reign supreme.

Authorized Airport Taxis

The airport taxis provide a good, fast service, but are relatively expensive.

Here's how to use them: buy a taxi ticket at one of the several little booths in the arrivals hall. You must tell the ticket-seller your hotel or destination, as price is based on a zone system. Expect to pay around 2,000 pesos ($4) for a ticket to, say, the Plaza de la Republica, Jardín del Arte, or Zócalo. Then just walk out the terminal door and you'll be on your way at once.

Other Taxis

What about other taxis? You'll be approached in the arrivals hall by men offering taxis. These are usually nonlicensed, unauthorized and often suspicious types. Ignore them. If you take a cab from the terminal, take an authorized cab with all the familiar markings: yellow car, white taxi light on the roof, "Transportacion Terrestre" painted on the doors.

Cheaper Cabs

The authorized cabbies try to maintain a monopoly of the airport business by not allowing any regular Mexico City cabs into their plush domain. This is bad for you, because a yellow VW Beetle taxi running its meter charges between 800 and 1,000 pesos ($1.60 to $2) for the trip between the airport and the center of town. You can beat the system by doing this: walk to the Terminal Aerea Metro station (see below), at the intersection of the busy Bulevar Aeropuerto and the airport entrance. When you see a yellow VW Beetle or little yellow Datsun cab, flag it down. You will save at least 25% and perhaps 50% by doing so.

To make sure you get a proper, trustworthy cab, be sure to read the information on taxis in the following section, "Public Transportation."

The Metro

The absolutely, positively cheapest way to get downtown is to take Mexico City's modern subway system, the **Metro.** As you come from your plane into the arrivals hall, turn left, walk all the way through the terminal and out the doors. Soon you'll see the distinctive Metro logo that identifies the Terminal Aerea station. The station is on Metro Line 5. Follow the signs for trains to Pantitlán. At Pantitlán, change for Line 1 ("Observatorio"), which will take you to stations that are just a few blocks south of the Zócalo and the Alameda Central: Pino Suárez, Isabel la Católica, Salto del Agua, Balderas. The ride costs an astoundingly low 1 peso (a fraction of a penny), but wait! You may not be able to go by Metro if you have luggage. Read carefully the Metro section below under "Public Transportation."

If you find that you can get on the Metro with luggage, you should not plan to take a Metro route that requires you to change trains at La Raza station. The walk between lines there is a good ten minutes, and you'll be carrying your luggage.

The trip by Metro from the airport to downtown may be as fast as a taxi ride, but it's unlikely to be as comfortable. The Metro is often very, very crowded downtown.

2. Public Transportation

Luckily for budget travelers, Mexico City has a highly developed and remarkably cheap public transportation system. The Metro, first- and second-class buses, minibuses *(colectivos),* and yellow VW taxis will take you anywhere you want to go for very little money.

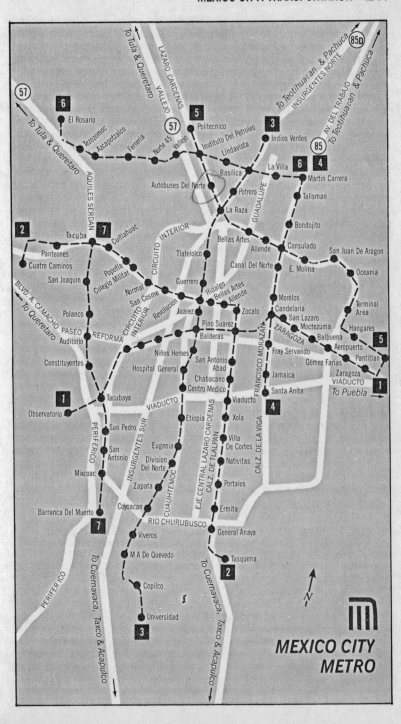

MEXICO CITY METRO

THE METRO: The subway system in Mexico City offers one of the smoothest rides for about the cheapest fare anywhere in the world. Seven lines are completed in the sprawling system.

As you enter the station, buy a *boleto* (ticket) at the glass *caja* (ticket office). Insert your ticket into the slot at the turnstile and pass through; once inside you'll see two large signs designating the destination of the line (for example, for Line 1, it's Observatorio and Pantitlán). Follow the signs in the direction you want, and *know where you're going,* since there is usually only one map of the routes, at the entrance to the station. There are, however, two signs you'll see everywhere: *Salida,* which means "exit"; and *Andenes,* which means "platforms." Once inside the train, you'll see above each door a map of the station stops for that line, with symbols and names.

Transfer of lines is indicated by *Correspondencias.* The ride is smooth, fast, and efficient (although hot and crowded during rush hours). The stations are clean and beautifully designed with lots of stone, tiles, piped-in music—and the added attraction of several archeological ruins unearthed during construction. There is also a subterranean passage that goes between the Pino Suárez and Zócalo stations so you can avoid the crowds and the rain along Pino Suárez. The Zócalo station has dioramas and large photographs of the different periods in the history of the Valley of Mexico, and at Pino Suárez there is the foundation of a pyramid from the Aztec empire.

Important Notes: The Metro system runs between 5 or 6 a.m. and midnight or 1 a.m. *only;* it is not an all-night operation. Also, heavy baggage is not allowed into the system at busy times, especially during rush hours on weekdays. In practice this means that bulky suitcases or backpacks sometimes make you *persona non grata,* but a large shoulder-bag such as I use is not classed as luggage; nor is an attaché case, or even a case that's slightly bigger. The reason is that Mexico City's Metro on an average day handles over 5,000,000 riders and that leaves precious little room for bags! But, in effect, if no one stops you as you enter, you're in.

You should note that Metro travel is usually very crowded during daylight hours on weekdays, and consequently pretty hot and muggy in summer. In fact, you may find (as I have) that between 4 and 7 p.m. on weekdays the Metro downtown is virtually unusable because of sardine-can conditions. At some stations there are even separate lanes roped off for women and children because the press of the crowd is so great someone might get hurt. Buses, colectivos, and taxis are all heavily used during these hours. The trick is to leave yourself some time and energy to walk during these hours. On weekends and holidays, the Metro is a joy to ride.

READER'S TRANSPORTATION TIP: "The **Metro** is the fastest way to get around. If it is treated as a game or a challenge, it becomes one of those unforgettable experiences that stick in your memory and provide dozens of boring stories to tell your friends back home. You can spend a fortune to run with the bulls at Pamplona; or for only one peso, you can ride the Metro at rush hour in Mexico City!" (Prof. Irwin Rovner, Raleigh, N.C.).

BUSES: Moving millions of people through this sprawling urban mass is a gargantuan task, but the city fathers do a pretty good job of it, though they tend to change bus numbers and routes too frequently. The municipal bus system, operated by the DDF (Departamento del Distrito Federal, or Federal District Department), is run on an enormous grid plan. Odd-numbered buses run roughly north-south, even-numbered buses go east-west, and a special express service runs along the main routes downtown. Maps of the system are difficult to find. I'll provide you with most of the routes and numbers you'll need, however.

The buses themselves are modern but they age very rapidly. They tend to be crowded or very crowded. The fare is very inexpensive—3 pesos (less than 1¢) at this writing. Downtown bus stops bear signs with full route descriptions.

One of the most important bus routes is the one that runs between the Zócalo and the Auditorio (National Auditorium in Chapultepec Park) or the Observatorio Metro station. The route is via Avenida Madero or Cinco (5) de Mayo, Avenida Juárez, Paseo de la Reforma; maps of the route are posted at each bus stop. At present, no. 76, **"Zócalo-km. 13,"** runs along this route.

Watch for Pickpockets!

Mexico City is unique in many ways, but in one matter it resembles any big city anywhere: pickpockets. Crowded subway cars and buses provide the perfect workplace for petty thieves, as do thronged outdoor markets and bullfights, or indoor theaters. The "touch" can range from lightfingered wallet lifting or purse opening to a fairly rough shoving by two or three petty thieves. Sometimes the ploy is this: someone drops a coin, and while everyone is looking, pushing, and shoving, your wallet disappears. Watch out for them anyplace tourists go in numbers: on the Metro, in Reforma buses, in crowded hotel elevators, at the Ballet Folklorico.

Luckily, violent muggings are pretty infrequent in Mexico City. But if you find yourself up against a handful of these guys in a crowded spot, the best thing to do is to raise a fuss—no matter whether you do it in Spanish or in English. Just a few shouts of "Robo! Robo!" ("Robbery!") or "Robador!" ("Thief!"), or anything loud, should put them off.

Another important route is no. 17, **"Indios Verdes-Tlalpan,"** which runs along Avenida Insurgentes connecting the northern bus terminal (Terminal Norte), Buena Vista Railroad Station, Reforma, the Zona Rosa, and—far to the south—San Angel and University City. Also, trolleybuses run from the Terminal de Autobuses del Norte down Avenida Lázaro Cárdenas to the Tasqueña Metro station.

TAXIS: Mexico City is pretty easy to get around by Metro and bus, and these methods bring you few hassles. Taxis are another matter, but there are times when nothing else will do. Cabs operate under several distinct sets of rules, one of them being highway robbery. The others are as follows:

The Cheap Cabs

Yellow Volkswagen Beetle and **Datsun** cabs are your best bet for low cost and good service. Though you will occasionally encounter a gouging driver ("Ah, the meter just broke yesterday; I'll have it fixed tomorrow!"), most of the service will be excellent. If the driver doesn't start the meter, get him to quote a fare, and then bargain him down, or get out of the cab.

Inflation always outpaces the taxi meters, so the driver often uses a printed table to find the actual fare. Thus, if the meter reads 100 pesos, the table will show that a 100-peso meter reading equals an 800-peso fare.

Other Cabs

There are other sorts of legitimate cabs, including pink ones and light blue ones. "Turismo" cabs have black bags over their meters, and charge what the traffic will bear. They often provide luxury service (in large late-model American cars) at luxury prices. If you use one, agree on a price before setting foot in the cab.

Tipping

There is no need to tip any taxi driver in Mexico. It's not the custom here, unless the driver has gone beyond the call of duty in his service.

Official/Unofficial Taxis

Do not use a car that is not an official taxi. Though most of the unauthorized drivers are just guys trying to earn some extra money and make ends meet, others are crooks. Here's how you tell an official, authorized taxi:

All official taxis (except those expensive "Turismo" cabs) are painted **yellow, orange, pink, or light blue,** and they have white plastic roof signs bearing the word taxi, and they have "Taxi" or "Sitio" painted on the doors, and they have several official-looking stickers (decals, transfers) on their windshields, and they have meters. Look for all of these indications, not just one or two of them.

COLECTIVOS: Also called *peseros,* these are sedans or minibuses, usually white, that run along major arteries. They pick up and discharge passengers along the route, charge established fares, and provide more comfort and speed than the bus. Routes are displayed on cards in the windshield; often a Metro station will be the destination. One of the most useful routes for tourists is Ruta 2, which runs from the Zócalo along Avenida Juárez, along Reforma to Chapultepec, and back again. Get a colectivo with a sign saying "Zócalo," not "Villa."

Note that some of the minibuses on this route have automatic sliding doors —you don't have to shut them, a motor does.

As the driver approaches a stop, he may put his hand out the window and hold up one or more figures. This is the number of passengers he's willing to take on (vacant seats are difficult to see if you're outside the car).

CAR RENTALS: For information on renting a car, see Chapter XVII under "Car Rentals."

3. Organized Tours

I've already mentioned that Mexico City is a great place for looking around on your own, and in general this is the cheapest way to see whatever you like. However, if your time is limited, you may wish to acclimate yourself quickly by taking a tour or two.

The most popular tours are: the four-hour city tour that includes such sites as the National Cathedral, the National Palace, and Chapultepec Park and Castle; the four- to six-hour tour of the Shrine of Guadelupe and the nearby pyramids in the Teotihuacán archeological zone; and the Sunday tour that begins with the Ballet Folklorico, moves on to the floating gardens of Xochimilco, and may or may not incorporate lunch and the afternoon bullfights. Almost as popular are the one-day and overnight tours to Cuernavaca and Taxco. There are also several popular nightclub tours.

I feel that I must give some caveats. Many readers have written to say that they were unhappy with the sightseeing tours of this or that company. The reasons are myriad: the tour was too rushed, or the guide knew nothing and made up fairy stories about the sights, or the tour spent most of its time in a handcrafts shop (chosen by the tour company) rather than seeing the sights. Do tour companies get a kickback from souvenir shops? You bet they do! If you meet someone who has recently taken a guided tour and liked it, go with the same company. Otherwise, you might do well to see the sights on your own, following the detailed guidance in this book.

4. Tourism Information

The Departamento del Distrito Federal (Federal District government) provides several information services for visitors. First of all there are **Tourist Information** offices, the most convenient of which is in the Zona Rosa at the corner of Londres and Amberes (tel. 905/528-9469 or 528-9289). Others are at the bus terminals, airport, and railroad station.

The DDF also has a **special telephone number** to call for information on performances, sporting events, festivals and other such activities: tel. 525-9380.

If you need **legal help,** call Protectur, the DDF's special legal-services agency for tourists at 516-0490.

The **Secretaría de Turismo,** Avenida Presidente Masaryk 172, north of Chapultepec Park in the district known as Polanco, is a bit out of the way. But any telephone will serve to get you information if you dial 250-0123. They'll speak English.

Downtown near the intersection of Avenida Juárez and Paseo de la Reforma, at Juárez 92, is an **information desk** of sorts. It's in the lobby of the Migración (Immigration) building.

The **Mexico City Chamber of Commerce** (tel. 546-5645) maintains an information office with a very friendly, helpful staff who can provide you with a detailed map of the city (or country) and answer some of your questions. It's conveniently located at Reforma 42—look for the Camara Nacional de Comercio de la Ciudad de México, open from 9 a.m. to 2 p.m. and 4 to 7 p.m. Monday through Thursday, to 6 p.m. on Friday; closed Saturday and Sunday.

MAPS: Should you want more detailed maps of Mexico City than the ones included in this book, you can obtain them easily. Most bookstores, and many street vendors and newsstands, sell a booklet of maps called the **Guia Amarilla** (also spelled *GuiAmarilla)* for about $2. There's an index of street names, and the index guides you through the 14 separate maps that cover the entire extent of this huge city's sprawl. The guide is excellent, if a bit *too* detailed for the normal visitor's purposes.

A map similar in greatness of detail is also sold at many outlets. Called simply the **Plano de la Ciudad de México y Area Metropolitana,** it's over two feet wide and three feet long, and thus a bit awkward to use on the street. But it's got all the detail, and it sells for only about $1.25.

A simpler map is the yellow **Mapa Turistico de la Ciudad de México,** put out by Ammex Asociados, S.A., and sold in Sanborn's stores (among other places) for about $1. Though not the easiest map to read, it is admirably simple (that seems like a contradiction, but look at the map and you'll see what I mean). It has a Metro map superimposed on the downtown street plan, so you can figure out where you are at once when you ascend from a Metro station.

And now you're ready to get down to the serious business of finding a good, reasonably priced place to stay in the world's largest city.

MEXICO CITY: ROOMS ON A BUDGET

IT COSTS LESS to stay in Mexico City than in most European capitals, or in almost any U.S. city of any size. The city is truly a bargain when you consider that for $15 to $20 you can find a double room in a fairly central hotel complete with bathroom, decent furnishings, often with extras such as air conditioning, television set, or a balcony. Many hotels have their own garages where guests can park for free. Most of the new construction in the last decade has been of more luxurious hotels with central air conditioning, elevators, restaurants, and the like; these are usually at the top of our budget. Cheaper hotels tend to be the older ones, well kept up but built in less affluent times without all the extras that tend to inflate prices.

The earthquake of September 1985, destroyed several Mexico City hotels, and damaged a number of others. For the most part, the city's hotels are now fixed up and are back in business. Among the recommendations given below, I have included several trusted hotels which are still undergoing repairs as of this writing, but which should be open and ready to receive guests by the time you arrive.

Here first are some tips on how to save money in the hotel you select from my recommendations.

1. Getting the Most for Your Money

First, remember that Mexican hotels have an assortment of rooms, and that those with a view of the street may be more expensive (and noisier!) than those with windows opening onto an airshaft. Second, rooms are usually furnished with one single bed, one double bed, or two twin beds; the best buy is for two people to take the double bed—twins are almost always more expensive. To get the double bed ask for *una cama matrimonial*. Third, although all rates are supposedly controlled by the Mexican government, these rates are the *maximum* allowable, and in many cases a desk clerk will quote you a lower price if business is slack or if you suggest a slight reduction. By the way, the room rates are required to be posted in plain view near the reception desk and as a rule they generally are, places like Acapulco being the exceptions. Ask the clerk to show you the *Tarifa*, and get to recognize the official form it's on to help you locate it in other hotels. Fourth, *test the beds* if you intend to stay any length of time. Price often has nothing to do with the comfort of the beds. Why pay good money for something that's going to give you a backache? Often the cheaper hotels will have beds bought at different times, so one room may have a bad bed but another one a good bed. Remember also that the 15% IVA tax will be included in your bill. When you register, remember to ask if it's been included in the rate quoted to you, or will be added later.

2. Choosing a Hotel Location

My recommendations below are grouped around major landmarks in Mexico City, places that are well known by every city-dweller and easily identifiable by first-time visitors. To find your chosen hotel area, or to get a bus going in that direction, all you need do is collar any passerby and ask, "Donde es . . ." *(Dohn-*deh ess) and then the name of the place: "El Monumento a la Revolución," "El Zócalo," "La Zona Rosa," etc. You'll know your way home in no time at all.

Here's a summary of the major areas. The **Zona Rosa** is Mexico City's Mayfair, Faubourg St-Honoré, or Gramercy Park: the status address. The chic boutiques, fancy restaurants and cafés, and expensive hotels are here. My hotel choices, in and near the Zona Rosa, are thus at the top of our daily budget.

The **Jardín del Arte (Sullivan Park)** is a wedge-shaped park extending west from the intersection of Paseo de la Reforma and Avenida Insurgentes. It has a wonderful range of hotels, old and new, colonial and modern, flashy and humble. Many are on quiet streets, some have views of the park, all are close to the Zona Rosa and to transportation.

The **Revolución Monument (Monumento a la Revolución)** is in the large Plaza de la República, at the very western end of Avenida Juárez. Here you're centrally located, about equidistant from the Zona Rosa and the Zócalo, and you're near major transportation routes, but most of the hotel streets are quiet.

The **Alameda Central,** right next to the Palacio de Bellas Artes, is closer to the downtown shopping district, a bit farther from the Zona Rosa. Transportation is still good. Most of the hotels are well-used modern structures on streets to the south of the Alameda.

The **Zócalo** is the heart of historic Mexico City, surrounded by colonial buildings and Aztec ruins. It's also the heart of the downtown shopping district, with interesting small stores to the west, and the gigantic Mercado Merced to the east.

For those arriving tired, or late at night, there is a section describing lodging possibilities near the major termini.

Finally, I list and describe some of Mexico City's apartment hotels, establishments (mostly in or near the Zona Rosa) where you can rent a fully furnished studio or one-bedroom apartment with kitchen by the week or month, at rates similar to or lower than those in a hotel. If you're traveling with a small group or a family, if you're staying for a week or more, apartment hotels may be the way to save money.

3. Hotels in the Zona Rosa

It's very difficult to find a hotel within our budget range in the posh Zona Rosa, but there are undoubtedly some readers who will want to throw budget and caution to the wind when they hit this glamorous city. For these fortunate travelers, I suggest the following hostelries within and on the fringes of the Zona Rosa.

The dowager of Mexico City's tourist hotels, the 378-room **Hotel Geneve,** Londres 130 (at the corner of Genova), México, D.F. 06600 (tel. 905/525-1500), bears the exhausting name of Hotel Geneve Calinda Quality Inn. Although the hotel has undergone extensive facelifting recently, its rather grand lobby ringed by fancy shops, dotted with richly carved furniture, and decorated with dark-hued Spanish paintings still whispers opulence. You'll love "El Jardín," the incredibly long glass-topped and plant-filled breakfast room, restaurant, and cocktail lounge. Rooms here come with two double beds (good for families), color TV, and servi-bar refrigerator, and are priced at 20,000 pesos ($40) for singles; doubles are 22,000 pesos ($44); kids 16 and under stay free. You can even reserve a room in the U.S. by calling Quality Inns toll free at 800/228-5151. As everywhere, watch out for street noise when you select your room.

ON THE FRINGES OF THE ZONA ROSA: Several hotels are a short walk from the Zona Rosa, and give you the convenience of being almost right there. The **Hotel Viena,** Marsella 28 between Dinamarca and Berlin (tel. 905/566-0700), is actually an older hotel but you wouldn't know it from its sleek, modern exterior. The 60 rooms are all well kept, although a bit older than the façade would indicate; some have a bathroom with tub and twin beds, and cost 6,125 pesos ($12.25) double. The cheaper rooms have one double bed and cost a dollar or two less. Blown-up color photos of forest scenes and Alpine views abound. There's a parking lot beneath the hotel, and a little Swiss-style restaurant at sidewalk level. The rooms at the Viena may be the quietest in the downtown area.

Across Reforma from the Zona Rosa is the **Hotel Bristol,** Plaza Necaxa 17, México, D.F. 06500 (tel. 905/533-6060), which is at the intersection of Panuco and Sena. Although many of its rooms are filled with sedate tour groups or long-term residents, the eight-story structure usually has rooms to spare for about 6,000 pesos ($12) single, 7,000 pesos ($14) double. Although bright and modern, shiny and clean, the Bristol is a fairly somnolent place. (Under repair.)

The **Casa Gonzalez,** Río Sena 69 (near the corner of Río Lerma), México, D.F. 06500 (tel. 905/514-3302), is a congenial hostelry made up of two mansions that have been converted to hold 22 guest rooms, each one unique. The houses, with little grassy patios out back and a huge shady tree, make an extremely pleasant and quiet oasis in the middle of the city. Meals (optional) are taken in a dining room bright with stained glass. All the rooms have a private bath (some with tub). The owner, Sr. Jorge E. Ortiz Gonzalez, speaks flawless and effortless English, and always seems to be smiling. Prices are quoted in U.S. dollars: $10.35 to $18.40 for a single or $13.80 to $18.40 for a double room. A suite for four costs $30. There's limited parking in the driveway. The Casa Gonzalez is highly recommended, especially for young women traveling alone.

4. Hotels Near the Jardín del Arte

The Jardín del Arte, also called Jardín Sullivan or Sullivan Park, extends westward from the intersection of Reforma and Insurgentes. A broad open

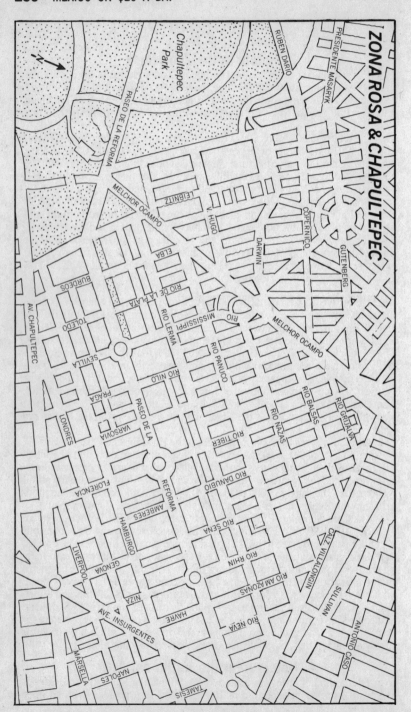

plaza is actually the roof of a subterranean parking garage. At the end of the plaza is a grand monument to motherhood, and behind that a green park filled with artists displaying their wares on Sunday afternoons. The streets off the park, especially Calle Río Lerma, have numerous hotels—a real assortment.

The **Hotel Mallorca,** Serapio Rendon 119, México, D.F. 06470 (tel. 905/ 566-4833), just off the Jardín del Arte, charges a bit more than I'd like to pay, but it's modern and even luxurious, with wall-to-wall carpeting almost everywhere, Muzak, air conditioning, a parking garage, coffeeshop, bar, and restaurant. Every room has its own TV (good for Spanish practice). If two get a *matrimonial* (double bed) the cost is 3,750 pesos ($7.50); twin beds cost 4,490 pesos ($9); singles, 3,350 pesos ($6.70).

Should the Hotel Mallorca be full, you can go across the street to the **Hotel Sevilla,** a similar hotel, at Sullivan and Serapio Rendon 126, México, D.F. 06470 (tel. 905/566-1866), with rooms and prices very similar to those at the Mallorca. Here your room will have a telephone, television, FM radio, purified water; the hotel sits atop its own parking garage, and has a central air-conditioning system. There's a restaurant and bar, which will provide room service too. The daily set-price lunches are incredible bargains at 750 and 900 pesos ($1.50 and $1.80).

Too much? The 17-room **Hotel Maria Angelo's,** Lerma 11 at Río Marne, México, D.F. 06500 (tel. 905/546-6705), is everything the Mallorca's not. An older place with rooms of all sizes and shapes, it's recently undergone some renovation, although many of the bathrooms remain unredeemed. The tiny lobby adjoins a small reading lounge to which departing guests sometimes contribute (you'll find English magazines, Spanish paperbacks). There's no elevator, and only one telephone per floor, but each room has a private bath with a tub and windows so wide that the sun streams in each morning. Single rooms cost 2,200 pesos ($4.40) doubles are 2,500 pesos ($5) and some rooms are large enough to accommodate three or four persons; an extra bed is 500 pesos ($1) per night. In addition, there are eight suites. The suites are quite large and have their own terraces—a fine extra.

The **Hotel Maria Cristina,** Río Lerma 31 (between Río Neva and Río Amazonas), México, D.F. 06500 (tel. 905/546-9880), is another of those lovely places that was once out of the range of this book but is now within our budget. It is quiet, shady, green, and colonial in feeling. The lobby shows rich use of blue-and-white tiles, leather and dark wood, and wrought iron. A lounge off the lobby has a nice big fireplace, but you will probably want to spend your spare minutes on the pretty lawn outside. The comfy, refurbished rooms with bath cost 4,600 pesos ($9.20) single, 5,175 pesos ($10.35) double.

The **Hotel Doral,** Sullivan 9 (just off the intersection of Insurgentes and Reforma), México, D.F. 06470 (tel. 905/592-2866), is a good example of the sort of medium-priced hotels seen throughout Mexico City. A high-riser of almost 20 stories, it overlooks the Jardín del Arte, and from its swimming pool, sundeck, and bar on the roof one can see most of the city. Rooms are close to the standard motel or medium-priced hotel in the U.S. or Canada, with fine bathrooms. The location couldn't be better. The price isn't bad: 8,000 pesos ($16) single, 9,000 pesos ($18) double.

At the **Hotel Stella Maris,** Sullivan 69, México, D.F. 06470 (tel. 905/566-6088), the starfish motif is carried to the lengths of having a brass effigy of this sea creature attached to each room key. Other than this, though, there's little nautical about the place except the small rooftop swimming pool. The rooms in this new building are sort of small and some are a bit dark, but part of this is due to the agreeable subdued colors. TV, radio, bathrooms with separate washbasin cubicle, bottles of pure water in each room, and (from front rooms) views of the

Jardín and its Sunday art exhibitions are the extras. Prices are good, and you get your money's worth, for sure: single rooms cost 4,370 pesos ($8.74) and doubles are 4,830 pesos ($9.66); junior suites are somewhat more. The hotel's restaurant serves a good set-price lunch for only 1,000 pesos ($2). This is a fine, modern hotel, not all that far from Reforma.

The small triangle formed by Insurgentes Centro, Antonio Caso, and Reforma has other good hotel choices, most more expensive than the Hotel Maria Angelo, but much more deluxe. Try the **Hotel Regente,** at Paris 9, México, D.F. 06030 (tel. 905/566-8933), between Madrid and the three-way intersection of Antonio Caso, Insurgentes, and Paris. Over 100 rooms plus a garage fill this modern building. Bold-patterned bedspreads and flowered drapes, plus wall-to-wall carpeting, make the rooms lively and comfortable. Bathrooms with showers are pretty small but quite adequate. A restaurant and travel agent desk are at your disposal in the lobby. Here one person pays 3,450 pesos ($6.90); two pay 3,680 pesos ($7.36). Again, the location and transportation possibilities are excellent.

5. Hotels Near the Revolución Monument

From the intersection of Avenida Juárez and Paseo de la Reforma, the western extension of Avenida Juárez (actually named Calle Ignacio Ramírez) leads to the large Plaza de la República. The plaza was chosen by Porfirio Díaz as the site of a Chamber of Deputies, and the mammoth dome was under construction when the Mexican Revolution (1910) interrupted Díaz's plans, not to mention Díaz himself. After the dictator fled the country, the building was restructured as a monument and two heroes of the revolution, Venustiano Carranza and Francisco Madero, were buried in its pillars.

The Monument to the Revolution is an odd, stolid, massive structure which I find peculiarly fascinating, and very art deco. The monument is illuminated at night; even during the day its somber dome is visible from many points in the city.

This is a fairly quiet area, near the major arteries and a Metro station (Revolución). You're about the same distance from the Zona Rosa as from the Zócalo, and next door to the Jardín del Arte and the Alameda—an excellent area.

With the fall of the peso, the comfortable, modern **Hotel Corinto** (tel. 905/566-6555 or 566-9711) has come back within our budget range. Located at Calle Vallarta 24, México, D.F. 06030, it is just a few steps north of Antonio Caso. The modern 90-room hotel caters to both tourists and businessmen with clean, shiny rooms with coordinated drapes and bedspreads, reproductions of paintings by modern Mexican artists, tiled showers, TV sets, piped-in music, and special taps for purified water. Just off the lobby is a little restaurant, and on the ninth floor is a small swimming pool, sunning area, and patch of grass, plus a bar. Most rooms have either twin single beds or one double bed, and cost 5,060 pesos ($10.12) single, 5,580 pesos ($11.16) double.

Considering its appointments, the five-story **Hotel Jena** (pronounced "haynah"), Jesus Teran 12 (at Puente de Alvarado), México, D.F. 06030 (tel. 905/566-0277), is a good medium-priced choice. From the swanky exterior, recently remodeled, you might think it expensive, but not so. The 60 rooms, nicely furnished with "Hotel Formica," each with large mirror, telephone, and glistening tile bath, cost 4,025 to 4,600 pesos ($8.05 to $9.20) single, 4,600 to 5,750 pesos ($9.20 to $11.50) double, the higher double price being for a huge room with a couch, rather like a junior suite. The hotel has a restaurant and free parking.

Less fancy than the Jena, and also less expensive, the **Hotel New York,** Edison 45, México, D.F. 06030 (tel. 905/566-9700), is a large four-story building, a cubist's dream of mosaic tile, grass-green paneling, and glass. The 45 rooms are

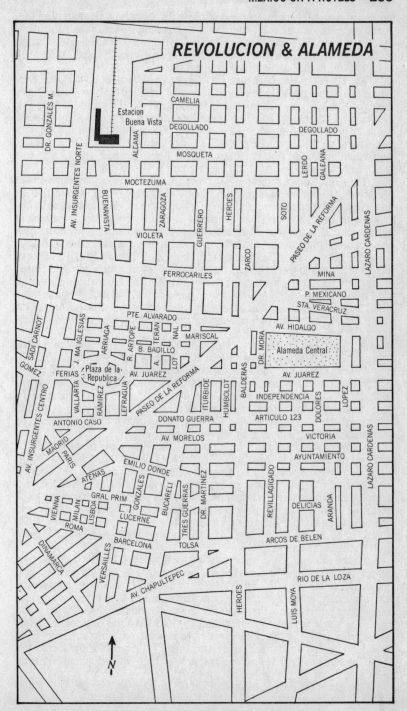

REVOLUCION & ALAMEDA

equipped with telephones, televisions, tile baths, carpeting, Formica furniture, wood paneling on one wall, and hanging glass lamps—very pleasant. Prices: 3,450 pesos ($6.90) single, 3,680 pesos ($7.36) double. The small restaurant off the lobby solves the breakfast problem. It's open every day from 7 a.m. to 10 p.m. Parking in the hotel's locked garage is free.

The 100-room **Hotel Frimont,** Jesus Teran 35, México, D.F. 06030 (tel. 905/546-2580), stands up well when compared to the Jena and the New York. Singles here rent for 2,530 pesos ($5.06), doubles for 2,790 to 3,000 pesos ($5.60 to $6), triples for 3,450 pesos ($6.90), four-to-a-room for 4,000 pesos ($8)—that's a mere $2 per person—all with telephone and private bath. But it is a pleasant hotel boasting a slick marble lobby, 72 nicely decorated rooms, free parking, and a medium-priced restaurant just off the lobby, open daily from 7 a.m. to 1 a.m., featuring a 600-peso ($1.20) lunch from 1 p.m. to 5 p.m.

The **Hotel Edison,** Edison 106 (a block from the Revolución Monument at the corner of Iglesias), México, D.F. 06030 (tel. 905/566-0933), is a real find. In the midst of the city's noise and bustle, its odd construction around a narrow court with grass and trees gives a sense of sanctuary. Some rooms are built in tiers overlooking the court, and even larger ones are hidden away down hallways. These latter rooms tend to be dark, but big and comfortable with huge king-size beds, and cost 3,000 pesos ($6) single, 3,400 pesos ($6.80) double; of the other rooms, a few singles go for a few pesos less; most are a bit higher; other doubles go for slightly more, with a few extra-luxurious rooms costing a good deal more. Blond wood and light colors, piped music, and sunlight make this a cheerful place. Services include bathrooms with separate washbasin areas, and some even have bidets, plus tub-shower combinations. The location is fairly quiet and near downtown.

Another hotel choice convenient to the Monument to the Revolution is the 75-room **Hotel Arizona,** Gómez Farías 20 at Insurgentes, México, D.F. 06030 (tel. 905/546-2855). For the very reasonable prices of 3,000 pesos ($6) single, 3,350 pesos ($6.70) double, 3,750 pesos ($7.50) triple, you get very clean rooms with tile showers, black-and-white TV sets, telephones, air conditioning, and a large covered parking garage right next door. Color TVs are yours at a small additional charge. Try not to get a room that looks onto busy Insurgentes. The Arizona is only half a block from the Monument.

Going to the top of the price scale, the **Hotel Palace,** at Ignacio Ramírez 7 (just off the Plaza de la Revolución), México, D.F. 06030 (tel. 905/566-2400), was one of Mexico's outstanding luxury hotels only a few decades ago. Today it retains its comfort, its good location, its experienced staff, and over 200 well-kept rooms. The bustle of a large hotel surrounds you here, with tobacco kiosk and travel desk in the lobby, bag-bearing bellboys scurrying here and there, and the occasional busload of tourists. Of the rooms, about half are priced at 4,830 pesos ($9.66) single, 5,520 pesos ($11.04) double; the rest are about 1,500 pesos ($3) higher in price.

At the low end of the price scale is a small, modest hotel which gets very high marks for effort. The **Gran Hotel Texas,** Ignacio Mariscal 129 near Arriaga, México, D.F. 06030, (tel. 905/546-4626 or 546-4627), has been consistently clean, friendly, and low-priced for more than a decade. Don't look for anything fancy here; rather, notice the smiles that greet you and the tidiness of the premises. The street is relatively quiet, and the location quite convenient. While some other hotels in this price range have become unrespectable, the Texas maintains its high standards. Single rooms cost 2,530 pesos ($5.06); doubles are 2,875 pesos ($5.75). Every room has private bath and telephone. Recommended.

The **Hotel Oxford,** Ignacio Mariscal 67, at Alcazar, México, D.F. 06030 (tel. 905/566-0500), overlooks the little park next to the Museo de San Carlos—a lovely, quiet setting. The hotel rooms, though "experienced," are decently kept and equipped in most cases with television. For a room with one double bed, the price is 2,450 pesos ($4.90); for two beds in a room, you pay 3,500 pesos ($7).

READER'S HOTEL SELECTION—REVOLUCIÓN: "The **Hotel Carlton** (tel. 905/566-2911), Mariscal 32-B, facing the park at the Museo de San Carlos, is rather shopworn; however, the rooms were clean, the beds comfortable, and we had a view of the pretty park. Our rate was only 2,300 pesos ($4.60) double. We had a small-screen color TV and the staff was very friendly and cooperative" (Richard C. Bradley, Springdale, Ariz.).

6. Hotels Near Alameda Central

The Alameda Central is Mexico City's downtown park, always filled with strollers, lovers, newspaper-readers, loafers, children playing in the fountains, and vendors hawking everything from dried pumpkin seeds to serapes. It's a pleasant place, right next to the marble Palacio de Bellas Artes (Fine Arts Palace) and only a block from the skyscraping Latin American Tower.

Most of my recommended hotels here are actually on the streets to the south of the Alameda. Hotels with views of the park itself tend to be out of our price range.

Having said that, let me recommend the wonderful old colonial **Best Western Hotel de Cortés,** Avenida Hidalgo 85, right at the northwest corner of the Alameda (tel. 905/518-2181). An authentic structure from Mexico City's Spanish past, it has very comfortable guest rooms, a good restaurant, and a lovely courtyard set with patio tables and chairs. Though prices stretch our budget, and though the traffic on busy Avenida Hidalgo is fierce, you can't do better in terms of location or charm. Expect to pay 8,855 pesos ($17.71) single, 10,120 pesos ($20.24) for a room with double bed or twin beds. Reservations are available in the U.S. and Canada through Best Western hotels.

The streets south of the Alameda harbor a cross-section of downtown life: little eateries and juice bars, shops selling pumps, sinks, car parts, blenders, electrical gear, homeopathic remedies, you name it. Not particularly beautiful, the area still manages to be sympathetic as a real slice of life. Its hotels are mostly of the modern type, well used and decently priced. Some specialize in tour groups because of the central location.

On the street with the unpronounceable name of Revillagigedo, the **Hotel Guadalupe,** at no. 36, México, D.F. 06050 (tel. 905/518-5240), has colonial touches such as lamps on chains and prints of an equestrian Bolívar. The staff is young and mostly English-speaking, and is used to handling tour groups (which the hotel does frequently). Prices are 2,600 pesos ($5.20) single, 3,400 pesos ($6.80) double. The restaurant features a 900-peso ($1.80) lunch; garage parking is free. (Under repair.)

Also on Revillagigedo, at no. 35, is the **Hotel Fleming,** México, D.F. 06050 (tel. 905/510-4530), a building of 100 rooms from which I've had good reports that were borne out by my inspection. Although well used, the heavy service has still left the rooms quite presentable, and the bathrooms are larger than most. Elevators take you to the upper floors. Singles at the Fleming cost 2,870 pesos ($5.74); doubles are 3,320 pesos ($6.64) in a double bed, 3,860 pesos ($7.72) in twin beds. A blindingly colorful coffeeshop-restaurant is located next to the lobby, and offers a set-price lunch daily.

STARVATION-BUDGET HOTELS: Although the **Hotel Conde,** Pescaditos 15, México, D.F. 06070 (tel. 905/585-2388), is five blocks off Juárez and equally far from Reforma, it offers the best rooms for the best price in this area. The hotel's entrance is at Pescaditos 15, but the building is on the corner of Revillagigedo, and would be numbered about Revillagigedo 56. It's fairly new with clean bathrooms, a small marbled lobby, wall-to-wall carpet, TV, and FM in the rooms, free garage parking. Rates are 2,000 pesos ($4), single or double.

FOR WOMEN ONLY: The **Asociación Cristiana Femenina** translates as the **YWCA,** and the association's headquarters at Humboldt 62, México, D.F. 06040 (tel. 905/510-9479 or 512-0499), a mere block off Avenida Juárez, holds very clean and respectable single rooms for women costing $8 (U.S.) per day without bath, $10 per day with private bath. A budget-priced restaurant is in the same building.

READER'S HOTEL SELECTION—ALAMEDA: "Our favorite hotel was the **Hotel Marlowe,** Independencia 17, just off the Alameda. For 6,000 pesos ($12) we got a lovely room with a balcony, TV, and private bath. It is a modern building with a rooftop restaurant. Cheaper rooms have no balconies" (John Veillette, Victoria, B.C., Canada).

7. Hotels Near the Zócalo

The center of the city's shopping and banking district is a great place to stay for many reasons, but most of all for location. Here you are a short walk from the Alameda Central, Bellas Artes, Latin American Tower, the art and craft stores, and the Zócalo. Transportation by bus, Metro, and *colectivo* to other parts of the city is easy and inexpensive. Hotels tend to be older ones with little of the glitter and flash of the more expensive places in the aforementioned areas, but this makes them even better bargains as prices are kept low. Many of the hotels east of Avenida Lázaro Cárdenas have their own garages and restaurants, and other good restaurants are scattered throughout the district. Staying here will permit you to stretch your budget dollars and stay a longer time in Mexico City.

I'll describe first of all the moderately priced hostelries west and south of the Zócalo, then a few tips for the Big Splurge: staying right on the Zócalo. Finally, I'll look at the lodging possibilities north and east of Mexico City's main square.

HOTELS WEST AND SOUTH OF THE ZÓCALO: The new **Hotel Canada,** Avenida Cinco de Mayo 47, México, D.F. 06000 (tel. 905/518-2106), near the intersection with Avenida Isabel la Católica, opened in 1984. Its location is very good, its decor and comforts right up-to-date. The 85 new rooms come with TV sets, piped-in music, double beds (one or two of them), tile showers, and telephones, all for 3,000 pesos ($6) single, 3,300 pesos ($6.60) for two persons in a double bed, 3,600 pesos ($7.20) for two in two double beds. You should definitely take a look at this shiny new place, so different from the rest of the downtown hotels, which tend to be older and somewhat worn.

Midway between the Zócalo and the Alameda Central, that's the location of the 140-room **Best Western Hotel Ritz,** at Avenida Madero 30, México, D.F. 06000 (tel. 915/518-1340). Rooms, priced right at the top of our budget, come with television, private baths (tubs), and a comfy feeling. There's no parking right in or near the hotel, but a valet will take your car and store it for a fee. If you don't have a car, or like to walk, you're well-situated here as the Ritz is within walking distance of half of Mexico City's points of interest. Rooms cost 6,500 pesos ($13) single, 7,000 pesos ($14) double, tax included.

Bronze statuettes cradling cut-glass lamps set the tone at the entrance of the **Hotel Gillow,** Isabel la Católica 17 at the corner of Cinco de Mayo, México, D.F. 06000 (tel. 905/518-1440). It's a dignified old establishment built during an

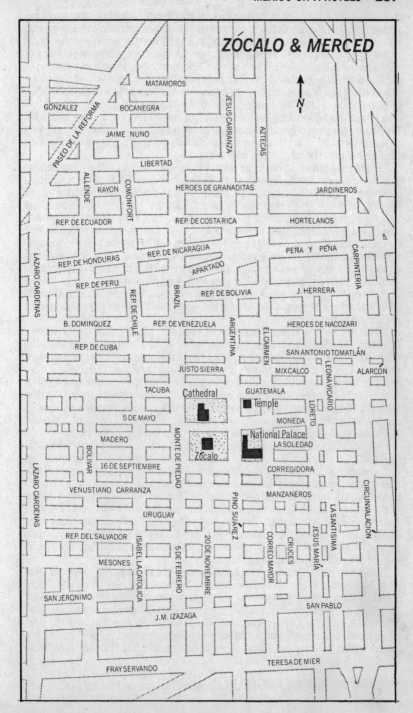

ZÓCALO & MERCED

N

MATAMOROS

GONZALEZ   BOCANEGRA

PASEO DE LA REFORMA

JAIME NUNO

JESUS CARRANZA

AZTECAS

LIBERTAD

ALLENDE

RAYON

COMONFORT

HEROES DE GRANADITAS

JARDINEROS

REP. DE ECUADOR   REP. DE COSTA RICA   HORTELANOS

LAZARO CARDENAS

REP. DE HONDURAS   REP. DE NICARAGUA   PEÑA Y PEÑA

CARPINTERIA

APARTADO

REP. DE PERU

REP. DE CHILE

BRAZIL

REP. DE BOLIVIA   J. HERRERA

B. DOMINQUEZ   REP. DE VENEZUELA

ARGENTINA

HEROES DE NACOZARI

REP. DE CUBA

EL CARMEN

SAN ANTONIO TOMATLÁN

JUSTO SIERRA   MIXCALCO   LEONA VICARIO   ALARCON

TACUBA

Cathedral   GUATEMALA

Temple

LORETO

5 DE MAYO   MONEDA

MADERO

BOLIVAR

National Palace

LA SOLEDAD

Zócalo

16 DE SEPTIEMBRE   CORREGIDORA

MONTE DE PIEDAD

VENUSTIANO CARRANZA   MANZANEROS

LAZARO CARDENAS

URUGUAY

CIRCUNNVALACION

PINO SUAREZ

LA SANTISIMA

REP. DEL SALVADOR

ISABEL LA CATOLICA

CRUCES

CORREO MAYOR

JESUS MARIA

MESONES

5 DE FEBRERO

20 DE NOVIEMBRE

SAN JERONIMO

SAN PABLO

J.M. IZAZAGA

FRAY SERVANDO   TERESA DE MIER

era when space was not at a premium: nearly every room boasts a small entrance hall. Tall French doors open onto tiny balconies from the exterior rooms. All 115 rooms are comfortably furnished in a modern style with carpeting, boldly patterned bedspreads, newish furniture, and telephone, and a good many of the bathrooms are equipped with a tub. They even follow the curious custom of putting a white paper band bearing the words "Sterilized for your Protection" across toilet and washbasin. Rooms come in several sizes and prices, from 3,500 to 3,750 pesos ($7 to $7.50) single, 3,750 to 4,370 pesos ($7.50 to $8.74) double, which puts the Gillow well within our budget range. The restaurant, handy for breakfast eggs and coffee, also serves a six-course comida corrida featuring such delectables as oyster cocktail, enchiladas suizas, and paella a la valenciana for a reasonable 1,600 pesos ($3.20), plus tax and tip.

Farther south along the same street (and therefore not quite so convenient) you'll come upon the four-story **Hotel Isabel,** Isabel la Católica 63 at Calle El Salvador, México, D.F. 06000 (tel. 905/518-1213), an older place with a mix of Mexican and foreign clientele. In the lobby, a somber painting of Queen Isabel gazes out over the vast lobby while guests gaze at the TV set on the mantelpiece just below the queen. (You can rent a set for your room for an extra charge.) Comforts include an elevator, a good restaurant and bar, and all-day room service. Each of the 72 rooms is old-fashioned and spacious, with dark wood or painted furniture, carpeting, telephone, and tile bath. Larger rooms have tubs as well as showers, little tiled entrance halls, and frosted-glass doors opening onto wrought-iron balconies. No garage, sad to say. Rates are 2,980 pesos ($5.96) single, 3,220 pesos ($6.44) double, with bath. You can wangle yourself a reduction if they're not full.

The four-story **Hotel Concordia,** Uruguay 13 just off Avenida Lázaro Cárdenas, México, D.F. 06000 (tel. 905/510-4100), is only two blocks from the Latin American Tower, the Bellas Artes, and the Alameda—a very convenient location. The multipillared lobby is at the end of a corridor. The 55 rooms are old but decently kept, all have a bath, some have both a tub and shower. The hotel boasts that it is *"totalmente alfombrado"* ("completely carpeted"). Besides the ubiquitous carpeting, there is an elevator and a garage for guests with cars. Rates at the Concordia are 1,800 pesos ($3.60) single, 2,000 to 2,300 pesos ($4 to $4.60) double, the latter double-room price being for twin beds.

Next choice is the **Hotel El Salvador,** República del Salvador 16, México, D.F. 06000 (tel. 905/510-0870 or 512-5267), a five-story hotel of 91 rooms just half a block off Lázaro Cárdenas. Look for a glass front broken by marble balconies. Inside, up a few marble steps, the monastically bare lobby is a world of red carpeting, low furniture, and wood paneling. The rooms, all sunny, are suffused in a pleasantly soothing monochromatic tan color scheme—TV sets, Formica furnishings, tan bed throws, drapes, and carpeting. Naturally there are telephones, hot and cold bathrooms. Rates are 4,200 pesos ($8.40) single, 4,600 pesos ($9.20) double. There's a good though simple little restaurant. Free parking in the hotel's subterranean garage.

Just two blocks south of the Zócalo stands the **Hotel Roble,** Avenida Uruguay 109 near the corner of Pino Suárez, México, D.F. 06060 (tel. 905/518-1000). It's not a place for sybaritic sorts and its accommodations could best be described as functional, but the odd-shaped rooms all have private shower and TV, and even manage to be cheerful. The hotel has an elevator, and the area nearby has lots of restaurants and several parking garages. The 40 rooms are well priced at 2,300 to 2,500 pesos ($4.60 to $5) single, 2,500 to 2,800 pesos ($5 to $5.60) double.

STARVATION-BUDGET HOTELS: Between Bolívar and Isabel la Católica, and parallel to these streets, is a short street named Motolinía. At Motolinía 40, near the corner with 16 de Septiembre, is the **Hotel Lafayette,** México, D.F. 06000 (tel. 905/521-9640), an older building kept up-to-date through renovation and patronized mostly by Mexican travelers. Not much English is spoken here, but with patience the staff will figure out your wants. You're right in the center of shopping here, on a pedestrians-only street. Rooms cost 1,800 pesos ($3.60) single, 2,100 to 2,400 pesos ($4.20 to $4.80) double.

One of the funniest looking hotels in all of Mexico is the **Hotel Monte Carlo,** Uruguay 69, México, D.F. 06000 (tel. 905/585-1222), where you once could drive through the front doors and the lobby to reach the garage. An old place with an interior courtyard, red iron stair railings, and a curved marble stairway, it was built about 1772 as an Augustinian monastery, and afterward was the residence of D. H. Lawrence for a time. The 35 rooms with bath are quite large and are equipped with telephones; some have little balconies. The 25 rooms without bath—they're small, perhaps built as cells or prayer rooms—have hot running water, and are furnished with whatever odd bits and pieces will fit in. Prices at the Monte Carlo are 1,400 pesos ($2.80) single, 1,650 pesos ($3.30) double for a room without bath; 1,750 pesos ($3.50) single, 1,950 pesos ($3.90) double for a room with bath. The manager won't take reservations over the phone—you have to show up in person to claim a room. (Under repair.)

The **Hotel Ontario,** República de Uruguay 87 at the corner of 5 de Febrero, México, D.F. 06000 (tel. 905/521-0952 or 521-0593), is a plainish and modest place, although the entryway and lobby seem to heighten the tone somewhat. You have a choice of rooms and suites here, priced at 2,000 pesos ($4) for a double bed (one or two persons), and 2,200 pesos ($4.40) for twin beds. The location isn't bad.

READER'S HOTEL SELECTION—ZÓCALO: "Without a doubt, the **Hotel Juárez,** Cerradas Cinco de Mayo 17, between Isabel la Católica and Palma (tel. 905/510-3175), is the best find in town for 3,800 pesos ($7.60) double. Broadloom carpet, televisions, telephones, marble bathrooms, pine furniture—but ask for a room with windows" (Catherine Parker-Nance, Hawkestone, Ontario, Canada).

THE BIG SPLURGE—STAYING RIGHT ON THE ZÓCALO: If you're feeling flush, the full amount of our $20-a-day budget will get you a room overlooking the Zócalo at the **Hotel Majestic,** Avenida Madero 73, México, D.F. 06000 (tel. 905/521-8600). A hotel of the Hostales de México group, the Majestic has 85 rooms that look onto Mexico City's main square, the Avenida Madero, or the hotel's own inner court. The attractiveness of the hotel starts with its lobby, a place of stone arches, brilliant tiles, and warm colors, plus a pleasantly gurgling little stone fountain at the far end. On the second floor is the courtyard, with a floor of glass blocks (actually the ceiling of the lobby) set with sofas, tables, and chairs, and decorated with pots of vines and hanging plants all the way up to the glass roof six stories above.

Nice touches of art and color are everywhere: each room doorway has a border of blue-and-white tiles to lighten the darkness of the heavy, colonial-style doors. Inside the rooms, however, colonialism is left behind in favor of pastel colors, simple and attractive decors, and newly redone tile bathrooms with tubs. On the lower floors facing the Avenida Madero noise from the street may be a problem—and you may not go for the rooms that look out onto the interior court (because people look in on *you!*)—but on the upper floors and in the rooms that front on the Zócalo you needn't worry. The finishing touch to the Majestic's luxury offering is a rooftop café-restaurant in which you can choose a table shaded by a bright-yellow umbrella for breakfast or just a drink or a cup of tea. For all this comfort and class, the prices are surprisingly moderate: single rooms cost 7,700 pesos ($15.40); double rooms are 8,800 pesos ($17.60).

HOTELS NORTH AND EAST OF THE ZÓCALO: Although not quite so convenient as my other accommodations areas, this one can be said to harbor the best of the bargains—hotels that would cost sometimes twice as much if they were located in a classier neighborhood. This is by no means a classy neighborhood, but no one can say it's not interesting: hardware stores, record shops, used-book stores, and pharmacies specializing in herbal and homeopathic remedies abound. There are enough tiny *taquerías* to feed the entire *Ejercito Nacional* (Mexican army) at one sitting, and enough streetlife to keep a squad of urban sociologists busy for years. Ignore the chipping paint and crumbling plaster here —everybody else does—and concentrate on the surprising bargains to be had in the way of accommodations and parking.

Urban renewal is slowly coming to this section, and besides new government offices going up you will see work crews restoring ancient churches, monasteries, and houses affected by sinkage. Calle de la Moneda is now a nice pedestrians-only street. The lake bottom upon which Mexico City was built is particularly soft here, and so huge old façades, steeples, and bell-towers lean and lurch at crazy angles. Somehow it reminds one of Venice (which has a similar problem with sinkage) and adds to the area's interest.

One block north of Tacuba is Calle Donceles, a street noted for its gunsmith shops. Here, set back from the street by a passageway lined with stores, is the six-story **Hotel Catedral,** Donceles 95, México, D.F. 06010 (tel. 905/518-5232), very popular with Mexico's middle class. Behind the big cool lobby is the hotel's restaurant-bar, bustling with white-jacketed waiters and featuring a special luncheon at around $2. The 140 rooms are well kept, equipped with telephones and private baths, some of which have tubs. Rates are 3,100 pesos ($6.20) single, 3,400 pesos ($6.80) double. Bonuses here are a parking garage next door, exceptionally high housekeeping standards, and rooms on the upper floors with views of the great rockpile which is Mexico City's cathedral.

Another fantastic bargain is the **Hotel Antillas,** Belisario Dominguez 34, México, D.F. 06010 (tel. 905/526-5674), with rooms priced at 2,875 pesos ($5.75) single, 3,150 pesos ($6.30) double. The Antillas is rather old-world, a five-story study in burnished red lava block with huge plate-glass windows hung with rust drapes. Inside, the lobby is lit by black wrought-iron chandeliers. It has a lot of charm. The 70 rooms, all with telephone and private bath, are extraordinarily large and very clean, with lots of new paint and new furniture. Parking is free, making it an excellent choice if you have a car. Without, it's a short walk to a main transportation artery.

The Antillas is a top choice of Mexican families, and is one of the best hotels—for the price—anywhere in the city. Prices are low because the area is dingy—but urban renewal has already begun.

8. Hotels Near Bus, Train, and Air Terminals

It might just happen that you'll arrive in this dauntingly large city late at night, or very tired, or both. In this case, you might want to go directly to the nearest suitable hotel, stay a night or two, and then find a better or more conveniently located place to stay. Well, here are the good places near the bustling terminals.

HOTELS NEAR THE AIRPORT: Mexico City's Benito Juárez International Airport is big, new, shiny-clean, and well run, but it's no place to spend the night. You can turn left out the terminal doors and walk a block to the local

Holiday Inn Mexico City–Airport, Boulevard Puerto Aereo 502 (tel. 905/762-4088). Do this only if you want to blow half a week's budget on one night's lodging, however, as the Holiday Inn charges about $50 single, $65 double for a room.

The **Hotel Riazor,** Viaducto Miguel Aleman 297 (tel. 905/657-4470), is only a short cab ride from the airport. You can take shelter in any of their 175 modern, comfy rooms complete with king-size bed, television set, telephone, tile shower, and perhaps even a view of the city. For the privilege, you'll pay 8,000 pesos ($16), single or double.

A HOTEL NEAR BUENA VISTA RAILROAD STATION: An excellent value,

that's the fairly new **Hotel La Riviera,** Calle Aldama 9 at Orozco y Berra (tel. 905/566-3611), half a block from Puente de Alvarado and only three blocks south of Buena Vista station. It offers a good many features of larger and more expensive establishments: air conditioning and heating, music in every room, and free parking. Look for a pink tile façade; inside, the lobby glistens with marble and one wall is given over to a mosaic mural of the Mediterranean coast. The hallways are laid with red carpets, as are the rooms, which are furnished in "motel Formica." Everything is light and airy. The hotel's restaurant—the only hotel that has one for blocks around, incidentally—serves combination breakfasts, a special set-price lunch, and is open from 7 a.m. to 11 p.m. every day. Rates are 4,500 pesos ($9) single, 5,500 pesos ($11) double.

A HOTEL NEAR THE TERMINAL NORTE: Say you've just arrived in the bus

terminal after a trip of 1,000 miles and you emerge from your bus in almost a liquid state, unable to face the prospect of searching for a hotel. Good news: The **Hotel Brasilia** (tel. 905/587-8577) provides luxurious refuge for travelers only 2½ blocks from the terminal. The modern V-shaped hotel is at Avenida de los Cien Metros 4823—go out the doors of the terminal, turn left, and walk the short distance. The hotel sign is visible from the terminal and assures you of the proper direction. Up the flashy black-and-white marble steps is a haven of piped-in FM music (three channels), air conditioning, polite service, hot baths, and a well-stocked bar and restaurant. You may even have color TV in your room. Prices for the 200 rooms and suites vary with sleeping accommodations, and run 5,000 pesos ($10) single, 7,000 pesos ($14) double (for two people in a double bed). You may even consider spending two nights here if you're just passing through Mexico City, but for any longer stays you should move downtown.

9. Apartment Hotels

Years ago Mexico City could boast of several apartment hotels, a type of establishment just now catching on up north. Apartment hotels have the best of both worlds: the privacy, space, and cooking facilities of an apartment, and the convenience and services of a hotel.

Apartment hotels, often called *suites* (soo-*wee*-tess) are found in several city districts, but mostly in and near the Zona Rosa. Who stays here? Families, businessmen, and consultants on extended stays; people waiting to find houses or permanent apartments; tourists staying for a week or more. Some apartment hotels rent by the day, but preferential rates really come into play with stays of a week or more.

The **Hotel Suites Michelangelo,** Río Amazonas 78 (between Calle Río Lerma and Paseo de la Reforma), México, D.F. 06500 (tel. 905/566-9877), has 40 suites with one or two bedrooms, living room, dining area, television, private telephone line, kitchenette with refrigerator, bathroom, and closet. The area, just north of the Zona Rosa and near the British and American embassies, is quiet and residential. By the day, rates are 11,270 pesos ($22.54) per day for two persons; the rate drops 5% if you stay two weeks, and 35% or 40% if you stay a month. Two people can pay as little as 5,850 pesos ($11.70) per day for a month's stay, depending on the size of the apartment. You can rent by the day if you wish too.

The **Suites Imperiales Niza,** Calle Niza 73, México, D.F. 06600 (tel. 905/511-9540), right in the Zona Rosa, is quite deluxe. A high-rise with balconies on each room, the decor stresses dark wood paneling and a "formal" feel of luxury. Complete apartments for two people cost about 9,000 pesos ($18) per day (by the day), or 7,000 pesos ($14) per day (by the month). (Under repair.)

FINDING A REAL APARTMENT: What if you're planning a truly lengthy stay, of several months? The first place to look is in the classified ads section of *The News*. This will give you an idea of the choice neighborhoods and the going rates. To save money, you might then dust off your Spanish and look at the similar sections in the Spanish-language dailies. As landlords advertising in *The News* will obviously be catering to foreigners, their rents may well be higher than the norm.

Another good idea is to make the rounds of the bulletin boards at the various language schools, cultural centers, and other places where foreigners congregate. Sublet and rental notices often find permanent places on such bulletin boards.

READER'S APARTMENT HOTEL SELECTION: "For our first month in Mexico we found the **Suites Riviera,** Juan de la Barrera 66, off Av. Mazatlán, near Metro Chapultepec. We paid $20 a day (on a monthly basis) for two bedrooms, a combination kitchenette–dining room–sitting room, and tile bathroom with shower. Telephone, maid service, and underground parking were included. Accommodations were spartan but functional and efficient" (Prof. Irwin Rovner, Raleigh, N.C.).

Chapter VIII

MEXICO CITY: MEALS ON A BUDGET

**1. About Mexican Restaurants
2. In and Near the Zona Rosa
3. Near Jardín del Arte/Revolución
4. Near the Alameda and Bellas Artes
5. In the Zócalo Area**

EVERYBODY EATS OUT in Mexico, from the wealthy executive to the peasant. Consequently you can find restaurants of every type, size, and price range scattered across the city. There are so many restaurants here, most of them good, that to cover all of them would be impossible. I get numerous letters each year from readers who have discovered another great restaurant, and indeed they have and so can you. Therefore, what I have tried to do in this section is give you a list of some of the tried-and-true establishments, on side streets and behind café curtains; I have sifted through a myriad of restaurants and have listed those that will give you the best food for the best price within the appropriate class: medium-priced, splurge, budget, and specialty.

I have not included here the various American-type chains such as Burger Boy, Pizza Hut, Vip's, Denny's, Woolworth's, and Tastee-Freez, as they have standard and familiar fare which, although good to cure a bout of homesickness, tends to be a good deal more expensive than Mexican food for what you get.

1. About Mexican Restaurants

Mexico City is a diner's delight, but to enjoy it fully, and at the best possible price, one must know about Mexican restaurants and dining habits.

The best bet for breakfast is a place which offers a set price for bacon and eggs, juice, toast, and coffee, for example. Breakfast can be very expensive if you end up ordering your hotcakes, or eggs, or cereal à la carte.

THE COMIDA CORRIDA: Remember that Mexicans have their biggest meal of the day in the afternoon between 1 and 4 p.m., and that many restaurants offer a set-price lunch called a *comida corrida,* or *cubierto,* at a price much, much lower than the four or five courses would cost if priced à la carte. Take advantage of the comida corrida for it's the biggest money-saver in Mexico, and then have a light supper in the evening. Be sure to get to the restaurant between about 1 and 4, or they won't serve you at the special price.

Comidas corridas can range in price anywhere from about $1 to $4 or $5, but by no means are all comidas the same. For the ultimate in high-level dining and low-level spending, you've got to compare menus. A $3 comida that starts with oyster stew and goes on to sautéed trout and carne asada, finishing up with fettuccine Alfredo and pêche Melba with coffee, is an indisputable bargain. But a meal for the same price that lists chicken broth, enchiladas, rice, pudding, and a soft drink is clearly a rip-off. Read carefully.

TAXES AND TIPPING: Mexico's 15% IVA tax, levied on everything from diapers to dirigibles, is now hidden in the price of every menu item, by law. You will probably see a notice on the menu such as "IVA Incluido" or "Estos precios incluyen el Impuesto de Valor Agregado." What this means is that the waiter is no longer authorized to add that 15% tax to the total of your bill. Businesses don't like this provision of the law; they want the customer to see what they charge for food, and what the government charges in tax. A few protest the law by refusing to comply with it. But others hide the IVA in their prices and then also charge unsuspecting tourists an extra 15%. If you see such an extra charge on your restaurant bill, question it.

Want a rule of thumb to estimate your restaurant tab? Select your main course, double its price, and—excluding wine and drinks—you've got a pretty fair estimate of the total bill you'll pay.

In the more expensive restaurants, particularly in the Zona Rosa, you'll be able to pay with a major credit card. Bonus: The charge won't show up on your bill at home for a month or more.

For tipping suggestions, see Chapter XVII under "Tipping."

2. In and Near the Zona Rosa

The select area known as the Zona Rosa is clearly defined: bounded by Insurgentes, Chapultepec, and the Reforma. Within this compound there are more charming restaurants than almost anywhere else in the world. You can find any type of food or ambience from the café set to the taco stand. As someone once remarked about the Zona Rosa, it reminds everyone of somewhere back home.

Shirley's (tel. 514-7760), famous for its very pleasant and successful main location on Reforma, has a branch in the Pink Zone at Londres 102, open 7:30 a.m. to 11:30 p.m. daily, Friday and Saturday nights till 1 a.m. Vaguely western in decor following that at the main restaurant, diners sit in red booths or captain's chairs as they pore over the long menu of appetizers, soups, salads, sandwiches, Mexican specialties, meats, fish, side orders, and desserts. There's a daily luncheon buffet for only 1,500 pesos ($3), slightly more on Sunday. Although it appears very American, Shirley's is patronized most heavily by Mexicans who know good food and service, and who want it at a reasonable price. Note that here in the Pink Zone you can order wine or beer with your dinner.

If you wander around the Zona Rosa long enough, eventually you'll discover the **passageway**, entered at Londres 104 or Genova 74, which harbors a half-dozen restaurants. Most of these have some sidewalk tables, and all benefit from the lack of street noise.

The long-running favorite in the passage is **Alfredo** (tel. 511-3864), where lowly pasta takes on noble proportions, and other Italian specialties crowd the menu. The clientele is mostly from the business community, the service is polished, and the food is delicious. Pasta dishes (huge portions) go for around 1,200 pesos ($2.40), items like veal scaloppine or fresh seafood for about 2,000 to

2,500 pesos ($4 to $5). You'll like it here. By the way, Alfredo also owns La Trucha Vagabunda, right by the passage entrance at Londres 104, but I prefer the original restaurant deep in the passage.

The **Mesón del Perro Andaluz** (tel. 533-5306), Copenhague 28, very near the Hotel Aristos, has two levels inside, a few outdoor tables (always crowded in the evenings), and a very loyal clientele. Although prices in the evening are fairly high, with such delicious things as duck in olive sauce *(pato a la aceituna)* and similar items going for 2,000 to 3,700 pesos ($4 to $7.40), the luncheon specials at 1,500 to 2,400 pesos ($3 to $4.80) make it especially attractive for a midday meal. Try the tuna and avocado salad or a bowl of the hearty minestrone soup. Note that entrees come ungarnished (without vegetables or salad). They have wine, both Mexican and imported. The Mesón del Perro Andaluz is open from 1 p.m. to 1 a.m. daily; arrive early in the evening if you want a seat at one of the café tables out front.

FOR MEXICAN SPECIALTIES: The **Fonda El Refugio** (tel. 528-5823), Liverpool 166, near the corner of Liverpool and Florencia, is a very special place to dine *a la mexicana*. Although small, it's unusually congenial with natural blond wood floors, a large fireplace decorated with gleaming copper pots and pans, and rows and rows of culinary awards and citations behind the desk. It manages the almost impossible task of being elegant and informal at the same time.

Service is careful, efficient, and extremely polite, and the menu is one that runs the gamut of Mexican cuisine. You can run part way by having a sopa de verduras (vegetable soup), then perhaps arroz con plátanos (rice with fried bananas), or perhaps tamales de elote con pollo (fresh corn tamales with chicken); for a main course, you can try the chalupas poblanas (tortillas topped with chicken, onions, cheese, lettuce, and green chile sauce), or perhaps enchiladas con mole poblano, topped with the rich, thick, spicy chocolate sauce of Puebla. Desserts are the authentic traditional ones, like sweet marzipan figurines and "camotes" (delicate cylinders of a flavorful sweet potato paste). Wine, liquor, and beer are served, and if you go all-out and order whatever you like, plus a half bottle of wine, the check should come to something like 3,500 to 5,000 pesos ($7 to $10) per person. You can dine for not much more than half that, though, if you like. The Fonda El Refugio is very popular, especially on a Saturday night, so get there early—remember, it's small.

Close by is another popular place with a very reasonable menu; it's **La Carretta Rosa** (tel. 514-3444), Hamburgo 96—you'll recognize it by the painting of the wagon over the pink door and two large wagon wheels that flank the tiled entrance. This is a down-home place patronized by Mexicans homesick for real country cooking: menudo (tripe soup), pozole (meat-and-hominy stew), chicharrón (pork crackling), and tacos of grilled or roasted meat. Specialty plates abound, mostly featuring northern cuisine. You can spend as little as 1,100 pesos ($2.20) or as much as 3,500 pesos ($7), but the average bill is more like 2,000 pesos ($4). Jukebox, fluorescent lights, hefty señoras—you might as well be in some small Sonoran ranching town.

FOR CRÊPES: The specialty at **La Crepa Suiza** (tel. 511-3734), Florencia 33 between Hamburgo and Londres, is crêpes, of course, but that's not all. Diners crowd the few tables set out in the courtyard off Florencia, and the cozy indoor dining room, for a plentiful luncheon buffet costing 1,900 pesos ($1.80), served from 1 to 5 p.m. After that, you must order à la carte: dinner crêpes with various delicious stuffings (including cactus or pumpkin flower!) cost 800 to 1,400 pesos ($1.60 to $2.80), dessert crêpes are half that price. For more filling fare, you can't miss with the fondue bourguinonne: succulent morsels of beef which you

can cook yourself in a pot of hot oil, and then dip into any of six different sauces. With garlic bread, the fondue is 2,000 pesos ($4) for two people. La Crepa Suiza is open for breakfast daily, as well.

JAPANESE FOOD: Mexico's trade with Japan is burgeoning, as is the number of Japanese businessmen who visit the city. This has led to a healthy, and very welcome, growth in the number of restaurants serving Japanese cuisine. My favorite is the **Restaurant Tokyo** (tel. 525-3775), at Hamburgo 134, corner of Amberes, on the second floor. Be sure to glance at the "models" of sample meals set out in the glass cabinet by the entryway. Upstairs, the mood is soothing, with quiet Japanese Muzak and a spare but comely decor. You may not believe how friendly the staff is. Start with a "Princess Kiku," a refined rocket fuel made of sake and cherry liqueur, the sweetness of the liqueur being cut by the sake's salt-bitterness. Sukiyaki, shabu-shabu (vegetables in beef broth, cooked at your table), tempura, and sashimi (raw fish) are all offered. For best value, order one of the set meals at 1,500 to 2,200 pesos ($3 to $4.40). Even the cheapest is a treat. Open every day from 12:30 p.m. to midnight, Sunday from 2 to 10 p.m.

FOR DANISH DESSERTS: Café Konditori (tel. 511-1589), Genova 61, near Londres in the Zona Rosa, advertises itself as a Danish restaurant and coffee shop. Though it's not what you'd call aggressively Danish, it does have a very pleasant sidewalk café section. In good weather (which is nearly always), you can sit out in the open air; if there's a shower, sit under the tent, or by a window in the restaurant proper. The cappuccino comes in a glass with a metal holder— very European—and the perfect accompaniment for it is one of the Konditori's luscious cakes or tarts. Be sure to inspect the dessert display before you sit down. Coffee and dessert will set you back about 1,000 pesos ($2). They have a full restaurant menu here as well. The café is open for breakfast, lunch, and dinner every day.

FOR PIZZA: Pizza Real, Genova 28 (tel. 511-8834), at the corner of Estrasburgo, boasts that it serves 50 different varieties of pizza, priced at 300 to 2,500 pesos (60¢ to $5), depending on size and toppings. The "Infante" size is enough for one person. They even serve a selection of five comidas corridas featuring soup, fruit salad, pizza, dessert, and coffee, or in the more expensive comidas, an Italian entree such as ravioli. Although it is billed as a pizza joint, Pizza Real is half pizza parlor, half Italian restaurant, with wide black-and-white stripes on the brick walls, yellow tablecloths, and a pizza-cutting counter by the front door. It's open from 8 a.m. to 11:30 p.m. Monday through Saturday, 1 to 11:30 p.m. on Sunday. Liquor is served.

FOR AFTERNOON TEA: The Zona Rosa would have to have some fine places for afternoon tea as they serve it on the continent, and the finest I've found yet is **Auseba,** Hamburgo 159-B at Florencia (tel. 511-3769), which serves pastries and candies along with its tea and coffee. The glass cases hold the most delicious-looking display of cookies, meringues, bonbons, cakes, pies, puddings, and *tortas* I've ever seen in the city. Paintings decorate one wall, fancy candy boxes another, and the little circular tables with white cloths all have modern black plastic chairs—eclectic, but comfortable. Pastries cost about 450 to 550 pesos (90¢ to $1.10), coffee or tea is about half that much; you can get away with spending only 550 pesos ($1.10) for coffee and croissants or you can spend twice as much for a rich pastry and Viennese coffee. Auseba is open daily for breakfast, and stays open until about 10:30 p.m. On Sunday, the hours are 11 a.m. to 10:30 p.m.

Very near Auseba, right on the corner of Florencia and Hamburgo, is the **Duca d'Este,** another *salon de té* with a rich decor, and prices to match.

SPECIALTY RESTAURANTS: At least half of my friends in Mexico swear that **Chalet Suizo,** Niza 37, between Hamburgo and Londres (tel. 511-7529), is the most dependable restaurant around. The decor is Swiss, of course, with checked tablecloths, enormous wooden horns, and Alpine landscapes; the service is good. The menu features hearty French onion soup for 800 pesos ($1.60), and a wide range of interesting entrees, some of which are changed daily, for 1,200 to 1,500 pesos ($2.40 to $3); among these are sausages with sauerkraut, smoked pork chops, baby veal tongue, sauerbraten, and excellent fondue. Wine is served. Open from about 12:30 p.m. to midnight daily. Menu in English.

Of the café-restaurants on the pedestrian street called Copenhague, in the Zona Rosa, the one with the best prices is **La Camello Rosa** (tel. 528-5108), Copenhague 25. As Copenhague developed into a place to see and be seen, prices climbed ever upward. But sit at one of the Camello Rosa's sidewalk tables, order filet mignon with mushrooms, or jumbo shrimp, and you'll pay only 3,200 pesos ($6.40) for your entree—and these are the most expensive dishes on the menu. Most of the seafood, meats, and Mexican specialties cost a good deal less, so you can lunch or dine here for about 3,500 pesos ($7), all included.

The place to go for steak is the **Restaurant Angus** (tel. 525-3825), in the Zona Rosa at Copenhague 21, corner of Hamburgo. If you're not lucky enough to grab one of the sidewalk tables on the café-street of Copenhague, take a seat in the woody bar behind, or in the attractive dining rooms upstairs. The decor is western, but restrained and refined. The steaks range from T-bone at 1,800 pesos ($3.60) to prime rib at 3,600 pesos ($7.20), and there are delights such as barbecued spare ribs at 1,500 pesos ($3) as well. The Angus is open every day for lunch and dinner.

Luau (tel. 525-7474), Niza 38, is a Chinese-Polynesian restaurant in the heart of the Zona Rosa and its prices reflect it. But the food is excellent and sometimes nothing else will taste as good as sweet-and-sour pork spare ribs or wonton soup. Combination dinners cost anywhere from 1,500 to 2,500 pesos ($3 to $5). It's an attractive restaurant with a goldfish pond, rock garden with a waterfall, and other amusements. Open noon to midnight.

Mexicans are fond of vegetarian and health-food restaurants. The most convenient one in the Zona Rosa is the **Restaurante Vegetariano Yug** (tel. 533-3296), Varsovia 3 at Reforma. This upbeat, modern place offers several set-price breakfasts, a dozen fantastic salads (the "Africa" features spinach and nuts), plus crêpes, spinach lasagne, and soya "meat" Mexican style. Portions are huge, prices are low. Figure to spend 500 to 1,000 pesos ($1 to $2) for breakfast, 1,000 to 2,000 ($2 to $4) for lunch or dinner. Closed Sunday.

STARVATION-BUDGET FOOD: You can eat for very little, even in the fashionable and pricey Zona Rosa, by pointing your appetite in the direction of the noble taco. **Tacos Beatriz** (no phone), Londres 179 at Florencia, sells them for 120 to 200 pesos (24¢ to 40¢) apiece, depending on filling. Choose chicken or steak, or more adventurous delights such as chicharron guisado (stewed pork crackling), barbacoa (barbecue), or nopales (tender prickly pear cactus leaves). They serve soups here as well. Closed Sunday.

NORTH OF REFORMA: The area north of Reforma and south of Melchor Ocampo is mostly residential, so there is not a great number of restaurants. Among the few, the best for your money is the **Restaurant Rhin** (no phone), Río

Rhin 49 at Río Panuco, one of those terrific little neighborhood restaurants every travel writer dreams of discovering. The Rhin is a modern place. The tables are dressed in red, the waiters are in natty black-and-white uniforms. I always try to order the 600- to 750- peso ($1.20 to $1.50) comida, but one look at the menu and I invariably weaken in favor of the Rhin's enchiladas Suizas, a little triumph of tortillas in a creamy sauce stuffed with Swiss cheese for 500 pesos ($1). Needless to say, they're soothing to pepper-pricked tummies, besides being delightfully tasty. There are plenty of other Mexican plates—lots of tacos, etc.—as well as such comforts as soup, and even filet mignon. Open 8:30 a.m. to 9:30 p.m.

On the same street, tucked away in the area of the British Embassy, is the little **Cafetería Marianne,** Río Rhin 63, a few blocks north of the Reforma-Insurgentes intersection (tel. 528-7289), where the atmosphere is European-coffeehouse and the specialty is pastries and cappuccino, but they also serve an excellent three-course lunch for 590 pesos ($1.18). Open 9 a.m. to 9 p.m. daily.

Las Fuentes (tel. 525-0629), Panuco 127 at Tiber, two blocks north of the Angel Monument, is another branch of the "Restaurant Vegetariano y Dietetico." This is the most modern and luxurious of the three, on the ground floor of a large building. More expensive than the other two, it's still well worth the money you pay for what you get. The daily set-price lunch costs 2,200 pesos ($4.40), but huge portions are the rule, and for that price you may enjoy lentil soup, carrot- and potato-filled tacos with apple salad, a side order of peas or beans, then coffee or tea and whole-wheat-and-honey cookies. Las Fuentes is open daily from 8:30 a.m. to 11:30 p.m., till 10:30 p.m. on Sunday. Highly recommended.

A Pastelería-Deli

North of Reforma, at the corner of Río Lerma and Río Sena, is a handy pastryshop-deli, just the thing for do-it-yourself breakfasts and snacks. The **Del Angel** has one of the best assortments of rolls, danish, cookies, cold meats, and drinks I've encountered in the capital. Prices are a bit higher than at pastelerías in less wealthy sections, but you can still make a paper bag heavy with goodies here and pay less than 600 pesos ($1.20). By the way, the full name of this place has got to establish some sort of record for length. According to the sign, it's the "Dulcería, Pastelería, Bizcochería, Salchichonería, Abarrotes Vinos y Licores Gastronómica Del Angel"!

3. Near Jardín del Arte/Revolución

The Pink Zone siphons off the carriage trade from surrounding areas, and what's left are mostly little eateries good for breakfast or incredibly inexpensive comidas corridas. Out of Reforma are a few classier places, including the dependably satisfying Shirley's—but more of that later. First, for some cheap lunches.

NEAR THE JARDÍN: The **Restaurant America** (no phone), on Villalongin facing the Jardín del Arte, half a block in from Insurgentes, serves a 800-peso ($1.60) comida that's worth every centavo and more. The small room (eight tables only) is almost always close to full with diners-who-know. My test meal started with delicious mushroom soup, went on to "espaguetti ala francesa" (spaghetti with a sauce of cheese and butter), a choice of three main-course dishes—beef, pork, or chicken—ice cream or good pastry, and coffee or tea. Such a feast is served daily between 1 and 5:15 p.m.

If you're staying in this area, or find yourself near the intersection of Reforma and Insurgentes, walk west along Villalongin (which skirts the southern edge of the Jardín del Arte), turn left and walk through the little plaza bearing a bust of Giuseppe Verdi, and you'll come to the Calle Río Lerma. A half block southwest of Lerma, on the right-hand side, is the **Restaurant Nucleo,** Río Lerma 5 at the corner of Río Marne, a small and simple restaurant worth a walk because of its two daily comidas corridas, one costing 550 pesos ($1.10), the other 650 pesos ($1.30). For the lower price you might get a cream soup, rice, charcoal-grilled beef, frijoles, and dessert; for the higher price you get a wider selection of main courses and slightly larger portions. The Nucleo is very popular with young office workers, and is sometimes crowded, but seats seem to come available quickly, and sharing tables with strangers is the custom here. The restaurant is open for breakfast and supper as well, but it's closed Sunday.

A Good Little Japanese Place

Daruma (tel. 546-3467), a Japanese restaurant not far from the intersection of Insurgentes and Reforma at Río Tamesis 6 (where Tamesis meets Finlay and Villalongin), is a bit hard to find but worth the effort. Informal as can be, the boys cook behind the sashimi bar while mom totals up the bills and makes change. The lunch counter and small tables are of heavy natural wood, however, and like the rest of the simple furnishings impart a good deal of dignity to the proceedings. The food is good, and even if you're not familiar with Japanese cuisine, here you can safely order what your neighbor's having and come out all right. The specialty of the house is tori-katsu, boned chicken breast stuffed with vegetables and with noodles. Sashimi (raw fish) and curry dishes with chicken and shrimp fill out the menu. Prices are moderate: about 1,000 to 2,000 pesos ($2 to $4). There are nine set-price meals priced under 2,000 pesos ($4). You can dine at Daruma from 1 p.m. to 10:30 p.m. every day.

NEAR REVOLUCIÓN MONUMENT: Located near the Plaza de la República at Edison 57, on the corner of Alcazar, the **Restaurant Covadonga** (no phone) offers friendly service as well as a very good comida for 720 pesos ($1.44). They're open for breakfast as early as 7 a.m.: a full breakfast is 380 to 560 pesos (76¢ to $1.12).

A bit of alpine Europe is yours just off the Plaza de la República at the **Cafetería Monique** (no phone), Vallarta 7. An Austrian ambience, a lofty ceiling with lots of light, a glass case full of cookies and cakes, and various sorts of coffee make this a good spot for an afternoon refresher. You can buy the cookies by the kilo if you're starving, but just a few, plus a cup of brew, will come to 450 pesos (90¢); light breakfasts are priced at 350 to 500 pesos (60¢ to $1).

Taco Row

Antonio Caso, a street running east and west between Insurgentes and Vallarta, is loaded with little *fogatas,* or hole-in-the-wall eateries, where you can pick up a cheap breakfast or a luncheon snack of tacos or tortas. The typical joint is run by an efficient señora and several young fellows who keep their customers happy with a 500-peso ($1) breakfast of two eggs, a choice of ham, sausage, or bacon, a bizcocho (croissant-type roll), and coffee. For lunch or supper they sell positively huge tacos (two is all you'll need) made with meat, tomato, onion, lettuce, and *hot* chiles for 200 to 600 pesos (40¢ to $1.20)—ask for yours *sin chiles,* without peppers—a smaller version of the same for a bit less. Tortas are similar concoctions made with bolillos (bread rolls). The torta especial comes with the works (avocado included). Closed Sunday.

ALONG REFORMA: Right on Reforma, northeast of the Insurgentes intersection, are two cafeteria-type restaurants, both noted for their good food and comfortable atmosphere. First of these is **Shirley's** (no phone), on the east side of the street at Reforma 108. Shirley's is the epitome of efficiency, from the navy-blazer'd maître d' to the light-blue-uniformed waiters and waitresses; everything runs smoothly, and the atmosphere is one of order and friendliness —a good bet for anyone who's homesick. In fact, from first to last (the check says "Please Pay the Cashier") Shirley's shows its American heritage. You can start the day with the bounteous breakfast buffet for 1,250 pesos ($2.50), tax and tip included, or the house special, English muffins with cheese and ham for even less. For lunch the best deal is the 1,500-peso ($3) buffet, or try a hamburger, or a Reuben sandwich with french fries for about 1,000 pesos ($2). Air-conditioned, open 7:30 a.m. to 11:30 p.m. daily, on Saturday till 1 a.m.—a very pleasant place!

On your way to a day's sightseeing, you might want to drop in at **La Calesa** (no phone), Reforma 36 near the intersection with Guerra, for a spot of breakfast. The huevos motulenos, for instance, consists of two tortillas topped by two eggs covered with ham, cheese, peas, frijoles, and fried bananas. This costs 600 pesos ($1.20), but most other items are somewhat less. A simply enormous glass of fresh-squeezed fruit juice costs 300 pesos (60¢). The daily comida corrida is a budget-pleasing 800 pesos ($1.60), and with it comes the view of the action on busy Reforma, seen through plate-glass windows. La Calesa's open Monday through Friday from 8 a.m. to 9 p.m., on Saturday to 5 p.m.; closed Sunday.

4. Near the Alameda and Bellas Artes

The center of the downtown area is a particularly good place to look for a good, inexpensive comida corrida. The rich concentration of banks and businesses means that lots and lots of hungry office workers must be served. Competition for the trade is stiff.

Along the south side of the Alameda, on the bank streets between Bucareli and Lázaro Cárdenas, are numerous restaurants, some old and well established, others new and modern. For a pleasant, relaxing comida corrida in the moderate price range I can recommend these special places.

THE BEST ALL-AROUND PLACES: The **Lincoln Restaurant** (tel. 510-1468 or 510-1102), 24 Revillagigedo at Independencia across from the Hotel Monte Real, is plush in decor but very moderate in price. Snowy tablecloths contrast with the dark paneling, and a portrait of Honest Abe lends dignity. Go here for a full lunch rather than a quick snack, for you'll find yourself wanting to settle in and order soup or perhaps a shrimp cocktail, then something like huachinanguito (baby red snapper), osso buco, or beef brochettes Mexican style. With one of their elaborate desserts, beverage, tax and tip, you can pay anywhere from 3,000 to 4,000 pesos ($6 to $8) for a full meal. The Lincoln is open for lunch and dinner from Monday through Saturday.

In contrast to the plushness of the Lincoln, right next door at 28 Revillagigedo is the **Restaurante Sac's** (tel. 521-2028), a place unabashedly light, modern, and upbeat. Useful for any meal, any day (it's open from 8 a.m. to 10 p.m., seven days a week), Sac's features five set-price breakfasts from 300 to 750 pesos (60¢ to $1.50), antojitos (Mexican specialties) such as burritos, enchiladas, and chilaquiles for 600 pesos ($1.20). The most expensive item on the menu is filete Tampiqueña (filet steak in a piquant tomato sauce) at 1,400 pesos ($2.80).

The little **Fonda Santa Anita** (tel. 518-4609), Calle Humboldt 48, half a block south of Avenida Juárez near the Hotel Ambassador, doesn't look like much from the outside. But it is one of the city's longest established and most dependable places with moderate prices. There's an English-language menu, and on it you'll find lots of dishes you may not have heard of before. For instance, you can order peppers stuffed with cheese, or bean soup with tortilla strips, or chongos zamoranos (a yogurt-like dessert). The food is quite good, but the prices are even better: for the set-price *menu turistico,* a four-course meal including a Mexican combination plate, you pay less than 2,000 pesos ($4), tax and tip included. Other daily special plates cost even less. The restaurant is not fancy, and it's quite small, but it's nice, with tablecloths and polite service. The Fonda Santa Anita is open for lunch and dinner daily, but closed Sunday and holidays.

One of the most teeming restaurants during comida-time (1 to 4 p.m.) is the **Restaurant Danubio** (tel. 512-0912), Uruguay 3 at Lázaro Cárdenas, which has a huge 1500-peso ($3) lunch that is practically an institution. A typical comida consists of a shrimp or oyster cocktail, maybe Valencia soup or tomato consommé, boiled lentils, a choice of a hot or cold fish dish, a choice of three entrees, custard or fruit, and coffee or tea. The à la carte menu is extensive, but you get better service during the busy time if you stick to the comida corrida. They serve cocktails, wine, and beer. There is also a room upstairs to accommodate the lunchtime overflow, although many in the overflow don't know it, so you may find more breathing space aloft. Open 1 p.m. to midnight daily.

Note: The house specialty is langostinos (baby crawfish) and well worth the splurge!

Walk down Calle Luis Moya from Avenida Juárez, cross Independencia, and on the right-hand side at no. 41 you'll see the **Restaurant Los Faroles** (no phone). Through the brick arches you'll see a firepit filled with cazuelas, the big earthenware cooking-pots, and a bevy of white-aproned señoras toiling to serve up some of the city's cheapest and most authentic Mexican food. Tacos, enchiladas, caldos (stews), and other truly Mexican dishes are the forte here, and low prices are the rule. The daily comidas corridas, for instance, are priced at merely 600 and 750 pesos ($1.20 and $1.50). Los Faroles is darkish, and not air-conditioned (at those prices?), but good, and it's open every day of the year.

OTHER GOOD PLACES:
The above are my favorites, having a special flavor of Mexico City not found everywhere. Now I'll describe a few more finds which, while they don't have the special feeling of the aforementioned establishments, still give you good, inexpensive, food in clean, although perhaps mundane, surroundings.

A very busy café that serves the office community all day long is **Mi Pebeta Cafetería** (no phone), Humbolt 62, just north of Guerra in the YWCA building. I like this place every time I go back; it's nothing fancy but the red-and-white-checkered tablecloths give a bit of a European flair. The service is friendly and the food is good. The comida costs 450 pesos (90¢) and includes soup, main course, refried beans, dessert, and coffee. Most à la carte items range between 450 and 600 pesos (90¢ and $1.20). The cheese omelet is good. Also open for breakfast. Closed Thursday.

The **Restaurant Guajalote** (no phone), a half block south of Juárez on Dolores, which is just one street west of López, has an ordinary atmosphere—just a number of booths and tables covered with tablecloths. On the right is a food bar and the smells are certainly tempting. The 1,000-peso ($2) comida includes juice, soup, rice, main dish, dessert, and coffee; most Mexican plates are fairly expensive, but breakfasts are cheap. No English menu. Long hours: from 8 a.m. to 2 a.m. daily.

SPECIALTY RESTAURANTS:
For something out of the ordinary, this is a rich area as well. Herewith, my recommendations for dining places when you crave something a little different.

For Chinese Fare

There is a small Chinese section in Mexico City located on Dolores between Independencia and Articulo 123.

One of the better restaurants here is **Hong King** (tel. 512-6703), Dolores 25-A at Independencia, a block and a half south of Avenida Juárez. Small and tidy like a luncheonette, the Hong King offers a nice selection of those incredible bargains, the set-price Chinese meals for two. You can choose a menu priced anywhere from 1,000 pesos ($2—for two people!) to 2,500 pesos ($5). A platter of assorted Chinese dishes is priced at 1,500 pesos ($3), and most à la carte entrees are even less than this. It's not elegant, but it's neat and clean, conveniently located, and you certainly can't beat those prices! The Hong King is open daily for lunch and dinner.

An Architectural Landmark

From the Bellas Artes, walk to Avenida Madero and the **Sanborn House of Tiles** ("Casa de Azulejos"; tel. 521-9100). This gorgeous antique building was once the palace of the Counts of the Valley of Orizaba, but now houses a branch of the Sanborn's restaurant-and-variety store chain. Dining tables are set in an elaborate courtyard complete with carved stone pillars, tiles, and peacock frescoes. It's a lovely place for a rest and a cup of coffee with some apple pie à la mode, but even this modest snack is relatively expensive here, costing about 850 pesos ($1.70). If you dine, order a daily special, which for 1,100 to 1,600 pesos ($2.20 to $3.20) gives you the best value.

A Vegetarian Place

I can't say enough good things about the food at the **Restaurante Vegeteriano y Dietetico** (tel. 521-6880 or 585-4191), Madero 56 not far from the Zócalo. There's no sign on the sidewalk, so look for a stairway marked Penella, or the menu posted outside on the entrance, walk one flight up, and you'll enter the restaurant. The decor is nothing special but the food is fantastic, and they have a piano player who plunks out Oldies-but-Goodies while you feast on the 990-peso ($1.98) comida. As the name implies, they serve no meat, but you can easily have your fill starting with a huge salad (watercress, tomato, radishes, grated carrot, and beets), followed by superb cream of tomato soup, a choice of two entrees (berengena empanizada, or breaded eggplant; ensalada trigo, or bulghur salad), a delicious cake made of whole wheat and honey, served with coffee or tea. This place is good—you must try it yourself to appreciate it. Menu in Spanish only; open every day except Sunday, from noon to 6 p.m. There's another Vegeteriano at Filomata 17, between 5 de Mayo and Madero, five blocks west of the Zócalo. Also closed Sunday.

Hot Chocolate and Churros

Those interested only in a snack at lunchtime should head for **El More** (no phone), Avenida Lázaro Cárdenas 42, at Uruguay. A man in the window turns out fresh doughnut-type treats called churros or estillos, which he then smothers in sugar and serves piping hot. The churros are offered in combination with hot chocolate (the best and richest chocolate I've ever tasted): 425 pesos (85¢) for the delectable hot chocolate and a plate of four churros, or 375 pesos (75¢) for the plate of churros plus coffee and milk. Try it—an authentic *churrería* is a bit of true Mexico City daily life. Open 24 hours.

Best Coffee in Town

One of the oldest establishments in town is the **Café La Habana** (tel. 535-2620), on the corner of Morelos (no. 62) and Bucareli. The cavernous interior reverberates with the sound of clinking glasses and tinkling silver as business-men and local folk have breakfast and enjoy the best coffee in town. In the front as you enter is a coffee-roasting machine that is whirling to ensure that the coffee is the freshest. I always bring home bags of their coffee to the delight of my friends.

For Upscale Pastry

Kiss your willpower goodbye when you enter the glittering precincts of the **Pastelería Ideal** (tel. 585-8099), Avenida 16 de Septiembre no. 14, between Avenida Lázaro Cárdenas and Gante. This classy place with moderate prices and a constant stream of loyal customers is sure to charm you with its assortment of confections. Brown-bag your next breakfast from here—if you can resist that long.

READER'S RESTAURANT SELECTION—ALAMEDA: "You should recommend the **Restaurant Centro Castellano** (tel. 518-6080), Uruguay 16. It has a very plain entrance, but you walk up a flight of stairs to a huge dining room always jumping with people. I had melon with ham, paella, fish filet, beefsteak a la cacerola, fresh pineapple, and coffee, all for only 1,600 pesos ($3.20)! The restaurant is open from 1 to 10 p.m. daily, including Sunday. There is full bar service. The family that runs the place owns a winery, and they sell a full jarrito of red or white wine for 750 pesos ($1.50). I drank a whole one thinking it would not be so much, and I found the walk back to my hotel a bit difficult" (John R. Hill, Los Angeles, Calif.).

5. In the Zócalo Area

Here's my roundup of restaurants and cafés in and near the Zócalo, an area extending westward almost to Avenida Lázaro Cárdenas.

The **Café La Blanca** (tel. 510-0399), on the north side of Cinco de Mayo at no. 40, between Motolinía and Isabel la Católica, is a large cafeteria-style place with two levels. There is no decor to speak of but the fare is good as is attested by the teeming business they do from 7 a.m. to midnight, every day of the week. They serve only à la carte items but with daily specials: huachinango (red snapper) or jumbo shrimp for about 700 to 800 pesos ($1.40 to $1.60), meat dishes for 500 to 700 pesos ($1 to $1.20), sandwiches and salads for 300 to 500 pesos (60¢ to $1). You cannot go wrong eating here.

The **Café de Tacuba,** on Tacuba at no. 28 (tel. 512-8482), very near the Metro station Allende, looks as though it's been here on this street in Mexico City since the city began—or at least for a hundred years or so. The wainscoting in the two long dining rooms is of orange, white, blue faïence; the lamps are of brass; dark and brooding oil paintings share wall space with a large mural of several nuns working in a kitchen (maybe it was here from the time of Cortés, at least?). The waitresses wear white uniforms with matching caps, and they're on duty every day from 8 a.m. to midnight. Soups here are excellent, with the top price going to cream of asparagus with biscuits; grilled chicken costs about 900 to 1,200 pesos ($1.80 to $2.40), and most meat dishes are 1,600 pesos ($3.20), but such things as enchiladas and chilaquiles con crema are cheaper. Rather than the customary comida corrida, the Café de Tacuba offers a selection of daily lunch plates, served with soup, costing 1,900 to 3,000 pesos ($3.80 to $6). The best is the last, however, as a tempting selection of what certainly look to be homemade cakes and pastries waits in a glass case near the front of the restaurant. Wine, beer, and liquor are served. You won't believe it, but the Tacuba dates from 1912.

PASTRYLAND'S PEARLY GATES: Imagine this: you walk into a vast, well-lighted room; the walls are lined with deep shelves, and each one of these shelves is filled with absolutely fresh, light puffy pastries, sweet rolls, danish, cookies, biscuits, fresh breads, jam-filled goodies, custards. Okay, now here's the good part: you pick up a circular aluminum tray and a pair of tongs, you feast your eyes on all the goodies, you pile your tray full (too much!) of what you want. Then you entrust it to a young lady who deftly transfers the mountain of pastries to a paper bag, totting up the tab at the same time. Then she says, "That'll be 600 pesos ($1.10), please." Sound like heaven? Actually, it's the **Pastelería Madrid** (tel. 521-3378), at Calle 5 (Cinco) de Febrero no. 25, corner of Calle República del Salvador, two blocks south of the Zócalo. There are other, similar pastryshops in the city, but the Madrid is about the best. It's open every day from early in the morning till late at night. Come for breakfast (coffee or tea, yogurt, and pastries). Here's a tip: as you pass along the shelves, you'll see several trays of the same pastry. Take your choices from the fullest tray as those are the freshest.

Another place to get fresh pastries is the **Panificadora Novedades,** Bolívar 78. It opens early in the morning so you can get your pastries as soon as necessary.

STARVATION BUDGET: For those after an adventure while keeping to a tight budget I have an ideal spot: the **Comedor Familiar,** located at Carranza 105 just off Pino Suárez. To get to the restaurant walk through the leather shop arcade, turn right, go through a double door, climb a flight of stairs, walk past the busy kitchen, and wait for a seat (this place gets a lot of business). There are three rooms packed with Mexicans (not a single foreigner) after 1 p.m. waiting for their 510-peso ($1.02) comida that includes soup, rice, main course, frijoles, pastry, and coffee. You can't beat it!

It's difficult to imagine a traveler who can't afford a comida corrida priced at 550 or 600 pesos ($1.10 or $1.20), but if that's you, take comfort. The **Rincon Mexicano** (tel. 573-4180), Uruguay 27 between Avenida Lázaro Cárdenas and Bolívar, is a tiny place with a full set-price lunch for a mere 400 pesos (80¢)! Don't expect foie gras and truffles, but don't expect to go away hungry and unhappy either. Breakfast, lunch, and supper are served (till 8 p.m.) every day. The menu lists numerous à la carte items at comparable, ridiculously low prices.

TWO SPECIAL PLACES: Walk northeast of the Zócalo, through dingy streets, to find **Las Cazuelas** (tel. 522-0689), Colómbia 69 (just down from Carmen), housed in a beautiful 18th-century tiled mansion. The dreariness of the street disappears as you enter Las Cazuelas, for you are surrounded by beautiful wall tiles, hand-painted chairs, and a lively group of mariachis. The kitchen, which is immediately visible when you enter, is lined with large earthen pots and casseroles, and thus the name *las cazuelas*. This place is always swinging (especially on a Sunday when the whole family is out for a good time) and it's no wonder, considering the dishes, which are distinctly Mexican, like costilla de res (grilled beef ribs), cabrito al horno (roast kid), chicharrón (pork crackling) with guacamole. There is no English menu here and the waiters do not speak English, so you'll have to know your Spanish menu. A full meal, with drinks, will be between 2,500 and 3,500 pesos ($5 and $7), including tip. Order a song from the mariachis, and you'll pay 1,000 pesos ($2). Highly recommended! Open daily noon to midnight, but the best time to come is late afternoon between 2 and 6 p.m.

A bit higher in class and price is the **Hostería de Santo Domingo** (tel. 510-1434), said to be the oldest restaurant in the city still in operation (established 1860). It is located at Dominguez 72 just east of República de Chile. The place has been redecorated in recent times so a lot of the antiquity is gone, replaced by bright walls, a few plants, and 20th-century murals. The à la carte prices are low—many entrees between 1,000 and 1,500 pesos ($2 and $3)—and the food's excellent. Try, for example, the stuffed peppers with cheese, pork loin, or the unusual bread soup. Note that the Santo Domingo is best for lunch when there's free live music—it's dead in the evening.

A DELICATESSEN: The Mexican equivalent of a deli is a shop that sells *productos ultramarinos* (imported goods). Although it's not a deli as we know it, **La Villa de Madrid** (tel. 512-3782), Uruguay 36 at the corner of Bolívar, still has a tempting assortment of hard-to-find goodies in its sidewalk windows, with more inside. (Don't confuse the deli entrance with the nearby grubby cantina of the same name.) Imported liquor—everything from Schlitz to Dom Perignon—cookies, crackers, nuts, cheese, and cold meats are sold daily, 9 a.m. to 9 p.m.; closed Sunday.

READERS' RESTAURANT SELECTIONS—ZÓCALO: "I want to report a real find, **El Cardenal,** Moneda 2, just off the Zócalo. Walk east about 20 paces down Moneda; on the left, just before the taqueria, take the stairs to the upper floor. There are no signs to indicate the upstairs facility, but it's a full-fledged restaurant in a corner room of this colonial building overlooking the Zócalo. It's very popular with government officials who fill the place to overflowing by 2 p.m. No comida corrida is offered, but there are daily specials. With cerveza, I got a fabulous meal for 1,750 pesos ($3.50). This place is mandatory!" (Prof. Irwin Rovner, Raleigh, N.C.) . . . "Down a short alley between Avenida Madero nos. 27 and 29, we found the **Restaurant Borda.** It has a small, old wood-paneled dining room which is pleasant and quiet. The service is friendly and attentive, and the short comida gives a well-cooked, filling if unexciting four courses for 1,500 pesos ($3)" (David Morris, London, England).

Chapter IX

MEXICO CITY: DAYTIME ACTIVITIES

1. Sights Near the Zócalo
2. Sights Near the Alameda
3. Chapultepec Park and Its Museums
4. Sights South of the Center
5. Sights North of the Center
6. Crafts Shops and Markets
7. For Excitement: Bullfights and Horseraces

NOW THAT YOU'RE comfortably installed in one of the world's most exciting cities, and you have absorbed enough of the preceding chapters to be able to find your way around, you'll be eager to begin delving into the life of Mexico City. This chapter will concentrate on the inexpensive activities available to you, or at least the more inexpensive ways to do those things that inevitably cost money.

You'll find that in Mexico even such routine activities as walking in the park are fraught with unexpected and delightful surprises, and even an ordinary stroll around any of the city's markets will offer you the opportunity to admire dozens of exotic items unavailable in the markets at home.

A final point: In the summer, always take along a raincoat when you venture out in the afternoon. The rain comes between 2 and 4 p.m. every day, so predictably that you can almost set your watch by it. In winter carry a jacket or sweater: stone-built museums are cold inside, and when the sun goes down, the outside air gets chilly. I'll start in the most economical way possible, on a do-it-yourself tour, on foot. And the place to begin your tour is where the ancient city of Tenochtitlán was founded, and later the City of Mexico was built on its ruins.

1. Sights Near the Zócalo

Every Spanish colonial city in North America was laid out according to a textbook plan, with a plaza at the center surrounded by a church, government buildings, and military headquarters. As capital of New Spain, Mexico City's Zócalo is one of the grandest, and is graced on all sides by darkened 17th-century buildings.

There's a wonderful view of the Zócalo from the seventh-floor restaurant, partly open air, of the Hotel Majestic, which is on the corner of the Zócalo and Madero. You can start your trip with breakfast here, or pay a late visit to the bar, which adjoins the restaurant. From this vantage point, the people strolling casually in the vast expanse of the square below look as though they have been choreographed by some omnipotent chess player, as indeed they may have been.

The odd Indian word *zócalo* actually means "pedestal," or "plinth." A grand monument to Mexico's independence was planned, and the pedestal built, but the project was never completed. The pedestal became a landmark for visiting out-of-towners, and pretty soon everyone was calling the square after the pedestal, even though the pedestal was later removed. Its official name is Plaza de la Constitución. In imitation, the main square in any other Mexican town is often called "el zócalo," whether it ever bore a pedestal or not!

METROPOLITANO: Take a look inside the cathedral, begun in 1573 and finished in 1667. If you wander quietly around past the innumerable small chapels, you'll almost certainly come across a guide who is busily demonstrating some of the cathedral's more outstanding features: the tomb of Agustín Iturbide perhaps, placed here in 1838, or the fact that the holy water fonts ring like metal when tapped with a coin. Like all good big churches it has catacombs underneath; unlike some churches it is immense, brilliant almost to blinding, overpowering.

Next to the cathedral, and communicating with it, is the chapel known as **El Sagrario,** another tour de force of Spanish baroque built in the mid-1700s.

In your look around the cathedral and the Sagrario, be sure to note the sinkage of the great building into the soft lake bottom beneath. The base of the façade is far from being level and straight, and when one considers the weight of the immense towers, the sinkage is no surprise.

Around to the east side of the cathedral is a quaint reminder of medieval trade life. Here is where carpenters, plasterers, plumbers, painters, and electricians gather who have no shops of their own—modern journeymen. Each has his tool box and may display the tools of his trade along with pictures of his work, paint color charts, and various other attractions.

TEMPLO MAYOR: In 1978 a workman accidentally discovered the very center of Aztec religious life. His digging, on the east side of the Metropolitan Cathedral, unearthed an Aztec votive stone. Mexican archeologists followed up the discovery enthusiastically with major excavations, and what they uncovered was the **Pyramid of Huitzilopochtli,** also called in the Templo Mayor (Great Temple). It was apparently the most important religious structure in the Aztec capital.

Archeological theory has it that the sacred ground of one religion often becomes the sacred ground of its successor. It makes sense that the Spanish missionaries who accompanied Cortés would want to distract their new Aztec converts by pulling down the pagan temples and using much of the stone to construct a church on the same spot. The church they built was not the present Metropolitan Cathedral, but rather a smaller edifice, which was pulled down in 1573 so that the cathedral could be built on the sacred site.

You'll see the extensive excavation site when you walk around to the east of the cathedral, on the side by the National Palace. Walkways allow you to see much of the Aztec construction without even entering the site. But to see it all, go to the corner of Calle República de Guatemala and Calle Verdad, on the south side of the excavations. There's also a small museum, on the northeast side at Calle Justo Sierra and Calle Correo Mayor. Hours are Tuesday through Sunday from 10 a.m. to 1 p.m.

The surrounding district, one of the oldest in the city, has suffered long neglect, but a project inaugurated in 1980 should restore much of its colonial charm. Designated a Historical Zone, the district is eligible for urban-renewal funds. The first product of the plan is the beautifully restored mansion at the corner of Donceles and República de Chile. Built as the home of Don Manuel de Heras y Soto in the 18th century, it is now the **Mexico City Historical Center.** Take a look in through the gates. Don Manuel, by the way, was one of the notables who signed Mexico's Act of National Independence.

PALACIO NACIONAL: On the east side of the Zócalo stands the impressive National Palace, begun in 1692, the last addition completed late in the 1920s. A complex of countless rooms, reached by wide stone stairways and adorned with carved brass balconies opening onto a series of courtyards, the National Palace is where the president works from 8 a.m. to 2:30 p.m. (regular hours for government employees in Mexico). Enter by the central door any day from 8 to 6. The guards will let you by if you ask.

Continue across the courtyard to the biggest attraction here, for Mexicans and tourists alike, the enormous murals painted over a 25-year period by Diego Rivera. All the murals are quite easy to understand. There is, for instance, *The Legend of Quetzalcóatl,* depicting the famous legend of the flying serpent bringing a white man with a blond beard to the country; when Cortés arrived, many of the Aztecs remembered this legend, and believed the newcomer to be Quetzalcóatl. Another mural tells of the *American Intervention,* during the War of 1847, when American invaders marched into Mexico City. It was on this occasion that the military cadets of Chapultepec Castle (then a military school) fought bravely to the last man; the final six wrapped themselves in Mexican flags and leaped from the windows to avoid surrendering. (You'll see a monument to the boy heroes later, in Chapultepec Park.) The pride and joy of palace murals is one called the *Great City of Tenochtitlán,* a pictorial study of the original settlement in the Valley of Mexico. The city takes up only a small part of the mural, and the remainder is filled with what appears to be four million extras left over from a Cecil B. De Mille epic. In fact, no matter what their themes, most of the murals incorporate a piece of ancient Mexican history, usually featuring Cortés and a cast of thousands.

The **Municipal Palace,** seat of government for the Federal District (Departamento del Distrito Federal), is the structure on the south side of the Zócalo.

Juárez Museum

A comparatively little-discovered (by tourists) museum in the Zócalo area (Metro: Zócalo) is the one dedicated to Benito Juárez, and situated in the National Palace. When facing the palace, take the farthest left of the three entrances, walk across the courtyard to the statue of Benito Juárez and then up the stairs to the left. The Juárez Museum (tel. 522-5646) consists of the well-preserved home of the former president of Mexico, and is usually bustling with school children studying the handwritten letters and papers that are carefully kept in glass cases around the room. In other cases are tablecloths, silverware, medals, shirts, watches, a briefcase, and symbolic keys to the city—all personal effects of the much-loved former president.

There's a beautiful library here (same hours as the museum), with lots of wood paneling, desks, history books arranged around the walls, and the wonderfully musty smell of mellow leather and aging paper that's indigenous to all respectable libraries. Anyone may study the books.

The last room at the rear is Juárez's bedroom, which gives one the eerie feeling that the former president might walk in at any moment; his dressing gown is laid out on the four-poster bed, and a chamber pot peeks from beneath the coverlet. Authenticity to the nth degree.

The museum is open from 10 a.m. to 7 p.m. Monday through Friday, to 3 p.m. on Saturday and Sunday. Admission is free after signing the registry books.

CALLE DE LA MONEDA: The pedestrian street just to the left of the National Palace, on the east side of the Zócalo (Metro: Zócalo) is Calle de la Moneda, or Street of the Treasury or Mint. The street is lined with aged buildings constructed of *tezontle,* the local volcanic rock. At the corner of Calle Verdad is the Edificio Arzobispal, the former archbishop's palace. True to Spanish tradition, the chief ecclesiastical official's power base was built smack on top of the Aztec's Temple of Tezcatlipoca, the multi-faceted god who gave life and governed a host of lesser gods.

The building from which the street takes its name is at no. 13. La Casa de Moneda was built in the 1500s and expanded over the centuries, but it now houses the Museum of Cultures. Restored after the earthquake of September 1985, the museum houses an eclectic assortment of exhibits relating to other cultures of Asia, Africa, and Europe. Hours are 9:30 a.m. to 6 p.m., till 4 p.m. on Saturday, closed Sunday.

RIVERA MURALS: From the northeast corner of the Zócalo, Calle República de Argentina heads north. If you head north too, you'll soon cross Calle González Obregón, and on your left will be the headquarters of the Secretaría de Educación Publica. The building is open during normal working hours (9 a.m. to 2 p.m.), and the attraction is its courtyards. The walls are decorated with a great series of over 200 murals by Diego Rivera, painted in 1923 and 1924. Other artists did a panel here and there, but it's the Riveras that are superb. The building itself dates from 1922.

On your way back to the Zócalo, take a peek at the murals in the Escuela Nacional Preparatoria, a block south of the Secretaría, at the corner of Argentina and Donceles. Here the murals are by the three Mexican greats: Rivera, Orozco, and Siqueiros.

For a look at more murals by Rivera's contemporary, José Clemente Orozco, drop in at the Suprema Corte de Justicia (Supreme Court of Justice), beside the National Palace on Avenida Pino Suárez at the southeastern corner of the Zócalo. The main staircase and its landings hold the murals.

MUSEO DE LA CIUDAD DE MÉXICO: Walk south on Pino Suárez from the Zócalo to reach the Museum of the City of Mexico (tel. 542-0487). Just before the corner of Calle El Salvador and Pino Suárez, pop through a stone doorway and you'll find yourself in the courtyard of a mansion built in 1528, and known originally as the House of the Counts of Santiago de Calimaya. Back in 1964 this classic old building, with its massive stone staircase and crumbling walls, was converted into the Museum of the City of Mexico (Metro: Pino Suárez or Zócalo—equal distance).

This museum is underrated, and should be visited by any newcomer to Mexico who wants to get the historical and prehistorical outlines of a fascinating culture. It deals solely with the Mexico Valley. The first arrival of man in the valley was in 8000 B.C. There are some fine maps and pictographic presentations of the initial settlements, outlines of the social organization as it developed, and a huge mock-up of Tenochtitlán, the city of the Aztecs. The conquest and destruction of Tenochtitlán by the Spaniards is fantastically portrayed with a mural of Capdevila that appears to have been painted in fire.

After a brief inspection of the elegant old carriage in the courtyard and the little room behind it devoted to the history of transportation in Mexico City, ascend the broad stairs and turn right. The second-floor exhibits begin with a potpourri of beautiful religious paintings, then continue the story of the city's history. Portrayals and notes on the "founding fathers," a fine picture of the Plaza of Mexico, and a series of figures clad in period costumes bring you up to the 1857 revolution. Among the tributes to Juárez and photos of the Villa/ Zapata insurrection, there's a marvelously fierce and slightly cross-eyed painting of "the agrarian martyr," Emiliano Zapata, with so much artillery strapped to his chest that he could have won a good-size battle single-handedly. (He probably did!)

Calmer, but no less interesting, are the photos and sketches of Mexico City in the present and the future. And on the third floor, you'll find the sun-drenched studio of Mexican impressionist Joaquin Clausell (1866–1935). The walls are completely covered with his fragmentary works, and two easel paintings still stand.

The Museum of the City of Mexico is open from 9:30 a.m. to 7:30 p.m. Tuesday through Sunday; closed Monday; admission is free. Every Thursday evening at 7 p.m. there is a scheduled lecture at the museum.

NATIONAL PAWN SHOP (Nacional Monte de Piedad): Who ever heard of touring a pawn shop? In Mexico City it's done all the time, for the Nacional Monte de Piedad, across the street (Monte de Piedad) from the west side of the cathedral, is a huge and rather imposing building, which turns out to be a department store for used items—the world's largest and most elegant Good Will/ Morgan Memorial thrift store. Electric power tools, jewelry, antique furniture, heavy machine tools, sofa beds, and a bewildering array of other things from trash to treasure are all on display. Buying is not required, but taking a look is recommended.

TIME FOR A REFRESHER: Want a refresher before you head on? We have just the place to recoup. For sunshine and a view of the Zócalo, it's the rooftop café-restaurant of the aforementioned **Hotel Majestic.** But if you don't mind being inside, make your way past the jewelry shops on the west side of the Zócalo to the southwest corner of the square and the beginning of Avenida 16 de Septiembre. A few steps west on this street (in the direction of the Alameda, more or less) will bring you to no. 82 and the entrance of the **Gran Hotel Ciudad de México.** The lavishly old-fashioned lobby, topped with its breathtaking stained-glass canopy, is served by a bar off in one corner, and a restaurant off in another. Both are sort of expensive, but a drink in the bar, about 750 or 1,000 pesos ($1.50 or $2), is a real pleasure. Beer or a soft drink will be cheaper; you should get a bowl of peanuts, *gratuito.* Even if you don't want to stop, and even if you don't plan to stay here, you should have a look at the magnificent lobby. By the way, the reason the birds in their splendid cages aren't flitting here and there is because they're stuffed. The bird calls you hear are electronic simulations!

Refreshed by a cup of coffee or a drink in the Gran Hotel, head back into the Zócalo and then west down Avenida Madero to take in some of its colonial buildings.

PALACIO DE ITURBIDE: Head west along Avenida Madero to reach the Alameda, our next grouping of sights-to-see. Along the way, stop at no. 17, a beautiful ornate stone palace with huge hand-carved wooden doors and a wildly baroque 40-foot-high carved stone archway. The mansion was built in the 1780s for a wealthy Mexican family, but was ceded in 1821 to Don Agustín de Iturbide, who later became the self-proclaimed Agustín I, Emperor of Mexico (1822–1823). His reign lasted only a matter of months, for although he was a partisan of Mexican independence, his political outlook was basically royalist and conservative, and the future of Mexico lay in the liberal social reforms advocated by the great revolutionaries Hidalgo and Morelos.

Financiera Banamex, present owner of the building, undertook restoration of the palace in 1972 and the result is beautiful, if a bit stark. Enter a courtyard with three tiers of balconies: the ground floor is a banking office; the upper floors have executive offices. Period paintings and statues grace walls and corners, and the second-floor chapel has been beautifully restored. Banamex has had a brief guide to the building printed up, and this leaflet, like your guided tour of the palace, is free of charge. Come in and have a look anytime Monday through Friday from 9 a.m. to 5 p.m. Closed holidays.

2. Sights Near the Alameda

Long ago, the **Alameda Central** was an Aztec marketplace. When the conquistadores took over in the mid-1500s, it became the place where heretics were burned at the stake under the Spanish Inquisition. In 1592 the governor of New Spain, Viceroy Luis de Velasco, converted it to a public park.

It's difficult to imagine this lovely spot thronged with Aztec traders, or lit by the horrid flames of an auto-da-fé witnessed by grim-faced churchmen, but so it was. For a vivid portrayal of the park's entire history, cross Avenida Juárez to the Hotel Del Prado. In the hotel's lobby is Diego Rivera's mural, *A Sunday Dream at the Alameda Park,* painted in 1947. The huge picture, 50 feet long and 13 feet high, chronicles the history of the park from the time of Cortés onward.

(**Note:** As of this writing the hotel is closed for restoration of damage caused by the earthquake of September, 1985. Check to see if work has been completed and the hotel reopened.)

As you make your pilgrimage to the Hotel Del Prado, you're bound to notice the Juárez Monument, sometimes called the Hemiciclo (hemicycle, half-circle). Juárez, enthroned as the hero he was, here assumes his proper place in the pantheon of Mexican patriots.

Most of the other statuary in the park was done by European sculptors (mostly French) in the late 19th and early 20th centuries.

There are lots of places to visit near the Alameda. If you've walked along Avenida Madero from the Zócalo, you've already admired the Palacio de Iturbide (see above). Next, head for the Palacio de Bellas Artes, then the Latin American Tower and the House of Tiles. North of the House of Tiles is the National Museum of Art. Two other museums lie to the west of the Alameda: the Pinacoteca Virreynal de San Diego, and the Museo de San Carlos. After touring the San Carlos, head south a few blocks to admire the Monument to the Revolution.

THE BELLAS ARTES: At the east end of the Alameda is the Palacio de Bellas Artes, that's *bey*-ahs *arr*-tess (tel. 526-7805), the supreme achievement of art deco lyricism, which, aside from being the concert hall, also houses permanent and traveling art shows. You can take a look around in the building Tuesday through Sunday from 10:30 a.m. to 6:30 p.m., for free.

Your first look at the building from the outside will tell you that it is impressive, lyrical, beautiful, ostentatious, eye-catching, and fun. But there's much more than first meets the eye. The theater is very turn-of-the-century Italian on the outside, but completely 1930s art deco inside. You may also be curious to know that it is made of Carrara marble, and that it has sunk into the soft belly of Lake Texcoco some 12 feet (4 meters) since construction was begun in 1900 (it was opened in 1934). Someday, perhaps, it will be the world's most ornate concert-hall-and-subway-station.

The palacio is the work of several masters: Italian architect Adam Boari, who made the original plans; Antonio Muñoz and Federico Mariscal, who modified Boari's plans considerably; and Louis Comfort Tiffany of New York, whose Tiffany Studios designed and constructed (from work by Mexican painter Gerardo Murillo, "Doctor Atl") the fabulous art nouveau glass curtain in the main theater.

The glass curtain, made from nearly a million irridescent pieces of colored glass, portrays the Valley of Mexico with its two great volcanoes. Lit from behind, it's easy to imagine the "sun" rising over the valley. You can see the curtain before important performances at the theater, and on Sunday mornings.

The palacio harbors several galleries of paintings, including a permanent collection of works by Mexican artists, and those on traveling exhibit.

On the third level are the famous murals by Rivera, Orozco, and Siqueiros. The Rivera mural on the western wall is justly famous, not only because of the artist's well-deserved fame, but because of the controversy surrounding it. The mural *Man in Control of His Universe* was commissioned in 1933 for Rockefeller Center in New York. Rivera completed the work there just as you see it: a giant vacuum sucks up the riches of the earth to feed the factories of callous, card-playing, hard-drinking white capitalist bullies, while the noble workers of the earth, of all races, rally behind the red flag of socialism and its standard-bearer, Lenin. Needless to say, the Rockefellers didn't enjoy their new purchase. Much to their discredit, however, they had it painted over—destroyed. Rivera duplicated the mural here as *Man at the Crossing of the Ways* to preserve it.

LA TORRE LATINOAMERICANA (Latin American Tower): A true bird's-eye view of the city is to be had from the Observation Deck of the Torre Latinoamericana, the Latin American Tower, soaring above the intersection of Juárez and Lázaro Cárdenas.

Buy a ticket for the deck (open 10 a.m. to midnight every day) at the booth as you approach the elevators—admission fee is 200 pesos (40¢) half price for children. Tokens for the telescope up top are on sale here too. You then take an elevator to the 37th floor, cross the hall, and take another elevator to the 42nd floor. A man will ask for your ticket as you get off.

The view is magnificent. Mountains surround the capital on all sides, but those to the north are the nearest, and Avenida Lázaro Cárdenas seems to head for them straight as an arrow. To the north just below is the marble pile of the Bellas Artes, and west of it, the green patch of the Alameda. Due west is the Monument to the Revolution, just beyond the intersection of Juárez and Reforma. You can't see Reforma too well because it's hidden by the buildings that line it, but the green swath of Chapultepec Park and its palace on the hilltop are easy to spot. To the east is the Zócalo, dominated by the cathedral. To the south is an area densely packed with homes, factories, and tall apartment buildings.

Climb the spiral staircase two flights—if it's open—and you're on the open roof. Now you've seen it all!

THE HOUSE OF TILES ("Casa de Azulejos"): Just past the Bellas Artes and the Latin American Tower, Avenida Juárez runs into (and becomes) the Avenida Madero, a one-way street going all the way to the city's main plaza. As

you proceed down Madero from the intersection with Avenida Lázaro Cárdenas, you can't fail to notice the mammoth Banco de México buildings (main building and Guardiola Annex) to your left, and behind these giants a small and wizened oldtimer decked out in gorgeous blue-and-white tiles. This building is one of Mexico City's most precious colonial gems, and was built at the very end of the 1500s for the Counts of the Valley of Orizaba. The tiles are a fine example of Puebla's craftsmen's work, and the making of faïence is still one of Puebla's outstanding crafts. Today the House of Tiles is used as a branch of the Sanborn's restaurant-newsstand-gift shop chain. You can stroll through to admire the interior (and it's air-conditioned!) or sit and have a refreshing drink or a cup of something hot.

NATIONAL MUSEUM OF ART: The next street to the north of Avenida Cinco de Mayo is Calzada Tacuba. Just east of the corner with Avenida Lázaro Cárdenas is the **Museo Nacional de Arte** (tel. 512-3224), housed in the old Secretaría de Communicaciones y Obras Públicas building. As you approach the museum, note the equestrian statue of King Carlos IV of Spain (1788–1808), by the Mexican sculptor Manuel Tolsa. Mexicans call the statue *El Caballito* ("The Little Horse"), and the name reveals a lot: they don't even mention Carlos, who was king shortly before the outbreak (1810) of the rebellion that gained Mexico its independence from Spain; and the statue is actually one of the largest equestrian statues in the world. Erected first in the Zócalo, it was later moved (1852) to a *glorieta* (traffic circle) in the Paseo de la Reforma. A few years ago *El Caballito,* unable to compete with the swirling traffic, rode over here to a more dignified and appropriate position in front of the museum.

Manuel Tolsa's sculpture is only the first Mexican work of art you'll see here. Within the museum, open from 10 a.m. to 6 p.m. Tuesday through Sunday, are exhibits that outline the development of Mexican art of the national period. Colonial works, from about 1525 to 1810, are in the Pinacoteca Virreynal de San Diego (see below); modern Mexican works are in the Museo de Arte Moderno and other museums. But for Mexican works of art from 1810 to 1950, this is the place to look.

PINACOTECA VIRREYNAL DE SAN DIEGO: As mentioned above, the Palacio de Bellas Artes is an art gallery as well as a concert hall. The same administration responsible for the Bellas Artes's shows is in charge of the Pinacoteca Virreynal de San Diego, Dr. Mora no. 7, at the northwest corner of the Alameda near the Hotel de Cortés (Metro: Hidalgo). This former church is now a gallery of paintings, mostly from the 16th and 17th centuries, and mostly ecclesiastical in theme. Highlights are apparent immediately as you walk around: in the wing to the right of where the altar would have been is a room with a gorgeous blue-and-gilt ceiling with gleaming rosettes and a striking mural by Federico Cantu (1959), one of the few modern works. Upstairs in a cloister are many small paintings by Hipolito de Rioja (who worked in the second half of the 17th century), by Baltazar de Echave Ibia (1610–1640), and others. By the way, the tremendous painting on the cloister wall called *Glorificación de la Inmaculada,* by Francisco Antonio Vallejo (1756–1783), should be viewed from upstairs—the lighting is better.

The Pinacoteca is open Tuesday through Sunday from 10 a.m. to 5 p.m.; entry is free.

MUSEO DE SAN CARLOS: The San Carlos Academy is Mexico's foremost school for artists, and most of the country's great painters—Diego Rivera among them—count it as their Alma Mater. Connected with the academy is the

San Carlos Museum, Alvarado at Arizpe, a few blocks west of the Alameda. The converted mansion that now houses the museum is very fine indeed, having been built in the early 1800s by architect Manuel Tolsa for the Marques de Buena Vista.

In the mansion's elliptical court you'll first come to displays of 19th-century Mexican statuary and busts by Manuel Vilar and his pupils, and off to one side is a pretty garden court shaded by rubber trees.

The various rooms on the first and second floors hold some of Mexico's best paintings, by both Mexican and European artists. In Sala IV, for instance, you can view *Christ in Limbo* by Mostaert (ca. 1534–1598), and also two paintings by Lucas Cranach the Elder: *Adam and Eve,* and *Federico de Sajonia.* Upstairs treats include *La Coqueta y el Jovenzuelo* by Fragonard and a portrait of Sir William Stanhope attributed to Sir Joshua Reynolds.

Admission to the Museum of San Carlos costs 25 pesos (5¢) and it's open from 10 a.m. to 3 p.m. and from 4 to 7 p.m. daily; closed Tuesday.

MONUMENTO A LA REVOLUCIÓN: A short three blocks south of the Museo de San Carlos along Calle Ramos Arizpe is the stocky art deco **Monument to the Revolution,** set in the large Plaza de la República. It has a curious and ironic history.

Porfirio Díaz, perennially "re-elected" as president of Mexico, wanted to dress up his dictatorship with a large and striking new legislative chamber. His government began construction, but only the dome was raised by the time the Mexican Revolution (1910) put an end to his plans—not to mention his dictatorship. After the turmoil of the revolution died down (1930s), the dome was finished off as a monument; the mortal remains of two revolutionary presidents, Francisco Madero and Venustiano Carranza, were entombed in two of its pillars; and it was dedicated to the memory of the revolution. Here it stands.

In the earthquake of September, 1985, the hefty monument suffered not so much as a broken brick.

LOTERÍA NACIONAL: Walk due east along Juárez toward Reforma. When you reach the wide boulevard, on your left will be the headquarters of the National Lottery. The building is a fine example of the art deco style, inside and out. You can visit during business hours, and most evenings. (See the Nightlife section for details on attending the lottery drawing).

Go up the front stairs, in the door, and up another short flight. Gleaming brass, marble, and rich stonework surround you. In the lobby is a small art gallery for changing shows. The auditorium is a 1930s masterpiece. No one will bother you as you look around. Admission is free.

CRAFTS SHOPS: At this point, you might want to cross Reforma, heading toward the Alameda on Avenida Juárez, for a stroll through the several excellent crafts shops located here. For details, jump ahead to Section 6, "Markets and Crafts Shops."

If it's Sunday, however, there's an alternative. Read on.

JARDÍN DEL ARTE: Though it's not strictly "near the Alameda," you might want to continue your tour southwest along Reforma to the Jardín del Arte, about a ten-minute walk. This pretty park, at the intersection of Insurgentes and Reforma, begins with the Monumento a la Maternidad (Monument to Motherhood), and continues with trees, shrubs and benches, fountains and sculpture. On Sunday, the park is crowded with artists displaying their wares for sale. Browsing is fun (in many cases, more fun than buying!)

3. Chapultepec Park and Its Museums

One of the biggest city parks in the world, Chapultepec Park is more than a playground: it's a whole way of life. Every day of the week the number of holidaying Mexican families that it can accommodate must be seen to be believed. They swarm over the grass, picnic under the century-old trees, stroll around the *lago* (lake) or crowd into rowboats, buy colorful balloons, trinkets, and eats from the numerous vendors, and file through the beautiful 18th-century castle that tops the 200-foot hill. It's here that you can really begin to understand the diversity and enormity of the population of Mexico City.

If you want to see this wonderful conglomeration of people at play amid nature, then head for Chapultepec by colectivo or bus heading west on Reforma. The park opens daily at 9 a.m. and closes promptly at 6 p.m.

The following sites are all within Chapultepec Park. A map (not drawn to scale) is included to help you find your way.

CHAPULTEPEC CASTLE: As you come down Reforma, at the foot of Chapultepec hill you'll notice six marble shafts carved as stylized torches placed in a semicircle around a small plaza. This is the Monument to the Boy Heroes (Niños Héroes)—the six cadets who jumped to their death rather than surrender to the U.S. Marines who attacked the castle during the war with Mexico in 1847. You can walk up the hill from here by following the right fork at the small castle-like gatehouse (now a house of mirrors) or take the elevator that is on the left a short way up the hill (usually a very long line on Sunday). Better to take the minibus to the top, which runs daily from 9 a.m. to 4:45 p.m. Catch it at the foot of the hill where the road begins its ascent.

Note about Chapultepec Park Map

Chapultepec Park, which covers about three square miles, is divided into three areas: (1) Chapultepec Castle (Museum of Modern Art, Historical Museum); (2) Anthropological Museum (National Auditorium and Galería, Zoo); (3) New Bosque (Technological Museum, Natural History Museum, Amusement Park). The map is meant solely as a graphic representation of these areas. *It is not drawn to scale.* The immensity of the park plus barriers such as fences and the Periferico Highway make it more time-consuming to get around on foot than one might suppose from a glance at the map.

Although on the site of Chapultepec Castle there had been a fortress since the days of the Aztecs, the present palace was not built until the 1780s. At the time of the previously mentioned U.S. invasion, it was in use as a military college, which is how it came about that Mexican army youths, including the unlucky sextet, were defending it.

The castle offers a beautiful view of Mexico which, from the balconies, appears to be covered solid with trees. It's reported that in the days of the French occupation during the 1860s, Carlotta could sit up in bed and watch her husband Maximilian proceeding down the Reforma on his way to work. Carlotta, incidentally, designed the lovely garden surrounding the palace, and until recent times it was still the official home of Mexico's president.

Today the palace houses the **Museum of National History** (tel. 553-6379), which covers the post-Hispanic period to the present—large paintings and statues of the Spanish leaders and heroes. On the second floor are rooms displaying jewelry, colonial art objects, and the impressive malachite vases. It's an intriguing place through which to stroll, from the elaborate furnishings brought over from Europe by Maximilian and Carlotta, to the patios and fountains and the

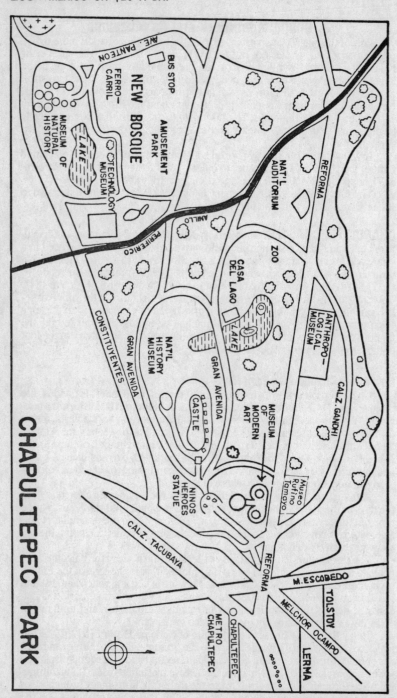

panorama of the city spread out below. Open from 9 a.m. to 5:40 p.m. (last ticket sold at 5 p.m.) every day except Tuesday. Admission is 50 pesos (10¢), except Sunday when it's half-price. Note: Hold onto the ticket the entire time you're on the hill—you may be asked to show it.

MUSEO DEL CARACOL: On your way up the hill, about 200 yards below the castle you probably noticed the circular glass building that spirals down the hillside. This is the **Galería de la Lucha del Pueblo Mexicano** (Gallery of the Struggle of the Mexican People), also called, because of its spiral shape, Museo del Caracol (Snail-shell Museum). In content it's a condensed history of Mexico complete with portraits, reproductions of documents, and dramatic montages —in three dimensions—of famous scenes from Mexico's past. The more recent years are also represented, with large photographic blowups, and some of the scenes, such as the execution of Maximilian, are staged with a great sense of drama and imagination.

Admission to the museum is free, and all the way down you're torn between how attractive it is inside and how beautiful the park looks outside through the big picture windows. The museum is open every day except Monday, from 10 a.m. to 5 p.m.

THE BOSQUE (WOODLAND): Going down the hill from the castle, turn left and follow the Gran Avenida through a landscape of trees, flowers, rock gardens, fountains, and hills. There is a beautiful man-made lake (although a bit mucky on my last visit), complete with an island, a geyser-like fountain, and boats that can be rented. On the west side of the lake is the **Casa del Lago,** originally built as a restaurant and now housing exhibits of local artists from the various art schools in and around Mexico City. There are four galleries (currently under restoration) with exhibits of the works of sundry artists in oil, lithograph, sculpture, etc. I found it very interesting to see the type of art that is currently being produced in Mexico. Most of the art is for sale. Nearby is the Galería del Bosque with similar exhibits. There is no entrance fee for any of the galleries, so stroll around as you please. Hours are from 11 a.m. to 5 p.m., Wednesday through Sunday only.

ZOO: Continue down the Gran Avenida, and off to your right you'll spot the spacious zoo. A good way to see the animals without much effort is to join the line of kids waiting to ride the miniature railway. For a few pesos you can ride in comfort around the whole zoo, catching tantalizing glimpses of monkeys, hippos, herons, polar bears, zebras, and most of the other creatures. Admission to the zoo is free.

AMUSEMENT PARK: This, complete with roller coaster (named the "Montana Rusa," or Russian Mountain) and ferris wheel, is in **New Chapultepec Park** —the area at the far western end. Continue in a southwesterly direction from the zoo and you'll come to the Periferico Highway (about half a mile or a 20-minute walk); the Amusement Park is just on the other side. If you are coming straight from downtown, you can take bus 30 along Servando Teresa de Mier, Río de la Loza, and Avenida Chapultepec to Avenida Constituyentes. Alight at the Natural History Museum, and it's a 15-minute walk to the concessions (for walking directions, see under "Technological Museum," below).

Admission is 20 pesos (4¢); children under 3, free. The gates are open Wednesday and Thursday from 11 a.m. to 6:30 p.m., on Saturday and Sunday from 10:30 a.m. to 7 p.m. The two large buildings to the right of the Amusement

Park are the Technological Museum, open everyday except Monday, 9 a.m. to 5 p.m. (See below.)

THE MUSEUMS: The nicest things about Chapultepec Park are its timelessness and spaciousness; it is big enough to accommodate almost anything that can be designed for it. Within this complex have been built five varied, beautiful, and exciting museums. They combine a superb sense of proportion with an equally good sense of design.

National Museum of Anthropology

By general consent, the finest museum of its kind in the world is Mexico's National Museum of Anthropology (tel. 553-6266), which was built by architect Pedro Ramírez Vasquez and a team of worthy helpers in 1964. If Sr. Ramírez never did another thing, he'd still deserve the fame of centuries.

Any Ruta 76 "Auditorio" or "Km. 13" bus up Reforma will drop you right outside the museum, which is situated off the broad boulevard about half a mile past the Diana statue, opposite Chapultepec Park Zoo. Line 1 of the Metro will take you to just outside the park; walk through the park, past the Museum of Modern Art, along Reforma, and you're there in 15 minutes. The museum is open Tuesday through Saturday from 9 a.m. to 7 p.m., on Sunday from 10 a.m. until 6 p.m.; closed all day Monday. Admission on Sunday is only 25 pesos (5¢), 50 pesos (10¢) all other days.

The museum, breathtaking in its splendor, with a massive patio half-sheltered by a tremendous stone umbrella, will take at least two or three hours to look around even if you are a dedicated museum rusher.

There are three sections, to all intents and purposes. First of all is the entrance hall to the museum proper. Here you'll find a check room. The museum shop, off the entry hall, has a nice collection of souvenirs and an excellent collection of guidebooks, large and small, to cultural, culinary, and archeological attractions in Mexico.

Inside the museum proper is an open courtyard with beautifully designed spacious rooms running around three sides at two levels. The ground-floor rooms are theoretically the most significant, and they are the most popular among studious visitors, devoted as they are to history and prehistoric days all the way up to the most recently explored archeological sites. These rooms include dioramas of the way Mexico City looked when the Spaniards first arrived, and reproductions of part of a pyramid at Teotihuacán. The Aztec calendar stone "wheel" takes a proud place here.

Save some of your time and energy, though, for the livelier and more readily understandable upstairs rooms. They're devoted to the way people throughout Mexico live today, complete with straw-covered huts, tape recordings of songs and dances, and lifelike models of village activities.

There is a lovely restaurant in the museum. Prices are moderate, the air-conditioned dining room and cheerful patio tables are inviting; all in all, it's a perfect place for a break.

After you pass by the ticket-taker into the courtyard, here are the museum's highlights, room (sala) by room:

Introducción a la Antropología: The entrance to this section is graced by a mural by Z. González Camarena depicting women of various nations. Exhibits deal with the various races of Man throughout the world, their progress and development, and how these aspects are studied by anthropologists.

A mural in the Mesoamerican room, by Raúl Anguiano, shows the Maya cosmogony: 13 heavens are held up by a giant ceiba tree; nine hells are beneath. The mural is directly above an exhibit of burial customs.

The next sign you'll see, *Salas de Etnografía en la Planta Alta,* means "Ethnographic Rooms on the Upper Floor." There's a stairway here so you can reach those rooms. But for now, continue around the courtyard on the main level.

Sala Origenes: This Room of Origins traces the history of the earliest men and women in the Americas.

Salas Preclasica y Teotihuacana: Exhibits here are of preclassic times (2000 B.C. to A.D. 300). You'll be fascinated by the models of the great ceremonial center at Teotihuacan, outside Mexico City.

Sala Tolteca: Toltec and Chichimec cultures are preserved here. There's a huge Atlantean Man statue from the Temple of Tlahuizcalpantecutli, at Tula, and other great monoliths, and pottery.

Sala Mexica: At the far end of the courtyard, lettering on the lintel reads "CEM ANAHUAC TENOCHCA TLALPAN," and beneath it is the entrance to one of the most important rooms in the museum. Among the amazing carved stones are these: the Aztec Calendar Stone, which bears symbols for all the ages of man (as the Aztecs saw them); the Piedra de Tizoc; Xiuhcóatl, the fire-serpent; a Tzompantli, or wall of skulls; and the terrifying monolith of Coatlicue, the goddess of earth and death.

Amid all this ominous dark volcanic rock, the irridescent feathered head-dress of Moctezuma blazes away, as impressive today (a copy) as when the Aztec emperor proceeded regally through the streets of Tenochtitlán. Near the glass case holding the headdress is a large model of Moctezuma's rich capital city; a mural echoes the city's grandeur as well.

Sala Oaxaca: After the Mexica room comes that of Oaxaca, with many exhibits from the Monte Albán excavations. Take time to admire the reproduction of Tomb no. 105 from Monte Albán. Go down the stairs to a reproduction of Tomb no. 104. Also look for the exquisite small heads carved from jade, in the glass cases.

Sala Golfo de Mexico: The highlight here is the enormous Olmec head, and models of El Tajín. The collection includes artifacts from both the Olmec and Huaxtec cultures, many of them looking distinctly Egyptian in inspiration.

Sala Maya: Don't miss this room! Not only are the exhibits here wonderful, but Maya art and culture itself has tremendous intrinsic interest. Displays here include a fine collection of well-preserved, beautiful Mayan carvings, not just from Mexican territory, but from other parts of Mesoamerica (Central America) as well.

Models of ancient cities include Copán (Honduras), Yaxchilán (Chiapas), Tulum (Quintana Roo), and Uaxactún (Guatemala). Downstairs is a model of the fabulous tomb discovered in the Temple of the Inscriptions at Palenque, complete with a rich jade mask for the deceased monarch. Outside the exhibit room is a full-scale replica of a temple at Hochob (Campeche), and another of the Temple of Paintings at Bonampak, plus replicas of stele from Quirigua (Guatemala).

Notice especially in all these examples the finesse of the carving. In the Tablero de la Cruz Enramada, from Palenque, note the fine work in all those wonderful glyphs.

Restaurant: After the Maya room, descend a wide staircase to reach the restaurant. No liquor (not even wine or beer) is served, but you can order breakfast, soup and salad, or a sandwich for 800 to 1,200 pesos ($1.60 to $2.40), more substantial main courses for about twice that amount.

Salas Norte y Occidente: These rooms deal with the "culture of the desert" from northern Mexico. If you're familiar with the culture of the American Indians of the southwestern United States, you'll notice many similarities here.

Many of the artifacts are from the Casas Grandes pueblo in the state of Chihuahua.

The occidental (western) exhibits hold echoes of the great civilization of the Valley of Mexico, mostly from sites such as Tzintzuntzan (Michoacan), Ixtlán (Nayarit), Ixtépete (Jalisco), and Chupicuaro (Guanajuato). The chac-mool from Ihuatzio, for instance, looks like a bad copy, or a stylized rendering, of the great chac-mools of Tula and Chichén-Itzá. There's also a model of a yacata, or vast stepped ceremonial platform, as found at many sites in the western zone.

Before leaving the museum, remember to take a look at those ethnographic exhibits on the upper floor.

Rufino Tamayo Museum

Oaxaca-born painter Rufino Tamayo not only contributed a great deal to modern Mexican painting. Over the years, the artist collected pre-Hispanic, Mexican, and foreign works of art. His collections are marvelous, and the attractive, boldly modern **Museo Rufino Tamayo** (tel. 286-5839) is the perfect place to display them. You'll see the museum in Chapultepec Park, on the right (north) side of Reforma, just before the National Museum of Anthropology.

Tamayo's pre-Hispanic collection is in a separate museum in the city of Oaxaca. Here in Mexico City you can see his collection of works gathered from many countries, unless there's a special exhibit on display. The museum staff brings world-class exhibits here frequently. If you see one advertised (in *The News,* for instance), don't miss it, for it's sure to be excellent. Hours are usually Tuesday through Sunday, 10 a.m. to 6 p.m.

Museum of Modern Art

The Museum of Modern Art (tel. 553-6211) is actually two buildings, set together in a statue-dotted section of grassy park, with two entrances: one on Reforma, the other across from—sort of behind—the Niños Héroes monument. The museum's interior is the perfect vehicle for showing works of art, simple with its handsome parquet floors, marble and stone walls, wood slatted ceiling, and circular windows (always covered by heavy drapes, presumably so the pictures don't get bleached by the sun).

The museum is open daily except Monday from 10 a.m. to 6 p.m., for an admission of 30 pesos (6¢). You get to it just through the entrance to Chapultepec Park at the western end of Reforma.

The museum section at the Reforma entrance has four salons, two on each level, around a central dome of incredible acoustic properties. The salons are attractive in their spaciousness, and give you the nice feeling that you're the only person in the museum. Exhibits in Salons I, II, and III are temporary, and have featured both Mexican and foreign artists including greats such as Magritte, Delvaux, Antonia Guerrero, Bissier, and Nay.

Salon IV houses a permanent collection of contemporary art, which seems to get even better each year. Most of the works are by Latin American artists and I—very critical when it comes to modern art—find most of them very palatable, and a few exceptional, such as Juan O'Gorman, Moro Hideo, and others.

In the circular rooms across the garden, near the Niños Héroes entrance to the museum, are more temporary exhibits. Note that the permanent collection of works by Mexican artists that used to be here has been moved to the Museo de Arte Carrillo Gil, in San Angel (see Section 4 of this chapter for details). This exceptionally fine collection encompasses works by Rivera, Kahlo, O'Gorman, Siquieros, Tamayo, Merida, Orozco, Gerszo, Romero, and others, and deserves a visit by all devotees of modern Mexican painting.

Museum of Natural History

An outstanding part of **New Chapultepec Park,** mentioned above, is the series of ten interconnecting domes that comprises the Museum of Natural History. From a distance the museum looks like a set of "topes" or brightly colored inverted bowls surrounded by foliage and flowers.

You can get there by bus 30 (see above, "Amusement Park"). Although it takes longer and costs more, you can also take the Metro to "Chapultepec" and get the no. 30 bus there.

Inside the museum, you'll see stuffed and preserved animals and birds, tableaux of different environments such as desert, seashore, tropical forest, and arctic tundra with the appropriate wildlife. Other domes contain exhibits relating to geology, astronomy, biology, the origin of life, and such displays as a relief map of the world's mountains and an illuminated map of Mexico showing the origin of various minerals.

The museum, fascinating for anyone with the slightest curiosity about nature and totally absorbing for youngsters, is open from 10 a.m. to 5 p.m. daily except Monday. There is no admission fee. Note: The large display cases of arctic bears and moose have pushbutton lighting (on the left)—a good idea in our age of conservation.

Just outside the museum and to the left is the **Ferrocarril,** a rubber-wheeled train, on which for a few pesos you can ride around this area. From here you can take the 15-minute walk to the Amusement Park or the Technological Museum, or if returning to the downtown area catch any of the no. 30 buses outside the museum.

Technological Museum

This museum is located in the western end of Chapultepec Park between the Amusement Park and Avenida Constituyentes. The best way to get there is to follow the directions to the Museum of Natural History given in the preceding section; from there it is only a 15-minute walk through very pleasant surroundings, as follows: take a northeasterly direction, past the Ferrocarril station on your left and then the lake on your right. When you come to a fork, bear left (downhill) to the large fountain and domed building on the left. Turn left at this rather weird fountain, then right through a series of fountains with circular snake reliefs. The Amusement Park and Technological Museum are a short distance straight ahead.

The museum is open from 9 a.m. to 5 p.m. daily; closed Monday. Entrance is free. The polyhedral dome outside is the **Planetarium,** which has scheduled shows at 10 a.m., noon, and 2 p.m. daily.

The museum is educational, to say the least. It is always filled with students madly taking notes on scientific developments through the ages. Inside and outside there are trains and planes, mockup factories, experiments of Morse and Edison, and various energy exhibits. When you're thoroughly exhausted, head for the basement, wherein a cafeteria for food or refrescas.

Galería del Auditorio

There is a newly opened galería for art exhibits on the second and third floors in the National Auditorium, across from the Hotel El Presidente Chapultepec. It is free and open from 9 a.m. to 5 p.m. Tuesday through Sunday. The exhibits change three or four times a year with works by local and internationally acclaimed artists. In 1980 they sponsored a weaving exhibit with some absolutely extraordinary display of cloths from Mexico and Central America. To get to the galería, you enter on the ground level of the National auditorium just off Reforma.

4. Sights South of the Center

Now that you've seen some of Mexico City's best downtown attractions, you might want to take an adventure farther afield. We'll look now at sights and activities in the southern reaches of the city which you can explore in a day or less.

You should make your trip to San Angel on Saturday if possible, as that's the day for the famous Bazar Sábado ("Saturday Bazaar"). On Saturday, Coyoacán has a small market as well. For many other sights—the Polyforum, University City—the day of the week doesn't matter. As for Xochimilco, it's busiest on Sunday, which is good if you like colorful crowds and activity, but bad if you hate crowded buses and haggling over prices. Don't go south on Monday, as most museums are closed then.

TRANSPORTATION: It might be best to plan two days for southern Mexico city. On a Saturday, catch a *colectivo* ("San Angel") or bus no. 17 ("Indios Verdes–Tlalpan") or no. 17-B ("Central Norte–Villa Olimpica") south along Insurgentes near the Zona Rosa. It will take you past the Polyforum Cultural Siqueiros to San Angel and its Bazar Sábado. After you visit these places, hop the same bus south to University City, Pedregal, and the Cuicuilco Pyramid. The bus trip takes almost an hour, straight through.

The Metro from the "Universidad" or "Coyoacán" station will give you a fast way to get back into town.

Heading south along Insurgentes, your first stop is at the mindboggling edifice called the Polyforum.

THE POLYFORUM CULTURAL SIQUEIROS: This gleaming new arts center is quite controversial: some say it's bold and imaginative, others say it's a modern monstrosity with overpowering murals, low claustrophobic ceilings, and poor acoustics that echo the slightest sound. Whichever it is, it does contain the world's largest mural (90,655 square feet) by a very well-known muralist, David Alfaro Siqueiros.

The polyforum (tel. 536-4524) is open from 10 a.m. to 2:30 p.m. and from 3:30 to 9 p.m. every day and costs 400 pesos (80¢) if you want to see the overambitious sculptured murals, *The March of Humanity on Earth* and *Toward the Cosmos,* by Siqueiros. They also stage a Sound and Light show here in English, for 1,000 pesos ($2) a head. Call for details.

Most of the Polyforum is devoted to art: on the floor that you enter is a small exhibition of visiting artists; on the two floors below are handcrafts from Mexico that you can purchase, although the prices are a bit high: the first level down has some art objects in glass display cases, while the floor below is basically the basement and things are just here and there in a wide open space.

After boggling your mind at the Polyforum, get back on Insurgentes and escape south in another colectivo or bus to San Angel.

IN SAN ANGEL: In the suburb of San Angel there are several famous colonial houses and the convent of the Carmelites. If you go on Saturday, you can combine your museum tour with a visit to San Angel's Bazar Sábado—see Section 6 of this chapter for details.

The nearest Metro station is M.A. Quevedo. A colectivo will terminate at the intersection of Insurgentes and Avenida La Paz; as for the bus, ask to get off at La Paz. There's a pretty park here, to the east, and on the west side of Insurgentes is a Sanborn's store and restaurant, good for a quick, moderately priced lunch. (My favorite is the fruit-and-sherbet salad plate, with a soft drink, for 1,000 pesos, $2.)

Walk west, up the hill on **La Paz,** and in a block you'll come to Avenida de la Revolución. To the left (south) is the dark colonial stone bulk of the Museo Colonial del Carmen. To the right, a few blocks north, is the Museo de Arte Carrillo Gil. And straight ahead across Revolución is the shady Plaza del Carmen.

The **Museo Colonial del Carmen** (tel. 548-5312), Av. Revolución 4, is a former Carmelite convent, now filled with religious paintings, other ancient artifacts, and a batch of mummified nuns in glass cases in the cellar! The museum, a maze of interlocking halls, corridors, stairways, chapels, and pretty flower-filled patios, is very pleasant to look around and is open from 10 a.m. to 5 p.m. every day for a few pesos admission.

San Angel's outstanding contribution to Mexican painting is the **Museo de Arte Alvar y Carmen T. Carrillo Gil** (tel. 548-7467), sometimes called the Museo de la Esquina (Museum on the Corner) as it is at a major intersection on the Avenida de la Revolución, at no. 1608. This modern gallery's collection of exhibit rooms include those dedicated to the works of José Clemente Orozco (1883–1942), Diego Rivera (1886–1957), David Alfaro Siqueiros (1896–1974), and rooms with works by a variety of Mexican painters. It's open 11 a.m. to 7 p.m. daily except Monday; admission is 50 pesos (10¢).

Having filled yourself with Mexican culture, both colonial and modern, head up the hill through the Plaza del Carmen on Calle Dr. Calvez. Soon you'll come to the beautiful **Plaza San Jacinto,** filled with artists and their paintings on Saturday. Many of the old buildings surrounding the Plaza San Jacinto have fine courtyards where crafts are sold. The Centro Cultural Isidro Fábela, at no. 15, deserves special mention.

Many famous personalities of show business, government, and social life maintain homes in San Angel, but the most famous house now belongs to the nation, to which it was recently donated by Isidro Fábela, an international jurist, statesman, and art collector. His house, the **Casa del Risco** ("House of Broken Porcelain"), was built during the 17th century and furnished in magnificent colonial style with ornate doors, fireplaces, coats-of-arms, statues, portraits, chairs, chests, and as the pièce de résistance, a fantastically decorated fountain that sits against one wall of the open patio. You'll have to see this fountain to believe it, for the decorative tiling consists of broken and unbroken pieces of porcelain that once comprised half a dozen banquet-size sets of porcelain. The Casa del Risco is open 10 a.m. to 6 p.m. every day except Monday, and entrance is free.

Two doors away from the Casa del Risco is the famous **Bazar Sábado,** in another colonial building. Be sure to take a turn through the building, whether or not you intend to buy. The crafts, the crowds, and the building itself are all wonderfully colorful.

Leaving the bazaar, spend some time in the plaza examining paintings. Some are excellent, others are quite good, and still others are, well, rather unfortunate. Prices are open to haggling.

Up the hill a few more steps from the Plaza San Jacinto is another, smaller plaza crowded with sellers of crafts, art objects, souvenirs, and tourist junk. The square is shady and interesting, festooned with printed and woven wall hangings.

After your shopping, are you up for a stroll? Continue uphill past the aforementioned little plaza on Calle Juárez. Soon you'll see a big old house—now a school—on your right at an intersection. Turn left, then left again, and you'll find your way to the gorgeous little **Plaza de los Archangelos.** Filled with bougainvillea (and often with adolescents in love), the plaza is a peaceful, flower-filled refuge away from the market bustle. The houses all around have high walls, exotic gardens, enormous gateways, and breathtaking price tags. When you're ready, retrace your steps; if you take that other road out down the hill you'll walk farther, and in traffic, to get back to the plaza.

Ready for lunch? The **Sanborn's** on Insurgentes (mentioned above) is a good, inexpensive bet. You can also have the buffet in the courtyard of the Bazar Sábado for about 3,500 pesos ($7), all in. Or you can dine in a marvelous colonial setting at the **San Angel Inn** (tel. 548-6746), at the corner of Palmas and Altavista. To get to the inn, walk up Calle Juárez out of the Plaza San Jacinto, past the little plaza, and turn right on Calle Reyna (or Reina). At the end of Calle Reyna, turn left onto Avenida Altavista. The inn is four blocks up—you can see it in the distance where the road curves.

The inn's courtyard is, well, like heaven I guess. Lush, green, peaceful, tasteful, a quiet refuge absolutely essential for anyone touring Mexico City. You can order a drink to be brought to one of the small, low tables here, or you can dine. The luncheon *menu turistico,* with tax, tip, and beverage all in, will run you 6,000 pesos ($12) or so.

All done in San Angel? Catch a no. 56 bus ("Alcantarilla–Col. Agrarista") at the San Angel Inn, or along Altavista, to get to Coyoacán or the Anahuacalli (see below). For University City, get back to Insurgentes and catch anything, colectivo or bus, with "Ciudad Universitaria," or simply "C.U.," in the window.

UNIVERSITY CITY: This is the site of the world's most flamboyant college campus and, indeed, of one of the world's most flamboyant architectural groupings. Appropriately enough, it is located on the avenue named Insurgentes, about 11 miles south of the Alameda Central.

University City (it houses Mexico's National Autonomous University) was planned to be the last and grandest achievement of the regime of former president Miguel Aleman. The original university is said to date back to 1551, which would make it the oldest university in the Western Hemisphere.

It's an astonishing place and well worth going out to see for its gigantic and brilliantly colored mosaics and murals. The most outstanding of these, by Juan O'Gorman, covers all four sides and ten complete stories of the library building. Fittingly, the mosaic wall depicts the history of Mexican culture and covers a space in which 2½ million books can be stored. The two lower stories are glass-enclosed and are used as the library's reading rooms.

The administration building, closest to the road, is mostly travertine onyx but also has an immense outer mural. This was executed by David Alfaro Siqueiros and depicts Mexican students returning the fruits of their labors to the nation. Diego Rivera's famous contribution is a sculpture-painting, which adorns the world's largest stadium (capacity: 102,000) across the highway.

Nobody will object if you wander at random around the campus, which accommodates 300,000 enrollment. There is a cafeteria on the ground floor of the humanities building and this, especially in summer, is well patronized by American students attending classes. All the university cafeterias are open to the public, and charge very reasonable prices.

Upstairs in the humanities building, you will find various notice boards. They merit a few moments' study, as their signs sometimes offer low-priced excursions or rides back to the States on a cost-sharing basis.

The university has its own Metro station ("Universidad"), but it's more than a mile from the library, so you should catch a no. 17-A, 17-B, 19, or 19-A bus along Insurgentes to go to and from the city center. Are you interested in seeing another pyramid? Then catch a no. 17 bus heading south on Insurgentes, and just after it crosses the Anillo Periferico Sur, hop off. You're only a 15-minute walk (go southeast) from the Museo y Ruinas de Cuicuilco.

The pyramid, open to visitors at all hours, represents some of the earliest civilization in the Valley of Mexico. Built in the Preclassic Period, around 1800 B.C., it was completely covered by a volcanic eruption (in A.D. 300), surviving only because it was protected by a strong outer wall. The museum closes at 5 p.m.

THE PEDREGAL: Near University City is Mexico's most luxurious housing development, the **Jardines del Pedregal de San Angel.** The word *pedregal* means lava, and that's precisely what this enormous area, stretching well beyond the university, consists of. In the Jardines del Pedregal, the only restriction placed upon homeowners is that they have enough money to buy at least 2,000 square meters of land and hire an architect to design their home. The result is that all the houses are exceptionally lavish, with swimming pools scooped out of the rock, split levels with indoor gardens, solid glass walls, and in one case, an all-glass sunroom on a narrow stilt above the house—like an airport's observation tower.

The pedregal, or lava, all came from the now-extinct volcano Xitle, whose eruption covered the above-mentioned Cuicuilco Pyramid. Only in recent times has the pedregal been regarded as anything but a nuisance; at one time, many of its caves hid bandits. Today, all kinds of odd plants and shrubs grow from its nooks and crevices, and if you are interested in botany, you'll want to take a good look around. The main street is the north-south Avenida Paseo del Pedregal.

TWO IN COYOACÁN: There are two interesting museums in the suburb of Coyoacán, near San Angel. If you have an extra morning I would strongly recommend a visit to the House and Museum of Trotsky and the Museo Frida Kahlo, the latter the former home of muralist Diego Rivera and his painter wife, whose name the house bears.

Coyoacán is a pretty, and wealthy, suburb with many old houses and cobbled streets. At the center are two large, graceful plazas, the Plaza Hidalgo and Jardín Centenario, and the Church of San Juan Bautista (1583). Once the capital of the Tepanec kingdom, Coyoacán was later conquered by the Aztecs, then by Cortés. The great conquistador had a palace here for a while.

The Metro, Line 3, can take you to "Coyoacán" station, within walking distance of Coyoacán's museums. Or buses 23 and 23-A ("Iztacala-Coyoacán") will get you from the center to this suburb. Catch the no. 23 going south on Bucareli, or the no. 23-A on Miguel Schultz, Antonio Caso, Río Rhin, or Niza.

Coming from San Angel, catch a no. 56 bus ("Alcantarilla–Col. Agrarista") heading east along the Camino al Desierto de los Leones or Avenida Altavista, near the San Angel Inn. When the bus gets to the corner of Avenida México and Xicoténcatl in Coyoacán, descend. Or, simpler, take a cab for the 15-minute ride.

Museo Frida Kahlo

The museum (tel. 677-2984) is about six blocks north of the plazas (ten blocks from the "Coyoacán" Metro station). There is a sign pointing east off Calle Centenario to the museum; follow this one block east to Allende. The house is on the corner of Allende and Londres—you can't miss it, for it's painted a brilliant blue with red trim.

Frida was born here on July 7, 1910, and occupied the house with Rivera from 1929 to 1954. The house is basically as she left it, and as you wander through the rooms you will get an overwhelming feeling for the life that they led. Their mementos are in every room, from the kitchen, where the names Diego and Frida are written on the walls, to the studio upstairs, where a wheelchair sits next to the easel with a partially completed painting surrounded by paint brushes, palettes, books, photographs, and other paraphernalia of the couple's art-centered lives.

The bookshelves are filled with books in many languages, nestled against a few of Rivera's files bearing such inscriptions as "Protest Rockefeller Vandalism," "Amigos Diego Personales," and "Varios Interesantes y Curiosos." Frida's paintings hang in every room, some of them dominated by the exposed human organs and dripping blood that apparently obsessed her in the final surgery-filled years of her life.

Frida was a collector of pre-Columbian art, so many of the rooms contain jewelry and terracotta figurines from Teotihuacán and Tlatelolco. She even went to the extreme of having a mockup of a temple built in the garden where she could exhibit her numerous pots and statues. On the back side of the temple are several skulls from Chichén-Itzá.

You will no doubt be spurred on to learn more about the lives of this remarkable couple. I can recommend Bertram D. Wolfe's *Diego Rivera: His Life and Times* and Hayden Herrara's *Frida: A Biography of Frida Kahlo*.

House and Museum of Trotsky

This most interesting place (tel. 554-4482) is located two blocks north and 2½ blocks east of the Frida Kahlo house, at Viena 45 between Gómez Farías and Morelos. You will recognize the house by the brick watchtowers on top of the high stone walls. There is a thick steel door, which more than likely will not be open, but will be opened for you by the caretaker from 10 a.m. to 2 p.m. and 3 to 5:30 p.m., Tuesday through Friday, 10:30 a.m. to 4 p.m. on weekends; closed Monday.

During Lenin's last days, when he was confined to bed, Stalin and Trotsky fought a silent battle for leadership of the Communist Party in the Soviet Union. Trotsky stuck to ideology, while Stalin took control of the party mechanism. Stalin won, and Trotsky was exiled, to continue his ideological struggle elsewhere. He settled here on the outskirts of Mexico City (this area was mostly fields then) to continue his work and writing on political topics and communist ideology. His ideas clashed with those of Stalin in many respects, and Stalin, wanting no opposition or dissension in world communist ranks, set out to have Trotsky assassinated. A first attempt failed but it served to give warning to Trotsky and his household, and from then on the house became a veritable fortress, with riflemen's watchtowers on the corners of the walls, steel doors (Trotsky's bedroom was entered only by thick steel doors), and round-the-clock guards, several of whom were Americans who sympathized with Trotsky's philosophies. Finally a man thought to have been paid, cajoled, or blackmailed by Stalin directly or indirectly was able to get himself admitted to the house by posing as a friend of Trotsky's and of his political views. On August 20, 1940, he put a mountaineer's axe into the philosopher's head. He was, of course, caught, but Trotsky died of his wounds shortly after.

If you saw the film *The Death of Trotsky* with Richard Burton, you already have a good idea of what the house looks like, for although the movie was not made here, the set that was used was a very good replica of the house and gardens. You can visit Natalia's (Trotsky's wife's) study, the communal dining room, Trotsky's study (with worksheets, newspaper clippings, books, and cylindrical wax dictating records still spread around), and his fortress-like bedroom.

Some of the walls still have the bullet holes left during the first attempt on his life. Trotsky's tomb, designed by Juan O'Gorman, is in the garden of the house.

Once you've seen Coyoacán, find your way to Avenida México-Coyoacán, and follow it northwest to the Metro station. If you're heading west to San Angel, catch a no. 56 on Calle Cuauhtémoc; going east to the Anahuacalli, catch a no. 56 on Calle Xicoténcatl, then transfer to a no. 25 ("Zacatenco-Tlalpan") or no. 59 ("El Rosario-Xochimilco") going south on the avenue called División del Norte.

DIEGO RIVERA MUSEUM (THE ANAHUACALLI): Probably the most unusual museum in the city is that designed by Diego Rivera before his death in 1957 and devoted to his works as well as to his extensive collection of pre-Columbian art. Called the Anahuacalli ("House of Mexico") Museum and constructed of pedregal (lava rock with which the area abounds), it is similar in style to Mayan and Aztec architecture. The name Anáhuac was the old name for the ancient Valley of Mexico.

The museum, admission free (tel. 677-2984), is open daily from 10 a.m. to 6 p.m. (closed Monday), and is situated on the southern outskirts of the city in the suburb of **San Pablo Tepetlapán,** at Calle Tecuila 150, off Calle del Museo. Take the Metro (Line 2) to the Tasqueña terminal. From the terminal, catch a SARO bus no. 136 ("Tasqueña-Peña Pobre") west, and it'll take you right past the museum.

Another way to get there is bus no. 25 ("Zacatenco-Tlalpan") south along Balderas, or no. 59 ("El Rosario-Xochimilco") south along Avenida Vasconcelos, Nuevo León, and Avenida División del Norte. Hop off at the Calle del Museo stop.

The museum is a ten-minute walk west along Calle del Museo from Avenida División del Norte. Signs point the way. If you see the no. 136 bus coming, you might as well hop aboard.

In front of the museum is a reproduction of a Toltec ball court, and the entrance to the museum itself is via a coffin-shaped door. Light filters in through translucent onyx slabs and is supplemented by lights inside niches and wall cases containing the exhibits. Rivera was a great collector of pre-Columbian artifacts and the museum includes literally hundreds of them, stashed on the shelves, tucked away in corners, and peeking from behind glass cases.

Upstairs, a replica of Rivera's studio has been constructed, and there you'll find the original sketches for some of his murals and two in-progress canvases. His first sketch (of a train) was done at the age of three, and there's a photo of it, plus a color photograph of him at work later in life in a pair of baggy pants and a blue denim jacket. Rivera (1886–1957) studied in Europe for 15 years, and spent much of his life as a devoted Marxist. Yet he came through political scrapes and personal tragedies with no apparent diminution of creative energy, and a plaque in the museum proclaims him "A man of genius who is among the greatest painters of all time."

XOCHIMILCO: As you might guess from its name, Xochimilco (pronounced "so-chee-*meel*-co") is a survival from the civilization of the Aztecs. They built gardens on rafts called *chinampas,* then set them afloat on a series of canals. Now, of course, the gardens are gone, but flower-bedecked boats still run to and fro.

Sad to say, Xochimilco is not in the best of shape today. Aside from the fact that it's become badly commercialized (from the moment you arrive, you'll be pestered by people trying to sell you something or persuade you to take one boat over another), the canals themselves are a bit polluted. On Sunday the place is jammed with foreign tourists and Mexican families with babies and picnic hampers; on weekdays, it's nearly deserted.

To reach Xochimilco, take the Metro to Tasqueña and then a bus. The buses run all the way across the city from north to south to end up at Xochimilco, but they take longer than the Metro. Of the buses coming from the center, the most convenient are nos. 31 and 33 ("La Villa–Xochimilco"), which you catch going south on Correo Mayor and Pino Suárez near the Zócalo; or no. 59, which you catch near Chapultepec on Avenida Vasconcelos, Avenida Nuevo León, and Avenida División del Norte.

When you get to the town of Xochimilco, you'll find a busy market in operation, specializing in garish, brightly decorated pottery. Turn along Madero and follow signs that say "Los Embarcaderos." If you can resist the blandishment of the inevitable salesmen and shills, you will eventually arrive at the docks.

The boats are priced according to their size and the number of people they can hold, plus your skill as a bargainer. The going rate for a medium-size boat which can hold five or six persons is about 2,000 pesos ($4) per hour. If you have a group of four or five people, a picnic lunch, and a few six-packs of beer or soft drinks, the ride can be a pleasure. Xochimilco is definitely the sort of place that is best enjoyed in a small group.

5. Sights North of the Center

Within the northern city limits are two more interesting locations, and another is just a short ride outside. You can take the Metro to the Plaza de las Tres Culturas (Tlatelolco station), and then continue up the same line to the Basilica de Guadalupe (Basilica station). Finally, the "Tacuba" station on Lines 2 and 7 (not the "Tacubaya" station!) is the place to catch a bus for the short ride to Tepotzotlán.

PLAZA DE LAS TRES CULTURAS: A few miles north of the Alameda, in **Tlatelolco,** stands this monument to the long and varied history of Mexico: all three cultures—Aztec, Spanish, and contemporary—are architecturally represented here.

During the Aztec Empire, Tlatelolco was on the northern edge of Lake Texcoco and for a long time it maintained its autonomy, independent of the Aztecs. In May of 1521 it was to Tlatelolco that Cuauhtémoc and his army withdrew when Cortés marched for the second time on the great city of Tenochtitlán. Cuauhtémoc would not surrender and after a three-month siege, with thousands of his army dead from starvation or wounds, he was finally captured. Reduced to a wretched state of captivity, he grabbed Cortés's dagger and fell upon it. The Plaza de las Tres Culturas is where this heroic siege took place, and a plaque commemorates it.

Afterward, Tlatelolco was officially abandoned, and it remained so until 1960 when the government began a redevelopment program to clean up the slum area that had grown during the years of neglect. Tlatelolco today is a suburb of housing projects, and not a very attractive one at that, but these tall building complexes represent the "contemporary" aspect.

The beautiful Spanish church that stands in the plaza, albeit at a slight angle as a result of sinking into the lake bed, is the famous **Cathedral of Santiago Tlatelolco.** Built in the 16th century entirely of volcanic stone, it echoes Aztec construction, which was made from the same stone. Inside, most of the frescoes have been badly damaged over the years; the interior has been tastefully restored, preserving little patches of fresco in stark white plaster walls, with a few deep-blue stained-glass windows and an unadorned stone altar.

To get to the plaza, take the Metro (Line 3) to Tlatelolco, leave the terminal by the exit to Manuel González, and turn right on this street. Walk two blocks to Avenida Lázaro Cárdenas and turn right again. The plaza is about half a block south, on the left, just past the Clinico Hospital. The walk takes less than 15 minutes.

BASILICA OF GUADALUPE: The Basilica of Our Lady of Guadalupe (Metro: Basilica) is on the site of the spot where a poor Indian named Juan Diego is reputed to have seen a vision, on December 9, 1531, of a beautiful lady in a blue mantle. The local bishop was reticent to confirm that Juan had indeed seen the Virgin Mary, and so he asked the peasant for some evidence. Juan saw the vision a second time, and it became miraculously emblazoned on the poor peasant's cloak. The bishop immediately ordered the building of a church on the spot, and upon its completion the image was hung in the place of honor, framed in gold. Since that time millions upon millions of the devout and the curious have come to this spot to view the miraculous image that experts, it is said, are at a loss to explain. The blue-mantled Virgin of Guadalupe is the patron saint of Mexico.

So heavy was the flow of visitors—many of whom approached for hundreds of yards on their knees—that the old church became insufficient to handle it, and an audacious new basilica was built, designed by the same architect who did the breathtaking National Museum of Anthropology.

To get to the basilica, take the Metro Line 3 to the "Basilica" station and take the exit marked "Salida Av. Montiel." A half-block or so north of the Metro station, turn right onto Avenida Montiel. The street is crowded with food and trinket vendors who know that floods of people will be passing along the street all day to get to the basilica. After about 15 minutes' walk, you'll see the great church looming ahead.

For a view of the miraculous cloak, which hangs at the altar, you should make your way to the lower level of the church. The architect has designed it so that you can look up from below through an opening at the image.

At the top of the hill, behind the basilica, is a cemetery and also several gift shops specializing in trinkets encased in seashells and other folk art. The steps up this hill are lined with flowers, shrubs, and waterfalls, and the climb, although tiring, is worthwhile for the view from the top.

Should you be lucky enough to visit Mexico City on December 12, you can witness the grand festival in honor of the Virgin of Guadalupe. The square in front of the basilica fills up with the pious and the party-minded as prayers, dances, and a carnival atmosphere attract thousands of the devout.

TEPOTZOTLÁN: Interested in baroque architecture? Want a close-up view of small-town Mexican daily life. Set aside a morning or afternoon for an excursion to the colonial town of Tepotzotlán, 24 miles north of Mexico City. Tepotzotlán's fine church (1682) is among the finest examples of churrigueresque (Mexican baroque) architecture, and the museum attached to it has a rich collection of paintings (including a Tintoretto), church ceremonial objects, vestments, pottery, and carving. Plan your visit for any day Wednesday through Sunday; the church is closed on Monday, and the museum is closed on Tuesday.

You can make the trip in a morning or an afternoon by taking the Metro to the "Tacuba" (*not* "Tacubaya"!) station, walking over Aquiles Serdan on the pedestrian bridge, and then catching a bus (one-hour trip) to Tepotzotlán. If you drive, go west on Paseo de la Reforma, and shortly after you pass the Auditorio Municipal (on your left) in Chapultepec Park, turn right (north) onto the Anillo Periferico. This soon becomes the Avenida Manuel Avila Camacho, which in turn becomes Hwy. 57D, the toll road to Querétaro. About 35 kilometers (22½ miles) out of the city, look for the turn to Tepotzotlán, which is about 2 kilometers west of the highway.

Whether you come by bus or car, you'll soon end up in the town's main square, where you'll spot the church's extravagantly elaborate façade at once. This is considered one of the three finest examples of churrigueresque decoration, the other two being the Santa Prisca in Taxco, and La Valenciana in Guanajuato.

The grand extravagance of the façade is echoed inside the church, which is richly decorated with carved altarpieces and paintings. When your senses start to reel from the power and weight of it all, stroll outside, turn right, and enjoy the shady park standing in front of the museum.

The **National Viceroy's Museum** (Museo Nacional del Virrienato) Plaza Hidalgo 99 (tel. 987-0332), was once the Novitiate of the Company of Jesus (1585). Besides the dozens of rooms with displays of colonial treasures, be sure to inspect the Domestic Chapel, dating from about the same time as the neighboring church.

The main church, the **Templo de San Francisco Javier,** has ten altars in the exaggerated baroque churrigueresque style, bearing paintings by Miguel Cabrera. There are also 22 canvases by Cristóbal de Villalpando outlining the life of San Ignacio de Loyola, as well as a rich collection of colonial furnishings and artifacts.

Hours for the museum are Tuesday through Sunday from 11 to 6; admission costs 40 pesos (8¢), half-price for students. On Saturday and Sunday, admission is free.

After you've seen Tepotzotlán's colonial monuments, you might want to have a look at the market, or simply wander the cobbled streets for a while. The bus back to Mexico City passes right through the main square. Those with cars might want to continue on (north) along Hwy. 57D, the Querétaro toll road, to the ruined Toltec city of Tula (see Chapter XI).

6. Crafts Shops and Markets

Mexico is a marvelous place to buy crafts of all types. You'll come across numerous places displaying fascinating native products, and you're certain to find something you want as a souvenir. Here's the rundown on the best places to shop, from small, selective crafts shops to vast general markets. But first, a few words about the fine art of haggling.

HOW TO BARGAIN: First and foremost, *never start bargaining unless you intend to buy*. Once you've looked around the shop or shops (at leisure and never showing too much enthusiasm over any one object, especially the one you're thinking of purchasing), ask the price. After the shopkeeper has answered, you might respond with *"es muy caro"* (it's very expensive), or better yet with no response at all. He will probably lower his price or ask you, *"¿Cuanto quiere pagar?"* (How much do you want to pay?). Don't answer at this point, just keep looking around, asking prices of things you're interested in. Once you have an idea of his prices and have decided the price you're willing to pay, then you can begin to bargain.

There are two approaches I've used—the first is probably the best: I set a price I want to pay for the goods (never wanting it so much that I can't leave without buying it). I look around a bit more (perhaps there's something else, and it's always easier to bargain a "two-for-one" price), then I state my price *"a la mas, tres mil pesos"* (at the most, 3,000 pesos). Simple: No bargaining, just state the price you want to pay. This approach, of course, is good only if you're a fair judge of quality and know the going prices around town. Obviously, if he asks 4,000 pesos for a hand-embroidered shirt and you tell him 400 pesos, then all you've accomplished is an insult!

The second approach is to halve the quoted price (depending on the product) and work on up to a compromise: He asks 10,000 pesos, you say 5,000, and you end up at 7,500—plus or minus 500 depending on who's the more adept at bargaining.

CRAFTS SHOPS: Mexico is famous the world over for the quality and variety of its arts and crafts. Today it often costs only a little more money to buy these things in the capital than at the source, if one knows a good shop. Several government-run shops and a few excellent privately run shops have exceptionally good collections of Mexico's arts and crafts. As fascinating as a fine art gallery, these shops deserve a visit whether you intend to buy or not.

The city is loaded with **Artes Populares** (handcrafts) shops. Two of the nicest shops with the most varied assortment of gifts are those run by the government, and the *prices are fixed* so you can avoid haggling. The **Exposición Nacional de Arte Popular** (Metro: Hidalgo or Juárez), located at Juárez 89, has simply everything! There are two floors of papier-mâché figurines, woven goods, earthenware, colorfully painted candelabras, hand-carved wooden masks, straw goods, beads, bangles, and glass.

When you're finished here, walk down a few blocks to the **National Museum of Popular Industrial Arts,** located across the street from the Benito Juárez statue in Alameda Park at Juárez 44. They have similar Mexican crafts from all over, and because the prices are fixed you can get an idea of quality vs. cost for later use in market bargaining. Even if you don't buy anything you should visit the shop, as it displays an enormous selection of crafts. Both government shops are open every day except Sunday, from 10 a.m. to 6 p.m.

The first store described above, the Exposición Nacional, and also the attractive store at Juárez 70 (in the Hotel Del Prado), plus the store at Juárez 92, are all operated by the quasi-governmental body known as FONART (Fondo Nacional para el Fomento de las Artesanías). FONART helps village craftsmen with problems of quality control and marketing.

The State of Mexico has gotten into the crafts shop act by opening the **Casa de las Artesanías del Estado de México,** or CASART for short, at Juárez 18-C. Look in this small shop for crafts produced in the state of Mexico, which surrounds the Federal District. Hours are Monday through Saturday from 10 a.m. to 7 p.m.

Victor's Artes Populares Mexicanas (tel. 512-1263) is a shop for serious buyers and art collectors. The Fosado family has been in the folk art business for 60 years and is a reputable authority. The store is located near the Alameda at Madero 10, second floor, Room 305 (Metro: Bellas Artes). They buy most of their crafts from the Indian villages near and far, and supply various exhibits with native craftworks.

CRAFTS MARKETS: These outdoor/indoor places have a lively village air about them.

Centro Artesanal (Mercado de Curiosidades)

This is a rather modern building set back off a plaza on the corner of Ayuntamiento and Dolores (Metro: Salto del Agua). It's comprised of a number of stalls on two levels selling everything from leather to tiles. They have some lovely silver jewelry and, as in most non-fixed-price stores, the asking price is high but the bargained result is often very reasonable.

Mercado de Artesanías "La Ciudadela"

An interesting market (Metro: Juárez), large, clean, and with numerous little streets, it rambles on forever just off Balderas and Ayuntamiento in the Plaza de la Ciudadela. The merchandise is of good quality, well displayed, and bartering is a must. I think this is probably the best place for buying; anything you want is here. The shops don't really get going until 11 a.m. or noon so it's best to save your shopping in this area until the afternoon. Open until 8 p.m. You might want to come for lunch before shopping; if so I can highly recommend the restaurant in the market called **Fonda Lupita,** Local no. 89 (ask someone). It has Spanish decor, and it's immaculately clean. A very handsome white-haired lady keeps the place shipshape and also prepares the very tasty food. A set lunch costs only 325 pesos (65¢); a plate of enchiladas, a mere 250 pesos (50¢).

Central Crafts Market

Not far from Buena Vista Railroad Station (Estación Buena Vista) is the Central Crafts Market, a commercial concern with a lot of floor space and an uninspired collection of crafts at rather high prices. If you want to take a look, get a no. 17 bus going north on Insurgentes to the railroad station. Get off and walk in front of the station—you'll be heading east. The first real north-south street you will come to is Calle Aldama, and the Central Crafts Market is at Aldama 187, just a few steps away. Or you can hop a no. 4 bus going west on Juárez, and it'll drop you right at the market.

Note: The Central Crafts Market employs undercover agents who prowl the length of Avenida Juárez and other tourist-frequented areas to tout the excellence of the market's wares. Offering "free tourist information" or "free guide service," they are friendly and helpful, but their goal is to persuade you to visit the market.

THE BAZAR SÁBADO: The Bazar Sábado in San Angel, a suburb a few miles south of the city, is held on Saturday, as its names indicates. If you like outdoor markets, you'll like this one. Plan to spend all of Saturday touring the attractions on the southern outskirts of the city, guided by Section 4, above.

OTHER SHOPS: Mexico City has thousands of other shops selling everything imaginable. The two best districts for browsing are on and off Avenida Madero and the streets parallel to it, and in the Zona Rosa (for jewelry, Calle Amberes is the place, for instance). A few unique shops deserve particular mention.

A Sweet Shoppe

Here's a crafts shop of a completely different kind. The **Dulcería de Celaya,** Motolinia 36, between Madero and 16 de Septiembre, is a beautiful old confectioner's shop founded in 1874. In its 19th-century windows you'll see a mouthwatering selection of the sweets for which the city of Celaya is famous: candied fruits of all varieties, jars of sweetened goat milk, sugar-coated almonds, fudge, pecan candies. Even if your diet doesn't allow you to buy, you should at least take a look at the lovely shop, open Monday through Saturday during business hours.

Mexican Wines

Oenophiles will be pleased to know that Mexico now produces a surprisingly good selection of palatable wines. About the best shop for surveying this selection is **La Puerta del Sol,** Avenida 16 de Septiembre no. 10, near the corner with Avenida Lázaro Cárdenas.

LARGE GENERAL MARKETS: Try your bargaining skill at the **Merced Market,** the biggest in the city (Metro: Merced). Continue down Fray Servando about six blocks and take a left on the Avenida Anillo de Circunvalación. The market is three or four blocks up this street.

The Merced Market consists of sesveral modern buildings. The first is mainly for fruits and vegetables; the others contain just about everything you would find if a department store joined forces with a discount warehouse—a good place to go looking for almost anything.

The area to the north of the market is a tangled confusion of trucks and stores, in which cascades of oranges spill gloriously down onto sidewalks. At the corner of Circunvalación and Calle Gómez Pedraza, a crowd has gathered to watch a street entertainer do his tricks. His rolled-up handkerchief lies on the ground and, as he beckons it toward him, in a cracked voice, interruptions come from a small figure in a battered fedora hat. The crowd roars, as much at the incongruity of the urchin's painted cheeks, oversize black mustache, and baggy pants, as at anything he says. Finally, feigning uncontrolled indignation, the entertainer seizes his straight "man" by the tie and drags him around the circle. But the boy (who can't be older than seven) has slipped out of the noose, which hangs limply from the entertainer's hand, and continues blithely on his way. A shower of coins testifies to the crowd's appreciation.

These street entertainers, the equivalent of Europe's age-old buskers, can be found everywhere in the capital. Many of them are strolling musicians or mariachis, but sometimesthey are youthful crosswalk teams with amazing mass appeal. It isn't necessary to speak Spanish to appreciate the down-to-earth humor of, say, a pair who can sometimes be found doing a "Knock, knock, who's there?" routine at the head of the Calle Talavera, which goes into the Plaza Merced.

To return to the Zócalo or anywhere else within the city, take the Metro from the Merced station, which is just outside the enclosed market. You can change at Pino Suárez (first shop) to take you to the Zócalo.

A few blocks north of the Plaza de Garibaldi (Metro: Allende) is another market well worth visiting. The **Lagunilla Market,** whose two enclosed sections, separated by a short street, Calle Juan Alvarez, have different specialties, is noted for clothes, rebozos, and blankets to the north, and tools, pottery, and household goods, such as attractive copper hanging lamps, to the south. This is also the area for old and rare books, many at a ridiculously low cost, if you're willing to hunt and bargain. Most, however, are in Spanish.

7. For Excitement: Bullfights and Horse Races

THE BULLFIGHTS: The capital's **Plaza México** (Metro: San Antonio on Line 7) is among the largest bullrings in the world. It seats 64,000 people and on Sunday during the professional season (usually December through April, but no fixed dates) most seats are taken. On other sundays through the year, the arena is given over to the beginners or *nouvilleros;* most of them are as bad as the beginners in any other sport. Six fights make up a *corrida,* which begins precisely at 4 p.m. and is one of the few things in Mexico that's always on time.

There are several ways to reach the Plaza México, which is situated two or three miles south along Insurgentes. Any big hotel or tour agency will be happy to book you onto a tour with transportation, 4,000 to 5,000 pesos ($8 to $10) and up—and that's real luxury living. Alternatively, you can take the Metro, or colectivo; the meager number of colectivos that normally roam Insurgentes is supplemented by Sunday afternoon taxis headed for the plaza, and they'll often pick up extra passengers going their way. Or you can catch the buses marked

"Plaza México" that travel down Insurgentes on Sunday afternoon. Finally, you can catch a no. 17 bus along Insurgentes.

Roughly 25 minutes after you start out, the bus will pass the bullring on the right. At the point at which you should alight, the ring is hidden by buildings, so you'll have to watch for a gray, modern apartment building to your right, its exterior more windows than walls. (This is Insurgentes 949, and its owners are so proud of it that, as in many cases of modern buildings in Mexico, they have listed the architect's name, Francisco Artigas, above the entrance.)

Most of the people on the bus will alight here, so you'll know you're at the bullring, which is just around the corner ahead. On the way you'll see dozens of men and women squatting on blankets selling nuts, hats, and all kinds of whatnots. Look for a woman or muchacha selling chewing gum and waving small "programs." If you buy the chewing gum, she'll give you (free) the one-page sheet that lists the names of the day's toreros.

Unless you want to pay more, take your place in the line at one of the windows marked *"Sol General."* It will be in the sun and it will be high up. But the sun isn't too strong (it sets soon, anyway), and you won't see many other tourists that way. Try to avoid the seats numbered 1 to 100; for some reason, the roughnecks prefer to gather in this section. Seats in *la sombra* (shade) are more expensive, of course.

Usually, there are six separate bulls to be killed (two by each matador) in a corrida, but I'd suggest that you leave just before the last bull gets his—to avoid the crowds. Outside, around two sides of the bullring is a scene of frantic activity. Hundreds of tiny stalls have masses of food frying, cold beer stacked high, and radios blaring with a commentary on the action inside the ring.

A DAY AT THE RACES: Mexico City's racetrack, the **Hipodromo de las Americas,** is as extraordinarily beautiful as many of its other tourist-popular spots. Approached by way of a tree-lined boulevard and containing a small lake on which an occasional swan or heron basks, it has stands built on the hillside for a good view of the track.

The track operates on Tuesday (in winter only), Thursday, Saturday and Sunday for 11 months of the year; it is closed only for part of September and October. Take a colectivo marked "Hipodromo" along Reforma, which takes you through Chapultepec to the Anillo Periferico (also called Avenida Manuel Avila Camacho). The track is just off this main entry, near the intersection with Calzada Legaria. You can also take the Metro to Toreo Quatro Caminos (Line 2), and then a taxi.

Once at the track, you may enter through a special (free) tourist gate, paying only the applicable tax. The normal price of admission is through purchase of a program. If you don't get a program, you won't have much idea what's going on, so you'd better buy one at the gate. Two or more people may enter on one program, but each must pay the program's tax. Inside, head for the stands and grab a seat. If you're willing to spend the extra loot, you can climb one level higher and sit at a table where the view is excellent and a minimum amount must be consumed in either food or drink. Racing begins at 2:15 p.m.

Betting: You can bet either to win *(primera),* to place *(segunda),* or to show *(tercera).* All windows have signs in both English and Spanish. On certain races, marked on the program with bold letters—"**SELECCIÓN 1-2**"—you can win a substantial sum by picking the horses that will come in first and second and placing a bet on your selections. In some races, there is an alternative way of betting called the *quiniela.* This operates on a similar principle, except that your choices for first and second can come in second and first.

Chapter X

MEXICO CITY: BUDGET NIGHTTIME ACTIVITIES

1. Nightlife in the Zona Rosa
2. Mariachis, Music, and Margaritas
3. High Culture
4. Movies and Theaters
5. The Ballet Folklorico
6. Jai Alai
7. The National Lottery Drawing

MEXICO CITY POSITIVELY SHINES with the glimmer of a billion lamps as night comes on. A torrent of headlamps floods rapidly along the Paseo de la Reforma in each direction of traffic, whizzing in circles around the Angel Monument which itself is dazzlingly illuminated by powerful floodlamps. At the foot of the monument lies the Zona Rosa, the city's brightest nighttime quarter.

Survey all this from the top of a tall hotel, or from the Latin American Tower, and it is certainly a captivating sight. Launch out into this glimmering sea for an evening's amusement and you can easily—*easily*—end up tens of thousands of pesos poorer. If your entertainments are of the contrived type (say, a supper club at a fancy hotel, with drinks and a show, cover charges, minimums, service charges, tips) you can enjoy them here at a price that compares favorably with any other major city, but that is still a lot of money. On the other hand, if you're willing to let *la vida Mexicana* put on its own fascinating show for you, the bill will be no more than a few dollars, or even nothing at all.

People-watching, café-sitting, music, even a dozen mariachi bands all playing at once, can be yours for next to nothing. To start, let's go straight to the heart of the city's nocturnal brouhaha, the famous Pink Zone.

1. Nightlife in the Zona Rosa
Although the Zona Rosa has a well-deserved reputation as Mexico City's high-priced playground, it is also true that the Zona Rosa by night in summer is

an unending carnival of people and places, lights and sights. You can enjoy yourself here for zero-dollars-and-zero-cents by window-shopping, people-watching, and generally taking it all in. Or you can spend a few pesos and have dessert and a cup of coffee, or perhaps a drink, and watch the ebb and flow of traffic. It's worth saving up some extra money to have at least one dinner here (see Chapter VIII for detailed suggestions). Whichever way you decide to take in the Pink Zone, you'll be glad you came to see this slice of life (taken from the upper crust, of course). Here are some prime locales for Pink Zone promenades:

The streets named Genova, Copenhague, and Oslo have been turned into pedestrian-only streets (save for the occasional car zipping in to the Aristos hotel), and sidewalk café-restaurants have sprung up making Copenhague one of Mexico City's most delightful "in" places. Tables are usually packed unless you come early. Some establishments are selected by the cognoscenti as "in," and chairs are then at a premium; while other places do a slower business and have tables more readily available. On Oslo the attraction is the several coffee-houses with coffee, pastries, and fortunetellers. Try, for instance, the **Elite Café Turco,** at no. 3, where coffee and pastry costs about 750 pesos ($1.50), plus a reading of the Tarot deck just-for-you at 900 pesos ($1.80). The low, mod decor here draws mostly people in love and people who are looking to fall in love.

Another such crossroads for live entertainment is in the arcade located at Londres 104, just off Genova. Half a dozen restaurants here (Alfredo, La Trucha Vagabunda, Toulouse-Lautrec) also serve as cafés, and some have live entertainment most evenings. Come for a margarita at 1,000 pesos ($2), a shrimp cocktail, or a full meal—by sitting in the outdoor section of one restaurant, you get to enjoy what's going on in neighboring places as well.

2. Mariachis, Music, and Margaritas

MARIACHIS: At some time or other, everybody—Mexicans and turistas alike—goes to see and hear the mariachi players. The mariachis are strolling musicians who wear distinctive costumes, which make them look like cowboys dressed up for a special occasion. Their costume—tight spangled trousers, fancy jackets, and big floppy bow ties—dates back to the French occupation of Mexico in the mid-19th century, as, indeed, does their name. Mariachi is the Mexican mispronunciation of the French word for marriage, which is where they were often on call for music.

In Mexico City, the mariachis make their headquarters around the **Plaza de Garibaldi,** which is a ten-minute stroll north of the Palacio de Bellas Artes up Avenida Lázaro Cárdenas, at Avenida República de Honduras. You pass dozens of stores and a couple of burlesque houses.

In the Plaza de Garibaldi itself, mariachi players swarm all over. Wherever there's a corner, guitars are stacked together like rifles in an army training camp. For music, see what there is of it in the square itself (hottest about 9 or 10 o'clock in the evening, especially on Sunday). Young musicians strut proudly in their flashy outfits, on the lookout for señoritas to impress. They play when they feel like it, or when there seems to be a good chance to gather in some tips, or when someone orders a song—the going rate seems to be around 2,000 pesos ($4) per song.

After all that singing, a man's got to wet his whistle, and so the plaza is surrounded with places for drinking and singing. Most famous of these is the **Tenampa,** once an all-male preserve but now open to men and women (no children, though), tourist and local alike. Across the plaza is the **Tlaquepaque,** a rather fancy restaurant where you can dine to strolling mariachis. But perhaps the most adventurous spot for newcomers to Mexico City is the **Pulquería Hermana Hortensia,** near the northeast corner of the plaza at the corner of Amargura and República de Honduras. Unlike most pulque bars, La Hermana Hortensia is a *pulquería familiar* (a "family" bar, that is, you can bring your wife—but not your kids). Pulque (that's "*pool*-keh") is a thick and flavorsome drink made by fermenting the juice of a maguey (century) plant. Discovered by the ancient Toltecs and shared with the Aztecs, pulque was a sacred drink forbidden to the common people for centuries. One of the effects of the Spanish Conquest was to liberate pulque for the masses. Was this good or bad? Ask your neighbor in La Hermana Hortensia as you quaff the thick brew. Pulque packs a whallop, although it's not nearly so strong as those other maguey-based drinks, tequila and mezcal. By the way, the pulque here can be ordered with nuts blended in for a different flavor.

In any of the eating and drinking establishments around the plaza you can enjoy the mariachi music that swirls through the air. But remember—if you give a bandleader the high sign, you're the one who pays the piper for the song, just like outside in the square.

Don't get the idea that you'll see only your countrymen in the Plaza Garibaldi, for it is indeed a Mexican phenomenon. As evening falls, lots of people from the neighborhood come to stroll or sit, catching some of the music or trying their hand at one of the stands where they can bust a balloon with a dart to win a prize.

MUSIC: The plushest circumstances under which I've ever listened to a pianist were at the **Hotel Maria Isabel,** Reforma 325, near the Angel (tel. 525-9060). A split-level fountain tips you off as to the quality of this hotel even before you enter. Once inside, you'll sink ankle-deep into lush red or blue carpets, admire hunks of Mayan architecture spotlighted in corridors, and eventually find your way to an elegant, second-floor cocktail bar. Drinks here cost about 1,500 to 2,000 pesos ($3 to $4) each, and for this you'll hear some marvelous arrangements from whichever "musica romantica" group happens to be featured— usually dreamy Latin stuff.

For contrast and high decibels, try **Le Rendezvous** at Madero 29 (tel. 518-3955), across from the Ritz Hotel several blocks west of Zócalo. From about 7 p.m. until midnight the place has jazz and rock groups that change hourly. There is a 400-peso (80¢) cover. Drinks run about 750 pesos ($1.50). A popular place—I've returned on several occasions always to find a jolly atmosphere.

MARGARITAS: The ubiquitous **cantinas** are more or less off limits for the average American tourist, especially women (they're usually not allowed inside). It is in the cantinas that you see the liveliest side of the Mexican male; it can be bawdy as the men "let loose" after a few tequilas. The **Bar Negresco,** on the corner of Balderas and Victoria (Morelos), is one such cantina, and even though it hangs out the "women welcome" sign the liveliness of the gatherings has not been refined. It's a grand ol' place, and dates back a long time. In fact, it was in the 1940s that an American correspondent, Alma Reed, entered the cantina and broke the sex barrier. The drinks cost 500 to 1,000 pesos ($1 to $2), and if you arrive in late afternoon you'll be treated to a free plate of entremeses (hors d'oeuvres).

Until a few years ago **La Opera Bar** (tel. 512-8959) was a staunchly masculine drinking and dining establishment at 5 de Mayo no. 14, corner of Filomeno Mata (a block from the Bellas Artes if you're heading toward the Zócalo). But now both men and women may enter and enjoy the gilded baroque ceilings, the dark wood booths with patches of beveled mirror and exquisite small oil paintings of pastoral scenes, or sidle up to the heavy carved wooden bar for some tequila and lime. La Opera used to be the Mexican's equivalent of a Londoner's club, and men in shirtsleeves or dark suits will be playing dominoes or cards, drinking beer at 440 pesos (88¢) or *copas* (hard liquor of whatever sort) at 550 to 1,100 pesos ($1.10 to $2.22), and perhaps having supper from the selective menu. Now the men are better dressed and even better behaved. La Opera Bar is open every day, but it closes early (9 p.m.) on Saturday night.

3. High Culture

Mexico City has much to offer in the way of opera, ballet, symphony, chamber music, and recitals. The quality of the performances is very high, and ticket prices—by North American standards—are delightfully low.

OPERA AND BALLET: Opera performances are usually held in either the **Palacio de Bellas Artes** or in the **Auditorio Nacional** (across from the Hotel El Presidente Chapultepec, in Chapultepec Park). Ballet is often performed in these two places as well, perhaps more frequently in the Auditorio. Sometimes they stage *Swan Lake* on the island in the lake in Chapultepec Park!

CLASSICAL MUSIC: Besides the Bellas Artes and the Auditorio Nacional, another popular venue for concerts is the **University Cultural Center,** near the university campus at Insurgentes Sur 3000, at the southern limits of the city. The two most popular halls here are the **Netzahualcóyotl Concert Hall** and **Miguel Covarrubias Hall.** These are a bit out of the way (though you can get there quickly by Metro). However, there's another chamber music hall less than a block from the Bellas Artes, right in the center of town. It's the **Palacio de Minería,** Calzada Tacuba no. 5, just off Avenida Lázaro Cárdenas.

For current information on cultural offerings, pick up the Friday edition of *The News,* which has a full listing of culture events. The *Mexico City Daily Bulletin,* a free daily newspaper found in hotel lobbies, is also a good source of current information.

4. Movies and Theaters

MOVIES: You'll find many current first-run hits playing in Mexico City, usually in the original-language version with Spanish subtitles, and usually under the same title (although the title will be translated into Spanish).

The best place to check for what's currently being shown is in the entertainment section of Mexico City's English-language paper, *The News.* Note that various cinema clubs, and the National Museum of Anthropology, also screen films from time to time.

Tickets cost about 250 to 400 pesos (50¢ to 80¢), even at the fancy movie houses along Reforma. At the gigantic Cine Diana, near the Angel Monument, there's a bonus: an enormous mural stretching the entire length of one wall, which is almost worth the price of admission alone.

THEATERS: There are a few theaters near the Plaza de la República, centered on Calle Antonio Caso. Bright marquees advertise the plays or vaudeville shows currently running, and box offices sell reserved-seat tickets in advance. It's all in Spanish, of course, but still very entertaining. As ticket prices are low, you have little to lose by trying an evening at the theater. Check the entertainment listings in the daily Spanish-language newspapers for current theater offerings.

The English-language community in Mexico City sponsors plays and shows in English from time to time, and *The News* will always carry details.

The **National Auditorium** (Auditorio Nacional) in Chapultepec Park, fronting onto Reforma, is usually the biggest bargain in town. International ballet, opera, and theater companies play here at prices as low as 300 pesos (60¢) per seat. Often they are the same companies that played at the elegant Bellas Artes theater with a 1750-peso ($3.50) minimum. The newspapers list performances at both.

5. The Ballet Folklorico

A combination of religious ceremony, can-can, pantomime, low comedy, and sheer beauty of color, design, and choreography—that's the **Ballet Folklorico de México.** There are two companies—three, if you count the one usually on tour—and their performances are given at the Palacio de Bellas Artes (tel. 585-4888, ext. 29).

Performances are on Sunday at 9:30 a.m. and 9 p.m. and on Wednesday at 9 p.m.; you cannot buy your tickets before Monday for the Wednesday performance, or Thursday for Sunday. The box office is open 10:30 a.m. to 1 p.m. and 4 to 7 p.m.; tickets range from galería seats on the third floor, at 1,500 pesos ($3), to 4,000 pesos ($8) for second-floor and 5,000 pesos ($10) for first-floor seats. The show is popular and tickets are bought up rapidly (especially by tour companies) so if you want a seat go early, or book seats through a tour agency (at twice the cost). The box office is on the ground floor of the Bellas Artes, main entrance.

A typical program will include Aztec ritual dances, agricultural dances from Jalisco, a fiesta in Veracruz, a Christmas celebration—all welded together with mariachis, marimba players, singers, and dancers.

As many other events are held in the Bellas Artes—visits by foreign opera companies, for instance—there are times when the Ballet Folklorico is moved. Usually, it reappears in the National Auditorium in Chapultepec Park. Check at the Bellas Artes box office, if it's at the "Auditorio," catch a Reforma bus for "Auditorio" from the Juárez Monument on Avenida Juárez. **Note:** The theater tends to be very cold so you may want to bring a sweater.

An alternative to the Ballet Folklorico de México is the Ballet Folclórico Nacional Aztlán, in the beautiful turn-of-the-century Teatro de la Ciudad at Donceles 36, between Xicotencatl and Allende, a block northeast of the Bellas Artes. Performances here are as good as the better known ones in the Bellas Artes, but tickets are a lot cheaper and much easier to get hold of. Shows are at 9:30 a.m. and 9 p.m. on Sunday, and 8:30 on Tuesday evenings. Call 521-2355 or 510-2942 for information.

6. Jai Alai

Jai alai (pronounced "hi-lie") must be the fastest game in the world, and is exciting to watch even without prior knowledge of how it is played. Games take place most Tuesday, Wednesday, Thursday, Saturday, and Sunday nights throughout the year in the Fronton México, on the Plaza de la República, which is the plaza dominated by the Monument to the Revolution. The plaza is a few blocks along Juárez west of Reforma. Any bus going west along Juárez will take you to the Juárez–Reforma intersection, and it's a short walk from there, or you can take the Metro to the "Revolución" station, and walk three blocks down Arriaga (south) to the plaza. Actually, many of my recommended hotels are so close to the fronton that you can walk there easily. It doesn't much matter what time you arrive. The box office opens at 6:30 p.m., and there are several games on each night's card.

As you walk into the fronton, the ticket office is to your left; pay 125 pesos (25¢) at the "Admision General" window, pick up a program, and then take a seat—the game will probably already be under way.

Jai alai players wear small baskets on their right arms, with which they catch and sling a fantastically resilient ball against the wall to the right of where you're sitting. In the best games, four players, two with blue armbands and two with red ones, are competing with each other in a fashion similar to tennis, but even more similar to squash. The member of one team throws the ball against the wall, and the other team has to return it. The whole thing is done at an incredible speed, and how they manage to see, much less catch, a ball traveling at about 80 miles per hour is just bloody marvelous.

The most fun, of course, is in the betting; you'd be amazed at how much more exciting a game seems to you when you have money riding on the result. Wait until the program announces a game of 30 points *(partido a treinta tantos)* and watch the bookies. These colorful gentlemen, who all wear white jackets and bright-red berets, carry little pads of betting slips edged in red *(rojo)* or blue *(azul)*, and when the game begins, they'll be offering only a slight edge on one team or another—say, 900 to 1,000 pesos ($1.80 to $2). When the scoring starts, however, the odds will change. If you're as good a mathematician as most jai alai aficionados, you'll be able to bet with impunity on both sides at different points of the game—and still finish up ahead.

7. The National Lottery Drawing

Any Monday, Wednesday, or Friday, walk in the front door of the older National Lottery Building, where Juárez meets Reforma, go straight up the steps, and take a seat in the small auditorium that faces you. Sharp at 8 p.m. a dozen pages, clad in maroon uniforms, enter to begin the ceremony of picking small wooden balls from two revolving cages. One cage contains 50,000 balls (or more, depending on the number of tickets issued for the lottery), the other contains balls relating to the number of prizes with the total of each prize on it. As each ball is picked and dropped into cages, the pages keep up a sing-song patter of the winning numbers. The big-money winners are posted on a board at the end of the stage. The whole ceremony is broadcast, and the winning numbers are also printed in the papers next morning and listed at all the stands where lottery tickets are sold. Attendance at the lottery takes on a whole different element of suspense if you are clutching a ticket in your hand as the numbers are called.

Chapter XI

ONE-DAY TRIPS FROM THE CAPITAL

1. Pyramids of San Juan Teotihuacán
2. Tula
3. Toluca
4. The Volcanoes
5. Cuernavaca
6. Taxco

JUST AS PARIS has its Versailles and Rome its Villa d'Este, so Mexico City is surrounded by suburban areas that are every bit as fascinating as the city itself—and all of them can be reached by a bus ride that is ridiculously cheap. Each of the places described in this chapter can be visited within a couple-of-hours journey, making each of them suitable for one-day trips that can be followed by an evening back in town (although for Taxco you may want to make an exception and stay overnight).

First stop is the most exciting trip on the outskirts of the capital: the breathtaking, ancient pyramids of Teotihuacán. Later I take you farther afield, southwest from University City over the mountains to Cuernavaca; and thence to the silver city of Taxco, on the road to Acapulco.

1. Pyramids of San Juan Teotihuacán

The pyramids of San Juan Teotihuacán were built about 300 B.C., the time when the Classical Greeks were building their great monuments on the other side of the world. Teotihuacán was the dominant city during the Classic Period, with its magnificent pyramids, palaces, and houses covering eight square miles. At its zenith around A.D. 500 there were 125,000 inhabitants, more than in contemporary Rome. But little is known about the city's inhabitants or about why they abandoned the place in A.D. 700. Today what remains are the rough stone structures of the three pyramids and sacrificial altars, and some of the grand houses. This is one of Mexico's most remarkable ruins, and you shouldn't miss it.

You may want to pack a lunch to take to the ruins. Restaurants exist, but they are expensive, or disappointing, or a long walk from the ruins, or all of the above. Almost any hotel or restaurant in the city can prepare a box lunch for you, if you like. Places like Sanborn's and Shirley's are well set up to do it, and charge only about 1,500 pesos ($3) for a plenteous repast. If you forget your box lunch, don't panic. Drinks and snacks are sold by vendors, so you needn't starve. For further recommendations on meals at Teotihuacán, see below.

GETTING THERE BY CAR: Driving to San Juan Teotihuacán on the toll Hwys. 85D and 132D will take about an hour. Head north on Insurgentes to get out of the city. There are two roads to the pyramids: one passes through picturesque villages and the like, but is excruciatingly slow, due to the surfeit of trucks and buses; the other is the toll road, which is a little duller but considerably faster. However, if you're in the mood for a leisurely drive, you might as well take the old two-lane road, slow as it is. And now I'll mention a few of the sights you'll pass.

About 15 miles from town, the village of **San Cristóbal Ecatepec** looms off to the left. Note, also on the left, an old wall built centuries ago to keep what was then a lake from flooding the area. When the road forks a mile or so farther north, take the road to the right.

Three miles farther along this road is the ancient **Convent of San Agustín Acolman** (1539–1560). Not long ago the monastery was in ruins, the only sounds being the ticking of a modern clock, the faint braying of sheep from the fields outside, and the chatter of birds building nests on the roof. Now, however, the monastery and church are restored.

GETTING THERE BY BUS: Don't let *anyone* tell you that it's difficult to get to the pyramids by bus, and that you should take a tour or a cab! It's simple, relatively fast, and very inexpensive to go by bus. Two different lines serve the route between Mexico City and San Juan Teotihuacán.

Buses leave every half hour (5 a.m. to 10 p.m.) every day of the week from the Terminal Central de Autobuses del Norte. Cost for a one-way ticket is 335 pesos (67¢), and the trip takes one hour. To get to the Terminal Norte, take bus 17 ("Indios Verdes"), or bus 17-B ("Central Camionera del Norte") going north on Insurgentes. Or take the Metro (Line 5) to "Autobuses Norte."

When you reach the Terminal Norte, look for the Autobuses Teotihuacán desk, located at the far northwest end (in the center door, turn left and walk all the way down to the sign "8 Espera"). Try to go early in the morning and give yourself plenty of time to wander around the ruins, for there is a lot to see. While you're waiting for your bus, strike up a conversation with other readers of this book who may be waiting there as well (if they've avoided the shills and misinformants who railroad tourists into tours and cabs, they're most likely readers like yourself). You may be surprised by how much your Mexican experiences coincide. When you've compared notes, write me a letter—I love getting feedback. Your letter, with its suggestions, experiences, complaints, and praise will help literally thousands of other readers have better trips south of the border. But to get back to the pyramids. . . .

Another way to get to the pyramids by bus is to take the Metro (Line 3) to Indios Verdes, and catch a bus from there. When you arrive at the Indios Verdes station, head for the exit *(Salida)* and you'll see arrows pointing to the various bus platforms. Buses to the ruins at Teotihuacán depart (as of this writing) from Platform "E." Look for a bus bearing the destination name "Pirámides." They leave every 15 minutes throughout the day, and charge 325 pesos (65¢) for the hour-long trip.

For the return journey, catch the same bus at the main gate to the museum or take a bus at the traffic circle near the pyramids entrance closest to the museum. The "Mexico-Metro" bus will drop you off at the Indios Verdes Metro station, from which it is a short ride to any other point in the city.

SEEING THE PYRAMIDS: During your visit to the pyramids and temples of Teotihuacán, please keep in mind these important points:

—You will be doing a great deal of walking, and perhaps some climbing. It is a full mile from the Pyramid of the Moon to the Unidad Cultural (Museum) and Ciudadela; and there are 248 steep steps up to the top of the Pyramid of the Sun.

—Because the site is so vast, I'll describe it in sections. Whichever entrance you use to the site, locate the section nearest you and visit it first. Backtracking takes too much time and energy.

—Remember always that you're at an altitude of more than 7,000 feet, and you will tire more easily than usual. Take it slowly. Also, the sun and heat can get you. Protect yourself.

—In the summer rainy season, it rains almost every afternoon. Plan to be in the museum or a restaurant when the showers come at 2 or 3 o'clock.

Admission

Teotihuacán is open every day of the week from 8 a.m. to 5 p.m. (you must be off the site by 6 p.m.); admission is 75 pesos (15¢) and there's a parking fee if you have a car. On Sunday and holidays you pay less admission, but the same for the car.

The Layout

The grand buildings of Teotihuacán were laid out on a cosmic plan. The front wall of the Pyramid of the Sun is exactly square to (facing) the point on the horizon where the sun sets on the day it reaches its zenith. So if a line were drawn from the pyramid to the sun at noon on the day when the sun reaches its highest point (that is, it seems to be directly overhead), and another line were drawn from the pyramid to the sun when the sun reaches the horizon later that same day, then the pyramid would be exactly square to these lines. The rest of the ceremonial buildings were laid out at right angles to the Pyramid of the Sun.

The main thoroughfare, called by archeologists the Avenue of the Dead, runs roughly north-south. The Pyramid of the Moon is at the northern end, and the Unidad Cultural (Museum) and Ciudadela are on the southern part of the thoroughfare. Actually, the great street was several miles long in its heyday, but only a mile or so has been uncovered and restored.

The Pyramid of the Sun is on the east side of the Avenue of the Dead.

Pyramid of the Sun

As pyramids go, this one is Number Three. The Great Pyramid of Cholula, on the Mexico City–Puebla road, is the largest structure ever built by man. Today it's so ruined that it appears as a muddy hill with a church built on top. Second largest is the Pyramid of Cheops on the outskirts of Cairo. In third place is Teotihuacán's Pyramid of the Sun, which is almost—at 730 feet per side—as large as Cheops at the base. But at 210 feet high, the Sun pyramid is only about half as high as its Egyptian rival. No matter. It's still the biggest restored pyramid in the Western Hemisphere, and an awesome sight.

Although the Pyramid of the Sun was not built as a great king's tomb, it does have secret tunnels and chambers beneath it. A natural grotto was enlarged and restructured into a four-room chamber that was used for some occult purpose—no one knows what. The tunnels are not open to the public.

The first structure of the pyramid was probably built a century before

Christ, and the temple that used to crown the pyramid was finished about 400 years later (A.D. 300). By the time the pyramid was discovered and restoration was begun (early in our century), the temple had completely disappeared, and the pyramid was just a mass of rubble covered with bushes and trees.

If you're game, trudge up the 248 steps to the top. The view is marvelous, if the smog's not too thick.

Avenue of the Dead

As you stroll north along the Avenue of the Dead toward the Pyramid of the Moon, look on the right for a bit of wall sheltered by a modern corrugated roof. Beneath the shelter, the wall still bears a painting of a jaguar. From this fragment, build a picture of the breathtaking spectacle that must have met the eye when all the paintings along the avenue were intact.

The Avenue of the Dead got its strange and forbidding name from the Aztecs, who mistook the little temples that line both sides of the avenue for tombs of kings or priests.

Pyramid of the Moon

The Pyramid of the Moon faces an interesting plaza at the northern end of the avenue. The plaza is surrounded by little temples, and by the Palace of Quetzal-Mariposa (or Quetzal-Butterfly), on the left (west) side. You get about the same range of view from the top of the Pyramid of the Moon as you do from its larger neighbor, because the moon pyramid is built on higher ground. So if the prospect of dragging yourself up the sun pyramid was just too much, you can go up the 150-foot-high moon pyramid with less effort. There's a bonus too: the magnificent perspective straight down the Avenue of the Dead.

Palace of Quetzal-Mariposa

The Palace of Quetzal-Mariposa lay in ruins until the 1960s, when restoration work began. Today it echoes wonderfully with its former glory, as figures of Quetzal-Mariposa (a mythical exotic bird-butterfly) appear painted on walls or carved in the pillars of the inner court.

Behind the Palace of Quetzal-Mariposa is the **Palace of the Jaguars,** complete with murals showing a lively jaguar musical combo, and some frescoes.

Cuidadela and Unidad Cultural

Along the southern reaches of the Avenue of the Dead, a 15-minute stroll from the Pyramid of the Moon, are two more important Teotihuacán sights.

The **Unidad Cultural** is the only modern building of any size on the grounds of Teotihuacán. It houses an entrance to the grounds, rows of little shops, a restaurant, a book and souvenir shop, and the **museum,** which is worth a look.

First thing you'll notice as you wander into the museum is an enormous statue (a copy, actually) of the goddess Chalchiuhtlicue. She stands in a small pool, which is appropriate as she was the goddess of water. Behind, around, and above her are various exhibits outlining the culture of Teotihuacán, as well as some artifacts found during excavations on the site. Useful in planning the rest of your visit is a scale model of the city of Teotihuacán.

Across the Avenue of the Dead from the Unidad Cultural is the **Ciudadela,** or Citadel, so named by the Spaniards. Actually, this immense sunken square was not a fortress at all, although the impressive walls make it look like one. It was the grand setting for a temple to Quetzalcóatl, the famed "plumed serpent" who appears so often in Mexican folklore. Once you've admired the great scale of the Ciudadela, go down the steps into the massive court and head for the ruined temple, in the middle.

The **Temple of Quetzalcóatl** was covered over by an even larger structure, a pyramid. As you walk toward the center of the Ciudadela's court, you'll be approaching the pyramid. Walk around to the right of it, and soon you'll see the reconstructed temple close behind the pyramid. There's a narrow passage between the two structures, and traffic is supposed to be one way—which is why I directed you to the right.

It wasn't unusual for early temples to be covered over by later ones in Mexico and Central America. Rather, it was a very common practice. The Pyramid of the Sun may even have been built up in this way. As for the Temple of Quetzalcóatl, you'll notice at once the fine big carved serpents' heads jutting out from aureoles of feathers carved in the stone walls. Other feathered serpents are carved in relief low on the walls. The temple provides a vivid example of pre-Columbian public decoration. The decoration at Chichén-Itzá, Uxmal, and Tikal is certainly more elaborate, but these sites are thousands of miles from Mexico City. Luckily, you can still get a good idea of the glory of Mexico's ancient cities from this temple. Don't miss it.

Where to Have Lunch

If you heeded my earlier advice to bring a box lunch, you can take a break wherever you like: in the shade of a tree or a palace, or atop a pyramid. Vendors sell soft drinks and various snacks, wandering with their wares throughout the ruins.

Outside the Unidad Cultural there are often primitive cookshops set up by local señoras, and you can sit at a rustic table under a shady tree and partake of whatever rough-and-ready fare is being served up. People prone to stomach grumbles had better head for a bona-fide restaurant, however.

There is a restaurant in the Unidad Cultural, but more suitable places exist along the road that rings the archeological site. **La Gruta** (tel. 595/6-0127 or 6-0104), for instance, is a ten-minute walk east of the Pyramid of the Sun (go out the gate behind the pyramid and follow the signs). Open from 10 a.m. to 9 p.m. every day, La Gruta is just that—a huge, delightfully cool natural grotto filled with table and chairs, natty waiters, and the sound of clinking glasses. Soft drinks and beer are served till 3 p.m., and then the full bar opens. As for food, the set-price lunch of five courses will cost you about 3,000 pesos ($6), all in, although you can have lunch for about half that price if you order a hamburger and soft drink. La Gruta is exactly three-tenths of a mile from the Pyramid of the Sun, but after the blazing heat, the delicious coolness makes you think you're at the center of the earth.

Behind the Pyramid of the Moon, to the north, is the modest **Restaurant Tepantitla,** where your lunch will be a bit cheaper than at La Gruta, but without the delightful coolness. Next door to the Tepantitla are the fairly uninteresting ruins of Tepantitla. **El Chinanco,** on the ring road between the entrances of Pyramid of the Sun and Pyramid of the Moon, is a similar place.

Yet another classy place is **Pirámides Charlie's** (tel. 595/6-0472), which has all the marks of a Carlos Anderson restaurant (you'll meet with others in various Mexican cities). Expect to pay 2,600 to 3,300 pesos ($5.20 to $6.60) for a good, full lunch here. Pirámides Charlie's is on the ring road between the two highways to Mexico City, the "México Libre" (Hwy. 132) and "México Cuota" (Hwy. 132D). It's not all that far from the Unidad Cultural.

SOUND AND LIGHT SHOW: The Mexican Tourist Office has organized a spectacle of sound and light nightly October to May, except Monday, in English at 7 p.m. and in Spanish at 8:15 p.m. For 1,000 pesos ($2) you can relive some of the Aztec legends; it's splendidly engineered and very impressive. **Note:** Warm clothing is a must with that cold night wind howling around the pyramids!

2. Tula

In A.D. 900 or thereabouts, Teotihuacán was overrun by a people called the Chichimecs. Many Teotihuacanos, or Toltecs, fled northward to found the city of Tula, which flourished from 900 to 1156. In that year the Chichimecs caught up with their former enemies the Toltecs again, and wiped out Tula. But the one-time Toltec capital's impressive pyramids, giant statues, and curious three-legged pottery survived to be uncovered by modern archeologists.

The city's remains are memorably beautiful, although its history is a sad story. The peace-loving king of the Toltecs, Quetzalcóatl (the "feathered serpent" in later lore) sought to purge his people of such things as human sacrifice and to direct their efforts to peaceful agriculture. The warlike party in Tula disagreed with the king's aims, and forced him and a band of his followers to flee the city in about 987. They wandered as far as the Yucatán and Chichén-Itzá, spreading Toltec culture along the way and giving birth to the legend of Quetzalcóatl (see the "Brief History" in Chapter I).

The Chichimecs seized Tula in 1156, but in 1200 a drought drove them out. They were succeeded by the Aztecs by 1325, and by the Spaniards in 1519, but Tula never regained its former glory.

Most striking of the city's remains are the 15-foot-high "Atlantean men," gigantic basalt figures mounted atop the Temple of Tlahuizcalpantecutli (that Toltec mouthful means "Morning Star"). At one time they supported the roof of the temple. The city's ball court, said to be the earliest ball court built on the continent, has been restored beautifully. To the west of the temple is the Burnt Palace (Quemado) where you'll be able to see several painted reliefs and a statue of Chac Mool, the reclining figure with head turned to one side. Between the temple and the ball court is a large wall with fantastic reliefs of the feathered serpent, skulls, eagles, and jaguars.

There's a small museum at the site containing a few Toltec artifacts as well as some Aztec pottery. The most interesting items here are the two stone figures once thought to be standard holders. The ruins and museum are open daily from 8 a.m. to 6 p.m.; there is a small admission fee.

GETTING TO TULA: Tula is about 50 miles due north of Mexico City along Hwys. 57D (a toll road) and 126. If you take the bus, you'll be obliged to walk out from town (about 15 minutes), or take a cab.

You won't find any food or drink at the ruins, not even soft drinks, so you might want to have a bite or a sip in town before you hike out. The **Café "El Cisne,"** on Tula's tidy main street, can fill your light lunch wishes admirably and cheaply. Assuming you won't eat heavily before walking to the ruins, you'll end up paying about 850 pesos ($1.70) for the daily set-price lunch, a bit more if you order à la carte.

By Bus

Buses leave every quarter hour from Mexico City's Terminal Central de Autobuses del Norte, reached by a no. 17 city bus ("Indios Verdes") going north along Insurgentes or by Metro to "Autobuses Norte." When you enter the giant bus station, turn left and walk down to the far (western) end to the Tula ticket counter, marked "Autotransportes Valle del Mezquital." Other companies run buses to Tula, but this one has the most frequent departures, every 15 minutes from 5 a.m. to 11 p.m. The trip takes about an hour and 20 minutes, and you should ask to get off the bus before it gets to the center of town. Cross the railroad tracks and the junction of Hwys. 22 and 87, and, going along 87, follow signs as mentioned above. The walk will take about 15 minutes.

By Car

Driving north on the fast toll road (57D), there are no fewer than three turnoffs for Tula, at km. 58 ("Petrolera-Tula"), km. 69 ("Tepeji del Río-Tula"), and km. 84 ("Jilotepec-Tula"). Take the first, most southerly one at km. 58 to avoid a toll.

When you reach the modern town of Tula, ask for directions to the Zona Arqueológica (there may be scattered signs), or follow signs to—get this—Tlahuelilpan. The ruins are about a mile from the center of town. Watch out for a sharp left turn just past a Pemex housing development.

3. Toluca

At 8,760 feet, Toluca is the highest city in Mexico, and the hour-long trip there from Mexico City offers spectacular scenic views. Pine trees and icy-looking blue lakes dot the landscape, and only an occasional cactus plant or brightly colored painting, drying in the sun, will remind you that you're in Mexico. Toluca isn't a particularly exciting city, but it has an immense market you'll want to visit on a Friday, as early as possible in the day before the tour buses roll in.

It's easy to get to the market by bus from Mexico City. Take the Metro to the "Observatorio" station, and look for the Terminal Poniente bus station. Buses ("Toluca Directo") of various companies depart every five or ten minutes on the hour-long trip.

Don't expect a small, backward Indian town at the other end of the bus trip. Toluca (pop. 200,000) is the capital of the state of México, and has been an important town since the Aztec times. You enter town along a beautiful parkway.

The gigantic **Mercado Juárez,** at the edge of town on the highway to Mexico City has both market buildings and open-air grounds. Shops in the buildings are open all week, but it's on Friday that the people from surrounding villages come and crowd the plaza. The bus from Mexico City pulls into a terminal right across the street from the Mercado Juárez. You'll recognize the market by the pair of slender concrete slabs that tower above it to serve as a landmark.

Because of the natives' bargaining powers, a peaceful walk around the market is not an easy matter. Every time you pause to admire such unfamiliar sights as a boxful of chattering chickens, a two-foot-high pile of assorted shoelaces, or an array of framed saints' pictures, some man or young boy will accost you with cries of *"Serapes, rebozos, Señor, very cheap."* And sooner or later the heat and crowdedness of the market will begin to get you down; you will barely raise your head as the man with the pig under his arm or the woman with a turkey sticking its head from the back of her shawl brushes past.

Some sights will make you pause—a marimba band banging away cheerfully between the stalls, and a little, open-fronted bakery where chains of tortillas can be seen pouring off a conveyor belt into a basket.

Finding a place for lunch is never a problem in such a huge market, but if none of the little market eateries appeals to you, there is an alternative. Search the skyline for the red-and-yellow star sign that identifies the local branch of

VIP'S (pronounced "beeps"), a clean, bright, and cheery American-style restaurant.

4. The Volcanoes

One of the nicest picnic spots in all of Mexico is the **Ixta-Popo National Park,** whose raison d'être are the volcanoes of **Popocatepetl** and **Ixtacchihuatl.** These snow-capped peaks are usually associated with the city of Puebla, a three-hour trip from Mexico City, but it is by no means necessary to go all the way to Puebla to see them.

GETTING THERE: Take Metro Line 1 east, in the direction of Pantatlán, to the San Lázaro stop. As you come to the surface, you'll see the green-domed TAPO ("Terminal de Autobuses de Pasajeros de Oriente"), Mexico City's eastern bus terminal. Walk along "Tunel 1," the corridor to the central domed area, and look for "Lineas Unidas–Cristóbal Colón" buses to Amecameca and Popo Park. Buses leave every half hour, every day, on the two-hour trip.

The bus will take the Puebla road (Rte. 190) out of Mexico City, turning off to the right (Rte. 115) at the village of Chalco. A few miles farther on is Amecameca (pop. 22,000), from which the best view of the volcanoes can be obtained. Situated at a height of 7,500 feet, Amecameca is a fresh, clear town, with a big square and a 200-year-old parish church. Behind it are the two lovely mountains, neither of which has erupted in this century.

READER'S TRANSPORTATION TIP: "We used the colectivos, the green VW vans that leave from near the Metro Candelaría in Mexico City and also the main square in Amecameca. The vans are stuffed to the gills, but are very convenient. It is cheap, not too much more than the bus, and vans are constantly arriving and departing" (Nancy Strom, Seattle, Wash.).

AMECAMECA: About the best hotel in Amecameca is the very plain but clean **Hotel San Carlos,** right on the main square to the right of the church, at Plaza de la Constitución 10 (tel. 597/8-0344). A room with one double bed costs 2,400 pesos ($4.80); with twin beds, 3,200 pesos ($6.40). All rooms have bath and hot water. The San Carlos's restaurant serves light meals.

ONWARD AND UPWARD: Getting to Ixta-Popo National Park from Amecameca takes some doing. You can hitchhike, or try to catch one of the rickety old village buses that leaves from the main square—look for the *camioneta azul* (blue minibus) marked "San Pedro—Los Volcanes." Otherwise, to get to the mountain lodge at Tlamacas you'll have to hire a taxi for about 5,000 pesos ($10) one way. Check at the Hotel San Carlos for other passengers, and perhaps you'll be able to split the cost. Make a deal with the taxi driver to come pick you up at a later time as there's no telephone at the lodge; or you can take a chance and try to thumb a ride down the mountain, which is often easily done.

THE LODGE: The **Albergue Vicente Guerrero,** at Tlamacas (alt. 12,800 feet, or 3,900 meters), Parque Nacional Ixta-Popo, was opened in 1978. It's beautiful: an ultramodern mountain lodge done in native stone and natural wood, complete with bunkrooms, showers, a cafeteria, and a restaurant. If you want to stay the night, especially on a weekend, it's best to call or drop by the Mexico City office of the lodge for a reservation: the address is Avenida Lázaro Cárdenas 661 (tel. 590-7694). A bunk with sheets, blankets, and pillow costs 1,100 pesos ($2.20).

Outside the Albergue is the snow-covered summit of Popocatepetl, 17,887 feet (5,452 meters) at the rim. In the morning the clouds may drift away for an hour, yielding an incomparable closeup view. Across the valley, Popo's sister volcano, Ixtacchihuatl, may be exposed as well. When you see them gleaming in the morning sun, surrounded by the chilly morning air, you'll remember the moment for a lifetime.

THE TRAILS: Please take me in dead seriousness when I say that Popocatepetl is no mountain for rookie climbers, or for any expert climber who's not in top shape. At the lodge trailhead, the air is so thin that even walking makes a normal, healthy person dizzy—and the air's considerably thinner at 17,887 feet! And it's *cold* up here, even in the sweltering heat of summer. But if you're an expert climber, pack your down sleeping bag, crampons, and what-not, and check in at the rescue hut next to the lodge. You'll have to pass an equipment check, and sign your name in the hikers' register, before you set out. Maps of the various trails to the summit, showing the several huts and shelters, are on view in the rescue hut. The trek to the summit takes from 9 to 12 hours, depending on what shape you're in and which trail you choose. You must camp at the summit that night, and return the next day.

When you return to the lodge, if all the bunks are taken, no one will mind if you pitch your hiking tent in the pine grove just below the lodge.

Guide Service
You can hire a mountain guide to take you from your hotel in Mexico City to one of the three nearby volcanoes, Popocatépetl (17,887 feet), Iztaccihuatl (17,332 feet) or the Pico de Orizaba (18,770 feet). The cost is about $100 to $150, depending upon the mountain and the climbing equipment which the guide must furnish (crampons, axes, down jackets, gloves, gaiters, glacier goggles, etc.). For full information, contact Mr. Bernard Wyns at the Compañia de Guías de Montaña (tel. 905/584-4695, 584-8997, or 689-0414), Apdo. Postal 21-413, México, D.F. 04000.

5. Cuernavaca
Cuernavaca (alt. 5,058 feet; pop. 360,000), capital of the state of Morelos, has been popular as a resort for people from Mexico City ever since the time of Moctezuma. Emperor Maximilian built a retreat here over a century ago. Mexicans say the town has a climate of "eternal spring," and on weekends the city is crowded with day-trippers from surrounding cities, especially from the capital. On weekends the roads between Mexico City and Cuernavaca are jammed, and so are restaurants and hotels in this city. Cuernavaca has a large American colony, consisting mostly of well-to-do retired people, plus students attending one of the myriad language and cultural institutes which crowd the city.

The Indian name for this town was Cuauhnáhuac, which means "at the edge of the forest." The city's symbol today is an Indian pictogram of a tree speaking. People have lived here, next to the whispering trees, since about A.D. 1200, but only in the early 1400s did it come under the sway of the Aztecs.

After the Aztec emperors of México conquered this country, they established huge hunting parks for themselves. They began a tradition of Cuauhnáhuac being a resort for the wealthy and powerful which continues to this day.

The conquistadores, when they arrived, heard "Cuauhnáhuac" but said "Cuernavaca", so the whispering tree became a cow's horn.

Emperor Charles V gave Cuernavaca to Cortés as a fief, and the conquistador built a mansion here in 1532 and lived here on and off for a half-dozen years before returning to Spain. Cortés introduced sugarcane cultivation to the area, and also black Caribbean slaves to work in the cane fields. Cortés's innovations destined Cuernavaca and Morelos to be a hotbed of insurrection and revolution, as the economics of sugarcane worked against the interests of the indigenous farmers. There were numerous uprisings in colonial times.

After independence, mighty landowners from Mexico City gradually dispossessed the remaining small landholders, converting them to virtual serfdom. It was this condition which led to the rise of Emiliano Zapata, the great champion of agrarian reform, who battled the forces of wealth and power, defending the small farmer with the cry of "Tierra y Libertad!" (Land and Liberty!) during the Mexican Revolution following 1910.

In this century, Cuernavaca has seen the influx of wealthy foreigners, and also the influx of industrial capital. The giant CIVAC industrial complex on the outskirts has brought wealth to the city, but also the curse of increased traffic, noise and air pollution.

GETTING TO CUERNAVACA: The Mexico City **Central de Autobuses del Sur's** reason for being is the route Mexico City–Cuernavaca–Taxco–Acapulco–Zihuatanejo: 90% of the buses leaving that terminal ply this route, and they do it with great frequency, so you'll have little trouble getting a bus.

Several lines serve the city, including Estrella de Oro and Lineas Unidas del Sur / Flecha Roja, but the line with the most frequent departures and the most convenient downtown terminal in Cuernavaca is Autobuses Pullman de Morelos.

If you plan to visit Cuernavaca on a day trip from Mexico City, the best days to do so are Tuesday, Wednesday, or Thursday (and perhaps Friday). On weekends, the roads, the city, its hotels and restaurants are filled with people from Mexico City, and prices jump dramatically. On Monday, the museum—which you definitely must see—is closed. So make it Tuesday through Friday.

Autobuses Pullman de Morelos

Buses leave Mexico City's Central del Sur every ten minutes throughout the day, so reservations are not really necessary. Buy a ticket for the "Centro," not for "La Selva," which is a bus stop at the northern edge of Cuernavaca. Be careful not to get off at La Selva, as some buses will stop there. When you arrive in Cuernavaca after the hour-long ride, you'll alight at the last stop, in the Autobuses Pullman de Morelos bus station (tel. 731/12-6001) at the corner of Abasolo and Netzahualcóyotl. Walk up the hill (north) on Netzahualcóyotl two blocks to Hidalgo, then turn right onto that street to reach the center of town.

Estrella de Oro

The Autobuses Estrella de Oro terminal (2) in Cuernavaca is at Morelos Sur 900 (tel. 731/12-3055), corner of Veracruz, about a 15- or 20-minute walk south of the center of town. If you arrive at this terminal (say, from Acapulco or Taxco), you should know that the tourist office is less than a block up Morelos (see below). Take any bus going north (uphill) on Morelos to reach the center of town, near the cathedral.

Flecha Roja

The second-class bus line Autobuses Unidas del Sur / Flecha Roja has its Cuernavaca terminal (tel. 731/12-5797) at Morelos 255, right in the center of town.

ORIENTATION: Coming into town from Mexico City, you'll pass La Selva (The

Woods), where there's a fancy hotel and a vast overambitious resort complex called the Casino de la Selva, begun in the 1960s, which was never really completed.

As your bus swings onto Avenida Morelos, you'll pass a dramatic **equestrian statue** of the popular hero Emiliano Zapata, galloping at full tilt in defense of the simple campesino. In the center of the city, Cuernavaca has two contiguous plazas. The smaller and more formal of the two is square, with a Victorian gazebo (designed by Monsieur Eiffel of Tour Eiffel fame) at its center. This is the **Jardín Juárez.** The larger, rectangular plaza planted with trees, shrubs, and benches is the **Jardín de los Héroes,** also sometimes called the Plaza de Armas or the Alameda. At the eastern end of the Alameda is the **Cortés Palace,** the conquistador's residence which now serves as the Museo de Cuauhnáhuac.

You should be aware that this city's street numbering system—or, rather, systems—are extremely confusing. It appears that the city fathers, during the past century or so, have become dissatisfied with the street numbers every 10 or 20 years, and have imposed a new numbering system each time. Thus, you may find an address given as "no. 5" only to find that the building itself bears the number "506." One grand gateway I know bears no less than five different and various street numbers, ranging from 2 to 567! In my descriptions of hotels, restaurants, and sights, I'll note the nearest cross-street so you can find your way to your chosen destination with a minimum of fuss.

Useful Facts

The **Post Office** (7) (tel. 731/12-4379) is on the Jardín de los Héroes, right next door to the Café Los Arcos.

There's a handy **bookstore** with English-language books and periodicals just off the main squares in the Centro Las Plazas shopping center. It's the Anglo-American Bookstore, also called the Librería Las Plazas, at Local 10 within the complex.

Tourist Information

Cuernavaca's tourist office used to be in the entrance to the Jardín Borda, but since the gardens have been closed for renovation, the office has been closed as well. I'll wager that when the gardens reopen, the tourist office will be back in its accustomed place. Until then, however, the **state tourist office (2)** (tel. 731/14-3860 or 14-3920) is at Avenida Morelos Sur 802, between Jalisco and Veracruz, a half-block north of the Estrella de Oro bus station, and about a 10- or 15-minute walk south of the cathedral. Hours are Monday through Friday, 9 a.m. to 8 p.m.; Saturday till 6 p.m.; Sunday till 3 p.m.

WHERE TO STAY: Cuernavaca's lodging situation is not normal. Because so many *capitalinos* come down from Mexico City for the day, or for the weekend (perhaps illicit?), the hotel trade here tends to be heavy on weekends and holidays, light at other times. Local hoteliers adapt their policies and prices to these weird shifts.

The 22-room **Hotel Iberia (3),** Rayon 9 at Alarcón, Cuernavaca, Morelos 62000 (tel. 731/12-6040), is tidy and convenient. Rooms in this richly tiled old building are simple but presentable, arranged around a small courtyard where you can park your car (if it's small). The hard-working señoras who run the hotel keep everything in top shape, and charge 3,789 pesos ($7.57) single, 4,186 pesos ($8.37) double in two beds. Watch out, there is some street noise in the evenings.

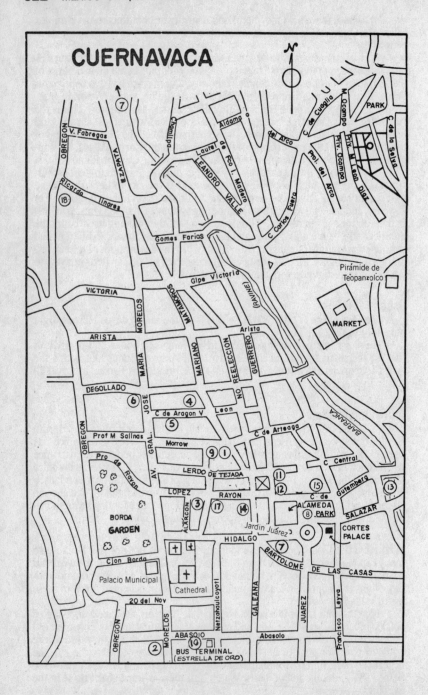

The **Hotel Palacio (1),** Morrow 204 at Matamoros, Cuernavaca, Morelos 62000 (tel. 731/12-0553), is only a block or so from the Jardín Juárez. Its 16 rooms positively shout 19th-century Mexican town house, which is what the building was. The glass-topped courtyard is a nice restaurant, popular for its low-priced but bounteous luncheon comida corrida. Single guests pay 3,450 pesos ($6.90) for a room, couples pay 4,025 pesos ($8.05). Big families, take note: you can rent rooms with beds for up to five people; top price is 5,750 pesos ($11.50).

The **Hotel Colonial (5),** Aragón y León 104, Cuernavaca, Morelos 62000 (tel. 731/12-0099), between Matamoros and Morelos, is only a few blocks from the Jardín Juárez on a quiet street known for its budget lodgings. The very nice, simple little rooms at the Colonial are the best buys on the street, going for 2,350 pesos ($4.70) for one bed (one or two people), 2,500 pesos ($5) for two beds. The dozen or so rooms with shower are arranged around a cheery courtyard. Recommended.

The Big Splurge

La Posada de Xochiquétzal (6) (tel. 731/12-0220), pronounced "so-chee-*ket*-zahl," charges 11,550 pesos ($23.10) single, and 13,455 pesos ($26.91) double. You get your money's worth in beauty, for the Posada's high walls harbor many delights: a small pool, lush gardens with fountains, tasteful colonial furnishings, a good restaurant, patios, and spacious guest rooms with attractive baths. It's a real haven in the midst of the city, and gives you a glimpse of what life must be like behind other high walls. Even so, the sooty buses roar by its door at Leyva 200, corner of Abasolo, just two blocks south of the Cortés Palace. The mail address is Apdo. Postal 203. Even if you don't come to stay, come for a meal (see below).

Near the Bus Station

The rambling **Hotel Papagayo (10),** at Motolinía 13 (tel. 731/14-1711 or 14-1924), is only a block from the Autobuses Pullman de Morelos terminal, but this is a disadvantage as well as an advantage. Walk south from the bus a block, and there's the hotel (ignore the ugly façade and dinky sign—there's a much nicer entryway at the address given above). The Papagayo's scores of rooms must be picked over to find a good, quiet one (remember those buses passing outside), but once you've located a good room, you can enjoy the bonus: a big swimming pool. Prices are moderate: 6,049 pesos ($12.09) double on weekdays; on weekends, it's 14,330 pesos ($28.66) double for a room with shower, breakfast included.

Starvation Budget Lodgings

If the budget blues have got you, head straight for Calle Aragón y León, at Matamoros, for this is the center of the district of casas de huespedes, simple little lodging places with the best prices in town.

Try the **Casa Marilú (4),** Aragón y León 12 (tel. 731/12-1057), with 25 plain but passable rooms, mostly without private bath, priced at 1,650 pesos ($3.30) single, 1,850 pesos ($3.70) double.

Nearby at no. 10 is the **Casa de Huespedes La Paz (4)** (no phone), with similar rooms at similar rock-bottom prices.

WHERE TO EAT: Because of the huge influx of visitors from out of town, Cuernavaca is well equipped with places to dine. Here are my favorites.

Everybody loves a sidewalk café, and Cuernavaca's best is the **Restaurant Los Arcos (7)** (tel. 12-4486), Jardín de los Héroes 4, right next to the Post Office on the larger of the city's two plazas. Wrought-iron tables and chairs, shaded by umbrellas, are set out within view of the Cortés Palace, and all three meals are served, everyday. The menu runs the gamut from sandwiches and enchiladas (400 to 700 pesos, 80¢ to $1.40) to fish, shrimp, and steaks (1,500 to 2,200 pesos, $3 to $4.40). There's even a set-price lunch, called the menu del dia, for 1,200 pesos ($2.40). Recommended.

The **Fonda Los Molcajetes** (no phone) is a bit difficult to find, even though it's virtually next to the Cortés Palace. Facing the palace, walk to your left, passing along with the cars underneath a pedestrian bridge. On your right you'll see the lovely little courtyard, shaded by a huge rubber tree, with pots of savory concoctions simmering to one side. Besides the quiet court, there's a glass-enclosed "greenhouse" room. Though it looks to be upscale, prices are surprisingly low: for soup, steak with salad, and pie for dessert, the total is only 1,600 pesos ($3.20). For a "meal in a bowl," try their pozole (after 6 p.m.). Open daily.

The **Restaurant La India Bonita (9)** (tel. 12-1266), Morrow 6B near Matamoros, boasts that it has been here since 1945. Though it has changed hands several times, it is still a cheery, pleasant restaurant specializing in mole poblano (chicken with a sauce of bitter chocolate and fiery chiles) and filete a la parrilla (charcoal-grilled steak). An appealing choice is the Mexican plate with seven different foods for 1,400 pesos ($2.80). Breakfast can be had for under 1,000 pesos ($2), unless you want the gigantic desayuno maximiliano, a huge tuck-in based on enchiladas. Open every day.

On the east side of the Jardín Juárez is the **Viena Cafetería (11),** Guerrero 104, where the specialty—besides people-watching—is excellent pastry, coffee, and ice cream. The cappuccino here is reputedly the best in town. Ice cream or pastry will put you out about 450 to 675 pesos (90¢ to $1.35), but for slightly more you can have a hot or cold luncheon plate at 900 to 1,600 pesos ($1.80 to $3.20), which is a full meal in itself.

A few doors down from the Viena Cafetería is **La Parroquía (12),** off the Jardín Juárez, at Guerrero 102. They have an open-air restaurant as well as a few outdoor café tables. This place does a teeming business, partly because of its great location right off the jardín and partly because they have fairly reasonable prices for Cuernavaca. Four quesadillas con pollo (with chicken) go for 575 pesos ($1.15), or you can just sip a beer for 300 pesos (60¢).

The Big Splurge

Cuernavaca has a number of very posh restaurants housed in those old mansions surrounded by high walls. The most famous, perhaps, and also the most pricey is **Las Mañanitas (13)** (tel. 12-4646), Linares 107, in the Hostería Las Quintas. You'll need a taxi to get to it, and you'll need enough money to pay moderate American prices.

A mere two blocks south of the Cortés Palace is **La Posada de Xochiquetzal (6)** (tel. 12-0220), Leyva 200 at Abasolo, where you enter an unimpressive doorway to find a quiet haven of greenery cascading down a hillside. The restaurant is open for breakfast, lunch, and dinner, seven days a week, and features a set-price buffet on Sunday. Specialties include Cornish game hen, spare ribs, osso buco, and steaks. Lunch or dinner will set you back about 6,000 to 7,000 pesos ($12 to $14) per person, all included. Note that Thursday afternoon is Happy Hour, when you get two drinks for the price of one.

Starvation Budget Restaurants

There are two restaurants right next to each other at no. 2 Galeana, corner of Rayón: **La Cueva** (tel. 12-6732) and **El Portal** (tel. 12-3449) **(14).** I put them together because there seems to be stiff competition between them, with each one vying daily to offer the lower prices. They both offer four-course comidas between 600 and 750 pesos ($1.20 and $1.50) that include soup, rice, fish or meat filet, dessert, and coffee. They also have à la carte items. The comida menus are written on blackboards in front of the restaurant so your best bet is to check to see which menu and which price agrees with you.

WHAT TO SEE: You can spend one or two days sightseeing in Cuernavaca pleasantly enough. If you've come on a day-trip from Mexico City, you may not have time to make all of the excursions listed below, but you'll have enough time to see the sights in town.

First place to visit is the former home of the greatest of the conquistadores, Hernán Cortés.

Cortés Palace

The Cortés Palace is right at the eastern end of the Jardín de los Héroes. Begun by Hernán Cortés in 1530, it was finished by the conquistador's son Martín, and later served as the legislative headquarters for the state of Morelos. It now houses the **Museo de Cuauhnáhuac,** open from 9:30 a.m. to 7 p.m. Tuesday through Sunday; closed Monday. As you tour the museum, remember to look at and "experience" the building, where Cortés once brooded over his adventures.

Inside the main door, go to the right. If you've recently visited the National Museum of Anthropology in Mexico City, these displays of Man's early times will be familiar. Passing through these exhibits, you come to a little court in which are the ruins of a Tlahuica temple. In keeping with conquistador policy, Cortés had his mansion built right on top of an older structure.

The Northern Wing: The northern wing of the palace, on the ground floor, houses exhibits from the colonial era: suits of armor juxtaposed with the arrows, spears, and maces used by the Indians. Upstairs in the northern wing are costumes, domestic furnishings, carriages, and farm implements from Mexico of the 1800s, mostly from *haciendas azucareras* (sugar plantations). There are also mementos of the great revolutionaries Francisco Madero and Emiliano Zapata.

The Rivera Mural: When you get to the east portico on the upper floor, you're in for a treat. A large mural commissioned from Diego Rivera by Dwight Morrow, U.S. ambassador to Mexico in the 1920s, depicts the history of Cuernavaca from the coming of the Spaniards to the rise of Zapata (1910). It's fascinating to examine the mural in detail. Above the north door, the Spaniards and their Indian allies, armed with firearms, crossbows, and cannon battle the Aztecs, who have clubs, spears, slings, and bows and arrows. Above the door is a scene of Aztec human sacrifice (remember this).

Moving southward along the wall, men struggle with a huge tree, perhaps symbolizing the Aztec "universe." Next, the inhabitants of Mexico are enslaved, branded, and made to yield their gold. The figure in a white headscarf is José María Morelos, one of the leaders in Mexico's fight for independence from Spain.

Moving along, malevolent priests, backed by lancers, subjugate the Indians spiritually; the Indians, dressed in white, stand peaceably and respectfully, at the orders of the priests. The Spaniards build a new society using the Indians as slave labor.

The scenes on the sugar plantations are from the time after independence when the wealthy and powerful dispossessed the Indians of their land in order to create the huge sugar haciendas. While the Indians slave away, the *blancos* recline in hammocks. Nearby, priests and friars direct the building of churches and monasteries by Indian labor; the churchmen accept gold from the Indians; and only one poor friar sits with the Indian women and children, teaching them the doctrines of the church.

Above the south door is an auto-da-fé, or burning of heretics, from the Spanish Inquisition. The scene is chronologically out of place, but Rivera obviously meant to contrast it to the Aztec sacrifice over the north door, opposite. He's saying, "Aztecs or Catholics, the more it changes, the more it stays the same." Rivera firmly believed that communism would break the cycle of man's inhumanity to man, but the Stalinist purges of the 1930s were yet in the future when Rivera painted this superb mural. It's ironic that his "religion" (communist ideology) led to the same horrors of ideological fanaticism as Aztec cosmology and Catholic Inquisition.

In the upper left corner of the southern door, Indian revolutionaries are hanged by slave-drivers. In the lower left, Zapata leads a group of revolutionary campesinos brandishing their farming tools as weapons.

The frieze beneath the mural is interesting as well, done in a chunky 1930s style which is very art deco, but also very Rivera. It looks to me as though he was inspired by the many Aztec friezes.

The Southern Wing: Through the southern door are more exhibits from colonial times, including several fascinating "painted books," or Indian codices, which survived the book burnings of the Spaniards. There's also a clock mechanism *(reloj)* from Cuernavaca's cathedral, thought to be the first public clock on the American continent.

Catedral de la Asunción

Cuernavaca's ancient cathedral is at the corner of Hidalgo and Morelos, three blocks southwest of the Jardí de los Héroes. As you enter the church precincts and pass down the walk between the rows of beggars to the main building, try to imagine what life in Mexico was like in the old days. Construction on the church was begun in 1533, a mere 12 years after Cortés conquered Tenochtitlán (Mexico City) from the Aztecs. The churchmen could hardly trust their safety to the tenuous allegiance of their new Indian converts, so they built a fortress as a church. The skull-and-crossbones above the main door is not a comment on their feelings about the future, however, but rather a symbol for the Franciscan order, which had its monastery here in the church precincts.

Inside, the church is stark, even severe, having been refurnished in the 1960s. The most curious aspect of the interior is the mystery of the frescoes. Discovered during the refurnishing, they depict Christian missionary activity and persecution in Japan, and are painted in Japanese style. No one is certain who painted them here, or why.

Palacio Municipal

Directly west of the cathedral, across Avenida Morelos at the corner of Callejon Borda, is Cuernavaca's Palacio Municipal, or Town Hall. A ceramic tile plaque to the right of the door says "Honorable Ayuntamiento de Cuernavaca" (town council); to the left, "Cuauhnáhuac," with the city's tree symbol. Walk into the pretty brick, stone, and stucco courtyard anytime the building is open (which tends to be Monday through Friday, 9 a.m. to 2 p.m. and 4 to 6 p.m., but often at other times as well). Besides the unusual and attractive building, you should tour the large old oil paintings hung in the arcades on the ground floor and upper floor.

On the north wall, ground floor, paintings explain the making of "feathered mosaics."

In the north arcade, on the upper floor, are scenes from Cuernavaca's pre-

Hispanic culture: Tlahuicans making pottery, storing corn (maize), being shaken down by an Aztec tax collector, and harvesting cotton.

On the east wall, the scenes continue: the Indians gather maguey leaves, pound them to release the fibers, and weave cloth; a priest offers a chicken to the god Tepuztecatl. The Aztec goldsmiths' craft is explained in a canvas with 17 smaller panels. In the southeast corner are two murals, done by R. Cueva in 1962, with scenes from the revolution.

On the south wall of the upper floor are scenes from the French Intervention: Emperor Maximilian and Empress Carlotta arrive in Cuernavaca for the first time; Maximilian, while out for a ride, gets his first glimpse of La India Bonita (Margarita Leguisamo Sedano), who was to become his lover. The next scene is of court festivities in the Borda Gardens, with courtiers taking turns rowing little boats. Finally, Maximilian's niece pleads with President Benito Juárez, after the siege of Querétaro, to spare the emperor's life. (At the time, Carlotta was off in Europe, trying to round up support for her husband's cause, without result). Juárez, urged on by Melchor Ocampo, refused her request, and Maximilian, along with two of his generals, was executed by firing squad on the Hill of Bells in Querétaro a few days thereafter.

Jardín Borda

On Morelos at Hidalgo, right near the cathedral and the Palacio Municipal, is the entrance to the Jardín Borda, or Borda Gardens. Cuernavaca, as I've noted, was (and is) a place where the wealthy and powerful built lavish resort homes ever since Moctezuma's time. One such builder was José de la Borda, the Taxco silver magnate, who ordered a sumptuous vacation house to be built here in the late 1700s. The large enclosed garden next to the house was actually a huge private park, laid out in Andalusian style with little kiosks and an artificial pond. Maximilian found it worthy of an emperor, and took it over as his private preserve in the mid-1800s. But after Max, the Borda Gardens fell on hard times. Decades of neglect followed.

The Borda Gardens are closed as of this writing, and are being restored to a semblance of their early glory. The work will take some time, but you should stop by and see if the gardens have been opened to visitors yet.

Museo de la Herbolaria (13)

This museum of traditional herbal medicine, in the southern suburb of Acapantzingo (take a taxi for about 650 pesos, $1.30), has been set up in a former resort residence built by Maximilian, the Casa del Olindo, or Casa del Olvido. It was here, during his brief reign, that the Austrian-born emperor would come for trysts with La India Bonita, his Cuernavacan lover. Restored in 1960, the house and gardens now preserve the local wisdom in folk medicine. Admission is free, and the museum is open from 9 to 5 every day.

Pirámide de Teopanzoloco

You'll need a taxi to reach the curious Teopanzolco pyramid, northeast of the center of town. Now set in a park, the pyramid was excavated beginning in 1921. As with most Mesoamerican cultures, the local Tlahuicans reconstructed their principal religious monuments at the end of a major calendar cycle by building a new, larger structure right on top of the older one. Here you can clearly see the two different structures of the older and newer.

CUERNAVACA NIGHTLIFE: After spending the day shopping and touring the city, it might be a good idea to return to your hotel and rest up for the evening's activities. This town has a number of cafés right off the Jardín Juárez where people gather to sip coffee or drinks till the wee hours of the morning. the best of the cafés are **La Parroquia** and the Cafetería Viena, previously mentioned in the restaurant section. There are band concerts in the Jardín Juárez on Thursday and Sunday evenings.

Another addition to the Carlos Anderson chain (Anderson's in Mexico City, Carlos 'n Charlie's in Acapulco), is **Harry's Bar (15),** Gutenberg 3 (tel. 2-7679). Their with-it atmosphere includes stereo, long-haired waiters, and Mexican revolutionary posters. Although they serve full dinners here, I'd recommend that you go for drinks—500 to 1,250 pesos ($1 to $2.50). Open Tuesday to Thursday from 6 p.m. to 1 a.m., Friday and Saturday from 1:30 p.m. to 1:30 a.m., on Sunday from 1:30 p.m. to midnight.

EXCURSIONS FROM CUERNAVACA: If you have enough time, you should try to make some side trips around Cuernavaca. To the north you'll find pine trees and an alpine setting; to the east, lush hills and valleys. On the road north to Mexico City you will climb several thousand feet within a half hour into some gorgeous mountain air. If you have a car you can go for a brisk morning hike (it's cold up there) or a lazy afternoon picnic lunch.

Tepoztlán

Take a bus from the Flecha Roja bus station (see above), leaving every 20 minutes or so, for the 12-mile ride to Tepoztlán. This Tlahuica Indian village predates the Conquest, and still holds the ruins of a temple, plus a Dominican monastery (1580) and the thatched huts of the residents. It's a slice of village life only minutes from the big city.

Xochicalco Ruins

About 26 kilometers (16 miles) south of Cuernavaca along Hwy. 95 (the "Libre"—no-toll—road to Taxco) is the town of Alpuyeca; 15 kilometers (9½ miles) northeast of Alpuyeca are the ruins of Xochicalco, the "House of Flowers." High on a mountaintop, Xochicalco boasts a magnificent situation, and an interesting complex of buildings dating from the 600s through the 900s A.D. Most interesting is the **Temple of the Feathered Serpents,** with beautiful bas reliefs. There's also a ballcourt, some underground passages, and other temples. Xochicalco is of interest to archeologists because it seems to have been the point at which the Teotihuacán, Toltec, Zapotec, and Maya cultures met and interacted. You can visit the ruins from 8 a.m. to 5 p.m. daily, but you'll need a car to get there.

Cacahuamilpa Caves

The Grutas de Cacahuamilpa lie some 74 kilometers (46 miles) southwest of Cuernavaca, 8 kilometers (5 miles) north of the Taxco road, Hwy. 95. You can join the group tour (every hour on the hour) of these mammoth caverns, said to stretch some 43 miles within the earth (don't worry—you don't get to see the entire 43 miles!). If you have a car and are driving to Taxco, this makes a nice detour. To go by bus, head for the Autobuses Pullman de Morelos station (see above) in Cuernavaca. You can also get to the caves from Taxco by Lineas Unidas/Flecha Roja bus.

The caves are truly awesome, worth a visit even if you're not generally a cave fancier. Judging by the graffiti in the caves, everyone important, from Empress Carlotta to Mexican presidents, has come to admire them. Hours are 10 a.m. to 5 p.m.; admission costs 350 pesos (70¢). Tours are in Spanish only, but you'll pick up the salient points, and the geologic grandeur and beauty speak for themselves.

Ixtapan de la Sal

The road to Cacahuamilpa, Hwy. 55, is also the road to Toluca, which is 127 kilometers (79 miles) north from Hwy. 95. On the way, 45 kilometers (28 miles) from Hwy. 95, is the pretty spa town of **Ixtapan de la Sal,** with a dozen hotels specializing in the cure: bathing in the natural mineral waters of the area.

6. Taxco

Taxco (pronounced "*tahs*-ko"; alt. 5,850 feet; pop. 70,000), famous for its silver, sits on a hill among hills, and almost everywhere you walk in the city there are fantastic views. The famous church of **Santa Prisca,** with its twin spires, was built by a French miner. José de la Borda, who made a packet in the 18th century. It is illuminated at night.

Taxco's renowned silver mines, first worked in the time of Cortés, four centuries ago, were revived, for all practical purposes, by an American, William Spratling, about 50 years ago. Today its fame rests more on the 180 silver shops, most of them little one-man factories, that line the cobbled streets all the way up into the hills. It is no place to come for bargains, with some silver prices actually higher than in Mexico City because of the magnitude of the tourist trade. In some cases, though, the bracelets and other items are heavier and this accounts for the difference in price. The artistry and imagination of the local silversmiths are evident in each piece.

You can get the idea of what Taxco's like by spending an afternoon there, but there's much more to this picturesque town than just the Plaza Borda and the shops surrounding it. You'll have to stay overnight if you want more time to climb up and down its steep streets, discovering little plazas and fine churches. The main part of town stretches up the hillside from the main highway, and although it's a steep walk it's not a particularly long one. But you don't have to walk: vehicles make the circuit through the town, up the hill and down, picking up and dropping passengers along the route. There are *burritos,* VW minibuses that run the route, and small city buses as well. Both these vehicles run from about 7 a.m. until 9 p.m.

Beware of self-appointed guides, who will undoubtedly approach you in the zócalo (Plaza Borda) and offer their services—they get a cut (up to 25%) of all you buy in the shops they take you to. Should you want a guide, however, ask to see his Departamento de Turismo credentials. Call 732/2-0579 or go to the Department of Tourism office on the highway at the north end of town to engage a licensed guide, about 2,000 to 3,000 pesos ($4 to $6) per hour.

GETTING TO TAXCO: The drive from Mexico City takes about 3½ hours, with a toll road at each side of Cuernavaca, the halfway point. Fill up with gas at Cuernavaca.

By Bus

Estrella de Oro, Calz. de Tlalpan 2205, at the Central de Autobuses del Sur in Mexico City (Metro: Tasqueña; tel. 549-8520), has five buses a day to Taxco (three hours), both first class and deluxe. Lineas Unidas del Sur/Flecha Roja also has several buses a day from the Central de Autobuses del Sur, but is a second choice to Estrella de Oro. From Cuernavaca you can catch an Estrella de Oro bus as it passes through, if there are seats. It is also possible to stop in Taxco on your way back from Acapulco or Zihuatanejo; two buses per day will drop you in Taxco after the 5½-hour ride.

USEFUL FACTS: For **tourist information,** you've got to find the Dirección de

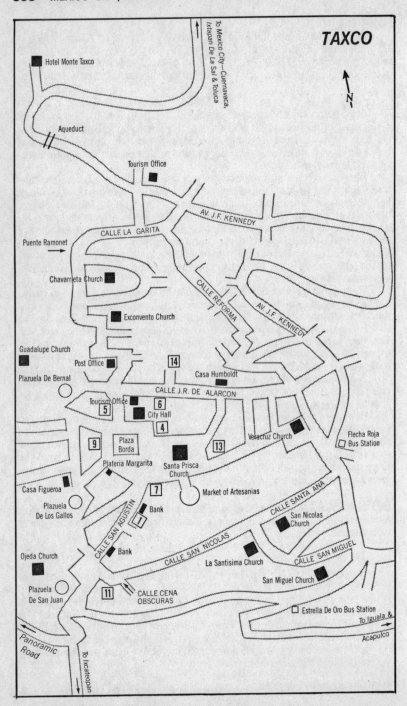

TAXCO

N

Hotel Monte Taxco

To Mexico City—Cuernavaca,
Ixtapan De La Sal & Toluca

Aqueduct

Tourism Office

AV. J.F. KENNEDY

CALLE LA GARITA

Puente Ramonet

CALLE REFORMA

AV. J.F. KENNEDY

Chavarrieta Church

Exconvento Church

Guadalupe Church

Post Office

14

Casa Humboldt

Plazuela De Bernal

CALLE J.R. DE ALARCON

Tourism Office

5

6

City Hall

4

Veracruz Church

Flecha Roja
Bus Station

9

Plaza
Borda

13

Platería Margarita

Santa Prisca
Church

Casa Figueroa

7

Market of Artesanias

Plazuela
De Los Gallos

Bank

CALLE SANTA ANA

San Nicolas
Church

CALLE SAN AGUSTIN

Bank

CALLE SAN NICOLAS

CALLE SAN MIGUEL

Ojeda Church

La Santisima Church

San Miguel Church

Plazuela
De San Juan

11

CALLE CENA
OBSCURAS

Estrella De Oro Bus Station

To Iguala &

Panoramic
Road

To Ixcateopan

Acapulco

Turismo (tel. 732/2-1705), run by the State of Guerrero. Find your way to the main square, the Plaza Borda, then look for the military headquarters bearing a sign, "Cuartel de Hidalgo No. 1." This is the Palacio Municipal (Town Hall). The tourist office is in a lower floor of this building, around the back. To get to it, go around the Cuartel to the left, then right. The tourist office's official address is Plazuela de Bernal 2. Hours are Monday through Saturday 9 a.m. to 3 p.m. and 5 to 7 p.m., Sunday from 9 a.m. to 3 p.m.

There's another office (tel. 732/2-0709) down on the main highway, at the north end of town, useful if you're driving into town from Mexico City.

The **post office** (Correos) is not far from the Dirección de Turismo. Head down the hill from the Plaza Borda as though going to the back of the Cuartel, but instead of turning right, go straight, and the post office is on the left-hand side of the street.

WHERE TO STAY: Compared to Cuernavaca, Taxco is an overnight-stop visitor's dream: charming and picturesque, not noisy or polluted, with a respectable selection of well-kept and delightful budget hotels. The prices aren't even that bad, although they do tend to "bulge" in the heavy summer season and at holiday times. Here are my favorite places to stay:

On a quiet side street just down the hill from the zócalo are two charming hotels at very reasonable rates. The **Posada de Los Castillo (6),** at Juan Ruíz de Alarcón 3 (tel. 732/2-1396), is a beautiful colonial mansion completely restored in 1980. Boasting lots and lots of plants (some even in planters in the bathrooms!), its "new colonial" rooms surround a courtyard on four levels—like a 17th-century Hyatt Regency, let's say. The 15 rooms are small, but equipped with private baths, some with tubs. One person pays 3,950 pesos ($7.90); two pay 4,450 pesos ($8.90), whether in one bed or two.

Right across the street from Los Castillo is its more luxurious and expensive sister hotel, the **Hotel Los Arcos (14),** Juan Ruíz de Alarcón 12 (tel. 732/2-1836). Larger and more sumptuously fitted out, Los Arcos is in fact a converted monastery (1620), and the monks never had it this good: swimming pool (small but nice), a courtyard restaurant-bar, and a maze of little courts and passages hiding 28 very comfortable rooms-with-bath. Prices are 4,700 pesos ($9.40) single, 5,000 pesos ($10) double, 5,300 pesos ($10.60) triple. Whichever of these two hotels you pick, you'll be immersed in colonial charm, blissful quiet, and you'll still be only a five-minute walk from the zócalo.

The **Hotel Melendez (1),** Cuauhtémoc 6 (tel. 732/2-0006, has 42 rooms with baths, all renting at 4,750 pesos ($9.50) single, 5,000 pesos ($10) double. It's a nice hotel just off the zócalo, and its airy bedrooms have blue tile walls and ornate glass and metalwork doors on the bathrooms. Several have terrific views. However, don't take rooms 5, 6, 7, or 8 unless you're desperate. The hotel's restaurant has fairly reasonable prices—a complete dinner for 1,400 pesos ($2.80), or a breakfast of fruit, soft-boiled eggs, coffee, and toast for even less.

The **Hotel Posada del Jardín (4),** Celso Muñoz 4 (tel. 732/2-0027), on the north side of Santa Prisca church just off the main square, is also a fine choice. The hotel is marked only by a small sign above the door, and resembles very much a European pension. You'll really enjoy meeting the super-friendly owners, Manuel and Malena Camacho. It's surprisingly peaceful inside, with a fine view of the mountains from the flower-filled balcony patio. Clean, large rooms rent for 2,950 pesos ($5.90) single, and 3,250 pesos ($6.50) for two people, each of the seven rooms having a private bathroom.

The **Hotel Agua Escondida (5),** Plaza Borda 4 (or Calle Spratling 4) (tel. 732/2-0726 or 2-0736), on one corner of the zócalo, is an exceptionally clean and well-tended establishment. Prices are 6,000 pesos ($12) single, 7,000 pesos ($14) double; rooms have extra touches such as vases of fresh flowers and bottles of mineral water at each bedside.

One of the older and nicer hotels in town is the **Hotel Santa Prisca (11),** Cena Obscuras no. 1, Apdo. Postal 42 (tel. 732/2-0080), in the Plazuela de San Juan. There are 37 cozy comfortable rooms with couch, tile floors, wood beams, and a colonial atmosphere. There are two lush patios with fountains, and a lovely dining room done in mustard and blue. They offer room and breakfast in singles for 7,050 pesos ($14.10), and in doubles for 7,590 pesos ($15.18). An excellent choice for those wishing a splurge.

WHERE TO EAT: Taxco gets a lot of people down from the capital for the day, or passing through on their way to Acapulco, and so there are a lot of restaurants to fill the demand for lunch. But the demand is so great that prices are high for what you get. If you have a big breakfast and pack a lunch you'll save money. Otherwise, the cheapest meals near the zócalo are these:

In the building called El Patio de las Artesanías you'll find a small pizza parlor called the **Pizzaría Dama (2).** Walk through the courtyard and to the left. The small outdoor tables enjoy a fine Taxco view, plus lots of peace and quiet. The medium-size pizza will feed two people, if you're not terribly hungry. A *grande* (large) will feed two hungry souls. Pizza prices range from 600 to 2,200 pesos ($1.20 to $4.40). Beer and soft drinks are served. For a soft drink that's not cloyingly sweet, order *manzanita,* a carbonated apple soda pop.

A good comida bargain these days is the 1,400-peso ($2.80) lunch at the **Hotel Melendez (1)** (tel. 2-0006), served in an attractive tiled dining room overlooking the town and the valley. You pour the soup from the tureen yourself (no need to skimp!). There follow rice-and-vegetables, a meat-and-vegetable plate, melon or pudding, and coffee or tea. For Taxco, you get your money's worth here.

The **Restaurant Arnoldo's (9)** (tel. 2-1272), Plazuela de los Gallos 2, overlooks the main square (it's directly across the square from the Santa Prisca church, but you enter by a little side street that runs around back of the restaurant), and offers a 1,200-peso ($2.40) comida as well as à la carte items. The señora who runs it is interested in pleasing her customers and will make sure everything is up to expectations.

The **Restaurant La Hacienda (5)** (tel. 2-0726), on Calle Bailar, just behind (and connected to) the Hotel Agua Escondida, has been completely redone, and now boasts white linen, colorful table settings, a simple colonial decor, and an extensive menu—everything from enchiladas to steak, from pasta to hamburgers. Despite its fancy (for Taxco) trappings, it's a small family-run operation, so the service is friendly if a little slow. Having had my fill of enchiladas for a while, I ordered a delicious cream of tomato soup and the deluxe hamburger platter. It was good, complete, and filling. With a beer, tax, and tip, the bill was less than 2,000 pesos ($4).

On the attractive Plazuela de San Juan (the one with the fountain) you'll spot the **Restaurante Ethel (8)** (no phone). A family-run place, it's kept clean and tidy, with cloths on the tables and a hometown atmosphere. The hearty daily comida corrida consists of soup or pasta, meat (perhaps a small steak), dessert, and coffee for 1,300 pesos ($2.60), tax and tip included. And if that modest amount seems like too much, you should check out the **Restaurant Santa Fe (10)** (tel. 2-1170), Hidalgo 2, just down the street from the Ethel, and even less expensive.

The **Restaurant El Triángulo del Sol (3)** (tel. 2-1721), Plazuela de los Gallos, Calle Delicias 4, serves diners from 8:30 a.m. to 10 p.m. every day in a pleasant room overlooking the Hotel Melendez. The family of Antonio Arce

Bahena provides quiet and attentive service, though they're relatively new to the restaurant business. Prices are moderate: a club sandwich, for instance, costs 620 pesos ($1.24), steaks range from 1,000 to 1,500 pesos ($2 to $3).

Cielito Lindo (tel. 2-0603), Plaza Borda 14, is on the main square at the corner near where the Calle San Agustín begins. The tables clad in white are usually packed, and plates of food disappear as fast as the waiters can bring them. For an à la carte feast of soup, roast chicken with two vegetables, pineapple pie, and coffee, tax, and tip, expect to pay 3,000 pesos ($6).

DAYTIME ACTIVITIES: In a word—shopping! When you're tired of that, perhaps you'd like to snoop through some colonial houses. **Casa de las Lágrimas** (House of Tears), also known as Casa Figueroa, Calle Guadalupe 2, above the zócalo, has been turned into a private art gallery and charges a few pesos for a look around. Next door, incidentally, is the local art school.

Or you might sneak in for a look at Juan O'Gorman's mural beside the swimming pool at the **Hotel Posada de la Misión** (on the highway; go via burrito).

Taxco has a fine little museum, called the **Museo de Taxco Guillermo Spratling (13)**, almost directly behind the Santa Prisca church, open every day but Monday, from 10 a.m. to 2 p.m. and 3 to 6 p.m. for an admission charge of 30 pesos (6¢). Don't write it off. The building and displays are of the high quality that's normal in Mexico. The entrance floor and the one above display a good collection of pre-Columbian statues and implements in clay, stone, and jade. A quote in Spanish by Gordon Willey sets the mood for this pre-Columbian exhibit: "Man speaks to man through art and emotional effect that does not change with the passing of centuries." The lower floor has a display on the history of Taxco. Documents, clippings, letters, engravings, and photographs give you an idea of what it was like a century or two ago in this mountain mining town: miners' implements, helmets, lanterns, and such add a touch of realism to the display. Look for the samples of silver ore, Taxco's raison d'être. A plaque (in Spanish) explains that most of the collection and the funds for the museum came from William Spratling, an American born in 1900 who studied architecture in the U.S., later settled in Taxco, and organized the first workshops to turn out high-quality silver jewelry. From this first effort in 1931 the town's reputation as a center of artistic silver work grew to what it is today. In a real sense, Spratling "put Taxco on the map." He died in 1967 in a car accident.

After your visit to the museum, stroll along Ruíz de Alarcón street right near the museum, looking for the richly decorated façade of the **Von Humboldt house.** The renowned German scientist and explorer Baron Alexander von Humboldt (1769-1859) visited Taxco and stayed in this beautiful house in 1803.

After shopping, a walk around town, and a visit to the museum, drag yourself back to the zócalo and up the flight of cobbled steps lined with geraniums to **Paco's Bar (9)** overlooking the zócalo. Drinks are anywhere from 200 pesos (40¢) for soft drinks, through beer at 350 to 450 pesos (70¢ to 90¢), with more sophisticated concoctions costing up to 1,000 pesos ($2). In the summer there's live music at Paco's from 5 to 9 p.m.

TAXCO NIGHTLIFE: Taxco's nighttime action is centered in the luxury hotels that have sprung up to catch the influx of well-heeled tourists. The **Holiday Inn** (tel. 732/2-1300), **Posada de la Misión** (tel. 732/2-0063), and **Hotel de la Borda** (tel. 732/2/0025) all have their clubs and nighttime shows. You'll need a taxi to get to any one of these, and then there will be the inevitable cover charge. La Borda's nightclub, El Bocanal, operates on a two-drink minimum. It features a marimba orchestra from 6:30 to 11 p.m.

Completely different in tone is **Berta's (7),** right next to Santa Prisca church. Open since the early '30s by a lady named Berta who made her fame on a drink of the same name (tequila, soda, lime, and sugar syrup), Berta's is traditionally the gathering place of the local gentry. Spurs and old swords decorate the walls, and a saddle is casually slung over the banister of the stairs leading to the second-floor room where tin masks leer from the walls. A Berta costs 400 pesos (80¢), rum the same. Open 9 a.m. to around midnight.

Chapter XII

TO THE GULF

1. Orizaba and Cordoba
2. Jalapa
3. Veracruz
4. Papantla, Tuxpan, and Tajín
5. Lake Catemaco

THE BOOM IN TRAVEL to the Yucatán has benefited the towns of the Gulf Coast, somewhat neglected in earlier years by the hordes rushing to Acapulco. Veracruz, chief among these, does not make its living from tourism—it's Mexico's biggest and most active port, and always has been—but it welcomes tourists (especially Mexican tourists on weekends) and has a great deal to offer. If you've come by land from the north to Mexico City you'll probably consider continuing on to the Yucatán, in which case you can make a convenient and rewarding stop in Veracruz. The toll road, although expensive, is advisable, for the old mountain road that twists and turns is neither as safe nor as fast. The bus will take the toll road, passing through the towns of Puebla (see Chapter XIII), Orizaba, and Cordoba along the way. From Veracruz it is possible to drive or take a bus to the nearby lake resort of Catemaco, and from there to the Isthmus of Tehuantepec. Jalapa, capital city of the state of Veracruz, can make an interesting detour if you're not in a blind rush to get to the coast.

1. Orizaba and Cordoba

ORIZABA: Famous as a manufacturing city, Orizaba, Veracruz (alt. 4,000 feet; pop. 300,000), sits at the foot of Mexico's highest mountain, Citlaltépetl (18,275 feet), and has a pleasant, cool climate that does little to encourage consumption of its most well-known product: various brands of Moctezuma beer. Maximilian and Carlotta had a hacienda on the outskirts of the town (now ruined and hardly worth seeing), but the major architectural attraction these days is the fanciful **Palacio Municipal.** The style might be called Victorian gingerbread, but the construction is all steel. Fabricated in Belgium during the 1800s, it was later taken apart, shipped across the Atlantic, and bolted together here in Orizaba.

The drive from Mexico City to Veracruz can easily be done in a day, but should you find it necessary to stop in Orizaba, the **Hotel Aries,** at Oriente 6 no. 265 (tel. 272/5-3699), will put you up in style. Restaurant and bar are all at your service, rooms are modern—even stylish, almost—and feature wall-to-wall carpets, telephones, and spanking-clean bathrooms. One person pays 5,500 pesos ($11); two people sharing the same bed pay 6,000 pesos ($12); two people in two beds pay 6,500 pesos ($13). The hotel is only about two blocks up the street from the A.D.O. bus station. The city tourist office is in the lobby here.

Almost across the street from the Aries is the older and less expensive **Grand Hotel de France,** at Oriente 6 no. 186, corner of Sur 5 (tel. 272/5-2311). The France, although well-worn, is still quite respectable and has a very agreeable staff. It seems as though no two rooms are alike, and you would do well to inspect several before choosing one. Singles are 4,000 pesos ($8), and doubles are 4,750 pesos ($9.50).

What to Do

The **tourist office,** in the lobby of the Hotel Aries, is a very helpful place to stop in Orizaba. Many of the attractions here center on the availability of cold, clear water like Laguna de Nogales or Ojo de Agua or the hydroelectric plants. Two other attractions may have more appeal. The **Moctezuma Brewery** is open for tours Monday through Friday from 10 a.m. to noon and 4:30 to 5:30 p.m.

The second attraction is Mexico's highest mountain, Citlaltépetl. It is possible to hire a Jeep and driver in Tlachichuca for 6,000 pesos ($12) to drive up to four people to the 14,000-foot-plus point—a rare opportunity for us normally earthbound souls to do some very high climbing. In Tlachichuca, see Mr. José Reyes, who controls alpine service to the mountain. He can give you information on the shelters at the 14,000-foot level and also information on the climb to the summit. Remember that the summit is covered with snow year round. The best time to climb is from the middle of November through the middle of January.

CORDOBA: This is a bustling city (alt. 3,000 feet; pop. 190,000), with a huge market district, an imposing cathedral with a famous set of bells, and a pretty main square complete with Muzak (everything from Hawaiian guitars to Scott Joplin). Cordoba, Veracruz, is a center for Mexico's coffee industry, and several brands proudly claim origin in the hills surrounding the town.

If you stay here, try the **Hotel Virreynal,** Avenida 1 and Calle 5 (tel. 272/2-2377), at the side of the cathedral off the main square. The façade is baroque, the lobby brilliant with tiles, but the three floors of rooms are fairly modern and comfortable—providing you don't get a room in the front, where the traffic noise and the famous churchbells can disturb your sleep. Prices are very reasonable: 2,600 pesos ($5.20) single, 4,400 pesos ($8.80) double, with free parking in the hotel garage.

The Virreynal has a restaurant, attractive in an old-fashioned way with wood furniture and white tablecloths. There's a daily comida for 1,000 pesos ($2).

Prime activity for the traveler laying over a night in Cordoba is people-watching, coffee- or cocktail-drinking, and dining on the main square. The **Hotel Zevallos,** fronted by an arcade along one side of the square, is famous for having seen the signing of Mexico's Pact of Cordoba (1821), which granted independence from Spain. Today the Portal Zevallos (the arcade proper) is lined with café-restaurants, each having a different character: there is the one for gilded youth, the one for ma and pa out to dinner, the one for an all-male cast of domino-players, etc. The **Restaurant & Café Parroquía,** Avenida 1 and Calle 1, in the Portal Zevallos, is a general mix of people and offers a varied menu. The end of the arcade is a good vantage point for ogling the other cafés and the square while having a sandwich for 300 to 500 pesos (60¢ to $1). Beer, wine, and cocktails are served. You can also get an early breakfast at the Parroquía.

2. Jalapa

Capital of the state of Veracruz, Jalapa (or Xalapa; alt. 4,500 feet; pop. 300,000) is an interesting town to explore for a day. Although modern, the city is riddled with old and narrow streets that wind downhill, apparently to nowhere in particular.

The center of town is midway down the mountainside. The cathedral (1773), Palacio de Gobierno, and the pretty, formal Parque Juárez are here, perched on a terrace beyond which the town continues its downward tumble. The view from the park, of the red tile roofs, orange trees, and the Cofre de Perote volcano in the far distance, is the finest memory you'll take with you from Jalapa.

Arriving by A.D.O. bus, you'll be about ten minutes' walk from the center of town. Turn left out the bus station door, and walk down the slope on the road named Enriquez, which will bring you to the park. By A.U. bus, you'll arrive a bit farther up the hillside, at Revolución 279. Walk downhill on Avenida de la Revolución (the street in front of the bus station) to reach the Palacio de Gobierno.

WHERE TO STAY AND EAT: Two favorites with business and government travelers have become too expensive for most of us, but are worth mentioning. The **Hotel Maria Victoria,** right behind the Palacio de Gobierno on Calle Zaragoza 6 (tel. 281/7-5600), charges 7,245 pesos ($14.49) single, 8,050 pesos ($16.10) double, plus 253 pesos (51¢) for parking. The clean but worn rooms and excellent location cannot compensate for the less than helpful staff and high prices. The gleaming **Hotel Xelapa,** at Victoria and Bustamante (tel. 281/8-2552), is the second. Singles cost 9,488 pesos ($18.98) and doubles are 10,695 pesos ($21.39). With the center of state power here in Jalapa, there seems to be no shortage of people willing to pay these prices.

The above prices may send you scurrying to my first choice, the 22-room **Hotel Continental,** Zamora 4 near the intersection with Enriquez (tel. 281/7-3530). There are tables, chairs, and potted plants in the central courtyard. The rooms are clean and have small bathrooms; since each is quite different, be sure to look at several. Prices are very reasonable, at 1,400 pesos ($2.80) single and 1,600 pesos ($3.20) double (one or two beds).

A higher priced alternative is the older **Hotel México,** Dr. Lucio 4 (tel. 281/7-5030), just across the street diagonally from the cathedral. Rooms are grouped around the central courtyard (which serves as parking lot) on three floors, and some peek through frosted glass onto the plaza out front. Accommodations are a little plain, but the prices aren't fancy either: 2,800 pesos ($5.60) single, 3,100 pesos ($6.20) double with one bed and 3,400 pesos ($6.80) with two beds, complete. Parking costs 100 pesos (20¢).

As for dining, the town favorite, good for all occasions, is the **Cafetería Terraza Jardín,** on Enriquez—that's the street that runs in front of the cathedral and Palacio. Right across from the Parque Juárez, the Jardín has three huge tiers of indoor seating, plain tables and chairs, no decor to speak of. Despite its name and the self-service line on the top tier, the Jardín is a waiter-service restaurant serving full breakfasts, lunches, and dinners. Just a sandwich? You can get away spending 300 to 480 pesos (60¢ to 96¢) or less. Something more substantial? I can recommend the carne asada con chilaquiles (a strip of broiled beef served with sliced tortillas and onions in a spicy tomato sauce). With a bottle of beer, you'll pay 975 pesos ($1.95) for such a tuck-in. A six-course comida corrida, which includes a choice of fish or meat, costs 1,000 pesos ($2.00). You can order more expensive items, but you shouldn't.

At Enriquez 31 is the old Hotel Regis, and beside it a little alley called the Calle Antonio Maria de Rivera. One block up this street on the right, at no. 16, is the **Restaurante El Diamante** (tel. 7-1326), a clean, modern place tastefully decorated with local pottery. Prices are roughly half those of the more centrally located Cafetería Terraza Jardín; for example, the midday comida of four courses goes for 700 pesos ($1.40). Other restaurants on this street invite experimentation as well.

Several small eateries are located right along Enriquez and entice the casual passerby with an assortment of scents and sights. **Enricos** (tel. 7-6447), at Enriquez 6, has big windows, an open grill, and an espresso machine. Try to ignore the cafeteria trays and try the tacos (four) for 420 pesos (84¢), or meats for 970 to 1,310 pesos ($1.94 to $2.62), or the five-course comida for 750 pesos ($1.50).

The café **Nuevo Chap Suy** at Enriquez 14 is another of the alluring eateries with an amazing assortment of pastries in the front window. Sandwiches are 250 pesos (50¢), and nothing on the menu is more than 750 pesos ($1.50)! The five-course comida wins the midday competition at 600 pesos ($1.20). Open 7 a.m. to midnight.

La Parroquía (tel. 7-4436), at Zaragoza 18 near the Hotel Maria Victora, has the same wonderful coffee but different owners than the restaurant with the same name in Veracruz. If the main floor is full here, there are more tables upstairs that look out over the street. Typical Mexican plates are 360 to 800 pesos (72¢ to $1.60), and the daily comida is 800 pesos ($1.60), or 950 pesos ($1.90) on Sunday. Open 7:30 a.m. to 10:30 p.m.

La Casona del Beaterio (tel. 8-2119), Calle Zaragoza 20, is like a jewel among the many cafeteria-style eateries in Jalapa. The restaurant has many rooms around a courtyard with flowering plants and a fountain. The comida corrida offers a selection of several different meat or fish dishes for 1,000 pesos ($2.00). A chicken meal costs 1,150 pesos ($2.30), while the meat dishes hover in the 900- to 1,700-peso ($1.80 to $3.40) range. This is a beautiful place to see the hundreds of old photographs of Jalapa's history and enjoy the cut-glass chandeliers and sound of trickling water. Open from 8 a.m. to 10 p.m. daily.

WHAT TO DO: Take a look at the murals by José Chávez Morado in the Palacio de Gobierno, and also a glance in the massive cathedral. Walk through the streets and admire the bougainvillea, fruit trees, and flowers. Jalapa is halfway between the mountains and the tropics, so they have coffee plantations and sultry breezes at the same time.

The **state tourism office** is on the corner Zaragoza and Bravo. No English is spoken, but these people know Jalapa and are helpful in a very friendly way. If you need assistance locating a particular place or getting to a specific destination, they can help.

The **Agora,** a hang-out for artists, students, and other cosmopolitan types, is just off the main park. Books, records, films, conversation, concerts—look here first. Afterward check out the **Teatro del Estado,** at Manuel Avila Camacho and Ignacio de la Llave. This is Jalapa's official cultural center, always with something going on.

Many people come to Jalapa just to visit the **Veracruz State Museum,** on the road to Mexico City, in a university complex on the left (southwest) side. The museum is well worth the visit. It contains many pieces that are noteworthy besides its gigantic Olmec head. The giant stone tortoise and the torso of an Olmec monumental figure are two exquisite pieces. The Olmec art from the 1500 B.C. to A.D. 500 period is particularly noteworthy for its power and expressiveness. The head, and other pieces of sculpture, are in a park surrounding the museum, while the interior rooms hold some 25,000 pieces of Huastec, Totonac, and Olmec art. The museum was temporarily closed for reconstruction during 1986. Huge new display halls are scheduled for completion in December 1986, although actual completion may trickle into 1987. Anticipated hours are 9 a.m. to 5 p.m. daily, 50 peso (10¢) admission. If the museum is your only reason to travel to Jalapa, do check ahead to be sure it is open.

From Jalapa, the first 20 kilometers (12 miles) of the fine new road to the coast are lined with roses, bougainvillea, and recently transplanted mature trees. The 110-kilometer (68-mile) trip to Veracruz will take about 1½ hours.

The weather gets hotter and the air gets thicker and muggier with each foot you descend.

3. Veracruz

From Cordoba or Jalapa, Veracruz is less than a two-hour ride. Veracruz (that's "bay-rah-*croos*"; pop. 550,000) is Mexico's principal port and has been since Hernán Cortés landed there on Good Friday in 1519. His name for the town he founded was Villa Rica de la Vera Cruz (the Rich Town of the True Cross). The Spaniards used to ship most of their gold and silver out of the port, so it became a popular calling point for pirates, who periodically would shut up the townfolk in the parish church, or abandon them on an island in the bay, while they methodically ransacked the town. The citizens took two major precautions: they built a high wall around the old town (around the **Plaza de Armas**) and they constructed a massive fort, **San Juan de Ulua (15)**, on what was then an island in the harbor but is now connected to the mainland by a curving pier. Neither precaution was entirely effective; the port was pillaged by pirates in 1654 and 1712, invaded by the French in 1832 and 1861, and by the Americans in 1847 and 1914.

Veracruz, a raucous, swinging port town, has an intriguing combination of European and African influences, and an impressive shoreline. Near the sea, the **Bank of Mexico (16)** building, all glass, steel, and gray stone, does double-duty as a lighthouse (Faro).

Important Note: Veracruz has become a favorite weekending spot for tourists from the capital city. Every Friday afternoon and evening, buses, trains (especially the sleepers), and planes fill up in Mexico City and empty out in Veracruz. The flood back up into the mountains is reversed on Sunday. In addition, ponderous Customs procedures in this, Mexico's largest port, demand that importers and exporters come to the city often, and they fill hotel rooms. Arrive as early in the week, and as early in the day, as possible. You will find a room in any case, but unless you arrive early, it may not be the room you want.

ORIENTATION: The **Tourism Office** (tel. 29/32-9942) is right downtown in the main square, the Plaza de Armas, in the Palacio Municipal (Town Hall) (1), on the east side of the square, open daily from 9 a.m. to 8 p.m., although sparsely staffed from 1 to 4 p.m. Tips for getting to and from the bus station are given below; the railroad station is only a few blocks from the Plaza de Armas, on the Plaza de la República right near the water (see map).

GETTING TO AND FROM VERACRUZ: Most northern Mexican cities, the capital itself, Oaxaca, Tehuantepec, and the cities and towns of the Yucatán are accessible by direct bus from Veracruz. Veracruz's **Central Camionera (17)** is about 15 blocks from downtown on Avenida S. Díaz Mirón at Calle Orizaba. Buses running along Díaz Mirón pass the Parque Zamora and then head downtown on various routes. Look for "Camionera" painted on the bus windshield to get back to the terminal from downtown. Two of the easiest to use are the "Díaz Mirón" and "20 de Noviembre," which can be caught running along Avenida 5 de Mayo. These buses pass the second-class bus station as well as the first-class

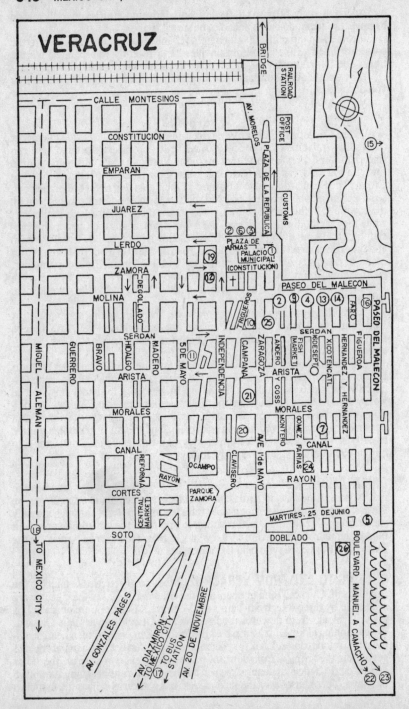

VERACRUZ

Central Camionera for a 40-peso (8¢) fare. The railroad station is right downtown on the Plaza de la República.

By Bus

From the Central Camionera (also called A.D.O., for the main company operating here) buses head from Veracruz to Mexico City (scores of buses every day, a seven-hour trip), to Oaxaca (one night bus), and Merida (three a day). As the bus station is a good distance from downtown, try to make your onward reservations when you arrive in Veracruz. Other buses leave for Tuxpan, Brownsville, Reynosa, Matamoras, and Cardel (for Zamora).

By Rail

Two trains a day leave from Mexico City to Veracruz, one evening (night) train and one day train, which leaves about 7:34 a.m. The trip takes about 12 hours. You can reserve a sleeper on the evening trains. One day train runs in each direction between Tapachula and Veracruz. Trains running between Mexico City and Veracruz tend to be good, although not without the occasional annoyance. But onward from Veracruz into the Yucatán or to the Guatemalan border, train quality suffers considerably. I recommend that you *not* take these trains.

By Air

You can fly between Veracruz and Mexico City (five flights daily). Although direct fares apply to all destinations, all flights go to Mexico City first. Mexicana runs most of these flights, as well as three flights a week to Los Angeles (with a stopover in Mexico City) on which special low excursion rates are available. The airport is indicated by (**18**) on the map. A taxi to the airport costs about 1,600 pesos ($3.20). There is a minibus service of sorts, operated by people working out of a dress shop two doors down from the Mexicana Airlines office (5 de Mayo, corner of Serdan). The green minibuses of Transportación Terrestre Aeropuerto (tel. 29/32-3520) don't go out for every departing flight, but if you're lucky enough to get one, you'll pay only a half of the cab fare for a seat.

WHERE TO STAY: Veracruz has a fairly good assortment of hotels, but you must be especially careful of noise in this town—auto and truck noise to be sure, but also *marimba* noise, for this is a gay, raucous town and the enthusiasts among the musicians keep it up until the early morning hours.

As a rule of thumb, you should plan to pay for air conditioning if you stay on or very near the Plaza de Armas. Hotels six or seven blocks away from the plaza are quieter, and you probably won't have to keep your windows closed as you would have to on the square.

Newest of Veracruz's moderately priced hotels is the **Hotel Baluarte (7),** Canal 265, corner of 16 de Septiembre (tel. 29/36-0844). Five stories high, modern, and very attractive, it has a location that helps to make it my first choice, for it's right on the square dominated by the romantic Baluarte de Santiago, now a museum. It's very quiet here, and although you're five blocks from downtown, the walk is a pleasant and brief one. The 73 rooms all have individual air conditioners, and each machine is thoughtfully equipped with a plastic tube so that condensation doesn't drip onto sidewalk passersby. Guests can use the hotel's own parking lot across the street, and a small air-conditioned restaurant off the lobby is good for breakfast (402 to 632 pesos, 81¢ to $1.27) or a light meal if you don't feel like going out. Singles go for 3,680 pesos ($7.36), doubles for 4,255 pesos ($8.51), and are excellent values.

One of the more centrally located hotels in town is the four-story **Hotel Oriente (1)**, Miguel Lerdo 6, at the south end of the Plaza de la República (tel. 29/32-0100). The Oriente's lobby is rather bare, furnished only with a few plants and low seats, and the rooms are quite noisy, but the manager is a kindly gentleman and the 57 rooms are clean if well worn and contain telephones, private showers, ceiling fans, and terraces. Rates are 3,838 pesos ($7.68) single, 4,200 pesos ($8.40) double in one bed, 4,514 pesos ($9.03) double in two beds, plus 517 pesos ($1.04) more for air conditioning.

Still in the same area is the **Hotel Prendes (2),** Independencia 88 at Lerdo (tel. 29/31-0241), whose three floors of recently renovated plush guest rooms are garnished with wood balconies and wood-louvered French doors. There's a little tiled lobby with several iron chandeliers and a stained-glass railroad mural above the desk. Rooms are very well kept and comfortable, spacious, and most outside rooms have balconies. Rooms cost 4,441 pesos ($8.89) single and 5,548 pesos ($11.10) double.

Newest addition to the collection of hotels located on the Plaza de Armas is the **Hotel Concha Dorada (3)**, officially located at Lerdo de Tejada 77 (tel. 29/31-2996), almost next door to the Hotel Colonial and Hotel Ruiz. The tiny reception desk might make one think this is a starvation-budget hotel, but in fact the smallish rooms, although somewhat dark, have some of the better touches: tile bathrooms, radio, telephone, air conditioning, and all-new furniture. Prices are in line with the modernization, and are a bit high (but consider the location): 2,100 pesos ($4.20) single with fan; 4,000 pesos ($8), single or double, with air conditioning; 2,100 pesos ($4.20) double with fan; or 6,300 pesos ($12.60) for a suite with air conditioning. The small inner rooms, while a bit claustrophobic, are bound to be quiet.

The **Hotel Colonial (6),** right on the Plaza de la Constitución (tel. 29/32-0193), has two sections, the older with ceiling fans or air conditioning and the newer with air conditioning. All the expensive hotel services are here, including private, covered parking and swimming pool for guests. You pay 3,608 pesos ($7.22) single, 4,245 pesos ($8.49) double for one of the older rooms (still very nice, mind you), 7,553 pesos ($15.11) single, and 8,888 pesos ($17.78) double for the air-conditioned rooms with TV. This is a pleasant place to stay.

Prices are slightly less in the imposing 132-room **Gran Hotel Diligencias (19),** facing the Plaza de Armas (tel. 29/31-2116), where air-conditioned rooms cost 5,790 pesos ($11.58) single and 6,957 pesos ($13.92) double; but in my opinion the Hotel Colonial offers the best value-for-money.

Hotel Santillana, at 209 Landero y Coss (tel. 29/32-3116), is directly opposite the fish market. The 42 tiny rooms with ceiling fans are wrapped around a small courtyard and rent for 3,250 pesos ($6.50) single, 4,500 pesos ($9) double. Cold soft drinks are available in the lobby.

The Big Splurge

The **Hotel Emporio (14),** out on the Malecón near the Banco de México tower (tel. 29/32-7520), is a huge, newly remodeled place with a garage, two swimming pools, and sundeck. Nowadays the good location, sea view, and air conditioning will cost 10,850 pesos ($21.70) single, 11,845 pesos ($23.69) double. The management offers a 10% to 15% reduction (or more) during the slow months, so feel free to bargain for a better rate.

Feel like spending some money? The **Hotel Puerto Bello Centro (9),** 458 Malecón, (tel. 29/38-0354), is a dramatic modern tower with posh, air-conditioned rooms and a gleaming second-floor swimming pool, plus private parking for guests (which costs extra). A big room here goes for 7,500 pesos

($15.00) single, 8,000 pesos ($16) double. On weekends, they probably get it too.

With the hope of avoiding confusion, I want to mention that this chain operates a twin establishment, Hotel Bello Boulevard at Camacho No. 1263 (tel. 29/31-0011). Rooms are identical, prices are not. Singles are 11,540 pesos ($23.08), doubles 12,190 pesos ($24.38); prices are raised to 13,800 pesos ($27.60) single or double during holidays.

On the Starvation Budget

It's probably only a matter of time before the musty old **Hotel Imperial,** on the north side of the Plaza de Armas at Lerdo No. 153 (tel. 29/31-1741), is gutted, renovated, and catapulted out of our price range. But at present you can get a double room here for 4,500 pesos ($9), and if you get one of the rooms overlooking the square—which are better kept—it might just be worth it, although I doubt it. Beware of street noise when selecting a room.

Two blocks south of the Plaza de Armas is the street named after Aquiles Serdan. The **Hotel Amparo (10),** Serdan 482 near the corner with Zaragoza (tel. 29/32-2738), has a tile façade, a tiled lobby, and a stone-lined corridor leading to an inner court. All this stonework won't keep you cooler—you'll need the windows open here if it's hot, and the street noise can be fierce. Take a room in the back of the building. They cost 3,337 pesos ($6.68) single, 3,925 pesos ($7.85) double, and are a better value than the Imperial.

Right across from the Amparo at Serdan No. 451 is the recently remodeled **Hotel Santo Domingo (10)** (tel. 29/32-8285). The tiny rooms are barely sufficient for the double bed, but all are clean, air-conditioned, and have television. The staff seems eager to help and even has a map of the city for guests. The cost of rooms here is 3,050 pesos ($6.10) single and 3,825 pesos ($7.65) double, which should give the non-air-conditioned Amparo all the competition it needs.

Near the Beach

Right at the northern (beginning) end of the Boulevard Manuel Avila Camacho is the **Hotel Villa Rica (26),** at no. 7 (tel. 29/32-0782). Mexican families and young people on vacation choose this neat-and-tidy little place as a favorite because it's near the beach and not all that far from downtown, either. Rooms are simple and clean with tile showers; prices are 3,000 pesos ($6) single, 3,500 pesos ($7) double, with ceiling fans, no air conditioning available. A small mom-and-pop restaurant on the ground floor offers a 625-peso ($1.25) comida corrida. Next door at Camacho no. 165-A is Tridente (tel. 29/2-7924), a scuba-diving outfitter.

The **Hotel Villa del Mar (23),** farther south and east along Boulevard Camacho (tel. 29/31-3366), is a large and rambling older place with modernized, air-conditioned rooms renting for 6,325 pesos ($12.65) single, or 7,475 pesos ($14.95) double. A very good value is one of the bungalows with ceiling fan and kitchen, which rents for 9,200 pesos ($18.40) and 1,150 pesos ($2.30) for additional beds up to six. The reason the prices are this high is obvious: the hotel has its own private little swimming pool, and the public beach is just across the busy boulevard.

Right next door is the **Hostal de Cortés (23)** (tel. 29/32-0065), a new six-floor hotel boasting an elevator, sea views from little balconies attached to some rooms, color television sets, and servi-bars, a restaurant, bar, and swimming pool. One pays for all this posh, though, as the 113 rooms go for 13,800 pesos ($27.60), single or double—a bit out of our range.

Much better in terms of price, although quite a bit older, is the **Hotel Mar y**

Tierra (5) ("sea and land"; tel. 29/32-0260), right at the junction of the Malecón, Boulevard Camacho, and Avenida Figueroa near the aforementioned Hotel Villa Rica. A towering new addition, complete with garage, brings the total number of rooms to 160. The older (cheaper) section has tile rooms with individual window air-conditioners; while rooms in the new section have carpeting, central air conditioning, and television. Many rooms have excellent views, so be sure to look before you lease. Room cost is reasonable at 3,220 to 4,600 pesos ($6.44 to $9.22) single, 3,680 to 5,750 pesos ($7.36 to $11.50) double. The more expensive rooms are in the new section.

Out of Town—On Mocambo Beach

The **Hotel Mocambo (22)** (tel. 29/37-1500) is quite a way out of town to the east, right on one of Veracruz's best stretches of beach. A palatial layout with rooms, halls, terraces, pools, grounds, etc., it must qualify as a splurge hotel. All 110 rooms have air conditioning, private bath, and sea views, and you can use their huge filtered pool or the beach, the Ping-Pong tables, tennis court, or other facilities. Cost is a cool 13,100 pesos ($26.20) single, 14,750 pesos ($29.50) double. **Warning:** Poolside and rooms with views cost more. Even if you don't decide to stay here, you might want to come out for a look and a swim. The beach is public—you needn't stay at the hotel. Buses stop right outside the front gate of the hotel and will take you into town for 75 pesos (15¢).

Next to the Bus Station

Right next door to Veracruz's Central Camionera, at Avenida Díaz Mirón 1612, is the **Hotel Central (17)** (tel. 29/37-2222). Although hardly central as its name implies, it is indeed convenient for those arriving by bus as long as you follow my caution about noise. The marbled halls of the Central lead to very worn rooms with tile showers and well-used furnishings; some rooms come with fans, for 3,000 pesos ($6) double, and some come with air conditioning for 3,450 pesos ($6.90) double. Air conditioning allows you to keep the louvered windows closed and thus the noise out. When choosing a room, remember the buses. This place is for emergencies only, because of noise.

WHERE TO EAT: Now that the Plaza de Armas, the main square, has been turned into a pedestrian zone, the restaurants under the portals that surround it have become even more attractive, and, sadly, more expensive. But you needn't wander far from downtown to enjoy what Veracruzans love best: seafood.

You get more than a meal when you dine at **El Chato Moyo (8)** (tel. 29/2-5078), down on the waterfront at Landero y Coss 142, corner of Insurgentes Veracruzanos. Sit outside on the Calle Prof. J. S. Montero, and you'll be treated to a view of a hundred itinerant peddlers (none of whom will give you a hard time); or at least two marimba or mariachi bands, competing for the scarce silence by trying to drown one another out. Shoeshine boys, beggars, sellers of tasteless model ships and cheap jewelry make up an endless procession. Sound like a horror? Somehow it's all great fun at the Chato Moyo. The food is quite good, the service all right for the size of the place, and the prices very competitive. Fish is ordered by size and costs 850 to 1,200 pesos ($1.70 to $2.40), depending. Meat plates are 700 pesos ($1.40), but you should try seafood here. Start with an oyster, shrimp, or octopus cocktail for 350 pesos (70¢). Special plates go as high as 1,250 pesos ($2.50), but you needn't spend that much. If the Chato Moyo's crowded, you might try one of the two other similar restaurants next door.

Devotees of Spanish food will undoubtedly like **La Paella,** Zamora 138

(Plaza de Armas), where a five-course comida goes for 950 pesos ($1.90), and most other meals are in the 400- to 700-peso (80¢ to $1.40) range. Three of the courses include such internationally known Spanish specialties as caldo gallego (a fish broth), paella valenciana, and Basque-style sea bass. The walls are festooned with bullfight posters—all Spanish, none Mexican. La Paella is right at one corner (the southeast) of the Plaza de Armas near the tourism office—look for its tiled, very colonial façade.

The **Hotel Prendes (2)** restaurant is still *número uno* in the plaza area—especially where seafood is concerned. Premises are spacious, well lighted, air-conditioned, and—rare for Veracruz—free from excessive noise. Supplementing a 1,000-peso ($2) comida are à la carte dishes ranging from 975 to 3,200 pesos ($1.95 to $6.40) for seafood dishes.

The aptly named **Restaurant El Unico (10)** may in fact be the only place where you can get such a good, filling comida corrida for a really low price anymore. For 450 pesos (90¢) the señora will bring you soup, rice, a choice of meat or fish, dessert, and coffee. The comida corrida is just about all anyone orders during the afternoon, but you can also get plates of fish for 450 to 550 pesos (90¢ to $1.10), with most dishes in the 250- to 450-peso (50¢ to 90¢) range. The decor is nothing much, of course, but the food is very tasty indeed, and can't be beaten at the price—or higher. The restaurant is located at the corner of Aquiles Serdan (no. 493) and Trigueros (a small street parallel to and in between Zaragoza and Independencia).

You might take a look at one of Veracruz's newer seafood restaurants, **La Olímpica del Puerto (4)** (tel. 29/34-7451), at Malecón 376. Big, bare, and bright, La Olímpica may take its name from the fact that it seems big as a football field. The cloth-covered tables are rarely full, nor is every dish on the endless menu ever offered all at once. But of the fish they have, you may pay 950 to 3,000 pesos ($1.90 to $6) for a full meal; other seafood is in the 2,500- to 3,500-peso ($5 to $7) range. When I tried it last, La Olímpica still had a way to run before it equaled, say, El Chato Moyo in quality, price, and ambience. Perhaps it will have reached its goal by the time you arrive. Open every day for lunch and dinner.

The best pizza place in town is **Pizzas El Padrino** (no phone), next to the Hotel Oriente (1). The pizza is the draw here from 1 p.m. to 1 a.m., as the restaurant is clean but without decor unless one considers a mural of the ruins in Athens "decor." Pizzas cost 600 to 850 pesos ($1.20 to $1.70) for a small and 1,300 to 1,800 pesos ($2.60 to $3.60) for a large, and come complete with an extra bowl of chiles. Beer is a reasonable 150 pesos (30¢).

Restaurant El Pescador (21) (tel. 29/32-5252) has all the decor that can be packed into one establishment. Eclectic sea decor is the best way to describe the sharks' jaws, blowfish, and fully rigged sailing ships (I always wondered who bought those things) that adorn every nook. As you may have guessed, seafood is the mainstay of the menu, with a shrimp cocktail for 700 pesos ($1.40), turtle stew for 1,650 pesos ($3.30), and a wide selection of fish for 1,200 to 3,500 pesos ($2.40 to $7). Just when you think you have fully digested all the nautical decorations, look into a low cage at the live crocodiles. Wow! El Pescador is open daily from 10 a.m. to 7 p.m.

Starvation Budget—Seafood

Market areas are famous the world over for providing hearty, inexpensive fare, and because Veracruz is on the water, the market fare here includes seafood. On Landero y Coss between Arista and Serdan is the **Municipal Fish Market,** its street level chock-a-block with little *ostionerías* (oyster bars) and shrimp stands. Take a stool, ask the price, and order a plate of boiled shrimp, fresh oysters, octopus, or conch. The price per plate should be about 300 pesos (60¢). Look upstairs for even more good places.

A Splurge Restaurant

If you're in the mood for a splurge, a great place to eat is **Garlics** (tel. 29/35-1034), on the Boulevard Camacho just past Hotel Villa del Mar (23). The manager, Mario Espinosa Absalon, speaks English and stresses good service. The restaurant is air-conditioned and affords a fine view of the ocean and Boulevard Camacho. Red snapper prepared as you wish is 2,500 to 3,800 pesos ($5 to $7.60), depending on size, and shrimp is 3,750 to 4,500 pesos ($7.50 to $9)—the chef claims he can cook these 30 different ways. The specialty of the house is a 4,000-peso ($8) paella for two which contains generous portions of shrimp, oysters, crabmeat, snails, and chicken. Recommended. A midday comida is also available for 1,800 pesos ($3.60). The restaurant and bar are open from 1 p.m. to 1 a.m., but I recommend Garlics for a late-afternoon meal with a view.

A Pastry Shop or Two

You should eat a big lunch as the Mexicans do to save money, so you won't want too much for breakfast. The cheapest way to get going in the morning is to seek out a pastry shop and pick up some sweet rolls or cakes (they're incredibly cheap and good in Mexico) and then find a café, order a cup of coffee, tea, or chocolate, and you'll have a good, tasty breakfast for less than a dollar. **El Fenix (11)** is a *panadería/pastelería* (bakery and pastry shop) which has a very wide selection of Mexican rolls and pastries for prices ranging from 5 to 100 pesos (1¢ to 20¢). You can't miss the assortment and the smell at Avenida 5 de Mayo 1362, corner of Arista. A similar establishment is the **Paris** at 5 de Mayo and Molina. By the way, neither of these places has tables where you can consume their wares on the spot. Rather, take a tray and a pair of tongs, select your pastries, and take them to the counter to be counted. Pay the total to the cashier.

A Café

One of Veracruz's most successful and popular places to while away the hours over coffee is the **Gran Café de la Parroquía (12)**, open 7 a.m. to 1 a.m., right across the street from the parish church *(Parroquía)* just off the Plaza de Armas on the Avenida Independencia. Bright, bare, always busy, with music at any hour, it takes its character from its clients, an assortment from most facets of Veracruz's daily life. Cappuccino is 200 pesos (40¢) small or 300 pesos (60¢) large; desserts are 300 pesos (60¢); breakfasts go for 300 to 500 pesos (60¢ to $1). So popular is the Parroquía, in fact, that the management has opened up a new and shiny branch of the café **(13)** on the Paseo del Malecón out toward the Bank of Mexico building, open 6 p.m. to 1 a.m. only. Take your newspaper and try out both.

Here's an interesting bit of Parroquía lore: notice the two waiters scurrying about with big aluminum kettles? One kettle has thick black coffee, the other has hot milk. Order the rich café con leche and you'll get a few fingers of coffee in the bottom of your glass. Then, pick up your spoon and bang on the glass to call the waiter with the milk—that spoon-banging is a constant chime in La Parroquía.

WHAT TO DO: Veracruz has beaches, but none of them is very good because the sand is a dirty brown color and the water tends to be shallow. There are points all along the waterfront downtown where people swim, but the nearest legitimate beach is at the **Villa del Mar (23)**, an open-air terrace and palm-lined promenade at the southern end of town. (To orient yourself, north is on your left as you look toward the gulf from town.) To get to the beach, take the bus marked "Playa V. del Mar" which travels south on Zaragoza. The trip takes about 15 minutes and costs 40 pesos (8¢).

The better beach is the one in front of the Hotel Mocambo, mentioned above.

Take a walk around town. Veracruz has a special affinity for lighthouses (no surprise), and they are to be found everywhere. In fact, the **Bank of Mexico** building **(16),** mentioned in the introduction to this section, is also called *El Faro Nuevo* (the new lighthouse), and indeed it is so equipped, as you'll see if you walk down that way in the evening. Other lighthouses include the Faro Juárez, on the Plaza de la República, and the one named for Venustiano Carranza, part museum and part Naval Headquarters, down past the Hotel Emporio on the way to the Bank of Mexico. The museum part, called the **Museo Historico de la Revolución "Venustiano Carranza"** is open Tuesday through Friday from 9 a.m. to 1 p.m. and 4 to 6 p.m., on Saturday to 1 p.m., Sunday and holidays to noon; closed Monday. Admission is free.

You can go out and look at the fort of **San Juan de Ulúa (15)** either by driving across the bridge that heads north out of the Plaza de Armas between Avenidas República and Morelos and then turning right past the piers—a bus from the corner of Landero y Coss and Lerdo marked "San Juan de Ulúa" also takes this route; fare: 40 pesos (8¢)—or by taking one of the boats that run from the Malecón (pier) to the left of the big Bank of Mexico building on the waterfront. There isn't much to see in the castle, by the way, except a pleasant view of the city across the still waters of the harbor.

Another interesting trip is to the **Isla de Sacrificios,** so named because the Spaniards are said to have witnessed human sacrifices there. Boats leave from the docks in front of the Hotel Emporium, but during the winter, between October and February, boat schedules depend on the winds, which can be pretty strong and unpredictable—in other words don't plan a trip to the Isla de Sacrificios from October to February. The only sure way to be safe is to inquire at the Tourism Office (1) before your journey (tel. 29/32-9942).

The **Fort of Santiago (24),** located on the corner of Rayón and Gómez Farías, is open to the public Monday to Saturday from 10 a.m. to 1 p.m. and 4 to 7 p.m., on Sunday from 4 to 7 p.m., for an admission charge of 10 pesos (2¢). The fort was built in 1636 as part of the city fortifications against the pirates; this bastion is all that is left of the old city walls. It's remarkable to see the type of construction that was used in those days: solid, to say the least!

Finally, the recently restored **City Museum Building (20),** Zaragoza 397, is 120 years old, and was built originally as an orphanage. Some years ago it was converted into a museum, and recently it was completely renovated. There is a beautiful courtyard with fountain, and about 12 rooms off the courtyard (on two levels) that house archeological relics from the Gulf Coast pre-Columbian sites. The collection is small compared to the museum in Jalapa or Villahermosa, but the displays are attractive and the setting is lovely. The Indian cultures represented here are the Olmecs (a civilization of the Preclassic period from around the Villahermosa area); the Totonacs (the Classic civilizations of Tajín and Zempoala, north of Veracruz and south of Tuxpan); and the Huastecas.

There are several rooms displaying regional costumes and crafts. Off the courtyard, there are gardens and split-level terraces with hanging plants and flower pots, bare stone arches, and white stucco walls, all architecturally very soothing. There is a very enthusiastic fellow who has worked in the museum for about 17 years, loves to speak English, and will be only too happy to show you around: ask for Luis Aguilar. The museum is open daily except Monday, from 10 a.m. to 6 p.m.; admission is free.

More than anything about Veracruz, you'll remember its gaiety. There is a certain carefree spirit about this bustling seaport. From 1 or 2 p.m. on you'll hear mariachi and marimba bands playing in the Plaza de Armas, and on Thursday and Sunday from 7 to 10 p.m. you can hear the band play in front of the Palacio Municipal. Up and down the Malecón and in the square, people gather to socialize, listen to the music, or sell knickknacks. It's a gay town, especially on a Sunday, which seems to be the big socializing day.

Carnival in Veracruz

If swinging parties are your thing, go to Veracruz at Mardi Gras time. The carnival, which takes place in March, is one of the best in the hemisphere—friendlier than New Orleans, less frantic than Rio. The 1985 carnival was the 60th anniversary. You'll find the town packed with visitors from the capital, and the impassive Indians who've walked a day's journey from their villages. Regional dancers, including the Voleadores, will perform. Even the townspeople, normally attentive to their own affairs, join the crowds in the music-filled streets. You'll see a local beauty crowned as queen and, although the government discourages the practice, you may see the Spanish equivalent of the Lord of Misrule being tied to a lamp post (a stuffed figure, of course, not a man).

There are fabulous floats (in Spanish, *carros Alegoricos*, "allegorical cars") made with the Mexican flair: bright colors, papier-mâché figures (even the Muppets showed up on a float), large flowers, and live entertainment. Groups from the neighboring villages don their peacock- and pheasant-feathered headdress in preparation for the dances which they will perform during the festivities. There are costumed Draculas and drag queens and girls in sparkling dresses parading down the streets.

Most of the activities center in the Plaza de Armas, and begin around noon, lasting well into the night, of course.

Do remember that if you plan to be in Veracruz for the week to ten days of carnival, reserve hotel space months in advance, for everything's jammed full at this time.

BOCA DEL RÍO AND MOCAMBO BEACH: About five miles south of Veracruz along the Gulf Coast is the beautiful beach of Mocambo; a little farther on at the mouth of the Jamapa River is the fishing village of Boca del Río. Both of these can easily be reached by taking the buses that leave every 30 minutes (on the hour and half hour) from the corner of Serdan and Zaragoza (**25**) near the municipal fish market. The bus stop is marked with a sign "Costa Verde" or "Boca del Río"; the trip takes 30 minutes and costs 75 pesos (15¢). Boats, snorkeling equipment, and water skis can be rented at Mocambo beach.

4. Papantla, Tuxpan, and Tajín

The coastal country to the northwest of Veracruz is particularly lush and beautiful, and the town of Tuxpan is very pretty in a tropical way. Along the road to Tuxpan from Veracruz one can visit the Totonac ruins at Zempoala, take a look at the vanilla-growing town of Papantla, stop for a look at the marvelous Totonac city of Tajín, and whiz as fast as possible through the oil boom town of Poza Rica.

HEADING NORTH—ZEMPOALA: Both Zempoala and Tajín are pre-Columbian ruins of the Totonac Indians. Both cities flourished during the Classic Period (A.D. 300–900), but Tajín was burned and abandoned in the 13th century when the barbarian warriors (the Chichimecs) from the north invaded the city, while Zempoala continued to thrive and was the capital of the Totonacs at the time of the Spanish Conquest. It was, in fact, the Totonacs at Zempoala who helped Cortés and his men make the journey inland to capture the Aztec capital of Tenochtitlán.

A 16th-century Spanish scholar described the Totonacs as "fun loving with no affront of words, no ugly or unjust things . . . calm and amiable." If you look at the artwork of these people you can see the joyfulness which he described. The figurines are delightful, most of them in animated positions with large smiles across their faces.

The ruins at Zempoala are not quite as impressive as those at Tajín but still very interesting. Zempoala means "place of the twenty waters," and was so named for the many rivers that converged at the site. This area is really gorgeous with lush foliage and rich agricultural land.

Most of the buildings at Zempoala date from the 14th and 15th centuries— quite late for pre-Columbian structures. This city was, however, inhabited before the time of Christ. The great temple is interesting because it resembles the Temple of the Sun in Tenochtitlán, probably a result of Aztec influence during the 15th century. There are several other temples. One of the most unusual is the Temple of the Little Faces, which has many stuccoed faces set into the walls, along with hieroglyphs painted on the lower parts of the walls. Then there is the Temple of Quetzalcóatl and Ehecatl (the gods of the feathered serpent and the wind, respectively). Both gods are represented in the building structure: Quetzalcóatl by the rectangular portion, Ehecatl by the round structure.

Zempoala is about 25 miles north of Veracruz. Driving time is 30 minutes on Hwy. 180 to Cardel. The ruins of Zempoala are just north of Cardel. There are buses on the La Fuega line (second-class bus), which is located just behind the Veracruz first-class A.D.O. terminal. The trip takes 1½ hours, and is truly a beautiful trip through tropical forests. Entrance to the ruins is 50 pesos (10¢).

PAPANTLA: Papantla (pop. 70,000), the former vanilla capital of the world, is 140 miles northwest of Veracruz on Hwy. 180. The hybrid symbol of the community, displayed at both entrances to the city, is a very large concrete vanilla bean with inscribed hieroglyphs. Vanilla extract can be purchased here for about one-half the cost in the States—650 pesos ($1.30) for 90 milliliters. Plain vanilla beans or figurines made from the beans, at 300 to 1,500 pesos (60¢ to $3.00), may also be purchased. Papantla's fame has diminished considerably with the advent of artificial vanilla flavoring, but is still noteworthy because of its proximity to the ruins of El Tajín and also because of the festivities around Corpus Christi Day. The Feast of Corpus Christi, the ninth Sunday after Easter, is surrounded by a very special week in Papantla. Well-known entertainers and matadors perform. Also the native *voladores* make special appearances. Lodging is scarce during this week, so be sure to book ahead.

The zócalo is lovely in Papantla. Ceramic tile is used throughout and the cathedral wall facing the square is covered with an artist's impression of El Tajín in concrete.

Where to Stay and Eat

Walk along the cathedral wall up the hill to the thriving **El Tajín Hotel,** at 104 Nuñez (tel. 784/2-1062). The 60 rooms here are small and tidy, and cost 2,300 to 2,588 pesos ($4.60 to $5.18) single, and 3,000 to 3,565 pesos ($6.00 to $7.13) double. The more expensive rooms are air-conditioned. The El Tajín Hotel sign is clearly visible alongside the cathedral spires if you are coming from the A.D.O. bus depot on Hwy. 180. Just walk toward it.

Hotel Pulido, advertised on the billboard north of town, is located at Enriquez 205, downhill from the zócalo (tel. 874/2-0036). You enter into a parking lot-type courtyard with walls entirely dotted with small colorful ceramic tile, which hopefully were purchased in sheets and not glued down individually! The 23 rooms are quite plain and worn, but clean and sport ceiling fans and private bathrooms. A single is 1,400 pesos ($2.80); doubles with one bed are 1,750 pesos ($3.50), and with two beds 2,300 pesos ($4.60); triples are 2,550 pesos ($5.10), and rooms for four are 3,000 pesos ($6.00). The downstairs restaurant is open 7 a.m. to 11 p.m., but closed on Monday.

The **Restaurant Tajín** is in the El Tajín Hotel and is clean and inexpensive. The comida corrida costs 400 pesos (80¢). Sandwiches are 130 to 190 pesos (26¢ to 38¢); shrimp, 700 pesos ($1.40); and meat dishes even less.

Across Nuñez from the hotel is the very plain restaurant **Meche,** which serves very good, inexpensive food also. The comida here is 500 pesos ($1.00).

TAJÍN: Papantla provides the easiest access to the El Tajín archeological site. Catch a Transporte Papantla bus one block from the zócalo at 20 de Noviembre 900 (tel. 2-0015) for the trip to the ruins; fare is 120 pesos (24¢). Board a bus marked "Agua Dulce" which will go to El Chote, then change to another local bus which will deliver you to El Tajín. One-way taxi fare will run you about 3,000 pesos ($6.00).

If you're going on to the ruins of El Tajín from Tuxpan, take a bus to **Poza Rica** (run every half hour, trip takes 1½ hours). The driver will drop you off at a place, and then you catch another bus to "las ruinas"; they're blue and are marked "La Marguarita," and they drop you off right outside the entrance. Later on, you can flag down a bus that goes to Papantla.

The ruins at Tajín are divided into those in the old section *(Tajín viejo)* and those in the new section *(Tajín chico)*. The most impressive structure is the **Pyramid of the Niches,** which is found in the old section. The pyramid is made of stone and adobe, with 365 recesses on all four sides of the building. The pyramid was once covered in painted stucco, and is today one of the most unusual pre-Columbian structures in Mesoamerica. Near this pyramid is the ball court with beautiful carved reliefs on the vertical playing sides depicting religious scenes and sacrifices.

The **Temple of the Columns** is in the new section. A stairway divides the columns, three on either side, each one decorated with reliefs of priests and warriors plus hieroglyphic dates. There are many mounds that are still uncovered; the view from on top of one of the pyramids overlooking the rich green forests, dotted with these mounds, is quite impressive. This is definitely worth a stop if you are driving the Gulf Coast Highway. From Veracruz take Rte. 180 to Papantla; from there take Rte. 127, which is a back road to Poza Rica, going through Tajín. It is not a well-publicized site and there is not much traffic. A.D.O. runs daily buses to Papantla. The entrance fee is 100 pesos (20¢); parking is 50 pesos (10¢). A small refreshment stand serves cool drinks; there is also a cafeteria inside the site.

An additional attraction on Saturday and Sunday (and also during the Corpus Christi festivities) is the *voladores* (fliers). These are local Totonac Indians who perform their flying upside-down pole dance.

TUXPAN: Although coming of age now, not long ago Tuxpan, Veracruz (that's "*Toosh*-pahn"; pop. 100,000), was the best example on the Gulf Coast of an unspoiled fishing town. The fishing boats are still moored in town at the mouth of the Río Tuxpan, and a fishing festival is held in early summer, but Tuxpan is growing. One of the benefits of this growth is the presence of several very good places to stay and to dine. Why stay in Tuxpan? It's simple: for the unhurried, tropical ambience, great seafood, and for the magnificent beach, about six miles from town.

Where to Stay and Eat

Avenida Juárez, Tuxpan's main downtown street, holds the three prime hotels, which in an unusual turn of events are all charging exactly the same rates. At the **Hotel Plaza,** Juárez 39 (tel. 783/4-0738), a modern air-conditioned room goes for 3,220 pesos ($6.44) single, 4,600 pesos ($9.20) double. All the conveniences are here: elevator, coordinated wood furniture and headboards, individual room thermostats, tile baths. Rooms are functional rather than fancy, but offer good accommodation. The Plaza's restaurant is one of the town's more popular places to dine, partly because it is air-conditioned. A large huachinango is a good buy at 2,000 pesos ($4), and most other seafood costs 1,600 to 1,815 pesos ($3.20 to $3.63), with lighter meals in the 575- to 905-peso ($1.15 to $1.81) range. You can order seafood at 9 a.m. here! A number of photographs of Tuxpan in the 1920s and '30s spice up the restaurant's otherwise unremarkable modern decor.

The **Hotel Florida,** Juárez 23 (tel. 783/4-0650 or 4-0602), is perhaps the best budget choice on Juárez as it has some rooms with fans for 2,530 pesos ($5.06) single, 3,450 pesos ($6.90) double; rooms with air conditioning cost 3,220 pesos ($6.44) single, 4,600 pesos ($9.20) double. The Florida is Tuxpan's older and well-used but still sturdy and serviceable hotel. An elevator serves the several floors, and as some rooms have been remodeled more recently than others it would be good to look before you buy; another reason to look is that the Florida is one of the few hotels with river views—only a few rooms offer this.

Although it looks old-fashioned from the outside, the **Hotel Reforma,** Juárez 25 (tel. 783/4-0210), is in fact Tuxpan's most modern place to stay. Actually, the building dates back some time, and the lofty inner court has been preserved and is now furnished with cast-iron tables, chairs, a little pool with a fountain, and bar service. The court is not air-conditioned but the lobby and guest rooms are. All rooms have been modernized, and cost 3,220 pesos ($6.44) single, 4,600 pesos ($9.20) double in one or two beds. The Reforma has its own restaurant (open 7 a.m. to 11 p.m.), entered from either the court or the street.

The best value in an air-conditioned room is the **Huasteco Hotel,** at Morelos 41 (tel. 783/4-1859), right next to the parking lot (Iberia). This clean, functional hotel has a concrete-block exterior and not much class save ceramic tile walls. By all means check out a room here to see if it's to your liking. Singles are 1,900 pesos ($3.80); doubles, 2,760 pesos ($5.52).

The **Hotel Tuxpan,** at Juárez and Mina (tel. 783/4-4110), is a small family-type hotel with reasonable prices. Rooms with ceiling fans are 1,886 pesos ($3.77) single and 2,360 pesos ($4.72) double.

If you are wondering what the white building on the other side of the river past the Pemex yard is, it's the expensive **Hotel Tajín,** where doubles start at 10,130 pesos ($20.26).

Look at the **Hotel Parque,** Humboldt 11 right on Parque Reforma (tel. 783/4-0812). Rooms with ceiling fans cost 1,610 pesos ($3.22), single or double, and air-conditioned rooms are 2,520 pesos ($5.04) for two to four persons.

If you are staying in one of the downtown hotels, parking is available one block off Juárez at Mina and Morelos for the reasonable rate of 435 pesos (87¢) per 24-hour period at Parking Iberia.

Many travelers staying in Tuxpan eat in the hotel restaurants in Hotel Plaza, Hotel Reforma, or Hotel Florida. There are more exciting places to eat!

If you are looking for a seafood meal in the evening, stroll along the palm-lined river bank to **Fisher's** at Boulevard Palmas 61. (This is the real reason I stop in Tuxpan!) You'll notice the neon pizza sign, but fear not, good food is available. Sit outside and look across the river while enjoying a 2,200-peso ($4.40) seafood platter, the 1,650-peso ($3.30) shrimp brochette (shish kebab), or the 1,100-peso ($2.20) grilled fish. Excellent.

Finish off this perfect meal with a pastry from the gleaming **Pastelísimo** on the main plaza, next to the church. You can buy a slice of cake from the mouth-watering window display for the sweet price of 250 to 280 pesos (50¢ to 56¢), a piece of pie for 250 to 320 pesos (50¢ to 64¢), and coffee for 140 pesos (28¢).

Other good places to eat at midday are the eateries along the hard-sand beach. All of these are about the same, so see which one is the busiest. Try a fish filete stuffed with seafood or a torta marisco (seafood fried with egg). Either of these meals will be in the 1,500- to 1,875-peso ($3.00 to $3.75) range.

Getting to the Beach

Now that you've cased the town and sniffed its tropical ambience, take a run out to the beach. Bring your bathing suit, and catch a red-and-white bus marked "La Playa" from near the first-class A.D.O. terminal, down by the bridge. The bus will drop you right on the hard-sand beach, where you'll find changing cubicles and showers. The bus comes by every now and then to buzz you back into town.

5. Lake Catemaco

Ninety miles southeast of Veracruz over good roads is the lake and town called Catemaco (alt. 1,100 feet; pop. 40,000). The ten-mile-long lake formed by the eruption of volcanoes long ago has been described by some as the most beautiful body of water in Mexico. The lake region is located between the only mountains on the steaming coastal plain that reaches from Tampico to Yucatán. Both peaks are named **San Martín** and are in the neighborhood of 7,000 feet; one is a volcano while the other is not. North of Catemaco is Monte Cerro Blanco, where it is rumored wizards, or *brujos,* meet each year. The Catemaco area is a balmy oasis in a region where the rule is muggy heat. Free from extremes of heat and cold, this is another region of the eternal spring so typical of Mexico's highlands.

The Catemaco area is richly endowed with bird and animal life. Many varieties of bird life are apparent upon even a brief walk along the lake. Many hunters in the area supplement their diets by taking squirrels, armadillos, iguanas, and wild pigs.

Lake Catemaco is highly recommended if you need a place to rest or a respite from the coastal heat. It has beauty, serenity, and good food!

GETTING TO AND FROM CATEMACO: There is daily first-class bus service from the A.D.O. terminal in Veracruz. You have your choice of 18 daily departures, but most of these will be going only as far as the cigar-making town of San Andres Tuxtla, 7½ miles short of Catemaco. Two or three buses a day go directly to Catemaco from Veracruz, however, and you should try for one of these. Otherwise, go to San Andres, and catch a local bus for the last short leg, or hire a taxi (bargaining like mad).

The next leg of your journey, whether your destination be the Yucatán or San Cristóbal de las Casas and Guatemala, is along the Gulf Coast past Coatzacoalcos to Villahermosa. This is the route to the Yucatán, but from Villahermosa buses cross the mountains on Hwy. 195 to Tuxtla Gutierrez and San Cristóbal. There is no reason to travel via Hwy. 185 which traverses the Isthmus of Tehuantepec, for the isthmus is flat, unscenic, full of traffic, and hot and muggy.

WHERE TO STAY AND EAT: My favorite place to stay in Catemaco is the **Posada (Motel) Koniapan** (tel. 294/3-0063), right on the lakeshore at the intersection of Malecón and Revolución (as you go down the hill toward the lake from the plaza and come to the shore, turn left onto the lakefront Malecón and walk along till you come to the Koniapan). Bright, and clean, the Koniapan provides a fan in each room, screens on the windows, and small but spotless tile bathrooms. The furniture is heavy neocolonial, but not bad for all that. There's a small, clean swimming pool in the front yard; sometimes a small restaurant next to it is open and serving. Rooms cost 3,795 pesos ($7.59) single, 4,365 pesos ($8.73) double with fan; with air conditioning, the prices are 1,130 pesos ($2.26) higher. The rooms with ceiling fans are upstairs, and have two double beds, a private balcony with chairs, and a view of the lake. Good value. Room prices may be 600 pesos ($1.20) higher in July and August when Catemaco is usually busy.

At the top of the budget range—but worth every peso—is the lush and expansive **Motel Playa Azul** (tel. 294/3-0001 or 3-0042; Apdo. Postal 26), east along the lakeshore from town 2 kilometers (1¼ miles). Take a bus marked "La Marguarita" from the town square, or hire a taxi for the short ride over a paved but rather bumpy road. At the end of it is a bit of paradise: stately palms, verdant and flower-filled gardens, a fine swimming pool overlooking the lake, a big restaurant, and modernish rooms renting for 5,320 pesos ($10.64) single, 6,400 pesos ($12.80) double with ceiling fan; 8,194 pesos ($16.39) single, 8,390 pesos ($16.78) double with air conditioning (which you should not need). The loudest noise here is that of the birds.

Too expensive for what it is, the **Hotel Catemaco,** at Carranza 8 (tel. 294/3-0203 or 3-0045), is the next choice in town. It's located right on the plaza, has a small pool out back, long-distance service, free parking, and features two double beds and air conditioning, which accounts for its rather high prices: 4,945 pesos ($9.89) single, 5,589 pesos ($11.18) double. It can't fill up at these Mexico City rates, so try offering a lower price and see if they'll go for it.

A good, plain, but serviceable budget choice is the **Hotel Tío Tin,** right down on the water at Avenida Playa 14 (tel. 294/3-0084). Some of the older rooms here have lake views, and several beds (good for families). Showers are tile, and there's lots of hot water (although it may take a while for it to come up). One person pays 1,500 pesos ($3), two persons pay 2,000 pesos ($4); a few very modern rooms with very fine lake views go for a bit more. Free parking in the yard.

One block from the plaza is the **Hotel Los Arcos** (tel. 294/3-0003), a small place with boldly colored rooms, each equipped with ceiling fan—there's good cross-ventilation too—and motel-style walkways to the rooms which also serve as balconies for the lake view. Prices are surprisingly moderate: 1,955 pesos ($3.91) single, 2,300 pesos ($4.60) double, and that's for a room with two double beds. Secure parking. Bargain for a lower price.

Down on the shore are several restaurants, my favorite being **La Ola.** A thatched roof, fish net decorations, and a beautiful view put you in the mood, and other attractions such as a small zoo containing turtles and alligators, or concerts of *jarocho* (Veracruz-style) guitar music are sometimes offered. The set lunch or dinner at La Ola is offered whenever the custom warrants, which it usually does in summer and on holiday weekends. Otherwise, try barbecued chicken for 650 pesos ($1.30) or the famous whitefish (mojarra) of the lake for 700 to 750 pesos ($1.40 to $1.50), depending on size.

La Luna, across the street from La Ola, is a similar restaurant without some of the sideshows of the Ola. Prices are virtually the same. As enthusiasm of cooks and staff wax and wane through the seasons, the best plan is to head for whichever restaurant seems the busier at the moment.

Although the lake is famed for its whitefish, gastronomy is not always of the highest quality in Catemaco. Perhaps the best all-around restaurant, good for breakfast, lunch, and dinner, is the dining room of the **Hotel Catemaco.** A view of the town's busy plaza adds to the pleasant, if simple, decor. For a light lunch of salad or a sandwich you'll pay from 460 to 805 pesos (92¢ to $1.61); for a full-course dinner based on anything from chicken to seafood, 920 to 1,495 pesos ($1.84 to $3).

If the street market is in operation around the Hotel Los Arcos, little cook-shops will be set up throughout. Here's the cheapest and most colorful place to sample the lake's mojarra, or any of a dozen other sorts of rough-and-ready fare. Prices are not set, and will depend on how the fishing season's going, how much money has been made that day, and how prosperous you look to be.

WHAT TO SEE AND DO: If you're sports-minded, boats are available for waterskiing or fishing. If sightseeing is your preference, you can just about choose the trip to fit your budget. The cheapest way to get to Playa Azul and Playa Hermosa beaches is by bus. Look for the bus marked "La Marguarita" from the town square. The same bus goes out to the Cuetzalapan River, known for its transparently clear waters, flowers, bird life, and interesting rock forma-tions.

You can take a tour of the lake by boat, stopping at the aforementioned beaches, the river, a mineral spring called Arroyo Agrio (sour) for its acid con-tent, and another called Coyame—you may have seen its water bottled and on your dinner table. Cost for the 1¼-hour lake tour is about 4,500 pesos ($9) per boatload of up to six persons. Talk to the boatmen down at the wharf on the Malecón right below the zócalo. Look for posted prices.

The **El Carmen Church** on the zócalo is visited by thousands of pilgrims each year around July 16, the feast day for El Carmen. Look for testimonial drawings around the portals.

READERS' HOTEL SELECTION FOR TUXTLA: "The **Hotel Castellanos** (tel. 294/7-0300) in San-tiago Tuxtla is a new hotel that overlooks the town square in the center of which is a gigan-tic Olmec head found on the hotel grounds during construction. The hotel is a family operation set in a tropical oasis: warm in the day, cool at night. The hotel has an excellent restaurant, huge pool, gorgeous rooms in tile and cherrywood. Rooms without meals are 3,335 pesos ($6.67) single, 3,795 pesos ($7.59) double" (Pat and Dave Schouweiler, Min-neapolis, Minn.).[*Note from T.B.:* The archeological museum is also an attraction here, open Tuesday to Saturday from 9 a.m. to 7 p.m. and Sunday 9 a.m. to 3 p.m.; admission is 30 pesos, 6¢. The Olmec head comes from Tres Zapotes.]

Chapter XIII

SOUTH OVER THE MOUNTAINS

1. Puebla
2. Tehuacán
3. Oaxaca
4. Tehuantepec

SHOULD YOU HAVE the time to go deeper into the country south and east of Mexico City, one of the best ways you can spend that time is by traveling to Oaxaca. It's a ten-hour, 325-mile ride over a road that sometimes winds through the mountains cutting your speed considerably, so it's unlikely you'll try to do it in one day. The flight is only 50 minutes; the train is an overnight trip. Oaxaca, like the Yucatán, is a center of Indian culture and archeology besides being an interesting city in its own right. Sometimes you can witness Indian ceremonies in the villages surrounding Oaxaca (always you can see the Indian costumes) and it is in Oaxaca and the area around it that you find the finest heavy blankets—almost rugs—of traditional design; and only a few miles out of the city are the Zapotec ruins of Monte Albán, and a bit farther afield are the ruins of Mitla. From Oaxaca you can go southeast to the mountains of Chiapas and San Cristóbal de Las Casas, and on to Guatemala; or you can go northeast to the gulf and to the Yucatán, or back to Veracruz.

If you can take the ten-hour ride on the bus, do so. Those driving will have to spend a night along the way. Figure that you'll drive two hours to get to Puebla, and three more hours to get to Tehuacán, another possible overnight stop.

There are now two roads to Puebla from the capital: an old, winding one that you'll drive with great frustration, following strings of lumbering trucks, with no chance to pass; and a classy, new toll road that is faster. The bus usually follows the new highway.

Whichever road you choose, you'll find that the route is unusually scenic, with many distractions to keep your eyes occupied. You'll see little shrines built into the sides of the road at intervals, roadside stands with fruit elaborately piled into pyramids, and occasionally, the passengers of a decrepit, second-class bus sitting patiently while the driver crawls underneath to effect repairs. Weather permitting, you'll also see the beautiful snow-capped volcano peaks of Popocatepetl and Ixtaccihuatl (the former dormant, the latter extinct), and dozens of enormous churches. Many of these have brightly painted domes of blue or gold and look very grand. Mostly, however, they are not as impressive inside. There are said to be 365 churches on this drive—one for every day of the year.

The border between the states of México and Puebla is reached halfway at Río Frío, in wild, mountainous country that was once heavily infested with bandits. Río Frío, where the buses now make a brief stop, was a renowned bandit town, but even more so was Huejotzingo, about 65 miles out of Mexico City on the Puebla road. Huejotzingo was the headquarters of a guerrilla named Augustin Lorenzo, whose capture is still celebrated every Shrove Tuesday with a colorful, firecracker-filled carnival.

A STOP IN HUEJOTZINGO: You might find yourself able and willing to stop in this pleasant town, especially if you're driving. Huejotzingo, Puebla (alt. 7,550 feet; pop. 25,000) has a fine big main square where the open-air market is held on Saturday. Even if you don't come for market day, you can stop and enjoy a glass or two of the local sparkling (alcoholic) cider, a specialty.

For sights, Huejotzingo has a prizewinner. The **Franciscan monastery,** right across the main road from the town plaza, was built between 1529 and 1570. As you walk up the stairs from the main road and enter the monastery compound, notice the little square chapels topped by pyramidal roofs that stand at each corner of the enclosure. They're nicely decorated. The cross mounted on a pedestal in the courtyard dates from the 1500s as well.

The church, very austere on the outside, has a wonderfully lacy Gothic vault inside, and a dazzling altar in the Plateresque style. The monastery proper is next door, entered through the double-arch doorway. The monastery has a lovely chapel, a cloister for the monks, and the necessary places: kitchens, dining room, etc.

The Franciscan monastery, one of the oldest in Mexico, is open from 10 a.m. to 5 p.m. Tuesday through Sunday; you pay 40 pesos (8¢) for admission.

Should you be in town on market day, be sure to look over the woolen goods, especially the serapes and blankets.

If you continue along Hwy. 190 (not the toll highway, 190-D), you'll pass through the colonial town of **Cholula,** 9 miles (14 kilometers) from Huejotzingo and 6 miles (10 kilometers) from Puebla. The **Great Pyramid of Cholula,** perhaps the largest man-made structure in the world, is on the southern outskirts of the town. The Great Pyramid is not much to look at these days, having become merely a huge mound or small mountain with a church perched on top. But in the depths of the mound are some interesting frescoes that you can visit. For details, see below in the Puebla section under "Day Trip to Cholula."

1. Puebla

Puebla (alt. 7,049 feet; pop. 1,250,000) has retained a lot of the wealth and the architecture from the 19th century when it was the principal stopping point on the way to Veracruz, Mexico's main port. The rich and famous built themselves mansions here so they could rest overnight in style. And like San Luis Potosí and Oaxaca, the church chose Puebla as a center of its activities. A full 99 churches remain from this time, along with numerous grand monasteries, convents, and a magnificent Bishop's Palace next to the cathedral.

Today Puebla is growing at an amazing rate, and it shows: the streets teem with people walking or people selling things, everything from tacos to kitchen utensils. Cars jam the streets, and the ever-present buses, spewing fumes, trumpet and roar. The overcrowding and fumes and noise make it unpleasant to stay in this otherwise graceful and architecturally fascinating city for more than a day. The city fathers are trying to deal with the problems by closing off downtown streets to all but pedestrian traffic. But a lot remains to be done. The best time to visit this city may be in June and July when evening rains frequently wash the oppressive pollution from the air.

Not to discourage you further, but I have never—well, almost *never*—in 14 years of looking, found a well-run, good value-for-money hotel in this city. Puebla has lots of hotels, but none that meets those simple criteria. Perhaps it's Puebla's industrial wealth, such as that gigantic Volkswagen plant on the main highway, cement plants, faïence works, etc., that keep the hotels full at inflated prices.

But you really should see Puebla. Get an early start from Mexico City, tour Puebla for a few hours and perhaps sample the famous Poblano cuisine at lunch, then head on to Oaxaca, or Tehuacán, or Veracruz.

GETTING TO AND FROM PUEBLA: Because it's so close to Mexico City, and because it's astride the main routes to Veracruz and Oaxaca, transportation to and from Puebla is a snap, both by bus and by train.

By Bus

The first-class line to take to Puebla is A.D.O. (Autobuses del Oriente). Besides many buses each day between the capital and Puebla, the A.D.O. line also runs six buses a day from Puebla to Veracruz and back, seven a day to Villahermosa, five a day to Oaxaca, and seven a day to Tehuacán. The A.D.O. terminal (tel. 41-2444) is downtown at the corner of Avenida Gral. Maximino Avila Camacho and Calle 6 Norte, as of this writing. It is probably only a matter of time until all bus traffic is moved to a central terminal outside the city, as has been done in most other large Mexican towns.

Another line, Autobuses Unidos (tel. 46-6500) also provides convenient second-class service from Mexico City to Puebla, from Puebla to Tehuacán (nine buses a day), and to Orizaba, Cordoba, and Veracruz, at rates slightly cheaper than those of the A.D.O.; service and equipment are pretty good. The A.U. terminal is presently at the corner of Avenida 10 Oriente and Calle 4 Norte, about seven blocks from the main square.

Autobuses Estrella Roja (tel. 41-7671), with its gleaming terminal located at Avenida 3 Pte. Calle 5 Sur, provides similar second-class services to Mexico City.

The trip from Mexico City to Puebla takes about two hours by bus, and it's another three hours from Puebla to Tehuacán.

By Train

The fastest train from Mexico City to Puebla leaves at 5:32 p.m. from Buena Vista Station, arriving in Puebla at 10:55 p.m. Bus service is much preferable. Leaving Puebla by rail is equally time-consuming as the train departs Puebla at 3:30 a.m. and arrives in Mexico City at 8:52 a.m.

Puebla's railroad station is at the far northern end of Calle 9 Norte, some distance from downtown. City buses ("Estación Nueva") ply between the station and the downtown area for a fare of 40 pesos (8¢). Catch one downtown at a sign that lists the Estación bus as stopping there.

By Car

From Puebla you have a choice of roads to Oaxaca, whether you go by bus or car. One route (Hwy. 190) goes south through Izucar de Matamoros, famed for black pottery (not much in evidence in the town—most of it's shipped to the big cities for sale!), and Acatlán, famous for its red animal pottery; then to Huajuapan de León, where the road becomes full of curves as it twists through the mountains to Oaxaca. Another route, taking about the same time to negotiate, runs southeast to Tehuacán, the mineral bath town, along Hwy. 150 which is now completed and paved all the way to Oaxaca, the Tehuacán-Oaxaca portion bearing the designation Hwy. 131. This road also is full of twists and turns, and although it's slow it does afford fine mountain vistas and curious stands of cactus. But before you wind up into the mountains, you might want to stop for lunch, or even overnight, in Tehuacán, Mexico's most famous spa.

ORIENTATION: The one indispensable fact, essential to finding one's way around the city, is that most streets running east and west are *avenidas,* and those running north and south are *calles.* Avenida de la Reforma divides the city north and south, with even-numbered avenues to the north and odd-numbered avenues to the south. Calle de 16 de Septiembre, which changes its name to 5 de Mayo north of Reforma, is the east-west dividing line, with even-numbered streets to the east.

USEFUL FACTS: The Tourist Office (20) is at Avenida 5 Oriente no. 3, at the side of the cathedral and next door to the Biblioteca Palafoxiana (tel. 46-1285). They're very friendly here, have a good map of the city, and are open from 8 a.m. to 8 p.m. Monday through Friday, from 9 a.m. to 4 p.m. on Saturday, and from 9 a.m. to 2 p.m. on Sunday. . . . The post office is in the Archbishop's Palace (17) beside the cathedral at the corner of Avenida 5 Ote. and Calle 16 de Septiembre (no sign!). . . . Puebla's big market day is Sunday. All shops, even Woolworth's, close for lunch and siesta from 1:30 to 4 p.m.

WHERE TO STAY: The 70-room Hotel Colonial (3), Calle 4 Sur no. 105 (tel. 22/42-4950), 1½ blocks from the bus station, is a decent choice. It has a good supply of character, with statue-filled alcoves, elevators, garage, roof garden, and all the appurtenances of its type. It's surprisingly reasonable too, for what it offers: single rooms (about 19 of them) for 3,680 pesos ($7.36); double rooms, 4,945 pesos ($9.89). There's a good restaurant in the hotel, where lunch costs 1,150 pesos ($2.30).

My next choice is near the upper edge of our budget. The 92-room Gilfer Hotel (4), Avenida 2 Ote. no. 11 (tel. 22/46-4199), is all glass and marble with large potted plants in the lobby, and large and quite comfy rooms for 6,325 pesos ($12.65) single, 6,900 pesos ($13.80) double. Extras include a very good location, covered garage, restaurant, bar, and a fairly well-to-do Mexican and foreign clientele. The attached restaurant offers a five-course comida for 1,050 pesos ($2.10). The Gilfer even has its own nightclub.

Similarly modern, although not quite so posh, is the Hotel Senorial (5), Calle 4 Norte no. 602 (tel. 22/42-4930), an edifice of aluminum, glass, and shiny black stone. Here, besides 72 rooms with bathrooms, wall-to-wall carpeting, and telephones, guests can use the hotel's garage, beauty and barber shops, and even their Turkish baths. Be careful with bus noise in street-side rooms. Singles are 3,900 pesos ($7.80) and doubles are 4,700 pesos ($9.40) in one bed, 5,160 pesos ($10.32) for twin beds.

For the blue-ribbon budget choice walk 3½ rather long blocks from the cathedral to the Hotel San Miguel (13) at Avenida 3 Poniente no. 721 (tel. 22/42-4860). What the rooms lack in colonial flavor, having none, is made up for in gleaming tile hallways and large, clean rooms. Despite the tempting balconies the wise choice is a serenely quiet interior room. The only drawback here is the limited supply of hot water; but unless you shower at midday, the 6 a.m. to 11 a.m. and 5 p.m. to 11 p.m. hot water schedule should suffice. With a single for 3,000 pesos ($6.00) or a double at 3,400 pesos ($6.80), one bed or two, the San Miguel is a winner.

Two Expensive Neocolonial Favorites

Two of Puebla's "colonial" hostelries have shown different ways of providing modern services without losing the feeling of Old Mexico. At the **Hotel Posada San Pedro (6),** Avenida 2 Oriente no. 202 (tel. 22/46-5077), the solution to the problem is unabashed neocolonialism: the rough walls and dark wood here are accented by bright blues and oranges in the spreads, drapes, and carpets. A small but very beautiful swimming pool is the centerpiece for a grassy inner courtyard open to the sky; on the first floor is a bar that features an organist or combo nightly. Rooms (all have TV) on the pretty, quiet inner court cost 7,613 pesos ($15.23) single, 8,911 pesos ($17.82) double.

The **Hotel Palacio San Leonardo (21),** Avenida 2 Oriente no. 211 (tel. 22/46-0555), almost across the street from the San Pedro, has another solution to the problem of antiquity-versus-modernity: the lobby is entered by massive wooden doors, a crystal chandelier hangs from the ceiling, and as you register, the 18th century is all around you. But once the bellboy takes your bags to the elevator, it's all 20th century: rooms have carpeting, TVs, and modern furnishings throughout. Try for a room on the sixth floor for a great view. On the roof is a tiny swimming pool and a terrace with a fine view of the city's church domes and the surrounding mountains. There are 75 rooms, over-priced at 6,325 pesos ($12.65) single, 6,960 pesos ($13.92) double.

Right on the Plaza

While you're staying in Puebla, you might as well stay right next to its prettiest spot, the zócalo. The **Hotel Royalty Centro (8),** is on the north side of the plaza, at Portal Hidalgo 8 (tel. 22/42-0202 or 42-4740). A 46-room colonial hotel, the Royalty boasts tasteful old-fashioned rooms with TV and bath or shower, and even a few rooms with little refrigerators (these cost extra). Basic prices are 6,325 pesos ($12.65) single, 6,900 pesos ($13.80) double, 8,740 pesos ($17.48) triple. The slightly larger rooms are a bit more expensive. The passable hotel restaurant/bar features a "two for one" Happy Hour (la Hora del Amigo) from 1:30 p.m. to 2:30 p.m. and 6:30 p.m. to 7:30 p.m.

Near the A.U. (Second-Class) Bus Station

Here's the scenario: you've just arrived at the Autobuses Unidos (A.U.) second-class bus station on Avenida 10 Oriente, it's late, and you just want to find a room—quick. Walk out the door onto Avenida 10 Oriente, turn right (west), and walk past Calle 2 Norte. Soon, on the right-hand side at 10 Oriente no. 6, you'll see a hardware store. Walk into the passage, and that big stairway will take you up to the **Hotel Cabrera (2)** (tel. 22/41-8897). It's no beauty anymore, but it tends to be quiet, inexpensive, fairly clean, and good for one night. The prices are the best part: 3,841 to 3,956 pesos ($7.68 to $7.91) single, 4,830 to 4,945 pesos ($9.66 to $9.89) double, and 5,796 to 5,934 pesos ($11.87 to $11.92) triple.

WHERE TO EAT: Right at the center of town where the two main boulevards intersect is the main square, or zócalo. Several restaurants on this main square offer good food and good value, and have the extra advantage of allowing you to dine and to watch the action in the square at the same time. The **Hostería de los Angelos (7),** at the corner of Camacho and Portal Morelos (tel. 46-0211), is one of Puebla's most popular places for lunch. Hungry *poblanos* come not for the setting—which, while modern and nice, is nothing special—but for the set-price lunches of four courses at 1,495 pesos ($2.99) and six courses at 1,845 pesos ($3.69). Besides the two extra courses in the latter meal, you get, for the higher price, a higher quality entree such as roast beef with onions. One of the Hoste-

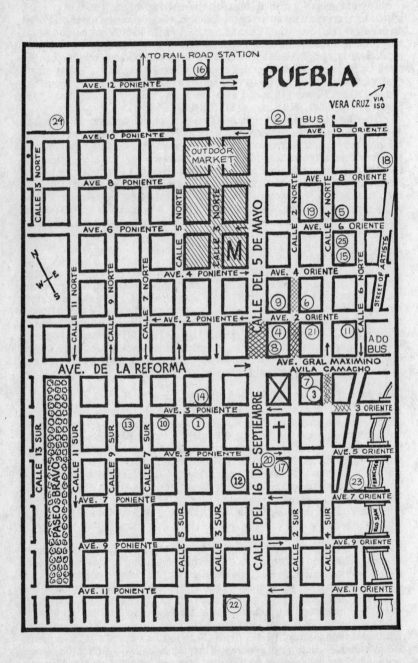

ría's lunches will last you the rest of the day. This is a pleasant place to stop in the evening to enjoy the live organ music.

All the way across the square are two more places worthy of mention. First is the **Café La Princesa,** at Portal Juárez 101 (tel. 42-1195), a brightly lit large room filled with tables draped in colorful cloths, all spic-and-span and offering a 850-peso ($1.70) comida corrida that gives you a good number of appetizers and main dishes to choose from. Other meals are in the 950- to 1,450-peso ($1.90 to $2.90) range, with breakfasts for 250 to 330 pesos (50¢ to 66¢). The other place on the square is Puebla's businessmen's café, the **Café El Vasco** (tel. 41-8689), at Portal Juárez 105. Tables outside on the sidewalk are in the midst of activity, but inside the restaurant all is somber and medieval, the decor using a Crusades motif: swords, maces, and paintings of Crusaders off to the Holy Land. The food is good and service is attentive, but prices are high: soups, about 420 to 600 pesos (84¢ to $1.20); red snapper 910 pesos ($1.82); chateaubriand, 1,700 pesos ($3.40). You can have enchiladas Suizas for only 520 pesos ($1.04), but most other entrees are in the 860- to 1,700-peso ($1.72 to $3.40) range.

Too much? Then a few steps from the zócalo at Calle 5 de Mayo no. 4 is the **Café Aguirre (8),** part of a photo shop advertised by a big yellow-and-white Kodak sign. The clientele is of all ages, the food largely snacks, sandwiches, and ice cream, with the notable exception of the daily 810-peso ($1.62) fixed-price lunch, served from 1 p.m. on. Breakfasts are good—and cheap—here.

Mixed Mexican-American ambience is what you get at the local **Sanborn's (9),** set up just like those in Mexico City with sales counters for magazines, cameras, and what-not, and a rather plush dining room in a fine colonial courtyard, with tables set out around a stone fountain—you wouldn't believe it from the store's modern façade on Avenida 2 Ote. no. 6 (tel. 42-9436). Enjoy the atmosphere, which is cool and quiet (a treat in Puebla). Stay away from the tenderloin tips, and order the breaded pork cutlet with chilaquiles at 2,000 pesos ($4.00) instead. Sanborn's is not particularly cheap, with even a hamburger and fries recently increasing to 1,200 pesos ($2.40); but it is very restful. Open daily 7:30 a.m. to 11 p.m., until midnight on Saturday.

The **Café Venecia** (tel. 46-2306), next to Hotel Palacio San Leonardo (21), is a clean, cheery, but simple place with a good variety of items for a lunch or light dinner at decent prices. For instance, a hamburger, ham sandwich, fruit cocktail, enchiladas, and chicken casserole are all priced between 400 and 700 pesos (80¢ to $1.40). Comidas are 400 pesos (80¢). Food is served on two levels, the second floor being a balcony or loft overlooking the first floor. The Venecia is at Avenida 2 Ote. no. 207, in the same building as another little place called **La Grecia** (tel. 46-2781), which also has good food—the roast meat smell from the sidewalk is enough to draw you in by the nose—and good prices. The featured item is tacos con tortilla arabe, which translates as a falafel sandwich, for 170 pesos (34¢), tortas (sandwiches) for about the same, and nothing on the menu costs more than 480 pesos (96¢), including the comida. They have yogurt also.

Head in the opposite direction to **El Vegetariano (10)** at Avenida 3 Poniente no. 525 (tel. 56-5462) for vegetarian fare, Puebla style. The place is sparsely furnished with plain pine boards reminiscent of an unpretentious Scandinavian kitchen, but the refreshing yogurt with fruit, honey, and granola for 400 pesos (80¢) is distraction enough. The 700-peso ($1.40) vegetarian comida is served either downstairs or on the mezzanine. El Vegetariano is open 8 a.m. to 8 p.m.

Regional Restaurants

Want to try some Puebla-style food? I can recommend two interesting places. First is the **Restaurante Del Parian (11)** (tel. 46-4798), corner of 6 Norte at Avenida 2 Oriente no. 415, decorated in what a Puebla city dweller must think is rustic country style: high clay pots line an old-fashioned charcoal range, tiles and carved wood abound, and the menus are on slices of plywood. Puebla cuisine is very complex, based on chile sauces articulated with dozens of other ingredients. *Pipian* sauces, made from pumpkin seed, are usually not super-spicy; *adobos* are dark wine-colored concoctions made with chiles, and can be very hot; *mole poblano* is a dark and very spicy sauce with a bitter chocolate base and a variety of other ingredients, including raisins, chile peppers, onions, and nuts. As the kitchen area is right by the door in El Parian, you might take a look at what's cooking, ask what it is, then be sure to ask, *"¿Es muy picante?"* ("Is it very spicy?") and take your pick. (No English spoken.) Prices are reasonable, with Puebla-style enchiladas at 600 pesos ($1.20), chalupas (boat-shaped tortillas that are filled with a meat mixture) at 400 pesos (80¢). Most other meals are 600 to 850 pesos ($1.20 to $1.70).

Second is the **Fonda Santa Clara (1)** (tel. 42-2659); across from the Bello Museum at Avenida 3 Pte. no. 307, a bit more formal place, although still in the "cozy little restaurant" class. Again, the cuisine is pure Puebla: pollo mole poblano, with the spicy chocolate sauce, is a standard choice for those unfamiliar with Puebla's complex cuisine. Remember, always, that the "chocolate sauce" is not sweet, but savory and spicy, even slightly bitter. It's hearty and delicious, once you've acquired the taste, but it's definitely not "chocolate-covered chicken" in the American sense. Expect to spend 1,670 to 1,950 pesos ($3.34 to $3.90) for a full meal here. Open noon to 11 p.m.; closed Monday.

One of the mom-and-pop-style restaurants in the area is the **Fonda Típica Angelopolis,** at Avenida 2 Ote. no. 407. This small, spotless establishment is attractively decorated with ceramic tile and offers the opportunity to examine the contents of the bubbling clay pots. The comida is 700 pesos ($1.40) for a typical Pueblan meal, with other dishes priced between 500 and 800 pesos ($1.00 and $1.60).

On Calle 6 Norte, up in the region of the A.D.O. bus station, are many more little Puebla-style eateries, all pretty cheap, and all doing their part to uphold the reputation Puebla bears as a culinary fount. In fact, the entire block of restaurants opposite the A.D.O. terminal offer memorable experiences. Great pots of boiling mole and other mysteriously delectable regional sauces bubble temptingly, yours for the price of a 400-peso (80¢) comida. The kitchens are right in front so when you see a good one dive in.

A Splurge Restaurant

El Cortijo (12) (tel. 42-0503), near the corner of Avenida 7 Pte. at 16 de Septiembre no. 506, is a closed patio charmingly decorated and always crowded. Lest you walk by, watch for the large wooden doors. The atmosphere is comfortable, the food tasty, the prices not too high, ranging from 1,100 pesos ($2.20) for pork chops to a delicious jumbo shrimp at 2,300 pesos ($4.60). The cubierto (or comida corrida) is a filling five courses with a choice of four different main dishes, for 1,300 pesos ($2.60). This is also a good place for that large afternoon meal and a bottle of wine. Open 1 p.m. to 6 p.m.

Starvation Budget

If you want to prepare your own picnic, you'll find two roast chicken places with cheap bottled drinks opposite the Cine Coliseo at Calles 2 Pte. and 3 Nte.

La Posada del Coyote Restaurant (25) at 4 Norte 402 (tel. 46-5175) is a rather small affair of ten tables arranged around an upstairs patio. The comida merits attention with a choice of camarones (shrimp) in mole, mojarra (fish) in garlic, or chicken for 450 pesos (90¢), 600 pesos ($1.20) on Sunday and during holidays. Other local dishes range from 400 to 600 pesos (80¢ to $1.20).

At the **Nevería Hermilo,** Avenida 2 Ote. and Calle 4 Nte. no. 9 (tel. 41-7963), the sandwiches are many and varied, being made from a long hot table. The hot table fits in with the modern-cafeteria mood of the place, and the prices are pretty low: 350 pesos (70¢) per sandwich, 690 pesos ($1.38) for the monster club sandwich. "Nevería" means "ice-cream parlor," and so dessert is—you guessed it!

For Dessert

Besides the famous mole poblano chocolate sauce, Puebla is also known throughout Mexico for its *dulces* (sweets). Scattered about in the city are small shops with display windows brim-full of marzipan crafted into various shapes and designs, candied figs, guava paste, and *camotes,* which are little cylinders of a fruity, sweet potato paste wrapped in wax paper. Camotes are fairly bland and fairly expensive; or buy one small one at a time in the market for 20 pesos (4¢). Beware! Your diet could suffer irreparable damage in Puebla's sweetshops.

WHAT TO DO IN PUEBLA: Puebla is a fascinating place to explore, but unfortunately the army of polluting buses makes it quite unpleasant to walk the streets. If you are here, however, bear the smog and venture out to see some of these really marvelous colonial monuments to a period when Puebla was the residential way station between the major port of Veracruz and the seat of finance, Mexico City.

The **Bello Museum (14),** now called the Museum of Art, is located at Avenida 3 Pte. no. 302 on the corner of Calle 3 Sur. It is open from 10 a.m. to 5 p.m. daily except Monday for 30 pesos (6¢) admission. (This is the standard cost of admission to all museums in Puebla, and these are the hours when the museums are open.) This museum is rarely visited, even though the house has some of the finest 17th-, 18th-, and 19th-century art I've seen anywhere. Señor Bello made his fortune in tobacco and, having no children to leave his money to, began to collect art from all over the world. (He, himself, never traveled, but he had art dealers who did.) Later, Señor Bello, who was himself a fine artist and an accomplished organist, organized a museum, which he left to the state when he died. His taste is evident throughout the house: velvet curtains, French porcelain, beautiful hand-carved furniture, several very fine organs, and numerous paintings. A worthy museum! Be sure to visit it when you are here.

The **Casa de Alfeñique (15),** which looks like an elaborate wedding cake and in fact means "the sugar-cake house," now houses the State Regional Museum, (open 10 a.m. to 5 p.m. every day except Monday for an admission charge of 30 pesos, 6¢). The 18th-century house is the most interesting part of the museum, but inside there is a small collection of pre-Hispanic artifacts and pottery as well as displays of regional crafts.

Puebla was a religious center like San Luis Potosí and Oaxaca, and today you can see several of the beautiful churches and convents left from that period. Most of the churches date back to the 17th and 18th centuries. A burgeoning anti-religious movement climaxed in 1767 when most of the orders were thrown out of the country and their convents closed. The **Convent of Santa Monica,** Avenida 18 Poniente no. 103, holds a certain amount of curiosity value. When the convents were closed in 1767, this one and two others operated secretly, using entrances through private homes, which hid the convent from public view. Very few people knew this convent existed; in fact, it was not discovered until 1935! Today this convent is a museum, kept as it was found. It is open 10 a.m. to 5 p.m. daily, except Monday, for 30 pesos (6¢) admission.

The largest convent in Puebla was of the Dominican order, called Santa Rosa, located at Calle 3 Norte no. 1203. It now houses the **Museum of Popular Arts** and the **Cocina** (kitchen) **de Santa Rosa (16).** It was in this kitchen that many native Mexican dishes were first devised. Both the museum and the kitchen can be visited every day from 10 a.m. to 5 p.m. (closed Monday) for 30 pesos (6¢) admission. The convent has been beautifully restored, and you can wander through two levels of rooms filled with elaborate examples of Mexican arts and crafts. This is a government-operated museum and the displays include some of the finest crafts around Oaxaca: six-foot earthenware candelabras, regional costumes, minute scenes made of straw and clay, hand-tooled leather objects, and so on. A small shop sells crafts of the area, but it is not as good as the government shops in other cities.

The **cathedral,** which is absolutely immense, is also worth inspection, especially for its interesting paintings. Begun in 1562 on the orders of King Philip of Spain, it was finished in 1649, before Mexico City's cathedral. Bells hang only in the tower closer to the zócalo (the other tower has none). Contemporary legend holds that at the time of construction Pueblans believed the weight of additional bells would make the cathedral sink into an underground sea. You can visit the still high and dry cathedral every day for free.

Just across the street from the cathedral, on the corner of Avenida 5 Oriente and Calle 16 de Septiembre, is the old **Archbishop's Palace (17),** which now houses the **Casa de la Cultura** and the **Biblioteca Palafoxiana.** The entrance to the Cultural Center and the Library is about halfway down the block on Avenida 5 Ote. You enter a courtyard; the marble stairs to the right will take you up to the second floor and the Biblioteca Palafoxiana. This library, which is the oldest one in the Americas (also the most beautiful), was built in 1646 by Juan de Palafoxe y Mendoza, then archbishop and founder of the College of SS. Peter and Paul. It bespeaks the glory of this period with its elegant tile floor, hand-carved wood walls and ceiling, inlaid tables, and gilded wooden statues. Bookcases are filled with 17th-century books and manuscripts in Spanish, Créole, French, English, etc. A lofty place!

The **Mercado Victoria (M)** is one of those Victorian railroad-station-like monsters covering an entire block between Avenidas 4 and 8 Poniente on Calle 3 Norte. The market and the entire area from Avenidas 4 to 10 Pte. and Calle 5 north to Calle 5 de Mayo (shaded area on the map) is teeming with unimaginable activity. You literally cannot walk on the sidewalks for the number of vendors on mats and knees selling vegetables and plastic trinkets—it's a maze of narrow pathways, blocked by old women in ill-fitting brightly colored clothes, who squat over piles of withered fruit. This is one of the most hectic and exciting markets you'll see in all of Mexico. **Note:** Puebla is a place to buy onyx, for most of the onyx of Mexico is shipped into Puebla where skilled craftsmen carve the stone.

While you're in the market area, stop in for a look at the **Iglesia de Santo Domingo,** on Calle 5 de Mayo between Avenidas 6 Ote. and 4 Ote. Finished in 1611, the church was part of a monastery at first. Be sure to see the Capilla del Rosario, a symphony of gilt and beautiful stone dedicated to the Virgin of the Rosary and built in 1690.

For a more systematic approach to your marketing, why not head for the **Barrio del Artistica,** Calle 8 Norte between Avenidas 2 and 6 Oriente. The Barrio (also called the "Mercado El Parian") looks for all the world like a colonial shopping mall, with neat brick shops in rows. Designed originally for artisans, the shops are run now by entrepreneurs who sell various crafts/products, much of which is standard souvenir stuff. Bargain to get a good price. While you're in this area you might take a look at the **Principal Theater (18),** which is said to be the oldest theater in the Americas. The interior has been restored and is being used for concerts (see the Tourism Office for schedules). The theater is only open when there is a scheduled event.

Another 18th-century house, now a museum, is the **Casa de Aquiles Serdan (19)**, Avenida 6 Oriente no. 206, which houses the Regional Mexican Revolutionary Museum, complete with bullet holes in the front façade of the house! It has collections of arms and photos of the great turmoil of the mid-19th century: the battle between the Juarists (liberals) and those who followed the imperialists (conservatives). Since Puebla lies between the main seaport of Veracruz and the capital, it was often under bombardment by besieging armies. The records and mementos of the various battles are here. Standard Puebla visiting hours apply, 10 a.m. to 5 p.m. daily, closed Monday, admission fee 30 pesos (6¢).

Two forts, about two miles from the zócalo, are worth a look. A cab will take you there for 300 pesos (60¢), or you can take a "Fuerte" bus for 40 pesos (8¢), catching it either at the corner of 16 de Septiembre and Avenida 9 Ote. or at Calle 2 Sur and Avenida 6 Ote., to **Fort Loreto** and **Fort Guadalupe.** Admission to the first of these costs 30 pesos (6¢), and the latter is free. The forts commemorate the defeat of the French here—2,000 Mexicans against 6,000 Frenchmen—on May 5, 1862, during Maximilian's attempt to dominate all of Mexico. You can buy a booklet for 350 pesos (70¢, and not worth it) at Fort Loreto telling the whole story. The battle's date is the origin of the street name "Cinco de Mayo" that pops up in almost every Mexican city and town.

The tourism office recently recommended the book *Guia de Cordero y Torres,* a bilingual guide to Puebla's main attractions, selling for 1,500 pesos ($3.00). You might obtain a copy at the Bello Museum.

The Game Preserve

There's a game preserve called African Safari, located ten miles southeast of town at Avenida 11 Oriente no. 2405, 15 minutes by car from downtown. They have a good collection of African animals: gazelle, antelope, lions, ostriches, and elephants, to name but a few; entrance fee is 900 pesos ($1.80) for adults, 700 pesos ($1.40) for children. A bus departs Terminal African at Avenida 12 Ote. and Calle 4 Nte. for the safari, charging 250 pesos (50¢) for the round trip.

DAY TRIP TO CHOLULA: The town of Cholula (pop. 36,000), located about six miles northwest of Puebla, is one of the most holy places in Mexico. It was here that Quetzalcóatl, the famed feathered serpent, lived in exile after he was forced to leave his city of Tula, capital of the Toltecs, in A.D. 900. Even during pre-Hispanic days pilgrims came here to pay their respects to this great leader.

The Cholulans organized some of the toughest resistance to Cortés and his men: one plot might have succeeded in wiping the Spaniards out, but Cortés found out about it, and instead some 3,000 Cholulans lost their lives.

Today Cholula has, so they say, a church for every day of the year, as well as the famed University of the Americas—the only U.S.-accredited university in Mexico. The great pyramid of Cholula, left from pre-Hispanic times, is slowly being excavated and restored, but as this is not a major archeological site it's hard to find a guidebook to the area. You'd do best to hire a guide if you care to see the hidden tunnels and the famous frescoes that are deep within the pyramid. The frescoes are some of the most famous in Mexico, and date back to the Classic period. And before you leave the site, climb to the top of the pyramid for the fine view of the town's steeples and spacious plaza. Admission to the ruins of the pyramid is 40 pesos (8¢); open daily from 10 a.m. to 5 p.m.

To get to Cholula take the red-and-white buses marked "Cholula" at the corner of Avenida 8 Pte. and Calle 7 Nte. in Puebla; fare, 50 pesos (10¢). Wednesday and Sunday are market days so you may want to schedule your trip accordingly.

READERS' SIGHTSEEING TIP: "If you do a day-trip to Cholula, don't miss the two churches **Santa María Tonantzintla** and **San Francisco Acatepec,** gems of Indian baroque architecture, only about 5 kilometers outside Cholula and easy to reach by bus. There is also a bus from Puebla, from the Central Market bus stop" (Verena Baumgartner and Markus Vogel, Zollikerberg, Switzerland). [*Note from T.B.:* Yes! These examples of local craftsmanship take full advantage of the beautifully colored Puebla tiles, and the woodcarving skills of local artisans. You'll enjoy seeing these churrigueresque tours de force.]

PUEBLA NIGHTLIFE: The mariachis play nightly from about 6 p.m. on in the **Plaza de Santa Inés (22)** at Avenida 11 Poniente and Calle 3 Sur. They stroll through the crowds gathered at a number of cozy sidewalk cafés. Another square which attracts mariachis is the **Plaza de los Sapos (23),** Avenida 7 Oriente near Calle 6 Sur. To get there, walk two blocks south from the zócalo and take a left onto 7 Oriente, toward the river. Keep your ears open and you can't miss the plaza. A third site where the mariachis perform nightly is the **Plaza de Los Trabajos** at Calle 11 Nte. and Avenida 10 Pte. (24).

2. Tehuacán

Tehuacán (alt. 5,409 feet; pop. 90,000) is a clean, attractive town that is popular with the wealthy and the unhealthy, its bigger hotels being pretty expensive and its mineral waters said to be good for hepatitis and for kidney and stomach ailments. Apart from drinking the waters (no charge) at **El Riego,** to the west of town, and **San Lorenzo,** off the road to Mexico City in the northwest, there isn't too much to do. Matter of fact, it isn't even necessary to go out of town because next door to the posh **Hacienda Spa Peñafiel,** at the northern end of town, is a luxurious cave with tile walls and silvered wrought-iron gates. Actually, it's not really a cave, but rather a long, downward-sloping hallway with plaster of Paris "rocks" on the ceiling. At the foot of this Dr. Caligari-type passage is a little modern patio with the waters gushing out of spigots on the wall and on the floor. There's nothing to drink from, so bring an empty bottle. No charge is made for all you can guzzle. The cave is apparently maintained by the Peñafiel bottling company, whose plant adjoins it. It is open to the public from 7:30 a.m. to 2:30 p.m. daily. About two blocks north, on the highway, is the post office and, adjoining it, a small tower that can sometimes be climbed to give a limited view of the tree-filled town.

ORIENTATION: Happily for visitors, several of Tehuacán's more regrettable faults have been swept away in recent years. The town's two main streets used to be named after two men with names identical except for their middle names, and so if someone sent you to the Avenida Camacho you didn't know which avenue they meant: Avila Camacho or Maximino Camacho. Now the two main thoroughfares are named Reforma (north-south) and Independencia (east-west).

Also, the A.D.O. company (tel. 2-0096) has a new and shiny bus station for first-class traffic at Independencia 119. It serves 16 buses a day each way between Tehuacán and Puebla, 15 to Oaxaca, and 3 per day to and from Veracruz. The bus station has its own cafeteria, but you can walk easily to other restaurants: just head out the front door of the station, turn right, and in a few minutes you'll be at the center of town, the intersection of Independencia and Reforma.

The second-class bus station, serving Autobuses Unidos lines, has yet to be redeemed. It's at Calle 2 Oriente no. 311 or 509 (depending on which building number you believe), near the corner with Calle 3 Norte, 2½ blocks east of Avenida Reforma and the Templo del Carmen. Six buses run to Puebla daily, four to Veracruz. If you have the misfortune to arrive here, walk out of the terminal, turn right, and walk to Reforma and the Carmen church. Turn left to reach the center of town.

WHERE TO STAY AND EAT: The posh **Hacienda Spa Peñafiel** (tel. 238/2-0190), for many years mentioned in this book as "The Impossible Dream" place to stay, is still just that. In fact, the dream is a bit faded these days. Many of the 150 rooms are just weary enough (threadbare carpet, chipped paint) to have lost their colonial charm. However the shady trees, verdant grounds, and larger than Olympic-size pools are as lovely as ever. If you have scheduled a stop at the spring right next door, do plan to take a stroll through the grounds and lobby of the Peñafiel. For all outward appearances this is still a fine example of the grand hotels of another era. One person pays 7,360 pesos ($14.72); two pay 7,935 pesos ($15.87). The hotel is on the Avenida José Garci-Crespa, the continuation of Avenida Reforma Norte (also Hwy. 150 north of town, going toward Puebla).

The **Hotel México,** right at the intersection of Reforma and Independencia (tel. 238/2-2319), is another colonial wonder, without the same full measure of grace as the Peñafiel, but very plush nonetheless. Prices, though, are a bit lower than the aforementioned hotel. Singles are pegged at 5,980 pesos ($11.96); doubles, 7,475 pesos ($14.95); and triples, 8,970 pesos ($17.94). There's also a neat-looking restaurant on the premises with many meals in the 690- to 1,380-peso ($1.38 to $2.76) range and a comida for 1,000 pesos ($2.00).

The **Casa Fagoaga,** at Reforma Nte. 213 (tel. 238/2-0220), is a cheerful little pension built around several small courtyards that catch lots of sun. The rooms, by contrast, tend to be dark, but the señora keeps them very clean. The price is very reasonable, but the difficulty here is that the eight rooms are now usually rented only by the month. You might stop by, though, on the outside chance that there'd be a short-term vacancy and negotiate a nightly rate.

A more solid prospect right next door to the Fagoaga is a functional establishment called the **Posada de Tehuacán,** at Reforma Nte. 211 (tel. 238/2-0491). In this modern, kelly-green building, trimmed with black and white ceramic stripes, are plain but suitable rooms for 1,600 pesos ($3.20) single, 2,200 pesos ($4.40) double with one bed and 3,100 pesos ($6.20) with two beds, and 3,700 pesos ($7.40) triple. The restaurant on the ground floor is well within the budget range too, with most entrees being in the 360- to 700-peso (72¢ to $1.40) range, plus a 600-peso ($1.20) comida. Service is pleasant and the food—although hardly delicate fare—is well worth the reasonable price. The señora in the kitchen will do her best to accommodate your whims and wishes.

From the intersection of Reforma and Independencia, walk east (oriente) on Independencia and after a block you'll reach the exceptionally pleasant Parque Juárez, shaded by grand old trees. The **Hotel Iberia,** (tel. 238/2-1122), a newly painted colonial mammoth of a place just a bit past the park on the left-hand side of Independencia, has become my leading choice. The Iberia has had a facelift and has managed to reverse its sagging image. Even the courtyard has been rejuvenated with a variety of potted plants. Another improvement is the addition of a delightfully quiet restaurant offering a 1,000-peso ($2.00) comida and no entree over 1,500 pesos ($3.00). The upstairs rooms center around a nice patio with singles for 3,956 pesos ($7.91) and doubles for 4,255 pesos ($8.51).

With lodging a bit scarce in Tehuacán these days, ask around for a recommended pension. This type of hotel has a habit of disappearing when the host family's relatives come for a visit. One that's been around for a while is **Pension Covadonga** (tel. 238/2-0842), on a narrow side street off Reforma (Ricardo Cacho), opposite the Banco de México. The place is clean, the atmosphere friendly, and a bed goes for 15,000 pesos ($30.00) per month.

Of the places to dine along the Parque Juárez, the most elegant and expensive is the **Restaurant Peñafiel,** on the eastern side (tel. 238/2-1005). Meat and fowl entrees here cost from 700 to 1,800 pesos ($1.40 to $3.60), egg dishes about 400 pesos (80¢), and you must plan on spending 900 pesos ($1.80) for a comida. But across the park on the west side are several much less expensive places. Meal prices here are, in general, 25% to 35% lower, and comidas corridas are in the 600- to 800-peso ($1.20 to $1.60) range.

WHAT TO SEE: Once you've quaffed some mineral water and strolled through the Parque Juárez, the only thing left to do is to walk up Avenida Reforma Norte to the **Templo del Carmen,** finished in 1783. Its dazzling domes are covered in polychrome faïence, which you probably noticed when you came into town. Hidden in the former convent (monastery) connected to the church is the **Museo del Valle de Tehuacán,** open from 10 a.m. to 5 p.m. every day but Monday; admission costs 40 pesos (8¢).

Some frescoes remain from the time the monks were in residence, but the exhibits on the lower floor go back much farther in time. In the early 1960s, Dr. Richard MacNeish discovered that the valley of Tehuacán had been the earliest maize (corn) growing center in the world—dating from 5000 B.C. You can trace the development of sculpture in the valley, from primitive pointy-chin female figurines to beautiful obsidian knives.

ON TO OAXACA: If you've chosen to go to Tehuacán, your best bet for the next leg of the journey to Oaxaca is the new Hwy. 131, which takes 4½ hours to negotiate by car, slightly more by bus, as the bus stops at Teotitlán en route. Five buses a day of the A.D.O. line pass through Tehuacán on their way to Oaxaca; the route is also served by several more local lines originating in Tehuacán.

On the road to Oaxaca, you wind through beautiful mountain country, dipping down into valleys filled with mango trees and climbing hillsides crowded with more gigantic cacti than you'd think possible.

3. Oaxaca

Oaxaca (pronounced "Wa-*hah*-kah"; alt. 5,070 feet; pop. 300,000) is a mountain city, and its location in a valley high in rugged mountains has determined its character. Oaxaqueños (pronounced "Wah-hah-*kehn*-yos") think of their native city as someplace special and unique, set off from the rest of the world—something of the feeling island dwellers have for their turf. Industrial and commercial development is making Oaxaca a booming, busy, wealthy town with a cosmopolitan touch, but local people are careful to preserve the beauty and special feeling of the city.

Local people include descendants of the Zapotec Indians who came to this high valley about 800 years before the birth of Christ and built a beautiful city and a flourishing culture at Monte Albán, six miles from the modern town. There had been people in the valley since 8000 B.C., but these early inhabitants were very primitive. It wasn't until the Preclassic period that cities were built, about the same time as they were in Teotihuacán. This building was the beginning of Monte Albán. There is speculation about who these early peoples were. Some authorities see a distinct resemblance in their art and calendar system to the Olmecs of the Gulf Coast. In any case, it was certainly the Zapotecs who raised the city's cultural life to a high level and built the monuments visible at the

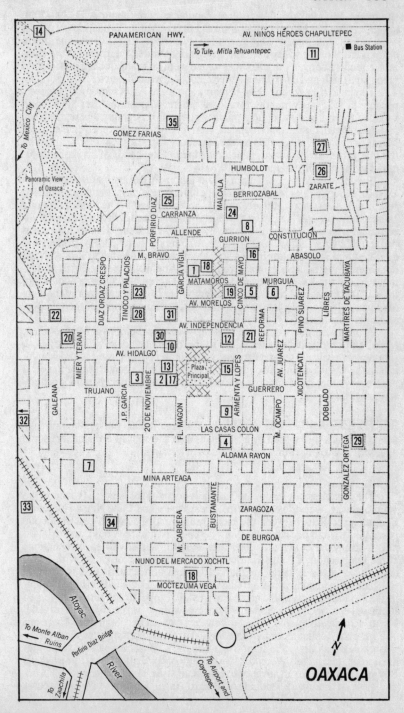

OAXACA

site today. But after this flowering of Zapotec culture (about A.D. 300–700), another tribe, the Mixtecs, built a rival center at Mitla, 36 miles away on the other side of what is today Oaxaca, and the two tribes struggled with one another for control of the valley until the Aztec threat united them against the common enemy. But even the two tribes united were no match for the Aztecs, and in the late 1400s and early 1500s Aztec influence predominated.

The local tribes didn't have to worry about the Aztecs for long, however, because in 1521 an even more formidable enemy appeared. After the Spanish subdued the valley they set up a military post called Antequers here; six years later the town of Oaxaca was founded. Hernán Cortés was later given the title of Marques del Valle de Oaxaca by the Hapsburg Emperor Charles V, and with the title came grants of land, which remained in the hands of his descendants until the Mexican Revolution in 1910.

Two of Mexico's presidents, Porfirio Díaz and Benito Juárez, came from Oaxaca. Nobody does much to remember Díaz these days, but monuments to Juárez are everywhere: statues, murals, streets named for him, even a Benita Juárez University. In fact, the city's official name is **Oaxaca de Juárez.** A Zapotec Indian who was born in the nearby village of Guelatao, Benito Juárez was "adopted" by a wealthy Oaxacan family who taught him Spanish, clothed and educated him in return for his services as a houseboy. He fell in love with the daughter of the household, and promised that he would become rich and famous and return to marry her. He managed all three, and Oaxaca adores him for it. After law school his experiences led him to become governor of the state of Oaxaca (1847–1852), later a resistance leader and president of the republic, and a national hero.

There's plenty to do and see in Oaxaca—visits to the ruins at Monte Albán, Mitla, and other smaller sites, visits to the outlying Indian villages for cloth shopping or festivals, several very good museums, convents, and colonial buildings in the city itself, and a wonderful zócalo at the city's center where the band plays every other night and sidewalk cafés provide the perfect perch for people-watching.

GETTING TO AND FROM OAXACA: Although hidden in its mountain fastness, Oaxaca is well served by bus, rail, and air transportation. Here are some tips, with advice on getting to and from each terminal.

By Bus

The first-class bus station in Oaxaca is north of the center of town on the main highway, which, as a city street, bears the name Calle Niños Héroes de Chapultepec. Taxis between the bus terminal and the zócalo cost about 500 pesos ($1.00), and perhaps this is your best bet, as direct city bus transportation must be caught several blocks down the street (turn left as you leave the station) at the intersection of Niños Héroes and Vasconcelos, a long walk with a suitcase. Buses, if you're game, are marked "Col. America" and "Col. Reforma."

The main first-class lines serving Oaxaca are A.D.O. and Cristóbal Colón; A.D.O. handles most traffic north and west, Cristóbal Colón serves the region south and east of Oaxaca. Some 28 buses a day run to Mexico City's Central del Norte, 10 a day to Puebla, 17 a day between Oaxaca and Tehuacán. There are also buses to Tehuantepec (seven a day), Tuxtla Gutierrez (three a day), San Cristóbal de las Casas, a 13-hour trip (one a day), Tapachula and the Guatemalan border (two a day), Veracruz (two a day), and Villahermosa (three a day). Buy your tickets a day in advance to be sure of space and a good seat.

Buses to Puerto Escondido and Puerto Angel, Oaxaca's two Pacific coast resorts (see Chapter III), leave from the second-class terminal. The Sociedad Cooperativa "Estrella del Valle" has three buses a day that bash over the mountains to Puerto Escondido, seven a day to Puerto Angel. Leave an entire day for this exhausting trip.

For second-class buses, head west out Trujano and cross the railroad tracks. The new Central Camionera de Segunda Clase (second-class bus terminal) is near the railroad station and the new market buildings. Take an "Estación" bus along Hidalgo.

By Train

Oaxaca's main station is west of the Cerro del Fortin hill, some distance from the center of town. Taxis to the Plaza Principal cost about 600 pesos ($1.20), or you can take the "Estación" bus that runs along Avenida Hidalgo between the station and the plaza.

There's a night train with sleeping cars that leaves Oaxaca at 6:20 p.m., arriving in Puebla at 3:30 a.m., and Mexico City at 8:52 a.m. From Mexico City the schedules are as follows: depart the capital at 5:32 p.m., arrive in Puebla at 10:45 p.m., Oaxaca at 8:05 a.m. Make your reservations for these trains as far in advance as possible.

By Air

Transportaciones Aeropuerto Oaxaca (tel. 951/6-7878) operates an airport minibus service between the center of town and the airport (a 15- or 20-minute trip) for 600 pesos ($1.20) per passenger, one way—a considerable saving over the 1,800 peso ($3.60) taxi fare. Drop by their office on the Alameda de León (in front of the cathedral), between the Hotel Monte Albán and the Correos (post office).

AeroMéxico (tel. 951/6-3765), Avenida Hidalgo 513, has nonstop flights between Oaxaca and Acapulco, Mexico City, Tapachula, and Villahermosa; other cities by connection. Mexicana Airlines has many daily nonstops between Oaxaca and the capital, plus a nonstop to Tuxtla Gutierrez three days a week. Contact them at Fiallo 102 at Avenida Independencia (tel. 951/6-8414).

Flights between Puerto Escondido and Oaxaca are operated in 28-passenger DC-3s by both of these little airlines: **Aerovias Oaxaqueñas S.A.**, Armenta y López 209, between Hidalgo and Guerrero (tel. 951/6-3824 or 6-3833 in Oaxaca; at the airport 951/6-1600; in Mexico City, Balderas 32, no. 514, tel. 905/510-0162); or **Lineas Aereas Oaxaqueñas,** Avenida Hidalgo 503, Oaxaca (tel. 951/6-5362 or 6-5243; in Mexico City at Calle 28 no. 20, Colonia Federal, tel. 905/571-2882 or 784-4043). The first-mentioned airline has two flights to Puerto Escondido each day with slightly different times on Sunday, the second airline only one flight a day, seven days a week. Cost for a one-way ticket is 7,900 pesos ($15.80). By the way, the plane may touch down in Pinotepa Nacional on the way to Puerto Escondido—don't get off there by mistake!

ORIENTATION: Questions out of the ordinary can be taken to the **Federal Tourism Office (1)** at the corner of Matamoros and G. Vigil, (tel. 951/6-0144). The office is open Monday to Saturday from 9 a.m. to 3 p.m. and 5 to 7 p.m.

The state of Oaxaca maintains a **State Tourism Office (5)** (Oficina de Turismo del Estado) at the corner of Morelos and Cinco de Mayo (tel. 951/6-0123 or 6-4828), open Monday through Saturday from 8 a.m. to 3 p.m. and 6 to 8 p.m. This office is well stocked with information and enthusiastic, competent advocates of Oaxaca. If you need information be sure to ask here.

USEFUL FACTS: The main **post office (30)** or *Correos* is at the corner of Independencia and the Alameda Park. . . . There is a good Spanish-English **book-store,** just off the southeast corner of the Plaza Principal at Guerrero 108, called Librería Universitaria. They carry mostly new books, but there is a small corner that has some used English books for sale. . . . The English **newspaper,** *The News,* is sold by enterprising children for 200 pesos (40¢) or by the newstands for 120 pesos (24¢). . . . For some reason, tourists seem to have more intestinal problems in Oaxaca than in most of the other states. Speaking of illnesses I might mention that the number of malaria cases has increased on the Pacific coast, and, in fact, it is becoming quite a problem. There have even been cases of typhoid fever, a deadly disease. There are clinics that distribute free quinine tablets in Puerto Escondido, Salina Cruz, and Potchutla. The Spanish word for malaria is *paludismo.* See the Introduction to this book under "Health and Medicaments" for more information.

I feel I must tell you about one of Oaxaca's few flaws. **Petty crime** is on the increase everywhere, and it seems to have come to Oaxaca. Take the normal precautions and you should have no trouble: park your car in a lot overnight, don't leave anything in the car within view, don't leave your things unattended one second in bus stations, and be especially careful of very professional pickpockets in the markets and buses—they'll have a wallet out of your back pocket, or out of your handbag, or out of your knapsack, and you won't know it until the time comes to pay for dinner. Luckily, violent crime (mugging and the like) is still very rare here. In any case, the police are no help at all.

WHERE TO STAY: Oaxaca is a boom town as far as the tourism industry goes, and this means that there is often a shortage of rooms. The rooms one does find are all priced about the same, no matter what they look like (the managers can get their price because the demand is so great), and budget rooms are not too common. But the middle range of hostelries offers some decent buys, outlined herewith:

Few hotels can be said to be run superbly these days, but one of those few is Sr. Raul Rodriguez's **Hotel Plaza (2),** Trujano 112 (tel. 951/6-2200), a half block from the zócalo. The hotel is not large (only 14 rooms and 5 junior suites), but it is maintained with meticulous care. Rooms are beautifully kept up, and the service is perfect: rooms are polished, fresh sheets spread, blankets changed and aired, all with an expert touch and a smile. But the hotel's greatest asset is Sr. Rodriguez himself, who receives and aids you with the greatest consideration, and just seems to make questions and problems vanish. Rates are reasonable: 3,779 pesos ($7.56) single, (4,715 to 5,658) pesos ($9.43 to $11.32) double (higher prices are for the junior suites), especially considering that once you bed down at the Plaza, you don't want to leave; 500 pesos ($1.00) extra for breakfast. Considering the prices at other hotels in Oaxaca—rising fearfully these days—I can state with conviction that the Plaza is one of the few hotels where you can get more than your money's worth.

Location and colonial charm are but two of the reasons to consider staying at the **Hotel Monte Albán (10),** right on the Alameda de León, a stone's throw from the main square (tel. 951/6-2777). The large, airy rooms in the front of the hotel are the ones closest to colonial times in their atmosphere, but the smaller interior rooms (servants' quarters?) are also fine, and a bit lower in price. All rooms have a tile shower and colonial-style touches. Prices are 4,913 to 6,141 pesos ($9.83 to $12.28) single, 6,141 to 7,666 pesos ($12.28 to $15.33) double. The courtyard is topped by a glass canopy that shelters a restaurant. Here on the Alameda you're in the best of company: the cathedral, the regional headquarters of the P.R.I., and the post office are right next door.

The **Hotel Francia (3),** at Calle 20 de Noviembre no. 212, at Calle Trujano (tel. 951/6-4811), is your next choice. Rooms are full of ancient furniture, and all have a bathroom. The court around which the rooms are built has been roofed over. The Francia is not fancy, but functional and quite pleasant. Single rooms cost 3,220 pesos ($6.44), doubles, 4,600 pesos ($9.20). The Francia has expanded from its original hotel building to engulf adjoining buildings, and so you can avail yourself of a wide choice of rooms. Watch out for street noise when choosing your chamber. The hotel restaurant, open 7:30 a.m. to 10 p.m., has an excellent comida (which is even better on Sunday) for 1,265 pesos ($2.53).

The **Hotel Principal (5),** Calle Cinco de Mayo 208 (tel. 951/6-2535), has no restaurant, but even the smallest of the 16 rooms is clean and attractive. Recent remodeling has done something for the lobby and the courtyard, but nothing much for the rooms or their prices. Still, it's reasonable and very popular with young travelers. Rates are 2,020 pesos ($4.04) for a single with bath, 2,525 pesos ($5.05) for a double with bath.

The **Hotel Virreyes (6),** at the corner of Morelos and Reforma (tel. 951/6-5555), has its courtyard covered with painted glass which lets in such a mellow light that the air seems to be colored beige. The whole hotel is mellow in a way, quiet, solid, functional, from its cool blue walls to the white tablecloths on the tables in the court. Most of the 31 rooms are quite big, all have tile bathrooms, and all are priced at 3,100 pesos ($6.20) single, 3,760 pesos ($7.52) double. Discounts of up to 20% are offered during slow times, which is usually winter. Be sure to look at your room before signing in as the rooms are quite individual ranging from well furnished to simply functional.

The **Hotel Antequera (12),** Avenida Hidalgo 807, (tel. 951/6-4020), has a location that is especially good, right off the Plaza Principal. The 29 rooms tend to be darkish but cool, with high ceilings and fans, television sets, and modernized showers. A cafeteria fills one side of the courtyard. The price: 3,772 pesos ($7.55) single, 5,313 pesos ($10.63) double.

The **Hotel Isabel (19),** Murguía 104 between Cinco de Mayo and Alcala (tel. 951/6-4053 or 6-4900), has some rooms that are good and others that are unsuitable—the only way to know what you're getting is to look beforehand. If they have a good room available, you'll be happy at the price: 2,000 pesos ($4.00) single, 3,000 pesos ($6.00) double. There are 64 rooms in all, with a private shower and telephone in each.

Most reasonably priced of the hotels right near the zócalo is the 35-room **Hotel Ruíz (9),** three doors down Calle Bustamante, at no. 103 (tel. 951/6-3660), from the southeast corner of the zócalo. The rooms are okay for the price, and have showers. Look at several before you move in. Single rooms cost 3,772 pesos ($7.55); doubles are 4,715 pesos ($9.43).

Most recent entry to the list of Oaxaca's colonial hostelries is the **Posada San Pablo (21),** at De Fiallo 102, near the corner of Avenida Independencia (tel. 951/6-4914). Completely restored now, this was in olden times the Convent of Saint Paul. Today the rooms are simple (as befits a former convent, perhaps), but very nice and certainly comfortable. All rooms have a two-burner stove, refrigerator, and private bath. The only drawback here is that most have no exterior windows. Prices depend on the length of your stay—each day gets less expensive the longer you stay—but for just a night or two you'll pay 3,910 pesos ($7.82) per day, or 90,000 pesos ($180) per month double and 75,000 pesos ($150) single. The San Pablo is just around the corner from the interesting little Plazuela Reforma.

Near the Francia in location, price, and comfort of accommodations is the **Hotel Meson del Rey (3),** at Trujano 212, two blocks from the main square (tel. 951/6-0033). The hotel's restaurant is always occupied by a few Oaxaqueños waiting for their long-distance phone calls to go through as this is the location of a convenient *caseta de larga distancia,* but they won't disturb you. The rooms are plain but comfy, with good clean bathrooms and sound-absorbent carpet on the floors. Prices are 3,772 pesos ($7.55) single, 4,715 pesos ($9.43) double.

Near the First-Class (A.D.O.) Bus Terminal

Those arriving by bus late at night could try the **Hotel Veracruz (11)**, virtually next door to the terminal at Avenida Niños Héroes de Chapultepec 1020 (tel. 951/5-0511). The Veracruz is modern and kept pretty clean; room decor is uninspired but neat and functional. Although they're allowed to charge more for the 30 rooms, the going rates are 3,105 pesos ($6.21) single, 4,232 pesos ($8.47) double. To get to the Veracruz, leave the terminal by the front door, turn left and walk a few steps, and you'll find it on the same side of the street.

Near the Second-Class Bus Terminal

The 34-room **Hotel Meson del Angel (7)** (tel. 951/6-6666) has an odd location—not in town and not out—which is good for you if you're arriving at Oaxaca's second-class bus terminal, west of downtown. It's at Mina 518, corner of Mier y Teran, a big modern building with louvered windows and *screens,* a restaurant, bar, and even a swimming pool. You pay a bit extra for the pool, but prices are still good: 4,120 pesos ($8.24) single, 6,200 pesos ($12.40) double, 5,150 pesos ($10.30) triple. This hotel is the departure point for buses to Monte Albán.

A Moderate Splurge

If the Plaza's full, and you want a touch of the posh life, you might try the **Hotel Señorial (13)**, Portal de Flores 6 (tel. 951/6-3933), right on the zócalo. It's less expensive than Oaxaca's other luxury places, but it provides several expensive services to its patrons such as a small private swimming pool, and 127 rather luxurious rooms, all with telephone, private bath, and reproductions of Diego Rivera paintings. Prices are high, though: 5,462 to 7,188 pesos ($10.93 to $14.38) single, 5,750 to 7,820 pesos ($11.50 to $15.64) double in season (mid-July to mid-September); reductions are offered off-season. The lower-priced rooms are in the older part of the hotel and are quite satisfactory. There's a roof-garden and bar.

I can't help mentioning Oaxaca's **Hotel El Presidente (16)** (tel. 951/6-0611) because it's so uncharacteristic of the establishments in this mammoth quasi-governmental chain. Rather than have a tall, modern shaft towering over this colonial city, El Presidente's directors chose (thank goodness) to convert the former four-centuries-old Convent of Santa Catalina to a hotel, and it has been recently designated a "national treasure." Two floors still adorned with some frescoes and colonial relics now hold 100 guest rooms, plus a swimming pool, laundry, souvenir shops, and all the other paraphernalia of a top-class hotel. Prices are 17,825 pesos ($35.65) single, 18,975 pesos ($37.95) double, 23,000 pesos ($46) triple. An extra bed costs another 4,600 pesos ($9.20). Children 12 and under stay for free in their parents' room. Even if this is way out of our range, you would enjoy a turn through the corridors and public rooms, or perhaps the buffet breakfast, at 1,575 pesos ($3.15), or a sandwich, at 750 to 1,200 pesos ($1.50 to $2.40), in the restaurant. You'll find El Presidente at Avenida 5 de Mayo no. 300, corner of the Plazoleta Labastida.

Starvation-Budget Hotels

The **Hotel Colón (4)**, Avenida Colón 120, between Bustamante and Armenta y López (tel. 951/6-4726), has about the cheapest rates in town for a respectable hotel: 1,900 pesos ($3.80) single, 2,900 pesos ($5.80) double. The big old rooms, each with a quaint add-on shower, are grouped about a flower-filled courtyard. The whole place is not at all fancy, but it's quite sympathetic. Give it a look if you're really out to save money.

Oaxaca's low-budget hotels are near the market and the red-light district, which is either an advantage or a disadvantage, depending on how you look at it. Adventurous but impecunious types should look them over: go to the corner of Trujano and Díaz Ordaz, and start your explorations.

WHERE TO EAT: Finding good restaurants with reasonable prices and good service is difficult in Oaxaca; dining here, in other words, is not the big attraction. Even though the afternoon hours from two to four o'clock are set aside for the comida corrida, and most shops and museums close for these hours, one must pick carefully to choose a good comida.

On the Plaza Principal

A special note is in order for restaurants and cafés in the arcades surrounding the main square. Sitting in one of these places, having a leisurely meal or snack and watching the action in the plaza—this is a prime attraction to Oaxaca. Consequently, prices in plaza eateries tend to be high for what you get, and service less attentive than it should be. You'll get more for your money if you go off the plaza, but you lose the bustle and excitement as well.

Of the places to dine on the plaza, my first choice is the **Guelatao (15),** (tel. 6-2311), Portal Benito Juárez 2, one of several restaurants located right next to one another in the arcade on the east side of the plaza. The Guelatao, open 9 a.m. to 11 p.m., offers a daily set-price lunch for 500 pesos ($1): soup, pasta, meat or fish, frijoles or salad, dessert, and coffee. If you don't want that much, just order a portion of lomo de cerdo (roast pork with potato salad) at 780 pesos ($1.56), or perhaps tamales oaxaqueños de mole (corn dough wrapped around bits of chicken, in a dark, rich mole sauce, the whole thing wrapped in banana leaves) at 540 pesos ($1.08). Prices, food, and service seem better here than at the neighboring establishments. By the way, the outdoor tables at the Guelatao are distinguished from the tables of neighboring next-door restaurants only by the color of the cloth—be sure you're sitting in the right section.

Across the main square, on the west side, are more café-restaurants, and the "in" place here for both gringo and Oaxaqueño is the **Restaurant del Jardín (17),** (no phone), open 7:30 a.m. to 11 p.m. The beautiful marble tables are always crowded with a varied crowd sipping beer or coffee and watching the action. This is the prime place to wait out one of Oaxaca's brief but intense afternoon thundershowers, provided you get a table when the first drops come down (after that they fill up fast). To dine, they recommend that you enter their indoor room—they say the service is faster there, but I suspect they want to keep the sidewalk portion a café rather than a restaurant. They offer a selection of set-priced breakfasts available all day, a half-dozen Oaxacan specialities, and such dinner entrees as tamale oaxaqueño at 430 pesos (86¢) and carne asada Oaxaca style at 1,480 pesos ($2.96).

Gerd and Elisabeth Wegemer of Hamburg, West Germany, were among several readers who wrote to recommend the **Restaurant El Meson** (tel. 6-2729), just off the Plaza Principal, around the corner from the Guelatao on Avenida Hidalgo. I've checked it out, and everything they say is true: the pozole is hearty, filling, spicy, delicious, and a bargain at 490 pesos (98¢)—it could easily be a full meal. A printed list of dishes serves as menu, order blank, and bill. The prices are printed on it, and the taco prices, 120 pesos (24¢), are *per taco,* so if you want more than one, you must indicate such when you order. From your seat at one of the bright wooden tables in this clean, attractive place, you can watch the señoritas prepare your tacos at what can only be described as the Mexican equivalent of a sushi bar. If you order the chorizo oaxaqueño, make sure you have a frosty beer for chaser, and that your fire insurance is up to date. El Meson is open seven days a week, but only for dinner (from 6 p.m.).

The **Asador Vasco (17)**, on the west side of the Plaza Principal (tel. 6-9719), open 1:30 to 11:30 p.m., is an old Oaxaca standard. It has its strong points: the second-floor location, with balcony tables overlooking the plaza; a menu listing lots of steaks, fish, and chicken, plus some familiar Mexican favorites. Prices are not bad: for a full three-course dinner, one might pay 3,000 to 4,000 pesos ($6 to $8), or try the fish filet served in a bubbling earthenware dish for 1,940 pesos ($3.88). Service is polite and fairly polished.

Best in Town

Perhaps the most delightful restaurant in all Oaxaca is **La Fontana (8),** on Gurrion near the corner of Cinco de Mayo, only a few steps from the Hotel El Presidente. My friends Harry and Catherine Gold, of Denver, Colorado, gave me the tip on this one. You enter a quiet courtyard with a fountain at its center, several shady trees beside it, a kitchen in the rear. A local family does the cooking and serving, with style and smile. A delightful dinner of pollo jardinera (chicken with vegetables) or huachinango (red snapper), plus a beer or a margarita, will cost 1,750 pesos ($3.50). For a more elaborate three- or four-course dinner you might pay 2,500 pesos ($5.00), which is unbeatable. For a light meal try the sopa de ajo, a fish-base soup with tomato. La Fontana is closed Sunday, but is open every other day from 1:30 to 11:30 p.m.

Elsewhere

At the **Café El Sol y La Luna,** Murguía 105 near Alcala, opposite Hotel Isabel (19), (tel. 6-2933), you can actually eat by the light of the sun from 8 a.m. to 4 p.m. or by the light of the moon from 7 p.m. until midnight, Monday through Saturday. A live band plays from 9 p.m. until closing and a cover of 200 pesos (40¢) per person is charged. You'll come for the food and not the lighting when you discover what they serve: yogurt with granola and honey, avocado salads, crêpes, pasta, hamburgers with salad and french fries, melted cheese plates. Prices range from 500 to 600 pesos ($1 to $1.20) for the light meals, 750 to 900 pesos ($1.50 to $1.80) for the latter items. Wine and beer are served at competitive prices.

The **Restaurant Bar Cathedral (31)** (tel. 6-3285) located one block off the zócalo at Vigil 105, is open from noon until 1 a.m. Here is a cool place to enjoy a leisurely midday meal. A few tables are near the fountain in the small courtyard while others are in two large rooms to your left and right as you enter. One can sense the touches of elegance here; waiters in jackets and ties, cloth napkins, and more than one fork. The restaurant is known for its excellent cuts of beef for 1,080 to 2,000 pesos ($2.16 to $4). The flan here for 280 pesos (56¢) may be the best I have had anywhere!

An Institution

The restaurant of **Doña Elpidia (18)** is virtually an institution in Oaxaca, for Doña Elpidia has been catering to a refined and selective local clientele for more than 40 years. Walking past Miguel Cabrera 413 (Cabrera's the southern entension of Garcia Vigil; no. 413 is about six blocks south of the main square), you'd hardly think it housed a restaurant, but inside the shabby-looking door is a beautiful courtyard filled with birds and plants. Two large dogs on the roof keep watch. Five tables are set out in the arcade, and about a dozen more fill the indoor dining rooms. Last time I visited, the five-course comida corrida cost 1,200 pesos ($2.40) and included small portions of an appetizer of chicharrón (delicious deep-fried pork rind), empanadas, and pork spare ribs, vegetable soup, roast chicken with a garnish of warm pickled vegetables, delicately seasoned pork with rice, a dessert of cinnamon rice pudding, and Mexican coffee (with cinnamon). Lunch only is served, from 1:30 to 4 p.m. daily; menu only in Spanish.

The Best of the Rest

Down the price range a bit—but with no sacrifice in quality—are several good places without flair or fanfare (no piped-in music, either), but with very good food at very agreeable prices. First place on this list goes to the **Cafetería Tito's** (tel. 6-7379), Garcia Vigil 116 about a half block north of the cathedral (which itself is on the north side of the main square): look for the green-and-black-striped awning that marks Tito's doorway. Always busy with a young student crowd happily drinking coffee or consuming one of the chickens cooked in the rotisserie next to the front door, Tito's offers mostly light meals such as sandwiches, hamburgers, and traditional dishes priced from 60 to 700 pesos (12¢ to $1.40). I tried the pozole, the famous rich stew of hominy with meat or chicken, at 350 pesos (70¢), tortilla chips included, and it was the best I've ever tasted—and very filling. You might also try the burritos with ham, cheese, and a side order of guacamole, also excellent. Tito's is a good place for breakfast at 350 pesos (70¢). The restaurant is open daily from 8 in the morning till midnight; it closes early on Sunday, at 4 p.m.

Gino's Pizza (28) (tel. 6-0580), on Independencia between 20 de Noviembre and J. P. Garcia, is a tiny place with three wooden benches and a large beer keg. Small, medium, or large pizzas are offered (pan sizes are on the wall), and the general wisdom has it that a small cheese pizza at 800 pesos ($1.60) will feed two people, while a large ham pizza at 1,900 pesos ($3.80) will do for three. The beer costs 200 to 240 pesos (40¢ to 48¢). Gino's is open from 2 to 11 p.m. Closed Monday.

The **Pizzeria Alfredo Da Roma** (tel. 6-5058), at 400 Alcala near the north end of the new mall, offers a little bit of Italy daily from 1:30 to 11:30 p.m. The small tables covered with the obligatory red-and-white-checkered table cloths are full of locals as well as tourists. Many people who stop for take-out pizza spend their time examining the Italian prints that are clustered together on the walls or simply stare out the ankle-level window at the passing shoppers. All prices are posted on a board in the entrance. They include pizzas for 1,300 to 1,680 pesos ($2.60 to $3.36), lasagna 800 pesos ($1.80), and spaghetti 700 pesos ($1.40). *Buono appetito*.

The Comedor Familiar

Of the inexpensive dining places in Mexico, the *comedor familiar* ("family dining room") is the institution that usually proves to be cheapest and best. Usually a plain little place with a minimum of decor and a señora with children in attendance, comedors serve what is basically home cooking at very modest prices. One of my favorites is the **Restaurant Pisces (20)**, which offers vegetarian fare on a menu that changes daily. The comida corrida, at 700 pesos ($1.40) gives an example of the offerings: vegetable soup, a plate of lentil stew with carrots and pineapple, frijoles, fruit salad, and tea. You'll find the Pisces at Avenida Hidalgo 119, five blocks west of the zócalo. It's open every day except Sunday, only from 1 to 4 p.m. despite what the sign says about evening hours.

Out in search of the city's cheapest comida corrida? Walk west on **Trujano** until you come to the two-block section between 20 de Noviembre and Díaz Ordaz. These little hole-in-the-wall eateries are very basic, but very cheap, a four-course meal costing only about 460 pesos (92¢).

Pastries and Snacks

At festival time in Oaxaca, sidewalk stands are set up in the market area and near the cathedral to sell *buñuelos,* the Mexican equivalent of a pappadum, only sweet. You'll be served your buñuelo in a cracked or otherwise flawed dish or bowl, and after you're finished you smash the crockery on the sidewalk for good luck. Don't be timid! After a while, you may find yourself buying more and more buñuelos—about 300 pesos (60¢) apiece—just for the fun of smashing plates.

For a more conventional snack or light breakfast, pick up your fill of pastries, cookies, sweet rolls, and breads from the large **Panificadora Bamby,** at the corner of Morelos and Garcia Vigil, two blocks north from the Plaza Principal.

The Big Splurge

I got a surprise the last time I was in Oaxaca. The price of a room at the **Hotel El Presidente (16)** (tel. 951/6-0611), Avenida 5 de Mayo no. 300, was way up, and the price of a meal was way down. If you choose carefully here, you can even have a pleasant dinner in rich surroundings. Consider this: sopa de frijole (bean soup), tasajo a la oaxaqueña (a beef dish), pie, pastry or ice cream, a bottle of beer, with tax and tip, came to 3,454 pesos ($6.91) for one person— hardly what one would call outrageous. The breakfast buffet, all you can eat for 1,575 pesos ($3.15), is an incredible bargain, especially for big eaters.

READERS' RESTAURANT SELECTIONS:
"I can recommend the **Restaurant Típico de Oaxaca** (no phone), Plaza Labastida, corner of Cinco de Mayo, around the corner from the Hotel El Presidente, opposite the Restaurant La Fontana. This restaurant serves authentic Oaxacan food, some of it not seen elsewhere. The Oaxaca platter (1,100 pesos, $2.20) gives one a chance to sample many regional dishes. Service and prices are friendly. They're open for all three meals" (Bruce D. Wagner, Middletown, N.J.). . . . . "Once we discovered the **Casa de Chocolate,** Independencia 501 near 20 de Noviembre, we went there at least once a day. A three- or four-course breakfast, including a bowl—that's right, a bowl—of the best hot chocolate I've ever had anywhere, ran 675 pesos ($1.35). Several of the staffers speak English. The only caution is that the coffee is terrible" (Shel Horowitz, Northampton, Mass.).

WHAT TO DO: There's plenty in Oaxaca to keep you busy: some 27 churches, lots of colonial buildings, two excellent museums, the market, and the sidewalk cafés on the Plaza Principal. Remember that Oaxaqueños observe the siesta from 2 to 4 p.m. and most shops and museums will be closed. To get a feel for this lovely city I would recommend a walking tour of the churches and monuments and then (mañana) a visit to the Regional Museum and the Rufino Tamayo Museum of pre-Hispanic art. You may want to visit the market and the various popular art shops around town: the craftwork of this state is some of the finest.

Start your tour in the Plaza Principal with a look at the **cathedral** (begun in 1544) with its 18th-century baroque façade and glittering interior of five naves and a bronze altar.

Go one block north to Independencia, turn right, and on the southeast corner of the intersection with Armenta y López is the beautiful belle époque **Teatro Macedonio de Alcala (21),** built in 1903. The theater holds 1,300 persons and is still used for concerts and such, and therefore is not usually open during the day. Peek through the doors to see the marble stairway, Louis XV vestibule, and other such flourishes, and come back for an event in the evening—a list of happenings is posted by the doors.

Walking west along Independencia, you pass the University of Oaxaca on your right between Calle López and G. Vigil (look for the graffiti). Two streets past G. Vigil is the **Church of San Felipe,** on the corner of Tinoco y Palacio and Independencia. The church was built in 1636 and mirrors all the architectural opulence of that period: the altar and nave are covered with ornately carved and gilded wood; the walls are frescoed. Somehow, although it's ornate, there seems to be enough free wall space to keep the feeling from being overpowering.

The **Basilica de la Soledad (22),** corner of Independencia and Galeana, is probably one of the most important religious centers in Oaxaca. Here is where you'll find an effigy of the town's patron saint carved in black stone. The basilica is in fact a huge complex of buildings including a garden, convent, and a smaller theater where spectators can witness the famous Fiesta de la Soledad (see below under "Festivals"). The basilica was built in 1682–1690, and has four levels on the outside, each displaying several niches inhabited by carvings of saints. Although it's handsome on the outside, the basilica inside is overpowering with chandeliers, lunging angels, gilt ceiling, paintings, and statues. The statue of the Virgin de la Soledad (the patron saint of Oaxaca) is in the museum around the back of the church, to the right as you exit. The statue is draped in black velvet and placed in a chapel filled with white bouquets made of glass, pearl, and plastic. The museum is open from 10 a.m. to 2 p.m. Monday through Saturday, admission free. Other than the display of the Virgin, the only item of interest is a three-foot-square case of innumerable miniature glass figurines (birds, angels, animals, and flowers) surrounding the Christ Child—if you like miniature glass figurines you'll love this. From the basilica you can walk east to visit the Rufino Tamayo Museum, the House of Benito Juárez, and the Santo Domingo Convent, or you can head south to see the oldest church in Oaxaca (San Juan de Díos) and the teeming market.

The **Rufino Tamayo Museum of Pre-Hispanic Art (23),** Avenida Morelos 503, is one of the most beautiful museums in all Mexico. It prides itself on being unique in that the artifacts are displayed "solely for the aesthetic rank of the works, their beauty, power, and originality," rather than as curious geegaws left from a dead way of life. The collection was amassed over a 20-year period by the artist Rufino Tamayo, born in Oaxaca. The museum itself is very attractive— pink, blue, lavender, green, and orange rooms follow in succession, holding a wealth of sculpture from the Preclassical period up to the Aztecs: terracotta figurines, scenes of daily life, lots of female fertility figures, Olmecan and Totonac sculpture from the Gulf Coast, Zapotec long-nosed god figures, and such. Plaques in Spanish give the period, culture, and location of each find, but you find yourself ignoring this information and just admiring the works and the displays, which are works of art in themselves. The museum is open from 10 a.m. to 2 p.m. and 4 to 7 p.m.; closed Tuesday. Admission is 50 pesos (10¢).

Whatever your interest or lack of it in churches, you should make a special effort to see the **Santo Domingo Church (24)** at the corner of Constitución and Cinco de Mayo. Started in the 1550s by Dominican Friars and not finished until a century later, it contains the work of all the best artists of that period. Walls and ceiling are covered with ornate plaster statues and flowers, most of them gilded, and two stained-glass panels at one end are particularly attractive. The church has recently undergone complete restoration—inside and out. Everything glistens, especially the large gilded rosary chapel to the right as you enter. Also, be sure to notice the genealogical tree of the Guzman family in the apse as you enter. Don Feliz de Guzman was the founder of the church.

Next to the Santo Domingo is the convent that now houses the **Regional Museum of Oaxaca (24).** The admission is 50 pesos (10¢), 25 pesos (5¢) on Sunday and holidays; it's open Tuesday through Friday from 10 a.m. to 6 p.m. and from 10 a.m. to 5 p.m. on Saturday and Sunday; closed on Monday. The interior is an arched courtyard somewhat restored with faint traces of elaborate frescoes along the walls and ceilings. The building must have been magnificent, judging from what remains. You can still feel the pervasive peacefulness of the place: all the rooms open onto the courtyard, where the only sound is that of the fountain. On the top floor, first room to the right, are objects left from the Dominican convent. Counterclockwise, the next three rooms are dedicated to finds from Monte Albán, a nearby Zapotec city, which flourished from 800 B.C. until it was abandoned in A.D. 900; following this was the Mixtec domination in the 14th century. Unfortunately there's no guidebook to the museum, and all the plaques are in Spanish, so you'll have to rely on information picked up elsewhere. Here are a few hints: the Zapotecs had a numbering system of bars and dots, similar to that of the Olmecs and the Maya, and a collection of glyphs which, perhaps, represent a calendar; another thing to note is that most of the ceramic sculpture here has the characteristic Zapotec touches of prominent teeth, proboscises, elaborate headgear (often as an eagle or jaguar mask), and large earplugs. Many of the figures have mouths similar to the one found in Olmec sculpture—it's thought that the Olmecs influenced the early development of Monte Albán. Be sure not to miss the room holding the incredible treasures found in Tomb 7 at Monte Albán, in 1932. The tomb contained seven bodies (hence its name) and dated from A.D. 500. Whether the tomb was Zapotec or Mixtec is still being debated. The beauty of the jewelry in gold, turquoise, conch shell, amber, obsidian, and the bowls of onyx and glass—this is no subject of dispute! Some 500 pieces of jewelry and art objects were found. The lower floor holds crafts and costumes of the Oaxaca region: mannequins dressed in authentic regional dress portray facets of religious, social, and cultural life.

The **House of Benito Juárez (25)** is located one block west and one block north of the Santo Domingo convent, on Garcia Vigil, left-hand side of the street across from the church. Look for the small plaque over the door which indicates that this was the residence of the local hero from 1818 to 1820. The house and museum are only moderately interesting. (Open 10 a.m. to 2 p.m. and 4 to 7 p.m. every day except Monday; 50 pesos, 10¢, admission.) Four rooms around a courtyard are set up to show the style in which the great man lived. The school across the street—it looks like a fortress—was once the convent-church of **El Carmen,** run by the Carmelite order. Next to the convent-church is the nice Plazuela del Carmen Alto, a good place to rest.

The earliest church in Oaxaca, built 1525–1530, is the **San Juan de Díos,** in the market area on the corner of Aldama and 20 de Noviembre. The exterior is nothing special but the interior has an ornate altar and paintings on the ceiling by Urbano Olivera. A glass shrine to the Virgin near the entrance and one to Christ (off to the right) are especially revered by Oaxaqueños, and much visited. Because it's in the market, many of the people who visit the church are villagers who've come in to buy and sell.

MARKETS AND SHOPS: Oaxaca's **Benito Juárez Market** is big and busy every day, but especially on Saturday when the villagers come in droves bringing their wares. The covered market is the "M" on our map, and the shaded area around it is all open street market teeming with vendors of chiles, string, parrots, talismans, food, spices, cloth, blankets—absolutely everything! It is the most exciting and probably the best market in all of Mexico, partially because the people who come to sell are so colorful and partially because the food and crafts are so colorful.

This used to be Oaxaca's central produce market, but the center of food trading has been relocated to a new building west of downtown called the **Abastos Market (33),** across the railroad tracks and near the second-class bus station. Both places are now filled with market-day hubbub, but if generalizations can be made, I'd say that the downtown market has mostly clothing while the new market specializes in food. The Abastos Market is open daily but erupts with goods and vendors on Saturdays. The huge mounds of dried chiles, herbs, and vegetables make an intriguing backdrop for the bustling market drama.

Two blocks south of the Benito Juárez Market at the corner of Garcia and Zaragoza is the **Mercado de Artesanías (34).** This is one sure place to see Indian women weaving on backstrap looms. A very interesting selection of woven goods are for sale including huipils and serapes.

If all this is too mind-boggling and you desire a more essential collection of crafts, there are a number of Casas de Artes Populares or Curiosidades, shops specializing in popular arts and crafts. The prices will be distinctly higher, but then you save haggling. Two I can recommend for their quality, prices, and attitude to customers are Victor's Artes Regionales and Yalalag de Oaxaca.

Victor's, at Porfirio Díaz 111, open 9 a.m. to 2 p.m. and 4 to 8 p.m., is housed in a 17th-century monastery and run by Sr. Ramon Fosado. Ramon goes to the villages himself in search of the best Indian art. He speaks English, and is very pleasant. **Yalalag de Oaxaca,** corner of Morelos and Alcala (no. 104), (tel. 6-2108), open 9 a.m. to 1:30 p.m. and 4 to 7:30 p.m., is in an old mansion, and displays a multifarious collection of black pottery, terracotta figurines, tin sculpture, jewelry, rugs, beads, necklaces, papier-mâché sculpture, and lots more. Owner Enriqua de la Lanza speaks English, as do most of her staff, and her prices seem okay. Yalalag has the widest assortment of stuff I've seen in one shop.

The **Casa Brena (26),** across the street from the park at Pino Suárez 58, (tel. 5-3890), which recently celebrated its 50th anniversary of operation, is mostly a textile shop with some pottery sold. Inside is a large courtyard with a tienda (store) off to the left, and looms in the back. You'll hear the slapping of the wooden paddles as the men tighten the shuttled thread between the warp. Walk back and look around. The boys are dying the wool in bright colors from fluorescent pink to canary yellow, the young girls spinning the thread, and the men working the looms. All in all, it's an impressive operation and I can almost guarantee you'll want to buy something. The prices here are about as low as you'll find anywhere, and the quality is the best. The "Colonia Reforma" bus will take you to the corner at Pino Suárez and San Martín. Casa Brena's looms work from 8 a.m. to 4:30 p.m. Monday through Friday, 8 a.m. to 2 p.m. on Saturday; the shop is open from 9 a.m. to 2 p.m. and from 4 to 7:30 p.m. Monday through Friday and is open the same hours as the looms on Saturday. Closed Sunday.

The state of Oaxaca runs **Aripo (35)** (an acronym for *Artesanías y Industrías Populares del Estado de Oaxaca),* which is located two blocks further up the hill beyond the Benito Juárez house at Vigil 809 (tel. 6-9211). The shop is open Monday through Saturday from 9 a.m. to 1:30 p.m. and 4 to 7:30 p.m.; Sunday from 9 a.m. to 1 p.m. You can hear looms working in the back as you browse through the handcrafts expertly displayed in the many rooms. Aripo has possibly the widest selection of black pottery in the city, some of which is sure to be as yet unpacked, still in the large woven shipping baskets. Masks, typical clothing, and cutlery are also in good supply here.

Oaxaca now has a branch of the quasi-governmental **FONART** shops ("Fondo Nacional para el Fomento de las Artesanías), at the corner of M.

Bravo and Garcia Vigil, open Monday through Saturday from 9 a.m. to 2 p.m. and from 4 to 7 p.m.; closed Sunday. Quality and selection are good here, and prices are fixed.

Three blocks of Alcala, from Morelos to Allende, have recently been closed to auto traffic and converted into an attractive colonial-style **mall.** Many quality shops have sprung up along this delightful strip. Compliments to you Oaxaca, well done!

A word about buying sarapes and blankets in Oaxaca: There is so much variance in quality and prices on both these items that I strongly recommend that you do a little research before buying. If you don't know what to look for in quality, I would recommend the friendly *patrons* in Victor's, as they are willing to tell you about the differences in materials (wool vs. synthetic), dyes (natural and chemical), and designs. You can also scout around and compare the various products in the open markets.

While you're in the neighborhood you might be interested in the **Oaxaca Lending Library (27)** at Pino Suárez 802. It was started over a decade ago by a group of American residents and they now have a good-size collection of books in English, Spanish, and French. There is a membership fee if you plan to be here any length of time; otherwise they welcome visitors, but ask them to leave a deposit, which is refunded when all borrowed books are returned. The library is a quiet, relaxing place for an afternoon stop to read about Benito Juárez. The hours are 10 a.m. to 1 p.m. and 4 to 6 p.m. Monday through Friday. They also accept and appreciate any books you may want to donate.

Market days for the surrounding villages are as follows:

Wednesday: Etla, 15 kilometers north
Thursday: Zaachila, 18 kilometers southwest; Ejutla, 65 kilometers south
Friday: Ocotlan, 30 kilometers south
Saturday: Oaxaca itself; Tlaxiaco
Sunday: Tlacolula, 32 kilometers southeast—visit the chapel as well.

To take all this sightseeing in at a glance, those with cars can drive to the **Cerro del Fortin,** a hill to the west of town from which you can get a panoramic view of the city, especially good just before sunset. Recognize the hill by a statue of—who else?—Benito Juárez, and a stadium built to hold 15,000 spectators.

You can walk to the hill as well. Head up Díaz Ordaz / Crespo, and look for the *Escaleras del Fortin* ("Stairway to the Fortress") shortly after you cross Calle Delmonte.

The Tourist Office will give you a map showing the nearby villages where beautiful handcrafts are made. It's a fun excursion by car or bus through luxuriant countryside and very interesting to wander the rutted street. At **Teotitlán del Valle,** you can see rug weavers at their loom, sheep in the yards. In **San Bartolo de Coyotepec,** home of the famous black pottery, you can see one of the frequent demonstrations on the method used to make these distinctive ceramics, which are in vast quantities at reasonable prices.

READER'S TIP—MAILING PARCELS: "**Mailing packages** from Oaxaca to the U.S. involves a side trip to the Ministry of Commerce, corner of Hidalgo and Tacubaya. Bring your goods there, fill out the paperwork, wrap your packages to weigh 10 kilos (22 lbs.) or less, go back across town to the post office and deal with more bureaucracy. It took us six hours to go through this process for three packages! However, our boxes were home before we were, even with rail shipping instead of the far more costly air freight" (Shel Horowitz, Northampton, Mass.).

FESTIVALS: Oaxaca is famous for its festivals, filled with the color and exuberance of traditional life. The three most important ones are during Holy Week at Eastertime, in July, and in December. Plan ahead and get hotel reservations if you're thinking of coming to any of the festivities.

During the week preceding Palm Sunday (the Sunday before Easter), figurines made of palm leaves are made and sold on the streets by village women. On Palm Sunday itself there are colorful street processions, and on the Thursday after that, Oaxaqueños follow the Procession of the Seven Churches. Hundreds of the pious move from church to church, taking communion in each one to ensure a prosperous year. Throughout the week each church sponsors concerts, fireworks, fairs, and other entertainments. On the day before Easter the famous *guelaguetza* is danced in the Plaza de la Soledad, followed by a candle-light service in the Santo Domingo church.

In mid-July you can witness the **Fiesta Guelaguetza** (offering) of the Virgin Carmen. From this day through the following two Mondays there are fairs, exhibits, and of course the much talked-about regional dances performed in the stadium on the Cerro del Fortin each Monday. It is a marvelous spectacle of color, costumes, music, and dance. Some 350 different *huipils* and dresses can be seen during the performance as the villages of the seven regions of Oaxaca present their traditional dances. This is definitely worth seeing. Admission ranges from 1,500 to 1,800 pesos ($3 to $3.60) and *must* be reserved in advance (no later than May). A travel agency could handle this for you, although the Tourism Office (5) will try to help if you do not have reservations. I recommend sections 5 and 6 in Palco A for the best seating in the Cerro del Fortin Auditorium. The color of your ticket matches the color of your seat. You will be sitting in strong sunlight so wear a hat and long sleeves. On Sunday night before the Guelaguetza, the university students present an excellent program in the Plaza de la Soledad. It is called the Bani Stui Gulal. The programs begin at 8 p.m., but since the event is free you should get there no later than 5:30 if you hope to get a seat.

The December festivals begin on the 18th with the **Fiesta de la Soledad** in honor of the patron saint of Oaxaca. On that night there is a cascade of fire from a "castle" erected for the occasion in the Plaza de la Soledad. December 23rd is the **Night of the Radishes** when the Oaxaqueños build fantastic scenes and sculptures out of radishes (the most prized vegetable cultivated during the colonial period), flowers, leaves, and fruits. They are on display in the garden off the zócalo. On December 24th each Oaxacan church organizes a procession with music, floats, and crowds bearing candles. New Year's Eve is celebrated with the **Petition of the Cross** where villagers from all over come to a forlorn chapel on the hill beyond Tlacolula (about 35 kilometers southeast of Oaxaca near Mitla) to light candles and express their wishes for the coming New Year. Mock bargaining, with sticks and stones to represent livestock and produce, is part of the serious game of expressing hopes for the New Year: tiny symbolic farms and fields are built and their wealth traded, enlivening hopes that the year to come will see the same prosperity, only for real.

OAXACAN NIGHTLIFE: The cheapest, and perhaps the best, evening entertainment is, of course, in the Plaza Principal, where band concerts are scheduled on Tuesday, Thursday, and Sunday, but more often than not during the summer some sort of musical group will be holding forth every night. Oaxaca's is perhaps the jolliest and most active zócalo in all Mexico, enjoyed by everyone in town from 3-year-olds to octogenarians, from those who can't afford a Chiclet to those who could ransom the whole city. Don't miss it.

The Guelaguetza, famous regional dance of Oaxaca, is performed at Hotel

El Presidente (16) on Friday evenings at 7:00 p.m. During the summer months, folk dances are also performed in the **Teatro Alcala** (mentioned above) and at the hotel Monte Albán. Check at the theater or at the Tourism Office for schedules.

As mentioned above, the **Teatro Macedonio de Alcala** has concerts, dance programs, and the like all year long. Schedules are posted by the front doors of the theater, located at Independencia and Armenta y López. The **Casa de la Cultura (29),** corner of Colón and G. Ortega, offers exhibits, lectures, films, and various art and music classes. Anyone staying in Oaxaca for some length of time should certainly check it out.

Cine Oaxaca is on Calle Morelos two blocks south of the zócalo; **Cine Mitla** is east of the plaza on G. Vigil.

The **Cinema Ariel 2000** is new, clean, and modern; films change every two or three days. Look for it at the corner of Juárez and Liceaga (that's the continuation of Berriozabal, six blocks north of the Plaza Principal).

On my last visit, Oaxaca's hottest disco was the one in the **Hotel Victoria (14),** on the Cerro del Fortin northwest of the center of town (tel. 5-2633). You'll need a taxi to reach it, however.

SIDE TRIPS FROM OAXACA:
Monte Albán and Mitla are the two most important archeological sites near Oaxaca, but there are several smaller ruins that are also interesting, so I have included a word about them too. Following this I mention a few day trips to the more interesting villages outside Oaxaca. (For Puerto Escondido, see Chapter III.) If you don't have a car, you can get to any of these places by taking a bus, the information for which will be given under the individual headings. It is also possible to hire a taxi. The rates are fixed and printed on the board for all to see and if you get a party together (cabs will take five people), it can work out cheaply. The trip to Monte Albán, about six miles outside the city, will cost 1,500 pesos ($3) by cab; to Mitla, 3,500 pesos ($7).

Monte Albán
Autobuses Turisticos at the Hotel Meson del Angel (7), Mina 518 at Mier y Teran, runs three daily buses to Monte Albán, leaving at 9:30 and 11:30 a.m., 12:30 and 3:45 p.m. Return service runs at noon, 2, 4, and 5:45 p.m. Round-trip fare is 500 pesos ($1)—you must choose a return time when you buy your ticket —and it's a 15-minute ride. Admission to the ruins is 50 pesos (10¢), 25 pesos (5¢) on Sunday.

Monte Albán is a beautiful ancient city dating from 1500 B.C. to A.D. 1400, almost 3,000 years of occupation. This site was first inhabited by Olmecan descendants who used this as a "city of the gods." What is left from this period are the Danzantes friezes, which are believed by Mario Perez Ramirez, in his book *El Enigma del Arte Hispanica,* to indicate the beginning of pre-Hispanic medicine. He thinks that Monte Albán at this time was used as a medical center to study pathological conditions.

The Zapotecs began to build their ceremonial center in 500 B.C. Later on, this site was used by the invading Mixtecs who came into the valley of Oaxaca from the west in the 11th century. Most of the excavated ruins represent the Zapotec culture, as the Mixtecs did little building; rather, they just occupied what was left of the abandoned city. It is thought that Monte Albán was an elite center of Zapotec merchants and artists, who were greatly influenced by contemporary cultures outside of the valley of Mexico. You can see a resemblance to Mayan art in many of the masks and sculptures. When Monte Albán was at its zenith in A.D. 300, Teotihuacán was the most influential city; you can see borrowed ideas from that site in the architecture of the Zapotecs.

The site of Monte Albán is about 40 square kilometers centered on the Great Plaza, a large grassy area that was once a mountaintop that was flattened by the Zapotecs in 600 B.C. From this plaza, aligned north-south, you can overlook the luxuriant green land of the Oaxacan valley, a gorgeous setting for any civilization. The excavations at Monte Albán have revealed some 170 tombs, numerous ceremonial altars, stelae, pyramids, and palaces.

Begin on the eastern side of the Great Plaza where the I-shaped ball court is. This ball court differs slightly from Mayan and Toltec ball courts in that there are no goal rings and the sides of the court are sloped. Also on the east side of the plaza are several altars and pyramids constructed with ocher stone that was once covered with stucco. Note the sloping walls and the wide stairs and ramps which are typical of Zapotec architecture and resemble the architecture of Teotihuacán. The building slightly out of line with the plaza (not on the north-south axis) is thought to be the observatory and was probably aligned with the heavenly bodies rather than with the points of the compass.

The south side of the plaza has a large platform that bore several stelae, most of which are now in the Museum of Anthropology in Mexico City. There is a good view of the surrounding area from the top of this platform.

The west side has more ceremonial platforms and pyramids. On top of the pyramid substructure are four columns that probably held the roof of the temple at one time.

The famous building of the Dancers (Danzantes) is on the west side of the plaza. This is the earliest structure at Monte Albán, dating back to around 800 B.C., perhaps a little later. This building is covered with large stone slabs carved into distorted, naked figures. There is speculation as to who carved these figures and what they represent. There is certainly a distinct resemblance to the Olmec "baby faces" seen at La Venta. The distorted bodies and pained expressions of the faces perhaps imply disease. There are clear examples of figures representing childbirth, dwarfism, and infantilism. Because of the fluidity of the figures, they became known as the Danzantes, but this is only a modern label for these ancient and mysterious carvings.

The Northern Platform is a maze of temples and palaces interwoven with subterranean tunnels and sanctuaries. Wander around here, for there are numerous reliefs, glyphs, paintings, and friezes along the lintels and jams as well as the walls.

Leaving the Great Plaza, head north to the cemetery and tombs. Of the 170 tombs so far excavated the most famous is Tomb 7, to the east of the cemetery. Inside were found some 500 pieces of gold, amber, and turquoise jewelry as well as silver, alabaster, and bone art objects—a most amazing collection, which is now housed in the Regional Museum of Oaxaca.

If you have more than one day to spend at Monte Albán, be sure to visit some of the tombs, for they contain some really magnificent glyphs, paintings, and stone carvings of gods, goddesses, birds, and serpents. Two of the tombs that are especially absorbing, tombs 104 and 105, are now locked and inaccessible.

A new museum, a shop selling guidebooks to the ruins, and a crafts shop now serve visitors to Monte Albán. The guidebook to this site is well worth purchasing.

Mitla, with a Stop at Santa Maria del Tule

The **Fletes y Pasajes** bus line **(32)** (tel. 951/6-5824), located in the second-class terminal, five blocks west of the Plaza Principal on Aldama, across the railroad tracks, runs buses every 20 minutes from 6 a.m. to 8 p.m. to and from Mitla. The trip takes an hour and 15 minutes and costs 622.6 pesos ($1.25) round trip. En route you can visit the famous El Tule tree, eight miles outside of Oaxaca. Bring your flashlight—there are some tunnels at Mitla.

Santa Maria del Tule is a small town that appears to be filled with turkeys, children, and rug vendors. This town is famous for the immense ahuehuete tree (water cypress) in a churchyard just off the main road. Some idea of the size of this 2,000-year-old tree can be gained by the fact that it takes about 33 seconds just to walk around it! Unfortunately, there is now a fence around the tree that will keep you from timing it yourself—as if a tree that has survived 2,000 years needs protection! This tree is still growing today, as is evidenced by the foliage, and will likely continue to do so as long as the water level remains high. This whole region around Santa Maria del Tule was once very marshy; in fact, the word *tule* means reed.

Beside the tree is a small stall selling refreshments, postcards, Mitla rugs, and some of the famous black pottery of the region.

Beyond El Tule is agricultural country, and at siesta time you'll see whole families sitting in the shade of giant cacti resting from the day's work. Mexican farmers and their wives don't bother with babysitters; they take the kids with them into the fields.

It's 22 miles farther southeast to Mitla. The turnoff comes at a very obvious fork in the road.

The road to **Mitla,** which stretches for 2¾ miles from the highway, eventually terminates in the dusty town square. If you've come here by bus, it's only half a mile up the road to the ruins; if you want to hire a cab, there are some available in the square. You'll probably find the drivers anxious to act as guides, and that isn't a bad idea, if you can fix a suitable price in advance. Admission to the ruins is 50 pesos (10¢), 25 pesos (5¢) on Sunday and holidays. The ruins are open every day from 9 a.m. to 5 p.m.

Mitla was contemporary with Monte Albán, being settled by the Zapotecs as early as 800 B.C. However, it never reached the excellence that Monte Albán did during the Classic period. In fact, it wasn't until after the Zapotecs had abandoned Mitla (in A.D. 900) and the Mixtec tribe from the west had arrived (in the late 10th century) that the city began to flourish. This city of the Mixtecs was still flourishing at the time of the Spanish Conquest, and many of the buildings were used through the 16th century.

Mixtec architecture is based on a quadrangle surrounded on three or four sides by patios and chambers, usually rectangular in shape. The chambers are provided with a low roof, which is excellent for defense but which makes the rooms dark and close. The buildings are constructed of stone, covered with mud, and inlaid with small stones cut in geometric patterns. It has been estimated that there are over 100,000 pieces used in the mosaics at Mitla.

There are five groups of buildings divided by the Mitla River. The most important buildings are on the east side of the ravine. The Group of the Columns consisted of two quadrangles, connected at the corners with palaces fronting on the rectangles. The building to the north has a long chamber with six columns and numerous rooms decorated with geometric designs. The most common motif is the zigzag pattern, the same one seen repeatedly on the Mitla blankets. It's uncommon to find human or animal depictions in Mixtec art; in fact, there is only one surviving frieze left at Mitla, and this is found in the Group of the Church, in the north patio. Here, you'll see a series of figures painted with their name glyphs.

Mitla is not a very large site and you can easily see the most important buildings in an hour or so. You might spend the rest of your day seeing Yaagul or Tlacolula. (See below for more information.)

Outside the ruins you will be bombarded by vendors. The moment you step out of a car or taxi, every able-bodied woman and child for ten miles around comes charging over with shrill cries and a basket full of bargains. Heavily embroidered belts, small pieces of pottery, ungenuine archeological relics, cheap earrings—all may be picked up invariably for half the price at which they are originally offered. By the way, prices are lower in town than in the modern handcrafts market near the ruins.

In the town of Mitla, the University of the Americas maintains a small museum which contains some Zapotec and Mixtec relics. Admission is a few pesos. Next door to the museum is the delightful **Posada La Sorpresa,** Avenida Independencia no. 40 (tel. 4), an old hacienda with six rooms, which rent from 1,200 pesos ($2.40) single, 2,100 pesos ($4.20) double. The restaurant serves breakfast and a comida daily. The Posada La Sorpresa is not a good late-afternoon gamble as it is frequently filled with students.

Another thing you'll notice in the town of Mitla, and out on the highway going south, are "expendios de mezcal," actually "factory outlets" for little distilleries that produce the fiery cactus *aguardiente*. To be authentic, a bottle of mezcal must have a worm floating in it—presumably in a highly advanced state of alcoholic bliss. The liquor is surprisingly cheap, the bottle labels are surprisingly colorful, and the taste is astoundingly horrible. But mix a shot of mezcal with a glass of grapefruit or pomegranate juice, and you've got a cocktail that will make you forget the heat, even in Mitla (remember that worm!).

Yaagul, Dainzu, and Zaachila

Yaagul is about 20 miles southeast of Oaxaca on the road to Mitla. There is a small sign indicating the turnoff to the left (a dirt road, but fairly good). This was a fortress city on a small hill overlooking the valley. The setting is absolutely gorgeous, and although the ruins are not nearly as magnificent as Monte Albán, there is still a lot that is of interest. (Admission is a few pesos.)

The city was divided into two sections: the fortress on the hill, and the area of palaces lower down the hill. The center of the palace complex is the plaza, surrounded by four temples. In the center is a ceremonial platform, under which is what's known as the Triple Tomb. The door of the tomb is a large stone slab decorated on both sides with beautiful hieroglyphs.

Look for the beautifully restored ball court, typical of Zapotec ball courts (which are without goal rings). North of the plaza is the incredible palace structure built for the chiefs of the city, a maze of huge rooms off six patios, decorated with painted stucco and stone mosaics. Here and there you can see ceremonial mounds and tombs decorated in the same geometric meanderings that are found in Mitla. This is one of the most interesting palace structures in Oaxaca.

The view from the fortress is worth the rather exhausting climb: it offers a whole panorama of the Oaxaca valley.

Dainzu, which is a more recently excavated site, is not terribly interesting to the layman because very little restoration has been done on the buildings. A caretaker on the premises will be happy to show you some of the more interesting points; he has a storeroom of relics unearthed during the excavation that are fascinating: massive stone carvings that resemble the Danzante carvings seen in Monte Albán. Admission is a few pesos. The site is located on a dirt road heading southwest from the highway (190) to Tehuantepec. Sixteen miles from Oaxaca, look for the turnoff to Teotitlán. Almost directly across the road will be an unmarked dirt road that will take you to Dainzu, approximately four miles in from Hwy. 190.

Zaachila, at the time of the Spanish Conquest, was the last surviving city of the Zapotec rulers. When Cortés marched on their city, they did not resist and instead formed an alliance with him, which outraged the Mixtecs, who invaded

Zaachila shortly after. Only a few pyramids and mounds plus some very interesting tombs of the Zapotecs and Mixtecs remain. These can be visited from 9 a.m. to 1 p.m. and 2 to 6 p.m. daily. Several of the tombs have been cleared of rubble, but the buried have been left as they were found. The tombs are elaborately decorated with mosaics and carved figures. You'll find the tombs and the pyramids near the church in the main plaza of the town of Zaachila. Most of the art objects found in the tombs have been moved to the Museum of Anthropology in Mexico City.

Zaachila is located 12 miles southwest of Oaxaca. You might want to plan your trip to Zaachila on a Thursday, since this is market day, and to stop in Cuilapam, a nearby village which has a 16th-century Dominican monastery.

Some Interesting Village Side Trips

Gueletao is a wonderful town about 65 kilometers north of Oaxaca. It's the birthplace of Benito Juárez, and there's a beautiful monument in his honor. The town is situated in the mountains, and the scenery from Oaxaca to Gueletao makes it well worth the trip.

Cuilapam is located about seven miles southwest of Oaxaca. Follow the road out of town that goes to Monte Albán, take the left fork after crossing the Atoyac River, and follow the signs to Cuilapam. Here, the Dominican friars built their second monastery in 1555. Parts of the convent and church were never completed, because of financial problems. The roof of the monastery has fallen, but the cloister remains, as does that portion of the church that was finished and later restored. The church is still used today. There are three naves with lofty arches and large stone columns plus many frescoes.

Tlacolula is 32 kilometers from Oaxaca southeast on the road to Tehuantepec. It is famous for its Dominican chapel, which is considered by many to be the most beautiful of the Dominican churches in the Americas. Note the wrought-iron gates, choir loft, and bannisters of the pulpit, plus the frescoes and paintings in relief. A few years ago a secret passage was found, leading to a room that contained valuable silver religious pieces. The silver had been hidden during the Revolution of 1916 when there was a tide of anti-religious sentiment; the articles are now back in place in the church. Sunday is market day in Tlacolula.

READER'S MOTEL SELECTION IN ARRIAGA: "A very complete and comfortable motel at Arriaga, on the road from Oaxaca to Tapachula, is **El Parador** (tel. 966/2-0135). Although it is not inexpensive, doubles cost 10,500 pesos ($21), it has a swimming pool and restaurant and can be a lifesaver for those following this route" (Mrs. R. E. Maret, Calgary, Alberta, Canada).

4. Tehuantepec

From Oaxaca to Tehuantepec is a comparatively short trip of 155 miles, but a fairly arduous one if you're driving, since you'll have to negotiate dozens of S-turns and innumerable climbs and descents.

The first thing you'll notice about Tehuantepec (alt. 200 feet; pop. 102,000) is that it's hot and the women wear long trailing skirts with heavy velvet embroidered huipils. I can't figure it out! The town of Tehuantepec itself has very little to offer, and I wouldn't recommend that anybody stay there. Should you want to surprise your wife or girlfriend with one of those magnificent Tehuana costumes, they're sometimes obtainable in the market. Although beautiful, a full-length skirt seems the last thing one would want to wear in this humid heat.

The oil boom in Tabasco and Chiapas has had its spinoffs here in Tehuantepec, most notably out on the highway past the Pemex station on the way to Tuxtla Gutierrez. Here the formerly dowdy **Hotel Calli** (or Cally; tel. 971/5-0085) has had an incredible facelift, its air-conditioned but fly-blown rooms having been superseded by a spiffy new addition à la Conrad Hilton. Part of the old hotel has been turned into a restaurant, and the new addition positively shines, keeping its air-conditioned cool. But you pay to escape Tehuantepec's mugginess: singles are 6,325 pesos ($12.65); doubles, 7,878 pesos ($15.16); triples, 10,120 pesos ($20.24). Outrageous for Tehuantepec? Not for the oilfield foremen, bank vice-presidents, and Pemex executives driving from the capital to the oil regions.

Tehuantepec's hotels and restaurants have, as you will see, little to offer, and you might be best advised to move on to your next destination if possible. It is a long haul to San Cristóbal de las Casas, or Palenque, or Veracruz if you leave from Oaxaca. Consider it, though. An alternative overnight stop can be made in Acayucan, at the northern end of Hwy. 185 near the Gulf Coast, if you're off to Villahermosa, Palenque, and the Yucatán. See Chapter XIV for details.

READER'S HOTEL SELECTIONS—TEHUANTEPEC AND JUCHITÁN: "You will find the **Posada Colonial** (tel. 5-0353) just across the railroad tracks from the main plaza, in the first block from the main highway. It's all bright and clean, 1,500 pesos ($3.00) per person, single or double room, with fans and bath. There is no real office so inquire for rooms at the desk in the restaurant downstairs. By the way, the Hotel Calli won't accept traveler's checks—you have to pay in cash (and plenty of it!).

"There is a new hotel at Juchitán, the **Hotel La Mansion** (tel. 941/2-1055), on the main road into town about two blocks from the highway; official address is Prolongacion de 16 de Septiembre no. 11. Rooms are 4,485 pesos ($8.97) single, 5,635 pesos ($11.27) double, and 6,727 pesos ($13.45) triple; there's a walled parking lot, a third-floor restaurant, an elevator, ladies' bar, and a whole lot of door hinges installed wrong. The owner's kid got a bang out of waiting until the elevator started down, then running down the stairs and pushing the button at each floor so that the passengers got the milk run with lots of stops. It must be the first elevator in town" (Rodolphe de Mordaigle, Pacific Palisades, Calif.).

READERS' HOTEL SELECTION—SALINA CRUZ: "They told us that Salina Cruz is a rather dull port city, but even if there is nothing to see, it is at least full of lively and original Mexican daily life. We spent a night in the **Hotel Guasti** (tel. 971/4-0755), Calle Guaymas 24, in the center, two blocks from the first-class bus station, in a big clean room with tile shower and fan; 3,500 pesos ($7) per night, tax included" (Verena Baumgartner and Markus Vogel, Zollickerberg, Switzerland).

Chapter XIV

THE ISTHMUS AND CHIAPAS

1. Acayucan
2. Villahermosa
3. Palenque
4. Tuxtla Gutierrez
5. San Cristóbal de las Casas
6. Tapachula

THE ISTHMUS OF TEHUANTEPEC occupies an interesting place in Mexican history, for it was across this narrow, flat band of land that a railroad was built and operated by an American firm before the opening of the Panama Canal. Tehuantepec was to be the site of the Atlantic-Pacific canal at one time, but the choice finally fell on Panama, and once the canal was opened, all the trade that had crossed at Tehuantepec switched to the Panama route (the earliest route had been all the way around South America) and Tehuantepec fell back into the muggy torpor it had known previously.

Just east of the isthmus are the states of Tabasco (on the gulf) and Chiapas (on the Pacific). Three routes traverse this area to take you into Mesoamerica, the Maya homeland; to the north, Hwy. 180/186 comes from Veracruz and Lake Catemaco past Acayucan to Villahermosa, capital of the state of Tabasco, and then to the fabulous Maya ruins at Palenque before heading for the Yucatán (see Chapters XV and XVI); Hwy. 190 comes from Oaxaca past the town of Tehuantepec (see Chapter XIII), meets the transisthmian highway, and then climbs into the mountains (where it's cool!) to Tuxtla Gutierrez and San Cristóbal de las Casas before going down to the Guatemalan border; and Hwy. 200 heads southeast to Tapachula and the Guatemalan border on the Pacific Slope. Going through the isthmus straight to the Yucatán you'll want to take the first of these routes; if you plan to go to Guatemala, take the second route; if you're in a great hurry to get to Guatemala City and don't care about scenery or keeping cool, take the third route, via Tapachula.

It's a longish drive, and an even longer bus trip (about nine or ten hours) to cover the 300 miles (500 kilometers) from Veracruz to Villahermosa in a day, but I recommend doing it if you have the stamina as it's hot, muggy, and uninteresting in the low-lying isthmus. For those who want to stop over I've included some tips on the way-station town of Acayucan.

From Oaxaca there are seven buses a day to Tehuantepec, three buses a day to Tuxtla Gutierrez, and one bus that takes you all the way to San Cristóbal and even farther on to the Guatemalan border. The trip to Tehuantepec takes about four to five hours, to Tuxtla another four to five, and to San Cristóbal another two hours. Unless you can't stand long bus rides, I'd recommend that you take the bus straight to San Cristóbal. All these buses belong to either the Cristóbal Colón or A.D.O. lines. It's best to reserve a day in advance for all bus travel in Mexico.

Those driving can do the trip a bit faster, but not much, for most of the road is winding, although fairly good and all paved. Luckily, you can zoom through the isthmus over flat, straight roads at high speed. Plan at least ten hours if you intend to go straight from Oaxaca to San Cristóbal.

These days you can expect to be held up for a half hour or so in the bridge-traffic at Coatzacoalcos, and after that, the traffic on Hwy. 180 to Villahermosa will be pretty heavy.

Several readers have written to report that train travel east of the isthmus (that is, beyond Veracruz) is slow, uncomfortable, and dangerous. Take buses here and in Yucatán, not trains.

1. Acayucan

The city of Acayucan (pronounced "Ah-ka-*yoo*-kan"; pop. 100,000), Veracruz, at the intersection of Hwys. 180 and 185, is a pleasant emergency stop during a long drive. At the center of town, a small but beautiful main plaza has as its centerpiece a Spanish gazebo with Chinese overtones; the plaza abounds in shrubs and trees.

Besides being pleasant and manageable, Acayucan has another advantage: rooms are often still available here when the oil-boom towns of Coatzacoalcos and Villahermosa are brim-full of visitors, with not a hotel room to be had (this happens very frequently in summer). Although Lake Catemaco is a much nicer place to stay, if you plan a stop in Acayucan, you will be able easily to make it to Palenque, Oaxaca, or Veracruz the next day.

The **Hotel Joalicia,** just off the main plaza at Zaragoza 4 (tel. 924/5-0877), is used to receiving lots of one-night guests because it has served as a way station on Hwy. 180 since it was built a few years ago. It's Acayucan's best budget hotel, and can usually offer you a choice of rooms, with fans or air conditioners, at 1,495 pesos ($2.99) single and 2,242.5 pesos ($4.49) double with shower and fan, or 2,530 pesos ($5.06) single or double with shower and air conditioner. Besides the 42 rooms, the Joalicia has an elevator and a garage, and also a bright and modern little restaurant off the lobby. Many of the meat and chicken entrees cost 700 to 900 pesos ($1.40 to $1.80). A four-course comida costs 600 pesos ($1.20). For postprandial coffee, an espresso machine (out here in the wilderness!) stands ready to hand.

Directly across the plaza from the Joalicia is the **Hotel San Miguel** (tel. 924/5-0018), at Avenida Hidalgo 8 (look for the address because all of the tubes are out of the neon sign). Rooms here are plainer and less congenial than at the Joalicia, but are still suitable. Prices are 1,150 pesos ($2.30) single or double in one bed, 1,840 pesos ($3.68) double in two beds. Prices, as you can see, are pre-oil-boom. The restaurant here is good, as well.

The seven-story **Hotel Kinaku,** at Ocampo Sur no. 7 (tel. 924/5-0410), glowers over the much lower buildings of downtown Acayucan as well as the zócalo. The large rooms are air-conditioned, have floral print curtains, and two double beds. The hotel has its own garage and elevator which was not working the day I looked at the hotel; consider this when selecting a room. Singles rent for 5,400 pesos ($10.80) and doubles for 6,750 pesos ($13.50).

The **Restaurant San Miguel** is a virtual air-conditioned oasis on a hot afternoon. Even the fish in the aquarium look content. A generous 600-peso ($1.20) comida corrida is served, with all meats on the à la carte menu at 700 pesos ($1.40) or less and fish and shrimp around 780 pesos ($1.56).

The A.D.O. bus station is about six blocks from the zócalo on Enríquez. If you are walking to the Centro, be sure to ask directions as there are very few street signs. Strolling up Enríquez, be sure to observe some of the eateries along the way like the **Happy Chicken** (Pollo Feliz). I wonder how pleased the chicken is about being cooked.

2. Villahermosa

Villahermosa (pop. 250,000), the capital of the state of Tabasco, is right at the center of Mexico's oil boom, and seems to grow in size visibly every day. From a somewhat dowdy provincial town, the oil wealth has helped transform it into a fairly attractive and obviously prosperous modern city.

The boom has brought difficulties as well, and the major one you'll encounter is a shortage of hotel rooms. This is bad enough, but the upshot of the shortage is that hotels can charge what they want for rooms, and not bother about maintenance or service, and they'll still get customers—the oilmen have to sleep somewhere. When they come in from the fields, they're ready to let loose too. Villahermosa thus has something of a frontier town mood about it.

I'd tell you to whiz by Villahermosa, except that it's a long ride to the next stop, Palenque or San Cristóbal de las Casas, and you really shouldn't miss the fabulous Parque La Venta. Tabasco is where many of the most important Olmec relics were discovered, including the mammoth heads. Parque La Venta holds significant Olmec displays in a beautiful setting, and the beautiful new Regional Museum of Anthropology holds others from all over Mexico.

If you want like anything to avoid the considerable hassle of locating a hotel room here—any hotel room, let alone one that's cheap and decent—there is a way. Take an early bus from wherever you're coming, and when you hit Villahermosa, check the schedules for your onward journey in the bus station. Locate a bus leaving in an hour or two, buy a ticket for it, and then grab a taxi to the Parque La Venta, a short buzz up the highway from the bus station (either first or second class). Allow at least an hour for the park. If there's time to spare, grab another cab to the Museo Regional de Antropología Carlos Pellicer Cámara (open Tuesday through Sunday from 9 a.m. to 8 p.m.; admission 150 pesos, 30¢). Allow a minimum half hour here, and then race back to catch your bus. This is no way to run a vacation, but, then again, hot, muggy, expensive Villahermosa is no place to spend one.

ORIENTATION: The hotels and restaurants I recommend are located off the three main streets running north and south: Madero, Pino Suárez, and the Malecón. Highway 180 skirts the city, so a turn onto Madero or Pino Suárez will take you into the center of town.

Coming in from Villahermosa's new airport, which is 6½ miles east of town, you'll cross a bridge over the Río Grijalva and turn left to reach downtown. The airport minibuses charge 750 pesos ($1.50), whereas a taxi will want a hefty 3,000 pesos ($6) at least.

Your point of focus in town can be the **Plaza de Armas,** or main square, bounded by the streets named Zaragoza, Madero, and Juárez. The plaza is the center of the downtown district, with the Río Grijalva to its west and Hwy. 186 to its north. If Villahermosa can be said to have a main downtown thoroughfare, then it is **Avenida Madero,** running south from Hwy. 186 past the Plaza de Armas to the river, where it intersects with the riverside avenue, the **Malecón.**

The **Central Camionera de Primera Clase** (first-class bus station, sometimes called the **A.D.O. terminal**) is on Avenida Javier Mina. To get to the Plaza de Armas, go out and turn right on Javier Mina, then go left for about six blocks to Avenida Madero. Turn right onto Madero, and the Plaza de Armas is about four blocks along.

The **Central Camionera de Segunda Clase** (second-class bus station) is on Hwy. 180/186 near the traffic circle bearing a statue of a fisherman. Buses marked "Mercado—C. Camionera" leave frequently from the bus station for the center of town.

Villahermosa is attempting to overcome the negative consequences of the oil boom. They have done well: the beautiful park which surrounds the Parque Museo La Venta; Tabasco 2000, with its gleaming office buildings, convention center, golf course, and exclusive residences; the CICOM development with its theaters and the Carlos Pellicer Cámara Regional Museum; the creation of a walking mall along Avenida Benito Juárez. All of this has greatly enhanced the beauty of Villahermosa.

USEFUL FACTS: The **Tourist Office** (tel. 931/2-3171 or 3-5762) has recently relocated to the mall at Juárez no. 111. A large sign in front trumpets TURISMO in green letters; you cannot miss it. The office has an excellent map of the city and an enthusiastic, helpful staff. Hours are 9 a.m. to 3 p.m. and 3:30 to 8 p.m., Monday through Saturday. . . . **Parking** is available underneath the Plaza de Armas for 500 pesos ($1) for 24 hours. Enter on the Avenida Vasquez Norte side of the plaza.

WHERE TO STAY: The area around the intersections of Avenidas Juárez and Lerdo is now one of the best places to stay, for these two streets have been closed to cars and made into pedestrian malls. A modest place here is the **Hotel San Miguel,** Lerdo 315 (tel. 931/2-1500), where 30 rooms have been renovated, each with tile bathrooms and ceiling fans, and going for 2,900 pesos ($5.80) single, 3,350 pesos ($6.70) double with air conditioning. The lobby of the San Mieguel is plain, but graced by one very important appliance: a super-cold water dispenser.

The aforementioned hotel, while adequate, may not be up to what you want after a long, tiring trip, so here are the alternatives. The fanciest place right downtown is the **Hotel Miraflores,** Reforma 304 (tel. 931/2-0054, 2-0486, or 2-0022), a modern establishment of glass, aluminum, and brightly colored plastic furniture equipped with elevator and central air conditioning. Price for all this luxury is high at 6,670 pesos ($13.34) single, 6,900 pesos ($13.80) double, 7,475 pesos ($14.95) triple, but the hotel situation in Villahermosa is not good.

The older **Hotel Manzur,** Madero 14 (tel. 931/2-2566), has older but well-kept accommodations, all air-conditioned of course. A double room here costs 6,095 pesos ($12.19).

Near the Bus Stations

Just off Hwy. 186, not far from the first- and second-class bus stations, is the **Hotel Ritz,** Avenida Madero 1013, one block in from the highway (tel. 931/2-1836). Its three modern stories hold 40 good rooms at 4,313 pesos ($8.63) single, 4,859 pesos ($9.72) double, all rooms with their own window air conditioner. While it's a block off the highway, the Ritz is not subject to any more noise than other Villahermosa hotels. Note, however, that this is not a choice particularly for those arriving late at night by bus—like other hotels in this city, it's almost sure to be full by early evening, at the latest.

High-Budget Motels

The **Hotel Villahermosa Viva** (tel. 931/2-5555), the **Hotel Maya Tabasco** (tel. 931/2-1111), and other luxurious establishments on Hwy. 180/186 will put you up if you can find no other place to stay, but it will cost you dearly: plan on spending in the range of 12,167 pesos ($24.34) for a very posh air-conditioned double. Another high-comfort, high-cost hostelry is the new **Exelaris Hyatt Regency Villahermosa** (tel. 931/3-4444), with double rooms going for 17,854 pesos ($35.71).

READER'S HOTEL SELECTION: "I would recommend **Choco's Hotel,** Avenida Constitución at Lino Merino (tel. 931/2-9444 or 2-9649). A double room cost us 9,625 pesos ($19.25). For that price we had a nice if smallish room with bathroom, air conditioning, and elevator. The restaurant provided decent food at reasonable prices. The hotel staff was extremely helpful and cheerful. I certainly would recommend it as an alternative to grim budget or very expensive luxury hotels" (Marie-Caroline Sainpy, New York, N.Y.).

WHERE TO EAT: The **Restaurant Los Pepes** (tel. 2-0154), Madero 610, near the Plaza de Armas, is probably the cleanest of Villahermosa's open cafés, and highly recommended by the townspeople. Each of the tables is covered in colorful placements, it's fairly cool with large ceiling fans. Almost every dish here costs between 800 to 1,300 pesos ($1.60 to $2.60), for liver, pork chops, chicken, shrimp, and the menu is fairly extensive. One of the tastiest dishes is the filet tampiqueño at 1,300 pesos ($2.60), but starvation-budget devotees might stick to the turkey tamales—you get three good-size ones for 400 pesos (80¢). Open daily 7 a.m. to 11 p.m.; closed Sunday.

PARQUE MUSEO LA VENTA: This is a lovely outdoor museum park located outside Villahermosa on Rte. 180 (take Paseo Tabasco northeast to Hwy. 180, turn right, and it's less than a mile on your right, next to the Exposition Park). As you walk through on a self-guided tour you'll see Olmec relics, sculptures, mosaics, a mockup of the original La Venta, and of course the colossal Olmec heads. These heads were carved around 1000 B.C., are 6½ feet high, and weigh around 40 tons. The faces seem to be half-adult, half-infantile with that fleshy "jaguar mouth" that is characteristic of Olmecan art. Even stranger is the fact that the basalt, for carving, had to be transported from the nearest source, which was over 70 miles from La Venta! A total of 13 heads has been found: five at La Venta, six at San Lorenzo, one at Tres Zapotes, and one at Santiago Tuxtla—all cities of the Olmecs. On your tour through the park, notice the fine stone sculptures and artistic achievements of the Olmecs, who set forth the first art style in Mesoamerica. Their exquisite figurines in jade and serpentine, which can be seen in the Regional Museum of Anthropology, far excelled any other craft of this period.

La Venta, by the way, was one of three major Olmec cities during the pre-Classic period (2000 B.C. to A.D. 300). The ruins were discovered in 1938, and there in the tall grasses were the mammoth heads. Today all that remains of the once-impressive city are some grass-covered mounds—once pyramids—some 84 miles west of Villahermosa. All of the gigantic heads have been moved from the site. You'll see three heads in Parque La Venta.

Parque Museo La Venta is open from 8 a.m. to 5 p.m. every day; admission is 40 pesos (8¢) to nonresidents, 20 pesos (4¢) to residents.

REGIONAL MUSEUM OF ANTHROPOLOGY: Tabasco's shiny new Museo Regional de Antropología Carlos Pellicer Cámara was opened in February 1980 to replace the older Tabasco Museum. The new museum is architecturally bold and attractive, and very well organized inside. There is more space and therefore the number of pre-Hispanic artifacts on display has greatly increased to include not only the Tabascan finds (Totonac, Zapotec, and Olmec), but the rest of the Mexican and Central American cultures as well.

The museum is beautiful, with parquet floors, wood dividers, and numerous plants. There is a very open and airy feeling about this place. Take the elevator to the top of the museum and walk down past large maps showing the Olmec and Mayan lands. Photographs and diagrams make it all easier to comprehend, but the explanatory signs are all in Spanish. Look especially for the figurines that were found in this area and for the colorful *Codex* (an early book of pictographs).

The Regional Museum is a mile south of the center of town, right along the river's west bank, open Tuesday to Sunday from 9 a.m. to 8 p.m.; admission is 150 pesos (30¢).

READER'S SIGHTSEEING SUGGESTION: "I recommend a visit to the **ruins of Comalcalco,** where you can see a very nice pyramid similar to the ones at Zempoala, Veracruz. It is easy to reach with the buses going to Paraíso, then about 15 minutes (one kilometer) on foot" (Walter Dufour, Brussels, Belgium).

GETTING OUT OF VILLAHERMOSA: If you're driving, you already know how you're going to get out of town. If not, you have two choices.

By Air

Mexicana (tel. 931/3-5044), Tabasco 2000: Avenida 4 and Calle 13, has four flights a day to Mexico City. AeroMéxico (tel. 931/2-6991), Periférico Carlos Pellicer 511, has nonstop flights to Cancún, Merida, Mexico City (2), Oaxaca, and Tuxtla Gutierrez every day.

Small regional carriers operate out of Villahermosa's old and new airports, starting up and then going bankrupt at irregular intervals. At the moment, Transporte Aereo de Tabasco (tel. 931/2-1645) flies from the new airport to Tuxtula Gutierrez and Tapachula every midmorning, except Sunday. Aviación de Chiapas has a daily (except Sunday) flight to Tuxtla Gutierrez from the new airport.

By Bus

From the first-class bus station (see above under "Orientation"), **A.D.O.** and Cristóbal Colón buses depart daily for Veracruz, Mexico City, and points along that route, to Oaxaca, and to Merida (18 buses a day) via Campeche.

To Palenque, there are two first-class A.D.O. buses a day, leaving at 8 a.m., and 5:30 p.m., and returning at 12:15 and 5:00 p.m. Buy your reserved-seat ticket as far in advance as possible; fare, 915 pesos ($1.83).

If you take a second-class bus, be sure to ask about arrival times. Sometimes these buses take hours and hours because of all the stops en route.

From Villahermosa to Tuxtla/San Cristóbal

Highway 195 connects the Tabascan capital of Villahermosa with Tuxtla Gutierrez, the capital of the state of Chiapas. Daily Cristóbal Colón buses ply the route from the tropical savannahs into the rugged Chiapan mountains, and the trip takes most of a day. The road is paved all the way, and although curvy and hilly, is fantastically scenic—a real treat.

An alternate route that has recently become practicable is that running between Palenque and San Cristóbal de las Casas, a road that as yet has no highway number. See below in the Palenque section for details on this jungle road.

3. Palenque

Certainly some of the most fascinating and beautiful Mayan ruins are those on the edge of the jungle at Palenque, in the state of Chiapas.

GETTING TO AND FROM PALENQUE: Highway 186 from Villahermosa passes the turnoff to Palenque, and there are daily first-class (A.D.O.) and second-class buses to take you the 90 miles from Villahermosa to the site. (Make sure you tell them *which* Palenque—the town or the Zona Arqueológica—you want a ticket to.) You can return to Villahermosa the same day, or stay overnight in Palenque village, or go on to Campeche and Merida by bus. Buy your tickets in advance.

Important: The trip by first-class bus takes 2½ hours, but it can take almost the whole day to get from Villahermosa to Palenque on a second-class bus. Be sure to ask about arrival times.

From a Pemex station on Hwy. 186, a road turns right and heads for Palenque, 27 kilometers (17 miles) off the main road. First you'll come to Palenque Junction (the railroad station), then a few miles later to a fork in the road—there's an incredibly dramatic statue of a Mayan here, so you can't miss it. Left at the fork takes you a mile or so into Palenque village with its bank, restaurants, hotels, stores, and ice house. A right at the fork takes you past several motels to Palenque ruins. A municipal bus is supposed to run between the town and the ruins every hour on the hour starting at 6 a.m., but in practice it's not very dependable. A taxi costs only about 750 pesos ($1.50), and might just be worth it. "Colectivos," minibuses or sedans, are the best buy, and charge 100 pesos (20¢) per person.

The first-class (A.D.O.) bus station is on the main square, more or less across the street from the Hotel Lacroix. Second-class buses have an office on Avenida Juárez near the Pemex station in town, across the street from the Hotel Avenida and not far from the Mayan statue.

WHERE TO STAY AND EAT: You must decide where you want to stay: at the fork in the road, in the village, or on the road to the ruins. Here are the possibilities, in that order.

Near the Mayan Statue

If you stand staring head-on in rapture (or horror) at the Mayan statue at the fork in the road, just off to your left will be a wooded area, a partially paved road (Calle Merle Green), and three lodging places. First is a camping area, the **Trailer Park Tulipanes,** with full hookups, and rather primitive showers and toilets for 600 pesos ($1.20) per person per night.

Just behind the camping area down Calle Merle Green, also called Calle La Cañada, is the **Hotel Tulipanes** (tel. 934/5-0230), run by the same family as the camping area. The "hotel" is actually several small buildings with very simple but adequate rooms-and-baths renting for 4,000 pesos ($8.00) double. There's a ceiling fan in each room.

Down along the road a bit farther, on the left, is **La Selva** (tel. 5-0363) perhaps the best restaurant in Palenque. Though the restaurant has a thatched roof, this shelters a fairly refined and accommodating place to dine. Main-course dishes such as carne asada (grilled beef) and lomo de cerdo (pork chops) cost only 1,000 pesos ($2). Figure that a full meal will cost twice that amount. Surprise of surprises, La Selva has a very respectable (for Palenque) assortment of Mexican wines. You'll enjoy your meal here. Frequently live music is provided for diners' enjoyment. The rooms you can see from your table are operated by Hotel La Cañada next door.

At the far end of the road, the **Hotel La Cañada** (tel. 934/5-0102), is a group of cottages surrounded by dense woods and thus pretty secluded. Rooms can be a bit musty, but aren't bad. Price is 3,500 pesos ($7) single or 4,500 pesos ($9) double. Rooms 7,8,9, and 10 across the street from the office are particularly good values. Each is equipped with air conditioning and a huge ceramic bathtub. The jungle surrounding the rooms looks like the set of a Tarzan movie. In the quaint dirt-floored restaurant, you can get a tasty supper of chicken tacos or quesadillas, with a cold bottle of beer, for 950 pesos ($1.90); meat entrees cost twice that amount. Near the restaurant, a two-story thatched "club" throbs to disco music. It never seems to be crowded, although it's the ideal setting for a *Night of the Iguana* romance.

Even if you do not stay along Calle Merle Green, a stroll along this shady street is enjoyable. Several interesting shops are busy making and selling quality reproductions of Mayan art.

A short distance back toward Villahermosa—only a half mile from the Maya-statue fork in the road, really—is the **Hotel Tulija** (tel. 934/5-0165), one of Palenque's more modern hotels with air-conditioned rooms going for 3,473 pesos ($6.95) single, 4,168 pesos ($8.34) double, 5,002 pesos ($10.01) triple. The hotel restaurant offers a six-course comida at midday for 1,200 pesos ($2.40), but the large-screen television may be more than one can endure. The hotel has a very nice swimming pool, and they take credit cards. Mailing address, by the way, is Apdo. Postal 57, Palenque, Chiapas, México.

In Palenque Village

The fanciest place to stay in Palenque Village is a bright new mini-hotel called the **Hotel Casa de Pakal** (no phone), on the main street (Avenida Juárez) near the central park. Each of the rather small rooms here comes with a TV set, servi-bar, and piped-in music, plus that blessed air conditioning, for 3,900 pesos ($7.80) single, 4,950 pesos ($9.90) double. The hotel has a fancy restaurant called **El Castellano.**

Very near the Casa de Pakal is the slightly older **Hotel Misol-Ha** (tel. 934/5-0092), with a dozen or so small rooms still well kept. With a ceiling fan, you pay 2,570 pesos ($5.14) single; 3,150 pesos ($6.30), for two people 3,650 pesos ($7.30) with air conditioning. Many readers think this is the best lodging bargain in all Palenque.

A good choice for the starvation-budget reader is the **Hotel Lacroix,** Hidalgo no. 18 (no phone), facing the main square or park (as you come up Avenida Juárez into the center of town, turn left at the park, then right, and the hotel is down a block on the left-hand side, opposite the church). Darkish and simple rooms are kept cool by shady trees, fans, and breezes, and each opens onto a cool veranda overlooking lush gardens of palms and banana plants. Primitive murals decorate the place, and prices are low: 2,500 pesos ($5) single or double. As you might imagine, the eight-room Lacroix is often full-up.

The **Hotel Vaca Vieja,** Avenida Cinco de Mayo no. 42 at the corner of Calle de Chiapas (tel. 934/5-0377), is one of Palenque's newer hotels. A small, modern 12-room place on the far side of the park (walk around the park and past the big old Hotel Palenque), it is one of Palenque's best places to stay. Each room has a fan and nice tile shower and is immaculate. A little restaurant on the ground floor provides breakfast and dinner. The price is a reasonable 2,750 pesos ($5.50) single, 3,440 pesos ($6.88) double. There's only one mystery about this place: how did it get the name "old cow"?

On the other side of the church from the Lacroix is Palenque's oldest hotel, the **Hotel Palenque,** Avenida Cinco de Mayo no. 15 (tel. 934/5-0188). It has had its ups and downs over the years; currently it seems to be up, because of the increased competition from newer hotels. Some of the Hotel Palenque's ancient rooms have been redeemed with paint, paper, and air conditioners, and the courtyard garden can be pleasant enough, but be sure you *inspect your room* before you take it—this is an "iffy" place. Rates are 3,284 pesos ($6.57) single, 4,200 pesos ($8.40) double, 4,996 pesos ($9.96) triple, with air conditioning and private shower. Thirty new rooms are being added along the courtyard and may be completed soon.

Village Restaurants: Downtown Palenque's restaurants are located near the central park. The **Restaurant Maya,** on the park near the Correos (post office), is breezy, open, and family run, but tends to be expensive for what you get: midday comida for 800 pesos ($1.60); entrees, 650 to 990 pesos ($1.30 to $1.98).

Next door to the Maya is the **Restaurant Nicté-Ha,** less cool but with advantages of its own: more food for less money—main courses for about 400 to 700 pesos (80¢ to $1.40), or a choice of two daily specials for 700 pesos ($1.40). The dishes seem to be about the same in both places, so choose on the basis of coolness, attractiveness, and price.

On the Road to Palenque Ruins

Closest hotel to the ruins is actually a motel-style place named the **Hotel Las Ruinas** (tel. 934/5-0352), Monday through Friday, 4 to 7 p.m.), Apdo. Postal 49 (that's the mailing address), operated by a friendly gentleman named Prof. Ismael Corzo. A nice swimming pool serves as the motel's centerpiece; 32 rooms are arranged around it, all modern, bathroom-equipped, and all with ceiling fans for 4,000 pesos ($8) single, 5,000 pesos ($10) double. Here you're only a half mile from the ruins.

Two camping areas are near the ruins, on the left-hand side of the road as you head out from town. The first one is very plain, simple, and cheap, but somewhat unappealing. You'd do better to continue to the next one, **Camping Mayabell,** within the grounds of the National Park. Here you're only two kilometers from the ruins proper, accessible by colectivo or on foot (about 30 minutes). Mayabell has hookups, showers, and palapas in which to hang your hammock. The price is 300 pesos (60¢) per person.

I'll mention the prices for rooms at the 18-room **Chan-Kah** (no phone), at km. 31 on the road to the ruins (2.5 miles from them), because you'll wonder what they are if I don't tell you. The very nicely done little bungalows, made of wood and stone, rustic but at the same time modern and comfortable, are fitted with ceiling fans and cost 11,500 pesos ($23) double. They're nice, but that's a lot to pay.

Last of all, the **Motel Nututum** (or Nututun; tel. 934/5-0100) is about three kilometers (two miles) from the Mayan statue along the road to the ruins, and then left on the road through the jungle to Ocosingo, Agua Azul, and San Cristóbal. The setting is beautiful, right on the Río Usumacinta, which provides excellent swimming in the cool river waters. The 40 air-conditioned rooms are huge, each with two double beds. The tiled rooms have large closets, bathtub, and shower. Although prices are in the splurge category, swimming in the river after a hot day at the ruins may be worth it. Singles cost 7,556 pesos ($15.11), doubles 9,143 pesos ($18.29), and triples 10,730 pesos ($21.46). You can camp on the riverbank with your own equipment for 2,000 pesos ($4) per person. The hotel restaurant is a bit expensive for what you get; most meals cost 1,500 to 3,000 pesos ($3 to $6), breakfasts cost 1,000 pesos ($2). The colectivo will take you to the ruins from the hotel for 100 pesos (20¢).

PALENQUE RUINS: Palenque, now protected in the Parque Nacional Palenque, is one of the most spectacular of the Maya ruins with its roof-combed temples ensconced in lush vegetation high above the savannahs. It was a ceremonial center for the high priests during the Classic period (A.D. 300–900), with the peak of its civilization being somewhere around A.D. 600–700. Pottery found during the excavations shows that there was a very early, Preclassic people living here as early as 300 B.C. Alberto Ruíz Lhuillier, the archeologist who directed some of the explorations, states that because of "the style of its structures, its hieroglyphic inscriptions, its sculptures, its works in stucco and its pottery, Palenque undoubtedly fell within the great Maya culture. Yet its artistic expressions have a character all their own which is evident in the absolute mastery of craftsmanship, turning the art of Palenque into the most refined of Indian America."

As you enter the ruins, the building to the right is the Temple of the Inscriptions, named for the great stone hieroglyphic panels found inside (most of them are now in the Archeological Museum in Mexico City) and famous for the tomb, or Crypt of Pacal, that was discovered in its depths in 1949. It took four seasons of digging to clear out the rubble that was put there by the Mayas to conceal the crypt. The crypt itself is some 80 feet below the floor of the temple and was covered by a monolithic sepulchral slab ten feet long and seven feet wide. You can visit the tomb, and so long as you're not a claustrophobe, you shouldn't miss it. The way down is lighted, but the steps can be slippery due to condensed humidity—watch it! This is the only such temple-pyramid (resembling the Egyptian pyramids) in the Americas!

Besides the Temple of the Inscriptions, there is the Palace with its unique watchtower, the northern group (Temple of the Count and Ball Court) and the group of temples beyond the Palace (Temple of the Sun, Temple of the Foliated Cross). The official guidebook has a detailed description of this site and is well worth the money. (For a summary of pre-Columbian history, see the Introduction of the book you're now reading.) A licensed guide will charge about 3,500 to 4,000 pesos ($7 to $8) for a two-hour tour.

Plan to spend a whole day in these wonderful surroundings. When you're tired of looking at ruins, grab your bathing suit and head for the gorgeous stream and falls near the tiny museum at the end of the dirt track that goes past the "Grupo del Norte" complex of structures. A sign by the stream informs you (in Spanish) that there is no bathing allowed, but downstream a ways is a large pool out of view.

The small museum (open 3 to 5 p.m.) has a chronological chart of Maya history, and a modest collection of votive figurines, pieces of statuary, and stones with calendar glyphs. Entrance is free once you have paid for access to the park. Be sure you save your ticket.

The Palenque ruins are open from 8 a.m. to 5 p.m., although the crypt closes at 4 p.m. The entrance fee to the National Park is 50 pesos (10¢), on Sunday 25 pesos (5¢) and it will cost you another 25 to 50 pesos (5¢ to 10¢) to park your car. By the way, a quarter mile back toward town from the parking lot, on the right-hand side (as you approach from town) is a path leading into the Cascada Motiepa, a cool, beautiful waterfall good for cooling the feet and resting the soul. Watch the mosquitos, though.

READER'S SIGHTSEEING TIP—GUIDES: "Guides at the **Zona Arqueológica** get a standard 3,500 ($10) for a two- or three-hour tour. We had a real winner in Sr. Victor Damas Hernándos. He has 18 years of experience working for the archeologists, and as a guide. He has learned a lot of archeology, and has taught himself English, French, and German" (Dr. Wilber E. Scoville, Oshkosh, Wis.).

A Note on Bonampak

The ruins of Bonampak, southeast of Palenque on the Guatemalan border, were discovered in 1946 and constituted a very important find. Reproductions of the vivid murals found here, deep in the jungle, are on view in the Regional Archeology Museum in Villahermosa. To see the real thing at Bonampak you'll have to hire a small plane to buzz you in, or else hire a sturdy car or Jeep to take you the five hours into the jungle. You can visit nearby Yaxchilán on the same trip. Plan to camp overnight, or go and return in a day.

For airplane charters, try contacting the **Sociedad Cooperativo Transporte Aereo de Tabasco, S.C.L.** (tel. 934/4-0035 or 4-2023), at the little Palenque Airport on the road in from Hwy. 186.

Curiously, it seems easier to arrange charter flights to Bonampak from San Cristóbal de las Casas with Aero Chiapas (tel. 8-0037 in San Cristóbal). The tourist office in San Cristóbal will coordinate the effort as groups of four or nine are most economical. The round-trip fare is approximately $100 U.S. per person, and should include an hour lay-over at Bonampak and two hours at Yaxchilán. If you also land at Agua Azul the rates go up accordingly. It is imperative that all financial matters are agreed upon in advance. Charters leave between 8:30 and 9 a.m., depending on weather conditions. Tickets may be purchased most cheaply directly from the Aero Chiapas office which is located at the airport in San Cristóbal.

Aero Chiapas also flies from San Cristóbal to Palenque for 10,000 pesos ($20.00) one way.

READERS' WARNING—TRAIN DANGER: "A band of robbers operates at La Candelaría, between Palenque and Campeche. They come at 3 a.m., looking for cameras, and they sell them in Campeche, even to the police, who tend to be very corrupt. We heard about four cases of this sort, including ourselves, unfortunately" (Wilma van de Werken and Ben Schippers, Utrecht, Holland).

FROM PALENQUE TO SAN CRISTÓBAL DE LAS CASAS: There are two
ways you can make this trip: by air or by road. Each has its advantages, and each shows you the vivid jungle scenery of Chiapas from a different vantage point.

By Air

Aviación de Chiapas and **Aero Chiapas** share an office on Palenque's main street, Avenida Benito Juárez. The office is equidistant between the park, in the center of town, and the Pemex gas station, on the left-hand side as you come from the Pemex. Here you can sign up for the flight to San Cristóbal. Aero Chiapas (tel. 5-0273 in Palenque) makes the trip three to five times a week for 10,000 pesos ($20.00), one way. Though this is expensive for our budget, you must consider that the views of the rugged Chiapan landscape, its canyons and mountains and rivers, are alone worth the price of the flight. If you can afford this flight, you won't regret it. The Aero Chiapas flights from Palenque to Tuxtla Gutierrez have been discontinued, but flights from Palenque to San Cristóbal, and San Cristóbal to Tuxtla still exist.

By Road

The road between Palenque and San Cristóbal de las Casas is an adventure in jungle scenery, with some fascinating hideaways to discover on the way. The 230-kilometer (143-mile) trip takes four or five hours by car, five or six hours by bus. You may want to spend some time swimming at Misol-Ha or Agua Azul, so perhaps you should leave early in the morning.

Two second-class bus lines serve this route, Autobuses Lacandonia and Autobuses Tuxtla. Look for their ticket offices in Palenque village near the Pemex gas station, across the road from the Hotel Avenida. Buy your ticket the day before your planned departure, if possible. Bus fare is about 1,200 pesos ($2.40).

On the road from Palenque, you pass the Motel Nututum (see above) and then climb into the Chiapan mountains. Your intermediate destination is the town of Ocosingo. Ten kilometers out of Palenque, at a fork in the road, take the right fork for Ocosingo. After 20 kilometers (12½ miles) from Palenque (km. 47 of the official highway marking system), look for signs to **Parque Natural Ejidal Misol-Ha** on the right. A mile down this road, on the grounds of an *ejido* (collective farm), is this heavenly spot. You must pay 200 pesos (40¢) admission or 250 pesos (50¢) per car, then walk down the shady lane to a spot where a stream leaps over a cliff and plunges into a deep, cool pool below. Tall jungle trees cluttered with vines permit a few rays of sun to filter through, but otherwise it's delightfully, refreshingly cool and serene here. You can swim if you like, though there are no changing or shower facilities.

Back on the road, the surface may change from macadam to stabilized dirt now and then, but you will still be able to make good time, except perhaps in the rainy season. Landslides and washouts sometimes slow traffic during the rains.

Sixty-two kilometers from Palenque is the well-marked turnoff, on the right, to **Agua Azul.** From the main road, you must go 4½ kilometers (2¾ miles) on a painfully broken road down the hill into the valley to reach the ejido and the swimming area. You can sometimes hitchhike, but if you're traveling by bus it usually means a walk. The walk down is not so bad; the walk back up, in the jungle heat, after that delightful cooling swim, is torture!

The park at Agua Azul is owned and operated by the ejido. You pass through a little gateway and pay the person on duty an admission fee of 100 pesos (20¢) per person, 250 pesos (50¢) per car. Past the gateway is a parking lot, a shaded snack-and-soft-drink place, and a camping area, charging 250 pesos (50¢) for two.

Behind this paraphernalia of civilization are the falls, a long, broad series of cascades with sunny spots and shady spots perfect for swimming. The water is delightfully cool and is the most striking shade of pale blue (azul) I have ever seen in fresh water. The water turns a slightly milky color during the rainy season but remains oh, so cool. Wander up and down the river, but heed the signs about where to swim—some places are dangerous.

After Agua Azul, it's about an hour's ride (64 kilometers, 40 miles) to Ocosingo, which has a few shops and small restaurants right on the highway. From Ocosingo, you have yet to travel 84 kilometers (52 miles), half of which is unpaved and may be some of the worst road in all of Mexico, to reach the junction with the Pan American Highway (Mexican Hwy. 190). From the junction, it's 7 kilometers (4½ miles) into San Cristóbal.

4. Tuxtla Gutierrez

Tuxtla (alt. 1,838 feet; pop. 300,000) is the boom-town capital of the state of Chiapas, long Mexico's coffee-growing center, but more recently an oil prospector's mecca. The mammoth reserves discovered in this wild, mountainous state several years ago have brought people, business, and wealth to Tuxtla. It's not an unpleasant town, but it's modern, hectic, and business oriented, so you'd best stop here only if necessary, as it offers little in the way of tourist sights.

ORIENTATION: It's a 40-minute ride into town from Tuxtla's new, main airport; driving or coming by bus from Oaxaca or Veracruz, you enter the same way, along Hwy. 190. From Villahermosa or San Cristóbal, you'll enter at the opposite end of town. Either way, you will end up at the big main square, Plaza Civica, with its gleaming white church (note the clockwork figures in the tower!) and modern buildings.

Tuxtla has another airport, a small one called the Aeropuerto Francisco Sarabia, in the suburb of Terán only 15 minutes from the center. You'll fly in here if you take Aviación de Chiapas (downtown office: 4a Calle Poniente and la Avenida Norte; tel. 2-1524).

The street systems bears a note of explanation. The city is divided by two "Central" streets: Calle Central, running north to south; and Avenida Central, running east to west—the main highway is the Avenida Central, also named Boulevard Dominguez (west of downtown). Streets are numbered from these central arteries, with the suffix *norte, sur, oriente,* or *poniente* designating the direction of progress from the central arteries.

The **Tourist Office** (tel. 961/3-3079) is at the western end of town on the Avenida Central (Boulevard Dominguez), just near the Hotel Bonampak Tuxtla, mentioned below.

The Cristóbal Colón bus terminal is at 2a Avenida Norte and 2a Calle Poniente, two blocks west of Calle Central.

WHERE TO STAY AND EAT: As Tuxtla booms, the center of the hotel industry has moved out of town, west to Hwy. 190. As you come in from the airport you'll notice the new motel-style hostelries, all of which charge rates out of our range: the Hotel Flamboyant (it's just that too), the Palace Inn, Hotel Laganja, La Hacienda, and the older Hotel Bonampak Tuxtla.

Those driving can splurge at the **Hotel Bonampak Tuxtla,** Avenida Central, Boulevard Dominguez 180, on the western edge of town (tel. 961/3-2101). The Bonampak's a lavish layout with over 100 rooms, air conditioning, swimming pool, barbershop, beauty parlor, and restaurant. Rooms are not cheap at 5,520 pesos ($11.04) single, 6,900 pesos ($13.80) double, but in booming Tuxtla that's about the norm. The hotel's cafeteria is open from 6 a.m. to midnight (air-conditioned), and has hotcakes, sandwiches, and hot entrees. Prices are better, the food as good, and the air conditioning just as cool at the Flamingo Cafeteria downtown, which is described below.

About your best bet in booming Tuxtla is the older **Gran Hotel Humberto,** very near the plaza at Avenida Central 180 Pte., corner of la Calle Pte. (tel. 961/2-2080). Enter from Avenida Central (the entrance on la Calle is for another—unsuitable—hotel). Over 100 rooms here, with air conditioning, adequate bathrooms, and elevators. The single rooms cost 4,840 pesos ($9.68), double rooms with one bed go for 5,635 pesos ($11.27) and rooms with two beds are 6,727 ($13.45).

The **Flamingo Cafetería** (tel. 2-0922) is the place to eat downtown. Not far from the Plaza Civica, it's modern, air-conditioned, open from 7 a.m. to 11 p.m., and features a wide selection of dishes (and prices) served with dispatch. It's located in the Zardain Building, Calle 1 Poniente no. 17 (go down the passageway to the Flamingo's entrance). From the bus station, turn left, then take the first right. Walk up and across the Avenida Central, and the Zardain Building is on the right-hand side. At the Flamingo, Mexican dishes cost anywhere from 695 to 1,100 pesos ($1.39 to $2.20), with sandwiches below this range and meat entrees above it. Seafood specialties are flown in frequently, so the oysters, shrimp, and fish may even be sort of fresh here. The daily comida corrida costs 1,200 pesos ($2.40).

A Peripatetic Breakfast

Up early to catch a bus or plane? Before the Flamingo opens at 7 a.m., you can grab something to eat by visiting the panadería (bakery) farther up the same street (la Calle Pte., up from the Avenida Central). Sweet rolls and danish in hand, walk back down toward the Flamingo and stop at the Jugos California stand for a huge glass of fresh-squeezed orange juice.

For Coffee Purists

There's not much to do in Tuxtla, but whenever I'm in town I drop by the **Cafe Avenida** (no sign), Avenida Central 230 at la Calle Pte., for a cup or two of the only thing they serve: freshly ground and brewed Chiapan coffee. Huge sacks of beans lean against the counter, the grinder hums away, producing wonderful coffee aromas. The Formica tables have been cleaned so often that the decorative pattern is wearing off. No tea, no sweets, just coffee, dark roasted (almost burnt), rough flavored, and hearty, at 70 pesos (14¢) the cup.

WHAT TO DO: It's possible to take a couple of out-of-town excursions, one being the small town of **Chiapa de Corzo,** a 30-minute, eight-mile ride by bus from the main square (buses leave every 15 minutes in the morning, every 30 minutes in the afternoon), or 10 to 15 minutes by taxi. Those going on to San Cristóbal or over the mountains to the Yucatán (see below) will pass through Chiapa de Corso on their way.

Chiapa has a small museum dedicated to lacquered wood items, and also a small pyramid, pretty well restored and visible from the road.

Another more spectacular trip is to the canyon of **El Sumidero,** ten miles from the center of town along a country road. The canyon can be reached by taxi—you must strike a bargain with a driver, who will want about 7,500 to 10,000 pesos ($15.00 to $20.00) a carload for the round trip.

If the canyon is the only side trip you intend to take, a better deal would be to book a tour with Sr. Ramón Marroquín Escodar at 1a Avenida Norte Oriente no. 1121 (tel. 2-0649), for 300 pesos (60¢) per person.

Eleven blocks east of the central plaza on the way to El Sumidero is **Madero Park,** which harbors the **Regional Museum of Anthropology,** open Tuesday through Sunday from 9 a.m. to 7 p.m.; the **Botanical Gardens** with the same approximate visiting hours; a **children's area** open Tuesday through Sunday from 10 a.m. to 10 p.m.; and a **city theater.** In one short stop you can pick up lots of information here on Chiapas's past civilizations, her flora, and her present-day accomplishments. As the Parque Madero and these attractions are on the way to El Sumidero, you can see it all in the course of one trip.

On the southeast side of town is the zoo, considered to be one of the best in Mexico. You may be able to spot jaguars, monkeys, and other creatures native to the area during visiting hours which are from 8:30 a.m. to 5:30 p.m. daily; closed on Monday.

If your time and budget are limited (and even if they aren't) the tourism office offers the most extensive and economical **tour** of all of the above attractions. The six-hour tour begins with pick-up service at most of the better hotels in town, including the Gran Hotel Huberto. At 1,500 pesos ($3.00) this is an excellent value. Call the tourism office at 3-4837 or Transportadora Turistica Mexicorama at 3-4293 for reservations.

Bazar Ishcanal (tel. 3-3478), located on the first floor of Plaza de las Instituciones, the same building housing the tourism office, is worthy of your time. This government-operated shop features a fine and extensive collection of the craft articles of the state of Chiapas, including representations of both the indigenous and Mexican populations. Pottery, weaving, jewelry, and wooden articles are grouped by area and type. The displays are informative as well as for sale. The shop is open from 9 a.m. to 2 p.m. and 5 p.m. to 9 p.m. Monday through Saturday, and 10 a.m. to 2 p.m. on Sunday.

Other than these, the best thing you can do in Tuxtla is go to the Cristóbal Colón bus station and book passage for San Cristóbal de las Casas or Villahermosa, gateway to Yucatán.

SHORTCUT TO YUCATÁN: A road runs between San Cristóbal and Palenque; see Section 3 of this chapter for full details. Otherwise, you don't have to go all the way back to Tehuantepec to cross the mountains as Hwy. 195 is open and completely paved from Chiapa de Corzo (near Tuxtla) to Pichucalco and Villahermosa. It's a winding mountain road that can't be taken fast, and shouldn't be anyway as the road meanders through some of the most gorgeous scenery in all Mexico: emerald-green mountains, thick banana groves, citrus trees growing wild by the roadside, quaint villages, and breathtaking vistas come one after the other as you wind along. It's important to get an early start on this road, especially if you're driving from San Cristóbal, for patches of fog often slow traffic until you climb above the clouds. The trip from San Cristóbal to Villahermosa takes about six to seven hours by car, seven to eight by bus. Autobuses Cristóbal Colón runs six daily buses from Tuxtla to Villahermosa.

BUSES FROM TUXTLA: Besides the six buses mentioned above going to Villahermosa, the Cristóbal Colón line also runs ten daily buses to San Cristóbal, two to Oaxaca, and eight to Comitán, on the way to the Guatemalan border at Ciudad Cuauhtémoc.

The buses to San Cristóbal leave at 5, 6, 8:45, 9:30, and 11:30 a.m., and 2, 3:30, 5:45, 6, and 7:45 p.m. on the 84 kilometer (52-mile), 1½- to 2-hour trip. Some of these are *autobuses de paso,* meaning that they've originated somewhere else, and that seats on them may or may not be available. Don't depend on these schedules, though—check what's current, as these things change.

FLIGHTS FROM TUXTLA: For flights to Palenque, see the Palenque section, above. Aero Chiapas (tel. 3-2798 or 2-9668) flies to San Cristóbal three to five times weekly. **Aviación de Chiapas** (tel. 961/3-2101), la Avenida Norte at 4a Calle Poniente, has a daily flight (except Sunday) between Tuxtla's smaller Aeropuerto Francisco Sarabia (not the main airport) and Villahermosa. The schedule says now that it departs Tuxtla at 2:20 p.m.

The following flights depart from Tuxtla's main airport, a 40-minute ride from the center of town.

AeroMéxico (tel. 961/2-2155 or 3-1000), relocating shortly to a site near Hotel Bonampak Tuxtla, operates direct, nonstop flights to Mexico City, Tapachula, and Villahermosa.

Mexicana (tel. 961/2-0020 or 2-1692), Avenida Central Poniente no. 206, has direct, nonstop flights to Mexico City and Oaxaca.

5. San Cristóbal de las Casas

The highway between Tuxtla and San Cristóbal de las Casas climbs to almost 7,000 feet in a matter of 50 miles and the scenery is spectacular. San Cristóbal itself (alt. 6,855 feet; pop. 60,000) is a colonial town set in a lovely valley. (Note: It's chilly every evening of the year there, so bring a sweater.) The town is the major market center for Indians of various tribes from the surrounding mountains, chiefly the Chamulas, who wear baggy thigh-length trousers and white or black serapes; the Zinacantes, who dress in light-pink blouses and extremely short pants, whose hat ribbons are tied on the married men and dangling loose on the bachelors; and the Tenahapa, with knee-length black tunics and flat straw hats. In a way, Indian life in Chiapas is an introduction to that of Guatemala, for San Cristóbal is deep in Mesoamerica where the Mayas flourished. In fact, nearly all the Indians around these parts speak languages derived from ancient Mayan. Some don't come into town at all—ever—and one group, the Lacandons (who number only 450), live so far off in the forests of eastern Chiapas that it takes six days on horseback to get to their territory. There are some Indian villages within access to San Cristóbal by road—Chilil, a Tuixtan village, where the Indian Institute maintains a clinic, reached via a drive through a beautiful forest; Amatenango del Valle, whose inhabitants make pots without a potter's wheel; Zinacantan, whose men weave hats; Contehuitz, Arcotete, and Tenajapa, the last village accessible only by Jeep. Without a guide who knows the area, however, there's not much to see. Most Indian "villages" consist of little more than a church and the municipal government, with homes scattered for miles around and a general gathering only for church and market days (usually Sunday).

In recent years San Cristóbal has become a popular vacation spot for Mexicans, not to mention North Americans and Europeans in search of a charming, cool, "unspoiled," traditional town to visit or to settle down in for a few years. Hotels and restaurants do a good business, but at times they're not very well run—a reminder that San Cristóbal is, at heart, a small country town high in the mountains.

ORIENTATION: Highway 190, the **Pan American Highway,** runs through the southern reaches of San Cristóbal. The first-class (Cristóbal Colón) bus station is right on the highway. The street that intersects the highway in front of the bus station is the Avenida de los Insurgentes, and nine blocks north along Insurgentes (a 10- or 15-minute walk) will bring you to the main plaza, complete with cathedral. Another nine blocks along the same street, in the same direction, will bring you to the public market, at the northern edge of town. From the market, minibuses (colectivos) trundle to outlying villages.

The second-class bus stations (Tuxtla and Lacandonia) are on Calle Pedro Moreno, three or four blocks from the first-class terminal. Walk east along Moreno to get to Insurgentes, then turn left (north).

Take note that this town has at least three streets named "Dominguez." There's Hermanos Dominguez, Belisario Dominguez, and Pantaleón Dominguez. Maybe more, who knows?

The **municipal tourism office** (tel. 967/8-0414), on the main square in the town hall next to the cathedral, is well organized, with a friendly, helpful staff. The office keeps especially convenient hours, open from 8 a.m. to 8 p.m. on weekdays; 8 a.m. to 1 p.m. and 3 p.m. to 7 p.m. on Saturday; and 9 a.m. to 2 p.m. on Sunday.

Note that it is illegal to park your car on the streets of San Cristóbal during the night. You will have to find off-street parking. If your hotel doesn't have it, go to the **public parking lot** (Estacionamiento) in front of the cathedral, just off the main square, on 16 de Septiembre. This is a pay lot, but rates are low, 20 pesos (4¢) per hour or 150 pesos (30¢) for ten hours. After this point the rate schedule gets complicated, but no more expensive.

USEFUL FACTS: The **post office** (Correos), open from Monday through Saturday 8 a.m. to 7 p.m. for purchasing stamps and mailing letters, 9 a.m. to 1 p.m.

and 4 to 5 p.m. for mailing packages, is on Avenida 16 de Septiembre, one block south of the main square. The **telegraph office** is on Calle Diego de Mazariegos, just past Avenida 5 de Mayo. . . . **Baths** (Baños Mercedarios), 1 de Marzo no. 56, are open 7 a.m. to 7 p.m., no more than 500 pesos ($1.00) for steam or Turkish.

WHERE TO STAY: San Cristóbal is no longer the quiet little village of ten years ago; in fact, it is presently at the boom stage when new hotels and restaurants spring up overnight.

You'll like the **Hotel Español,** 1 de Marzo at 16 de Septiembre (that's *primero de Marzo y dieciseis de Septiembre),* two blocks north of the cathedral (tel. 967/8-0045 or 8-0412). For one thing, it has the prettiest courtyard in the entire city. For another, you can get a good price if you take room and meals together. The old-fashioned rooms are comfortable and well kept, with private baths. The prices, for room alone, tax included, are 3,956 pesos ($7.91) single, 4,945 pesos ($9.89) double, and 5,934 pesos ($11.87) triple.

The **Posada Diego de Mazariegos,** Maria Adelina Flores 2 (this street also seems to be called Cinco de Febrero), corner of Utrilla, one block from the main plaza (tel. 967/8-0513 or 8-1825), is fairly fancy, with a nightclub, travel agency, bar, and café-restaurant called El Patio. It is aggressively colonial, but not unpleasantly so (baroque goes well in these mountain towns). Rooms tend to have a bit more "decor" than at less expensive hotels, yet prices here are not bad: 5,566 pesos ($11.13) single, 6,958 pesos ($13.92) double, 8,349 pesos ($16.70) triple, tax included.

The **Hotel Ciudad Real,** on the zócalo (tel. 967/8-0187), is one of the snazzier hotels in town, but the prices are still pretty reasonable: 3,404 pesos ($6.81) for a single, 4,255 pesos ($8.51) double. The 31 rooms are new and rather small, but you are paying for the decor and the central courtyard complete with a large fireplace, which is always blazing away on those cold (or cool) evenings. And here smolders the only problem with the Ciudad Real. This fireplace, its greatest asset, may also be its greatest debit. A crackling fire attracts people, who converse sometimes not quietly, late into the night, while upstairs guests catch every word as it reverberates through the courtyard.

Next door to the Ciudad Real is the **Hotel Santa Clara** (tel. 967/8-1140), a very similar establishment that tends to charge slightly more for its peaceful rooms: 3,460 pesos ($6.92) single, 4,450 pesos ($8.90) double; parking free.

The **Hotel Fray Bartolomé de las Casas,** on the corner of Niños Héroes (no. 2) and Insurgentes, next to the Pemex station (tel. 967/8-0932), is a nice old colonial inn with 18 rooms. If you are looking for a quiet abode this is the place, and although the rooms are plain, they are clean and in good condition with tile showers. The courtyard has numerous planters and bentwood furniture as well as parking. Singles are 2,622 pesos ($5.24); doubles cost 3,277 pesos ($6.55). **Note:** Hot water is only available between 7 and 10 in the morning and 7 and 10 in the evening.

At Avenida Juárez 16, corner of León, is the **Hotel Palacio de Moctezuma** (tel. 967/8-0352), a modern, clean, and neat hostelry with small rooms arranged around a series of small courtyards with pretty fountains, trees, or potted shrubs. A restaurant featuring good food and a fireplace is situated in one corner, and nestled throughout are unique sitting rooms. The 33 rooms are small and somewhat expensive: 2,960 pesos ($5.92) single, 3,700 pesos ($17.40) double. It's a decent place to stay.

The **Hotel San Martín,** Calle Real de Guadelupe 16 (tel. 967/8-0533), is a family-run operation, and is thus very clean. The 27 rooms are on three floors in the long, narrow building with balcony-type walkways. Each room has a private tile bath and a firm bed. Rates are 2,100 pesos ($4.20) single, 2,860 pesos ($5.72) double, 3,430 pesos ($6.86) triple. Ask about hot water availability before you register.

Casa de Huespedes Margarita, at Calle Real de Guadelupe no. 34 (tel. 967/ 8-0957), offers more than a hostel, but less than a hotel. The "more" are the private rooms positioned around a typical courtyard; the "less" is the lack of private bathrooms. An informative bulletin board hangs near the reception area and the restaurant resounds with a medley of languages as younger folks from everywhere congregate for the evening. A single room costs 1,200 pesos ($2.40); and doubles are 1,600 pesos ($3.20).

Students staying in San Cristóbal for any length of time find basic but acceptable **hospedajes** which charge 750 to 1,000 pesos ($1.50 to $2.00) per person per day or less. Usually these places are unadvertised, and were I to include names and addresses here the prices would surely skyrocket. If you're interested in a cheap, cheap hospedaje, ask around in a restaurant or café and you're sure to find one.

To get you started, I suggest looking on Calle Real de Guadalupe, east out of the main square. Some of the best hospedajes are here. Other ones, on Insurgentes near the bus stations, tend to be noisy.

READERS' HOTEL SELECTIONS: "We stayed at **Posada del Abuelita,** Tapachula 18 (tel. 967/ 8-1741), near the market about 20 minutes from the bus station. The Posada is rather a youth hostel. They rent rooms around a patio for 700 pesos ($1.40) per person. They have lots of clean showers and toilets and a kitchen with open chimney" (Dr. Hugo Lanz, Munich, West Germany). . . . "The **Posada Tepeyac,** on Calle Real de Guadalupe no. 40, has no bath or water in the rooms, but it's a friendly and inexpensive place: 1,500 pesos ($3.00) double, or 2,000 pesos ($4.00) for a room (Maren Sagvaag and P. H. Keim Börresen, Bergen, Norway). . . . "The Casa Huespedes Lupita, 12 Juárez, is friendly and clean; 1,000 pesos ($2.00) per person" (Monique Willemsen and Marcel Nijenhuis, Apeldoorn, Holland).

WHERE TO EAT: Remember now, this is a country town, and so service may be fairly slow.

There's a double treat waiting at **La Galería** (tel. 8-1547), Avenida Hidalgo no. 3. Open daily from 9 a.m. to 9 p.m., the street-level part of La Galería is a shop displaying folk art, weaving, pottery, and painting. The little two-room café-restaurant upstairs over the shop thrums to cool, hip music while the efficient staff serves up chiles rellenos (stuffed green peppers), wholewheat sandwiches, big fruit salads, and the like for 250 to 300 pesos (50¢ to 60¢)—good place. Additional attractions are the original exhibits, sometimes local crafts, now a showing of black-and-white photographs depicting the Mexico City earthquake; and on the way up the stairs there's a bulletin board which in itself makes interesting reading.

Ernest Hemingway called Paris "a moveable feast." San Cristóbal has its own, in the shape of the **Restaurant Normita,** at the corner of Juárez and Flores. The Normita has moved no fewer than three times in the past few years, and I keep following it around because the food and the prices are good. For 650 to 750 pesos ($1.30 to $1.50) you can get a Mexican specialty such as enchiladas that is sure to fill you up, as will the 750-pesos ($1.50) comida served from 1 to 3 p.m. Pozole, the thick, rich hominy stew, is also a good choice for 750 pesos ($1.50), or perhaps the cochinita (suckling pig) appeals to you. Come to the Normita from 1 to 10 p.m. daily; closed on Sunday.

San Cristóbal has a vegetarian restaurant and food shop named **El Trigal.** A pretty courtyard in an old house has been furnished with tables, plants, and a pyramid (to furnish digestive powers?), all at Calle 1 de Marzo no. 13, corner of

20 de Noviembre, on the north side of the Cine Las Casas. For breakfast, have granola with milk and bananas; for lunch, an alfalfa-and-lettuce salad with a bowl of lentil soup; for dinner, perhaps cream of carrot soup and chilaquiles made with tomatoes and cheese. The bill will be only 700 to 1,250 pesos ($1.50 to $2.50), only a bit more for a glass of wine (the only liquor served). When I tried it out, the food was excellent, the service very friendly.

El Fandango, Mazariegos 24 at the corner of Allende, is a recent addition to the restaurant/café scene. The fresh bread is great as is the coffee at 100 pesos (20¢) a cup. The Fandango's forte may well be its light meals such as two quesadillas and a bowl of vegetable soup for 700 pesos ($1.40), stuffed green pepper with vegetables, or a hamburger and fries for 600 pesos ($1.20).

In this same price range but with heartier fare and even less decor is the also new Los Angeles, across the street (1 de Marzo) from the Hotel Español. There is truth in the sign over the door advertising "cocina economica". A breakfast of eggs costs 150 pesos (30¢), chicken prepared in any number of ways is 450 to 500 pesos (90¢ to $1.00); but the not so economical comida stretches the budget unnecessarily at 850 pesos ($1.70). Open 9 a.m. to 5 p.m.

The small family-run Pizza Villa Real (tel. 8-0534), Dr. José Felipe Flores no. 1-A, between Insurgentes and Juárez, will make you a fresh pizza that you can eat at one of the few tables, or take out. Pizzas come in all sizes, from the small for 700 to 870 pesos ($1.40 to $1.74) to the gigantic *familiar* ("family-size") for 1,450 to 1,700 pesos ($2.90 to $3.40). The Villa Real is open every day from 10:30 a.m. to 11:30 p.m.

The best for last. . . . The Restaurant Tuluc (tel. 8-2090) is an epicure's delight, and presents a constant dilemma to those not totally ravenous (and therefore unable to consume the entire comida). The 950-peso ($1.90) comida is an exceptional value. This five-course feast begins with a plentiful fruit plate or a tropical drink, followed by a serving of fresh baked rolls and a generous bowl of vegetable-beef soup. You next work your way through a heaping plate of rice and a main dish of your choice (meat, chicken, or fish). Even though that's already five courses, you still get dessert (try pastel tres leches) and a fine cup of coffee! You will locate Restaurant Tuluc by following the crowd at 1:30 p.m. or racing over to Francisco Madero 9C at 1 p.m. to be ensured of a booth. The evening à la carte menu is equally popular, with huachinango for 750 pesos ($1.50) and most meat entrees for 650 to 920 pesos ($1.30 to $1.84). The owner speaks several languages and is a most agreeable host. By the way, El Tuluc's namesake, the turkey, is displayed in portrait over the espresso machine. El Tuluc is closed on Tuesday but open every other day from 9 to 11 a.m., 1 to 5 p.m., and 7 to 10 p.m.

Coffeehouses

A rather pleasant discovery is the great number of coffeehouses concealed in the nooks and crannies of San Cristóbal's side streets. Cafetería El Mural, at Crescencia Rosas 4 (around the corner from the post office), is a quietly classy place. There's nothing fancy here, but after you've eased into one of the comfortable chairs clustered around a small pine table, a nice feeling just settles in around you. I like to drop in during the evening to sample the local coffee brewed 14 different ways. There's a snack-time crowd also that favors the cheese fondue, hamburgers, or crêpes for about 300 pesos (60¢), or dessert for 180 to 230 pesos (35¢ to 46¢). One loyal patron with quick humor has penned a set of "coffeehouse" cartoons, displayed near the door, that overcome any language barrier. El Mural is open from 10 a.m. to 2 p.m. and 5 to 10 p.m.

The Café San Cristóbal at Cuauhtémoc no. 1 may be an answer to the cravings of the coffee aficionado. What you'll be served here is local coffee—that's all. If you like the brew, the beans are in glass display cases and are sold by the kilogram (2.20 lbs.) for 1,100 pesos ($2.20). There are even more beans in burlap bags stacked up along the wall. This little café is open from 9 a.m. to 2 p.m. and 4:30 to 8:30 p.m.

Open later into the evening is **Cafetería El Rinconcito de Pedro** located at Real de Guadalupe no. 9. Reflecting its name this "little corner" is packed with six tiny tables and a local crowd with a purpose—dominoes. Eleven types of coffee, espresso for 70 pesos (14¢), cappuccino for 100 pesos (20¢), sandwiches for 150 pesos (30¢), or premier desserts fail to break the concentration of the domino players. So important are these games that even the richest of coffee ends up cooling on a stool beside the table. Open 10 a.m. to 3 p.m. and 5 to 10:30 p.m.; dominoes provided!

WHAT TO DO: Although San Cristóbal is a mountain town, it has drawn more and more visitors. They come to enjoy the scenery, the air, hikes in the mountains, and to look at the Indians in the zócalo. I have no doubt that the Indians come down from the mountains to look at them. In any case, the town is now showing signs of "progress."

The **Bellas Artes building,** on Hidalgo three blocks south of the plaza to the arch), is one of the more active centers in San Cristóbal. Be sure to check in if you are interested in the arts. I recently saw a fine show of batiks and painting here and another of folkloric dance. There should be a schedule of events and shows posted on the door, if the Bellas Artes is not open. By the way, there's a public library right next door.

Just being in San Cristóbal is good for mind and body. For the soul I can recommend heartily a hike to some of the churches throughout the town. Very near the Bellas Artes, where the arch towers over Avenida Hidalgo at the intersection of Hermanos Dominguez, is the **Templo del Carmen.** It's a favorite of the townspeople despite its rather plain interior (some gilded work, paintings, and statues). It's over two centuries old. At the other end of town is the **Templo de Santo Domingo** (1560), on Avenida 20 de Noviembre, five blocks from the zócalo. The carved stone façade is in a style called "Plateresque," and there's a beautiful gilded wooden altarpiece inside. The **Templo de San Francisco** is near the aforementioned Carmen church, at the corner of Insurgentes and Callejón Libertad. During Holy Week you might walk through the pleasant square, enter the church with its dark, somber oil paintings and softly glowing gilt altarpieces, and hear the exquisitely simple sounds of a primitive flute and bells breaking the silence at intervals.

Get your wind up, because the next church visit takes stamina. From the hill which holds the **Templo de San Cristóbal** you will have a very fine panorama of the town—but you pay. Leave the zócalo on Avenida Hidalgo, turn right onto the third street (Hermanos Dominguez), and there at the end of the street are the steps you've got to climb. Take it slowly.

An easier church to visit is the **cathedral,** right on the zócalo, dating from the 1500s and boasting some fine timberwork and a very fancy pulpit.

FESTIVALS: San Cristóbal explodes with lights, excitement, and hordes of visitors during Holy Week, when the annual **Fería de Primavera** (Spring Festival) is held. Carnival rides, food stalls, handcraft shops, parades, and band concerts fill an entire week. Hotel rooms get hard to find, and room prices rise accordingly.

Another spectacular is staged **July 24th,** date for the annual fiesta. The steps up to the San Cristóbal church are lit with torches at night.

MARKETS AND SHOPS: Because of the many Indian villages near San Cristóbal where traditional crafts are still practiced, this is a good town in which to shop for pottery and woven goods. One of the best selections I've seen is at **Sna Jolobil** (means "the weaver's house" in Tzotzil Maya), in the former convent (monastery) of Santo Domingo, next to the Templo de Santo Domingo, Avenida 20 de Noviembre between Navarro and Nicaragua. It's a cooperative store operated by groups of Tzotzil and Tzeltal craftspeople, with about 3,000 members who contribute products, help in running the store, and share in the moderate profits. Their works are simply beautiful; prices are set, and are moderate, and quality is high. Be sure to take a look. The Sna Jolobil is open daily from 9 a.m. to 2 p.m. and 4 to 7 p.m.

San Cristóbal's **central market** is farther along Avenida Gral. Utrilla from the Santo Domingo church, about nine blocks from the zócalo. The market buildings, and the streets surrounding them, offer just about anything you'd have need of.

Market day in San Cristóbal is every morning except Sunday (when each village has its own local market), and you'll probably enjoy looking at the sellers as much as at the things they sell. This area is especially good for woven and leather products. They make and sell beautiful serapes, colorful native shirts, and rebozos in vivid geometric patterns. In leather they are craftsmen of the highest rating, making the sandals and men's handbags indigenous to this region. There are numerous shops up and down the streets leading to the market, all of them willing to sell you anything from string bags and pottery to colorfully patterned ponchos. Shop here: the products are good and the prices are right.

NA BOLOM: Those interested in the anthropology of this region will want to visit the museum and library called **Na Bolom** (tel. 8-1418). The home, and headquarters, of noted anthropologists Franz and Trudy Blom for many years, it is now a focal point for serious study of the region. You can take a tour of the house from 4 to 5:30 p.m. Tuesday through Sunday, 100-peso (20¢) fee; the museum is open from 4 to 6 p.m. every day but Monday. (For the museum, a donation is asked.) Na Bolom offers limited accommodations to serious visitors, with all meals included. Prices are well out of our range, though. Na Bolom is nine blocks from the zócalo. Leave the square on Real de Gaudalupe, walk four blocks to Avenida Vicente Guerrero, and turn left. Five and a half blocks up Guerrero, just past the intersection with Comitán, is Na Bolom.

SIDE TRIPS: A side trip to the village of **San Juan Chamula** really gets one into the spirit of Chiapas. The village, eight kilometers northeast of San Cristóbal, is the cultural and ceremonial center of the Chamula Indians. Activity centers on the huge church, the plaza, and the municipal building; each year a new group of citizens is chosen to live in the municipal center as caretakers of the saints. Carnival, just before Lent, is the big annual festival, and turns out to be a fascinating mingling of the Christian pre-Lenten ceremonies and an ancient Maya celebration of the five "lost days" that arise at the end of the 360-day Maya agricultural cycle. The Chamulas are not a very wealthy people as their economy is based on agriculture. Absolutely no photography is permitted during these ceremonies. Those who choose not to observe this local custom may find themselves in physical danger. At no time is photography allowed in the church.

Colectivos (minibuses) to San Juan Chamula leave the municipal market in San Cristóbal about every half hour, and charge 100 pesos (20¢).

Zinacantán is another small village in the region where visitors are required to observe certain local customs: before seeing the church, one must ask permission of the Presidente Municipal, seated to the right of the church. Once permission is granted and you have purchased a ticket for 50 pesos (10¢), an escort will show you the church. Note also that no cameras are allowed in the town at any time.

HORSEBACK RIDES: Tired of riding buses? You can make arrangements to rent a horse at various places in town, including at your hotel; or check the bulletin board in the Casa de Huespedes Margarita. Cost is between 2,500 and 3,000 pesos ($5.00 and $6.00) for an afternoon, more if you want to have a guide accompany you. Reserve your steed after 7 p.m. at least a day before you want to ride. You could, for instance, ride over to San Juan Chamula, or just up into the hills.

NIGHTLIFE: I think of San Cristóbal as a do-it-yourself nightlife town. Friendly conversation at several of my recommended restaurants, particularly the coffeehouses with their international clientele, is a favorite evening pastime. The Normita frequently has a guitarist at night. And if it's just a cozy fire and a comfortable chair you crave, have a drink by the blaze in the Hotel Ciudad Real.

Otherwise, hang around one of the two movie theaters in town. There's a slim chance they'll be showing a film in English, or one that you might not mind watching in Spanish; and even if you don't want to see the movie, that's where many of the local citizens will be hanging out, for better or worse.

COMITÁN: Southeast from San Cristóbal, another 75 km, lies Comitán (alt. 5,018 feet; pop. 40,000), a pretty town on a hillside, whose chief distinction, apart from the production of a sugarcane-based fire water called *comitecho*, is that it's the last big town along the Pan American Highway before the Guatemalan border.

What do you do with a free day in Comitán? You take a side trip to the **Monte Bello National Park** and enjoy the multicolored lakes and exuberant tropical vegetation. Buses run out to the park, but schedules change with the seasons so check for the latest information at the office of Transportes Montebello, on 5a Avenida Sur. Plan to see the park in a day as there are no places to stay overnight.

READER'S HOTEL SELECTION: "Getting off the bus in Comitán, I inquired as to the location of the **Hotel Lagos Montebello** (tel. 963/2-1145 or 2-0657), Carretera Internacional Km 1257, and it was just across the street. The rate was 3,800 pesos ($7.60) per night. We paid for two nights after examining the rooms which were fairly large and clean" (Richard C. Bradley, Springdale, Ariz.).

6. Tapachula

Although I prefer entering Guatemala via San Cristóbal (see above), you can go via the Mexican town of Tapachula (El Carmen on the Guatemalan side), a pleasant enough town of 120,000 people at the base of a 13,000-foot volcano. This is the Pacific Slope of Middle America, covered with plantations growing sugarcane, coffee, rubber, and bananas, many of them run by Germans or German-speaking people; the Slope is much the same in both Mexico and Guatemala. The drive to Tapachula is a long, hot one from Tehuantepec—almost 300 miles—and even longer and hotter from Coatzacoalcos or Veracruz. When you arrive, take refuge in Tapachula's main square, shaded by fine trees.

Tapachula's layout is logical if a bit confusing, so take a moment to consider it. Two central streets divide the town, the Avenida Central which goes from north to south, and the Calle Central which goes from east to west. All streets parallel to Avenida Central are also called avenidas, and are numbered (Avenidas 1, 3, 5, etc., are *east* of the Avenida Central; Avenidas 2, 4, 6, etc., are *west* of Avenida Central). The same arrangement applies for the calles: Calles 1, 3, 5, etc., are *north* of Calle Central; Calles 2, 4, 6, etc., are *south* of Calle Central.

WHERE TO STAY: Most people will only stay one night in Tapachula, then head for Guatemala.

At 4th Avenida Norte no. 19 is the 51-room **Hotel Fenix** (tel. 962/6-1464), a slightly snazzier place than nearby hotels, featuring its own restaurant and bar, plus a tobacco stand and a parking garage. About a third of the rooms are air-conditioned. Rates are 4,125 pesos ($8.25) single, 5,250 pesos ($10.50) double (one bed), 6,375 pesos ($12.75) double (two beds); add 1,000 pesos ($2) for air conditioning.

Chapter XV

MÉRIDA AND THE MAYA CITIES

1. Yucatán's Fascinating History
2. Touring the Yucatán: Itineraries
3. Mérida
4. Mayapán and Ticul
5. Uxmal
6. Kabah, Sayil, Xlapak, Labná, Loltún
7. Campeche
8. Chichén-Itzá and Balankanché
9. Valladolid

YUCATÁN IS A WORLD APART from the rest of Mexico, and always has been. Legend has it that when the great man-god Quetzalcóatl was driven from the Valley of Mexico by the people he had hoped to save, he took refuge in Yucatán. His adopted people, the Mayas, built one of the world's great civilizations here in the flat jungle sprawl of Mesoamerica. They had little contact with the peoples of the Valley of Mexico, and that's the way they liked it.

Yucatán took little part in the Mexican War of Independence (1810–1821), and in fact the power elite here considered declaring their own independence from Mexico. But in 1847 began a revolt of the Mayan tribes against both the local powers and the government in Mexico City. Battles in this "War of the Castes" raged off and on until 1901, when Mexican government troops finally quashed it and united Yucatán definitively to the rest of Mexico.

For some fascinating insights into Yucatecan history and culture, read Fray Diego de Landa's *Yucatán Before and After the Conquest,* the travel diaries of John Stevens, and the book on the Maya codices by Maria Sten, as noted in the Introduction to this book.

ABOUT YUCATÁN: Contrary to popular belief, which places the Yucatán in the extreme southeast of Mexico, the land of the Mayas forms the far east-central part of the Republic. A look at the map reveals that the Yucatecan capital, Mérida, is north of such major population centers as Mexico City, Guadalajara, Puebla, and Veracruz. Mérida is also surprisingly close to the tip of Florida: from Mexico City to Mérida it's about 600 miles as the crow flies, and from Mérida to Miami it's a mere 675 miles.

Actually there are two Yucatáns—the peninsula and the state. The peninsula is the piece of land north of Hwy. 186 which extends from Francisco Es-cárcega to Chetumal, and includes part of the state of Campeche and all of the state of Yucatán, plus most of the state of Quintana Roo. The Yucatán state is a wedge-shaped entity that includes Mérida and many of the best archeological sites.

1. Yucatán's Fascinating History

Yucatán's history has fascinated the rest of the world since Lord Kingsbor-ough published a study of its ruins in 1831. Just a few years later, New York lawyer John L. Stephens and artist Frederick Catherwood made several trips through Yucatán and Central America. Stephens recorded his adventures in a fascinating series of travel books, decorated by Catherwood's superb drawings, which achieved great, immediate, and lasting popularity. The books still make for wonderful reading, and are available from Dover Publications, 31 E. 2nd Street, Mineola, NY 11501, or through bookstores in North America and Mex-ico.

Ever since Stephens's adventures, foreigners have been touring Yucatán to view its vast crumbling cities and ponder the fall of a once truly great civiliza-tion. The Mayas, though they practiced human sacrifice and self-mutilation, de-veloped mathematical theories far in advance of European thought, and perfected a calendar even more accurate than the Gregorian one which we use today.

Here is a summary of Maya history so you can comprehend the importance of the archeological sites you're about to visit.

THE EARLY TIMES: The years 1500 B.C. to A.D. 320, the Preclassic Period, are thought to be the time when Maya civilization began and was shaped. It may be that the Mayas learned a good deal from the mysterious Olmecs, whose great monolithic head sculptures are preserved in the Parque La Venta at Villahermo-sa and in the Museo de Anthropología in Mexico City. Or it may be that the Mayas developed from wandering tribes in what is now Guatemala's vast low-lying jungle province of El Petén.

Little is known about the first thousand years of Maya culture, except that they discovered how to cultivate corn (maize), the food—to them even a reli-gious symbol—which was to shape their lives fo thousands of years, and which still influences them strongly today. In any case, by 500 B.C. the Mayas were making great strides.

The Formative Period

The time from 500 B.C. until the end of the Preclassic Period is sometimes called the Formative Period because this is when the Mayas developed their cal-endar, their complex and beautiful system of hieroglyphic writing, and their early architecture. The Maya religion, with its 166 known deities, was also being shaped in these early centuries.

While the Mayas were doing these things in the yet-to-be-"discovered" New World, the following events took place in the Old World: the Second Tem-ple was built in Jerusalem; the Roman Empire reached the height of its power and influence; Jesus carried out his ministry; Jerusalem was destroyed and the Jewish Diaspora took place; and Constantine the Great was preparing to found his new imperial capital of Constantinople, now Istanbul.

THE CLASSIC YEARS: The great years of Maya culture were from A.D. 320 to 925, called the Classic Period. When Rome was falling to the barbarians and the Dark Ages were spreading over Europe, the Mayas were consolidating their cultural gains, wiping out pockets of backwardness, and connecting their ceremonial centers by means of great roads. The finest examples of Mayan architecture were conceived and constructed during these years, well before the Gothic style made its appearance in Europe. You can see these supreme achievements of Mayan art at Palenque (near Villahermosa), at Copán in Honduras, and at Quirigua in Guatemala. All these sites flourished during the last part of the Classic Period, in the 700s.

The End of the Great Era

The Classic Period closes with a century of degradation and collapse, roughly equivalent to the A.D. 800s. By the early 900s, the great ceremonial centers mentioned above were abandoned, the jungle moving in to cover them after not much more than one short century of florescence. Why classic Maya culture collapsed so quickly we don't really know. Epidemic? Earthquake? Overpopulation? A breakdown of society?

In Europe at the time of the Maya collapse, it was the Middle Ages. Charlemagne was building his empire, an Umayyad Muslim prince reigned in Spain, the Anglo-Saxon King Alfred the Great ruled England, and the iconoclastic controversy raged in the Byzantine Middle East.

INTERREGNUM: With the collapse of Maya civilization, the Mayas seem to have migrated from their historic home in Guatemala and Chiapas into the northern lowlands of Yucatán, roughly the modern states of Yucatán and Campeche. After their arrival around A.D. 900, they spent three centuries (till 1200) growing into an inferior copy of their former greatness.

Puuc Architecture

The cities near Yucatán's low western hills were built in this period in the style now called Puuc ("hills"). These include Kabah, Sayil, Labná and Xlapak. Even though Mayan architecture never regained the heights achieved at Palenque or Tikal, the Puuc buildings, such as the Codz Poop at Kabah and the palaces at Sayil and Labná are quite beautiful and impressive.

The Putún Maya

After the Puuc period in architecture, Yucatán was profoundly affected by a strong influence from mainland Mexico. Some theories now hold that a distantly related branch of the Mayan people, called the Putún Maya, were the ones who came from the borders of Mexico and crowded into Yucatán during the Interregnum, developing a civilization of their own, heavily influenced by the cultures of mainland Mexico. The Putún Maya had been traders and navigators, controlling the coastal and riverine trade routes between mainland Mexico and the classic Mayan lands in Petén and Chiapas. They spoke the Mayan language badly, using many Nahuatl (Aztec) words.

The Itzáes

When the Putún Maya left their ships and joined the Toltecs to overrun Yucatán, the invaders became known as the Itzáes. It is thought that the semilegendary god-man Quetzalcóatl (in Nahuatl; Kukulcán in Maya) was the leader of the invasion. With a band of Toltecs, and the support of the Putún Maya, he conquered the town which he called Chichén-Itzá ("In the mouth of the well of the Itzá"). It became his chief city until he founded Mayapán.

Uxmal was founded during this same period (around A.D. 1000), according to some authorities, by the tribe known as the Tutul Xiú. Other scholars think that the Xiú took over from some earlier builders.

The three great centers of Chichén-Itzá, Mayapán and Uxmal lived in peace under a confederation: the Itzá ruled in Chichén-Itzá, the Cocom tribe in Mayapán, and the Xiú in Uxmal. But in 1194 the people of Mayapán overthrew the confederation, sacked Chichén-Itzá, conquered Uxmal, and captured the leaders of the Itzá and the Xiú. Held in Mayapán, the Itzá and Xiú princes reigned over, but did not rule, their former cities.

The Xiú took their revenge in 1441 when they marched from Uxmal on Mayapán, capturing the city, destroying it, and putting the Cocom rulers to death. They thereupon founded a new city at Maní. Thereafter the Mayan lands suffered from a series of battles and skirmishes, and were to know no peace until it was brought forcibly by the Spanish Conquistadores.

THE SPANISH CONQUEST: Francisco de Montejo, the Spaniard who led the conquest of Yucatán, was actually three men. The adventure was begun by Francisco de Montejo the Elder, a member of the lesser Spanish nobility who had petitioned the crown for the right to conquer Yucatán at his own expense in exchange for a lifetime appointment as its governor.

"El Adelantado"

The conquest of Yucatán took a full 20 years. Montejo sailed from Spain in 1527 with 400 soldiers, landed at Cozumel, then proceeded to the mainland at Xel-ha. After scouting the terrain and plumbing the depths of the Mayas' wrath, he decided to relaunch his campaign from the western coast, where he could more easily receive supplies from New Spain (Mexico).

Having regrouped in Mexico, Montejo the Elder (El Adelantado, "the pioneer") conquered what is now the state of Tabasco (1530), and then pushed onward to Yucatán. At first his campaign was successful, but Maya resistance increased along with his success, and after four difficult years (1531–1535) he was forced to return to Mexico a failure, out of money and out of energy. His soldiers had found little in the way of gold, and when stories began to arrive of the vast treasures up for grabs in newly conquered Peru, they deserted the Montejo cause en masse.

"El Mozo"

Montejo's son, Francisco Montejo the Younger (El Mozo, "the lad"), had accompanied him on this expedition, and in 1540 the father turned over his cause and his hope to the son. Montejo the Younger, bringing new vigor and his cousin (another Francisco de Montejo) to the cause, was successful in firmly establishing a town at Campeche, and another at Mérida (1542), and by 1546 (the year Martin Luther died in Germany) virtually all of the peninsula was under his control.

A few weeks after the founding of Mérida, the greatest of the several Maya leaders, Ah Kukum Xiú, head of the Xiú people, offered himself as Montejo's vassal, and was baptised. As was the custom, upon being baptised he took a new Christian name. Choosing what must have been the most popular name in the entire 16th century, he became—yes!—Francisco de Montejo Xiú. With the help of Montejo's troops he then accomplished his real objective, the defeat of the Cocoms. By allying his people with the Spaniards, Xiú signed the Cocoms' death warrant—but also his own and that of the Yucatecan Mayas as a free people.

The Fruits of Conquest

The population of the peninsula declined drastically in the following centuries as the result of warfare, disease, slavery, and emigration.

Fray Diego de Landa, second bishop of Yucatán, studied the Mayan culture and language and, thus equipped, used this knowledge to eradicate as much of it as possible. It was he who ordered the mass destruction of the priceless Mayan codices, or "painted books" at Maní in 1562, only three of which survived.

INDEPENDENCE: Yucatán, controlled directly from Spain rather than from Mexico City, struggled along under the heavy yoke of Spanish colonial administration until the era of Mexican independence. In 1810 the Mexican War of Independence began with Father Hidalgo's famous "Cry of Dolores." With the success of the revolutionary effort in 1821, Spain signed a treaty with the newly independent country of Mexico. In that same year, the Spanish governor of Yucatán resigned, and Yucatán too became an independent country. Though it decided to join in a union with Mexico two years later, this period of Yucatecan sovereignty is an indication of the local spirit. That same spirit arose again in 1845, when Yucatán seceded from Mexico, unhappy with close control from Mexico City.

Rise of the Haciendas

With independence came important changes in landholding practices, and thus in the economy. Sugarcane and henequen cultivation were introduced on a large scale, and soon there arose a culture of vast landed estates, each of which employed hundreds of Mayas. The trick, according to the hacienda owners, was to keep them in debt, so much debt that they could never work their way out of it, and that is precisely what the owners did.

The same Mayas who provided virtual slave labor on the haciendas also served in Yucatán's armed forces which, in the light of later events, was very poor planning on the part of the oppressive hacienda owners. Having been issued weapons with which to defend independent Yucatán against attack from Mexico or the United States, the Mayas instead attacked their local oppressors. Thus, in 1847, began the War of the Castes.

WAR OF THE CASTES: The first target was Valladolid, which was attacked, looted and sacked by the rebellious Mayas in the most horrible manner. It soon became apparent to all concerned that this was a race war, and the line was drawn between the Mayas on one side and those of Spanish blood on the other.

The Mayas, increasing their numbers with every victory, bought more guns and ammunition from British merchants in Belize (British Honduras). By June 1848 they held virtually all of Yucatán except Mérida and Campeche—and Mérida's governor had already decided to abandon the city. Feeling sure they had won the war, the rebel fighters went off to do something equally important: plant the corn. In the meantime reinforcements arrived from Mexico, which sent this aid in exchange for Yucatán's resubmission to Mexican authority. Government troops took the offensive, and things went badly for the Mayas. Many retreated to the wilds of Quintana Roo, in the southeastern reaches of the peninsula.

The Talking Crosses

Then came the Talking Crosses. Massed in southern Quintana Roo, the Mayas needed inspiration in their war effort. It came in the form of a cross that "spoke." The cult was begun in 1850 by a Mayan ventriloquist and a mestizo "priest," and carried on a tradition of "talking idols" which had flourished for centuries in several places, including on the sacred Mayan island of Cozumel. The first appearance of the loquacious symbol was at a place which later became the town of Chan Santa Cruz, named "Little Holy Cross" in its honor. Soon several crosses were talking, inspiring the Mayas to go out and get the whites.

This worked pretty well until about 1866, when the fighting subsided. The Yucatecan authorities seemed content to let the rebels and their talking crosses rule the southern Caribbean coast, which they did with only minor skirmishes until the late 1800s. The rebel government received arms from the British in Belize, and in return allowed the British to cut lumber in rebel territory.

The End
But at the turn of the century, Mexican troops with modern weapons penetrated the rebel territory, soon putting an end to this bizarre, if romantic, episode of Yucatecan history. The town of Chan Santa Cruz was renamed in honor of a Yucatecan governor, Felipe Carrillo Puerto, and Yucatán was finally a full and integral part of Mexico.

2. Touring Yucatán: Itineraries
Any good itinerary of Yucatán would involve the following elements:

Mérida: Spend at least overnight here; two full days to see the city would be much better. You can also use Mérida as your base for visits to Chichén-Itzá, Uxmal, Kabah, Sayil, Xlapak, Labná and Loltún, taking organized tours or renting a car to tour on your own.

Uxmal: If you get as far as Mérida, seeing Uxmal is an absolute must! Traveling from Mérida, touring the ruins, and returning to the city will take the best part of a day. There are hotels at Uxmal where you can spend the night. Though well worth the money, they do exceed our daily budget limit.

Kabah, Sayil, Labná, Xlapak, Loltún: These Maya cities, south of Uxmal, demand another full day of touring time. If you stay overnight at Uxmal, you'll save travel time from Mérida.

Campeche, Edzná, Dzibilnocac, Hochob: Campeche, capital of the state of the same name, is a pleasant city with a charming walled colonial center. It's not a necessity on your Yucatán itinerary, but you may want to stay the night here if you're enroute between Palenque and Mérida. Campeche is also the most convenient place to stay for those visiting the Maya sites at Edzná and Dzibalchén (Dzibilnocac and Hochob).

Chichén-Itzá: This is another must-see, the most impressive Maya city in Yucatán. You'd be well-advised to spend the night here, as there is a good range of hotels, with several in the budget category. If you take a day tour from Mérida or Cancún, you'll arrive and begin to climb pyramids at the very hottest, most crowded time of day, and you'll climb back into your bus for the two-hour return ride just when the light on the ruins is prettiest and the heat is abating. Plan to spend the night at Chichén-Itzá.

Cancún: You'll want to see this world-class resort, but you needn't plan to spend all of your beach time here. Prices are lower on nearby Isla Mujeres, and the skin diving and snorkeling are best on Cozumel (though Cozumel prices rival—even exceed—those of Cancún at times).

Isla Mujeres: Easily accessible from Cancún by city bus and ferry boat, this small island is great for a day-trip, or even for a stay of several days.

Caribbean coast: You'll certainly want to take a trip along the coast south of Cancún, certainly as far as the beautiful cove of Xel-ha and the Mayan seaport of Tulum. Inland from Tulum lies the ancient city of Cobá, well worth the detour if you have the time.

Cozumel: Mexico's entry into the Caribbean islands competition, it's a skindiver's paradise, which drives up prices in winter. Though larger than Isla

Mujeres, Cozumel does not offer more variety of activities, and it's farther from the mainland.

TIME AND DISTANCE: You must become aware of the distances involved in a trip to Yucatán. Mérida, for instance, is 900 miles (1,450 km) by road from Mexico City, 400 miles (650 km) from Villahermosa, 125 miles (200 km) from Campeche, and 200 miles (325 km) from Cancún. A trip from Yucatán's nicest colonial city, Mérida, to the peninsula's premier resort, Cancún, thus involves a bus ride of five or six hours.

You can touch at all the high points of Yucatán in a week of touring by rental car, but you'll be traveling fast. Ten days is a more reasonable period to spend, and two weeks is excellent. You can easily spend three weeks and even more if you plan to explore ruined Maya cities off the beaten track, or put in several hours of beach or pool time every day.

ITINERARY—TEN DAYS TO TWO WEEKS: Here is a sample itinerary for a visit of ten days to two weeks, starting on the day you arrive in Mérida:

Day 1, Mérida: On the day of arrival, plan to settle in, get your bearings, perhaps change some money and adjust to the heat.

Day 2, Mérida: Tour the city, stopping at each of the historic buildings near the Plaza Mayor, and along the Paseo de Montejo. Save some time for the market!

Day 3, Uxmal: If you're driving, you can stop at Mayapán on your way to Uxmal. These two sites, and perhaps a quick stop in Ticul, will fill your day. Return to Mérida for the night, or stay at Uxmal.

Day 4, Kabah etc.: Spend the day touring sites of Kabah, Sayil, Labná, Xlapak, and the Grutas (caves) de Loltún. If you're absolutely fascinated by ruins and can't get enough, head for Campeche to spend the night, then spend the next day at Edzná, Dzibilnocac, and Hochob. Otherwise return to Mérida.

Day 5, Chichén-Itzá: Ride from Mérida through henequen country to Chichén-Itzá. Find a hotel room, have lunch, perhaps take a nap, then hike out to the ruins and tour until closing time.

Day 6, Cancún: Spend the morning at the ruins of Chichén-Itzá, then ride to Cancún in the afternoon. Find a hotel and settle in.

Day 7, Cancún: Put on your bathing suit, catch a city bus, and head out to the Zona Hotelera. Spend the day on one of Cancún's fine beaches. In the evening, wander around the restaurants in town.

Day 8, Isla Mujeres: Get an early start, and spend the day on Isla Mujeres's beaches, especially Garrafón, with its good snorkeling and diving. Perhaps stay the night.

Day 9, Caribbean coast: Using Cancún or Cozumel as your base, visit Tulum, Xel-ha, and perhaps other beaches and sites along the coast between Tulum and Cancún. If you have a car, drive inland to Cobá also. By bus or hitchhiking, Cobá will take at least a full day by itself.

Day 10, Cozumel: Spend a day on Cozumel, taking the passenger ferry or the shuttle flight from Playa del Carmen, or a flight from Cancún.

BEST MEANS OF TRANSPORT: Touring Yucatán is best done by car, though this presents several problems. First and foremost, rental cars in Mexico as of this writing are breathtakingly expensive. For a week's rental of a VW Beetle, adding in the costs of unlimited mileage, insurance, tax and gas, you might pay $300 to $350! If you have several people to share the cost, if you shop around and haggle a bit, and if it's not high season, the price becomes more reasonable.

Another caution is that roads are narrow, with virtually no shoulders or rest stops—just jungle on both sides. Though all right for daytime driving, you should not drive at night. I mean this! A way to cut the high cost of renting a car is to rent one only on certain days. For instance, touring from Mérida to Uxmal and Kabah, rent a car. But from Mérida to Chichén-Itzá and Cancún, take the bus—or even fly. From Cancún, take the ferry to Isla Mujeres, or the bus to the ferry for Cozumel, but rent a car for a day to see Xel-ha, Tulum, and Cobá. This involves more paperwork, but if a car costs $50 or $60 per day, you don't want it sitting around unused.

Of course, the bus is by far the most economical transport. Prices are incredibly low, less than $1 for an hour's travel. Although the buses go everywhere, you will spend a lot of time waiting at highway intersections, particularly near Uxmal, Kabah, etc., and along the Caribbean coast. Hitchhiking doesn't help too much, as traffic is usually light. If you plan to take buses exclusively, you must allow at least two weeks to see Yucatán thoroughly.

OFF WE GO: Most visitors head directly for Mérida, Cancún or Cozumel, and use those places as home base for further explorations. We'll start our Yucatecan tour in the Yucatecan capital—Mérida—using that city as a base to explore the ancient Maya cities of Uxmal, Mayapán, Kabah, Sayil, Xlapak and Labná, plus the walled Spanish city of Campeche. Then we'll head east, passing Chichén-Itzá and Valladolid on our way (in the next chapter) to Puerto Juárez, Cancún, and Isla Mujeres. Finally, we'll head down the Caribbean coast for a tour of Cozumel, Tulum, Cobá, Lago de Bacalar, and the brash new city of Chetumal, on the Belizean border.

3. Mérida

Mérida (pop. 500,000) is the capital of Yucatán, and has been its major city ever since the Spanish founded it in the mid-1500s on the site of the defeated Mayan city of Tiho. Although it's changing due to general growth and increased tourism, you'll still see examples of its ancient culture around.

In the market and elsewhere, you'll notice items woven of a sisal fiber called **henequen**. The raising of henequen is Yucatán's main industry, apart from tourists, and it is used to make hammocks, baskets, shoes, tablemats, twine, and rope.

The tourist season is busiest in July and August, when the weather is very hot and humid. A far more pleasant time to visit is in December, January, and February. You'll need a light jacket or sweater for winter, cool clothes for summer days. Light raingear is suggested for the brief showers of late May, June, and July.

GETTING TO AND FROM MÉRIDA: Unless you have a private car, it's simple: arrive by air or by bus. As mentioned before, I do not recommend the passenger trains in this part of Mexico because they're uncomfortable and slow, and foreign tourists riding in them tend to be a mark for thieves. If you must take the train, you'd be well advised to get a special reserved first-class seat *(primera especial),* or a private sleeping compartment. For information on the types of sleeping accommodations, see Chapter I, "Getting There," Section 2.

Arriving (and Departing) by Air: Mérida enjoys nonstop air connections with the following cities (with flights per day listed): Cancún (two), Chetumal (one), Cozumel (two), Havana (three flights per week), Houston (two flights per week), Mexico City (eight or nine per day), Miami (two), Veracruz (four per week), and Villahermosa (one per day).

Flying into Mérida's modern airport, you'll find yourself on the southwestern outskirts of town, where Hwy. 180 enters the city. Taxis between the airport and downtown hotels cost about 1,500 pesos ($3). The "Transporte Terrestre" minibuses charge 720 pesos ($1.44) per person for the ride downtown, so if you're travelling in a group, take a cab as it'll work out to be cheaper.

City bus no. 79 ("Aviación") operates between the center and the airport. This is the cheapest way to go, of course, with a one-way ticket costing only 40 pesos (8¢), though the buses are not all that frequent. Other city buses run along the Avenida de los Itzáes, just out of the airport precincts, heading for downtown.

You can make reservations and buy air tickets from one of the many travel agencies in Mérida. The two national carriers have offices downtown as well: **Aeroméxico** is at Av. Paseo de Montejo no. 460 (tel. 27-9000) and at Calle 60 no. 499-A (tel. 24-4786 or 24-4692). At the airport, phone them at 24-8554 or 24-8576. **Mexicana** is at Calle 58 no. 500 (tel. 24-6623) and Calle 56-A no. 493, at Paseo de Montejo (tel. 24-7421 or 23-0508). At the airport, their number is 23-8602 or 23-6986.

Arriving (and Departing) by Bus: Mérida's main bus station (BUS), run by the Unión de Camioneros de Yucatán, is on Calle 69 between Calles 68 and 70, about six blocks southwest of the Plaza Mayor. The **ADO** line runs from here, as do **Unión de Camioneros** buses. The station has a travel agency with tours to the ruins, a newsstand, a bank, and various stalls selling souvenirs and snacks.

Coming from the west (Cancún, Chichén-Itzá, Valladolid), your bus may make a stop at the old bus station on Calle 50 between 65 and 67. If you're headed for the Plaza Mayor, you'd might as well get off here. It's six blocks to the plaza from here as well.

As for departures, buses to Uxmal depart at 6, 7, and 9 a.m., 12 noon, and 3 and 5 p.m.; return trips are at 8:30 and 11:30 a.m., and 2:30, 5:30 and 7:30 p.m.

Going via Mayapán, catch a bus to Oxcutzcab, which will take you through Kanasin and Acanceh, to Ruinas de Mayapán, and then through the villages of Mayapán, Mama, etc. Be sure to tell the driver you want to get off at the ruins, or he'll assume you want to go to the village, several kilometers farther on.

For Chichén-Itzá there are buses at 6:30 and 8:30 a.m. and 4:30 p.m. If you're planning to go out and back in a day (something I don't recommend if you enjoy seeing impressive ruins), take the 8:30 bus and reserve a seat on the 3 p.m. bus returning from Chichén. A one-way ticket on the 2- to 2½-hour trip costs 731 pesos ($1.46), by the way; a round-trip ticket is precisely twice as much.

To Cancún and Puerto Juárez (the dock for boats to Isla Mujeres), there are buses almost every hour on the hour throughout the day, from 7 a.m. to just past midnight. The trip takes about five hours and costs 1,970 pesos ($4).

For buses north to Progreso, you must go to a special bus terminal at Calle 62 no. 524, between Calles 65 and 67. Buses leave every five or ten minutes or so throughout the day on the 45-minute trip.

There are buses to Campeche from the main bus station about every 30 minutes or so throughout the day on the three- or four-hour trip (the duration depends partly on which route you pick, the short way via Hwy. 180, or the longer route past Uxmal and Kabah via Hwy. 261).

About 18 ADO buses per day head out to Villahermosa via the Palenque junction, a trip of about 11 or 12 hours.

Seven buses a day make the long grind all the way to Mexico City.

Arriving (and Departing) By Train: Just in case you arrive by train, you should know that the station is about eight blocks northeast of the Plaza Mayor on Calle 55 between Calles 48 and 46.

To make a reservation for a primera especial seat or sleeping car berth, something you should do several days before you hope to depart, go to the ticket office between 11 a.m. and 1 p.m. any day. Then go off to the market and pick up plenty of food and drink, as there are no restaurant cars on the trains in this area.

ORIENTATION: As with most colonial Mexican cities, Mérida's streets were laid out in a grid. Even-numbered streets run north-south, odd-numbered streets run east-west. In the last few decades, the city has expanded well beyond the grid, and several grand boulevards have been added on the outskirts to ease traffic flow.

A word of warning about street numbers: What with unnumbered dwellings and -A, -B, and -C additions, these progress agonizingly slowly. Example: I wanted to get from 504 to 615D on Calle 59 and did—after walking 12 blocks! Otherwise, the street grid is fairly easy to find your way in.

Plaza Mayor

The center of town is the very pretty Plaza Mayor, sometimes called the Plaza Principal, the main square, with its shapely, shady trees, benches, vendors, and a social life all its own. Around the plaza are the massive cathedral, the Palacio de Gobierno (state government headquarters), the Palacio Municipal, and the Casa de Montejo, a mansion built by the founder of Mérida, now occupied by a bank. Within a few blocks of the Plaza Mayor are several smaller plazas, each next to a church; the University of Yucatán; and the sprawling market district.

Paseo de Montejo

Mérida's most fashionable address, however, is over seven blocks northwest of the Plaza Mayor. It's the Paseo de Montejo, a wide tree-lined boulevard laid out during the 19th century and lined with houses and mansions built by politicos and henequen barons. The Paseo, which extends northward for over a dozen blocks, is home to Yucatán's anthropological museum, several upscale hotels and auto dealerships, and the American Consulate.

GETTING AROUND: Most of the time, you'll walk, because many of the most attractive sites are within a handful of blocks from the Plaza Mayor.

Taxis are usually easy to find in the center of town. A short ride, perhaps between the Plaza Mayor and the bus station or the Paseo de Montejo, might cost 600 or 700 pesos ($1.20) or $1.40).

Another way to tour the town is in a horse-drawn carriage. Look for a rank of them near the cathedral, then haggle for a good price. An hour's tour might cost 2,000 to 2,500 pesos ($4 to $5).

City buses are the cheapest of all, charging only 40 pesos (8¢) for a ride. You might conceivably take one to the large, shady Parque Centenario on the western outskirts. Look for the bus of the same name ("Centenario") on Calle 64.

As for rental cars, you may well want one of these for your explorations of Mayapán, Uxmal, Kabah, etc. You don't really need one to get around Mérida, or to Chichén-Itzá or Cancún.

The bad news is that rental cars are very expensive these days in Yucatán, averaging out to $50 or $60 per day for a VW Beetle. The good news is that you can often haggle for a lower price. You should, in any case, shop around among the local agencies for a good price. Unlike the situation in many other cities, I have not had a rash of complaints about the little local businesses in Mérida.

Keep these tips in mind as you scour the city for a rental car deal: kilometers and insurance are the most expensive charges, daily rental and fuel are the least. Don't be impressed by a very low daily charge, unless it includes unlimited kilometrage. In every single case, get the absolutely final figure for a rental before you decide; if you can't get kilometers included, estimate the distance you'll travel by adding up the highway mileages, then add 15% for wrong turns and detours. Keep in mind that you can often get lower rates if you rent for more than a day or two, and if you promise to pay at the end of the rental in cash dollars (you'll need a credit card at first for the paperwork, though). For more information on car rental, see Chapter XVI, "Latin Listings," under "Car Rentals."

Here are some of the local agencies that seem to be good. Please write and tell me about your car-rental experiences, both good and bad.

México Rent-A-Car (tel. 992/21-7840), Calle 60 no. 495, between 59 and 57, across from the Parque de la Madre, in the garage entrance of the Hotel del Parque, is a small, dependably friendly firm with prices a good deal lower than the big international firms.

Rentadora "Lol-tún" (tel. 992/23-3637), Calle 62 no. 483-A, between 61 and 59, is operated by two brothers, José Alberto and Victor González Loeza, who readily adjust their prices according to demand. I was quoted a flat price of $72 for two days' rental, unlimited kilometers, tax and insurance all included.

Budget Rent-A-Car (tel. 992/27-8755), on the northern reaches of the Paseo de Montejo (Prolongación no. 497), and at the airport, also offers an unlimited mileage rate which works out to about $51 per day, all included except gas.

You might also try **Volkswagen Rent** (tel. 992/21-8128), Calle 60 no. 486-F, between 57 and 55, which tends to be competitive with (usually slightly higher than) Lol-tún.

TOURIST INFORMATION: The most convenient source is the office operated by the **Estado de Yucatán** (tel. 24-9290 or 24-9389), in the hulking edifice known as the Teatro Peón Contreras, on Calle 60 between 57 and 59, open Monday through Friday from 9 a.m. to 9 p.m., Saturday from 9 a.m. to 4 p.m., Sunday from 9 a.m. to 12 noon.

You can also try the **Palacio Municipal,** on the western side of the Plaza Mayor (opposite side from the cathedral), which has a tourism office open daily from 8 a.m. to 8 p.m., Sunday from 11 a.m. to 5 p.m.

The **Secretaría de Turismo** (SECTUR) building (tel. 24-9431 or 24-9542), where not much seems to be happening, is at the corner of Calles 54 and 61.

USEFUL FACTS: Banamex, in the Palacio Montejo on the Plaza Mayor, has its own casa de cambio which usually provides a better rate of exchange than the banks. Other banks are located on and off Calle 65 between Calles 62 and 60.

The **American Consulate** (17) is at Paseo de Montejo no. 453, corner of Avenida Colón (tel. 992/25-5011 or 25-5409), next to the Holiday Inn; hours are 8 a.m. to 1 p.m. and 2 to 5:30 p.m., Monday through Friday, closed on Mexican and American holidays. The telephone number of a duty officer is posted at the entrance. The **British Vice-Consulate** is at Calle 53 no. 489, corner of Calle 58 (tel. 992/21-6799). Open in principle from 9:30 a.m. to 1 p.m., you may find no one there. The vice-consul fields questions about travel to Belize as well as British matters. The **Canadian Consulate** is at Calle 62 no. 309-D-19 (tel. 992/25-6299). The **Alliance Française** has a branch at Calle 56 no. 476 (tel. 992/21-6013).

Medical care: If "Montezuma's Revenge" has got you, see the Introduction to this book for tips. If it gets serious, ask your hotel to call a doctor after you've got an estimate of his fee. The city's **Hospital O'Horan** is on Avenida de los Itzáes at Calle 59A (tel. 992/23-8711), north of the Parque Centenario.

Mérida's **main post office** (22) is at the corner of Calles 65 and 56, in the midst of the market, open from 8 a.m. to 7 p.m. Monday through Friday, on Saturday from 9 a.m. to 1 p.m.; closed Sunday.

Telephones: Long-distance casetas are at the airport, the bus station, at Calles 59 and 62, and Calles 59 and 64, on Calle 60 between 55 and 53 in "El Calendario Maya," and at the intersection of Avenidas Reforma and Colón in a farmacia. Remember that international calls are extremely expensive, but at least from a caseta you won't pay a hotel's gross "service charge."

WHERE TO STAY: Mérida's line-up of hotels is a budget traveler's dream-come-true. From the very expensive to the very low-priced, from the modern to the romantically old-fashioned, everyone can find a place that suits. Most hotels offer at least a few air-conditioned rooms (and current weather reports will tell you whether or not you'll need this), and a few of the places in the budget line-up even have swimming pools! Although Mérida, and the Yucatán in general, are in the midst of a tourism boom, it is only in August that you may find absolutely every room taken. If you cannot find exactly what you want when you first arrive, take an available room for a night or two, and spend an hour the next morning pinpointing and reserving your chosen room.

Modern, with Colonial Touches

As in many Mexican towns, the hotel lineup in Mérida includes numerous establishments which are basically modern in amenities and construction, but colonial in inspiration and decor. Mérida has quite a few of these, in a nice range of prices. Expect a serviceable and comfortable if not particularly charming room, and a fairly central location, in any of these places.

At the corner of Calles 59 and 60, a mere half-block northeast of the Plaza Mayor, is the 43-room **Hotel Caribe (2)** (tel. 992/21-9232), with three floors arranged around a quiet central courtyard. The restaurant's tables are set out in a portico surrounding the court; on the top floor is a small but quite serviceable swimming pool, a sundeck, and a vantage point for views of the cathedral and the town. Most of the rooms here have an air conditioner, television set, phone, ceiling fan, and modern tile bathroom, usually with a walk-in shower. Attached to the hotel is a sidewalk cafe with wrought-iron tables set out in the shady Parque Cepeda Peraza. Prices for a room with ceiling fan are 4,600 pesos ($9.20) single, 5,520 pesos ($11.04) double, 6,440 pesos ($12.88) triple; with air conditioning, you pay 5,060 pesos ($10.12) single, 5,980 pesos ($11.96) double, 6,900 pesos ($13.80) triple. Suites cost about 2,000 pesos ($4) more per room.

For the price and location, it's hard to beat the **Hotel Colonial (4)**, at Calle 62 no. 476, corner of Calle 57 (tel. 992/23-6444). This bright and modern five-story hotel has over 50 rooms, a small swimming pool, and central air conditioning. But the prices are the best part: singles cost 5,540 pesos ($11.08) and doubles go for 6,680 pesos ($13.36), representing good value for what you get. Here you're right next door to the University of Yucatán.

The new **Hotel del Gobernador (24), Calle** 59 no. 535 at the corner of Calle 66, Mérida 97000-8 (tel. 992/23-7133), qualifies as among Mérida's most modern. Sleek but small (43 rooms and 16 junior suites), the hotel features air conditioning and telephone in each room, a swimming pool, cafeteria, bar, laundry, and parking lot for guests' cars. Rooms cost 8,590 pesos ($17.18) single, 10,350 pesos ($20.70) double, 1,500 pesos ($3) for each extra person. As for the junior suites, they have two double beds each, and cost about 2,000 pesos ($4) more per room than the standard accommodations.

The **Hotel Dolores Alba (25),** Calle 63 no. 464 between Calles 52 and 54 (tel.

992/21-3745), is an old Merida house converted to receive guests. Twenty rooms here come with air conditioning, ceiling fans, and showers, plus decorations of local crafts. A big open court and another court with a nice clean swimming pool give a sense of space. You'll pay 3,000 pesos ($6) single, 4,500 pesos ($9) double, 5,500 pesos ($11) triple, for a room with a fan. Air conditioning costs a bit more. The Dolores Alba is run by the Sanchez family, who also have the Hotel Janeiro, plus the Hotel Dolores Alba at Chichén-Itzá. Make reservations at one hotel for space at the other hotel, if you like.

The **Hotel Janeiro (21),** Calle 57 no. 435, between Calles 48 and 50, about seven blocks from the Plaza Mayor (tel. 992/23-3602), is owned by the same family as the Dolores Alba. Since buying the Janeiro, they've spruced up the rooms and added a nice little swimming pool and patio tables for breakfast or snacks. Rooms come with ceiling fan for 3,320 pesos ($6.64) single, 4,000 pesos ($8) double; with air conditioning and TV for 4,400 ($8.80) single, 5,300 ($10.60) double. They have parking places for a few cars.

The **Hotel Reforma (7),** Calle 59 no. 508, just off Calle 62 (tel. 992/24-7922, is another of those grand old establishments embellished with flowered tiles and tortured wrought-iron staircase. The high-ceilinged rooms, most with ceiling fans, open on two floors off the central patio where there are rubber plants in huge pots. Furnishings are old but well kept: singles with ceiling fan are 3,675 pesos ($7.35); doubles, 4,430 pesos ($8.86). Add 850 pesos ($1.70) for air conditioning. The few rooms upstairs in the back around a separate little court are among the nicest in the hotel. A small swimming pool is open for guests' use.

Only a block and a half north of the Plaza Mayor is the small **Hotel del Parque (3),** Calle 60 no. 495, at Calle 59 (tel. 992/24-7844). The hotel entrance and restaurant are quite colonial, but the 21 rooms are actually in the modern structure next door. The rooms are quite small, but bright with floral wallpaper, tiled baths, and ceiling fans. The hotel has its own large enclosed parking lot. Figure to pay 3,000 pesos ($6) single, 3,565 pesos ($7.13) double here.

Budget Rooms

The aforementioned hotels offer excellent value for money, but if your budget is even slimmer, consider the following ones which offer suitable if spartan accommodations for unbeatable prices.

The **Hotel Peninsular (13),** Calle 58 no. 519, between 65 and 67 (tel. 992/23-6996 or 23-6902), is right in the heart of the market district less than three blocks southeast of the Plaza Mayor. In such a busy district, you'll be surprised to find this warren of tidy, quiet little rooms at the end of the long entrance corridor. There's even a small restaurant. Prices are 2,160 pesos ($4.31) single, 2,600 ($5.20) double with ceiling fan; 2,900 ($5.80) single, 3,500 ($7) double with air conditioning.

Four blocks northeast of the Plaza Mayor is the **Hotel Mucuy (5),** Calle 56 no. 481 (between Calles 56 and 58; tel. 992/21-1037). The hotel is named for a small dove said to bring good luck to places where it alights, and you should have good luck, as many alight here. The two floors of rooms, with window screens, tile showers, and ceiling fans, are lined up on one side of a garden with fine grass and bougainvillea; you can park your car within the hotel gates for free. The owners are Sr. Alfredo and Sra. Ofelia Comin, who live on the premises. Señora Comin speaks English. Rates are 2,400 pesos ($4.80) single, 3,000 pesos ($6) double, 3,600 pesos ($7.20) for three persons. A laundry sink and clothesline are available for guests' use. The roses and bougainvillea seem to be in bloom all summer here.

The **Casa Bowen (9)** (tel. 992/21-8112) is actually two buildings. The original old building, with small, bare rooms around a courtyard, has been supple-

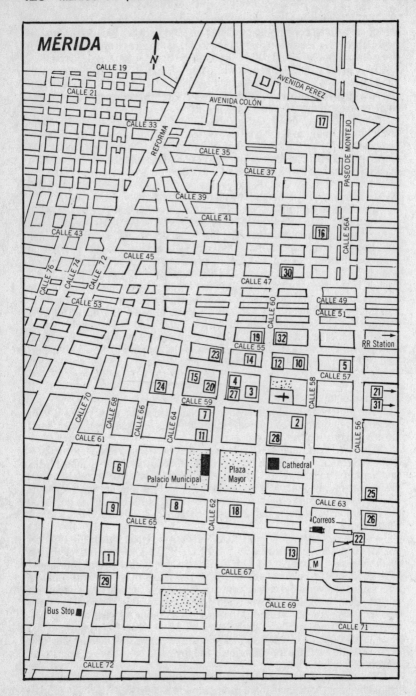

mented with a big new addition next door. Rooms come with tile showers and ceiling fans for 3,000 to 3,500 pesos ($6 to $7). Rooms in the old building are cheaper, but well used. The location is good, though: Calle 66 no. 521-B, near Calle 65.

Another budget hotel is the **Hotel Latino (6),** Calle 66 no. 505, between Calles 61 and 63 (tel. 992/21-4831). Inside, all 25 rooms have private bath, hot and cold water, built-in headboards and bed tables, the only furniture in the rooms being the beds themselves and a chair. Nevertheless, it's okay for the price. Singles are 2,600 to 2,870 pesos ($5.20 to $5.74), doubles are 2,870 to 3,120 pesos ($5.74 to $6.24), air conditioning and two beds are included in the higher priced rooms. This makes the Latino the best choice for low-budget readers who really want the comfort of a cooled room.

The **Hotel Lord (8),** a block out of the Plaza Mayor on Calle 63 at no. 516 (tel. 992/23-9371), is a rather sterile place that somehow looks as if it should be a barracks, except that it's painted a cheerful yellow. Although it's a newish building, the rooms are arranged in several tiers around a central court that serves as a parking lot for guests. All rooms have screens and ceiling fans, and cost 2,575 pesos ($5.15) single, 3,100 pesos ($6.20) double. Rooms with air conditioning rent for 750 pesos ($1.50) more. Don't let the hotel's architecture fool you: it's a fine place to stay, with a very friendly management.

Colonial Inns

A few of Mérida's lodging places have an authentic colonial ambience, somewhat faded, it's true, but still charming.

I'm very fond of the hotel **Posada Toledo (10),** Calle 58 no. 487 (at the corner of Calle 57) (tel. 992/23-2256), once a private mansion but now run as an inn with 19 rooms and a rooftop deck, good for sitting and viewing the city in the cool of the evening. The place seems to be a cross between a garden and a museum with antique furnishings and lots of verdure. Rates are 6,000 pesos ($12) single and 7,000 pesos ($14) double with ceiling fan, 6,500 pesos ($13) single and 7,500 pesos ($15) double with air conditioning.

You're sure to notice the crumbling façade of the **Gran Hotel (28),** overlooking the Parque Cepeda Peraza at Calle 60 no. 496, between 59 and 61, a half-block north of the Plaza Mayor (tel. 992/24-7622). It has obviously seen better days, but those in search of faded splendor will like its fancy woodwork, wrought-iron balustrades, and marble staircases. Everyone likes its prime location, and some go for its restaurant. Room prices, with private bath and ceiling fan, are 3,150 pesos ($6.30) single, 3,800 pesos ($7.60) double.

Near the Bus Station

The **Hotel Posada del Angel (1),** Calle 67 no. 535, between Calles 66 and 68, Mérida 97000 (tel. 992/23-2754), is a mere 1½ blocks from Mérida's main bus station, and thus a good choice for late arrivals. It's a tidy, modern white place with red tile accents and semicircular windows, two floors, and 26 rooms. The few rooms on the front are very noisy due to the bus thrumming, but most rooms are in the back. Make sure yours is. Prices are 2,865 pesos ($5.73) single, 3,450 pesos ($6.90) double, for a room with bath and fan. There's free parking if you've come by car, not bus.

Right across the street from the aforementioned place is the **Casa Becil (29),** Calle 67 no. 550-C, between 66 and 68, Mérida 97000 (tel. 992/21-2957), a homey casa de huespedes where you pretty much live with a pleasant family. Most of the 12 rooms are around a tiny court in back where it's quiet. They're plain, but suitable, and go for 2,200 pesos ($4.40) for one bed (one or two people), 2,500 pesos ($5) for a room with two beds.

The Big Splurge

Although the Yucatán is unquestionably one of Mexico's great delights, there's no denying that it can be hot and even frustrating to travel here, now and then. When you get the feeling you owe yourself a bit of luxury, head for the **Hotel Los Aluxes (30),** Calle 60 no. 444, at Calle 49 (tel. 992/24-2199). Pronounced "ah-*loo*-shes," the name refers to the magical elves who acted as guardian angels to the ancient Mayas. This modern 109-room hotel is Mérida's newest, and offers you a patio café with thatch-shaded tables, a coffee shop, a posh restaurant, a swimming pool and sundeck on the mezzanine level, and a staff ready to please. Air-conditioned rooms are priced at 11,500 pesos ($23) single or double, 12,650 pesos ($25.30) triple, all included. The hotel has its own parking lot.

Another good choice is the **Hotel Panamericana (31),** Calle 59 no. 455, between 52 and 54 (tel. 992/23-9111 or 23-9444). The Panamericana has a secret: you enter an ornate 19-century doorway to register at the front desk. Then you pass through a classic Spanish atrium with its fancy stone and woodwork, and head for a modern annex which holds the up-to-date guest rooms, the restaurant, and the swimming pool. The old building is quite charming, the new one quite efficient. For one of the 90 rooms with bath, air conditioning, television (with satellite programming), and perhaps a fine city view, you pay 11,500 pesos ($23) single or double. Twelve junior suites cost about 2,500 pesos ($5) more per room; six suites yet another 1,500 pesos ($3).

Those in mind for a real splurge will want to know that Mérida has a **Holiday Inn (17),** Av. Colón no. 498, between Calle 60 and the Paseo de Montejo (tel. 992/25-6877). The lavish low-rise layout, right next to the American Consulate, includes all the comforts and conveniences, including a big swimming pool, of course. Rooms are priced at 23,000 pesos ($46) single or double.

READERS' HOTEL SELECTIONS: "The **Hotel Nacional,** Calle 61 no. 474, between 54 and 56 (tel. 992/4-9255 or 4-9463), has quiet rooms at the back, hot water, cafeteria and pool and costs 4,500 pesos ($9) per person per night. The staff speaks very little English, and the clientele is mostly Spanish-speaking" (Mike Wei, Victoria, B.C., Canada).

WHERE TO EAT: As with hotels, Mérida is a budget-traveler's delight when it comes to mealtime. American, Mexican, and Yucatecan meals from snacks to banquets are all easy to find. Some of the best dining you'll experience during your Mexican trip will be had here in the capital of Yucatán, and it will cost you anywhere from 200 pesos (40¢) for a sandwich to 3,500 pesos ($7) for a complete and embarrassingly bountiful repast.

You should make a point of trying some of the special dishes of Yucatán during your stay in Mérida. I'll give you a few suggestions.

Yucatecan Food

First you must know how things are seasoned. The hot pepper of Yucatán, called *chile habanero,* is among the hottest in all Mexico, and if you tangle with one, you won't soon forget it. But you needn't worry, as dishes are not heavily doused in habanero, although it is used. Often it lurks in a fiery sauce served on the side.

A popular sauce is *achiote,* made of sour orange juice, salt, onion relish, habanero peppers, and cilantro (fresh coriander leaf). There's also *pipián,* a sauce made with pumpkin or sunflower seeds, and *escabeche,* a thick, mildly piquant concoction reminiscent of a stew, though the word means "pickle."

Here are some Yucatecan favorites:

Huevos motuleños: Said to have originated in the Yucatecan town of

Motul, these breakfast eggs come atop a tortilla, garnished with beans, peas, ham, sausage, and grated cheese.

Sopa de lima: Lime soup is tangy and flavorful, made with chicken stock.

Cochinita pibil: Suckling pig is wrapped in banana leaves and baked in a barbecue pit (if it's authentic), flavored with achiote. Look also for the similar pollo pibil, made with chicken.

Papadzules: Tortillas are stuffed with hard-boiled eggs and seeds (cucumber or sunflower) in a tomato sauce.

Pavo relleno negro: Pavo means turkey, and Yucatán was the original home (along with New England) of this marvelous bird. Stuffed turkey, Yucatán style, is filled with chopped pork and beef and cooked in a rich, dark sauce.

Poc-chuc: Slices of pork with onion are served in a tangy sauce of sour oranges or limes.

Venado: Venison (deer) is a popular dish served numerous ways, perhaps as pipián de venado, steamed in banana leaves and served with a sauce of ground squash seeds.

Queso relleno: "Stuffed cheese" is a mild yellow cheese stuffed with minced meat and spices.

Beer: As for drinks, Yucatecan beers such as Carta Clara and Montejo (lager) and León Negro (dark) are delicious, but harder and harder to find as the gigantic brewing companies from central Mexico move in and crowd the market.

Liquor: *Xtabentún (Shtah*-ben-*toon)* is the local high-octane firewater, traditionally made by fermenting honey, then flavoring the brew with anise. Today the xtabentún you buy in the market may have a lot of grain neutral spirits in it instead of fermented honey. Think of the drink as Yucatecan ouzo or pastis. It comes *seco* (dry), or *crema* (sweet).

Here, then, is the rundown on Mérida's restaurants. Write and tell me if you find any new good ones.

Full Service, Moderate Prices

Probably the most popular meeting place in town is the **Café-Restaurant Express (3)** (tel. 21-3738), facing the park at Calles 59 and 60. Here, hordes of townspeople—mainly men—sit and ogle the hours away, totally oblivious of surroundings, with all attention focused on the sidewalk or at least a newspaper. The menu is vast—lengua a la Mexicana (Mexican-style tongue), pollo pibil (the chef wraps and marinates the chicken in banana leaves before cooking), huachinango milanesa (red snapper). Top off whatever you choose with pasta de guayaba con queso (guava paste with cheese). Or simply while away some time here with coffee, good and strong. Plan to spend 800 pesos ($1.60) for breakfast, about 1,250 pesos ($2.50) for the set-price lunch, and 2,600 pesos ($5.20) for dinner. Open 6 a.m. to 1 a.m. every day.

I used to recommend a number of restaurants on Calle 62 just north of the main plaza, but in recent years the traffic noise and fumes (particularly from the buses) have become overwhelming. Nowadays one is much better off dining right on the plaza, at the **Restaurant Nicté-Ha,** for instance, Calle 61 no. 500 (tel. 23-0784). Although very plain, the Nicté-Ha is pretty quiet and pollution free, and prices are low: tacos, hamburgers, even carne asada and chicken dishes cost 750 to 1,300 pesos ($1.50 to $2.60).

Soon after your arrival in Mérida you'll discover **El Mesón** (tel. 21-9232), the tiny place just to the left of the Hotel Caribe's entrance. Wrought-iron tables are set out in the shady Parque Cepeda Peraza (alias Parque Hidalgo), and they're often full. The food is usually pretty good; I especially enjoy the sopa de verduras (vegetable soup), and prices are great: the set-price meal, usually served right into the evening hours, is only 1,050 pesos ($2.10). El Mesón is open for three meals a day, every day.

For a light lunch, try **Pop (14)** (tel. 21-6844), on Calle 57 between Calles 60 and 62, next to the university. The little place is air-conditioned, clean, bright, and modern, and seems to be where the gilded youth of Mérida have their afternoon snack. Apple pie, Bavarian fudge cake, the best hamburgers in town, and air conditioning are the attractions. Prices are okay: 400 to 500 pesos (80¢ to $1) for a hamburger, 500 pesos ($1) for a fruit salad with ice cream. "Pop," by the way, is the first month of the 18-month Maya calendar.

For Yucatecan Cuisine

As Yucatecan cuisine spreads throughout Mexico, the fame of poc-chuc pork goes with it. The dish, a delectable concoction of grilled pork, tomatoes, onions, *cilantro* (fresh coriander leaves), and salt, was created in Mérida at **Los Almendros (21)** (tel. 21-2851), Calle 50 no. 493, between Calles 57 and 59, facing the Plaza de Mejorada. Actually, the first Los Almendros is deep in the Maya hinterland, at Ticul, but the branch in Mérida has become the favorite spot to sample local delicacies. Start with venison broth (sopa Mestiza), then have poc-chuc, pollo pibil, or pavo relleno negro (baked turkey with a black stuffing of ground pork, roasted peppers, and Yucatecan spices). You'll find lots of similarly exotic and delicious entrees, all for about 900 to 1,050 pesos ($1.80 to $2.10)—with descriptions in English! The daily special plate, always a good bargain, costs about 1,250 pesos ($2.50) and constitutes a full meal. Over the years, I've been alternately delighted and mildly disappointed at Los Almendros. You must try it, though.

For Lebanese Cuisine

In Yucatán? A Middle Eastern restaurant? Why? Because 19th-century Mexico, and particularly Yucatán, had a significant population of Ottoman traders, mostly from the sultan's province of Lebanon. The Restaurant **Cedro del Libano (24)** (tel. 23-7531), Calle 59 no. 529, between Calles 64 and 66, is a simple but tidy place with experienced waiters and a menu that lists berenjena con tijini (eggplant with tahini), labne (yogurt), labin (like buttermilk), tabule, kibi, and alambre de kafta (ground meat grilled on skewers). I had the fatta Cedro del Libano, which turned out to be chicken topped with chick-peas, yogurt, and sliced almonds. Meat dishes cost about 1,400 to 1,500 pesos ($2.80 to $3), and a full meal can be had for 2,500 pesos ($5) or so. Hours are 11:30 a.m. to 11:30 p.m. every day.

Vegetarian Fare

Any Mexican town of considerable size has a vegetarian restaurant, and Mérida is no exception. Here it's the **Restaurante Vegetariano La Guaya (32)** (tel. 23-2144), Calle 60 no. 472, between 55 and 53, just a few steps north of the Parque Santa Lucia. Enter to find a little patio cafe in a courtyard, combined with a bookstore featuring health-related titles. Lots of different salads are offered here, as well as a Hindu dish of oats, wheat, and fish, named Kama Sutra! The daily set-price meal costs 900 pesos ($1.80). Come any day for lunch or dinner.

A Plaza Café

For after-dinner ice cream or Mexican pastries and cakes, the **Dulcería y Sorbetería Colón** sets out bent-wire café tables and chairs in the portico on the

Plaza Mayor (Calle 61 side). Besides serving dessert at budget prices—320 pesos (64¢) for ice cream, 100 to 150 pesos (20¢ to 30¢) for cake—it provides the best vantage point for people-watching in the late afternoon or evening. Try some of their exotic tropical fruit ice creams such as coconut or papaya. Open 8 a.m. to midnight daily. Try to pick a time of day when auto traffic (with its noise and smelly fumes) is not so heavy in the square.

For Breakfast

A good breakfast choice, particularly if the day is already hot, is the aforementioned **Pop,** which is air-conditioned and has set breakfasts priced at 400 pesos (80¢) for a continental breakfast, 520 pesos ($1.04) with two eggs, and 620 pesos ($1.24) with two eggs plus bacon or ham.

To make your own breakfast, feast your eyes (and later your appetite) on pastries and sweet rolls from the **Panificadora Montejo,** at the corner of Calles 62 and 63, which is the southwest corner of the main plaza. It's hard not to over-eat with your eyes as you choose from a dozen or more delectable breakfast treats. With a hot drink a suitable light breakfast can be thrown together for about 400 pesos (80¢).

For those (like me) who simply cannot start a day without fresh orange juice, here's good news. Juice bars with the name of **Jugos California** or Jugos Florida have sprouted up all over Mérida. Three of these thirst-quenching establishments are on or just off the main plaza: one on Calle 62 near Calle 61, one on the Calle 63 side of the plaza, and another just across the corner from it on Calle 62! Demand is brisk, and prices are not high for what you get: a tall ice-cream-soda glass of juice squeezed right before your eyes for 200 to 450 pesos (40¢ to 90¢).

Starvation-Budget Restaurants

Cafetería Erik's (11) (no phone), Calle 62 no. 499A, just off the main plaza, among the various other Erik's restaurants in town belonging to the chain, has the reputation for the best tortas—fried sandwiches stuffed with ham and cheese, turkey, roast pork—for 350 to 675 pesos (70¢ to $1.35) apiece. A few of these are very filling. A pleasant wood-paneled place with tablecloths, it features smooth jazz in the background.

El Louvre (11) (tel. 21-3271), Calle 62 no. 499, right next door to Erik's off the main plaza at Calles 61 and 62, is rather inaptly named unless you consider it a gallery of people. Open 24 hours a day, this big open place probably feeds everybody who comes to Mérida at one time or another—chicle workers, laborers from the henequen fields, planters, and townspeople. Prices are low: sandwiches for 300 to 425 pesos (60¢ to 85¢), eggs motuleños (Yucatán style on a fried tortilla with fried beans and chopped ham) for 475 pesos (95¢), lots of combination plates, and a daily set-price lunch for a mere 700 pesos ($1.40). Calle 62 between the main plaza and Calle 57 is a riot of such small, rock-bottom food shops offering everything from chalupas to chow mein. Starvation-budgeteers are sure to find things to fit the appetite and the wallet all along the street.

Where the Students Eat

Mérida is the home of the Yucatán's university, and thus of student throngs deep into plain living and high thinking. Living plainly does not mean badly, however, for the humble torta (sandwich) always provides tasty and nutritious fare at a rock-bottom price. The mecca for this time- and budget-saver is **Las Mil Tortas (23)** (no phone), on Calle 62 between Calles 57 and 55. Very small, this shop-of-a-thousand-sandwiches sports a long list of sandwiches priced from 200 to 380 pesos (40¢ to 76¢). The few small tables are often filled with the student crowd, but you can get your tortas and *refresco* (soft drink) to go, all for less than 500 pesos ($1). By the way, Las Mil Tortas is branching out now, and you may see similar shops in other parts of the city. There's one on Calle 56 near Calle 57, around the corner from the Hotel Mucuy.

Romantic Dinners

A place to try if you're feeling only moderately wealthy is the **Restaurante Portico del Peregrino (14)** (tel. 21-6844), Calle 57 no. 501, right next door to the ever-popular Pop and across the street from the university. The restaurant aims to recapture the 19th century in Mexico, and does this rather well. You enter through a little garden court—a good place to take a bench seat and wait for laggers in your party—then through a cross-topped gateway into another little courtyard set with tables and shaded by vines and trees. If the weather is too warm for outdoor dining, escape to the air-conditioned bliss of the two enclosed dining rooms which are well stocked with antique beveled mirrors and elegant sideboards. Table settings are done with white cloths and decent glassware. For less than 3,500 pesos ($7) you can have soup, fish filet, a brochette of beef, or pollo pibil, plus rum raisin ice cream for dessert. The Peregrino is open for lunch and dinner, noon to 3 p.m. and 6 to 11 p.m., every day of the week.

Those in the mood for French cuisine will want to try the **Yannig Restaurante (4)** (tel. 21-8468), Calle 62 no. 480, between 57 and 59. Chef Yannig Oliviéro was trained in France, and serves up the old favorites and some of his own creations: onion or garlic soup, roquefort salads and crêpes, pâté maison, beef with unripe pepper sauce, fish amandine, coq au vin, pêche Melba. The bright, cheery, cozy little restaurant is a pleasant change from the normal fluorescent lighting. Plan to spend 2,000 pesos ($4) for a light meal, 4,500 pesos ($9) for a feast with wine. Only dinner is served, Monday through Saturday from 5 to 11:30 p.m., Sunday from 1 to 10:30 p.m.

READERS' RESTAURANT SELECTIONS: "I'd like to highly recommend a new Lebanese restaurant, the **Restaurante Hazbaya,** Calle 72 no. 416-E. The atmosphere is very plain, but the air conditioning is nice on a hot day. The food is excellent (eggplant and garbanzo appetizers, cream of garlic soup, etc.) and prices moderate" (Judith Ludy, Chapel Hill, N.C.). . . . "An ideal place for speakers of Spanish to enjoy an inexpensive lunch is at the **Chapur department store,** Calle 63 at 58. The second-floor cafeteria is pleasantly air-conditioned. We had one hamburger (ground beef and a slice of ham in a bun), one plate of achiote rice with plantains and bits of chicken, a slice of pecan pie, a glass of watermelon juice, a soft drink, and an espresso all for under 2,000 pesos ($4)" (Robert and Janice Titiev, Detroit, Mich.).

WHAT TO DO: Mérida is pretty, congenial, friendly, and in summer it's also very, very hot. Just before the coming of the muggy rainy months (June through September), Mérida can get up to 108° F (42° C). You'd do well to arise early, snatch a quick breakfast, and do your walking well before the noonday sun does its worst. Then have lunch, and a siesta, and issue forth in the evening, refreshed and ready for the next round.

If you're lucky enough to be visiting in January or February, you'll be able to spend most of the day outdoors without discomfort.

Start your explorations of old Mérida at the city's focal point, the Plaza Mayor.

Plaza Mayor

This beautiful town square, now shaded by topiary laurel trees, began its history as the Plaza de Armas, a training field for Montejo's troops. Later called the Plaza Mayor, it was renamed the Plaza de la Constitución in 1812, then the Plaza de la Independencia in 1821. Other common names for it include Plaza Grande, Plaza Principal, and even (sometimes) zócalo.

The city was laid out by the conquering Montejos on the classic Spanish colonial plan. Surrounding the plaza were the cathedral, the archbishop's palace, the governor's palace, and the mansions of notables. Let's examine each in turn.

The cathedral: On the east side of the plaza, the cathedral was under construction from 1561 to 1598. It looks like a fortress, as do many other early churches in Yucatán. That was actually their function in part for several centuries, as the Mayas did not take kindly to white domination. Much of the stone in the cathedral's walls came from the ruined buildings of Maya Tihó. Inside, decoration is sparse and simple, the most notable feature being a picture over a side door of Ah Kukum Tutul Xiú visiting the Montejo camp.

To the left of the main altar is a smaller shrine with a curious burnt cross, recovered from the church in the town of Ichmul, which burned down. The figure was carved by a local artist in the 1500s from a miraculous tree which burned but did not char. The figure burned, though, along with the church, and broke out in blisters as it did. The local people named it Cristo de las Ampollas (Christ of the Blisters).

Also take a look in the side chapel (open 8 to 11 a.m. and 4:30 to 7 p.m.), which has a life-sized diorama of the Last Supper. The Mexican Jesus is covered with prayer crosses brought by supplicants asking for intercession.

The archbishop's palace and a seminary used to stand to the right (south) of the cathedral. The palace was torn down during the Mexican Revolution (1915); part of the seminary remains, but is now used for shops.

Palacio de Gobierno: on the north side of the plaza, this site was first occupied by a mansion built for the colonial administrators; the present building dates from 1892.

Between 8 a.m. and 8 p.m. (Sundays 9 to 5) you can visit the palace and view the large murals painted mostly between 1971 and 1973. Scenes from Mayan and Mexican history abound, the painting over the stairway combining the Mayan spirit with ears of sacred corn, the "sunbeams of the gods." Nearby is a painting of the mustached benevolent dictator Lázaro Cárdenas, who in 1938 expropriated 17 foreign oil companies and was hailed as a new Mexican liberator.

Palacio Municipal: Facing the cathedral across the plaza from the west side is the Palacio Municipal, or City Hall, with its familiar clock tower. It started out as the cabildo, the colonial town hall and lock-up, in 1542. It had to be rebuilt in the 1730s, and rebuilt again in the 1850s, when it took on its present romantic aspect.

Palacio Montejo (18): Also called the Casa de Montejo, it was begun in 1549 by Francisco Montejo, "El Mozo," and was occupied by Montejo descendants until the 1970s. It now houses a bank branch (Banamex), which means you can get a look at parts of the palace just by wandering in during banking hours (9 a.m. to 1:30 p.m., Monday through Friday). Note the arms of the Spanish kings and of the Montejo family on the Plateresque façade, along with figures of the Conquistadores standing on the heads of "barbarians" overcome by their exploits. Look closely and you'll find the bust of Francisco Montejo the Elder, his wife, and his daughter.

Shopping in the Market

Mérida's bustling market district is just a few blocks southeast of the Plaza Mayor, roughly the area bounded by Calles 63 to 69, and 62 to 54. The market proper is right next to the post office, at the corner of Calles 56 and 65. Wade into the clamor and activity, browsing for leather goods, hammocks, Panama hats, Mayan embroidered dresses, men's formal guayabera shirts, and hand-craft items of all kinds. A few tips and pointers might be helpful.

Buying hammocks: The supremely comfortable Yucatecan fine mesh ham-mocks (hamacas) are made of string from several materials. Silk is wonderful, but extremely expensive, and only for truly serious hammock-sleepers. Nylon is long-lasting. Cotton is attractive, fairly strong, and inexpensive, but it wears out sooner than nylon. There are several grades of cotton string used in hammocks. What will probably serve your needs best is a cotton hammock of good quality string. Here's how to find it:

First, look at the string itself. Is it fine and tightly spun? Are the end loops well made and tight? Grasp the hammock at the point where the body and the end strings meet, and hold your hand level with the top of your head. The body should touch the floor; if not, the hammock is too short for you.

Next, open the hammock and look at the weave. Are the strings soiled? Are there many mistakes in the pattern of the weave?

Then, decide on size. Keep in mind that any of these hammocks is going to look big when you stretch it open, but many will seem small when you actually lie in them, so you want a hammock as big as you can afford. Hammocks are sold as *sencillo* (single, 50 pairs of end strings, about $5), *doble* (double, 100 pairs of end strings, about $8 to $10), *matrimonial* (larger than doble, 150 pairs of end strings, about $12 to $15). The biggest hammock of all is called *una hama-ca de quatro cajas,* or sometimes *matrimonial especial,* and it is simply enor-mous, with 175 pairs of end strings; if you can find one, it'll cost you about $16 to $18. Buy the biggest hammock you think you can afford. You'll be glad you did. The bigger ones take up no more room, and are so much more comfortable, even for just one person.

Where should you buy your hammock? Street vendors will approach you at every turn, "¿Hamacas, Señor, Señorita?" Their prices will be low, but so may be their quality. Buy from these guys if you're willing to take the time and go through all the steps listed above. Otherwise, booths in the market will have a larger selection to choose from, at only slightly higher prices.

I've been recommending the store called **La Poblana, S.A.** (tel. 21-6503), Calle 65 no. 492, between 60 and 62, for years with no complaints. Sr. William Razu C., the owner, is usually on the job and ready to whip out dozens of ham-mocks for your inspection. Prices are marked, and bargaining is not encour aged. If you've spent some time in the market for hammocks, and you seem to know what you're talking about, Sr. Razu may usher you upstairs to a room wall-to-wall with hammocks, where you can give your prospective purchase a test-run. La Poblana sells ropes and mosquito nets for hammocks as well, and also Mayan women's dresses and men's guayaberas.

Panama hats: Another very popular item are these soft, pliable hats made from the palm fibers and fibers of the jipijapa plant in several towns along Hwy. 180 in the neighboring state of Campeche. If you travel through Becal, for in-stance, you'll see a sculpture in the main square composed of several enormous concrete hats tipped up against one another. It's a fitting monument to a town-folk who have made their wealth (such as it is) weaving the pliant fibers into handsome headgear while sitting in humid limestone grottoes and caves. The caves provide just the right atmosphere for shaping the fibers. Stop and ask for a demonstration, and any citizen will be glad to oblige.

There's no need to journey all the way to Becal, however, as Mérida has the hats in abundance. Just the thing to shade you from the fierce Yucatecan sun, the hats can be rolled up and carried in a suitcase for the trip home. They retain their shape quite well.

Jipi hats come in three grades, judged by the quality (pliability and fineness) of the fibers and closeness of the weave. The coarser, more open weave of fairly large fibers will be sold for a few dollars (or by street vendors in Cancún and Cozumel for up to $10!). The middle grade, a fairly fine, close weave of good fibers, should cost about $10 in a responsible shop. The finest weave, truly a beautiful hat, can cost twice this much. For most people, the middle grade is fine.

A tried and true sombrería is **La Casa de los Jipis** (no phone), Calle 56 no. 526, near Calle 65, where a phlegmatic señora will show you the three grades of hats, grumping the while. Find your size, more or less, and the señora will tie a ribbon around the hat for final adjustment. If you'd like to see how the hats are blocked, wander into the shady depths of the rear of the store.

Handcraft: For a look at the best of Yucatán's crafts and handiwork, drop by the **Museo Regional de Artesanías,** Calle 59 between 50 and 48, open for free from Tuesday through Saturday, 8 a.m. to 8 p.m., Sunday till 2 p.m., closed Monday. Another place to examine crafts is at **La Casa de la Cultura,** Calle 63 no. 513, between 64 and 66, a beautiful restored monastery with exhibits of crafts, and a shop where you can buy. There are also two galleries here with changing exhibits, plus a bookstore, a bulletin board listing cultural events, and an inexpensive cafeteria.

Exploring Calle 60

Many of Mérida's old churches and little parks are located along Calle 60 north of the Plaza Mayor. Plan a stroll along this street, perhaps continuing to the Paseo de Montejo and its Museo Regional de Antropología.

Parque Cepeda Peraza: As you leave the Plaza Mayor, you'll pass the site of the Seminario de San Ildefonso, an early hospital, on your right. You then come to the little Parque Cepeda Peraza (also called the Parque Hidalgo), named for the 19th-century General Manuel Cepeda Peraza. Part of Montejo's original plan for the city, the parque borders the church called La Iglesia de Jesus, or El Tercer Orden (the Third Order), built by the Jesuit order in 1618. The entire city block in which the church stands was part of the Jesuit establishment, and the early schools started by these worthies ended up being the Universidad de Yucatán. The Biblioteca (library) Cepeda Peraza, founded by the general in 1867, is beside the church.

Down Calle 59 a few steps past the park and the church is the former Convento de la Mejorada, a late-1600s work of the Franciscans.

Parque de la Madre: This little park is sometimes called the Parque Morelos. By its statue shall you know it, this little park with its modern madonna and child. The statue is a copy of the work by Lenoir which stands in the Luxembourg Gardens in Paris.

Teatro Peón Contreras: Designed by Italian architect Enrico Deserti in the beginning of the present century, the enormous yellow building holds the state Tourist Information Office (facing the park). The main entrance, with its Carrara marble staircase and frescoed dome, is closed most of the time, unfortunately. Try for a look at 11 a.m. on Sunday.

Universidad de Yucatán: On the west side of Calle 60, at the corner of Calle 57, is the university, founded in the 19th century by Felipe Carrillo Puerto with the help of the aforementioned General Cepeda Peraza. Wander in, ask directions to the fresco (1961) by Manuel Lizama, and it will show you the whole story of the founding.

Heading north on Calle 60, you'll see the Hotel Mérida Misión on your left, the Hotel Casa del Balam on your right. Soon you'll come to the Parque Santa Lucia.

Parque Santa Lucia: Facing the park is the ancient Iglesia de Santa Lucia (1575). The plaza itself, surrounded by an arcade on the north and west sides, used to be the place at which visitors first alighted in Mérida from their stagecoaches. The plaza is floodlit at night, and on Thursday there are concerts of local music at 9 p.m. On Sunday afternoons, the plaza fills up with vendors and browsers during the weekly Antiques and Crafts Bazaar.

To reach the Paseo de Montejo, walk up Calle 60 to Calle 47, turn right, and the Paseo is two blocks away.

Paseo de Montejo

Most guidebooks compare the Paseo to Paris's Champs-Élysées, but you'll see at once that they're pretty different. Even so, it is a broad, tree-lined thoroughfare lined with imposing banks, hotels, and a number of the old 19th-century mansions put up by henequen barons, generals, and other Yucatecan potentates.

Museo Regional de Antropología (16): Most impressive mansion of all is that occupied by the local anthropology museum, at the corner of Calle 43. The Palacio Cantón (1909–1911) was designed by Enrico Deserti, the architect who designed the Teatro Peón Contreras, and built during the last years of the Porfiriato as the home of General Francisco Cantón Rosado (1833–1917). The general got to enjoy his palace for only six years, until his death. After this short occupancy the imposing edifice began a new career as a school, then as the official residence of Yucatán's governor, before becoming first the archeological museum, and now the Regional Museum of Anthropology.

Don't neglect to admire the building itself as you walk around. It's the only Paseo mansion that you'll get to visit. Note especially a great luxury of the time: the little art deco elevator. The museum is open from 8 a.m. to 8 p.m. Tuesday through Saturday, to 2 p.m. on Sunday, closed Monday. Entry costs 40 pesos (8¢).

On the right as you enter is a room for changing shows. After that are the permanent exhibits, with captions in Spanish only. Starting with fossil mastodon teeth, the exhibits take you down through the ages of Yucatán's history, giving special attention to the daily life of its inhabitants. You'll see how the Mayas tied boards to babys' skulls in order to reshape the heads, giving them the slanting forehead which was then a mark of great beauty, and how they filed teeth to sharpen them, or drilled teeth to implant jewels. Enlarged photos show the archeological sites. The one of Mayapán, for instance, clearly shows the city's ancient walls. Even if you know little Spanish, the museum provides a good background for your Mayan explorations.

Monumento a la Patria: Continue your stroll along the Paseo, and you'll walk by the Parque de las Americas, planted with trees and shrubs from throughout the New World, to the grandiose Monumento a la Patria (Monument to the Fatherland), done by Rómulo Rozo in the 1950s in neo-Mayan style.

Parque Centenario

Due west of the Plaza Mayor along Calle 61 or 65, lies the large Parque Centenario, bordered by the Avenida de los Itzáes, which leads to the airport and Campeche. The parque is a fine place for an afternoon stroll, especially with children. There's a small zoo with Yucatecan animals; the deer, for instance, are quite graceful and nimble.

A Side Trip to Progreso

Want to zoom out to Progreso for a day? There's a good beach, not touristy but very Mexican, a fantastically long *muelle* ("mu-*wey*-yeh," or pier) that shoots out into the bay to reach water deep enough for ocean-going ships, and a few seafood restaurants (nothing great, though).

To get there, go to the special Progreso bus station on Calle 62 at no. 524, between Calles 65 and 67. Buses leave every five or ten minutes during the day, starting at 5 a.m. The trip takes 45 minutes.

Once in Progreso, Calle 19 runs along the beach. The bus station is about four blocks south of this street. The beach seems endless, and is crowded with coconut palms (and on weekends, with Mexican families). The **Restaurant Carabela,** Calle 69 no. 146, on the seashore Avenida Malecon, will serve you a fish platter for 1,450 pesos ($2.90), shrimp for just a bit more.

MÉRIDA NIGHTLIFE: There are band concerts every Sunday at 9 p.m. in the Plaza Mayor. Every Thursday in **Santa Lucia Park (19),** on the corner of Calles 60 and 55, you can hear some festive music and serenades by different maria-chis. They begin at 9 p.m. and stop when their enthusiasm turns to thirst.

Take a stroll past the **Jardín de los Compositores** (Garden of Composers), behind the Palacio Municipal, to see what's happening. This is the venue for many concerts, movies, and general happenings.

Another good place to check is the **Teatro Peón Contreras** at Calles 60 and 57. Ask at the Tourist Information Office right in the building about current shows. They often have Yucatán's own ballet folklorico in performance, but usually on Sunday mornings at 11 rather than at night.

Hotel bars, lounges, and discos depend largely upon the crowd of custom-ers presently staying at each hotel. Most of Mérida's downtown hotels are filled with tour groups whose members, after an exhausting day, seek to rest rather than rock.

For a cross-cultural experience, you might want to try the club named **Tulipanes** (tel. 27-2009 or 27-0967), Calle 42 no. 462-A, which has a restaurant, bar, and disco. Every evening from 8:30 to 10 they put on a floor show inspired, however remotely, by Mayan customs, ancient and modern. Cover charge is 3,000 pesos ($6); the restaurant menu tends toward Yucatecan specialties such as pollo pibil, venison steaks, and chuleta yucateca (pork chops with achiote).

ONWARD TO MAYALAND: Uxmal ("Oosh-*mahl")* is about 80 kilometers (50 miles) to the south of Mérida. Uxmal and Chichén-Itzá (see below) are the two must-not-miss sites in Yucatán, but there are many other sites of beauty and significance. Depending on how you travel, you may be able to visit some of these other sites on your way to Uxmal.

Want the full rundown? First there's Mayapán, the ancient Maya capital city, badly ruined now but in a lush setting. It's difficult to reach, but thrilling to consider yourself walking among the ruins of the great Maya capital. Then there's Uxmal, with several of the most beautiful and awe-inspiring buildings ever constructed by man. Then 27 kilometers (17 miles) southeast of Uxmal is Kabah, with a unique palace, several other grand buildings, and a decorative style very different from that at Uxmal. From Kabah it's only a few kilometers to Sayil, with its immense palace reminiscent of Minoan structures. Xlapak ("Shla-*pahk")* is almost walking distance (through the jungle) from Sayil, and Labná just a bit farther east. A short drive east from Labná brings you to the caves of Loltún. Backtrack to the main road (Hwy. 180) and you can head west to spend the night in Campeche.

Those with only a little time and/or money will have to limit themselves to seeing Uxmal on a day-trip by bus (see above, "Getting To and From Mérida," for details). The ideal but more expensive way to tour the ruined cities south of Mérida is to rent a car, plan to stay the night in a fairly expensive hotel at Uxmal (that's all there is), and allow two full days to sightseeing before hitting Campeche or returning to Mérida, or driving on toward Tulum and Cancún. How interested are you in Mayan archeology? If you enjoy it as much as I do, then find some friends to share expenses, rent a car in Mérida, ignore your daily hotel budget in Uxmal, and enjoy yourself. You can save money on hotels at Chichén, where you'll find an assortment of inexpensive and moderate hostelries. At Uxmal, there's no such choice.

Another way to do it is to ignore Mayapán, get an early start in your rental car, and head south on Hwy. 180 directly to Uxmal. Spend the morning there, and the afternoon at Kabah, Sayil, Xlapak, and Labná, and then head on to find an inexpensive hotel in Campeche, or return to Mérida. This tour would be about 445 kilometers (275 miles) round trip.

Here, then, is a stone-by-stone description of the ruined Maya cities south of Mérida, starting with Mayapán, and the old pottery-making town of Ticul.

4. Mayapán and Ticul

MAYAPÁN: Founded by the semilegendary Quetzalcóatl (Kukulcán in Maya) in about 1007, Mayapán ranked in importance with Chichén-Itzá and Uxmal. It was a vast city, and for almost two centuries it was the capital of a Maya confederation of city-states that included Chichén and Uxmal. But before the year 1200 the rulers of Mayapán put an end to the confederation by attacking and conquering Chichén, and by forcing the rulers of Uxmal to live as vassals in Mayapán. For almost 250 years Mayapán was the center of power in Yucatán.

You can take a village bus to the Ruinas de Mayapán (not to be confused with the village of Mayapán; see above, "Getting To and From Mérida," for details). But the easiest way is to drive. Ask directions frequently—it's very easy to take wrong turns or to get onto unmarked roads by mistake.

Head out of Mérida toward Kanasin and Acanceh ("Ah-kahn-*keh*"), about 20 kilometers. This is not as easy as it sounds, as signs are few and sometimes mistaken. Here are some hints: get to Calle 65 in the Mérida *colonia* (suburb) named Miraflores, on the eastern edge of the city. Head east on 65, bear right at its end, then take an easy left at a big intersection. Follow the wide, divided highway complete with speed bumps, cross Mérida's *circunvalación* (ring road)—you'll see signs to Cancún (left) and Campeche (right)—and continue straight on. Soon you'll enter Kanasin. Watch for signs that say *desviación* (detour) as you approach the town. As in many Yucatán towns, you're being redirected to follow a one-way street through the urban area. Go through the market, pass the church on your right, the main square on your left, and continue straight out of town.

The next village you come to, at Km. 10, is San Antonio Tehuitz, an old henequen hacienda. At Km. 13 is Tepich, another hacienda village, with those funny little henequen-cart tracks crisscrossing the main road. After Tepich comes Petectunich, and finally Acanceh.

ACANCEH: In Acanceh there's a partially restored pyramid to the left of the church, overlooking the main square, and several others tucked away in back yards. Should you need sustenance, Acanceh's market, complete with little loncherías, is just to the right of the church.

Turn right in the main square (around that statue of a smiling deer) and head for Tecoh (9 kilometers) and Telchaquillo (11 kilometers). This route takes you past several old Yucatecan haciendas, each complete with its big house, chapel, factory with smokestack, and workers' houses. Shortly after the village of Telchaquillo, a sign on the right-hand side of the road will point to the entrance of the ruins, on the right.

A hundred yards in from the road, after passing the guards' hut, are the remains of Mayapán. The main pyramid is ruined but still lofty and impressive. Next to it is a large cenote (natural limestone cavern, used as a well), now full of trees, bushes, and banana plants. A small temple with columns and a fine high-relief mask of Tlaloc, the hook-nosed rain god, are beside the cenote. Other small temples, including El Caracol, with its circular tower, are in the nearby jungle, reached by paths.

These piles of stones, though impressive, give one no idea of what the walled city of Mayapán must have been like in its heyday. Supplied with water from 20 cenotes, it had over 3,000 buildings in its enclosed boundaries of several square miles. Today, all is covered in dense, limitless jungle.

Sr. Fausto Uc Flores, the guard, or his wife Sra. Magdalena, whom you may meet as you enter the ruins, will sell you the requisite admission ticket for 40 pesos (8¢), and help you with any bits of information you may need.

Heading onward, continue along the main road to Tekit (8 kilometers), turn right and go to Mama (7 kilometers), turn right again for Chapab (13 kilometers), and finally you'll reach Ticul (10 kilometers), the largest town in the region.

TICUL: You can have an excellent lunch here, or get a soft drink, or change some money, or pick up snacks in the market, or even stay the night in modest comfort if necessary.

This sprawling town actually has only 20,000 inhabitants, many of whom make their living embroidering huipiles (the Mayan ladies' costume), weaving straw hats, and shaping pottery. Workshops and stores throughout the town, and especially in the market area, feature these items.

The main street is Calle 23, also sometimes called the Calle Principal. It's where you'll find the market, a hotel, and Ticul's best-known restaurant.

Where to Stay and Eat

The nicest hotel in town is actually a motel on the outskirts. The **Hotel-Motel Cerro Inn** (no phone), is just at the edge of town, two kilometers from the market, on the highway to Muna and Mérida. Its nine rooms, dark but cool, with showers and fans, face a shady grove and a nice palapa restaurant. Prices are 2,500 pesos ($5) for a double bed (single or double), 6,000 pesos ($6) for two beds. This place doesn't look so great as you enter, but it's not bad at all.

Right downtown, mere steps from the market, is the little **Hotel San Miguel** (no phone), Calle 28 no. 195, at the intersection with Calle 23. The 20 very simple rooms here with showers and fans, arranged along a corridor in what can only be called Mexican cell-block fashion, cost 1,300 pesos ($2.60) double in a double bed, 1,600 pesos ($3.20) double in twin beds.

The **Hotel Sierra** (no phone), on the main square, charges about a dollar more than the San Miguel for its tidy rooms.

The restaurant called **Los Almendros** (tel. 2-0021) is on Calle 23 not far from the market. Set in the courtyard of a big old Andalusian-style house, this is the original of the chain with branches now in Mérida and Cancún. The specialties are Mayan, such as papadzules (the stuffed tortillas) and poc-chuc. The illustrated menu in English explains the dishes in detail, so you're not in for a mystery meal. Stop in any day for lunch or dinner, and your bill will come to about 1,500 or 1,900 pesos ($3 or $3.80).

near the market there's a cantina called **Bar "Tu Hermana"** (Your
can't recommend it, but as a veiled insult or the punch-line to a ribald
unbeatable!

R'S RESTAURANT SELECTION: "Our find is just off the Plaza Principal, called **Restau-
Los Delfines**, Calle 26 no. 195, between Calles 21 and 23 (tel. 2-0070). It's a wonderful
ce run by Miguel Angel Cachon Lara and his wife, Aida. Most main courses cost
ound 1,000 pesos ($2), and the comida corrida costs 800 pesos ($1.60); liquor is served,
and it's open from 8 a.m. to 11 p.m. every day" (Malcolm Cochran, Sutton Mills, N.H.).

What to Do

Ticul's annual festival, complete with bullfights, dancing, and carnival
games, is held during the first few days of April.

Besides a look at the pottery shops, Ticul offers a look at some impressive
caves, those called Yaxnic (Yash-neek), on the grounds of the old Hacienda Yo-
toliin, within the city limits. Virtually undeveloped and full of colored stalactites
and stalagmites, the caves are visited by means of a perilous descent in a basket
let down on a rope.

Onward

It's 22 km (14 miles) from Ticul to Muna. At Muna, turn left and head
south on Hwy. 180 to Uxmal, 16 km away. Buses depart Ticul for Muna almost
hourly during the day. At Muna, change to a bus heading south to Uxmal.

5. Uxmal

Prepare yourself for one of the highlights of your Yucatán vacation, for the
ruins of Uxmal are truly breathtaking.

If you've decided to come directly from Mérida on Hwys. 180 and 261, you
get a bonus: the chance to tour a real Yucatecan hacienda.

YAXCOPOIL: This unpronounceable Maya name designates a fascinating old
hacienda on the road between Mérida and Uxmal. It's difficult to reach by bus,
but if you're driving, look for it on the right side of the road 33 kilometers (21
miles) south of Mérida, 16 kilometers (10 miles) south of Uman, on Hwy. 261.

Take a half hour to tour the house, factory, outbuildings, and museum.
You'll see that such haciendas were the administrative, commercial, and social
centers of vast private domains, almost little principalities, carved out of the
Yucatecan jungle.

When you leave Yaxcopoil, you still have 45 kilometers (28 miles) to drive
to reach Uxmal.

UXMAL: Although the ruins of Uxmal are visible from the highway, the im-
pressiveness of this site will not strike you until you enter the archeological zone
and walk around. Coming from the north along Hwy. 261, you'll pass four
hotels—three of them moderately expensive—before you reach the ruins proper. Here's what to expect.

Where to Stay and Eat

Unlike Chichén-Itzá, which has several classes of hotels from which to
choose, Uxmal has mostly one class: comfortable, but expensive. But at Uxmal,
"expensive" doesn't mean prices like at the Ritz, so you should be able to absorb
a night's stay in your budget without too much pain.

Each of these hotels is willing to offer you room-with-meals plans, and you should look into them. Buying your dinner and breakfast—and perhaps even lunch—with your room in a package will ultimately save you money, because there's nowhere to eat but at the three hotels. Buying the meals separately adds up to more than buying the package. For savings, pack a box lunch in Mérida and bring it along.

My favorite of the hotels here is the oldest one, the **Hotel Hacienda Uxmal,** Uxmal, Yucatán 97844 (tel. 4-7142; for reservations, contact Mérida Travel Service in the Hotel Casa del Balam in Mérida, Calle 60 no. 488; tel. 992/21-9212). Right on the highway across from the ruins, the Hacienda Uxmal was built as the headquarters for the archeological staff years ago. Rooms are large and airy, with equally large bathrooms, screens on the windows, ceiling fans, and blocky, substantial furniture. The rambling building groups many rooms around a central garden courtyard complete with fine swimming pool and bar. A dining room and gift shop fill out the spare rooms. Singles cost 15,075 pesos ($30.15); doubles are 16,400 pesos ($32.80); huge triple rooms are 17,700 pesos ($35.40). For dinner and breakfast, add 8,200 pesos ($16.40) per person to these prices. You should definitely take the meal package here, as dinner alone costs almost as much as the entire meal plan if you buy it separately. In effect, you get a full breakfast for no extra charge when you take the meal plan. It's a five-minute walk to the ruins from the hotel. Check-out time is 2 p.m., so you can spend the morning at the ruins and take a cooling dip (you'll need it!) before you check out and head out on the road again.

Even closer to the ruins is the **Villa Arqueológica** (no phone)—the hotel driveway starts at the ruins parking lot. A Club Med operation, the Villa Arqueológica has a swimming pool, tennis court, library, audio-visual show on the ruins in English, French, and Spanish, and 40 air-conditioned rooms that are fully modern. The layout is posh and tasteful—it's the "designer" version of the Hacienda Uxmal. Room prices here are 8,625 pesos ($17.25) single, 10,810 pesos ($21.62) double; meals are à la carte only.

Farther out, north of the ruins two kilometers on the highway is the **Hotel Misión Uxmal** (no phone), a new and modern 40-room hotel that you can't help but notice as you drive. Same services here: restaurant, bar, pool, etc. The comfortable, air-conditioned rooms sell for 11,660 pesos ($23.30) double.

Now there is an exception to the high-priced places near Uxmal, but only if you have strong legs and a sun hat, or a car. The **Rancho Uxmal** (no phone), on Hwy. 261 north of the ruins 3½ kilometers (2¼ miles), is a modest little place with a thatched-roof restaurant, a few primitive camping spots, and four comfy rooms with showers and fans. If the rooms were in Mérida they'd rent for much less, but as they're here in a high-rent district near the ruins, they go for 4,500 pesos ($9) double. Camping is very cheap: 500 pesos ($1) per person, with electrical hookup and use of a shower. In the restaurant, most main-course plates cost less than 900 pesos ($1.80). It should take you about 30 minutes to walk to the ruins from here, but remember—that sun gets awfully hot.

Food at or near the Ruins

There is now a new service center at the ruins, called the **Unidad Uxmal.** Within the modern complex are toilets, a first-aid station, a small museum, a cafeteria, and shops for publications, photo supplies, and craftwork. This is the most convenient place to get a snack or light lunch for about 1,000 pesos ($2).

Otherwise, the Hacienda Uxmal has a little lunchroom and bar called the **Posada Uxmal, Café-Bar Nicté-Ha,** in a building right across the highway from the turnoff to the ruins. A ham-and-cheese sandwich costs about 750 pesos ($1.50), a fruit salad only slightly less. This is a lot for what you get, but it's less to spend than the 3,000 pesos ($6) or so you'd spend on the set-price full lunch in the hotel. The café-bar is open from 12:30 p.m. to 7 p.m.

Seeing the Ruins

The ruins of Uxmal are open from 8 a.m. to 5 p.m. every day. Admission is 50 pesos (10¢); on Sunday and holidays admission is 30 pesos (6¢).

A 45-minute sound-and-light show is staged each evening, in Spanish for 300 pesos (60¢) at 7 p.m., and in English for 800 pesos ($1.60) at 9 p.m. The special sound-and-light bus from Mérida only stays for the Spanish show. If you stay for the English, you've got to find your own ride back to Mérida.

The Pyramid of the Magician: As you enter the ruins, note first of all the *chultún* (cistern) just inside the fence to the right, the ticket booth being to your left. Besides the natural underground cisterns (such as cenotes) formed in the porous limestone, these chultúnes were the principal source of water for Maya civilization. You'll see more of them at Sayil and at sites near it.

After buying your ticket and walking a few steps farther, you'll be confronted with Uxmal's dominant building, the Pyramid of the Magician. Legend has it that a mystical dwarf who had hatched from an egg built this pyramid in one night, which is where it gets its name. Actually, there are several temples underneath the one you see. It was common practice for the Maya to build new structures atop old ones, even before the old structures were ruined.

The pyramid is unique because of its oval shape, its height and steepness (wait till you see the steps on the other side!), and its odd doorway. The doorway is on the opposite (west) side near the top, and is actually a remnant of the fourth temple built on this site (what you see today is the fifth). In contrast to the clean, simple style of the rest of the pyramid, the doorway is in Chenes style, with elaborate decoration featuring stylized masks of the rain god Chac. In fact, the doorway is a huge Chac mask, with the door as mouth.

The View from the Top: It's a tiring and even dangerous climb, but what a view! You're now in an ideal position to survey the rest of Uxmal. Next to the Pyramid of the Magician, to the west, is the Nunnery Quadrangle, so called because it resembles a monastery or convent. To the left (south) of the Nunnery is the ruined ball court, and south of that are several large complexes. The biggest building, with a 320-foot-long façade, is called the Governor's Palace. Near it is the small House of the Turtles. Behind the Governor's Palace is the Great Pyramid, only partly restored, and beyond that the Dovecote, a palace with a lacy roofcomb that looks as though it'd be a perfect apartment complex for pigeons.

These are the main structures you'll notice from atop the Pyramid of the Magician, but there are others. For instance, the small ruined pyramid directly south is called the Pyramid of the Old Woman, which may be the oldest building at Uxmal. Due west of the pyramid is the Cemetery Complex, a temple with roofcomb that's pretty ruined. There's also a Northern Group, mostly covered with jungle and in ruins.

Uxmal is special among Maya sites because of the broad terraces or platforms constructed to support the building complexes—look closely and you'll see that the Governor's Palace is not on a hill or rise, but on a huge square terrace, as is the Nunnery Quadrangle.

Now that you've got your breath, prepare for the climb down. If you came up the east side, try going down the west.

The Nunnery: No nuns lived here. It's more likely this was a military academy or a training school for princes, who may have lived in the 70-odd rooms. The buildings were constructed at different times: the northern one was first, then the southern one, then east, then west. The western building has the most richly decorated façade, with interesting motifs of intertwined snakes. Masks of the rain god Chac, with his hooked nose, are everywhere. The richness of the geometric patterns on the façades is one of the outstanding features of Uxmal.

As you head toward the archway out of the quadrangle to the south, notice that above each doorway in the south building is a motif showing a Maya cottage, or *na,* looking just like you see them today. All of this wonderful decoration has been restored, of course—it didn't look this good when the archeologists discovered it.

The Ball Court: The ball court is ruined, and not so impressive. Keep it in mind, and compare it to the magnificent restored court at Chichén-Itzá.

The Turtle House: Up on the terrace south of the ball court is a little temple decorated with colonnade motif on the façade, and a border of turtles. It's small, but simple and harmonious—one of the gems of Uxmal.

The Governor's Palace: This is Uxmal's masterwork, an imposing edifice with a huge mural façade richly decorated in mosaic designs of the Puuc style. "Puuc" means "hilly country" and Uxmal has many examples of this rich decoration. The Puuc hills, which you passed over coming from Mérida, are the Mayan "Alps," a staggering 350 feet high! Mayan towns near the hills favored this style of geometric patterns and masks of Chac, giving the style its name.

The Governor's Palace may have been just that: the administrative center of the Xiú principality, which included the region around Uxmal. The Xiú rulers later conquered the emperors at Mayapán, and became supreme in the region. The fall of Mayapán allowed Yucatán to split up into smaller principalities. It was just great for the conquistadores, who arrived less than a century after the fall of Mayapán and mopped up the principalities one by one. The great princes of Xiú, as it turns out, did the Maya people no favor by breaking up the hegemony of Mayapán.

Before you leave the Governor's Palace, note the elaborate stylized headdress patterned in stone over the central doorway.

The Great Pyramid: A massive structure partially restored, it has interesting motifs of birds, probably macaws, on its façade, as well as a huge mask—the Uxmalians went in for masks in a big way. The view from the top is wonderful.

The Dovecote: It wasn't built to house doves, but it could well do the job in its lacy roofcomb. The building is remarkable in that roofcombs weren't a common feature of temples in the Puuc hills, although you will see one (of a very different style) on El Mirador at Sayil if you visit that site.

Leaving Uxmal

It can give you quite a thrill to ponder what Uxmal must have been like in its heyday: great lords and ladies clad in white embroidered robes and feathered headdresses moving here and there; market day, when the common people would come from their thatched huts and gather nearby in a tumultuous scene of barter and brouhaha. Uxmal flourished in the Late Classic period, about A.D. 600 to 900, and then became subject to the Xiú princes (who may have come from the Valley of Mexico) after the year 1000. Four and a half centuries later, the Xiú conquered Mayapán (1440s). The conquistadores moved in shortly after, ending forever the glories of Mayan cultural independence.

If you're off to Kabah, head southwest on Hwy. 261 to Santa Elena (14 kilometers), then south to Kabah (13 kilometers).

6. Kabah, Sayil, Xlapak, Labná, Loltún

South and west of Uxmal are several other Maya cities well worth your exploration. Though the scale of these smaller cities is not as grand as that of Uxmal or Chichén-Itzá, each has its gems of Maya architecture. You will not be spending your time looking at the same old pyramids and temples. Rather, the great façade of masks on the Codz Poop at Kabah, the enormous palace at Sayil, the fantastic caverns of Loltún may be among the highpoints of your trip.

Transportation to these sights is not easy. Though buses do run occasionally along the road south from Uxmal to Kabah, it is difficult to reach the other sites without a private car. Consider renting one in Mérida, if just for a day or two.

KABAH: The ancient city of Kabah sits astride the highway, but you turn left into the parking lot. Buy your ticket from 8 a.m. to 5 p.m. daily for 40 pesos (8¢), the same to park your car.

The most outstanding building at Kabah is the one you notice first: that huge palace up on a terrace. It's called the Palace of Masks, or **Codz Poop** ("rolled-up mat") from a motif in its decoration. Its outstanding feature is the façade, completely covered in masks of the hook-nosed rain god Chac. All those eyes, hooked noses, and grimacing mouths, used as a repeated pattern on a huge façade, have an incredible effect. There's nothing like this façade in all of Maya architecture.

Once you've seen the Palace of Masks, you've seen the best of Kabah. But you should take a quick look at the other buildings, and follow the paths into the jungle, for a look at the **Tercera Casa** (Third House), or Las Columnas. This temple has fine colonnaded façades on both front and, even better, back.

Across the highway, you'll pass a conical mound (on your right) that was once the **Great Temple,** or Teocalli. Past it is a great arch. This triumphal arch was much wider at one time, and may have been a monumental gate into the city. For all their architectural achievements, the Maya never discovered the principle of the true arch made of many small fitted stones and a keystone. Instead, they used this corbelled arch, which is simply two flat stones leaned at an angle against one another. Compare this ruined arch to the one at Labná (below), which is in much better shape.

SAYIL: Just short of five kilometers south of Kabah is the turnoff (left, east) to Sayil, Xlapak, Labná, Loltún, and Oxkutzcab. Four kilometers along this road are the ruins of Sayil, just off the road. The ruins are open from 8 a.m. to 5 p.m., and the admission cost is 40 pesos (8¢), half price on Sunday and holidays.

Sayil is famous for **El Palacio,** the tremendous 100-room palace that is a masterpiece of Mayan architecture. The rows and rows of columns and colonnettes give the building a Minoan appearance. There are some nice decorative details, but for the most part El Palacio impresses one by its grandeur and simplicity.

Off in the jungle past El Palacio is **El Mirador,** a small temple with a slotted roofcomb, an odd structure. Beyond El Mirador, a crude stele has a phallic idol carved on it, with greatly exaggerated proportions. The Maya didn't normally go in for this sort of thing, and this crude sculpture may well be unique.

Climb to the top of El Palacio if the heat is not too intense. The breeze up here is cooling, and the view of the Puuc hills delightful. Sometimes it's difficult to tell which are hills and which are unrestored pyramids, as little temples and galleries peep out at unlikely places from the jungle foliage. That large circular basin on the ground below the palace is a catch basin for a chultún (cistern). This region has no natural cenotes (wells) to catch rainwater, so the natives had to make their own.

XLAPAK: Back on the road, it's 5½ kilometers to Xlapak ("Shla-*pahk*"), a small site with one building. The Palace at Xlapak bears the inevitable rain god masks. If you do this tour of the ruins in the summer rainy season, it may be at this point that Chac responds to your earnest pleas for a break from the heat. When I was there, Chac let loose a downpour. It soaked through. Cool, though.

LABNÁ: Labná is only three kilometers past Xlapak, open 8 a.m. to 5 p.m. Admission is 40 pesos (8¢). The first thing you should look at here is the monumental arch. Good old Chac takes his place on the corners of one façade, and stylized Mayan huts are fashioned in stone above the doorways. El Mirador, or **El Castillo** as it is also called, stands near the arch, with its roofcomb towering above it.

The **Palacio** at Labná is much like the one at Sayil: huge, restrained, monumental. It's not in quite as good shape as that at Sayil, but still impressive. In the decoration, find the enormous mask of Chac over a doorway, and also the highly stylized serpent's mouth, out of which pops a human head.

LOLTÚN: About 30 kilometers (18½ miles) past Labná on the way to Oxkutzcab (that's "Oaks-kootz-*kahb*") are the caverns of Loltún, on the left-hand side of the road.

No sign marks the entrance to the caves, so look for a tidy fence with a small park behind it, entered by a gravel drive. Wander in, and someone will fetch a guide. If they tell you that you've missed the last tour of the day, offer to pay a substantial tip (a few dollars) and you will get your tour.

You will have to pay a small admission fee—about 50 pesos (10¢)—and also tip the guide at the end of the hour-long tour; I'd suggest a dollar or two if the tour has been a good one.

The caves are fascinating. Not only were they the home of ancient Mayas, but they were used as a refuge and fortress during the War of the Castes (1847-1901). You can examine statuary, wall carvings and paintings, chultúnes (cisterns), and other signs of Maya habitation. Besides the Mayan artifacts, you'll be impressed by the sheer grandeur and beauty of the caverns themselves.

HEADING NORTH, SOUTH, EAST, WEST: From Loltún, you can drive the few kilometers to Oxkutzcab, and from there north on Hwy. 184 to Ticul, Muna, and Mérida (100 kilometers, 62 miles). Or you can head back past Sayil, then south on Hwy. 261 to Campeche. Those intrepid souls out to do a circuit of the northern peninsula can strike out southeast toward Tekax, Tzucacab, and Polguc on Hwy. 184. After about 200 kilometers (124 miles) you'll arrive in the town of Felipe Carrillo Puerto, where there are restaurants, hotels, banks, and gas stations. Carrillo Puerto thus serves as your jumping-off point for the tour north to Tulum, Xel-ha, Cozumel, and Cancún. See Chapter XVI for more information.

THE ROAD TO CAMPECHE: Highway 261 heads south for several kilometers, then beneath a lofty arch which marks the boundary between the states of Yucatán and Campeche. You then pass through Bolonchén de Rejón (*bolonchén* means "nine wells").

Three kilometers south of Bolonchén you'll notice a sign on the side of the road pointing west to the Grutas de Xtacumbilxuna (though the sign spells it "Xtacumbinxunan"). Another sign says that these "Caves of the Hidden Girl" are 300 meters along the dirt track, and yet a third says they're 500 meters. In fact, the parking area is four-fifths of a kilometer west of the highway, only a ten-minute walk.

Legend has it that a Mayan girl, to escape an unhappy love affair, hid her-

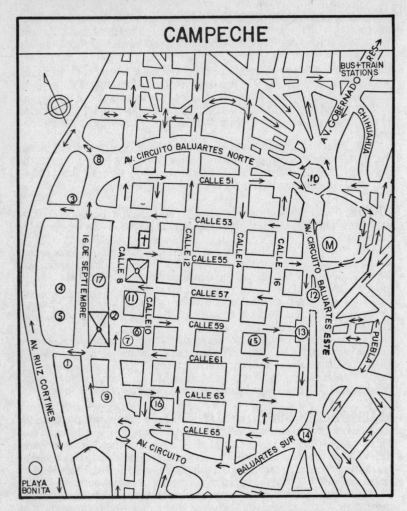

CAMPECHE

self in these vast limestone caverns. It wouldn't be hard to do, as you'll see if you sign the guest register and follow the guide down for the 30- or 45-minute tour in Spanish (tip the guide at the end).

But if she did hide down here, the girl left no trace. Unlike the fascinating caves at Loltún, filled with traces of Mayan occupation, these have only the standard bestiary of limestone shapes: a dog, an eagle, a penguin, madonna and child, snake, and so on, the fruit of the guide's imagination. The caves are open whenever the guide is around, which is most of the time.

Chenes Ruins

At Hopelchén there's a turn-off for Dzibalchén, near which you can see several unspoiled, unexcavated, all but undiscovered ruined cities in the Chenes style. You've got to be an explorer for these. It's good if you have some food and water. Head for Dzibalchén, 41 kilometers from Hopelchén, then begin asking for the way to Hochob, San Pedro, Dzehkabtun, El Tabasqueño, and Dzibilnocac.

From Hopelchén, Hwy. 261 heads west, and after 42 kilometers you'll find yourself at the turn-off for the ruined city of Edzná, 20 kilometers farther along to the south.

Edzná

At one time, a network of Mayan canals crisscrossed this entire area, making intensive cultivation possible, and no doubt contributing to Edzná's wealth as a ceremonial center. But today what you'll see at this "House of Wry Faces" (that's what *edzná* means) is a unique pyramid of five levels with a fine temple, complete with roof-comb, on top.

The buildings at Edzná were mostly in the Chenes, or "well country" style, so named because of the many wells found in the region.

Back on Hwy. 261, it's 14 kilometers to the intersection with Hwy. 180, and then another 31 kilometers to the very center of Campeche.

7. Campeche

Campeche (pop. 121,000), capital of the state bearing the same name, is a pleasant coastal town with a smooth, leisurely pace. Founded by Cordoba in 1517 and officially claimed for the Spanish crown by the soldier Francisco de Montejo the Elder in 1531, Campeche was hounded for years by pirates who plied the gulf. To protect themselves, the townspeople finally built a wall around the city in the late 1600s. Remnants of these walls, called *baluartes* ("bulwarks"), are among the city's proudest links with the past.

Sad to say, the flow of tourists passing through Campeche on their way to Mérida has dried up in recent years. With the road now open via Kabah and Uxmal to Mérida, virtually everyone travels that way (for good reason) and bypasses old Campeche. With the drying up of the tourist flow, good and inexpensive tourist establishments have mostly gone as well.

ORIENTATION: Virtually all of your time in Campeche will be spent within the confines of the old city walls. You'll certainly pass one of the old baluartes as you come toward the center of town, which is the modernistic Plaza Moch-Couoh on the waterfront, next to which rises the modern office tower called the Edificio Poderes or Palacio de Gobierno, headquarters for the State of Campeche. Next to this is the futuristic Cámara de Diputados, or Casa de Congresso (state legislature's chamber), which looks somewhat like an enormous square clam.

The city's two best hotels are within sight of the Palacio de Gobierno on the waterfront.

Arriving by Air

Campeche's connections by air are minimal, with one daily flight to and from Mexico City. Sometimes there is a shuttle service to Mérida. If you happen to arrive by air, you'll have to take a taxi (1,500 pesos, $3), or walk from the airport out to the intersection of Avenidas Héroes de Nacozari and López Portillo, where you can catch a bus ("China Campeche") for the trip into town.

Arriving by Bus

First- and second-class buses arrive and depart from the terminal on Avenida Gobernadores, corner of Calle de Chile, about four blocks northeast of the Baluarte de San Pedro (10). You can walk to the center of town from here if your bags are not too heavy (turn left as you leave the station). Otherwise, a taxi to the hotels will cost a little over a dollar.

Arriving by Train

Campeche's train station is about two kilometers northeast of the downtown waterfront, on Avenida Héroes de Nacozari, which intersects Avenida de los Gobernadores. A taxi should cost about 1,200 pesos ($2.40) to the center.

Tourist Information

The State of Campeche operates a convenient and helpful **Tourist Office** (1) (tel. 981/6-6068 or 6-6767) on the waterfront near the Palacio de Gobierno. Look for the modernistic bulwark with a slender vertical sign ("Turismo") on top. When you get to the structure, don't walk up the ramp toward the sign, but rather walk around to the right to reach the entrance, which faces the sea. Hours are 8 a.m. to 2:30 p.m. and 4 to 8:30 p.m., closed Sunday. They speak some English and are very helpful.

Useful Facts

Look for the **post office** (Correos) (3) in the Edificio Federal (tel. 981/6-2134) at the corner of Av. 16 de Septiembre and Calle 53, near the Baluarte de Santiago. The telegraph office is here as well.

Finding an Address

Unlike most towns in Mexico, Campeche boasts a systematic street-naming plan whereby streets that run roughly north to south have even numbers, and those running east to west have odd numbers. Thus along Calle 14 you will cross in succession Calles 51, 53, 55, 57, etc., and if you turn right off Calle 14 onto Calle 51 you will cross Calles 12, 10, 8, etc., in your course down 51. Not to confuse you further, but the streets are numbered so that numbers ascend toward the south and west. After you get downtown and walk around for five minutes you'll have the system down pat. Bus, train, and airport terminals are all a good distance from downtown, and as Campeche is hardly a good town to negotiate by bus, I would recommend a taxi to get you from the various depots to the center.

WHERE TO STAY: Though Campeche's tourist trade has largely dried up, there are still some good places to stay. With the peso's fall in value, even the forbidden luxury of El Presidente comes very close to our budget range.

Right at the center of town, on the waterfront, are the city's two best hotels.

The **Hotel El Presidente Campeche (4)**, P. O. Box 251, Campeche 24000 (tel. 981/6-2233 or 6-4611), is officially at Avenida Ruiz Cortines no. 51. Most of the 120 rooms and suites have views of the sea, and all have the four-star luxuries: air conditioning, color television, servi-bar, and a terrace for sunrise-watching. Other luxuries include a swimming pool, fenced parking lot, plus a nice restaurant, bar, coffeeshop, and discothèque. Prices are quite happily low for all this: 11,385 pesos ($22.77) single, 12,535 pesos ($25.07) double, 14,835 pesos ($29.67) triple, tax included. Junior suites cost $3 to $5 more per room.

Just south of El Presidente is Campeche's old standby, the 100-room **Hotel Baluartes (5)**, Av. Ruiz Cortines no. 61, Campeche 24000 (tel. 981/6-3911). This was the city's original luxury digs, but it's been extensively modernized, and now has all of the posh services of its neighbor, including air conditioning, swimming pool, and many rooms with sea views. Prices are less: 9,660 pesos ($19.32) single, 10,695 pesos ($21.39) double, 12,650 pesos ($25.30) triple, tax included.

At the other end of the price spectrum is the convenient **Hotel America (6)**, Calle 10 no. 252, near the corner with Calle 59, a block east of the picturesque "Sea Gate" of the former city walls (tel. 981/6-4588 or 6-4576). The hotel charges 3,853 pesos ($7.70) for a double room overlooking the interior court, equipped with screens against the bugs, and a private shower.

WHERE TO EAT: The best all-around restaurant choice in Campeche is the **Restaurant Miramar (7),** Calles 8 and 61, very near the town hall building (tel. 6-2883). The decor is simple but pleasant, with lots of light-colored stone and some dark wood and ironwork. The menu offers typical Campeche seafood dishes: fried, breaded shrimp (ask for "camarones empanizadas") for 1,450 pesos ($2.90), ceviche or fish and vegetable cocktail for 1,000 pesos ($2), arroz con calamares (squid and rice) for slightly more, and for dessert, queso napolitana, a sort of very rich, thick flan.

The **Restaurant del Parque (11),** overlooking the zócalo on Calle 57, is a beautifully white, cool, open place with a cozy air about it, due in part to use of incandescent (not fluorescent) lighting. Stereo music, caned chairs, and a tempting menu add to the attractions. Have soup, a fish dinner, and dessert for about 2,900 pesos ($5.80); or dine for less on enchiladas or crêpes. Shrimp platters are available, but they'll run your meal tab up.

WHAT TO SEE: Campeche's dearth of tourists is a blessing, in a way, because it allows you to see this charming old city without the crowds.

City Walls and Bulwarks

Campeche gets its name from the Mayan name Ah Kim Pech. Founded in 1531, later abandoned, and refounded by Montejo the Younger in 1540, it became the springboard for the Montejo's conquest of Yucatán. As the busiest port in the region during the 1600s and 1700s, Campeche was a choice prize to pirates, who attacked it repeatedly starting as early as 1546. The Campechanos, eventually tired of the depredations, began construction of the city's impressive defenses in 1668. By 1704, all of the walls, gates, and bulwarks were in place. Today, seven of the bulwarks remain, and four are worthy of a visit. Here's the rundown:

Baluarte de San Carlos: Southernmost of the seaside bulwarks, the Baluarte San Carlos (9) is near the modern Palacio de Gobierno at the intersection of the Circuito Baluartes and the Avenida Justo Sierra, near where Calles 63 and 8 meet. It's a good place to begin your tour, as it is now set up as the Sala de las Fortificaciónes (Chamber of Fortifications). Models within the heavy stone walls, where once Campechano soldiers and militia held off the pirates, show you how the city looked in its glory days during the 1700s. Admission is free after you sign the guest book. Hours are 9 a.m. to 1 p.m. and 5 to 7:30 p.m., every day.

Baluarte de la Soledad: Walk north along Calle 8, and you'll pass the Puerta de Mar, or Sea Gate, the ancient entry to the city enclosure from the port area. Just beyond the Puerta de Mar is the Baluarte de la Soledad (17), or Bulwark of Solitude, just off the zócalo where Calles 57 and 8 meet. This bastion now houses the Sala de Estelas, or Chamber of Steles. The Mayan votive stones were brought from various sites in this ruin-rich state. Many are badly worn, but the excellent line drawings beside the stones allow you to admire their former glory. Admission is free, and hours are the same as for the Baluarte de San Carlos.

While you're in the area, take a stroll through Campeche's pretty little zócalo, or Plaza de la Independencia, complete with cathedral. Construction of the church was begun in 1650, though it was frequently interrupted, and not completed for over a century and a half.

Baluarte de Santiago: Walk north along Calle 8 and at Calle 51 you'll come to the Baluarte de Santiago (8), northernmost of the seaside bulwarks, now fixed up as Campeche's Jardín Botánico (Botanical Gardens). This is the perfect place to take a breather in your walking tour, among the plants both common and exotic, on a bench in the cool shade. Want to learn about what you're seeing? The garden offers tours in English at 12 noon and at 4 p.m., Tuesday through Saturday; in Spanish almost every hour in the morning and evening. Admission to the Jardín Botánico is 50 pesos (10¢). It's open Tuesday through Saturday from 9 a.m. to 8 p.m., Sunday from 9 a.m. to 1 p.m., closed Monday.

Baluarte de San Pedro: Head inland (east) on Calle 51, and at Calle 18 you'll see the Baluarte de San Pedro (10), where there's a crafts showroom called the Exposición Permanente de Artesanías. Besides the bastion itself, you can look over the products of Campechano craftspeople. Hours are the same as at the Baluarte de San Carlos.

Other Baluartes: If you're not tired yet, make the complete circuit of the bulwarks. Follow Calle 18 south, passing the Baluarte de San Francisco (12) at Calle 57, then the Puerta de Tierra (13) (Land Gate) at Calle 59. The Baluarte de San Juan (14), at Calle 65, is where you turn west toward the sea. The Baluarte de Santa Rosa (18), at Calles 14 and 67 (Circuito Baluartes) is now a library.

Three blocks' walking brings you back to the Baluarte de San Carlos.

Museo Regional de Campeche

Over the years, Campeche has moved its museum collections around quite a bit. The best of the lot have now come to rest in the Museo Regional de Campeche (15), in the former mansion of the Teniente de Rey (Royal Governor) at Calle 59 no. 36, between Calles 14 and 16. The museum's displays are similar to those in the Palacio Cantón in Mérida. Pictures, drawings, and models are combined with original artifacts, bringing to life the ancient Mayan culture. The curious skull-flattening deformation of babies is shown in the most direct way: with an exhibit of the actual deformed skulls. Another highlight is the Late Classic (A.D. 600–900) Maya stele carved in a metamorphic rock which does not exist in Yucatán, but was brought hundreds of miles from its quarry.

A model of the archeological site at Becán shows Maya society in daily life. Other displays demonstrate Mayan architecture, techniques of water conservation, aspects of their religion, commerce, art, and their considerable scientific knowledge.

Hours for the museum are 9 a.m. to 8 p.m. Tuesday through Saturday, 9 a.m. to 1 p.m. Sunday, closed Monday. Admission costs 100 pesos (20¢).

Museo de Campeche

For colonial glitter with a touch of modern art, drop in at the **Museo de Campeche (16)**, entered from Calle 10 at the corner of Calle 63. The museum is actually the nicely restored Templo de San José (1640), a fine place in which to display traveling exhibits of Mexican art. I saw one made up of the works of Mexican painter Joaquin Clausell (died 1935). The museum is free to all, open from 10 a.m. to 1 p.m. and 5 to 9 p.m. daily.

Strolling Through Campeche

Besides visiting the museums, the most enjoyable pastime is to walk around the streets (especially Calles 55, 57, and 59), for the structures are in typical Mexican-colonial style. A glance through the large doorways will give you a glimpse into the colonial past with high-beamed ceilings, Moorish stone arches, interior courtyards, and lots and lots of peeling paint. Even the most luxurious establishment seems to give in to the humidity and accept the flaking walls.

You'll probably hear about **Playa Bonita,** about four miles west out of town, but unless you're in need of some cooler air I recommend going to the Caribbean for your swimming. The last time I was there the beach was pretty dirty and the water was not so appetizing.

8. Chichén-Itzá and Balankanché

The fabled pyramids and temples of Chichén-Itzá are Yucatán's best-known ancient monuments. You can't really say you've seen Yucatán until you've gazed at towering El Castillo, sighted the sun from the Maya observatory called El Caracol, or shivered on the brink of the gaping cenote that served as the sacrificial well. Luckily for travelers on a budget, Chichén-Itzá is well and frequently served by buses, as it's on the main highway (no. 180) between Mérida and Cancún. Also, being on the main highway, Chichén-Itzá has a decent selection of hotels in all price ranges, so you needn't bend your budget here as you may have done at Uxmal.

HOW TO SEE CHICHÉN: I strongly urge you to spend the night at Chichén-Itzá. No matter what the time of year, it will be hot in the middle of the day, and instead of clambering up pyramids you should be taking a siesta after lunch, in a cool hotel room. If you come on a day-trip, you'll arrive just in time to hike the pyramids in the heat of the day. You'll have to rush through this marvelous ancient city in order to catch another bus, which will take you away just as the once-fierce sun is softening to a benevolent gold and burnishing the temples.

Here's the plan: get a bus from Mérida or Cancún in the morning, find your hotel room, then head for the ruins. After an hour or two, have some lunch, take that siesta, then return to the ruins for a few more hours. The next morning, get to the ruins early, before the intense heat. When the heat of the day approaches, climb on a bus to your next destination. This may involve paying the admission fee more than once, but the fee is minimal, the experience maximal!

Note that it's possible (but not probable) that your chosen hotel at Chichén-Itzá might be booked up. If you want to make a reservation, be advised that it is difficult to reach Chichén by phone; however, most hotels have a means by which you can make reservations in Mérida. Read the hotel descriptions for details.

READERS' TOUR SELECTION: "We used the **Agencia de Viajes Gonzáles,** Calle 59 no. 476, Mérida, Yuc. 97000 (tel. 992/21-0197 or 21-0865), for the Chichén-Itzá tour. We also found this company had the lowest prices for the Uxmal Sound and Light show, the best such show I've seen" (Jane Bogner, Miami Beach, Fla.). . . . "We were extremely satisfied with the attention, coverage, and facilities on our tour of Chichén-Itzá, operated by Ricardo Gonzáles of **Agencia de Viajes González,** Avenida Tulum 26 (Hotel Parador), Cancún, Q. Roo (tel. 988/4-1310 or 4-1043). Sr. González has an agency in Mérida as well" (Carol Rosenwinkel, Stillwater, Minn.).

ON THE ROAD: See the section above, "Getting To and From Mérida," for bus information. Once you're on the road, it'll take between 1½ and 2 hours to reach Chichén (120 kilometers, 75 miles).

Along the way, tiny Maya hamlets with thatched houses (called *na*) dot the highway. Sometimes the frames of sticks are covered in mud plaster and white-washed. The women take pride in wearing the traditional white *huipil*, which always has embroidery around the neckline, and several inches of lacy slip showing at the hem.

This is henequen country, and you'll pass a big Cordemex plant that gathers in the leaves from the surrounding fields. Tied in bundles, the leaves form huge piles by the plant, waiting to have the sisal fibers extracted and made into rope and cloth. Henequen has been the principal industry of Yucatán for centuries, and the vast henequen haciendas were owned by absentee landlords and worked by peasants who were little better than slaves. The great haciendas have been split up in recent years, but the hacienda complexes—house, smokestack, factory, chapel, workers' houses, gateway, narrow-gauge railways—still stand along the road. In every direction stretch the numberless stone-walled fields where the spiny henequen plants grow, taking years to reach maturity.

After an hour's musing on antique economics, you pass through the village of Pisté, which is only a mile or so west of Chichén-Itzá. There's a sidewalk all the way from Pisté to the archeological zone. As long as you don't do it in the heat of the day, the walk is a comfortable 15 or 20 minutes.

CHICHÉN-ITZÁ: You can see all there is to see at Chichén-Itzá in a day, but you may not want to continue your journey after a tiring round of the ruins. Because rooms at Chichén are sometimes difficult to find in the busy season, here is a rundown on all the hotels near the ruins, whether budget priced or not.

Where to Stay

A good place to stay overnight is the **Hotel Dolores Alba,** 1½ miles (2.4 kilometers) past the ruins on the road going east to Cancún. (If you go to Chichén-Itzá by bus from Mérida, ask for a ticket on a bus that is going *past* the ruins—to Valladolid or Puerto Juárez—and then ask the bus driver to stop at the Dolores Alba; he will be glad to do so. Or take a taxi from the ruins to the hotel.) The 12 rooms are kept clean and neat, and several of them have been equipped with air conditioners to help the ceiling fans. Besides the motel-style rooms, which are older, you'll find two modern, air-conditioned rooms and a separate cottage that sleeps four in two bedrooms. Prices are 3,000 pesos ($6) single, 4,500 pesos ($9) double, 5,500 pesos ($11) triple, and 6,500 pesos ($13) for four (in the cottage). All rooms have a shower, of course, and there's a pretty little swimming pool besides. Good meals are available here at decent prices, but you should realize that when it comes to dining you have little choice—the nearest alternative restaurant, or tienda to buy your own supplies, is several miles away. For your trips to the ruins, the Dolores Alba provides free transportation to guests without cars. By the way, this hotel is run by the same family that runs the Dolores Alba in Mérida (tel. 992/21-3745) at Calle 63 no. 464. Either hotel will help you to make reservations at the other one.

The **Hotel Hacienda Chichén** is a short walk from the ruins, and guests stay in the bungalows built for those excavating the ruins some years ago. There's a fine pool—which, by the way, is open also to those who drop in for the 2,000-peso ($4) lunch—and all is quite plush. It should be for 12,500 pesos ($25) single, 14,300 pesos ($28.60) double. If I had to "upgrade" for a night, this romantic and sympathetic place is where I'd stay. Each cottage is named for an early archeologist working at Chichén. You can make reservations for the Hacienda by contacting the Mérida Travel Service, in the Hotel Casa del Balam at Calle 60 no. 488, corner of Calle 57 (Apdo. Postal 407, Mérida, Yucatán; tel. 922/21-9212).

Of the various hostelries at the ruins that are out of our price range, the **Pirámide Inn** (tel. Pisté 5) is among the least far out. Less than a mile from the ruins near Pisté, the Pirámide boasts near-luxurious large rooms equipped with king-size beds, air conditioning, wall hangings of local handcrafts, plus the bonuses of a pool and absolutely gorgeous landscaped gardens and grounds. A number of people on the staff speak English. For all this comfort one pays 6,555 pesos ($13.11) single, 7,705 pesos ($15.41) double. Besides the 42 rooms, the Pirámide has ten bungalow suites, priced higher, and there's a trailer park on the other side of the highway. You can make reservations in Mérida by contacting the Pirámide's sister hotel, the Principe Maya Airport Inn, Avenida Aviación km. 4.5, Apdo. Postal 433 (tel. 992/24-0411).

The **Hotel Misión Chichén-Itzán** (tel. Pisté 4) is a fancy establishment that's right in the town of Pisté. With two floors of rooms, a pretty pool, a shopping arcade, and a restaurant-bar, the Misión is the compleat place to stay, but it's not cheap: double rooms cost 11,660 pesos ($23.32). Meal plans are available, or you can drop in for breakfast, lunch, or dinner. For reservations in Mexico City, go to Florencia 15-A in the Pink Zone, or call 533-5953 or 553-3560.

The **Hotel Villa Arqueológica** (tel. 985/6-2830) is part of the Club Méditerranée operation, as you might guess by a glance at the lavishness of the layout: tennis courts, a pool, and garden-like grounds. On my last inspection tour I was quoted rates of 9,775 pesos ($19.55) for one person, 10,925 pesos ($21.85) for two—a very reasonable price for what you get. Meals are more expensive here than at a nearby Hacienda Chichén or at the Hotel Misión. For reservations in Mexico City, contact the office at Liebnitz 34, or telephone 514-4995 or 511-1284.

The **Hotel Mayaland,** sister hotel to the Hacienda Chichén and very close to it, is perhaps the most genteel and sumptuous of Chichén-Itzá hotels. Built positively to reek of jungle adventure, it boasts such subtle touches as a front doorway that frames perfectly El Caracol (the observatory) as you walk from the lobby outside. It has a swimming pool and restaurant-bar, of course, and very attractive rooms for 14,300 pesos ($28.60) double. Make reservations as at the Hacienda Chichén.

The budget choice in the village of Pisté, next to the Pirámide Inn, is the very basic **Posada Novelo** (phone the Pirámide Inn), with adequate if bare rooms, all with shower, for 2,200 pesos ($4.40) single, 2,600 pesos ($5.20) double.

Where to Eat

Food is available near the ruins in the expensive hotels, but for the budget traveler I recommend the little restaurants in the town of Pisté. Actually, these days Pisté's restaurants are pushing their prices up and standardizing their fare so that there is little difference among them. Expect to find your silverware encased in a plastic bag, and mood music (old Swingle Singers records, etc.) pulsing in the background—whether you like it or not. In any of the restaurants—El Carrusel, La Fiesta, or the Poxil—they'll try to sell you an entire lunch of four or five courses, and will balk at à la carte orders. The cost will be about 1,700 pesos ($3.40); that's a bit high, considering that the Hotel Misión, also in Pisté and very posh, charges only 1,950 pesos ($3.90) for lunch. About the cheapest of the town's restaurants are the Nicté-Ha and the Parador Maya. The Restaurant Xaybe, across from the Hotel Misión, is air-conditioned and rather fancy.

Luckily for us, Pisté still retains a few operating **loncherías,** where sandwiches, bowls of soup, and similar light-lunch fare are offered at low prices. One lonchería is right next to the Fiesta restaurant, another is in the small arcade by the highway, across from the church. Shops in the same arcade sell biscuits, drinks, and similar supplies.

The Mayan Sense of Time

To understand Chichén-Itzá fully, you've got to know something about the unique way in which the Mayas kept time.

The amazingly exact and intricate Maya calendar system begins with the year 3113 B.C., before Maya culture even existed. From that date, the Mayas could measure time—and their life cycle—to a point 90,000,000 years in the future! Needless to say, they haven't felt the need for the whole system yet. For now, just note that they conceived of world history as a series of cycles moving within cycles.

The Solar Year: The Mayan solar year was very precisely measured, and consisted of 365.24 days. Within that solar year there were 18 "months" of twenty days each (total: 360 days) plus a special five-day period.

The Ceremonial Year: A ceremonial calendar, completely different from the solar calendar, ran its "annual" cycle at the same time. But this was not a crude system like our Gregorian calendar which has saints' days, some fixed feast days, and some moveable feasts. The Maya ceremonial calendar "interlaced" exactly with the solar calendar. Each date of the solar calendar had a name, and each date of the ceremonial calendar also had a name; so every single day in Maya history has two names, which were always quoted together. The ceremonial calendar was a very complex and ingenious system with 13 "months" of 20 days, but running within that cycle of 260 days was another of twenty "weeks" of thirteen days!

The Double Cycle: After 52 solar years and 73 ceremonial "years," during which each day had its unique, unduplicated double name, these calendars ended their respective cycles simultaneously on the very same day, and a brandnew, identical double cycle began. Thus, in the longer scheme of things, a day would be identified by the name of the 52-year cycle, the name of the solar day, and the name of the ceremonial day.

Mystic Numbers: As you can see, several numbers were of great significance to the system. The number 20 was perhaps most important, as calendar calculations were done with a number system with base 20. There were 20 "suns" (days) to a "month," 20 years to a *katun,* and 20 katuns (20 times 20, or 400 years) to a *baktun.*

The number 52 was of tremendous importance, for it signified, literally, the "end of time," the end of the double cycle of solar and ceremonial calendars. At the beginning of a new cycle, temples were rebuilt for the "new age," which is why so many Maya temples and pyramids hold within them the structures of earlier, smaller temples and pyramids.

The Mayas, obviously, were obsessed by time. (You'd have to be, to deal with such a system!) Time for them was not "progress," but the Wheel of Fate, spinning endlessly, determining one's destiny by the combinations of attributes given to days in the solar and ceremonial calendars. The rains came on schedule, the corn was planted on schedule, and the celestial bodies moved in their great dance under the watchful eye of Maya astronomers and astrologers.

It's no wonder that Chichén's most impressive structure, El Castillo, is in fact an enormous "time machine," and that this imperial city included a huge and impressive astronomical observatory.

Touring the Ruins

The archeological zone at Chichén is open from 6 a.m. to 6 p.m. daily. Admission costs 100 pesos (20¢), less on Sunday and holidays.

This Mayan city was absorbed by the Toltecs in A.D. 987, when, as legend has it, a man named Kukulcán, who was the same as Quetzalcóatl from the Toltec capital of Tula, arrived from the west "for the redemption of his people." Here he built a magnificent metropolis combining the Maya Puuc style with Toltec motifs of the feathered serpent, warriors, eagles, and jaguars. There are actually two parts of Chichén-Itzá: the northern zone, which is distinctly Toltec;

and the southern zone, which is of an early period with mostly Puuc architecture. A day is needed to see all the ruins here, preferably from 6 or 7 a.m. to 1 p.m., and 3 or 4 p.m. to 6 p.m.

El Castillo: Begin with the beautiful 75-foot El Castillo pyramid, built with the calendar in mind: there is a total of 364 stairs plus platform, which makes 365 (days of the year), 52 panels on each side which represent the 52-year cycle of the Maya calendars, and nine terraces on each side of the stairways, a total of 18 terraces to represent the 18-month Maya solar calendar. If this isn't proof enough of the mathematical precision of this temple, come for the spring equinox (March 21), and when the sun goes down you'll see the seven stairs of the northern stairway plus the serpent head carving at the base touched with the last rays of the fading sun; within a 34-minute period the "serpent" formed by this play of light and shadow appears to descend into the earth as the sun leaves each stair, going from the top to the bottom, ending with the serpent head. To the Maya this is a fertility symbol: the golden sun has entered the earth; time to plant the corn.

El Castillo, also called the Pyramid of Kukulcán, was built over an earlier structure of Toltec design. A narrow stairway entered at the western edge of the north staircase leads into the structure, where there is a sacrificial altar-throne encrusted with jade, and a Chac-mool figure. The stairway is open at odd and irregular hours, is claustrophobic, usually crowded, and very humid and uncomfortable. Plan your visit for early in the day, if possible. By the way, you can indeed reach the top of the pyramid via the interior staircase.

Main Ball Court (Juego de Pelota): Northwest of El Castillo is Chichén's main ball court, the largest and best-preserved anywhere. This is only one of nine ball courts built in this city.

The game was played with a hard rubbery ball. Players on two teams tried to knock the ball through one or the other of the two stone rings placed high on either wall, using only their elbows, knees, and hips (no hands). The losing players, so it is said, paid for defeat with their lives. The game must have been an exciting event, heightened by the marvelous acoustics of the ball court. Have someone walk to the North Temple at the far end, and speak or clap hands. You'll hear the sound quite clearly at the opposite end, about 450 feet away.

The North Temple has sculptured pillars, and more sculptures inside. For a look at the teams after a game, walk along the bas-reliefs on each wall. Two opposing teams are facing the center. At the mid-point in the wall, Death accepts the sacrifice of one team's captain, who has been decapitated by the captain of the other team, who wields an obsidian knife.

Temple of Jaguars (Tigres): Near the southeastern corner of the main ball court is a small temple with serpent-columns and carved panels showing jaguars *(tigres)*. Up the flight of steps and inside the temple, a mural was found which chronicles a battle between Mayas and Toltecs. The Toltecs are the ones with the feathered serpents, attacking a Maya village of nas.

Tzompantli (Temple of Skulls): When a sacrificial victim's head was cut off (some unlucky ball player, for instance), it was stuck on a pole and displayed here, in a tidy row with others. Just in case the skull population dropped, the architects have provided rows of skulls carved into the platform. Also carved into the stone are pictures of eagles tearing hearts from human victims. The word Tzompantli is not Mayan, but came from central Mexico with the Toltecs.

Platform of the Eagles: Next to the Tzompantli, this small platform has reliefs showing eagles and jaguars clutching human hearts in their talons and claws.

Platform of Venus: East of the Tzompantli and north of El Castillo, near the road to the Sacred Cenote, is the Platform of Venus. Don't look for beauty, for the planet Venus, in Maya-Toltec lore, is thought to have been represented by a feathered monster, or a feathered serpent with a human head in its mouth, not a luscious lady. A Chac-mool figure was discovered "buried" within the structure, which is why it is sometimes called the Tomb of Chac-Mool.

The Sacred Cenote: Follow the dirt road that heads north from the Platform of Venus, and after five minutes you'll come to the great natural well which may have given Chichén-Itzá ("The Well of the Itzáes") its name. By now you must have heard the sacrificial virgin lore. It seems that the priests herded a rather different breed of person to death in the watery depths here. Anatomical research done in the earlier part of this century by Earnest A. Hooten suggests that children and adults, male and female, were used as sacrificial victims. Judging from Hooten's evidence, the victims may have been outcasts: diseased, feeble-minded, or generally disliked.

Whatever the worth of the sacrificial victims, the worth of other presents to the rain god Chac was very considerable. Edward Thompson, American consul in Mérida and a Harvard professor, bought the hacienda of Chichén in the beginning of this century, explored the bottom of the cenote with dredges and divers, and brought up a fortune in gold and jade. Most of this he spirited out of the country and lodged in Harvard's Peabody Museum of Archeology and Ethnology. Later excavations, in the 1960s, brought up more treasure. It appears, from studies of the objects recovered, that offerings were brought from throughout Yucatán, and even farther away.

Temple of the Warriors: One of the most impressive structures at Chichén, the Temple of the Warriors (Templo de los Guerreros), also called the Group of the Thousand Columns, is due east of El Castillo. Climb up the steep stairs at the front to reach a figure of Chac-mool, and several impressive columns carved in relief to look like enormous feathered serpents. The building gets its name from the carvings of warriors marching along its walls. Other motifs, as you may have guessed by now, include feathered serpents, jaguars, and eagles.

South of the temple was a square building called by archeologists the market (mercado). Its central court, surrounded by a colonnade, may well have been just that. Beyond the temple and the market, in the jungle, are mounds of rubble that have yet to be uncovered, excavated, analyzed, or reconstructed.

The main Mérida-Cancún highway used to cut straight through the ruins of Chichén, and though it has now been diverted, you can still see the great swath it cut. South and west of the old highway's path are more impressive ruined buildings. On the way to these buildings is a shady little stand selling cold drinks.

Tomb of the High Priest: Past the refreshment stand, to the right of the path, is the Tomb of the High Priest (Tumba del Gran Sacerdote), which stood atop a natural limestone cave in which skeletons and offerings were found, giving the temple its name.

Next building along, on your right, is the House of Metates (Casa de los Metates), named after the concave corn-grinding stones used until recently by the Mayas. Past it is the Temple of the Stag (Templo del Venado), fairly tall though ruined. The relief of a stag which gave the temple its name is long gone.

Chichán-chob ("Little Holes"), the next temple, has a roof comb with little holes, three masks of rain-god Chac, three rooms, and a good view of the surrounding structures. It's one of the older buildings at Chichén, built in the Puuc style during the Late Classic period.

El Caracol: Construction of the Observatory (El Caracol), a complex building with a circular tower, was carried out over quite a long period of time. No doubt the additions and modifications reflected the Mayas' increasing knowledge of celestial movements, and their need for ever more exact measurements. Through slits in the tower's walls, Mayan astronomers could observe the cardinal directions and the approach of the all-important spring and autumn equinoxes, and the summer solstice. The temple's name, which means "snail," comes from a spiral staircase within the structure.

On the east side of El Caracol, a path leads north into the bush to the Cenote Xtoloc, another natural limestone well. The Sacred Cenote of Chichén was reserved for sacrifices; its water was not used for drinking (good thing!). The city's daily water supply came from Xtoloc.

Temple of Panels: Just to the south of El Caracol are the ruins of a steambath (Temazcalli), and the Templo de los Tableros, named for the carved panels on top. This was once covered by a much larger structure, only traces of which remain.

Edifice of the Nuns: If you've visited the Puuc sites of Kabah, Sayil, Labná, and Xlapak, the Nunnery here (Edificio de las Monjas) will remind you at once of the "palaces" at the other sites. It is enormous, and was built in the Late Classic period. Like so many other Mayan buildings, a new edifice was built right over an older one. Suspecting that this was so, an archeologist named Le Plongeon, working earlier in this century, put dynamite in between the two and blew part of the newer building to smithereens, thereby revealing part of the old. You can still see the results of Le Plongeon's delicate exploratory methods.

On the eastern side of the Nunnery is an annex (Anexo Este) in highly ornate Chenes style, with, as usual, lots of Chac masks and serpents.

The Church: Next to the annex is one of the oldest buildings at Chichén, ridiculously named The Church (La Iglesia). Masks of Chac decorate two upper stories. Look closely and you'll see among the crowd of Chacs an armadillo, a crab, a snail, and a tortoise. These represent the Mayan gods called *bacab,* whose job it was to hold up the sky.

Akab Dzib: The Temple of Obscure Writing (Akab Dzib) is due east of the Edifice of the Nuns along a path into the bush. Above a door in one of the rooms are some Mayan glyphs, which gave the temple its name. In other rooms, traces of red hand-prints are still visible. The earliest part of this building is very old, and may well be the oldest at Chichén. It was reconstructed and expanded over the centuries.

Old Chichén: For a look at more of Chichén's oldest buildings, constructed well before the Toltecs arrived, follow signs from the Nunnery southwest into the bush to Old Chichén (Chichén Viejo), about half a mile away. Be prepared for this trek with long trousers, insect repellant, and a local guide. The attractions here are the Temple of the First Inscriptions (Templo de los Inscripciones Iniciales), with the oldest inscriptions discovered at Chichén, and the restored Temple of the Lintels (Templo de los Dinteles), a fine Puuc building.

Grutas de Balankanché

Spelunkers take note: the Grutas (caves) de Balankanché are 4½ kilometers from Chichén-Itzá on the road to Puerto Juárez. You can see them with a guide only. Guides begin their tours at 9, 10, and 11 a.m. and 2, 3, and 4 p.m. (Sunday at 8, 9, 10, and 11 a.m. only). Admission costs 20 pesos (4¢).

Getting down into the caves takes some doing as you will probably end up taking a taxi to the caves, and having it wait for your return. The entire excursion takes about two hours. Check at the main entrance to the Chichén ruins for current tour hours at the caves, which may or may not prove to be fully accurate. The Chichén entrance is also the place to ask about hiring guides, should you want one.

The natural caves became wartime hideaways after the Toltec invasion of Yucatán. You can still see traces of carving and incense-burning, as well as an underground stream which served as the sanctuary's water supply.

9. Valladolid

An attractive, and money-saving, alternative to staying at Chichén is to stay in the sleepy town of Valladolid (that's "Bye-ah-doh-*leet*')), 40 kilometers (25 miles) east of the ruins. You can get an early bus from Mérida, spend the day at the ruins, then trundle on to Valladolid in a half hour. In recent years Valladolid has acquired some nice, modern hotels, and since they're a distance from the ruins, prices are very reasonable and crowds are not a problem.

The highway goes right past the main square in town, and it's here, or very nearby, that you'll find good hotels and restaurants.

Although it remained untouched by tourism for centuries, Valladolid is no newcomer to Yucatán. It was founded in 1543 near the site of a Maya religious center called Zací. The Franciscans built an impressive monastery here, called the **Convento de San Bernardino de Siena** (1552), and the town can boast of half a dozen colonial churches and two cenotes.

The main square is called the **Parque Francisco Cantón Rosado,** and when you find your way there, you'll be just a few steps from a variety of acceptable hotels and restaurants.

WHERE TO STAY: Walking around the main square, here's what you'll find: El Parroquía de San Servasio (the parish church) on the south, the Palacio Municipal (Town Hall) on the west (with a little tourism information desk out front, open from 9 a.m. to noon daily).

Near El Parroquía, at the southwest corner of the square, is the **Hotel San Clemente** (tel. 985/6-2208 or 6-2065), a modern, colonial-style building covered in white stucco. The 64 rooms, each with air conditioning, ceiling fan, and tidy bath, are located on two floors around a central garden quadrangle complete with swimming pool (which may or may not have water in it). Rates, compared to those at Chichén or Cancún, are very low: 3,300 pesos ($6.60) double, all included.

On the west side of the square is the **Hotel Maria de la Luz** (tel. 985/6-2070), which is well known for its breezy restaurant overlooking the square. A daily set-price lunch is featured for only 600 pesos ($1.20), beverage included. The food is hearty rather than delicate, but filling. A heaping fruit salad and a cold soft drink costs less than 500 pesos ($1). The rooms at the Luz are similar to those of the aforementioned hotel in accoutrements, although they're a bit more worn, and cost 3,000 pesos ($6) double. The swimming pool at the Luz is definitely not crystal clear.

The north side of the square holds the **Hotel El Mesón del Marqués,** a nice old colonial building at Calle 39 no. 203 (tel. 985/6-2073). Signs in English advertise the restaurant (very tidy) and gift shop. Most of the rooms are in a modern addition, however, and come with air conditioning for 4,370 pesos ($8.74) single, 4,974 pesos ($9.94) double, 6,124 pesos ($12.24) triple, 7,274 pesos ($14.54) for four people. The addition is behind the pretty tree-shaded courtyard, and therefore away from street noise. There's a nice little swimming pool here, and even a small zoo!

Valladolid has even cheaper places to spend the night. For instance, the **Hotel Zací,** Calle 44 no. 191, near Calle 37 (tel. 985/6-2167), charges 2,400 pesos ($4.80) for its double rooms with showers and fans. As some of the rooms around the long, quiet little courtyard are newer than others, you'd do well to look at a few rooms before moving in.

Other small hotels on the same street—Calle 44—have even·lower prices.

My favorite hotel in Valladolid is not on the main square proper, but just a block off it. It's the relatively new **Hotel Don Luis,** Calle 39 no. 191, at Calle 38 (tel. 985/6-2024). From the north side of the square (which is Calle 39) go east (that's away from the Hotel Maria de la Luz) one block, and the Hotel Don Luis is on the left-hand side: you'll spot the sign. Despite its being on a busy street, the Don Luis's rooms are quiet, big, and air-conditioned. All are doubles, many with two double beds. A thoughtful touch is that the washbasin is located *outside* the bathroom, so one can wash while another showers. The swimming pool in the courtyard is attractive and very clean, and prices are good: 2,484 pesos ($4.96) single, 3,266 pesos ($6.53) double for a room with fan; or 3,266 pesos ($6.53) single, 3,864 pesos ($7.72) double for a room with air conditioning; an extra person in a room pays 750 pesos ($1.50).

WHERE TO EAT: The hotel restaurants are not bad here. I especially like the one at the aforementioned Hotel Maria de la Luz, because you can watch the activity in the plaza as you dine.

But for a real Valladolid adventure, and the lowest prices of all, take a stroll through the **Bazar Municipal,** that little arcade of shops beside the Hotel El Mesón del Marqués. The little cookshops here open at mealtimes, and their family-owners set out tables and chairs in the courtyard. Local farmers and traders in town on business come to chow down. You won't find a printed menu often, let alone one in English. But a quick look around at nearby tables will tell you what's cooking, and a discreet point of a finger will order it. Ask the price as you order, for the record, so you won't be charged something exorbitant when it's too late.

My favorite cookshops here are the **Doña Mary** and **El Amigo Panfilo.** A three-course meal of soup, enchiladas, and dessert in either one should cost no more than 750 pesos ($1.50).

TINUM, A MAYAN VILLAGE: Valladolid is the jumping-off place for a visit to a unique adventure: a stay in a real Mayan village. This is only for the intrepid, but if you're one, read on.

Some years ago, Ms. Bettina McMakin Erdman left Miami to settle in the tiny village of Tinum, to get away from it all. She learned the Mayan language, got to know many of the villagers, and soon had visitors. At first they were just friends from back home, but later her "visitors" included those interested in discovering exactly what it's like to live as the Mayas did—and do.

Ms. Erdman doesn't spend a lot of time in Tinum anymore, but the 15-year tradition of hospitality survives, carried on by her village friends, especially Don Chivo.

Here's what you do: twice daily, buses run from Valladolid to Tinum in 40 minutes. Or you can take the daily 3 p.m. train from Mérida to Tinum, arriving at 7:15 p.m. (or thereabouts). Bring a hammock with you, or write ahead to arrange to have one made and waiting for you in Tinum. Don Chivo will arrange for you to board with a Maya family in their *na* (house of sticks with a thatched roof), and to eat with them and share their daily life. The cost, paid directly to the family, is US$7 per day. Be sure you realize that this is the real thing: you sleep in your hammock, live with a dirt floor, cook on a fire, and use one of the two bathrooms in Doña Bettina's house. You're welcome for two or three nights.

ONWARD TO CANCÚN: Having refreshed yourself with a stop in Valladolid, you're ready to head onward to Cancún and Isla Mujeres. These two favorite resort destinations are only a handful of miles apart in distance, but worlds apart in ambience. The 160-kilometer (100-mile) ride from Valladolid to Cancún or Puerto Juárez will take about two hours.

CANCÚN AND THE CARIBBEAN COAST

ONLY A DECADE AGO, the name Cancún would have meant little to anyone. Perhaps a resident of Puerto Juárez or Isla Mujeres would have linked the name to a hook-shaped sandy island a few hundred feet off the Yucatecan coast, a desert island of powdery limestone sand, surrounded by coral reefs. Today Cancún is the magic word in Mexican vacations.

Looking to expand tourism, the Mexican government did a study to find the best location for a new jet-age resort, and Cancún came out on top. From a tiny mainland hamlet, Ciudad Cancún soon grew to a city of 30,000; its projected size is 70,000, to be reached in a few years. Engineers, construction crews, shopkeepers, and restaurateurs all flocked to the new development, and as the luxury hotels began to increase on the deserted sand island, so did the vacationers in search of warm sun and cool waters.

But that's not the end of the story. As the wide-body jets brought more and more vacationers into Cancún's convenient international airport, the government decided to expand its development along Mexico's beautiful palm-lined Caribbean coast. The once sparsely populated state of Quintana Roo is booming these days, with public and private investment causing modern towns and lush resorts to spring up in the jungle almost overnight.

What makes Cancún the perfect site for a resort? The land is the beautiful Yucatecan jungle, the long sand spit is perfect for seaside hotels, and the beaches are covered in a very fine sand that has been called "air-conditioned" by its ingenious promoters. Mayan ruins at Tulum, Chichén-Itzá, and Cobá are a short drive away, and for a change of scene the older resorts of Isla Mujeres and Cozumel are close at hand. The Caribbean waters are incredibly blue and limpid, temperatures (both air and water) are just right, and the coral reefs and tropical climate guarantee brilliant underwater life, good snorkeling, and fine scuba-diving.

Nevertheless, this region is still underdeveloped compared to the rest of Mexico. It is big, and transportation services are not as convenient as in, say, the Valley of Mexico. So you must give special consideration to your means of transport here.

After exploring the delights of modern Cancún and Isla Mujeres, I'll take you south along the coast to the newer resorts—and also some timeless Maya cities recently unearthed in the jungle. To get you set for your travels, here's a summary of transport in and out of Cancún so you can plan your travels wisely.

TRANSPORTATION: If you're beginning your Yucatecan adventure in Cancún or Cozumel, you'd be well advised to read the first two sections in the preceding chapter, "Yucatán's Fascinating History" and "Touring Yucatán: Itineraries."

To help specifically in planning your trips, here are some **distances from Cancún** to other Yucatecan points: to Belize City, 610 km (378 miles); Chetumal, 390 km (242 miles); Chichén-Itzá, 200 km (124 miles); Cobá, 175 km (109 miles); Felipe Carrillo Puerto, 230 km (143 miles); Isla Mujeres Ferry Dock (Punta Sam), 10 km (6 miles); Mérida, 320 km (199 miles); Palenque, via Chetumal, 895 km (555 miles); Palenque, via Mérida, 940 km (583 miles); Playa del Carmen (Cozumel passenger dock), 68 km (42 miles); Puerto Morelos (Cozumel car ferry dock), 36 km (22 miles); Tulum and Xel-Ha, 130 km (81 miles); Uxmal, 400 km (248 miles); Valladolid, 160 km (99 miles); Villahermosa, via Chetumal, 1200 km (744 miles); Villahermosa, via Mérida, 1240 km (769 miles).

By Air

AeroMéxico (tel. 988/4-2728 or 4-2639) is located at Avenida Tulum, corner of Avenida Uxmal, and they also have an office in the Centro Comercial El Parián, near the Convention Center; they operate daily flights between Cancún and Houston, Mérida, Mexico City, Monterrey, New York, and Villahermosa.

Mexicana (tel. 988/4-1423) at Avenida Cobá 13, has daily nonstops between Cancún and Chicago, Dallas/Fort Worth, Guadalajara, Miami, Mexico City, and Philadelphia.

AeroCaribe (tel. 988/4-1231 or 4-1364), in the same building as AeroMéxico, has six daily flights to Cozumel, so you can whiz over and back in a day easily. Round-trip fare is 14,000 pesos ($28).

Aero Cozumel (tel. 988/4-2562 at the airport) has a number of small prop planes that make trips between Cozumel and Cancún. See the section on Cozumel (below) for full details.

Lacsa, the Costa Rican airline, has offices at Avenida Yaxchilán 5 (tel. 988/4-1276), in the Centro Comercial El Parián (tel. 988/4-2617), and at the airport (tel. 988/3-0103). Go there for flights to Central American destinations.

By Bus

Autotransportes del Caribe (BUS) is located across the street from the Hotel Plaza Caribe, downtown in Ciudad Cancún at the intersection of Avenidas Tulum and Uxmal. They run buses almost hourly from 6 a.m. to midnight on the route between Cancún and Mérida, stopping at Valladolid and Chichén-Itzá. There are both first- and second-class buses (each has its own ticket window and waiting room). Though second class is a bit cheaper, the buses are slower.

Here are some sample first-class fares from Cancún, to give you an idea what travel by bus costs; second-class fares are about 8% lower: Chichén-Itzá, 1,239 pesos ($2.47); Playa del Carmen, 422 pesos (84¢); Valladolid, 985 pesos ($1.97).

This company also runs three buses a day on the *long* (1,800-kilometer, 1,100-mile) trip to Mexico City.

Twelve buses a day run down the coast to Chetumal, stopping at Puerto Morelos (car and passenger ferry for Cozumel), Playa del Carmen (passenger boat and shuttle flights for Cozumel), Akumal, Tulum, Felipe Carrillo Puerto, and finally Chetumal, on the Belizean border.

By Rental Car

There are very few areas in Mexico for which I would recommend this, but for the Yucatán I think you should consider renting a car. Those traveling alone will find it expensive, but a couple or a family will find it reasonable. Unlike most areas of Mexico, Yucatán lends itself to pleasant car travel: the roads are good and straight, traffic is light, sights are spread out, bus service is not as frequent or as comfortable as one might wish. You could easily spend several weeks trying to get to all the major ruins, cities, and beaches in Yucatán by bus, but you can cover them all quite well in one hassle-free week with a car.

The way to do it is to rent the cheapest car, a VW Beetle, for a week at the unlimited-mileage rate. Total cost for the week, including gas, insurance, rental fee, and IVA tax, might be $300, which comes out to $42.85 per day. As of this writing, only two companies—**Budget Rent-A-Car** and **Dollar Rent-A-Car**—offer this weekly unlimited-mileage rate, and in fact both of these franchises are owned and operated by the same Mexican firm. They have an office at the airport, and another downtown at the corner of Avenidas Tulum and Uxmal (tel. 988/4-1709), across from the Autobuses del Caribe bus terminal.

If you don't rent your car in Cancún, consider renting it in Mérida.

1. Cancún

Mexico's second most famous resort (after Acapulco), Cancún (pop. 100,000) was definitely not developed with the cost-conscious budget traveler in mind. Rather, its lavish layout and posh luxury hotels were meant to attract charter-travel crowds and bottomless-pocket types.

But don't let this worry you. Following the philosophy of this book, you'll be able to stay in expensive Cancún, enjoy its fabulous beaches and water sports, take side trips to nearby Maya archeological sites, and to the islands of Isla Mujeres and Cozumel, and *still* remain within our proposed budget. The trick is to spend your nights, and most of your daily budget, in businesslike Ciudad Cancún, and *not* in the posh Zona Turística (also called the Zona Hotelera). Hotels in Ciudad Cancún are comfortable without being flashy, moderately priced, and convenient to everything. The beaches are a short, cheap bus ride away, which brings me to the subject of . . .

GETTING AROUND: Though it costs more here than in most Mexican cities, there's plenty of transport available.

From the Airport

Special minibuses run from Cancún's international airport into town for 830 pesos ($1.66) per person. As of this writing, minibus service is one way only, and you'll have to hire a taxi for twice that amount to get back to the airport. Note that if you are in a group or family of more than two people, you can do better by taking a taxi instead of a minibus. Rates for a cab from the airport to the Zona Hotelera are 1,800 pesos ($3.60) for one person, 2,000 pesos ($4) for up to four persons.

By Bus

In town, almost everything's within easy walking distance. The only places you need take buses to are the beaches near the luxury hotels in the Zona Turística, and to Puerto Juárez/Punta Sam for ferries to Isla Mujeres. City buses will trundle you from your in-town hotel out to the beaches of the Zona Turística for a ridiculously low fare. These "Ruta 1" buses operate every 15 minutes or so along the Avenida Tulum, Ciudad Cancún's main street, all the way to Punta Nizuc at the far end of the Zona Turística.

As for Puerto Juárez/Punta Sam, catch a Ruta 8 (to Puerto Juárez and Punta Sam) bus along Cancún's main street, Avenida Tulum, and the bus will take you straight to the ferry docks for 80 pesos (16¢); a taxi costs 600 pesos ($1.20).

By Taxi

The city fathers have instituted an authorized table of taxi fares, but in any case it's best to make a deal on a fare in advance. From Ciudad Cancún out to, say, the Hotel Camino Real should cost 500 pesos ($1); a short ride between two of the big hotels, less than 350 pesos (70¢); from Ciudad Cancún to the airport, 1,450 pesos ($2.90).

By Moped

You'll see lots of moped (motorbike) rental places in Cancún, particularly out in the Zona Hotelera. Fees for a day's rental can range from 3,000 to 6,000 pesos ($6 to $12). The lowest rates come from the guys who have set up shop on a piece of sidewalk: no phone, no desk, no address, just a few mopeds and a folding chair. Highest rates are from legitimate agencies with a phone number you can call in case of emergency or breakdown. They usually have newer bikes in better repair.

When you rent, try to get a discount if it looks like business is slow. You will have to pay the estimated rental in advance, and perhaps leave your driver's license as security for the moped. You should receive a crash helmet and a lock and chain with the rental.

Mopeds are a fine way to cruise around the Zona Hotelera, but they're not really good for trips to and from town, or for any distances over a few kilometers. The bike path which borders the roadway between the Zona Hotelera and the town is in bad disrepair in many spots, so you must ride cautiously and slowly. The alternative—riding in the roadway itself—pits you against hundreds of would-be Latin Grand Prix racers in beat-up Datsuns, not a cheery prospect.

By Calesa

An alternative to the expensive car and the somewhat dangerous and unwieldy moped is the "calesa," which in Cancún means a little two- or four-person horseless carriage. These antique-style putt-putts rent for 5,800 or 7,650 pesos ($11.60 or $15.30) per hour, up to 15,750 or 21,150 pesos ($31.50 or $42.30) for a full day until 6 p.m. These prices, for two- and four-seat models respectively, includes gas, mileage, tax, and insurance. Rent one in the parking lot next to the Plaza Caracol shopping mall, between the Viva and Krystal hotels (no phone).

ORIENTATION: Here's the layout. Ciudad Cancún, the new town on the main-

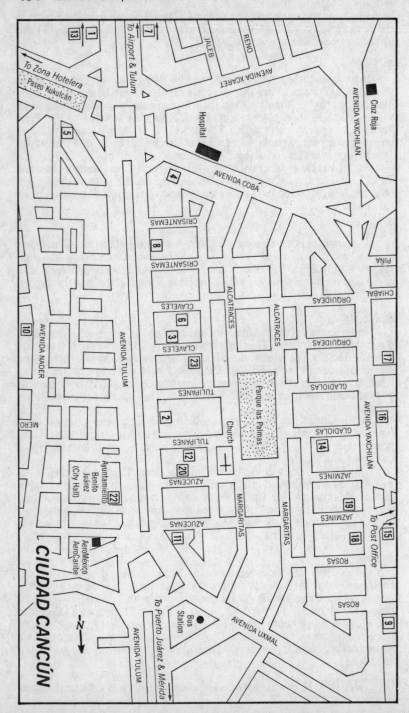

CIUDAD CANCÚN

land, has banks, travel and airline agencies, car rental firms, restaurants, hotels, and shops, all within an area about nine blocks square. The main thoroughfare is Avenida Tulum. Heading south, Avenida Tulum becomes the highway to the airport, Tulum, and Chetumal; heading north, it joins the Mérida–Puerto Juárez highway.

The Zona Hotelera, or Zona Turística, stretches out along the former Isla Cancún (Cancún Island), a sandy strip 14 miles long, shaped like a "7." Now joined by bridges to the mainland at north and south, it is an island no longer. Cancún's international airport is just inland from the base of the "7."

Useful Facts

Banks: Most are downtown along the Avenida Tulum. There are also a few casas de cambio (exchange houses). In addition, you'll find downtown merchants particularly eager to change cash dollars, sometimes at very advantageous rates. In Cancún it's important to shop around for a good exchange rate. Many places, particularly hotels, will offer you absolutely terrible rates of exchange.

Consulates: The **U.S. Consular Agent** (tel. 988/4-2411) is in the office of Intercaribe Real Estate, Avenida Cobá 86, a block off Avenida Tulum going toward the Zona Hotelera. The agent's hours are Tuesday through Saturday 10 a.m. to 2 p.m.; the office is open from 9 a.m. to 2 p.m. and from 4 to 8 p.m., Monday through Friday. In an emergency, call the U.S. Consulate in Mérida (tel. 992/5-5011).

Medical Care: Cruz Roja (Red Cross, tel. 4-1616), good for first aid, is on Avenida Yaxchilán near the intersection with Avenida Xcaret. For more serious ailments, head for the IMSS (Mexican Social Security Institute) Hospital (tel. 4-1108 or 4-1907), on Avenida Cobá at Avenida Tulum.

Post Office: The main post office (tel. 4-1418) is at the intersection of Avenida Sunyaxchén and Avenida Xel-Ha, open 9 a.m. to 7 p.m. except Sunday.

Tourist Information

The official **tourist office** is in the City Hall ("Ayuntamiento Benito Juárez") on Avenida Tulum. You may find one of the several little information kiosks set up on busy sidewalks downtown attended by a helpful person as well.

Lots of other people will offer to give you information, usually in exchange for listening to a spiel about the wonders of a Cancún time-sharing or condo purchase.

Pick up a copy of the monthly *Reader's Digest*-sized publication called **Cancún Tips.** They're handed out for free at the airport when you arrive, and are available downtown in several places. It's got lots of useful information, as well as fine maps. The publication sponsors information offices in several locations, stocked with well-informed personnel, brochures, and a collection of restaurant menus for browsing. The scheme is designed to benefit the publication's advertisers, of course, but these people and their booklet are very helpful nonetheless.

A Note on Addresses

Starting with a clean slate, one would think the city fathers of Ciudad Cancún would have laid out a street-numbering system that was simple and easy to use, but such has not been the case. Addresses are still often given by the number of the building lot and by the *manzana* (city block). Some streets have signs with names on, although the establishments along the street may refer to the street only by its number, as Retorno 3, etc. In short, it is very difficult to find a place in Ciudad Cancún just by the numbers. Luckily, the city is still relatively small and the downtown section can easily be covered on foot. I've tried to be very specific in my directions to recommended establishments. Your best companion in confusing Cancún is the map in this book, with numbers keyed to places I mention.

WHERE TO STAY: Ciudad Cancún has a good collection of moderate- and budget-priced hotels, just as does Acapulco, Cozumel, or any other Mexican resort town. Prices are a bit higher than in, say, Mérida, which is not right next door to a fabulous resort, but you can stay overnight comfortably and inexpensively in Ciudad Cancún. Off-season (April and November), bargain for a price reduction. Here are Cancún's recommended hotels, by location.

On and Off Avenida Tulum

Just off Avenida Tulum, entered from Calle Claveles 37, is the new **Antillano Hotel (6)** (tel. 988/4-1532 or 4-1244). Modern wood-and-stucco in design, the Antillano has air-conditioned rooms that overlook the busy Avenida Tulum and also the side streets. Being one of the newer hotels downtown, it's decidedly a bit fancier, and includes a swimming pool. Consider that when you study the prices: 9,200 pesos ($18.40) single, 9,775 pesos ($19.55) double, 10,580 pesos ($21.16) triple, all in.

The seafood restaurant chain of Soberanis has both a restaurant and a hotel in Cancún. The **Hotel Soberanis (4)**, Cobá 5, near the corner with Avenida Tulum (tel. 988/4-1125 or 4-1858), has a bright white-and-orange color scheme and some other touches such as elegant table lamps, two double beds to a room, and little balconies. All rooms are air-conditioned, of course, and are priced at 9,750 pesos ($19.50) single, 10,750 pesos ($21.50) double with one double or two twin beds, 11,250 pesos ($22.50) double with two double beds.

An outstanding choice all around is the attractive **Novotel en Cancún (11)**, Apdo. 70, Cancún Q. Roo 77500 (tel. 988/4-2999), on Avenida Tulum at Azucenas, near the intersection with Avenida Uxmal. Though modern, it has enough traditional touches such as white stucco walls, metalwork, and colorful craft decorations, to give it a truly Mexican spirit. The 40 air-conditioned rooms are often booked solid, and are priced at 7,130 pesos ($14.26) single, 7,333 pesos ($14.66) double, 8,740 pesos ($17.48) triple, 9,890 pesos ($19.78) for four.

Carrillo's (6) (tel. 988/4-1227) is on a side street called Calle Claveles which meets Avenida Tulum at two places (Claveles forms a loop). Look for the intersection of Claveles and Tulum that's right across from the Banco Nacional de México and its large statues of Tula's Atlantean men; official address is Retorno 3, Manzana 22. Now that you're there, you'll find Carrillo's to be one of the strangest places in Cancún. Although a few of the hotel's rooms are older and more standard, most are finished—walls and ceiling—in a nubbly white stucco that gives the entire place a troglodytic quality. Add plywood vanities, tiled showers, and individual air conditioning units and you have the standard rooms at Carrillo's, which rents for 7,015 pesos ($14.03) single, 8,280 pesos ($16.56) double. Besides the two-story hotel, Carrillo's building houses a seafood restaurant.

The **Hotel Cancún Handall (7)** (tel. 988/4-1122 or 4-1976) opened in 1980. Two wings of two floors each hold a variety of single rooms, doubles, and suites, and a pool awaits your pleasure outside. Most of the modern rooms have two double beds, and cost 11,500 pesos ($23) single, 13,800 pesos ($27.60) double, and 15,000 pesos ($30) triple. The Handall is at the intersection of Avenidas Tulum and Cobá.

On the Avenida Tulum right downtown is the **Hotel Rivemar (8)** (tel. 988/4-1199), a modern but heavily used establishment right in the midst of downtown.

Rooms are air-conditioned, of course, with private baths, and are priced at 5,315 pesos ($10.63) single, 6,855 pesos ($13.71) double, 8,275 pesos ($16.55) triple.

It's strange to imagine a colonial hotel in brand-new Cancún, but there is such a thing. Aptly enough, it's named the **Hotel Colonial (12),** Tulipanes 22 at Avenida Tulum, on a quiet side street (tel. 988/4-1535). Furnishings of the rooms around the little courtyard are, not surprisingly, colonial in inspiration. But the colonists didn't have private baths or air conditioning, yet every room in the hotel does. Price for a room, single or double, is 5,000 pesos ($10) with a fan, 5,400 pesos ($10.80) with air-conditioning.

On and Off Avenida Yaxchilán

Avenida Yaxchilán, west of and parallel to Avenida Tulum, also has a good selection of hotels in all price ranges.

My favorite place in this area is the tidy, quaint little **Posada Lucy (14),** Calle Gladiolas 25, a half-block off Avenida Yaxchilán near the Plaza del Sol hotel and shopping complex (tel. 988/4-4165). The dozen rooms here are jammed into a tiny space, on two levels, painted cheery blue and white, with red tile floors. It's quiet, though, and the rooms have aluminum screens on the windows, air conditioners, and even kitchenettes in some. Rates are 6,000 pesos ($12) single, 8,000 pesos ($16) double for a room, 12,000 pesos ($24) double for a room with kitchenette. Weekly rates are even cheaper.

The **Hotel Komvaser (9),** Avenida Yaxchilán 15 (tel. 988/4-1650), is a surprisingly open-air place with pool, bar, reception desk, etc. all right out next to the sidewalk. No big sign announces the hotel's presence, and you may find yourself waltzing right by it. The rooms, all air-conditioned and set back from the street, have one double and one single bed, and rent for 8,500 pesos ($17) single or double, 9,500 pesos ($19) triple.

For big families, the place is the **Hotel Hacienda Cancún (15),** Avenida Sunyaxchén 39-40, at Avenida Yaxchilán (tel. 988/4-1208 or 4-3672). The building gives a whole new dimension to the word "stucco," but some of the rooms can hold up to six persons, for 15,000 pesos ($30) total. Other rates are 6,210 pesos ($12.42) single, 7,475 pesos ($14.95) double, 8,855 pesos ($17.71) triple; continental breakfast is included in these rates. The hotel has its own parking lot, swimming pool, and restaurant.

The simple, modern **Hotel Canto (17),** Avenida Yaxchilán at Retorno 5 (tel. 988/4-1267), is tall enough to stand out, modern enough to satisfy, and cheap enough to please. Double rooms with ceiling fans here go for 5,570 pesos ($11.14).

The **Hotel Yaxchilán (18),** Avenida Yaxchilán 41-43, at the intersection with Sunyaxchén (tel. 988/4-1324), has several dozen quite plain rooms with ceiling fans for 4,500 pesos ($9) single, 5,075 pesos ($10.15) double. Avoid rooms overlooking the busy street. Housekeeping here is sporadic, but the hot water always seems to be hot.

Right around the corner is the **Hotel Marrufo (19),** on Calle Rosas at Avenida Yaxchilán (tel. 988/4-1334). The plain but clean rooms here cost even less: 3,900 pesos ($7.80) single, 4,400 pesos ($8.80) double, 5,000 pesos ($10) triple with fan; about 600 or 700 pesos ($1.20 or $1.40) more for a room with air conditioning, hot plate, and refrigerator.

Starvation Budget Digs

The lowest-priced decent lodgings in Cancún are to be found at **La Carreta (20)** (no phone), Calle Azucenas 17 next to El Pirata Restaurant (turn off Avenida Tulum at the Bananas Restaurant). For 2,000 pesos ($4) double per day you can rent an extremely basic room without plumbing; the same room by the month costs 35,000 pesos ($70), not including towels, bed linen, or cleaning. All rooms share baths.

The Youth Hostel

Cancún now has a big, beautiful, comfortable, modern youth hostel right out in the expensive Zona Turística. Look for the sign that says **Albergue de la Juventud,** on the left-hand (north) side of the road as you bus out from town. The address is: Paseo Kukulkan km. 3.2, Apdo. 849 (tel. 988/3-1337). Backpackers will want to know that the hostel is 4 kilometers (2½ miles) from the bus station. Inexpensive city buses ("Hoteles") go right by it. The hostel has 612 beds, a swimming pool, a fine location right near the beach, and prices like this: 1,050 pesos ($2.10) for a bed, 420 pesos (84¢) for breakfast, 540 pesos ($1.08) for lunch or dinner. It's fabulous!

The Big Splurge

Were I to upgrade in pricey Cancún, it wouldn't be to one of the skyscrapers out on the beach, but to the new **Hotel America (1),** on Avenida Tulum at Avenida Brisa, Apdo. 600 (tel. 988/4-1500). From here you can walk into the center of town and yet stay in a top-class, luxurious, air-conditioned hotel. The America has its own beach club, with a free shuttle bus to take you there, plus its own swimming pools right in the hotel. Prices are moderate, for what you get: 27,600 pesos ($55.20) single, 29,900 pesos ($59.80) double, 31,625 pesos ($63.25) triple.

A Different Kind of Place

The **Suites Residencial "Flamboyanes" (10),** is a different and delightful place (tel. 988/4-1503; for reservations in Mérida, call 992/1-0603 or go to Calle 65 no. 514). Here at Avenida Carlos J. Nader, no. 101–103, Super Manzana 3, just off Avenida Cobá, are 80 suites in a number of attractive two-story buildings surrounded by grass and trees, and equipped with a private swimming pool. All suites are air-conditioned and include a bedroom, a living room with couches to sleep two more people, fully equipped kitchen with dining area, bathroom, and terrace/porch. A suite for one or two persons costs 10,925 pesos ($21.85), plus 2,300 pesos ($4.60) for each additional person. The daily rate goes down for extended stays, of course. Remember that you are renting an *apartment* here, and not just a hotel room, and thus the prices are very reasonable for what you get.

READER'S HOTEL SELECTION: "We stayed at the **Hotel Plaza Caribe** (tel. 988/4-1252 or 4-1796), at Tulum and Uxmal, facing the bus terminal. Don't get badly impressed by the shabby outside, for the standard is medium-high with a beautiful tropical garden including bird cages, swimming pool, pool bar, another bar with music in the evening, an attractive cafeteria-restaurant, and arctic air conditioning everywhere. The 200 rooms are modern, reasonably large, with two double beds. The price is 8,855 pesos ($32.20) double, which is good for what you get. They sometimes have special package offers that make it even more attractive" (Leonardo Scalfi, Besana Brianza, Italy).

WHERE TO EAT: One must be cautious in accepting the extravagant claims made by the luxury hotels for their own restaurants. The very economics of the situation are against them: package tours must be offered at a competitive low price, and so the meals included in the tour must be fancy but not expensive to prepare. Guest must go away satisfied, but it must be remembered that guests have prepaid their meals, which puts them in a difficult position if they don't like the food! I've had letters from readers who have stayed at the fancy hotels and have found the food so mediocre they made the trip into Ciudad Cancún every day and paid extra just to have tasty meals.

Living by the philosophy of this book does away with the luxury-hotel-restaurant problem, as I'll recommend only small independent restaurants in downtown Cancún that must compete nightly for clients, and that therefore are careful that price *and quality* are competitive.

For Yucatecan Specialties

The first **Restaurant Los Almendros** was located deep in the Maya heartland at Ticul. Then a branch opened in Mérida, and now one has been opened in Cancún **(13)**. Los Almendros specializes in Maya cooking, and the big restaurant on Avenida Bonampak, at Calle Saíl (tel. 4-0807), is meant to look something like a large Mayan palapa inside. Get in a cab, and for about 500 pesos ($1) the driver will take you south on Avenida Tulum, past the Hotel America and toward the airport, and will turn left onto Avenida Bonampak. The restaurant is a few blocks down, on the left-hand side. The menu here has explanations of all the dishes (in English too), and you'll see lime soup; roast venison with radishes, onions, and sour oranges (tzic de venado); and the house specialty, which is grilled pork served with onions, chiles, and beans (poc-chuc). The combinado yucateco is a sampler with small portions of four typically Yucatecan main courses. Wine and beer are served. You can dine at Los Almendros any day of the week, and you may spend 2,500 pesos ($5) per person, or even less.

The **Restaurant Papagayo** (no phone), Claveles 31, off Avenida Tulum, has a lush tropical-garden layout complete with straw-thatched palapa. It's a proper setting for Yucatecan dishes such as lime soup or tikinchik, but the menu goes beyond Yucatecan specialties to more familiar fare. Expect to spend 2,500 to 3,500 ($5 to $7) for a full lunch or dinner; breakfast is served as well. Closed Sunday.

For Seafood

There always seems to be a line for dinner at the **Restaurant El Pescador** (tel. 4-2673), Tulipanes 5, off of Avenida Tulum. Fresh seafood excellently prepared and moderately priced (for Cancún) is the drawing card. You can sit on the rustic porch at streetside, or in an interior dining room, and feast on cocktails of shrimp, conch, lobster, fish, or octopus for 1,200 to 1,525 pesos ($2.40 to $3.05), and main fish courses priced between 2,150 and 3,000 pesos ($4.30 to $6). The specialty here is Créole cuisine, such as Créole-style shrimp (camarones alla criolla), or charcoal-broiled lobster, but these cost more. Open for dinner only, El Pescador is closed Monday.

The **Restaurant El Pirata** (no phone), Azucenas 19 off Avenida Tulum, has the proper nautical motif, long dinner hours (3 to 11 p.m., seven days a week), and seafood prices that are moderate for Cancún. For a dinner based on grilled filet of fish, expect to spend about 4,000 pesos ($8), half again as much for fancy items such as a brochette of shrimp and steak.

The local incarnation of the Soberanis seafood restaurant group is at Avenida Cobá 5 and 7, in the **Hotel Soberanis (4)** (tel. 4-1125). The patio dining area is shaded by large awnings, and although you're not far from Avenida Tulum here, it's fairly quiet. Service is attentive, and prices are moderate considering the general range of prices in Cancún for seafood. Fish entrees are a moderate 1,750 to 3,000 ($3.50 to $6), and are the best things to have. Soberanis opens about 9 in the morning (good for breakfast), and closes at 11 p.m. or midnight.

Carrillo's Restaurant (6) (tel. 4-1227), in the hotel of the same name on Calle Claveles (see above), is a good place, whether you want to put together a light lunch for a couple of dollars, or to go all-out and have lobster. A nice filet of red snapper (huachinango) will cost about 2,100 pesos ($4.20), depending on style of preparation, while a steak will cost a few dollars more. For a full meal, with wine, tax, and tip, expect to pay 4,500 to 6,000 pesos ($9 to $12) per person. The big bonus at Carillo's, fairly rare in Cancún restaurants, is air conditioning. There's piano music every evening. In winter it's fun to sit at one of the outdoor tables, but in the heat of summer almost everyone opts for the cool indoor dining room.

Dinner Is the Show

Many restaurants in Cancún provide the customary entertainments of Mexican seaside resorts: sassy waiters, strolling mariachis, perhaps a charro lasso-twirler. There's no extra charge for the lively atmosphere, though dinner prices do tend to be a bit higher than in places which offer less distraction.

A place that was booming on my last visit was **Perico's (16)** (tel. 4-3152), Avenida Yaxchilán 71, at Calle Marañón. Made of sticks to resemble a large Maya house, Perico's has a western decor that includes a few saddles on display here and there. The restaurant is open for dinner only, and features steaks, Cancún seafood, and the more traditional Mexican dishes for very moderate rates. You should be able to choose whatever you like from the menu (except lobster) and still get out for under 5,000 pesos ($10) per person.

A very popular sidewalk restaurant on Avenida Tulum is popular for its food, its ambience, and its clientele—all three. It's **Blackbeard's Taberna (2)**. The food might consist of ceviche, the marinated fish cocktail, followed by a brochette (the specialty) of beef, chicken, shrimp, lobster, or all of the above. Finish with cheesecake, or ice cream topped with a liqueur, accompany your meal with a full carafe of the house wine, and the entire bill for two people might come to 14,000 pesos ($28). You can dine for less, though: say, 5,000 pesos ($10) per person. The decor is rustic Mexican wooden shanty, the clientele mostly international sun-seekers. Open every day.

Across the street from the aforementioned Carrillo's at Calle Claveles 13 is **Chocko's & Tere (8)** (tel. 4-1394), a ramshackle, semi-open-air collection of brightly lit dining rooms where the noise level is high, but the fun level is even higher. Something is always going on here—mariachis, a lasso-twirling *charro* (cowboy), or a solo guitarist—to liven up the already-lively crowd. The food seems to be of second interest here, and the service is, well, casual. But you can have soup, main course, dessert, and a bottle of beer, tax and tip included, for 4,200 pesos ($8.40). And don't forget all that free entertainment. By the way, the "tip" is a *required* 15%.

If you've enjoyed restaurants of the Carlos Anderson chain in other cities, you can in Cancún too. **Carlos & Charlie's** (no phone) is out in the Zona Hotelera, on the right as you ride out the peninsula. Same upbeat atmosphere, same menu, and price that will put you out about 4,500 to 6,000 pesos ($9 to $12) per person for a full evening.

Modern and Air-Conditioned

The popular **Restaurant Pop (12)**, (tel. 4-1991), famous in Mérida for a number of years now, has a branch in Cancún at Avenida Tulum 26, near the corner of Avenida Uxmal and the Hotel Parador. As in Mérida the fare tends to the light, simple, and delicious rather than the elaborate and expensive. Breakfast or a light lunch can be had in the cool comfort of Pop's air-conditioned dining room for 750 to 1,250 pesos ($1.50 to $2.50); a more substantial dinner should be in the range of 2,000 to 3,000 pesos ($4 to $6). Wine and beer are served.

For Pizza

Is there no place to get a good, inexpensive (under $4) meal in Cancún? There is. At **Pizza Rolandi (5)** (tel. 4-4047), Avenida Cobá 12, between Tulum and Nader, you can get the basic cheese-and-tomato pizza for 1,140 pesos ($2.28), which, with a drink, will satisfy your hunger very pleasantly. The super-special pizza costs 2,750 pesos ($5.50), which isn't bad, and Italian specialties like spaghetti and fettucine cost about that as well. Italian desserts are offered. Pizza Rolandi is usually crowded, its outdoor patio tables busy with the hungry, thirsty (beer is served), thrifty set.

READER'S RESTAURANT SELECTION: "**La Parrilla**, at Av. Yaxchilán no. 51, serves Mexican food (no seafood). The taco al pastor, with pork, pineapple, onion, cilantro, and hot sauce, was especially great for 140 pesos (28¢)" (Mike and Lynn Miller, Anchorage, Alaska).

WHAT TO DO: First thing to do is to explore the sandy, once-deserted island (now actually a peninsula) that is this billion-dollar-resort's reason for being. Perhaps the best thing to do is to take a ride on a Ruta 1 or Ruta 2 bus to the end of the line just to see the fabulous resort and get your bearings. On the return trip, get off the bus at El Parián Centro Comercial, next to the Convention Center, and wander along the beaches from there. The best stretches of each are dominated by the big hotels, of course, but all beaches are public property in Mexico. Note well, though: on the sea (as opposed to the lagoon) side of the sand spit, *undertow is a potentially deadly problem.* Swim where there's a life-guard.

If you'd rather not insinuate yourself onto a hotel beach, the public beach called **Playa Tortugas** is a short walk from the Convention Center bus stop. Both swimming and underwater observation are fine from Playa Tortugas, "Turtle Beach."

You can rent a windsurfer and take lessons on it at Playa Tortugas. Telephone **Windsurfing Cancún** (tel. 988/4-2023) for more information, or wander out to the beach.

Yacht Excursions

Yacht excursions are a favorite pastime here. Modern motor yachts, trimarans, even oldtime sloops take swimmers, sunners, and snorkelers out into the limpid waters, often dropping anchor at Isla Mujeres' Garrafon Beach for lunch and snorkeling around the coral reef. Trips tend to leave at 10 or 11 a.m., last for five hours, include lunch (and sometimes drinks), and cost 7,500 to 15,000 pesos ($15 to $30) per person.

The **Corsario** (tel. 3-0200), an "18th-century pirate sloop," leaves from the marina next to the Hotel El Presidente.

The glass-bottom trimaran **Manta** (tel. 3-1676 or 3-0348) departs the marina next to the Club Caribe Cancún, and several readers have written to recommend it as a fine experience.

The motor yacht **Fiesta Maya** leaves from its dock near the Hotel El Presidente; the boat has a glass-bottom area for watching fish.

The motor yacht **Antares** (tel. 4-1543 or 4-0386) departs from its dock next to the Hotel Casa Maya.

The motor yacht **Tropical** (tel. 3-1488) will take you from the Naval Dock to Isla Mujeres and Garrafon on a cruise from 9 a.m. to 3:15 p.m. daily.

Any of these trips can be booked through a travel agent in Ciudad Cancún —no need to hassle with the phones or trek out to the Zona Turística.

Ruinas El Rey

Cancún has its own Mayan ruins. Though they're unimpressive compared to Tulum, Cobá, or Chichén-Itzá, the Ruinas El Rey are still of interest. The ruins are about 13 miles from town, at the southern reaches of the Zona Hotelera, almost to Punta Nizuc. Look for the Royal Mayan Beach Club on the left (east), and then the ruins on the right (west). Admission is free daily from 8 a.m. to 5 p.m.; write your name in the register after you pass through the gate.

This was a small ceremonial center and settlement for Maya fishermen built very early in the history of Maya culture, then abandoned, and later resettled near the end of the Postclassic Period, not long before the arrival of the Conquistadores. The platforms of numerous small temples are visible amid the banana plants, papayas, and wildflowers.

Archeological Museum

It started out as a fake, more or less, a few bits of Maya flotsam and jetsam meant to entice people to the nearby ruins. But the collection has been expanded now, and though all the truly great stuff is still in greater museums, you can enjoy a visit here. The Museo Arqueológico de Cancún is right next to the convention center (Centro de Convenciónes) near Punta Cancún and the Hotel Krystal. Visit from Tuesday through Saturday from 10 a.m. to 5 p.m.; admission costs 50 pesos (10¢).

Bullfights

Cancún has its own small bullring near the northern (town) end of Paseo Kukulcán. Any Wednesday at 3:30 p.m. during the winter tourist season you can witness this Spanish spectacle. There are usually four bulls.

Farther Afield

Day-long excursions, or perhaps even an overnight stay, are easy using Cancún as a base. The Mayan ruins at Tulum should be your first goal, then perhaps the *caleta* (cove) of Xel-ha, and later to nearby Isla Mujeres. By driving fast or catching the buses right, one can get to Chichén-Itzá, explore the ruins, and return in a day, but it's much better to make a trip of several days and include Mérida and Uxmal on the same trip. If you plan to go south to the island of Cozumel, think of staying on the island at least one night. See below for transportation details and further information on all of these destinations.

NIGHTLIFE: Ciudad Cancún has hardly been in existence long enough to have developed an indigenous nightlife, although there are a few lively spots that are offshoots of clubs in Mérida or Mexico City. But the real action is in the Zona Turística at the big hotels. Part of the thrill of getting away to the Caribbean is the intrigue of meeting new people either on the beach or in the cool, dark depths of a disco or nightclub.

Clubs and Discos

All the big hotels have night places, usually both a disco and a supper club with a floor show or at least live music for dancing. Expect to pay a cover charge of about 2,000 pesos ($4) per person in the discos or show bars, or be subjected to a 1,500-peso minimum—(since drinks cost 1,000 to 1,400 pesos, $2 to $2.80),

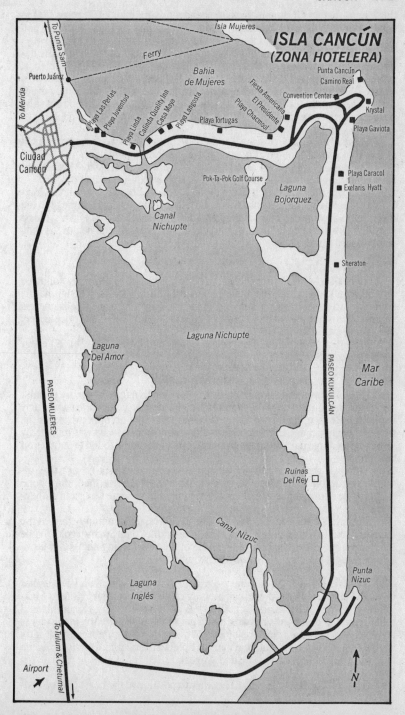

ISLA CANCÚN
(ZONA HOTELERA)

To Punta Sam

Isla Mujeres

Ferry

Puerto Juárez

Bahía
de Mujeres

To Mérida

Punta Cancún
Camino Real
Convention Center
Fiesta Americana
El Presidente
Playa Chacmool
Playa Las Perlas
Playa Juventud
Playa Linda
Calinda Quality Inn
Casa Maya
Playa Langosta
Playa Tortugas

Krystal
Playa Gaviota

Ciudad
Cancún

Playa Caracol
Exelaris Hyatt

Pok-Ta-Pok Golf Course

Laguna
Bojorquez

Canal
Nichupte

Sheraton

Laguna Nichupte

Laguna
Del Amor

PASEO KUKULCÁN

Mar
Caribe

PASEO MUJERES

Ruinas
Del Rey

Canal Nizuc

Punta
Nizuc

Laguna
Inglés

To Tulum & Chetumal

Airport

N

this means that you'll actually have to spend a minimum of 2,000 pesos ($4) to cover your "1,500-peso" minimum. Add 15% tax and tip to these prices, and you'll see that a night out in fabulous Cancún is not all that cheap.

Believe it or not, one of the least expensive evenings can be had at the deluxe **Hotel El Presidente,** in the Zona Hotelera (tel. 3-0200). In the lobby bar, groups entertain each night except Wednesday, and no cover or minimum is charged. The music is traditional—mariachis, jarocho, etc.—and changes every half hour. In the hotel's club, called **Bum Bum Cancún,** the thatched roof shivers every night except Monday to the cool jive of salsa music, for dancing, of course.

At the **Hotel Cancún Caribe** (tel. 3-0044), dancers can work out every night of the week except Monday. Look for a two-drink minimum here.

The posh **Camino Real Hotel** (tel. 3-1200) hosts a Mexican Music Night each Friday, and lays on as much rhythm as anyone could handle.

The **Lone Star Bar** is next to the Hotel Maria de Lourdes on Avenida Yaxchilán. The cover charge is only about 500 pesos ($1), beer is the same, and the music is live country. The Lone Star advertises itself as "Cancún's oldest (1980)"! The bar opens at 9 p.m. every night but Monday, and begins to really go at about 11 p.m.

The Ballet Folklorico

Dinner-and-a-show here includes a table d'hôte dinner at 7 p.m., followed at 8:30 by a show with more than 30 dancers and musicians. Though hardly equivalent to the extravaganza staged in Mexico City's Palacio de Bellas Artes, you may consider it worth the price of 10,000 pesos ($20). That price covers everything except drinks.

Shows are staged in the **Convention Center** auditorium (tel. 3-0199) every evening except Sunday.

2. Isla Mujeres

There are two versions of how Isla Mujeres got its name. The more popular one states that pirates used the island as a place to park their women while they were off buccaneering on the Spanish Main. The other account attributes the name to conquistador Francisco Hernandez de Córdoba, who was reportedly struck by the large number of female terracotta figurines he found in temples on the island.

Although the more prosaic version is probably correct (aren't they always?), incurable romantics such as myself continue to nurse the forlorn hope that the tale about pirates and their women might have some vestige of authenticity.

Modern Isla Mujeres has happily displayed a healthy immunity toward the latter-day pirate whose prey is American green rather than Spanish gold. While there are a few expensive hotels, you'll encounter a satisfying number of facilities for budget travelers and even beachcombers.

GET THERE EARLY: In the busy seasons, June to August and December through February, Isla Mujeres can literally fill up with overnight visitors. Making reservations at the island's small hotels does not always go smoothly and reliably, so the best thing you can do is to get to the island as early in the day as possible. You may even have to stay a night in Cancún so that you can arise early for the first ferry. Check-out time in most hotels is 1 or 2 p.m. Plan to arrive no later than that in February, July, and August.

GETTING TO ISLA MUJERES: The island's position at the heart of the Mexican Caribbean's resort area, as well as its location just a few miles from the mainland, makes it easily accessible.

From Mérida

Buses leave from the bus station several times a day, and you can travel either first or second class depending on the bus. Your destination is Puerto Juárez, from which you take a ferryboat to the island. You can also fly from Mérida to Cancún, and proceed from there (see below).

From Cozumel

Aerocaribe operates daily flights between Cozumel and Isla Mujeres; telephone them for schedules and rates at 2-0503 or 2-0928 in Cozumel, 4-1231 in Cancún. If you don't fly, you must take a ferry to the mainland, then a bus to Puerto Juárez, then another ferry to Isla Mujeres (see below, and also in the Cozumel section).

From Cancún

Take a Ruta 8 city bus (80 pesos, 16¢) to Puerto Juárez or Punta Sam to get the boat. Buses can be caught along the Avenida Tulum or Cancún, running about every 15 minutes.

From Puerto Juárez

Puerto Juárez is the dock for the slightly more expensive passenger boats to Isla Mujeres. Boats depart Puerto Juárez at 6:30, 9:30, and 11:30 a.m., 1:30, 3:30, and 5:30 p.m. on the half-hour trip; one-way fare is 200 pesos (40¢) for a scheduled trip. Boats may run at other than scheduled departure times, but these are *especiales* (special trips), and fares may be considerably higher. Make sure you know the fare before you board.

From Punta Sam

The car ferry to Isla Mujeres accepts passengers as well, and charges only 25 pesos (5¢) per person for the 40-minute ride; cars cost 170 pesos (34¢). To reach Punta Sam, stay on the Ruta 8 bus past Puerto Juárez, all the way to the end of the line at the ferry dock. A taxi from Cancún to the Punta Sam dock costs about 600 pesos ($1.20); make sure the driver understands that he is to take you all the way to the car ferry *(transbordador)* dock, not just to Puerto Juárez.

Note that the car ferries do not run on Monday mornings due to boat maintenance. The first ferry on Monday is at 1:30 p.m., the next at 5:45 p.m. On all other days of the week, departures from Punta Sam are at 8:30 and 11:30 a.m., 1:30, 5:45, and 8:30 p.m. Departures from Isla Mujeres on the return trip are at 7:15 and 10 a.m., 12:15, 4:30, 7:30, and 10 p.m.

ORIENTATION: Isla Mujeres is about 5 miles long and 2½ miles wide. At the northern tip is Playa Cocos (Coconut Beach) and the Hotel El Presidente Caribe. Just a few yards south of these is the small town. The ferry docks right at the edge of the town, walking distance from all hotels except (if your luggage is heavy) the Hotel El Presidente.

USEFUL FACTS: The post office, telegraph office, and market (Mercado Municipal) are all in a row on Calle Guerrero, an inland street at the north edge of town, which, like most streets in the town, is unmarked by signs.

WHERE TO STAY: Isla Mujeres has a varied assortment of places to put up for the night, in all price ranges. Quality of housekeeping seems to be on a roller-coaster, however: if a hotel fills up, the manager tends to sit back, fire the house-keeping staff, put off repairs, and take it easy. When business drops off, he gets back to work. That's life in these island towns.

The **Hotel Rocamar** (tel. 988/2-0101) is perched on the higher ground at the opposite side of town from the ferry dock, and thus has a commanding view of the sea. Everything's done in nautical style here, with every conch shell ever opened in the restaurant going to line the garden walkways; ropes and hawsers are employed as trim; even the bathroom sinks are mounted in Lucite tops, and the Lucite is chock full of small seashells. The sea breezes keep the rooms cool, assisted by ceiling fans. Although definitely among the most well-used rooms on the island, the Rocamar's collection of *quartos* has the breeze and the view. Prices are 8,200 pesos ($16.40) single, 8,600 pesos ($17.20) double. If they're not busy, you can make a deal for a lower price.

The **Hotel Martinez**, Avenida Madero 14, (tel. 988/2-0154), two blocks from the ferry dock (turn left as you debark, go two blocks, and turn right), has been around for years and years, and satisfied guests keep returning because here the basics are rigidly observed: rooms are spotless, sheets and towels are gleaming white (although perhaps a bit frayed here and there), and little luxu-ries such as soap are provided. Prices are fair, at 4,500 pesos ($9) single, 4,000 pesos ($8) double per day, ceiling fans (but no air conditioning) included.

Just up Avenida Madero from the Martinez is the **Hotel Osorio** (tel. 988/2-0018), which has similar comforts at about the same price: 5,000 pesos ($10) double, with fan.

A new addition to Isla Mujeres's collection of small, basic hotels is the **Hotel Caribe Maya**, Avenida Madero 9 (tel. 988/2-0190), west of the Restaurant Gomar, where the showers are tile, although a few bits and pieces of furniture (the bedside tables, for instance) may have seen service in some older and now long-gone establishment. The three floors are set up motel style, and rooms rent for 4,500 pesos ($9) single, 5,000 pesos ($10) double.

The **Hotel Berny**, Avenidas Juárez and Abasolo (tel. 988/2-0025), is fancier than its prices would suggest: a modern stucco building with handsome red tile floors and an interior court with a pretty swimming pool. Each room has one queen-size bed and one single bed, plus either a ceiling fan or an air conditioner; some have balconies with sea views. The tradition here is to include a continen-tal breakfast in the room prices, which are 6,210 pesos ($12.42) single, 7,475 pesos ($14.95) double, 8,855 pesos ($17.71) triple.

The **Hotel Vistalmar**, Avenida Rueda Medina between Abasolo and Mata-moros (tel. 988/2-0096), has a name which means "sea view," and that's exactly what you get from the pleasant verandah. Rooms, with private showers and ceiling fans, are simple but well kept by a resident family, and decently priced at 5,000 pesos ($10) single, 5,400 pesos ($10.80) double. The hotel is just north of the Pemex gas station on Rueda Medina, the waterfront street.

Even more basic than the above choices is the **Hotel Caracol**, Avenida Ma-dero 5 (tel. 988/2-0150), which charges 5,000 pesos ($10) single, 5,500 pesos ($11) for its spartan rooms with ceiling fans.

The modest little **Posada San Jorge**, Avenida Juárez 31, near Playa Coco-teros (tel. 988/2-0052), has decent rooms (and more abuilding), a good location, and excellent prices. For a room with two double beds, fan, and shower, you pay only 4,000 pesos ($8). Can't beat it.

For Beachcombers

Poc-na (tel. 988/2-0090 or 2-0053) bills itself as "a basic clean place to stay at the lowest price possible," and it's just that. The reception desk just inside the door will rent you a sheet, towel and soap, or blanket, and a canvas bunk or nylon hammock (plus you get your own private locker). The open bunk rooms are arranged around a central palapa-shaded dining area provided with picnic tables and served by a small kitchen. Meals are served cafeteria-style. The location is excellent, only a short walk from the beaches at the northern tip of the island, at the end of Calle Matamoros. If you have your own hammock or sleeping bag, the basic charge is 1,300 pesos ($2.60) per person per night. But if you're unequipped, you'll have to rent a mattress to put on top of the rope hammock for 85 pesos (17¢), a sheet, pillow, blanket, and towel for 80 pesos (16¢) each, for a total one-time charge of 405 pesos (81¢). You'll have to put down deposits on all these items, refundable at the end of your stay.

Just So You'll Know

Wonder what it costs to stay at El Presidente's dramatic addition to their hotel chain? Well, the daringly designed **Hotel El Presidente Caribe** (tel. 988/2-0029), which you admired during the voyage to the island by ferry boat, rents its 101 air-conditioned rooms for 19,000 pesos ($38) single, 20,000 pesos ($40) double, with a junior suite even more. These are winter prices, and in the summer you'll pay less.

WHERE TO EAT: Dining on Isla Mujeres is not wildly cheap, but it is certainly easier to keep to a budget here than in, say, Cancún or Cozumel. The first thing you must learn is the password: **Avenida Hidalgo.** Going north out of the town's main square, this street is lined with small and inexpensive or moderately priced places to have a meal. With the coming of Cancún's prosperity, Avenida Hidalgo has undergone a facelift and now boasts lots of trees and shrubs. Many houses have rustic gardens in pseudo-Caribbean style. All these decorations were laid out by a landscape architect to make Isla Mujeres "more authentic," and although authenticity may in fact have been driven out, beauty and quaintness have been ushered in. It's a pleasant street.

I will start our culinary excursion in the main square, head north on Avenido Hidalgo, and then afterward mention some places for waterfront dining.

Among Isla Mujeres's most dependable old standbys is the **Restaurant Gomar** (no phone), which has two outdoor tables on Avenida Hidalgo and about 16 indoors. Decor is modern, warm, and nice, with lots of natural wood and the quaint touch of hand-woven tablecloths (protected under glass). In general, prices here are among the highest on the avenida, but this means that meat, fish, or shrimp meals come to about 2,000 to 3,500 pesos ($4 to $7), complete.

The **Restaurant La Peña** (no phone), behind (east of) the town-square bandstand, near the water tower at Calle Guerrero 5, gives you a choice on where to hang out: streetside porch, interior room, or seaside terrace. You get an even greater choice of what to eat, from pizzas (three sizes, many varieties, 600 to 2,900 pesos, ($1.20 to $5.80) through seafood to mole poblano. Prices are low to moderate, drinks are served (happy hour from 6 to 7 p.m.). No choice on the music, though. It's rock.

Look for the cozy little **Restaurant El Peregrino** (tel. 2-0190) next to the Hotel Caribe Maya at Avenida Madero 8. The tiny streetside porch has a few tables; the interior is darker but cooler. The draw here is meals at prices lower than the better-known restaurants nearby. Shrimp, for instance, can be had for only 1,200 pesos ($2.40), fish or meat for even less.

Should you be dying of the heat, a few restaurants have air conditioning.

You pay for it in meal prices which are 35% to 45% higher than in comparable establishments. For instance, at the **Villa del Mar** or **Martita's** on Avenida Rueda Medina near the ferry dock, a meal that costs 1,500 pesos ($3) at an open-air place will cost 2,200 to 2,500 pesos ($4.40 to $5). On a very hot day, the coolness is well worth it, though.

Of the other restaurants on Hidalgo, most are very similar in price and atmosphere to the **Restaurant La Mano de Dios,** on Hidalgo at the corner of Matamoros. A family operation, one suspects the family beds down for the night right in the dining room after the last dish has been washed. You can have lentil soup—delicious—and the filet of fish, plus a large fruit salad and a soft drink for a total bill of 1,750 pesos ($3.50), although in the hot weather you might not have the appetite needed to finish it all. Shrimp cocktail, fried bananas, and other such delicacies are offered, along with the regulation chicken tacos, omelets, and breakfast huevos rancheros. Tablecloths are of plastic, the air is moved by ceiling fans, and the whole front of the restaurant is open to the street.

Right next to the plain Hotel Caracol is the fancy restaurant called **Ciro's** (tel. 2-0102), very much like the aforementioned Gomar in decor, and also in price. Various omelets cost 550 pesos ($1.10); turtle, shrimp, or roast meat as an entree will cost about 1,500 pesos ($3); chicken dishes cost a bit less as a rule. At Ciro's, the bonus is air conditioning.

The **Restaurant Estrellita Marinera,** on Hidalgo, always has a collection of café tables enclosed by groups of ardent people-watchers. In the afternoon, it's usually a busy spot as the comida costs a mere 1,000 pesos ($2) and comprises fried fish, rice, frijoles, and salad.

Across the street from the Estrellita Marinera is that essential establishment for fixing your own breakfast and picnics, the **Panadería La Gloria,** filled with fresh bread and sweet rolls.

Near the Ferry Dock

The **Restaurant Tropicana** (no phone), Avenida Rueda Medina at Bravo, directly opposite the car-ferry dock, has a heavy patronage of local people. You couldn't call its Formica furniture romantic, nor its fluorescent lights, but the prices aren't bad: sopa de pollo, the island favorites of beef, turtle, or chicken, plus dessert and drink, might cost 2,200 pesos ($4.40), twice that for shrimp. Note that the Tropicana is open from 8 a.m. to 10 p.m. daily.

WHAT TO DO: Isla Mujeres is a sun and sea haven with all the attractions: snorkeling, swimming, fishing, or just plain relaxing. There are two beautiful beaches, one in town called the **Playa Cocos,** to your left as you get off the boat, and **Garrafón National Park** about five kilometers to your right. Playa Cocos is quite shallow and is better for swimming, while Garrafón beach with its coral reef is excellent for snorkeling.

There are several agencies that offer tours around the island as well as lessons in scuba-diving and deep-sea fishing. Included in this adventure is a visit to the large turtles, and the biological station, swimming and snorkeling at Garrafón beach, and a lunch of fish or shrimp from the day's catch at the little Idios Beach. (Note: Make your boating arrangements a day in advance as they like to get an early start at about 8 a.m.) Getting to Garrafón beach on your own is difficult as there are no buses. You can walk (takes 1½ hours), hitch, rent a bicycle or a moped, or take a taxi. While at Garrafón you might like to take a walk to the south end of the island and its lighthouse. Just beyond the lighthouse is a Maya ruin believed to have been an observatory built to the moon goddess Ix-Chel.

The **Fortress of Mundaca** is about four kilometers in the same direction as

Garrafón, off about half a kilometer to your left. The fortress was built by the pirate Mundaca Marecheaga who in the early 19th century arrived at Isla Mujeres and proceeded to set up a blissful paradise while making money from selling slaves to Cuba and Belize. The fortress is set in a pretty, shady park, and is a nice trip if you are suffering from too much sun.

Playa Lancheros, south of town a few miles, has shady palapas, a snack stand, and a good sandy beach.

Ask around at the docks, and you'll find a boatman who is willing to ferry you over to **Isla Contoy,** an uninhabited National Park island north of Isla Mujeres where the beaches are very fine, the bird life rich and colorful, and life is blissfully peaceful.

SOUTH ALONG THE COAST: After Isla Mujeres, what next? To enjoy fully
the wealth of attractions that Yucatán has to offer, you must wander farther from your Cancún base. The previous chapter has full information on points west of Cancún such as Chichén-Itzá and Mérida. Let's look now at what lies south of Cancún, on the way to—and beyond—that other Mexican Caribbean resort, the island of Cozumel.

If you don't have your own car, transport along the Caribbean coast presents problems. Though there are about a dozen buses a day down the coast (see the introduction to this chapter), you may end up waiting along the sweltering highway for an hour or more only to have a jam-packed bus roar right by you. The difficulty of transport has given rise to a lively practice of hitchhiking. Be prepared to hitch whenever the opportunity presents itself; and if you're driving, why not give rides to hitchers?

3. Puerto Morelos

Only a short ride (36 kilometers, 21 miles) south of Cancún along Hwy. 307 lies the village of Puerto Morelos. Its reason for being is the car ferry, which departs from a dock here on its voyage to Cozumel, several hours away. So far, Puerto Morelos has not shared measurably in the building boom that has swept this coast, so there are not many recommendable lodging places or restaurants. You need not go without a bed and a meal, however.

WHERE TO STAY AND EAT: The little **Posada Amor** (no phone), on the inland
road to the ferry dock (right-hand side as you approach the dock), rents simple rooms with screens on the windows and a common bathroom for 4,500 pesos ($9) double. The rooms are quite plain, but adequate.

The Posada's restaurant is rustic and very amusing: a big thatched hut is decorated with painted wooden masks, craft items, and a motorcycle helmet in each corner. Ask what's cooking, as the "menu" is liable to be limited to one or two items. Prices are reasonable, and an entire meal need cost only 1,500 pesos ($3) or so. No alcohol is served.

As you come into Puerto Morelos from the main highway, you turn right for the Posada Amor and the ferry dock. But if you go well into town and turn left, you'll see the **Cabañas Playa Ojo de Agua** (reservations in Mérida at Calle 65 no. 254-B, Apdo. Postal 709; tel. 992/3-0841 or 1-5150). The Cabañas is very popular with the scuba-diving set, with 21 rooms in little cabañas and bungalows renting for 13,500 pesos ($27). Rooms have fans and good cross-ventilation which, with the sea breeze, renders air conditioning unnecessary. There's a restaurant. Ojo de Agua strains our budget, but there are few lodgings in this town, so you should know about it.

THE CAR FERRY: You won't have trouble finding the car-ferry dock (tel. 988/

2-0916, 2-0938, or 2-0849), as it's the largest establishment in town. The ferry schedule does change now and then, so you should call in advance if possible. Note that there is no car-ferry service on Monday. That being said, I must also say that the ferries are rarely on schedule. Even so, you must act as though they will be on time, and do the following: arrive at the ferry dock any day but Monday, between 5 and 6 a.m. to buy your ticket for the ferry that will leave (you hope) at 7 a.m. Boarding of vehicles begins at 6 a.m. if all goes according to plan. The journey (not counting the wait onshore) takes between 2½ and 4 hours, depending upon sea and wind. Passenger cars and small campers take precedence over larger vehicles, and so there's hardly ever a problem getting a ticket if you're there on time. The return voyage from Cozumel leaves the car-ferry dock, south of town near the Hotel Sol Caribe, at 12 noon or so, but be there early to buy your ticket and get in line. Recheck these schedules upon arrival in Cozumel. The fares are 160 pesos (32¢) per person, 830 pesos ($1.66) per vehicle. Of course, you don't have to have a car to use this ferry (which is closer to Cancún than is the strictly passenger boat from Playa del Carmen). Passengers on foot are welcome aboard.

ONWARD: Heading south on Hwy. 307 from Puerto Morelos, the village of **Muchi** is the next landmark. It's only 32 kilometers (20 miles) from Puerto Morelos to Playa del Carmen, so you'll be there in a half hour or less.

4. Playa del Carmen

This little Caribbean village came into being because of the passenger boat service to Cozumel, but recently it has developed a tourist trade of its own. Intrepid travelers have discovered that Playa del Carmen's beaches are far better than those on Cozumel, as much of Cozumel's coast is covered by sharp coral or is pounded by dangerous surf.

As of this writing, Playa del Carmen's lodgings consist of several plush and expensive hotels, and a handful of very inexpensive but basic hostelries; there is as yet very little in the way of a comfortable middle ground. But it will come.

WHERE TO STAY AND EAT: The town's most prominent hotels are also its most expensive. Right down by the Cozumel boat dock is the **Hotel Molcas** (reservations in Mérida at Turismo Aviomar; tel. 992/1-6661 or 1-6620). The very comfortable hotel cascades down the hillside, giving many rooms and the dockside restaurant fine ocean views. But the price for a double room is a daunting 24,700 pesos ($49.40). You may well get a reduction in price if you try.

On the other (south) side of the boat dock from the Molcas is another lavish place, the **Hotel Playacar** (tel. in Cancún, 988/3-0935), with even higher prices.

Many of the town's inexpensive hostelries are placed along the road that comes into town from Hwy. 307. For instance, right by the highway junction is the **Hotel Maranatha** (no phone), on the left just after you turn from the highway, with double rooms for 8,500 pesos ($17). They tell me that the hot and cold water is always available, as are meals in the little restaurant.

Closer in toward the center of town, along the same road, is the **Posada Lily,** on the right-hand (south) side. Double rooms with shower cost 4,500 pesos ($9). You can walk to the boat dock in 15 or 20 minutes if your luggage is not impossibly heavy.

More or less across the road from the Lily are two more places. The **Posada Marinelly** charges 5,000 pesos ($10) for its simple rooms, set back from the road a bit and relatively quiet.

Right next door is the **Hotel Playa del Carmen** (no phone, no sign), with a collection of rooms to rent above a shop. Talk to the shopkeeper and you'll probably be quoted a price identical to that of the Marinelly.

You may be glad to know that Playa del Carmen has many little camping areas down along the water (turn to the left as you come to the center of town). There are also many small, inexpensive restaurants in this same area.

Starvation Budget Lodgings

The little **camping areas** in Playa del Carmen afford the absolute cheapest lodgings, provided you have your own equipment. Otherwise, head for the **Camping-Cabañas Brisas del Mar** (no phone), right on the beach next to a cenote (pool) alive with turtles and fish. This shady, laid-back place charges 3,000 pesos ($6) double for its sympathetic if ramshackle huts, without fan or private plumbing. A shady palapa serves as restaurant and general gathering area. Coming in from the highway, turn left (north) on the town's main street, go two blocks, and turn right.

BOATS TO COZUMEL: Passenger boats leave Playa del Carmen's dock for Cozumel three times daily, at 6 a.m., noon, and 6 p.m., on the 45-minute trip. Return trips depart Cozumel at 4 and 9:30 a.m. and 4 p.m. A one-way ticket costs 430 pesos (86¢). Anyone subject to seasickness will be happy to know that there is an alternative method for getting between Playa del Carmen and Cozumel. If it's a windy day, consider flying.

SHUTTLE FLIGHTS TO COZUMEL: AeroCozumel operates an air shuttle service from Playa del Carmen's airstrip at the south edge of town to Cozumel's international airport. The modern twin-engine, eight-seat planes take off about every two hours throughout the day on the ten-minute trip. The price is 2,685 pesos ($5.37) one way. At Cozumel's airport, you will need to pay an additional 280 pesos (56¢) for a minibus ride into town.

It's nice to have this alternative to the ferry ride, which can be noisy, windy, and fraught with the hassles of seasickness.

5. Cozumel

In Mexico's Caribbean resort area, if Cancún is the jet-set's port of call and Isla Mujeres belongs to the beachcombers, Cozumel, 44 miles south of Cancún, is a little bit of both. More remote than either of the other two resorts, this island (pop. 30,000) becomes more of a world unto itself, a place where people come to get away from the day-tripping atmosphere of Isla Mujeres or the megadevelopment feeling of Cancún, a place to take each day as it comes for a week or more without moving very far from the hotel or the beach. There is actually little reason to leave the island as all the necessaries for a good vacation are here: excellent snorkeling and scuba places, sailing and water sports, fancy hotels and modest hotels, elegant restaurants and taco shops, even a Mayan ruin or two. If, after a while, you do get restless, the ancient Maya city of Tulum and the lagoon of Xel-ha provide convenient and exciting goals for excursions.

Many visitors complain about Cozumel's price structure, which seems high for what you get. But if you're diving at Palancar Reef, it all seems worth it.

GETTING TO COZUMEL: Daily bus service from Mérida via Puerto Juárez and Cancún provides easy access to the aforementioned towns of Puerto Morelos, the dock for the car ferry to Cozumel, and to Playa del Carmen, the dock for the strictly passenger boat to the island. Autobuses del Caribe runs buses that arrive in time to catch departing ferries, and to meet returning ferries.

The Ferryboats

See the sections on Puerto Morelos and Playa del Carmen (above) for details on boats to Cozumel.

Flights

Cozumel has an international airport with a surprising number of direct flights from distant cities.

AeroMéxico, downtown in Cozumel at Avenida Rafael Melgar 13 (tel. 987/2-0251 or 2-0422), in the Cine Cozumel building near Calle 4 Norte, has nonstop flights to Houston, Mérida, and Mexico City.

Mexicana, Avenida Rafael Melgar Sur 17 (tel. 987/2-0157 or 2-0263) offers nonstops to Miami, Mérida, and Mexico City. Several other international airlines such as Eastern, American, United, and Continental have flights as well.

AeroCaribe and **AeroCozumel** (tel. 987/2-0928 at Cozumel's airport) both run flights between Cozumel and Cancún at 8 and 10 a.m., noon, and 2, 4, and 6 p.m. A one-way ticket costs 6,385 pesos ($12.77). In addition, AeroCozumel runs a shuttle-type operation between Cozumel and Playa del Carmen. See the beginning of this chapter, and also the section on Playa del Carmen, for more details.

The minibus from Cozumel's airport into town costs 275 pesos (55¢).

ORIENTATION: Cozumel lies some 12 miles (20 km) out in the Caribbean from Playa del Carmen. The island is roughly 28 miles (45 km) long and 11 miles (18 km) wide. Its only town is San Miguel de Cozumel, usually just called Cozumel.

San Miguel's main waterfront street is called Avenida Rafael Melgar, running along the western shore of the island. Passenger ferries dock right in the center, near the main plaza. Car ferries dock south of town near the hotels Sol Caribe, La Ceiba, and El Presidente.

The town is laid out on a grid, with avenidas running north and south, calles running east and west. The exception is Avenida Juárez, which runs right from the passenger ferry dock through the main square and inland. Juárez divides the town into northern and southern halves.

Heading inland from the dock along Juárez, you'll find that the avenidas you cross are numbered by fives for some reason: "5a Avenida," "10a Avenida," "15a Avenida." If you turn left and head north, you'll discover that calles are numbered evenly: 2a Norte, 4a Norte, 6a Norte. Turning right from Juárez heads you south, where the streets are numbered oddly: 1a Sur (also called Adolfo Salas), 3a Sur, 5a Sur. The scheme is more systematic than it is practical.

The northern part of the island has no paved roads. It's scattered with small Mayan sites, badly ruined, from the age when "Cuzamil" was a land sacred to the moon goddess Ixchel. The sites are best visited by Jeep or boat.

North and south of town are many hotels, moderate to expensive in price; many cater to divers. Beyond the hotels to the south is Chancanab National Park, centered on the beautiful lagoon of the same name. Beyond Chancanab is Playa Palancar, and, offshore, the Palancar Reef *(arrecife)*. At the southern tip of the island is Punta Celarain, which bears a lighthouse.

The eastern, seaward shore of the island is mostly surf beach, beautiful for walking but dangerous for swimming. There is safe swimming in a few coves.

GETTING AROUND: In the town itself, everything is within walking distance. Though there is limited bus service along Avenida Rafael Melgar from north of town as far south as Palancar, you may find yourself taking taxis in Cozumel. In general, figure about 1,000 pesos ($2) for 15 or 20 minutes of travel. For a day at the beach, finding some like-minded fellow travelers and sharing the cost of a cab is the easy, quick way to go. But for exploring the island, you should consider renting a car or a moped (motorbike).

Car rentals are as expensive here as in other parts of Mexico. See Chapter XVI, "Latin Listings," under "Car Rentals" for specifics.

As for motorbikes, it seems as though every shop, garage, restaurant, street cleaner, and mortician in Cozumel is also in the business of renting them. Terms and prices vary from place to place: one renter may only rent by the day or half-day, another may rent you a moped for a minimum three-hour period. One may charge 3,000 pesos ($6) for three hours, most will charge 5,000 to 6,000 pesos ($10 to $12) for a full day (8 a.m. to 5 p.m.); some time the rental period from 12 noon to 12 noon the next day.

As part of your bargaining, carefully inspect the actual moped you'll be renting. Early in the morning, with most of the bikes waiting there to be rented, you can choose one on which all the gizmos are in good shape: horn, light, starter, seat, mirror. Later in the day you'll get the clunker on which everything is broken and you'll pay the same full price for it. Rent early.

One final note: Be aware that riding a moped is like sunbathing. No matter how much you cover up, your head, neck, hands, and perhaps legs will be exposed to hours and hours of intense midday sun. Protect yourself. There's a tendency to forget that riding in the sun all day is like lying on the beach all day.

Here's a price comparison to keep in mind: a couple renting two mopeds for a day will pay 10,000 to 12,000 pesos ($20 to $24). Car rental for a day may total $40. Hiring a taxi for two hours of chauffeured riding costs about 6,000 pesos ($12).

USEFUL FACTS: The **post office** (Correos) is on Avenida Rafael Melgar at Calle 7 Sur, at the southern edge of town. . . . There's a little **Tourist Information** booth on Melgar in the main plaza, open at odd hours. They sell the best map of the town and the island, *The Brown Map of Cozumel*, for about $1. The SECTUR (Secretaria de Turismo) headquarters is south of the post office on Melgar (tel. 2-0357). . . . There's a **long-distance telephone office** on the main plaza. . . . As for **medical care,** Cozumel has a number of English-speaking American and Mexican doctors in residence. Your hotel or the police can help you contact one.

WHERE TO STAY: These days Cozumel has a good selection of hotels in all price ranges. In summer there is usually little trouble finding a room. In the high-season months of December, January, February, and March, it's good to call or write ahead for reservations. (Postal Code for all of Cozumel is 77600.) Prices are higher in those months as well.

First I'll detail the better, moderately priced hotels, and then move on to the very low-priced places.

You can hardly do better than the **Hotel Vista del Mar,** on the shoreline promenade called Avenida Rafael Melgar at no. 45 (tel. 987/2-0545). Large rooms here shine with white paint and a joyful decor, which includes, in many rooms, a sea-view wall entirely of glass opening onto a small balcony from which you can gaze at the public beach just across the street, and far out to sea. Each room has its own air conditioner, and prices are set according to the season and whether or not the room has a view: off-season the rooms cost 9,500 pesos ($19) double without the view, 10,500 pesos ($21) with; during high-season months of mid-November to mid-April prices are slightly higher. If you can afford it, try this place first.

Whether or not you will feel "Comfortable as In Your Own Home," as advertised in the brochure, you are certain to admire the **Hotel Elizabeth,** Calle

Salas no. 3-A (tel. 987/2-0330), for its cleanliness and the helpfulness of the staff. A minute and manicured garden plot adds a splash of green. You have two choices for accommodations: suites come with kitchen, living room, and bedroom, a refrigerator and all utensils, and cost 10,000 pesos ($20) double; the double rooms (no kitchen) cost 8,000 pesos ($16).

A downtown hotel with great appeal is the **Hotel Mary-Carmen,** 5a Avenida Sur 4 (tel. 987/2-0356 or 2-0581), half a block from the zócalo (main square). Watched over by a conscientious collection of matronly señoras, the hotel specializes in cleanliness and some elegant touches: brocade couches in the lobby, extra decoration in the rooms, screens on the windows, and a mammoth *mamey* tree in the courtyard. The two-story structure harbors 27 rooms priced at 7,600 pesos ($15.20) single or double (with two beds, good for families). All rooms have beautiful tile baths and also air conditioning.

A hotel on the southern edge of town is the **Hotel Maya Cozumel,** Calle 5a Sur no. 4 (tel. 987/2-0011). The upbeat rooms are painted in white and orange and have odd triangular showers. Comfy leather deck chairs add another touch of class. In the rear court is a small swimming pool surrounded by thick lawn and bougainvillea; a small restaurant/bar looks onto the lawn and pool. Rooms come with air conditioning and the price is okay: 10,235 pesos ($20.47) double.

The **Hotel El Marques,** 5a Avenida Sur no. 12, right downtown (tel. 987/2-0537), has several surprising touches that make it a delight. The rooms have quaint formal-ish touches such as ersatz gold trim and Formica-marble countertops, but the air conditioning is genuine, the baths are kept quite clean, and the staff is attentive. The big surprise is the tiny swimming pool (you won't expect the hotel to have one when you see it) and the ingenious wall-waterfall behind it, next to a minuscule bar. Rates are 10,000 pesos ($20) single, 11,500 pesos ($23) double, less per day if you stay awhile. A great place!

Right across the street from the El Marques is a mini-mall of shops, and also the **Hotel Suites Bazar Colonial,** Avenida 5 Sur no. 9, Apdo. 286 (tel. 987/2-0506). Prices at this nice, new hostelry might seem high at 17,000 pesos ($34) double in the junior suites, and 19,000 pesos ($38) double in the master suites, but you get a nicely appointed studio or one-bedroom apartment, with complete kitchenette, for the cost. Pay in cash, get a discount. It's certainly one of the few hotels on the island to have an elevator, which serves its four floors. Rooms are quiet, and air-conditioned.

The **Posada Letty** (tel. 987/2-0257) is hard to find because there's nothing to tell you it's a hotel except for a tiny sign: no lobby, reception desk, potted palms. But the rooms are there, each with louvered wooden shutters on the windows to let in the breeze and ceiling fans to whirl it around. Rooms have tile showers and ceiling fans; single travelers pay 3,500 pesos ($7) and two persons pay 4,000 pesos ($8) for any of the eight rooms on two floors. To get to the Letty, walk from the main square up Calle 1 Sur past the Banco del Atlantico until you see the small sign on the right-hand side of the street. The man who runs the Letty works in the little store on the corner just past the pension. Official address: Calle 1 Sur at 15a Avenida Sur.

The **Hotel Pepita,** 15a Avenida Sur no. 6 (or no. 120, by a later numbering system), corner of Calle 1 Sur (tel. 987/2-0098), is more like a pension than a hotel. Rooms, some old, some new, some abuilding, have been fixed up with ceiling fans and tile baths and rent for 6,800 pesos ($13.60) single, 7,200 pesos ($14.40) double, 7,500 pesos ($15) triple, but this may include such luxuries as a mammoth bottle of purified water *in the room,* as well as a small refrigerator to keep it cool. It's very quiet here on the back street, and if your room gets stuffy you can relax in the very beautiful garden terrace to one side of the hotel. For reservations, write to Apdo. Postal 56.

A quiet downtown choice is the **Hotel El Pirata,** 5a Avenida Sur no. 3-A (tel. 987/2-0051), a small place with quite acceptable standard rooms going for 4,500 pesos ($9) single and 5,000 pesos ($10) double with ceiling fan, or 5,500 pesos ($11) single and 6,000 pesos ($12) double with air conditioning. Here you're only two blocks from the ferry dock and a stone's throw from the main square.

The very simple **Hotel Yoli** (or Yoly), Calle 1 Sur no. 164, between the main plaza and 10a Avenida Sur (tel. 987/2-0024), has plain and rather dark rooms, nothing to write home about, but clean. The price, however, is great: 3,500 pesos ($7) double, in expensive Cozumel.

The **Posada Edem,** Calle 2 Norte no. 12, near 5a Avenida Norte and the Sports Page Restaurant (tel. 987/2-1166), is a newish, modest hostelry where you can get a room with fan, shower, and one bed or two for 4,000 pesos ($8) double.

The **Hotel Aguilar,** 5a Avenida Sur and Calle 3 Sur (tel. 987/2-0307), sounds good when you hear about it: air-conditioned rooms, filtered swimming pool, interior gardens, reasonable rates. The management seems a bit bewildered by the hotel business, but if the gardens are blooming, the air conditioning working, and the pool full, it's well worth the 7,500 pesos ($15) asked for a double room.

If everything else in town is full, take a look at the **Hotel Flores,** Calle Adolfo Rosado Salas 72, a few doors down from the Suites Elizabeth (tel. 987/2-1429). The Flores is hardly florid in its decoration; in fact, it could use some paint. But prices are remarkably good at 4,000 pesos ($8) single or double, 4,500 pesos ($9) triple, 5,000 pesos ($10) for four, in a room with private shower. The location is convenient.

WHERE TO EAT: Cozumel is well provided with places to dine, but one must be careful in choosing a place because "resort food" is a problem here, as it is in most seaside resorts. Proprietors think that hungry customers will show up whether the food is good or not, and they're not far from wrong. A number of places sometimes rise above this level of thinking, though, and here they are:

Best all around is a restaurant suitable for breakfast, lunch, dinner, or just a late-night dish of ice cream. The **Restaurant Las Palmeras** (tel. 2-0532) is only a few steps from the zócalo at the corner of Avenidas Juárez and Rafael Melgar, very near the ferry dock. Las Palmeras is open to the four winds, although tables are shaded from the sun. Always busy, service is nonetheless fairly efficient, and prices are moderate. A breakfast of bacon, eggs, and strong coffee will cost 800 pesos ($1.60); a light lunch of enchiladas suizas followed by guayaba con queso (guava paste with a slice of cheese, and crackers—delicious!) will be only about 1,400 pesos ($2.80). Dinner can be light as lunch, or can run to seafood at 1,200 or 1,500 pesos ($2.40 or $3) per plate, or even lobster.

To escape Cozumel's high prices, escape the town itself. On Avenida Rafael Melgar at the southern outskirts of town, a few steps south of the lighthouse, is the **Restaurant Costa Brava** (no phone). Modest but certainly not plain, the Costa Brava has lots of local decoration, decent service, and fairly good food at exceptionally low prices. Set-price breakfasts, served till 9 a.m., cost 360 to 450 pesos (72¢ to 90¢) and include good coffee with a dash of cinnamon; don't bother with the "orange juice." Lunch or dinner can be bistec or filet of fish, and a three-course repast won't cost more than 2,000 or 2,500 pesos ($4 or $5) unless you have lobster. Wine and beer are served, and the restaurant is open every day from 6:30 a.m. to 11:30 p.m.

Cozumel, heavily populated with North Americans, finally has its own unabashedly North American restaurant. Called **The Sports Page** (tel. 2-1199), it features a satellite TV antenna on the roof to snag all the stateside network sports action, team pennants and T-shirts on the walls. It's air-conditioned. It serves burgers ($3.70). Its prices are in dollars. It has "all-you-can-eat" nights (shrimp, $9). In short, though Mexican-owned, it is very American. Hours are every day from 10 a.m. to 2 a.m.

Pepe's Grill (tel. 2-0213) south of the main square on the waterfront drive (Avenida Rafael Melgar), is deluxe: low lights, soft music, solicitous waiters. Tables are open to sea breezes; failing that, ceiling fans move the air. The menu is short and not cheap, with most meat and fish courses costing about 2,500 pesos ($5), although a Mexican combination plate is 2,000 pesos ($4). Despite the prices, it's a very popular place. Open for dinner only, 5 p.m. to 12 midnight.

B.B.Q's (tel. 2-1569), on Melgar north of the square between Calles 4 and 6 Norte, is a newer Pepe place. The specialty is barbecued spare ribs, chicken, and roast beef. The decor and service is beach-bum hideaway, with live country and western dance music accompaniment: old wagon wheels, plants, funky-posh design of wood beams and paraphernalia. There's a view of the bay, and a menu (in English) with prices of 1,100 pesos ($2.20) for chicken or ribs, 2,600 pesos ($5.20) for shrimp kebab.

For Pizza

When Cozumel has a pizza joint, it's no dive, and so **Pizza Rolandi,** four blocks north of the main square along Avenida Rafael Melgar, is about as elegant a pizzeria as you're likely to run into anywhere. Deck chairs and red-and-white-checkered tablecloths make the interior garden very mod, and candle lamps add romance. The Four Seasons pizza, at 1,600 pesos ($3.20), is eight inches in diameter and serves only one person, but what a serving: it comes topped with black olives, tomatoes, asparagus, cheese, and ham. The pizza margarita costs only 1,100 pesos ($2.20), but others (six kinds) are all priced the same as the Four Seasons. Wine, beer, and mixed drinks are all served. Rolandi is open from noon to midnight daily.

Starvation-Budget Restaurants

Although you may doubt it, there are possibilities for dining on Cozumel that will leave your budget not only intact, but robustly healthy. On Calle 2 Norte, half a block in from the waterfront, is the **Panificadora Cozumel,** excellent for a do-it-yourself breakfast, or for picnic supplies.

Few eateries are cheaper than a Mexican lunchroom, and Cozumel's version is the **Restaurant Los Moros,** 10a Avenida Norte at Avenida Juárez, a block east of the main plaza. Lunch can be soup, Mexican-style bistec or breaded fish filet; with lemonade and a tip, the total comes to 1,300 pesos ($2.60). Though there are fans, it can be hot in here because the kitchen and dining room are one. Open for breakfast, lunch, and dinner, except Monday.

For a quick, healthful pick-me-up on a hot day, drop by the **Fruit and Juice Bar** at the corner of Calle 1 Sur and 5a Avenida Sur, just a few steps from the Hotel El Marques. The sweet smell of fruit greets you as you enter. Juices, liquados, "the best coffee in town," yogurt, and pastries are served in stark surroundings, at low prices. The señora squeezes fruit, not you.

WHAT TO DO: What is there to do on Cozumel? Tour the island, swim, snorkel, scuba-dive, that's what. Let's start with a tour so you can get the lay of the land.

Touring the Island

The question of tours brings us back to rentals, as there is no good reason to take an organized tour. You can rent a bicycle, motorbike, or car, and the motorized vehicles will take you around the southern part of the island easily in a half day, although it will take all day to cover the 70 kilometers (42 miles) on a bicycle.

Head south along Avenida Melgar out of town, past the Hotel Barracuda. The Hotel La Perla is next, then the Villa Blanca. Remember that no hotel in Mexico "owns" the beach—by law, all beaches are public property, so feel free to use a "hotel" beach. On Cozumel this public ownership is more important than ever, as most of the island is surrounded by coral reefs difficult to walk across (that coral is sharp!) let alone lie on.

About eight kilometers (five miles) south of town you'll come to the big Sol Caribe and La Ceiba hotels, and also the car-ferry dock, for ferries to Puerto Morelos. Go snorkeling out in the water by the Hotel La Ceiba and you might spot a sunken airplane. No, it's not the wreckage of a disaster; it was put there for an underwater movie.

Chancanab: A mile past the big hotels is this lagoon, which has long been famous for the color and variety of its sea life. Actually, it became too famous. It was discovered that the intrusion of sightseers was ruining the marine habitat, and that if swimming were not controlled, snorkelers would soon have only one another to look at. So now you must swim in the open sea, not in the lagoon, which is just as well. If you don't have snorkeling gear with you, it's rentable right here.

Good Beaches: Next beach you'll come to, 16 km (10 miles) is **Playa San Francisco,** and south of it, **Playa Palancar.** By Cancún standards they're not much, but on Cozumel they're the best, so plan most of your beach time for here. Food (usually overpriced) and equipment rentals are available.

The underwater wonders of famous Palancar Reef are offshore from Playa Palancar, and you'll need a boat to see them. Numerous vessels on the island operate daily diving and snorkeling tours to Palancar, so the best plan is to shop around and sign up for one of those.

Punta Celarain: After Playa San Francisco, the drive becomes boring as you plow through the jungle on a straight road for miles. The only distraction is the turnoff (on the left) to Cedral, a tiny market hamlet that is deserted most of the time. Otherwise, all you see is jungle until you're 28 kilometers (17½ miles) from town. Finally, though, you emerge near the southern reaches of the island on the east coast. The lighthouse you see to the south is at Punta Celarain, the island's southernmost tip. The sand track is not suitable for motorbikes, but in a car you can drive to the lighthouse in about 25 minutes.

The Eastern Shore: The road along the east coast of the island is wonderful. Views of the sea and the rocky shore, surf pounding into it, on the land side are little farms and hamlets. Exotic birds take flight as you approach, and monstrous (but harmless) iguanas skitter off into the undergrowth. Most of the east coast is unsafe for swimming because the surf can create a deadly *undertow, which will have you far out to sea in a matter of minutes.* But at a few places on this coast there are headlands and breakers that create safe swimming areas. At **Chan Río** you can swim, and also at **Punta Morena,** where there is even a small motel and restaurant. **Playa Chiqueros** is also safe, and has a little restaurant.

Halfway up the east coast, the paved road meets the transversal road back to town, 15 kilometers (9½ miles) away.

Heading On: Not ready to go back to town yet? For adventure, start out on the sand track that continues north from this junction. Follow this road for 18 very rough and rocky kilometers through the jungle, past little abandoned farms, along the rocky shore to **El Castillo Real,** an unimpressive but authentic Maya ruin in the middle of nowhere. The trip from the paved road to the Castillo takes 1½ hours, and then the same amount of time to return, but the time is spent watching hermit crabs scutter through the sand, watching lizards watch you, and listening to pairs of parrots squawk as they wing overhead. Don't attempt this trip in a large or a low car, or on a motorbike. Best thing to have is a VW Safari.

A scattering of other vestiges from Cozumel's Maya religious past can be found throughout the northern reaches of the island. One of the most popular trips is to **San Gervasio.** A road leads there from the airport, but you'll find it rough going. When it comes to Cozumel's Mayan remains, getting there is most of the fun, and you should do it for the trip, not for the ruins. For real Mayan cities, visit Tulum and Coba, on the mainland.

Head north of town along the west coast and you'll pass a yacht marina and several older hotels as well as some new condominiums. A few of the hotels sit atop nice beaches. Feel free to use them (the beaches, not the hotels).

Back in Town

The adventure over, spend some time strolling along the Avenida Rafael Melgar admiring the unique black coral found in Cozumel's waters, and made into all sorts of fanciful jewelry.

At night, check out what's playing at the Cine Cozumel, Avenida Rafael Melgar between 2 Norte and 4 Norte. It's probably in Spanish, but when it comes to the light melodrama usually offered here, that's just as well.

Snorkeling and Scuba-Diving

Anyone who can swim can go snorkeling. Rental of the snorkel (breathing pipe), goggles, and flippers should only cost about 1,250 pesos ($2.50) for a half day. The brilliantly colored tropical fish provide a dazzling show for free.

Various establishments on the island rent scuba gear—tanks, regulator with pressure guage, buoyancy compensator, mask, snorkel, and flippers. Many will also arrange a half-day expedition in a boat complete with lunch for a set price. Sign up the day before, if you're interested.

Sailboards are for rent at several hotels south of town, including the Divers' Inn and the Villa Blanca.

Boat Excursions

Another popular Cozumel pastime is the boat excursion, by yourself or as part of a group, with snorkeling or scuba-diving or without. Various types of tours are offered, including a glass-bottom boat tour lasting 1½ hours and costing 3,000 pesos ($6) per person.

6. Akumal, Tulum, and Cobá

Of the fledgling resorts south of Cancún, Akumal is perhaps the most developed, with moderately priced bungalows scattered among the graceful palms that line the beautiful, soft beach.

But the beach south of the ancient Maya port city of Tulum is coming along. Though Tulum's specialty is now the laid-back beach bums' locale, where the generator shuts down at 10 p.m. (or dies much earlier), the several cabaña establishments along the beach will no doubt lay on reliable power, telephones, and hot showers in the not-too-distant future. If the beach-bum life is what you're after, grab it now before it disappears. If it's not, you'll want to visit Tulum in any case, and you will also thoroughly enjoy a swim in the nearby lagoon of Xel-ha, one of the coast's prettiest spots.

The impressive Maya ruins at Cobá, deep in the jungle, are a worthy detour from your route south. You needn't stay overnight in order to see the ruins, but there are accommodations if you'd prefer to. Here are details.

SOUTH FROM PLAYA DEL CARMEN: Bus transportation from Playa del Carmen south is a chancey thing. In principle, buses meet each boat arriving from Cozumel and whisk passengers north to Cancún, but this may not happen. And to catch a bus south along the highway, you have to walk out to the highway (about 20 minutes) and wait for whatever may come by.

Once in a vehicle, however, you will come to Xcaret, eight kilometers (five miles) south of Playa del Carmen.

Xcaret

As of this writing, Xcaret is someplace magical, a touch of Mayan romance. But the bulldozers have already entered the woods, so it won't last long. Get there soon.

One-and-a-half kilometers (one mile) in from the highway brings you to the little **Rancho Xcaret,** a turkey farm which is so authentic with its rail fences and thatched Mayan *na* houses that you'll think its a Yucatecan theme park. But pay the tiny admission charge (50 pesos, 10¢) and walk eastward toward the sea along a path into the bush. Soon you'll pass some tumbledown little Mayan temples overgrown with jungle, and then get a glimpse of the sea.

At the end of the path is a narrow inlet, or *caleta,* bright with sun and flashing with tropical fish. The inlet has already been discovered by snorkelers, who come on foot or in boats, and by one intrepid souvenir seller who has set up shop in a *na*.

On your way back to the rancho, turn right at the Mayan ruins and take a path down a slope into the jungle. Pass several caves on your left, and after a few dozen yards you will see a crystalline pool in a great cave mouth, or grotto, its lightly salted water clear as glass. Though it's not well-known to tourists, it's a favorite with local people, who come for a dip and a picnic. It can get busy. Come early or late in the day if you can.

Pamul

Sixteen kilometers (10 miles) south of Xcaret and seven-tenths of a kilometer (one-half mile) east of the highway is Pamul, a safe cove for swimming. Little bungalows with hot-water showers face the beach. You can rent one for 6,000 pesos ($12) double, or camp for much less. Several pet monkeys preside at the simple restaurant-bar, and a sign warns, "They bite."

For information in Cancún, contact Sr. Humberto Rosado Loria at Apdo. Postal 1143, Cancún, Q. Roo.

In a very short time you come to Akumal, one of Mexico's newest stars in Caribbean tourism.

AKUMAL: Signs point the way in from the highway, and less than half a kilometer toward the sea you will come to the Akumal gateway. The resort complex here consists of three distinct establishments which share the same wonderful, smooth palm-lined beach protected by a breakwater.

The **Hotel-Club Akumal Caribe Villas Maya** (P.O. Box 1976, El Paso, TX 79950, tel. 915/584-3552; outside Texas, toll free 800/351-1622) rents bungalows easily capable of sleeping two couples or a family. Each is equipped with bath and air conditioner, and costs 20,000 pesos ($40) double.

Las Casitas Akumal (in Cancún at Apdo. Postal 714; tel. 988/4-1945 or 4-1689) is a collection of villas or bungalows rented by the day, week, or month. Each faces the sea, has two bedrooms, two baths, a living room, fan, and refrigerator, and can accommodate up to five people. A small store and restaurant nearby take care of the food problem, and a diving shop caters to the scuba set. The price for up to five people is 28,000 pesos ($56), or $11.20 per person, daily.

Just 300 yards/meters south of these two places is the **Hotel Akumal Caribe Ina Yana Kin** (tel. in Cancún 988/4-2272), a very nice and modern 116-room, two-story hotel in a palm grove by the beach. Rates for its comfy rooms-with-bath are 21,200 pesos ($42.40) double, 27,000 pesos ($54) triple. This is beyond our budget at the moment, but prices may come down as competition builds along this coast.

READER'S DIVING TIP: "Six kilometers south of Akumal is the resort complex of **Las Aventuras;** a diving franchise called **Yucatan Diving Adventures** is part of it. It's run by an American couple, Mike and Kathy Madden, who, between them, have every diving credential imaginable. They'll take people out snorkeling and deep-sea diving, and are reliable, efficient, dependable, and very sensitive to safety factors. Anyone who's encountered 'bad air' will appreciate the latter" (Dr. and Mrs. E. M. Beekman, Northampton, Mass.).

Xcacel

Next down the highway is **Aventuras,** a posh hotel and condominium complex. After that, three miles (4.5 km) along, comes the beach and camping area at Chemuyil, developed by the government as "the most beautiful beach in the world." Though sleepy and deserted in the summer, it's active in winter, with a snack bar, free medical clinic, and an admission fee for cars. Two-and-a-half kilometers (1½ miles) south of Chemuyil lies Xcacel.

Xcacel, one-half kilometer (one-quarter mile) east of the highway, is a gorgeous palm-shaded spot where you can pitch your tent or park your van for 250 pesos (50¢) per person per night, including use of changing rooms, toilets, and showers. There's a small restaurant here as well.

After traveling less than 13 kilometers (8 miles) south of Akumal, you come to Xel-ha.

XEL-HA: The Caribbean coast of the Yucatán is carved by the sea into hundreds of small *caletas* (coves) that form the perfect habitat for tropical marine life, both flora and fauna. Many caletas remain undiscovered and pristine along the coast, but one caleta 117 kilometers south of Cancún is enjoyed daily by snorkelers and scuba-divers who come to luxuriate in its warm waters, palm-lined shore, and brilliant fish. Xel-ha (that's "*shell*-hah") is a bit of paradise for swimming, with no threat of undertow or pollution. Being close to the ruins at Tulum makes Xel-ha the best place for a dip when you've finished clambering around the Maya castles. The short 8½-mile hop north from Tulum to Xel-ha is hard to do by bus, but you may have luck hitchhiking. Those who don't have a car and who don't want to chance missing Xel-ha can sign up for a tour from either Cancún or Cozumel: most companies include a trip to Tulum and a swim at Xel-ha in the same journey.

The entrance to Xel-ha is half a mile in from the highway. You'll be asked to pay a 200-peso (40¢) "contribution" to the upkeep and preservation of the site.

Once in the park, you can rent snorkeling equipment, buy a drink or a meal, change clothes, and take showers—facilities for all these are available. When you swim, be careful to observe the "swim here" and "no swimming" signs. *(Hint:* In the swimming areas, the greatest variety of fish are to be seen right near the ropes marking off the "no swimming" areas, and near any groups of rocks.) Xel-ha is an exceptionally beautiful place!

Just south of the Xel-ha turnoff on the west side of the highway, don't miss the Mayan ruins of ancient Xel-ha.

Thirteen kilometers (8 miles) south of Xel-ha is the Maya seaport of Tulum.

TULUM: At the end of the Classic period in A.D. 900 the Maya civilization began to decline and most of the large ceremonial centers were deserted. The Postclassic Period (A.D. 900 to the Spanish Conquest) in the Yucatán is one of small rival states, Maya in culture but with some imported traditions from the Mexicans. Tulum is one such city-state, built in the 10th century as a fortress city overlooking the Caribbean. Aside from the spectacular setting, Tulum is not otherwise an impressive city. There are no magnificent pyramidal structures as are found in the Classic Maya ruins. The most imposing building in Tulum is the large stone structure on the cliff called the **Castillo** (castle), actually a temple-cum-fortress. At one time this was covered with stucco and painted.

The view from on top of the Castillo is quite grand. From here you get a good view of the city walls, which are constructed of limestone. In front of the Castillo are several palace-like buildings: unrestored stone structures partially covered with stucco. The **Temple of the Frescoes** is directly in front of the Castillo and contains some 13th-century wall paintings, which are quite interesting. They are inside the temple and the lighting is bad, so if you have a flashlight it would be helpful to bring it along. Most of the frescoes are hard to see, but they are distinctly Maya in content: representing the gods Chac (rain god) and Ix Chel (the goddess of the moon and of medicine). On the cornice of this temple is a relief of the head of a god. If you get a slight distance from the building you will see the eyes, nose, mouth, and chin. Notice the remains of the red-painted stucco on this building—at one time all the buildings at Tulum were painted a bright red.

Much of what we know of Tulum at the time of the Spanish Conquest comes from the writings of Diego de Landa, third bishop of Yucatán. He wrote that Tulum was a small city inhabited by about 600 people, who lived in dwellings situated on platforms along a street. The town commanded a strategic point on the Caribbean and thus supervised the trade traffic from Honduras to the Yucatán. Tulum survived about 70 years after the Conquest, when it was finally abandoned.

The ruins are open 8 a.m. to 5 p.m. Admission is 50 pesos (10¢).

Where to Stay and Eat

It's useful to know that Tulum consists of four distinct areas. First there's the junction of Hwy. 307 and the Tulum access road, where you'll find a small hotel, two restaurants, and a Pemex gas station. Then, a kilometer down the access road, are the ruins of Tulum and a collection of small restaurants, snack shops, and souvenir stands. Past the ruins, the road heads south along a narrow strip of sand to Boca de Paila and Punta Allen. Though most of this 60-mile stretch of bad road is uninhabited, you will find a few beachcombers' settlements a few kilometers south of the ruins. The fourth area is the Mexican village of Tulum, right on Hwy. 307 about 2 kilometers (1½ miles) south of the Hwy. 307–Tulum access road junction. There's nothing much in the way of services in Tulum village. Let's look at what the first three areas have to offer, in order.

Tulum Junction: Right at the junction of Hwy. 307 and the Tulum access road is the aptly named **Motel El Crucero,** which has rooms for rent plus a small restaurant. The rooms, though very basic, come with ceiling fans, hot and cold water, and cost 3,000 pesos ($6) double. In the thatched restaurant, rough-and-ready simple meals are yours for 1,500 to 1,800 pesos ($3 to $3.60). Beer is served, and a counter at one side of the restaurant serves as a tiny "convenience store."

Across the street from El Crucero is the **Restaurant El Faisan y El Venado,** with similar meals and prices.

At the Ruins: In at the entrance to the ruins are small soft-drink stands and eateries serving up things at resort prices. Not much you can do about it, though, if you're hungry. The **Centro Chac-Mool**—it's that modern palapa on the beach north of the ruins—gives more, but charges more as well.

Boca de Paila: Down the road past the ruins are some lodgings that might be good for the intrepid traveler. Hitchhiking is the only transport. The paved road ends 4½ kilometers (3 miles) south of the ruins. Here's where you'll see the **Cabañas Chac-Mool** (no phone), a thatched-hut-and-campsite establishment. Though you can rent a very basic thatched-hut cabaña with bedding for an expensive 5,000 pesos ($10), you may find that you need mosquito netting. In effect, this is a place to come if you already have the camping gear you'll need.

The **Cabañas Los Arrecifes** (no phone), south of the Chac-Mool, about 5½ kilometers (3½ miles) south of Tulum, are about the nicest on this stretch of beach, though still quite simple. A room set back from the beach, without a sea view and without a private bath, costs 4,500 pesos ($9) double; one right on the beach with bath goes for 7,500 pesos ($15) double. The ambience here is very laid-back.

The **Cabañas Tulum** (no phone), six kilometers (4 miles) south of the Tulum ruins, are little thatched bungalows facing a heavenly stretch of ocean beach (deadly surf). Each bungalow comes with well-used cold-water shower, two equally well-used beds, screens on the windows, rickety table, one electric light, and a veranda good for hanging a hammock. The cost is 4,000 pesos ($8) double per night. The electricity is on from 5 to 10 p.m. only, so bring candles or a flashlight. A small restaurant serves three meals a day at fairly low prices; beer and soft drinks are on sale. Bring your own towels, soap, and blankets.

Onward to Cobá: About a mile south of the turnoff to Tulum, on Hwy. 307, is the road to Cobá, another fascinating Maya city. Less than a mile past the Cobá road is Tulum village, with little to offer the tourist. If you're driving, turn right when you see the signs to Cobá, and continue on that road for 50 kilometers (30 miles).

COBÁ: The Yucatán is rich in breathtaking Mayan cities, but in its time, fewer were grander than Cobá. Linked to important cities many miles distant by excellent, straight roads through the jungle, Cobá itself covered numerous square miles on the shores of two Yucatecan lakes.

Today the city's principal monuments are on display again, but unless you take a tour or rent a car, they're difficult to reach.

Pay the 50-peso (10¢) admission fee at the little entrance shack, and stroll into the ruins. Keep your bearings as it's very easy to get lost on the maze of dirt roads in the jungle.

The Grupo Cobá boasts a large, impressive pyramid just in the entry gate to the right. Were you to go straight, you'd pass near the badly ruined *juego de pelota* (ball court).

Straight in from the entry gate, walk for 10 or 15 minutes to a fork in the road. The left fork leads to Nohoch Mul group, which contains El Castillo, the highest pyramid in the Yucatán (higher than the great El Castillo at Chichén-Itzá and the Pyramid of the Magician at Umal). The right fork (more or less straight on) goes to the Conjunto Las Pinturas. Here, the main attraction is the Pyramid of the Painted Lintel, a small structure with traces of the original bright colors above the door. You can climb up to get a close look.

Throughout the area, intricately carved stelae stand by pathways, or lie forlornly in the jungle underbrush.

It can be hot here deep in the jungle. You'd be well advised to visit Cobá in the morning, or after the heat of the day has passed.

Where to Stay and Eat

Staying at Cobá entails a choice between rags or riches. The very nice **Villa Arqueológica Cobá** (tel. in Cancún 988/4-2574), a Club Med operation, is here, right at lakeside a five-minute walk from the ruins. The hotel has a French polish because of the Club Med affiliation and, as you might expect, the restaurant is top-notch, though expensive, with full meals for about 4,600 pesos ($9.20). Comfortable rooms have private bath and air conditioning, and cost 9,000 pesos ($18) single, 13,200 pesos ($26.40) double, tax included. Besides rooms, the hotel has a library of books on Mesoamerican archeology (with books in French, English, and Spanish), and a swimming pool. You can make reservations in Mexico City at Hoteles Villas Arqueológicas, Avenida Masaryk 183, México, D.F. 11570 (tel. 905/203-3886).

Then there's the **Hotel Isabel,** a five-minute walk from the ruins back along the road to the highway. At the Isabel you can rent a bed for 1,900 pesos ($3.80), and I mean *a bed*. There's no bath, no washbasin, no running water, no linens, no blankets, no privacy, no screens; just a place to lie down and sleep. The place will no doubt get fancier in years to come, but right now it's pretty darn basic.

El Bocadito (no phone) is a restaurant and lodging near the Isabel with a handful of rooms priced at 3,000 pesos ($6) double. For this you get modern construction, washbasin and shower, and use of an electric lantern. There are only a handful of these rooms, and they may well be full unless you arrive to claim one early in the day. Don't expect anything fancy; but the proprietors do their best.

7. Felipe Carrillo Puerto

From the Cobá turnoff, the main highway (no. 307) heads southwest through Tulum village. About 23 kilometers south of the village are the ruins of **Chunyaxche,** on the left-hand side (look for the little restaurant and camping area called "El Caminero"). The ruins aren't very exciting, but the price is right: admission is free after you sign the register. In exploring Chunyaxche, I was virtually eaten alive by mosquitos in the beautiful jungle. You may have better luck, though.

After Chunyaxche, the highway passes 72 kilometers (45 miles) of jungle-bordered road with few distractions. Then comes an oasis of sorts.

Felipe Carrillo Puerto (pop. 15,000) is the only oasis in the jungle along the road to Ciudad Chetumal, and has this to offer: several banks (off the zócalo), gas stations, a market, a small ice plant, a bus terminal, the intersection with the road back to Mérida, and a presentable handful of modest hotels and restaurants to serve the traveler's needs. Carrillo Puerto is the turning point for those making a "short circuit" of the Yucatán peninsula, as Hwy. 184 heads west from here to Ticul, Uxmal, Campeche, and Mérida. It is quite possible you may have to spend the night here, and very probably that you will arrive in town hungry.

As you spend your hour or your overnight in Carrillo Puerto, recall its strange history: this was where the rebels in the War of the Castes took their stand, guided by the "Talking Crosses." Some remnants of that town—Chan Santa Cruz—and that time are still extant. Look for signs in town pointing the way. For the full story, refer to Chapter XV, Section 1, "Yucatán's Fascinating History."

WHERE TO STAY: The highway goes right through the town, becoming Avenida Benito Juárez in town. Coming from the north, you will pass a traffic circle with a bust of the great Juárez. The town market is here.

Turn right (west) at the traffic circle, and you will immediately see, on the left-hand side of the road, the **Hotel La Colina** (no phone). Plain rooms, the only type to be found in town, rent for 2,500 pesos ($5) double. Watch out for the street noise when you choose a room.

Head south from the traffic circle to get to the other hotels and restaurants in town.

A few blocks south of the traffic circle, on the left-hand side of the road, just past the Restaurant Zona Maya is the small **Hotel San Ignacio,** a simple place with an interior court (for parking), and clean if very bare rooms. Prices are 1,500 pesos ($3) single, 2,000 pesos ($4) double, 2,300 pesos ($4.60) triple, with private bath and ceiling fan. Get to bed early—this town wakes with the dawn.

The street that crosses Avenida Juárez at the Hotel San Ignacio is Calle 67. Turn right onto it, go up past the banks (Banobras, Banamex, and Banrural), and you will see the main square. Turn right just before the square for the Hotel Chan Santa Cruz (tel. 983/4-0170), located more or less behind the bank buildings. The plain rooms here, grouped around a courtyard in older buildings, cost 2,600 pesos ($5.20) double with fan, 4,200 pesos ($8.40) double with air conditioning.

On the main square, diagonal to the church, is an old Caribbean-style building—look for the wooden gallery on the second story. This houses the **Hotel Esquivel,** an odd collection of rooms, many with added-on showers, all neat and well kept if basic. Ceiling fans keep you cool; in some cases, double-knit sheets and pillowslips keep you hot. The lamp tables are sections of Mayan columns from temples. Original oil paintings decorate some walls. As for prices, the Esquivel is similar to the other places in town: 2,200 pesos ($4.40) double, for a room with a fan. Parking in the rear.

WHERE TO EAT: Starting from the traffic circle again, and heading south, the **Restaurant El Faisan y El Venado** is on the left-hand side. This is one of the townfolks' favorites, with a modern, airy dining room equipped with ceiling fans, and even a small air-conditioned section (used mostly for private parties). Chances are that many tables will be filled at mealtimes, and people will happily be chowing down from the standard Mexican menu for only about 1,500 pesos ($3) per meal, all in.

Just down the street a few steps are two more dining choices, one of them air-conditioned. With a Pemex gas station on your right, the **Restaurant 24 Horas** will be on your left. Similar to El Faisan y El Venado, and priced about the same, the 24 Horas has long hours—24 of them, in fact—to recommend it, plus decent food at moderate prices. Also, it has a breathtaking Mayan glyph picture stone gracing the wall of its dining room. Be sure to take a look. This is the place to come for breakfast especially, as it'll be the only place in town open early. Scrambled eggs, ham, instant coffee, and watermelon slices will cost 850 pesos ($1.70). Beef entrees are priced about 1,100 pesos ($2.20). For cheaper fare, you can wait until the little café across the street opens up.

The aforementioned restaurant is not bad, although it tends to fill up in the evening with beer drinkers rather than diners. For a nice dinner, the pillars of local society go to the place right next door, the **Restaurant Zona Maya.** Open for lunch and dinner only, the Zona Maya is wonderfully air-conditioned, be-Muzak'd, and supplied with provisions. A good hamburger or sandwich, with a soft drink, will cost 975 pesos ($1.95); a pizza big enough for two people will be 1,950 pesos ($3.90); a plate of roast chicken with french fries, 1,075 pesos ($2.15). Decor (as though it mattered, with that heavenly air conditioning) is a leopard skin, some crossed machetes, and a bug zapper. And double-knit table-cloths. Felipe Carrillo Puerto, it has been noted by this observer, is a town dedicated to the creative use of double-knit synthetic fabrics. By the way, beer—and wine!—are served, and the beer-only crowd is kept at bay by a sign that says "We reserve—strictly—the right of admission."

8. Lago de Bacalar

From Carrillo Puerto to Chetumal is another 2½ hours' ride. About 100 kilometers (64 miles) past Carrillo Puerto you'll sight the limpid waters of Lake Bacalar, a crystal-clear body of water fed by swamps and streams. It's a heavenly place to swim, and the perfect place for a resort, but so far progress in building facilities has been painfully slow. If you're in your own car, take a detour through the village of Bacalar and down along the lakeshore drive. You'll pass the **Hotel Laguna,** which has been under construction for a decade, and will probably be that way for another decade. Rooms here (there are only a few complete) are overpriced at 7,600 pesos ($15.20) for two, but this is all there is. Past the Laguna a way is a small, extremely primitive camping area on the shore.

As you approach the end of the lake, Hwy. 307 intersects Hwy. 186. Turn right, and you're headed west to Escárcega, Palenque, and Villahermosa; turn left, and you'll be going toward Chetumal. The turnoff to Belize is on the road *before* you enter Chetumal, but you may need to stop in the town for a meal or a bed.

9. Chetumal

Quintana Roo became a state only in 1974, and Chetumal (pop. 50,000) is the capital of the new state. While Quintana Roo was still a territory, it was a free-trade zone to encourage trade and immigration, and as the free-trade regulation is still in effect, much of the town is given over to small shops selling a strange assortment of imported junk and treasures at pretty inflated prices. The old part of town, down by the river (Río Hondo), preserves a Caribbean atmosphere with its wooden buildings (and sticky heat), but the newer parts are modern (and rather raw) Mexican. Lots of noise and heat, so your best plan would be not to stay—vacant rooms are difficult to find—but if you must, here are some hints.

WHERE TO STAY: Behind the Central Bus Station is the **Hotel Real Azteca,** Calle Belize 186 (tel. 983/2-0666). Walking out the front door of the bus station, turn left and walk past the market (on your left), turn left again (so the large CFE plant is on your right), and go down a block to the Calle Belize. Turn right, and the hotel is on the left-hand side of the street. It's all air-conditioned, and costs 4,200 pesos ($8.40) single, 5,450 pesos ($10.90) double. This is your first choice. If it's full, the **Hotel Continental Caribe,** across the street from the bus station entrance, at Avenida Héroes 71 (tel. 983/2-1100), is a luxury palace, a modern Sheraton-type establishment with central air conditioning, a series of swimming pools in the courtyard, a restaurant large as a basketball court (and cold as a cave), and prices to match: 12,500 pesos ($25) single, 14,000 pesos ($28) double. It rents a lot of rooms though, even at those prices, because Chetumal is booming and rooms are scarce—particularly comfortable, air-conditioned rooms.

Down the hill from the bus station on Avenida Héroes, 1½ blocks in toward the center of town, is the Continental Caribe's competition. The **Hotel El Presidente** (tel. 983/2-0542 or 2-0544) has similar central air, pool, and restaurant, and is presently attempting to swipe the Continental's business by charging 11,500 pesos ($23) single, 13,000 pesos ($26) double.

Still farther down along Avenida Héroes at the corner of Avenida Obregón, four longish blocks from the bus station, is the **Hotel Jacaranda** (tel. 983/2-1155), a modernish two-story hostelry which is undistinguished except for its prices, which are a pleasure to relate: 2,300 to 3,400 pesos ($4.60 to $6.80) single, 3,600 to 4,900 pesos ($7.20 to $9.80) double, the higher prices being for rooms with that blessed air conditioning. Many similarly priced hotels are right nearby.

READERS' HOTEL SELECTION: "We stayed at the **Hotel Quintana Roo,** Avenida Obregón 41 (tel. 983/2-0212), for 2,500 pesos ($5) with fan and shower. You might have some difficulty understanding the boss for he has no upper teeth" (Mary Ann Jongenelen and Wouter van Furth, Utrecht, Netherlands).

WHERE TO EAT: As for places to dine, there are many little market eateries (and indeed the produce-filled market itself) right next door to the bus station. Across the street from the station, the **Hotel Continental Caribe's** immense restaurant puts out a mammoth breakfast buffet until 11 a.m. for 2,400 pesos ($4.80)—hardly cheap. For better prices, you'll have to walk a way.

Two blocks down the hill on Avenida Héroes is the **Restaurant Grijalva,** just past the Hotel El Presidente on the left-hand side of the street. Three señoras bustle about, one hands you an impossibly inclusive menu, and then chirps *¡No hay!* ("We don't have it!") to most of your selections. Nevertheless, they always have the makings for enchiladas or quesadillas, and the charge will be only 460 to 750 pesos (92¢ to $1.50). Chicken and fish dinners cost twice that figure.

The **Restaurant Baalbek,** in the middle of the block past 9a Calle (or Calle Plutarco Elias), demonstrates by its name that some of the immigrants were Lebanese—not unusual in the Yucatán. Prices are a bit high here, but the bills must pay for the wrought-iron café furniture out front and the tablecloths inside. A big refrigerator keeps the food fresh until it's served. A plate of eggs or a fruit salad costs only 440 pesos (88¢), but heartier fare—fried chicken, grilled meat, fish—is in the 1,400- to 1,800-peso ($2.80 to $3.60) bracket. Tacos and enchiladas are in between.

All the way down by the Rio Hondo, in the old Caribbean section of town, is the incongruously modern **Restaurant Chetumal,** on Calle 5 de Mayo a block northwest of Avenida Héroes, on the riverbank. Open to cooling sea breezes from the Bay of Chetumal, it's a fine place for a refreshing salad of chicken or fruit for 525 to 1,000 pesos ($1.05 to $2), or a big Mexican combination plate for 1500 pesos ($3). Look around at the quaint wooden buildings nearby before hiking back to the bus station.

TRANSPORTATION FROM CHETUMAL: Lots of bus service, a few flights.

By Bus

From the bus station in Chetumal you can get a seat to Tulum, Playa del Carmen, or Puerto Juárez to the north; Villahermosa, Veracruz, and Mexico City to the west; or to Belize City in the country to the south, once called British Honduras but (since 1973) officially named Belize.

Twelve direct first-class buses a day go to Cancún via Tulum, Playa del Carmen, and Puerto Morelos. With changes en route, four first-class buses a day go to Mexico City, seven a day go to Villahermosa.

Second-class bus service includes routes daily to Tulum and the coast (two buses), Mérida (four buses), Campeche (two buses), Villahermosa (four buses), San Andres Tuxtla, Veracruz, and Mexico City (one bus).

To Belize, a bus runs daily, departing at 4 p.m. and making the run through Corozal, Orange Walk, and roadside villages to Belize City. If you're coming from Puerto Juárez, get an early bus (before 10 a.m.) in order to make this connection.

By Air

One daily flight by AeroMéxico links Chetumal with Mérida, and thus with Mexico's major cities.

Leaving Chetumal

From Chetumal you can make the long, hot trip due west to Escárcega and Palenque: you can cut diagonally across the peninsula to Mérida; you can retrace your steps to Cancún; or you can go on south to Belize and even Guatemala.

Chapter XVII

LATIN LISTINGS

The ABCs of Life South of the Border

WHENEVER I HAVE found myself in some foreign country, dozens of questions have always come up that guidebooks neglected to answer. Often these questions concerned very minor things—how to make a phone call—except that no question is minor when you don't have the answer to it.

In this section, I have tried to anticipate some of the questions that you may find yourself asking. You will probably think of many other listings yourself; if so, I would appreciate hearing about them. Such listings will be included in future versions of this book. For the present, here's my own collection of vital statistics, from A to Y.

ABBREVIATIONS: Dept.—apartments; **Apdo.**—post office box; **Av.**—Avenida; **Calz.**—calzada or boulevard. **C.P.** stands for *Codigo Postal* (Postal Code). **C** on faucets stands for *caliente* (hot), and **F** stands *fría* (cold). In elevators, **PB** *(planta baja)* means "ground floor."

ALTITUDE: Remember as you stroll around Mexico City that you are now at an altitude of 7,240 feet—almost a mile and a half in the sky—and that there is a lot less oxygen in the air here than what you're used to. If you run for a bus and feel dizzy when you sit down, that's the altitude; if you think you're in shape, but all the same you puff and puff getting up Chapultepec hill, that's the altitude. It takes about ten days or so to acquire the extra red blood cells you need to adjust to the scarcity of oxygen.

At very high-altitude places such as Ixta-Popo Park outside Mexico City (13,000 feet), your car won't run very well, you may have trouble starting it, and you may not even sleep well at night.

AMERICAN EXPRESS: The Mexico City office is at Reforma 234 (tel. 905/533-0180), in the Zona Rosa. It's open for banking, the pickup of clients' mail, and travel advice from 9 a.m. to 2 p.m. and 4 to 6 p.m. Monday through Friday, and also 9 a.m. to 1 p.m. on Saturday. If it's mail you're going for, remember that they charge $1 if you have no American Express credit card, travelers check, or tour ticket to prove that you're a client of theirs.

The Acapulco office is at Costera Alemán 709A (tel. 748/4-1095).

AUTO MECHANICS: Your best guide is the **Yellow Pages.** For specific makes and shops that repair them, look under *Automoviles y Camiones: Talleres de Reparación y Servicio;* auto-parts stores are listed under *Refacciones y Accesorios para Automoviles.*

I've found the Ford and Volkswagen dealerships in Mexico to give prompt, courteous attention to my car problems, and prices for repairs are, in general, much lower than in the U.S. or Canada. I suspect that other big-name dealerships—General Motors, Chrysler, and American Motors—give similar, very satisfactory service. Oftentimes they will take your car right away and service it in a few hours—a thing almost unheard of at home.

Mexico imports lots of American cars of all makes, and the country manufactures a tremendous number of Volkswagens (using the old 1600 engine).

BANKS (See also "Money"):
In Mexico, banks tend to be open from 9 a.m. to 1:30 p.m., Monday through Friday.

Large airports have currency-exchange counters that stay open as long as flights are arriving or departing.

Many banks south of the border have an employee who speaks English.

For the fastest and least complicated service, travelers checks or cash are the best things to carry. You can usually get a cash advance on your credit card in 20 minutes or less. Personal checks may delay you for weeks—the bank will wait for it to clear before giving you your money. For money by wire, see "Money."

BOOKSTORES:
In Mexico City, **Sanborn's** and **Woolworth's** always have books in English, as well as magazines and newspapers. So does the **American Bookstore,** Madero 25 off Bolívar (tel. 512-7284). The **American Benevolent Society's Caza Libros** (tel. 540-5123) at Monte Athos 355, 2½ blocks off Reforma *west* of Chapultepec Park in the section called Lomas Barrilaco, has used books in Spanish and English, hardback and paperback, plus magazines. Hours are 10 a.m. to 5 p.m. Monday through Saturday. All profits go to charity projects of the society.

French and English books and magazines, especially those dealing with Mexico, its history, archeology, and people, are the specialty of the **Cia. Internacional de Publicaciónes,** or Libererías C.I.P. for short. Branches of this firm in Mexico City are located at Serapio Rendon 125 (just off the Jardín del Arte, near the Hotel Sevilla), at Avenida Madero 30 not far from the House of Tiles, and also in Polanco, San Angel, Guadalajara, and Mérida.

About the most convenient foreign- and Spanish-language bookstore in Mexico City, with a good selection of guides and books on Mexico, is **Central de Publicaciónes—Librería Mizrachi,** (tel. 510-4231), Juárez 4 near Avenida Lázaro Cárdenas, right across from the Bellas Artes. Another shop, nearby, is the **Librería Británica,** Madero 30-1, in the Hotel Ritz building (tel. 521-0180). The Museo Nacional de Antropología in Chapultepec Park also has a shop with a good selection of books on Mexico, particularly special-interest guides (birds, flowers, geology and mineralogy, cuisine, etc.).

BRIBES:
Called *propina* (tip), *mordida* (bite), or worse, the custom is probably almost as old as mankind. Bribes exist in every country—as one sees upon picking up a daily newspaper—but in Third World countries the amounts tend to be smaller and collected more often. You will meet with bribery, so you should know how to deal with it.

At the Mexican border, the Customs officials have it down to an art. If you don't offer a tip of a few dollars to the man who inspects your car (if you're driving), he'll come right out and ask for it, as in "Give me a tip." Some officials, at the Mexican, Guatemalan, and Honduran borders, will do what they're supposed to do (stamp your passport or birth certificate, inspect your luggage, etc.) and then say, "Two dollars, please." If it's an official fee, you'll get a receipt. If you get no receipt, you've paid a bribe.

You can avoid some bribes, and after paying the umpteenth one, you'll want very badly to do so. Here's how: officials don't put the touch on everybody, and they don't always put it on in the same amount. Those dressed in suit-and-tie formality, with pitch-black sunglasses and a scowl on the face, rarely get touched at all. Those who are dressed for vacation fun, seem good-natured and accommodating, are touched every time and for ever-larger amounts. You may not want the bother of dressing up for border crossings (in that heat!), but you should at least act formal, rather cold and businesslike, perhaps preoccupied with Important Affairs on your mind. Wear those dark sunglasses. Scowl. But whatever you do, avoid impoliteness, and *absolutely never insult a Latin American official!* When an official's sense of *machismo* is roused, he can and will throw the book at you, and you may be in trouble. On the other hand, you must stand your ground (although always politely). Various means by which I, in my long experience, have cut down the high cost of bribing is by ignoring completely a request for "one dollar, please" (the request was not repeated); by plunking down less than the desired amount; or by politely requesting a receipt (in which case the request was dropped). Remember, only certain people pay bribes. What you want to do is be among that group who do not. The border official will request a bribe only after he has sized you up. Make him think you're dignified and important.

BUSES: Bus travel is the most popular form of transportation in Mexico. More and more foreign tourists are choosing to travel this way, and so here's a glossary of bus terms you'll find useful:

Autobus	Bus
Camión	Bus or Truck
Directo	Nonstop
Equipajes	Baggage (claim area)
Foraneo	Intercity
Llegadas	Gates
Local	Bus that originates at this station (see "Paso")
Paso, de paso	Bus originating somewhere else that will pass through this station; stops if seats are available.
Primera	First (class)
Recibo de Equipajes	Baggage claim area
Sala de Espera	Waiting Room
Sanitaríos	Toilets
Segunda	Second (class)
Sin Escala	Nonstop
Taquilla	Ticket window

When traveling by bus, it's best to buy your ticket (and thus reserve your seat) a day in advance, or even more than a day in the case of very long-distance and international buses, and those running on holidays.

CAMERAS AND FILM: Both are more expensive than in the States; take full advantage of your 12-roll film allowance, and bring extra batteries. A few places in resort areas advertise developing for color film, but it might be cheaper to wait till you get home.

If you're really into the sport, bring an assortment of films at various ASA/DIN speeds as you will be photographing against glaring sand, in gloomy Mayan temples, in dusky jungles, through hazy humidity. The proper filters are a help, as well.

CAMPING: It's easy and relatively cheap south of the border if you have a recreational vehicle or trailer, a bit less easy if you're tenting. Some agencies selling Mexican car insurance in the U.S. will give you a free list of campsites if you ask. The AAA has lists of sites. The *Rand McNally Campground & Trailer Park Guide* covers Mexico.

Campgrounds here tend to be slightly below the standards of northern ones (with many attractive exceptions to this rule, though). Remember that campgrounds fill up just like hotels during the winter rush-to-the-sun and at holiday times. Get there early.

CAR RENTALS: The car-rental business in Mexico is as far flung and well developed as in Europe and the U.S., with the usual problems and procedures. As elsewhere, it's good to reserve your car in advance in Mexico, an easy task when you fly into the country, as most airlines will gladly make the reservations for you. Mexico City and most other Mexican cities of any size have several rental offices representing the various big firms and some smaller ones. Rent-here/leave-there arrangements are usually simple to make.

With a credit card (American Express, VISA, MasterCard, and so forth) rentals are simple if you're over 25, in possession of a valid driver's license, and have your passport with you. Without a credit card you must leave a cash deposit, usually a big one.

Driving in Mexico City, and especially in and out of it (to sights a day's drive out of town) is a pretty big hassle, and parking's certainly a problem, so I can't recommend a rental car. But if you have enough people to fill one and to share the cost, and if this is your preference, the information below may help you out.

You can save yourself some money by renting only as much car as you *need:* make sure that the company you select offers the VW Beetle or Datsun—usually the cheapest car—if that will do, and make sure they will have one on hand to rent you. (Sometimes they'll say they do over the phone, but when you arrive at the office the cheapest cars will be "all booked up" for two weeks, etc.)

Don't underestimate the cost of renting a car. The total amount you'll be out-of-pocket for a short one-day trip to, say, Cuernavaca (85 kilometers, or 50 miles, from Mexico City) might be in the range of $50. Take your time when you look over the company's brochure, estimate the distance and time, allowing a generous margin for wrong turns, side trips, etc.—those kilometers are expensive!—and then add up *all* the charges you'll have to pay *before* the clerk starts filling out an order form.

Your completed estimate should look something like this, based on a total of 170 kilometers for the very cheapest car offered:

Basic daily charge	7,000
Kilometers, 170 @ 60 pesos each	10,200
Full nondeductible insurance	2,750
Subtotal	19,950
IVA tax @ 15%	2,993
Gas @ 95 pesos per liter	2,090
Tolls and parking	1,000
Grand Total	26,033 pesos ($52.06)

This estimate is for Mexico City; in a resort, a one-day rental would be slightly cheaper as the custom there is to include 200 free kilometers in every rental deal. But longer rentals in resorts turn out to be even more expensive than in Mexico City. An average three-day rental in a resort might be $175, a few dollars cheaper in Mexico City. For a week, the figures might be $365 for a resort, $340 for Mexico City—and these are for the very cheapest car offered, Group "A." Add about 15% to these estimates for Group "B" cars (VW Caribe—that's the Mexican version of the Rabbit, VW Safari), about 30% for Group "D" cars (Jeep, Ford Fairmont, VW Bus or Combi).

Recently, the larger firms in the big cities and resorts have been offering weekly unlimited-mileage rates. If you plan to do a lot of traveling, these can be great bargains. Plan your route, work out the mileage, then add about 15% to your mileage total to compensate for wrong turns, detours, and side trips. The unlimited-mileage price, plus the insurance charges, should then be compared to the "subtotal" above; remember, gas, 15% tax, tolls, and parking will still come out of your pocket. You'll find that it still costs about $50 a day, all in.

Once you've made up your mind to rent a car, finding a rental office is a snap. Rental desks are set up in the airports, in all major hotels, and in many travel agencies. The large firms like Avis, Hertz, National, and Budget have rental offices on main streets as well.

CLOTHES FOR TRAVEL:
Mexico tends to be a bit more conservative in dress (except for the capital) so shorts and halter tops are not generally acceptable except at seaside resorts. Cool clothes are needed at all times for the lowlands (the Yucatán, and coastal areas). In the highlands where you reach 7,000 or so feet you will need warmer clothes (a warm sweater and jacket). A raincoat is a good idea (a fold-up plastic one will do) for the rainy season (middle of May through September) when it rains almost every afternoon for an hour or so. For more hints on clothing, see the Introduction to this book.

CONSULATES (See "Embassies").

CRIME:
It's getting to be more of a problem in Mexico—which is to say that there was not much of a crime problem before. Although you will feel physically safer in most Mexican cities than in comparable big cities at home, you must take some basic, sensible precautions.

First, remember that you're a tourist, and a tourist is a mark. Beware of pickpockets on crowded buses, the Metro, in markets. Guard your possessions very carefully at all times; don't let packs or bags out of sight even for a second (the big first-class bus lines will store your bag in the luggage compartment under the bus, and that's generally all right, but keep your things with you on the less responsible village and some second-class buses on country routes).

Next, if you have a car, park it in an enclosed or guarded lot at night. Vans are a special mark. Don't depend on "major downtown streets" to protect your car—park it in a private lot with a guard, or at least a fence.

Women must be careful in cities when walking alone, night or day. Busy streets are no problem, but empty streets (even if empty just for afternoon siesta) are lonely places.

As to the police, in the past they have been part of the problem, not part of the solution. Although Mexico no doubt has dedicated and responsible officers, the general impression is that police have little training and fewer scruples. If you have the misfortune to be robbed, you should go to the police and report it, and get them to certify a report of the loss (you may have to write up the report yourself). But don't expect much sympathy, and even less action.

All these warnings having been stated, let me repeat that the prudent person need feel no more danger in Mexico than at home; most of the time you'll feel in less danger.

CUSTOMS AND DUTY-FREE GOODS: Coming to Mexico, Customs officials are very tolerant as long as you have no drugs (that is, marijuana, cocaine, etc.) or firearms. You're allowed to bring two cartons of cigarettes, or 50 cigars, plus a kilogram (2.2 pounds) of smoking tobacco; the liquor allowance is two bottles of anything, wine or hard liquor.

Reentering the U.S., you're allowed by **federal law** to bring in a carton (200) of cigarettes, *or* 50 cigars, *or* two kilograms (total, 4.4 pounds) of smoking tobacco, or proportional amounts of these items, plus one liter of alcoholic beverage (wine, beer, or spirits). If you bring larger amounts of these things, you will have to pay federal duty and internal revenue tax. *But wait!* Your quotas will also be subject to **state laws** (that is, of the state in which you reenter the U.S.). The state law may not allow you to bring back *any* liquor, which means *you will have to pour it out.* It's not simply a matter of paying duty, it's a matter of absolute quotas—or no quotas at all—for some states. This liquor quota is most strictly applied at the border posts, less strictly at airports not near the border.

Here are the limits for liquor in the states that border Mexico, from information supplied by the Distilled Spirits Council, Washington, D.C.:

Arizona: You may not import more than the federal duty-free limit; any amounts over the limit will be destroyed.

California: You may bring in a "reasonable amount" of liquor for each adult, for personal use only (not for resale or as gifts).

New Mexico: You may bring in a reasonable amount duty-free.

Texas: All liquor brought into Texas is subject to state tax; for amounts of hard liquor over one quart, you must have a permit from the state liquor authorities.

Canadian returning-resident regulations are similar to the U.S. ones: a carton of cigarettes, 50 cigars, two pounds (not kilos) of smoking tobacco, 1.1 liters (40 ounces) of wine or liquor, *or* a case of beer (8.2 liters). All provinces except P.E.I. and the Northwest Territories allow you to bring in more liquor and beer —up to two gallons (nine liters) more—but the taxes are quite high.

DOCTORS AND DENTISTS: Every embassy and consulate is prepared to recommend local doctors and dentists with good training and up-to-date equipment; some of the doctors and dentists even speak English. See the list of embassies and consulates under "Embassies" (below), and remember that at the larger ones a duty officer is on call at all times. See also "Hospitals," below.

DRUGSTORES: The word is *farmacia,* and they will sell you just about anything you want, with prescription or without. Most are open every day but Sunday from 8 a.m. to 8 p.m. The Sanborn's chain has a drug counter in many of their establishments.

If you need to buy medicines outside of normal hours, you'll have to search for the *farmacia de turno*—pharmacies take turns staying open during the off hours. Find any drugstore, and in its window should be a card showing the schedule of which farmacia will be open at what time.

ELECTRICITY: Current in Mexico is 110 volts, 60 cycles, as in the U.S. and Canada, with the same flat-prong plugs and sockets. Light bulbs may have bayonet bases, though.

EMBASSIES: They provide valuable lists of doctors, lawyers, regulations concerning marriages in Mexico, etc. Contrary to popular belief, your embassy cannot get you out of a Mexican jail, provide postal or banking services, or fly you home when you run out of money. Consular officers can provide you with advice on most matters and problems, however. Here's a list.

Australia

The Australian Embassy in Mexico City is at Paseo de la Reforma 195 (tel. 905/566-3055); hours are Monday through Friday from 9 a.m. to 5 p.m.

Canada

The Canadian Embassy in **Mexico City** is at Schiller 529, in Polanco (tel. 905/254-3288). Hours are Monday through Friday from 9 a.m. to 1 p.m. and 3 to 5 p.m.; at other times the name of a duty officer is posted on the embassy door. In **Acapulco,** the Canadian consulate is in the Hotel Club del Sal, Costera Miguel Alemán Reyes Católicos (tel. 748/5-6621). Hours are 9 a.m. to 1 p.m. and 3 to 5:30 p.m.

Denmark

The Embajada Real de Dinamarca (tel. 905/545-5376 or 250-8577) is at Tres Picos 43, México, D.F. 11570.

France

The French Embassy (tel. 905/525-0183) is at Liverpool 67; the Consulate-General (tel. 905/533-4480 or 533-1360) is at Havre 15, between Reforma and Hamburgo, in the Zona Rosa.

Germany (Federal)

The Embajada de la República Federal de Alemánia (tel. 905/545-6655) is at Lord Byron 737.

Netherlands

The Embajada Real de los Países Bajos (tel. 905/557-9588) is at Bulevar M. Avila Camacho 1-806.

New Zealand

The New Zealand Embassy (tel. 905/250-5999) is on the eighth floor of the building at Homero 229, México, D.F. 11570. Hours are 9 a.m. to 2 p.m. and 3 to 5:30 p.m., Monday through Friday.

Norway

The Norwegian Embassy (tel. 905/540-3486 or 540-5220) is at Virreyes 1460.

Sweden

The Embajada de Suecia (tel. 905/540-6393 or 531-9089) is at Bulevar M. Avila Camacho 1, sixth floor; and at Homero 136, México, D.F. 11550, ninth floor.

Switzerland

The Embajada de Suiza (tel. 905/533-0735) is in the Zona Rosa at Hamburgo 66, México, D.F. 06600, on the fifth and sixth floors.

United Kingdom

The British Embassy in **Mexico City** is at Lerma 71, at Río Sena (tel. 905/511-4880 or 514-3327). There are honorary consuls in the following cities: **Acapulco,** Hotel Las Brisas, Apdo. Postal 281 (tel. 748/4-6605); **Ciudad Juárez,** Calle Fresno 185 (tel. 7-5791 or 6-0750); **Mérida,** Calle 58 no. 450 (tel. 992/1-6799); **Monterrey,** Privada de Tamazunchale 104 (tel. 83/56-9114); **Veracruz,** Avenida Morelos 145 (tel. 293/2-4323).

United States

The American Embassy in **Mexico City** is right next to the Hotel Maria Isabel Sheraton at Paseo de la Reforma 305, corner of Río Danubio (tel. 905/211-0042). There are U.S. consulates in **Guadalajara** at Progreso 175 (tel. 36/25-2998); in **Mazatlán** at Circunvalación 6, corner of Carranza (tel. 678/1-2685 or 1-4488); and in **Monterrey** at Avenida Constitución 411 Poniente (tel. 83/43-0650). In addition, consular agents are resident in **Acapulco** (tel. 748/2-1906); **Cancún** (tel. 988/3-0178); **Oaxaca** (tel. 951/6-0654); **Puerto Vallarta** (tel. 322/2-1143); **San Luis Potosí** (tel. 481/2-5327); and **Veracruz** (tel. 293/2-6921).

HOLIDAYS, PUBLIC: Banks, stores, and businesses are closed on national holidays, hotels fill up quickly, and transportation is crowded. Here are the holidays celebrated in Mexico:

January 1	New Year's Day
February 5	Constitution Day
March 21	Birthday of Benito Juárez
March-April (moveable)	Holy Week (closures usually Good Friday through Easter Sunday)
May 1	Labor Day
May 5	Battle of Pueblo, 1862 (Cinco de Mayo)
September 1	President's Message to Congress
September 16	Independence Day
October 12	Columbus Day (Mexico: Day of the Race)
November 20	Mexican Revolution Anniversary
December 24-25	Christmas Eve (evening); Christmas Day

HOSPITAL: In Mexico City there is a hospital staffed by English-speaking personnel. It's the **American-British Cowdray ("A.B.C.") Hospital,** located at Calle Sur 132136, corner of Avenida Observatorio ("Sur 132" is the name of the street; tel. 905/515-8500). Take the Metro (Line 1) to "Observatorio," and the hospital is a short taxi ride from there. Have your insurance up to date as the hospital bills at Stateside prices.

Clinics and hospitals with English-speaking doctors exist in other major areas visited by tourists. Call your consulate (see "Embassies") for a list of telephone numbers.

INFORMATION: Before you leave home, you can get tourist information from any of the Mexican government tourist offices listed in the Introduction to this book. Once you're in Mexico, drop in to the tourism information offices mentioned in the text for each city or area.

The **Secretariat of Tourism,** once located right downtown in Mexico City at the intersection of Juárez and Reforma, is now at Avenida Presidente Masaryk

172, north of Chapultepec Park in the section called Polanco. To replace their handy downtown info booth there is now a special Tourist Information telephone number (the person on the other end will speak English): dial 905/250-0123.

LAUNDRY: All hotels can make some arrangements to have your laundry taken care of. Small laundries can be found in all but the tiniest villages. Coin laundries exist in all cities of any size—just ask at your hotel or a tourism information office.

LIBRARIES: Mexico City has several libraries of English-language books connected with her diplomatic missions. Check out the **Benjamin Franklin (American) Library,** on Niza between Londres and Liverpool. The **Canadian Embassy Library** (Canadian books and periodicals in French and English) is at Schiller 529, in Polanco (tel. 254-3288, ext. 248), open Monday through Friday from 9 a.m. to 5 p.m. The British Embassy, Consular Section, has British periodicals in the waiting room. See also "Bookstores," above.

MAIL: Mail service south of the border tends to be slow (sometimes glacial in its movements) and erratic. If you're on a two-week vacation, it's not a bad idea to buy and mail your postcards in the Arrivals lounge at the airport to give them maximum time to get home before you do.

For the most reliable and convenient mail service, have your letters sent to you c/o the **American Express** Mexico City office at Reforma 234, México, D.F. 06600 (open Monday through Friday from 9 a.m. to 2 p.m. and 4 to 6 p.m., on Saturday from 9 a.m. to 1 p.m.), which will receive and forward mail for you if you are one of their clients (a travel club card or an American Express travelers check is proof). They charge a small fee if you wish them to forward your mail.

General Delivery (Poste Restante)

If you don't use American Express, have your mail sent to you care of *Lista de Correos*, (City), (State), (Country). In Mexican post offices there may actually be a "lista" posted near the Lista de Correos window bearing the names of all those for whom mail has been received. If there's no list, ask, and show them your passport so they can riffle through and look for your letters.

You'll have to go to the central post office—not a branch—to get your mail, if the city has more than one office.

READERS' MAIL TIP: "If you make the mistake of having your mail sent to Poste Restante rather than Lista de Correos, make sure the people at the post office in Mexico know that your mail has arrived addressed to 'Poste Restante.' Most of the time they will wave you away if your name is not on the Lista. By the way, in many post offices they return your mail to sender if it has been there for more than ten days. Make sure people don't send you letters too early" (Mary Ann Jongenelen and Wouter van Furth, Utrecht, Netherlands).

Post Offices

The main one in **Mexico City** is located at the corner of Tacuba/Hidalgo and Lázaro Cárdenas, across the street from the Bellas Artes. It's open from 8 a.m. to midnight weekdays, 8 a.m. to 8 p.m. on Saturday, 8 a.m. to 3:45 p.m. on Sunday. On the third floor is an interesting philatelic exhibit, open for free from 9 a.m. to 1 p.m. weekdays, 9 a.m. to noon on Saturday.

Branch post offices in Mexico City are located at the following places you might find yourself: **Zócalo**—beneath the Hotel Majestic, in the arcade running along the west side of the square, at no. 7, down the passage bearing a sign,

"Almacenes Nacionales de México"; **Plaza de la República**—just north of the Monument to the Revolution at the corner of Arriaga and Mariscal; **Insurgentes/Reforma Intersection**—off Sullivan Park on Río Lerma near the intersection of Río Marne, almost across the street from the Hotel Maria Angelo's; **Buenavista Railroad Station**—in the railroad office building adjoining the station to the east; **Zona Rosa**—at the corner of Londres and Varsovia.

Parcel Post

In Mexico City you'll have to take parcels to the special post office called Correo Internacional no. 2, Calle Dr. Andrade and Río de la Loza (Metro: Balderas or Salto del Agua), open Monday through Friday from 8 a.m. to noon. Don't wrap up your package securely until an inspector examines it.

Glossary

Words you'll need to know include these:

Aduana	Customs
Buxon	Mailbox
Correo Aereo	Airmail
Correos	Postal Service
Entrega Immediate	Special Delivery, Express
Estampillas	Stamps
Giros Postales	Money Orders
Lista de Correos	General Delivery, Poste Restante
Oficina de Correos	Post Office
Paquetes	Parcels
Por avión	Airmail
Registrado	Registered Mail
Seguros	Insurance (insured mail)
Sellos	Stamps (sometimes rubber stamps)
Timbres	Stamps

MONEY (See also "Banks"): The dollar sign ($) is used to indicate pesos in Mexico. As many establishments dealing with tourists also quote prices in dollars, confusion is cleared up by the use of the abbreviations "Dlls." for dollars, and "m.n." (*moneda nacional*—national currency) for pesos, so "$1,000.00 m.n." means 1,000 pesos. Banks often charge a fee for changing travelers checks, or give a rate of exchange below the official daily rate. Hotels usually exchange below the official daily rate as well. The bank that writes your travelers checks (American Express, First National City, etc.) will give you the best rate of exchange.

In recent years it has been normal for the exchange rate on travelers checks to be better than that for cash dollars—you actually get something back for your penny-on-the-dollar investment in safety.

Canadian dollars seem to be most easily exchanged for pesos at branches of Banamex and Bancomer.

Credit Cards

You'll be glad to know that Mexico is well into the age of living on the little plastic card, and that you will be able to charge some hotel and restaurant bills, almost all airline tickets, and many store purchases. You can get cash advances of several hundred dollars on your card. You can't charge gasoline purchases in Mexico at all.

VISA, MasterCard (which is "Carnet" in Mexico), American Express, and their affiliates are the most widely accepted cards. You may not see your card's logo in a shop window or on a travel agency door, but don't worry—the Mexican equivalents such as Bancomer and/or Bancomatico will do just as well.

Money by Wire

If you need to get money from your bank at home, don't try to clear a check through a Mexican bank—it takes too long. Instead, go to the office of **Telegramas Internacionales** in Mexico City (tel. 905/519-5920), Balderas 14-18, near Colón and just off the west end of the Alameda look for the sign saying "Telex"). Have the money remitted to that office, and pick it up about four days later with your passport and Tourist Card. If there's any chance you'll leave Mexico City before the money arrives, try to get cash somewhere else. It takes up to six months for your home bank to track down an unclaimed international money order. Hours for *giros internacionales* (international money wires) are 9 a.m. to 1 p.m. and 2:30 to 6:30 p.m. Monday through Friday, 9 a.m. to 1 p.m. on Saturday, and 9 to 11 a.m. on Sunday. (Under repair.)

NEWSPAPERS AND MAGAZINES: For American travelers in Mexico the English-language newspaper *The News* is an excellent buy at about 25¢, more on Saturday. It carries many Stateside columnists as well as newsworthy commentaries, and a calendar of the day's events including concerts, art shows, plays, etc. A Spanish-language paper, *Excelsior,* has a daily partial page in English. Most Mexico City hotels carry the *Mexico City Daily Bulletin,* a free throw-away sheet in English with a list of events in the city and environs. **Note:** Not all the information is correct (for example, museum hours). Sanborn's, and newsstands in the large hotels, carry many United States papers, usually a day old.

Newspaper kiosks in larger Mexican cities will carry a selection of English-language magazines—*Time, Newsweek,* and the like.

POST OFFICE (See "Mail").

RADIO STATIONS: There are lots of stations in Mexico City, on both AM and FM, all in Spanish. Station XELA, 800 kHz AM and 98.5 mHz FM, broadcasts classical music, as do several university stations.

RELIGIOUS SERVICES: Services in English in Mexico City are at the following times and places:

Baptist: Capital City Baptist Church, Bondojito corner of Calle Sur 138, Colonia Las Americas (tel. 516-1862), one block from the Observatorio Metro station, across from the American School and A.B.C. Hospital. Services at 10:45 a.m. Evening worship in Spanish at 6 p.m.

Catholic: St. Patrick's Church, Bondojito 248, Colonia Hidalgo (tel. 515-1993). Sunday mass given at 10 and 11 a.m.

Christian Science: First Church of Christ Scientist, Calle Dante 21, Colonia Anzures. Service at 11 a.m. Bilingual meeting on Wednesday at 7:30 p.m. Reading room open Monday to Saturday from 4 to 7:30 p.m.

Church of Christ: Central Church of Christ, Calle 13 de Septiembre no. 26 in Colonia Condesa (tel. 562-2344 or 529-7385). (It's on a one-block, one-way street between Tacubaya and Chapultepec.) Worship and communion at 9 a.m.; Bible classes for all at 10 a.m.

Episcopal: Christ Church Episcopal, Articulo 123 no. 134 (tel. 521-0389), Communion at 8 a.m. Morning prayer or Communion and sermon at 10 a.m. St. Andrews at San Jeronímo 117 in San Angel.

Greek Orthodox: St. Sophia Church, Agua Caliente corner of Saratoga, Colonia Lomas Hipódromo (tel. 540-0080), Orthros at 10 a.m.; liturgy (in Greek and Spanish) at 11 a.m.

Interdenominational: Central Church, Balderas 47 at Independencia (tel. 560-9223), special worship service for tourists at 8:30 a.m. on Sunday. (Held in sanctuary of Messiah Methodist Church.)

Jewish: Hebrew Synagogue, Justo Sierra 71 (tel. 522-48-28). Beth Israel Community Center, Virreyes 1140, Lomas (tel. 520-8515), services at 8:30 p.m. on Friday and 10:30 a.m. on Saturday.

Lutheran: Lutheran Church of the Good Shepherd, (La Iglesia Luterana del Buen Pastor), Paseo de las Palmas 1910, Colonia Lomas de Chapultepec (tel. 596-1034), services at 9:45 a.m.

Methodist: Messiah Methodist Church, Balderas 47 (tel. 560-92-23), service at 8:30 a.m.

Mormon: Church of Jesus Christ of Latter Day Saints (tel. 540-2790 or 540-3797), Cerro de Jesus 75, Colonia Campestre Churubusco (same block as Tasqueña Metro station on Tlalpan Line 2); SS and Sacrament at 9:30 a.m. to 1 p.m.

Presbyterian: Gethsemane Presbyterian Church, Allende and Cuauhtémoc in Coyoacán (tel. 524-49-28), services in English at 9 a.m. on Sunday.

Quaker: The Quaker Center is at I. Mariscal 132 (tel. 535-2752). Meetings are Sunday at 11 a.m.

Union Evangelical Church: (Protestant Interdenominational): Located at Reforma 1870, in Lomas (tel. 520-0436). Sunday school at 9:45 a.m., worship at 11 a.m.

Unitarian Church: Herodoto 46 (tel. 531-7166), meetings at 11 a.m. on Sunday and 8 p.m. on Wednesday.

SIESTA: The custom of having a copious, long lunch and taking a rest during the heat of the day is still well entrenched south of the border. You may notice it less in mountainous areas and in the big cities, where life seems to plow onward from morning to evening without a break. But in coastal towns and hot climates, expect banks, offices, consulates, and museums to take a somewhat lengthy break for lunch. You'd be well advised to do the same.

SPANISH LESSONS: A dozen towns south of the border are famous for their Spanish-language programs. In Mexico City, there's the **Mexican-North American Institute of Cultural Relations,** Hamburgo 115 and Varsovia 43 (tel. 905/511-4720) in the Pink Zone. You can sign up for courses in University City as well. Also, consult Mexican National Tourist Council offices (listed in the Introduction to this book) about schools in Cholula, Cuernavaca, Guadalajara, Mérida, and San Miguel de Allende.

Reader John Donahue, of Dalton, Minnesota, has the following tips for those contemplating a Spanish course in Mexico:

Use language tapes before you go. Many U.S. libraries have excellent tapes you can check out and listen to in your car or on your portable cassette player.

Go anytime of year—you needn't really wait for a "semester" or course year to start. It's best to begin on a Monday, however.

Try living with a Mexican family. Pay only a week or ten days in advance, and if things are going well, continue. If your "family stay" ends up being little more than a room rental, feel free to go elsewhere. Family stays are not particularly cheap, by the way, so you should get your money's worth in terms of interaction and language practice.

Don't expect the best and latest in terms of language texts and materials. Many are well out of date. Teachers tend to be underpaid and perhaps undertrained, but very friendly and extremely patient.

Seek out Mexican students of English, and exchange conversation with them. Look for them carrying English-language books. This is how the best friendships are made.

READER'S TIP—SPANISH LESSONS: "The National Registration Center for Studies Abroad (NRCSA), 823 North Second St., Milwaukee, WI 53203 (tel. toll free 800/558-9988) has a catalogue ($4) of schools in Mexico. They will register you at the school of your choice, arrange for room and board with a Mexican family, and make your airline reservations, all for no extra fee. The school I attended was **CECEMMAC,** Apdo. Postal 56, Morelia, Michoacan. I would recommend it for intensive Spanish courses, courses in local arts and crafts, and for regular college courses. Credits earned here are accepted at many colleges in California (and probably in other states as well)" (Sonia Fraser, Independence, Calif.).

STUDENT INFORMATION OFFICES: Students traveling on a budget may want to contact the student headquarters in the various cities that can supply information on student hostels, organized tours, charter flights, as well as free maps and printed materials about the area. The office in **Mexico City** is at Hamburgo 273 (tel. 905/514-4213 or 511-6691); in **Guadalajara,** it's Pedro Moreno 1328 (tel. 36/25-3226), and in **Monterrey,** at Plaza Zaragoza (tel. 83/40-5236).

TAXIS: Taxis are dealt with in each separate section of this book.

TELEGRAMS: Note that the telegraph office may be in a different place from the post office in many cities. For the address of the international telegraph office in Mexico City (open 8 a.m. to 11 p.m. every day), see "Money."

TELEPHONES: Local calls in Mexico are very inexpensive. There are two types of coin phones: in one the slot at the top holds your coin (20 or 50 centavos, or one peso) in a gentle grip until your party answers, then it drops; if there's no answer or a busy signal you can pluck your coin from the slot. The other type is the sort where you insert a coin which disappears into the bowels of the machine, and drops into the cashbox when your call goes through, or into the return slot if it doesn't (after you hang up). This type of phone is often jammed, and your coin won't drop, so that when your party answers you will hear them but they won't hear you. Try from another pay phone.

Long Distance

Long-distance calls in Mexico are as expensive as local calls are cheap. And *international long distance calls tend to be outrageously expensive,* even if you are calling *collect* to the U.S., Canada, or Britain: a 20-minute call from a Mexican hotel to the U.S. or Canada can easily cost $50 or $60! To find out estimated charges *(tarifas)* and area codes *(claves)* you don't know, dial 07 in Mexico City.

To call the U.S. or Canada collect, dial 09, and tell the *operadora* that you want *una llamada por cobrar* (a collect call), *teléfono a teléfono* (station-to-station), or *persona a persona* (person-to-person).

If you don't want to call collect; you'll have to go to a *caseta de larga distancia,* or call from your hotel, as it's impracticable to load hundreds of small coins into a pay phone. Your hotel will levy a service charge—perhaps a percentage! —on top of the already exorbitant rate. Ask in advance what they'll add on. At a caseta you pay just the call charge.

From a caseta or hotel, dial 95 + Area Code + number for the U.S. and

Canada, or 98 + Area Code + number for anywhere else in the world. If you need the international (English-speaking) operator after all, dial 09 in Mexico City. Casetas in Mexico City are at the airport (two), Buenavista Station, Terminal Norte de Autobuses, in the Insurgentes and Merced Metro stations, at Donceles 20, and at Sullivan 143.

To call long distance (abbreviated "lada") within Mexico, dial 91 + Area Code + number. Mexican area codes *(claves)* are listed in the front of the telephone directories, and in the hotel listings for each area in this book. For Mexico City, it's 905/; for Acapulco, 748/.

Calling to Mexico from Abroad

I've included Mexican Area Codes in all important telephone numbers so that you can call long distance within Mexico, or to Mexico from the U.S. and Canada (and, for that matter, from the rest of the world). Mexico's *claves* (Area Codes) and numbers are sometimes shorter than those up north, but they work just as well. Until the Mexican system is fully integrated with that in the U.S. and Canada, you may have to ask the operator for assistance in calling.

Saving Money in Mexico

You can save up to 29% by calling in off-peak periods. The cheapest times to call are after 11 p.m. and before 8 a.m. any day, and all day Saturday and Sunday; the most expensive times are 8 a.m. to 5 p.m. weekdays.

TIME: Central Standard Time prevails throughout most of Mexico. The states of Sonora, Sinaloa, and parts of Nayarit on the western coast are on Mountain Standard Time. The state of Baja California Norte is on Pacific Standard Time, but Baja California Sur is on Mountain Time.

Note that Daylight Saving Time is *not* used in Mexico, except in Baja California Norte (late April to late October).

TIPPING: When it comes to tipping, you should throw out the iron 15% rule right away south of the border, no matter what other travel literature may say. Do as the locals do: for meals costing $2 to $3 or under, leave the loose change; for meals costing around $4 or $5, leave from 6% to 10%, depending on service. Above $6 to $7, you're into the 10% to 15% bracket. Some of the more crass high-priced restaurants will actually add a 15% "tip" to your bill. Leave nothing extra if they do.

Bellboys and porters will expect about 25¢ per bag. You needn't tip taxi drivers unless they've rendered some special service—carrying bags or trunks, for instance.

TURISTA: This is the common name for diarrhea from which many tourists suffer, although others seem immune. It's not only unclean food or water that's to blame, but also the change of eating habits and environment. If your condition becomes serious—fever and chills, stomach pains—do *not* hesitate to call a doctor. Diseases far more serious than Turista are on the loose down here. To neglect a potentially serious ailment, because of the belief that Turista is painful but not dangerous, could be an unhappy mistake. Also, it is advisable, no matter how serious your illness, to consult a doctor before buying or taking any kind of drug. For more information on Turista, refer to the Introduction to this book, Section 3, "Health and Medicaments."

WATER: Most hotels have decanters or bottles of purified water in the rooms and the snazzier hotels have special taps marked *"Aqua Purificada."* Virtually any hotel, restaurant, or bar will bring you purified water if you specifically request it.

YOUTH HOSTELS: Mexico has some beautiful government-built and supported hostels, at very low prices. For a list, write to—or drop in at—**SETEJ,** Hamburgo 273 in Mexico City (tel. 905/211-0743). A source of information on inexpensive youth hostel tours is the **Agencia Nacional de Turismo Juvenil,** Glorieta del Metro Insurgentes, Local C-11, México 6, D.F. (tel. 905/525-2699 or 525-2974), at the Insurgentes Metro plaza.

Part Two: Special Supplement

BELIZE AND GUATEMALA

Special Supplement: Belize & Guatemala

Belize and Guatemala are beautiful, friendly, wonderful places. In the recent past, political difficulties in these countries have kept me from recommending that you go there. I've looked forward to the day when I could again include coverage of Belize and Guatemala in this guide. And now that day has come!

I've been writing guidebooks long enough to know that political situations can change overnight from good to bad—or bad to good. Right now, the outlook for travel to these countries is very encouraging and getting better every day. North American and European travelers are again returning home from Guatemala and Belize with stories of beautiful landscapes, friendly people, fascinating ruins, wonderful handcrafts, and incredibly low prices. And it looks as though the good news will continue to arrive as thousands of travelers rediscover the joys of travel here.

The revised manuscript of this guidebook was approaching its deadline, and was almost under the copy editor's skillful hand, when I decided it was all right to again recommend travel to Belize and Guatemala. There was no way I could do my normal in-depth, on-the-spot research and still get this book to the printer on schedule. But I didn't want to leave you without any information, so I quickly put together the material available to me at this time. For the next edition of this guide, I look forward to providing you with complete information for travel in Guatemala and Belize.

I believe that inaccurate or out-of-date information is *worse* than no information at all. Wrong information leads you to think that you know something, when in fact you really don't. Thus, I have only included information here which I believe to be up-to-date and accurate. I have not been able to confirm prices and quality of the many very inexpensive lodgings and restaurants to be found throughout Guatemala, though I know they exist in every town and village. You'll find them. In the meantime, I've provided several lodging and dining choices closer to the top of our $20-a-Day budget, information which I could confirm.

You can help pave the way for future travelers. Drop me a note on your experiences in Guatemala and Belize, mentioning the details on your favorite hotel, restaurant, and transportation discoveries. If I confirm that your tips can help other travelers, I'll include them, with your name, as "Reader's Selections" in the next edition of this book. And thanks!

Chapter XVIII

BELIZE

1. Getting to Belize
2. Corozal Town
3. Belize City
4. Belmopan and San Ignacio

ACROSS THE RÍO HONDO from Chetumal lies Belize (formerly British Honduras), a British colony which has been self-governing (Britain still handles defense and foreign affairs) since 1964. Belizean history is similar to that of neighboring Mexico and Guatemala for the Maya period and early colonial times, but the Spanish were driven out by the British in 1798, and the land became a British colony in 1862. Modern Belize is a very unlikely mixture of peoples and cultures, for although the descendants of the Maya still populate the western jungle areas, the majority of Belizeans are black Caribs or Créoles, descendants of slaves shipwrecked in transit from Africa, who established their own African-type culture in the Caribbean. The first Europeans to settle in Belize were pirates-turned-farmers, but today they have been joined by Britons and North Americans, Chinese, Lebanese, and adherents of a German Protestant sect called Mennonites. All these peoples live in apparent harmony and mutual self-respect, divided by no great differences in wealth or power. English is the official language of the country, but Indian languages, Spanish, German, Arabic, Chinese, and Créole patois or Pidgin English are also current, depending on the district in question. Sound impossible? To understand Belize, you have to go see for yourself.

1. Getting to Belize

Besides the buses to Belize City from Chetumal, there are daily flights to Belize City from Miami and New Orleans, and also flights from Mexico City, and from Guatemala City via San Salvador. But most people who visit Belize are either going to the "cayes" and islands off the coast for deep-sea fishing or scuba diving (marvelous, but very expensive), or are taking the overland jungle route to Tikal in Guatemala. For the purposes of this book we'll assume you're going through Belize to Tikal.

VIA BELIZE TO TIKAL: Ambitious readers of this book who want to make the entire "Maya circuit" and save themselves backtracking in Yucatán and Guatemala might consider the route Chetumal—Corozal—Belize City—San Ignacio —Melchor de Mencos—Tikal—Flores—Guatemala City, but we hasten to warn you that this is not an easy trip by car, and is a downright miserable one by bus: roads are bad, accommodations scarce and chancy, border officials unpredictable, and the weather is either hot and dusty or hot and muggy. We have

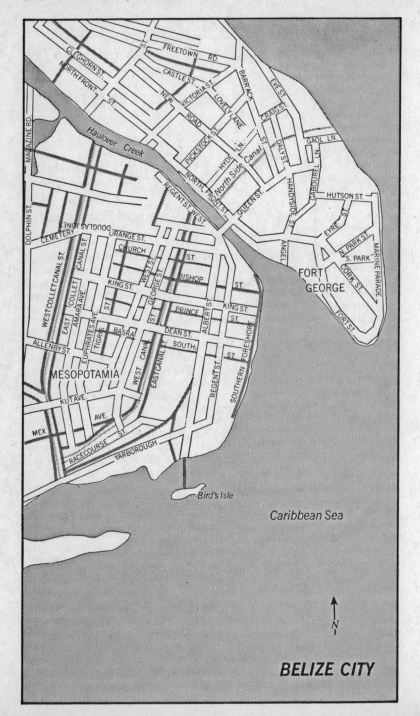

BELIZE CITY

traveled a good deal, and we found this particular road to be pretty rough. But if you're determined, you're in for an unforgettable adventure. Be sure your car is in top condition; cars which are very low-slung should *not* be taken over this road. Vans do pretty well; large cars must proceed carefully.

MONEY: The unit of currency in Belize is the Belizean dollar, abbreviated "B$." US $1 equals about B$2. The B$-Mexican peso rate fluctuates greatly, and those with pesos are always at a disadvantage.

CROSSING THE BORDER: Hand in your Mexican Tourist Card (and car papers, if you have them) at the Mexican border station. You'll be issued new ones when you reenter Mexico. The official may ask you to pay an "Exit tax." There is no such tax. He's ripping you off. Ignore him. If you have Mexican auto insurance, get the policy stamped by an official so you get a rebate for the days you're outside Mexican territory. You'll buy Belizean insurance across the river. Cross the bridge over the Río Hondo and you're in Belize.

Both Mexican and Belizean border stations seem to be open during daylight hours all week, with no breaks for lunch.

Your entry permit is the rubber stamp put in your passport, birth certificate, or other proof of nationality, and it will show the length of time you're allowed to stay. Ask for a week and you'll probably get it. Be sure to get a Temporary Import Permit for your car, even if no one tells you a thing about it. *Ask* for the Customs official if he's not there, and *get the permit* or you'll be held up at the border when you leave the country. Also, auto insurance is required. You buy it in the restaurant across the road from the border station.

After they've stamped your passport or birth certificate, issued your auto permit and inspected your car (a process which ranges from a glance through the window to a good going-over), and after you've bought auto insurance, you're on your way. *Don't* change money at the border unless you're forced to; if you have to, change cash dollars, *not pesos,* for you lose a tremendous amount on peso exchange. There are banks in Corozal Town (open 8 a.m. to noon Monday through Friday, 8 to 11 a.m. on Saturday) seven miles down the road, where you'll get the full rate for your dollars or travelers checks.

2. Corozal Town

The road to Corozal Town from the border station of Santa Elena is paved and quite good. Local buses make the run into town from the border several times a day. Three miles in from the border you bear left at a fork for Corozal Town.

WHERE TO STAY AND EAT: The traditional place to stay is the **Caribbean Motel, Cabins and Trailer Park,** right on the bay in an idyllic location shaded by lofty palms and with a swimming dock only steps away. Price for double accommodations in quaint and primitive thatched bungalows is B$20 (US$10) for two.

Just past the Caribbean Motel on the shore road south of town is the 18-room **Tony's Motel,** newer and more comfortable than the aforementioned hostelry, with double room-and-shower renting for B$50 (US$25) per night.

For an after-dinner nightcap, don't miss a visit to the **Capri Hotel, Bar and Dance Hall,** between the intersection of the main streets and the bay, which looks for all the world like a set for a Tennessee Williams play. The paint's cracking on the old wooden structure, and the dance hall floor may be dusty and deserted, but the bar in the back is usually open. At twilight you can catch a glimpse of palm trees on the bay through a rear window, at other times admire the unique collection of decorations and geegaws above the bottles. A bottle of

"Charger," the local light lager, costs only B50¢ (US25¢), and drinks made with rum such as rum-and-Coke or rum-and-fruit-juice are only B$1 (US50¢) apiece.

WHAT TO DO: Swim in the bay, or walk around town and marvel at the difference between Mexican culture and Belizean culture, so close and yet worlds apart. Belize is truly a Caribbean country, the frame houses built on high stilts for coolness, protection from floods, and to give storage room and shade for sitting. Farming and sugarcane are what Corozal gets along on, plus perhaps a little fishing.

MOVING ON: Two roads head south to Orange Walk. One is the shore road which travels past the Caribbean Motel and Tony's Motel. The other road is the main road from the border station south. Pavement is better on this one, and there's more traffic, which is what you want if you're hitching.

You may find yourself hitching whether or not it's your normal means of transport as buses leave Corozal for Belize City infrequently. Otherwise, there are the trucks: a cross between a farm truck and a military transport, they're uncomfortable but dependable.

ALTUN-HA RUINS: Sixty miles south of the Mexican-Belizean border on the main road is the turnoff to Altun-Ha, an ancient Mayan city thought to have existed here since about 250 A.D. Look for a small and rather inconspicuous sign on the right-hand side of the road. From the highway, it's a bumpy 2³⁄₁₀ miles to the ruins. About 1½ miles in, the road forks; take the right fork.

Altun-Ha flourished during the Classic Period of Maya civilization, up to the 800s. Only a few of the most imposing temples, tombs, and pyramids have been uncovered and rebuilt; hundreds more lie under the rich jungle foliage. The archeological work was done principally by the Royal Ontario Museum beginning in 1964. Even though restoration has resulted in a scene that's anachronistic—various parts of the temples built at different periods are all seen together—it's a beautiful ruined city, well worth the visit.

Altun-Ha is open during daylight hours, every day of the week. A soft-drink stand and picnic area are open for your use.

BELIZE CITY BY-PASS: Readers with their own cars who are on a lickety-split trip through Belize to Tikal can cut out Belize City altogether by watching for the Burrell Boom road, off to the right about ten miles north of Belize City. You must take your car across the Belize River on a hand-cranked ferry, but you'll cut 25 miles off the border-to-border trip. This route is preferable if the river floods during the rainy season's early months as the main highway can be covered in water.

If you choose to visit Belize City, it's only 30½ miles south of the turnoff to Altun-Ha.

3. Belize City

Although Belmopan, along the Western Highway, is the new capital of Belize, the cultural and commercial center is still Belize City (pop. 40,000), founded three centuries ago by pirates who decided to give up the sea for the land. It's a strange, fascinating warren of narrow streets and canals (the later pretty pungent in hot weather), modern stores, and quaint wooden mansions. The Supreme Court building, off the small Central Park, is a real prize of English colonial architecture (à la Caribbean). The town's central landmark is the Swing Bridge over the Haulover Creek, and everything you'll need in Belize

City—stores, consulates, hotels, and restaurants—will be a short walk from this bridge.

WHERE TO STAY AND EAT: Accommodations and restaurants in Belize City are definitely a problem, even more so than in the rest of the country. Local police advise that the cheapest hotels are not recommendable because of the danger of theft, and the expensive hotels often commit a similar offense by charging too much for what you get. Be cautious looking for a room here.

Ms. Mara Cantor of Carmel Valley, California, archeologist, leader of tours for her company called Expanding Horizons, and noted Belizophile, makes these recommendations for Belize City:

"The **Fort George** is *the* luxury hotel in Belize. Rooms are expensive, but you can drop in for lunch, which costs only B$10 to B$12 (US$5 to US$6). Perhaps the best place to stay in Belize City is the **Hotel Mopan** (tel. 7351 or 3356), 55 Regent St., Belize City, where the most interesting people in Belize congregate at the bar. Owners Jean and Tom Shaw are delightful. Rooms cost B$50 (US$25) double.

"As for restaurants, **Mama's** is a gathering-place for young North Americans. Other places worth a try are the **Upstairs Café** near the post office, and the **Golden Dragon Chinese Restaurant,** across the street from the Hotel Mopan. For a big splurge, try **The Villa,** or the **Chateau Caribbean,** near the Fort George Hotel.

"If you're interested in renting a car, check with **Smith and Sons Auto Rental** (tel. 02-3779). Ask for 'Smitty' (Dennis Smith). The cost is about B$100 (US$50) per day."

WHAT TO DO: A walk around town is all you need to entertain you in Belize City, for the fascination never seems to end. Turn right as you come off the northeast end of the Swing Bridge before the post office and follow the street southeast to the Fort George Lighthouse and Baron Bliss Memorial. Baron Bliss, who visited Belize in his yacht in the 1920s, left Belize City most of his fortune (a few million dollars, in fact) when he died on the yacht in the harbor, and the town has been able to build and endow many public buildings and foundations with the income from the bequest.

Banks are all around the Central Park, as are the major department stores, many of which close for lunch. The American Consulate is on Gabourel Lane. To find it, walk along Queen Street from the Swing Bridge to the end of that street and turn right. The consulate is a block down on the left-hand side—it's a big, white wooden building, very well kept. The market, right next to the Swing Bridge on the Central Park side, is the seamiest one we have ever seen.

A Trip to the Cayes

Almost everyone who visits Belize for more than a day or two takes a trip out to the cayes, or offshore islands. Snorkeling, scuba-diving, fishing, sunbathing, and sloth are the prime occupations in this laid-back Caribbean paradise.

Small hotels and pensions, from fairly inexpensive to very pricey, are scattered here and there on the islands. You can fly out in a little place, or take a boat from the Swing Bridge in the center of Belize City. My friend Mara Cantor writes, "The boats will take you out to **St. George's Caye** or **Caye Caulker** for a day of snorkeling for about B$48 (US$24) roundtrip. Choose a boat carefully, as some are better than others. A good thing to look for is a boat with two outboard motors; if one fails, the other can get you to shore."

BUSES OUT: Belize City's bus station is about ten blocks from the Swing

Bridge. From Albert Street between the Swing Bridge and the Central Park, walk up Orange Street, cross a canal, veer left, and the bus station will be on your right-hand side. Apparently, not all buses leave right from the station; there are other bus stops nearby. Ask in the station for current details.

Buses depart several times daily for Belmopan and San Ignacio. The bus trip takes 1½ hours to Belmopan, where there's a brief stop; then another 1½ hours to San Ignacio, where you either stay overnight or grab a taxi to the border station at Benque Viejo.

4. Belmopan and San Ignacio

The Western Highway to Belmopan (about 50 miles) is sometimes good, other times bad. The road to the new capital takes you into the foothills of the Maya Mountains and through farming country that's quite pretty. Belmopan itself is a model city designed and built from scratch in the jungle at the geographical center of the country. It's still under construction, and like all such new-founded capitals, it will be a while before it becomes the cultural center of the country.

BELMOPAN: Conceived as the dynamic center of a growing Belize, Belmopan is actually a sleepy place 2½ miles in from the Western Highway. Modest government buildings are laid out according to a master plan, and small residential areas are enclosed by a ring road. Business seems limited to a gas station, a few little food shops, and a very modest hostelry.

Under a 20-year development plan, Belmopan will be a pulsating metropolis of 30,000 before the end of the century. That may well come to be, but there remains a tremendous amount to be done.

Facilities here which you may find useful are a bank, post office, hospital, and microwave telephone installation.

Onward from Belmopan, the road climbs slowly into the Maya Mountains, and one gets the feeling that the seamy, ramshackle way of life in Belize's coastal towns gives way to cooler, less humid air, a workaday mood inspired by strenuous farm labor, and greater natural beauty.

SAN IGNACIO (CAYO): In the foothills of the mountains, the road runs through the twin towns of Santa Elena and San Ignacio on either side of a beautiful calm, clear river (good for a swim). From Linda Vista, a small gazebo perched on a hill above Santa Elena (walk up the hill on a dirt road near the Santa Elena end of the suspension bridge), the towns look like a picture book scene of a tropical village. White town hall, bridge over the river, parrots squawking as they fly overhead in pairs: no one living here seems to have a care about the outside world.

Accommodations in San Ignacio are scarce, but the first place to look is the **Hotel San Ignacio** (tel. 09-2034), up the hill just past the police station at the west end of the bridge. Although it's a bit expensive, with doubles at B$70 (US$35), it's clean, comfortable, and about the only such place to be had for miles— includes a good restaurant and bar with decent food. The Hotel San Ignacio is a very welcome oasis in this country of generally substandard accommodations.

Little hotels down in the main part of town charge much less, and give you much less. You can get a very basic, plain room for as little as B$6 (US$3) double.

Those with camping gear can get permission to camp down by the river in a town park, or up at the gazebo on Linda Vista, although the latter has in recent years been woefully neglected. No services are available in either place, however.

XUNANTUNICH: Although you may not be able to pronounce it, you can visit it. Xunantunich is a Maya ruin 6½ miles past San Ignacio on the road to Benque Viejo. Look for the small wooden sign, park, and cross the river on the quaint hand-drawn ferry (no charge) which operates daily from 8 a.m. to 5 p.m. You can walk the mile to the ruins, or take your car on the ferry if you want to drive. The site is open whenever the ferry is running. By the way, if you walk to the ruins, it's all uphill.

Archeologists from Cambridge University did the first important reconstruction work here in 1959-60, but the effects of weather and jungle plants have done more damage even since that time. Preservation efforts are still being carried on, especially on El Castillo, a tall temple with a fascinating frieze of calendar gods on its east side. (During a period of tension between Belize and Guatemala, British soldiers on sentry duty mounted the temple for the view, hanging their hammocks in the chamber at the top!) The entire countryside is a panoramic picture from up here. Don't miss it.

Under the protection of a thatched palapa in the temple forecourt are three magnificent stelae portraying rulers of the region. Xunantunich was a thriving Mayan city about the same time as Altun-Ha, in the Classic Period about 600 to 900 A.D.

MOUNTAIN PINE RIDGE: Another note from Ms Mara Cantor raves about this 3,400-foot ridge complete with Maya reminders, secret waterfall, wild orchids, parrots, keel-billed toucans and other exotic flora and fauna. Mountain Pine Ridge, Hidden Valley Falls, the Río On and Río Frío Caves are off the Western Highway near Georgeville.

ON TO THE BORDER: Benque Viejo, the town nearest the border, ten miles up the road from San Ignacio, is a good place to stop for a soft drink if you've driven from Belize City. Then it's a short ride of less than a mile to the border.

The Belizean officials will ask to see your passport or other proof of nationality and will give you an exit card to fill out. If you have a car, you'll have to turn in your Temporary Entry Permit.

As you cross the border, notice the signs: "Belize for the Belizeans" on one side, "Belice es Guatemala" (Belize is part of Guatemala) on the other. Guatemala has a long-standing claim to all of Belize, but British protection keeps the controversy to a diplomatic squabble.

The officials at the Guatemalan border station keep the place open most of the time—including weekends—but charge extra if you demand their services outside of business hours (8 a.m. to noon and 2 to 6 p.m. Monday through Friday). In fact, they may demand a minimal amount from you even during business hours. You will have to pay for your Tourist Card ($1 U.S.). Car papers should be free, but the fumigation of your tires, required by law, will cost $2 and you'll be given a receipt for it.

A bank is in operation at the Guatemalan border station, and *you should not fail to change money here,* particularly if you're going straight to Tikal. There are no banks in Tikal, and *travelers checks are not accepted* (although cash US dollars are) by establishments at Tikal. Flores has banks, but they close by 2 p.m., 2:30 p.m. on Friday. Guatemalan currency, the Quetzal, is exactly equal to the US dollar, and so if you change US $50, you should receive a full Q50.

ON TO TIKAL: Walk out of the border station toward Melchor de Mencos, and head up the main street on the right. The center of this dusty border town is up the hill, a mile from the border station. Here you'll come across a few modest hotels.

Shops and a small market sell provisions in central Melchor.

Now you've got to do some planning, as getting to see Tikal can be tricky. First, find out when the next bus leaves Melchor for points west. It's two hours at least to Las Cruces (also called El Cruce), the turnoff for Tikal. If you can make it there by 7 a.m., you should be able to catch the bus from Flores which heads to Tikal daily. Once you get on the bus, it's another 37 km. (24 miles, or 45 minutes) to Tikal. If you can't make it from Melchor to Las Cruces by 7, you can get off there anyway and try to hitch a ride, or hope for another bus. Las Cruces has no facilities except a gas station.

The journey straight to Tikal may seem chancy to you, in which case you should hop a bus from Melchor directly to Flores, three hours of bumping and wheezing away. You will have to backtrack a bit to reach Tikal.

There is an alternative: if you can get together with some other Tikal travelers to split the cost, you can attempt to hire a taxi in Melchor. The cabby will take you straight to Tikal, or to Flores if you prefer.

Okay, hop on your bus or cab out of Melchor. Just outside of town the bus may stop at an army checkpoint, where the curious troops will look you and your belongings over. Be courteous, formal, and haughty. Once the bus chugs into motion again, flip to the next page and begin reading Chapter XIX, "Introducing Guatemala."

INTRODUCING GUATEMALA

1. Background Information
2. The Road to Guatemala

BEYOND THE ISTHMUS of Tehuantepec lie the tropical savannahs of the Yucatán and the wild mountains of Chiapas. Beyond these, the North American continent ends, politically as well as geographically, and you enter Central America. But in the past the Yucatán peninsula, Chiapas, Belize (British Honduras), and Guatemala made up "Mesoamerica," the wild and unlikely area in which Mayan civilization flourished over 1,200 years ago. Today Mexico and Guatemala are very different countries—you'll feel the contrast as soon as you cross the border. There is less industrial and technological development in Guatemala, few cars outside the cities, and the Indians, proud of their descent from the ancient Mayas, live a more peaceful and unspoiled, if primitive, life.

1. Background Information

A CAPSULE HISTORY: The earliest Mayan culture dates back to the Formative Period (in Mesoamerican civilizations) from 300 B.C. to 100 A.D. But it did not really achieve full flowering until the Classic Period (200–925 A.D.). By 600 A.D., the Mayas were the most important culture in Mesoamerica. The advanced culture of Teotihuacan was declining while the Mayas were rising intellectually and artistically to a height never before reached by the natives of the New World. In Guatemala and the Yucatan peninsula, the Mayas built magnificent ceremonial centers, carved intricate hieroglyphic stelae, and developed superior astronomical, calendrical, and mathematical systems.

Then in the Late Classic Period, around 790 A.D., the Mayan civilization began to decline. Over the next 40 to 100 years one village after another was abandoned, until by the end of the 9th century the last chapter of this brilliant civilization was closed. Why? No one is certain. Was it the population explosion, the misuse of land, the northern barbarians who were roaming Mesoamerica? Whatever, the Postclassic Period, from 900 A.D. up to the Spanish Conquest, shows the loss of splendor and the beginning of a polity of class systems (priests, merchants, serfs), government regulation and taxation, trade guilds, and a primitive but productive agriculture.

In 1519 Hernán Cortés conquered Mexico and in 1523 he sent his chief lieutenant, Pedro de Alvarado, to explore the region of Guatemala. Alvarado led an expedition against the Quiché people (then the most powerful and wealthy

GUATEMALA & BELIZE

MEXICO

Chetumal

Corozal

Orange Walk

BELIZE

Tikal

Altun-Ha

Lake Petén-Itzá

Belize City

Xunantunich

Flores

Belmopan

Dolores

Melchor De Mencos

San Ignacio (Cayo)

MEXICO

San Cristobal de las Casas

Poptún

San Luis

GULF OF HONDURAS

Comitan

Livingston

Ciudad, Cuauhtemoc

Castillo De San Felipe

Puerto Barrios

La Mesilla

GUATEMALA

Lake Izabal

Quirigua

Pan American Highway

Zaculeu

Huehuetenango

Tapachula

Santa Cruz del Quiche

Zacapa

HONDURAS

Cd. Tecun Uman

Totoni- capan

Chichicastenango

Chiquimula

Copán

Atlantic Highway

Quetzal- tenango

Solola Panajachel

EL Progreso

Esquipulas

Retalhuleu

Lake Atitlán

Guatemala City

Mazatenango

Antigua

Siquinalá

Lake Amatitlán

Pan American Highway

EL SALVADOR

La Democracia

Escuintla

PACIFIC OCEAN

Sacapulas

San Salvador

CARIBBEAN SEA

tribe in Guatemala). In the words of a 16th-century Spanish historian, Alvarado was "reckless, merciless and impetuous, lacking in veracity if not common honesty, but zealous and courageous." It wasn't long before Alvarado had conquered the indigenous peoples and was named representative of the sovereign power of Spain. He set about establishing a typical Spanish colonial empire, founding cities and towns throughout Central America and converting the Indians to Catholicism. But unlike Mexico, Central America did not yield vast amounts of gold and silver for the conquerors and was thus somewhat of a disappointment. Many of the Spaniards stayed on, however, to carve out large coffee plantations using the Indians as laborers.

Early in the 19th century, Guatemalan and other Central American leaders followed the lead of other Latin America states and declared their independence from Spain. The captain-general of Guatemala became the chief executive. But in Mexico, the empire of Agustín Iturbide had been formed and conservative Guatemalan leaders voted for annexation to the empire. This political arrangement didn't last, and a republican Federation of Central American States was formed in 1823. The federation lasted some 15 years, but was continually torn by internecine battles, both political and military. By 1840 Central America had taken the political form it has today, and political struggles were confined to the large towns. As a result, except for Guatemala City and the provincial capitals, "progress" is a stranger to much of the country, leaving it untouched and incredibly beautiful.

MONEY: The Guatemalan unit of currency is the *quetzal,* named after the freedom-loving bird of the ancient Mayas. Officially, it's worth exactly one American dollar, and is divided into 100 centavos, equivalent to U.S. cents. Proud of the fact that the quetzal has retained parity with the U.S. dollar since 1926, the Guatemalan government is loath to admit officially that the quetzal's value has dropped dramatically in recent years. But you will find many legal opportunities—even in banks!—to buy quetzals at rates up to Q3.50 or even Q4 for US$1. So officially the quetzal is at par with the dollar, but unofficially you get far more than one quetzal for each dollar you exchange.

Prices in this book are given in quetzals only. Thus, if you pay Q20 for a double room in a hotel, and changed dollars at the official rate, you will have paid US$20 for the room. But if you changed money at US$1 = Q3, the room will have cost you only US$6.66!

You can change money at the border or at the bank in town—no charge for the transaction. In many places small denomination dollars are accepted along with quetzals. The one-to-one rate of dollar to quetzal is helpful but deceptive: after spending pesos for so long, there's a tendency to think foreign money is cheap. Remember that when you spend 25 Guatamalan centavos for something it's not a fraction of a U.S. or Canadian penny (as in pesos), but US25¢.

By the way, in Guatemalan villages you may hear the Maya words *pisto* for money (quetzals) and *leng* for centavos.

It's good to have $25 or so in cash U.S. dollars of small denominations with you at all times for emergencies (most places will take them if you don't have the proper local currency).

GUATEMALAN HOTELS AND RESTAURANTS: The division between luxury and squalor which used to reign throughout Guatemala's hostelries has been modified in most towns, so that now wherever you go you'll find a selection of hotels in all price categories, from Q2.50 per person to Q18 or Q20. At Christmas, New Year's, and especially Holy Week (the week before Easter), most hotels are fully booked weeks in advance, so plan accordingly.

In the higher priced hotels expect pretty good service, comfortable and sometimes wonderfully quaint and picturesque accommodations, private baths, a fairly good restaurant, and extras like 24-hour hot water and a garage or parking lot. In the inexpensive places you usually get only a very small room, one light bulb, two beds, a small nightstand, and a plastic pitcher of drinking water. But there's always a shower nearby, often hot, and most of these little places have a *comedor,* or dining room, where the señora's home-cooked meals are served for something like Q1 or Q2. By our reckoning, the expensive places, although often charming, are slightly too expensive for what you get, while the low-priced places are sensational bargains.

By the way, taxi drivers in some Guatemalan towns may receive commissions from certain hotels for bringing new customers. If your taxi driver suggests strongly that your chosen hotel is "bad," or "too expensive," and wants to take you to another, think twice. Have him go to your chosen hotel first, so you can at least get a price and inspect a room.

Room Tax

The Guatemala Tourist Commission, INGUAT, levies a 10% room tax on each night spent in a Guatemalan hotel. When a hotel receptionist quotes you the room price, the tax will probably *not* be included in the quotation. Ask to make sure.

In this book we will quote room prices with the tax included, so that you'll know the total charge you will have to pay for a room.

FINDING AN ADDRESS: After Mexico, the street-numbering system in Guatemala is a dream come true; it is logical, systematic, easy to use, and is found in every Guatemalan town. In fact, it's so good there's almost no excuse for getting lost anywhere but in Guatemala City! Once you get the hang of it, you're on your way to the exact location of any hotel or restaurant. Here's how it works: every town is planned on a grid with *avenidas* running roughly north-south, and *calles* running east-west. Addresses are given in the following form: 2a. Av. 4-17, which means that the place you're after is on 2nd Avenue, at 4th Calle, number 17 (2a is "Spanish" for 2nd, 3a for 3rd, etc.) You can even tell what side of the street it will be on. If the street number is even, it'll be on the right side, if odd on the left, as you walk along the avenida toward higher and higher numbered Calles. You can guess, then, that 3a. Av. 5-78 will be on 3rd Avenue between 5th and 6th Calles (closer to 6th as the house number is a high one), on the right-hand side. Once you get the hang of it, it's a marvelous system.

The only exceptions are in Antigua and Guatemala City. In Antigua, avenidas and calles are also designated *Norte, Sur, Oriente,* and *Poniente,* the central point being the main square. All you need do, however, if, say, the address reads "5a. Av. Norte 9," is make sure you're not on the Sur, or southern half of 5th Avenue. In Guatemala City the system works in the downtown section, but the city sprawls beyond the practical limits of the plan, so you find within the downtown area such addresses as 14 av. "A" 2-31, 14 "A" being a short street or alley between, and parallel to, 14th and 15th Avenues. Outside the downtown area of the capital you also run into *diagonales, rutas, vias,* and other designations.

One last note: Each town is also divided into zones, but in the smaller towns (everywhere but Guatemala City) almost every important place is in Zona 1. If a zone number does not appear as a part of any address given in this book, you can assume that the place you're looking for is in Zona 1.

TRAVELING IN GUATEMALA: The main roads in Guatemala are better than the main roads in Mexico, with smoother, harder surfaces, gentler curves, and better maintenance. Big, comfortable buses run from various points in Mexico (including Mexico City) to both border stations (Tapachula-Talisman and Ciudad Cuauhtémoc-La Mesilla), where they connect with similar Guatemalan buses for the onward journey. Within Guatemala every town of any size has several bus companies which operate to surrounding towns and to the capital; minibus services connect the smaller villages or run the very frequent services between towns a short distance apart. Therefore, driving your own car or taking the bus is the best way to see Guatemala, except when it comes to ruins. Tikal is best reached by air, and even less accessible ruins are normally reached by chartered light plane, which can work out fairly cheaply, if you have enough people to fill the plane and you are very interested in the ruins.

For those driving, note that Mexican auto insurance is not valid in Guatemala. Buy Guatemalan insurance through your agent at home, or through the AAA, or within Guatemala.

WEATHER AND CLOTHING: Conditions in Guatemala are similar to those in Mexico, with basically two seasons: the rainy season from May to October, and the dry season from November to April. In the rainy season it will be chillier in the highlands, muggier in the lowlands. Bring extra warm clothes for the mountain towns, extra insect repellant for the lowland towns.

Average annual temperatures in Guatemala's highlands are 64 to 68 degrees Fahrenheit; in Guatemala City, 68 to 72 degrees; in El Peten and along the Atlantic Highway, 77 to 86 degrees.

IMPORTANT FOR BRITISH READERS: British subjects must have a Guatemalan visa, available in any Guatemalan consulate, plus three photographs. Be sure you have yours when you hit the border. It's all because of that little disagreement over Belize . . .

2. The Road to Guatemala

Actually, there are two roads to Guatemala from Mexico and one from Belize (see Chapter XVIII). From Tehuantepec you can head (by bus or car) either to Tapachula and the Pacific Slope road to Guatemala City, or to Tuxtla Gutierrez and San Cristóbal de las Casas for the high mountain road to Guatemala City. The low road along the Pacific Slope goes through lush tropical country and a few pretty towns. It's straighter and faster than the high road, but has several disadvantages. It is heavily trafficked (especially when the sugarcane harvest is on), it is hot and muggy all the time, the border officials at Tapachula-Talisman have a reputation for unpleasantness and extortion, and except for the lushness there's not much to stop and see along the road. The high road, by contrast, is reached by going through San Cristóbal, one of the prettiest places in Mexico; the border officials are somewhat better (although not efficient), there is virtually no traffic for the first 100 miles into Guatemala, the mountain scenery is breathtaking, and interesting towns and villages abound all along the road. Perhaps you can see that we prefer the high road despite its disadvantages: some landslides in the rainy season (late May to October), although they are cleared away pretty quickly by road crews; and a curvy (although very good and safe) 40 m.p.h. mountain road.

Should you change your mind once you've entered Guatemala you can switch roads by taking the paved road between Retalhuleu and Quezaltenango (by bus or car).

We'll give you information on both roads. The border-crossing procedures are the same at both posts (although, as mentioned, there are more hassles at

Tapachula-Talisman on the low road), so we'll only go through them once. You can shorten procedures at the border a bit by getting your Tourist Card in advance at a Guatemalan consulate, but don't spend a day doing it. If you're near a consulate (hours are usually 9 a.m. to 2 p.m. weekdays) it's a good plan; if not, you can always get one at the border. Best place to get a card in advance is the Guatemalan Embassy in Mexico City.

CROSSING THE BORDER, BY BUS OR ON YOUR OWN: Buses leave San Cristóbal de las Casas for the border station at Ciudad Cuauhtémoc. After border formalities, passengers board a Guatemalan bus for the rest of the journey. This bus leaves the Guatemalan border station at La Mesilla and heads for Huehuetenango and Guatemala City. The bus from the border will drop you at transfer points for Chichicastenango or Quezaltenango if you wish. Other buses go to Huehuetenango. Take your pick.

The road from San Cristóbal is fairly fast. It's slightly over 100 miles from San Cristóbal to Ciudad Cuauhtémoc, the border station, and you should be able to cover it in about 2½ hours. After winding through the mountains east of San Cristóbal, you descend to a plain before heading into the mountains that mark the border. The first Customs post you'll come to is where you hand in your car papers and Tourist Card (you fill out a new one when you return from Guatemala). Go on to the border proper, about a mile down the road, and pass the barrier into Guatemala.

You must get a Guatemalan Tourist Card right across the border, if you don't already have one, and a policeman will take great pains and much time to register your car in his big book. After getting your card (have your passport or birth certificate ready), drive on for a miles or so to the Customs inspection station, where you'll get your car papers, usually after a fairly serious look at the car and its contents. You may have to open a few bags, but it's wise just to follow the inspector around and do exactly *and only* what he asks. You may also be asked to take a bag or two into the station for a quick inspection.

While you're getting your car papers, someone will wash your tires with a disinfectant solution. This fumigation is required and costs a dollar, and is a bothersome but fairly minor nuisance. The entire border crossing, from the Mexican who takes your car papers to a slosh with disinfectant, takes about an hour. The officials are business-like, sometimes even friendly (especially if you show an interest in Guatemala), and the whole procedure is quite painless. The Guatemalan border stations keep regular business hours: 8 a.m. to noon and 2 to 6 p.m. Monday through Friday, and 8 to noon on Saturday. You can cross at other hours and on Sunday, but you end up paying a little extra.

Chapter XX

THE MOUNTAIN ROAD

1. Huehuetenango
2. Quezaltenango
3. Chichicastenango
4. Lake Atitlán and Panajachel
5. Antigua

ON THE MOUNTAIN ROAD, you're headed for some of the most spectacular scenery south of the Rio Grande. The road follows the course of a river through a magnificent gorge walled by craggy rock faces and steep mountain slopes that have been cultivated clear to the top. In summer, the rainy season, the weather is balmy and everything is beautifully lush. Cornfields are everywhere, usually with farmhouses nestled in their midst. One of the first things you'll notice is that everyone walks. There's almost no real traffic until you approach Guatemala City, not even horses. Women always seem to be carrying something on their heads while they walk, and you may see them carry huge loads of produce to an informal crossroads market that is miles away. Everyone seems shy, happy, friendly. The country is beautiful, the pace is relaxed, so drive slowly. You'll see a great deal more, and a slow speed seems to fit in with the culture. It's a small country, and there's no barren territory that has to be covered to get to a point of interest.

1. Huehuetenango

The first settlement on the road into Guatemala is the provincial capital of Huehuetenango (alt. 6,240 feet; pop. 35,000), a clean, quiet town high up in mountain pastures. The ruins of Zaculeu are only a few kilometers from town and there's an assortment of hotels and restaurants, all within our price range. If you've driven from San Cristóbal, this is the logical place to spend the night.

Now that you've read "Finding an Address" in the previous chapter, it will help you to know that Huehuetenango's main square, reference point for everything in town, is bounded by 2a and 3a Calles, and 4a and 5a Avenidas.

WHERE TO STAY AND EAT: The town's dowager is the **Hotel Zaculeu**, 5a Av I-14 (tel. 064-1050 or 064-1575), which bills itself as a "rustic mountain inn." It almost makes it, for its 19 rooms are decorated with local handcrafts—handwoven cloth, tin candlesticks, clay water pitchers. Some rooms are truly charming, others so-so. Rooms open onto a beautiful courtyard filled with flowers, bordered by a colonial arcade. Additional facilities include a private parking lot and the best restaurant in town. Rooms come with or without bath, and cost Q8 to Q10 single, Q14 to Q20 double. In the restaurant, meals are good. Huehuetenango gets a lot of travelers coming from or going to the border, and many stay at the Zaculeu, lending it an old-time roadhouse character. It's a good place to strike up a conversation and gather information for the trip ahead.

Besides these hotels, the town has half a dozen little hostelries, none more than a few blocks from the main square. Virtually all are built around a courtyard and have bare but clean rooms, which cost a few dollars per person.

WHAT TO DO: First of all there's the **market**, a nice one busy every day. It's located at 2a Av. and Calle 3, and its four great walls hold a busy collection of fruit stands, candle sellers, cloth shops, piles of baskets, bales of dried chili, and even an old bottle shop where you can purchase an old instant-coffee jar (nothing goes to waste in this town)! The sturdy shopping basket you paid $5 for in Oaxaca can be had here, with a minimum of bargaining, for $1. Shopkeepers are very obliging, most friendly, all curious, and they expect you to bargain for their merchandise.

Besides the market, you'll want to take a look at the **ruins of Zaculeu.** Avoid self-appointed "guides" and take a minibus which departs from a stand across from the volunteer fire company right downtown. You can even walk—it's a pleasant hike of about 45 minutes—and chances are better than not someone will stop to give you a lift.

If you drive, head out of town on 6a Avenida, and keep asking people the way, as there are few signs. It's a 2½-mile ride. The ruins at Zaculeu date from the Postclassic Period just before the Spanish Conquest. The Postclassic Period begins in 900 A.D. when the Maya civilization began to fade out and become absorbed by the Mexican tribes that were moving down from the north. Out of this assimilation of Mexican and Maya cultures arose three powerful nations, one of which was the Mam, who settled in the area around Huehuetenango and made their capital at Zaculeu. The Maya culture had been greatly diffused by this time so you will see very little similarity between the Maya ruins of Yucatán and Peten and those at Zaculeu.

This site was restored in 1940 by the United Fruit Company "as a contribution to Guatemalan culture." The site is small, however, and there are several mounds which have not been uncovered; at present there are no further plans for excavation. The restoration was so complete, down to the coat of mortar which covered the temples, that it appears as a reconstruction rather than a restoration: "perfect temples" down to the manicured lawns. The surroundings are beautiful and the ruins are worth a visit. There is a small but interesting museum on the premises. Entrance is free to the ruins and museum, courtesy of the United Fruit Company.

Then you can always take a walk around town. No doubt a local boy will appoint himself your guide and expect a quarter for pointing out the obvious. It's all very friendly, but you can ignore him politely if you wish. In the evening everybody gathers in the main square, especially the young, to see and be seen. If there are no festivities the night you're there, the next best attraction at night is the **movie theater** on Calle 4, half a block out of the square.

HUEHUETENANGO MISCELLANY: This town might be your first glimpse of Guatemalan culture, and you'll be pleasantly surprised the farther you go into the country. The costumes seem to get more and more colorful and unusual as you head southeast. Notice that in Huehuetenango it's traditional for women to wear aprons all the time. They come in all sizes, shapes, and colors, but no matter what sort of apron she has, every woman must have one.

BACK TO THE HIGHWAY: On the road from Huehuetenango the vistas continue: old men, young boys, teenage girls—literally everyone is on foot and carrying something. The men use a "tump line" (a rope or strap from the backpack load to the forehead) to distribute the weight of the huge bundles they carry, or they put their packs in a large piece of cloth, tying the ends so that they can loop it over the forehead and carry the load on the back. It's a constant reminder that horses were not found in this hemisphere before the Conquest, and that the Indian civilizations knew nothing about the wheel. It also shows how little Indian culture has changed from that day to this.

2. Quezaltenango

An easy 50 miles down the highway from Huehuetenango toward Guatemala City lies the country's second-largest town (alt. 7,800 feet; pop. 270,000), named by the Aztecs for what is now the national bird. It's on the site of the Quiché Indians' ancient capital of Xelaju, and the Indians still call it by this name. (You may even see "Xelaju" on the destination signs on buses, or just the abbreviation "Xela.") Quezaltenango is a booming, growing city—but the countryside surrounding it is marvelously beautiful. In the marketplace, men and women wear traditional costumes of heavily embroidered cloth. These are not costumes in the sense that they're put on for special occasions, but rather the normal, everyday clothing in the traditional rural culture. The Indian garb contrasts strikingly with the Italinate columns and monuments in the main square, which is called the Parque Centroamerica. The Parque is the center of town; most of the principal buildings face it, including the new municipal market, the Tourism Office and town hall, the church, the museum, and several hotel and restaurant choices. Streets are not well-marked in this town, so keep track of where you're going.

WHERE TO STAY: Top of the list in Quezaltenango is the **Pension Bonifaz,** on the main square (tel. 061-4241), a fairly luxurious place with all the trappings: 50 rooms, all with bath, a bar with live music and dancing, a smoking room, a color television in its own lounge, lots of flowers and plants—and steep prices. Singles cost Q20, doubles are Q24 to Q29. Many of the rooms are new and are furnished in Danish modern with lots of fake wood paneling. The older rooms are cozier and more congenial. You can have all three meals for Q15 per day.

A DINING NOTE: Eating in Quezaltenango will give you a chance to observe a curious phenomenon: a Central American Chinese restaurant! Believe it or not, almost every city in Guatemala of any size has at least one Chinese restaurant. Quezaltenango has several, and they add welcome relief from Guatemalan fare, which, while good, tends to get monotonous.

WHAT TO DO: Quezaltenango has two prime points of interest. The **Museum** is located on the south side of the Parque Centroamerica. On the ground level to your left is a room of objects from the revolution of 1781 when there were feuds between the government (captain-general) and the church. The discontent of the people here followed the revolutionary trend that was sweeping Europe at this time. There are letters, photographs, and memorabilia of one Don Marcelo Molino, leading light in Quezaltenango's history.

From the entrance hall a stairway leads off to your right to the museum of Indian artifacts. Unfortunately very few of the objects have been classified, dated, or systematically displayed. There are thousands of terracotta figurines, mostly primitive, bunched together in a case along with obsidian tools, ceramic pots, and local craftwork. It could be a very interesting museum if everything weren't displayed in such a haphazard manner. If you're here, it is worth a look, especially to see the huge number of pre-Columbian artifacts, which have been found by the local Indians while plowing their land. Most of what is here is not from an organized dig but rather from donations of *fincas* (plantations) whose owners have found the artifacts on their soil. Also on the second floor is a natural history room with stuffed birds and a few animals, a botanical room with dried plants and herbs, and a school of art.

The **National Theater,** built in 1835 when there was a flourishing colonial population, still operates today. They have musical productions as well as theater so check with the Tourism Office for schedules of events. If you want to take a look inside, which you should, it is open all day, every day, from 9 a.m. to 5 p.m. It is a small theater, typically European. There are three tiers of seats, the first two having boxes, which were rented by families for the season or year. The boxes were comfortable—for the ladies, each is furnished with a vanity. Some of the chairs you see are the originals.

NIGHTLIFE: There's not a lot to do at night in Quezaltenango, unless you want to see what's cooking at the Bonifaz or sneak into their TV room. You can go to a movie: the cinema at 13a Av. and 7a Calle sometimes shows films in English. It's pretty chilly sitting in the square unless it's been an exceptionally warm day.

SAN FRANCISCO AND MOMOSTENANGO: Quezaltenango is high in the mountains, but you can go even higher (660 feet higher, to be exact) and visit the small town of San Francisco El Alto, famous for its Friday market featuring hand-woven wool blankets. The town is only a mile off the Panamerican Highway over a paved road (or two miles over a dirt road, the back way). Buses run from Quezaltenango three or four times a day. The view from the large, cobbled municipal plaza where the market is held is fabulous (if you get a clear day). The town itself is very quiet, with virtually no action and very few people in evidence, except on Friday.

Past San Francisco El Alto, 16 kilometers (10 miles) from the Pan American Highway, is the small town of Momostenango (market day: Sunday), famous throughout Guatemala for its *chamarras* (woolen blankets). Buses from Quezaltenango chug and bash over the rough dirt road daily, winding up through the forests and down through the valleys. The road may well be impassable during parts of the rainy season. On the way into town the road passes little shops advertising blankets and woolen goods for sale, retail and wholesale.

The somewhat forlorn town square has near it two very plain pensions, the **Roxana** and the **Casa de Huespedes Paclom.** For meals there are several modest cafés, one attached to the Paclom. There is little to do here but interact awkwardly with the citizenry, and buy blankets. Chamarras, serapes, and other fine things are all made by hand here, and the local people in this high-altitude place know what warm blankets mean at night. Look for comely designs and fine-quality wool. Depending on size and fineness, you might pay Q20 to Q40 for a marvelous blanket.

BACK ON THE ROAD: Heading east to Guatemala City, the road brings you to more sights. The local costumes here include kilts for the men, held up by large leather belts. Herds of black sheep and boys hawking fertility charms made of straw turn up at intervals along the way. At the turnoff to Chichicastenango, there's a small open market where people from the surrounding hills sell vegetables and other produce, and entrepreneurs from the towns sell locally made cloth. There's also a gas station and a postal and telephone office. The road to Chichi curves through pretty country, then careens down into a gorge and shoots up the other side—one of the steepest grades our old car ever managed to wheeze up.

3. Chichicastenango

You enter the town through narrow, cobblestoned streets, up and down steep grades and around sharp, blind turns. At least a few village boys will come out and want to act as guides, with all the good will in the world, but actually there's hardly anything to show off. One comes to Santo Tomás Chichicastenango (alt. 6,650 feet; pop. 6,500) for the setting and the scenery, to walk around the old town and look at the local wares, and a guide is more a hindrance than a help. Once into the main square, everything is only a few blocks' walk. The main square is the scene of the frantic markets on Thursday and Sunday, and also the site of the Santo Tomás church which figures prominently in the religion, both pagan and Christian, of the region.

Tour companies have discovered Chichi, and on market days huge buses roar into town to deliver several hundred curious cloth-buyers, who are often promised a bonus: a peek at "pagan ceremonies" performed by local people. The "ceremonies" are not much more than a guy lighting a few candles, with not even so much as the decapitation of a chicken. You can avoid the crowds and still see the local weaving by coming on a nonmarket day, for a few stands are always open and the whole town is a lot quieter. But still, the town's been "discovered." Signs are in English: "Bar and Steak House," "Handwoven Indian Costumes," "Typical Souvenirs." It's mostly for the day-trippers, though; it must be, for there are only four hotels in town.

Note that Chichicastenango is a small town, with no street signs or numbers, so you have to ask around to find everything.

WHERE TO STAY: The super-duper is the **Hotel Mayan Inn** (tel. 056-1176), but at Q30 to Q42 single, Q36 to Q46 double, it's a bit high for this book. (Don't confuse the snazzy Mayan Inn with the less satisfactory Maya Lodge, right on the main square.)

Our favorite hostelry in Chichi, and perhaps in all Guatemala, is the **Pension Chuguila** (no phone), which has 25 very nice rooms set in nooks and crannies around a cobbled court, really a series of courts. Flowers and plants are everywhere. The rooms themselves range from quaint and simple to quite comfy; some have little parlors with fireplaces, marble-topped tables, and handwoven bedspreads of native cloth. Prices run Q5 to Q7 per person in bathless rooms, Q9 to Q10 per person in rooms with bath. Meals are good but pedestrian, but the coffee is a marvel. The waiter brings a pitcher of boiling-hot water and a little crystal flask of coffee essence, made by rendering strong coffee. You mix the two to suit your taste, and you need very little of the essence because it's so concentrated. The coffee is very good indeed. The Chuguila fills up quickly on weekends with people from the capital, so get there early in the day, or better still, write ahead.

The **Hotel Santo Tomás** (tel. 056-1061) is new only in a sense. Most recently opened of Chichi's hostelries, in fact it's a colonial-style place with two large courtyards filled with pools, plants, and birds. All 43 rooms have shower and fireplace (firewood included), and some have magnificent views of the woods and hills surrounding Chichi. There's a dining room and bar. Prices are not bad, for what you get: Q26 single, Q32 double.

WHAT TO DO: Chichi certainly isn't what you'd call an exciting place, except on market days, and that's its very fascination. Unless you're an anthropologist or textile expert, you won't spend more than an afternoon looking over the marvelous hand-woven and embroidered cloths for which the district is famous. Chichi's other claim to fame, it's much-vaunted survivals of paganism, involves things that you can't look for, although you may happen upon them: on a rainy night, a young man swings a censer swiftly back and forth before the locked doors of the Santo Tomás church, barking admonitions and chants at a woman kneeling on the bare stones praying. The symbols, paraphernalia, and words are Christian, but the inspiration is clearly pagan.

On Sunday the service in the Church of Santo Tomás presents a fascinating vignette of life in Chichi: within the church a Christian Mass is in progress, while behind the church pagan rites are being held.

In the rainy season it's a pleasure to go to the corner grocery, buy some firewood, and make a fire in the fireplace (if your room has one), and read, think, or talk.

A SIDE TRIP TO SANTA CRUZ DEL QUICHÉ AND NEBAJ: Called simply Quiché by the natives, the provincial capital is only 20 miles farther along the road from Chichi. A day trip will hold no great thrills, but you can take a look at its famous church, watch the local women weave straw hats as they walk (distances here are measured in hat-making time!), or have a shave and a haircut in the barbershop by the market. There are some ruins two miles from town at **Ciudad Gumarcaan** (no public transportation), once the royal city of King Quiché. Nothing's been excavated or rebuilt, and the grass-covered stone mounds give one the eerie feeling of walking in a dead city.

You can continue past Quiché by bus over a bumpy and dusty (or muddy) road for a good number of miles to Nebaj, a more-or-less remote village in which your arrival will be the day's big event. Of the few norteamericanos who venture into Nebaj, most come to see the exquisitely beautiful costumes and headdresses of the Nebaj women, said by crafts experts to be the most beautiful in all of Guatemala. The trip is a fairly long one.

BUSES FROM CHICHI: Buses leave from Chichi's main square quite early each morning for Guatemala City, both first-class and second-class service. Your next stop may be Lake Atitlán and Panajachel, however, in which case you can catch a truck or minibus from the square out to the Pan American Highway, and from there catch another to **Panajachel.**

4. Lake Atitlán and Panajachel

The road from the main highway winds through the mountains and then descends to the lake through the provincial capital of **Sololá** (alt. 6,825 feet; pop. 9,000). Before you reach this town, however, you get glimpses of one of the most beautiful lakes in the world, a clear blue mirror more than a mile above sea level, ringed by near-perfect-shaped volcanoes. The lake is not heavily settled or developed, so that much of its natural beauty remains in its pristine state. Fishing, swimming, boating (some waterskiing), and hiking along the shore keep most lake visitors busy, and there are some restaurants and even a nightspot or two (they open and fold every two weeks, it seems) to keep people from going to bed too early. A good selection of hotels in all price ranges completes the picture.

Sololá has been here a long time, since 1547 to be exact. Even earlier than that, it was a Maya town. Stop to inspect the ornate church façade (Sololá has a bishop), and for the fabulous market (on Tuesday and Friday). The most exciting day of the year in Sololá is August 15, date of the annual festival. If you're anywhere nearby on that date, don't miss it.

From Sololá, head down the hill for Panajachel (that's pahn-ah-*ha*-chell; alt. 5,150 feet; pop. 12,000), the resort town on the lakeshore. This is where you'll want to make your headquarters, not in Sololá. Market day in Panajachel is Sunday.

WHERE TO STAY IN PANAJACHEL: The town of Panajachel has two parts: there's the center of the old, with the post office, church, municipal building, and several good, cheaper hotel choices; and there's the string of new hotels and motels stretching along the road out of town toward Sololá. As you enter the town from Sololá, the *last* place you come to is the old town center. First you pass the **Hotel Atitlán** (tel. 062-1429; Q32 double) and the **Cacique Inn** (tel. 062-1205; Q$18 double).

But don't let these prices get you down, for almost every other hotel in town charges rates way below the top class, and you won't be hard up for a reasonable place to stay.

On a back street off Panajachel's main drag we came across the **Rancho Grande Inn** (tel. 062-1554). At first glance, the whitewashed bungalows surrounded by bougainvillaea, emerald lawns, and thatched porches for sitting looked to be quite expensive. Surprisingly, a room with bath costs only Q20 double, breakfast included. Only seven rooms here, though.

Besides these places, Panajachel has numerous tiny pensions of one or two rooms opening (and closing down) constantly whenever a family decides a little extra cash would come in handy. The only way to find such rooms is to ask around. Price per person for a room is usually about Q2 to Q4.

WHAT TO DO: It's only a 10- or 15-minute walk to the beach from any of the hotels mentioned above, and it's hardly ever crowded, perhaps because the water's a little chilly. There are beach cubicles for changing clothes and several little eateries and soft-drink stands serve up snacks advertised on signboard menus. Nearby is a dock where you can rent a launch for a ride to another town on the lake, such as San Luca or Santiago Atitlán. The one indispensable activity in Panajachel is to sit at one of the picnic tables along the beach, sip a cool drink, and look out over the water to the clouds scraping the tops of the volcanoes—you'll never forget the scene.

The town has a modern **market** building located up the street from the Hotel Panajachel and the town hall (walk along the southeast road out of town past the Hotel Panajachel on your left hand, the town hall on your right), but the Indians in surrounding villages come into town on Sunday for the weekly market and display their wares near the church. The church is across a side street from the Hotel Panajachel; walk down the side street to find the front entrance. Inside the church there's little gaudy decoration. Someone is usually praying or meditating at any given time of day, and often you will see groups praying together with an intensity that seems unusual even for the deeply religious. The post office is also in this area, down the side street which borders the Hotel Panajachel, on the right-hand side of the street.

Keep your eyes open as you walk around town and you'll come across little pathways leading through the shrubs and trees, past whole communities of little straw huts and woodstick houses with pigs grunting and chickens cackling in the yard, laundry out to dry, a dark smile from a shy young girl, a baby at play with some stones. It's a whole world, the real Guatemala, hidden away off the streets and side roads, private, quiet, peaceful, and secure. Everyone is friendly: no one will pass you on the path without a smile and a word—"Buenos días!" Evening is the best time to enjoy the mood of these semisecret places.

BUSES FROM PANAJACHEL: Besides the buses which penetrate the hinterland around the lake, such as the one to Santiago Atitlán mentioned above, Pa-

najachel is a way station for national-route buses. First-class Rutas Lima buses will take you onward to Guatemala City. If you're heading out for Antigua you will have to catch a bus to Chimaltenango, out on the Pan American Highway, and then transfer to another bus or minibus going in to Antigua. The ride to Chimaltenango takes about 2½ hours; that to Antigua, 30 minutes.

5. Antigua

Officially called Antigua Guatemala, this well-preserved colonial city (alt. 5,020 feet; pop. 27,000) was the capital of the country from 1543 to 1773. Even before it was the capital, however, it was on the way to becoming the cultural and religious center of the country. Pedro de Alvarado encouraged the Dominican, Mercedarian, and Franciscan friars to come and teach here, and the church spent a great deal of money in subsequent centuries to make this the most impressive city in Central America.

As the capital of the Captaincy-General of Guatemala, Antigua's official name was *La muy Noble y muy Leal Ciudad de Santiago de los Caballeros de Goathemala*, or Santiago for short, and from here orders went out to all parts of the region (which included the present-day states of Guatemala, Belize, Honduras, El Salvador, and Costa Rica). The city's population peaked at 55,000, and the citizens could boast that they lived in the third-oldest Spanish city in America (founded 1542), and that they had the first Pontifical University in the hemisphere (founded 1675). It remains impressive to this day, still beautiful and much-visited by tourists, even though the ravages of the earthquakes of 1773 and 1976 are plain to see, not to mention the effects of 14 smaller quakes, fires, and floods which damaged the city between 1540 and 1717. Some buildings have been in ruins since the quake of 1773, and in the one of 1976 some of the finest churches were badly damaged: reconstruction efforts are now well under way. The San Francisco church, virtually ruined in earlier quakes, was barely touched in the recent one, and if you look at the photographs of the reconstruction work on display in the church you'll see why: modern construction methods using steel reinforcing rods kept everything in place.

SPECIAL NOTE: Antigua is packed full on Good Friday because of its unique pageantry during Holy Week, so if you plan to be here at that time be sure to reserve your room weeks (even months) in advance.

At other times of year, Antigua is one of the most delightful towns to make your base, greatly preferable in all ways to Guatemala City. We highly recommend that you settle in at Antigua and make day trips to the capital, rather than vice-versa.

Coming down into the valley of Antigua from Guatemala City you see Antigua's impressive situation, surrounded by three magnificent volcanoes named Agua, Fuego, and Acatenango—Agua is the grand one to the south, visible from throughout the town.

WHERE TO STAY: Antigua is the premier tourist attraction in Guatemala apart from the magnificent ruins at Tikal, so there is a good selection of hotels. The range in prices is not so great as in either Panajachel or Guatemala City, most places charging between Q3.50 and Q8 per person, but there are several very suitable choices in this range, and at least one place that's even cheaper.

The vast colonial mansions of noble Antigua convert nicely into small hotels and pensions. But this dignified city has luxurious hostelries as befits its noble character. The **Hotel Antigua** (tel. 032-0331 or 032-0288), Callejón San Jose El Viejo, and the new **Ramada Antigua** (tel. 032-0659 or 032-0237), 9a Calle and Carretera Ciudad Vieja, charge Q39 to Q41 for a double room. But

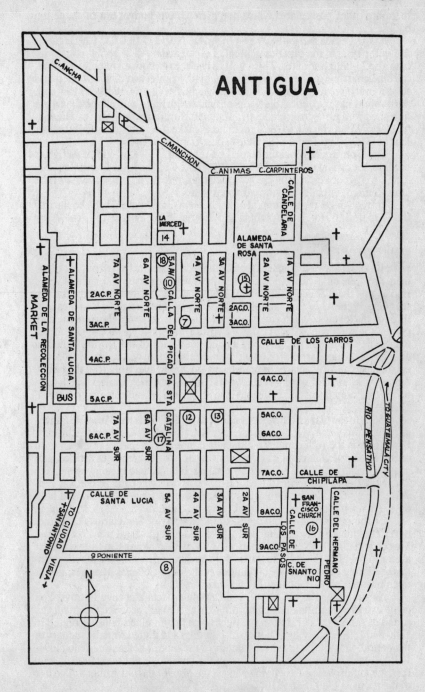

there are other posh places which don't stretch our budget out of shape too badly.

At the **Posada de Don Rodrigo (7)**, 5a Av. Norte 17 (tel. 032-0291), guests live in the style of the captains-general of Guatemala. All 27 rooms come with bath and 24-hour hot water. The hotel has two courts, both extremely beautiful, the hind court having a pretty tinkling fountain to entertain diners at the tables set out in the arcade. Some rooms have beamed ceilings, one has a brass bed, most rooms have beautiful tile floors or fine woven mats, and all the rooms are furnished with plenty of antiques or "antiqued" furniture. In short, it's a beautiful place. When you ask to see a room here, make sure you see at least three or four before you take your pick. Singles cost Q30; doubles cost Q35.

The Don Rodrigo's sister hotel is on the road to Ciudad Vieja, Antigua's predecessor capital of Guatemala. It's the **Hotel Cortijo de las Flores** (tel. 032-1285), a 31-room establishment which charges prices identical to those at the Don Rodrigo, but adds countrified atmosphere.

You can make reservations at either hotel in Guatemala City by contacting the Corporación Hotelera, Avenida La Reforma 15-00, Zona 9 (tel. 31-28-07 or 31-27-88).

WHAT TO DO: Antigua is one of the nicest towns to stroll around in. The reasons: It's quiet because there are few cars and the buses are routed outside of the main area, the air is clean (no exhaust fumes) with an occasional smell of wood smoke, and there are beautiful colonial buildings around every corner. You can see some 35 churches and monasteries in Antigua. The best thing is to meander through the lovely cobbled streets and see what you discover. Here are the high points: On the main square (Parque Central), you have to take a look at the **Palacio de Gobierno (12)**, officially named the Palace of the Royal Audiencia and the Captaincy-General of Guatemala. Construction was begun in 1543, but earthquakes and the ravages of time destroyed almost everything but the façade on the park. Most of what you see was rebuilt about 100 years ago. The façade bears the insignia of the Bourbons and the name of the reigning monarch, Charles III.

Also on the plaza on the north side at 4a Calle Ote. is the **Museo de Santiago,** which was set up a few years ago to preserve some of Guatemala's history. On display in the 16th-century building that once was the palace of the Council of the Realm of Guatemala, are cannons, guns, swords, religious articles, and an old Quiché marimba. Not terribly exciting, but nice and certainly worth the 25¢. Note the barred rooms which were used as cells when the palace was converted to a prison in the 19th century. Admission is free on Sunday and holidays. It's open 9 a.m. to 1 p.m. and 2 to 6 p.m. daily.

Of the other notable buildings, the **University of San Carlos (13)** comes next. The university was founded in 1676 and was the third university (after Mexico and Lima) in Spanish America. Much of the building you'll see was built around 1763 after the previous structure was damaged by the inevitable earthquake. Today the university building serves as the **Colonial Museum,** and is open from 9 a.m. to noon and 2 to 6 p.m. every day.

As you enter the university, you can almost feel a change in time. You come first to a beautiful open courtyard with a fountain, peaceful except for the sound of running water. Off to the right is the first of nine salons decorated in 17th- and 18th-century style, hung with paintings and dotted with the statuary of the period. One of the foremost painters of the time, Thomas de Meilo (1694-1739), is well represented, and although the museum is not slick, or even well run, the atmosphere succeeds in giving you a taste of the old Antigua. The last of the rooms is the Library (Biblioteca).

Of the churches, one of the best is the **Convent and Church of Our Lady of Mercy (14),** called simply **La Merced** by local people. It's at the end of 5a Av. Norte, and the façade is something to behold—you'll see what I mean. Legend has it that the 12 sprays in the church's foundation are symbolic of the Apostles, which makes sense. La Merced is much more of an attraction than the **cathedral** on the main square, but the latter has the distinction of being the church in which were buried such illustrious figures of Guatemalan history as Pedro de Alvarado, discoverer of the country, and one of his wives; and Bernal Díaz de Castillo, whose day-to-day account of the conquest of Mexico and Guatemala has become a classic (it's available in Penguin paperback). Back in the 16th century some 180,000 gold pieces went toward the construction of this cathedral. Inside are 68 vaulted arches carved with angels and coats-of-arms. The dome is 70 feet high; the altar is decorated with gold and lacquer. Unfortunately very little remains intact of this once-opulent cathedral, but it is presently under reconstruction to repair the sections that collapsed with the earthquakes. Since the 'quake of 1976, entrance to the cathedral has been limited to the hours of 8 a.m. to noon, daily except Monday, when it's closed.

The **Convent of the Capuchinas (15),** 2a Av. Norte and 2a Calle Oriente, was built by the monastic order for the sisterhood of the Capuchins in 1736. The nuns were invited to come here from Madrid by the bishop of Santiago (Antigua). Earthquakes have destroyed a good part of the building, but what remains is fascinating. As you enter there's a plan of the convent to your right, and the central court to your left. Notice the unusual pillars, rather squat and wider at the base than the top. At the west end of the court is the bath and laundry room, made of beautiful pink stone, and next to it a stairway leading down into the crypt. There's a small museum, on the right as you enter, where you can see tiles and ceramics from excavations done in 1974-75 on several churches in Antigua; some of the relics found in these excavations date as far back as 400 B.C.

From the museum, turn right and walk through a small patio and take the first left to where a large white tunnel leads to a lower-level room which must be seen to be believed: ring-shaped, with a large concave pillar in the middle. Any sound reverberates for a long time. Although we'd like to think some sort of religious rite took place here, it seems this was a bodega (wine cellar).

Go back upstairs and turn right to the central courtyard, turn left, and go upstairs to get to the monastic cells complete with mockup of a nun saying her vespers. Back in the central courtyard, two stairways lead to an upper level from which you can get a good idea of the layout of the convent and the surrounding area.

The **Church of San Francisco (16)** was once a very beautiful building, and is still fine, but earthquakes destroyed a lot of the best work on the façade. The church was built through the wish of one Fray Toribio de Benavente Motolinia, a Franciscan friar who arrived in Guatemala in 1544. Of the original church, about all that survives is a single chapel, and that houses the remains of Hermano Pedro. Hermano Pedro de Betancourt was a Franciscan who came to Antigua in about 1650 and later established a hospital where he cared for the sick and the poor for 15 years. He is remembered as an unselfish and saintly man, and people still come to solicit his help for cures. The walls around his resting place hold the most fantastic array of testimonial plaques, letters, photos, and memorabilia. You may see someone quietly praying before his crypt, gently knocking on it to let Hermano Pedro know he's needed.

The church was restored in 1961 using modern methods and this helped it to survive the 1976 'quake; only rubble remains of the convent of the Franciscans, south of the church. The church is at 7a Calle Oriente and 2a Avenida Sur.

The **market** is located between Alameda de Santa Lucia and Alameda de la

Recolección. It is a busy market selling everything from vegetables and baskets to huipils (the Guatemalan hand-woven, embroidered blouses) and beautiful cloth. The village women file in early every day (except Sunday when the market is closed) with their wares of jackets, huipils, and rugs. The only better place to shop for the handsome Guatemalan clothes is in **San Antonio,** eight kilometers south of town. (Principal market days here are Monday, Thursday, and Saturday.) You can get there easily by taking any of the numerous buses outside the market going to San Antonio; the trip takes 15 minutes. As you wind down into that town you'll see a number of stands hung with bright-colored items. The prices for the women's handwork have gone up considerably in the past years and, frankly, it's about time. The prices they used to ask were just not fair compensation for the work involved. Anyway, someone got smart and there now seems to be a type of cooperative among the village women, for all the prices seem to be pretty much fixed.

To buy local silverwork you must go to the nearby village of **San Felipe,** where there's a silver factory. Catch a bus near the market in Antigua for the two-kilometer ride, and when you get to the village ask for the factory—no street signs.

Buying Jade

Buying jade is a tricky business, for unless you're an expert there can be low-quality stones pawned off as the real thing. Antigua has recently become a very reputable jade center: an ancient Mayan quarry near Nejar was rediscovered in 1958 and has been opened; the jade from this quarry that was sent to the Smithsonian Institution has verified that the stones are jadite, the highest quality of jade and equal to Chinese jade. Jadite is characterized by its hardness (6.5 to 7) which differs from many other stones and can easily be distinguished from softer stones. If a stone can be scratched with a pocketknife, then it isn't jadite.

The quality of jade is also differentiated as gemstones and carving stones. The gemstones are the most valuable and are rated as to purity and intensity of color and translucency. A good gemstone jade can be more valuable than a diamond, and because of its hardness it can take a jade carver half a day just to carve one simple pendant. Therefore, know that if you go looking at the real things you will be looking at price tags in the $100-and-up bracket.

Two dealers in jade with good reputations and experience, not to mention beautiful collections, are **La Casa de Jade** (that's pronounced "*Ha*-deh," not "jayd"), 4a Calle Ote. 3; and **Jades** ("*Ha*-dess"), 4a Calle Ote. 34.

Visiting Ciudad Vieja

You can also visit Ciudad Vieja, which is actually midway along the route to San Antonio. Although there's not much to see there now (an old church), this was once the capital of Guatemala, but a flood destroyed it in 1541 and the city was moved to a new site, which is today Antigua. Buses to Ciudad Vieja leave the market (Alameda de Sta. Lucia and 5 Poniente) for the ten-minute ride.

VIEWS OF THE CITY: You can get a fine panorama of the city of Antigua by walking along la Av. Norte northward to the outskirts of town. Pretty soon you'll come to a path leading uphill to a small park and a cross mounted on a pedestal. The walk takes only 20 minutes to a half hour, and is well worth it for the view. Go around to the back of the hill and you can see Ciudad Vieja, the town which was the forerunner of Antigua.

Ambitious mountaineers can climb up **Agua,** the impressive volcano which seems to be right on the outskirts of town. Start by taking the bus from behind the Antigua market to Santa Maria de Jesus. After a 20-minute ride, the bus will drop you in the main square of the village of that name; right from the square a road leads out of town and up the volcano. It's a fairly easy hike (not a climb) to the top for someone who's used to hiking, and the free bonuses are everywhere: lovely wildflowers, good smells, lots of forest, and more and more mist the higher up you get. You can reach the top in four hours if you push it, five hours if you don't. (Remember: The air's thinner here than at sea level.) When you reach the top you'll see the crater, a magnificent view (if it's a clear day and the cloud doesn't shut you off) and—of all things—a soccer field. Teams actually *run* up here to play!

HOLY WEEK: From Palm Sunday until Easter, Antigua celebrates—and celebrates in style! This is perhaps one of the best pageantries of Holy Week anywhere in Central America and they claim it's "comparable to the one held in Seville." There are large processions on Palm Sunday, Holy Thursday, and Good Friday, each involving hundreds of men and boys dressed in deep-purple robes (cucuruchos) rhythmically swaying under the heavy load of the 40-foot wooden casket-like platform topped with a statue of Christ carrying the cross. It is a most awesome sight as the incense and rhythmic silence pervades the procession that lasts all day long and often into the night. On Good Friday, *not to be missed,* are the numerous *alfombras* (sawdust rugs) made by each neighborhood which line the processional streets. They are made with colored sawdust, pine needles, coroso (large two- to three-foot slender yellow flower-like seeds), and flowers in beautiful patterns and scenes.

This festival is very popular and is packed with Guatemaleans and foreigners who have come to enjoy the ceremonies. You'll need hotel reservations well in advance.

A brochure listing the events during Holy Week can be obtained through the Tourism Office, but below is a quick rundown on the processional times:

Palm Sunday—3 to 10 p.m., leaves from La Merced.

Holy Thursday—4 to 9:30 p.m., leaves from the Church of San Francisco.

Good Friday—8 a.m. to 3 p.m., leaves from La Merced; and 4:30 to 11:30 p.m., leaves from Escuela de Cristo.

ANTIGUA MISCELLANY: The **Tourist Office (10)** is located a half block west of the Plaza on 5a Calle Poniente. . . . **Banks** are open 8:30 a.m. to 2 p.m. Monday through Thursday, until 2:30 on Friday; closed weekends. . . . The **post office (17) (Correos)** (open 8 a.m. to noon and 2 to 8 p.m.; closed Sunday), is at 4a Calle Pte. and the Alameda de Sta. Lucia, near the market at the western edge of town. . . . **Public toilets** are located on the main square at the corner of 4a Calle and 5a Avenida.

Chapter XXI

THE PACIFIC SLOPE ROAD

1. Retalhuleu
2. La Democracia
3. Lake Amatitlán

ONCE ACROSS THE BORDER at Talisman you're off along the tropical highway. The first big town along the road is Retalhuleu, a clean and pleasant farming town good for an overnight stop if you've crossed the border in late afternoon.

1. Retalhuleu

Like most towns on the Pacific Slope, Retalhuleu is agricultural and industrial. The town proper is a mile or two off the main road. When you get into town, you should be able to find a decent place to stay.

There's nothing to hold you in Retalhuleu, so set off early. Just three miles out of town is the junction with the toll road to Quezaltenango, an exciting drive which winds up two miles in altitude in only an hour's time. The road's good, and the scenery is exceptional: four of the highest volcanoes in Guatemala flank the macadam strip, two on either side. At the cloth-weaving town of Zunil there's a turnoff to the famous hot springs at Georgina, unfortunately up the side of the volcano on a rough dirt road.

But the Pacific Slope road itself bears right at the junction and heads out to Mazatenango, a bustling farm and industrial town right astride the highway with lots of activity. From there the highway goes up hill and down through sugarcane fields and by little *fincas* (farms or plantations). Every now and then an exceptionally beautiful *ceiba* tree will catch your eye, huge but of fine proportion, its blade-like roots standing two or three feet high at the base.

2. La Democracia

About 125 miles along this road from the border you come to the small town of Siquinalá. By the main plaza in this town is a macadam road which heads south to the coastal town of Sipacate, but long before you reach the coast —in fact, only five miles from Siquinalá, is the town of La Democracia, famous for some strange Preclassic Maya (sometimes called pre-Olmec) statues and artifacts found at Monte Alto. If you don't have a car, take a Sipacate bus from the square in Siquinalá; or if you're coming from the capital, take a bus from Guatemala City for Escuintla, and transfer in Escuintla for the Sipacate bus. When you get to La Democracia, ask frequently for "El Museo," as there are no signs. The museum is on the town's main square (two blocks east of the main road through town). The plaza is simple but has a nice wooden gazebo built around a large ceibo tree and several of the large stone sculptures decorate the square.

La Democracia Museum was built in 1967 to house the numerous objects found during excavations at Finca Monte Alto and the smaller fincas of Río Seco, La Gomera, and Ora Blanca. The museum is not large, so an hour or so should give you enough time to see everything. Unfortunately, organization and classification are not the museum's high points, so you'll see primitive pottery and terracotta figurines (mostly female), obsidian blades, spears and knives, and curious zoomorphic jars all mixed together, the primitive with the sophisticated. Some of the figurines have elaborate headdresses similar to those found in Zapotec Monte Albán (Mexico). There are several stone "yokes," and also replicas in stone of mushrooms, which immediately suggest that hallucinogenic mushrooms, and their replicas, were used in ceremonies by these people.

Outside the museum, in front of it and in the plaza, are the great Buddhalike stone figures and heads carved from boulders—11 of these have been found to date. Just what they represent is a mystery: similar crude carvings have been found in El Salvador and as far northwest as Chiapas in Mexico, but are they deities, chiefs, or local dignitaries? Professor Edwin Shook, who headed the excavations here in 1968–70 under the auspices of the National Geographic Society and Harvard's Peabody Museum, says they were made during the period from 300 B.C. to the birth of Christ. He maintains they were carved by a Maya people, not "pre-Olmecs" as many others thought: the Olmecs carved much more sophisticated heads, complete with headbands and ornaments, while these are really very crude images chipped out of the sides of boulders. His theory is that they were carved by a Preclassic Maya people who settled at Monte Alto about 1000 B.C., reached the peak of their civilization from 300 B.C. to 1 A.D., and then declined by about 300 A.D. If this is so, these people would be very early Mayas, earlier than the people who settled at Tikal and Palenque, but so far no Maya glyphs—which would be proof of their race—have been found at Monte Alto. Perhaps some will turn up, for glyphs were found at Kaminaljuyú (in Guatemala City) which predate those found at Tikal, therefore it's thought that Maya hieroglyphic writing may have started here on the Pacific Slope and then moved north and east to the Petén and Yucatán.

The town of La Democracia itself is not what we'd call wildly interesting, unless you're an anthropologist who loves sticky heat, so plan on a quick visit to the museum and the plaza, and then a quick retreat to the mountains.

From Siquinalá it's only about 45 miles up into the mountains to Guatemala City. On the way you go through Esquintla, a largish town (flat, hot, and humid) with virtually nothing to recommend it, and later you pass near Lake Amatitlán, a popular haven with weekenders from the capital.

3. Lake Amatitlán

Don't confuse this small lake with Lake Atitlán to the northwest, for the latter is a spectacular sight, whereas this one, Lake Amatitlán, is not all that interesting. After the exit from the highway, bear left at a gas station, then left again at a "T," then right down a wide, straight street to the lakefront.

The government has built a park here on the shore with little stone thatched-roof changing cubicles, picnic tables, and the like. The swimming from this beach is not great as the water tends to be dirty, so your best bet for a dip would be either to walk along the road to the left past the villas and cottages to a rock outcrop, or to rent a rowboat for an hour, row out a ways, and swim. Near the entry road where you came in are various little restaurants and soft-drink stands which will do nicely for lunch. As for hotels, the one that's here is more on the order of a thermal spa, and not really suitable for one-night stays. As we said, the lake is mostly a place for denizens of the capital to cool off in for a day. Don't plan an extended stay, for in fact it is not all that recommendable.

Chapter XXII

GUATEMALA CITY

1. Transportation Tips
2. Where to Stay
3. Dining Notes
4. What to Do
5. Useful Information

THE CAPITAL OF THE COUNTRY is a city of over a million souls. Needless to say, it's the biggest and most modern city in the country—indeed, in all Central America—and is the headquarters for companies, airlines, and government. Some things about it remind one of Mexico City: it has a Paseo de la Reforma, a Hippodrome, a National Palace on the main plaza, an ultra-plush residential district, a University City. But that's where the similarity ends, for Guatemala City has none of the charm of its big sister to the north; in fact, it is not a major point of attraction for anyone who visits Guatemala for pleasure rather than for business. After the spectacular beauty of the countryside, the clean air and relative quiet of the provincial towns, the capital almost puts one off: the decibel level and pollution index go up almost as soon as you leave Antigua and start on the Guatemala road.

But since all roads lead to the capital, it's the transportation hub of the nation, and chances are you'll find occasion to pass through. Here's the information you'll need to make a short visit pleasant.

1. Transportation Tips

From the **bus terminal** in Zona 4, catch a bus to downtown along 5a Avenida, which runs behind the terminal. Ask the driver for "Parque Central," which will be near most of our hotel choices. To return to the terminal, catch any bus running along 4a or 8a Avenida with "6," "7," "17 Terminal," "BC," or "10 Terminal" written on the destination sign or posted in the front window.

Guatemala city has **two airports,** the international one for flights abroad and the national one where you hop the plane to Tikal. For the Aurora International Airport, use bus 6 to get downtown; catch the same bus along 8a Avenida to return to the airport. For the national airport, use bus 20, which you catch along 4a Calle. A taxi costs Q5 to Q7.

2. Where to Stay

The price for a room in the city is, naturally, above that which you'd pay in a smaller town, and in many cases the rooms are quite presentable, if slightly expensive for what you get. Most of the newer hotels are even more expensive,

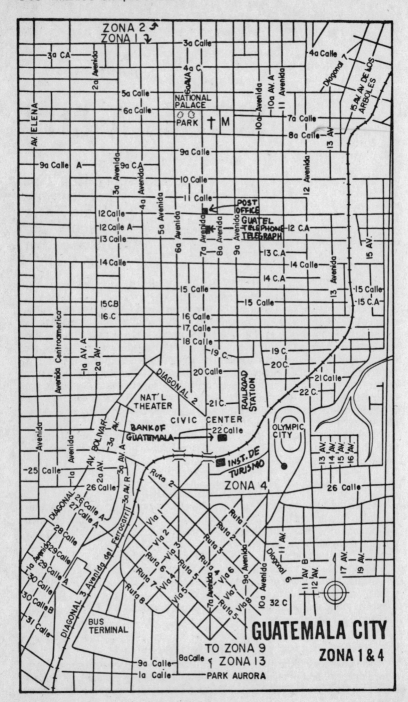

GUATEMALA CITY
ZONA 1 & 4

so expect furnishings that are not exactly right up to date. Unless otherwise indicated, all the hotel choices listed below are downtown in Zona 1. By the way, a hotel on a *calle* will be less noisy than one on an *avenida*.

A bit high in price, but well worth it, is the **Posada Belén** (tel. 2/2-9226 or 2-9401), a beautiful colonial building converted into an intimate hotel with a lush central courtyard. The beds are good quality and the rooms are tastefully decorated. Singles are Q18; doubles, Q22; triples, Q26. They have a dining room which serves breakfast, lunch, and dinner. The Posada is located about six blocks south of the National Palace at 13a Calle "A" 10-30, Zona 1.

The capital city has its very expensive hotels, like the Camino Real Biltmore, the Conquistador Sheraton, and the Guatemala Fiesta. But there's no reason to pay upward of Q53 for a double room (which is what these places cost) for a dose of luxury.

The **Hotel del Centro (8)** (tel. 8-0639, 8-1519, or 2-5980) is right downtown in Guatemala City, and has enough luxury features to please anyone except the unabashed sybarite. For a single room, you pay only Q29; for a double, Q38 and this gets you two double beds, central air conditioning, wall-to-wall carpeting, ice machine in the hallway, tile combination shower-and-tub bathroom, elevators, smiling staff, etc. You even get to watch Guatemalan TV in your room. The del Centro is at 13a Calle 4-55 in Zona 1, right near the corner with 5a Avenida.

3. Dining Notes

Guatemala City has a number of good dining places ranging from the purely "Americano" to those with a local or international cuisine and ambience.

Guatemala is not noted for the richness and delicacy of its cuisine. Although Guatemala City has lots of restaurants, and some good ones, don't expect the high standards of taste, service, and delicacy found in Mexico City.

But Guatemala City has the bonus of low prices. Except for that special evening when you decide to blow some money in a big splurge, you can easily stay within our daily budget here.

The Chinese and the Central Europeans in particular were drawn to Guatemala's beautiful mountain highlands, which to them closely resembled the topography of the Old Country. They've left their culinary imprint on the city.

4. What to Do

The sights of Guatemala City described below are arranged in five sections, beginning with the downtown area around the National Palace.

North of the city is the much-talked-about Relief Map. South of the city is the Civic Center and Olympic City, and farther south the museums centered on the Parque Aurora. Finally we devote some space to Kaminaljuyú. **Note:** The earthquake of 1976 caused a fair amount of damage to some of the buildings and they are still undergoing extensive repair and restoration.

NATIONAL PALACE: This should not be missed, it's beautiful! It was built 1939–1943 by the past president, General José Ubico to the tune of Q2,800,000.

Located on 6a Calle, on the main square, it has three entrances: the lower central one which houses exhibits now and then, and the two side entrances which will take you inside the palace. The mood of the palace is set as you climb the brass and wood stairways upward through three levels of beautiful wood-beamed ceilings, hand-carved stone and wood columns, frescoed arches, large wrought-iron and glass lanterns, tile floors, and numerous murals by Alfredo Galvez Auarez. It's fascinating, with all the interest of a museum yet not so overpowering as to be unlivable. There's a sense of harmony about the palace

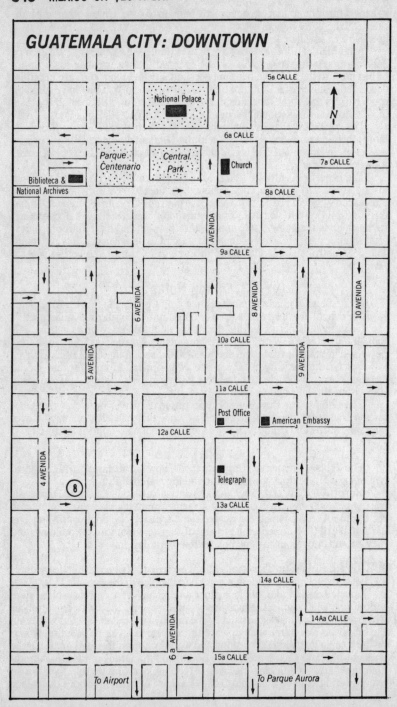

GUATEMALA CITY: DOWNTOWN

5a CALLE

National Palace

N

6a CALLE

Parque Centenario

Central Park

Church

7a CALLE

Biblioteca & National Archives

8a CALLE

7 AVENIDA

9a CALLE

6 AVENIDA

8 AVENIDA

10 AVENIDA

10a CALLE

5 AVENIDA

9 AVENIDA

11a CALLE

Post Office

American Embassy

12a CALLE

4 AVENIDA

⑧

Telegraph

13a CALLE

14a CALLE

6 a AVENIDA

14Aa CALLE

15a CALLE

To Airport

To Parque Aurora

that you don't often find in government buildings. The two side entrances lead up to symmetrical floors, both of which overlook separate courtyards on the ground floor. Visit for free any weekday from 9 a.m. to 5 p.m.

CATHEDRAL: As you leave the palace the cathedral is to your left, surrounded on all sides by a wrought-iron gate, locked from 1 to 3 p.m. daily (the caretaker's lunch, I suppose). Its quite simple interior has the standard arches, white walls, and some quite lovely oil paintings. If you're here in July, don't miss the feast of the Virgin Carmen, featuring a large procession and much fanfare.

BIBLIOTECA AND NATIONAL ARCHIVES: There is not much to interest you here unless you're a student who wants to do research. It's an incredibly large building, the archives entered from 4a Avenida off 8a Calle. The student library is on the 5a Avenida side off 8a Calle, and as you enter you'll notice a rather controversial, high-relief sculpture done by artist Efrain Recinos. To the right is Centenario Park, where the Declaration of Independence was signed.

MUSEO POPOL VUH: Named for the Quiché Maya's sacred book, the Museo Popol Vuh (tel. 31-8921) is an appropriate place to find a wealth of Mayan and religious artifacts. Displays are housed on two floors of a newly renovated colonial building. The immense collection of Mayan art is arranged by region and period, as is a smaller collection of colonial religious and secular art.

Some of the Mayan pieces are simply gorgeous: polychrome vases, huge burial urns, incense urns, and ceramic figurines. The religious art, mostly of the 16th to 18th centuries, includes some handsome altars in wood with silver trim. You will come across folk art here as well: facemasks, which are still made and used in the Morerias region, and mockups showing regional costumes. It'll take you about 1½ to 3 hours to see everything, depending on your interest. Hours are Monday through Saturday from 9 a.m. to 12 noon and 3 to 6 p.m. Museo Popol Vuh is south of the downtown area, in Zona 9, at Av. La Reforma 8-60. Take either a no. 2 or a no. 14 bus traveling south along 6a Avenida.

MUSEO IXCHEL: The Ixchel Museum is walking distance from the Museo Popol Vuh, three blocks east of Av. La Reforma at 4a Av. 16-27, (walk east on 16a Calle, turn right onto 4a Avenida). Hours are 9 a.m. to 12 noon and 3 to 6 p.m. every day except Sunday.

The museum is private, but nonprofit, established to preserve Guatemala's cultural heritage, especially that of the Mayas. There are two floors of really excellent displays showing indigenous dress and woven work of the 20th-century Mayas. Artful use of mannequins has created very lifelike situations which really give you a feeling for these creative, hardworking people. Several figures represent *cofradías,* the village church leaders who are chosen annually to direct church affairs and religious festivals—a high honor in every Guatemalan village. You'll see also figures demonstrating the weaving process from wool to finished cloth. An example of the characteristic cloth worn by the inhabitants of Huehuetenango shows a primitive but successful method of tie-dying.

A small shop on the grounds sells textiles and huipils.

Ixchel, by the way, was the Mayan wife of the sky god Itzamná. She was goddess of the moon, and protector of women in childbirth.

RELIEF MAP OF GUATEMALA: You'll probably hear a lot about the **Mapa en Relieve** built in 1904. It's 80 by 40 meters large with a depth of 2 meters. It is interesting to trace your route from the border through the mountains, but unless you're really interested in topography you'd probably not find it worth the

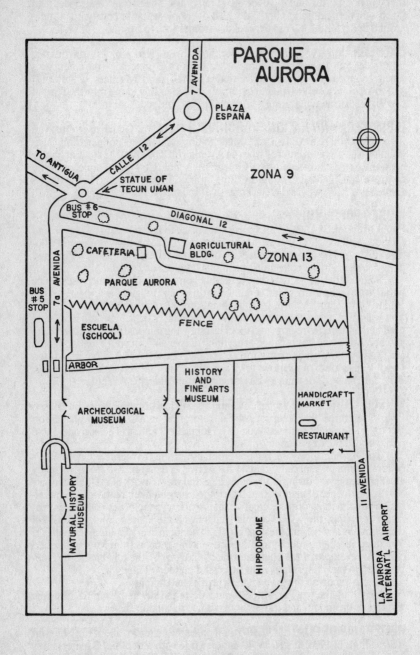

PARQUE
AURORA

7 AVENIDA

PLAZA
ESPAÑA

TO ANTIGUA

CALLE 12

STATUE OF
TECUN UMAN

ZONA 9

BUS #6
STOP

DIAGONAL 12

CAFETERIA

AGRICULTURAL
BLDG.

ZONA 13

7a AVENIDA

PARQUE AURORA

BUS
#5
STOP

FENCE

ESCUELA
(SCHOOL)

ARBOR

HISTORY
AND
FINE ARTS
MUSEUM

HANDICRAFT
MARKET

ARCHEOLOGICAL
MUSEUM

RESTAURANT

NATURAL HISTORY MUSEUM

HIPPODROME

11 AVENIDA

LA AURORA INTERNAT'L AIRPORT

trip. If you go, however, the **Parque Minerva** is just beyond the map and is good for a quiet stroll. The map is north of the center of town in Zona 2 at the end of Avenida Simeon Canas.

CIVIC CENTER AND OLYMPIC CITY:
This is the pride of Guatemala City because of its modern architecture. The city fathers claim it is "the most advanced architecture in Latin America." The center includes the well-known (and always hopelessly crowded) Bank of Guatemala building, the Social Security building (IGSS), and Olympic City. Much of the exterior relief sculpture is the work of artists Efrain Recinos and Carlos Mérida. As you enter the complex (at the intersection of 6a Avenida and Diagonal 2), you'll see a statue of a wolf with Romulus and Remus underneath; the statue is inscribed "From Eternal Rome to Immortal Guatemala." To the right as you face the statue is City Hall, and directly ahead of you in the distance is the Bank of Guatemala building, constructed in 1962–1966. The high-relief murals in concrete are by Dagoberto Vasquez and depict the history of Guatemala. The Social Security Building behind City Hall was designed by Roberto Aycinena and Jorge Montes; the enormous mosaic, completed in 1959, is by Carlos Mérida. On the hill behind you is the Fortress of San José and the National Theater, which looks a lot like a blue-and-white ocean liner. Olympic City, farther to the east, is an enormous building which houses the Mateo Flores Stadium (named after the athlete who won the Boston Marathon in 1952), the National Gymnasium, a swimming pool, tennis courts, and a Boxing Palace.

PARQUE AURORA:
Located in Zona 13 along with the museums of fine arts, archeology, and natural history, the zoo, the hippodrome, and the handcrafts market, this park is cool and quiet, full of green grass and trees, and for Guatemala City that's quite a treat. To help you find your way around, we've drawn a map of this area showing locations of the various museums and sights.

If you're driving, go south on 6a Avenida until you reach Zona 13, turn right on Diagonal 12 and take a left on 7a Avenida. This brings you directly to the front of the park. For those using public transportation (5¢), take bus 6 which leaves from 8a Calle across the park from the National Palace. The bus travels down 8a Avenida to 18a Calle, and you can pick it up anywhere along its route. Bus 5 ("Parque Aurora,"), which travels up and down Avenidas 5, 7, and 8, will also get you there. It's a 20-minute trip; two stops after you pass the park and the zoo, get off the bus and you'll find the museums on your left. The beautiful stark white Moorish building is the **Archeological Museum** (Museo Nacional de Arqueología y Etnología) and is open 9 a.m. to 4 p.m. Tuesday through Friday.

The museum now boasts the largest and most spectacular collection of Mayan carvings in the world. One of the more famous pieces now on display is the throne from Piedras Negras, which you should not miss seeing. The throne had been in storage for a decade, while the museum was being renovated.

As you wander through the archeological section of the museum you'll see beautiful black ceramic vessels from excavations in Zaculeu (Preclassic Period, 200 A.D.), the Dieseldorff collection of clay masks from the Postclassic Period (925–1200 A.D.), and artifacts of shell, alabaster, obsidian, and flint belonging to the Classic Period (200–925 A.D.).

There is also an ethnological section in the museum, with a textile room in which are displayed 150 native costumes. Moving through the other ethnological rooms you'll see a glass rotunda exhibiting the types of dwellings the Indians used, exhibits of nutrition (foods which originated in America), and industry (baskets, ceramics, weaving, etc.). There's a lot to see here, so plan at least a half day or more. To return to Zona 1, catch bus 5 to the right and across the street from the museum, or bus 6 outside the museum where it dropped you off.

Directly across from the Archeological Museum is the **National Museum of Modern Art** (Museo Nacional de Arte Moderno) (tel. 31-0703). The interior of this building is striking with a high wooden rosette ceiling and white plaster walls. The museum was founded in 1934 and contains paintings and sculpture from the late 18th century up to the present. Some well-known Guatemalan painters, such as Carlos Mérida and Garavito, are represented here. The historical section is smaller, the exhibit of greatest interest here being a collection of coins from the colonial period.

The **Handcrafts Market** is an outdoor area with vendors' stalls, a small courtyard, and a modern restaurant. The products on sale represent a good portion of Guatemala and the prices are surprisingly good. They have leather goods, woven cloth, huipils, ceramics, baskets, and hand-painted terracotta figurines. If you're traveling extensively throughout Guatemala you will find these products elsewhere but, regardless, it's probably worth a trip to see what they have here. Although prices are a little higher here than at the shops in front of the railroad station, this is a very pleasant place to shop, and you may even be entertained by a marimba band as we were. As for quality of merchandise, it's good, with the exception of woven goods—especially huipils—which are of higher quality in the villages.

The **Aurora Park Zoo** is a pleasant place to stroll and to look at the birds, monkeys, elephants, and lions. You'll find a number of little stands offering cold drinks and sandwiches.

East of 7a Avenida is the **Hippodrome,** where the Sunday horse races are held.

THE RUINS OF KAMINALJUYÚ: West of the city in Zona 7 is the Maya ruin of Kaminaljuyú (tel. 51-3224). To get there, take bus 2, 6, 14, or 17 Kaminal BC to the intersection of Diagonal 24 and 24a Avenida; the entrance is just west of Diagonal 24.

Kaminaljuyú was a very early Maya city (300 B.C.–900 A.D.), flourishing before the Classic Maya cities of Tikal and Palenque. The earliest people here (called the Miraflores people) planted crops and made excellent ceramics and carved jade. They seem to have been dominated by the priestly class which held all the power. By 300 A.D. Kaminaljuyú had been conquered by the people of Teotihuacán (near Mexico City), but the rulers who came here from Mexico were "Mayanized" over the years. The remains of the intermediate period (called the Esperanza Phase), before they were completely assimilated, show a strange mixture of Maya and Teotihuacán art and culture.

The Spanish conquerors who came in the 1500s make no mention of Kaminaljuyú, probably because the city had been burned and destroyed when it was abandoned in 900 A.D. It wasn't until the late 18th century that mounds were discovered, and only in 1899 did Maudslay begin the first excavations. About 200 mounds have been found here, some from the Miraflores time when structures were built of adobe and pumice, others from the later Esperanza period when the inhabitants built pyramids and temples of limestone. Archeologists have found traces of Teotihuacán influence such as stepped temple platforms called "tablero y talud" covered in red stucco, slit-eyed figurines, and three-legged pottery cylinders, and also of influence from Monte Albán (Tlaloc figures with large headdresses). In the tombs here were the finest jade objects found in all Guatemala, and in fact these people valued fine jade more than they did gold. The objects found in the tombs, which include precious stones, pottery and terracotta figurines, and incense burners, are in the Archeological Museum and the popol-vuh in Guatemala City, as are the stelae carved with hieroglyphs, earlier than any stelae found in the Petén (pre-290 A.D.).

Urban development has covered or destroyed much of the ancient city, and what you see today are substructures of buildings from various periods, mostly built of ordinary clay and rubble. There are a few of limestone covered in a lime wash: not too impressive a site.

TOURS: Several sights in Guatemala are well suited to guided tours because of the knowledge needed to appreciate them or the hassles involved in transportation. Guatemala City itself is one of these, and for around Q10, depending on the agency, you can have a guided tour of the city's principal attractions. We can't recommend a tour of Antigua as it's the sort of place you should go to, stay in, and explore yourself. The same thing goes for Lake Atitlán and Chichicastenango. But the Mayan ruins at **Copán, Honduras,** are troublesome to get to by private car or bus and taxi, so a tour might be a good thing. The cost does not include entrance fees to the ruins nor the "fees" which may be charged by border officials (see below where we discuss making this trip). Still, on a tour you have a guide to do the hassling for you. As for Tikal, if you must "do" the ruins in a day it might be best to take a tour, as the organizers help you get through fast: pick you up at your hotel, put you on the plane, show you around the ruins, provide lunch, and bring you back again all for about Q15 or Q20 more than the price of the air fare alone. Air fare, round trip, is Q80. But we would recommend that you spend at least one night at Tikal, buy an archeological guidebook, and do it yourself if you have the time.

5. Useful Information

Most **banks** are open Monday through Thursday from 8:30 a.m. to 2 p.m., on Friday till 2:30, but some have small sidewalk offices which stay open longer. . . . The **post office** is at the corner of 12a Calle and 7a Avenida, and has no sign to identify it. Look for the men selling postcards in large racks—that's the front door . . . Two English-language publications distributed free in hotel lobbies, the Tourist Office, and similar places are called *Headlines* and *Guatemala Bulletin.* The first has the usual ads and what to see info, plus selections from the latest wire service reports; the latter has no current news. *The Guatemala News,* an English-language newspaper published each Friday, contains local political information with a smattering of international news.

The **Tourism Office** (tel. 31-1333) is in the Civic Center, 7a Av. 1-17, Zona 4. The officials are helpful and have numerous brochures and maps. The place is a bit hard to find, however. Get off the bus at the Civic Center, walk down the slight grade past the Banco de Guatemala (on your left), under a small stone railroad bridge. The next big building on the left is the Turismo headquarters— no sign, no number, but it's a gray-and-white place with horizontal bands. Walk up the steps just after passing under the railroad bridge.

Embassies and Consulates

Here's a list of the diplomatic missions in Guatemala City which you might want to know about:

Austria: Embassy, 6 Av. 20-25, Zona 10, Edificio Plaza Marítima, tel. 68-1134 or 68-2324; consulate, 6 Av. 11–00, Zona 10, tel. 6-4314.

Belgium: Embassy and consulate, Av. La Reforma 13–70, Zona 9, Edificio Real Reforma, tel. 31-6597 or 31-5608.

Canada: Embassy and consulate, 7 Av. 11–59, Zona 9, Edificio Galerías España, tel. 32-1411 or 32-1413.

Denmark: Consulate, 7 Av. 20–36, Zona 1, tel. 8-1091 or 51-4547.

Finland: Consulate, 10 C. 6–47, Zona 1, tel. 51-3387.

France: Embassy and consulate, 16 C. 4–53, Zona 10, tel. 37-4080 or 37-3639.

Germany, West: Embassy, 20 C. 6–20, Zona 10, Edificio Plaza Marítima, tel. 37-0028 or 37-0029.

Israel: Embassy, 13 Av. 14–07, Zona 10, tel. 37-1334 or 32-5305.

Italy: Embassy and consulate, 8 C. 3–14, Zona 10, tel. 6-2128 or 6-5432.

Mexico: Embassy, 16 C. 0–51, Zona 14, tel. 68-0769 or 68-2495; consulate, 13 C. 7–30, Zona 9, tel. 6-6504.

Netherlands: Consulate, 15 C. 1–91, Zona 10, tel. 32-4092.

Norway: Consulate, 10 C. 3–17, Zona 10.

South Africa: Consulate, 10 Av. 30–57m Zona 5, tel. 6-2890.

Spain: Consulate, 4 C. 7–73, Zona 9, Edificio Seguros Universales, tel. 6-5382.

Sweden: Embassy, 4 Av. 12–70, Zona 10, tel. 6-2467 or 31-8375.

Switzerland: Embassy and consulate, 4 C. 7–73, Zona 9, Edificio Seguros Universales, Apdo. Postal 1426, tel. 6-5726 or 31-3725.

United Kingdom: Consulate, 7 Av. 4–13, Zona 9, tel. 6-3302 or 6-5726.

U.S.A.: Embassy and consulate, Av. La Reforma 7–01, Zona 10, tel. 31-1541.

Chapter XXIII

THE ATLANTIC HIGHWAY

1. Copán (Honduras)
2. Esquipulas
3. Quiriguá
4. Lake Izabal
5. Livingston and Puerto Barrios

FROM GUATEMALA CITY the "Carretera al Atlántico" (Highway to the Atlantic) opens up several more interesting destinations, including the Maya ruins at Copán, Honduras; the great church at Esquipulas, which is a place of pilgrimage; the marvelous Maya stelae at Quiriguá; and Lake Izabal on the road to Tikal.

WHERE TO STAY: For the first two of these excursions we would recommend using as a base the **Motel Longarone** (tel. 41-0314 in Guatemala City) at km. 126 of the Atlantic Highway near the little town of **Río Hondo,** Zacapa. The motel has pretty, shaded grounds behind the restaurant (which protects the rooms from the noise of the road) and one of the largest swimming pools we have ever seen at a motel. Rooms with bath and air conditioning go for Q20 single and Q27 double.

1. Copán (Honduras)

GETTING THERE: If you're driving, turn off the Atlantic Highway at Río Hondo and take CA 12 south past Zacapa and Chiquimula. By bus you make your way to Chiquimula, then take a bus or hire a taxi for the 40-mile ride to the ruins.

Just south of Chiquimula is a small sign pointing to a dirt road on the left. Take it—it may be a bad road, but it's all you've got. The distance to the border is 40 miles, over mountains, through streams and villages.

You will have to go through a good deal of border formality (and cash) on both sides of the border before you are finally allowed to proceed, and we would recommend that only those with a rather intense interest in Maya ruins attempt it. The charge for a car and driver—all costs included—can be as much as $10 before you're actually in the ruins (the $1 charge for admission to the ruins is included in this figure). If you're game, here's the gamut: Guatemalan Immigration, police, Customs, Hacienda (Finance Ministry) guards (at three separate stations); Honduran Immigration, fumigation, and Customs (two stations), then the ruins. (The Honduran dollar, by the way, is worth 50¢ U.S.) On your way back through it's easier (and cheaper). Pick up your Guatemalan Tourist Card at the immigration office, and the exit stamp will be canceled.

THE RUINS AT COPÁN: Copán is in a valley about 2,000 feet high, right on the Copán River. The area is lush and fertile, good for growing tobacco, but cooler than most Maya sites (which are in sea-level jungle). As with most early cities, Copán has had several locations in its 1500 years of existence. The first settlement (Early Classic, about 400 A.D.) was where the village of Copán is today. By the Late Classic Period (about 700 A.D.) most of the area in the Copán valley had been occupied at one time or another. But the Main Structure, about one mile east of Copán village, did not become the religious and governmental center until the middle of the 8th century A.D.; and not until this time did the Maya artisans of Copán reach their highest level of achievement.

As you enter the village you'll see signs to the parking lot and a bit further on a booth where you buy a ticket for the ruins and museum. The museum is on the main plaza in town and has the standard collection of stelae, sculptures, a tomb complete with skulls, and many small jade and stone objects. You can purchase a guidebook to the ruins here, which is not really worth it, but the area is so large that a guide is almost a necessity.

From the museum it's about a half-hour walk to the Main Structure, one mile east, and you'll need at least a full day to see these ruins. Plan to spend another day if you want to dig around the other sites: Copán cemetery, quarry beds, and the stone buildings outside Santa Rita. There are vestiges of settlement everywhere in the valley.

The Main Structure is in the center of the valley, north of the Copán River, and covers 62 acres: five plazas surrounded by temples, pyramids, and platforms, all built at different times between 730 and 850 A.D. The largest complex, 130 feet high from the plaza floor, is at the southern end. It's called the Acropolis, and was the center for religious life in the city. On the Acropolis's northeast corner (left as you face it from the plaza) is the famous Hieroglyphic Stairway, decorated with some 2,500 glyphs on the 63 stairs which lead up to Temple 26. (The stairs have been restored—a landslide in the 19th century toppled all but 15 of them). Unfortunately, they won't let you get close enough to the stairs to have a good look at the glyphs.

The stairs on the north side of the Acropolis lead to the Eastern and Western Courts. Archeologists think the Eastern Court was the most sacred spot at Copán because it contains Temple 22 (north side of the court), the most magnificent structure in Copán. Much of the work on the façade has been destroyed; but you can tell from the vestiges of mosaic and sculpture how grand it was. Note the two giant death's-heads intermeshed with squatting figures and grotesque monsters over the door to the sanctuary. The Western Court is less impressive, although Temple 16, a stepped-platform type, is impressive enough. When Maudslay began excavations in 1885 he found fragments of sculpture, which had once decorated this temple, strewn all over the Western Court.

The Great Plaza at the northern end of the Main Structure is similar in layout to the Great Plaza at Tikal. From dates on the 20 stelae and 14 altars found here, archeologists think the Great Plaza was the first complex built in the Main Structure. The center of life may have shifted to the Acropolis area once that part was finished.

Be sure to notice the special artistry which Copán's sculptors exhibited in carving the glyphs here, for Copán's glyphs are the finest examples of this Maya "writing." Also, the unusual sculptures, unique in Maya art, owe a lot of their beauty to the greenish volcanic stone found only here at Copán.

2. Esquipulas

The scenery is beautiful on the CA12 highway down from Chiquimula, and the town of Esquipulas with its church comes into view while you're still high above it. The church looks altogether too big for such a small town, and it is, in fact, famous as a place of pilgrimage. Buses run frequently from Chiquimula all day. Direct buses from the capital run about every 30 minutes, returning just as frequently. These buses stop in Zacapa and Chiquimula on the way.

Esquipulas is not much different from any other Guatemalan town, except for the basilica—but the basilica is very special indeed. Called by some the "Basilica of all Central America," it was ordered built by the first archbishop of Guatemala, Pedro Pardo de Figueroa, in 1759. The archbishop wanted such a grand place to house the sacred statue of Christ Crucified which had been made in 1594 by one Quirio Cantano. The statue had had a long history of miraculous events connected with it even before the church was built: in 1740 it was said to have perspired profusely, a miracle authenticated by the then bishop of Guatemala.

Devout Catholics visit the basilica throughout the year, but the rites during Holy Week attract a larger than average crowd, as does the Festival of the Holy Name of Jesus (January 6–15). At times like these it's possible for visitors to file past the statue and even to kiss it.

Besides the statue, in the glass case above the altar, the church boasts the largest bell in Central America, installed in 1946. And the building itself is impressive, simple (for the style of the time), but harmonious with four tall towers, one at each corner, and beautiful grounds.

The market just outside the church is especially active during the two festivals mentioned, and in fact takes on a carnival atmosphere: stalls selling snacks such as fried banana slices, games of skill and chance, as well as the normal market activities of selling hand-woven blankets and—here in religious Esquipulas—religious articles and trinkets.

3. Quiriguá

The Maya stelae in a beautiful jungle park at Quiriguá are among the most impressive Maya relics, and well worth a visit. With a car one can visit Quiriguá using Río Hondo as a base. But if you're traveling by bus you'll have to stay in the nearby village of Quiriguá.

THE RUINS: Quiriguá is a Late Classic Maya city, dating from 692 to 900 A.D. It was a dependency of Copán, and it was here that the Maya methods of quarrying and carving great pieces of stone reached the height of excellence. The area around Quiriguá was once dense forest of ceiba, mahogany, and palm, but at the turn of this century trees and bush were cleared to make way for the farms and plantations of the United Fruit Company. All that remains of the forest is the 75-acre park in which the ruins are set.

The ruins were discovered in 1840, and Maudslay took an interest in them later (1881–1894); after the turn of the century several teams came and excavated at Quiriguá. The site is now being restored by the University of Pennsylvania, sponsored by the National Geographic Society.

Quiriguá has three sites, but only the one most lately occupied (751–900 A.D.) is of interest. This is the one in the excellent park, reached by crossing the railroad tracks, going through the parking lot, and then walking along a path to the southwest. From the great plaza (about 1,500 feet long, north to south), it's an awesome sight: a lofty, lush grove with a gigantic ceiba tree in the middle; a yellow-billed *ticu* may poke his head out of a hole in a dead tree, or you may see a brilliant-green iguana two feet long moving slowly in the grass.

Restoration work is still in progress. At the southern end of the plaza is the largest of the complexes, a temple plaza raised above ground level and surrounded by six temple-palace structures built at different times between 750 and 810 A.D. Take a look at the structure on the east side of the plaza which has two altars, designated Q and R by archeologists, in front of the west doorway. Both these altars represent human figures seated cross-legged. Also look at the nine-foot-high mosaic head over the doorway in the north façade of "Structure 2," on the southwest corner of the plaza. Another sculptured mask with huge teeth is on the southwest corner of the same structure. And on Structure 1, at the far southern end of the plaza, look at the beautiful heiroglyphic inscriptions around the doors.

But to us Quiriguá is synonymous with the grand stelae the Mayas did so well. As you enter the park you pass several of these, carved from brown sandstone, 13 to 35 feet tall. The most famous is 35-foot Stela "E," the tallest stone shaft in Mesoamerica, which is about one-fourth of the way down the plaza as you walk south (there are two stelae side by side here; facing south, "E" is the one on your right). Both front and back are carved with a man standing on a platform and holding a manikin scepter in his right hand (this scepter is a Maya ceremonial wand depicting a long-nosed god). The northern face is the best preserved. On the sides are glyphs which archeologists have used to date this stela at 771 A.D. Most of the other stelae here have similar figures, many having beards which seemed to come into fashion with the Maya for a 30-year period. Stela "D," at the far north end of the plaza, has a figure with a beard, and some of the glyphs on the sides have been deciphered, indicating that this figure is "Two-armed Sky," a ruler of Quiriguá in 766 A.D., a native of Copán.

Look also at the "zoomorphs," huge boulders carved into monsters. Zoomorph "B," behind Stela E, is one such monster who has a human torso and head protruding from (or, rather, disappearing into) his mouth. Another good one is at the far southern end of the plaza, east side: a crouched man covered by a shield (looks like a human turtle): the shield, seen from the top, is clearly the face of a deity with two large ear plugs, and the crouched figure has a face at each end. There are several more of these zoomorphs; to see them well you have to take your time and look at them from every possible angle.

A note on the sandstone used here: The Mayas were lucky in that the beds of this stone in the nearby River Motagua had cleavage planes good for cutting large pieces; and the stone when freshly cut was very soft, hardening only after some exposure to the air. No wonder the highly skilled Maya craftsmen picked Quiriguá for their most impressive sculpture!

4. Lake Izabal

Thirty miles northwest of the Atlantic Highway over a dirt road lie Lake Izabal and the Río Dulce, which connects the lake with the Gulf of Honduras and the Caribbean Sea. The lake and its jungle-forest setting are quite beautiful, but swimming is not so good in the reaches near the road as the water's not too clean. It's very good for power-boating, however, and on weekends the wealthier citizens of the capital come to the lake and exercise the glittering craft stored on the shore. The lake was famous as a refuge for pirates in days gone by, and its entrance was protected by the picturesque fortress called the **Castillo de San Felipe,** on the northern shore a short walk from the ferry landing. Nowadays most people who come to the lake, if not out for the boating, are on their way to Tikal by road.

Before tearing off to Tikal, take a boat ride on the river. Ask down at the docks, and you're sure to find a boatman who's willing to ferry you to the Castillo de San Felipe. Minimum for a trip is two fares, and the boatman will rarely rush you to get through the castle. Plan to spend about a half hour there, about two hours for the entire trip.

The castle was built in the 1600s by the Spaniards to keep pirates out. Today it is famous more for its beautiful setting—which does just the opposite of keeping people away.

Another boat trip you can make is down the Río Dulce to Livingston or Puerto Barrios. It takes about 1½ hours to get there, with a minimum of five fares.

If you take a boat through the marvelous jungle scenery to Livingston, read on below. If not, you must be heading into El Petén, destined for Flores and Tikal, in which case you should turn to Chapter XXIV, which takes up the journey from the other end of the Río Dulce toll bridge.

5. Livingston and Puerto Barrios

On the Bahía de Amatique, at the end of the Atlantic Highway, are several towns and settlements, mostly devoted to shipping bananas and entertaining the workmen, navvies, and sailors who do the shipping. Puerto Barrios and Santo Tomás de Castilla (also called Matias de Galvez) are port towns next door to one another, Barrios being the original town, Santo Tomás the new planned port. Not much to do here unless you're into studying the shipment of bananas, but across the mouth of the Río Dulce is a different sort of place.

Livingston, on the easternmost tip of the Río Dulce's northern bank, is a world unto itself, somewhat difficult of access, primitive, quiet. Like parts of neighboring Belize, it is friendly and informal to the utmost degree, very Caribbean, and, well, just very comfortable, although one has few of the "modern" comforts. There is little to "do" in Livingston except swim, sunbathe, explore the tropical surroundings by boat or on foot, read, talk, get to know the people. Somehow these activities quickly become all one wants to do, and every day is deliciously half-full of activity, and half-full of just taking it easy.

EL PETÉN

EL PETÉN IS GUATEMALA'S huge, wild, low-lying jungle province. Its capital town is Flores, and here's where you'll find banks, gas stations, repair garages, and an ice house, besides the usual selection of hotels and restaurants. Tikal, the site of the magnificent Maya ruins, is really no more than a jungle settlement, with hotels and restaurants only. Have cash with you to pay your bills in Tikal—no one there will accept your travelers checks or credit card. Cash dollars circulate about as easily as quetzals. Have either, but have cash. The nearest bank is in Flores.

Recently, gargantuan road machines have been plowing through the jungle between Flores and Tikal to smooth out the incredibly bad road. By the time you arrive there, the road will be smooth and 60-m.p.h. all the way from Flores to Tikal National Park. The road between Flores and Río Dulce, on the other hand, may not be as good.

By the way, if you do go by bus, be sure to go by first-class bus ("Pullman"), without fail. You save five hours on the road.

INTO THE PETÉN BY ROAD: Those with more stamina and patience than money might consider going to Tikal by road, although the dust in the dry season or the mugginess in the wet season, plus the incessant jostling and banging, maybe enough to wear anyone down. Be sure your car is in good condition, for although you won't be stranded in the jungle if you break down (there's traffic periodically on the road, and villages scattered along it), you'll be a long way from a mechanic or a garage.

Still game? Then start out early from Río Dulce. The road is 126 miles long to Flores.

1. Flores

The town itself is on an island in Lake Petén-Iztá, connected to the shore by a causeway. It's only a short walk (ten minutes) from Flores to the shore towns of Santa Elena and San Benito, and in fact the three towns actually form one settlement. You can find all essential services here, although this is certainly no cosmopolitan center. Aviateca has daily flights (except Monday and Wednesday) to Flores, Q40 one way.

The Guatemalan government is developing Flores into the tourism center of the Petén, doing away with hotels at Tikal and having all visits to the Maya monuments originating from Flores. Construction of buildings at Parque Nacional Tikal is booming, and the road from Flores is nicely paved; new luxury hotels are opening in Flores. The master plan progresses apace. But Flores still has a lot of work to do before it is a bustling tourist metropolis.

The settlement on the shores of Lake Petén-Itzá is actually three settlements in one. Santa Elena is the name of the town in which you'll find the airport. San Benito, right next to Santa Elena, is the commercial center and holds the bus station. And Flores, an island in the lake linked to San Benito by a short causeway, is the capital of the province, with banks, government offices, and a traditional town square set on a hill.

Santa Elena

You can bed down in comfort at the **Hotel Maya Internacional** (tel. 121-352), a nice layout on the lakeshore with little thatched four-room cottages. Each room has a tile bath, pleasant decor, screens on glass-louvered windows, and balcony sitting porches. The swimming pool is filled and in operation most of the time, although at the end of the dry season (around April) it may not be. A huge thatched and air-conditioned restaurant completes the estate. How much do you pay? You pay Q15 single, Q25 double. Note that the rooms are not air-conditioned, but there is a good cross-breeze at most times.

Across from the Maya Internacional is the **Hotel El Patio** (tel. 121-229), a shiny neocolonial place with the same prices as the Maya Internacional. El Patio's construction is largely of stone, which helps keep things cool during the hot months.

Flores

Out on the island, you're not really cut off from things. Even with a suitcase, it's not all that far to the shore. As with the other communities, addresses mean little here so ask directions frequently.

The 16-room **Hotel Yun Kax** (tel. 121-811-368) is a nice airy place with fairly bare rooms, each equipped with a shower. The price is a moderate Q12 single, Q22 double.

BUSES FROM FLORES: In the confusing world of Guatemalan jungle transport, you must check on your proposed travel the day before you leave. Ask for the Terminal de Autobuses in San Benito, find out the schedule, buy your ticket if possible, and then get there early to claim your seat.

To Tikal

At least two buses a day go to Tikal. If you can't hit it off right with the bus schedules, consider getting together a group of people and hiring a taxi. Bargain with the driver vociferously.

The road from Flores to Tikal is good. The 40-mile stretch of road should take only about an hour to do, less if you go by car or in a taxi.

To Belize

Several buses run daily from San Benito, near Flores, to Melchor de Mencos on the Belizean border. You can walk to the border from Melchor's bus station, and then take a taxi on the other side to San Ignacio, Belize. See Chapter XVIII for details. The ride from San Benito to the border takes about three hours over a roughish, but not impossible, dirt road.

2. Tikal

The most spectacular of the many Mayan ceremonial centers is at Tikal, in the huge wild jungle province of El Petén. Over 3,000 buildings have been located and mapped in the immediate area of the famous Great Plaza, and there must be thousands more in the rest of the 200-square-mile Tikal National Park. Almost as impressive as the ruins is the jungle setting of Tikal, filled with exotic birds, spider monkeys, apes, ocelots, and other wildlife. Tikal is a "must" for visitors to Guatemala.

In a few years the installations at Parque Nacional Tikal will be completed, and you'll find a spanking-new cafeteria, museum, administration building, rental bungalows, etc.

You must have *cash* money to pay your bills at Tikal. There are no banks here, and the hotels won't change travelers checks for you. Have quetzals, or, failing that, cash U.S. dollars. If you don't, you'll have to bus down to Flores, 40 miles away, to cash a check.

Another thing you should bring with you to Tikal is *insect repellant*. All year round, but especially in the rainy season (May to October) you'll need the stuff all the time. Don't come without it.

Because all of Tikal is a National Park, you will have to pay an entry fee, either on the road in or on the plane. The ticket is normally good for one overnight stay, 24 hours.

THE RUINS AT TIKAL: Tikal is the largest of the Maya ceremonial centers. So far archeologists have mapped about 3,000 constructions, 10,000 earlier foundations beneath surviving structures, 250 stone monuments (stelae and altars) and thousands of art objects found in tombs and cached offerings. There is evidence of continuous construction at Tikal from 200 B.C. through the 9th century A.D., with some suggestion of occupation as early as 600 B.C. The Maya reached their zenith in art and architecture during the Classic Period, which began in about 250 A.D. and ended abruptly about 900 A.D., when for some unknown reason Tikal was abandoned. Most of the visible structures at Tikal date from the Late Classic Period, 500–900 A.D.

No one's sure just what role Tikal played in the history of the Maya: was it mostly a ceremonial center for priests, artisans, and the elite; or was it a city of industry and commerce as well? In the six square miles of Tikal which have been mapped and excavated only a few of the buildings found have been domestic structures. Most of the buildings are temples, palaces, ceremonial platforms, and shrines. Workers are now beginning to excavate the innumerable mounds lying on the periphery of the six-square-mile mapped area, and they have been finding modest houses of stone and plaster with thatched roofs. Just how far these settlements extended beyond the ceremonial center and how many people lived within the domain of Tikal is still to be determined. At its height, Tikal may have covered as much as 25 square miles.

Tikal is such an immense site that several days are needed to see it thoroughly, but you can visit many of the greatest temples and palaces in one day. To do it properly you should have a copy of the excellent guidebook to the ruins entitled *Tikal*, by William Coe, written under the auspices of the University Museum of the University of Pennsylvania. Archeologists from Penn, working in conjunction with Guatemalan officials, did most of the excellent excavation work at Tikal from 1956 to 1969. Write to the museum in Philadelphia for a copy of the guide, or pick one up in the museum at Tikal. One of the best features of the guide, and a real necessity given the size of the Tikal complex, is a very detailed map of the area. Don't take a chance on getting lost from site to site.

The best time to visit the ruins is early in the morning if you can manage it. The ruins open at 6 a.m., and from then until 11 a.m. they're uncrowded. The ruins close at 5:30 p.m., but on moonlit nights you can sometimes get a special pass to visit the temples bathed in moonlight—an unforgettable vision.

Walking along the road which goes west from the museum toward the ruins, turn right at the first intersection to get to Twin Complexes Q and R. Seven of these twin complexes are known at Tikal, but their exact purpose is still a mystery. Each complex has two pyramids facing east and west; at the north is an unroofed enclosure entered by a vaulted doorway and containing a single stela and altar; at the south is a small palace-like structure. Of the two pyramids here, one has been restored and one has been left as it was found, and the latter will give you an idea of just how overgrown and ensconced in the jungle these structures had become.

At the end of the Twin Complexes is a wide road called the Maler Causeway. Turn right (north) onto this causeway to get to Group "P," another twin complex, a 15-minute walk; turn left (south) onto the causeway to get to the Great Plaza.

Some restoration has been done at Complex P, but the most interesting points are the stela (no. 20) and altar (no. 8) in the north enclosure. Look for the beautiful glyphs next to the carving of a warrior on the stela, all in very good condition. The altar shows a captive bound to a carved-stone altar, his hands tied behind his back—a common scene in carvings at Tikal. Both these monuments date from about 751 A.D. As for Temple IV, it's said to be the tallest structure surviving from the pre-Columbian era, standing 212 feet from the base of its platform to the top. The first glimpse you get of the temple from the Maudslay Causeway is awesome, for the temple has not been restored, and all but the temple proper (the enclosure) and its roof comb are covered in foliage. The stairway is occluded by earth and roots, but if you're adept at scrambling you can make your way to the top of the temple from its northeast corner. Do it if you can, for the view of the setting and layout of Tikal—and all of the Great Plaza—is magnificent. From the platform of the temple you can see in all directions and get an idea of the extent of the Petén jungle, an ocean of lush greenery. Temple III is in the foreground to the east, Temples I and II further on at the Great Plaza. To the right of these is the South Acropolis and Temple V. The courageous and nonacrophobic can get even a better view by clambering up a metal ladder on the south side of the temple which goes up to the base of the roof comb.

Temple IV, and all the other temples at Tikal, are built on this plan: a pyramid is built first, and on top of it a platform. The temple proper rests on this platform and is composed of one to three rooms, usually long and narrow and not for habitation, but rather for priestly rites. Most temples have beautifully carved wooden lintels above the doorways, but the one from Temple IV is now in a museum in Basel, Switzerland. The temple is thought to date from about 741 A.D.

From Temple IV walk east along the Tozzer Causeway to get to the Great Plaza, about a ten-minute walk. Along the way you'll pass the twin-pyramid Complex N, the Bat Palace, and Temple III. Take a look at the altar and stela in the complex's northern enclosure—two of the finest monuments at Tikal—and also the altar in front of Temple III showing the head of a deity resting on a plate. By the way, the criss-cross pattern shown here represents a woven mat, a symbol of authority to the Mayas.

The Great Plaza

Entering the Great Plaza from the Tozzer Causeway one is struck by the towering stone structure which is Temple II, seen from the back. It measures 125 feet tall now, although it is thought to have been 140 feet high when the roof comb was intact. Called also the Temple of the Masks, from a large face carved in the roof comb, the temple dates from about 700.

Temple I reaches 145 feet above the plaza floor, the most striking structure in Tikal. The temple proper has three narrow rooms with high corbeled vaults (the Maya "arch") and carved wooden lintels made of zapote wood, which is rot-resistant. One of the lintels has been removed for preservation in a museum. The whole structure, as are most others at Tikal, is made of limestone. It was within this pyramid that one of the richest tombs in Tikal was discovered, containing some 180 pieces of jade, 90 bone artifacts carved with hieroglyphic inscriptions, numerous pearls, and objects in alabaster and shell.

The North Acropolis (north side of the Great Plaza) is a maze of structures from various periods covering an area of 2½ acres. Standing today 30 feet above the limestone bedrock, it contains vestiges of a hundred different constructions, dating from 200 B.C. to 800 A.D. At the front-center of the acropolis (at the top of the stairs up from the Great Plaza) is a temple numbered 5D-33. Although much of the 8th-century temple has been destroyed during the excavations to get to the Early Classic Period temple (300 A.D.) underneath, it's still a fascinating building. Toward the rear of it is a tunnel leading to the stairway of the Early Classic temple, embellished with two ten-foot-high plaster polychrome masks of a god—don't miss these.

Directly across the plaza from the North Acropolis is the Central Acropolis, which covers about four acres. It's a maze of courtyards and palaces on several levels, all connected by an intricate system of passageways. Some of the palaces had five floors, connected by exterior stairways, and each floor had as many as nine rooms arranged like a maze. Look for the graffiti on some of the palace walls.

Before you leave the Great Plaza, be sure to examine some of the 70 beautiful stelae and altars right in the plaza. You can see the full development of Mayan art in them, for they date from the Early Classic Period right through to the Late Classic. There are three major stylistic groups: the stelae with wraparound carving, on the front and sides with a text on the back; those with a figure carved on the front and a text in glyphs on the back; and those with a simple carved figure on the front, a text in hieroglyphs on the sides, and a plain back. The oldest stela is no. 29 (now in the Tikal museum) dating from 292 A.D.; the most recent is no. 11 in the Great Plaza, dating from 879 A.D.

THE MUSEUM: The museum contains a good collection of pottery, mosaic masks, incense burners, etched bone, and stelae which is chronologically displayed beginning with the pre-Classic objects on up to the Late Classic ones. Of note are the delicate three-to five-inch mosaic masks made of jade, turquoise, shell, and stucco. There is a beautiful cylindrical jar from about 700 A.D. depicting a male and female seated in a typical Maya pose. The drawing is of fine quality and the slip colors are red, brown, and black. There are a number of jade pendants, beads, and earplugs. Also on exhibit is the famous Stela no. 31 which has all four sides carved: the two sides are of spear-throwers, each wearing a large feathered headdress and carrying a shield in his left hand. The front is a complicated carving of an individual carrying a head in his left arm and a chair in his right—a most amazing stela from the Early Classic Period, considered one of the finest.

Appendix

FOR YOUR INFORMATION

1. Shopping Guide
2. Conversion Tables
3. Basic Vocabulary
4. Useful Phrases
5. Menu Terms

1. Shopping Guide

The charm of Mexico is no better expressed than in arts and crafts. Hardly a tourist will leave this country without having bought at least one of these hand-crafted items. Mexico is famous for textiles, ceramics, baskets, and onyx and silver jewelry, to mention only a few.

This guide is designed to help the traveler know some of the crafts and the regions where they can be found. I have listed the cities or villages where the item is sold (and often crafted), the first place listed being the best place to buy. The larger cities, especially Mexico City and Oaxaca, will have many crafts from other regions but, in general, a greater variety and better prices are still to be found in the areas where the items are made. Also included in Section 2 of this chapter are tables of metric conversions and clothing sizes. I have not listed any prices for the crafts since this is really dependent on one's bargaining ability. For some hints on bargaining see Chapter IX, Section 6. I would add that it is very helpful to visit a government fixed-price shop (every major Mexican city has one, usually called the **Artes Populares** or **FONART**) before attempting to bargain. This will give you an idea of the cost versus quality of the various crafts. Following, now, are the various crafts, in alphabetical order.

BASKETS: Woven of reed or straw—Oaxaca, Guanajuato, Mexico City. Cost depends on the tightness of the weave and the size of the basket.

BLANKETS: Oaxaca and Mitla (made of soft wool with some synthetic dyes; they use a lot of bird motifs). Make sure that the blanket you pick out is in fact the one you take since often the "same" blanket in the wrapper is *not* the same.

CERAMICS: Tlaquepaque, Guadalajara, Mexico City (hand-painted dishes and bowls); Puebla, Oaxaca, Mexico City (clay figurines and scenes—glazed, unglazed, and painted); Coyotepec and Oaxaca (black pottery, especially bells and animal jars); Puebla and Izupa de Matamoras (colorful folk-art earthenware candelabras, hand-painted and unglazed).

GLASS: Hand-blown and molded—Monterrey; Mexico City at the Avalos Brothers glass factory, Carretones 5 (Metro: Pino Suárez).

GORANGOS: Knitted wool pullover ponchos, hip length—Santa Ana Chiautempan, 49 kilometers north of Puebla near Tlaxcala. A good selection for a slightly higher price can be found in Puebla and Mexico City; also Chiconcoac, one hour's drive northeast of Mexico City, a few miles east of Texcoco.

GUITARS: Made in Paracho, 25 miles north of Uruapán on Hwy. 37.

HAMMOCKS AND MOSQUITO NETTING: Mérida, Campeche, Mazatlán. See market section in Mérida (Chapter XV) for details on buying.

HATS: Durango (woven straw); Mérida (Panama), made of sisal from the Maguey cactus; finest quality weaving; easy to pack and wash. See market section in Mérida (Chapter XV) for more information.

HUARACHES: Leather sandals with rubber-tire soles—San Blas, Mérida, Mexico City, Hermosillo, and in fact most states.

HUIPILS: Hand-woven and embroidered blouses indigenous to Yucatán and Chiapas. Huipils can also be found in most major towns in these states, with a good selection in Mérida and San Cristóbal de las Casas. Most of the better huipils are in fact used ones that have been bought from the village women and cleaned. The new huipils that are made for the tourist are often of inferior quality since they are made with synthetic dyes and a coarser weave. Note that huipils can be distinguished by villages; for instance, in Chiapas the pattern is very floral using bright colors, while in San Antonio, Guatemala, the predominant color is red with interesting lattice and geometric designs. Look around before buying; you'll be amazed at the variety.

LACQUER GOODS: Uruapán, 300 miles west of Mexico City, where they are made; also can be bought in Morelia and Pátzcuaro.

LEATHER GOODS: Mexico City along Calle Pino Suárez, San Cristóbal de Las Casas, Oaxaca.

ONYX: Puebla (where onyx is carved), Querétaro, Mexico City.

REBOZOS: Woman's or man's rectangular woven cloth to be worn around the shoulders or waist, similar to a shawl—Oaxaca, Mitla, San Cristóbal de las Casas, Mexico City, Pátzcuaro. Rebozos are generally made of wool or a blend of wool and cotton. Nowadays they are using synthetic fibers, so check the material carefully before buying. Also, compare the weave from different cloths since the fineness of the weave is proportional to the cost.

SERAPES: Heavy woolen or cotton blankets with a slit for the head, to be worn as a poncho—Santa Ana Chiautempan (49 kilometers north of Pueblo near Tlaxcala), San Luis Potosí, Santa Maria del Río (25 miles south of San Luis Potosí), Chiconcoac (one hour's drive northeast from Mexico City, near Texcoco), Saltillo, Toluca, Mexico City.

SILVER: Taxco, Saltillo, Mexico City. Copper and tin masks are found in Oaxaca and Mexico City. Sterling silver is indicated by "925" on the silver, which certifies that there are 925 grams of pure silver per kilogram, or that the silver is 92.5% pure. In Mexico they also use a spread-eagle hallmark to indicate sterling. Look for these marks for otherwise you may be paying a high price for an inferior quality that is mostly nickel, or even silver plate.

STONES: Chalcedony, turquoise, lapis lazuli, amethyst—Querétaro, San Miguel del Allende, Durango, Saltillo, San Luis Potosí. The cost of turquoise is computed by weight, so many pesos per carat.

TEXTILES: Oaxaca, Santa Ana, and Tlaxcala are known for their excellent weaving, each culturally distinct and different. The Oaxaqueños are famous for their hand-loomed woven tablecloths.

TORTOISE SHELL: Veracruz, Campeche.

2. Conversion Tables

Mexico uses the metric system, as in Canada, Europe, and the rest of the world. Here are some conversion tables to help you in your shopping and traveling.

METRIC EQUIVALENTS: Here are the metric equivalents for units of length, weight, and liquid measure.

1 inch = 2.54 centimeters
1 foot = 30.5 centimeters
1 meter = 39.37 inches
1 mile = 1.6 kilometers
1 kilometer = 0.62 miles
1 pound = 0.4536 kilograms
1 kilogram = 2.2 pounds
1 U.S. gallon = 3.79 liters
1 liter = 0.26 U.S. gallons

Approximations

Here are a few handy rules of thumb. A pound is slightly less than half a kilogram. A meter is a little more than a yard (three feet). A gallon is almost four liters.

An easy way to convert kilometer distances into miles is to multiply the kilometer distance by 0.6; another way of doing the same thing is to think in 3s and 5s, 6s and 10s; 3 miles is about 5 kilometers, 6 miles is about 10 kilometers, so 100 kilometers is about 60 miles.

Temperature

Use of the metric system includes use of the Celsius (centigrade) thermometer. Here are some reference points:

Fahrenheit		Celsius
−40		−40
0		−18
32	Water freezes	0
50	Cool weather	10
68	Comfortable weather	20
88	Hot weather	30
98.6	Body temperature	37
104	Very hot weather	40
212	Water boils	100

CLOTHING SIZE EQUIVALENTS: You'll want to try on any clothing you intend to buy, but here are some equivalents in case you're buying gifts for friends. Note that women's blouse sizes are the same in the U.S. and Mexico.

Woman's				Man's					
Dress		Shoes		Collar		Jacket		Shoes	
U.S.	Mex.	U.S.	Mex.	U.S.	Mex.	U.S.	Mex.	U.S.	Mex.
6	36	5	35	14	36	38	48	8	41
8	38	5.5	35.5	14.5	37	40	50	8.5	41.5
10	40	6	36	15	38	42	52	9	42
12	42	6.5	36.5	15.5	39	44	54	9.5	42.5
14	44	7	37	16	40	46	56	10	43
16	46	7.5	37.5	16.5	41	48	58	10.5	43.5
18	48	8	38	17	42	50	60	11	44
20	50	8.5	38.5	17.5	43	52	62	11.5	44.5
22	52	9	39	18	44	54	64	12	45

3. Basic Vocabulary

Let me now deal with the omnipresent, unavoidable, unfortunate fact that not everyone in Mexico speaks English (this isn't as silly as it sounds; these days, English is taught in most Mexican schools).

Berlitz's *Latin American Spanish for Travellers,* available at most bookstores for $4, cannot be recommended highly enough. But for added convenience, I've included a list of certain simple phrases for expressing basic needs, followed by some menu items presented in the same order in which they'd be found on a Mexican menu.

		Pronounced
Hello	**Buenos días**	bway-nohss dee-ahss
How are you?	**¿Cómo está usted?**	koh-moh ess-tah oo-sted
Very well	**Muy bien**	mwee byen
Thank you	**Gracias**	grah-see-ahss
You're welcome	**De nada**	day nah-dah

Goodbye	**Adiós**	ah-dyohss
Please	**Por favor**	pohr fah-bohr
Yes	**Sí**	see
No	**No**	noh
Excuse	**Perdóneme**	pehr-doh-neh-may
Give me	**Déme**	day-may
Where is?	**¿Dónde está?**	dohn-day ess-tah
the station	**la estación**	la ess-tah-see-own
a hotel	**un hotel**	oon oh-tel
a gas station	**una gasolinera**	oon-nuh gah-so lee-nay-rah
a restaurant	**un restaurante**	oon res-tow-rahn-tay
the toilet	**el baño**	el bahn-yoh
a good doctor	**un buen médico**	oon bwayn may-dee-co
the road to . . .	**el camino a . . .**	el cah-mee-noh ah . . .
To the right	**A la derecha**	ah lah day-ray-chuh
To the left	**A la izquierda**	ah lah ees-ky-ehr dah
Straight ahead	**Derecho**	day-ray-cho
I would like	**Quisiera**	keyh-see-air-ah
I want	**Quiero**	kyehr-oh
to eat	**comer**	ko-mayr
a room	**una habitación**	oon-nuh hab-bee-tah-see-own
Do you have?	**¿Tiene usted?**	tyah-nay oos-ted
a book	**un libro**	oon lee-bro
a dictionary	**un diccionario**	oon deek-see-own-ar-eo
How much is it?	**¿Cuánto cuesta?**	kwahn-toh kwess-tah
When	**¿Cuando?**	kwahn-doh
What	**¿Qué?**	kay
There is (Is there?)	**¿Hay . . .**	eye
Yesterday	**Ayer**	ah-yer
Today	**Hoy**	oy
Tomorrow	**Mañana**	mahn-yawn-ah
Good	**Bueno**	bway-no
Bad	**Malo**	mah-lo
Better (best)	**(Lo) Mejor**	meh-hor
More	**Más**	mahs
Less	**Menos**	may-noss
No Smoking	**Se prohibe fumar**	seh pro-hee-beh foo mahr
Postcard	**Tarjeta postal**	tahr-hay-tah pohs-tahl
Insect repellant	**Rapellante contra insectos**	rah-pey-yahn-te cohn-trah een-sehk-tos

1	uno (ooh-noh)	15	quince (keen-say)		kwen-tah)
2	dos (dose)	16	dieciseis (de-ess-ee-	60	sesenta (say-sen-
3	tres (trayss)		sayss)		tah)
4	cuatro (kwah-troh)	17	diecisiete (de-ess-ee-	70	setenta (say-ten-tah)
5	cinco (seen-koh)		see-ay-tay)	80	ochenta (oh-chen-
6	seis (sayss)	18	dieciocho (dee-ess-ee-		tah)
7	siete (syeh-tay)		oh-choh)	90	noventa (noh-ben-
8	ocho (oh-choh)	19	diecinueve (dee-ess-		tah)
9	nueve (nway-bay)		ee-nway-bay)	100	cien (see-en)
10	diez (dee-ess)	20	veinte (bayn-tay)	200	doscientos (dos-se
11	once (ohn-say)	30	treinta (trayn-tah)		en-tos)
12	doce (doh-say)	40	cuarenta (kwah-ren-	500	quinientos (keen-ee
13	trece (tray-say)		tah)		ehn-tos)
14	catorce (kah-tor-say)	50	cincuenta (seen-	1000	mil (meal)

4. Useful Phrases

Do you speak English?	¿Habla usted Inglés?
Is there anyone here who speaks English?	¿Hay alguien aquí qué hable Inglés?
I speak a little Spanish	Hablo un poco de Español.
I don't understand Spanish very well.	No lo entiendo muy bien el Español.
The meal is good.	Me gusta la comida.
What time is it?	¿Qué hora es?
May I see your menu?	¿Puedo ver su menú?
What did you say?	¿Mande? (colloquial expression for American "Eh?")
I want (to see) a room	Quiero (ver) un carto (una habitación)
for two persons	para dos persones
with (without) bath	con (sin) baño
We are staying here only one night (one week)	Nos quedaremos aquí solamente una noche (una semana).
We are leaving tomorrow.	Partimos mañana.
Do you accept travelers checks?	¿Acepta Usted cheques de viajero?
Is there a laundromat near here	¿Hay una lavandería cerca de aquí?
Please send these clothes to the laundry.	Hágame el favor de mandar esta ropa a la lavandería.

5. Menu Terms

almuerzo		lunch	frito	fried
cena		supper	poco cocido	rare
comida		dinner	asado	roast

desayuno	breakfast	**bien cocido**	well done
el menu	the menu	**milanesa**	breaded
la cuenta	the check	**veracruzana**	tomato and green
tampiqueña	thinly sliced meat		olive sauce
cocido	boiled	**pibil**	roasted
empanado	breaded		

BREAKFAST (DESAYUNO)

jugo de naranja	orange juice	**huevos motuleños**	egg on ham
café con crema	coffee with		with tortilla,
	cream		cheese, and
pan tostado	toast		tomato sauce
mermelada	jam	**huevos poches**	poached eggs
leche	milk	**huevos fritos**	fried eggs
té	tea	**huevos pasados al agua**	
huevos	eggs		soft-boiled eggs
huevos rancheros	fried eggs	**huevos revueltos**	scrambled
	on a tortilla, covered with		eggs
	tomato sauce	**tocino**	bacon
huevos cocidos	hard-boiled	**jamón**	ham
	eggs		

LUNCH AND DINNER

antojitos	Mexican specialties	**caldo de pollo**	chicken broth
caldo	broth	**frijoles refritos**	refried beans
sopa	soup	**menudo**	tripe soup
sopa de ajo	garlic soup with egg	**médula**	bone marrow soup
sopa clara	consommé	**salchichas**	knockwurst
sopa de lentejas	lentil soup	**taco**	filled fried tortilla
sopa de chicaros	pea soup	**torta**	sandwich
sopao de arroz	rice pilaf (not	**tostada**	crisp fried tortilla
	soup!)	**enchilada**	filled tortilla
pozole	meat-hominy stew	**tamales russos**	cabbage rolls

SEAFOOD (MARISCOS)

almejas	clams	**caviare**	caviar
anchoas	anchovies	**corvina**	bass
arenques	herring	**huachinango**	red snapper
atún	tuna	**jaiba**	crab
calamares	squid	**langosta**	lobster
camarones	shrimp	**lenguado**	sole
caracoles	snails		

merluza	hake (type of cod)	salmon ahumado	smoked salmon
ostiones	oysters		
pescado	fish	sardinas	sardines
mojarra	perch	solo	pike
pez espada	swordfish	trucha	trout
robalo	sea bass		
salmon	salmon		

MEATS (CARNES)

ahumado	smoked	callos	tripe
alambre	shish kebab	venado	venison
albondigas	meatballs	conejo	rabbit
aves	poultry	cordero	lamb
bistek	steak	costillas de cerdo	spare ribs
cabeza de ternera	calf's head	faisan	pheasant
cabrito	kid (goat)	filete milanesa	breaded veal chops
carne	meat		
carne fría	cold cuts	filete de ternera	filet of veal
cerdo	pork	ganso	goose
chiles rellenos	stuffed peppers	pavo	turkey
chicharrón	pigskin cracklings	higado	liver
chorizo	spicy sausage	jamón	ham
chuleta	chop	lengua	tongue
chuleta de carnero	mutton chop	lomo	loin
chuletas de cordero	lamp chops	mole	chicken in spicy bitter chocolate sauce
chuletas de puerco	pork chops		
paloma	pigeon	pollo	chicken
pato	duck	res	beef
pechuga	chicken breast	riñones	kidneys
perdiz	partridge	ternera	veal
pierna	leg	tocino	bacon

VEGETABLES (LEGUMBRES)

aguacate	avocado	espinaca	spinach
aceitunas	olives	frijoles	beans
arroz	rice	hongos	mushroom
betabeles	beets	jicame	sweet yellow turnip
cebolla	onions		
champiñones	mushrooms	lechuga	lettuce
chicharos	peas	lentejas	lentils
col	cabbage	papas	potatoes
col fermentada	sauerkraut	pepino	cucumber
coliflor	cauliflower	rabanos	radishes
ejotes	string beans	tomate	tomato
elote	corn (maize)	verduras	greens, vegetables
entremeses	hors d'oeuvres	zanahorías	carrots
esparragos	asparagus		

SALADS (ENSALADAS)

ensalada de apio	celery salad		
ensalada de frutas	fruit salad	guacamole	avocado salad
ensalada mixta	mixed salad	lechuga	lettuce salad
ensalada de pepinos	cucumber salad		

FRUITS (FRUTAS)

chavacanos	apricots	higos	figs
ciruelas	yellow plums	limon	lime
coco	coconut	mamey	sweet orange fruit
duraznos	peaches	mango	mango
frambuesas	raspberries	manzanas	apples
fresas	strawberries	naranjas	oranges
con crema	with cream	pera	pear
fruta cocida	stewed fruit	piña	pineapple
granada	pomegranate	plátanos	bananas
guanabana	green pear-like fruit	tuña	prickly pear fruit
		uvas	grapes
guayabas	guavas	zapote	maple-sugary fruit

DESSERTS (POSTRES)

arroz con leche	rice pudding	helado, nieve	ice cream
brunelos de fruta	fruit tart	macedonia	fruit salad
coctel de aguacate	avocado cocktail	nieve	sherbet
		pastel	cake or pastry
coctel de frutas	fruit cocktail	queso	cheese
compota	stewed fruit	torta	cake
flan	custard	leche tipo bulgar, lavin	yogurt
galletas	crackers or cookies		

BEVERAGES (BEBIDAS)

agua	water	café negro	black coffee
brandy	brandy	cerveza	beer
café	coffee	ginebra	gin
café con crema	coffee with cream	hielo	ice
		jerez	sherry

jugo de naranja	orange juice	sidra	cider
jugo de tomate	tomato juice	sifon	soda
jugo de toronja	grapefruit juice	té	tea
leche	milk	vaso de leche	glass of milk
licores	liqueurs	vino blanco	white wine
manzanita	apple juice	vino tinto	red wine
refrescas	soft drinks	refresco	soft drink
ron	rum		

CONDIMENTS AND CUTLERY

aceite	oil	pan	bread
azucar	sugar	bolillo	roll
copa	goblet	pimienta	pepper
cilantro	coriander	sal	salt
cuchara	spoon	taza	cup
cuchillo	knife	tenedor	fork
epazote	Mexican tea	tostada	toast
mantequilla	butter	vinagre	vinegar
mostaza	mustard	vaso	glass

PREPARATION AND SAUCES

asado	roasted	poc-chuc	pork leg cooked with onions, cilantro, sour oranges, and served with black beans
cocido	cooked		
bien cocido	well-done		
poco cocido	rare		
empanado	breaded	relleno negro	stuffed ground pork pimiento, olives, eggs, epazote, salt, vinegar, and tomato stuffing
frito	fried		
al horno	baked		
milanesa	Italian breaded		
mole poblano	hot red peppers and cocoa sauce with raisins and spices	blanco	the above with raisins, cinnamon, and capers
a la parilla	grilled	tampiqueño	thinly sliced meat
pibil	sauce of tomato, onion, red pepper (hot), cilantro, vinegar; wrapped in a banana leaf	veracruzana	tomato and green olive sauce